Handbook of Research on Digital Communications, Internet of Things, and the Future of Cultural Tourism

Lídia Oliveira
University of Aveiro, Portugal

A volume in the Advances in Hospitality, Tourism, and the Services Industry (AHTSI) Book Series

Published in the United States of America by
  IGI Global
  Business Science Reference (an imprint of IGI Global)
  701 E. Chocolate Avenue
  Hershey PA, USA 17033
  Tel: 717-533-8845
  Fax: 717-533-8661
  E-mail: cust@igi-global.com
  Web site: http://www.igi-global.com

Library of Congress Cataloging-in-Publication Data

Names: Oliveira, Lidia, 1968- editor.
Title: Handbook of Research on Digital Communications, Internet of Things,
  and the Future of Cultural Tourism / Lídia Oliveira, editor.
Description: Hershey PA : Business Science Reference, [2022] | Includes
  bibliographical references and index. | Summary: "This book is aimed at
  researchers who want to improve their understanding of the strategic
  role of new digital technologies in the field of cultural tourism,
  offering innovative research results within the scope of the
  interdisciplinary cross between Digital Communications, Internet of
  Things, and Cultural Tourism"-- Provided by publisher.
Identifiers: LCCN 2021031859 (print) | LCCN 2021031860 (ebook) | ISBN
  9781799885283 (hardcover) | ISBN 9781799885306 (ebook)
Subjects: LCSH: Heritage tourism--Information technology. | Heritage
  tourism--Data processing. | Digital communications. | Internet of
  things.
Classification: LCC G156.5.H47 H355 2022 (print) | LCC G156.5.H47 (ebook)
  | DDC 338.4/791--dc23
LC record available at https://lccn.loc.gov/2021031859
LC ebook record available at https://lccn.loc.gov/2021031860

This book is published in the IGI Global book series Advances in Hospitality, Tourism, and the Services Industry (AHTSI) (ISSN: 2475-6547; eISSN: 2475-6555)

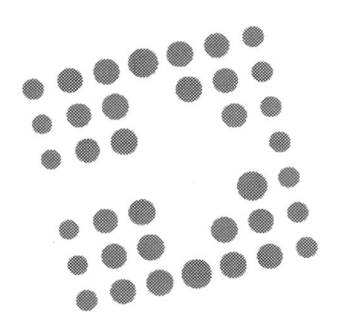

Advances in Hospitality, Tourism, and the Services Industry (AHTSI) Book Series

Maximiliano Korstanje
University of Palermo, Argentina

ISSN:2475-6547
EISSN:2475-6555

MISSION

Globally, the hospitality, travel, tourism, and services industries generate a significant percentage of revenue and represent a large portion of the business world. Even in tough economic times, these industries thrive as individuals continue to spend on leisure and recreation activities as well as services.

The Advances in Hospitality, Tourism, and the Services Industry (AHTSI) book series offers diverse publications relating to the management, promotion, and profitability of the leisure, recreation, and services industries. Highlighting current research pertaining to various topics within the realm of hospitality, travel, tourism, and services management, the titles found within the AHTSI book series are pertinent to the research and professional needs of managers, business practitioners, researchers, and upper-level students studying in the field.

COVERAGE

- Tourism and the Environment
- Sustainable Tourism
- Food and Beverage Management
- Customer Service Issues
- Leisure & Business Travel
- Cruise Marketing and Sales
- Casino Management
- Destination Marketing and Management
- Service Management
- Service Design

IGI Global is currently accepting manuscripts for publication within this series. To submit a proposal for a volume in this series, please contact our Acquisition Editors at Acquisitions@igi-global.com or visit: http://www.igi-global.com/publish/.

Titles in this Series

For a list of additional titles in this series, please visit: http://www.igi-global.com/book-series/advances-hospitality-tourism-services-industry/121014

Planning and Managing the Experience Economy in Tourism
Rui Augusto Costa (GOVCOPP, University of Aveiro, Portugal) Filipa Brandão (GOVCOPP, University of Aveiro, Portugal) Zelia Breda (GOVCOPP, University of Aveiro, Portugal) and Carlos Costa (GOVCOPP, University of Aveiro, ortugal)
Business Science Reference • © 2022 • 407pp • H/C (ISBN: 9781799887751) • US $195.00

Food Safety Practices in the Restaurant Industry
Siti Nurhayati Khairatun (Universiti Putra Malaysia, Malaysia) Ainul Zakiah Abu Bakar (Universiti Putra Malaysia, Malaysia) Noor Azira Abdul Mutalib (Universiti Putra Malaysia, Malaysia) and Ungku Fatimah Ungku Zainal Abidin (Universiti Putra Malaysia, Malaysia)
Business Science Reference • © 2022 • 334pp • H/C (ISBN: 9781799874157) • US $215.00

Prospects and Challenges of Community-Based Tourism and Changing Demographics
Ishmael Mensah (University of Cape Coast, Ghana) and Ewoenam Afenyo-Agbe (University of Cape Coast, Ghana)
Business Science Reference • © 2022 • 300pp • H/C (ISBN: 9781799873358) • US $195.00

Challenges and New Opportunities for Tourism in Inland Territories Ecocultural Resources and Sustainable Initiatives
Gonçalo Poeta Fernandes (CITUR, Polytechnic Institute of Guarda, Portugal)
Business Science Reference • © 2022 • 295pp • H/C (ISBN: 9781799873396) • US $195.00

Rebuilding and Restructuring the Tourism Industry Infusion of Happiness and Quality of Life
André Riani Costa Perinotto (Universidade Federal do Delta do Parnaíba, Brazil) Verônica Feder Mayer (Federal Fluminense University, Brazil) and Jakson Renner Rodrigues Soares (Universidade da Coruña, Spain & Universidade Estadual do Ceará, Brazil)
Business Science Reference • © 2021 • 330pp • H/C (ISBN: 9781799872399) • US $195.00

Handbook of Research on the Impacts and Implications of COVID-19 on the Tourism Industry
Mahmut Demir (Isparta University of Applied Sciences, Turkey) Ali Dalgıç (Isparta University of Applied Sciences, Turkey) and Fatma Doğanay Ergen (Isparta University of Applied Sciences, Turkey)
Business Science Reference • © 2021 • 906pp • H/C (ISBN: 9781799882312) • US $415.00

701 East Chocolate Avenue, Hershey, PA 17033, USA
Tel: 717-533-8845 x100 • Fax: 717-533-8661
E-Mail: cust@igi-global.com • www.igi-global.com

Editorial Advisory Board

List of Contributors

Table of Contents

Detailed Table of Contents

Eunice Ramos Lopes, Instituto Politécnico de Tomar, Portugal
Paulo Alexandre Santos, Instituto Politécnico de Tomar, Portugal
João Tomaz Simões, Instituto Politécnico de Tomar, Portugal

This chapter aims to reveal the growing importance of cultural tourism, reflected in the cultural heritage of cities and its concrete tourist experience in a digital age society. One of the stipulated goals was to understand the existing relationship between tourist and cultural appropriation with the mediation of the digital. The chapter focuses on a city located in the central region of Portugal and followed a quantitative and qualitative analysis methodology. The digital era has been fostering a fundamental capital in the promotion of the existing resources in cities to attract visitors and to reveal the tourist experiences developed in the visited tourist destinations. The main conclusion is the interactions that take place between heritage, tourist experience and ICT implying connections that tourists spontaneously comment through online resources. When making their comments they end up demarcating their tourist experience classifying it according to their expectations in relation to the heritage resources they visit.

Yunus Topsakal, Adana Alparslan Türkes Science and Technology University, Turkey
Onur Icoz, Aydın Adnan Menderes University, Turkey
Orhan Icoz, Yasar University, Turkey

Technology has transformed the tourism industry over time, and today, this transformation has accelerated with digitalization and Industry 4.0. With the application of new generation technologies that shape Industry 4.0 to the tourism industry, the concept of smart tourism has entered the literature and digitalization has accelerated in tourism. It can be said that digital transformation has had an impact on tourist experiences. In this context, this chapter aims to describe the potential impact of digital transformation on the tourist experience. For this purpose, the following topics and concepts will be studied: uses of Industry 4.0 technologies in tourism industry, digital transformation, tourist experiences, and effects of digital transformation on tourist experience.

Business enterprises have gained leverage through artificial intelligence (AI) in the tourism and hospitality industry. The roots of the concept and its link with big data environment has drawn a lot of interest from researchers. The employment of technology has increased economic viability of tourism enterprises due to the efficiency, effectiveness, and transparency it creates for tourism and hospitality organizations. The chapter views the emergence of smart tourism in destination management in accordance with sustainable tourism concept and evaluates the issue both in supply side and demand side of tourism. Moreover, it aims to discuss the use of such a paradigm. If the destinations have a viable ground for motivational change to adapt, this philosophy will also be high lightened. For this reason, value creation will be evaluated in accordance with cost-benefit assessment.

Chapter 4

In this study, a review of the future of VR technologies for digital tourism alternatives will be presented. The general purpose of the research is to contribute to VR technologies, which are developing and integrating with new systems with each passing day from the point of view of providing a general perspective in tourism. VR application information to deepen understanding of the scope of the digital future of tourism alternatives will be presented in a systematic framework. In general, VR technologies express the behavioral experiences of individuals in virtual environments. When tourism and VR technologies are combined, the composition of the product in which these virtual experiences are directed towards a purpose emerges. Every new development that occurs from a technological point of VR technology will make it possible to be used in every field of tourism. The contribution of this research is to provide suggestions for future studies as well as practical implications for the tourism industry regarding VR systems, which are among the digital tourism alternatives.

Chapter 5

The last point reached in today's technology revolutions is the fourth level industrial revolution. This revolution is called Industry 4.0. Many new generation technologies such as the internet of things, artificial intelligence, internet services, augmented reality, smart objects, and business sector branches have been included in human life. Industry 4.0 technologies have an effective use in many areas of our lives. The tourism sector, which is in constant interaction with people, is also affected by these technological developments. For this reason, businesses should perceive the internet of things well and need to introduce various applications to their businesses to provide the best service to their potential customers. In this chapter, after giving information about the internet of things, cultural heritage, digital transformation practices in the tourism sector, and smart tourists are discussed.

As technology affects the tourism sector as it does all sectors, smart tourism has emerged. The ultimate goal of smart tourism is to improve the efficiency of resource management, maximize competitiveness, and increase sustainability through technological innovations and practices. The digital transformation of the tourism sector, especially in recent years, has greatly affected the tourist experience by completely changing the supply-demand interaction in the industry. The spread of information and communication technologies, the development of the web, and the growing technology use skills in the population, in general, have helped increase the level of self-organization of tourists and have led to smart tourists. This new tourist profile created by smart tourism technologies frequently benefits from technology before, during, and after their travels.

Big data enriches the experiences of cultural tourism visitors as well as being used in the management, presentation, and protection of cultural heritage. Technological innovations and the production of more data every day have increased the importance of data and information in competition in the tourism industry. For this, since it is seen that it is important to examine issues such as big data and analytics in cultural tourism, this book chapter presents the studies in the related research area in detail. As a result of the systematic literature review, data types that can be the basis for the formation of big data in cultural tourism and technologies that can support are specified. In addition, researches on cultural heritage and cultural tourism were examined, and theoretical and practical suggestions were presented.

Underwater cultural heritage and deep diving are important attractions for tourism. Using cutting-edge technology tools for cultural heritage became more important for tourism destinations. The purpose of this chapter is to evaluate the use of virtual reality (VR) and augmented reality (AR) in tourism from the perspective of cultural heritage and deep diving. This chapter will contribute to the literature to show a new way of sustainable tourism. Commercial diving to an underwater heritage site a is popular touristic activity. Sometimes shipwreck recovery can be hazardous for cultural heritage. The review results indicate that these underwater cultural heritage sites need to be protected for sustainable tourism development. Virtual tours contribute to the sustainability of cultural heritage. On the other hand, treasure hunting trips and recreational diving may cause damage to the archaeological sites. Underwater cultural heritage sites should be protected for sustainable tourism. VR and AR applications can be used to promote a touristic destination by tourism marketers for experimental marketing.

This chapter will initially introduce the concept of intangible cultural heritage. After establishing the relationship between intangible cultural heritage and tourism, changes in intangible cultural heritage components will be expressed through the digitization and COVID-19 processes. "Digital intangible cultural heritage," "digital cultural heritage," "digital safeguarding" concepts will be described because they attracted great attention during this time. Additionally, the other aspect of the research is the use of digital applications to safeguard the intangible cultural heritage. In the final part, the pilot projects concerning the safeguarding and promoting the intangible cultural heritage implemented by the Ministry of Culture and Tourism of Turkey will be discussed.

This chapter aims to give information about how the digitalization process is using technologies suitable for today's conditions in the transmission of cultural heritage to future generations and its preservation, what methods are being employed, the concept of digital heritage, the developments that took place and the projects that were carried out in the digitization of cultural heritage. In addition, it is also aimed in this chapter to evaluate the cultural heritage sites within the framework of this new understanding and to examine how these areas can be redefined with new technical possibilities. At this point, after reviewing the literature about the cultural and digital heritage, the importance of cultural heritage is referred to in detail. Finally, a case study is conducted by the authors via compiling the V-must.net website established to develop virtual museums, blog comments, and academic studies carried out in respect to this project.

With the rapidly developing technology, the tourism experience has started to enrich and innovative/personalized services and competitive advantage in tourism have started to gain importance. Smartness in tourism refers to tourism activities supported by technology. This study aims to classify the current literature on the subject of smartness in tourism. First of all, a qualitative research was carried out by explaining the concepts of smart tourism and smart tourism destination in the literature. Within the scope of the research, a qualitative research was conducted using systematic literature review method. In the research, 264 academic publications related to smartness in tourism were analyzed in terms of the destinations where they were applied, the scope of the journals they were published, the language of the publication, the methods and approaches, and suggestions were made for further studies.

This chapter aims at understanding the Rooster of Barcelos (Galo de Barcelos) as local intangible cultural heritage, being the case study of a research leading to the proposal of this explanatory model for developing and implementing tourism creative destinations. The Barcelos Rooster is the result of two ancestral customs of this territory, namely handicrafts and the Jacobin legend of the miracle of the rooster. These two customs, eternalized in time, were associated by the intervention of tourism. In addition, handicrafts, the Camino de Santiago, gastronomy (roast rooster from this legend), wine (vinho verde) and the traditional market, and heritage associated with the Rooster of Barcelos emerge as the main tourist attractions of this territory. It might be concluded that the Rooster of Barcelos, as one of the main symbols of Portuguese tourism, local heritage, and tourism product honey pot has the potential to leverage the sustainable development of this territory as a creative tourist destination.

Chapter 13

This chapter aims to know the experience of the public in the use of virtual visits to museums. For that, the authors developed a survey and gave it, through social media, between December 22, 2020 and January 5, 2021. Ninety-one valid responses were obtained. The results indicate that although most respondents say that they are aware of the possibility of carrying out virtual visits to museums, very few carry out this type of visit. One of the advantages most mentioned by respondents was the fact that it is not necessary to leave the house for the visit.

In this chapter, the author explores the application of the internet of things (IoT) in museums. IoT technology typically combines physical objects with hardware and software. For museums, the simplest example is 3D virtual tours, which need a computer and an internet connection. Today, however, museums have become more complicated with virtual and augmented technologies. Virtual and augmented reality devices, such as virtual reality (VR) glasses, and related applications, such as Google Arts and Culture, provide interactive museum tour experiences for visitors. For all these experiences, they only need to connect to the internet with their devices. Virtual museum tours range from history to space technologies. This chapter explores the nature of using IoT technologies in cultural tourism, especially in museums.

Chapter 15
Digital Communication in Museums and Museological Spaces: Diagnosis of Baixo Alentejo, Portugal 271

Victor Figueira, Polytechinc Institude of Beja, Portugal & CiTUR, Portugal

João Arnedo Rolha, Polytechnic Institute of Beja, Portugal

Bruno Barbosa Sousa, Polytechnic Institute of Cávado and Ave (IPCA), Portugal & CiTUR, Portugal

SMM (social media marketing) aims to produce content that users share in their various social media applications in order to increase brand exposure and broaden customer reach. There are numerous marketing techniques to apply in social media in order to involve the customer, some of which have costs and others that do not. Digitization was a real challenge for any museum, requiring cautious and well-planned action to be successful. In this sense, the nature of social networks demands the adoption of a constructivist perspective, that is, a perspective that involves affirmations of knowledge based on individual and collective experiences. Presently, being present in social networks presents itself as a high value advantage, allowing the exposure of the brand, product, or idea at a low cost to a large audience. This chapter aims to systematize some relational marketing best practices that are identified in the museums and museum spaces in "Baixo Alentejo" (Portugal). Specifically, some examples of relational marketing in terms of communication will be identified and analysed.

Chapter 16
Using New Tools to Attract Visitors to Museums and Heritage Sites 291

Lia Bassa, Budapest Metropolitan University, Hungary

Melanie Kay Smith, Budapest Metropolitan University, Hungary

Árpád Ferenc Papp-Váry, Budapest Metropolitan University, Hungary

This chapter discusses the ways in which museums and heritage sites have adapted to the need to create technology-based experiences in recent decades culminating in the intensive online provision during the COVID period. The aim of both online and live visits should be as inclusive as possible of different audiences, stimulating interesting, rich, multi-cultural experiences that encourage re-visitation or at least recommendation to others. Ideally, sites should create meaningful as well as memorable experiences. This process includes several aspects and is very complex requiring the combination and harmonisation of education, heritage interpretation, marketing skills, and local initiatives. This chapter uses case studies to analyse the extent to which museums are rising to these challenges above, including the principles of the so-called 'new museology', the need for more innovative technology to create visitor experiences, and COVID-19.

Chapter 17
An Exploratory Study on the Role of Websites in Gastronomy Museum Dialogic Communication 311

Eray Polat, Gumushane University, Turkey

Rooted in the dialogic communication model, the main objective of this study is to analyse the interactivity level of websites of gastronomy museums in Turkey. Thus, it will be unearthed whether gastronomy museums are progressing towards more dialogic or are staying informative systems with the relationship with their target audience. Via content analysis on websites, two questions were sought: (1) What kind of tools are utilized to present information? (2) What tools or resources are utilized on websites to interact with virtual visitors? The data were analysed by comparing private and public museums. The results indicate that the websites of gastronomy museums in Turkey have a medium level of interaction in presenting information and a low level of interaction in the tools available to virtual visitors. And thus, it can be said that museums use their websites for one-way communication, which are not fit for dialogic communication. This is valid for both private and public museums. Managerial implications were discussed, and future research directions are presented.

Chapter 18
Mahmut Baltaci, Silifke Tasucu Vocational School, Selcuk University, Turkey
A. Celil Cakici, Tourism Faculty, Mersin University, Turkey

Factors such as technological developments, increasing population growth, social opportunities, the right to paid vacation, increase in leisure time, increase in income level have provided tourism development and rapid acceleration in recent years. In addition, factors such as culture and education level have gained importance in the development of tourism. The prominence of cultural values in the destination management is proportional to the satisfaction of the tourists coming to the region. The aim of this chapter is to explain and give knowledge about the "serendipitous cultural tourist" typology, which is one of the types of tourists who do not come for cultural motivations. Although tourists do not participate in tourism for cultural purposes, the fact that they visit cultural attractions causes them to be named as cultural tourist type. Destination management organizers providing better service and more detailed information to the tourists improve the likelihood of them visiting the destination again.

Chapter 19
Aruditya Jasrotia, Amity University, Noida, India

Virtual reality, also known as computer-based reality, is an advanced technology that has the capability to upsurge destination accessibility and to increase the popularity of lesser-known destinations. The objective of the current study is to understand the latest trends in virtual reality and to discover the future scope of implementation of virtual reality in the tourism industry across the world. The potential and the employment of virtual reality is not entirely understood and comprehended by many destinations. The present study identifies that there is a continuous development in popularity of virtual reality, and it is the need of the hour today. This disruptive technology has led to the phenomenon of virtual tourism, which gives people a preview and understanding of what they will experience if they visit a place physically. Virtual reality is becoming an outstanding way to showcase information and to gain relevant response from the tourists to enhance the services and overall tourist experience in the tourism destination.

Chapter 20
Murat Koçyiğit, Necmettin Erbakan University, Turkey
Büşra Küçükcivil, Necmettin Erbakan University, Turkey

The development of digital communication technologies and the increase in the use of digital platforms by individuals have increased the tendency towards touristic activities. Cultural tourism, which is carried out for certain purposes within the diversity of tourism, is one of the rising tourism activities of recent times. In this context, tourism management benefits from social media platforms as a tool in marketing their products and services related to cultural tourism. Social media platforms are important here for two aspects. The first of these is the use of social media by tourism management in the marketing of products and services by organizing individual and mass cultural tours and communicating with target audiences. The second is that individuals benefit from social media platforms in participating in cultural tourism and decision making. In this direction, it is important to evaluate conceptually the relationship between social media platforms, one of the most important digital communication technologies, and cultural tourism.

The rise of social media allowed greater people participation online. Platforms such as Facebook, Twitter, Instagram, or TikTok enable visitors to share their thoughts, opinions, photos, locations. All those interactions create a vast amount of data. Social media analytics, as a way of application of big data, can provide excellent insights and create new information for stakeholders involved in the management and development of cultural tourism destinations. This chapter advocates for the employment of the big data concept through social media analytics that can contribute to the management of visitors in cultural tourism destinations. In this chapter, the authors highlight the principles of big data and review the most influential social media platforms – Facebook, Twitter, Instagram, and TikTok. On that basis, they disclose opportunities for the management and marketing of cultural tourism destinations.

New technological requirements and needs of today's world are forcing cities to transform into smart cities and smart destinations in tourism cases. Smart destinations are focused on enhancing the tourist experience while also supporting the decision-making process, sustaining effective usage of resources, and maintaining sustainability. Big data has started to act as a reliable resource that assists these processes and offers alternative solution methods. Improvements in the usage of big data within the framework of smart destination management systems will also provide new insights and understandings about heritage sites and their management. Istanbul and the Sultanahmet region, which were included in the UNESCO World Heritage List, form the main domain of this chapter. This research aims to reveal any significant differences between Istanbul Wi-Fi data, Sultanahmet Wi-Fi data, and Istanbul Arrivals data. Kruskal-Wallis Test was conducted for comparing these data sets for 28 countries, and recommendations are presented.

The aim of the chapter is to provide recommendations for cities that are aiming to reposition themselves in the post-pandemic period in terms of image, product development, and the attraction of different segments of visitors. It is aimed at those readers who seek to understand the role that digital tools can play in the information provision and promotion of cities, especially for younger tourists who may have been more attracted by night-time activities in the pre-COVID period and who could be redirected to other activities or areas in future strategies. A case study of Budapest is presented that is typical of a European cultural tourism destination that has also suffered from overtourism in recent years. Primary data is used to identify tourists' preferred activities in the destination as well as their choice of digital tools for finding information and optimizing experiences. Both theory and primary data are used to make recommendations for repositioning cultural cities post pandemic with the assistance of appropriate digital tools.

Chapter 24

The tourism industry includes air, sea, and land transportation; food supply chain; accommodation; entertainment; recreation; etc. services. Hence, tourism businesses are proposing changes, and post-COVID tourists will not be the same as pre-COVID ones. Innovative solutions regarding safety and hygiene measures as well as the proximity of medical facilities will be of key importance in meeting the tourist expectations and sustainability of the tourism industry. In addition, it is possible to state that the COVID-19 pandemic has affected the whole world. This situation caused the economic balances of countries to deteriorate and some sectors to be adversely affected. The most affected sector is undoubtedly the tourism industry. Innovation has gained more importance in the tourism industry in the context of sustainability of tourism with the COVID-19 pandemic process. In this context, this chapter aimed to examine how innovation can contribute to the sustainability of post-COVID tourism.

Chapter 25

In today's competitive global environment, cities are striving to stand out and be attractive to investors, visitors, and residents. City branding is an important tool to differentiate the city from its competitors and to be preferred by visitors. Every city has its own characteristics resulting from its historical development, the influence of its geography, and its social, cultural, and economic past. Therefore, the tangible and intangible cultural heritage of cities is vital for their promotion and branding. This study aims to show the importance of their cultural heritage, which is the most fundamental feature to differentiate themselves from their competitors in city branding. It is emphasized that the cultural events organized in cities or the assets specific to cities, most of which are on the UNESCO World Heritage List, have a significant impact on city branding. In addition, the chapter explains the impact of digitalization, which is one of the most important developments of our time, on city branding and cultural heritage.

Preface

Digital communication opens up new opportunities and challenges in the field of tourism, in particular cultural tourism. The convergence of territory, culture, data and new media allows the generation of new experiences using the Internet of Things (IoT), augmented reality, virtual reality, mixed reality, giving tourists the opportunity to have an in-depth experience of the place they visit. Smart and sustainable tourism is a contemporary challenge that must be constantly investigated as it is a dynamic process (Quevedo, Samaniego, Vinueza, & Merino, 2022).

The tourist brings with him a smartphone that can be enhanced so that the tourist experience is enriched (Lan et al., 2021). Thus, researchers in the field of tourism, but also in history, archeology, literature. digital humanities, media studies, culture and communication should take advantage of this opportunity to propose new ways of reaching more and better content and experiences for tourists.

The cultural tourist is someone who is open and interested in understanding in detail the places and heritage he visits, so he is a motivated user of services and platforms that improve his tourist experience. Algorithms and big data, geolocation and the internet of things make it possible to generate personalized scenarios for the tourist to explore the socio-cultural territory, valuing the material and immaterial cultural heritage (Zhou, Tian, Peng, & Su, 2021).

Tourism investors, as well as stakeholders in territories with a tourist vocation, must be particularly attentive to the opportunities that the convergence between new media and tourism can generate. Namely, the role that digital media can play in building the brand of tourist places (Huertas, Moreno, & Pascual, 2021).

This book has a wide target audience, considering that it is important for students, professors and researchers in the field of tourism, who should consider in depth the role of digital technologies in the tourist experience and in the cultural tourism experience. Essentially all tourism is cultural tourism, and, in the contemporary world, all tourist experiences benefited from the contribution of digital communication, before, during and/or after the tourist experience. This is also a very important book for decision makers and stockholders in the area of tourism, because digital technologies (big data, data analysis, artificial intelligence) are essential tools for management and decision making, but also because they need to know the new trends in tourist experiences, so they can make informed decisions.

ORGANIZATION OF THE BOOK

The book is organized into 25 chapters. A brief description of each of the chapters follows:

Chapter 1, "Cultural Tourism and the Tourist Experience in the Digital Era," aims to understand the relationship between tourist and cultural appropriation with the mediation of the digital. The study is carried out in a city in central Portugal and concludes that the connections that tourists comment spontaneously through online resources are a reflection of the tourist's interactions with heritage and ICT, implying the tourist experience as a whole.

Chapter 2, "Digital Transformation and Tourist Experiences," is about how digitization has transformed the field of tourism and had an impact on tourism experiences. Namely, the uses of Industry 4.0 technologies in the tourism industry, digital transformation, tourism experiences and the effects of digital transformation on the tourism experience.

Chapter 3, "Smart Tourism in Destinations: Can It Be the Way Forward?" focuses on the emergence of smart tourism in the management of destinations in the context of sustainable tourism, namely with artificial intelligence and big data, as well as dealing with and evaluating the issue of the supply and demand side of tourism. Analyzes the paradigm shift and the assessment of value creation according to the cost-benefit assessment.

Chapter 4, "The Future of Digital Tourism Alternatives in Virtual Reality," focuses on the use of Virtual Reality technologies to enrich the digital tourism experience. Emphasizing that when tourism and Virtual Reality technologies are combined, the composition of the product emerges in which these virtual experiences are directed towards a purpose. Suggestions for future studies are presented, as well as practical implications for the tourism industry in relation to Virtual Reality systems, in the context of digital tourism.

Chapter 5, "The Internet of Things and Cultural Heritage," emphasizes the role of digital technologies, namely the internet of things, as promoters of a new dynamic in the tourism industry, in which the interaction between people and technological development must always be considered. In this context, cultural heritage, practices of digital transformation in the tourism sector and smart tourists are discussed.

Chapter 6, "Tourist Experience and Digital Transformation," presents the main objective of smart tourism: to improve the efficiency of resource management, maximize competitiveness and increase sustainability through practices and technological innovations. The digital transformation of the tourism sector has allowed the emergence of a new tourist profile, which is capable of incorporating technologies into all phases of the tourist experience: before, during and after their trips.

Chapter 7, "Understanding the Big Data and Techniques in Cultural Tourism," presents the relevance of big data in the tourism industry, namely, in cultural tourism. Big data enriches the experiences of cultural tourism visitors as well as being used in the management, presentation, and protection of cultural heritage. In addition, research on cultural heritage and cultural tourism was examined and theoretical and practical suggestions were presented, from the perspective of the relevance of issues such as big data and analytics in cultural tourism.

Chapter 8, "The Use of Virtual Reality and Augmented Reality in Cultural Heritage and Deep-Diving Destinations," evaluates the use of virtual reality (VR) and augmented reality (AR) in tourism from the perspective of cultural heritage and deep diving, from the perspective of sustainable tourism. The analysis highlights that these underwater cultural heritages need to be protected for sustainable tourism development and VR and AR applications can be used to promote the tourism destination by tourism marketers.

Chapter 9, "Intangible Cultural Heritage in the Digitalization Process: The Case of Turkey," begins with the presentation of the concept of intangible cultural heritage, it continues with the relationship between intangible cultural heritage and tourism. Considers the use of digital applications to safeguard intangible cultural heritage. Ending with the presentation of pilot projects related to the safeguarding and promotion of intangible cultural heritage implemented by the Ministry of Culture and Tourism of Turkey.

Chapter 10, "Digital Cultural Heritage," presents the process of digitization and transmission of cultural heritage to future generations and its preservation, namely, the methods, the developments that have taken place and the projects carried out in the field of digitization of cultural heritage. A case study is presented with a focus on the development of virtual museums, blog comments and academic studies carried out regarding this project.

Chapter 11, "A Comprehensive Systematic Literature Review About Smartness in Tourism," presents a bibliographical research on technology, tourist experience, intelligence in tourism with a focus on the topic of smartness in tourism. Through the systematic literature review method, 264 academic publications related to intelligence in tourism were analyzed, and the results were presented.

Chapter 12, "Creative Destinations and the Rooster of Barcelos (Galo de Barcelos)," presents the Rooster of Barcelos (Galo de Barcelos-Portugal) as local intangible cultural heritage, being the case study of an investigation that leads to the proposition of this explanatory model for the development and implementation of creative tourist destinations. They conclude that Galo de Barcelos, as one of the main symbols of Portuguese tourism and local heritage, has potential for the sustainable development of the territory, as a creative tourist destination.

Chapter 13, "Cultural Tourism: Use of Virtual Visits to Museums," aims to learn about the experience of the public in the use of virtual visits to museums, through research on social networks, between December 22, 2020 and January 5, 2021. The results indicate that although most respondents claim to be aware of the possibility of carrying out of virtual visits to museums, very few do. Respondents presented as an advantage of virtual visits the fact that it is not necessary to leave their homes for the visit. At the time of the Covid-19 pandemic, in which people had to stay at home, the trend and interest in virtual visits was unleashed.

Chapter 14, "Cultural Tourism Internet of Things and Smart Technologies in Museums," presents the application of the Internet of Things (IoT) in cultural tourism, especially in museums. Notably, virtual and augmented reality devices such as virtual reality (VR) glasses and related apps such as Google Arts and Culture provide visitors with interactive museum tour experiences. For all these experiences, they just need to connect to the internet with their devices.

Chapter 15, "Digital Communication in Museums and Museological Spaces: Diagnosis of Baixo Alentejo (Portugal)," systematizes some good relational marketing practices that are identified in museums and museological spaces in Baixo Alentejo (Portugal). Whereas in the contemporary context social media marketing aims to produce content that users share across their various social media applications in order to increase brand exposure and extend customer reach. This digitization scenario is a real challenge for any museum.

Chapter 16, "Using New Tools to Attract Visitors to Museums and Heritage Sites," reviews the ways in which museums and heritage sites have adapted to the need to create technology-based experiences in recent decades, culminating in intensive online offerings during the COVID-19 period. To make the visits appealing it is necessary to consider several aspects: education, heritage interpretation, marketing skills and local initiatives. The chapter uses case studies to analyze the extent to which museums are facing the need for more innovative technology to create visitor experiences, and more recently, COVID-19.

Chapter 17, "An Exploratory Study on the Role of Websites in Gastronomy Museum Dialogic Communication," analyzes the level of interactivity of websites of gastronomy museums in Turkey, in order to understand if gastronomy museums are moving towards more dialogic or remain information systems with the relationship with their target audience. An analysis was carried out to understand what kind of tool is used to present information and what tools or resources are used on websites to interact with virtual visitors. The results indicate that the websites of gastronomy museums in Turkey present a medium level of interaction in the presentation of information and a low level of interaction in the tools available to virtual visitors.

Chapter 18, "Serendipitous Cultural Tourist," presents and explains the typology of the "random cultural tourist"/ "serendipitous cultural tourist", who is one of the types of tourists who do not travel for cultural reasons. However, these tourists visit cultural attractions which causes them to be named as a type of cultural tourist by chance. Given this situation, it is essential to provide a better service and more detailed information to tourists by the organizers of the destination management, helping them to visit the destination again.

Chapter 19, "Virtual Reality the Groundbreaking Smart Technology for Tourism and Service Industry," presents the latest trends in virtual reality, with a focus on the implementation of virtual reality in the tourism industry around the world. It emphasizes that there is a continuing development in the popularity of virtual reality leading to the phenomenon of Virtual Tourism, which gives people a preview and understanding of what they will experience if they visit a place physically. In short, virtual reality is changing the tourist experience.

Chapter 20, "Social Media and Cultural Tourism," underlines, on the one hand, the importance of social media for tourism management in the marketing of products and services, organizing individual and mass cultural trips and communicating with the target audience; on the other hand, individuals benefit from social media platforms by participating in cultural tourism and decision-making. In short, a conceptual assessment of the relationship between social media platforms, one of the most important digital communication technologies today, and cultural tourism is carried out.

Chapter 21, "Social Media Analytics: Opportunities and Challenges for Cultural Tourism Destinations," advocates the use of the big data concept through social media analytics that can contribute to visitor management in cultural tourism destinations. In this regard, we highlight big data principles and review the most influential social media platforms – Facebook, Twitter, Instagram and TikTok. From the analysis carried out, they conclude that there are opportunities for the management and commercialization of cultural tourism destinations.

Chapter 22, "Integrating Big Data to Smart Destination Heritage Management," focuses on the idea of smart destinations, which rely on big data to improve the tourist experience, decision making and promoting the efficient use of resources while maintaining sustainability. Namely, use of big data within the framework of intelligent destination management systems that will provide new insights and understandings about historic places and their management. The investigation focused on Istanbul and the Sultanahmet region, which were included in the UNESCO World Heritage List.

Chapter 23, "Post-Pandemic Re-Positioning in a Cultural Tourism City: From Overtourism to E-Tourism," presents recommendations for cities that intend to reposition themselves in the post-pandemic period in terms of image, product development and attraction of different visitor segments. A case study of Budapest is presented, typical of a European cultural tourism destination that has also suffered from over-tourism in recent years. Aiming to identify tourists' favorite activities, choosing digital tools to find information and optimize experiences.

Chapter 24, "Innovation in Sustainability of Tourism After the COVID-19 Pandemic," focuses on the changes that the COVID-19 pandemic situation has had in the tourism industry that includes air, maritime and land transport, food supply chain, accommodation, entertainment, recreation, etc., services. This new scenario highlights how innovation gained more importance in the tourism industry in the context of tourism sustainability with the Covid-19 pandemic process, with the objective of examining how innovation can contribute to the sustainability of tourism after COVID-19.

Chapter 25, "Cultural Heritage and Digitalization in City Branding," focuses on the importance of the city's brand as a means to differentiate itself and be attractive to investors, visitors and residents, through its specific characteristics that come from its historical development, the influence of its geography and its social, cultural and economic background, namely, with regard to tangible and intangible cultural heritage. The investigation presented aims to show the importance of cultural heritage, cultural events and how digitalization impacts the branding and cultural heritage of the city.

This set of chapters provides a broad overview of the challenges facing Digital Communications, the Internet of Things, and the Future of Cultural Tourism.

The development of digital technologies and the dynamics of tourists' desires are strongly related, making this area of investigation very challenging.

Lídia Oliveira
University of Aveiro, Portugal

REFERENCES

Huertas, A., Moreno, A., & Pascual, J. (2021). Place branding for smart cities and smart tourism destinations: Do they communicate their smartness? *Sustainability (Switzerland)*, *13*(19), 10953. Advance online publication. doi:10.3390u131910953

Lan, F., Huang, Q., Zeng, L., Guan, X., Xing, D., & Cheng, Z. (2021). Tourism Experience and Construction of Personalized Smart Tourism Program Under Tourist Psychology. *Frontiers in Psychology*, *12*, 691183. Advance online publication. doi:10.3389/fpsyg.2021.691183 PMID:34367015

Quevedo, L., Samaniego, N., Vinueza, P., & Merino, K. (2022). Analyzing Trends in Academic Papers about Sustainable Development and Smart Tourism using Text Mining. In *Smart Innovation* (Vol. 252). Systems and Technologies. doi:10.1007/978-981-16-4126-8_23

Zhou, X., Tian, J., Peng, J., & Su, M. (2021). A smart tourism recommendation algorithm based on cellular geospatial clustering and multivariate weighted collaborative filtering. *ISPRS International Journal of Geo-Information*, *10*(9), 628. Advance online publication. doi:10.3390/ijgi10090628

Acknowledgment

The editor would like to acknowledge the help of all the people involved in this project and, more specifically, to the authors and reviewers that took part in the review process. Without their support, this book would not have become a reality.

First, the editor would like to thank each one of the authors for their contributions. Our sincere gratitude goes to the chapters authors who contributed their time and expertise to this book.

Second, the editor wishes to acknowledge the valuable contributions of the reviewers regarding the improvement of quality, coherence, and content presentation of chapters. Most of the authors also served as referees; we highly appreciate their double task.

Lídia Oliveira
University of Aveiro, Portugal

Chapter 1
Cultural Tourism and the Tourist Experience in the Digital Era

Eunice Ramos Lopes
Instituto Politécnico de Tomar, Portugal

Paulo Alexandre Santos
Instituto Politécnico de Tomar, Portugal

João Tomaz Simões
ⓘ https://orcid.org/0000-0003-3923-5555
Instituto Politécnico de Tomar, Portugal

ABSTRACT

This chapter aims to reveal the growing importance of cultural tourism, reflected in the cultural heritage of cities and its concrete tourist experience in a digital age society. One of the stipulated goals was to understand the existing relationship between tourist and cultural appropriation with the mediation of the digital. The chapter focuses on a city located in the central region of Portugal and followed a quantitative and qualitative analysis methodology. The digital era has been fostering a fundamental capital in the promotion of the existing resources in cities to attract visitors and to reveal the tourist experiences developed in the visited tourist destinations. The main conclusion is the interactions that take place between heritage, tourist experience and ICT implying connections that tourists spontaneously comment through online resources. When making their comments they end up demarcating their tourist experience classifying it according to their expectations in relation to the heritage resources they visit.

INTRODUCTION

In cultural tourism and in the tourist experience that occurs in tourist destinations chosen by tourists, there is a set of factors that vary according to specific characteristics of that destination. These factors include cultural heritage (tangible and intangible) and natural heritage. Integrating culture are also

DOI: 10.4018/978-1-7998-8528-3.ch001

architectural heritage, arts, gastronomy, sports, education, pilgrimages, handicrafts, storytelling, and city life (UNWTO, 2004). In cultural tourism and the tourist experience there are factors that convey the social reality of a given community, this being constituted by heritage. The cultural heritage of a region or community is composed of a set of tangible and intangible manifestations which are intrinsic to it. It comprises knowledge, beliefs, art, laws, habits, and other abilities acquired by man as a member of a society. It encompasses all the tangible and intangible achievements produced by humanity, from artefacts to beliefs (UNWTO, 2004).

The development of cultural tourism and the experiences associated with them has been having a significant impact and according to the Organization for Economic Cooperation and Development (OECD, 2009), there are elements that justify it. On the demand side, there is the growing interest in culture; the desire for direct and immediate experiences; the extension of forms of mobility which creates greater access to other cultures; ageing populations in developed countries; growing levels of cultural capital, resulting from the increasing level of education and growing appreciation of intangible culture. On the supply side: the emergence of new regions with a distinct identity; the aspirations to project a differentiating external image; the growing offer of culture and tourism thanks to new information and communication technologies; the development of cultural tourism to stimulate employment and investment and as a growing and quality market.

Cultural tourism explores the uniqueness of a destination, based on the enhancement and preservation of heritage, and can be presented in two formats: tangible (examples: museums, monuments, historic sites, archaeological spaces, military spaces, etc.) and intangible (examples: traditions, festivals, rituals, music, etc.). It focuses on the movement of people seeking essentially cultural motivations. Cultural tourism provides entertainment, self-knowledge, and general culture, allowing it to satisfy the needs of tourists looking for new and unique experiences.

Tourists make their choices according to the experiences that the territory offers them or the existing cultural resources for cultural enjoyment (Roque, 2015). In this sense, cultural tourism products must be elaborated to lead for the fulfilment of tourist experiences, developing a tourism service that includes an emotional connection with the existing cultural resources (Sukanthasirikul & Trongpanich, 2016).

Portugal, due to its historical, gastronomic, literary, and artistic heritage is considered a destination of excellence and historical and cultural authenticity of national and international scope, supported by the sites classified as World Heritage Sites and by the diversified existing material and immaterial historical and cultural heritage. Within the scope of the tourism system, the nature of tourism activity turns out to be a complex set of interrelationships that evolve dynamically. Human behavior, the use of resources, the interaction between people and the relations of man with the environment are fundamental elements of the tourism system (Neves, 2012). The tourist experience in tourist destinations is fundamental to the attractiveness and development of cultural tourism. The experience is understood as a reality as a product or service, so it is not an indifferent construct (Pine & Gilmore, 1998). Tourism experiences encompass a set of memorable activities that comprise emotions and senses (Mitchell, at al 2000). Emotion and emotional experience can lead to personal change (Tarssanen & Kylänen, 2007).

Here, too, comes the importance of the authenticity of the place where the experiences take place, as the development of experiences is molded according to each community (Weyermuller et al., 2015). Cultural tourism and tourism experiences in the "digital age" have a strong impact on decision-making (Katsoni, 2015), and it is pertinent in this study to link these two themes.

Anchored in cultural tourism and tourist experiences, the connection of these two vectors is based on the digital age. The promotion of tourist destinations through digital information has transformed the media in the tourism sector, representing almost entirely the basis of all travel planning.

In the dynamics of tourism activity, the tourist demand for a particular product or service ceases to be, and begins to incorporate personal choices, cultural heritages, and sensations ((Dalton, Lynch & Lally, 2009), and there are eight vectors that may influence tourist demand (Table 1). These factors may influence tourists in their choice of tourist destination.

Table 1. Vectors of influence on tourism demand

Vector	Tourism demand - influences
Socioculture	Social attitudes delimit individual motivations, since they represent the beliefs and notions that people acquire throughout their lives and the social, economic, and cultural group they belong to.
Economical	The state of the economy where tourists live influence their decision-making and purchasing power, conditioning their choice.
Demographical	The composition of the household, age and qualifications of the tourist condition the selection of a destination.
Geographical	The climatic conditions play a decisive role in the choice of a destination.
Pricing	The economic power of tourists restricts the cost of their trips. Price is a constantly changing variable in tourism as it varies according to the cost of travel fees to certain countries and the level of inflation in the destination area.
Mobility	Tourists travel in line with their personal mobility, i.e., according to changes in their personal, professional and social lives.
Governmental	Governments intervene in the tourism market by imposing their laws and regulations to safeguard the welfare of their populations.
Communication	The media, through mass communication, expose possible tourist destinations, making them attractive through multiple promotion strategies.

Source: elaborated by the authors. Adapted from Middleton (2001).

The tourist experience can be evaluated through the comparison between tourists' expectations and the stimuli resulting from the interaction between the tourist and cultural offer of the destination visited. Tourism experience is the result of visiting a given tourist destination in a multidimensional dimension based on the willingness and ability of the tourist to be influenced by physical and/or human interaction dimensions (Walls et al., 2011). Tourist experiences can be classified into four categories (Table 2).

Table 2. Classification of tourist experiences

Experiences Category	Experience Rating
Entertainment Experience	Experiences in which tourists participate passively. The connection to the event is one of absorption.
Education experiences	Experiences that tend to involve more active participation. Tourists are more absorbed in the event than immersed in the action.
Circumvention experiences	Experiences that can teach as much as educational experiences or entertain as much as entertainment experiences. They imply greater immersion on the part of tourists.
Aesthetic experiences	Experiences where tourists are immersed in the activity or environment, but with little significant influence.

Source: elaborated by the authors. Adapted from Pine & Gilmore (1998).

The tourism experience adds value to the tourism product translating into a competitive advantage for tourism (Buhalis, 1999; Getz & Brown, 2006; Lawn, 2004). To encompass the tourist experience as a competitive advantage is fundamental to the provision of innovative tourism products, since tourists evaluate their experience as a whole and associate tourist destinations to the tourism product acquired in that destination (Buhalis, 1999). Tourism experiences are fundamental given that the success of a tourism destination is measured by its offer and the actions practiced affecting the enjoyment of tourism experiences (Bornhorst, Ritchie & Sheehan, 2010). The tourist experience based on cultural tourism can be understood through a set of criteria (Figure 1).

Figure 1. Criteria to consider in the tourist experience
Source: Prepared by the authors. Adapted from Soares (2009).

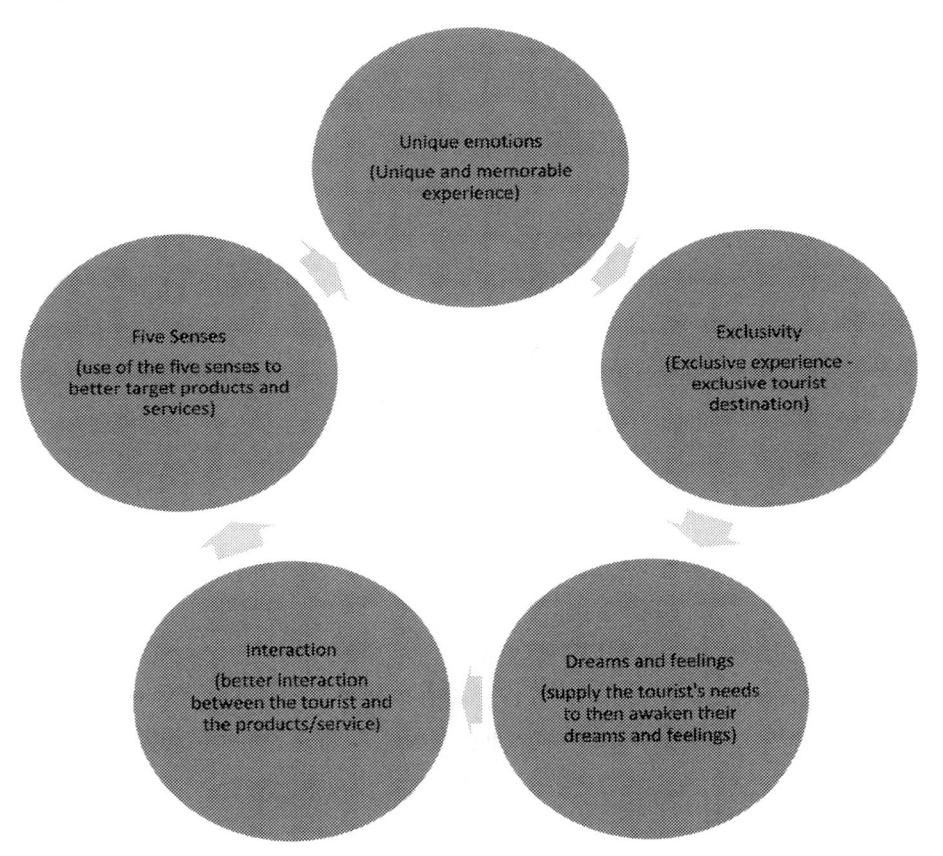

The relevance of cultural tourism and tourist experience in tourist destinations explains the relevance of this dynamic, even more in the digital age. The heritage resources combined with tourism activities promote a strong component of development in the territories, allowing tracing more consistent guidelines in economic, social, cultural, and environmental aspects, providing experiences to visitors and local people who interact in the cultural dynamics of the territories (Lopes, et al, 2020: 11). Therefore, the aim of this study is to understand the interactions that take place between heritage, tourist experience and ICTs and what these connections imply before the enjoyment of heritage resources (tangible and intangible). The case study of incidence of this study, is in the city of Tomar, holder of a diverse set of heritage resources (cultural and natural), geographically located in central Portugal.

TOURIST DESTINATIONS IN THE DIGITAL ERA

The digital approach applied to cultural tourism and tourist experiences arising from the visitation of a tourist destination are important means of understanding these destinations and the perception of the importance of using these tourist experiences in the digital age. The current relationship of tourism with other heritage activities also involves the ability to enter the environments of digitalization, taking advantage of the benefits for its dissemination in the markets and in attracting visitors.

ICTs are bringing about changes in society through the possibility of creating new ways of producing, communicating, and managing. They provide the development of the Internet, allowing the flow of information. The use of ICT in tourism has had an impact on both supply and demand. There have been several changes at the level of tourism activity operation, with advantages for tourism sector organizations and advantages for visitors to tourism destinations (Table 3).

Table 3. ICT use: benefits for organizations and tourists

Benefits for tourism sector organizations	Benefits for tourists in tourist destinations
Fast and effective communication with customers.	Greater efficiency in obtaining information (destinations, flights, accommodation, catering, exchange rates, events, etc.).
Manage the distribution system quickly and efficiently.	Access to information with greater variety and depth.
Enable the flow of information to be improved.	Greater control of choice.
To improve response times.	Ability to prepare, organise and directly purchase products and services.
Capacity to increase competitiveness.	Easier and quicker booking.
Business opportunity creation.	More confidence (there are no intermediaries).
Ability to adapt to the specific characteristics and needs of clients.	No travel is required.
Development in promotion.	They create their own experiences.
Strengthening and creation of strategies.	
Promotion of the tourist offer available.	
Providing market information.	

Source: prepared by the authors.

In general, all information systems in the tourism sector are necessary for decision-making and proper tourism management, and the online availability of complete and up-to-date market information is of vital importance. Currently, it is possible to witness a growing investment by tourism and cultural sector organizations and tourists in ICT for the distribution, marketing and acquisition of tourism products and services. The way a product, service or destination is communicated is a key factor in tourism because it allows creating unique experiences, thus satisfying the needs of tourists of a particular tourist destination. ICT emerges as a driver and fundamental in-service innovation (Lovelock & Wirtz, 2006). In the connection between the tourism sector and ICTs, virtual tourism is associated, which consequently creates experiences such as virtual trips. It is understood that in the "virtual trips", tourists assume a participatory role consequently seeking the development of new tourism products. It means that all tourism products and services within the cultural tourism segment and the technological sector, should involve innovation and creativity, enabling tourists to participate in experiences that enrich them in a memorable way. The emotional issue can be related to the emotion that certain tourist places convey. The place of memory in contemporary society is now widely discussed and, once again, virtual tourism could help preserve this very memory. Virtual tourism is seen as an innovative practice, which has emerged in technology and in the way, tourism is viewed. It provides changes at psychological level in the individual with visual, auditory, or even sensory elements, bearing in mind that experiences always cause certain emotions in those who experience them. Virtual tourism is more than seeing a destination through a computer, tablet, or smartphone, it is the ability to instigate desires and needs to seek and know more, and ultimately purchase a tourism product or service (Guttentag, 2010). Virtual travel enables tourists to enjoy an experience without being physically present at the location, providing an opportunity to satisfy their desire to disconnect from everyday life. They enable tourists to enjoy a product or service in the comfort of their home, in an innovative way and without financial expenses. Virtual travel is considered positive, not only because there is no need for actual travel, but also because it encompasses several activities that, in a traditional way, would not be carried out - that is, it allows a greater reach and growth by the target audience. ICTs have enabled the development of organizations contributing to the competitiveness of tourist destinations, caused by the increase in communication and access to information (Bhatt et al., 2005). Information on demand/tourists, tourist destinations, accessibility, prices, geographical information and climate, transport, are fundamental for understanding the relationship between tourists and the appropriation of heritage resources in tourist destinations. The information on these aspects is essential to meet the preferences of tourists, to improve the tourist offer of tourist destinations.

The tourism sector contributes to the development and competitiveness of destinations, being relevant to analyze the cultural image of the tourist destination. Tourism communication should be based on experiential strategies, to provide experiences that meet the needs and preferences of tourists (Smith, 2003). Tourism promotion through ICT is undoubtedly a key factor in the tourism sector. Most tourists are fans of new technologies and use the Internet intensively (Machado & Almeida, 2010). In this field, the trend of fruition in relation to culture and heritage resources gains more impact by the acquisition of tourism products and services based on the experience occurred in tourist destinations.

The approach in this study refers to virtual tourism and its contribution to tourist destinations. This perception of virtual tourism is important, including the opinions of tourists visiting the city of Tomar. The importance of digitization in the selection of travel and tourist destinations is highlighted.

METHODOLOGY

Tourists use ICT to constantly share their experiences and impressions of the places they visit, competing in this way with promotional materials and strongly influencing the decision-making process in the choice of the tourist destination to visit. One of the basic questions in tourism research on tourist destinations with strong impetus on heritage resources (as is the case of the historical city of Tomar, geographically located in Central Portugal), is to understand what motivates individuals and families to visit heritage cities, from their own testimonials or online travel comments. To understand the interactions that take place between cultural heritage, tourist experience and ICTs and what these connections imply before the fruition of the heritage resources (tangible and intangible) existing in the historical city of Tomar, this chapter was guided by three main research questions:

Q1: What perceptions and types of comments do tourists refer to about their tourist experience when visiting the heritage resources of the city of Tomar (Portugal)?

Q2: What is the incidence (season, months of the year), if any, of the highest number of comments in terms of geographical distribution?

Q3: What kind of appreciation and classification is attributed to the assets visited?

Tourists more than ever in the digital age, rely on strategies of choice through the internet and for tourist consumption this medium is fundamental in the decisions of the choice of tourist destinations. The comments of online travel, ends up reflecting the reviews and comments on the experience of the tourist himself, as well as on the tourist destination visited, itself.

In Tomar, exist a lot of different heritage. This is one of the oldest places in Portugal and was the Templars Headquarter for 200 years. We find a series of different heritage in this city, from romans to Swabians, Arabic and Jews, this is a culturally rich place. But, to answer the questions above, it was decided to collect the comments from the virtual platform TripAdvisor about the three most visited heritage resources in the destination Portugal (the Castle of Tomar where the Convent of Christ, the Synagogue and the Church Santa Maria do Olival are located), specifically in the city of Tomar (Figure 2).

Figure 2. Tomar City (Portugal)
Source: Google maps, 2020

The Synagogue of Tomar is the only Renaissance proto-Hebrew temple in our country. The quadrangular plant and vaulted cover based on columns and cordons embedded in the walls denote eastern influences. It was built in the 19th century. XV and closed in 1496, at the time of the expulsion of the Jews from Portugal, after which it was converted into prison, in the 19th century. XVII is referred to as Hermitage of St. Bartlomy and in the 19th century. XIX was used as a haystack, barn, grocery store and storage room. Only the year 1921 would give him back the possibility of reading lost dignity when it was classified as a National Monument. Samuel Schwarz a Polish Jew and hebrew culture researcher saved her from the chaotic state she was in, acquiring it in 1923 and donating it in 1939 to the Portuguese state for the Luso-Hebrew Museum of Abraham Zacuto. Excavations from 1985 showed water heating structures and hoists, proving the existence of a room for purifying baths. In the Middle Ages, like other merchants, the Jews also roamed the country, where their passages through Tomar would not go unnoticed to Infante D. Henrique, who stimulated his fixation in Rua da Judiaria. The most far-backreference in time to this community dates to 1315, and its contribution to the growth of Tomar in the 14th, 15th and 16th centuries is indisputable (Cm-Tomar, 2019b *apud* Lopes *et al.,* 2020).

The Church of Santa Maria dos Olivais was built "in the twelfth century, was the place of the Order of the Templars in the country, having served as pantheon of the masters of the Order. Faced with the extinction of the Order, this church became the head of the Order of Christ, becoming the matrix of all churches of the Portuguese Empire, with honors of The Cathedral. Classified as a National Monument since 1910, it is one of the most emblematic examples of Gothic art in Portugal having served as a model for the churches of three naves built until the Manueline period" (Olivais, 2019a apud Lopes et al, 2020).

The Castle of Tomar/Convent of Christ in Tomar is a monument dating from the 12th century, it was designated by UNESCO, in 1983, as a World Heritage Site. Characterized by various architectural styles, its main attractions are the Charola (original Church of the Templars) and the Chapter Window (Manueline style), decorated with marine motifs alluding to the Discoveries. The city of Tomar has about 40,677 inhabitants, and spreads over an area of 351 km^2. The municipality consists of 16 parishes and is located in the district of Santarém, in the province of Ribatejo. The streets and squares of the centre of Tomar are organized following a chessboard pattern. Scattered throughout the city there are many interesting houses with Renaissance, Baroque, and romantic facades (CM-Tomar, 2019a *apud* Lopes et al, 2020).

The data were collected using a web bot developed specifically for this study which at the end generated a report with several qualitative and quantitative variables such as the visitor's country of origin, a rating from 1 to 5 (on the heritage resource visited) and a descriptive comment on their tourist experience from 2012 to 2021. Based on the size of the results (n=750), it was decided to apply a mixed results analysis method in the present study. A descriptive statistical analysis was carried out, to identify the date of the visit (in this case the writing of the comment will be more appropriate), the country of origin, which of these three resources they visited and their appreciation score of the experience, expressed on a numerical scale (1-5). It was also decided to deepen this relationship between the numerical attribution of the value of the experience and the description of the experience (comments). To this end, a qualitative analysis of the comments left by visitors was carried out using the MaxQda® software, where a text mining type study was designed. Through the analysis of this text (especially the adjectives used), it was possible to ascertain and describe the feeling generated by the experience, especially regarding the city of Tomar.

The questions in the figures allow a quick comparison not only between heritage resources, with their frequency and distribution over the time they were collected, allowing the moment of evaluation to be compared and correlated with the grade given, which places received the most votes, what was the predominant classification and also the nationalities.

WEB BOT

Data are the basis of the knowledge generation process (Figure 3), so they are of vital importance in the business development of companies. TripAdvisor provides an API that allows access to some of its data, but given its importance, it does not allow access for some purposes, including research (TripAdvisor, 2021). However, all the information that is published on the Internet can be collected using other tools.

Figure 3. Knowledge pyramid (Ackoff, 1989)
Source: authors, 2021

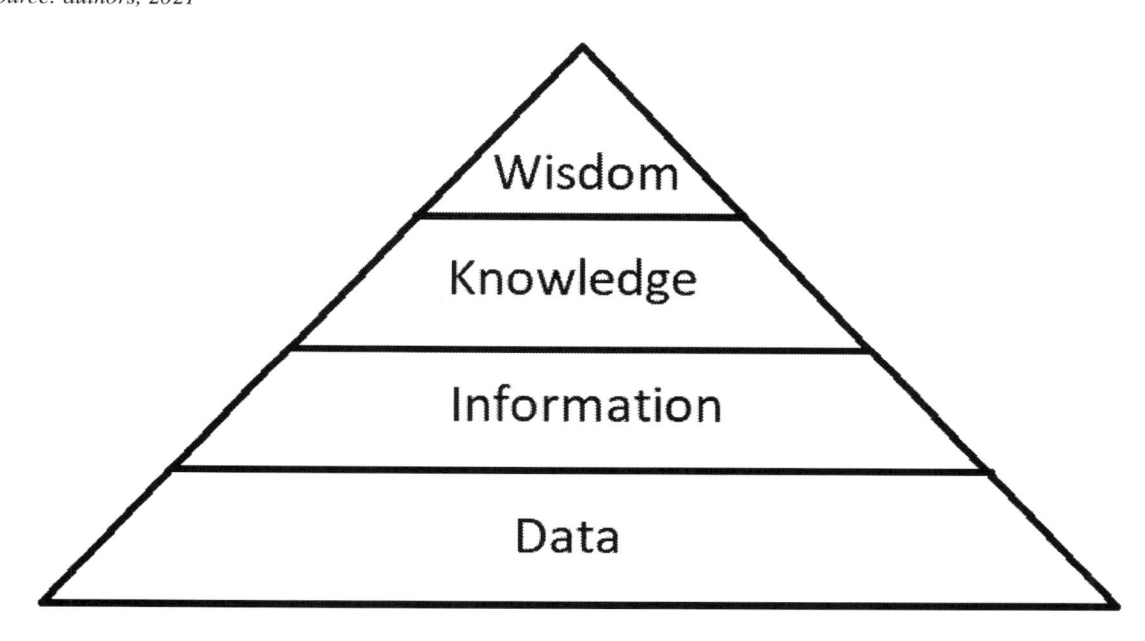

A Web Bot is a tool that simulates the behavior of a human being in a browser in order to automate tasks. A Web Bot was specifically developed to collect the information required for this work. This Web Bot was developed in Java programming language using Selenium WebDriver. The main disadvantage of this approach is that we are dependent on the HTML generated by the developers of the TripAdvisor site, so when they redesign the page our Web Bot may stop working. But certainly, the time spent developing this Web Bot was much less than the time that would be spent by a manual collection.

RESULTS PRESENTATION

The origin of the tourists to the three Tomar attractions under study, and who left a total of 750 comments on TripAdvisor, is geographically distributed over 22 locations (Graph 1)

Figure 4. Comments: geographical distribution
Source: authors, 2021

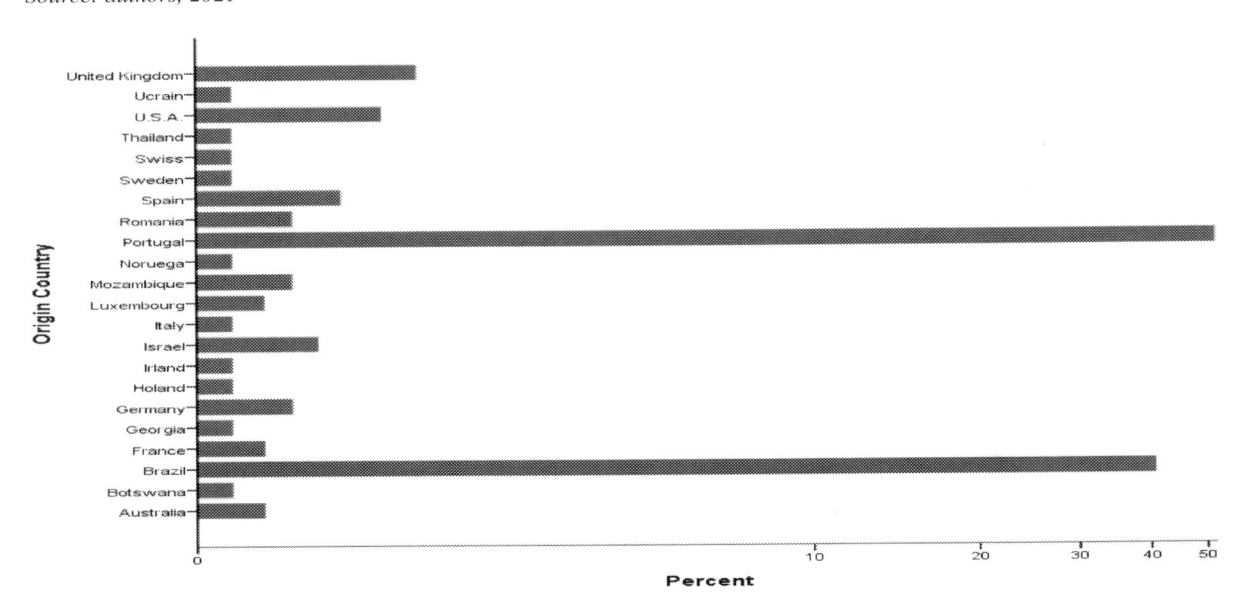

The results appear balanced when comparing the number of European visitors (56.2%) with those from outside the E. U. (43.8%). Each of these values is spread across 14 and 8 locations respectively, with Portugal (51.7%) and Brazil (40.6%) standing out.

The analysis reveals that Tomar Castle was the heritage resource that gathered the most comments (Graph 2). It was followed by the Synagogue and the Santa Maria do Olival Church.

Figure 5. Patrimonial resource
Source: authors, 2021

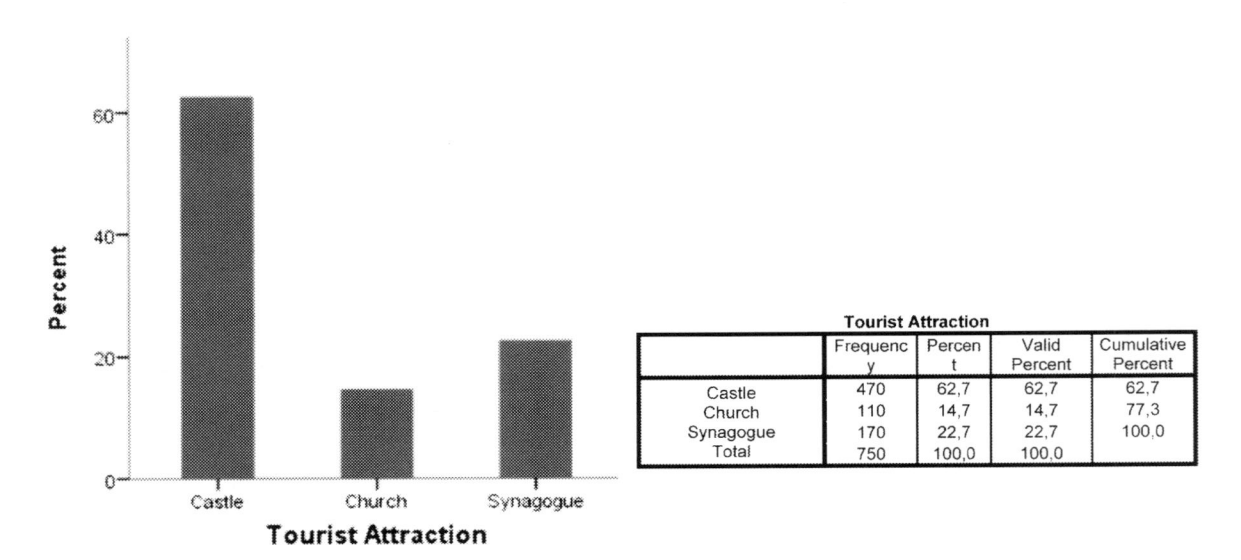

Tourist Attraction				
	Frequency	Percent	Valid Percent	Cumulative Percent
Castle	470	62,7	62,7	62,7
Church	110	14,7	14,7	77,3
Synagogue	170	22,7	22,7	100,0
Total	750	100,0	100,0	

We gather 470 comments about Tomar Castle which corresponds to a percentage of 62.7%. The remaining attractions are divided by the remaining 37.4% with 14.7% for the church and 22.7% for the Synagogue, which correspond respectively to 110 and 170 comments. The 733 comments validated regarding the date of their elaboration, these started in June 2012 and were collected until May 2021. As for the temporal distribution (Graph 3), the multimodal data is justified in relation to the peaks of the known tourist seasonality.

Figure 6. Temporal distribution
Source: authors, 2021

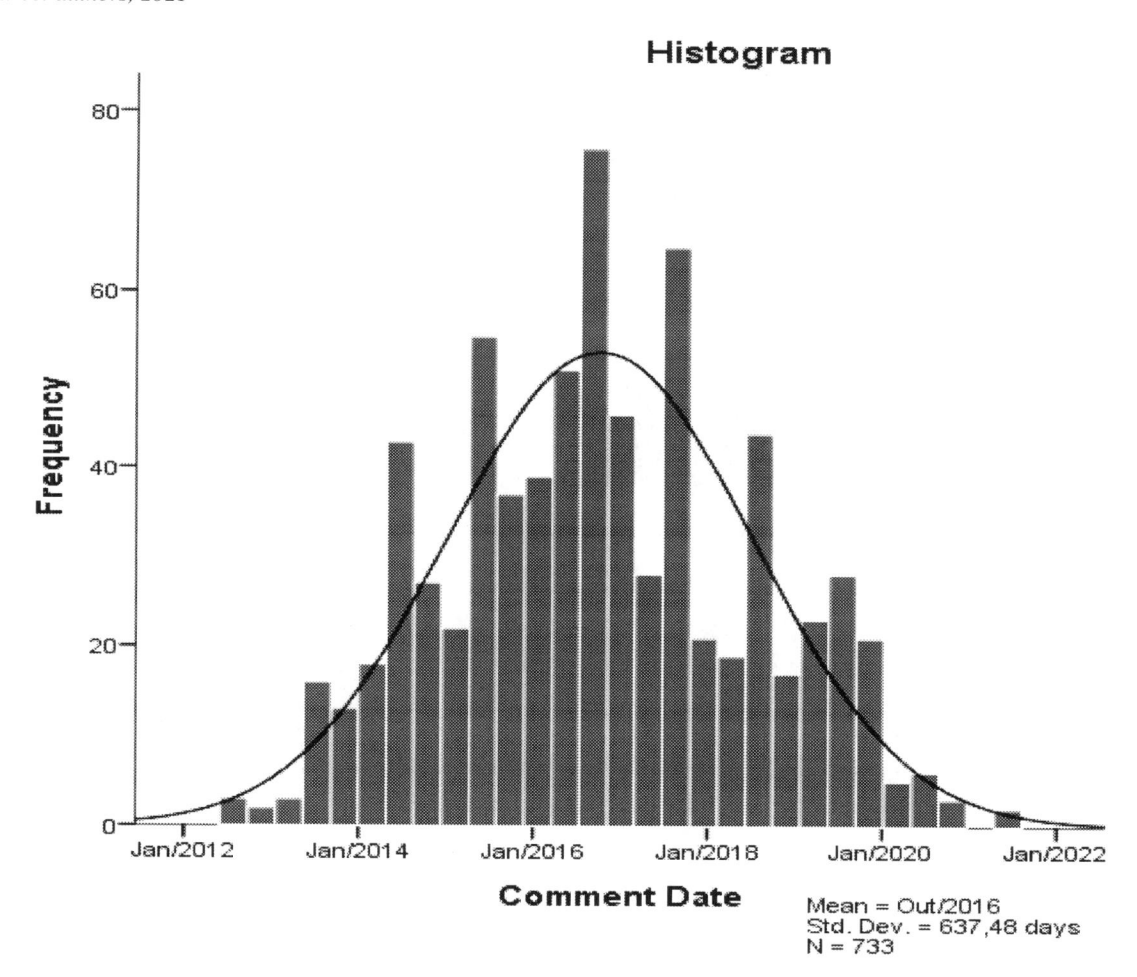

In this case, the highest number of comments took place in the month of October 2016. It is normal that from January 2020 onwards some outliers may occur, mainly related to the travel disruption caused by Covid-19. It is also possible to observe the date of the comments and the classification assigned to each of the three heritage resources (Graph 4), which allows a multivariate observation to be carried out and quite relevant conclusions to be drawn.

Figure 7. Comments and classification
Source: authors, 2021

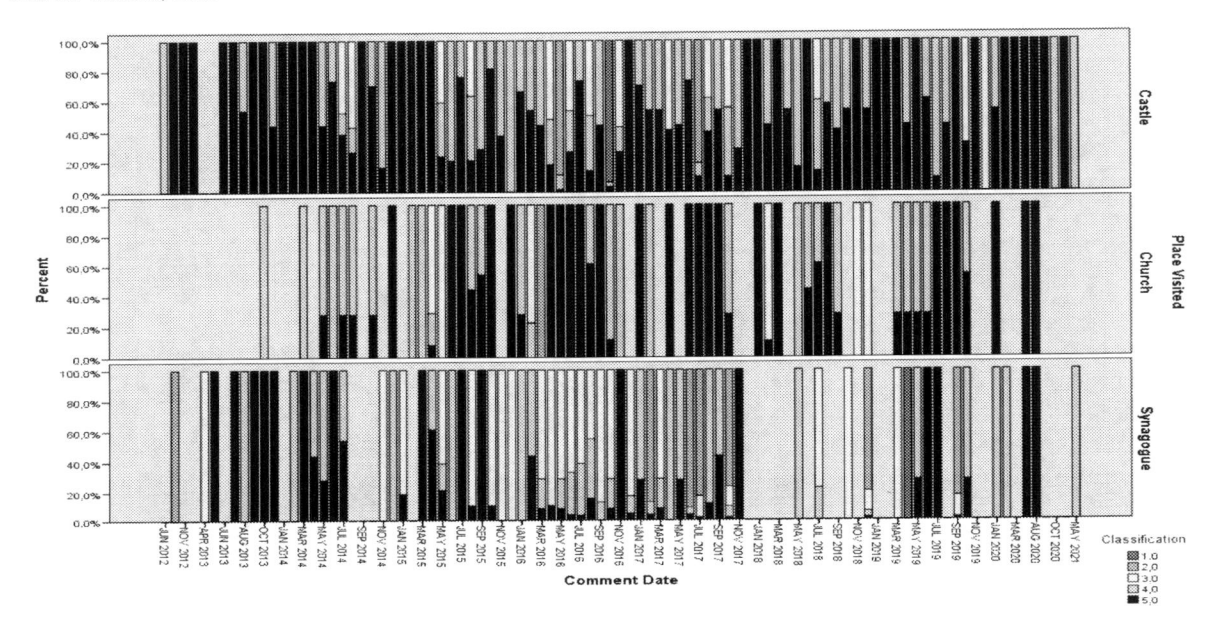

It is understood that the only two level 1 value ratings were assigned to Tomar Castle in October 2016 and the Synagogue in April 2019. The first related to the charging for the car park that the tourist indicates should be free and the second, referring to the Synagogue, related to the management of expectations in the heritage resource, where the tourist mentions that he was expecting more and better. As for rating levels 2 (1.5%), except for one vote for the Church, the remaining ten are divided between the Synagogue with eight and Tomar Castle with two. Levels 3 represent 7.7% of the total recorded, and their pre-eminence is clearly visible in the column for the Synagogue. Levels 4 and 5 are the most relevant in terms of frequency. Both represent around 90.5% of the total number of ratings obtained. This analysis allows one to perceive that the tourist experience was more in line with the tourists' expectations. It should be noted that the Synagogue presents some irregularity in comparison with the other heritage resources that is related to the closure of the heritage resource for rehabilitation works and construction of its Interpretive Centre.

After applying some techniques to the written comments of tourists, such as text mining for example, lexical synthesis and lemmatization, the results were obtained that may somehow deepen the interpretation of the results obtained in the quantitative analysis. The most repeated word throughout the 750 comments, referenced through the lexical search "church" and "beautiful" are the most highlighted. Both words appear about 168 times (Table 2).

Table 4. Most repeated word

Word	Word lenght	Frequencie	%	Ranking	Comments	Comments %
Church	6	110	4,65	1	69	70,41
Beautiful	9	58	2,45	2	38	38,78
Tomar	5	46	1,95	3	40	40,82
Templars	8	45	1,90	4	39	39,80
Order	5	41	1,73	5	21	21,43

Source: authors, 2021

From this analysis a word cloud was created (Scheme 1) to make the qualitative framing of this analysis more perceptible. Despite being the heritage resource with the lowest number of comments (14.7%), the word "church" was the most written. This is interesting since the comments related to Tomar Castle represent about 62.7% (470).

Figure 8. Word cloud
Source: authors, 2021

Through the search made by the "most used term", it was possible to see the set of most used words (Table 3).

Table 5. Set of most used words

Word Combination	Word	Frequencie	%	Ranking	Documents	Documents %
Of the Order	3	36	0,38	1	20	20,41
Of the Templars	3	31	0,33	2	28	28,57
Of the Order of	4	28	0,30	3	19	19,39
The Order of	3	28	0,30	3	19	19,39
Of the Order of the	5	24	0,25	5	18	18,37
Order of the	3	24	0,25	5	18	18,37
The Order of the	4	24	0,25	5	18	18,37
Order of the Templars	4	16	0,17	8	14	14,29
The Order of the Templars	5	16	0,17	8	14	14,29
The Church of	3	14	0,15	10	12	12,24
One of the	3	12	0,13	11	12	12,24
Church of Santa	3	11	0,12	12	9	9,18
Church of Santa Mare	4	11	0,12	12	9	9,18
City of Tomar	3	11	0,12	12	10	10,20
Master of the	3	11	0,12	12	9	9,18
Of Santa Mare	3	11	0,12	12	9	9,18
The 12th century	3	11	0,12	12	11	11,22
Of the Temple	3	10	0,11	18	6	6,12

Source: authors, 2021

The word cloud allows a more synthetic visual analysis, helping to achieve the objectives proposed in this study. There is also an affectionate connection to the history and cultural heritage linked to the Templar heritage (Scheme 2).

It is recognized that the major link to heritage resources is the theme of the Knights Templar. The Order of the Templars was established in Portugal in the century XII, to support the first Portuguese kings in the Christian Reconquest and continue the Crusades.

The Castle of Tomar, inspired by the fortifications of the Holy Land, was founded in the city of Tomar, in 1160. About two centuries later, in 1312, the Order was extinguished by Pope Clement V. In Portugal, the Order of Christ was created, maintaining the crusade spirit during the epic Discoveries.

Over time, in the culture of the Crusades, knights came to be known as Knights of the Temple of Solomon or simply Templars. They became defenders of the Christian states of the Holy Land. The Order will be maintained thanks to the numerous gifts given to them in Europe, grouped and methodically administered in Commendations (Templários, ConventoCristo.gov.pt).

It should be noted that in both word clouds elaborated for a more synthetic analysis of the analyzed results, it is possible to consider that the city of Tomar as a tourist and cultural destination, incorporates

Figure 9. Set of words cloud
Source: authors, 2021

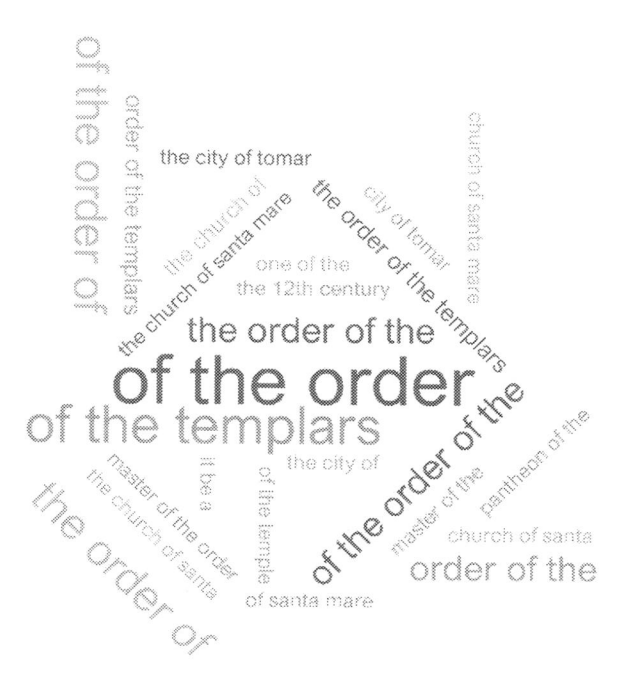

its cultural and tourist identity left by its founder, D. Gualdim Pais. The history surrounding the city of Tomar, the legacy of the Order of the Temple and the Order of Christ, the diversity of its global and intangible heritage, are elements referenced by tourists who express their tourist visitation experiences, recording them on online platforms.

FUTURE RESEARCH DIRECTIONS

In future research and consequent analysis, it is intended to carry out a comparative analysis between existing heritage resources. There are other heritage resources in the region of Tomar, in addition to those mentioned in this study, with tourist value and which will be considered in an upcoming thematic approach.

This chapter is a first exploratory study that is intended to open the way to new and better opportunities for exploration, using both the methodology and the similar objectives applied to other heritage sites and resources.

It is also pointed out as a future line, the inclusion of more recent international studies on the digital age in tourism.

CONCLUSION

In this study on cultural tourism and tourist experience in the digital age, it was possible to realize the existing dynamics between tourist and cultural appropriation with the mediation of the digital. The digital era has been intensifying the mobility of travel to visit various and specific tourist destinations according to the specific motivations of tourists. Tourist experiences developed in the visited tourist destinations are often recorded online through online resources. These comments are fundamental for understanding tourists' perceptions of the heritage resources (cultural and natural) visited.

Tourists, when making comments, point out their expectations in relation to the experiences they have in tourist destinations. They spontaneously classify and evaluate the heritage resources they visit, linking a set of information of "tourism consumption", fundamental for the implementation of tourism development strategies.

The tourist experience in the digital age recorded online allows not only to assess tourists' expectations regarding the heritage resources they visit, but also to compare the stimulated connections between cultural tourism, heritage, and ICT. It means comparing the tourism and cultural offer against the expectations (positive and negative). This comparison is advantageous at the level of the competitiveness of tourist destinations, as it may allow the creation and development of innovative tourism products that better adapt to the expectations of tourists, while considering those of residents as well. The tourist experience in the digital era allows a better analysis and understanding of the motivations and behaviors of tourists towards what they visit.

This understanding and the results perceived from it are important as tourists evaluate their experience as a whole and associate tourist destinations with the tourism product provided at the destination. The success of a tourist destination is ultimately measured by its tourism offer and in the positive and "memorable" evaluation of the experiences achieved.

Tourism promotion through ICT is undoubtedly a key factor in the tourism sector. The dynamics of tourism with heritage activities has a great impact on digitalization environments through the advantages related to the promotion of destinations and consequent tourist attractiveness.

Tourists, undoubtedly, are active users of ICT to record their comments and share them constantly their tourist experiences. By doing so spontaneously, they are active influencers of the decision-making process in the choice of visiting the tourist destination. From the testimonies or online travel comments, in addition to being able to interpret the tourist destination, it is also possible to understand the tourist seasonality of the destination, as well as the incidence of geographical distribution, nationality, and even other assessments recorded through the classification that is attributed to the heritage resources visited.

As the main contribution of this study, it is understood that it offers solutions to problems related to the theme, which relates cultural tourism with tourist experiences in the digital age. As a contribution, an attempt was made to highlight the evaluation of cultural heritage values and the experiences of tourists through the BIT.

This study also contributes to finding new and better exploration opportunities, using similar methodology and objectives applied to other heritage and resource sites. In addition, sharing experiences acquired in the destinations they visit on social platforms, which is one of the digital tools, is an important source of information for potential tourists who choose to visit this tourist destination.

More international and recent studies can also be included to provide information on the future use of these technologies. It can also be mentioned about the methods currently used to bring cultural values to tourism.

The relevance of cultural tourism and the tourist experience in tourist destinations explains the competitiveness of destinations in a digital age.

REFERENCES

Ackoff, R. L. (1989). From data to wisdom. *Journal of Applied Systems Analysis, 16*(1), 3–9.

Bhatt, G. D., & Grover, V. (2005). Types of information technology capabilities and their role in competitive advantage: An empirical study. *Journal of Management Information Systems, 22*(2), 253–277. doi:10.1080/07421222.2005.11045844

Bornhorst, T., Ritchie, J. B., & Sheehan, L. (2010). Determinants of tourism success for DMOs & destinations: An empirical examination of stakeholders' perspectives. *Tourism Management, 31*(5), 572–589. doi:10.1016/j.tourman.2009.06.008

Buhalis, D. (1999). Tourism on the Greek Islands: Issues of peripherality, competitiveness and development. *International Journal of Tourism Research, 1*(5), 341–358. doi:10.1002/(SICI)1522-1970(199909/10)1:5<341::AID-JTR201>3.0.CO;2-0

Convento de Cristo. (2021). Retrieved from: http://www.conventocristo.gov.pt

Dalton, R., Lynch, P., & Lally, A. M. (2009). *Towards an Understanding of Experience Concept Development in Tourism Service Design*. RIKON Group.

Guttentag, D. A. (2010). Virtual reality: Applications and implications for tourism. *Tourism Management, 31*(5), 637–651. doi:10.1016/j.tourman.2009.07.003

Katsoni, V. (Ed.). (2015). Cultural tourism in a digital era. In *First International Conference IACuDiT*. Springer. 10.1007/978-3-319-15859-4

Lawn, J. (2004). Innovation. *Food Management, 39*(7), 30–42. PMID:10164554

Lopes, E. R., Simões, J. T., & Nunes, M. R. (2020). Cultural Tourism and Heritage Resources: evolution of visitors to a municipality. In Heritage Tourism: The past as an experience. Pelotas.

Loverlock, C., & Wirtz, J. (2006). *Marketing de serviços: pessoas, tecnologia e resultados*. Pretice Hall.

Machado, L. P., & Almeida, A. (2010). *Inovação e Novas Tecnologias*. SPI Sociedade Portuguesa de Informação.

Middleton, V. (2001). *Marketing in Travel and Tourism* (3rd ed.). Taylor & Francis.

Mitchell, R., Hall, C. M., & McIntosh, A. (2009). Wine tourism and consumer behaviour. In *Wine tourism around the world* (pp. 115–135). Routledge. doi:10.4324/9780080521145-6

Neves, J. M. (2012). The attractiveness of Portugal as a tourist destination, by mature domestic travellers. *World Review of Entrepreneurship, Management and Sustainable Development, 8*(1), 37–52. doi:10.1504/WREMSD.2012.044486

OECD, Organization for Economic Cooperation and Development. (2009). Temple Stay Programme, Korea, The impact of culture. OECD.

Pine, B. J., & Gilmore, J. H. (1998). *Welcome to the experience economy*. Academic Press.

Roque, M. (2015). As humanidades digitais no cruzamento entre museus e turismo. *Revista Internacional de Ciências Humanas, 4*(2), 179–194. doi:10.37467/gka-revhuman.v4.748

Smith, M. K. (2003). *Issues in cultural tourism studies*. Routledge. doi:10.4324/9780203402825

Soares, T. C. (2009). *Características do Turismo de Experiência: Estudos de caso em Belo Horizonte e Sabará sobre inovação e diversidade na valorização dos clientes*. Minas Gerais–UFMG.

Sukanthasirikul, K., & Trongpanich, W. (2016). Cultural Tourism experience on customer satisfaction: Evidence from Thailand. *Journal of Economic and Social Development, 3*(1), 17–25.

Tarssanen, S., & Kylänen, M. (2007). A Theoretical Model for Producing Experiences – A Touristic Perspective. In *Lapland Centre of Expertise for the Experience Industry* (pp. 134–154). Lapland University Press.

TripAdvisor. (2021). *Request Developer API*. Retrieved from https://developer-tripadvisor.com/content-api/request-api-access/

UNWTO. (2004). *Tourism Market Trends*. World Tourism Organisation.

Walls, A. R., Okumus, F., Wang, Y. R., & Kwun, D. J. W. (2011). An epistemological view of consumer experiences. *International Journal of Hospitality Management, 30*(1), 10–21. doi:10.1016/j.ijhm.2010.03.008

Weyermuller, A., Jung, P., Rosa, M., & Kehl, L. (2015). A Indústria Criativa Verde e adaptação ambiental: O Turismo Criativo como Materialização. *Revista do Instituto de Ciências Sociais Aplicadas-Gestão e Desenvolvimento, 12*(2), 83–96.

KEY TERMS AND DEFINITIONS

API: Application Programming Interface. A way to interact with a computer application provided by the developers of the application.

Cultural Heritage: Cultural assets considered as historical and cultural testimonies of interest that can be preserved for future generations.

Cultural Tourism: Travel destinations with motivations based on cultural interest and understanding.

HTML: HyperText Markup Language. A language used in the creation of web pages.

Tourism Consumption: Products and services which are part of the tourism offer of a destination.

Tourism Destination: Places that have a set of heritage resources (cultural and natural), infrastructures and services that attract tourists.

Tourism Development: Cultural, economic, social, and environmental development strategies to meet the needs of tourists and residents.

Tourism Experience: Trips that integrate memories and emotions related to the destinations visited.

Chapter 2
Digital Transformation and Tourist Experiences

Yunus Topsakal
ⓘ https://orcid.org/0000-0003-3202-5539
Adana Alparslan Türkes Science and Technology University, Turkey

Onur Icoz
ⓘ https://orcid.org/0000-0002-0775-1451
Aydın Adnan Menderes University, Turkey

Orhan Icoz
ⓘ https://orcid.org/0000-0002-3077-8476
Yasar University, Turkey

ABSTRACT

Technology has transformed the tourism industry over time, and today, this transformation has accelerated with digitalization and Industry 4.0. With the application of new generation technologies that shape Industry 4.0 to the tourism industry, the concept of smart tourism has entered the literature and digitalization has accelerated in tourism. It can be said that digital transformation has had an impact on tourist experiences. In this context, this chapter aims to describe the potential impact of digital transformation on the tourist experience. For this purpose, the following topics and concepts will be studied: uses of Industry 4.0 technologies in tourism industry, digital transformation, tourist experiences, and effects of digital transformation on tourist experience.

INTRODUCTION

Historically, "technology" has played very crucial role in human life, and it has been driving force for socio-economic growth and development through the ages. In the course of history, human beings used variety of technological devices, means and instruments from primitive horse-pulled carts to supersonic aircrafts and spaceships for transportation and from primitive hammer to computers in order to facilitate human work and life. Nowadays, societies use the most contemporary devices, vehicles and equipment

DOI: 10.4018/978-1-7998-8528-3.ch002

including software in smart devices, as a result of technological progress. Moreover, latest technological progress permits artificial intelligence such as robots, self-controlled drones and driverless cars and other digital technologies. The word "technology" originally comes from old Greek language, as a combination of the words "τέχνη" (techno) - "craft, dexterity and handicrafts" and "-λογία" (-logy) "science", meaning "the science of craft or skill". According to this definition, all the skills, methods and processes used in the production of goods and/or services they needed and/or scientific investigation on these topics in the course of history are included into the meaning of this concept (Wikipedia, 2021).

Today, robotization, Internet of Things, smart networks technologies, 3D, big data, smart robots, smart signaling, wearable technologies, quantum computing, Internet of Services, nanotechnology, cognitive technologies, sensors, and artificial intelligence have led the fourth industrial revolution. Industry 4.0 can be said to be the intelligent automation of technology-based and cyber-physical systems (Cotteler and Sniderman, 2017). According to Hooijdonk (2015), although new generation technologies are accepted generally unnoticed by users, and the author also emphasized that they take place in almost all areas in life. Industry 4.0 technologies have started to change lifestyles and business environments by being used in areas such as business, education, and communication in our lives. Especially the Z generation consists of people who use and love technology intensively, socialize through the internet and interact with mobile technologies. This situation is expected to be even more intense in the Alpha generation, which is the generation of the next years. Although the Alpha generation, also defined as digital children and whose toys are electronic, are still in their childhood, they are very familiar with digital technologies, and it is thought that digital environments will become an inseparable part of their lives. The main reason for this is that the Z and Alpha generations were born in the digital world and internet era that are already present in social life (Bağçı ve İçöz, 2019).

The tourism industry is rapidly adopts technology. With the application of new generation technologies to tourism, the concept of smart tourism has emerged. "Smart tourism" is defined as tourism supported by initiatives provided at the destination to collect data from human minds about organizations, government institutions, physical social connections, and infrastructure. Smart tourism has a clear focus on experience enrichment, sustainability, and efficiency (Gretzel et al., 2015). Internet of Things (Gretzel, 2011), such as smart tour guide (Yüzbaşıoğlu et al., 2018), smart ticket and cards (Topsakal et al., 2018a), smart hotel management (Topsakal et al., 2018b), smart travel agency technologies and smart remote video monitoring systems are used to develop smart tourism. Industry 4.0 technologies work based on effective and efficient communication in real time.

End-user internet service systems, cloud computing, and Internet of Things are intangible resources such as human resources and information resources or technological tools. The real effects of smart technologies emerge with the combination of technology and existing infrastructure (Lopez de Avila, 2015). For example, near-field communication (NFC) is an important technology that has become very widespread in smartphones and offers many new applications for the tourism industry (Egger and Jooss, 2010). Internet of Things technology enables physical objects to be connected to each other via the Internet (machine-machine). Thus, machines can communicate and work together via remote controls (Holler et al., 2014). In addition, the use of smartphones and applications can be considered as a source of experience and reflective stage, as it provides useful information on the tourist's trip to the destination. Because smart phone users can access destination-specific applications via smart phones and send messages to tourists via technologies such as Beacon at the destination (Nabben et al., 2016). Beacon technology can locate place of tourists and send personalized messages (Toedt, 2016).

Artificial intelligent technology, on the other hand, improves accuracy and brings hotel managers a better understanding of tourist supply and demand. In this context, planning an effective marketing strategy result in human resource planning and financial management (Claveria et al., 2015). Sensors and Internet of Things installed in the hotel/around the city collect a significant amount of internal and external data such as the availability of amenities in the hotel, tourist location, weather, airport traffic, and road conditions. This information not only affect the experience of tourists, but also affects the overall satisfaction of tourists and impression (Jin et al., 2014). Considering the rapid progress of Industry 4.0 technologies that shape Industry 4.0, it can be said that these technologies will take more place in people's lives in the course of time. For example, robotic technology, which includes flying robots (drone), service robots and delivery robots, has been used in many areas of life during the COVID-19 pandemic that emerged in 2020 (Marr, 2020). Therefore, it can be said that digital transformation has had an impact on tourist experiences. In this context, this section focuses on the potential impact of digital transformation on the tourist experience. The chapter intends to constitute a review of scientific literature/state-of-the-art on the topic that constitutes the guiding thread of the analysis. The work is conceptual. First, Industry 4.0 technologies in the tourism industry are explained. Examples of the use of these technologies in tourism are given. Then, the topics of digital transformation and tourist experience was examined within the framework of the literature. Finally, the effect of digital transformation on the tourist experience has been examined and suggestions have been made.

BACKGROUND

Industry 4.0 Technologies in Tourism Industry

Internet of Things, virtual reality, NFC, mobile applications, QR codes, cloud computing, smart guidance systems, big data, artificial intelligence, smart tourist cards, the global positioning system (GPS), wearable technologies, electronic touch screens (kiosks), humanoid robots, and drones are the technologies that enable digital transformation in tourism industry. These technologies and their usage in tourism industry are briefly examined below.

Internet of Things

Internet of Things is the interconnection of everything over the Internet, without space, time, and presence limitations. Therefore, the Internet of Things enables the development of platforms that can transfer various and a wide range type of data using participatory detection systems (Gretzel et al., 2015). Internet of Things consists of radio frequency identification (RFID) tags, mobile devices, sensors, processors, smartphones, chips etc., which can collaborate and interact with each other to achieve common goals. It is the pervasive presence of various objects around us. These counted objects are connected to the Internet and therefore, the gap between digital world and real world is getting narrower everyday. In general, Internet of Things can provide advanced connectivity of systems, data sharing, object-to-object communication, physical objects, and services. For example, the control of heating, lighting, processing, and remote monitoring can be possible by Internet of Things (IoT) technologies (Zhong et al., 2017). The negative impacts of IoT will be security of data by the security breaches, and cyber-attacks (Pate and Adegbija, 2018), regulatory and technological challenges with the data sharing (Kaur and Kaur, 2016) and collection, installation cost, and replacement of devices if any, harsh uncontrolled environment, overdependence on sensors and self-sustainability of sensors (Evans, 2011).

Virtual Reality

Virtual reality is a live indirect or direct view of a new perception environment created by combining animated and computer-generated elements such as graphics, video, audio, or GPS data with the real-world, physical environment (Chavan, 2014). In the simplest definition, virtual reality is the combination of digital information with the real world (Pence, 2010). Virtual reality plays a huge role in the tourism industry. Tourists can make a virtual trip to existing or fictional places with virtual reality (Fes, 2018). Virtual reality technology contributes to tourists' experience in a smooth, simple, and interactive way. Many operations, such as making tourist hotel reservations, accessing information while at the destination, navigating touristic spots, translating spoken or written conversations and signs, and locating entertainment and food options, can be done with an application on mobile devices with virtual reality. For example, before a reservation, the tourist can visit the inside of hotel with virtual reality and book the room the likes. While navigating in the destination, tourists can increase their experience with the digital elements using virtual reality maps. Multimedia personalized interactive information is being designed to improve the virtual reality as a memorable tourist experience (Çelik and Topsakal, 2019). Virtual reality is used in tourism for promotional and marketing purposes through 360° virtual tours. The use of virtual tours developed within the scope of Tourism 4.0, especially in destination and museum visits, is increasing day by day. London British Museum and New York Metropolitan Museum, which are among the most important museums in the world, have reached large audiences and gained an international appeal by organizing virtual tours in digital environments (Durmaz et al., 2018).

Near-Field Communication

NFC is a wireless communication technology that provides data transfer in a certain distance range (Halaweh, 2013). NFC as a promising short wireless communication technology provides various services from the use of mobile phones to payment and loyalty applications to access keys to offices and homes (Coşkun et al., 2013). For example, with panels placed at bus stops and close field communication, the tourist can learn about transportation schedules, the waiting time for arrival, ticket purchases, etc. Tourists can learn about the exhibited artifacts by bringing their smart phones closer to an artifact exhibited in the museum, or they can pay with their phone at a restaurant where they dine as well (Çelik and Topsakal, 2019).

Mobile Applications

The emergence of smartphones and the development of fourth and fifth generation wireless data networks has allowed the emergence of new software. A mobile application is a software designed and developed for use on smartphones, tablet computers and other mobile devices (Purcell et al., 2010). With the applications developed through independent software, called mobile applications, smart phone users can access the services offered by the Internet from their mobile devices (Hoehle and Venkatesh, 2015). In addition to interacting with the target users expected from the mobile application, it works more like a computer program than a website. The first mobile applications were developed and presented to users for information and productivity purposes, including information such as e-mail, calendars, weather, and calculators. With the rapid development of technology and the increasing expectations of users, new mobile application categories, such as mobile games, mobile banking, mobile ticket purchasing, social media, video chat, location-based services, and mobile medical applications, have entered into our lives (Inukollu et al., 2014).

Quick Response Codes

Quick response (QR) codes offer a solution to users to provide information or access mobile services, linking to physical and virtual content (Canadi et al., 2010). QR codes are a variation of matrix codes. A QR code is a 2-dimensional barcode or matrix of dots that link to a specific web address, in the form of pixelated squares, which are loaded with strategic information for linking to reader applications for mobile devices. The use of QR codes in the tourism industry has increased because QR codes allow quick and simple interaction between the tourists and destination amenities. QR codes can enrich information boards and promotional materials, simplify processes and boost loyalty campaigns, etc. (Segittur, 2020). By scanning the QR code with their smartphones, tourists can access a variety of information about the destination or certain events in any language they want. Tourists can also access a wide range content (text, video, link, or web page) with the barcode reading mobile application. When it comes to its use in smart tourism, QR codes can be used in such areas as smart bus stops, museums, historical sites, hotels, ticketing system and much more.

Cloud Computing

The technology designed to access online data storage areas is called cloud computing. In other words, cloud computing makes it possible to store data and access the stored data at any time (Masseno and Santos, 2018). Cloud computing, that is able to reach the reliable network platforms and data stores in a certain network, also increases information sharing, which is the basis of smart tourism destinations (Yalçınkaya et al., 2018). Cloud computing promotes knowledge sharing, a key feature for smart tourism; that is, a sophisticated guide system can serve the maximum number of tourists without being installed on any personal device, although it allows for personalized experiences (Masseno and Santos, 2018).

Smart Tourist Guidance Systems

Today, there is a wide range of mobile solutions developed to support travelers before, during and after travel, for example, guides to city attractions, excursions, exhibitions, or museums (Smirnov et al., 2013). Smart travel guides, developed as mobile applications, allow users to get the tour guide information they need whenever and wherever they want (Jinendra et al., 2012). The basic function of smart guides is to convey information to the visitor and can often be an information communication tool that may replace tourist guides (Lee, 2017). These tools are installed on the smart devices by the visitors before their travel to the destination. In this way, tourists can explore the destination beforehand and can be familiar with major tourist attractions, as well as learn about the local resources (Yüzbaşıoğlu et al., 2018).

Smart tourist guidance systems can be incorporated with GPS and mobile applications to provide tourists with a more effective travel experience. With these applications, tourists can better understand the places they visit. In short, smart tour guide apps can enhance the tourist experience and provide more or different information for tourists. The multilingual options of the guidance service usually offered in archaeological sites and museums will also increase the popularity of these attractions (Wang et al., 2016).

Big Data and Artificial Intelligence

Big data refers to very large data sets that can be obtained, stored, and interpreted with artificial intelligence (Sheoran, 2017). The combination of the huge dimensions of big data and the complexity of the analysis required to benefit from it has led to the development of the tools and new technologies to manage them (Doğan and Arslantekin, 2016). Big data basically fulfills two basic tasks: data storage and data analysis (Sheoran, 2017).

Big data are collected from different sources where tourists leave their digital fingerprints behind (Dolgos, 2018) and it is an important tool of Tourism 4.0 (Manjari, 2018). In the tourism industry, big data can provide real-time information about behavior of tourists, their preferences, purchasing decisions, wishes, etc. (McCraken, 2018). Artificial intelligence technology analyzes big data. With smart tourism, the issue of destinations benefiting from big data comes to the fore more. Big data are obtained about restaurant services, entertainment, and accommodation, traveling tourists leave a digital trace in their use of web and mobile-based services, and external sources is shared through various social media applications in the process from the planning of the trip to the realization of the trip and in the entire subsequent process (Esen and Türkay, 2017). Destinations also offer a special experience and offers to customers by using the information they obtain about the big data, preferences, and behaviors of the customers (Akergar, 2012). The use of big data is one of the important tools to date for determining tourist behavior and increasing efficiency. In the tourism industry, probably the most important issue for the customer is satisfaction with the provided services, while for the businesses, keeping the expenses to a minimum while fulfilling the commitments and gaining a reputation (Sheoran, 2017). Kayıkçı and Bozkurt (2018) also stated that artificial intelligence applications will enable all tourists to receive services in their mother tongue, making their travel more comfortable. For example, Thomas Cook and Samsung Gear's augmented reality application together earned 17 thousand dollars (US$) additional income from accommodation and flights in the first three months of the application (Hughes, 2016).

Smart Tourist Card

Smart tourist card can standardize and facilitates tourists' learning of the diversity of the destination [transportation, performances, visits to museums, excursions, guides, etc.] (Segittur, 2020). Helping tourists to gain a unique experience for the destination, tourist cards not only provide users with several benefits in terms of cost and timesaving, but also stand out in the success of destinations. The tourist card, which combines various activities and services provided at the destination at a discounted price, is an important destination-marketing tool. Discounts are among the main benefits provided by tourist cards, such as free admission or discounts to enter historic sites, churches, museums, the use of public transport, inner city parking, bike rental, car rental, guided tour activities, restaurants, amusement parks, shops, etc. Considering the various tourist services and opportunities included in a tourist card, these cards can be important marketing tool for the destination (Topsakal, 2018).

Electronic Touch Screens - Kiosks

Electronic touch screens can be represented as a form of intelligent information systems. In smart tourism destinations, kiosks are mounted at certain points, such as tourist information centers, shopping centers, airports, and important touristic centers, provide tourists with a lot of information about the destination. Kiosk is a system that can improve the tourists experience and provide different information during their stay at the destination. The biggest advantage of electronic touch screens is that they provide 24/7 information to their users (Rodrigues et al., 2017). Touch screens created for tourists to access information provide a platform to promote the destination and businesses while improving visitor engagement and experience. In addition to presenting information about the destination, such as shops, entertainment centers, libraries, art museums and galleries, hotels, tourist information centers and restaurants, digital screens can also be aimed at organizing virtual tours. In addition, using the touch screen, tourists can browse the destination's attractions and businesses and send the information directly to their smartphones or tablets, so they can read the information about the destination on the go (Segittur, 2020).

Global Positioning Systems

Geographic information systems are generally defined as automated systems for capturing, storing, analyzing, and displaying spatial data (Epstein, 1995). One of the geographic information systems is the GPS. The GPS can be used to identify the best locations for a new tourist destination while trying to provide a sustainable natural area (Butler, 1993). GPS is used for purposes such as transportation, shopping, cargo and traffic services, choosing the most suitable location, tourist information, map or geographical information inquiry, and finding a place. New generation Web-based GPS applications such as Google Maps, GlobeXplore, and Yahoo Map provide detailed spatial information to users all over the world (Chang and Caneday, 2011). For example, GPS is used for treasure hunting activity in tourism. Treasure hunting is similar to the ancient activity Letterboxing. The important difference is the use of a navigation device in Letterboxing. Treasure hunting with GPS was made possible by Dave Ulmer (Beavercreek, Oregon) on May 1, 2000, with the further development of the GPS system and making it available to ordinary people outside of military work (Pelton and Pelton, 2011). Although GPS has some negative aspects such as not being able to calculate water depth, the fact that routes for tourism purposes are preformed eliminates such negative effects. GPS is very beneficial for the visitors who travel to unknown geographic places and for whom those travel independently in a foreign country or destination. They can easily find their way, or their geographic position when they are lost in nature. Perhaps these systems are the best and most useful devices for wanderlust tourists, eco-tourists, and nature seekers.

Drones

Drones are tiny helicopters that can fly without a pilot. The control of drones is carried out remotely by radio waves or independently [on a predetermined route] (Kardasz et al., 2016). With a drone, both businesses and destinations can display their tourist attractions from the sky in a creative and unique way and it can be used for promotional and marketing purposes. It can be predicted that event organizations in the tourism industry will also change via the use of drone light shows and races. In tourism, transportation services are provided to consumers by drones by food and beverage businesses. First, food delivery services with drone save time by avoiding traffic jams and provide food delivery services without any restrictions (Hwang et al., 2019). Drones can also be used to make room service and package deliveries faster in hotels located in large areas. On the traveler side, these devices are very useful for adventure-some visitors who would like to find out their environment where they cannot walk or climb themselves due to geographic barriers and some other difficulties. In other words, drones can encourage the tourists to travel easily to some risky places.

Wearable Technologies

Wearable technology (smart watches, bracelets, glasses, headphones, and foot and hand jewelry) has begun to be used in more and more applications in the tourism industry. For example, hotels work with Apple Watch to allow guests to check-in and unlock the doors (Dorsi, 2016). For example, Starwood Hotels has launched an app for the Apple Watch that enables wearers to tap their device to unlock hotel room doors via Bluetooth in 2014 (Boden, 2015).

Humanoid Robots

A robot is defined as a mechanism that moves within itself, has a degree of autonomy, can be programmed in two or more axes to perform its intended tasks (Ivanov and Webster, 2019). In the tourism industry, the robots are used to assist customers or tourists in tasks, such as guiding, serving food and beverages, providing cleaning, safety, and security services (Ivanov et al., 2017). For example, Henn-na Hotel in Japan operates entirely with automation and robot technology, check-in and check-out procedures are done by robots and guests do not encounter any employees. Henn-na hotel in Nagasaki, Japan, which is considered one of the first examples of the world, whose staff consists of robots, started its operations in 2015. The guests, who are greeted by dinosaur robots at the entrance to the hotel, are assisted by robots to find rooms (Ohlan, 2018). The robot named "Mario" at the Marriott Hotel in Belgium can speak 19 languages, give guests room keys, and inform guests about events inside or outside the hotel (Tuyed, 2016).

MAIN FOCUS OF THE CHAPTER

Digital Transformation

According to Gartner (2020), "digitization" is the process of transition from analog to digital, also known as digital activation. In other words, it is the way of taking an analog process and transforming it into a digital form without any change in the operation itself. In general, the digitization is the process of moving a non-digital process to digital environment. For example, it is a digitization process for a hotel to transfer the product stock records kept on paper to the computer environment. Digitization is directly related to new and up-to-date services, which enable different perspectives to be revealed in relation to customer satisfaction. Consumers are always in search of new and better service. Digitization aims to ensure maximum customer satisfaction. The increase in digital applications in businesses provides an increase in customer satisfaction rates (Keshab, 2018).

There is no single definition of "digitalization" (Kazandzhieva, 2021). Gartner (2020) states that digitalization is the use of digital technologies to change a business model and provide new revenue and value generating opportunities. It is the process of transitioning to a digital business. For example, seeing the product stock records kept in the computer environment of a hotel by the production units and shaping the production program according to these data is a digitalization process. Digitization has benefits for an organization such as increased profitability, speed, and flexibility (Gartner, 2020). Digitalization moves beyond digitization, leveraging digital information technology to entirely transform a business' operation (evaluating, re-engineering, and reimagining the way you do business). If digitization is a conversion of data and processes, digitalization is a transformation. More than just making existing data digital, digitalization embraces the ability of digital technology to collect data, establish trends and make better business decisions. Different authors have made different definitions for digitalization (Henriette et al., 2016). As Löwgren and Stolterman (2004) stated digitalization is a social phenomenon. Stolterman and Fors (2004) stated that digitalization is related to the change of digital technology applications on human beings. Rogers et al. (2011) defined digitalization as cultural progress. Digitalization has six components, which comprise data, numbers, business culture, innovation in workflow, and customer-centeredness (Keshab, 2018). Digitalization affects the working and functioning structure of organizations. In today's competitive environment, inaccurate digital applications pose a great threat to businesses. On the other hand, if digitalization is applied correctly within a business, it turns into an opportunity for businesses. The widespread use of mobile devices with the rapid development of technology enables consumers to reach suppliers directly (Parviainen et al., 2017). Digitalization aims to develop business models and provide a unique customer experience by integrating information and company resources with digital technologies. The main purpose of digitalization is the creation of new products and services and the effective use of company resources. In order to use business resources more effectively, resources need to be transformed into technology (Accenture Digitization Index, 2015).

The concept of digital transformation has recently become one of the most frequently used concepts. Patel and McCarthy (2000) are the first scientists to use digital transformation. The research of Westerman et al. (2011) on digital transformation showed that the use of technology directly improves performance or facilitates access to businesses. Brooks and McCormack (2020) defined digital transformation as a concept that refers to everything from information technology modernization to digital optimization and the invention of new digital business models. For example, the fact that the product stock records of a hotel are visible in real time by all stakeholders in a computer environment, this data is used by algorithms for real-time optimization, and suppliers can plan the optimum shipment order based on this data can be described as a digital transformation process. According to Stolterman and Fors (2014), digital transformation means the changes that occur as a result of the application of digital technologies for the development of society. Digital transformation is the process of using digital technologies to develop new customer experiences and business processes or replace existing ones in order to meet changing market needs (Bencheva and Manevsky, 2019). Digital transformation encompasses changes in value creation brought about by the adoption of digital technologies and changes in existing business models (Mitroulis and Kitsios, 2019).

Although there are contradictions regarding the interpretation of the concept, there is a clear difference between the concepts of business transformation and digital transformation. In the past, the concept of digital transformation was considered to be improvements in business practice. After the Industry 4.0, it has been understood that the concept of digital transformation has a meaning contrary to what is known (Lee et al., 2014). Digital transformation refers to the organizational change that occurs through digital technologies. In addition, it describes the business models developed to increase performance and customer experience (Wade, 2015). Digital transformation is the process of transforming the big data provided by smart machines into better services or products. These developments, artificial intelligence, and robot technologies will change our current lives and habits. It is a situation that should be accepted that these developments will carry human beings to a post-reality world (Büyükuslu, 2018).

Tourist Experiences

While the customer's emotions, perceptions and attitudes form the concept of customer experience, this concept is a process that includes all operations from the first moment the customer sees the business to communication (Seyitoğlu, 2019). Businesses that want to provide their customers with a unique and unforgettable experience follow the process of experience dimensions (Güney, 2015). According to Schmitt (1999), there are five different experiences that customers will experience, which comprise sensory experience, emotional experience, intellectual experience, behavioral experience, and relational experience.

The sensory dimension aims to provide an experience by appealing to the senses and activating the customer's senses, such as hearing, touching, and seeing. The *sensory dimension* is the first dimension of experience encountered during the experience (Tsaur et al., 2006). The *intellectual experience* dimension supports the detailed and creative thinking of the consumer about the business and its products (Kır, 2014). The *behavioral experience* dimension adds excitement to the lives of customers by examining their lifestyles in detail and to create experiences that can be offered to customers in advance (Deligöz, 2014). The *relational experience* dimension allows for the establishment of a relationship with the customer, to strive to emphasize the difference, uniqueness, and personality of everyone. Experience and relationship are an inseparable whole and are an important factor that businesses care about (Batı, 2017).

When looking at the definitions of the tourist experience, Selstad (2007) defined this concept as a combination of novelty/familiarity that includes the search for individual identity and self-actualization. According to Otto and Ritchie (1996), the tourist experience is a subjective mental state felt by the participants. Prentice et al. (1998) claim that tourist experience includes enjoying nature, avoiding physical stressors, learning, and sharing similar values, and creativity. Quan and Wang (2004) defined tourist experience as a way of experiencing things different from daily life. Tung and Ritchie (2011) assert that tourist experience includes a person's subjective evaluations (affective, cognitive, and behavioral) of tourism activities before (planning and preparation), during (destination), and after (remembering) participating in a tourism activity. Tourists may forget the destinations and dates they visited, but they do not forget the experiences they had in the activities they participated. The motivation for designing and staging the memorable tourist experience comes from the focus of an experience that is subjectively felt by individuals associated with an event on an emotional, physical, spiritual and/or intellectual level (Tung and Ritchie, 2011).

Experiencing the tourism event starts with the travel planning and preparation period and continues with the process of remembering and transferring the event that took place after the tourist returns to his place of residence. According to another definition, touristic experience (Büyükkuru and Aslan, 2016) is the sum of an individual's pre-trip experiences, experiences during the trip, and post-trip experiences. Therefore, the tourist experience model of Craig-Smith and French (1994) consists of three stages, which comprise before experience, during experience, and after experience. Clawson and Knetsch (1966) stated that the tourist experience consists of five consecutive stages. In the *first stage*, there is an expectation. At this stage, there are the thoughts that tourists have about their holidays before they go on vacation. The *second stage* is the travel stage to the destination. At this stage, there are events that tourists experience until they reach their destination. In the *third stage*, there are some activities they perform at the destination. The *fourth stage* is the return stage, and the last stage includes remembering what happened during the holiday. Aho (2001) stated that distinguishing the stages of the touristic experience basically consists of three stages: *pre-trip, on-the-trip, and post-trip*. The first stage is planning and decision making, the second stage is the touristic act itself, and the third stage is all thoughts. The experience can be enriched with digital transformation at every stage of the tourist experience. Therefore, the potential effects of digital transformation on the tourist experience have been examined in detail with examples under a next heading.

Due to the dynamic nature of the tourism industry, experiences are constantly evolving and changing. One of the most important developments regarding experiences is the increasing level of integration of ICTs in tourism industry (Neuhofer et al., 2014). The latest technological developments such as online booking tools, virtual tourist communities (e.g., tripadvisor), and mobile devices are improving the experiences of tourism firms and tourists. For example, tourists can create new experiences by adopting mobile devices while on the move and by attaching personal meanings to them (Gretzel and Jamal, 2009).

The literature states that ICTs are important in the tourism experience (Huang et al., 2010). There are studies focusing on technologies that affect the tourist experience, such as virtual communities (Binkhorst and Den Dekker, 2009), social networking sites such as Facebook, YouTube, or Wikipedia (Ramaswamy, 2009), social networking platforms, blogs, or microblogs such as Twitter (Wang and Fesenmaier, 2004), and virtual worlds (Shaw et al., 2011). Social media such as Facebook, Twitter, YouTube, or Flickr play an important role in empowering for enhanced levels of interaction between multiple parties. Fotis et al. (2011) affirmed the importance of social media as a platform for tourism providers and tourist consumers to engage and share experiences throughout the entire journey (Dwivedi et al., 2012).

Effects of Digital Transformation on Tourist Experience

Dubey (2017) stated that the preferences and experiences of tourists have changed, and that with the support of virtual reality concept and 3D printers, tourists can experience different experiences (stroking animal skin, hugging a tiger, etc.) with these technologies. Smart applications used in the tourism industry, augmented reality, e-agency, 3D printers, holograms and artificial intelligence supported applications that allow tourists to try before purchasing tours and digital smart travel companions are mentioned (Soava, 2015).

In the tourism context, there are various mobile applications, such as those that help users to translate written texts and verbal communication. Some mobile apps can improve the pre-trip experience by helping tourists plan their stay by creating an event schedule (Benckendorff et al., 2019). Tourists can see mobile applications as useful, easy to use, and compatible with themselves (Lu et al., 2015) on issues such as obtaining information about their travels (No and Kim, 2014), purchasing various services related to their travel (Morosan and DeFranco, 2014), booking a hotel room (Park and Huang, 2017), and enriching their experience while at the destination (Jung et al., 2015). Tourists want to improve their experience by using mobile apps and saving time (Bader et al., 2012). Since mobile apps are located on smartphones, they are always with the tourists. Therefore, mobile apps help to increase the efficiency and experience of tourists in their daily work (Kim et al., 2013). Mobile applications provide many benefits to tourists, such as comparing prices, gaining discounts, researching products, looking at restaurant menus, accessing transportation timetables and instant locations of local transportation, and booking (Wang and Wang, 2010). In terms of tourism businesses, mobile applications can increase the tourist experience by providing businesses with the opportunity to increase customer loyalty, use discounts more effectively, and interact with those who make purchases through mobile applications, anytime and anywhere (Cameron et al., 2012).

Drone technology is used as a new marketing tool for touristic destinations and tourism businesses. In destination marketing and promotion, drone technology is used to create images with aerial shots (Stankov et al., 2019). Potential tourists can enhance their experience by viewing drone videos before traveling or booking. In addition, intermediaries such as travel agencies offer drone aerial images to tourists with a virtual tour experience (Marasco et al., 2017). Drone technology also plays an important role in destination management. Drone technology is recognized as a useful tool for exploring wildlife on land tours, whale watching tours, and fishing trips. The use of drones reduces the fuel and vehicle maintenance costs of tour operators. Thus, the tourist experience can be improved, and business costs can be reduced at the same time. For example, in Taiwan, drones are used to monitor the landscape change at Penghu Kuibishan Geopark, and monitor the number of visitors and their routes to carry out maintenance in the park, providing tourists with an improved experience (Lu, 2018).

Social media applications can be seen as a marketing tool to convey that the destination managers and businesses offer a better tourism experience to tourists (Li et al., 2017). Since social media is an interactive platform, it is used extensively by users and thus enables the process of co-creating a tourism product. Businesses and destination management organizations can improve products by following tourist experiences through social media (Zhang, 2020). Social media can affect the virtual acculturation process of a tourist before visiting to the destination. This refers to acculturation that takes place while tourists learn and acquire culturally relevant skills for sociological adaptation before to their travel (Cuomo et al., 2021).

GPSs and smartphones provide a sense of security to tourists, especially those involved in tourism activities in wildlife areas. Geographic information systems offer tourism destination managers the opportunity to develop efficient and effective tools for planning, managing, and monitoring. While at the destination, tourists can use geographic information systems especially for direction finding. Therefore, geographic information systems, such as the GPS, have the potential to enrich the experiences of tourists at the destination.

Wearable technologies can be used in tourism activities such as hearing and translation. Wearable technologies are also an important technology for the collection and analysis of big data. It can be predicted that robots will perform tasks such as welcoming the visitors, selling tickets, informing them about important attractions, guiding visitors by checking the density in tourism destinations, and humanoid guide robots will even accompany tourists during tourism activities. With artificial intelligence, factors such as road conditions, weather conditions, visibility, maximum speed, following distance can be determined instantly and various directions can be made. Creative tourism activities are communicated to potential tourists through mobile applications supported by artificial intelligence technology. For example, the destinations where these activities are offered to tourists who are interested in ecotourism activities such as mushroom picking can be communicated via mobile applications. In fact, tourists can be attracted to destinations by providing an online experience through 3D videos about mushroom picking activities in the selected destination. Before traveling, tourists can gain experience related to tourism destinations by using virtual tours prepared with virtual reality. Therefore, it can be claimed that the digital transformation realized by the use of technologies in tourism activities affects the experiences of tourists in various ways.

SOLUTIONS AND RECOMMENDATIONS

Technology has transformed the tourism industry over time, and today, this transformation has accelerated with digitization and Industry 4.0. With the application of new generation technologies that shape Industry 4.0 to the tourism industry, the concept of smart tourism has entered the literature and digitalization has accelerated in tourism. Another reason for the acceleration of digitalization in tourism is that the Z generation, has started to participate in tourism activities. Tourists can have a pre-travel virtual experience about destinations by watching videos prepared with virtual reality in the process before they travel. Therefore, pre-travel virtual experience can be effective in tourists' destination selection. During their travel, tourists can obtain data such as managing the tickets they buy with mobile applications and instant weather conditions about their destination. While at the destination, tourists can enrich their experiences by receiving personalized services prepared with artificial intelligence. After the trip, tourists can create electronic word-of-mouth communication by sharing their experiences in interactive social media applications. In this context, the following recommendations can be claimed:

- Tourists can experience the destination with photos, videos, and 3D images in virtual environments or by visiting mobile applications. Therefore, destinations and tourism product providers should introduce their tourism products in an interesting way with virtual and reality that has been prepared with 3D images, videos, photographs,
- It is necessary to improve tourist experiences by using such technologies as robots and kiosks, especially at the airports in tourism destinations,
- Integration should be ensured between public transportation vehicles, such as railways, highways, and metros within the destination, and the information about the vehicles on this line should be provided in real-time via mobile applications,
- Smart tourist cards should be created for tourists in order to offer free admission or discounts to museums, churches, historical sites, and free use of public transport.
- Wearable technologies can be used to ensure the health and safety of tourists in hotels. Tourists can enrich their experience by accessing services such as ordering room service and getting information about activities in the hotel with wearable technologies. Similarly, opening the doors to the rooms with the tourist's phone with NFC technology can enrich the tourists' experience.

FUTURE RESEARCH DIRECTIONS

In this study, first, information was given about the technologies that have led the Industry 4.0 and were used for digitalization. Information on the use of these technologies from the tourism industry is presented. Then, the effect of digital transformation on the tourist experience was examined and suggestions were made in this context. Today, the importance of digitalization in the tourism industry has been understood more. For future studies, the effect of digital technologies on the tourist experience can be investigated empirically based on generations in the tourism industry.

CONCLUSION

Digital technologies, which have become an integral part of the tourist experience, have resulted in digital transformation in the tourism industry. The reason why digital technology has become important in the tourist experience is that tourists have begun to use technological tools before, during and after travel (Wang et al., 2014). For example, based on the idea that the use of Tourism 4.0 in Malaysia will increase the use of digital technology in the tourism sector and that this will improve tourist experiences, it predicts that there will be an increase in the number of tourists coming from China, and that it will contribute to the economy by improving job opportunities in the tourism sector (Tüzünkan, 2019). Therefore, tourism destinations need to provide digital transformation with new generation technologies in order to be competitive and attract potential visitors to the destination. With the digital transformation carried out in the destination, positive word of mouth marketing can be realized by enriching the tourist experience.

REFERENCES

Accenture Digitization Index. (2015). *Accenture digitization index Turkey results*. Turkish Science Foundation.

Aho, S. K. (2001). Towards a general theory of touristic experiences: Modelling experience. *Tourism Review*, *56*(3), 33–37. doi:10.1108/eb058368

Akergar, R. (2012). *Big data and tourism*. Technomathematics Research Foundation.

Bader, A., Baldauf, M., Leinert, S., Fleck, M., & Liebrich, A. (2012). Mobile tourism services and technology acceptance in amature domestic tourism market: the case of Switzerland. In M. Fuchs, F. Ricci, & L. Cantoni (Eds.), *Information and communication technologies in tourism 2012* (pp. 296–307). Springer. doi:10.1007/978-3-7091-1142-0_26

Bağçı, E., & İçöz, O. (2019). Digitalized tourism through Z and Alpha generation. *Güncel Turizm Araştırmaları Dergisi*, *3*(2), 232–256.

Batı, U. (2017). *Markethink ya da Farkethink: Deneyimsel pazarlama ve duyusal markalama*. Kitap Kulübü.

Bencheva, N. & Manevsky, N. (2019). Digital transformation of the tourism industry. *Knowledge - International Jorunal*, *34*(1), 165-168.

Benckendorff, P. J., Xiang, Z., & Sheldon, P. (2019). *Tourism information technology*. CABI. doi:10.1079/9781786393432.0000

Binkhorst, E., & Den Dekker, T. (2009). Agenda for co-creation tourism experience research. *Journal of Hospitality Marketing & Management*, *18*(2/3), 311–327. doi:10.1080/19368620802594193

Boden. (2015). https://www.nfcw.com/2015/04/28/335007/starwood-guests-unlock-hotel-rooms-with-apple-watch-app/

Brooks, C., & McCormack. (2020). *Driving digital transformation in higher education.* Retrieved form https://www.educause.edu/ecar/research-publications/driving-digital-transformation-in-higher-education/2020/defining-digital-transformation

Butler, R. (1993). Alternative tourism: The thin edge of the wedge. In V. Smith & W. Eadington (Eds.), *Tourism alternatives: Potential and problems in the development of tourism* (pp. 31–36). University of Pennsylvania Press.

Büyükkuru, M., & Aslan, Z. (2016). The effect of communication skills of tourist guides on tourists' tour experiences: A research in Nevsehir. *Mustafa Kemal University Journal of Social Sciences Institute*, *13*(34), 338–354.

Büyükuslu, A. R. (2018). *Dijital dönüşüm.* D&R Yayınevi.

Cameron, D., Gregory, C., & Battaglia, D. (2012). Nielsen personalizes the mobile shopping app if you build the technology, they will come. *Journal of Advertising Research, 52*(3), 333–338. doi:10.2501/JAR-52-3-333-338

Canadi, M., Höpken, W., & Fuchs, M. (2010). Application of QR codes in online travel distribution. In U. Gretzel, R. Law, & M. Fuch (Eds.), Information and communication technologies in tourism 2010 (pp. 137-148). Springer. doi:10.1007/978-3-211-99407-8_12

Çelik, P., & Topsakal, Y. (2019). *Endüstri 4.0 ve Akıllı turizm.* Detay Yayıncılık.

Chang, G., & Caneday, L. (2011). Web-based GIS in tourism information search: Perceptions, tasks, and trip attributes. *Tourism Management, 32*(6), 1435–1437. doi:10.1016/j.tourman.2011.01.006

Chavan, S. R. (2014). Augmented reality vs. virtual reality: Differences and similarities. *International Journal of Advanced Research in Computer Engineering and Technology, 5*(6), 1947–1752.

Claveria, O., Monte, E., & Torra, S. (2015). A new forecasting approach for the hospitality industry. *International Journal of Contemporary Hospitality Management, 27*(7), 1520–1538. doi:10.1108/IJCHM-06-2014-0286

Clawson, M., & Knetsch, J. L. (1966). *Economics of outdoor recreation.* Johns Hopkins Press.

Coşkun, V., Özdenizci, B., & Ok, K. (2013). A survey on near field communication (NFC) technology. *Wireless Personal Communications, 71*(3), 2259–2294. doi:10.100711277-012-0935-5

Cotteler, M., & Sniderman, B. (2017). *Forces of change: Industry 4.0.* Deloitte Touche Tohmatsu Limited.

Craig-Smith, S., & French, C. (1994). *Learning to live with tourism.* Pitman.

Cuomo, M. T., Tortora, D., Foroudi, P., Giordano, A., Festa, G. & Metallo, G. (2021). Digital transformation and tourist experience co-design: Big social data for planning cultural tourism. *Technological Forecasting and Social Science, 162,* Article Number: 120345.

Deligöz, K. (2014). *A study on determining the effect of experiential marketing practices on brand preference (the case of coffee world and Starbucks)* (Master Thesis). Atatürk University, Erzurum, Turkey.

Doğan, K., & Arslantekin, S. (2016). Big data: Its importance, structure, and current status. *Ankara DTCF Journal, 56*(1), 15–36.

Dolgos, G. (2018). *Tourism industry benefit greatly from big data.* Retrieved from https://www.tourismreview.com/tourism-industry-relies-more-on-the-big-data-news10492

Dorsi, S. (2016). *Travel industry – wearables don't offer much.* Retrieved form https://www.tourismreview.com/hotel-of-the-future-would-include-lots-of-technologynews10616

Dubey, A. K. (2017). *Future technology and service industry: A case study of travel and tourism industry.* Informaticjournal.com

Durmaz, C., Bulut, Y., & Tankuş, E. (2018). The integration of virtual reality into tourism: Application in the hotels with five star in Samsun. *Turkish Journal of Marketing, 3*(1), 32–49. doi:10.30685/tujom.v3i1.27

Dwivedi, M., Yadav, A., & Venkatesh, U. (2012). Use of social media by national tourism organizations: A preliminary analysis. *Information Technology & Tourism, 13*(2), 93–103. doi:10.3727/109830512X13258778487353

Egger, R., & Jooss, M. (2010). mTourism. Wiesbaden: Gabler Springer.

Epstein, J. M. (1995). Global positioning system (GPS): Defining the legal issues of its expanding civil use. *Journal of Air Law and Commerce, 61*(1), 243–285.

Esen, F., & Türkay, B. (2017). Big data applications in tourism industries. *Journal of Tourism and Gastronomy Studies, 5*(4), 92–115. doi:10.21325/jotags.2017.140

Evans, D. (2011). *How the next evolution of the internet is changing everything.* https://www.cisco.com/c/dam/en_us/about/ac79/docs/innov/IoT_IBSG_0411FINAL.pdf

Fes, N. (2018). *Hotel 4.0 - what the hotel of the future looks like.* Retrieved from https://www.tourismreview.com/hotel-of-the-future-would-include-lots-of-technologynews10616

Fotis, J., Buhalis, D., & Rossides, N. (2011). Social media impact on holiday travel planning: The case of the Russian and the FSU markets. *International Journal of Online Marketing, 1*(4), 1–19. doi:10.4018/ijom.2011100101

Gartner. (2020). *Gartner glossary.* Retrieved from https://www.gartner.com/en/information-technology/glossary/digitalization

Gretzel, U. (2011). Intelligent systems in tourism: A social science perspective. *Annals of Tourism Research, 38*(3), 757–779. doi:10.1016/j.annals.2011.04.014

Gretzel, U., & Jamal, T. (2009). Conceptualizing the creative tourist class: Technology, mobility, and tourism experiences. *Tourism Analysis, 14*(4), 471–481. doi:10.3727/108354209X12596287114219

Gretzel, U., Sigala, M., Yiang, Z., & Koo, C. (2015). Smart tourism foundations and developments. *Electronic Markets, 25*(3), 179–188. doi:10.100712525-015-0196-8

Güney, D. (2015). *The effect of experiential marketing on customer loyalty: An application for boutique hotels in Muğla* (Master Thesis). Muğla Sıtkı Koçman University, Muğla, Turkey.

Halaweh, M. (2013). Emerging technology: What is it. *Journal of Technology Management & Innovation, 8*(3), 108–115. doi:10.4067/S0718-27242013000400010

Henriette, E., Feki, M., & Boughzala, I. (2016). Digital transformation challenges. In *Proceedings of the Tenth Mediterranean Conference on Information Systems* (p. 33). Paphos, Cyprus: Academic Press.

Hoehle, H., & Venkatesh, V. (2015). Mobile application usability: Conceptualization and instrument development. *Management Information Systems Quarterly, 39*(2), 435–472. doi:10.25300/MISQ/2015/39.2.08

Holler, J., Tsiatsis, V., Mulligan, C., Avesand, S., Karnouskos, S., & Boyle, D. (2014). *From machine-to-machine to the Internet of things: Introduction to a new age of intelligence.* Academic Press.

Hooijdonk, R. (2015). *Technology trends 2030.* Retrieved from https://www.richardvanhooijdonk.com/en/keynote/trends2030/

Huang, Y. C., Backman, S. J., & Backman, K. F. (2010). The impacts of virtual experiences on people's travel intentions. In U. Gretzel, R. Law, & M. Fuchs (Eds.), *ENTER 2010.* Springer-Verlag. doi:10.1007/978-3-211-99407-8_46

Hughes, N. C. (2016). *How virtual reality is about to transform the travel industry.* https://www.inc.com/neil-c-hughes/how-virtualreality-is-ab-transform-the-travel-industry.html

Hwang, J., Kim, H., & Kim, W. (2019). Investigating motivated consumer innovativeness in the context of drone food delivery services. *Journal of Hospitality and Tourism Management, 38*, 102–110. doi:10.1016/j.jhtm.2019.01.004

Inukollu, V. N., Keshamoni, D. D., Kang, T., & Inukollu, M. (2014). Factors influencing quality of mobile apps: Role of mobile app development life cycle. *International Journal of Software Engineering and Its Applications, 5*(5), 15–34. doi:10.5121/ijsea.2014.5502

Ivanov, S., & Webster, C. (2019). Conceptual framework of the use of robots, artificial intelligence and service automation in travel, tourism, and hospitality companies. In S. Ivanov & C. Webster (Eds.), *Robots, artificial intelligence, and service automation in travel, tourism and hospitality* (pp. 7–37). Emerald Publishing Limited. doi:10.1108/978-1-78756-687-320191002

Ivanov, S., Webster, C., & Berezina, K. (2017). Adoption of robots and service automation by tourism and hospitality companies. *Revista Turismo & Desenvolvimento, 27*(28), 1501–1517.

Jin, J., Gubbi, J., Marusic, S., & Palaniswami, M. (2014). An information framework for creating a smart city through Internet of things. *IEEE Internet of Things Journal, 1*(2), 112–121. doi:10.1109/JIOT.2013.2296516

Jinendra, D. R., Bhagyashri, J. R., Pranav, G. Y., Seema, V. U., & Parag, A. N. (2012). Smart travel guide: Application for Android mobile. *International Journal of Electronics, Communication and Soft Computing Science & Engineering, 2*, 115–120.

Jung, T., Chung, N., & Leue, M. C. (2015). The determinants of recommendations to use augmented reality technologies: The case of a Korean theme park. *Tourism Management, 49*(August), 75–86. doi:10.1016/j.tourman.2015.02.013

Kardasz, P., Doskocz, J., Hejduk, M., Wiejkut, P. & Zarzycki, H. (2016). Drones and possibilities of their using. *Journal of Civil & Environmental Engineering, 6,* Article Number: 233.

Kaur, K., & Kaur, R. (2016). Internet of Things to promote tourism: An insight into smart tourism. *International Journal of Recent Trends in Engineering & Research, 2,* 357–361.

Kayıkçı, M. Y., & Bozkurt, A. K. (2018). Generation Z and Alpha in digital age, artificial intellegence and reflections on tourism. *Sosyal Bilimler Metinleri, 1,* 54–64.

Kazandzhieva, V. (2021). Enhancing the competitiveness of destination Bulgaria through digital transformation in tourism. *Economic Studies Journal, 30*(2), 177–198.

Keshab, M. C. (2018). *Digitization study in industry: Requirements and considerations* (Master Thesis). Stavanger University Faculty of Science and Technology, Norway.

Kim, E., Lin, J. S., & Sung, Y. (2013). To app or not to app: Engaging consumers via branded mobile apps. *Journal of Interactive Advertising, 13*(1), 53–65. doi:10.1080/15252019.2013.782780

Kır, S. (2014). *Test drives in the context of experiential marketing* (Master Thesis). Selçuk University, Konya, Turkey.

Lee, J., Kao, H. A., & Yang, S. (2014). Service innovation and smart analytics for industry 4.0 and big data environment. *Procedia CIRP, 16,* 3–8. doi:10.1016/j.procir.2014.02.001

Lee, S. J. (2017). A review of audio guides in the era of smart tourism. *Information Systems Frontiers, 19*(4), 705–715. doi:10.100710796-016-9666-6

Li, Y., Hu, C., Huang, C., & Duan, L. (2017). The concept of smart tourism in the context of tourism information services. *Tourism Management, 58,* 293–300. doi:10.1016/j.tourman.2016.03.014

Lopez de Avila, A. (2015). Smart destinations: XXI century tourism. *Proceedings of the ENTER2015.*

Löwgren, J., & Stolterman, E. (2004). *Thoughtful interaction design: A design perspective on information technology.* MIT Press.

Lu, C. H. (2018). Uav-based photogrammetry for the application on geomorphic change-the case stydy of Penghu Kuibishan geopark, Taiwan. In *Proceedings of the IEEE International Geoscience and Remote Sensing Symposium* (pp. 7840-7842). IEEE.

Lu, J., Wang, M., Mao, Z., & Hu, L. (2015). Goodbye maps, hello apps? Exploring the influential determinants of travel app adoption. *Current Issues in Tourism, 18*(11), 1059–1079. doi:10.1080/136835 00.2015.1043248

Manjari, R. M. E. (2018). *Introducing tourism 4.0: What is it and how do we get here?* Retrieved from http://forbil.org/id/article/211/introducing-tourism-40-what-is-it-and-howdo-we-get-here

Marasco, A., Buonincontri, P., Van Niekerk, M., Orlowski, M., & Okumus, F. (2017). Exploring the role of next-generation virtual technologies in destination marketing. *Journal of Destination Marketing & Management, 9*, 138–148. doi:10.1016/j.jdmm.2017.12.002

Marr, B. (2020). *Robots and drones are now used to fight COVID-19.* Retrieved from https://www.forbes.com/sites/bernardmarr/2020/03/18/how-robots-and-drones-are-helping-to-fight-coronavirus/#f29aee32a12e

Masseno, M. D., & Santos, C. (2018). Smart tourism destinations privacy risks on data protection. *Revista Eletronica Sapere Aude, 1*(1), 125–149.

McCraken, S. (2018). *Hoteliers share insights on the industry's future.* Retrieved from http://www.hotelnewsnow.com/Articles/283839/Hoteliers-shareinsights-on-the-industrys-future

Mitroulis, D., & Kitsios, F. (2019). Evaluating digital transformation strategies: A MCDA analysis of Greek tourism smes. In *Proceedings of the European Conference on Innovation and Entrepreneurship*, (pp. 667-676), Kalamata, Greece: Academic Press.

Morosan, C., & DeFranco, A. (2014). Understanding the actual use of mobile devices in private clubs in the US. *Journal of Hospitality and Tourism Technology, 5*(3), 278–298. doi:10.1108/JHTT-07-2014-0022

Nabben, A., Wetzel, E., Oldani, E., Huyeng, J., Boel, M., & Fan, Z. (2016). Smart technologies in tourism: Case study on the influence of iBeacons on customer experience during the 2015 SAIL Amsterdam Event. In *Proceedings of the International Tourism Student Conference* (pp. 1-32). Madrid, Spain: Academic Press.

Neuhofer, B., Buhalis, D., & Ladkin, A. (2014). A typology of technology-enhanced tourism experiences. *International Journal of Tourism Research, 16*(4), 340–350. doi:10.1002/jtr.1958

No, E., & Kim, J. (2014). Determinants of the adoption for travel information on smartphone. *International Journal of Tourism Research, 16*(6), 534–545. doi:10.1002/jtr.1945

Ohlan, R. (2018). Role of information technology in hotel industry. *International Journal of Scientific Research in Computer Science, Engineering and Information Technology, 3*(2), 277–281.

Otto, J. E., & Ritchie, T. (1996). The service experience in tourism. *Tourism Management, 17*(3), 165–174. doi:10.1016/0261-5177(96)00003-9

Park, S., & Huang, Y. (2017). Motivators and inhibitors in booking a hotel via smartphones. *International Journal of Contemporary Hospitality Management, 29*(1), 161–178. doi:10.1108/IJCHM-03-2015-0103

Parviainen, P., Tihinen, M., Kääriäinen, J., & Teppola, S. (2017). Tackling the digitalization challenge: How to benefit from digitalization in practice. *International Journal of Information Systems and Project Management, 5*(1), 63–77.

Pate, J., & Adegbija, T. (2018). AMELIA: An application of the Internet of Things for aviation safety. 15th IEEE Annual Consumer Communications & Networking Conference, 1-6.

Patel, K., & McCarthy, M. (2000). *Digital transformation: the essentials of e-business leadership.* McGraw-Hill Professional.

Pelton, L. F., & Pelton, T. W. (2011). Outreach workshops, applications, and resources. In D. Lary (Ed.), *Pacific crystal centre for science, mathematics, and technology literacy: lessons learned* (pp. 113–129). Sense Publishers. doi:10.1007/978-94-6091-506-2_7

Pence, H. E. (2010). Smartphones, smart objects, and augmented reality. *The Reference Librarian, 52*(2), 136–145. doi:10.1080/02763877.2011.528281

Prentice, R. C., Witt, S. F., & Hamer, C. (1998). Tourism as experience: The case of heritage parks. *Annals of Tourism Research, 25*(1), 1–24. doi:10.1016/S0160-7383(98)00084-X

Purcell, K., Entner, R., & Henderson, N. (2010). *The rise of apps culture, internet and American life project.* Retrieved from https://www.pewresearch.org/internet/2010/09/14/the-rise-of-apps-culture/

Quan, S., & Wang, N. (2004). Towards a structural model of the tourist experience: An illustration from food experiences in tourism. *Tourism Management, 25*(3), 297–305. doi:10.1016/S0261-5177(03)00130-4

Ramaswamy, V. (2009). Co-creation of value - towards an expanded paradigm of value creation. *Marketing Review St. Gallen, 6*(6), 11–17. doi:10.100711621-009-0085-7

Rodrigues, J. M., Ramos, C. M., Cardoso, P. J., & Henriques, C. (2017). Handbook of research on technological developments for cultural heritage and eTourism applications. IGI Global.

Rogers, Y., Sharp, H., & Preece, J. (2011). *Interaction design: beyond human-computer interaction.* John Wiley & Sons.

Schmitt, B. H. (1999). *Experiential marketing: How to get customers to sense, feel, think, act, relate to your company and brands.* The Free Press.

Segittur. (2020). Retrieved from www.segittur.es

Selstad, L. (2007). The social anthropology of the tourist experience. Exploring the middle role. *Scandinavian Journal of Hospitality and Tourism, 7*(1), 19–33. doi:10.1080/15022250701256771

Seyitoğlu, Z. (2019). *Changing customer experience in digital public relations in Turkey: Chatbot applications* (Master Thesis). Istanbul Kultur University, İstanbul, Turkey.

Shaw, G., Bailey, A., & Williams, A. M. (2011). Service dominant logic and its implications for tourism management: The co-production of innovation in the hotel industry. *Tourism Management, 32*(2), 207–214. doi:10.1016/j.tourman.2010.05.020

Sheoran, S. K. (2017). Big data: A big boon for tourism sector. *International Journal of Research in Advanced Engineering and Technology, 3*, 10–13.

Smirnov, A., Kashevnik, A., Balandin, S. I., & Laizane, S. (2013). Intelligent mobile tourist guide. In S. Balandin, S. Andreev, & Y. Koucheryavy (Eds.), *Internet of things, smart spaces, and next generation networking.* Springer. doi:10.1007/978-3-642-40316-3_9

Soava, G. (2015). Development prospects of the tourism industry in the digital age. *Revista Tinerilor Economist, 1*, 101–116.

Stankov, U., Kennell, J., Morrison, A. M., & Vujicic, M. D. (2019). The view from above: The relevance of shared aerial drone videos for destination marketing. *Journal of Travel & Tourism Marketing, 36*(7), 808–822. doi:10.1080/10548408.2019.1575787

Stolterman, E., & Fors, A. C. (2004). Information technology and the good life. In B. Kaplan, D. P. Truex, D. Wastell, A. T. Wood-Harper, & J. I. DeGross (Eds.), *Information systems research* (pp. 687–692). Springer. doi:10.1007/1-4020-8095-6_45

Toedt, M. (2016). *Hospitality net - beacons - top or flop for the hospitality industry?* Retrieved from https://www.hospitalitynet.org/news/4073267.html

Topsakal, Y. (2018). Disabled-friendly mobile services in the context of smart tourism: Recommendations for Turkey 4.0. *Journal of Tourism Intelligence and Smartness, 1*(1), 1–13.

Topsakal, Y., Yüzbaşıoğlu, N., Çelik, P., & Bahar, M. (2018b). Tourism 4.0 - tourist 5.0: Why the human revolution is one number bigger than industrial revolutions? *Journal of Tourism Intelligence and Smartness, 1*(2), 1–11.

Topsakal, Y., Yüzbaşıoğlu, N., & Çuhadar, M. (2018a). Industrial revolutions and tourism: Turkey tourism 4.0 swot analysis and proposal for adaptation process. *Süleyman Demirel Üniversitesi İktisadi ve İdari Bilimler Fakültesi Dergisi, 23*, 1623–1638.

Tsaur, S., Chiu, Y., & Wang, C. (2006). The visitors behavioral consequences of experiential marketing: An empirical study on Taipei zoo. *Journal of Travel & Tourism Marketing, 21*(1), 47–64. doi:10.1300/J073v21n01_04

Tung, V. W., & Ritchie, J. R. (2011). Exploring the essence of memorable tourism experiences. *Annals of Tourism Research, 38*(4), 1367–1386. doi:10.1016/j.annals.2011.03.009

Tuyed. (2016). http://www.tuyed.org.tr/turizmde-insansi-robotlar-devri/

Tüzünkan, D. (2019). Turizm 4.0. In O. İçoz & M. Uysal (Eds.), *Turizm Ansiklopedisi - Türkiye: Turizmin ve Ağırlama Endüstrisinin Temel Kavramları* (p. 521). Detay Yayıncılık.

Wade, M. (2015). *A conceptual framework for digital business transformation.* Retrieved from https://www.imd.org/contentassets/d0a4d992d38a41ff85de509156475caa/framework

Wang, D., Xiang, Z., & Fesenmaier, D. (2014). Smartphone use in everyday life and travel. *Journal of Travel Research, 55*(1), 1–12.

Wang, H. Y., & Wang, S. H. (2010). Predicting mobile hotel reservation adoption: Insight from a perceived value standpoint. *International Journal of Hospitality Management, 29*(4), 598–608. doi:10.1016/j.ijhm.2009.11.001

Wang, X., Li, X. R., Zhen, F., & Zhang, J. (2016). How smart is your tourist attraction? Measuring tourist preferences of smart tourism attractions via a FCEM-AHP and IPA Approach. *Tourism Management, 54*, 309–320. doi:10.1016/j.tourman.2015.12.003

Wang, Y., & Fesenmaier, D. R. (2004). Towards understanding members' general participation in and active contribution to an online travel community. *Tourism Management, 25*(6), 709–722. doi:10.1016/j.tourman.2003.09.011

Westerman, G., Calmejane, C., & Bonnet, D. (2011). Digital transformation: A roadmap for billion-dollar organizations. MIT Center for Digital Business.

Wikipedia. (2021). https://en.wikipedia.org/wiki/Technology

Yalçınkaya, P., Atay, L., & Korkmaz, H. (2018). An evaluation on smart tourism. *China-USA Business Review, 17*(6), 308–315.

Yüzbaşıoğlu, N., Çelik, P., Topsakal, Y., & Bahar, M. (2018). Industry 4.0 and smart tourism: Antalya destination smart tourist guide application development. *Proceedings of the Innovation and Global Issues in Social Sciences III.*

Zhang, T. (2020). Co-creating tourism experiences through a traveler's journey: A perspective article. *Tourism Review, 75*(1), 56–60. doi:10.1108/TR-06-2019-0251

Zhong, R. Y., Wang, L. H., & Xuan, X. (2017). IoT-enabled real-time machine status monitoring approach for cloud manufacturing. *Procedia CIRP, 63*, 709–714. doi:10.1016/j.procir.2017.03.349

ADDITIONAL READING

Ang, S. C., & Zaphiris, P. (2009). *Human Computer Interaction: Concepts, Methodologies, Tools, and Applications* (Vols. 1–4). IGI Global. doi:10.4018/978-1-60566-052-3

Guerra, A. G. (Ed.). (2019). *Organizational transformation and managing innovation in the Fourth Industrial Revolution.* IGI Global. doi:10.4018/978-1-5225-7074-5

Mezghani, K., & Aloulou, W. (Eds.). (2019). *Business transformations in the era of digitalization.* IGI Global. doi:10.4018/978-1-5225-7262-6

Rodrigues, J. M., Ramos, C. M., Cardoso, P. J., & Henriques, C. (Eds.). (2017). *Handbook of research on technological developments for cultural heritage and etourism applications.* IGI Global.

Ruiz, G. R., & Hernandez, M. H. (Eds.). (2018). *Augmented Reality for Enhanced Learning Environments.* IGI Global. doi:10.4018/978-1-5225-5243-7

Sabri, E. (Ed.). (2019). *Technology optimization and change management for successful digital supply chains.* IGI Global. doi:10.4018/978-1-5225-7700-3

Shi, N. (Ed.). (2019). *Architectures and frameworks for developing and applying blockchain technology.* IGI Global. doi:10.4018/978-1-5225-9257-0

Thomason, J., Bernhardt, S., Kansara, T., & Cooper, N. (Eds.). (2019). *Blockchain technology for global social change.* IGI Global. doi:10.4018/978-1-5225-9578-6

KEY TERMS AND DEFINITIONS

Digitalization: The use of digital technologies to change a business model and provide new revenue and value-producing opportunities; it is the process of moving to a digital business.

Digitization: Digitization encompasses the integration of digital data and information technologies by making them meaningful.

Drone: Drone is aircraft that can fly without a pilot or passengers.

Industry 4.0: Industry 4.0 led by technologies such as intelligent networks, 3D technology, big data, humanoid robots, smart signaling, augmented reality, wearable technologies, quantum computing, Internet services, nanotechnology, cognitive technologies, sensors, artificial intelligence, the Internet of Things and robotization.

Tourist Experience: Tourist experience is a combination of novelty/familiarity that includes the search for individual identity and self-actualization.

Chapter 3
Smart Tourism in Destinations:
Can It Be the Way Forward?

Fisun Yüksel

https://orcid.org/0000-0002-4147-3889

Adnan Menderes University, Turkey

ABSTRACT

Business enterprises have gained leverage through artificial intelligence (AI) in the tourism and hospitality industry. The roots of the concept and its link with big data environment has drawn a lot of interest from researchers. The employment of technology has increased economic viability of tourism enterprises due to the efficiency, effectiveness, and transparency it creates for tourism and hospitality organizations. The chapter views the emergence of smart tourism in destination management in accordance with sustainable tourism concept and evaluates the issue both in supply side and demand side of tourism. Moreover, it aims to discuss the use of such a paradigm. If the destinations have a viable ground for motivational change to adapt, this philosophy will also be high lightened. For this reason, value creation will be evaluated in accordance with cost-benefit assessment.

INTRODUCTION

This chapter provides a theoretical overview of the impacts of smart applications have had on tourism industry, as well as how smart tourism transforms supply side and demand side of tourism sector in the digital era. In the first part of the chapter, evolution of artificial intelligence in smart tourism will be examined. Similarly, description of smart city and smart destinations will be explored. Besides, sustainable tourism concept a long with local tourism planning issue will be discussed within in the chapter. The second part will be devoted to the use of cost-benefit analysis within the chapter. Finally, this chapter will end with conclusion and recommendations as well as challenges that different stakeholders are facing when engaging with smart systems and conversion towards digitalized foundations.

DOI: 10.4018/978-1-7998-8528-3.ch003

BACKGROUND

Transport has a significant role in tourism as tourists cannot reach destinations without using it in tourism industry. Most of the time governments are concerned with transport infrastructure programs and therefore they need to counteract the negative and positive impacts of the policy choices. For example, a highway development may bring about saving time for users, by contrast noise can adversely affect local people (Mouter, 2014).

In the literature Cost Benefit Analysis is utilized in updating decision-making process about the advantageous and disadvantageous of a program, or a plan in tourism development. The benefits together with expenses are rated and evaluated in monetary terms of the concept in the literature. (Hayashi and Morisugi, 2000; Mouter, 2014, Hanson, 2007). Therefore, the chapter offers a theoretical review of pros and cons of smart tourism through cost-benefit analysis in order to put forward what part of the smart tourism is in line with sustainable tourism and what part is not within tourism planning issue.

EVOLUTION OF ARTIFICIAL INTELLIGENCE IN SMART TOURISM

Technology was predominantly being utilized in innovations with a critical effect of development on the tourism industry (Hjalager, 2010). Borras, Morreno & Vals (2014) recorded the surveys where these structures were applying some of the AI practices such as;

intelligent autonomous agents that can analyze the users behavior, learn about their profile and derive proactive recommendations in certain period of time, optimization in terms of a detailed timetable of the visit according to the opening hours of the site clustering or classifying tourists, with similar characteristics, inferring the preferences of the users through approximate reasoning methodologies, deducing users' preferences through reasoning of tourism domain knowledge by ontologies (Borras et all 2014, pp.7370-7371).

Big data and analytics has given rise to emergence of smart tourism ecosystem within large data sets in many different formats obtained from various stakeholders through the internet of things, artificial intelligence, cloud computing services, sensors, mobile devices and the Internet are processed with different analysis techniques such as emotion analytics, text analytics, and web analytics. Then this information is being transferred by algorithms into interpreted information to guide decision-making process.

Embarking on Industry 4.0 and the latest progress in communication and information technologies have given rise to improvement of new product and services in line with this paradigm modification. In the digitalization process we live in, the big data that emerges as a result of the widespread use of the internet, smart phones and social media applications is analyzed and then tried to be used in decision making process (Chen H, Chiang R H, Storey; 2012). Naturally, tourism as an industry is also one of the fields that try to keep up with this rapid change and start to benefit from the opportunities offered by big data and data analytics (Carigliu A, Del Bo; 2011).

The tourism industry, which has changed with a data oriented approach, has adopted the word "smart", which we have started to hear frequently in different areas, pointing to the use of the concept of Smart City and Smart tourism, and as a result, a paradigm shift triggered by digitalization in the field (Del Bo and Nijkamp, 2011; Boggia and Camarda 2014; Damari 2013; Albino, Berrardi and and Dangalico, 2015).

In the literature, description of smart city provides rich and on-site occurrences to beneficiaries through smart phones, and creates rates in terms of actions with mutual information, exchange, and that efficiency and sustainability are aimed throughout process through collecting, combining and processing data on destinations (Gretzel, Sigala, Xiang, Koo, 2015; Jastrotia and Gangotia, 2018). The recent industrial revolution Industry 4.0, abbreviated as, has revealed a more complex vision that includes technologies such as internet of things, robotics, cloud computing, augmented reality, cyber security, big data and analytics, machine learning, not alone but in integrated structures, simultaneous and real-time (I-Scoop, 2021; Höjer and Wangel, 2015). Industry 4.0, unlike previous revolutions, has features such as including more automation, bridging the internet of things and the physical and digital environment, providing more personalized products where smart products determine the production stage (I-Scoop, 2021). With these features, Industry 4.0 data, use it to increase efficiency, transform manufacturing process, disseminate knowledge along the value chain, and create commerce chain, products and enterprise models.

The concept of "smart", which is basically defined as the transformation of data into business intelligence for the processing, analysis and decision-making process with the opportunities offered by Industry 4.0 technologies, has started to be added to the factories, energy, manufacturing, buildings, services, cities and the tourism sector (Harrison, Eckman, Hamilton, Hartswick, Kalagnanam, Paraszczak, Williams 2010; Buhalis D, Amarenggana 2014). According to Gretzel, being smart stems from the fact that various technologies are interrelated with each other and can work simultaneously and harmoniously, rather than being a feature of a single technology (Gretzel U, Sigala M, Xiang Z, Koo; 2015).

Technologies for achieving this harmony and for the right decision-making mechanisms are the tolls for connections, and the big data and analytics are the resources that enable the data coming from different channels to be blended and turned into business intelligence (Arbib and Felleous, 2004).

THE CONCEPT OF SMART CITY

Digital communication and information technologies which are affecting the functioning of the metropolitan correct use of connected information from all stakeholders and smart systems finding flexible solutions to problems, sustainability for a better future, increasing the life quality and work, helping the surrounding and people sensitivity and economic development represent the blend of definition (Çelik & Topsakal 2017; Jasrotia A & Gangotia, 2018).

Smart cities are divided into six main components and directly related to economy, people, mobility, and living sub-components, and directly related to management and environment (Buhalis & Amarenggana 2014; Cohen 2021).

The concept of smart tourism is a complex structure comprising of smart experience, smart venture ecosystem and smart destination sub-components that exchange data with each other and operate in constant connection, identical to the smart city concept (Gretzel U, Sigala M, Xiang Z, Koo & 2015).

Different technical knowledge for example; RFID, NFC, artificial intelligence, internet of things cloud computing, AR, VR, QR codes, location-based services, geo-tag, beacon technology, social media applications etc. are involved in the production of tourist's smart experiences (Wang, 2014; Lopez de Avila, 2015).

Smart business ecosystems include an open data-oriented and sharing structure where all the stakeholders government, public and private companies are in co-operation of basic business steps supported by technology (Çelik & Topsakal, 2017).The smart destination component on the other hand is a structure that can be considered as smaller components of smart cities, where visitors are taken into account as well as visitors as smart city services applied to urban and rural area (Lopez de Avila; 2015). The concept of smart tourism is also used synonymously with smart destination in the literature (Yalçınkaya P, Atay L& Karakaş, 2018), and its definition in WTO (2017) keeps the two concepts together in the same direction.

For smart tourism adaptation, it is necessary to organize the technological and physical infrastructure, which is also called the platform, and to provide instant data flow from all components, as well as to examine this data with the right techniques and turn into quick managerial decisions and feedback (Chen H, Chiang R & Storey, 2012; Buhalis and Amarenggana, 2015).

Therefore, big data analytics are of great importance in determining current trends and developing a customer-oriented service approach by rapidly processing data from all kind of stakeholders from managers, employees, investors, customers to local people (Camilleri, 2020).

The synchronized digitalization and new technologies employment in the tourism industry has altered the behaviors of tourists, business and tourism centers, enabling them to anticipate the benefits of a smarter approach to achieve efficiency and sustainability.

Gretzel, Wethner, Sigala, Koo & Lensfus (2015) proposed a model which can be explored at diverse layers for instance;

- **Local level** which integrates crux of the business such as suppliers other related players in the business which connect through smart applications so as to generate enriched value.
- **Intermediary level**, that will utilize relevant elements within business ecosystems for instance; government bodies, markets, competition. Additionally, different kind of stakeholders should form a merger so as to form a platform for conserving and safeguarding resources of tourists by supporting participation among different participants.
- **The final level** is the global level with priority on supplementary elements affecting the ecosystem. These are global competition and global markets.

To co-create value, conceptualizing the essence of the units are connected in destinations (Buhalis & Amaranggana, 2014; Buhalis, 2015). Soft smartness concept will be based on soft power and smartness units in its employment of highly sophisticated technologies. It also reflects human capital from the tourist centric angle (Cizel and Ajanovic; 2019).

However, Singh (2019) puts forwards some contrasting view with smart tourism concept. The author suggests that as a remedy to individual connected problems of traffic, self-driving cars have been proposed even though it is not proven to be achievement. Besides, sixteen companies are in competition to sell those cars for extensive revenue (Hiltzik, 2018; Singh 2019,). In 2018, a woman was murdered by Uber self-driving car. Subsequently, driver owner of Tesla's x model car was killed on auto-pilot. However, perception and prediction seems to be problem that makes such cars unmanageable.

On the other hand, robots may take the responsibility of many tasks from individuals (I scoop, 2021). Robots are not very close in performing tasks including illustrating creativity (Singh, 2019) or showing emotions (Nictch & Popp, 2014). On the other hand, Ekman & Friesen (1978) states that a six essential emotions that are specified through facial interpretations in robots and these are hate, horror, surprise, satisfaction, grief, and dislike. Additionally, Kısmet, Leonardo and Paro robots which are developed to be social robots through using facial expressions to communicate with people. These robots can transmit various emotions eye brow, eye lids, lips and ears, head orientation (Nicthch and Popp, 2014). Leonardo, Kısmet's inherited have almost human-like facial expression abilities and can utilize body language (Breaeal, Buchsbaum, Gray, Gatenby& Blumberg; 2005). It is indicated that human attitude may transmit from human being to another one to human-robot communication and co-operation beyond the specific craving of human feelings. Having said that the relationship between emotional attitude and robot is rather complicated (Nitsch & Popp 2014). More specifically, if a robot behaves in a joyful manner, it would be chosen for a play, but an earnest robot would be selected for critical activities (Goetz and Kiesler and Powers; 2003).

Singh (2019) suggests that using self-driving cars would be beneficial to stop traffic problems for number of reasons. For instance; cab drivers would no longer take advantage of tourists. Furthermore, roads would be more secure for tourists because of potential car accidents. Additionally, digital money would be become more public, and radio taxis of the sort Uber and Lyft are encouraging would be a source of alleviation and comfort to exhausted tourists. Apart from that self-driving cars would be achievement story for developed countries as the roads are properly signposted and being mapped through geographical information system. In that case, the situation in developed countries is more promising because of the accurate signposting. Last but not least, machine- human communication with travelers via e.g. voice commands. These are the bright side of the coins regarding the advantages of smart tourism.

Downsides of smart tourism also exist in the literature. First, in developing countries road conditions are not suitable for self-driving cars due to missing road signs and infrastructures. Second if the traveler does not have the exact amount, this may lead to abuse of tourists. Third, digital money hoax would be more prevailing. Fourth self-driving cars may give rise to getting tourists lost by misleading road signs. Therefore, conveyers may be hijacked because of the previous condition. Accountability related to car accidents or hijacked vehicles would be serious danger. On the other hand, when companies earning a lot of money, the taxi drivers may lose their jobs (Sing; 2019).

There is also a school of thought that are favored using robots in smart tourism and the view has four dimensions to explain its usage and may change the perception towards robots in tourism. The emotional involvement of robots has four dimensions. First, emotional interpretation and body language, second, robots may have actually emotions, third the outcome should re-explore the neurobiology and fourth, emotion robots may offer and apply an original test-base for theories of biological emotion.

SUSTAINABLE TOURISM

Having debated Smart tourism issue, Sustainable tourism concept will be analyzed within three dimensions which are environmental impact, socio-economic impacts and the tourism product along with tourist markets. The connection of tourism with environment and local community and how to allocate resources for developing tourism are part of the searched issue. Sustainable tourism development accommodates the wishes of today's travelers and host locality while preserving and boosting opportunities for the future. It is also considered as prominent to governance of all resources in such a way that social, economic, and aesthetic needs can be accomplished while protecting cultural unity, fundamental biological diversity, ecological process and life support system.

United Nations defined Sustainable tourism development as "meets the needs of the present tourists and host regions while protecting and enhancing opportunities for the future. It is envisaged as leading to management of all resources in such a way that economic, social, and aesthetic needs can be fulfilled while maintaining cultural integrity, essential ecological process, biological diversity, and life support system" (WTO; 1998, p.19).

The Framework of Sustainable Tourism

Principles of Sustainable tourism are summarized as stated below.

- The authentic, physical, social and other kind of reserves for the industry are protected for ongoing application in the long run, while delivering gains to the local community.

The sustainable development concept is notably significant for the industry as the industry is relied upon tourist activities and attractions which are linked to the cultural, historic, natural and environment inheritance of an area. If these wealth and capabilities are destroyed or degenerated, then tourism industry may not be flourished. In fact, preservation of part of these richness may be strengthened by tourism development. Preservation of natural tourism reserves can assist residents of a regional area and making them feel appreciative of their inheritance and assist their conservation.

- Tourism growth t is arranged and being guided in order not to cause significant sociocultural or environmental crises in tourist destinations.

Environmental planning concept and carrying capacity technique are significant methods for preserving sociocultural and ecological problems resulting from tourism. Operation of environmentally safe technology is to be aided in diminishing the negative impacts of tourism development.

- The comprehensive ecological aspect of the industry is supported and enhanced when it is desired.

Many travelers want to visit areas that are interesting, non-polluted, functional. Tourism and hospitality industry can ensure motivation and instruments to protect when a need arises to enhance the physical quality of local region. A superior profile of conservationist standards is rather significant for the local inhabitants to benefit tourism. Tourism would aid inhabitants to become more conscious of the attribute of their surrounding and encourage its care.

- A superior profile of tourist contentment is provided so that the tourism destination will keep its marketable position.

If the travelers are not happy with the touristic localities, they cannot contain its tourist market and prevail as a feasible destination. Former destinations, for instance, generally require an occasional a regular regeneration to match marketing objectives and sustainability.

- The advantages of tourism are extensively disseminated all over the community.

Tourism development must be designed and governed so that its advantages are disseminated as extensively as possible by community of the tourist destination. Therefore, the advantages will be intensified and inhabitants will encourage tourism if they are having gains out of it. Community-based tourism plans and programs are a significant method for spreading advantages to inhabitants.

It should be noted that tourism politically recognizable and without compromising its feasibility. Political support and commitment should be provided for sustainable tourism. Therefore, tourism policies and plans should be based on sustainable tourism principles. Sustainable tourism can be feasible by careful organization and planning process. In this sense, Agenda 21 is a complete schedule of activity adopted by 182 governments at the Earth Summit in 1992 on predominant development and environment matters at the global level. Agenda 21 serves a blueprint for safeguarding the sustainable future of the world. In Agenda 21 Framework, World Tourism and Travel Council, Earth Council, World Tourism Organization formulated a plan as to be Agenda 21 for the travel and tourism sector in relation to Environmentally Sustainable tourism development. This schedule offers the specific role to travel and tourism industry towards Environmentally Sustainable Development. The program offers definite role that travel and tourism can have in attaining the objective of Agenda 21. According to Agenda 21 for tourism sector states that government departments, National Tourism Organizations and trade association, the objective is to set up systems and process to integrate sustainable development considerations at the central of the decision- making process and determine crucial actions to deliver sustainable tourism development. In sum, Agenda 21 sets up actions and priority areas (WTO;1998).

According to **UN Goal 17** refers to forming sustainable tourism that provides employment and encourages local civilization product. Tourism is a significant determinant of employment and foreign exchange. Thus the industry leads to social, environmental and economic welfare of many countries, notably in developing countries. Investments of local Tourism Businesses in sustainability promotes that to reinforce investments in sustainable tourism, including cultural tourism and eco-tourism, which may add forming small and medium sized companies and facilitating access to finance, including through initiatives for the poor, aboriginal and local communities in fields with high eco-tourism possibility. Resort related tourism and coastal tourism are for instance are crucial industries of the economy in resorts and coastal least developed countries (UN WTO, 2019, WTO 1998). For instance; community local products can be integrated into sustainability approach in the locality. In this regard, below represents a nice blend of sustainability and local agricultural development.

COMMUNITY AIDED AGRICULTURE

Community Aided Agriculture has its roots in the USA. The model consists of community members who are willing to sell their products on an annual subscription program. This allows them to plan in advance what their locality want them to grow. Additionally, through subscription payment earlier, the farmer is better able to manage the annual developing and cropping cycle.

The crucial issue here is that forming a harmony between environment and sustainable tourism development (UNDP, 2018).

TOURISM PLANNING FOR LOCAL TOURISM DEVELOPMENT

Local tourism planning focuses on delivering definite socio-economic benefits to society while observing sustainability of the tourism sector by protecting the environment and local culture. Planning is formulated within a generation framework and must apply an adjustable, integrated, extensive sustainable, environmental, implementable and community based approach. Similarly, strategic planning approach is sometimes employable since all the pieces of tourism must be regarded in planning: tourist activities and attractions, transportation, infrastructure and another element, accommodation, institutional alternative tourist services and facilities (Local Agenda 21).

Tourism planning is executed in accordance with a systematic process of continuous steps:

Step 1: Study preparation encompassing the terms of reference for the planning project.
Step 2: Decision of tourism development objectives.
Step 3: Evaluation off all the relevant elements and survey.
Step 4: Analysis and amalgamation of the survey information.
Step 5: Composition of the tourism plan and policy.
Step 6: Composition of other recommendations.
Step 7: Applications and management

Local governments must decide and alter site planning principles, design guidelines and development standards for tourist facilities so that they are combined with the environment and do not to cause environmental problems. Development standards relate to several factors: Site coverage landscaping, building height limits, off street parking, densities, public access, going through of utility lines. In coastal areas, asking sufficient setbacks of building from the shoreline is significant. Suitable architectural, landscaping and engineering design of facilities are rather significant. Quality standards for services and tourist facilities must be embraced and suitably managed to assure that facilities are off admissible standards and meet the expectations of tourists (WTO, 2018).

In recent years, tourism sector has witnessed wonderful alteration, new destinations with dissimilar appearance and holidays styles and the integration of different kind of technologies into its business. Environmental tourism, sustainability concept and ecotourism and its waves, preserves areas, resort destinations and other remarks have raised and been offered to tourism in previous years subsequent to awareness and required a sustainable tourism in globe.

COST BENEFIT ANALYSIS

This part of the chapter aims at investigating smart tourism issue through cost-benefit analysis. The study also carefully investigates the impacted areas of smart tourism in connection with sustainable tourism. Cost benefit analysis is lacking in tourism sector and fundamentally used for reviewing transport related infrastructure programs and policies within tourism industry. The concept is used to make inferences in line with smart tourism concept under the light of sustainable tourism point of view. Therefore, the study offers valuable insights for other researcher, practitioners and managers to assess the for and against views of smart tourism. The Value cost and benefit approach of policy, project or decision has been utilized for the study. Cost and benefit analysis is an analytical process that may be utilized to measure and differentiate the environmental and socio-economic costs and benefits in decision making process of demand side in destinations (Read; 2013). Marshall states that this approach is supposedly was introduced in midcentury and subsequently it was adjusted (Deput,1848). Nowadays, it is in use by governmental authorities and profit-making sector. However, cost benefit analysis is generally accumulating applicability since it is calculated by eagerness to pay of persons. It is important to state that there are winners and losers as an outcome of a project, a decision or a plan. If the defeater attains more than underprivileged lose in such case net benefit is assessed. How can a desirable outcome or net benefit be defined? Success degrees may be varied in line with the potential threats or confrontations.

Read (2013) identified a five-stage process initiated as follows. Inclusion of related studies, expansion of social, economic and environmental benefits and costs, forming an algorithms and measuring gratitude for all categories, a preliminary testing of the mechanism, and assembling results into a framework of investigation. A cost benefit investigation of tourism may comprise all behaviors of indirect effects notably, pollution attribute, pesticide use in products, fabricating transfer conveyance. Consequently, sensible bounds ought to be installed for the analysis and judgement of decision should be made regarding extensive impacts.

CBA analysis is extensively utilized for the assessment of transport and infrastructure proposals and programs for the last forty years. Despite the fact that some of the disadvantageous of CBA exists in the literature, it is still offers a value of constructing all side of effects. Their analysis is based on Internal Rate of Return approach. The Project highlights net benefit flow as a rule in decision making (Kocabaş & Kopurlu 2010).

On the other hand, this technique has had major criticism in non-merchantable costs and benefits of monetized projects (Hensher & Greene, 2003). Hence, value of life and ages draw analyst's attention. To assess the life there are two main paths which are willingness to pay approach and human capital approach. Henser et al. (2009) indicates that willingness to pay approach is being chosen in comparison to human capital approach and the latter is more suitable for safety issues for instance; the analysis of safety of a road in order to weigh the benefits of that road. Willingness to pay approach depends on income and how the segment ready for paying the cost. By contrast, to assess the significance of life is not a clear cut case and is full of various difficulties. Nevertheless, how human life should be assessed or valued has not been statistically provided as data. Similarly, willingness to pay concept means that in the case of death situation, danger should be avoided and the defeaters are ready to pay for the risks to avoid or overcome the possibility of a threat. (Heinzerling & Ackerman, 2002). It should be noted that it takes a lot of verbal disapprovals. Because of the fact that to value the life before or after implementing the project or program is not specifically set or decided. Even though advantageous and disadvantageous of the project or program are somehow counteracted, it is not certain to specify the impacts are underestimated or overestimated with regard to assessing value (Panayatou, 2000).

Similarly, the same school of thought on CBA is shared by many scholars. An interdisciplinary approach with inclusion of many experts in various domains unitedly with improvement from Value of life is generally core of the most studies of CBA analysis and there are couple of major concepts which are human capital approach and willingness to pay concept. The subsequent approach is rather convenient for the analysis of security benefits of highways. However, the problem in assessment of life is clear because of the fact that the absence of analytical life and human life cannot be estimated (Hensher, Rose, Ortuzar and Rissi, 2009; Heinzerling and Ackerman, 2002; Kocabaş and Kopurlu, 2010).

Syafinaz, Juni, İbrahim and Manaf (2017) states that it may suffer from the obstacles of CEA in selecting a suitable section of effect, on the other hand it contains downsides notably in relation to impact assessment. It grapples with the negative sides in assessing a changing grades of results of a program or interference for example; alteration in wellbeing and excellence of life in relation to monetary terms which can be hard an even corrupted or illegal (Mills and Gilson, 1998). Individual preferences should be defined well and when the benefit exceed the cost the project proposal is accepted (Drummond, Schulpher, Torrence, O'Brien & Stoddart, 2005).

Such analysis is represented by means of human prosperity, wellbeing or efficiency. It is being estimated by one's receiving the cost in order to gain the profit. While the crux of the CBA is based upon identifying one's choices; and social selection represents exceptional blended group of people. As a result of this process for a project to be deemed to be worthwhile or justified depends on how total expenses should exceed the total benefit (Ackerman & Heinzerling, 2002). Under this examination budgetary assessment raises some questions about inequality, discounting and appraisal. CBA analysis illustrates a justified preference (Ben-Amitai, 2006, p. 364 in Kwangseon) and Willingness to pay changes in accordance with income and consumption (Frank 2000). In some cases, values and options can be too computing. Overall social utilities and values may be contradictory. Ackerman and Heinzerling (2002) indicates that some group of people who are getting the benefits, the rest of the people's rights are not cared much.

The fundamental idea is economic wellbeing should supersede expenditures. There are different school of thought regarding CBA's output ratio for instance the "economic interval rate of return (EIRR), the net present value and the break-even point" (World Health Organization [WHO], 2006). The EIRR illustrates intervention's return on investment, which is the deduction rate at which the prospectus expected flow of benefits equals the prospectus expected flow of expenditure (WHO, 2006). In this case the net present value indicates that the net financial welfare earnings which was set at the beginning, anticipated from interference course. Whereas the break-even point reflects that the subsequent period of intervention's investment stage corresponds to economic benefit gained through interference. (WHO, 2006). Human capital approach is rather easy to run, however there are some ethical and budgetary drawbacks that reduces its employment. Such concept is employable in the labor market, where earnings are given to employees as incentive to take riskier jobs. Regardless that some other factor affects estimation of the programs or projects. More specifically, the contingent valuation technique utilizes samples in the valuation of its effect. That means what people conceive that they would pay may not actually, the amount that they would really pay in definite circumstances (Syafinaz, Juni, İbrahim, Manal, 2017). The authors explained different kind of fiscal analysis which are Cost Maximization Analysis (CMA), Cost Effectiveness Analysis (CEA), Cost Benefit Analysis (CBA), and Cost Utility Analysis (CUA). CEA analysis is utilized for monetary assessment as a technique in which objectives are the main criteria for limited assessment. The validity is based on a specific unit effect of a program (Mills and Gibson; 1988). CMA is suitable when the results for discrimination are equal and is employed to determine the minimum cost interference. CBA and CUA should be the selection technique. The concept of CBA is more extensive in terms of conversion of benefits and costs into economic terms. It is not limited to using this technique entirely within one different layer of economy (Drummond, Schulpher, Torrence, O'Brien & Stoddart, 1987).

The process of CBA can be summarized as stated. In phase 1 objectives of interference are described. In phase 2 baseline is defined in the case of if the intended action would not be taken. In phase 3 alternative choices to accomplish objective are defined. In phase 4 investment cost of every option is assessed. In phase 5 adverse and favorable benefit impact of every option alternative selection is determined. In phase 6 valuation of effects in fiscal terms are specified. In phase 7 current expenditure and assets value of costs and benefits utilizing discount rate are estimated. In phase 8 NPV OR BCR OF each of each option are determined. In phase 9 sensitivity analysis is performed. In phase 10 the most productive interference opportunity is selected.

SOLUTIONS AND RECOMMENDATIONS

Investments should be made in systems capable of collecting big data, namely smart tourism tools and infrastructure. Accurate interpretation of data enables informed and smart decisions. Data privacy and security should also be given importance. It should be stated that the boundaries laws and regulations that of complied with, and the privacy and security policies explaining where and how user data will be used should be clearly articulated. Ensuring that user data securely is likely to assist people's acceptance and adoption of such technologies. Use of digital technologies related to cooperation and data sharing without violating personal data security and privacy, destinations should be allowed to interact with tourists, leading to better communication between all stakeholders in destination marketing. This interaction is valuable for making real-time and on the spot decisions regarding efficiency, resource management and sustainability.

FUTURE RESEARCH DIRECTIONS

Since the robots have started to overtake people's jobs in tourism destinations at various degrees, there is a highly likely that they may cause some damage to a human being or not being able to take right action towards tourists where their help is mostly needed. At this point who would be the responsible part of this malfunctioned operation? Therefore, delineation of responsibility should be determined clearly and explicitly. Moreover, the developer of the algorithms should not be the only decision-maker in tourism destination in relation to service provision. Another issue which needs to be investigated is that security violation cases in which data is acquainted through tourist activities within big data environment. How can be data collection is provided without causing data security and data violation? Thus the employment of the robots in service provision instead of human actually contradicts with the sustainable tourism concept and its principles. Basically, tourism is supposed to generate income as a livelihood for residents rather than robots in destinations. As a result, their existence actually contradicts with Sustainable tourism development approach.

CONCLUSION

Describing carrying capacity in a locality in line with sustainable tourism will ensure a competitive advantage of a destination over smart tourism applications to create efficiency and effectiveness of resources. However, at this point, it should not be forgotten that the information to be obtained from big data during tourist activities my mean violating data security and data privacy of tourists. With respect to sustainable tourism principles, employment of smart applications in tourism destinations to some extent contradicts with the concept and to some degrees supports the concept even reinforces at varying degrees. These are, first, in marketing of destination attractions and tourist activities are supposed to deliver different kind of profits or gains as an income source to local people. So, if the residents are not being employed in the locality who would be taking advantage of tourism benefits as a livelihood? Second, sustainable tourism development is supposed to guide tourism development not to cause any sociocultural crises. Such notion contradicts with the applications at increasing level. Being physically distant to tourist may likely to cause antagonistic feelings towards tourist and tourism development.

Therefore, residents my hinder the development in different ways in retaliation. Third, comprehensive environmental aspect of tourism is supported and enhanced through sustainable tourism. In this regard, smart tourism concept may be a right aid in maintaining carrying capacity of a destination through collecting data over visitors unlike the previous conditions discussed earlier. Fourth, a high profile tourist satisfaction is provided through combination of utilizing smart tourism and sustainable tourism principles. This is largely because, AI applications is being employed in various marketing and tourist guiding activities in smart tourism so, it may be a right choice taking advantage of smart tourism. But, at some point human touch may be a good choice in service provision such as host and visitor interaction cases. Fifth, the advantageous of tourism are extensively disseminated all over the community. In sum, if the benefit taker would not be the local inhabitants, in this case who would be benefitting the advantageous of sustainable tourism in the locality.

To sum up, smart tourism may not be the sole data provider for tourists or residents for satisfaction of both sides. In fact, they should be used in combination, in accordance with the interrelated situation or cases determined by different stakeholders within destination. It should be appropriate to say that within cost-benefit analysis introducing smart tourism in destination it removes the significance of human capital approach within CBA. Consequently, the other approach in CBA analysis may be viable, willingness to pay approach. Since, the practice of this concept requires to have one side of sufficient income to pay for the cost in order to gain a higher benefit, unlike the disadvantaged groups. The critical question needs to be asked here, if the residents are removed from the stage, who would be paying for the cost in order to gain a higher benefit? What they are offering in return of a higher advantage?

REFERENCES

Ackerman, F., & Heinzerling, L. (2002). Pricing the Priceless: Cost-Benefit Analysis of Environmental Protection. *University of Pennsylvania Law Review*.

Albino, V., Berrardi, U., & Dangalico, R. M. (2015). Smart cities definitions; performance and initiatives. *Journal of Urban Technology*, *22*(1), 3–21. doi:10.1080/10630732.2014.942092

Arbib, M., & Fellous, J. M. (2004). Emotions: From brain to robot. *Trends in Cognitive Sciences*, *8*(12), 553–561. doi:10.1016/j.tics.2004.10.004 PMID:15556025

Borras, J., Morena, A., & Valls, A. (2014). Intelligent tourism recommender systems: A survey. *Expert Systems with Applications*, *41*(16), 7370–7389. doi:10.1016/j.eswa.2014.06.007

Breazeal, C., Buchsbaum, D., Gatenby, D., & Blumberg, B. (2005). Learning from and about others by robots. *Artificial Life*, *11*(1-2), 31–62. doi:10.1162/1064546053278955 PMID:15811219

Buhalis, D. (2015). *Working definitions of Smartness and Smart tourism destination*. http: buhalis. blogspot.com/2014/12/working-definitions-of-smartness-and.html

Buhalis, D., & Amaranggane, A. (2015). Smart Tourism Destinations Enhancing Tourism Experience through Personalisation of Services. In Proceedings of Information and Communication Technologies in Tourism (pp. 377-389). Springer International Publishing. doi:10.1007/978-3-319-14343-9_28

Camilleri, M. A. (2020). The Use of data-driven technologies for customer-centric marketing. *International Journal of Big Data Management*, *1*(1), 50–63. doi:10.1504/IJBDM.2020.106876

Caragliu, A., Del Bo, C., & Nijkamp, P. (2011). Smart cities in Europe. *Journal of Urban Technology*, *18*(2), 65–82. doi:10.1080/10630732.2011.601117

Çelik, P., & Topsakal, Y. (2017). Akıllı turizm destinasyonları: Antalya destinasyonunun akıllı turizm uygulamalarının incelenmesi. *Seyahat ve Otel İşletmeciliği Dergisi*, *14*(3), 149–166. doi:10.24010oid.369951

Chen, H., Chiang, R. H., & Storey, V. C. (2012). Business intelligence and analytics: From big data to big impact. *Management Information Systems Quarterly*, *36*(4), 1165–1188. doi:10.2307/41703503

Cizel, B., & Ajovic, E. (2019). Smart tourism Ecosystem Impacts. In D. Gursoy & R. Nunkoo (Eds.), *The Routledge Handbook of Tourism Impacts- Theoretical and Applied Perspectives* (pp. 403–417). Taylor and Francis. doi:10.4324/9781351025102-30

Cohen, B. (2018). *Blockchain cities and the smart cities wheel*. https://medium.com/iomob/blockchain-cities-and-the-smart-cities-wheel-9f65c2f32c36

Damari, R. P. (2013). Searching for smart city definition: A comprehensive proposal. *International Journal of Computers and Technology*, *11*(5), 2544–2551. doi:10.24297/ijct.v11i5.1142

Depuit, J. (1848). On the measurement of utility of public works. *International Economics Papers, 2*.

Drummond, M. F., O'Brien, B., & Stoddart, G. L. (2005). *Methods for the economic evaluation of health care programs*. Oxford University Press.

Frank, R. H. (2000). Why is Cost-Best Analysis So Controversial. *Journal of Legal Studies,* In Kwangseon, H. (2016). Cost-benefit analysis: Its usage and critiques. *Journal of Public Affairs*, *16*(1), 75–80.

Frank, R. H., & Sunstein, C. R. (2002). Why cost –Benefit Analysis and Relative Position. *The University of Chicago Law Review. University of Chicago. Law School*, (68), 323–374.

Goetz, J., Kiesler, S., & Powers, A. (2003). Matching robot appearance and behavior to tasks to improve human-robot cooperation, *Proceedings of the IEEE International Symposium on Robot and Human Interactive Communication*. 10.1109/ROMAN.2003.1251796

Gretzel, U., Sigala, M., Koo, C., & Lensfus, C. (2015). Smart tourism for understanding smart tourism ecosystems. *Computers in Human Behavior*, *50*, 558–563. doi:10.1016/j.chb.2015.03.043

Gretzel, U., Sigala, M., Xiang, Z., & Koo, C. (2015). Smart tourism: Foundations and developments. *Electronic Markets*, *25*(3), 179–188. doi:10.100712525-015-0196-8

Hansson, S. O. (2007). Philosophical problems in cost- benefit analysis. *Economics and Philosophy*, *23*(2), 163–183. doi:10.1017/S0266267107001356

Harrison, C., Eckman, B., Hamilton, R., Hartswick, P., Kalagnanam, J., Paraszczak, J., & Williams, P. (2010). Foundations for smarter cities. *IBM Journal of Research and Development*, *54*(4), 1–16. doi:10.1147/JRD.2010.2048257

Hayashi, Y., & Morisugi, H. (2000). International comparison of background concept and methodlogy of transportation project appraisal. *Transport Policy, 7*(1), 73–88. doi:10.1016/S0967-070X(00)00015-9

Heinzerling, L., & Ackerman, F. (2002). *Pricing the priceless: Cost-Benefit analysis of environmental protection.* Georgetown Environmental Law and Policy Institute.

Henser, D. A., Rose, M. J., Ortuzar, J. D., & Rizzi, L. I. (2009). Estimating the willingness to pay and value of risk reduction for car occupants in the road. *Transportation Research Part A, Policy and Practice, 43*(7), 692–707. doi:10.1016/j.tra.2009.06.001

Hensher, D. A., & Greene, W. H. (2003). Mixed logit models: The state of practice. *Transportation, 30*(2), 133–176. doi:10.1023/A:1022558715350

Hiltzic, M. (2018). Self driving car deaths raise the questions: Is society ready for us to take our hands off the wheel? *Los Angeles times.* www.latimes.com/business/ la-fi-hiltzik/la-fi-hiltzic-self-drive-20180403.-story.html

Hjalager, A. M. (2010). A review of innovation research in tourism. *Tourism Management, 31*(11), 1–12. doi:10.1016/j.tourman.2009.08.012

Höjer, M., & Wangel, J. (2015). Smart Sustainable Cities: Definition and Challenges. In L. M. Hilty & B. Aebischer (Eds.), *Proceedings of ICT Innovations for Sustainability, Advances in Intelligent Systems and Computing* (pp. 333–349). Springer. https://webunwto.s3.eu-west-1.amazonaws.com/s3fs-public/2020-01/final_nursultan_declaration_unwto_urban.pdf

I-Scoop. (2010). *Industry 4.0: the fourth industrial revolution – guide to Industry 4.0.* https://www.i-scoop.eu/industry-4-0/#origins-and-history-of-industry-40

Jasrotia, A., & Gangotia, A. (2018). Smart cities to smart tourism destinations: A review. *Journal of Tourism Intelligence and Smartness, 1*(1), 47–56.

Kocabaş, G., & Kopurlu, S. B. (2010). An Ex-Post–Benefit Analysis of Bolu Mountain Tunnel Project. *Ege Academic Review, 10*(4), 1279–1287. doi:10.21121/eab.2010419612

Kwangseon, H. (2016). Cost-benefit analysis: Its usage and critiques. *Journal of Public Affairs, 16*(1), 75–80. doi:10.1002/pa.1565

Lopez de Avila, A. (2015). Smart Destinations: XXI Century Tourism. Proceedings on Information and Communication Technologies in Tourism, 4-6.

Mills, A., & Gibson, L. (1998). *Health economies for developing countries: A survival kit.* HEFP working paper 01/88.

Mooter, N. (2014). *Cost- Benefit Analysis in Practice-A study of the way Cost-Benefit Analysis is perceived by key individuals in the Dutch CBA practice for spatial-infrastructure projects* [Unpublished master dissertation]. University of Delft.

Nitch, V., & Popp, M. (2014). Emotions in Robot Psychology. *Biological Cybernetics, 2*(9), 418–427.

Piro, G., Cianci, I., Grieco, L. A., Boggia, G., & Camarda, P. (2014). Information centric services in smart cities. *Journal of Systems and Software, 88*, 169–188. doi:10.1016/j.jss.2013.10.029

Read, M. (2013). Socio-economic and environmental cost-benefit analysis for tourism products-A protype tool to make holidays more sustainable. *Tourism Management Perspectives*, (8), 114–125.

Singh, S. (2019). The Onwards March of Technology and Its Impact on the World of Tourism. In D. Gursoy & R. Nunkoo (Eds.), *The Routledge Handbook of Tourism Impacts- Theoretical and Applied Perspectives* (pp. 418–427). Francis and Taylor. doi:10.4324/9781351025102-31

Syafina, I., Juni, M. H., İbrahim, F., & Abdul Manaf, R. (2017). Valuation of Impacts in Cost Benefit Analysis. *International Journal of Public Health and Clinical Sciences*, 4(4), 51–60.

UNDP. (2018). *Channel17 Partnership for the Goals*. https://pacificfilmfoundation.org/partnerships17 ?gclid=EAIaIQobChMIpKLNvbSw8QIVCdTtCh0MWATrEAAYAyAAEgKPy_D_BwE

UNWTO. (2019). *8th UNWTO Global Summit on Urban Tourism Smart Cities, Smart Destinations. Top Incredible Robots that Actually Exist*. https://www.youtube.com/watch?v=ZgtpUd5TsIg

Van Wee, B. (2007). Rail Infrastructure: Challenges for Cost-Benefit Analysis and Other ex-ante Evaluations. *Transportation Planning and Technology*, 30(1), 31–48. doi:10.1080/03081060701207995

Wang, N. (2014). Research on construction of smart tourism perception system and management platform. *Advances in Social Science, Education and Humanities Research*, 30, 1745–1748. doi:10.4028/www.scientific.net/AMM.687-691.1745

WHO. (2006). *Guidelines for conducting cost benefit analysis of household energy and health interventions*. https://www.who.int./indoorair/publications/

World Tourism Organization. (1998). *Guide for Local Authorities on Developing Sustainable Tourism*. WTO.

Yalçınkaya, P., Atay, L., & Karakaş, E. (2018). Akıllı turizm uygulamaları. *Gastroia: Journal of Gastronomy and Travel Research*, 2(2), 34–52.

ADDITIONAL READING

Polese, F., Botti, A., Grimaldi, M., Monda, A., & Vesci, M. (2018). Social innovation in smart tourism ecosystems: How technology and institutions shape sustainable value creation. *Sustainability*, 10(2), 1–24. doi:10.3390u10010140

Prahald, C. K., & Ramaswamy, V. (2004). Co-creation experiences: The next practice in value creation. *Journal of Interactive Marketing*, 18(3), 5–14. doi:10.1002/dir.20015

Singh, S. (2014). Anthropology, tourism and mobility: New directions for research. *The Eastern Anthropologist*, 67(1-2), 39–62.

Yu, G., & Schwartz, Z. (2006). Forecasting short time- series tourism demand with artificial intelligence models. *Journal of Travel Research*, 45(2), 194–203. doi:10.1177/0047287506291594

KEY TERMS AND DEFINITIONS

Big Data: Extensive amount of data which cannot be gathered, saved, or converted by traditional instruments such as word processor within a given time span.

Cost Benefit Analysis (CBA): It is an analytical approach that can be utilized to measure and differentiate the environmental and socio-economic costs and benefits in decision-making process of project or program assessment.

Human Capital Approach: Some ethical and economic concerns are attached to the approach since it is mainly utilized in the labor market earnings are given to employees for them to take more unsafe jobs.

Smart City: Finding solutions to tourism related problems of tourists by employing information and communication technologies in cities supported by different stakeholders.

Smart Tourism: Creating augmented tourist product through collecting, combining, or processing data smart or mobile phones in order to ensure sustainability and efficiency issues.

Sustainable Tourism: This concept fundamentally requires to create a balance between consumption and preservation pattern in counterbalancing future generations' needs along with current tourists' needs.

Willingness to Pay Approach: It is mainly used for securing improvement of highways related projects and plans and individuals are accepted to pay for a cost in order to receive a benefit.

Chapter 4
The Future of Digital Tourism Alternatives in Virtual Reality

Zuleyhan Baran

ⓘD https://orcid.org/0000-0003-4804-5622
Duzce Universtiy, Turkey

Huseyin Baran
Duzce University, Turkey

ABSTRACT

In this study, a review of the future of VR technologies for digital tourism alternatives will be presented. The general purpose of the research is to contribute to VR technologies, which are developing and integrating with new systems with each passing day from the point of view of providing a general perspective in tourism. VR application information to deepen understanding of the scope of the digital future of tourism alternatives will be presented in a systematic framework. In general, VR technologies express the behavioral experiences of individuals in virtual environments. When tourism and VR technologies are combined, the composition of the product in which these virtual experiences are directed towards a purpose emerges. Every new development that occurs from a technological point of VR technology will make it possible to be used in every field of tourism. The contribution of this research is to provide suggestions for future studies as well as practical implications for the tourism industry regarding VR systems, which are among the digital tourism alternatives.

INTRODUCTION

Humanity has important power like as curiosity and through this concept has gone to the path of overcoming all works that it could not be able to do biologically and physiologically with inventions. This process continues with humanity's material processing and development efforts have enabled it to reach the technological dimension. Humanity, which has managed to develop a technological product for every difficult task throughout history transitioned to the modern life process where life became easier with the industrial developments and technological progresess more appropriate over time. Social developments

DOI: 10.4018/978-1-7998-8528-3.ch004

affected by industrial developments and industrial developments also affected by social developments can be regarded as a paradoxical process. At this point development of humanity defining that using Society 1.0–hunter-gatherer, Society 2.0–agriculture, Society 3.0–industrial, Society 4.0–knowledge, Society 5.0–super smart society reflections of these concepts. On the other hand, it has been possible to observe these developments that Industry 1.0–steam power, Industry 2.0–electricity, Industry 3.0–mass production, Industry 4.0–digital technology and Industry 5.0–robotic manufacturing. The social and industrial developments experienced also have reflections on the tourism sector. Positive developments in the tourism sector, where innovative approaches have been experienced in meeting tourist demands in recent years, have left it to the process of overcoming the difficulties posed by the pandemic process, which continues to be effective today. While the issue of sustainability of tourism activities has gained more importance with the effect of the current pandemic, advances in technology have contributed to the development of concepts such as tourism 4.0, smart tourism and digital tourism. In this process, while the new generation advantages created by technological developments reveal important opportunities for tourism which has also made it important to introduce digital concepts such as virtual reality to the sector. This situation shows a two-way development, firstly it gains a whole new dimension in terms of tourist experiences and secondly it opens up brand new tourism investment opportunities for tourism businesses that can offer new experiences to tourists. Tourism evolves from its traditional structure to reality technologies as a result of social and industrial developments. Virtual Reality (VR) is an unreal environment that allows participants to have different experiences in simulation areas. Developing VR technologies are highly demanded in tourism. In general, VR technologies express the behavioral experiences of individuals in virtual environments. VR technology, which has used to promote travel products in first place, which is a marketing product, is now on the agenda in terms of new generation digital tourism alternatives. In this study, a review of the future of VR technologies for digital tourism alternatives and VR application information to deepen understanding of the scope of the digital future of tourism alternatives will be presented in a systematic framework.

VIRTUAL REALITY

History of Virtual Reality

The first and most important development started with the invention of the Stereoscope mechanism, which was developed by Wheatstone in 1838 and enables two-dimensional photographs to be perceived as three-dimensional in virtual reality technology. This process that formed the beginning of the 3D film industry continued with the development of Kinematoscope by Coleman Sellers in 1861 and Mutoscope devices by Herman Casler in 1894 (Brown, 2003). Then the US army used for pilot training called Trainer device that was invented by Link in 1929 in the First and Second World Wars and was the first example of a flight simulator in military field. These developments gained a new dimension in 1948 when Wiener stated that the concept of Cybernetics "human-machine interaction" would positively affect the quality of social life. Then Heilig invented Sensorama ifor the theater cabin, which appeals to all the senses and offers a realistic experience to the user in 1957 and the first head-mounted display (HMD) Telesphere Mask in 1960 (Angelo, 2000). Comeau and Bryan, two engineers, developed prototype of a modern-day HMD in 1961. Sutherland developed the Sketchpad software program, which transfers graphichs drawn to the computer environment in 1963, after that together with his two students they invented the goggles they called Sword of Damocles and hereby the foundation of the virtual reality system in 1968 (Huaman, 2018). Since the concept of virtual reality began to emerge, different concepts such as cyber-space and digital world have emerged. Krueger created systems that respond to gestures-mimics with human-computer interaction allowing the virtual reality artificial environment to be perceived as natural in 1969 and then developed which detects the movements of the participant and adds audio-visual combinations to these perceptions creating Videoplace system in 1974 (Praveen, 2021). Gibson introduced the concept of cyber-space, in which people direct the space in 1982. Later, scientist Lanier defined this concept as virtual reality for the first time and the use of this concept has been recognized since 1989 (Calin, 2018). After this process, game companies started to enter the virtual world. Nintendo first released Virtual Boy, a virtual reality goggle that aims to make the viewer feel like they are in the environment by creating a parallax depth effect in 1995 (Baran, 2020). A prototype of a virtual reality goggles Oculus device, which is a stereoscopic three-dimensional model, including technology, was designed by Luckey in 2010 (VRS, 2017). Today, still developing on virtual reality goggles continue to be updated and renewed by Oculus.

Definition of Virtual Reality

Virtual reality is one of the nine basic components of Industry 4.0 (Yıldırım, 2019a), and it is estimated that it will play an important role in the production of the future and in the creation of value-oriented marketing strategies (Yıldırım, 2019b). The concept of virtual reality, known as the technology that requires participation in the virtual environment produced by the computer, has been developed and reached today (Neuburger et al., 2018). In this environment, the external stimulant is transformed into mental activity with a focus on a different area marked by the illusion of the senses (Girvan, 2018). In the universe created by virtual reality goggles, simulation environments where personal avatars can interact in real time are meant (Guttentag, 2010), which is equipped with optical sensors, infrared emitters, electromagnetic tracking devices to monitor for body movement of user (Huang et al., 2010). It interacts with real-time simulation of the user with special clothes worn on the body, allowing sensory reactions to occur in its mind (Rebenitsch & Owen, 2016) that is a special technology. Virtual reality has basic features such as creating 3D computing environment and integration, intuitive, real-time interaction with this environment. The use of visuality is among the most effective methods for all tourism stakeholders in tourism industry. Virtual reality technology provides awareness enabling the visual presentation of declarations about touristic destinations (Mikropoulos & Bellou, 2006) and thus, it is an important technological product that can provide information about destinations' attractions, historical artifacts, museums and exhibitions in tourism industry (Öngider & Yazıcı, 2020).

Components of Virtual Reality Technology

Virtual reality consists of systems that transform the user into an interactive participant (Gigante, 1993:11). It is possible to say that all disciplines, economies and industries have been affected as the reflections of this transformation process (Yıldırım, 2020). The virtual reality elements that contribute to this are listed below (Ferhat, 2016):

Software

Software can be in the form of presenting an event or object directly to user or it can be in the form of pre-recording a real event or object with imaging devices and transferring it to user with 3D modeling.

Stereoscopic Display and Stereophonic Sound System

The provision of a 3D image is realized through a stereoscopic system in which the image is combined in the brain from a different angle for each eye possessed by human eyes in virtual reality systems. The quality and resolution of virtual images is the most important factor that helps to provide a sense of reality in the virtual environment. Likewise, stereophonic sound systems can be provided by the use of 360-degree surround sound systems that increase the user's perception of reality.

Imagers

In order to provide realistic perception of virtual reality images, the virtual reality goggles are equipped with systems that allow the user to see 360 degrees when turns head (Gigante, 1993).

Sensory Devices

This system is a system that has the most important effect of virtual reality elements and enables the user to become a participant. With the perception sensors used here, wearable technologies that enable the individual to perceive objects in the virtual environment as they are in reality are utilized (Erbaş & Demirer, 2014). Having a sense of touch in the user's perception of reality is important in terms of allowing interaction with virtual objects. Today, these sensory technologies are divided by haptic feedback (feel shape, size, roughness or vibration of the object with interacts through gloves, joysticks, smart clothes) and force feedback (feel movements, jolts, vibrations in the virtual environment) (Gigante, 1993).

Virtual Reality Technology Equipments

Tools that classify user experiences according to emotion, purpose and effectiveness are examined in 3 sections: Stage, Desktop and Mirror World (Kayabası, 2005):

Stage

It is a platform where users can watch, experience and discuss designs and arrangements as if they were real. Stage, real-time communication to users, offers an immersive visualization and awareness for the atmosphere. Stage environment can be explained with 3 virtual reality tools (VRON, 2019). These are described below as Head Mounted Display (HMD), Cab Simulators and Virtual Reality-Chambers:

Head Mounted Display, HMD

Since its inception, the virtual reality space has revolved around the head-mounted display (HMD) as the primary visual display device. Virtual reality futurists, on the other hand, define it as a personal experience in which users interact with a virtual environment and reality synonymously. Looking, pointing, walking are prime examples of this. Spatial immersive display (SID), which emerged as an alternative to HMD, is a screen that drags the user spatially. These screens physically surround the viewer through a panorama of images, usually produced by video projection. SIDs have advantages over HMDs in terms of group viewing and interaction, wide field of view high resolution, bulky headgear and low user fatigue. In addition, angular tracking is performed without head rotation tracking and associated response time requirements. (Bryson et al., 1997).

Cab Simulators

They are cabins connected to computers where users feel themselves in any object (plane, car, etc.). People experience training in these cabins, especially before driving a vehicle in real life. In the world created by reflecting the real environment on the screen, users are enabled to interact with the simulated world inside the cabin. Users immersed in the environment through the cabin interact with the tools such as joystick, remote control, button and steering wheel in the virtual world (Burnett et al., 2007).

Virtual Reality-Chambers

Virtual reality rooms immerse people in computer-generated worlds where they interact with avatars and with each other. These systems allow users to virtually walk on the surface of another planet, steal a laser tag with a friend on the other side of the world, or watch a cardiac surgeon perform an operation as if looking over their shoulder (Wadhwa, 2015).

Desktop World

The system, especially used in the gaming industry, developed to be used with a desktop computer monitor or interactive touch table. In this case, a virtual world is represented, but the user is not completely immersed in it, but only looks at the scene from the outside (Freina & Canessa, 2015).

Mirror World

In recent years, impressive hardware technologies have been developed that enable mobile and embedded devices to take better advantage of the internet and the web and enable users to interact better with the physical world. The world of mirrors, which is shown as one of them, is a technology that provides online multi-entity messaging communication by combining live sensor data in the environment with online 3D environments and participants. The vision of the world of mirrors is modeled by the physical world in which smart spaces, open communities, and software organizations play the role of smart city dwellers (Ricci et al., 2015).

Virtual Reality Types

Virtual reality types are evaluated in three environments according to the immersive level it provides and the differences in the hardware used (Daghestani, 2013):

Non-Immersive Desktop Systems

Desktop systems are display of two or three-dimensional images with the help of a standard high resolution monitor without using immersive elements in virtual reality environments (Mandal, 2013). Interaction in these environments takes place with traditional hardware elements such as keyboard and mouse, and the user is not physically and psychologically separated from the real world throughout the experience. Although these systems that provide a low sense of presence and interaction are mostly used in education, video and game applications, they also provide advantages in terms of adequate image quality, user comfort and low cost (Cox, 2003: 2821).

Semi-Immersive Projection Systems

It is a virtual experience environment where physical and virtual elements are used together without being completely disconnected from reality (Alqahtani et al., 2017). Usually used for training simulator systems have this kind of infrastructure (Yengin & Bayrak, 2017: 381).

Fully-Immersive Head Mounted Display Systems

It is a type of virtual reality that provides the user with the feeling of being a part of the virtual environment and enables them to transform the user into the participant (Mazuryk & Gervautz, 1996). In these environments, also called 'CAVE', a physically fully interactive experience is offered in a multidimensional environment by appealing to the user's multiple sensory perceptions (Muhanna, 2015). In order to create the environment, besides the basic software elements such as 360° shot and 3D models, wall and floor projections, stereophonic speakers, advanced HMD, motion sensors that display the instant perspective of the environment and haptic device (gloves, clothing, etc.) hardware are required (Mihelj et al., 2014).

VIRTUAL REALITY TECHNOLOGY IN TOURISM

Along with all these evaluations, there are some applications for virtual reality technology that are currently used in tourism. Virtual reality tourism applications used in cultural heritage, recreation, museums, travel and food-beverage management are explained below, respectively under the headings.

Virtual Reality in Cultural Heritage

Cultural heritage have a real existence and is defined as national values that contain elements express a community, inherited from the past and transferred to future generations. Cultural heritage sites consist of historical and national values that need to be protected (Vlahakis et al., 2002). At this point, one of the new generation reality technologies such "virtual reality technology" that is used as technology products that allow the original conditions of historical buildings in cultural heritage areas to be seen with virtual travel (Papagiannakis et al., 2005). Tourism activities related to cultural heritage sites carried out by using virtual reality technology is given below;

- Using "ARcheo-Guide" project developed for the Temple of Hera in the Ancient City of Olympia in Greece, the weathered archaeological structures are configured in accordance with their original form and 3D transfer of the ancient image is provided with virtual reality technology. Exhibiting reconstructions of important structures such as the Temples of Zeus and Hera and their objects such as statues, vases and bowls from the period; Olympic sports such as spear, wrestling and long jump are experienced in virtual environment (Vlahakis et al., 2002).
- Made for the Ancient City of Pompeii in Italy, Lifeplus software is combined with virtual reality and virtual storytelling technologies to experience it like it's real (Papagiannakis et al., 2005).
- Valencia Cathedral is designed with virtual reality technology and 3D transfer of old and a new image is provided (Portales et al., 2009).
- Made for the Ancient City of Knossos in Greece, "KnossosAR" mobile virtual reality guide developed for real-time transmission of virtual contents describing the architecture of the period, daily life and the collapse of civilization is provided.
- Made for the Sibenik Cathedral in Croatia, virtual reality app developed about historical buildings and the region is transferred with the 3D virtual animation of Juraj Dalmatinac, architect of this cathedral, by combining education and tourism activities.
- 3D transfer of original states of the cultural heritage sites of Athens Acropolis, Delos, Delphi, Knossos, Kos, Lindos and Olympia is provided with virtual reality technology developed by MOPTIL (Mobile Optical Illusions) company (Moptil, 2019).
- The Mardin Municipality in Turkey offers virtual reality technology service developed by local software developers who provide information about the cultural heritage points of the city during the destination visit. Users can have information with 3D visuals and videos before visiting the areas where they can be discovered about destination with this application (Akram & Kumar, 2017).

Apart from these, Canadian Rockies, The Abbey of Cluny, structuring of China-Beijing that was destroyed in French revolution, and the experimentation of the image of the new city in 3D virtual environments are among the virtual reality tourism applications as cultural.

Virtual Reality in Recreation

Recreation is any activity for leisure and non-compulsive participation in which demographic, sociological, psychological and economic factors are effective. It is thought that virtual reality technology will bring a new perspective to recreational alternatives and similar factors will be effective in the prevalence of recreational use. It is thought that virtual reality technology will bring a new perspective to recreational alternatives and similar factors will be effective in the spread of recreational use (Rainey, 2018). Recreational tourism activities carried out by using virtual reality technology is given below;

- Recreation service that can be experienced with virtual goggles is offered on the virtual reality train LEGOLAND Park in Florida (Legoland, 2018).
- At the Oriental Science Fiction Valley theme park, 35 different virtual reality and recreation activities are offered Guizhou in China (VRFocus, 2018).
- Crytek playground, which was founded by Turks in 1999, provides a recreation activity that enables dangerous sports simulations to be experienced on the game platform using virtual reality technology Coburg in Germany (Crytek, 2019).

- A virtual reality recreation activity with a realistic flight feeling is offered with simulations created with virtual reality software ICAROS that developed by the Hyve company Munich in Germany (Icaros, 2019).
- Serious Game developed for the promotion of the touristic city of Valladolid in Spain, a recreation activity is provided that allows the streets and directions of the city to be recognized accurately. It is thought that the developed virtual reality game system will contribute to the promotion of the tourism aspect of the city.

Virtual Reality in Museums

Although museums are educational, cultural and recreation-oriented institutions, they also have collection and exhibition functions. The International Council of Museums as "a non-profit institution that acquires, preserves and exhibits tangible and intangible heritage for the purposes of education, research, entertainment, and serves community development" defines a museum. It is an important part of the social culture mosaic and provides access to culture. In addition to providing cultural and social benefits for their current destinations, museums also play an important role in creating awareness of social identity, ensuring harmony and increasing the quality of life. Today, museums exhibit a visitor-oriented approach rather than being artifact-oriented institutions. For this reason, they are trying to provide experience-based service where entertainment and interaction will go together. In this context, the development of reality experiences to be offered by new generation reality technologies is considered as an important potential. In recent years, kiosk, beacon, gamification, 3D scanning and new generation reality technologies have been applied in museums. It is stated that new generation reality technologies have an important potential in ensuring interaction with the exhibited works (Dierking et al., 2019). Examples of the activities of museums using virtual reality applications in the modern century are given below;

- With "Virtual Reality Weekend" event brought to life by The British Museum in UK, a museum service that can be experienced with virtual goggles where the objects in the Bronze Age collection can be seen and interacted with in their 3D original states are offered. Since the end of 2018, in cooperation with Oculus, a 360 virtual reality tour with leaf interactive, in addition to the in-museum experience, the service of examining the Ancient Egyptian artifacts in another museum they are connected to online (Whistler, 2018).
- Natural History Museum London in UK undertook five different virtual reality projects in three years. An experience was presented that brings natural history to life with David Attenborough's First Life, created cinematic virtual reality by Atlantic Productions Alchemy VR studio in 2015. In this fifteen-minute experience, the oportinity of seeing the extinct sea creatures long time ago in the depths of the sea with virtual goggles was presented. In the same year, in the project called Great Barrier Reef Dive, a fifteen-minute virtual submarine tour to the Great Barrier Reef was carried out under the guidance of a famous nature broadcaster and the experience of life under the sea was presented. The experience of seeing the world through the eyes of mantis shrimp was presented with the application called Mantis Shrimps Vision Experience in 2016. At the end of the same year, the virtual reality experience "Rhomaleosaurus: Back to Life in Virtual Reality" was presented. The experience of closely examining the sea dragon Rhomaleosaurus Cramptoni, which disappeared 180 million years ago, is presented with this application. The experience of ex-

ploring certain artifacts of the museum was presented, accompanied by Sir David Attenborough, whose 3D animation was created with the Hold the World project in 2018.

- Presented the experience of discovering iconic life types and their relations with each other in the project named "Journey to the Heart of Evolution in the Virtual Reality Cabinet", which established in Muséum National D'histoire Naturelle in France in 2017 (Collins et al., 2015).
- Presented the experience of entering the Mona Lisa painting and interacting with the painting in the presence of multi-faceted sense with a temporary exhibition called "Mona Lisa: Beyond the Glass" in Louvre museum in France in 2019.
- The American Museum of Natural History in the USA offered the experience of discovering the work that was brought to life by combining parts of the dinosaur's skeleton in a virtual environment with a temporary exhibition called "T-Rex: Skeleton Crew".
- The Kremer Museum, with a private space in New York City, is the first virtual reality museum without a physical presence. The museum, which houses 74 Dutch and Flemish old artists' paintings, can only be accessed with virtual reality technology and the experience of examining the texture and colors of the artworks only with virtual reality technology is offered.

Virtual reality applications have been made in the field of archeology, which indirectly contributes to tourism. Niccolucci and Cantone wanted to demonstrate that by transferring a historical monument to a virtual environment, it could better reflect historical remains by integrating archeology and virtual reality. Throughout history, the remains of the tomb of the legendary Clusium king Porsenna, historians and archaeologists have tried to draw for years, but they have never been able to draw this impressive monument in detail. With their research, they managed to shape this ancient tomb in 3D in a virtual environment (Niccolucci & Cantone, 2002). A similar work has been adapted in the form of real-time animations of ancient historical settlements and Fauna-Flor (Papagiannakis et al., 2005).

Virtual Reality in Hospitality

Hospitality is trying to provide visually high quality and rich experiences in order to gain a competitive advantage. Examples hospitality benefiting from virtual reality technology is given below;

- USA Marriott Hotel Group has developed Teleporter virtual reality technology similar to a phone booth equipped with high technology called "Travel Brilliantly" campaign, which provides a four-dimensional (heat, wind, smell, feedback ground) travel experience accompanied by haptic technology (Relevent, 2020). It is offered 360° video-supported "Virtual Reality Postcards" experience of the destination with in-room virtual reality technology by "VRoom". It is brought together technology and tourism by allowing different parts of the world to be experienced through the eyes of specific travelers (Mariott, 2018).
- Arizona Best Western Hotel uses virtual reality technology to promote its hotels with 360° videos and special narration before booking and hosting (Bestwestern, 2018).
- Shangri-La Hotel Group enables the experience of their hotels and destinations through 360° videos; Hilton Hotel Group watch the beaches as if they are watching from the balcony of their rooms, to stroll in the forest, divin into the sea by snorkel with mobile devices; Holiday Inn hotel groups are among that use technological applications that allow them to see some celebrities who come to the hotel and have experience of taking photos with them. (Buhalis & Yovcheva, 2013).

Virtual Reality in Travel

The prevalence of virtual reality technology is classified as experiences before, during and after travel, which is the initial stage of tourism experience. It is designed as a system that allows the tourist who needs information before the trip to experience and evaluate the destination virtually before visiting, enrich the touristic experience by providing awareness of the content, time and place of the destination during the trip, and enable the development of technology by sharing the experiences after the trip (Neuhofer & Buhalis, 2012). Examples of travel businesses that mostly use virtual reality technology is given below;

- Thomas Cook offers helicopter and Egyptian pyramids trip experiences with virtual reality and 360° videos by "Try before you fly" campaign in Manhattan skies (Cook, 2020).
- By opening first of the world virtual airline facility, Tokyo First Airlines pioneered an important transformation that is predicted to take place in the industry. It offers local food service prepared by first-class chefs and unique to destinations during a two-hour 360° virtual travel experience with virtual reality goggles (First, 2020).
- Germany Lufthansa Airlines offers a flight conference experience in a real congress atmosphere, accompanied by experts on airline digitalization by establishing the "FlyingLab" innovation platform (Flyinglab, 2020).
- Jolly Tur organizes virtual tours through 360° videos about destinations and hotels with virtual reality goggles before booking, allowing the final decision to be shaped according to the experience (Global, 2020).
- Turkey Mersin Municipality and the Ministry of Culture and Tourism prepared in cooperation for the final decision with 360° video through the "VR Mersin" in website, important tourism centers as the historical and natural beauties of the city are introduced before visiting the destination (Mersin, 2020).

Virtual Reality in Food and Beverage

The perception of eating in physical life is a complex experience that requires not only the taste and smell of food, but also the perception of other sensory properties (Stelick et al., 2018). However, when it comes to virtual reality, the most important senses that increase the user's perception of presence and reality in the virtual environment are the sense of smell and taste (Guttentag, 2010). Although many studies have been conducted in the scientific literature to simulate the feeling of eating and drinking through virtual reality technology an adequate conclusion has not been reached yet (Ranasinghe et al., 2017).

Today's virtual reality technology, where the sense of smell and taste cannot be fully or partially satisfied, still finds some use in tourism (Guttentag, 2010). Virtual reality technology, which is mostly used in travel, recreation and partially hospitality management, has not yet been fully equipped in food and beverage businesses. Instead, it is tried to provide an immersive and dynamic context for the eating and drinking experience by changing the environment in which the sensory properties of the products are consumed with the developed virtual reality technology (Stelick et al., 2018).

Similar to the examples given before, it is seen that augmented reality technology is mostly used in food and beverage businesses, which allows virtual items to be added to the physical environment in real time. The primary reason for this situation is the lack of virtual reality technology to simulate the sense of taste, so a full immersion experience cannot be realized for the food and beverage industry.

VIRTUAL REALITY TECHNOLOGY REFLECTIONS IN TOURISM

Virtual reality technology and applications, which are becoming increasingly popular nowadays, have basically emerged from the expectation of consumers to experience the sense of reality for a certain product or service in a virtual environment. In recent years, the use of virtual reality technology in social and personal areas has become quite common. Virtual reality technology has advantages and disadvantages in terms of tourism applications, as well as positive and negative contributions.

Advantages

Digital technologies, one of the last products of the industrial revolution, are considered as a system that improves and modernizes life. Digital products, which have become widespread in daily and business life, also contribute to the development of social life, allowing tourism and communication to be experienced in a pleasant way.

Virtual Reality technology provide a significant benefit, especially in cases where the user does not have the time or financial power to perform in the real world, as well as some basic advantages (Li et al., 2011):

Virtual Reality technology can simulate real and unreal event, situation or object. This situation creates an important advantage in terms of providing full freedom to the user, especially in virtual designers (Baran, 2020).

- Since virtual reality technology has been developed to affect the user's perception of reality, the sensory channels that affect individual perception are simulated in real time and the virtual environment can be experienced interactively as if it were real.
- Since many risky situations in the real world do not exist in the virtual environment, it provides an advantage especially for educational purposes.
- Virtual reality technology provides users with the ability to make unlimited observations of any event or object. Thus, the margin of error regarding the situation is reduced and a faster and more effective process is realized.
- One of the most important advantages of virtual reality technology is the accessibility it provides. Thus, the user can reach any part of the world in a virtual environment quickly and smoothly.

Fictions can be made not only in the present time, but also through 3D models of the past and the future with virtual reality technology. A virtual Reality technology has the feature of integrating the real and the reality universe and offering a real-time interaction space (Azuma, 1997). It provides an advantage in promotion with innovative approaches in terms of marketing and advertising with this feature in the tourism sector (Weiss et al., 2004). Dependent behavior and learned helplessness patterns that may occur in tourism activities of elderly and disabled groups, which are relatively difficult to participate in entertainment organizations independently (Gandhi & Patel, 2018) thought that it will disappear with unlimited interaction to be provided through virtual environments (Jung & Han, 2014). When this situation is evaluated in terms of tourism activities, it makes us think that a new virtual reality environment can be created for all kinds of groups and individuals with special needs. The need for information about new destinations to be discovered can be made enjoyable with virtual reality technology, thus providing both intriguing and satisfying information (Buhalis & Yovcheva, 2013). Providing a personalized experience with the filtering method in line with the needs of demographic and social expectations (Selvam et al., 2016) that has the ability to create memorable experiences by enriching and modernizing the service quality with experiential elements such as "information - culture - entertainment" (Manuri & Sanna, 2016). It has a two-way interaction feature as it provides the opportunity to communicate with the real world at the same time while gaining new experiences in the virtual reality environment (Killians et al., 2012). In the communication of the new generations growing up in digital environments, it will be possible to communicate with the new generation digital language opportunities, even when speaking in the mother tongue (Kwok & Koh, 2020).

Virtual reality technology will make it possible to preserve and maintain historical structures for future generations by providing interesting experiences that allow historical events to be relived through time travel (Cranmer & Jung, 2017). It is known that there are different types of virtual reality technology in terms of some hardware and related immersive features. In this context, virtual reality technology can offer different content within the perception of reality that the user needs. Especially with the development and widespread use of mobile devices, virtual reality technology has become more accessible. As a result, it is very important to analyze and evaluate the advantages and opportunities offered by virtual reality technology, which is one of the most important and value-creating technologies of the future, both in terms of providing competitive advantage to technology manufacturers and improving user experience.

Disadvantages

It is very important for both users and technology and content producers to know the disadvantages that have created or have the potential to create as well as the advantages offered by virtual reality technology, which are rapidly entering every field of daily life with the developments in technology. In this context, the necessity of using and developing the said technologies without harming the freedom and legal rights of both the individual in real life and the user in the virtual environment is clear. Digital technologies, which are more and more involved in daily life, may have different disadvantages in different areas of tourism. These disadvantages are explained under the related headings below.

As Tourist: The possibility of changing the roles of real elements and reality elements (Baudrillard, 1994: 244).

As Technological: Technological infrastructure inadequacies, cost barriers, the fact that the tourism experience offered in reality is different from the real tourism experience (Sharples et al., 2008).

As Sociological: The lack of interaction of tourists and local people creates a lack of cultural and social interaction (Pantelidis, 2009).

As Economical: Reducing the economic effects of real tourism in terms of employment and economy for developing countries (Guttentag, 2010).

As Conceptual: Change in tourism definitions that limit touristic activities to physical movements due to the fact that reality experiences are very different from real experiences (Guttentag, 2010).

Apart from these consequences, many studies argue that virtual reality technology may have psychological, physical and social effects on users (Travis, 2010).

- In this sense, the effect of the first virtual reality Plato's Cave video game on human psychology was examined. The game is based on the interaction of a group of people with chains in the cave with their shadows. The game is a first reveals negative effects in that it is based on how immersion in the virtual world can break the connection (Karen & David, 2010) with the real world.

- During reality perception, the brain tends to expend more energy in integrating unusual stimulation. This situation can cause balance problems such as dizziness and nausea due to being different from the real-life environment and improper equipment (Nepal & Shiqi, 2017).
- Since the new generation reality technologies are not an essential need, it is not possible for the consumer to easily give up their purchasing behavior, and it is not possible for the companies selling the product to reduce the price. This situation can reveal a paradoxical loss-loss situation for both parties (Wolwort, 2019).

Virtual reality technology, which offers many applications that facilitate daily life, can cause problems, primarily due to some technical deficiencies, along with all their advantages. As a matter of fact, today's virtual reality technology need advanced technical features in terms of hardware (Yengin & Bayrak, 2017). From this point of view, the fact that computers used individually do not yet have powerful processors to be compatible with virtual reality technology or the cost of such hardware is high restricts the user-based development of these technologies. Again, although the weights of goggles and imaging heads, which are among the basic hardware elements of virtual reality technology, have been made more useful and ergonomic today compared to when they were first developed, they are not yet at a sufficient level for the user to dive into a fully immersive environment.

On the other hand, technical problems that may occur can cause short-term problems in elements such as motion tracking sensors, various sensors and haptic feedback devices that affect the user's perception of reality by increasing the sense of diving, immersion and presence, which are the basic components of virtual reality technology, can be harmful for human health such as dizziness, nausea and eye fatigue (Sharples et al., 2008). Therefore, the systems used should be well coordinated with each other and long-term use should be avoided.

The relationship between virtual reality technology and depersonalization can be explained by the fact that the individual is not affected by extreme behaviors such as violence in the virtual environment and loses the ability to empathize (Güdüm, 2016). Especially in game-based applications, the negative effects of some content on children (aggression, anti-social behavior, etc.) are expressed in different studies (Anderson et al., 2010: 355). However, the use of virtual reality technology in the treatment of some fear and anxiety-based phobias provides an important benefit under the name of systematic desensitization (Parsons & Rizzo, 2008), especially in fully immersive environments, the potential to normalize the user's violent tendencies, is an issue that needs careful attention (Funk et al., 2004).

Another disadvantage created by virtual reality technology is the virtual addiction experienced by individuals who spend more time in the virtual environment than they should, become increasingly addicted and eventually have difficulty in separating the real world from the virtual world (Suler, 2004). Another issue that VR developers and users are worried about is that the content presented with virtual reality technology can be used in a negative way to direct human perception due to the fact that it is realistic and immersive (Ericsson ConsumerLab, 2017). The effect of these situations, on the basis of which there is not only a technological but also a psychological problem, can create many negative physical and mental situations on the real life of the individual.

Advances in the Internet and other digital technologies also change the life and behavior patterns of individuals (Greenfield, 1999). Accessibility, immersion and sense of virtual presence, especially provided by virtual reality technology, increase individuals' enjoyment of this technology and virtual environment. However, virtual reality technology, which can lead to the confusion of virtual and reality day by day, may also be responsible for virtual criminal acts in this context (Grabosky, 2001).

Positive Effects

In recent years, the potential of virtual reality technology to transform the tourism industry has been frequently discussed. As in many areas, tourism is seen as one of the sectors that can benefit from the advantages of virtual reality technology. It is predicted that the tourism and especially the travel sector has a structure that is compatible with virtual reality applications and that its popularity will increase in the near future by reaching its full potential (Cheong, 1995).

For this reason, virtual reality technology can be used effectively in order to eliminate or reduce the effects of these fears by creating a safe environment for those who do not participate in touristic activities due to certain fears. On the other hand, when it is evaluated as the area where it is used, virtual reality technology in terms of tourism that will help to ensure environmental and economic sustainability by eliminating the negative effects, making an effective travel decision (Jung et al., 2017), added the entertainment experience (Guttentag, 2010), effective marketing and promotion of destinations (Williams & Hobson, 1995), creating alternative tourism experiences, creating new attraction centers, making tourism education more interactive and efficient (Roussou, 2004), elimination of travel-related bureaucracy, security and language problems (Dewailly, 1999), embody tourist information and provide accessibility (for disabled, elderly and economically disadvantaged individuals and for remote, unsafe, destroyed or no longer existing places) (Paquet & Viktor, 2005) etc. appears to have many positive effects.

Virtual reality, which offers a rich sensory experience to its users, gains importance with the role of this experience in shaping attitudes towards real touristic consumption (Tussyadiah et al., 2017). Tourism applications created with virtual reality are seen as an important tool for potential tourists to obtain all the information about a planned trip in advance and accordingly to take a more effective travel decision (Arat & Baltacıoğlu, 2016),

In today's digital society, where tourism applications based on tourism-technology cooperation are increasing rapidly, virtual reality offers advantages in terms of tourism development. If these advantages are implemented with the right projects, virtual reality will be an indispensable tool for the tourism sector. Therefore, especially for developing countries, turning to virtual reality and touristic applications in this context indicates that they can increase their share of tourism with innovative solutions (Sambhanthan & Good, 2013). From another point of view, there are relatively few opportunities for other people to participate in recreational activities of people living independent of physical constraints. This widespread lack of opportunity often leads to the development of dependent behavior patterns and learned helplessness (Weiss et al., 2004). Virtual reality, which allows users to interact in a three-dimensional virtual or artificial environment created by the designer, greatly reduces this disadvantage (Gandhi & Patel, 2018).

Negative Effects

Virtual Reality is increasingly taking place in our daily lives and may cause sociological, psychological, economic and conceptual problems.

As Tourist: A representative model is produced by combining virtual reality technology and the basic elements of reality, and this model plays the role of a past or future event - a situation. In this case, reality is destroyed for the benefit of this new reality of the model produced by it. For example Lascaux

Cave, located in Southern France, has been taken under protection and closed to visitors because it has an important historical and archaeological value. Then, an exact replica of the cave was built near the cave, where digital technologies were used, and it was opened to visitors. Scientists express this situation as the mental reality disappears and both caves become artificial as the copy replaces the original, although nothing is physically lost (Baudrillard, 1994: 244).

As Technological: Especially in developing countries, it is considered that there is a lack of technological infrastructure, prejudice against technology, the high cost of these technologies for the consumer, and although it offers a simulation of real experiences, it cannot be a substitute for a real holiday or travel experience (Musil & Pigel, 1994: 92). The impact of virtual reality technology on the tourism sector depends on how fast and well the technology develops, as well as its cost and its acceptability in society. As a matter of fact, tourism activities that can be experienced with current virtual reality technology require less cost than a real holiday or travel expenditure, and it is frequently discussed at the points that they cannot provide the opportunities that a real tourism experience will offer (mutual interaction, souvenir purchase, etc.) (Cheong, 1995).

As Sociological: The fact that the tourist-local interaction, which is one of the main components of the tourism phenomenon, cannot exist in the applications produced with virtual reality, creates a lack of cultural and social interaction, which constitutes an important negativity in terms of tourism (Cheong, 1995). Similarly, it reflects another factor of concern that digital technologies such as virtual reality may cause some physical and psychological disorders individually and negatively affects the socialization process (Sharples et al., 2008).

As Economical: With the use of virtual reality in tourism, the economic impact of real tourism decrease, negative effects on employment and economic, tax and tourism policies problems express the estimated negative effects on tourism sector (Guttentag, 2010).

As Conceptual: If the travel experienced with virtual reality technology is perceived and accepted as a real travel, how the current tourism definitions that limit touristic activities to physical movements will change (Guttentag, 2010). Different answers can be given to this question from different angles, but it seems inevitable that virtual reality technology will create significant changes in the tourism sector in the future.

Real and Reality Paradox

A new reality has emerged with the combination of virtual and real concepts, and this reality is an "immersive environment" due to the perception of human senses as real; "simulation" due to its implementation via computer; Because it is a different production stage, it is called "artificial reality" or "cyber reality" (Yücel, 2016). In this context, according to Baudrillard simulation theory, when today's TV world, games, Disneyland, virtual museums, tours are evaluated, it can be said that reality gradually disappears, becomes blurred and fictionalized lives paradoxically begin to replace reality (Baudrillard, 1994: 246).

The concept of experience defined for virtual environments, on the other hand, is accepted as a sense of being characterized by the feeling of being in a place (Steuer, 1992). From this point of view, the demand that the individual cannot experience in reality for various reasons, but is formed by the desire to experience it somehow, is tried to be met with the alternative reality world offered by virtual reality. Although the postmodern individual and the society rapidly adapt to this process technologically, it can be stated that this adaptation cannot be realized at the same speed psychologically. The most concrete example of this is when a young man in Tokyo made an official application to marry a video game character was a fan of in 2009. This situation reveals that in the digital age, people can do things that they cannot do in real life, thanks to the virtual world, and thus create a new reality space for themselves.

Virtual reality, which can create simulations and limitless simulation environments for the human mind indistinguishable from objective reality; It has the potential to create a new world that exists or is perceived by the individual even if it does not actually exist, and therefore considered to exist (Özgüneş & Bozok, 2017). According to the "Mixed Reality" report published to explain this complex situation, it is stated that virtual reality technology creates some paradoxes on the basis of the user. These paradoxes can be summarized given below (Ericsson ConsumerLab, 2017):

Mobility Paradox

According to the mobility paradox; although virtual reality allows the user to go virtually anywhere they want, in fact, the individual is not physically in motion. Although this situation is expressed as an illusion experienced by the individual, the person, place and events in the virtual world think and feel as if they are real, and this affects the user's perception of reality. For example, the fact that there is an abyss in front of the user in the virtual environment causes his heart to beat rapidly and pulls back in fear, even though he physically knows that there is no abyss in front of him. This paradox, observed by VR experts and neuroscientists in virtual reality laboratories, can be associated with many other concepts from perception to consciousness, primarily by referring to the concept of "being/virtual entity"

Isolation Paradox

Although it is possible to socialize with other people anywhere in the world with virtual reality technology, it refers to the isolation of the individual from the social environment due to virtual reality in real life. In other words, although the user is in an interactive virtual environment, he is actually isolated from the real world and cannot experience the sociality in the virtual environment in real life.

Social Paradox

It also reflects the psychological contradictions of the individual. The fact that someone who is against socialization in real life behaves more socially in virtual reality can explain this paradox. The social paradox of integration, which contrasts with the paradox of isolation, generally applies to virtual environments where individuals can interact with each other through avatars.

Virtual reality should reconcile these paradoxes as much as possible, which should be taken into account by both the producer and the consumer. When we look at the rapidly developing and life-changing technologies, physiological and psychological adaptation problems can be experienced. When this situation is evaluated in terms of the mobility paradox, the fact that users feel uncomfortable and uncomfortable with a virtual reality goggles on their heads can also affects the perception of reality about the experience. Again, social paradoxes emphasize that the individual can cause many social and psychological problems by mixing the objective reality and virtual reality environment. In this context, when the physical and mental problems that can be created by technological changes are evaluated by considering these paradoxes, it is thought that solutions can be considered more comprehensively (Sanchez-Vives & Slater, 2005).

Virtual Reality Tourism in Pandemic

New generation reality applications are considered as a solution for the negative effects of the global pandemic that has emerged in recent years. Digital technologies, which approach tourism activities with a new perspective, are formations that can enable tourism even during travel restrictions and quarantine processes. As potential solutions to government, business and tourists to overcome the global pandemic process (Cranmer & Jung, 2017).

Government: Policies aimed at reducing personal contact (travel restrictions, closure of borders, control of domestic movements, etc.) significantly affect tourism.

Tourist: The emergence of voluntary or compulsory social distance and isolation situations resulting from government policies will push tourists seeking hedonic experience to seek alternative forms of tourism access.

Business: Has to innovate for sustainability due to declining tourist demand and limited tourism products.

Virtual reality technology has the ability to offer tourists a personal, disabled and immersive experience from their seat (Yung & Khoo, 2019). It has the feature of offering businesses the opportunity to eliminate market restrictions, ensure sustainability and gain competitive advantage. In addition, since it is an emerging technology, the lack of established ethical rules and regulatory government restrictions reduces the barriers to virtual reality technology adoption in the short term. On the other hand, it shows that how governments will implement future virtual reality policy arrangements (privacy, authentication, data protection, etc.) will have a significant impact on the adoption of digital technologies (Slutter vd., 2020).

CONCLUSION

Virtual reality, which can enable its users to experience most of a real tourism experience interactively with multidimensional, immersive and various sensory stimuli, has started to increase in recent years with the development of user-based mobile applications. Today, the level of adoption of virtual reality is increasing and efforts are being made to make this technology more accessible. In this framework, many virtual reality applications are being developed and these applications are moving towards becoming an almost inseparable part of the tourism sector. Virtual reality can be considered the beginning of a new era for tourists who cannot participate in tourism activities for various reasons or who want to experience different experiences even.

Virtual reality technology is considered as a remarkable element for the tourism sector. When the tourism sector is evaluated in terms of innovative approaches, tourism elements affected by industry, informatics, communication and digital technologies come to mind. The new virtual reality that has emerged with the technological developments in recent years, especially in the period when a new lifestyle in which restrictions such as the pandemic began to become widespread, shows that there are innovative searches in tourism. It is a technology that allows to visit any destination purchased with online connections, accompanied by avatars, and to communicate during the visit, especially during periods such as pandemic, when the time spent at home increases.

Today, evaluations of current virtual reality applications are generally used to keep interest alive, to provide up-to-date information about potential tourism products and to inspire, rather than replacing real-life travel experiences. However, mixed and cross-reality technologies not only increase the tourism potential, but also contain features that can be presented as an innovative and remarkable tourism activity. Evaluating future investments in this context and integrating them with new generation technologies can be examined as an important element in terms of competitive advantage.

With virtual reality technology, it seems likely that the effects of future negative situations such as pandemics will be reduced. With this technology, many activities such as conferences, meetings, games, entertainment, parties, picnics, chats and recreation will be able to be offered with a service concept that is no different from the reality.

Although virtual reality technology is an innovative approach that arouses curiosity in all areas of tourism, they also have the ability to meet the needs of tourist searches in this direction. The presentation of three-dimensional tourism elements created in virtual environments to tourist experiences can be considered as interesting activities that will carry the perception of tourism to a completely new dimension. The realization of tourism activities within the framework of the new generation reality technology can be considered as very important developments, especially for the elderly, disabled, tourists who have problems in traveling, and for tourists who like to travel alone, and in processes that force them to close their homes, such as the global pandemic. For this reason, it seems likely that tourism activities will develop in the coming years, accompanied by new generation reality technologies suitable for the innovative and dynamic understanding of tourism.

When the national and international studies are examined, it is seen that there are not many studies especially in the field of tourism. The fact that the number of publications is quite low indicates that the adaptation of this technology, which is still in development, to tourism will be completed in the near future.

Especially on the international platform, within the scope of new generation reality technologies, tracks such as games, excursions and walking can be created and offered for sale, enabling people to meet their social needs. In addition, by encouraging the use of virtual reality technology, it seems possible to create a new tourism market and to sign new initiatives in this regard.

New generation reality technologies have integrated with reality and reality, enabling the creation of interactive virtual spaces that can be visited and included with avatars. Thus, it is possible to think of the utilitarian aspect of design as a brand new platform in the field of tourism by revealing a new vision of development in the reality environment where visual design and technology are intertwined. On this platform, it seems possible to provide brand new opportunities in tourism by integrating new generation reality technologies, traditional tourism understanding with the possibilities of the 21st century. Tourism continues to develop within the framework of new generation reality technologies that integrate the concepts of design, technology and society with a new perspective, social media brings communities together and manifests itself with innovations in communication platforms. This development is considered as one of the important achievements of the social and cultural heritage of humanity extending from the past to the future for the digital world.

On the other hand, new generation reality technologies continue to develop with 360 reality and real reality technologies. While virtual reality technology offers the opportunity to experience a fictional experience as if it were real with all the senses, on the other hand, it aims to be a technology that aims to preserve the separation of real and reality worlds. This situation can be considered as a development as a precaution taken considering that the time spent in the virtual environment will increase in the future. Thus, it seems to be a development that will give the individual the chance to realize the concepts of communicating and performing activities at their own free will, by gaining the ability to understand that they are in reality without losing their perception of reality. It is thought that the reality 'R' industry, which is expected to take place in life in the near future, will offer exciting experiences especially in the field of tourism for tourist and managers.

Recently, the lockdown process that has arisen due to the pandemic has paved the way for the development of tourism in the direction of VR technology. During the pandemic period, tourism activities have emerged with VR technology for those who do not want to give up tourism activities and who want to perform tourism activities from their environment. This is a feature that can be expressed as a technical success in terms of tourism, and at the same time, tourism experiences that cannot be distinguished from real tourism are presented by simulating in these tourism areas. This is an indication that tourism experiences will change for the tourist profile looking for different alternatives in future.

FUTURE RESEARCH DIRECTIONS

When the studies around the world are examined, it is seen that there are not many studies especially in the field of tourism. The fact that there has not been any study on the subject of new generation reality technologies in important and remarkable areas such as sports tourism among the national publications is considered as an important detail that is overlooked. In this regard, the ticket sales offered by the NBA and Premier Football Leagues using new generation reality technologies is a very important development. In this context, it is important to draw attention to the issue by making national publications. It can be ensured that any sports branch that can be evaluated on the subject is determined; the necessary infrastructure is created in this regard and presented as a tourism product.

According to the other results obtained from the publications, it is seen that there are studies on the use of virtual reality technology in areas such as historical places, museums and ruins. At this stage, increasing research on tourism investments and obtaining different data for presenting different tourism experiences will contribute positively to the development of this technology in the field of tourism. Thus, an important step will be taken not only by the tourists who come to visit physically, but also in the international context, in terms of offering alternative tourism opportunities for the disabled tourists who seek innovation during the global epidemic process. By including the subject of festivals in new studies on the subject, it can be ensured that the attention of the administrations in tourism activities is drawn to reality technologies. Especially on the international platform, within the scope of new generation reality technologies, tracks such as games, excursions and walking can be created and offered for sale, enabling people to meet their social needs. In addition, it seems possible to create a new market by encouraging the use of virtual reality technology in the field of tourism and to sign new initiatives in this regard.

New generation reality technologies have integrated with reality and reality, enabling the creation of interactive virtual spaces that can be visited and included with avatars. Thus, it is possible to think of the utilitarian aspect of design as a brand new platform in the field of tourism by revealing a new vision of development in the reality environment where visual design and technology are intertwined. On this platform, it seems possible to provide brand new opportunities in tourism by integrating new generation reality technologies, traditional tourism understanding with the possibilities of the 21st century. Tourism continues to develop within the framework of new generation reality technologies that integrate the concepts of design, technology and society with a new perspective, social media brings communities together and manifests itself with innovations in communication platforms. This development is considered as one of the important achievements of the social and cultural heritage of humanity extending from the past to the future for the digital world.

The main subject of tourism, which is a social phenomenon, is human. For this reason, it is recommended not to look at the tourism sector from the perspective of the business discipline due to its economic instrumentality in future studies, and to examine the situation, events or relations in the tourism sector from an interdisciplinary perspective such as philosophy, sociology, archeology and psychology. This interdisciplinary perspective also gains importance in order to better internalize the relationship between technology and tourism.

ACKNOWLEDGMENT

Would like to thank Lidia Oliveira for giving opportunity to publish a chapter in this book and patiently answering every question asked. This research didn't receive any specific grant from any non-profit funding agency, public, commercial or in any sector.

REFERENCES

Akram, W., & Kumar, R. (2017). A study on role and applications of augmented reality in tourism: Its challanges and future prospects. *International Journal of Advanced Research in Computer Science*, 8(8), 168–172. doi:10.26483/ijarcs.v8i8.4633

Alqahtani, H., Liu, C. Z., Thorne, M., & Kang, Y. (2019). An agent-based intelligent HCI information system in mixed reality. *Proceedings 28th International Conference On Information Systems Development*, 226-235.

Anderson, E. (2010). *The imperative of integration*. Princeton University Press. doi:10.1515/9781400836826

Angelo, J. (2000). The link flight trainer. *ASME Landmarks*, 12.

Arat, T., & Baltacıoğlu, S. (2016). Sanal gerçeklik ve turizm. *Selçuk Üniversitesi Sosyal Bilimler Meslek Yüksek Okulu Dergisi*, 19(1), 103–118.

Azuma, R. T. (1997). A survey of augmented reality. *Presence (Cambridge, Mass.)*, 6(4), 355–385. doi:10.1162/pres.1997.6.4.355

Baran, H. (2020). Technological development and art and design as a digital medium. *International Journal of Scientific and Technological Research.*, 6(13), 36–45.

Baudrillard, J. (1994). *Simulacra ve simulation*. University of Michigan press.

Bestwestern. (2018). *Innovative companies*. Retrieved from: https://www.bestwestern.com/en_US/about/press-media/ 2018-press-release/bw-named-one-of-top-10-most-innovative-companies.html

Brown, M. (2003). *Virtual reality training manual*. Retrieved from: https://oxford.universitypressscholarship.com/view/10.1093/acprof:oso/9780195167962.001.0001/acprof-9780195167962-chapter-11

Bryson, G., Bell, M., & Lysaker, P. (1997). Affect recognition in schizophrenia: A function of global impairment or a specific cognitive deficit. *Psychiatry Research*, 71(2), 105–113. doi:10.1016/S0165-1781(97)00050-4 PMID:9255855

Buhalis D. & Yovcheva, Z. (2013). Augmented reality in tourism: 10 Unique applications explained, digital tourism think tank reports and best practice. *Digital Tourism Think Tank*, 1-12.

Burnett, A., Yates, T., & Crane, R. (2007). Rights and the reality of healthcare charging in the United Kingdom. *Medicine, Conflict, and Survival*, *23*(4), 297–304. doi:10.1080/13623690701596775 PMID:17987981

Calin, R. A. (2018). Virtual reality, augmented reality and mixed reality-trends in pedagogy. *Social Sciences and Education Research Review*, *5*(1), 169–179.

Cheong, R. (1995). The virtual threat to travel and tourism. *Tourism Management*, *16*(6), 417–422. doi:10.1016/0261-5177(95)00049-T

Collins, L., Eylott, S., Leedale, J., & Graham, T. N. (2015). Alaska steve: Using virtual reality to enhance a 2nd platforming game. *Proceedings Annual Symposium on Computer-Human Interaction in Play*, 767-770.

Consumerlab, E. (2017). TV and media 2017. *A Consumer-Driven Future of Media*, 9.

Cook. (2020). *Thomascook*. Retrieved from: https://www.thomascook.com/

Cox, C. (2003). *The use of computer graphics and virtual reality for visual impact assessments* (Doctoral dissertation). University of Nottingham.

Cranmer, E. & Jung, T. (2017). The value of augmented reality from a business model perspective. *e-Review of Tourism Research*, 8.

Crytek. (2019). Retrieved from: https://www.crytek.com/

Daghestani, L. (2013). *The design, implementation and evaluation of a desktop virtual reality for teaching numeracy concepts via virtual manipulatives* (Doctoral dissertation). University of Huddersfield.

Dewailly, J. M. (1999). Sustainable tourist space: From reality to virtual reality? *Tourism Geographies Journal*, *1*(1), 41–55. doi:10.1080/14616689908721293

Dierking, L. D., Falk, J. H., & Storksdieck, M. (2013). 34 learning from neighboring fields: conceptualizing outcomes of environmental education within the framework of free-choice learning experiences. In International Handbook of Research on Environmental Education. Routledge.

Erbaş, Ç., & Demirer, V. (2014). Eğitimde artırılmış gerçeklik uygulamaları: Google Glass örneği. *Journal of Instructional Technologies and Teacher Education*, *3*(2), 8–16.

Ferhat, S. (2016). Dijital dünyanın gerçekliği, gerçek dünyanın sanallığı bir dijital medya ürünü olarak sanal gerçeklik. *Trt Akademi*, *1*(2), 724–746.

First. (2020). Retrieved from: https://firstairlines.jp/

Flayinglab. (2020). Retrieved from: https://www.flyinglab.aero/en/about/

Freina, L., & Canessa, A. (2015). Immersive vs desktop virtual reality in game based learning. *European Conference on Games Based Learning*, 195.

Funk, J. B., Baldacci, H. B., Pasold, T., & Baumgardner, J. (2004). Violence exposure in real-life, video games, television, movies, and the internet: Is there desensitization? *Journal of Adolescence, 27*(1), 23–39. doi:10.1016/j.adolescence.2003.10.005 PMID:15013258

Gandhi, R. D., & Patel, D. S. (2018). Virtual reality–opportunities and challenges. *Virtual Reality (Waltham Cross), 5*(1), 482–490.

Gigante, G., & Tomassini, G. (1993). *Deformations of complex structures on a real lie algebra in complex analysis and geometry.* Springer.

Girvan, C. (2018). What is a virtual world? definition and classification. *Educational Technology Research and Development, 66*(5), 1087–1100. doi:10.100711423-018-9577-y

Global. (2020). Retrieved from: https://www.turizmglobal.com/sanal-gerceklik-vr-jolly-tur-tarafindan-acentecilik- sektorune-girdi/

Grabosky, P. (2001). The prevention and control of economic crime. In Corruption and Anticorruption. Canberra: Asia Pacific Press.

Greenfield, D. N. (1999). *Virtual addiction: Sometimes new technology can create new problems.* Retrieved from: http://www.virtual-addiction.com/pdf/ nature_internet_addiction.pdf

Güdüm, S. (2016). Sanal yaşamlar ve bilgisayar oyunlarinda pazarlanan şiddet. *Journal of International Social Research, 9*(42), 1986. doi:10.17719/jisr.20164216306

Guttentag, D. A. (2010). Virtual reality: Applications and implications for tourism. *Tourism Management, 31*(5), 637–651. doi:10.1016/j.tourman.2009.07.003

Huaman, K. (2018). *The history of virtual reality: An escape to different worlds.* Retrieved from: https://www.colocationamerica.com/blog/history-of-virtual-reality

Huang, H. M., Rauch, U., & Liaw, S. S. (2010). Investigating learners' attitudes toward virtual reality learning environments: Based on a constructivist approach. *Computers & Education, 55*(3), 1171–1182. doi:10.1016/j.compedu.2010.05.014

Icaros. (2019). https://www.icaros.com/en/about/

Jung, T. & Han, D.D. (2014). Augmented reality (AR) in urban heritage tourism. *e-Review of Tourism Research, 5,* 1-7.

Jung, T., Tom Dieck, M. C., Moorhouse, N., & Tom Dieck, D. (2017). Tourists' experience of virtual reality applications. *IEEE International Conference on Consumer Electronics,* 208-210.

Karen, S., & David, G. (2010). *Ethics and game design: Teaching values through play.* IGI Global.

Kasapakis, V., Gavalas, D., & Galatis, P. (2016). Augmented reality in cultural heritage: Field of view awareness in an archaeological site mobile guide. *Journal of Ambient Intelligence and Smart Environments, 8*(5), 501–514. doi:10.3233/AIS-160394

Kayabaşı, Y. (2005). Virtual reality and use for education. *The Turkish Online Journal of Educational Technology, 4*(3), 151–158.

Killian, T., Hennigs, N., & Langner, S. (2012). Do Millennials read books or blogs? Introducing a media usage typology of the internet generation. *Journal of Consumer Marketing, 29*(2), 114–124. doi:10.1108/07363761211206366

Kwok, A. O., & Koh, S. G. (2020). COVID-19 and extended reality (XR). *Current Issues in Tourism,* 1–6.

Legoland. (2018). Retrieved from: https://www.legoland.com

Li, C., Wang, D., & Zhang, Y. (2011). iFeel3: a haptic device for virtual reality dental surgery simulation. *International Conference on Virtual Reality and Visualization,* 179-184. 10.1109/ICVRV.2011.32

Mandal, S. (2013). Brief introduction of virtual reality and its challenges. *International Journal of Scientific and Engineering Research, 4*(4), 304–309.

Manuri, F., & Sanna, A. (2016). A survey on applications of augmented reality. *ACSIJ Advances in Computer Science: An International Journal, 5*(1), 19–28.

Marriott. (2018). https://hotel-development.marriott.com/wp-content/uploads/2018/11/Marriott-Hotels-NoAm-November-2018-One-Pager.pdf

Mazuryk, T., & Gervautz, M. (1996). *Virtual reality-history, applications, technology and future.* Technical Report TR-186-2-96-06. Vienna: Institute of Computer Graphics Vienna University of Technology.

Mersin. (2020). Retrieved from: https://vr.mersin.bel.tr/

Mihelj, M., Novak, D., & Beguš, S. (2014). *Virtual reality technology and applications.* Springer. doi:10.1007/978-94-007-6910-6

Mikropoulos, T. A., & Bellou, J. (2006). The unique features of educational virtual environments. *International Association for Development of the Information Society, 1,* 122–128.

Mnhn. (2020). Retrieved from: https://www.mnhn.fr/en/explore/virtual-reality/journey-into-the-heart-of-evolution

Moptil. (2019). Retrieved from: http://www.moptil.com/sites_lindos

Muhanna, M. A. (2015). Virtual reality and the CAVE: Taxonomy, interaction challenges and research directions. *Journal of King Saud University-Computer and Information Sciences, 27*(3), 344–361. doi:10.1016/j.jksuci.2014.03.023

Musil, S., & Pigel, G. (1994). Can tourism be replaced by virtual reality technology? In *Information and Communications Technologies in Tourism.* Springer. doi:10.1007/978-3-7091-9343-3_14

Nepal, G. C., & Shiqi, T. (2017). Issues and challenges. *Virtual Reality Multimedia Communication.* Retrieved from: http: http://web.tecnico.ulisboa.pt/ist188480/cmul/issues.html

Neuburger, L., Beck, J., & Egger, R. (2018). The 'phygital' touristexperience: the use of augmentedand virtual reality in destination marketing. Tourism Planning and Destination Marketing, 1(2), 188–202.

Niccolucci, F., & Cantone, F. (2002, April). Legend and virtual reconstruction: Porsenna's mausoleum in x3d. In CAA (pp. 57-62). Academic Press.

North, M. M., North, S. M., & Coble, J. R. (1997). Virtual reality therapy: an effective treatment for psychological disorders. *Virtual Reality In Neuro-Psycho-Physiology*, 59-70.

Öngider, M. U., & Yazıcı, S. (2020). 360° sanal gerçeklik videolarının turistlerin seyahat motivasyonuna etkisi üzerine deneysel bir araştırma. *Türk Turizm Araştırmaları Dergisi*, 4(1), 121–136. doi:10.26677/TR1010.2020.303

Özgüneş, R. E., & Bozok, D. (2017). Turizm sektörünün sanal rakibi (mi?): Arttırılmış gerçeklik. *Uluslararası Türk Dünyası Turizm Araştırmaları Dergisi*, 2(2), 146–160.

Pantelidis, S. V. (2009). Reasons to Use virtual reality in education and training courses and a model to determine when to use virtual reality. *Themes in Science and Technology Education*, 2(1), 58–70.

Papagiannakis, G., Schertenleib, S., O'Kennedy, B., Arevalo, P. M., Magnenat, T. N., Stoddart, A., & Thalmann, D. (2005). Mixing virtual and real scenes in the site of ancient Pompeii. *Journal of Visualization and Computer Animation*, 16(1), 11–24. doi:10.1002/cav.53

Paquet, E., & Viktor, H. L. (2005). Anthropometric calibration of virtual mannequins through cluster analysis and content-based retrieval of 3-D body scans. *IEEE Instrumentationand Measurement Technology Conference Proceedings*, 2, 1458-1463. 10.1109/IMTC.2005.1604392

Parsons, T. D., & Rizzo, A. A. (2008). Affective outcomes of virtual reality exposure therapy for anxiety and specific phobias: A meta-analysis. *Journal of Behavior Therapy and Experimental Psychiatry*, 39(3), 250–261. doi:10.1016/j.jbtep.2007.07.007 PMID:17720136

Portales, C., Lerma, J. L., & Perez, C. (2009). Photogrammetry and augmented reality for cultural heritage applications. *The Photogrammetric Record*, 24(128), 316–331. doi:10.1111/j.1477-9730.2009.00549.x

Praveen. (2021). Retrieved from: https://amt.parsons.edu/~praveen/thesis/html/wk05_1.html

Rainey, A. (2018). *Using Technology in parks and recration: A new spectrum of reality*. Retrieved from: http://greenplayllc.com/wp-content/uploads/2018/06/AR-VR-Edited-F2.pdf

Ranasinghe, N., Jain, P., Karwita, S., Tolley, D., & Do, E. Y. L. (2017). Ambiotherm: enhancing sense of presence in virtual reality by simulating real-world environmental conditions. *Proceedings of the CHI Conference on Human Factors in Computing Systems*, 1731-1742.

Rebenitsch, L., & Owen, C. (2016). Review on cybersickness in applications and visual displays. *Virtual Reality (Waltham Cross)*, 20(2), 101–125. doi:10.100710055-016-0285-9

Relevant. (2020). Retrieved from: https://www.relevent.com/work/marriott/teleporter

Ricci, F., Rokach, L., & Shapira, B. (2015). Recommender systems: introduction and challenges. In *Recommender systems handbook* (pp. 1–34). Springer. doi:10.1007/978-1-4899-7637-6_1

Rockonit. (2020). Retrieved from: https://rockonit.weebly.com/blog/how-augmented-reality-is-revolutionizing-the-hospitality-industry

Roussou, M. (2004). Learning by doing and learning through play: An exploration of interactivity in virtual environments for children. *Computers in Entertainment*, 2(1), 10–29. doi:10.1145/973801.973818

Sambhanthan, A., & Good, A. (2013). Critical success factors for positive user experience in hotel websites: Applying Herzberg's two factor theory for user experience modeling. *International Journal of E-Services and Mobile Applications*, *5*(1), 1–25. doi:10.4018/jesma.2013010101

Sanchez-Vives, M. V., & Slater, M. (2005). From presence to consciousness through virtual reality. *Nature Reviews. Neuroscience*, *6*(4), 332–339. doi:10.1038/nrn1651 PMID:15803164

Selvam, A., Yap, T., Tzen-Vun, N., Tong, H., Hau, L., & Ho, C. C. (2016). Augmented reality for information retrieval aimed at museum exhibitions using smartphones. *Journal of Engineering and Applied Sciences (Asian Research Publishing Network)*, *100*(3), 635–639.

Sharples, S., Cobb, S., Moody, A., & Wilson, J. R. (2008). Virtual reality induced symptoms and effects (VRISE): Comparison of head mounted display (HMD). *Desktop and Projection Display Systems Displays*, *29*(2), 58–69. doi:10.1016/j.displa.2007.09.005

Slater, M., Gonzalez, L. C., Haggard, P., Vinkers, C., Gregory-Clarke, R., Jelley, S., Watson, Z., Breen, G., Schwarz, R., Steptoe, W., Szostak, D., Halan, S., Fox, D., & Silver, J. (2020). The ethics of realism in virtual and augmented reality. *Frontiers in Virtual Reality*, *1*(1), 84–96. doi:10.3389/frvir.2020.00001

Stelick, A., Penano, A. G., Riak, A. C., & Dando, R. (2018). Dynamic context sensory testing–A proof of concept study bringing virtual reality to the sensory booth. *Journal of Food Science*, *83*(8), 2047–2051. doi:10.1111/1750-3841.14275 PMID:30044500

Steuer, J. (1992). Defining Virtual Reality: Dimensions Determining Telepresence. *Journal of Communication*, *42*(4), 73–93. doi:10.1111/j.1460-2466.1992.tb00812.x

Suler, J. (2004). Computer and Cyberspace "Addiction". *International Journal of Applied Psychoanalytic Studies*, *1*(4), 359–362. doi:10.1002/aps.90

Travis, R. (2010). Bioshock in the cave: ethical education in plato and in video games. In K. Schrier & D. Gibson (Eds.), *Ethics and game design*. IGI Global. doi:10.4018/978-1-61520-845-6.ch006

Türkan, T. (2006). Televizyon Haber Yayıncılığında Tabloidleşme Olgusu: ATV ve Kanal 7 Haber Bültenlerinin Karşılaştırılması (Doktora tezi). Ege Üniversitesi Sosyal Bilimler Enstitüsü, İzmir.

Tussyadiah, I. P., Wang, D., & Jia, C. H. (2017). *Virtual reality and attitudes toward tourism destinations. In Information and communication technologies in tourism*. Springer.

UNWTO. (2007). *A Practical Guide to Tourism Destination Management*. Madrid, Spain: World Tourism Organization. Retrieved from https://www.e-unwto.org/doi/abs/10.18111/9789284412433

UNWTO. (2019). Retrieved from http://www.unwto.org

Vlahakis, V., Ioannidis, N., Karigiannis, J., Tsotros, M., Gounaris, M., Stricker, D., Gleue, T., Daehne, P., & Almeida, L. (2002). Archeoguide: An augmented reality guide for archaeological sites. *Computer Graphics in Art History and Archaeology*, *22*(5), 52–60. doi:10.1109/MCG.2002.1028726

VRfocus. (2018). Retrieved from https://www.vrfocus.com/2018/05/the-oriental-science-fiction-valley-is-chinas-first-vr-theme-park/

VRon. (2019). *Multi-user VR across industries made simple*. https://vr-on.com/stage-vr-collaboration.html

VRS - Virtual Reality Society. (2017). *Headsight first motion tracking HMD.* Retrieved from https://www.vrs.org.uk/virtual-reality/history.html

Wadhwa, V. (2015). How The Cutting Edge of Virtual Reality Is Making The Real World Seem Boring. *The Washington Post.* Retrieved from https://www.washingtonpost.com/news/innovations/wp/2015/10/21/how-the-cutting-edge-of-virtual-reality-is-making-the-real-world-seem-boring/

Weiss, P. L., Rand, D., Katz, N., & Kizony, R. (2004). Video capture virtual reality as a flexible and effective rehabilitation tool. *Journal of Neuroengineering and Rehabilitation, 1*(1), 1–12. doi:10.1186/1743-0003-1-12 PMID:15679949

Whistler, C. T. (2018). Fantasy and reality: Tiepolo's poetic language at Wutzburg, Verona and Madrid. *Verona Illustrata, 7*(3), 30–43.

Williams, A. P., & Hobson, J. P. (1995). Virtual Reality and Tourism: Fact or Fantasy? *Tourism Management, 16*(6), 423–427. doi:10.1016/0261-5177(95)00050-X

Wolwort, K. (2019). *5 Major challenges for the VR industry.* The Innovation Enterprise Channels. Retrieved from https://channels.theinnovationenterprise.com/articles/5-major-challenges-of-vr-industry

Yengin, D., & Bayrak, T. (2017). *Sanal Gerçeklik-VR.* Der Yayınları.

Yıldırım, Y. (2019a). Endüstri 4.0'a kapsamlı bir bakış: 2011'den bugüne. *Bilgi Dünyası, 20*(2), 217–249. doi:10.15612/BD.2019.754

Yıldırım, Y. (2019b). Industry 4.0, Marketing and Value Triplication. In A. Y. H. A. N. Fatih (Ed.), *Several Dimension of Innovation, Technology and Industry 4.0* (pp. 127–141). Peter Lang Pub.

Yıldırım, Y. (2020). Farklı disiplinlerde endüstri 4.0. *OPUS–Uluslararası Toplum Araştırmaları Dergisi, 15*(21), 756–789. doi:10.26466/opus.624938

Yücel, D. M. (2016). Farklı Bir Olay Yeri Olarak Sanal Gerçek. *Kırıkkale Üniversitesi Sosyal Bilimler Dergisi, 6*(2), 407–421.

Yung, R., & Khoo, L. C. (2019). New realities: A systematic literature review on virtual reality and augmented reality in tourism research. *Current Issues in Tourism, 22*(17), 2056–2081. doi:10.1080/13683500.2017.1417359

ADDITIONAL READING

Batiha, K., Al Salimeh, S., & Besoul, K. (2006). Dijital Art And Design. *Leonardo Journal of Sciences,* 1-8.

Caldwell, C. (2017). *Story Structure and Development: A Guide for Animators, VFX Artists, Game Designers, and Virtual Reality.* CRC Press. doi:10.1201/9781315155319

Jerald, J. (2015). *The VR book: Human-centered design for virtual reality.* Morgan & Claypool. doi:10.1145/2792790

Lanier, J. (2017). *Dawn of the new everything: Encounters with reality and virtual reality*. Henry Holt and Company.

Lévy, P. (1998). *Becoming virtual, reality in the digital age*. Plenum Trade.

Morrell, E. (2008). Review of Tourism, Culture, and Development: Hopes, Dreams, and Realities in East Indonesia. *Indonesia*, (86), 179.

Sutcliffe, A. (2003). *Multimedia and virtual reality: designing multisensory user interfaces*. Psychology Press. doi:10.4324/9781410607157

KEY TERMS AND DEFINITIONS

Augmented Reality: Augmented reality (AR) involves overlaying visual, auditory, or other sensory information onto the world in order to enhance one's experience. Retailers and other companies can use augmented reality to promote products or services, launch novel marketing campaigns, and collect unique user data.

Digital Tourism: The term "digital tourism" refers to how we use digital tools to organize, manage and even enjoy the travel experience. "Digital tourism" is therefore a set of systems that use all the tools of digital transformation to change the way we travel and the way the industry works.

Reality Technologies: Reality Technologies refers to the wide spectrum of technologies and affordances that include Augmented Reality, Virtual Reality and Mixed Reality that simulate reality in various ways.

Virtual Reality: Virtual reality (VR) is a computer-generated environment with scenes and objects that appear to be real, making the user feel they are immersed in their surroundings. This environment is perceived through a device known as a Virtual Reality headset or helmet.

Chapter 5
The Internet of Things and Cultural Heritage

Aybuke Ceyhun Sezgin
Tourism Faculty, Ankara Hacı Bayram Veli University, Turkey

Elif Esma Karaman
ⓘ https://orcid.org/0000-0002-5735-2504
Artvin Coruh University, Turkey

ABSTRACT

The last point reached in today's technology revolutions is the fourth level industrial revolution. This revolution is called Industry 4.0. Many new generation technologies such as the internet of things, artificial intelligence, internet services, augmented reality, smart objects, and business sector branches have been included in human life. Industry 4.0 technologies have an effective use in many areas of our lives. The tourism sector, which is in constant interaction with people, is also affected by these technological developments. For this reason, businesses should perceive the internet of things well and need to introduce various applications to their businesses to provide the best service to their potential customers. In this chapter, after giving information about the internet of things, cultural heritage, digital transformation practices in the tourism sector, and smart tourists are discussed.

INTRODUCTION

Human life is in a process of constant change and development in direct proportion to the time. Over time, some changes have a facilitating effect on human life. These changes are expressed as industrialization and are divided into revolutions. Industrialization is defined as "the process of replacing human power with machines" (Outman & Outman, 2003: 15). Today, as a result of the integration of the industrialization process with information and communication technologies, the Industry 4.0 revolution is mentioned. The Industry 4.0 revolution is also expressed as the 'internet of things' (IoT) (Karaman & Karaman, 2019). With Industry 4.0, the concept of 4.0 and smart concepts have emerged with the effect of digitalization in various sectors.

DOI: 10.4018/978-1-7998-8528-3.ch005

The concept of IoT is defined as the transfer of data produced from any object to other systems with the help of a network (Rouse, 2016). IoT has caused a cultural change with the effect of connecting many machines, sensors, devices, activators, and other objects with each other and strengthening communication. A lot of data can be provided in short time via objects (Tosun & Saglık, 2019). With this change, many concepts defined as 'smart' have entered the literature and various sectors. In the tourism sector, which is in constant interaction with human life, concepts such as tourism 4.0, smart tourism, smart tourism applications, and the use of smart objects have emerged through the effects of digitalization and objects Along with these concepts, some applications in the tourism sector have started to be used actively in destinations and businesses thanks to IoT.

While people benefit from the effect of digitalization and the ease of the internet of things, they also try to preserve the existing cultural textures of nations. Each nation has its own tangible and intangible cultural heritage items. These elements are protected by various institutions and organizations and their sustainability is supported. Nowadays, people in the globalizing world tend to experience local and locality rather than cosmopolitanism while participating in tourism activities. With the active use of the Internet in human life, tourists can get information about the destination and the business they will go to before participating in tourism activities and experience various applications during their visit. In addition, it contributes to the marketing activities of the enterprises by recommending destinations and businesses after the trip. Furthermore, people have the chance to experience many places with their sensorial properties (visual, auditory, tactile, etc.) through the internet of things, virtual reality, and augmented reality applications. While these practices enable tourists to have new experiences, they also have a positive effect on the marketing of businesses. In this part of the book, the concepts of the internet of things and cultural heritage are examined in detail in sub-titles. In addition, current practices used in the field of cultural heritage at the international, destination, and business levels are included through the Internet of Things. The aforementioned titles have been examined for information purposes and represent the current situation.

BACKGROUND

Internet of Things (IoT)

The Internet of Things is one of the known terminologies related to the development of today's technology and is technology-focused on providing solutions to the problems encountered in daily life (Kılıc, 2019). The concept of the Internet of Things is a phenomenon that rapidly changes and develops in information and communication technologies. Looking at the internet of things in the historical process, it started with the prediction by the German computer science pioneer Steinbuch in 1966 that "in a few decades, computers will be intertwined with almost every industrial product" (Elazhary, 2019: 128). In 1982, the Coke machine was invented at Carneige Mellon University that could report the temperature and the inventory in it. In the literature, it is thought that this machine is the first device invented with the internet. The term IoT, which expresses the internet of things, was used in 1985 by Lewis, one of the speakers of the United States Federal Communications Commission (FCC). Weiser, a scientist in the USA in 1991, used the term 'ubiquitous computing anytime, anywhere', published a seminal article on computing and the concept of IoT was produced in the academy (Kılıc, 2019; Elazhary, 2019).

The widespread use of the internet of things, which is a popular concept, in the literature was realized in 1999 when British technology pioneer Ashton (2009) established the Auto-ID Center at the Massachusetts Institute of Technology and defined Radio Frequency (RF). In 2013, emerging technologies such as wireless communication, Micro-ElectroMechanical System (MEMS) and embedded systems have evolved the concept of IoT (Kılıç, 2019). Ashton (2009) defined the concept of IoT as a network that provides the ability to connect to anything in any location at any time to identify, manage, locate and monitor real objects and places that can be defined as intelligent. The latter author also stated that computers know everything, the data they obtain without human beings, and the use of this data will reduce cost, loss of time, and waste. In another definition, IoT is defined as a worldwide network created by uniquely addressable objects among themselves, and a structure that enables objects to communicate with each other depending a specific protocol (Kutup, 2016).

As it can be understood from its historical past, the concept of the IoT is not new, but its history dates back to the 1980s. The concept is briefly expressed as "connecting different objects to the internet and communicating and interacting over the internet network" (Dokmetas, 2016: 2). The concept of IoT can be more broadly defined as "a network of uniquely addressable objects that are different from each other and that this network is used around the world, and the objects in this network are in communication with each other". In the concept of IoT, not only the connection of objects to the Internet should be understood, but also the production of information by Radio Frequency Identification System (RFID) and similar descriptive systems with some devices (Seker, 2018).

IoT is the widespread use of various objects that can interact with each other through unique addressing schemes and collaborate to achieve common goals. In this context, IoT provides convenience by providing the opportunity to prepare information, exchange information, monitor activities, reduce the gap between the real world and the digital region and conduct analysis (Buonincontri & Micera, 2016). On the other hand, Kranenburg (2008) defines IoT as a self-configurable dynamic global network infrastructure based on standard and interoperable communication protocols that use smart interfaces and can integrate seamlessly into the information network.

Miorandi, Sicari, De Pellegrini and Chlamtac (2012) evaluate IoT with three main features at the system level. These are in the way of communicating, identifying and interacting.

- **Communication:** Smart objects have the ability to communicate among themselves wirelessly and create private networks of interconnected objects.
- **Identification:** Smart objects are identified by digital name. Relationships between objects can be defined in the digital domain when physical interconnection cannot be established.
- **Interaction:** The local environment can be interacted with, thanks to their sensing and actuation capabilities when smart objects are present.

With all these advanced technologies, it is possible to see the active use of IoT applications in many sectors and fields from new mobile technologies for human life to wearable systems, electrical devices, smart home systems, and many more. Thanks to IoT system, while operating objects, it also has the potential to interact with the internet or other communication systems actively. Many components such as electronic networks, microprocessors, and microcontrollers that enable these systems to interact with each other are also part of IoT system (Akkurt, 2019).

Objects expressed in the concept of IoT: While the objects, humans, animals, and plants in our environment characterize the entities, the networks used in this technology refer to wired and wireless networks. The main support systems that provide secure data flow of wired and wireless networks with objects are Wi-Fi, Bluetooth, Zigbee, and 6LoWPAN. In addition, sensors, access devices, biochips, and monitoring devices are also considered objects. To be considered an object, a device must have a sensor, have a unique name (unique id), and be connectable. Thanks to these features, objects can be accessed, monitored, and controlled from anywhere in the world at any time. The data collected through the sensors are stored in Big Data Cloud Computing Systems by forming 'Big Data' (Tosun & Saglık, 2019). Companies that conduct big data analysis use cloud computing infrastructure. Cloud computing is defined as an infrastructure service that provides services to internet users with internet infrastructure, without the need for extra hardware and software, and allows information exchange through information tools (Soydas & Saclı, 2019).

The Internet and object concepts refer to a universal network system based on communication, networking, sensing, and information processing technologies. Internet of Things technology is a very comprehensive system that has social and technological effects by making use of objects in order to serve many different types of applications. For this reason, the International Telecommunication Union (ITU, 2005) referred to the 'communication dimensions of objects' in its internet reports and stated that any device can communicate with the communication facility at any time in any location. The communication dimensions of IoT are divided into three. These dimensions are (Dilek, 2017):

- **Communication at all times** (night, day, on the move),
- **Communication everywhere** (outside, inside, on the computer),
- **Communication with every object** (computer-to-computer, human-to-human, object-to-object, and object-to-people).

IoT developments are expected to continue at an accelerated pace in the future. In its vision for the future, IoT paved the way for artificial intelligence objects to perform difficult tasks and to cooperate with other objects by communicating. It is expected that cloud services will be needed more as a result of the analysis of data obtained from smart objects included in daily life with artificial intelligence methods and collaboration with other objects. With these developments, the impact of smart object applications will increase further and the widespread use of these applications will increase, and standards that can perform complex tasks with low power consumption, low cost, variety of functions, and easy programming feature will be formed (Simsek, 2019).

Technological infrastructure is needed at the stage of data collection, processing, and distribution in IoT applications. These sub-structures are divided into 4. These are as follows:

- **Radio Frequency Identification System**: It is one of the basic technologies that make up IoT system. The data received via radio frequencies of an object carrying an RFID tag is converted into digital information, transferred to the computer system, and automatically performs operations such as tracking and identifying objects (Maraslı & Çıbuk, 2015).
- **Wireless Sensor Networks**: These are wireless networks consisting of thousands of sensor nodes that can wirelessly interconnect and exchange information between independent objects. These sensors have system structure such as accuracy, flexibility, reliability, ease of installation, cost efficiency and data collection (Kalaycı, 2009).

- **Middleware**: It is the software layer that provides communication and enables data management in order to simplify, develop and make more useful IoT technologies with complex infrastructure (Muti, 2019).
- **Cloud Computing**: It is a model that allows access to a common pool of configurable computing resources, under appropriate conditions and on-demand, anytime and anywhere. In addition, it is the infrastructure system that enables the storage, processing, and use of data by providing access to remote computers over the internet (Yazıcı & Ayazlar, 2019).

CULTURAL HERITAGE

Since the concept of culture is interdisciplinary, it has broad meanings. It is a word that has been used since the 12th century and came from the Latin word 'cultura' to other languages. While the word expresses agricultural production and farming as its origin, it has started to define the arts, skills, traditions and lifestyles of societies since the 19th century. Today, culture is a concept that includes the elements that people think, do, and create (Tekin, et al., 2017). In the definition of culture by the United Nations Educational, Scientific and Cultural Organization (UNESCO, 2001), which is at the center of issues, such as identity, social cohesion, and the development of a knowledge-based economy, should be accepted as all of the material, spiritual, emotional, and intellectual characteristics specific to a society or a social group, and it should be accepted as a way of life in addition to art and literature. It emphasizes that the system of values, beliefs, and traditions also have an impact. As it can be understood from the definition, the concept of culture is divided into two: tangible and intangible elements. While the tools and materials created by people are considered concrete cultural elements, the practices, values, expressions, knowledge, and skills they produce are considered abstract cultural elements (Tekin et al., 2017).

The concept of inheritance is defined as "what a person or a society leaves to the next generation" (TDK, 2021). In a more comprehensive sense, from the artistic and daily used objects to landscape, architectural value and intangible cultural values, which are shared under the title of tangible culture, performances such as music, theater, ritual, and dance, as well as language and human memory are considered as general common benefits (Silverman & Ruggles, 2007). The concept of cultural heritage, which is expressed by the combination of the words 'natural heritage' and 'culture', refers to artistic and symbolic material symbols that belong to all cultures and humanity, transferred from generation to generation (UNESCO, 2001). Cultural heritage items, like culture, are divided into two being tangible and intangible cultural heritage items.

Tangible cultural heritage elements are expressed in three articles in the UNESCO (1972) Convention for the Protection of Natural and Cultural Heritage as monuments, building complexes, and sites. Monuments: Exceptional universal architectural works in terms of history, science, and art, works in the field of painting and sculpture, works of archaeological nature, caves, inscriptions, and element combinations. Building communities: These are separate or combined building groups that have exceptional value in terms of history, art, and science due to their harmony in terms of architectural features and their location on the land. Sites, on the other hand, are works of man or joint works of nature and man, and areas that include archaeological sites, which have universal value in terms of history, ethnology, aesthetics, or anthropology. Tangible cultural heritage items are divided into two: movable and immovable items (Kurtar, 2012: 19).

Intangible cultural heritage in the Convention for the Safeguarding of the Intangible Cultural

Heritage saw it as the crucible of cultural diversity and the assurance of sustainable development and explained it by taking expressions, skills, information, and related tools and cultural spaces (UNESCO, 2003). The establishment of documentation centers that will ensure the research, compilation, and protection of cultural heritage products is also considered within the main purpose and action plans of the contract.

Every nation and society have their own cultural values and cultural heritage elements that have managed to survive from the past to the present. These cultural heritage items are protected by national and international institutions and organizations and their sustainability is supported. In order to catch the difference in the globalizing world order and to protect cultural values, it is the most important factor that saves every country and region from being cosmopolitan. Cultural heritage assets around the world are damaged for various reasons. Conservation of destroyed cultural heritage sites and artifacts is an important issue for the entire world. For this reason, international organizations have drawn attention to the protection of cultural heritage with the statutes they have enacted and international agreements, and have stated the principles that determine the standards related to protection in their guides. International organizations, such as UNESCO, the International Council on Monuments and Sites (ICOMOS), the International Centre for the Study of the Preservation and Restoration of Cultural Property, and the International Maritime Organization, with their statutes, declarations and decisions, focus on the protection of cultural heritage, its management, structural assessment, archiving and documentation (UNESCO, 2005; Yigit, et al., 2020).

The preservation of cultural fabric is a function that separates countries and regions from each other and increases their attractiveness. For this reason, every nation should give due importance to its cultural heritage values and be able to perform effective marketing. Today, it is observed that tourists participating in tourism activities have a tendency towards alternative tourism activities besides the sea-sand-sun trio. Cultural tourism, which is one of the alternative tourism activities, also states that tourists tend to learn and experience the tangible and intangible cultural heritage elements of their own culture in the places they go, and cultural values are effective in the choice of destination (Mercan & Kazancı, 2019). Van Loon, et al. (2014) in their study in the Netherlands state that the high attractiveness of the cultural heritage items in the destination has a positive effect on the attractiveness of the cities in recreational trips. Even in regions where cultural and heritage values are not the main tourism product, they are used to increase product diversity and almost all types of tourism contain various elements related to cultural and heritage values (Gulcan, 2010).

Infrastructure systems and promotional pages are used in order to convey all the potential of the destination, such as tourism elements, all cultural heritage, local tastes, and activities, in the best way possible, based on the digitalization of destinations with the themes of accessibility and sustainability, in the promotion and marketing of existing tangible and intangible cultural heritage elements of countries and societies to tourists. Thanks to IoT, tourists who want to come to the region perform functions such as getting to know the destination, making plans, and preparing an effective travel route before their visit (Korkmaz, 2021). The inclusion of the concept of IoT in the tourism sector has enabled the active use of concepts such as tourism 4.0, smart destination, smart city, and then various applications that have an effective use in many areas of tourism with IoT.

INTERNET OF THINGS AND CULTURAL HERITAGE APPLICATIONS

In the global world order, the internet has many effects that facilitate human life with its inclusion in all areas of life. The tourism sector, which is in constant communication and interaction with people, is also affected by products and applications with internet infrastructure. This effect is expressed as tourism 4.0 or smart tourism in the tourism sector. The concept of smart tourism was defined by Gordon Philips in 2000 as a holistic, sustainable, and long-term approach to planning, processing, developing, and marketing tourism businesses and products (Li et al., 2017). In other words, smart tourism is the convergence of tourism with information technologies. In smart tourism, people work together to create social ecosystems using information exchange with the help of mobile devices connected to the Internet (Hunter et al., 2015: 106).

The technological factor in smart tourism supports real-time interaction of the person not only with the physical environment but also with the community and society, directly or indirectly with tourists. It has an increasingly complex dimension that includes ubiquitous infrastructures, mobile information systems, and dynamic connections (Gretzel et al., 2015: 182). While the tourism sector has good potential in terms of growth and job creation with the effect of its dynamics, it further increases its current potential with smart tourism and IoT (EU, 2021).

Technologies used for smart tourism affect guest experiences and enable new creative business models to emerge. Smart technologies, which have widespread use in the smart tourism sector, such as cloud computing, mobile applications, big data, beacon technology, location-based services, geotag services, augmented and virtual reality, social networking services are among the applications that shape tourism experience and services (Wang et al., 2012; Karaman & Karaman, 2019: 46).

Today, innovation, sustainability, and accessibility constitute the future of tourism. The cornerstones of the concept of smart tourism are accessibility, sustainability, digitalization, cultural heritage, and creativity. Accessibility does not only require being a barrier-free destination but also includes multilingual service delivery, allowing anyone to use it digitally without any physical barriers. Sustainability does not only mean protecting natural resources or the existing destination but also involving the local community by reducing seasonality. Creating a digital destination includes leveraging digital technologies to improve all functions of tourism experiences and leads the growth of local businesses. Focusing on cultural heritage and creativity means protecting cultural and creative assets as well as a local heritage for the benefit of the industry and tourists of the destination and using them by marketing them (EU, 2021; Korkmaz, 2021: 134).

Smart technologies used for smart tourism increase the competitiveness of destinations by providing the opportunity to enrich touristic experiences by adapting them to the destination environment (Buhalis and Amaranggana, 2014: 554). In addition, the use of smart tourism technologies such as websites, social media, and smartphones is increasing, as well as planning about the destination they want to go to (Huang et al., 2017: 757).

IoT, which has a widespread use network for smart tourism destinations and businesses, has an active use network among cultural heritage items. Today, IoT is used in the promotion and marketing of cultural heritage items in many countries. Tangible and intangible cultural heritage are digitized and transferred to virtual environments.

There are many initiatives at the international level for the digitization of cultural heritage items. Calimera Project (Cultural Applications: Local Institutions Mediating Electronic Resources), InterPARES (International Research on Permanent Authentic Records in Electronic Systems), which aims to develop approaches and application models for authenticity, reliability, and long-term preservation of documents in digital media, defines best practices on digital preservation. CEDARS (Curl Exemplars in Digital Archives) to provide strategic, methodological, and practical guidance, CAMILEON (Creative Archiving at Michigan & Leeds: Emulating the Old on The New), Networked European Compilation Libraries NEDLIB (Networked European Deposit Library), which aims to establish its core infrastructure, and PANDORA (Preserving and Accessing Networked Documentary Resources of Australia) and the Europeana project, which provides access to the cultural and scientific heritage of Europe (Ozdemiz, 2016: 23).

Applications of the Internet of Things Used in the Field of Cultural Heritage

Products that have become accessible and identifiable with digital means are referred to as 'digital cultural heritage'. With the rapid development of technology, digitalization studies in cultural memory institutions are gaining momentum. In this regard, it is necessary to digitize cultural memories and to reuse, protect, share and preserve digital objects in accordance with certain standards. The necessary standards ensure the spread of such studies and the formation of a controlled digital cultural heritage. The effective way to keep alive the digital cultural heritage created by standardization is archiving. Institutions such as the British Library, Rijksmuseum and Louvre Museum, which are examples of the digitization of cultural heritage at the international level, are also involved in the European Digital Library (Europeana) within the scope of digitization studies. In Turkey, in the 1970s, manuscripts in the 'National Library', one of the cultural memory institutions, began to be digitized. With the AccessIT (Accelerate the Circulation of Culture Through Exchange of Skills in Information Technology) project, digitalization studies were carried out for museums in Ankara Anatolian Civilizations Museum (Karadag, 2019: 30-33). In addition, as of 2016, the materials of 29 museums such as Hagia Sophia, Ankara Painting and Sculpture Museum, and Konya Mevlana Museum have been transferred to digital media and 360-degree panoramic views of some of them have been presented (Ministry of Culture and Tourism, 2021). CALIMERA (Cultural Applications: Local Institutions Mediating Electronic), NINCH (National Initiative for Networked Cultural Heritage), and Electronic Resources Preservation and Access Network (ERPANET) can be given as examples of successful projects in Europe in the field of digitalization of cultural heritage (Karadag, 2019: 36; NINCH, 2021; ERPANET, 2021).

On the other hand, at Walters Art Museum in the USA, 2642 works of art in the museum are offered open access through its website. Works protected by copyright 'creative commons' are registered by users. Similarly, open access museums include The Metropolitan Museum of Art, Los Angles Art Museum, Yale University Art Gallery, and National Art Gallery Washington (Terras, 2015: 13).

Another data-sharing network that makes digital cultural heritage data open and accessible in 3D is Open Heritage. Three-dimensional data acquisition technology is a widely used method for documenting cultural heritage. Open Heritage application presents open access heritage data in a simple and understandable way on the map with Google infrastructure. How many open access heritage products are available for each country, which ones are published or in the process of publication can be discovered through the interface. There are sets in which various information are given for each heritage through the application. The datasets collect the general characteristics of the heritage, downloadable data, point cloud viewers, data boundaries, background information, data types, contributors, and citations. Turkey - Ani Temple, Mexico - Chichen Itza, and Italy - Pomposa Abbey can be given as examples for point cloud in the application (Halac and Ogulmus, 2021: 526-527; Openheritage3d.org, 2021).

When the studies on cultural heritage are examined recently, context and supra-context expectations have started to evolve thanks to simulations of cultural heritage experts with digital platforms including exhibition kiosks, audio guides, mobile guides, augmented reality (AR), virtual reality (VR), games, and interactive stories (Nacak, 2020:18). Tourists visiting cultural heritage sites change the dimensions of the interaction between the museum and its visitors by accessing the objects and their stories from their devices connected to the internet instead of the integrated systems of the heritage sites. Thanks to the widespread use of smartphones and IoT, digital interactive systems that can be accessed through private and personal devices for everyone have been replaced by systems that serve users in heritage areas such as kiosks (Hudson-Smith et al., 2012: 1183-1184).

The widespread use of computer and communication technologies in many fields is also effective on cultural institutions. These technologies, which were used for purposes such as inventory recording, artifact tracking, and exhibition in museums, which are one of the cultural institutions, are now differentiated with an interactive museology approach. The concept of interactivity is a form of communication that means mutually influencing each other. With the new technology applications used in museums, visitors can get information about museums and artifacts in easier and more comfortable ways. Applications used in museums thanks to IoT are touch screens, 3D visuals, data matrix applications, digital photo archives, augmented reality (AR), virtual reality (VR) displays, animated boards, and simulators. Touch systems in museums were first used in the London War Museum in 1944 (Mutlu, 2017: 263).

In addition, web-based systems consisting of data entry, access and query modules for museums and 360-degree panoramic virtual tours, layered hologram, interactive examination system applications, archaeological excavation and mapping, land information system, interactive surface system E-catalogue, transparent LCD showcase application, virtual assistant, virtual objects, video mapping are also used. Objects that are not suitable for exhibition in museums in terms of space and location can be presented to visitors with 3D visual enrichment in both virtual and real environments thanks to virtual and augmented reality (AR) applications (Yıldırım and Ozbek, 2019: 170).

One of the applications used in museums is augmented reality. Augmented reality (AR) is expressed as a system that can present a live image of a physical real-world environment augmented with the help of computer-generated input such as information, video, audio, graphics, or GPS data (Demirezen, 2019: 3). There are two main difficulties in AR technologies used in museums. The first of these is the creation of 3D works in efficient ways and the second is the creation of virtual exhibitions based on these models. Visitors can easily interact with the exhibits through 3D presentations. Virtual Tour in the Ancient City of Hattusa in Turkey, Göbeklitepe, Ottoman Archives Museum, Casa Batlló Museum in Spain, Smithsonian National Museum of Natural History in the USA, England - London Natural History Museum, Italy - Svevo Museum are museums presented with these technologies. Singapore - Singapore National Museum can also be given as an example (Yıldırım and Ozbek, 2019: 170; Sucaklı and Tülay, 2020: 73).

One of the frequently preferred technology applications in culture and history museums is virtual museology and virtual reality (VR). Virtual reality (VR) technology is a device consisting of a head-mounted display and a glove called DataGlove. Thanks to the screen attached to the head, the user is provided with a 3D visuality, and the touch is provided by the glove (Demirezen, 2019: 4). These applications, which allow more people to learn about museum displays, are generally used in interactive applications within the museum as well as being presented on the web. These web-based applications, which are low in cost, are also easy to access (Yıldırım and Ozbek, 2019: 172).

Virtual technology museums, which have been used in various countries of the world in the last 20 years, have functions such as enriching the museum experiences of the visitors, integrating with the cultural heritage of the visited destination, and creating a sense of belonging with the interactive environment. The Museum of Pure Form, supported by the European Union and created by the joint work of 4 museums from Spain, Sweden, Italy, and England, is designed to provide an interactive experience to its visitors. In this context, by using the tactile wearable skeleton system and VR glasses, visitors are allowed to touch the works of art that are forbidden to touch virtually. Thus, visitors can perceive the works in 3D and examine them with a sense of touch. With this experience, visitors get the chance to experience works that are cultural heritage items both by touching and seeing them (Carrozzino and Bergamasco, 2010). In many places in the world, 3D digitalization has begun in the fields of cultural objects and cultural heritage. In this way, it has become a very important and applicable technology within the scope of urban heritage tourism by preventing the destruction of valuable historical objects and destinations by visitors (Demirezen, 2019: 13).

Another interactive application used in museums is robot guides. In robot guides, like professional guides, the visitors of the museum can be told about the museum sections, objects, and displays with the preferred language option. This application was first used in 1997 at the Deutsches Museum in Germany. Later, in 1998, it gave a lecture to the visitors of a history museum in the USA (Catlin-Legutko, 2012). Examples of robot tourist guide applications are the USA with 12 robots, Japan with 6 robots, Germany with 4 robots, Spain with 2 robots, and France, England, Australia, Switzerland, Italy, Korea, India, Taiwan and Greece with 1 robot each (Yıldız, 2019: 171). These are listed in Table 1.

Table 1. Robot tourist guide applications based on countries

Robot Name	Country Name	Museum Name
Minerva	USA	Smithsonian National Museum of American History
Sage and Chips	USA	Carnegie Museum of Natural History
Sweetlips	USA	North America Wildlife Center
Joe Historybot	USA	Heinz History Center
Robovie	Japan	Osaka Science Museum
Enon	Japan	Kyotaro Nishimura Museum
Tawabo	Japan	Tokyo Tower
Asimo	Japan	Miraikan National Museum of Science and Innovation
Rhino	German	Bonn German Museum
Care-o-bot	German	Communications Museum
Urbano	Spain	Prince Felipe Museum
Unnamed	France	Great War Museum
Unnamed	England	Tate Britain
Aggie	Australia	Western Australian Art Gallery
Cicerobot	İtaly	Agrigento Archaeological Museum
Jinny	Korea	National Science Museum
Unnamed Humanoid Robot	India	Jaipur Wax Museum
Indigo	Greece	Hellenistic World Foundation

Source: (Yıldız, 2019: 171)

Since AR and VR applications are actively used not only in cultural heritage areas but also in many areas of tourism, these applications contribute positively to the attractiveness, competitiveness, and marketing of the destination (Yovheva and Buhalis, 2013: 2). In addition, AR provides benefits such as promotion, obtaining information, encouraging the purchase decision, competitive advantage, efficiency, and performance (Han, 2016: 64-68). The first application example designed with AR is a hotel built by Holiday Inn. At the hotel, the guests were shown the Olympic and Paralympic athletes at the reception, in the hall, or the hotel rooms, as if they were there, thanks to their smartphones (Yovheva and Buhalis, 2013: 8). With AR application functions with smartphones, location-based information about the immediate environment can be accessed, timely and updated variables can be accessed, it can provide flexibility in presenting text, video, or images, and it has the opportunity to access interactive information that can be integrated into map-based additional information (Yovcheva et al., 2012: 66).

AR applications offer an effective visual interaction opportunity to access and understand cultural tourism information. It should be considered that these technological approaches provide added value, not an alternative to real environments, and thanks to this technology, visitors have the opportunity to customize and experience the story between them and the real environment (Fritz et al., 2005: 3). In Tuscany, Dublin, and Basel, tourist guides are created with AR to provide tourists with different language options about accommodation, city life, food and beverage, destination culture, people and markets in the destination, restaurants, shopping centers, events, historical and cultural places and filming places. Presentations are made at 360-degree angles. Another application, called Urban Sleuth, provides opportunities for visitors to explore interesting and historical places of the city and to get to know the destination by creating a sense of adventure. In Turkey, 3D ancient city sightseeing opportunities are available at the Temple of Zeus, Red Court, Asclepius and Athena in Bergama (Demirezen, 2019: 8).

Future Internet of Things and Cultural Heritage Trends

Technological developments in the tourism sector through IoT have caused changes in many areas. The tourism sector needs to keep up with these developments and changes. As technological developments provide many conveniences and benefits, augmented and VR technologies used for producers and consumers provide the attractiveness and preferability of all actors in the tourism sector (business, destination, tourist, museum) and meet their curiosity, interest, desire and needs (Demirezen, 2019: 2). With the VR technology, a simulation of the virtual, digital, or reality for each object is reflected, while AR blends the digital with the real. Digital information enhances users experience or understanding. Thus it provides to augment the truth with useful information (Berryman, 2012).

There are many future trends in the tourism sector and cultural heritage through IoT; Hjalager (2015) considered AR technology as one of the innovations that changed tourism. This technology is quite important for the animation method used in touristic trips, events and museums. In addition, these innovations will contribute to development and profitability by making tourism businesses and organizations more recognizable. In this way, tourism actors will be able to gather with new networks and systems. AR applications offer tourists the opportunity to experience the destination interactively with various functions (Jung et al., 2015). Thanks to AR technology, animations can perform in hotels, theme parks, museums and special event venues to provide a better impression and feeling about the service that purchased by the tourists. Thus, this technology can contribute to the profitability of businesses as an inclusive and persuasive power (Demirezen, 2019).

AR technology offers a visual and interactive opportunity to access and understand cultural tourism information. These technologies provide much more added value to real environments than alternative possibilities. These values provide the experience of personalizing the story behind the setting by the tourists (Fritz et al., 2005). AR applications in the tourism sector have positive effects on the destination, promoting of business or venue, eliciting and purchasing, outmaneuvering against competitors, efficiency and performance (Han, 2016).

VR technology in the tourism sector offers many possibilities, from management, planning, marketing, education, entertainment and preservation of history to the accessibility of tourism attractions or destinations (Jung, 2016). VR applications, especially used in cultural heritage areas, provide opportunities such as 3D touching objects that are not possible in real life, and visiting cultural heritage areas without damaging them. In this regard, museums can display virtual exhibitions and digital collections of cultural objects using different data presentations such as VR, AR and websites (Wojciechowski et al., 2004).

The concept of IoT, which is included in many points of daily life with the Industry 4.0 revolution, and the technological applications that develop with this concept will continue to shape the future without slowing down. These technologies, which are evaluated within the framework of the tourism sector and cultural heritage tourism, will promote cultural values more easily and fastly in the future. Furthermore, tourists will experience different presentation techniques before arriving at their destination. The tourist which is the main function of tourism activities does not have the opportunity to purchase and experience the service without going to the destination. Today, with the concept of IoT, tourists have the opportunity to experience the place they want to go and the service they want to receive beforehand. In the light of experience, it is thought cultural heritage values will gain more attractiveness and competitive edge with current technological applications.

DISCUSSION

The concept of the internet of things has an effective usage network with current applications on cultural heritage values. The widespread use of the Internet of Things and related applications all over the world has affected cultural heritage as well as in many areas. This effect is thought to increase over time. In the literature, some studies have been carried out on the Internet of Things applications used for cultural heritage sites and values.

A smartphone AR application was used to inform visitors at the National Palace Museum of Korea. It is stated that this technology has some benefits such as helping the decision-making process of tourists, saving time and effort in finding content, providing spatial indexability, less physical effort, and more confidence (Yovcheva, 2015).

Jung et al. (2015) stated that tourists visiting visiting a park in a theme park with an AR application in Jeju Island, South Korea, welcomed the application in terms of factors such as personal content, innovation, and personalized service quality.

Demirezen (2019) conducted a study on the benefits of AR and VR technologies to the tourism sector and their importance in tourism. These technologies support sustainability in the tourism sector, provide a competitive advantage, brand loyalty, convenience and professionalism in service delivery, increase service quality, marketing and security, sales and customer satisfaction, create an image, and contribute to marketing, promotion and retention.

Technologies used in the tourism sector and cultural heritage areas through IoT are interpreted very positively by industry leaders, especially scientific studies, and the positive features of these technologies are highlighted. These technological applications have many advantages such as offering ease of sales and marketing, providing different experiences to tourists, chance to experience the desired destination beforehand, providing trust, and saving time and effort

In the rapidly globalizing world order, the active use of technologies at many points of life is considered positive However, while AR and VR applications allow people to experience the destination places beforehand, they also bring up the idea that people can only be satisfied with these experiences and will not want to go to the destination place While these technologies create trust in people before purchasing services, on the other hand, they reveal the possibility that the real service may not be sold at all. In addition, the lack of the need for guidance services in touristic areas because of these technological developments can also pose a. Thus, a challenging situation arises for the service sector. For this reason, it is necessary to keep up with the technological evolution that develops over time, however keeping this evolution within certain limits for the tourism sector and cultural heritage areas will support sustainability more. As a result, it is necessary to keep up with the technological evolution that develops over time, however, keeping this evolution within certain limits for the tourism sector and cultural heritage areas will support sustainability more.

CONCLUSION

The last point of industrial revolutions, which develops in direct proportion to time, is Industry 4.0. With this revolution, many objects that have become an important part of human life and have an active use network are used by experiencing great developments in information technologies. Thanks to IoT in daily life, many jobs can be performed in a much shorter time, at less cost, and quite easily. The integration of IoT into human life has affected the tourism sector as well as many other sectors whose subjects are human. Thanks to Industry 4.0 and IoT, the tourism sector has started to be expressed with the concepts of tourism 4.0 or smart tourism. In the smart tourism sector, many technological applications are developed for important functions such as providing better experiences to its visitors, increasing the attractiveness of the destination, and providing a competitive advantage over its competitors, thanks to IoT.

Cultural heritage in the tourism sector is an important factor in promoting a country and increasing its preferability by clearly showing its difference from other countries. Visitors tend to learn and experience the culture of the destination they visit. For this reason, countries prefer various applications in order to offer their visitors the opportunity to transfer and experience the existing cultural heritage items in the best way through IoT. In the field of cultural heritage, AR and VR technology, which are included in technological developments and internet of things applications, provide information transfer in touristic places and destinations at anytime, anywhere, and in any condition. It can provide information and location services about places such as historical, cultural, and architectural sites, museums, restaurants, tourism businesses, and entertainment facilities of the destination, especially for the tourists who choose a new destination. With these applications, visitors are provided with the opportunity to experience the culture as well as to transfer information about the cultures of the country.

AR and VR applications, which are included in life with IoT technology, are used effectively in many areas in the tourism sector and provide positive contributions for businesses and visitors. The use of these technologies in cultural values and heritage areas provides opportunities such as the protection of cultural heritage, the promotion and experience of cultural heritage values. While visiting historical places or museums, visitors have the possibility to animate, 3D view and touch with AR or VR applications. The use of these applications provides a positive image of the business, destination, or place in the eyes of the visitors, providing a competitive advantage in important issues such as different experience satisfaction, energy and time savings. The use of technological developments by following closely has effects such as superiority over competitors, ease of marketing, attractiveness, image strengthening and productivity increase.

VR, AR and various website-based technological applications via IoT enable the preservation and sustainability of cultural areas and values, different and versatile experiences, and the transfer of information in various ways more easily and effectively. The positive aspects of AR and VR applications are emphasized in the literature and within the framework of sectoral applications. The framework of these technologies, which facilitate human life and contribute to time and energy, should be determined in detail. It is necessary to keep up with innovations and technologies. However, nowadays, with these technologies, information about the world's very valuable cultural heritage items can be obtained without traveling, it can be visited in a virtual environment and even the sense of being in that place is felt. These opportunities are likely to damage the vitality of tourism and destination visits over time. It is a matter of debate how long the destination without visitors can survive. Considering such important issues, it should be considered that the boundaries of technologies should be determined.

REFERENCES

Akkurt, M. (2019*). Simulation of Internet of Things Applications with Cupcarbon: Smart City Examples* (Master Thesis). Kocaeli University Institute of Science and Technology, Kocaeli.

Ashton, K. (2009). That 'Internet of Things' Thing. *RFID Journal.* Retrieved 05.05.2021 from https://www.rfidjournal.com/articles/pdf?4986

Berryman, D. R. (2012). Augmented Reality: A Review. *Medical Reference Services Quarterly, 31*(2), 212–218. doi:10.1080/02763869.2012.670604 PMID:22559183

Buhalis, D., & Amaranggana, A. (2014). Smart Tourism Destinations. In Z. Xiang & I. Tussyadiah (Eds.), *Information and Communication Technologies in Tourism* (pp. 553–564). Springer.

Buonincontri, P., & Micera, R. (2016). The Experience Co-Creation in Smart Tourism Destinations: A Multiple Case Analysis of European Destination. *Information Technology & Tourism, 16*(3), 285–315. doi:10.100740558-016-0060-5

Carrozzino, M., & Bergamasco, M. (2010). Beyond virtual museums: Experiencing immersive virtual reality in real museums. *Journal of Cultural Heritage, 11*(4), 452–458. doi:10.1016/j.culher.2010.04.001

Catlin-Legutko, C. (2012). *Interpretation: Education, Programs, and Exhibits Stacy.* Altamira Press.

Demirezen, B. (2019). A Literature Review on the Availability of Augmented Reality and Virtual Reality Technology in the Tourism Sector. *International Journal of Global Tourism Research, 3*(1), 1–26.

Dilek, S. (2017). *Internet of Things Based Remote Healthcare Monitoring Application* (Master Thesis). Gazi University Institute of Social Sciences, Ankara.

Dokmetas, G. (2016). *Internet of Things with Arduino and Raspberry PI, (1 st. Edition)*. Dikeyeksen Publications.

Elazhary, H. (2019). Internet of Things (IoT), Mobile Cloud, Cloudlet, Mobile IoT, IoT Cloud, Fog, Mobile Edge, and Edge Emerging Computing Paradigms. *Disambiguation and Research Directions Journal of Network and Computer Applications, 128*, 105–140. doi:10.1016/j.jnca.2018.10.021

Electronic Resources Preservation and Access Network (ERPANET). (2021). Retrieved 07.05.2021, from https://www.erpanet.org/

EU. (2021). https://smarttourismcapital.eu

Fritz, F., Susperregui, A., & Linaza, M. T. (2005). Enhancing Cultural Tourism Experiences with Augmented Reality Technologies. *The 6th International Symposium on Virtual Reality, Archaeology and Cultural Heritage VAST,* 1-6.

Gretzel, U., Sigala, M., Xiang, Z., & Koo, C. (2015). Smart Tourism: Foundations and Developments. *Electronic Markets, 25*(3), 179–188. doi:10.100712525-015-0196-8

Gülcan, B. (2010). Body of Cultural Tourism in Turkey and Need of Product Differentiation Based on Tangible Cultural Assets. *Journal of Business Studies, 2*(1), 99–120.

Halac, H. H., & Ogulmus, V. (2021). Digital Storage of Cultural Heritage Data: Openheritage3D Example. *The Turkish Online Journal of Design, Art and Communication, 11*(2), 521–540.

Han, D. (2016). *The Development of a Quality Function Deployment (QFD) Model for the Implementation of A Mobile Augmented Reality (AR) Tourism Application in the Context of Urban Heritage Tourism* (PhD thesis). Department of Food and Tourism Management, The Manchester Metropolitan University.

Hjalager, A. M. (2015). 100 Innovations that Transformed Tourism. *Journal of Travel Research, 54*(1), 3–21. doi:10.1177/0047287513516390

Huang, C. D., Goo, J., Nam, K., & Yoo, C. W. (2017). Smart Tourism Technologies in Travel Planning: The Role of Exploration and Exploitation. *Information & Management, 54*(6), 757–770. doi:10.1016/j.im.2016.11.010

Hudson-Smith, A., Gray, S., Ross, C., Barthel, R., De Jode, M., Warwick, C., & Terras, M. (2012). Experiments with the internet of things in museum space: QRator. *Proceedings of the 2012 ACM Conference on Ubiquitous Computing,* 1183-1184. 10.1145/2370216.2370469

Hunter, W. C., Chung, N., Gretzel, U., & Koo, C. (2015). Constructivist Research in Smart Tourism. *Asia Pacific Journal of Information Systems, 25*(1), 105–120. doi:10.14329/apjis.2015.25.1.105

Jung, T., Chung, N., & Leue, M. C. (2015). The Determinants of Recommendations to Use Augmented Reality Technologies: The Case of A Korean Theme Park. *Tourism Management, 49*, 75–86. doi:10.1016/j.tourman.2015.02.013

Jung, T., Dieck, T. M. C., Lee, H., & Chung, N. (2016). Effects of Virtual Reality and Augmented Reality on Visitor Experiences in Museum. In A. Inversini & R. Schegg (Eds.), *Information and Communication Technologies in Tourism*. Springer International Publishing.

Kalaycı, T. E. (2009), Wireless Sensor Networks and Applications. XI. In *Academic Informatics Conference Proceedings* (pp. 37-46). Harran University.

Karadag, D. K. (2019). *Developing Content Management Systems for Museums in Turkey Within the Frame of Digital Cultural Heritage Management's Digital Curation Applications* (Master Thesis). Hacettepe University Institute of Social Sciences, Department of Information and Records Management.

Karaman, E. E., & Karaman, A. (2019). Smart Hotel Management and Tourism 4.0. In Digital Tourism: The New Future of the Industry (pp. 41-62). Eğitim Publication.

Kılıc, A. (2019). *Internet of Things and Suggestions for Food and Beverage Sector, A Sample Practice* (Master Thesis). Haliç University Graduate Education Institute Management Information Systems, Istanbul.

Korkmaz, H. U. (2021). Cultural Heritage and Creativity For "Smart Tourism": A Qualitative Research on Konya. *Journal of Vocational and Social Scinces of Turkey*, *3*(5), 132–143.

Kranenburg, R. V. (2008). The Internet of Things: A critique of ambient technology and the all-seeing network of RFID. Institute of Network Cultures.

Kurtar, C. (2012). *Urban Cultural Heritage Management and Its Relationship with Recreation: The Case of Ankara Hamamönü* (Master's Thesis). Ankara University Institute of Social Sciences, Department of Geography, Human and Economic Geography.

Kutup, N. (2016). *Internet of Things; 4H Connection with Anywhere, Everyone, Anytime, Any object.* Internet Conference in Turkey.

Li, Y., Hu, C., Huang, C., & Duan, L. (2017). The Concept of Smart Tourism in the Context of Tourism Information Services. *Tourism Management*, *58*, 293–300. doi:10.1016/j.tourman.2016.03.014

Maraslı, F., & Cıbuk, M. (2015). RFID Technology and Application Areas. *BEU. Journal of Science*, *4*(2), 249–275.

Mercan, S. O., & Kazancı, M. (2019). Destination Selection for Cultural Values: A Research on Local Visitors to Çanakkale. *Academic Journal of Tourism*, *02*, 115–125.

Miorandi, D., Sicari, S., De Pellegrini, F., & Chlamtac, I. (2012). Internet of Things: Vision, Applications and Research Challenges. *Ad Hoc Networks*, *10*(7), 1497–1516. doi:10.1016/j.adhoc.2012.02.016

Muti, S. R. (2019). *Using Internet of Things and Big Data in Production Systems* (Master's Thesis). Gebze Technical University Social Sciences Institute, Gebze.

Mutlu, E. (2017). Education in Museums with New Generation Technologies. *National Education*, 214. https://dergipark.org.tr/en/download/article-file/441171

Nacak, E. (2020). *The Use of Digital Interactive Narrative Methods in the Context of Cultural Heritage* (Master's Thesis). Akdeniz University Institute of Social Sciences, Department of Tourism Guidance, Antalya.

NINCH. (2021). http://www.ninch.org/about/

OpenHeritage. (2021). https://openheritage3d.org/about

Outman, J. L., & Outman, E. M. (2003). *Industrial Revolution: Almanac.* Thomson Learning.

Oztemiz, S. (2016). *Open Access to Digitalized Cultural Heritage Products in Turkey: A Model Proposal* (PhD Thesis). Hacettepe University Institute of Social Sciences, Department of Information and Records Management.

Rouse, M. (2016). *Internet of Things (IoT).* https://internetofthingsagenda.techtarget.com/definition/Internet-of-ThingsIoT

Seker, S. (2018). *5G Internet of Things and Our Health* (1st ed.). Hayykitap Publications.

Silverman, H., & Ruggles, D. F. (2007). Cultural Heritage and Human Rights. In Cultural Heritage and Human Rights. Springer.

Simsek, E. (2019). *Edge Computing Based Intelligent Visual Perception Analysis for the Internet of Things* (Master's Thesis). Ataturk University Institute of Science and Technology, Erzurum.

Soydas, M. E., & Saclı, Ç. (2019). Big Data and Tourism 4.0. In Digital Tourism: The New Future of the Industry (pp. 91-101). Education Publishing.

Sucaklı, G., & Güzel, T. (2020). Augmented Reality Technology Applications in Museum Tourism; World and Turkey Examples. *Journal of Tourism Research Institute.*, *1*(2), 71–82.

TDK. (2021). https://sozluk.gov.tr/

Tekin, O., Bideci, M., & Aydın, A. (2017). Comparison of Mobile Guide Applications and Competence of Professional Tourist Guides in Transfer of Cultural Heritage (The Case of Konya Mevlana Museum). *Eurasia International Tourism Congress: Current Issues, Trends, and Indicators (EITOC-2015).*

Terras, M. (2015). Opening Access to Collections: The Making and Using of Open Digitized Cultural Content. *Online Information Review*, *39*(5), 1–30. doi:10.1108/OIR-06-2015-0193

Tosun, N., & Saglık, E. (2019). Internet of Things and Tourism 4.0. In Digital Tourism: The New Future of the Industry (pp. 91-101). Education Publishing House.

UNESCO. (1972). *Convention for the Protection of the Cultural and Natural Heritage.* www.unesco.org.tr

UNESCO. (2001). *UNESCO Universal Declaration on Cultural Diversity.* https://www.refworld.org/docid/435cbcd64.html

UNESCO. (2003). *Convention for the Safeguarding of the Intangible Cultural Heritage.* http://www.unesco.org/culture/ich/doc/src/00009-TR-PDF.pdf

UNESCO. (2005). *Venice Charter 1964.* https://www.international.icomos.org/charters/venice_e.htm

Van Loon, R., Gosens, T., & Rouwendal, J. (2014). Cultural Heritage and Attractiveness of Cities: Evidence from Recreation Trips. *Journal of Cultural Economics*, *38*(3), 253–285. doi:10.100710824-014-9222-5

Wang, D., Park, S., & Fesenmaier, D. (2012). The Role of Smartphones in Mediating the Tourism Experience. *Journal of Travel Research*, *51*(4), 371–387. doi:10.1177/0047287511426341

Wojciechowski, R., Walczak, K., White, M., & Cellary, W. (2004). Building virtual and Augmented Reality Museum Exhibitions. *Proceedings of the Ninth International Conference on 3D Web Technology-Web3D*, 135-144. 10.1145/985040.985060

Yazıcı, S., & Ayazlar, G. (2019). Cloud Computing and Tourism 4.0. In Digital Tourism: The New Future of the Industry (pp. 63-82). Education Publisher.

Yigit, A. Y., Ulvi, A., & Varol, F. (2020). 3D Documentation of Cultural Heritage with Augmented Reality Application: The Case of Chashma-Ayup Tomb in Uzbekistan. *Journal of Tourism and Gastronomy Studies*, 8(4), 3155–3172.

Yıldırım, G., & Ozbek, O. (2019). Tourist Guidance and Interactive Technologies in Museums. In Digital Tourism: The New Future of the Industry (pp.165-174). Education Publisher.

Yıldız, S. (2019). The Rise of Robot Guides in the Tourist Guiding Profession. *Süleyman Demirel University Visionary Journal*, 10(23), 164–177.

Yovcheva, Z., Buhalis, D., & Gatzidis, C. (2012). Overview of Smartphone Augmented Reality Applications for Tourism. *e-Review of Tourism Research (eRTR)*, 10(2), 63-66.

Yovcheva, Z., & Buhalis, D. (2013). Augmented Reality in Tourism: 10 Unique Applications Explained. *Digital Tourism Think Tank*, 1-12.

KEY TERMS AND DEFINITIONS

Augmented Reality (AR): A system that can present a live image of a physical real-world environment, augmented by computer-generated input such as information, video, audio, graphics or GPS data.

Cloud Computing: It is a model that allows access to a common pool of configurable computing resources, under appropriate conditions and on-demand, anytime and anywhere. In addition, it is an infrastructure system that enables the storage, processing and use of data by providing access to remote computers over the internet.

IoT/The Internet of Things: IoT is defined as all the systems that can transfer data over the network without the need for human beings provided with information processing devices, mechanical objects, digital machines, or identifiers that are related to each other.

Middleware: It is the software layer that provides communication and enables data management in order to simplify, develop and make more useful IoT technologies with complex infrastructure.

RFID/Radio Frequency Identification System: An object carrying an RFID tag converts the data received via radio frequencies into digital information, transfers it to the computer system, and automatically performs operations such as tracking and identifying objects.

Virtual Reality (VR): Virtual reality technology is a device consisting of a head-mounted display and a glove called DataGlove. Thanks to the screen attached to the head, the user is provided with a 3D visualization, while the tactile feeling is provided through the glove.

Wireless Sensor Networks: These are wireless networks consisting of thousands of sensor nodes that can wirelessly connect independent objects and exchange information.

Chapter 6
Tourist Experience and Digital Transformation

Ahmet Erdem
Harran University, Turkey

Ferhat Şeker
Adana Alparslan Türkeş Science and Technology University, Turkey

ABSTRACT

As technology affects the tourism sector as it does all sectors, smart tourism has emerged. The ultimate goal of smart tourism is to improve the efficiency of resource management, maximize competitiveness, and increase sustainability through technological innovations and practices. The digital transformation of the tourism sector, especially in recent years, has greatly affected the tourist experience by completely changing the supply-demand interaction in the industry. The spread of information and communication technologies, the development of the web, and the growing technology use skills in the population, in general, have helped increase the level of self-organization of tourists and have led to smart tourists. This new tourist profile created by smart tourism technologies frequently benefits from technology before, during, and after their travels.

INTRODUCTION

The Internet and other information technologies have had serious effects on consumer behavior (Huang et al., 2017). In 2021, the number of internet users reached approximately 5.1 billion in the world (Internetworldstats, 2021), 218 billion mobile applications were downloaded in 2020, and at the end of 2020, 46.45 percent of the world's population owned a smartphone (Statista, 2021). In addition, with digitalization, many economic sectors such as energy, construction, banking, transportation, retail trade, education, health, media and security have been transformed and the social vision of the world has changed (Okhrimenko et al, 2019). As technology affects the tourism sector as it does all sectors, smart tourism has emerged. The intensive use of information and communication technologies and the adoption of new ideas and approaches to the tourism sector have allowed new services and the re-transformation of

DOI: 10.4018/978-1-7998-8528-3.ch006

traditional services (Sigalat-Signes et al., 2020). In order to bring smartness to tourism destinations, it requires the use of a technological platform where information about local resources, tourists, activities/events and consumption habits can be gathered in a single center and presented to various stakeholders (Buonincontri & Micera, 2016).

The concept of smart tourism is defined as systems that coordinate all activities, information and services in real time with the intensive use of technology, connect all local organizations and allow to increase urban efficiency (Buhalis & Amaranggana, 2014). According to Molz (2012), smart tourism is;

- the establishment of connections via web-based applications with location features,
- the creation of shared value with tourists through the applications in the destination,
- the development of experiences through new technologies such as augmented reality and virtual reality,
- connecting and interacting with local communities and other tourists at the destination,
- the development of social and environmental sustainability.

Thus, it can be said that the ultimate goal of smart tourism is to increase the efficiency of resource management, maximize competitiveness, improve the quality of life for both local people and tourists, and increase sustainability by using technological innovations and practices (Lee et al., 2018). Buhalis and Amaranggana (2015) cite the four key dimensions of smart technology that can be found in a destination as information, access, interaction and personalization. First, the environments in which the technology is placed should allow information sharing among all users (locals, previous visitors and current visitors). Second, smart technology needs to be connected to a real-time communication system that can be much more interactive among all users. Third, it is necessary to contribute to the high accessibility of information with smart devices (smartphones and portable tablets). Finally, personalized service should be provided through data from various information sources. Technologies in tourism have played a critical role not only for the competitiveness of tourism organizations, but also for the tourist experience with personalized service delivery (Huang et al., 2017).

The primary purpose of offering tourists a particular tourist destination is to provide a memorable experience. For this purpose, it is necessary to re-establish the destination by making it attractive and exciting (da Costa Liberato et al., 2018). The spread of information and communication technologies, the development of the Web, and the growing technology use skills in the population in general have helped to increase the level of self-organization of tourists (Jacobsen & Munar, 2012) and have led to smart tourists. This new tourist profile, created by smart tourism technologies, frequently benefits from technology before, during and after their travels. For example, tourists can search for information about the price and places to visit before their travel. During travel, they can ask for directions, get digital guidance or make e-payment transactions. After travel, they can use various applications to share their experiences, make suggestions or warnings. Tourism service providers have to respond to these demands and produce value-added services. Hence, Information Communication Technologies (ICTs) have become an integral part of the experience, as tourists use technology to plan their travel, enjoy the destination experience and share it when they return (Wang, Li & Li, 2013).

When the scientific studies on the interaction between technologies and tourists are examined; Chung et al., (2015) investigated the relationships among quality, convenience, satisfaction, and intention to use consistently of destination websites, and the relations between these factors and the intention to visit destinations. According to the findings, website information has an impact on the destination preference decision of visitors. Pai et al., (2020) revealed that smart tourism technology experience is significantly associated with travel experience satisfaction, and travel experience satisfaction has a positive impact on both tourists' happiness and revisit intention. Tavitiyaman et al. (2021) assert that when tourists' travel experiences are enriched by advances in information technology, the quality of experience and perceived destination image are affected, which in turn triggers the intention to recommend or revisit the destination. Lastly, Shen, Sotiriadis and Zhang (2020) state that tourism destinations equipped with various technologies have a positive influence on obtaining an attractive and memorable visiting experience.

BACKGROUND

Information and communication technologies (ICTs) have undeniably changed human life (Egger, Lei & Wassler, 2020; Cuomo et al., 2021) and digital transformation has become inevitable in all areas of life. Digital transformation can be defined as the process of using digital technologies to create new business processes and customer experiences, or to change existing ones, to meet changing business and market needs (Bencheva & Manevsky, 2019).

Derzko (2006) defines technology in six realms (Gretzel, Werthner, Koo & Lamsfus, 2015):

1. Adaptation: changing behaviors to adapt to the environment,
2. Perception: bring awareness to everyday things,
3. Inference: drawing conclusions from rules and observations,
4. Learning: using experience to improve performance,
5. Forecasting: thinking and reasoning about what to do next,
6. Self-organizing: self-managing through various systems.

Technology, as in any sector, has affected tourism, which is a labor-intensive sector, has been included in business processes and has started to play a very important and central role. It is possible to say that ICT and tourism have interacted since the 1970s. After this period, change and transformation started in touristic products and services. Especially Computer Reservation Systems (CRS) in the 1970s, Global Distribution Systems (GDS) in the late 1980s, the Internet in the late 1990s and smart technologies in the 2010s were integrated and used in every stage and field of the tourism industry (Koo et al., 2015). Smartness optimizes collective performance and competitiveness. It also facilitates shaping products, actions, processes and services in real time, bringing together different stakeholders simultaneously, creating solutions and value for all (Jasrotia & Gangotia, 2018).

Digital transformation has led to the emergence of the concept of smart destination, where the information is accessible to all stakeholders, facilitating continuous innovation in performance and activities as much as possible (Jovicic, 2019). Smart tourism is a technology-tight phenomenon. Therefore, the first step in trying to define it is to define smart technology. Smart technology is a concise term for specific technologies and technology-driven phenomena that provide data and connectivity in ways that were not previously possible (Gretzel et al., 2015a). SEGITTUR (2015) defined smart tourism as an innovative tourism area built on a cutting-edge technological infrastructure, accessible to everyone, which guarantees the sustainable development of the region, facilitates the interaction of visitors and their integration with their environment, increases the quality of experience (Femenia-Serra, Neuhofer & Ivars-Baidal, 2019). As tourism sector has always been at the forefront of technology, similar pathways can be recognised, and the concept of "Tourism 4.0" is nowadays being introduced (Fig. 1). The advent of Industry 4.0 with new technologies have a profound impact on tourism, qualifying the current period as the "era of Tourism 4.0", wheretechnologies are modifying the behaviour of tourists, businesses and destinations, projecting them towards a smart perspective.

Figure 1. Development of Industry 4.0 and Tourism 4.0

Source: (Gajdošík & Orelová, 2020)

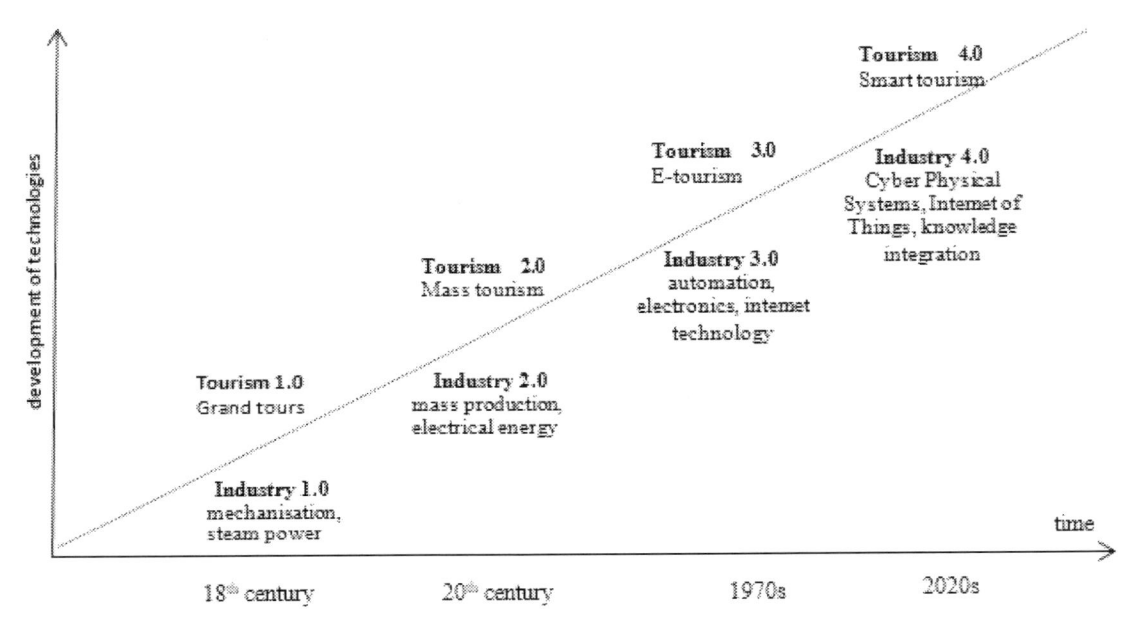

Technology benefits the tourism ecosystem in different ways, especially through applications such as the Internet of Things (IoT) and artificial intelligence to monitor, analyze and optimize the resource use of destinations (Fereidouni & Kawa, 2019). Among the applications used in the tourism sector, applications such as artificial intelligence, blockchain technology, sharing economy platforms in tourism, Internet of Things, virtual reality, augmented reality, mobile applications, QR code, chatbot can be counted (Konstantinova, 2019). Buhalis and Amaranggana (2015) suggest that there are various forms of ICT vital to smart tourism, particularly cloud computing, Internet of Things (IoT), and end-user service providers. Cloud computing services make accessible anytime and anywhere all data stored and managed virtually by cloud service providers from a customer (Thomas, 2011). IoT, on the other hand, refers to the widespread presence of various things or objects that can interact with each other through unique addressing schemes and collaborate to achieve common goals (Atzori, L., Iera, A., & Morabito, 2010). All systems, applications or sensors in the destination can be connected to each other and have the opportunity to interact through the Internet of Things. End-user service providers are information and communication technologies that enable visitors to use the technological infrastructure at the destination. Another major innovation affecting the structure of the industry is big data. Big data has played a crucial role in transforming global travel and providing significant challenges and opportunities for established companies and new entrants to the tourism industry. Industry stakeholders use big data to predict tourist demand, make better decisions, manage information flows and interaction with customers, and provide the best service more efficiently and effectively. This data obtained can result in increased customer satisfaction, personalized marketing campaigns and more efficient operations (Ardito et al., 2019).

Given the usage areas of technology in the tourism sector, it can be used in the promotion and marketing activities of the destinations. In addition, with the help of various applications and devices, the activities of tourists in the relevant destination can be examined, reservations can be made and virtual tours can be performed (da Costa Liberato et al., 2018). In this regard, technology is expected to emerge as a driving and fundamental force for tourism destinations (Kuflik et al., 2015). In addition to becoming an integral part of industry stakeholders, technology has also changed the way travel is planned and experiences are created for visitors (Neuhofer, Buhalis & Ladkin, 2014). Tourists now do preliminary research on the relevant destination before visiting it, search for content that will make them feel a part of the visited region and use the technology extensively (Cuomo et al., 2021). Tourist behavior has undergone a major transformation due to the fact that tourists use information and communication technologies during travel. Tourists have become more demanding, active, independent, knowledgeable and skilled and have discovered new ways to seek, compare, book, interact, share, complain, review and recommend information (Femenia-Serra, Neuhofer, & Ivars-Baidal, 2019).

As a result, ICTs have provided new tools for the tourism industry, leading to new experiences for tourists. The rapid adoption of technologies by visitors has enabled travelers to consume personalized information regardless of their location and situation (Sigalat-Signes et al., 2020). Smart tourism technology has a great impact on travel decision support satisfaction, especially in connection with information quality, resource reliability, interaction and accessibility (Yoo et al., 2017). Therefore, countries, destinations and especially commercial organizations need to undergo a rapid change and transformation process during this period of increased competition conditions (Pindžo & Brjaktarović, 2018).

Digital Experience Literature: A Brief Overview

While the customer's emotions, perceptions and attitudes form the concept of customer experience, this concept is a process that includes the customer's first contact with the business, even all subsequent processes. "Customer Experience" in the marketing literature goes back to the 1960s, there are also studies stating that the consumption experience should be considered as an experience that focuses only on the product (Olshavsky and Granbois, 1979). In addition to the fact that economy and business are in the majority in customer experience, it is seen that philosophy, psychology and ethics are also on the agenda. In addition to creating experience, it has been accepted that it provides benefits in terms of making profit in the long term, not losing customers that will generate profit, and reducing the factors that will cause expense, and it is a factor that increases profits.

With the customer experience, businesses can become indispensable with desires and emotions by revealing some situations that are hidden in customers. For this reason, the emotional bond that brands establish with their customers is very important for businesses today. Therefore, due to the emotional bond that most big brands create with their customers, the bonds established by customers are an important factor in becoming a big brand by putting price into the background and revealing more different aspects (Garg et al., 2014). Customer experience is the whole of the emotions and feelings that exist as a result of relationships established with customers at all points we reach.

In the digitalizing world, digitalization of digital customers and of course institutions has become inevitable, and in this process, the concept of customer experience has begun to gain importance for businesses. New main technological trends such as globalization, the effects of internet and mobile, changes in customer demands and expectations, social media, artificial intelligence, robotic and mechatronic developments, big data, internet of things affect every sector and of course the tourism sector.

In order for businesses to meet changing customer demands, Scmhitt (2003) has drawn attention to the following five stages for the realization of customer experience:

- *Analysis of the Customer Experience World:* Institutions should be able to analyze the customer's inner world well. Customers' requests should be evaluated according to their socio-cultural environment.
- *Establishing an Experiential Platform:* It is necessary to create a link between the strategies created and the practices. It is necessary to compare the experiences that customers want to live with the features that businesses want to offer to customers.
- *Brand Experience Design:* Bringing together products and services that will make customers feel special and meet their expectations.
- *Structuring Personal Relationships with the Customer:* It is necessary to be in constant communication with the customer and all communication channels should function actively.
- *Continuous Innovation Work:* All the experiences of the customers, whether positive or negative, should be taken seriously and customer reactions should be benefited from.

All these stages are important elements in digital transformation for businesses to fulfill the wishes and demands of customers who closely follow the digital environment. With the increasing use of technology and customer experience, it is now possible to provide customers with digital experiences.

MAIN FOCUS OF THE CHAPTER

Smart Tourists

Before explaining the effects of digitalization on the tourist experience, it is necessary to briefly touch on the smart tourists who use technology today. The rapid evolution of ICTs means that destinations, tourists and experiences can no longer be treated as they used to be. The latest technological developments such as smart systems, Internet of Things or cloud computing are all reshaping these concepts and forcing them to go one step further, to develop new viable models for an unprecedented situation for tourists (Femenia-Serra, Neuhofer and Ivars-Baidal, 2019) . The digital world is almost entirely dependent on humans for information captured in text, audio, video or images. Humans have a quite limited ability to obtain real-world information precisely because of limited time, accuracy, and attention. For this reason, smart devices have been developed in order to making the most accurate decisions and effective use of scarce resources. Smart devices collect and analyze information from people, thereby reducing the waste of time and money to a great extent (Kaur & Maheshwari, 2016: 30). It is necessary to improve the tourist experience by using smart technologies, to take more efficient and appropriate measures, and to contribute to the promotion of tourism experience (Wang, 2014). The relevant literature suggests that visitors use smart technologies to dynamically interact with other stakeholders and create their own experiences. Smart tourists are buyers and users of smart tourism destinations or services provided by tourism businesses (Shen, Sotiriadis & Zhang, 2020). Femenia-Serra, Neuhofer, and Ivars-Baidal, (2019) define the smart tourists as innovative, social, proactive, open to sharing their data and using smart technologies, interacting dynamically with other stakeholders, thus creating an enhanced and personalized smart experience. It is very important to understand the "new" tourists and their needs in the smart age in order to better understand the smart tourism destination preferences of tourists. Smart tourists who;

- Request personalized service,
- Are less willing to endure waits or delays,
- Research on travel,
- Use online booking and shopping
- Make price comparisons on different travel websites
- Communicate and actively use social media
- Have a keen profile in conveying their experiences (Wang et al, 2016).

It is an undeniable fact that the development of technology profoundly affects the entire lifestyle, preferences and expectations of touristic consumers. Therefore, it can be said that human beings and their comfort are at the heart of technological progress. Technology strives to effectively ensure efficiency and sustainability by taking the co-creation and personalization of tourism experiences to a new level (Gretzel, Reino, Kopera & Koo, 2015). The impact of technology on tourist experiences is evaluated in detail in the next section.

The Impact of Digitalization on Tourist Experiences

Digital transformation has greatly affected the journey of tourists in this area by completely altering the supply/demand interaction in the travel industry (Cuomo et al., 2021). The intensive use of technology in daily life and especially in the tourism sector changes the way they travel and diversifies the needs of tourists. The smart infrastructure in the destination effectively integrates physical spaces with virtual spaces, providing tourists with multiple experiences. These opportunities provide services that enrich the tourist experience and increase satisfaction (Wang et al., 2020).

Due to its dynamic nature, the tourism experience undergoes a continuous change, characterized by the increasing importance of consumer participation, co-creation and technology (Neuhofer, Buhalis & Ladkin, 2014). Digitalization opportunities in tourism aim to create new key initiatives. Among them; services such as digital competences and skills, changing thinking, creativity and innovation, creating new relationships between consumers and producers, developing new practices, creating new value chains, facilitating the personalization of tourist experiences, providing financing, contributing to new destination configurations, improving infrastructure and political support (Konstantinova, 2019). Information and communication technologies have made it possible to offer more special and richer services by enabling tourism service providers to create value together with tourists.

Especially since the 1990s, with the development of technology and its impact on the sector, a tourist profile has emerged who wants to obtain more informed, empowered, personalized and better designed experiences by transforming tourist behavior (Femenia-Serra, Neuhofer & Ivars-Baidal, 2019). In this respect, today smart tourists/contemporary travelers often carry mobile devices to make decisions on the go, manage travel plans, connect with the work and social world, and fill their spare time (Egger, Lei & Wassler, 2020). Also, Google Maps, mobility services, apps and accommodations (e.g. Airbnb) play an important role in making a city smarter and more accessible to people. This improves the quality of experience by enabling the fusion of tourists and residents (Chung et al., 2021). Technological advances have already changed the way tourists research, plan and purchase before their travels. Smart technologies are used by tourists in a wide variety of settings and contexts. At all stages of a visiting experience, it is open to external influences and smart technologies have become an increasingly important impact, especially in the very first phase (Shen, Sotiriadis & Zhang, 2020). Thanks to technological applications, it has become easier to influence the purchasing decision processes of tourists.

Evaluating smart tourism as a process would be the right approach. This process also includes the process that starts before the tourists arrive at the destination, continues during their stay at the destination, and covers to their place of residence. A possible disruption at any point in this chain may damage the basis of the smart tourism system. Therefore, if the destination managers want to offer a real smart tourism experience, they should make a comprehensive and holistic plan. Today, tourists receive help from technology in their purchasing decision processes and make their decisions to this extent. In this regard, at a time when competitive conditions are getting harder, destinations should get help from information and communication technologies and promote their destinations in the best possible way. Table 1 includes the stages that show the personalized service expectation of tourists'.

Table 1. Tourists Expectation on Personalised Services

Dimensons	Phases		
	Before	*During*	*After*
Transportation	1. Planning: navigation and information (duration, types of transportation, schedule and fare)	1. Real-time schedule	1. Feedback loop
	2. Recommender system: trail package and offerings	2. Personalised greetings	2. Promotional update
	3. Time savings: booking, check-in	3. Personalised meals	3. Luggage finder
		4. Suggest alternative	
		5. Universal card	
Accommodation	1. Planning: navigation and information (location, reviews, room type, price and surrounding events)	1. Personalised welcome message	1. Feedback
	2. Time savings: booking and check-in	2. Awareness on customer preference	2. Promotional offers
	3. Personalised welcome message	3. Personalised customer service	3. Maintaining engagement
		4. Room control over customer services	4. Post customer service
Gastronomical	Information (special dietary, variety of meals, navigation, food ingredients and restaurant information)	1. Integration service	1. Promotion
		2.Real-time information: customer awareness and social context	2. Prolong engagement
Attraction	1. Recommender system	1.Co-creation through digital maps	1. Sharing platform
	2. Information provider	2.Real-time information	2. Prolong experience
		3.Information on surrounding events	3. News update
			4. Recommender system
Ancillaries		1. Navigation	
		2.General information	
		3.Instantly exchanging information	

Source: (Buhalis & Amaranggana, 2015)

When the table is examined, the ways/methods of using technology at every stage of travel for new tourists or smart tourists are shown. Since environmental stimuli in smart destinations have a positive effect on tourist experiences (Wang et al., 2020), destinations and tourism service providers (hotels, restaurants, travel agencies, etc.) adopt innovative technological approaches to enhance and improve the tourism experience they offer. In addition, destinations or businesses using information and communication technologies (ICTs) gain an important competitive advantage as well as increasing the quality of tourist experience and satisfaction. As shown in Table 1, tourists use various e-notification platforms via smartphones, tablets or computers to receive comments and feedback on past experiences of other visitors before deciding on the destination they will travel to (Azis et al., 2020). Researches on the destination to be visited are directly effective in the purchasing decision process. Therefore, infrastructure activities required should be carried out in order to fully meet the demands of the new tourist profile.

Today, tourists are curious, inquisitive, knowledgeable, impatient, love to be seen and sharing (social media shares), uses technology and demands personalized service. Of course, technological developments are the main reason for this change of tourists (Pradhan, Oh, & Lee, 2018). For example, today's tourists want to be surprised by the novelty of the destination. With the help of technology, they are looking for up-to-date information about what to do, where to visit and how to reach a destination. Tourists also wonder whether there is internet and WiFi access in a particular destination, whether mobile devices and other communication channels are used frequently, and they conduct research. For this reason, a tourism destination should have certain characteristics such as being surrounded by modern and convenient communication facilities, equipped with excitement and innovation elements that can arouse the curiosity of tourists, being filled with desired and expected experiences of tourists and being easily accessible (da Costa Liberato et al., 2018).

Smart tourism is based on instant collection, processing and transfer of data to the site. In this way, it becomes possible to provide personalized service to visitors. Essentially, personalization is the process of collecting and using personal information about customers' needs and preferences to create offers and information that perfectly fits with customers' needs. In the service industry, personalization refers to a situation where consumers increasingly expect a service that suits them. Tourism service providers should gather appropriate information and adapt their approach to meet this expectation in order to present the right offer at exactly the right time (Buhalis & Amaranggana, 2015).

A smart tourist is an open/comfortable/free tourist who allows their data (for example, basic personal information, preferences, social media profile information, location, expenditures, etc.) to be transmitted to other stakeholders in the name of quality and personalized service to be provided to them. These tourists adopt the sharing of personal information as a usual practice, as long as they know that the benefits they will receive as a result of the data they share are valuable and that they are sure that there will be no privacy violations (assuming that their privacy and security will be protected). Therefore, smart tourists, aware of the value of their data and the need to protect them, tend to share their personal and preference-related data to receive special information and offers (Femenia-Serra, Neuhofer, & Ivars-Baidal, 2019).

While research on technology in tourism mostly explores the benefits and applications of digitalization, the risk of structural dependency and data control is mostly neglected in smart tourism research. When the studies on the subject are examined, it is stated that there are various concerns such as too much reliance on technology, less interaction with people, and errors in the information given, as well as concerns about data privacy. In addition, not being able to live the destination as it is, difficulties in using technology for the elderly and the possibility of losing the jobs of waiters, receptionists, cooks and guides working in the sector pose significant problems. One of the reasons for not fully benefiting from smart tourism applications is that the visitors do not have enough equipment to use the existing applications or the technology usage self-efficacy problem. Although destinations or hotels invest to increase the quality of experience of tourists, problems will arise if the visitors do not have the necessary devices to use the investment effectively. In order to overcome this problem, some hotels in Korea give the visitors smart phones during their stay, so they can benefit from the hotel's facilities (free internet, room control, service request, etc.). This not only gives extra value to the customer, but also offers managers the opportunity to analyze all visitor behavior (Put-van den Beemt and Smith, 2015).

One of the obstacles to the use of technology and to maximizing the quality of experience is that visitors ' level of technology use is low. Visitors should be willing and competent to use technology in order to use the applications in the destination correctly and effectively. Otherwise, the service provided may cause various problems for users. At this point, managers should act by thinking of the whole (all tourist profiles) instead of creating completely technology-embedded destinations that are expressed as rigid smartness. Besides, various mobile applications can share training videos for use in the region through information and communication technologies such as websites. In this way, visitors know what kind of applications they will encounter before visiting the destination and have the opportunity to make preliminary preparations.

Finally, it is noted that the intensive use of technology while traveling can potentially have negative effects on the tourist experience, and tourists may want to disconnect from the virtual world by moving away from technology while traveling (Egger, Lei & Wassler, 2020). An example of this is the concept of digital detox. Digital detox is a period in which a person voluntarily refrains from using mobile electronic devices such as a smartphone or computer, and this avoidance process is considered as an opportunity to reduce stress in the physical world or focus on social interaction (Jiang & Balaji, 2021). Another debate is over the definition of tourist. There are obvious conditions when looking at the definitions related to tourists. However, with developing technology, it is highly controversial how to define people who travel to different destinations through applications such as virtual reality, even if they are not physically present (Gajdošík, Maráková & Kučerová, 2020). Hence, there is much more work to be done in the field of tourism and technology, and there are gaps that need to be filled.

SOLUTIONS AND RECOMMENDATIONS

In recent years, the global prevalence of smart technologies and devices has fundamentally changed the way global urban cities are built, as well as mediated by technologies and tourism businesses (Chung et al., 2021). The basis of all investments made in the tourism sector is the enrichment of the experience quality of tourists. As stated before, it is possible to say that smart tourists now draw a profile that are more connected, curious, demanding, impatient, inquisitive, inclined to consume, prefer the original, give importance to quality and are willing to share their experiences. To look at the technologies used in the tourism sector in general, Internet of Things, 5G mobile network, radio frequency identification, mobile devices, wearables smartphones and devices, 3D printing, cryptocurrency and Blockchain, sensor and beacon networks, gamification, destination apps, augmented and virtual reality, sensors, near field communication, QR codes, iBeacons, ubiquitous connectivity through Wi-Fi, social networks, chatbots, big data, open data, etc. can be counted (Gajdošík & Orelová, 2020). Table 2, contains sample applications and their usage areas in the tourism sector.

Table 2. Smart Application Examples in the Tourism Industry

A Robot-Staffed Hotel – The Henn-na Hotel in Nagasaki, Japan	Using robots at the reception as customer information and storage points; It is considered as the world's first robotic hotel in terms of the use of voice, face recognition and artificial intelligence technology.
Connie, Hilton's Robot Concierge	In collaboration with IBM, Hilton launched Connie Robot, a smart concierge. Connie is able to communicate with visitors using speech recognition technology to answer questions.
A Staff-less restaurant in Beijing	In 2018, the world's first robotic, staffless restaurant with robot chefs and waiters opened in Beijing.
Travelmate: A Robotic Suitcase	It is one of the most innovative applications of robots in the travel industry. The suitcase can track its owner alone and rotate up to 360 degrees, using technology to avoid collisions.
Robot Assistants for Hotels and Airports	Robot assistants can ask questions, inform, and perform important tasks such as room service. Many of these robotic assistants are also able to understand and communicate in many languages.
Chatbots for Flight or Hotel Bookings	Online bookings have revolutionized tourism, now chatbots have the same effect. Chatbots assist customers by guiding them through the booking process.
Security Robots for Airports	Airport security robots are deployed in different places to assist security guards. For example, Knightscope robots are used at some airports to detect weapons and other prohibited items concealed during flight.
RFID (Radio Frequency Identification)	RFID applications are generally used in hotel businesses for monitoring textile products, providing convenience to guests in various services such as room service with RFID-based smart wristbands, tracking materials used in housekeeping and ensuring the security of guest rooms.
Voice Recognition	Smartphones and artificial intelligence assistants are among the most widely used applications in the travel industry, especially for booking. Tourists, in particular, use voice recognition to find and book flights or hotel rooms.
Contactless Payment	Another important form of travel technology is the ability to accept contactless payments. This is expressed as a method used when customers do not have access to cash, credit or debit cards.

Source: (Konstantinova, 2019)

In England, Premier Inn's the Hub Hotel has adapted augmented reality to wall maps in hotel rooms. When these maps are viewed through a smart device, these maps provide additional information about some local points of interest. The "Smart Dubai" application, on the other hand, is used in many areas of the city, from transportation to life and environment, such as e-door services at airports, smart parking application, smart taxi, smart homes and buildings, smart transportation system management, and makes the lives of users easier. Wynn, Las Vegas Hotel uses the "Amazon Echo" app, which allows controlling elements such as lighting and TV in their rooms. In this way, visitors can adjust the ambiance of the room as they wish. Located in Istanbul, Cloud 7 has a lobby area without a reception and check-in / check-out processes are done with a smartphone application. Finally, The Walt Disney Company has developed a wearable, customizable, RFID-equipped smart wristband called the MagicBand to reduce wait times and track guests' locations and activities. In addition, augmented and virtual reality, artificial intelligence, Internet of Things, audio technology, Wi-Fi connection, wearable devices (GlobalData Technology, 2018), mobile applications and hologram are shown as the most important applications that affect the tourist experience in the tourism sector.

Málaga (Spain) and Gothenburg (Sweden) were jointly awarded the title of European Capitals of Smart Tourism for 2020 – an award that recognizes outstanding achievements in smart tourism planning. Gothenburg, both citizens and visitors are able to benefit from this approach as the city aspires, in all its digital initiatives, to achieve equal access for all, affordable technology, effective long-term planning and the promotion of public-private partnerships. This has paved the way for abundant 4G coverage, smart grids for traffic and electricity, accessible and open government data, future-oriented public transport systems, optimised for all citizens and dedicated environmental protection platforms. Málaga has been incorporating the concepts of sustainability, innovation and culture into their strategic plans for many years. There is a constant exchange between visitors and the government's tourism services, so that Málaga can do more to meet the needs of visitors (European Commission, 2021).

In the study of Baser, Dogan, and Al-Turjman (2019) in which they examined Antalya (Turkey), tourists can get information about the destination before visiting the website, social media, blogs and augmented reality applications in tourism offices. During their visit, they can get information about payment transactions, entry/exit transactions, and transportation times with various mobile applications. In addition, it is stated that there are WiFi connections, QR codes, kiosks, augmented and virtual reality applications in certain parts of the city. Finally, after the visit, they can share via various feedback systems and social media.

Qatar is the world's first country to introduce a commercial 5G network. Free WIFI facilities are available at the Hamad International Airport and most public places including shopping malls, restaurants and parks. (2) The Accessible Qatar smartphone app provides information about accessibility and facilities at different public and touristic venues across the country. (3) Ooredoo Qatar has partnered with Wheel the World to offer accessible tourist experiences to differently abled visitors (visitqatar, 2021).

Pyeongchang, South Korea, one example of smart tourism cities is Pyeongchang, which hosted the 2018 Winter Olympic Games. The city became a live stage for cutting-edge 5G technology that opened new opportunities for visitors, like 4K video streaming, VR/MR broadcasting, and 360-degree video. The most tech-centric Olympics to date also featured AI-powered translation robots, self-driving buses, and patrolling drones. Dubai, United Arab Emirates: Driven by the ambitious goal to emerge as a world-leading city by 2021, Dubai has implemented over 1000 smart services and initiatives to promote technological advancements for the benefit of residents and visitors. One such example is the smart tourism guide solutions that leverage NFC tags to help tourists with effortless city navigation. Another initiative is the smart parks with VR learning centers and solar-powered smart benches that allow visitors to charge their mobile devices (intellias.com, 2020).

FUTURE RESEARCH DIRECTIONS

The speed of development of technology increases exponentially every year compared to the previous year. However, especially in the tourism sector, the competition conditions are getting heavier and this threatens the sustainability of destinations/businesses that cannot keep up with this change. The process of change in technology affects the sectors as well as making the change inevitable in tourist attitude, behaviour and consumption habits. In addition, smart technologies have a positive effect on the experience quality of visitors. Therefore, since tourism is a sector based on creating and/or selling experience, businesses have to constantly renew themselves. For example, it is mentioned that the concept of the metaverse, which has become very popular today, will eliminate borders, especially in the field of travel. In this context, investments in the metaverse, which is expressed as the technology of the future, are important in creating a competitive advantage for other businesses. At this point, getting help from such technologies at the point of sales of tourism businesses will affect the purchasing decision process of tourists and enrich their experiences. In this context, if it is necessary to offer suggestions for the sector and academia in further studies;

- Industry stakeholders (hotels, restaurants, travel agencies, etc.) must follow new technologies and make their investments accordingly in order to provide better quality and personalized service to tourists.
- From an academic point of view, in addition to issues such as ethics, legal regulations, user experience, and sustainability-related to digital transformation in the tourism sector, comprehensive studies can be conducted on marketing, management and worker rights.

CONCLUSION

Technologies applied to the tourism sector, the quality of pleasure and experience for tourists; the ability to reduce costs, profit and provide personalized service for organizations and destinations; sustainability for the natural environment; prosperity for the local people (Jasrotia & Gangotia, 2018). In this context, smart tourism bridges the virtual environment and the physical space to create a new information structure that covers the entire destination with a widespread connection. Thanks to this connection, it takes the co-creation and personalization of tourism experiences to a new level, effectively trying to provide efficiency and sustainability (Gretzel et al., 2015). The higher level of knowledge and socialization of people as a result of digital media effects will undoubtedly make them more aware of tourist attractions and increase the intensity and diversity of the needs of tourists seeking personalized service (Jovicic, 2019).

The rapid development of technology in tourism and the increasing interest of visitors in technology/ smartness has increased the interest of destination managers and policymakers in the opportunities offered by adopting a smart strategy at the tourism destination level (Buonincontri & Micera, 2016). Since the experiences gained from the visit have a direct impact on tourist satisfaction and revisit intention, it has become a critical issue for destination management organizations to examine the main structure of the tourism experience and how a positive tourism experience can be developed (Buhalis & Amaranggana, 2015).

New innovations and tools emerging more and more rapidly make it difficult for destinations to stay up-to-date in the context of global competition. Destinations need to adapt themselves to this new situation. Furthermore, destination management organizations (DMOs) play a critical role in managing these changes and ensuring the strong performance and collaboration required among all stakeholders to do so (Femenia-Serra, Neuhofer, & Ivars-Baidal, 2019).

The success of the smart tourism system can only be possible with the cooperation of all stakeholders on a macro and micro scale. The disruption of the smart tourism infrastructure in the country, in the city or in any attraction will affect the overall functioning of the system. Potential problems may have direct negative effects on tourist satisfaction. When the above-mentioned features of the new tourist type are taken into account, it is seen that there are sides that do not accept mistakes, are impatient, seek perfection. Therefore, it is necessary to provide the best service to the tourist profile that has adopted such a lifestyle.

The tourism market is changing rapidly due to the more complex requirements of tourists and the tough competition between tourism businesses and destinations. The use of smart technologies for tourism development is becoming more and more important for tourism stakeholders. If a business or a destination wants to be competitive and differentiate in terms of innovation and knowledge, it must adopt the smart approach. Moreover, if a tourist does not want to be confused in an unfamiliar environment and wants to have a personalized experience, the use of smart technologies is inevitable (Gajdošík

& Orelová, 2020). At this point, both tourists and destinations or businesses need to do their duties. If tourists want to explore the destination better, not deal with unnecessary details, eliminate waste of time, reduce costs, and support sustainable practices, they should both trust the system established in the destination at the point of data sharing and have minimum technological devices. When technology is used correctly, it is an indispensable element of human life. Considering the current conditions, it has become a necessity to make technological infrastructure investments in the tourism sector in order to keep up with the requirements of the era. The future is hidden in technology and scientific progress, hence, it is impossible to avoid it.

REFERENCES

Ardito, L., Cerchione, R., Del Vecchio, P., & Raguseo, E. (2019). Big data in smart tourism: Challenges, issues and opportunities. *Current Issues in Tourism, 22*(15), 1805–1809. doi:10.1080/13683500.2019.1612860

Atzori, L., Iera, A., & Morabito, G. (2010). The internet of things: A survey. *Computer Networks, 54*(15), 2787–2805. doi:10.1016/j.comnet.2010.05.010

Azis, N., Amin, M., Chan, S., & Aprilia, C. (2020). How smart tourism technologies affect tourist destination loyalty. *Journal of Hospitality and Tourism Technology, 11*(4), 603–625. doi:10.1108/JHTT-01-2020-0005

Başer, G., Doğan, O., & Al-Turjman, F. (2019). Smart Tourism Destination in Smart Cities Paradigm: A Model for Antalya. In F. Al-Turjman (Ed.), *Artificial Intelligence in IoT. Transactions on Computational Science and Computational Intelligence* (pp. 63–83). Springer.

Bencheva, N., & Manevsky, N. (2019). Digital transformation of the tourist industry. *Knowledge International Journal, 34*(1), 165–168.

Buhalis, D., & Amaranggana, A. (2014). Smart tourism destinations. In Z. Xiang & I. Tussyadiah (Eds.), *Information and communication technologies in tourism 2014 Springer* (pp. 553–564).

Buhalis, D., & Amaranggana, A. (2015). Smart tourism destinations enhancing tourism experience through personalisation of services. In *Information and communication technologies in tourism 2015* (pp. 377–389). Springer. doi:10.1007/978-3-319-14343-9_28

Buonincontri, P., & Micera, R. (2016). The experience co-creation in smart tourism destinations: A multiple case analysis of European destinations. *Information Technology & Tourism, 16*(3), 285–315. doi:10.100740558-016-0060-5

Chung, N., Lee, H., Ham, J., & Koo, C. (2021). Smart Tourism Cities' Competitiveness Index: A Conceptual Model. In *Information and Communication Technologies in Tourism 2021* (pp. 433–438). Springer. doi:10.1007/978-3-030-65785-7_42

Chung, N., Lee, H., Lee, S. J., & Koo, C. (2015). The influence of tourism website on tourists' behavior to determine destination selection: A case study of creative economy in Korea. *Technological Forecasting and Social Change, 96*, 130–143. doi:10.1016/j.techfore.2015.03.004

Cuomo, M. T., Tortora, D., Foroudi, P., Giordano, A., Festa, G., & Metallo, G. (2021). Digital transformation and tourist experience co-design: Big social data for planning cultural tourism. *Technological Forecasting and Social Change, 162*, 120345. doi:10.1016/j.techfore.2020.120345

da Costa Liberato, P. M., Alén-González, E., & de Azevedo Liberato, D. F. V. (2018). Digital technology in a smart tourist destination: The case of Porto. *Journal of Urban Technology, 25*(1), 75–97. doi:10.1080/10630732.2017.1413228

Egger, I., Lei, S. I., & Wassler, P. (2020). Digital free tourism–An exploratory study of tourist motivations. *Tourism Management, 79*, 104098. doi:10.1016/j.tourman.2020.104098

European Commission. (2021). *European Capitals of Smart Tourism*. Retrieved on 18.06.2021, https://smart-tourism-capital.ec.europa.eu/competition-winners-2020/malaga/malaga-winner-2020-european-capitals-smart-tourism_en

Femenia-Serra, F., Neuhofer, B., & Ivars-Baidal, J. A. (2019). Towards a conceptualisation of smart tourists and their role within the smart destination scenario. *Service Industries Journal, 39*(2), 109–133. doi:10.1080/02642069.2018.1508458

Fereidouni, M. A., & Kawa, A. (2019). Dark side of digital transformation in tourism. In *Asian Conference on Intelligent Information and Database Systems*. Springer. 10.1007/978-3-030-14802-7_44

Gajdošík, T., Maráková, V., & Kučerová, J. (2020). From mass tourists to smart tourists: A perspective article. *Tourism Review, 76*(1), 47–50. doi:10.1108/TR-07-2019-0285

Gajdošík, T., & Orelová, A. (2020). Smart Technologies for Smart Tourism Development. In *Computer Science On-line Conference*. Springer.

Garg, R., Rahman, Z., & Qureshi, M. N. (2014). Measuring customer experience in banks: Scale development and validation. *Journal of Modelling in Management, 9*(1), 87–117. doi:10.1108/JM2-07-2012-0023

GlobalData Technology. (2018). *Top 6 technology trends to watch out for in the travel and tourism industry in 2018*. Retrieved on 18.06.2021, https://www.globaldata.com/top-6-technology-trends-watch-travel-tourism-industry-2018/

Gretzel, U., Reino, S., Kopera, S., & Koo, C. (2015). Smart tourism challenges. *Journal of Tourism, 16*(1), 41–47.

Gretzel, U., Werthner, H., Koo, C., & Lamsfus, C. (2015). Conceptual foundations for understanding smart tourism ecosystems. *Computers in Human Behavior, 50*, 558–563. doi:10.1016/j.chb.2015.03.043

Huang, C. D., Goo, J., Nam, K., & Yoo, C. W. (2017). Smart tourism technologies in travel planning: The role of exploration and exploitation. *Information & Management, 54*(6), 757–770. doi:10.1016/j.im.2016.11.010

Intellias.com. (2020). Retrieved on 15.06.2021, https://www.intellias.com/from-smart-cities-to-smart-tourism/

Internetworldstats. (2021). Retrieved on 15.06.2021, https://www.internetworldstats.com/stats.htm

Jacobsen, J. K. S., & Munar, A. M. (2012). Tourist information search and destination choice in a digital age. *Tourism Management Perspectives*, *1*, 39–47. doi:10.1016/j.tmp.2011.12.005

Jasrotia, A., & Gangotia, A. (2018). Smart cities to smart tourism destinations: A review paper. *Journal of Tourism Intelligence and Smartness, 1*(1), 47-56.

Jiang, Y., & Balaji, M. S. (2021). Getting unwired: What drives travellers to take a digital detox holiday? *Tourism Recreation Research*, *2021*, 1–17. doi:10.1080/02508281.2021.1889801

Jovicic, D. Z. (2019). From the traditional understanding of tourism destination to the smart tourism destination. *Current Issues in Tourism*, *22*(3), 276–282. doi:10.1080/13683500.2017.1313203

Kaur, M. J., & Maheshwari, P. (2016). Smart tourist for dubai city. In *2016 2nd International Conference on Next Generation Computing Technologies (NGCT)* (pp. 30-34). IEEE. 10.1109/NGCT.2016.7877385

Konstantinova, S. (2019). Digital Transformation in Tourism. *Knowledge International Journal*, *35*(1), 188–193.

Koo, C., Gretzel, U., Hunter, W. C., & Chung, N. (2015). Editorial The Role of IT in Tourism. *Asia Pacific Journal of Information Systems*, *25*(1), 99–102. doi:10.14329/apjis.2015.25.1.099

Kuflik, T., Wecker, A. J., Lanir, J., & Stock, O. (2015). An integrative framework for extending the boundaries of the museum visit experience: Linking the pre, during and post visit phases. *Information Technology & Tourism*, *15*(1), 17–47. doi:10.100740558-014-0018-4

Lee, H., Lee, J., Chung, N., & Koo, C. (2018). Tourists' happiness: Are there smart tourism technology effects? *Asia Pacific Journal of Tourism Research*, *23*(5), 486–501. doi:10.1080/10941665.2018.1468344

Molz, J. G. (2012). *Travel connections: Tourism, technology, and togetherness in a mobile world*. Routledge. doi:10.4324/9780203123096

Neuhofer, B., Buhalis, D., & Ladkin, A. (2014). A typology of technology-enhanced tourism experiences. *International Journal of Tourism Research*, *16*(4), 340–350. doi:10.1002/jtr.1958

Okhrimenko, I., Sovık, I., Pyankova, S., & Lukyanova, A. (2019). Digital transformation of the socio-economic system: Prospects for digitalization in society. *Revista Espacios*, *40*(38), 26–35.

Olshavsky, R. W., & Granbois, D. H. (1979). Consumer Decision Making - Fact or Fiction? *The Journal of Consumer Research*, *6*(2), 93–100. doi:10.1086/208753

Pai, C. K., Liu, Y., Kang, S., & Dai, A. (2020). The role of perceived smart tourism technology experience for tourist satisfaction, happiness and revisit intention. *Sustainability*, *12*(16), 6592. doi:10.3390u12166592

Pindžo, R., & Brjaktarović, L. (2018). Digital transformation of tourism. *TISC-Tourism International Scientific Conference Vrnjačka Banja*, *3*(1), 340-355.

Pradhan, M. K., Oh, J., & Lee, H. (2018). Understanding travelers' behavior for sustainable smart tourism: A technology readiness perspective. *Sustainability*, *10*(11), 4259. doi:10.3390u10114259

Put-van den Beemt, W., & Smith, R. (2016). Smart tourism tools: linking technology to the touristic resources of a city. *Smart Tourism Congress Barcelona*, 1–12.

Schmitt, B. H. (2003). *Competitive Advantage Through The Customer Experience.* www.exgroup.com

Shen, S., Sotiriadis, M., & Zhang, Y. (2020). The influence of smart technologies on customer journey in tourist attractions within the smart tourism management framework. *Sustainability, 12*(10), 4157. doi:10.3390u12104157

Sigalat-Signes, E., Calvo-Palomares, R., Roig-Merino, B., & García-Adán, I. (2020). Transition towards a tourist innovation model: The smart tourism destination: Reality or territorial marketing? *Journal of Innovation & Knowledge, 5*(2), 96–104. doi:10.1016/j.jik.2019.06.002

Statista. (2021). Retrieved on 15.06.2021, https://www.statista.com

Tavitiyaman, P., Qu, H., Tsang, W. S. L., & Lam, C. W. R. (2021). The influence of smart tourism applications on perceived destination image and behavioral intention: The moderating role of information search behavior. *Journal of Hospitality and Tourism Management, 46*, 476–487. doi:10.1016/j.jhtm.2021.02.003

Thomas, P. Y. (2011). Cloud computing. *The Electronic Library, 29*(2), 214–224. doi:10.1108/02640471111125177

Visitqatar. (2021). Retrieved on 18.06.2021, https://www.visitqatar.qa/en/plan-your-trip/travel-tips

Wang, D., Li, X. R., & Li, Y. (2013). China's "smart tourism destination" initiative: A taste of the service-dominant logic. *Journal of Destination Marketing & Management, 2*(2), 59–61. doi:10.1016/j.jdmm.2013.05.004

Wang, J., Xie, C., Huang, Q., & Morrison, A. M. (2020). Smart tourism destination experiences: The mediating impact of arousal levels. *Tourism Management Perspectives, 35*, 100707. doi:10.1016/j.tmp.2020.100707

Wang, N. (2014). Research on construction of smart tourism perception system and management platform. *Applied Mechanics and Materials, 687*, 1745–1748. doi:10.4028/www.scientific.net/AMM.687-691.1745

Wang, X., Li, X. R., Zhen, F., & Zhang, J. (2016). How smart is your tourist attraction?: Measuring tourist preferences of smart tourism attractions via a FCEM-AHP and IPA approach. *Tourism Management, 54*, 309–320. doi:10.1016/j.tourman.2015.12.003

Yoo, C. W., Goo, J., Huang, C. D., Nam, K., & Woo, M. (2017). Improving travel decision support satisfaction with smart tourism technologies: A framework of tourist elaboration likelihood and self-efficacy. *Technological Forecasting and Social Change, 123*, 330–341. doi:10.1016/j.techfore.2016.10.071

KEY TERMS AND DEFINITIONS

Digitalization: It is the process of converting information into a digital (i.e. computer-readable) format.

Smart Destination: A smart destination is one with a strategy for technology, innovation, sustainability, accessibility, and inclusivity along the entire tourism cycle: before, during and after the trip. A smart destination is also one with residents as well as tourists in mind, factoring multilingualism, cultural idiosyncrasies, and seasonality into tourism planning.

Smart Tourism: It is reliant on core technologies such as ICT, mobile communication, cloud computing, artificial intelligence, and virtual reality. It supports integrated efforts at a destination to find innovative ways to collect and use data derived from physical infrastructure, social connectedness, and organizational sources (both government and non-government), and users in combination with advanced technologies to increase efficiency, sustainability, experiences.

Smart Tourist: Smart tourists are buyers and users of smart tourism destinations or services provided by tourism businesses.

Technology: It is the sum of any techniques, skills, methods, and processes used in the production of goods or services or in the accomplishment of objectives, such as scientific investigation.

Tourism: It is travel for pleasure or business; also, the theory and practice of touring, the business of attracting, accommodating, and entertaining tourists, and the business of operating tours.

Tourist Experience: It is a set of activities in which individuals engage on their personal terms, such as pleasant and memorable places, allowing each tourist to build his or her own travel experiences so that these satisfy a wide range of personal needs, from pleasure to a search for meaning.

Chapter 7
Understanding Big Data and Techniques in Cultural Tourism

Zafer Türkmendağ
ⓘ https://orcid.org/0000-0002-7712-1500
Atatürk University, Turkey

ABSTRACT

Big data enriches the experiences of cultural tourism visitors as well as being used in the management, presentation, and protection of cultural heritage. Technological innovations and the production of more data every day have increased the importance of data and information in competition in the tourism industry. For this, since it is seen that it is important to examine issues such as big data and analytics in cultural tourism, this book chapter presents the studies in the related research area in detail. As a result of the systematic literature review, data types that can be the basis for the formation of big data in cultural tourism and technologies that can support are specified. In addition, researches on cultural heritage and cultural tourism were examined, and theoretical and practical suggestions were presented.

INTRODUCTION

Big data provides serious benefits in all industries, but due to its information-intensive structure, having data, information, and knowledge about tourists in the tourism industry is the basis of competitive advantage. Emerging technologies led to an exponential increase in both user-generated and self-produced data in cultural tourism. The main reasons for this are the mobility of tourists and intangible and tangible assets of cultures. Tourism has arguably the biggest relationship with technology, and technological innovations add value to tourist services. Using these technologies, tourists can virtually experience and learn about the cultural assets of the destination before and during their travel. After traveling, tourists can share on the internet and through social media their media records of cultural assets and experiences which can be enriched and differentiated during the travel. Therefore, digitalization in cultural tourism has many important consequences for management and marketing fields. The tourists not only enter into cultural interaction with the local people during their travels but also learn about the cultural information about the region to be visited virtually before the travel (M. T. Cuomo et al., 2021). To pres-

DOI: 10.4018/978-1-7998-8528-3.ch007

ent cultural elements in a virtual environment, technologies such as augmented reality (AR) and virtual reality (VR), holograms, and digital twins are used in cultural sites to make them attractive for tourists (Frey & Briviba, 2021). In addition, new technologies and practices help preserve cultural heritage by strengthening communication with tourists while contributing to content creation (Richards, 2018) by improving visitors' experiences and interactions with history (Bec et al., 2019).

Discussions on digitalization in tourism have shown that big data presents challenges and opportunities for destinations to be competitive. Especially, with the development of mobile technologies, social media, content addition, and data obtained through sensors offer opportunities for businesses to create value (Del Vecchio et al., 2018b). Digitalization in the tourism sector allows businesses to get to know their customers better and to present their products by co-creating. One of the important factors that guide the marketing strategies that enable co-design and co-creation in the tourism experience has been the big social data approach. The industrial achievements and case studies presented in the literature show the importance of it in the design of the touristic experience (M. T. Cuomo et al., 2021). The integration of data collection and definition into various applications enable the analysis of data obtained from media such as social networks. These data not only include a wide variety of information such as feelings, opinions, preferences, and profiles of tourists but also allow analysts to reveal different relations by analyzing them. On the other hand, it enables them to strengthen decision-making processes for smart tourism destinations and businesses, develop new products, produce innovative solutions and enrich the touristic experience (Del Vecchio et al., 2018b). Previous big data studies have been conducted for the prediction of tourist arrivals (Liu et al., 2018), the planning of cultural tourism (M. T. Cuomo et al., 2021; Hu et al., 2021), the creation of a cultural tourism platform (Yin & Li, 2021), network analysis (X. Li & Law, 2020), the discovery of tourist behaviors (Ma et al., 2020), and tourist profiles (Centobelli & Ndou, 2019).

In addition, preserving cultural heritage and transferring it to future generations is possible by virtualizing it through applications like image storage, virtual recording, virtual simulations, 3D printing, etc. (J. Li, 2021). So much so that, thanks to the digital tour guidance platforms created on cultural tourism, students learn about the cultural characteristics and environment of any destination through virtual media (Chiao et al., 2018). In summary, technology radically changes all life and its effects can also be seen on cultural tourism. Recent studies have revealed the importance of data production and analysis in cultural tourism. In this respect, it is necessary to use effectively the big data resources created by tourists or consisted of intangible/tangible cultural heritage elements in order to ensure that cultural assets can be managed, promoted and protected within the tourism industry. Using daily technologies produce continuously more data which are stored through various programs. In addition to organizing and managing such large databases, industrial professionals should know about the advanced analysis techniques for revealing unseen relationships. In this context, this book chapter aimed to reveal out data types of big data technologies and their utilization areas in the context of cultural tourism. Studies on various methods and technologies used to present the virtual world created by intangible and tangible cultural assets and industrial applications were discussed and sectoral solutions were given with examples.

BACKGROUND

The Baselines of Culture, Data, and Technology

The definitions made on big data show that the subject is multidimensional and complex. Big data has attracted a lot of attention in the literature recently. All intangible or tangible entities and events around us have the potential to be transformed into data, and they can also be derived from their relationships. Therefore, data has gained importance with the development of new technologies. Sometimes one piece of data is very important on its own, and sometimes millions of data help to understand the nature of some facts or relationships. In this context, a definition of *big data analytics* phenomenon can be made as follows (Corea, 2019, p. 1): "big data analytics is an innovative approach that consists of different technologies and processes to extract worthy insights from low-value data that do not fit, for any reason, the conventional database systems". Moreover, the researches on database systems have found out 6Vs of databases which are volume, variety, velocity, veracity, volatility, and value (Alaei et al., 2019; Demunter, 2017). These initiatives are basic to understand and measure the nature of big data. Consequently, the database can be a measurement for real-time and private data generation. The increase in sectoral knowledge has also revealed the importance of big data. The size and quality of big data are also directly reflected in the performance of businesses because adapting businesses to the changing environment is related to investing in the constant development of information technologies. Further, the deployment of big data is a process that should be planned carefully. This process involves the basic definition of business process and analytical framework, creating the dataset, modelling and optimization (Figure 1).

Figure 1. Big data lean deployment approach
Source: Corea, 2019, p. 8

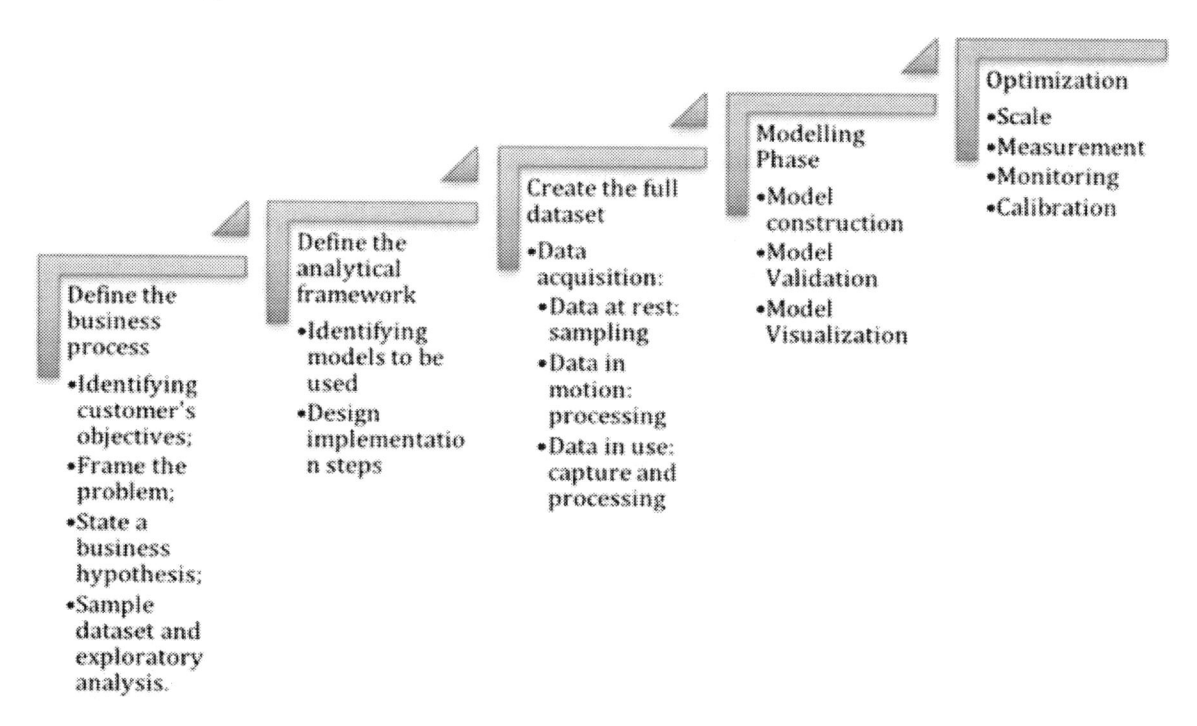

Big data analysis can be used to realize destination assets and goals by providing the foundations needed by smart tourism. It can provide a competitive advantage by providing sufficient technical support to understand the consumers especially in product changes and to predict new conditions. These analyzes can clarify many complex interpersonal issues, from local planning to enabling smart sustainable tourism (Balasaraswathi et al., 2020; Centobelli & Ndou, 2019). According to the research conducted in 2017 in the three big cities (Barcelona, Amsterdam, and London), which came first in smart city applications, it was seen that despite the technological advancements cultural heritage was not systematically included in smart city applications (Angelidou et al., 2017). However, in the comparative research conducted in the cities of Tarragona (Spain), Budapest (Hungary), and Karlsruhe (Germany), it has been observed that the smart city applications used in these cities have a rich cultural heritage content and strategic content for touristic branding and promotion. While these studies reveal the importance of cultural heritage in new generation smart city applications, they reveal three strategies: different players in smart cities, cultural heritage, and sustainable urban development (Angelidou & Stylianidis, 2020).

As a result of the increase in people's living standards and the use of technology, smart solutions are being developed in the tourism sector. Smart tourism is adopted by new tourists every day and many tourists, especially young people, prefer smart travel through IoT technologies. In particular, with the 5G mobile technology infrastructure coming to the fore, how to collect and classify the IoT and the big data has become a new discussion. This classification can help businesses and tourists make decisions (Gao, 2021). One of them is to measure the satisfaction of tourists and to report them by analyzing them with different variables. Thus, planners can identify areas that are missing or need improvement (Hwang et al., 2020). In a study to simulate the social interactions of visitors and the sharing of cultural heritage data at an event where cultural assets were exhibited, it was found that cultural heritage information shared by a visitor had an impact on others in his social network circle. This finding shows that it is important to develop cloud-based profiling, feedback, recommendation system in cultural events or tourism (S. Cuomo et al., 2015). Supporting consumers' data sharing not only provides benefits in all areas but also reciprocal big data value goes beyond value co-creating and provides new benefits. The reciprocal big data value can be specified as using big data to create data value. In addition, big data can increase cooperation as it develops a trust relationship based on equal benefit between consumers and businesses (Line et al., 2020). Moreover, social big data creates value in smart tourism by improving decision making, improving and differentiating the tourist experience, developing new business models or products/services, and providing connectivity in the business ecosystem. In addition, big data analysis creates a connected ecosystem between destination stakeholders, as well as by affecting, directly or indirectly, local experiences with certain characteristics based on nature and culture from existing facilities, products and services (Del Vecchio et al., 2018b). Further, among the obstacles to obtaining data in cultural tourism are differences in technology use, lack of sufficient data, legal obstacles, lack of trust, people's fear of being followed or their privacy being revealed, incomprehensible or unsolvable data, data on different platforms, problems arising from the right to use, difficulties in distinguishing between local people and tourist data, the inadequacy of technical infrastructure, data not easily accessible, model deficiencies, etc. (Kalvet et al., 2020).

Digital historical archives have led social scientists to develop new perspectives on the management of qualitative metadata with the development of big data and analysis methods. Considering the connection between theory and data, cultural sociologists have incorporated new techniques such as advanced text analysis into their work to try to balance the flow of big data. This gives cultural sociologists the chance to better recognize cultural assets and their evaluations over time, providing new perspectives on the change of culture over time (Bail, 2014). One of the most important aspects that provide big data about cultural heritage is networking efforts. While information technologies provide the circulation of data via local networks or the internet, they also provide data production. An exemplary project in this regard, *digitalmeetsculture.net* was established in 2011 and used as a tool for collecting and sharing digital culture. The most difficult issues in the project we're developing new relationships and collaborations. However, thanks to this portal, the common heritage has been enriched and the existing knowledge has been increased (Bachi et al., 2014). Moreover, museums use a variety of software integrated with data management system tools to manage their cultural heritage inventories and create catalogs. New technologies can be presented to the user with technologies such as VR and AR, as well as being realistic and cost-effective, including three-dimensional rendering and imaging. Digital cultural assets created like this can be stored, categorized and extracted with the content management system. These technologies are used both for the management and marketing of cultural heritage and for its long-term digital preservation (Belhi et al., 2017). Big data containing cultural heritage can be subjected to data analysis to be used for innovation and research.

Local and central government support for the collection and use of big data ensures the development of cultural tourism (Xu, 2020). Governments also have important roles in equipping a region with smart systems and providing the ability to circulate information. Governments can ensure the effective management of cultural knowledge by ensuring the correct dissemination of the synthesized information circulating in the region and by ensuring coordination and participation among stakeholders (Garau, 2014). Different languages are among the obstacles encountered in the management of cultural heritage data. Collaborative management-based multilingual approaches can make data accessible to different stakeholders (Dragoni et al., 2017). Further, social big data enables competitiveness as well as creating value for destinations and stakeholders through open and collaborative innovation. The cooperation in the destination contributes to the collection and effective use of big data and offers important opportunities for destinations to be successful at a global level (Del Vecchio et al., 2018a). The data obtained from the platforms (social media, search engines, etc.) and applications can be used in the planning of cultural sites and events to be organized there. In addition to determining cultural tour routes, it also provides success in revealing the most interesting attractions. With cultural tourism reaching more audiences, big data also offers opportunities for planning (Hu et al., 2021). In cultural tourism, route planning is necessary to present and market cultural assets at a sufficient level. To do this effectively, the use of technology and the acquisition of data are inevitable. However, since it is a new subject, the scarcity of data collection and scoring systems for route planning can be seen as a gap in the literature. A study on this subject was carried out on recreational navigation platforms (*RouteYou*). This program involved data analysis to automatically collect and develop information about cultural assets through arguments such as mobile sensors and geotagging. Points of interest were determined based on the places that users were most interested in on their trips. Finally, thanks to the program, the weights of the determined routes could be made and the experiential results could be presented to the end-user as a suggestion (Baker & Verstockt, 2017).

During the use of IoT technologies in culture preservation, the lack of a valid data model, security and privacy problems, the inadequacy of the technologies used (the tangible and intangible heritage can be handled more with video or audio recording), and the robustness of the applications (difficulties in connecting devices from many different places or synchronization problems, etc.) emerge as difficulties. The semantic data model can be used to understand and use the data collected in smart destinations. In addition, organizing heterogeneous data from IoT devices appears to be a major challenge. To achieve this, appropriate queries and operations must be carried out in the programs (Jara et al., 2015). In addition to all its benefits, big data also creates ethical, privacy, and security problems for individuals and organizations. For this, businesses and destinations need to pay special attention to data management and privacy (Yallop & Seraphin, 2020).

Data and Database Management in Cultural Tourism

Open, big and new data approaches can facilitate the data presented by consumption patterns in tourism, as well as changing socio-economic policy and research. Among the areas where the biggest change in cultural tourism is the presence of evidence, availability of open and big data, and improvements in intelligence and analytics. Mobile positioning data can be used to monitor tourist flow and behavior in cultural tourism. Thus, their relevance to certain cultural attractions can be determined. Big data obtained from social media or the web can be used to determine tourist use, perceptions, and interests, as well as to predict important issues and demand. Visitor data can be used to monitor and plan visit patterns and traffic in cultural tourism. Sharing economy data, on the other hand, helps cultural tourism planners to obtain more detailed information about their visits to certain sites by helping to reveal consumption data that are not reflected in official tourism statistics (Kalvet et al., 2020; Zhang & Dong, 2021). In a cultural event, it is important to present the cultural elements appropriate to the characteristics and needs of the participants. Therefore, the suggestions provided by analyzing their social information improve their experiences. For this matching to be efficient, it is essential to determine both the participants and the characteristics of the cultural property well and to organize the data accordingly. While the social data of the participant may be information such as age, position, independence, proximity to others; Cultural property data can be the type of cultural property, date of creation, technical material used, geographical information, artist and artist's birth/death date (Hong et al., 2017).

In time, there have been technological developments in databases that store cultural heritage data. Current databases have emerged due to the difficulties of traditional database systems in storing and managing big data. To present very large cultural heritage information quickly, a knowledge graph can be created and textual information can be obtained with natural language processing techniques. Thanks to these techniques, cultural heritage information can be obtained, managed, and protected more quickly (Dou et al., 2018). As a data source, big data related to tourism can be collected in three main categories (J. Li et al., 2018):

1. *User-generated data* is media content, such as online text, photos, or videos, that includes interactions such as product reviews or experience sharing on social media or the web.
2. *Device data*, positioning, mobile roaming, RFID, WIFI, meteorology, etc. generated during use or automatically. data produced by devices as hardware (electronic).
3. *Transaction data* consists of web search data, web page visit data, online reservation data, etc. that mostly occur in the background when users interact with certain programs in electronic devices or virtual environments. software data.

Studies on the big tourism data few theorized but involve general issues on social media and user-generated content (X. Li & Law, 2020). Very useful information can be obtained from the semantic tags and media data that cultural tourists process over social media during their trips. These data can then be classified according to the interests of the users and the label and media data important for each region can be determined (Nguyen et al., 2017). In addition, currents can be created through social media or web blogs by creating certain hashtags to collect data. To gather information about the local experience in Italy, nature (i.e #MygarganoExperience, etc.), culture (e.g. #InvasioniDigitaliNoci, etc.), agro-food (e.g. #Transumanza, etc.) hashtag were created, both to obtain information about a large ecosystem of destinations that make up activities, services and people on related topics, and to create networks among local stakeholders and visitors (Del Vecchio et al., 2018b). In their study, Piccialli and Jung (2017) classified the tweets of companies as three types in 8 concepts: providing information, advertising, and both. After this classification, it has been shown that tweets in the type of providing information and using the advertisement together rather than the type of advertisement spread faster. Thus, it has been revealed that the content is important in the dissemination of information.

Developed in Italy, DATABENC (a High Technology District for Cultural Heritage Management recently funded by Regione Campania) project has provided many application users with the opportunity to explore and manage cultural assets in the region with its IoT and hybrid cloud-based architecture. In the project, an interactive network was created thanks to the ability to share and analyze information via the mobile Android application, by keeping the participation of the users in the foreground. In the application, a questionnaire was applied to each user, and information about demographic information and other areas of interest was collected. In the light of this experiential information, a context dimension tree was created for the museum and categorized as the point of interest representing pictures of attractions, as shown in Figure 2, (Colace et al., 2014).

Figure 2. The context dimension tree considered for the museum scenario
Source: Colace et al., 2014, p. 472

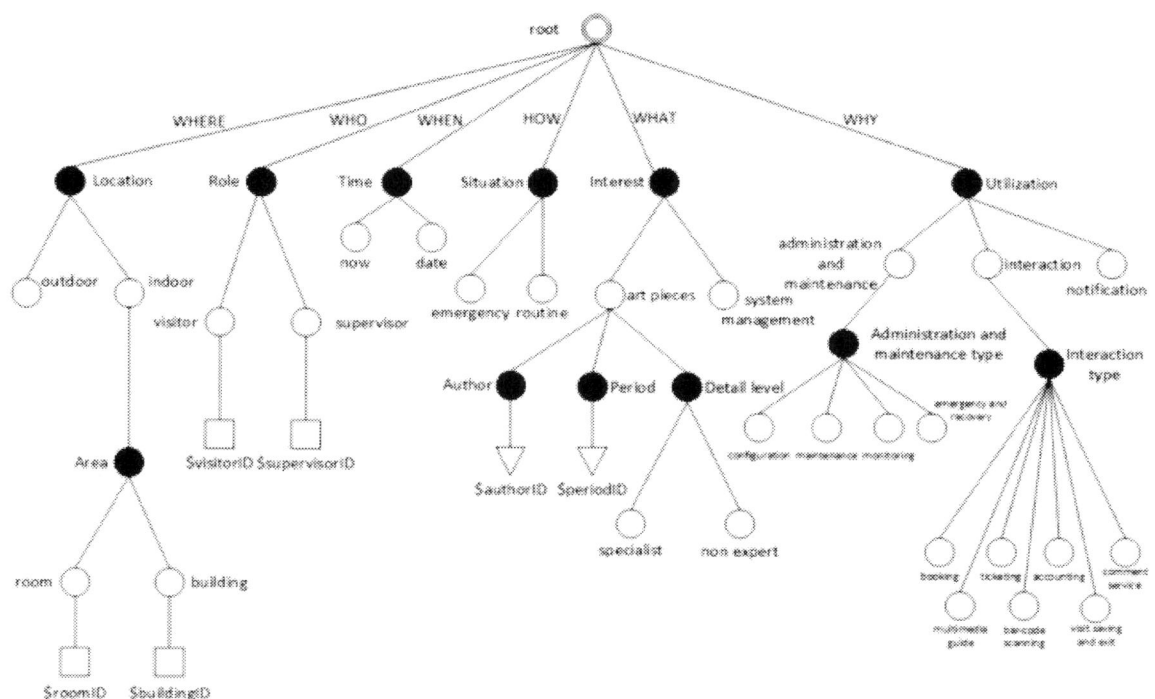

With HYDRIA, a program that can be used by those with weak information technology knowledge, it provides the use of large cultural data from dispersed sources/formats and heterogeneous data and is used in tasks like monitoring and mining. This system enables the creation of integrated datasets by extracting cultural knowledge from social networks (Deligiannis et al., 2020). The cultural heritage information system (CHIS), also created in Italy, is a cloud-based big data infrastructure created for querying, viewing, and analyzing digital content based on cultural heritage. This system can collect data from different and heterogeneous sources such as sensors networks, social media networks, digital libraries, web data services and generate user-specific information. In addition, thanks to many APIs, it supports different applications as well as data analytics and data processing, enabling the display of cultural assets on mobile, developing suggestions, and telling their stories (Castiglione et al., 2018). In addition, with passive mobile data, mobility and movement patterns within and between destinations can be determined. Big data generated by passive mobile data can be used in tourism research (Reif & Schmücker, 2020).

Many database systems have been developed to record and effectively use big data. Relational databases, one of them, are used extensively in the field. Meyer et al. (2007) set an example for the management of heritage objects by creating a class diagram as in Figure 3 in the cultural heritage web information system they created. For this, the data of the archaeological assets in terms of time and place were formulated and the relationships between these data were determined as in Figure 3.

Figure 3. UML class diagram of a web information system of cultural heritage data
Source: Meyer et al., 2007, p. 404

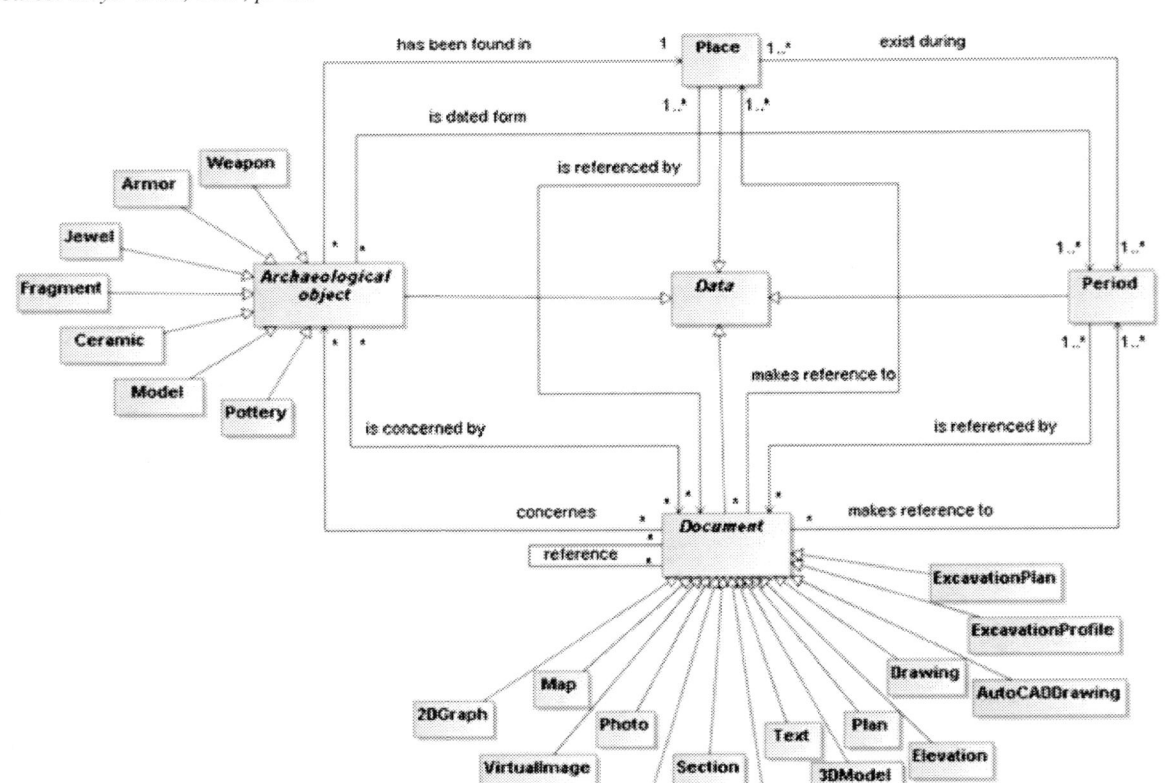

Big Data Techniques Used in Cultural Places

In the literature, data collection before and after the destination visit was generally made through social media research. Although there is limited work on collecting data during travel, the data collected by mobile sensors and positioning has added a vision to the subject. This approach not only goes beyond the research on social media but also offers innovative information for destinations and provides a better understanding of travel phenomena with data analysis (Park et al., 2020). In tourism, the internet and being connected provide the production of a lot of data in volume thanks to social networks and e-tourism-based websites. Especially for social media data, tourist behavior and demand forecasting can be made using the following four techniques (Boulaalam et al., 2018, p. 348):

1. Analysis of text meta-data processes for keyword identification,
2. Identifying popular places by classifying geographic data,
3. Tagging and analysis of photos according to their subject with photo analysis,
4. Time series analysis for tourism demand forecasting and determining tour patterns.

Interest in cultural assets can be increased by gamification through VR or AR technologies. AR applications can be gamified and offered to tourists via mobile devices, and their use can be increased, and it can cause a great increase in the amount of data that can be collected through the application (Kotsopoulos et al., 2019). By using cameras and sensors in mobile devices, the level of knowledge in cultural tourism can be increased to a large extent, and other users can benefit from this great information with VR/AR solutions integrated into mobile technologies. In these solutions, beyond two-dimensional, static three-dimensional (such as an ancient city) and dynamically animated three-dimensional (such as cultural elements) models can be provided via a head-mounted screen connected to mobile technologies (Cirulis et al., 2015). AR, VR, and 3D printing technologies can be used to enhance the visitor experience at cultural heritage sites. The use of multiple technologies similar to the aforementioned technologies can support the joint value creation efforts for cultural heritage sites and affect the pre-, during-, and post-visit experiences of businesses and tourists (Jung & tom Dieck, 2017). Thus, it provides a competitive advantage by ensuring the recognition of the sites where the heritage is located (Graziano & Privitera, 2020) and also contributes to data production by directing the use of more applications. Moreover, developments in the field of geometric shaping in the virtual environment have also led to developments in the modeling of cultural elements. Accordingly, 4D modeling has emerged by adding the concept of time to three-dimensional objects. Thus, historical mapping of three-dimensional tangible or intangible cultural objects in the virtual environment can be made and provides the user with a comparison opportunity (Doulamis et al., 2017).

Big data and artificial intelligence in tourism provide a very rich personalization opportunity and provide efficiency, productivity, and profitability in businesses. Tourists' travel experience can be enriched at every stage and respond to their needs (Samara et al., 2020; Zhang & Dong, 2021). IoT technologies and mobile technologies can be used in museums to measure interest in cultural assets and to model the behavior of visitors. Visitors' profile information, language preferences, duration of visit, first visited cultural asset, the total number of visited assets, which asset they visited for how long, which floors they visited, which assets they listened to can be analyzed by collecting proper information. Recommendation systems, decision support systems, artificial intelligence algorithms, marketing, and management strategies can be developed by performing analyzes with this kind of big data created by the museum. Since the management of cultural heritage sites is important, it supports the development of IoT data analytics techniques by providing efficiency with a technology-oriented approach (Piccialli et al., 2020). While big data support technologies such as artificial intelligence and the internet of things (IoT) in tourism, it also opens up new technological venture areas (Mariani, 2019).

In cultural heritage scenarios, smart tools with machine learning approaches such as voice recognition, automatic question answering, virtual assistant make their experience more enjoyable and enable them to learn more (S. Cuomo et al., 2021). For such intelligent systems to work well, machine learning algorithms must be trained with a sufficient number of data. In such cases, the most efficient solutions can be produced with big data and analysis. Sentiment analysis is one of the important topics developed in connection with big data. In thought analysis, the focus is on what is intended to be conveyed in the text, either conceptually or practically. Accordingly, words are analyzed using big data and new judgments are tried to be revealed. The majority of thought analysis in the tourism field has adopted the machine learning approach and is trained with small datasets (Alaei et al., 2019). Big data analysis in the field can be used for text summarization and text classification using NLP algorithms. Big data is needed to train artificial intelligence algorithms of recommendation systems in cultural tourism. The tourist's daily activities such as searching for destinations, determining a route, sharing experience, evaluating touristic businesses, booking a place, buying tickets, establishing social networks, etc., can be considered as a whole in the programs, which can improve the touristic experience holistically. For this, web or mobile apps can be used, and with an architectural structure integrated with artificial intelligence, the application can achieve the ability to collect and analyze information within itself. To give an example, the mobile application named *CHAT-BOT* in Italy, which was created to support the touristic experience with knowledge of cultural heritage, can develop tourist route suggestions for tourists via correspondence, identify touristic points of interest and suggest other services for tourists' expectations (Casillo et al., 2020). If sufficient information can be obtained about the profiles of tourists, machine learning-based recommendation systems can be trained with tourist typologies to develop more personal recommendations. Thus, the quality of the recommendation and the person's compliance can be ensured, and tourists can be helped to have a better experience (Konstantakis et al., 2020). Intelligent recommendation systems are widely used in tourism. For these systems to work effectively, machine learning and decision-making structures must be programmed with advanced techniques. Besides, the most important issue is how to train the created machine learning algorithms. For the algorithm to give good results and make the right decision and offer appropriate recommendations to the user, it must be trained with the right big data. When considered in the context of cultural tourism, smart assistants and smart natural language and audio processing models have an important place in the industry (Pavlidis, 2019).

SOLUTIONS AND RECOMMENDATIONS

In this context, the current book chapter deals with big data management in cultural tourism with new technological developments and new methods. For this purpose, a systematic literature review has been carried out, which includes sample studies that connect cultural heritage and data, the usage areas of big data in terms of tourism, and systematically address data management in cultural tourism.

In the light of the results obtained from the literature review, it is estimated that big data creates radical changes in cultural tourism and will increase its impact exponentially in the next period. Big data and analytics, which are frequently encountered in industrial applications, oblige stakeholders to compete on the data level in cultural tourism. From the point of view of knowledge economies, the economic value of data is variable but high, and for this, businesses need to take steps in knowledge management. Data hunting is not an easy activity, it is costly and requires good planning. For this, all businesses operating in cultural tourism and this type of tourism should continue their search for quality and useful data by adopting data-oriented approaches and adapting to new technologies. Organizations and those working in the field of cultural tourism cannot achieve the efficiency they want with a single channel (only the top manager) or information flow for a single person, instead, they should prefer two-way channels and ensure that the information is automatically generated through devices and autonomously created and circulated within the organization (Türkmendağ & Tuna, 2021).

The fact that there is a large area of use for new technologies in cultural tourism supports data production. Consumer-oriented AR/VR, AI-based recommendation development systems, IoT, etc. technologies both improve the travel experience of tourists and create virtual environments where data can be generated. It is a known fact that R&D investments in the tourism sector are seriously inadequate. Increasing the ability to innovate by increasing such investments is important for businesses to survive in a competitive environment. In addition to new investments, effective use of existing technologies by enterprises is also important. Communication with tourists can be increased by gamification of existing technologies in cultural tourism, or it can be made easier to use technology by organizing classroom training, seminars, or desk training within the organization. Studies in the literature have mentioned the importance of big data in tourism. For this reason, destination managers and businesses should search for ways to obtain data by following current technologies and turn to outsource or employment of employees with the technical capacity to analyze the data they obtain.

In recent years, especially the increase in the use of mobile phones offers great opportunities for businesses to obtain big data and to interact with customers instantly. With the use of 5G technology in daily life, there is an increase in the use of wearable and IoT technologies beyond mobile phones and an excessive increase in data. In addition, knowing the data types related to culture and cultural tourism provides a good system design. In this regard, in the light of the data obtained from the literature, the data types, potential uses, and difficulties encountered in obtaining the relevant data types are summarized in Table 1. The cultural assets presented in museums and ruins and the revealing of their characteristics shape the issue of what data will be kept in the databases and what kind of data will be used. In addition, the profile, travel patterns, and interests of the cultural tourists are also important in determining the data structures and the relationships between these data structures. Data collection or sharing is as important as data is important, and the use of encouraging new methods provides data saturation. For this, it is important to make promotions to provide the data necessary for the formation of big data, to take measures to facilitate the use of technology, and to develop automatic data collection systems through devices. In addition, methods such as data scraping can be used to collect data about cultural tourism or destination from widely used social media and web environments.

Table 1. Data types and their usage in cultural tourism

	Technology Used to Obtain	Used For	Challenges
Profile Data	Mobile devices, personal computers,	Personalization of products/ services	Privacy and security issues
Location (Routes) Data	Mobile devices, wearable devices, IoT devices	POI identification	Privacy and Security issues
Cultural Heritage Data	Mobile devices, IoT devices	Management, marketing, and protection of heritage	Misinformation
Social Media Data	Mobile devices, personal computer	Personalization of products/ services, marketing of cultural heritage	Privacy and security issues
Destination Information Data	Mobile devices, personal computers, IoT devices	Marketing and planning of cultural tourism destination	Misinformation

While developing a big data system, using cloud-based solutions and giving importance to API integration can provide efficiency. Dissemination of IoT technologies and increasing cooperation on a destination-based basis can provide support to data production and open innovation. In addition, open-source code should be used for such systems to be open to development, but measures should be taken for the security and protection of personal data. In the design of databases and connected technologies to be used in the system, it is recommended to design the data of cultural heritage and its characteristics in the fastest and most orderly manner. In addition to what needs to be done on technological issues, organizational approaches that provide efficiency in information management in enterprises or destinations should be adopted. In addition, it is necessary to show a more professional approach by giving importance to the training and getting expert support on big data analytics (statistical analysis and mathematical modeling techniques) in organizations.

FUTURE RESEARCH DIRECTIONS

Big data and analytics can be seen as a field that has started to be studied frequently in the literature and has many gaps in various aspects. Studies can focus on qualitative studies and quantification studies on cultural data and its use in the tourism industry. By examining the psychological foundations that guide tourists to data processing, it can be investigated how these affect tourists through technologies. In this respect, studies can be carried out on social networks and economic and marketing studies that examine the value of the data formed in these networks.

REFERENCES

Alaei, A. R., Becken, S., & Stantic, B. (2019). Sentiment analysis in tourism: Capitalizing on big data. *Journal of Travel Research*, 58(2), 175–191. doi:10.1177/0047287517747753

Angelidou, M., Karachaliou, E., Angelidou, T., & Stylianidis, E. (2017). Cultural Heritage In Smart City Environments. *The International Archives of the Photogrammetry, Remote Sensing and Spatial Information Sciences, XLII-2*(W5), 27–32. doi:10.5194/isprs-archives-XLII-2-W5-27-2017

AngelidouM.StylianidisE. (2020). Cultural Heritage In Smart City Environments: The Update. *ISPRS Annals of the Photogrammetry, Remote Sensing and Spatial Information Sciences, V-2–2020*, 957–964. doi:10.5194/isprs-annals-V-2-2020-957-2020

Bachi, V., Fresa, A., Pierotti, C., & Prandoni, C. (2014). The Digitization Age: Mass Culture Is Quality Culture. Challenges for Cultural Heritage and Society. In M. Ioannides, N. Magnenat-Thalmann, E. Fink, R. Žarnić, A.-Y. Yen, & E. Quak (Eds.), *Digital Heritage. Progress in Cultural Heritage: Documentation, Preservation, and Protection* (pp. 786–801). Springer International Publishing. doi:10.1007/978-3-319-13695-0_81

Bail, C. A. (2014). The cultural environment: Measuring culture with big data. *Theory and Society, 43*(3–4), 465–482. doi:10.100711186-014-9216-5

Baker, K., & Verstockt, S. (2017). Cultural heritage routing: A recreational navigation-based approach in exploring cultural heritage. *Journal on Computing and Cultural Heritage, 10*(4), 1–20. doi:10.1145/3040200

Balasaraswathi, M., Srinivasan, K., Udayakumar, L., Sivasakthiselvan, S., & Sumithra, M. G. (2020). Big data analytic of contexts and cascading tourism for smart city. *Materials Today: Proceedings*. Advance online publication. doi:10.1016/j.matpr.2020.10.132

Bec, A., Moyle, B., Timms, K., Schaffer, V., Skavronskaya, L., & Little, C. (2019). Management of immersive heritage tourism experiences: A conceptual model. *Tourism Management, 72*, 117–120. doi:10.1016/j.tourman.2018.10.033

Belhi, A., Bouras, A., & Foufou, S. (2017). Digitization and preservation of cultural heritage: The CEPROQHA approach. *11th International Conference on Software, Knowledge, Information Management and Applications (SKIMA)*, 1–7. 10.1109/SKIMA.2017.8294117

Boulaalam, O., Aghoutane, B., El Ouadghiri, D., Moumen, A., & Malinine, M. L. C. (2018). Proposal of a big data system based on the recommendation and profiling techniques for an intelligent management of moroccan tourism. *Procedia Computer Science, 134*, 346–351. doi:10.1016/j.procs.2018.07.200

Casillo, M., Clarizia, F., D'Aniello, G., De Santo, M., Lombardi, M., & Santaniello, D. (2020). CHAT-Bot: A cultural heritage aware teller-bot for supporting touristic experiences. *Pattern Recognition Letters, 131*, 234–243. doi:10.1016/j.patrec.2020.01.003

Castiglione, A., Colace, F., Moscato, V., & Palmieri, F. (2018). CHIS: A big data infrastructure to manage digital cultural items. *Future Generation Computer Systems, 86*, 1134–1145. doi:10.1016/j.future.2017.04.006

Centobelli, P., & Ndou, V. (2019). Managing customer knowledge through the use of big data analytics in tourism research. *Current Issues in Tourism, 22*(15), 1862–1882. doi:10.1080/13683500.2018.1564739

Chiao, H.-M., Chen, Y.-L., & Huang, W.-H. (2018). Examining the usability of an online virtual tour-guiding platform for cultural tourism education. *Journal of Hospitality, Leisure, Sport and Tourism Education, 23*, 29–38. doi:10.1016/j.jhlste.2018.05.002

Cirulis, A., De Paolis, L. T., & Tutberidze, M. (2015). Virtualization of digitalized cultural heritage and use case scenario modeling for sustainability promotion of national identity. *Procedia Computer Science, 77*, 199–206. doi:10.1016/j.procs.2015.12.384

Colace, F., De Santo, M., Greco, L., Lemma, S., Lombardi, M., Moscato, V., & Picariello, A. (2014). A context-aware framework for cultural heritage applications. *2014 Tenth International Conference on Signal-Image Technology and Internet-Based Systems*, 469–476. 10.1109/SITIS.2014.14

Corea, F. (2019). Introduction to Data. In F. Corea (Ed.), *An Introduction to Data: Everything You Need to Know About AI, Big Data and Data Science* (pp. 1–5). Springer International Publishing. doi:10.1007/978-3-030-04468-8_1

Cuomo, M. T., Tortora, D., Foroudi, P., Giordano, A., Festa, G., & Metallo, G. (2021). Digital transformation and tourist experience co-design: Big social data for planning cultural tourism. *Technological Forecasting and Social Change, 162*, 120345. doi:10.1016/j.techfore.2020.120345

Cuomo, S., Colecchia, G., Cola, V. S., & Chirico, U. (2021). A virtual assistant in cultural heritage scenarios. *Concurrency and Computation, 33*(3), e5331. doi:10.1002/cpe.5331

Cuomo, S., De Michele, P., Galletti, A., & Piccialli, F. (2015). A cultural heritage case study of visitor experiences shared on a social network. *2015 10th International Conference on P2P, Parallel, Grid, Cloud and Internet Computing (3PGCIC)*, 539–544.

Del Vecchio, P., Mele, G., Ndou, V., & Secundo, G. (2018a). Open innovation and social big data for sustainability: Evidence from the tourism industry. *Sustainability, 10*(9), 3215. doi:10.3390u10093215

Del Vecchio, P., Mele, G., Ndou, V., & Secundo, G. (2018b). Creating value from Social Big Data: Implications for Smart Tourism Destinations. *Information Processing & Management, 54*(5), 847–860. doi:10.1016/j.ipm.2017.10.006

Deligiannis, K., Raftopoulou, P., Tryfonopoulos, C., Platis, N., & Vassilakis, C. (2020). Hydria: An Online Data Lake for Multi-Faceted Analytics in the Cultural Heritage Domain. *Big Data and Cognitive Computing, 4*(2), 7. doi:10.3390/bdcc4020007

Demunter, C. (2017, June 21). Tourism statistics: Early Adopters of Big Data. *Sixth UNWTO International Conference on Tourism Statistics Measuring Sustainable Tourism.*

Dou, J., Qin, J., Jin, Z., & Li, Z. (2018). Knowledge graph based on domain ontology and natural language processing technology for Chinese intangible cultural heritage. *Journal of Visual Languages and Computing, 48*, 19–28. doi:10.1016/j.jvlc.2018.06.005

Doulamis, N., Doulamis, A., Ioannidis, C., Klein, M., & Ioannides, M. (2017). Modelling of static and moving objects: Digitizing tangible and intangible cultural heritage. In *Mixed reality and gamification for cultural heritage* (pp. 567–589). Springer. doi:10.1007/978-3-319-49607-8_23

Dragoni, M., Tonelli, S., & Moretti, G. (2017). A knowledge management architecture for digital cultural heritage. *Journal on Computing and Cultural Heritage*, *10*(3), 1–18. doi:10.1145/3012289

Frey, B. S., & Briviba, A. (2021). A policy proposal to deal with excessive cultural tourism. *European Planning Studies*, *29*(4), 601–618. doi:10.1080/09654313.2021.1903841

Gao, H. (2021). Big data development of tourism resources based on 5G network and internet of things system. *Microprocessors and Microsystems*, *80*, 103567. doi:10.1016/j.micpro.2020.103567

Garau, C. (2014). Smart paths for advanced management of cultural heritage. *Regional Studies, Regional Science*, *1*(1), 286–293. doi:10.1080/21681376.2014.973439

Graziano, T., & Privitera, D. (2020). Cultural heritage, tourist attractiveness and augmented reality: Insights from Italy. *Journal of Heritage Tourism*, *15*(6), 666–679. doi:10.1080/1743873X.2020.1719116

Hong, M., Jung, J. J., Piccialli, F., & Chianese, A. (2017). Social recommendation service for cultural heritage. *Personal and Ubiquitous Computing*, *21*(2), 191–201. doi:10.100700779-016-0985-x

Hu, I.-L., Chang, C.-C., & Lin, Y.-H. (2021). Using big data and social network analysis for cultural tourism planning in Hakka villages. *Tourism and Hospitality Research*, *21*(1), 99–114. doi:10.1177/1467358420957061

Hwang, J. S., Liu, C., Li, G., & Park, S. T. (2020). A Study on Problem Solution of Culture Tourism Festival Through Big Data Analysis. *International Journal of Emerging Multidisciplinary Research*, *4*(3), 17–21. doi:10.22662/IJEMR.2020.4.3.020

Jara, A. J., Sun, Y., Song, H., Bie, R., Genooud, D., & Bocchi, Y. (2015). Internet of Things for cultural heritage of smart cities and smart regions. *2015 IEEE 29th International Conference on Advanced Information Networking and Applications Workshops*, 668–675.

Jung, T. H., & tom Dieck, M. C. (2017). Augmented reality, virtual reality and 3D printing for the co-creation of value for the visitor experience at cultural heritage places. *Journal of Place Management and Development*, *10*(2), 140–151. Advance online publication. doi:10.1108/JPMD-07-2016-0045

Kalvet, T., Olesk, M., Tiits, M., & Raun, J. (2020). Innovative tools for tourism and cultural tourism impact assessment. *Sustainability*, *12*(18), 7470. doi:10.3390u12187470

Konstantakis, M., Alexandridis, G., & Caridakis, G. (2020). A personalized heritage-oriented recommender system based on extended cultural tourist typologies. *Big Data and Cognitive Computing*, *4*(2), 12. doi:10.3390/bdcc4020012

Kotsopoulos, K. I., Chourdaki, P., Tsolis, D., Antoniadis, R., Pavlidis, G., & Assimakopoulos, N. (2019). An authoring platform for developing smart apps which elevate cultural heritage experiences: A system dynamics approach in gamification. *Journal of Ambient Intelligence and Humanized Computing*, 1–17. doi:10.100712652-019-01505-w

Li, J. (2021). Digital Protection and Inheritance of Intangible Cultural Heritage in the Era of Big Data. *Cyber Security Intelligence and Analytics: 2021 International Conference on Cyber Security Intelligence and Analytics (CSIA2021)*, 1, 24–30. 10.1007/978-3-030-70042-3_4

Li, J., Xu, L., Tang, L., Wang, S., & Li, L. (2018). Big data in tourism research: A literature review. *Tourism Management, 68*, 301–323. doi:10.1016/j.tourman.2018.03.009

Li, X., & Law, R. (2020). Network analysis of big data research in tourism. *Tourism Management Perspectives, 33*, 100608. doi:10.1016/j.tmp.2019.100608

Line, N. D., Dogru, T., El-Manstrly, D., Buoye, A., Malthouse, E., & Kandampully, J. (2020). Control, use and ownership of big data: A reciprocal view of customer big data value in the hospitality and tourism industry. *Tourism Management, 80*, 104106. doi:10.1016/j.tourman.2020.104106

Liu, Y.-Y., Tseng, F.-M., & Tseng, Y.-H. (2018). Big Data analytics for forecasting tourism destination arrivals with the applied Vector Autoregression model. *Technological Forecasting and Social Change, 130*, 123–134. doi:10.1016/j.techfore.2018.01.018

Ma, S., Kirilenko, A. P., & Stepchenkova, S. (2020). Special interest tourism is not so special after all: Big data evidence from the 2017 Great American Solar Eclipse. *Tourism Management, 77*, 104021. doi:10.1016/j.tourman.2019.104021

Mariani, M. (2019). Big data and analytics in tourism and hospitality: A perspective article. *Tourism Review, 75*(1), 299–303. doi:10.1108/TR-06-2019-0259

Meyer, É., Grussenmeyer, P., Perrin, J.-P., Durand, A., & Drap, P. (2007). A web information system for the management and the dissemination of Cultural Heritage data. *Journal of Cultural Heritage, 8*(4), 396–411. doi:10.1016/j.culher.2007.07.003

Nguyen, T. T., Camacho, D., & Jung, J. E. (2017). Identifying and ranking cultural heritage resources on geotagged social media for smart cultural tourism services. *Personal and Ubiquitous Computing, 21*(2), 267–279. doi:10.100700779-016-0992-y

Park, S., Xu, Y., Jiang, L., Chen, Z., & Huang, S. (2020). Spatial structures of tourism destinations: A trajectory data mining approach leveraging mobile big data. *Annals of Tourism Research, 84*, 102973. doi:10.1016/j.annals.2020.102973

Pavlidis, G. (2019). Recommender systems, cultural heritage applications, and the way forward. *Journal of Cultural Heritage, 35*, 183–196. doi:10.1016/j.culher.2018.06.003

Piccialli, F., Benedusi, P., Carratore, L., & Colecchia, G. (2020). An IoT data analytics approach for cultural heritage. *Personal and Ubiquitous Computing, 24*(3), 1–8. doi:10.100700779-019-01323-z

Piccialli, F., & Jung, J. E. (2017). Understanding customer experience diffusion on social networking services by big data analytics. *Mobile Networks and Applications, 22*(4), 605–612. doi:10.100711036-016-0803-8

Reif, J., & Schmücker, D. (2020). Exploring new ways of visitor tracking using big data sources: Opportunities and limits of passive mobile data for tourism. *Journal of Destination Marketing & Management, 18*, 100481. doi:10.1016/j.jdmm.2020.100481

Richards, G. (2018). Cultural tourism: A review of recent research and trends. *Journal of Hospitality and Tourism Management, 36*, 12–21. doi:10.1016/j.jhtm.2018.03.005

Samara, D., Magnisalis, I., & Peristeras, V. (2020). Artificial intelligence and big data in tourism: A systematic literature review. *Journal of Hospitality and Tourism Technology*, *11*(2), 343–367. Advance online publication. doi:10.1108/JHTT-12-2018-0118

Türkmendağ, Z., & Tuna, M. (2021). Empowering leadership and knowledge management: The mediating role of followers' technology use. *Journal of Organizational Change Management*. doi:10.1108/JOCM-11-2020-0364

Xu, J. (2020). Research on the Construction of Cultural Tourism Market in Shenyang Based on Big Data. *Journal of Physics: Conference Series*, *1621*(1), 012104. doi:10.1088/1742-6596/1621/1/012104

Yallop, A., & Seraphin, H. (2020). Big data and analytics in tourism and hospitality: Opportunities and risks. *Journal of Tourism Futures*, *6*(3), 257–262. doi:10.1108/JTF-10-2019-0108

Yin, X., & Li, J. (2021). Development of cultural tourism platform based on FPGA and convolutional neural network. *Microprocessors and Microsystems*, *80*, 103579. doi:10.1016/j.micpro.2020.103579

Zhang, J., & Dong, L. (2021). Image monitoring and management of hot tourism destination based on data mining technology in big data environment. *Microprocessors and Microsystems*, *80*, 103515. doi:10.1016/j.micpro.2020.103515

KEY TERMS AND DEFINITIONS

Artificial Intelligence: Algorithms that act like an intelligent being.

Augmented Reality: Combining computer-generated data (image, text, etc.) with real-world photos or videos.

Big Data: Dataset with a very large number of units.

Cultural Heritage: The total of elements or assets related to the local culture such as archaeological, monumental sculpture, historic building, and town, paintings, etc.

Data: They are objects and subjects found around.

Internet of Things: Actuators and sensors distributed in physical environments.

Relational Database: A digital workspace that represents the data in tabular form.

Virtual Reality: Computer model that interacts user with artificial 3D visual environments.

Chapter 8
The Use of Virtual Reality and Augmented Reality in Cultural Heritage and Deep–Diving Destinations

Nihan Garipağaoğlu-Uğur
ⓘ https://orcid.org/0000-0003-2390-6940
Istanbul University, Turkey

Orhan Akova
ⓘ https://orcid.org/0000-0001-7740-2938
Istanbul University, Turkey

ABSTRACT

Underwater cultural heritage and deep diving are important attractions for tourism. Using cutting-edge technology tools for cultural heritage became more important for tourism destinations. The purpose of this chapter is to evaluate the use of virtual reality (VR) and augmented reality (AR) in tourism from the perspective of cultural heritage and deep diving. This chapter will contribute to the literature to show a new way of sustainable tourism. Commercial diving to an underwater heritage site a is popular touristic activity. Sometimes shipwreck recovery can be hazardous for cultural heritage. The review results indicate that these underwater cultural heritage sites need to be protected for sustainable tourism development. Virtual tours contribute to the sustainability of cultural heritage. On the other hand, treasure hunting trips and recreational diving may cause damage to the archaeological sites. Underwater cultural heritage sites should be protected for sustainable tourism. VR and AR applications can be used to promote a touristic destination by tourism marketers for experimental marketing.

DOI: 10.4018/978-1-7998-8528-3.ch008

INTRODUCTION

Cultural heritages and deep diving as a tourist attraction are important components for tourism marketers and using technological tools for cultural heritage became more important for tourism destinations. Virtual experiences and augmented reality (AR) gives the visitors feel that as if they were at the historical places and historical times (Magnenat-Thalmann, et al. 2002). Virtual reality (VR) systems show visitors historical places that do not exist. Most of the historical places are under ongoing construction or away from population. Therefore, using VR makes it easier to reach them. Virtual means "being something in essence or effect, though not actually or in fact" (Etymology Dictionary, 2021). VR is a visional experience which is different than real world or similar the real one. VR is applicable mostly in education, video games, business, entertainment and cultural heritage. VR is a simulation of a historical place which is really exist and also not real. VR includes augmented reality and mixed reality (Goode, 2019). One of the uses of VR is simulation based. Such as driving a car or deep diving. This really feels like driving a car or diving deep. The other VR is avatar which is image based and 3D virtual environment in the form of video that user can join the system with an avatar.

Augmented reality is the type of VR technology that mixes the user vision in real surroundings with digital content. There are different approaches about virtual and augmented reality in tourism. According to Cheong (1995) VR could be a virtual threat for tourism and it may substitute to travel. Williams (2006) concluded that using VR & AR is the new way to experimental marketing. tom Dieck & Jung (2018) studied British female tourists' acceptance of AR mobile applications. Their acceptance depended on different dimensions such as information quality, costs, recommendations, innovations and condition risks. Boboc et al. (2019) showed in their work mobile AR applications have great potential in cultural heritage sites. However, user acceptance is low. Güzel & Sucaklı (2020) emphasized AR implications use at different levels for each museum. According to Graziano & Privitera (2020) on the occasion of AR and VR applications do not work, tourists show their disappointment. Jingen et al. (2020), Yin et al. (2021) emphasized, AR tourism research literature is mature and growing fast.

AR is in use in many sectors such as education, music, gaming, art, commerce and tourism (Mesároš, et al. 2016). Food and beverage sector also use VR and AR implications for food safety (Georgakopoulos, 2008). VR and AR based virtual educational tours are sustainable for nature and cause less greenhouse emissions (Mohanty, Hassan, & Ekis, 2020). VR provides more effective for advertising than brochures (Guttentag, 2010).

AR technology originated to 1960's and still are used with mobile devices, live feed cameras into a headset or smart glasses. AR is able to bring together physical world and digital information. On the other hand, gamification technology uses the game elements in non-gaming environments. Gamification is new trend for tourism which attract all ages of customers (Xu et al. 2013). Gamification and AR can act as interface among cultural heritage, tourism companies and tourist in sustainable tourism. Using AR and gamification techniques in tourism are more sustainable (Negruşa, Toader, Sofică, Tutunea, & Rus, 2015). AR has been increasingly used for cultural heritage tourism (Cranmer, Tom Dieck, & Fountoulaki, 2020). Digital technology and AR offers new ways to discover cultural heritages so that people can learn the heritage, have fun and socialize with others. Cultural heritage organizations are using innovative applications, gamification and AR. Today many organizations use AR for turning fiction to real experiences to attract tourists.

Since the recovery of artefacts and possibility of finding a sunken treasure from shipwrecks on the seabed, diving has become a commercial activity in waters. Underwater cultural heritages are always threatened for commercial gain and irresponsible salvage operations (Fletcher-Tomenius & Forrest, 2000). Historical shipwrecks have a potential to attract more tourists. Sunken wreck mesmerizes tourists about the history of ships, what it had carried, crew on board and passengers. Also artefacts and treasures attract people with dazzling riches and glory. With the help of AR and VR, tourists can be a part of cultural heritage and learn the history of sunken wrecks. The aim of this chapter is to evaluate the use of VR and AR in tourism in the perspective of cultural heritage and deep diving. A literature review is conducted to evaluate the use of VR and AR in tourism.

BACKGROUND

VR and AR are growingly used as an information, experience and marketing tool within tourism sector (Cranmer et al. 2020). Digital marketing provide more opportunities via internet (Uğur, 2020). VR techniques are instruments of digital marketing which are used to provide interaction with customers (Meral, 2021). Cutting-edge technologies are used as a marketing tool for nearly all kinds of products. Users have accessible information and enhance their experiences via VR and AR applications. Tourism marketers may use VR and AR technologies especially young tourists (Özdemir, 2021). Tourism marketers use VR and AR to enhance visitor experiences, satisfaction. Cutting-edge technology increases social media effects and provides a positive destination image via VR and AR (Moorhouse, Jung, & tom Dieck, 2019). VR is almost used in every sector especially real estate and tourism. Virtual reality is not a new term. It was first mention by Myron Kruger in mid-1970's. He used the term "virtual reality" to describe to understand how human – computer interface (Williams & Hobson, 1995).

Williams A. (2006) indicated that virtual reality technologies assist marketers to create new memories and experiences on tourism. This provides brand loyalty and new memories for guests. Guttentag (2010:638) explains virtual reality in his study "Use of a computer-generated 3D environment – called a 'virtual environment' (VE) – that one can navigate and possibly interact with, resulting in real-time simulation of one or more of the user's five senses". Hsu (2012:113) described the VR "The proliferating applications of virtual reality (VR), which means to creating a real world within the context of the virtual environment (VE) or virtual world (VW)". In his definition, Çeltek (2021:237) states that virtual reality (VR) is a computer technology that allows users to copy a real or imaginary environment, and the simulation of the user in this environment allows users to see and hear using a "headset".

THE USE OF VIRTUAL REALITY AND AUGMENTED REALITY IN CULTURAL HERITAGE AND DEEP DIVING DESTINATIONS

VR means that interactive videos or images which allows people to see the whole scene. VR technology takes every part of the destination which has a unique ambient. For using VR technology special cameras, software rigs are needed. However, using VR content to view location is not required to use special devices. It can be viewed by any device and mobile phones. VR technology is utilized in tourism as a marketing tool. VR allows users to experience existence in a platform within a unique destination. Gaming industries uses VR, but a 360 degrees VR focused on the real world. That makes it perfect for tourism sector. Consumers can see the real location rather than the simulation. Applications of VR in tourism such as travel experiences, virtual hotel tours and sharing tourism experiences in social media.

Some travel agencies use VR technology to allow consumers to explore the destination as they were in there. Travel agencies can offer virtual travels experiences to consumers instead of brochures. Consumers use VR tours for searching hotels and can see extreme details. Using VR technology in tourism has some benefits such as, allowing the users to be in travel destination. Being able to see 360 degrees of the destination and enabling them to explore a scene. Also creating a unique experience. Making consumers to commitment towards the brand. Provide travel experiences to vulnerable destinations or somewhere which is hard to travel (Immersion VR, 2021). From the consumer's perspective the tourism experiences such as cultural heritage sites or museums have tree contexts.

- Personal context: Personal experiences, motivation, knowledge
- Social context: Social environments where the tourism destination
- Physical context: Cultural heritage or objects. Also agriculture of the buildings where object in (Kuchelmeister, 2018).

VR technology focus on physical context but not effect on personal context. Personnel context includes personnel motivations which are vary from person to person (Garipağaoğlu-Uğur, 2020). Tourism sector offers different venues which people can visit. Such as bars, restaurants, hotels, casinos, cruise, daily tours, cathedrals, mosques, theme parks (Williams A., 2006). These places are visited by different kind of people with diverse motivations. Social context plays a fundamental role during a visit to historical places or touristic destinations. Virtual places are also visited by tourist to share same experiences with others. Their avatars communicate with other avatars. Addition to that, recording instructions should let them have conversation each other (Kuchelmeister, 2018). Visiting a place in person gives different experiences than virtual visit. They both have different motives and pleasure. Therefore, both have different attributes and sometimes both can be visited, sometimes not. Especially if some place cannot be visited in person, the virtual visits are the best option (Schweibenz, 2012).

Virtual technology has potential to create events for users (Williams & Hobson, 1995). Some games such as "Second life" is the most active virtual platform which socialized by avatars and built their own life. This 3D (three-dimensional) virtual world has one million visitors each month (Huang, et al. 2016). Second life used in academic context such as computer studies, design, language and tourism. Second life enables users to have virtual socialization. Second life based tourism course was a complementary project for travel management students. The aim of second life based project was to show the usability of 3D innovative simulations for tourism (Hsu, 2012). VR offers interactivity and virtual experiences in tourism. Simulated trips influence the tourism sector. (Huang, el al. 2016). VR technologies help to promote and create tourist attractions and entertainments, in addition to that, this helps protecting cultural heritages (Guttentag, 2010).

A VR experience provides physical immersion, which means isolation from real world, and psychological presence. VR systems are classified as fully immersive that refer to use HMD (A head-mounted display). On the other hand, semi-immersive use large projection screens. Another VR system is non-immersive that refers desktop based VR system. The classification depends on how much user can interactive with real world at same time. Psychological presence is, when the simulations gets refined by the brain and accepted as a real environment. For instance, while playing a game, players knows that environments are not real, but players act similar to real world (Gutierrez, Vexo, & Thalmann, 2008). VR is used in tourism in many different ways. VR model is used for road planning, which goes through cultural heritage area process in Sweden (Heldal, 2007). This creates illustrated virtual environments on tourism plans and present to the public freely. This was used in Italy for transportation (Caneparo, 2001). Tourism companies use VR technology to attract tourist. Some hotels and destinations offers virtual trip for consumers (Guttentag, 2010). Travel agencies uses VR for communicating and sharing information with consumers. TripAdvisor is the most successful virtual community in tourism. All hotels reviews and experiences of guests are shared with others (Buhalis & Law, 2008). Theme parks offer VR entertainments such as Dreamworld in Australia. They offer "'V8 Supercars Redline" which are similar to the Cyber Speedway in Las Vegas. Also "The Future Is Wild" in which AR technology projects futuristic animals onto a real environment presented by Futuroscope theme park in France. Disney Quest Indoor Interactive Theme Park in Orlando presented on "Aladdin's Magic Carpet Ride". Users wear an HMD use a motorcycle-type apparatus to race on a virtual magic carpet. VR's can be used in museums, cultural heritage sites and other touristic venues. For instance, Foundation of the Hellenic World, a Greek cultural heritage institution has offered educational VR exhibits. Users feel like archaeologist and journey through the Miletus where ancient city (Guttentag, 2010). Table 1 shows some of the cultural heritage sites and objects that can be seen virtual.

Table 1. Heritages cites and objects as 3D models

Michelangelo's statues of David
Florentine Pieta
More than 150 sculptures from the Parthenon
The Great Buddha carving from Afghanistan
Angkor temples in Cambodia
Terra Cotta Warrior statues from China
castles in Northern Italy
Byzantine crypt in Italy
Frescoes from the House of the Vettii in Pompeii
Hawara pyramid complex from ancient Egypt
Hagia Sophia Mosque of Istanbul
the Dutch castle of Huys Hengelo
19th century aboriginal chief house in Canada
14th century Bosnian king's monumental gravestone

Source: Guttentag, 2010

As it is shown in Table 1, lots of heritage sites and objects have been digitalized as 3D VR models. Using 3D VR technology helps to preservation of cultural heritage for damages. In addition, that museums use VR to bring their collections to life. VR is being used to make interactive exhibits or create museum tours. Here below some of the museums use VR to bring dimension to collections (Coates, 2021):

- London V&A opened "Curious Alice" in summer of 2021.
- Louvre provides VR experiences for "Mona Lisa".

- The Peterson Automotive Museum in Los Angeles created exciting VR experiences with classic American sport car.
- The National Museum of Finland in Helsinki launched R. W. Ekman's painting *"The Opening of the Diet 1863 by Alexander II"*.
- Smithsonian Institution used VR to *"No Spectators: The Art of Burning Man"* exhibition
- London's Tate Modern created VR exhibit that visitors experience actual artist's studio *in Paris.*

There are also lots of museum, castle and mosque that can be visited as 3D modelling in Turkey. Table 2 shows name of 3D touristic places in Turkey.

Table 2. 3D VR places in Turkey

Mosques	Palaces	Museums	Castle	Nature	Ancient
Selimiye – Edirne	Topkapı Palace - Istanbul	Panaroma 1453 Istanbul	Alanya Catle – Alanya	Pamukkale - Denizli	Aspendos - Serik
Great Mosque- Bursa	Dolmabahce Palace - Istanbul	Submarine – Kocaeli	Rumeli Castle - Istanbul	Manavgat Waterfall - Manavgat	Ephesus - Izmir
Blue Mosque- Istanbul	Beylerbeyi Palace – Istanbul	Mevlana Museum – Konya	Kilitbahir Castle – Canakkale	Damlitas Cave- Alanya	Didymaion - Aydin
Suleymaniye- Istanbul	Yıldız Palace - Istanbul	Former Parliament Building – Ankara	Bodrum Castle - Bodrum	Dim Cave - Alanya	Theodosius Cistern - Istanbul
Fatih Mosque – Istanbul	Aynalikavak Pavilion - Istanbul	Archaeology Museum - Istanbul	Marmaris Castle - Marmaris	Lake Golcuk- Bolu	Basilica Cistern - Istanbul
Yeni Mosque – Istanbul	Ciragan Palace - Istanbul	Princes Museum – Amasya	Amasya Castle - Amasya	Zeus Cave - Aydin	Acropolis - Bergama
Eyup Sultan – Istanbul	Kucuksu Pavilion - Istanbul	Rahmi Koc Museum - Istanbul	Anatolian Castle - Istanbul	Kaklik Cave - Denizli	Aphrodisias - Aydin
Beyezid Mosque – Istanbul	Ihlamur Pavilion - Istanbul	Dervish Lodge of Galata - Istanbul	Ankara Castle - Ankara	Bulak Cave- Safranbolu	Hierapolis - Denizli
Green Mosque - Bursa	Imperial Kiosk - Istanbul	Kariye Museum - Istanbul	Yedikule Dungeons and walls- Istanbul	Thermal Woods - Yalova	Euromos - Milas
Mihrimah Sultan – Istanbul	Adile Sultan Pavilion and Palace -Istanbul	Health Museum – Edirne	Becin Castle - Milas	Karahayit Red Water - Denizli	Roman Temple - Ankara
Old Mosque – Edirne	Imperial Kiosk - Bursa	Bimarhane – Amasya	Ayvalik Castle - Ayvalık	Cal Kisik Canyon - Denizli	Karahayit Byzantine Jacuzzi - Denizli
Ahi Elvan Mosque – Ankara		Yoruk Ali Museum - Aydin	Güvercinada Castle - Kusadasi	Azmak River - Ula	Priene - Aydin
Big Selimiye Mosque – Istanbul		Iznik Museum - Iznik	Erzurum Castle – Erzurum	The Fairy Chimneys Cappadocia	Laodikeia - Denizli

Source: Sites in 3D, 2021

As it is shown in Table 2, there are lots of museums, mosques, palaces, castle and natural places that 3D VR technology is used in in Turkey. VR technology provide individual visitors to see cultural objectives and heritage. VR technology is a virtual trip to tourism destinations. In the meantime, AR lets users interact with real-world that improves visitor's experience.

AR increases an individual's digital senses of hearing and view. User reach the senses via head-mounted displays smart glasses, any kind of computers and mobile phones. Since 1960s AR has been researched in computer science field (Jingen Liang & Elliot, 2020). Azuma et al. (2001) describes AR "supplements the real world with virtual (computer-generated) objects that appear to coexist in the same space as the real world". AR system is combined of virtual objects and real one in real environment. AR system works interactively in real time. Real and virtual objects line up with each other (Azuma et al. 2001).

AR is location-based mobile implementation. AR games elements are attracting tourist into challenges and interactive game-play while they are exploring a destination or cultural heritage site. AR games are used for location-based storytelling, social interactions and personalized features. Tourism sector needs the entertainment of video games and exploring cultural heritage as well. Using AR techniques implementing the mobile devices allow tourists to have experiences in a way of fun (Weber, 2014). In AR, the user can see and feel as if he/she is in the real world. By using see-through displays virtual objects overlapping the real world can be seen (Bimber & Raskar, 2019). AR provide virtual context such as images or videos that make someone see or feel as if in the real world. AR technology helps consumers to try some different experiences (Loureiro, Guerreiro, & Ali, 2020). While VR is completely virtual and controlled by system, AR can control by users and uses a real world setting. AR improves both the virtual and real world experience (Tulane, 2021).

Tourists can explore the historical places of cultural heritage as it was the same as in the past, and see the location over the real world. For example, heritage sites as National Pantheon and the 12th century Pinhel Castle in Portuguese used AR devices to show them on a larger screen. Through the AR device, guests can get explanatory information over the location being seen (Guttentag, 2010).

Among all the touristic places, cultural heritage sites are the most popular destinations on the earth. Those places have rich historical, architectural, and cultural elements in which mesmerize the tourists. However, tourists need full information and knowledge about these cultural heritages. Usually, the original heritage is not solid and people who used to be live there no longer exist. Natural disasters cause corruption in these cultural heritages. Moreover, these heritages suffer from the inflow of tourists. Therefore, usually limited access to cultural heritage cites because of preservation or renovation (Chung, Lee, Kim, & Koo, 2018). AR mobile applications are providing useful tour information. It can navigate and give information about cultural heritage. AR mobile applications gives information about historical events that occurred in the past (Siang, Aziz, & Ahmad, 2020). While tourists use the AR application to visit cultural sites, they no longer have a language barrier and they can move beyond time. Some of museums using AR in the world are given in Table 3.

Table 3. Museums using augmented reality

Casa Batlló museum - Spain
Smithsonian National Museum of Natural History - USA
National Geographic Museum - USA
La Conciergerie - France
Cosmo Caixa -Spain
National History Museum - USA
Natural History Museum - England
Geneva art and history museum - Switzerland
The Franklin Institute Science Museum – USA
New Philadelphia - USA
London Museum - England
Pompeii – Italy
Berlin Museum - Germany
National Museum of Singapore
Royal Ontario Museum – Canada
Svevo Museum – Italy
Acropolis Museum – Greece
Parthenon temple - Greece
Van Gogh – Holland

Source: Güzel & Sucaklı, 2020; World Itineraries, 2020

As it is seen in Table 3, there are some of the museums which uses augmented reality.

- Casa Batlló is one of Barcelona's most successful tourism attractions in which designed by Antoni Gaudí. It can be visited via using AR implemented devices.
- Smithsonian's one of the oldest museum opened in 1981. Visitors using their smartphones, can see exotic creatures in action. These are a flying vampire bat, an anhinga catching fish and, a sea cow growing flesh.
- National Geographic Museum has special exhibition that named "Queens of Egypt". Visitors can see the inside of the tomb of Queen Nefertiti with special glasses.
- At La Conciergerie, visitors hire a Histopad[1] to explore the place digitally, including the Hall of the Soldiers and the Guards Room.
- Cosmo Caixa Barcelona is a science museum that focus on a special dinosaur named Triceratops.
- National History Museum at Utah illustrates how archaeologist discover fossils. Visitor can see the digging and have information about artefacts (World Itineraries, 2020).
- National History Museum at South Kensington presents magical beasts and full of fantastic real-life. Visitors can take a deep dive into the life of a blue whale (Nhm, 2021).
- Museum of Art and History at Geneva, visitors can get an audio guide and see via tablet.
- The Franklin Institute using AR to presents Terracotto Warriors (Güzel & Sucaklı, 2020).

- New Philadelphia museum at Illinois. Visitors get into the virtually reconstructed historic town with AR applications (Painter, 2015).
- London museum has augmented gallery, contend 20 life-sized colorful frames on walls (Museums and Heritage, 2021).
- VR and AR technologies provide a historical trip to Ancient city of Pompeii (Retro Futuro, 2021)
- Berlin museum presents eight sculptures by Berlin Artist which can be seen via mobile devices. Visitors can experience art virtually (Berlin, 2021).
- National Museum of Singapore is the oldest museum and focuses on history of Singapore. Museum provide virtual tour to different sections (Joy of museums virtual tours, 2021).

Some of museums using augmented reality in Turkey are given in Table 4.

Table 4. AR using museums at Turkey

Topkapı Carpet Museum - Istanbul	Virtual carpet is patterned on interactive floor
Yesil Efendi Konagi - Eskisehir	Visitors can take a photo with Ataturk
Bilgi Kultur ve Tanitim Merkezi – Mardin (Information, Culture and Publicity Center)	Visitors able to see 22 construction in Mardin
Saat (Watch) Museum – Bursa	Visitors interact with table clock
Anadolu Medeniyetleri (Anatolian Civilizations) Museum - Ankara	Take virtual tour in museum and get information about all objects
Sakıp Sabancı Museum - Istanbul	The rare manuscripts exhibition can be viewed in detail on the iPad

Source: Güzel & Sucaklı, 2020

Nowadays museums use AR implementations to enhance the visitor's experiences. Using AR in tourism is newish. However, many researchers have interested in this field and conducted many studies. Williams A. (2006) argue that tourism sector will change with virtual experiences. Alzua-Sorzabal, Linaza, & Abad (2007) concluded that tourists using AR on the tourist site agree that AR is beneficial and enhances interaction. They are willing to pay for the experience. Weber (2014) developed theoretical model for locational based AR games used by tourists. Cranmer, Jung, & Miller (2016) contended that sustainability plays important role for cultural heritage and AR implementations could contribute to increased attraction sustainability. According to Siang, Aziz, & Ahmad (2020) all tourism suppliers use AR technologies to provide more satisfaction to tourists. Especially, AR can help tourists in case of inability to travel. According to Graziano & Privitera (2020), AR applications are provided knowledge and interaction with cultural heritage.

Tourism companies have been using web technologies, including VR, and AR. Virtual visits are increasing. Some sites provide virtual tours to touristic sites and cultural heritages. Consumers also try virtual tours before pay for a tour. They prefer rather gets an ocean cruise, or dive into the aqua blue sea than seeing a promotional brochure (Williams A., 2006). As a new form of tourism AR applications can create cultural heritage sites or underwater archaeological places (tom Dieck & Jung, 2018). While AR applications mesmerizing people, it makes possible for tourists to visit cultural heritage sites (Siang, Aziz, & Ahmad, 2020) that cannot be reached. Virtual travel can make sunken wrecks or underwater archaeological sites reachable in addition it provides artefact or treasures in the deep sea to be seen for visitors looking for adventure and wish to discover new places into the mystery of historical lives.

SUNKEN WRECKS AS AN EXTREME CULTURAL TOURISM

Deep diving means to dive deeper than 20 meters. On the other hand, there are different definitions. In recreational diving, maximum dive limit is 40 meters. Diving deeper than 60 meters means deep dive which is technical diving. However commercial diving companies defines recreational diving as 18 meters and beyond (Lonne, 2020). Scuba diving means to dive around 18 meters. Scuba diving make it possible to explore the underwater for divers. Scuba diving is a recreational activity that someone can see shipwrecks, underwater caves, corals and habitats (Quora, 2020).

Deep diving for treasures in which lie on the bottom of the sea and sunken wrecks mesmerize thrill-seekers. Since scuba diving equipment has been developed in the 40s, underwater exploration such as shipwreck diving has become a popular recreational activity. The Japanese fleet in Chuuk Lagoon are popular areas for divers. Some of the sunken wrecks have been lying on deeper seas. British aircraft carrier Hermes lying at 60 meters off Sri Lanka or The Andrea Doria which is lying at 80 meters off New York are the sunken vessels that only professional deep divers can dive with special equipment (Spennemann, 2007).

Some famous vessels such as The Titanic, Bismarck, and USS Yorktown are resting in the deep sea in oceans. After permission was taken, mini submersibles have gone to the Titanic, and over 6000 artefacts salvaged at different years. These rescues have caused financial problems until fee-paying tourists visit victims' graves or artefacts exhibits. Private companies have interested in deep diving trips to these vessels. Since diving technology is becoming easier to get, more tourist activity is expected. America, Canada, United Kingdom and France have an agreement to protect the remains of Titanic (Spennemann, 2007). This agreement provides sustainability of cultural deep sea heritage. Protecting underwater cultural heritage from threats of commercial gain is a highly important issue for sustainability.

As recoveries from shipwreck can be highly valued, the artefacts from a shipwreck in the deep sea have become a commercial activity. It is possible to recover any archeological and historical object in the deep sea via new technology. While Titanic found in 4000 meters. Isis a 4th-century Roman wreck has been found in 800 meters. The Melkarth Phoenician wreck in 900 meters has been found recently. These recoveries provide valuable historical and archaeological resources. However, some of the wrecks have economically valuable cargo (Fletcher-Tomenius & Forrest, 2000). These cargos mesmerize the treasure hunters. Therefore, governments and UNESCO (United Nations Educational, Scientific and Cultural Organization) are trying to take care of these artefacts and protect cultural heritage.

Commercial diving to underwater heritages are happening in several regions of the world. Thus, it recovers some treasures or artefacts of shipwrecks which are taken back to land. Some of these artefacts are exhibited at the museums but some of them goes missing. Shipwreck recovery seems to be a hazardous industry for saving cultural heritages. Cultural heritages are limited assets. During the treasure hunting, hunters may destroy the site that can cause not to be restructured. Commercial recovery companies do not pay attention to these sites. Commercial deep diving companies usually focus on ancient shipwrecks. They focus to sellable artefacts and cargos. On the other hand, scientists research only for public benefit. Archeological excavations keep away the unnecessary disturbance of site. They respect to cultural heritage (UNESCO, 2001a). As a scientific view, artefacts recovered from historic wreck should not part of private collection or sell out.

Underwater cultural heritages are threatened by treasure hunters. But it is not the only threat. Some legal but unscientific salvages also cause harm to cultural heritage. In addition, that climate changes, natural disasters, trawling, and other exploitation of sea resources have a negative impact on underwater archaeological sites (UNESCO, 2001b). In Figure 1 it is shown the treats of underwater cultural heritage.

Figure 1. Threats of underwater heritages
Source: UNESCO (2001b)

Many historic shipwrecks and other cultural heritages have sunken into the oceans. In Figure 1 the threats to underwater cultural heritage are seen.

- Pillage: Historical artefacts are stolen from an archaeological site by looters. This treasure hunting pillage is desecrating the graveyards in shipwrecks.
- Commercial exploitation: The legal way to pick up artefacts from an archaeological site and put them up for sale. These operations usually do not have scientific standards and damage the archaeological sites.
- Irresponsible diving: Divers enjoy the underwater and usually protect underwater cultural heritages. Even so, there are some divers collecting souvenirs from archaeological sites and cause negative effects.
- Trawling: A major problem for the protection of underwater cultural heritage is trawling. Fishing nets and digging sea beds with trawling is destroy the shipwrecks on archaeological sites.
- Resource extraction: Some of the underwater prehistoric cultural heritage sites are under the sand. Stakeholders recover the metal from shipwrecks and sales. During the recovery shipwrecks are also destroyed.
- Lack of protection: Treasure hunters exploit the artefacts from underwater. In many countries, there is no legal protection for pillage. Besides this, during the recovering and bringing up on surface an artefact that has been plunged in saltwater for a long period, contacts with air and light. This contact carries the risk of rapid deterioration. For this reason, artefacts need to be properly recovered and proper conservation process (UNESCO, 2001b).

Museums presents objects, materials and artefacts. Many museums exhibit artefacts recovered from underwater shipwrecks or archaeological sites. Underwater cultural heritage exhibited in museums are shown in Table 5.

Table 5. Underwater cultural heritages exhibited in museums

Sweden's Vasa shipwreck	Sweden
Bodrum Museum of Underwater Archaeology	Turkey
Great Britain's Mary Rose shipwreck	Great Britain
The Greek National Museum	Greece
Danish National Museum	Denmark

Source: UNESCO, 2001b

- Vasa ship sunk in front of onlookers in 1628. Vasa set sail was the highest technological war ship in that days. Vasa sank because the weapons were too heavy. The remains of ship is in Stockholm's Vasa Museum (Eschner, 2017).
- Bodrum Museum of Underwater Archaeology have precious wreck collection recovered from Turkey's shores.
- Great Britain's Mary Rose shipwreck was discovered in 1971 and raised in 1982. The remains have been exhibited in Portsmouth.
- The Greek National Museum is largest archaeological museum in Greece. Museum hosts the Antikythera shipwreck collection.
- Danish National Museum in Copenhagen (UNESCO, 2001b).

Mediterranean Sea has been an important transportation route. Therefore, lots of ships have passed through Mediterranean Sea throughout the history. Some of them were sunken in the past and their wrecks, their cargos are still lying in deep down. Some of their remains are exhibited in museums, others are still underwater. These sunken wrecks need preservation for climate changes and marine pollution. Mediterranean Sea has high salinity and can decompose the sunken ships and its materials. An another problem is the lack of knowledge about the condition of artefact's (Argyropoulos & Stratigea, 2019). There have been lots of shipwrecks lying down the oceans with their treasures and artefacts. There are more historical artefacts in the oceans than all museums combined (Snyder, 2017). Since the ancient eras, ships have been used for transportation in the Mediterranean Sea. Turkey's coastal regions have been a transit route for many merchants and sailors from different empires and countries since ancient times. Black Sea, Aegean, and Southern Mediterranean routes were used by navies, merchant fleets, cruise ships, and explorers for a long time. The ancient Egyptian figures also indicated that the Anatolian coasts played an important role in the development of maritime trade. The world oldest sunken is explored in Turkey's coastal area. The world's oldest (3600 years old) sunken shipwreck, named "The West Antalya Shipwreck" was found in 50-meter-deep in Turkey's coastal area (Arkas News, 2020). Last three years, 125 shipwrecks have been found in the Mediterranean Sea nearby Turkey's shores. Many of them were carrying olive oil, wine, dried meat, fish, and legumes in amphorae (İHA, 2021). 37 land wrecks from the Byzantine Period have been found in the district of Yenikapı (Theodosius Harbor) in Istanbul (Mahsereci, 2013). Table 6 shows some ancient shipwrecks in Mediterranean Sea.

Table 6. Ancient era sunken vessels in Mediterranean

Vessel	Ancient era	Sunken place
Şeytan Deresi Batığı / Devil's Creek shipwreck	BC 17Th century	Gokova Bay (Kerameikos)
Uluburun Batığı / Uluburun shipwreck	BC 14th century	Uluburun (Grand Cape) – Kaş
Gelidonya Burnu batığı / Cape Gelidonya shipwreck	BC 13th century	Gelidonya Cape
Pabuç Burnu Batığı / Shoe Cape wreck	BC 6th century	Pabuç Burnu – Bodrum
Tektaş Burnu Batığı / Lone Rock Cape shipwreck	BC 5th century	Aegean coast – Turkey
Serçe Limanı Helenistik Batığı / Sparrow Harbor Hellenistic shipwreck	BC 3th century	Marmaris
Kızılburun Batığı / Kizilburun shipwreck	BC 1th century	Kızılburun
Yassıada Roma Batığı / Yassiada Roman shipwreck	AD 4th century	Bodrum (Halikarnassos)
Yassıada Bizans Batığı / Byzantine shipwreck in Yassıada	AD 7th century	Bodrum
Bozburun Bizans Batığı / Bozburun Byzantine shipwreck	AD 9-10th century	Marmaris
Yenikapı batıkları / Theodosius Harbor shipwrecks	AD 4-12th century	Istanbul
Serçe Limanı Cam Batığı / Sparrow Harbor glass wreck	AD 11th century	Marmaris
Çamaltı Burnu Batığı / Çamaltı Cape shipwreck	AD 13th century	Çamaltı Cape – Marmara island
Yassıada Osmanlı batığı / Yassiada Ottoman shipwreck	AD 16th century	Bodrum

Source: Mahsereci, 2013

As it is seen in Table 6, some of these shipwrecks and their artefacts are exhibited in Bodrum Museum of Underwater Archaeology. Uluburun shipwreck is a Bronze Age vessel in Kas (Mahsereci, 2013). Cape Gelidonya was the first ancient shipwreck excavated by archaeologists. The Classical Greek shipwreck which was one transporting wine and other foods in amphoraes is at Tektaş Burnu. Sparrow Harbor Hellenistic shipwreck is a Byzantine shipwreck at Yassıada. The ancient Roman vessel named Kizilburun shipwreck (Crimson Cape) is in the Aegean Sea. Sparrow Harbor glass wreck was discovered near Marmaris (INA, 2021). Recently new shipwreck has discovered approximately 3,5-meter-deep in the Marmara Sea. Underwater excavations at Limnae/Civetot show that the history of the excavation area dates back to the 4th century BC (Milliyet, 2021).

Underwater cultural heritage needs to be protected. In the literature there are many studies about underwater cultural heritage. Brice (1996) argue that underwater cultural heritage will be destroyed until new laws made. Zamora (2008) states that the cultural value of underwater cultural heritage is more than the commercial value of shipwrecked cargoes. Cultural managers and museums are aware of the potential for sustainable development linked to tourism around sunken cities and shipwrecks. In Ilgar's (2011) study about Çanakkale Boğazı (The Dardanelles) he propose protection of shipwrecks and navigation use for prevention of accidents in Dardanelles. Dromgoole (2013) studied the UNESCO Convention on the Protection of the Underwater Cultural Heritage. UNESCO offers international legal frame work for the protection of shipwrecks and other artefacts located in international seas. Huang (2013) concluded that lack of international conventions and inadequate domestic legislations, cannot provide protection of underwater cultural heritage. Huang (2014) decided that to identification of a shipwreck is a multi-disciplinary work. To identify a shipwreck, legal professionals and maritime archaeologist should work together. Yarmaci, Keleş, & Ergil (2017) researched diving in Turkey's marines and found that diving tourism is developing in Kaş and it affects sustainability.

Underwater cultural heritage has a great potential for sustainable tourism development. Underwater museums and museum aquariums, diving trips are important attractions for tourists who seeks for alternative tourism. For instance, Bodrum, The Vasa, Mary Rose, and Roskilde Museums have changed the cities (UNESCO, 2001a). Using cutting-edge technology on shipwrecks could provide new destinations for tourism. Marine sites and underwater cultural heritage are often pulled factors for tourists. Local authorities have been innovative to support local economies with cutting-edge technology (UNESCO, 2021c). Additionally, using VR and AR on underwater cultural heritage sites, sunken vessels, and museums provides sustainable tourism. There are lots of artefacts lying under the oceans in darkness and it is hard to reach them. Museums exhibits some of the treasures from different periods all around the world. Museums could use VR & AR technology to exhibit these unreachable treasures (Snyder, 2017). Museums can attract more visitors and enhance their experiences by using virtual and augmented reality. VR and AR applications can increase the recognition of mysterious places and visitors can feel as they are a part of ancient history. In addition to that, it helps to the preservation of archaeological sites. Virtual tours contribute to the sustainability of cultural heritages while tourists have satisfaction with their virtual exploration.

USING AUGMENTED REALITY AND VIRTUAL REALITY FOR UNDERWATER CULTURAL HERITAGE

The potential of underwater cultural heritage is enormous and exploring submerged sites always mesmerize people. Lots of historic cities and shipwrecks have sunken into the ocean in human history. There are more than 150 historical sunken cities in the Mediterranean Sea. Some of the prehistoric cultural landscapes have been submerged by rising sea levels. Flooded caves, lakes are unique collection of archaeological materials. Approximately more than three million shipwrecks are spread all around the oceans as well as ancient cities. For example, Pompeii in which discovered in the bay of Alexandria – Egypt. There are still ongoing legends about Atlantis. People always have close relationship with water, and always wonder about sacred places underwater (UNESCO, 2001b). There is relatively less study about using cutting-edge technology for underwater cultural heritage. Chapman, et al. (2008) introduces project "Venus" that provide VR and AR tools for exploring deep underwater archaeological sites out of reach of divers. Agrafiotis, et al. (2017) studied the effect of the radiometry of the underwater imagery and 3D reconstruction. Bruno, et al. (2019) investigated potential of underwater AR technologies.

Except divers, shipwrecks cannot be visited directly by visitors in underwater and can only be seen in museums. It is only possible if a shipwreck or its cargo is salvaged and restored. However, prehistoric cities and their recovered artefacts are exhibited in museums. Despite that some of the submerged archaeological sites are suitable to use as a museum sites in situ. For instance, Caeserea Maritima in Israel, the port of Ampurias in Spain, submerged city of Baia in Italy are the examples of submerged archaeological sites. These submerged cities have been transformed into underwater parks (Davidde, 2004).

- Since 1991, the port of Ceasarea Maritima has free access underwater archaeological park. Private diving club rents boats and organizes tours. University of Haifa supervised the park.
- There are square-shaped blocks that have been left underwater in the port of Ampurias. Archaeological site also visited by divers without scuba equipment.
- Since 2002, the submerged city of Baia has been an underwater park. The city contains lots of well-preserved buildings that decorated ancient motifs (Davidde, 2004).

Retain the underwater cultural heritage in situ is an important issue for preservation. Removing cultural heritage from its original natural environment, may cause political, scientific, or cultural conflict. When possible, underwater cultural heritage should be kept in situ for preservation. However, this is not suitable for every situation. Sometimes the best way is to remove artefacts or vulnerable heritage from where it is placed. Even in a museum or in situ preservation could help for sustainability to underwater cultural heritages (UNESCO, 2001b). Using virtual and augmented reality on submerged archaeological sites is improving the sustainability of underwater cultural heritage. However, VR and AR applications for improving diving experiences are still few. Even experienced divers miss their direction because of low visibility at underwater archaeological sites or sunken wrecks. Cutting-edge technologies could be useful tools to cope with this problem. VR and AR implementations could improve the diving experiences of archaeological sites (Bruno, et al. 2019).

People always wish to be witness of history. Development of new technologies provide opportunity of using cutting-edge information, implemented to improve tourist experiences of underwater cultural heritage (Graziano & Privitera, 2020). Using virtual and augmented reality improve divers' experiences in underwater and promote diving tourism. In addition, underwater cultural site VR & AR tours are innovative and can develop tourism product. Bruno et al (2016:2) reviewed the project Visas (Virtual and Augmented Exploitation of Submerged Archaeological Sites), and reported three main services:

- *"Underwater 3-D reconstruction*: This service exploits the combined use of optical and acoustic techniques for the generation of multiresolution textured 3-D models of underwater sites, obtained by merging the results of surveys carried out with these two types of systems.
- *Virtual dive experience*: A VR system allows users to live a virtual experience inside the reconstructed 3-D model of the underwater archaeological site. The software application also provides an interactive navigation within the virtual environment to plan the guided dives.
- *Augmented diving*: This service is intended for the divers who will visit the underwater site, allowing them to have a virtual guide that provides specific information about the artifacts and the area they are visiting. The service is based on a tablet properly equipped with a waterproof case and an integrated system for acoustic localization and inertial navigation".

VR technologies focus on to improve the visitor's experiences. It makes underwater cultural sites accessible and more interesting for them. These VR technology is not used only in submerged sites but also in many other cultural and archaeological sites on dry land. VR technology can be used by tourist and divers. It allows users to have virtual experiences and find out about underwater cultural heritage. AR providing information about artefact improve diving experience trough a special tablet that can be used in underwater (Bruno, et al. 2016). While using VR implementation, tourists and divers can discover the underwater cultural heritage, and AR application enriches the experiences by making it more charming.

SOLUTIONS AND RECOMMENDATIONS

Tourism companies use AR and VR technologies to conduct virtual tours to cultural heritage sites or in museums. Cutting-edge technology can create a new form of tourism. Using VR and AR make possible to reachable underwater archaeological places for everyone. As it is difficult for non-divers to visit underwater archaeological sites or shipwrecks. Visitors can have a time and space advantage by using virtual and AR in tourism. Tourists can visit an underwater cultural site with VR. In addition, that, AR provide an artefact to be seen as it was in the original. New technologies through special tablets or mobile devices superimpose virtual artefacts into the real image (Čejka, Zsíros, & Liarokapis, 2020).

Cutting-edge technology may provide new tourism products such as virtual tours to ancient vessels. An artefact may see at the original time and place via VR and AR applications. New destinations can be created and introduced to available and new tourist markets. Local authorities and stakeholders should consider using VR and AR as marketing tool to promote their destinations.

This study contributes literature that VR and AR implications on shipwrecks and underwater cultural heritage. New technologies provide to understand historical places and culture. Cutting-edge technology brings new trends to tourism. Tourists have new experiences by using technological implementations. VR and AR provide enhance tourist satisfaction. Especially somewhere such as "last chance" tourism heritage, sunken ships, submerged archaeological sites VR and AR applications are essential for sustainability.

FUTURE RESEARCH DIRECTIONS

In the future studies, researchers can investigate virtual tours in underwater cultural heritage. Software developers may improve gamification, VR, AR, and mixed realty applications on underwater cultural heritage or shipwrecks. AR devices, for example, waterproof tablets can be tested by divers in the underwater cultural heritage sites so that tourism marketers could supply the virtual tours for visitors. In addition, professional guidance and cutting-edge technology devices can provide visitors seeing underwater artefact in situ. Governments should preserve the underwater cultural heritage. There should be legal protection for archaeological sunken sites. Destination management organizations could strengthen to community's environmental senses for proper diving tours that can help for conservation, keep away from vandalism and also develop sustainable tourism.

CONCLUSION

Underwater cultural heritage sites should be protected for sustainable tourism. Recreational diving and treasure hunting trips cause damage the archaeological sites. Even so professional divers care about the environment and wants to protect underwater heritage but still many cultural heritage and artefacts are lost in the sea. Visitors can see sunken wrecks or historical site via VR, and able to see artefact on the original places with AR. The immersive underwater shipwreck site increase users' archeological knowledge of the underwater archeological site, amphorae, wood, rocks, and vegetation (Čejka, Zsíros, & Liarokapis, 2020). Especially Mediterranean Sea is like an open museum of European history (Argyropoulos & Stratigea, 2019). Underwater cultural heritage sites have their own value in situ. Developing AR applications and useful gamification techniques influence the visitor's experiences for underwater cultural heritage. Shipwrecks can attract tourists with the implementation of AR. Also, this technology can improve tourist experiences. One of the advantages of using AR in cultural heritage is the avoidance of damaging the artefact in which position (Yin, Jung, & Lee, 2021).

In tourism industry VR and AR make it possible for tourists to explore the underwater cultural heritages in an exciting way. AR interacts with cultural heritage and artefacts. Divers can see artefacts and ancient lost cities with AR. Many archaeological projects have developed many methods for 3D reconstructions of underwater cultural sites. Gamification techniques, virtual and augmented reality applies for underwater cultural heritage (Philbin-Briscoe et al. 2017) that provides visitors with joyful experiences while learning.

Tourism marketers and tourism suppliers may use VR and AR applications to promote a touristic destination. These implementations provide for experimental marketing. Cutting-edge technology could enhance tourist satisfaction. However, some of the studies show that, if the application does not work properly, tourists have disappointed. VR and AR implementations relatively newish in tourism but it is a trending topic. These applications can be a new form of tourism. Some of the places in which hard to reach could visit by VR implementation. However virtual tours may also cause losses for tourism suppliers. Therefore, it is better the use mixed reality and at the same time visiting cultural heritage onsite.

REFERENCES

Agrafiotis, P., Drakonakis, G., Georgopoulos, A., & Skarlatos, D. (2017). *The effect of underwater imagery radiometry on 3D reconstruction and orthoimagery*. International Society for Photogrammetry and Remote Sensing. doi:10.5194/isprs-archives-XLII-2-W3-25-2017

Alzua-Sorzabal, A., Linaza, M., & Abad, M. (2007). An experimental usability study for Augmented Reality technologies in the tourist sector. *IENTER*, 231-242.

Argyropoulos, V., & Stratigea, A. (2019). Sustainable management of underwater cultural heritage: The route from discovery to engagement—Open issues in the Mediterranean. *Heritage, 2*(2), 1588–1613. doi:10.3390/heritage2020098

Arkas News. (2020). *Dünyanın En Eski Batığı Türkiye'de Keşfedildi*. Arkas News (E.T.31.05.2021): https://arkasnews.com/dunyanin-en-eski-batigi-turkiyede-kesfedildi/

Azuma, R., Baillot, Y., Behringer, R., Feiner, S., Julier, S., & MacIntyre, B. (2001). Recent advances in augmented reality. *IEEE Computer Graphics and Applications, 21*(6), 34–47. doi:10.1109/38.963459

Berlin. (2021). *Augmented Reality by Highsnobiety*. Visit in Berlin (E.T.07.06.2021): https://www.visitberlin.de/en/event/berlin-berlin-augmented-reality-highsnobiety

Bimber, O., & Raskar, R. (2019). *Spatial augmented reality: merging real and virtual worlds*. AK Peters/CRC Press.

Boboc, R., Duguleană, M., Voinea, G., Postelnicu, C., Popovici, D., & Carrozzino, M. (2019). Mobile augmented reality for cultural heritage: Following the footsteps of Ovid among different locations in Europe. *Sustainability, 11*(4), 1167. doi:10.3390u11041167

Brice, Q. (1996). Salvage and the underwater cultural heritage. *Marine Policy, 20*(4), 337–342. doi:10.1016/0308-597X(96)00022-X

Bruno, F., Barbieri, L., Mangeruga, M., Cozza, M., Lagudi, A., Čejka, J., Liarokapis, F., & Skarlatos, D. (2019). Underwater augmented reality for improving the diving experience in submerged archaeological sites. *Ocean Engineering, 190*, 106487. doi:10.1016/j.oceaneng.2019.106487

Bruno, F., Lagudi, A., Muzzupappa, M., Lupia, M., Cario, G., Barbieri, L., Passaro, S., & Saggiomo, R. (2016). Project VISAS: Virtual and augmented exploitation of submerged archaeological sites-overview and first results. *Marine Technology Society Journal, 50*(4), 119–129. doi:10.4031/MTSJ.50.4.4

Buhalis, D., & Law, R. (2008). Progress in information technology and tourism management: 20 years on and 10 years after the Internet—The state of eTourism research. *Tourism Management, 29*(4), 609–623. doi:10.1016/j.tourman.2008.01.005

Caneparo, L. (2001). Shared virtual reality for design and management: The Porta Susa project. *Automation in Construction, 10*(2), 217–228. doi:10.1016/S0926-5805(99)00032-1

Čejka, J., Zsíros, A., & Liarokapis, F. (2020). A hybrid augmented reality guide for underwater cultural heritage sites. *Personal and Ubiquitous Computing*, 1–14.

Çeltek, E. (2021). Gamification: Augmented Reality, Virtual Reality Games and Tourism Marketing Applications. In *Gamification for Tourism* (pp. 237–279). Channel View Publications. doi:10.21832/9781845418236-014

Chapman, P., Roussel, D., Drap, P., & Haydar, M. (2008). Virtual exploration of underwater archaeological sites: visualization and interaction in mixed reality environments. In *The 9th International Symposium on Virtual Reality, Archaeology and Intelligent Cultural Heritage*. Braga, Portugal: VAST 2008.

Cheong, R. (1995). The virtual threat to travel and tourism. *Tourism Management, 16*(6), 417–422. doi:10.1016/0261-5177(95)00049-T

Chung, N., Lee, H., Kim, J., & Koo, C. (2018). The role of augmented reality for experience-influenced environments: The case of cultural heritage tourism in Korea. *Journal of Travel Research, 57*(5), 627–643. doi:10.1177/0047287517708255

Coates, C. (2021). *Virtual Reality is a big trend in museums, but what are the best examples of museums using VR?* Museum Next (E.T: 6.10.21): https://www.museumnext.com/article/how-museums-are-using-virtual-reality/

Cranmer, E., Jung, T., & Miller, A. (2016). Implementing Augmented Reality to Increase Tourist Attraction Sustainability. In *AR VR Innovate*. Dublin: Perspectives on Business Realities of AR and VR Conference.

Cranmer, E., Tom Dieck, M., & Fountoulaki, P. (2020). Exploring the value of augmented reality for tourism. *Tourism Management Perspectives, 35*, 100672. doi:10.1016/j.tmp.2020.100672

Davidde, B. (2004). Methods and strategies for the conservation and museum display in situ of underwater cultural heritage. *Archaeologia Maritima Mediterranea, 1*, 137–150.

Driver, F., & Martins, L. (2006). Shipwreck and salvage in the tropics: The case of HMS Thetis, 1830–1854. *Journal of Historical Geography, 32*(3), 539–562. doi:10.1016/j.jhg.2005.10.010

Dromgoole, S. (2013). Reflections on the position of the major maritime powers with respect to the UNESCO Convention on the Protection of the Underwater Cultural Heritage 2001. *Marine Policy, 38*, 116–123. doi:10.1016/j.marpol.2012.05.027

Eschner, K. (2017). The Bizarre Story of 'Vasa,' the Ship That Keeps On Giving. *Smithsonian Magazine*. https://www.smithsonianmag.com/smart-news/bizarre-story-vasa-ship-keeps-giving-180964328/

Etymology Dictionary. (2021). Virtual. *Online Etymology Dictionary*. https://www.etymonline.com/search?q=virtual

Fletcher-Tomenius, P., & Forrest, C. (2000). Historic wreck in international waters: Conflict or consensus? *Marine Policy, 24*(1), 1–10. doi:10.1016/S0308-597X(99)00019-6

Garipağaoğlu-Uğur, N. (2020). İçsel ve Dışsal Motivasyon Araçlarının Örgütsel Bağlılığa Etkisi: Turizm Sektöründe Bir Araştırma. *IBAD Sosyal Bilimler Dergisi*, 95-115.

Georgakopoulos, V. (2008). Food safety training: A model HACCP instructional technique. *TOURISMOS: An International Multidisciplinary Journal of Tourism, 5*(1), 55–72.

Goode, L. (2019). Get Ready to Hear a Lot More About 'XR'. *Wired.* https://www.wired.com/story/what-is-xr/

Graziano, T., & Privitera, D. (2020). Cultural heritage, tourist attractiveness and augmented reality: Insights from Italy. *Journal of Heritage Tourism, 15*(6), 666–679. doi:10.1080/1743873X.2020.1719116

Gutierrez, M., Vexo, F., & Thalmann, D. (2008). *Stepping into virtual reality.* Springer Science & Business Media. doi:10.1007/978-1-84800-117-6

Guttentag, D. (2010). Virtual reality: Applications and implications for tourism. *Tourism Management, 31*(5), 637–651. doi:10.1016/j.tourman.2009.07.003

Güzel, T., & Sucaklı, G. (2020). Müze turizminde artırılmış gerçeklik teknolojisi uygulamaları; Dünya ve Türkiye örnekleri. *Journal of Tourism Research Institute, 1*(2), 71–82.

Heldal, I. (2007). Supporting participation in planning new roads by using virtual reality systems. *Virtual Reality (Waltham Cross), 11*(2), 145–159. doi:10.100710055-006-0061-3

Hsu, L. (2012). Web 3D simulation-based application in tourism education: A case study with second life. *Journal of Hospitality, Leisure, Sport and Tourism Education, 11*(2), 113–124. doi:10.1016/j.jhlste.2012.02.013

Huang, J. (2013). Chasing provenance: Legal dilemmas for protecting states with a verifiable link to underwater culture heritage. *Ocean and Coastal Management, 84*, 220–225. doi:10.1016/j.ocecoaman.2012.11.007

Huang, J. (2014). Maritime archaeology and identification of historic shipwrecks: A legal perspective. *Marine Policy, 44*, 256–264. doi:10.1016/j.marpol.2013.09.017

Huang, Y., Backman, K., Backman, S., & Chang, L. (2016). Exploring the implications of virtual reality technology in tourism marketing: An integrated research framework. *International Journal of Tourism Research, 18*(2), 116–128. doi:10.1002/jtr.2038

İHA. (2021). *Antalya kıyılarında 3 yılda 125 batık bulundu.* NTV (E.T.31.05.2021): https://www.ntv.com.tr/galeri/sanat/antalya-kiyilarinda-3-yilda-125-batik-bulundu,7OmiL1LhOUSqcOP7ZZoKiQ/VzW1wCFDnkGpcI8R7Ea_JA

Ilgar, R. (2011). Çanakkale Boğazı Batıkları. *Türk Bilimsel Derlemeler Dergisi, 4*(2), 63–68.

Immersion, V. R. (2021). *What is virtual reality in travel?* VR for Tourism (E.T.02,05.2021): https://immersionvr.co.uk/about-360vr/vr-for-tourism/

INA. (2021). *Mediterranean.* Institute of Nautical Archaeology (E.T.31.05.2021): https://nauticalarch.org/about/

Jingen Liang, L., & Elliot, S. (2020). A systematic review of augmented reality tourism research: What is now and what is next? *Tourism and Hospitality Research.*

Joy of Museums Virtual Tours. (2021). *National Museum of Singapore – Virtual Tour.* Joy of museums virtual tours. Virtual Tours of Museums, Art Galleries, and Historic Sites (E.T. 07.06.2021): https://joyofmuseums.com/museums/asia-museums/singapore-museums/national-museum-of-singapore/

Kuchelmeister, V. (2018). The Virtual (Reality) Museum of Immersive Experiences. *Electronic Visualisation and the Arts*, 203-210.

Lonne, T. (2020). *Deep Diving: Rules, Recommendations And Fun Facts*. Divein.com (E.T.25.05.2021): https://www.divein.com/articles/deep-diving/#:~:text=In%20Recreational%20diving%2C%20the%20 maximum,to%2018%20meters%20and%20beyond

Loureiro, S., Guerreiro, J., & Ali, F. (2020). 20 years of research on virtual reality and augmented reality in tourism context: A text-mining approach. *Tourism Management*, 77, 104028. doi:10.1016/j.tourman.2019.104028

Magnenat-Thalmann, N., Papagiannakis, G., Ponder, M., Molet, T., Kshirsagar, S., Cordier, F., & Thalmann, D. (2002). LifePlus: Revival of life in ancient Pompeii. *Proc. VSMM (Virtual Systems and Multimedia)*. http://george.papagiannakis.org/wp-content/uploads/2011/10/Proc.-of-Virtual-Systems-and-Multimedia-VSMM02-Gyeongju-2002-Papagiannakis.pdf

Mahsereci, N. (2013). *Türkiye'de kazılmış arkeolojik batıklar*. Bilim ve Gelecek (E.T: 31.05.2021): https://bilimvegelecek.com.tr/index.php/2013/09/01/turkiyede-kazilmis-arkeolojik-batiklar/

Meral, K. (2021). *Strategic Social Media Marketing and Data Privacy. In Management Strategies to Survive in a Competitive Environment: How to Improve Company Performance*. Springer.

Mesároš, P., Mandičák, T., Mesárošová, A., Hernandez, M., Kršák, B., Sidor, C., & Delina, R. (2016). Use of Augmented Reality and Gamification techniques in tourism. *e-Review of Tourism Research*, 13(1/2), 366-381.

Milliyet. (2021). *Marmara Denizi'nde keşfedildi! 3,5 metrede gemi batığı*. Milliyet (E.T: 10.10.2021): https://www.milliyet.com.tr/galeri/marmara-denizinde-kesfedildi-3-5-metrede-gemi-batigi-6610713/1

Mohanty, P., Hassan, A., & Ekis, E. (2020). *Augmented reality for relaunching tourism post-COVID-19: socially distant, virtually connected*. Worldwide Hospitality and Tourism Themes.

Moorhouse, N., Jung, T., & tom Dieck, M. (2019). Tourism marketers perspectives on enriching visitors city experience with augmented reality: An exploratory study. In Augmented reality and virtual reality (pp. 129-144). Cham: Springer.

Museums and Heritage. (2021). *London museums join augmented reality art trail to tempt visitors back after reopening*. Museums and Heritage Advisor (E.T.07.06.2021): https://advisor.museumsandheritage.com/news/london-museums-join-augmented-reality-art-trail-to-tempt-visitors-back-after-reopening/

Negruşa, A., Toader, V., Sofică, A., Tutunea, M., & Rus, R. (2015). Exploring gamification techniques and applications for sustainable tourism. *Sustainability*, 7(8), 11160–11189. doi:10.3390u70811160

NHM. (2021). *Virtual Museum: 14 ways to expşore from home*. Natural History Museum (E.T: 20.05.2021): https://www.nhm.ac.uk/visit/virtual-museum.html

Özdemir, M. (2021). Virtual Reality (VR) and Augmented Reality (AR) Technologies for Accessibility and Marketing in the Tourism Industry. In *ICT Tools and Applications for Accessible Tourism* (pp. 227-301). IGI Global.

Painter, A. (2015). *The New Philadelphia Augmented Reality Tour App.* Cultural Heritage Informatics Initiative (E.T. 07.06.2021): http://chi.anthropology.msu.edu/2015/11/new-philadelphia-app/

Philbin-Briscoe, O., Simon, B., Mudur, S., Poullis, C., Rizvic, S., Boskovic, D., . . . Skarlatos, D. (2017). A serious game for understanding ancient seafaring in the Mediterranean sea. In *2017 9th international conference on virtual worlds and games for serious applications (VS-games)* (pp. 1-5). IEEE.

Quora. (2020). *What is the difference between scuba diving and deep diving?* Quora (E.T. 25.05.2021): https://www.quora.com/What-is-the-difference-between-scuba-diving-and-deep-diving

Retro Futuro. (2021). *Pompeii. Voice from the past.* Retro Futuro (E.T.07.06.2021): https://pompeii.refutur.com/en/

Schweibenz, W. (2012). Museum exhibitions-The real and the virtual ones: An account of a complex relation. *Uncommon Culture*, 38-52.

Siang, T., Aziz, K., & Ahmad, Z. (2020). Developing a Framework for Augmented Reality Mobile Application Success and World Heritage Sites Sustainability. *International Journal of Advance Science and Technology*, *29*(108), 287–296.

Sites in 3D. (2021). *360 Derece Panoramik Fotagraflarla Sanal Turlar.* 3D Mekanlar (E.T. 16.05.2021): http://www.3dmekanlar.com/index.html

Snyder, K. (2017). *Oceans Have More Historical Artifacts Than All Museums Combined.* Clipperton Project (E.T: 25.05.2021): https://www.clippertonproject.com/oceans-have-more-historical-artifacts-than-all-museums-combined/

Spennemann, D. (2007). Extreme cultural tourism from Antarctica to the Moon. *Annals of Tourism Research*, *34*(4), 898–918. doi:10.1016/j.annals.2007.04.003

tom Dieck, M., & Jung, T. (2018). A theoretical model of mobile augmented reality acceptance in urban heritage tourism. *Current Issues in Tourism*, *21*(2), 154–174. doi:10.1080/13683500.2015.1070801

Tulane. (2021). *What's the difference between AR and VR?* Tulane University (E.T: 6.10.21): https://sopa.tulane.edu/blog/whats-difference-between-ar-and-vr

Uğur, N. (2020). *Effects of Internet on Tourism Marketing: An Empirical Analysis About Online Tourism. In Tools and Techniques for Implementing International E-Trading Tactics for Competitive Advantage.* IGI Global.

UNESCO. (2001a). *Submerged Archaeological Sites: Commercial Exploitation Compared To Long-Term Protection.* http://www.unesco.org/new/en/culture/themes/underwater-cultural-heritage/2001-convention/

UNESCO. (2001b). *Protection of the Underwater Cultural Heritage.* Underwater Cultural Heritage. http://www.unesco.org/new/en/culture/themes/underwater-cultural-heritage/2001-convention/#:~:text=The%20UNESCO%20Convention%20on%20the,protect%20their%20submerged%20cultural%20heritage.&text=provides%20widely%20recognized%20practical%20rules,research%20of

UNESCO. (2021c). *Cutting Edge | Bringing cultural tourism back in the game.* https://en.unesco.org/news/cutting-edge-bringing-cultural-tourism-back-game

Weber, J. (2014). Augmented reality gaming: A new paradigm for tourist experiences. *Information and Communication Technologies in Tourism*, 57-67.

Williams, A. (2006). Tourism and hospitality marketing: Fantasy, feeling and fun. *International Journal of Contemporary Hospitality Management*, *18*(6), 482–495. doi:10.1108/09596110610681520

Williams, P., & Hobson, J. (1995). Virtual reality and tourism: Fact or fantasy? *Tourism Management*, *16*(6), 423–427. doi:10.1016/0261-5177(95)00050-X

World Itineraries. (2020). *Augmented reality ingites museum experiences. A Luxury Travel Blog.* World Itineraries (E.T. 2021.05.20): https://worlditineraries.co/2020/08/12/augmented-reality-ignites-museum-experiences/

Xu, F., Tian, F., Buhalis, D., & Weber, J. (2013). Marketing tourism via electronic games: understanding the motivation of tourist players. In *2013 5th International Conference on Games and Virtual Worlds for Serious Applications (VS-GAMES)* (pp. 1-8). IEEE.

Yarmaci, N., Keleş, M., & Ergil, B. (2017). Diving of underwater tourism current status, Problems and suggestions for the development: A case study of Kaş. *Güncel Turizm Araştırmaları Dergisi*, *1*(1), 66–87.

Yin, C., Jung, T., & Lee, M. (2021). Mobile Augmented Reality Heritage Applications: Meeting the Needs of Heritage Tourists. *Sustainability*, *13*(5), 2523. doi:10.3390u13052523

Zamora, T. (2008). The impact of commercial exploitation on the preservation of underwater cultural heritage. *Museum International*, *60*(4), 18–30. doi:10.1111/j.1468-0033.2008.00662.x

KEY TERMS AND DEFINITIONS

3D: Three-dimensional (subject has height, width, and depth).
AR: Augmented reality.
HMD: A head-mounted display.
VE: Virtual environment.
VR: Virtual reality.
VW: Virtual world.

ENDNOTE

[1]   Histopad is a new way of immersing visitors into their surroundings which is interactive, educational and fun, but is also at the cutting edge of technology (google.com)

Chapter 9
Intangible Cultural Heritage in the Digitalization Process:
The Case of Turkey

İsmail Çalık

ⓘ https://orcid.org/0000-0001-9815-5796

Gumushane University, Turkey

ABSTRACT

This chapter will initially introduce the concept of intangible cultural heritage. After establishing the relationship between intangible cultural heritage and tourism, changes in intangible cultural heritage components will be expressed through the digitization and COVID-19 processes. "Digital intangible cultural heritage," "digital cultural heritage," "digital safeguarding" concepts will be described because they attracted great attention during this time. Additionally, the other aspect of the research is the use of digital applications to safeguard the intangible cultural heritage. In the final part, the pilot projects concerning the safeguarding and promoting the intangible cultural heritage implemented by the Ministry of Culture and Tourism of Turkey will be discussed.

INTRODUCTION

Oral traditions and expressions, behaviors relating to nature and the universe, performing arts and crafts traditions are all examples of intangible cultural heritage. A vital role is played by strategies and policies for preserving intangible cultural heritage and transferring it to future generations. The first chapter of the book will explain world heritage and intangible cultural heritage, followed by a discussion of the relationship between intangible cultural heritage and tourism. Other key issues covered in the book chapter include explaining the basic dynamics of the Covid-19 process and the digitalized intangible cultural heritage process, as well as reporting on the role of mobile applications and platforms in the protection of intangible cultural heritage during the digitalization process. The book chapter will conclude with an overview of digital application projects that have been done in Turkey in recent years to protect intangible cultural heritage.

DOI: 10.4018/978-1-7998-8528-3.ch009

It has been shown that, as a direct consequence of the digitalization process, interest in intangible cultural heritage has started to wane, and that, as a result of modern people's habits of individualization and urbanization, they have not made sufficient efforts to protect and transfer intangible cultural heritage to future generations. Promotion and transmission of intangible cultural heritage elements guided by a sustainable tourism approach that considers the balance of protection and usage will help to raise awareness of these qualities.

For a period, access to intangible cultural heritage materials was curtailed as part of the Covid 19 process, making concerts, events, folk culture practices, and festivals impossible to organize. Barriers to accessing intangible cultural assets have been attempted to be overcome by digitalization through projects such as online events hosted by UNESCO and other international organizations. As a result, it is important to remember that, thanks to digitalization, intangible cultural material is accessible, albeit limited, during the epidemic.

In terms of protecting intangible cultural heritage elements in Turkey's digitalization process, it's worth noting that, while some digital projects have been completed in terms of storing data on digital platforms and introducing cultural heritage elements, digital transformation has not yet been fully realized. In this context, the book part discussed the types of digital projects that were implemented, as well as the menus and features of online and mobile digital projects.

BACKGROUND

World Heritage and Intangible Cultural Heritage

In the most basic sense, the values that people seek to pass on to future generations are referred to as heritage. Folk dances, oral traditions, monumental structures, archaeological sites, material culture and ideology structure are some of these values. Heritage is a fundamental element that reflects the depth of cultural expressions and creates cultural identity and distinctiveness between generations (Deacon et al., 2004). Heritage encompasses a variety of cultural forms that encapsulate the worth of a community's social, historical, or cultural dimensions (Throsby, 1997). In the Deschambault Declaration adopted in 1982 (ICOMOS Canada (Quebec)), the concept of heritage has been outlined as follows:

All of the natural and human-made things that make up the environment we live in are considered heritage. Heritage refers to the property and transferable wealth of the community that make a contribution to our recognition and participation (Icomos Canada, 1982)

In the historical process, people's interest in heritage items such as objects and relics from the past has continued to grow. Ashworth (1994) emphasizes that commodifying heritage values and turning them into modern consumption products that will satisfy people have been potent in the rise in this interest. In addition, it is asserted that concepts such as marketable product, heritage product, heritage consumer emerged in this context.

On the other hand, cultural heritage means all tangible and intangible assets that have survived from the past and are described as a reflection of people's values, beliefs, knowledge and traditions that are constantly changing without being in a bond of ownership. Cultural heritage refers to all aspects of the environment that have developed over time as a result of interactions between people and places (ICOMOS Turkey, 2013).

In the study named "Mid-Term Draft Plan 1990-1995" and prepared by UNESCO in 1989, the *"cultural heritage" is defined as:*

All of the creative or symbolic tangible indications that have been conveyed to each civilization can be defined as cultural heritage and therefore to all humanity from past to present. As a founding part of the affirmation and enrichment of cultural identities and a heritage of all humanity, it is the sum of human experiences, giving its recognizable features. The safeguarding and presentation of cultural heritage is the building block of cultural policy (UNESCO, 1990: 87-88)

The concept of cultural heritage is classified as tangible cultural heritage and intangible cultural heritage. Movable and immovable cultural heritage parts are two types of tangible cultural asset. Movable cultural heritage items are movable assets such as paintings, sculptures, manuscripts and coins. However, immovable cultural heritage elements are like monuments, archaeological sites. Underwater cultural heritage, which includes sunken ships, underwater city ruins, and so on, is another sort of cultural heritage. On the other side, intangible cultural heritage elements are values such as oral traditions, artistic performances and ceremonies. The concept of natural heritage is also something that needs to be articulated in this context. With the concept of natural heritage, cultural landscape, physical, biological and geological formations are referred (UNESCO, 2021).

Today, there are 1121 properties on the World Heritage List from 167 different countries. Of these assets, 213 are natural, 869 are cultural, and 39 are mixed (natural and cultural) (UNESCO, 2021a). Turkey has 16 assets in this list. Aphrodisias Ancient City (Aydın) (2017), Ani Archaeological Site (Kars) (2016), Historical Areas of Istanbul (1985), Divriği Grand Mosque and Hospital (Sivas) (1985), Hattusha (Bogazkoy)-Hittite Capital (Çorum) (1986), Diyarbakir Castle and Cultural Landscape Area of Hevsel Gardens (2015), Ephesus Ancient City (İzmir) (2015), Mount Nemrut (Adiyaman-Kahta) (1987), Xantos-Letoon (Antalya-Muğla) (1988), Göbeklitepe (Şanlıurfa) (2018), City of Safranbolu (Karabük) (1994), ancient city of Troy (Çanakkale) (1998), Edirne Selimiye Mosque and its Complex (2011), Neolithic City of Çatalhöyük (Konya) (2012), Multilayered Cultural Landscape Area of Bergama (İzmir) (2014), Bursa and Cumalıkızık: The Rise of the Ottoman Empire (2014) are on the cultural list. On the other side, Göreme National Park and Cappadocia (Nevşehir) (1985) and Pamukkale Hierapolis (Denizli) (1988) are on the list as both cultural and natural heritage. In addition to those, 85 assets of Turkey are on the interim list (UNESCO, 2021b).

Intangible cultural heritage means the practices, representations, expressions, knowledge, skills that groups, communities and sometimes individuals described as part of cultural heritage values and it implies the tools, equipment and cultural places belonging to them (UNESCO, 2003). According to Oğuz (2013), Since the 1970s, the phrase "intangible cultural heritage" has taken on new meaning according to UNESCO's expert assessments and has been named as a cultural heritage safeguarding program rather than a scientific discipline, and thus its meaning has expanded in this way.

UNESCO specified the intangible cultural heritage elements in the *"Convention for the Safeguarding of the Intangible Cultural Heritage"* accepted by the parties in 2003. These elements generally cover oral traditions and expressions transmitted through language, performing arts, social practices, rituals and feasts, knowledge and practices related to nature and the universe, and handicraft traditions.

Moreover, the safeguarding of intangible cultural heritage elements is deciphered as "*securing the survival of the cultural heritage*". These safeguarding activities include elements such as identification, documentation, research, preservation, safeguarding, educational activities and transfer from generation to generation (UNESCO, 2003). Intangible cultural heritage that can be passed down through generations is created and reconstructed as a result of communities' interactions with nature, the environment, and history and this cycle also contributes to cultural diversity in addition to creating a sense of identity and continuity (Akyıldız and Olğun, 2020).

With "The Law on Approval of the Convention for the Safeguarding of the Intangible Cultural Heritage" No. 5448 of 19 January 2006, Turkey accepted the "Convention for the Safeguarding of the Intangible Cultural Heritage" adopted in Paris on October 17, 2003 and officially became a party to the agreement on March 27, 2006. Intangible cultural heritage emerges and develops especially in the following areas below (Ministry of Culture and Tourism, 2021a):

- In the transfer of intangible cultural heritage, oral traditions and narratives in addition to the language functioning as a carrier (epics, legends, folk tales, proverbs, tales, anecdotes, etc.),
- Performing arts (Karagöz, meddah, puppetry, folk theater etc.),
- Social practices, rituals and feasts (celebrations such as engagement, wedding, birth, Nawruz, etc.),
- Knowledge and practices related to nature and the universe (traditional dishes, folk medicine, folk calendar, folk meteorology, etc.),
- Handicraft tradition (weaving, evil eye bead, filigree, copper work, folk architecture).

The countries that are party to the "Convention for the Safeguarding of the Intangible Cultural Heritage" and accepted by UNESCO (2003) Countries must take the required steps to conserve intangible cultural assets at the national level, as well as identify and define the various elements of intangible cultural heritage in the relevant country with the participation of all stakeholders. Also, they must carry out appropriate preparation and updating of national inventories, including the safeguarding of this heritage in planning programs, and carrying out scientific, technical and artistic studies for the practical safeguarding of the intangible cultural heritage in danger.

Articles 11 and 12 of the UNESCO Convention for the Safeguarding of the Intangible Cultural Heritage, to which Turkey became a party in 2006, demand that a national inventory of intangible cultural heritage shall be prepared by each state party to the convention. Inventory determination works in this context are carried out by the Ministry of Culture and Tourism General Directorate of Research and Development, under the coordination of the Provincial Culture and Tourism Directorates with the help of Provincial Determination Commissions set up in the provinces (T.C. Kültür ve Turizm Bakanlığı, 2021b).

"Commission for the Safeguarding of the Intangible Cultural Heritage" operating under UNESCO, in accordance with the terms of the contract adopted in 2003, meets annually to evaluate the nominations proposed by the state parties and determine the intangible cultural heritage elements to be added to the relevant list (UNESCO, 2021c). Intangible cultural heritage elements have been categorized by UNESCO in three distinct lists since 2008. The lists are "*Representative List of the Intangible Cultural Heritage of Humanity*", "*List of Intangible Cultural Heritage in Need of Urgent Safeguarding*" and "*Register for Good Safeguarding Practices*" (UNESCO, 2021c). There is a total of 584 intangible cultural heritage items around the world belonging to 131 countries in these lists mentioned (UNESCO, 2021d). Turkey has 20 intangible cultural heritage items that are listed on the above-mentioned lists, which are either

Turkey's own application or a combined application with other nations. 19 of these heritage elements are included in *"Representative List of the Intangible Cultural Heritage of Humanity"* while 1 of these heritage elements is in the *"List of Intangible Cultural Heritage in Need of Urgent Safeguarding"*. The indicated heritage elements are listed in Table 1:

Table 1. Elements of Turkey in UNESCO representative list of the intangible cultural heritage of humanity and list of intangible cultural heritage in need of urgent safeguarding

Representative List of the Intangible Cultural Heritage of Humanity	Type of Application	Date of Acceptance
Tradition of Meddah (eulogy show in Ottoman culture and entertainment life)	Single Application	2008
Mevlevi Whirling ceremonies	Single Application	2008
Tradition of minstrels	Single Application	2009
Karagöz (shadow play)	Single Application	2009
Nawruz (Joint file with Azerbaijan, Afghanistan, Azerbaijan, India, Iraq, Iran, Kazakhstan, Kyrgyzstan, Uzbekistan, Pakistan, Tajikistan and Turkmenistan)	Joint Application	2009
Traditional Talking Meetings (Yaren, Barana, Sıra Geceleri ve diğer)	Single Application	2010
Alevi-Bektaşi Ritual Semah	Single Application	2010
Kırkpınar Oil Wrestling Festival	Single Application	2010
Traditional Ceremonial Keşkek (a dish of mutton or chicken)	Single Application	2011
Mesir Paste Festival	Single Application	2012
Turkish Coffee and Tradition	Single Application	2013
Ebru: Turkish Paper Marbling Art	Single Application	2014
Tradition of Thin Bread Making and Sharing: Lavaş, Katrıma, Jupka, Yufka (Joint file with Azerbaijan, Iran, Kazakhstan, Kyrgyzstan and Turkey)	Joint Application	2016
Traditional Tile Art	Single Application	2016
Hıdırellez: Spring Festival (joint file with Macedonia)	Joint Application	2016
Dede Korkut-Legacy of Korkut Ata: Culture, Legends and Music (Joint file with Azerbaijan and Kazakhstan)	Joint Application	2018
Traditional Turkish Archery	Joint Application	2016
Miniature Art (Joint file with Azerbaijan, Iran and Uzbekistan)	Joint Application	2020
Traditional game of intelligence and strategy: Togyzqumalaq, Toguz Korgool, Mangala / Göçürme (Joint file with Kazakhstan and Kyrgyzstan)	Joint Application	2020
List of Intangible Cultural Heritage in Need of Urgent Safeguarding		
Whistled language	Single Application	2017

Source: UNESCO Turkish National Commission, 2021

Intangible Cultural Heritage and Tourism

In many times of history, people have speculated about the features of civilizations living in different geographies. Because one of the primary factors that satisfies our drive to learn and explore is the culture. When we look at the world history, it is seen that travels between geographies in the Middle Ages, Modern Ages and Contemporary Ages were mostly conducted for commercial, religious and educational purposes. However, travel within the purview of tourism rose following World War II as a result of factors such as globalization, technical advancements, and the worldwide peace atmosphere. As of 2019, it has exceeded 1.4 billion people. However, the Covid19 epidemic, which started in March 2020 and still continues today, has caused tourism movements to stagnate for a while.

Tourism encompasses various purposes and characteristics, including social, economic, cultural, environmental, and many more. It has also evolved into a global phenomenon (Alaeddinoğlu, 2007). Tourism is a pivotal step for preserving cultural diversity and uniqueness (Çetin, 2010: 182). It should be highlighted that tourism contributes to preserving of these values and their transmission to future generations.

In the concept of sustainable tourism, the necessity of planning tourism according to economic, socio-cultural and environmental principles is emphasized. Within the framework of the socio-cultural aspect of sustainable tourism, the importance of preserving living cultural heritage and traditional values is explained (UNEP&UNWTO, 2005). Among the Agenda 21 key sustainability measures is "defining and strengthening the role of local people in society" (UN, 2007). In addition, reference is made to the protection and development of tangible and intangible cultural heritage in key indicators and related sub-indicators of sustainable tourism, such as information on local culture and protection of intangible cultural heritage (Kuntay, 2004), sustainability of cultural assets and protection of structural cultural heritage (UNWTO, 2004). On the other hand, in the 2030 Sustainable Development Goals, issues such as the protection of cultural diversity, increasing intercultural understanding and tolerance, and the contribution of all cultures to sustainable development are mentioned. The contribution of cultural diversity to sustainable development has been referred to under the headings of providing inclusive and equitable quality education and promoting lifelong learning opportunities for all (UN, 2015).

During the interaction of tourists and locals, members of traditional local society can be influenced by the cultural objects, behavior, and values of modern societies. Therefore, the greater the difference between the two cultures, the bigger the cultural shock will be (Bal, 1995: 34). On the other hand, according to Languer (1991), the tourist who has cultural and monetary advantage will not make much effort to participate in the local culture. On the contrary, the locals will have to constantly smile and run around to show their hospitality and prove how inclined the tourist's values are to their behavior.

According to Bak (2007: 28), changes in cultural tourism are unavoidable as a result of interactions between tourists and locals. From the tourist's point of view, change is new cultural knowledge gained through tourist experience and can take the form of like(s), and these will likely be the intended result of the experiences. Albeit, in the case of local people, change may be more complex, diverse and possibly the opposite of what was planned. These and other related elements are examples of tourism's influence on traditional culture in the medium and long term. Dealt it from different perspectives, some problematic areas may arise such as the commodification of traditional culture, the change of socio-cultural values and rituals, the change of cultural heritage elements and the loss of their essence and spirit in addition to the socio-economic gain of the local people in the tourism-cultural heritage interaction.

In terms of tourism, cultural heritage aspects occupy a prominent position. In this instance, the conservation, development, and sustainability of intangible cultural heritage elements are challenges that must be addressed in terms of both the preservation of traditions and the creation of added value in the tourism industry (Alagöz et al., 2018). Although tourism has negative consequences, such as the loss of local people's cultural values, it is thought that within the context of sustainable tourism, cultural values can be better protected rather than being lost in planned tourism activities (Türker and Çelik, 2012).

All mankind has the right to see and enjoy intangible cultural heritage aspects of local civilizations. Tourism has a weighty function in the fulfillment of this right. This function includes firstly preventing the forgetting and disappearance of cultural heritage elements by considering the balance of protection/use, and then contributing socio-economically to underdeveloped or developing regions through tourism. To Çalık & Ödemiş (2018), the unregulated openness of intangible cultural heritage elements to tourists may result in the local culture's cultural values deteriorating and eventually disappearing. Accordingly, it must be targeted that sustainable tourism development should be supported and besides economic and environmental factors, the protection/use balance of socio-cultural assets should be considered, and then the region should be brought into tourism.

Satar & Güneş (2014) also looked at the issue from a sustainability standpoint and emphasized that Intangible Cultural Heritage is harmed by all tourism practices that disregard the notion of sustainability. According to the authors, many spiritual values such as customs and traditions have either vanished or died out as a result of the mass tourism strategy, which causes rapid consumption of natural and historical resources. According to Özünel (2011:259), "Turkish nights" organized in star hotels in the name of authenticity and locality, "Turkish baths" with navel stones and plastic slippers, "Turkish pancake tents" and restaurants with plastic and bamboo chairs on the beaches, "local and authentic" souvenirs made in China can be given as examples of these poor practices. Satar & Güneş (2014:11-12) put forward that successful eco-tourism examples, social tourism, and literary tourism activities that do not undermine the essence of traditions should be supported instead of these practices that threaten Intangible Cultural Heritage.

THE COVID-19 PROCESS AND THE DIGITALIZED INTANGIBLE CULTURAL HERITAGE

Identified on January 13, 2020, the Novel Coronavirus Disease (COVID-19) first came into our lives as a result of research conducted on a group of patients who developed respiratory symptoms (fever, cough, shortness of breath) in Wuhan Province, China, in late December 2019 (Ministry of Health of Turkish of Republic, 2021). On March 11, 2020, it was announced that Covid 19 can be described as a pandemic by the World Health Organization (WHO) due to the speed of its spread and the effect of the damage it causes (WHO, 2021a). As of June 3, 2021, Covid 19 cases were detected in 171,292,827 people, and 3,687,589 of these cases resulted in a fatality, and approximately 1.5 billion doses of Covid 19 jabs were applied to the cases worldwide. (WHO, 2021b).

It can be stated that the Covid-19 pandemic has caused many changes in our daily lives. Among these changes, the prevalence of working at home, the development of sports options in the home environment, the increase in the time we spend with video calling platforms due to remote education, the increase of companies that provide take-out meals to home can be counted (Fortune, 2021). The pandemic has had a significant influence on people's mental health and coping with pandemic stress has become extremely difficult due to factors such as isolation and social distance. In a study by Alzueta et al. (2021), it was reported that while the majority of the sample showed low and mild depression and anxiety symptoms, a significant portion of the participants showed moderate to severe depression (25.4%) and anxiety (19.5%). Divorce rates increased by 22% during the pandemic process. 15% of weddings were cancelled, airline traffic fell from 4.5 billion to 1.8 billion people (2019-2020). 77% of children aged 5 to 12 years spent at least 4 hours a day in front of electronic devices (35% before the pandemic). In 8% of these children, this rate increased to an average of 9 hours a day. When compared to the pre-pandemic period, average household television viewing time has increased by two times to 11 hours per day. These are some of the other significant events that have an impact on our daily life (Time, 2021).

The tourism industry is one of the industries that has been most impacted by the Covid 19 pandemic. In the first quarter of 2021, for example, international visitor arrivals fell by 83 percent on average compared to the same time in 2020. International tourism revenues decreased by 64% in 2020 compared to the previous year (approximately $900 billion), and when transit passenger transportation is added, the total loss reached $1.1 trillion (UNWTO, 2021). Before the pandemic, 319 million employees were employed in the tourism industry, and 1 out of every 10 employees was working in tourism and related jobs (WTTC, 2019). According to World Labor Organization estimates, roughly 305 million employees in all sectors lost their jobs as a result of the epidemic, with the tourism industry accounting for the majority of the job losses (ILO, 2020).

Following a summary of the Covid-19 pandemic's emergence, the changes it has wrought in our lives, and the impacts of Covid-19 on the tourism sector, which has a notable role in the preservation of intangible cultural heritage, this section will address the changes in intangible cultural heritage during the Covid 19 process. The Covid 19 epidemic process has brought new dimensions to the preservation, transfer and experience of intangible cultural heritage. This process necessitated the continuation of cultural heritage experiences in online spaces.

The Covid 19 process has brought with the closure of heritage sites, museums, theatres, cinemas, and other cultural institutions. According to UNESCO data, 89% of the world's cultural heritage sites have been partially or completely closed during the Covid 19 process (UNESCO, 2020a). "*Platform on Living Heritage and the Covid 19*" established by UNESCO highlighted that artists and craftsmen, who are carriers of cultural heritage, experience loss of income due to festivals and rituals canceled during the epidemic (UNESCO Turkey, 2020).

A number of initiatives have been launched in order to overcome the problems produced by the social isolation caused by the Covid-19 crisis and support the cultural heritage under the leadership of UNESCO (UNESCO, 2020b). The first of these initiatives is the preparation of a web application with online exhibitions of cultural heritage elements with the technical support of the "Google & Arts and Culture" platform. On this platform, there are digital experiences related to other cultural heritage such as museums, exhibitions, cultural heritage sites, music applications in many parts of the World (Google Arts & Culture, 2021). Another endeavor is the " *ResiliArt* " project, which attempts to encourage artists and ensure that everyone has access to culture. As part of the "*ResiliArt*" initiative, 270 artistic and cultural events were held online in 110 different countries (UNESCO, 2020c).

On the other hand, among the basic questions that seek answers during the epidemic are whether cultural heritage is detached from its essence in new contexts and spaces, and to what extent the threat of excessive commercialization exists (Tüzel, 2020). In this context, both because of the epidemic and for other reasons, it is noteworthy that concepts such as "*digital heritage*", "*digital intangible cultural heritage*" and "*digital safeguarding*" come to the fore in today's world where digitalization and individuality are intensified. "*Digital cultural heritage*" *is defined as* in the "*Guidelines for Preservation of Digital Heritage*" study put forward by UNESCO in 2003 *(UNESCO, 2003:1):*

Digital Heritage is made up of one-of-a-kind human knowledge and expressive resources. These resources include cultural, educational, scientific and administrative resources as well as technical, legal, medical and other types of information created digitally or converted from existing analogue sources into digital form.

In terms of safeguarding intangible cultural heritage pieces and conveying them to future generations, the concept of *"digital intangible cultural heritage"* is notable. According to Ertürk (2020), representations, expressions, knowledge, and oral traditions are all examples of digital intangible cultural heritage and they are protected through digital photography and other audio and visual recordings and applications. They may also include instruments, tools, artifacts and cultural sites associated with elements of cultural heritage practiced by members of a group or community.

To ensure the preservation of the digital cultural heritage of the member states, UNESCO argues that there is a need for appropriate legal and institutional framework practices. In this context, the main recommendations put forward are as follows (UNESCO, 2003):

- Access to legally held digital heritage artifacts should be guarded with acceptable limits while not obstructing their usage.
- The introduction of legal and technical regulations is deemed consequential in order to prevent the manipulation or deliberate alteration of the digital heritage, and in terms of ensuring the authenticity of the digital heritage.
- Maintaining the functionality of cultural heritage content and files and securing documents and records largely require the preservation of digital heritage.
- Archive legislation should be formulated as a key component of national preservation policy and legal or voluntary storage in libraries, museums and other public archives should be adopted.

It is cardinal in terms of effectively managing all processes, stages and elements and adopting a project management approach for digitalization processes, making plans for all transactions to be carried out. The processes, stages and elements required in the digitization of cultural heritage assets can be summarized as follows (Özel,2014: 161-162):

- *Planning of digitization projects:* Carrying out analyses such as why digitization will be made, what risks exist, and to which target audience the content will be presented.
- *Selection of materials:* Selecting cultural heritage assets to be digitized according to certain selection criteria.
- *Procuring of original copies:* Providing original copies of cultural heritage assets to be transferred to digital media.
- *Securing copyrights*: Before transferring cultural heritage assets to digital media and putting them into service, determining the institutions and organizations that will provide the service and looking after the legal rights of the owners of the cultural property.
- *Procuring of hardware and software:* Supplying appropriate tools and equipment to be used in the realization of digitization processes.
- *Realization of digitization processes:* Transferring cultural heritage assets to digital media using scanners, imaging devices and optical character recognition software.
- *Preservation of digitized materials:* Saving the images or other objects in digital form that is an output of the digitization process into appropriate media using appropriate file formats.

- *Identification of digitized materials:* Cataloguing and classifying digitized materials properly and defining the metadata required for these materials to ensure access to digitized materials.
- *Making digitized material available:* Providing the materials transferred to the digital environment to the service of users in a way that they can be accessed without limitation of time and place.
- *Managing digitization projects:* Within the scope of digitization processes, managing all processes effectively, encouraging teamwork, training individuals working on the project, realizing national/international cooperation for technical support and content sharing, taking into account the cost.

DIGITAL APPLICATIONS FOR THE SAFEGUARDING OF INTANGIBLE CULTURAL HERITAGE

Intangible cultural heritage aspects are at risk, it can be said. At an unprecedented rate, socio-technological changes are reshaping the forms of cultural relations all over the world. Experiencing a diverse range of cultural knowledge, oral histories, and customs results in a rich cultural ontology that connects people, places, and events. This entails a duty for the long-term preservation and safeguarding of intangible cultural heritage based on cultural knowledge (Hannewijk, 2020). Cultural values must be known and understood in order to encourage the preservation of intangible cultural heritage elements and the transmission of cultural values to future generations (Tzima et al., 2020). Increasing children's and young people's knowledge of cultural heritage is crucial to achieving this goal. Digital data, on the other hand, plays a critical role in the preservation and long-term viability of cultural heritage because it acts as a document (Halaç and Öğülmüş, 2021).

It is crucial to record and disseminate intangible cultural heritage elements through digitalization. Otherwise, it can be stated that Culture-specific cultural heritage information may be lost to current and future generations. It is obvious as to why choosing a sustainable and protective way about how to achieve this. Care should be taken to comply with the following principles and implementation steps in the digitization and protection of intangible cultural heritage elements and their representatives in the information age along with transmitting these values to future generations (Guan, 2021:1-6):

- Having determination as to protect and save intangible cultural heritage elements,
- Having awareness of the necessity of protecting the representative heirs of the intangible cultural heritage through digital technologies,
- Establishing digital protection/recovery mechanism,
- Creating database of representative heirs of intangible cultural heritage,
- Formulating national digital preservation /recovery standards and norms,
- Increasing investments in digital preservation /recovery projects.

Many programs are being conducted nowadays to protect intangible cultural heritage aspects. On the other hand, adopting mobile technologies to preserve heritage aspects is not very popular. Creating a platform and system using mobile technologies, on the other hand, will allow unrestricted access to content resources (Hannewijk, 2020). The rapidly rising costs, the transfer of scientific communication to large platforms, the increase in research impact and the need for protection of digital heritage form the reasons for the emergence of open access to cultural heritage elements (Halaç and Öğülmüş, 2021). On the other hand, with the use of digital technologies in intangible cultural heritage elements, it is resolved to document the element of cultural heritage as expressed by society and traditions within their unique contexts and transform traditions and expression styles into emerging technology-based designs and create collaborative designs to create meaningful experiences (Papangelis et al., 2016).

Game-based cultural heritage applications (Cosovic and Brkic, 2019), augmented reality-based mobile applications (Vargün and Nuhoğlu, 2019), applications that provide necessary tools for users to share their local knowledge and daily experiences (Pluggy etc.) (Lim et al., 2019), virtual museum applications, storytelling technologies focusing on cultural heritage education in early childhood (Tzima et al, 2020), three-dimensional visualization applications of intangible cultural heritage are essential mobile apps that may be mentioned in this context.

Figure 1.

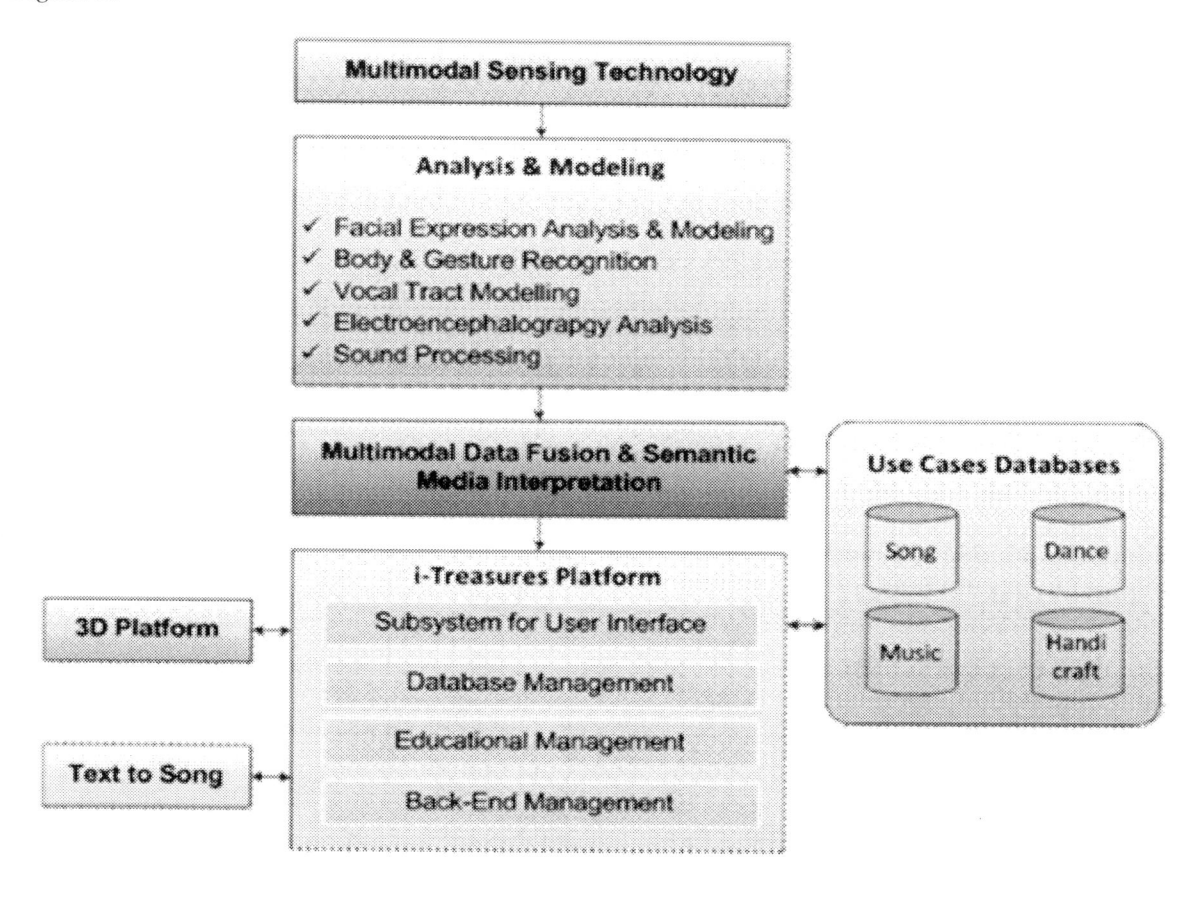

It is considered significant to meet the principles to be determined in the preservation of cultural heritage by digitizing and sample projects that will be prepared in line with the adoption stages. Certain projects in this scope will be provided in this section. Within the context of preservation of intangible cultural heritage, the *"i-Treasures"* project, financed by the EU between 2013-2017, hopes to enable new information and communication technologies to serve cultural heritage documentation and learning. The main themes within the scope of the project are inventory creation, virtual learning and community participation. First, digital repositories of cultural expressions were organized, and how this information adds meaning and value to intangible cultural heritage was examined. Later on, the way the document records and data are used in virtual learning environments was examined and online activities formed by heritage expressions were discussed. In the last section, how digital technologies regulate the relationship between communities and cultural heritage and to what extent they affect access and participation was explored (Alivizatou, 2021).

İ-Treasures Project was created with the goal of providing access to intangible cultural heritage treasures, allowing researchers to share information, and assisting in the transmission of rare knowledge between "Living Human Treasures" and apprentices, as well as developing an open and extensible platform (European Commission, 2016). The main stages of this platform are demonstrated in Figure 1:

DIGITAL APPLICATION PROJECTS WITHIN THE SCOPE OF SAFEGUARDING OF INTANGIBLE CULTURAL HERITAGE IN TURKEY

UNESCO adopted the Convention for the Safeguarding of the Intangible Cultural Heritage at its 32nd General Conference held in Paris on 17 October 2003. Turkey was included in this process with the Law on the Approval of the *Convention on the Safeguarding of Intangible Cultural Heritage* dated 19 January 2006 and numbered 5448 and officially became a party to the convention on 27 March 2006 (T.C. Kültür ve Turizm Bakanlığı, 2021a). As of this date, General Directorate of Research and Training continues its activities as the executive unit according to the 13th article of the Law No. 4848 on the Organization and Duties of the Ministry of Culture and Tourism. The Ministry of Culture and Tourism adjusts the list of potential SOKUM (*Intangible Cultural Heritage*) elements in our country through its provincial directorates and submits it to UNESCO to safeguard the cultural heritage elements selected from these lists every year as a result of the examinations of the General Directorate of Research and Training (Türker & Çelik, 2012).

Turkey carries out two different national inventory works in accordance with the article that was adopted by UNESCO in 2003 and accepted by the states parties saying in the "Convention for the Safeguarding of the Intangible Cultural Heritage" that "*it* needs to *prepare and update the inventory of intangible cultural heritage on its territory in accordance with its situation in order to protect it (UNESCO (2003)*". These studies are 1- National Inventory of Intangible Cultural Heritage and 2- National Inventory of Living Human Treasures (T.C. Kültür ve Turizm Bakanlığı, 2021c). Provincial inventories shape the basis of intangible cultural heritage national inventories. Inventory studies in the provinces are performed under the coordination of the Provincial Culture and Tourism Directorates.

In terms of cultural heritage elements, Turkey is a country with a lot to offer. The intangible cultural heritage elements of Turkey were mentioned in the other parts of the book section. The way to protect this richness is to initially record the tangible and intangible cultural heritage elements. Then spreading it to the general public through education and awareness activities. There are certain challenges in protecting intangible cultural heritage aspects in the digital age. Digital storage, archiving, and documenting, on the other hand, can be accomplished using today's technological capabilities. On the other hand, considering the extent of the time that today's generation spends on digital platforms, it should be noted that digital mobile applications have a momentous role in raising awareness of children and young people about intangible cultural heritage elements (such as handicrafts, traditional music culture, traditional dishes, jokes, legends, folk dances).

In this part of the study, projects related to the safeguarding, creating awareness, archiving, disseminating and promoting the intangible cultural heritage elements implemented by the Ministry of Culture and Tourism and the digital applications instructed in this context will be consulted.

Museum National Inventory System (MUES)

Museum National Inventory System (known as MUES in Turkish) module is a national data bank where detailed information about the artifacts in all museums affiliated to the Ministry of Culture and Tourism will be kept. In this project, it is endeavoured to realize general studies and scientific research to be carried out on inventories by expert personnel working in museums and the works and procedures for the exhibition organizations and the supply of visuals of the works mainly through the MUES inventory module. In this way, the continuous movement of original works will be prevented and risk factors such as breakage, abrasion and theft will be eliminated (T.C. Kültür ve Turizm Bakanlığı, 2021). The following outputs are proposed to be achieved in the MUES project (Information and Data Security Advanced Technologies Research Center, 2021):

- A national database where detailed information about the works in all museums will be kept,
- Artificial intelligence-based visual content search,
- Assisting in the detection of smuggling and counterfeit works,
- Accelerating decision making processes as a decision support system,
- Safeguarding artifacts against damage and risks by using digital media,
- Providing a national and standardized metadata model for artifacts and museums.

Figure 2.

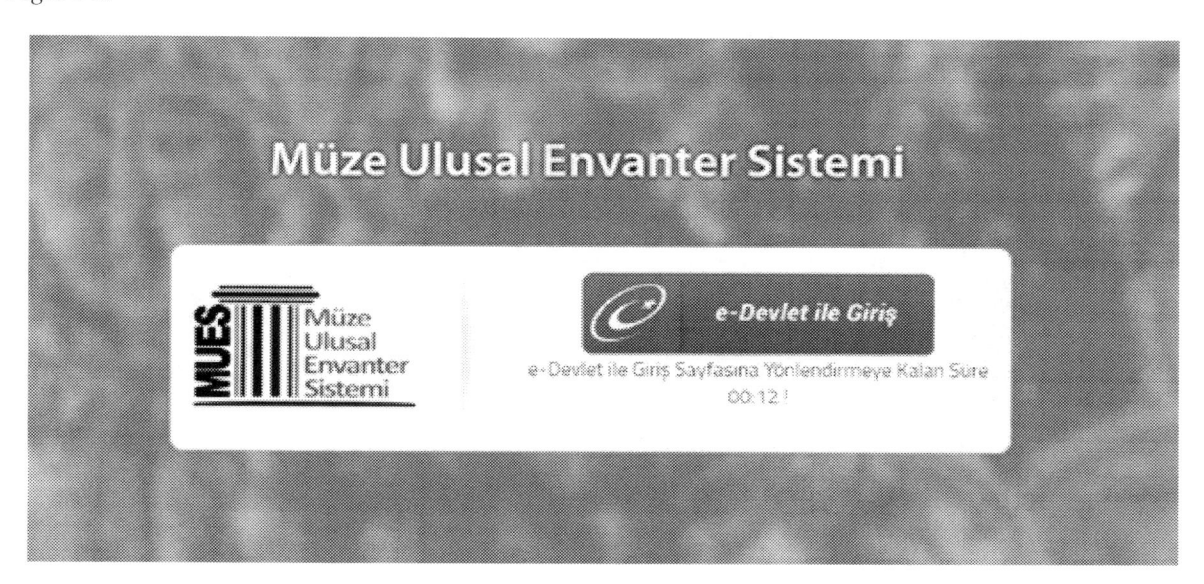

Digital Platform of Turkish Manuscripts

It is worth noting that during the 2000s, Turkey has begun to develop manuscript accessibility through electronic media. Manuscripts, audio-visual items, museum pieces, and archival documents at cultural heritage memory centers such as libraries, archives, and museums have begun to be made available online as a result of digitalization (Öztemiz and Yılmaz, 2017). *The union Catalogue of Manuscripts in Turkey* (known as TÜYATOK) is one of the first projects in Turkey in this context. The goal of this project is to catalog the existing Arabic script manuscripts in Turkey. Despite the fact that the project moved slowly for a variety of reasons, it was crucial in the bibliographic control of manuscripts in Turkey. This initiative can be considered the foundation for the "Turkish Manuscripts" project (Aynur, 2021).

In recent years, 28 libraries in Turkey have been working on digitizing these items in order to preserve them and pass them on to future generations, and they have cultural heritage materials such as "manuscripts" in their collections. 166.210 works in these libraries and 208.562 records consisting of works in the National Library archive are available in the system accessible from www.yazmalar.gov.tr (Öztemiz, 2016). A basic and extensive manuscript catalog search method is available on this platform. The works can be obtained in digital format after a person becomes a member of this portal. This site provides access to all manuscript libraries in Turkey's provinces. On this platform, the entire manuscript or a specific page range can be downloaded. Moreover, there are user guide, collections, libraries, legislation, browsing and information menus (TYEKB, 2021a).

Figure 3.

Figure 4.

Turkish Culture Portal

"Turkish Culture Portal" project prepared by the Ministry of Culture and Tourism is a digital platform including Turkish language literature, folk culture, archaeological heritage, geographically indicated products, information on traditional cuisine culture and other tangible and intangible cultural heritage elements. The portal established with the web address "kultürportali.gov.tr" contains the information and photographs about the cultural heritage elements mentioned below (Culture Portal, 2021a):

- Geographical Indications Products
- Archeology and History
- Language and Literature
- Folk Culture
- Traditional Cuisine
- Our Cultural Heritage
- Museums
- Art

- Activities Specific to Provinces
- Tourism Activities

Handicrafts, traditional cuisine, souvenirs, tourism activities and other cultural heritage information about the provinces in Turkey are also available (Culture Portal, 2021b). The portal also includes online e-books and other papers relating to folk culture, in addition to basic information concerning social customs, performing arts, oral expressions, and handicraft traditions. (Culture Portal, 2021c). In the detailed document menu, there are photos, videos, audio and other documents to be uploaded related to the relevant cultural heritage element (Culture Portal, 2021d).

Figure 5.

CONCLUSION

The safeguarding of intangible cultural heritage pieces and their transmission to future generations are essential considerations. Although advances in technology are reducing interest in cultural heritage aspects, it is claimed that digital technologies have become substantial in safeguarding these pieces, inventorying them, assimilating through education, and promoting awareness.

During the Covid 19 pandemic and other crises, access to cultural heritage assets has been restricted. This condition has unfavorable socio-economic consequences for artists, craftspeople, and other similar professions, who are often seen as primary carriers of the heritage. On the other hand, visitors may be deprived of the common cultural heritage elements of humanity for a certain period of time. In the Covid 19 process, the access obstacles to tangible and intangible cultural heritage have been attempted to be removed through online exhibitions, virtual museums, and online artistic performances. In order to safeguard, archive, and promote Turkey's intangible cultural heritage, significant projects have been implemented. Museum National Inventory System (MUES), "Digital Platform of Turkish Manuscripts" and "Turkish Culture Portal" projects have been put into practice by the Ministry of Culture and Tourism within the scope of digitalization. The safeguarding of intangible cultural heritage materials and their transfer to future generations may be ensured by these and other project efforts. In this context, other challenges that need to be addressed include preserving the authenticity of cultural heritage and avoiding the destruction of cultural asset's essence through digitalization.

The role of digitalization in preserving intangible cultural heritage is discussed. It is one of the main views that emerged in this context that digitalization harms the spirit and originality of cultural heritage. Another view is that intangible cultural heritage elements, which are difficult to store and archive physically, can be prevented from being lost by using digital mobile applications. On the other hand, the level of digital addiction is quite high, especially in children and young people today. Mobile applications that contain intangible cultural heritage elements instead of harmful content in digital environments will contribute to the development and cultural learning levels of children and young people. Adding practical lessons on intangible cultural heritage elements to education curricula and increasing awareness on digital heritage literacy are other suggestions to be put forward in this context.

SUGGESTIONS FOR FUTURE RESEARCH

It is suggested that researchers concentrate their efforts on challenges connected to the preservation and transmission of intangible cultural assets to future generations. Furthermore, cultural studies are required in order to preserve the authenticity of intangible cultural heritage while avoiding hurting its spirit, not commoditizing cultural heritage, and promoting sustainable tourism. Finally, research that explore both the positive and negative consequences of digitalization on intangible cultural resources are regarded to be necessary.

REFERENCES

Akyıldız, N. A., & Olğun, T. N. (2020). Somut olmayan kültürel mirasın Anadolu'da tarihî yerleşimlerin korunması ve sürdürülebilirliği bağlamında değerlendirilmesi [Evaluation of the intangible cultural heritage in the context of conservation and sustainability of historical settlements in Anatolia]. *Milli Folklor, 32*(16), 234–243.

Alaeddinoğlu, F. (2007). Van halkının turisti ve turizmi algılama şekli [Van community's perception of tourists and tourism]. *Coğrafi Bilimler Dergisi, 5*(1), 1–16.

Alagöz, G., Çalık, İ., & Güneş, E. (2018). Kültürel miras turizmi açısından Erzincan bakır işleme sanatının mevcut durumu ve sürdürülebilirliği [Current situation and sustainability of erzincan copper processing art in terms of cultural heritage tourism]. *Dumlupınar Üniversitesi Sosyal Bilimler Dergisi, 55*, 174–191.

Alivizatou, M. (2021). Digital ıntangible heritage: Inventories, virtual learning and participation. *Heritage & Society, 12*(2-3), 116–135. doi:10.1080/2159032X.2021.1883950

Alzueta, E., Perrin, P., Baker, F. C., Caffarra, S., Usuga, D. R., Yuksel, D., & Lasprilla, J. C. A. (2021). How the COVID-19 pandemic has changed our lives: A study of psychological correlates across 59 countries. *Journal of Clinical Psychology, 77*(3), 556–570. doi:10.1002/jclp.23082 PMID:33128795

Ashworth, G. J. (1994). From history to heritage–from heritage to identity.: In search of concepts and models. In G. J. Ashworth & P. J. Larkham (Eds.), *From history to heritage–from heritage to identity. Building a new heritage: Tourism, culture and identity in the new Europe* (pp. 13–30). Routledge.

Aynur, H. (2012). Türkiye Yazmaları Toplu Kataloğu [Collective catalog of Turkey manuscripts], DİA, İstanbul. *Türkiye Diyanet Vakfı Yayınları*, *41*, 597–598.

Bak, S. (2007). Domestic and International Cultural Tourism in the Context of Intangible Heritage. In Safeguarding Intangible Heritage and Sustainable Cultural Tourism: Opportunities and Challenges. Bangkok: UNESCO Bangkok.

Bal, H. (1991). *Turizmin Kırsal Toplumda Aile İçi İlişkilere Etkisi* [The effect of tourism on family relations in rural society]. Doğa İnsan Yayınları.

Bilişim ve Bilgi Güvenliği İleri Teknolojiler Araştırma Merkezi. (n.d.). *Müze Ulusal Envanter Sistemi Projesi* [Museum National Inventory System Project]. https://b3lab.org/sayfa/mues_muze_ulusal_envanter_sistemi_projesi-32

Çetin, T. (2010). Cumalıkızık köyünde kültürel miras ve turizm algısı [Perception of cultural heritage and tourism in Cumalıkızık village]. *Milli Folklor*, *22*(87), 181–190.

Cosovic, M., & Brkic, B. R. (2019). Game-based learning in museums—Cultural heritage applications. *Information (Basel)*, *11*(22), 3–13.

Deacon, H., Dondolo, L., Mrubata, M., & Prosalendis, S. (2004). *The subtle power of intangible heritage: Legal and financial instruments for safeguarding intangible heritage.* HSRC Publishing.

Dimitropoulos, K., Manitsaris, S., Tsalakanidou, F., Nikolopoulos, S., Denby, B., Al Kork, S., ... Grammalidis, N. (2014, January). Capturing the intangible an introduction to the i-Treasures project. In *Proceedings international conference on computer vision theory and applications (VISAPP)* (pp. 773-781). IEEE.

Ertürk, N. (2020). Preservation of digitized intangible cultural heritage in museum storage. *Milli Folklor*, *16*(128), 100–110.

European Commission. (2016*). İ-treasures: capturing the intangible cultural heritage and learning the rare know-how of living human treasures.* https://ec.europa.eu/digital-single-market/en/blog/i-treasures-capturing-intangible-cultural-heritage-and-learning-rare-know-how-living-human

Fortune. (2021). *One year later: 15 ways life has changed since the onset of the COVID pandemic.* https://fortune.com/2021/03/09/covid-pandemic-how-life-has-changed-coronavirus-one-year-later-march-2020/

General, A. (2015). *Transforming our world: the 2030 agenda for sustainable development.* UN.

Google Arts& Culture. (2021). https://artsandculture.google.com/

Guan, Z. (2021). Digital rescue protection of representative inheritors of intangible cultural heritage in the information age. *Journal of Physics: Conference Series*, *1744*(4), 042124. doi:10.1088/1742-6596/1744/4/042124

Halaç, H. H., & Öğülmüş, V. (2021). Kültürel miras verilerinin dijital olarak depolanması: Openheritage3d örneği [Digital storage of cultural heritage data: Openheritage3d example]. *The Turkish Online Journal of Design Art and Communication*, *11*(2), 521–540.

Hannewijk, B., Vinella, F. L., Khan, V. J., Lykourentzou, I., Papangelis, K., & Masthoff, J. (2020). Capturing the city's heritage on-the-go: Design requirements for mobile crowdsourced cultural heritage. *Sustainability*, *12*(6), 2–20. doi:10.3390u12062429

ICCROM Working Group. (1990). *Heritage and Society*. http://cif.icomos.org/pdf_docs/Documents%20 on%20line/Heritage%20definitions.pdf

ICOMOS Türkiye. (2013). *ICOMOS Türkiye Mimari Mirası Koruma Bildirgesi* [ICOMOS Turkey Architectural Heritage Protection Declaration]. http://www.icomos.org.tr/Dosyalar/ICOMOSTR_ tr0784192001542192602.pdf

ILO. (2020). *The impact of COVID-19 on the tourism sector. ILO Sectoral Briefs Mayıs 2020*. https:// www.ilo.org/wcmsp5/groups/public/---ed_dialogue/-- sector/documents/briefingnote/wcms_741468.pdf

Kuntay, O. (2004). *Sürdürülebilir turizm planlaması* [Sustainable tourism planning]. Alp Yayınevi.

Lim, V., Frangakis, N., Tanco, L. M., & Picinali, L. (2018). PLUGGY: A pluggable social platform for cultural heritage awareness and participation. In M. Ioannides, J. Martins, R. Žarnić, & V. Lim (Eds.), *Advances in Digital Cultural Heritage* (pp. 117–129). Springer. doi:10.1007/978-3-319-75789-6_9

MUES. (2021). *Müze ulusal envanter sistemi* [Museum national inventory system]. https://mues.kultur. gov.tr/giris

Oğuz, M. Ö. (2013). Terim Olarak Somut Olmayan Kültürel Miras [Intangible cultural heritage as a term]. *Milli Folklor*, *25*(100), 5–13.

Ölçer Özünel, E. (2011). Kültür turizminde "yöresel" ve "otantik" olanı sorgulamak ve tüketilmiş mekânları yeniden üretmek üzerine [Questioning the locality and authenticity in cultural tourism and arguing the space consuming]. *Turkish Studies*, *6*(4), 255–262.

Öztemiz, S. (2016). Türkiye'de dijitalleştirilen kültürel miras ürünlerine açık erişim: bir model önerisi [Open Access to digitized cultural heritage products in Turkey: A model offer] (Yayınlanmamış Doktora Tezi). Hacettepe Üniversitesi Sosyal Bilimler Enstitüsü, Bilgi ve Belge Yönetimi Anabilim Dalı, Ankara.

Öztemiz, S., & Yılmaz, B. (2017). Kültürel bellek kurumlarında dijitalleştirme: Kültürel miras ürünlerine yönelik uygulamalar üzerine bir araştırma [Digitization in cultural memory institutions: A study on applications for cultural heritage products]. *Ankara Üniversitesi Dil ve Tarih-Coğrafya Fakültesi Dergisi*, *57*(1), 493–523. doi:10.1501/Dtcfder_0000001524

Papangelis, K., Chamberlain, A., & Liang, H. N. (2016, September). New directions for preserving intangible cultural heritage through the use of mobile technologies. In *Proceedings of the 18th International Conference on Human-Computer Interaction with Mobile Devices and Services(MobileHCI '16)* (pp. 964-967). Adjunct. 10.1145/2957265.2962643

Sağlık Bakanlığı, T. C. (2021). *Covid 19 nedir?* [Whats Covid 19]. https://covid19.saglik.gov.tr/TR-66300/covid-19-nedir-.html

Satar, İ., & Güneş, G. (2014). *Türkiye'de somut olmayan kültürel mirasın korunmasında kültür turizmin önemi* [The importance of cultural tourism in the protection of intangible cultural heritage in Turkey] [Paper Presentation]. Quo Vadıs: Sosyal Bilimler – Artvin Çoruh Üniversitesi Hopa Uluslararası Sosyal Bilimler Konferansı.

T.C. Kültür ve Turizm Bakanlığı. (2014). *Müzeler Ulusal Envanter Sistemi (MUES)* [Museum National Inventory System]. https://kvmgm.ktb.gov.tr/TR-98489/muzeler-ulusal-envanter-sistemi-mues.html

T.C. Kültür ve Turizm Bakanlığı. (2021a). *Somut olmayan kültürel mirasın korunması sözleşmesi hakkında* [On the convention for the protection of the intangible cultural heritage]. https://aregem.ktb.gov.tr/TR-50837/somut-olmayan-kulturel-mirasin-korunmasi-sozlesmesi-hak-.html

T.C. Kültür ve Turizm Bakanlığı. (2021b). *Somut olmayan kültürel miras ulusal envanteri* [National inventory of intangible cultural heritage]. https://aregem.ktb.gov.tr/TR-159257/somut-olmayan-kulturel-miras-ulusal-envanteri.html

T.C. Kültür ve Turizm Bakanlığı. (2021c). *Somut olmayan kültürel miras envanter çalışmaları* [Intangible cultural heritage inventory works]. https://aregem.ktb.gov.tr/TR-50839/somut-olmayan-kulturel-miras-envanter-calismalari.html

Throsby, D. (1997). Seven questions in the economics of cultural heritage. In M. Hutter & I. Rizzo (Eds.), *Economic Perspectives on Cultural Heritage* (pp. 13–30). Macmillan. doi:10.1007/978-1-349-25824-6_2

Time. (2021). *These 29 numbers show how the covıd-19 pandemic changed our lives over the last year.* https://time.com/5947302/covid-19-data/

Türker, A., & Çelik, İ. (2012). Somut olmayan kültürel miras unsurlarının turistik ürün olarak geliştirilmesine yönelik alternatif öneriler [Alternative proposals for tourist product development of ıntangible cultural heritage elements]. *Yeni Fikir Dergisi*, (12), 86–98.

Türkiye Kültür Portalı. (2021). *Kültür atlası*. https://www.kulturportali.gov.tr/portal/halk-bilimi-ve-kultur-atlasi

Türkiye Yazma Eserler Kurumu Başkanlığı (TYEKB). (2021a). http://www.yazmalar.gov.tr/

Türkiye Yazma Eserler Kurumu Başkanlığı (TYEKB). (2021b). *Basit tarama* [Simple scan]. http://www.yazmalar.gov.tr/basit-arama?q=yazma

Türkiye Yazma Eserler Kurumu Başkanlığı (TYEKB). (2021c). *Keşfu'z-Zunûn 'an-Esâmî'l-Kutubi ve 'l-Fünûn*. http://www.yazmalar.gov.tr/eser/kesfuz-zun%C3%BBn-an-esam%C3%AEl-kutubi-ve-l-fun%C3%BBn/126743

Tüzel, B. (2020). Covid-19 salgını sürecinde el sanatları geleneği deneyimlerí [The experiences of traditional craftsmanship in the process of covid-19 pandemic]. *Milli Folklor*, *16*(127), 87–100.

Tzima, S., Styliaras, G., Bassounas, A., & Tzima, M. (2020). Harnessing the potential of storytelling and mobile technology in intangible cultural heritage: A case study in early childhood education in sustainability. *Sustainability*, *12*(22), 2–22. doi:10.3390u12229416

UNEP & UNWTO. (2005). *Making tourism more sustainable: a guide for policy makers*. Author.

UNESCO. (1990). *Third medium-term plan (1990-1995)*. UNESCO, General Conference, 25th session. https://unesdoc.unesco.org/ark:/48223/pf0000084697

UNESCO. (2003). *Charter on the Preservation of Digital Heritage*. http://portal.unesco.org/en/ev.php-URL_ID=17721&URL_DO=DO_TOPIC&URL_SECTION=201.html

UNESCO. (2003). *Somut Olmayan Kültürel Mirasın Korunması Sözleşmesi* [Convention for the Safeguarding of the Intangible Cultural Heritage]. https://ich.unesco.org/doc/src/00009-TR-PDF.pdf

UNESCO. (2020a). *Culture & covıd-19 impact & response tracker*. https://en.unesco.org/sites/default/files/issue_1_en_culture_covid-19_tracker.pdf

UNESCO. (2020b). *RESILIART Artists and Creativity beyond Crisis*. https://en.unesco.org/news/resiliart-artists-and-creativity-beyond-crisis#

UNESCO. (2020c). *UNESCO supports culture and heritage during COVID-19's shutdown*. https://whc.unesco.org/en/news/2099

UNESCO. (2021a). *Dünya miras listesi* [World heritage list]. http://whc.unesco.org/en/list/&order=country#alphaT

UNESCO. (2021b). *Dünya miras listesi (Türkiye)* [World heritage list (Turkey)]. http://whc.unesco.org/en/statesparties/tr

UNESCO. (2021c). *Purpose of the lists of intangible cultural heritage and of the register of good safeguarding practices*. https://ich.unesco.org/en/purpose-of-the-lists-00807

UNESCO. (2021d). *Browse the lists of intangible cultural heritage and the register of good safeguarding practices*. https://ich.unesco.org/en/lists

UNESCO. (n.d.). *What is meant by "cultural heritage"?* http://www.unesco.org/new/en/culture/themes/illicit-trafficking-of-cultural-property/unesco-database-of-national-cultural-heritage-laws/frequently-asked-questions/definition-of-the-cultural-heritage/

UNESCO Türkiye Milli Komisyonu. (2021). *Somut Olmayan Kültürel Miras Listelerinde Türkiye* [Turkey on Intangible Cultural Heritage Lists]. https://www.unesco.org.tr/Pages/126/123/UNESCO-%C4%B0nsanl%C4%B1%C4%9F%C4%B1n-Somut-Olmayan-K%C3%BClt%C3%BCrel-Miras%C4%B1-Temsil%C3%AE-Listesi

United Nations (UN). (2007). *Indicators of Sustainable Development: Guidelines and Medhodologies*. UN Publishing.

UNWTO. (2021). *Tourist numbers down 83% but confidence slowly rising*. https://www.unwto.org/news/tourist-numbers-down-83-but-confidence-slowly-rising

Vargün, Ö., & Nuhoğlu, M. (2019). Kültürel miras eğitiminde bilgi iletişim teknolojilerinin rolü ve mobil uygulamalar [The role of ICT in cultural heritage education and evaluation of mobile communication vehicle]. *UNIMUSEUM, 2*(2), 45–53.

WHO. (2021a). *Archived: WHO timeline - COVID-19*. https://www.who.int/news/item/27-04-2020-who-timeline---covid-19

WHO. (2021b). *WHO Coronavirus (COVID-19) dashboard*. https://covid19.who.int/

World Tourism Organisations (WTO). (2004). *Indicators of Sustainable Development for Tourism Destination: A Guide Book*. WTO Publishing.

WTTC. (2019). *Travel & tourism economic impact 2019 world*. https://www.slovenia.info/uploads/dokumenti/raziskave/raziskave/world2019.pdf

KEY TERMS AND DEFINITIONS

Cultural Heritage: Cultural heritage is the cultural resources available to all humanity from past to present.

Digital Cultural Heritage: This concept refers to cultural and scientific resources related to digitally created human knowledge and expression.

Digital Intangible Cultural Heritage: It is the representation, expression, information, and oral traditions protected by digital photography and other audio and visual recordings.

Intangible Cultural Heritage: It is all of the handicrafts, oral expressions and traditions, performing arts and expression, representation, knowledge and oral traditions related to nature and the universe that are hard to transfer to future generations.

Museum National Inventory System (Known as MUES in Turkey): It is a data bank where detailed information about the artifacts in all museums affiliated to the Ministry of Culture and Tourism in Turkey is recorded.

Treasures Project: It is a digital project that foresees inventory creation, virtual learning, and community participation.

Turkey Culture Portal: This is a digital platform that contains information on heritage elements such as Turkish language and literature, folk culture, archaeological heritage, geographically indicated products, traditional cuisine culture.

Chapter 10
Digital Cultural Heritage

F. Füsun İstanbullu Dinçer
https://orcid.org/0000-0003-2338-2462
Istanbul University, Turkey

Seda Özdemir Akgül
Selcuk University, Turkey

ABSTRACT

This chapter aims to give information about how the digitalization process is using technologies suitable for today's conditions in the transmission of cultural heritage to future generations and its preservation, what methods are being employed, the concept of digital heritage, the developments that took place and the projects that were carried out in the digitization of cultural heritage. In addition, it is also aimed in this chapter to evaluate the cultural heritage sites within the framework of this new understanding and to examine how these areas can be redefined with new technical possibilities. At this point, after reviewing the literature about the cultural and digital heritage, the importance of cultural heritage is referred to in detail. Finally, a case study is conducted by the authors via compiling the V-must.net website established to develop virtual museums, blog comments, and academic studies carried out in respect to this project.

INTRODUCTION

Heritage embodies values that remind the past and give clues about the future. Cultural heritage is a set of values that encompass the cuisines, beliefs, lifestyles, religious traditions, customs, and sense of art of the communities. The concept of cultural heritage that has been passed down from generation to generation, such as the traditions, customs, values, etc. of a society, is divided into two as tangible and intangible. Tangible heritage includes monuments, pictures, prints, archaeological sites, temples, mosaics, sculptures, landscapes, etc. and intangible elements include dance, beliefs, festivals, customs, and intangible elements include oral traditions, dance, beliefs, festivals, customs, ceremonies, rituals, traditional handicrafts and folklore, ceremonies, rituals, traditional handicrafts and folklore (Franchi, 2017). According to Silverman and Ruggles (2007), intangible cultural heritage values such as architecture, landscape forms, works of art, oral traditions, dance, theater, rituals, memories and languages

DOI: 10.4018/978-1-7998-8528-3.ch010

are values that must be preserved for next generations. The characteristics of individuals and the whole society are shaped by cultural heritage.

In order for cultural heritage to be preserved, passed on to the next generations and kept alive, values must be transformed by using contemporary technologies. From this point on, the concept of digital cultural heritage has emerged. According to Rahaman and Tan (2009), digital cultural heritage; is the reflections of archaeological, historical and attractive values in virtual environments. While cultural heritage can be defined as assets and areas of archaeological, aesthetic and historical value, digital heritage refers to examples of these assets and areas in a virtual environment (Roussou, 2002: 99). The cultural heritage found in digital environments can be easily accessed from all over the world and diversified through digital channels (Hancock, 2018: 10).

There are various cultural memory institutions (such as museums, libraries, archives, sculptures, botanical gardens) that take an active rolewalues in virtual environments, in the transmission and preservation of cultural heritage to next generations and carry out investment activities (Manžuch, 2009). In these institutions, artifacts, monuments, historical places and various values are digitized and digitally preserved. Digital storytelling, virtual reality (VR), augmented reality (AR), three-dimensional 3D reconstructions, mobile devices and virtual guidance, interactive computer games and simulations are among the methods used by institutions during the digitization phase to preserve cultural heritage and pass it to the next generations.

Digitalized cultural heritage elements are conveyed to visitors by using virtual technologies through various programs and by storytelling these experiences. Digital storytelling, which started to be used in the 90's and has become widespread with social media and smart phones today; is a narrative technique performed by using digital tools (Caffo and Canale, 2014: 5-14). The storytelling method created through digital technologies contributes to the conservation of cultural heritage directly and indirectly (Selmanovic et al., 2018: 57).

In the digitalization of cultural heritage, the use of 3D technologies has become widespread in recent years. With these technologies, the collection, storage, protection and reconstruction of data such as monuments, sites and works of art can be carried out more effectively and efficiently (Portales et al., 2018; Merchan et al., 2019). In addition, through these technologies, it is possible to produce and store copies of the original works (Katz and Tokovinine, 2017). Among the reasons for the 3D reconstruction of cultural heritage values in virtual environment are education, documentation in case of disaster, examination of the works in different dimensions, restoration of damaged or destroyed buildings (Noh et al., 2009). 3D digital tools provide various advantages in the areas of education, presentation, preservation, documentation and visualization (Addison, 2000). These tools provide accessibility for those both visiting museums and historical sites and researchers (Zarnowski et al., 2015).

In the documentation of the tangible heritage, 3D data is scanned by laser and the scanned objects are presented to public by virtual reality (VR), augmented reality (AR), exhibitions, etc (Bautista, 2013). Intangible heritage, on the other hand, is not easy to document. However, for a culture an object can be used as a tool to document where it takes place, oral traditions (Thwaites et al. 2019). Since it is now important not only to document the heritage, but also to convey the intangible part, which may include emotions, perceptions and motives, for conservation, successful integration of virtual and physical environments is required for the continuity of reality and for individuals to feel as if they are living the moment (Selmanovic, 2018: 65). Virtual heritage areas can be accessed both from applications that can be downloaded to smart devices and through related websites (Basaraba, 2018: 72). Virtual heritage projects aim to recreate cultures from the past to the present with digitalization, aiming to make users understand these cultures and feel themselves as if they lived in that period (Noh et al., 2009).

From this point of view, this chapter aims to give information about how the digitalization process is by using technologies suitable for today's conditions in the transmission of cultural heritage to future generations and its preservation, what methods are being employed, the concept of digital heritage, the developments that took place and the projects that were carried out in the digitization of cultural heritage.

THE CONCEPT OF CULTURAL HERITAGE

Culture; in particular, defined as the traditions and beliefs, arts and lifestyles of a certain society at a certain time (Cambridge, 2020). Inheritance is generally defined as the contemporary use of the past transferred from the past to the future (Emekli, 2012: 1). Based on the definitions of culture and heritage, cultural heritage can be defined as the transfer of cultural values, traditional knowledge, festivals, rituals, belief systems, clothes, arts to future generations in verbal and nonverbal forms (Shimray and Ramaiah, 2019: 1). "Cultural heritage", which brings together the concepts of culture and heritage, refers to the artistic or symbolic, material symbols of all cultures and humanity, passed down from generation to generation (UNESCO, 2001). The common heritage and values of humanity constitute its cultural heritage. Cultural heritage is defined as an expression of life styles that have been passed down from generation to generation, including traditions, objects, artistic expressions and values developed by a community (Cultural Heritage, 2002). The concept of cultural heritage refers to the accumulation of material or spiritual cultural values of a society from the past to the present. It is ensured that cultural heritage values are adopted and passed on to future generations by conventions prepared by international institutions such as UNESCO and ICOMOS. This situation is also important for different cultures to communicate with each other (Yılmaz, 2020: 158). Cultural heritage elements transferred from generation to generation are an output of the culture of the society in the historical process. For this reason, cultural heritage elements appear as resources of societies. According to the Council of Europe (2005), cultural heritage values are seen as being a resource for human development, cultural diversity and interaction, and providing economic development to the society by using these resources sustainably. Cultural heritage assets are a part of the dynamic system that is often subject to natural and human-induced changes and deterioration (Elfadaly et al., 2018: 1348). For this reason, taking the necessary measures for the protection of cultural heritage should be carried out within a planning.

The concept of cultural heritage that has been passed down from generation to generation is divided into two as tangible and intangible elements. Tangible elements include buildings, villages, structures, monuments, cities, art and museum works, historical gardens and objects, and intangible elements include oral traditions, dance, beliefs, festivals, customs, ceremonies, rituals, traditional handicrafts and folklore (Timothy, 2011: 3). Cultural heritage is also all of the tangible and intangible values related to identity of society, culture and history. Living but intangible values such as historical cities and textures, cultural landscapes, monumental structures, archaeological sites, language, tradition, dance, music and rituals also constitute cultural heritage (Kuşçuoğlu and Taş, 2017). In a simple comparison, tangible heritage values express the solid state of culture such as buildings, places and objects, while intangible cultural heritage values express the softer form of culture such as people, their traditions and knowledge (McKerher and du Cros, 2012). Tangible cultural heritage includes buildings, historical sites, monuments, and any artifacts made by human beings. These artifacts are important archaeological, architectural, technological and scientific structures that should be protected and preserved for future generations (UNESCO, 21 November 2014).

Intangible cultural heritage is the protection of the intangible cultural heritage that a society sees as a part of its own cultural identity and brought to the present day by transferring it from generation to generation, and to future generations, with the Convention on the Protection of the Intangible Cultural Heritage (ICH) accepted by UNESCO on October 17, 2003. It is defined as the ways, methods and possibilities that will contribute to the transfer of information (Oğuz 2009: 8). The preservation of intangible cultural heritage is equated with the preservation of cultural identities and thus the cultural diversity of humanity (UNESCO Intangible Culturel Heritage 2017). Intangible Cultural Heritage shows its existence in the following five areas (UNESCO, 2016): a) Oral traditions and expressions, together with the language that acts as a carrier for the transmission of intangible cultural heritage; b) performance arts; c) Social practices, rituals and feasts; d) Knowledge and practices related to nature and the universe; e) Craft tradition.

THE CONCEPT OF DIGITAL AND VIRTUAL HERITAGE

Cultural heritage studies objects and areas of historical, archaeological and original value. Digital heritage is the reflection of these objects and spaces in virtual environments (Roussou, 2002: 99; Rahaman and Tan, 2009). At this point, digital heritage includes the virtualization of cultural heritage (MacDonald, 2006).

According to UNESCO (2003), digital heritage includes human knowledge and historical resources as well as cultural, scientific, technical, administrative and other types of created data converted into digital form. In line with this definition, the digitalization process includes the transfer and interpretation process of intangible and tangible cultural heritage values to the virtual environment. According to Gasimova and Abbaslı (2020), these digitalized elements are important to maintain and preserve as they contain information that needs to be protected for future generations.

Virtual heritage, on the other hand, plays an important role in the preservation and documentation of cultural, historical and natural values with digital technologies (Özgan, 2012). It aims to reconstruct cultures by using digital tools within the scope of virtual heritage and to enable users to experience the moment and feel themselves as a part of that culture (Noh et al., 2009).

Virtual heritage is a new technology to preserve traditional cultures. Reasons to focus on virtual heritage: documenting historic buildings and objects against any kind of destruction, rebuilding ruined or damaged historical monuments, interacting without damaging objects, providing educational resources, scaling objects and structures from different angles, computing environments and giving individuals the opportunity to visit previously devastated objects virtually, eliminating travel costs (Noh et al., 2009; Kolivand et al., 2018). These virtual tools, especially used in archeology and architecture, have also provided advantages in the fields of documentation, presentation and visualization (Addison, 2000).

DIGITALIZING CULTURAL HERITAGE

The culture that is digitally copied and recreated in virtual environments is accessible from all over the world and can reach many people easily (Hancock, 2018: 10). Today, Digital Media plays an important role in re-establishing links between artifacts and different social groups and offers powerful tools for the digital acquisition, storage, preservation, recreation, reconstruction of both tangible and intangible cultural heritage assets (Portales et al., 2018). By using new virtual technology tools, cultural heritage not only provides access to individuals, but also provides information to researchers who have difficulties in finding the originals of artifacts. Cultural heritage uses these new virtual technology tools in the development of its techniques (Zarnowski et al., 2015).

Electronic copies of documents and works of art refer to digitization. Digitization is the conversion of any resource such as paper, prints, slides, and three-dimensional objects into a digital format (Astle and Muir, 2002). At this point, printed versions of documents or works are transferred to computers. In the digitization process, data, video and audio files are transferred to digital media. Digitization aims to protect library resources and improve access to resources and information. This technique will protect the materials that may be lost in the future (manuscripts, official newspapers, maps, music recordings, photographs, etc.) and prevent the originals from being damaged (Fabunmi et al., 2006).

Cultural Memory Institutions in the Digitalization of Cultural Heritage

Digitalization has a great importance for cultural memory institutions in conveying lifestyles, traditions and historical resources of societies (Fabunmi et al., 2006). Digitalization investments of cultural memory institutions increased in the 1990s. Cultural memory institutions such as libraries, archives and museums (Dalbello, 2004: 267; Valm, 2007) have important functions in protecting cultural heritage, forming cultural memory and presenting it for the benefit of society (Astle and Muir, 2002).

Many library organizations digitize materials that are in danger of being lost in the future, such as old manuscripts, photographic images, non-commercial live music recordings, theses (Liu, 2004; Fabunmi et al., 2006). In addition, these institutions not only digitize resources such as rare works and old manuscripts, but also digitize educational materials within the framework of copyright in order to increase access. Archives, on the other hand, provide another collection model with the role of preserving the information contained in the records, not generally as a content interpreter, as well as grouping large amounts of documents as digital records (Robinson, 2012). Archivists preserve the original order in the records, allowing users to interpret and analyze the records in a variety of ways (Bettington et al., 2008: 18). In the archive system, steps are taken to define, store and protect digital materials, and to develop strategies for their access (Lavoie, 2014). Digital archives created for the protection and access of cultural heritage materials carry out digital preservation processes through Open Archival Information Systems – OAIS functions (Holdsworth, 2007). Museums, one of the cultural memory institutions such as libraries and archives, are other institutions that carry out digitization studies. The fact that virtual museums are indefinitely accessible and carry a large collection to the digital platform makes it easier for them to be visited virtually by followers from different countries (Oksaar, 2008). Cultural memory institutions are trying to organize training, cooperation and projects on the subject by creating strategies that cover digitalization requirements (Çakmak and Yılmaz, 2012).

Virtual Technologies Used in the Digitization of Cultural Heritage

Virtual Reality (VR)

Virtual Reality (VR) is a computer-assisted environment for people to explore new worlds, share ideas and experience new experiences in the digital space (Craig et al., 2009). According to the American Heritage

Dictionary, virtual reality, which is a computer simulation of a real or imaginary system, enables users to operate in this system and shows its effect in real time (Brayton, 2003). This technology allows users to embody abstract objects through virtual experiences and to perceive actions as their own (Villalba et al., 2021). The concept of virtual reality defined by Guttentag (2010: 638) is an interactive model that creates unreal simulated content for users in a computer-generated environment. Gong (2021) defined virtual reality as: It is an elevated mobile platform that uses several platforms to simulate and communicate in real time. Also, Gomez et al. (1995: 198) defines virtual reality as the combination of technologies necessary to create interactive, versatile and immersive multidimensional computing environments.

With virtual reality technology, three-dimensional models and fictions can be made not only for the present time, but also for the past and the future (Jin, 2011: 2). Bringing heritage content to life digitally and simulating computer graphics technology using synthesis, preservation, reproduction, representation, digital reprocessing and VR technologies facilitate the display of cultural heritage (Merkx and Navijn, 2021).

Reconstruction of monuments and buildings belonging to the historical and cultural past lost over time is now possible with 3D modeling software and VR tools (Cirulis et al, 2015). At this point, the main reason for the use of virtual reality tools in heritage areas is that it allows the originals of the physically exhibited works to be viewed from every angle and presented in the closest and most interactive way to reality (Arnold and Geser, 2012: 17). Thanks to the virtual reality provided by cultural heritage sites, users can visit offline (Abraham, 2015). According to Guttentag (2010), tourists can visit destinations that have no means of transportation, dangerous or expensive transportation, with virtual reality technology without risk. VR applications designed for various purposes, entertainment, education, accessibility and heritage preservation can be experienced (Bogicevic et al., 2021). With regard to its use by tourism industry professionals, according to Merkx and Navijn (2021), VR tourism experiences should be designed to be enjoyable.

According to Gong (2021), with the advancement of science and technology, virtual reality technology emerges in accordance with the spirit of the time and its application in digital media art creation is becoming more and more extensive. The use of virtual reality technology in digital media art creation helps to enrich artistic tools and improve the quality of the creation process.

Augmented Reality (AR)

Augmented reality (AR) is a process where real world and virtual elements are brought together, virtual objects in the real world are enriched and harmonized with the real World (Azuma, 1993: 50; Burdea and Coiffet, 2003; Manuri and Sanna, 2016: 18). In the definition of Van Krevelen & Poelman (2010), augmented reality is a structure formed by simultaneously enriching the real image and the virtual image. According to Azuma (1997), augmented reality is a variation of virtual environments or virtual reality. (AR) is a system that presents the real world to the user with computer-provided input such as information, audio, video, graphics or GPS data (Marimon vd., 2010: 1; Johnston, 2014: 24; Jenny, 2017: 7; Nelson, 2016: 2; Yagol, 2018: 5). Also, AG also be defined as any situation where a real environment is augmented with virtual (computer graphic) objects. It refers to any system that combines real and virtual content, real-time interactive and recorded in three dimensions (Steffen et al., 2019).

AR data, created by transferring the images captured by the user in the real world to digital media via camera, camera glasses, smart watches, mobile phones or tablets (Neuburger et al., 2018). AR allows the user to see the real world combined with virtual objects. Thus, the user interacts with the real world in a natural way (Bellalouna, 2021). There are variations of AR, but what they all have in common are displays, input devices, monitoring and computers (Carmigniani et al., 2011). The AR system has three basic features. (1) It is combining real and virtual objects in a real environment, (2) aligning real and virtual objects, and (3) working interactively, in three dimensions and in real time (Azuma, 1997).

The first augmented reality prototype for tourism purposes called Touring Machine was prepared by Feiner et al. in 1997 as a graphical guide for Columbia University campus visitors (Azuma et al., 2001: 4). Application issues of augmented reality technologies in the field of cultural heritage; presentation, interpretation (archaeologists, art historians and architects who use AR as a research tool can conduct their research better), geographical information, various information, endangered heritage sites, documentation, visualization, education and individuals with physical disabilities (Özgan, 2012). Augmented reality offers an important opportunity to preserve heritage sites in destinations (Guttentag, 2010: 643-644; Jung et al., 2016: 622; Bec et al., 2019: 117). In addition, less harm is done to the environment by eliminating the use of paper in transactions such as reservations (Chiao et al., 2018: 31). With augmented reality, many touristic items such as museums, exhibitions and outdoor places offer unique experiences (He et al., 2018). In this way, tourists can experience the story behind the real environment in a personalized way.

Three Dimensional 3D Reconstructions

Digitalized cultural heritage elements are conveyed to visitors by using virtual technologies through various programs and by storytelling these experiences. Digital storytelling, which started to be used in the 90's and has become widespread with social media and smart phones today; is a narrative technique performed by using digital tools (Caffo and Canale, 2014: 5-14). The storytelling method created through digital technologies contributes to the conservation of cultural heritage directly and indirectly (Selmanovic et al., 2018: 57).

The use of 3D technologies, which are effective in transferring and protecting cultural heritage to digital media, is developing rapidly thanks to technological developments. Virtual museums have emerged with 3D models of structures such as sites, monuments, historical artifacts, sculptures (Guarnieri et al., 2010; Merchán, et al., 2019). With the digital imaging method 3D modeling, the entire shape of the digitally archived work is reconstructed virtually (Rizzi et al., 2007). Creating 3D models of objects is of great importance in preserving, maintaining and transferring historical artifacts to future generations. In addition to physical protection, 3D documentation also provides the protection of structures and culture. According to Bruno et al. (2010), this technology is of great importance in the preservation, reconstruction, documentation, research and promotion of cultural heritage.

Established modeling techniques such as laser scanning, closer range scanning, photogrammetry, mobile mapping or a combination of desired techniques can be used to produce 3D models of heritage assets (Aburamadan et al., 2021). 3D models in cultural heritage are used not only for documentation and visualization purposes, but also for producing copies of original works of art, preserving their original form and storing them permanently. In addition, 3D digital cultural heritage models are also used in other fields such as education, research, tourism, virtual and augmented reality (Scopigno et al., 2011; Rahaman et al., 2019; Nishanbaev, 2021).

The benefits of digital archiving of cultural heritage are listed as follows: Processing objects for different purposes in the digital environment (Haddad, 2010), ensuring that information about the shape and appearance of an object is not lost; To ensure the dissemination of 3D modeled objects to a wide audience through virtual museums; to ensure that objects are protected by making copies (Remondino,

2011), to ensure that information can be accessed when it is difficult to obtain data from real structures (Gomes et al., 2014). In addition, thanks to digital 3D modeling, damaged parts of structures or artifacts can be restored virtually and virtual restoration can be performed without compromising their original form (Farazis et al., 2019). 3D measuring tools and techniques allow 3D digitization of tangible values in cultural heritage from the smallest to the largest. This rapid evolution in technology has significantly advanced the preservation of cultural heritage in digital form (Nishanbaev, 2021).

Mobile Devices and Virtual Guidance

Mobile electronic devices are playing an increasingly common role in daily activities. Tourists are increasingly following the important places and activities related to their destinations via mobile applications (Feiner, 2002; Kyela and Štorková, 2015: 930). With the mobile application, cultural heritage sites are customized according to the preferences of people such as visual identity and general appearance, and interactive activities can be offered to visitors (Vrettakis, 2019). Tourists will be able to visualize historical sites and beautiful landscapes using 3D objects in real-time locations. At this point, mobile augmented reality (MobiAR) can provide location-based and personalized information to users while navigating somewhere, and can provide information according to visitors' special interests, demographics and wishes. Thus, the visits of tourists can be personalized according to their wishes (Akram and Kumar, 2017: 170; İlhan and Çeltek, 2016: 587; Marimon et al., 2010: 1).

Digital Storytelling Technique

Experiences are narrated to visitors through various programs using virtual technologies. Digital storytelling; It is a narrative technique performed using digital tools in digital environments such as social media and smartphones (Caffo and Canale, 2014: 5-14). According to Hartley and McWilliam (2009: 3), digital storytelling is digital-based tools used to create audio stories about any topic. Digital stories combine media and motifs to convey cultural heritage through narratives (Wong, 2015). Digital storytelling is an effective method of conveying important information by providing a way to send messages to the audience through multiple ways such as visual, verbal, and music that do not rely on a single method (Gray et al., 2015).

Digital stories divided into three types as personal stories, stories examining historical events, and informative or instructive stories (Robin, 2008). Personal stories are consisting of memories, lived events, places that are important in our lives, stories such as love and affection. Stories examining historical events tells about historical or fictional events and situations such as a historical figure, war, invention. Informative or instructive stories are prepared to inform listeners and viewers (Borneman & Gibson, 2011).

The technique of telling stories with digital tools is an action that reproduces and revives culture. At this point, it contributes to people re-living their heritage and feeling that they belong to a community (Abrahamson, 1998: 451). In addition, digital storytelling methods enable cultural heritage exhibitions to be personalized and offer different cultural experiences (Ardissono et al., 2012: 73). It helps visitors to have their own personal experience, blending cultural data and learning about ancient culture (Floch and Jiang, 2015: 504).

Narration in heritage sites is also an ideal strategy for visitors to create their own meanings by experiencing different experiences and to discover the intersection between the familiar and the unknown (Hein, 1998: 177). Digital storytelling methods used for cultural heritage presentations consist of stories and virtual environments that present interactive 3D models of artifacts (Rizvic, 2017: 50). Many museums use digital storytelling methods to attract more visitors and interact with people (Johnson et al., 2016: 31). Especially in heritage areas, mostly digital storytelling systems consist of voice guidance tools More extensive interaction has been achieved recently with the use of transmedia narration methods. Another feature of this method is that when a story is wanted to be told through digital media in places such as museums and open heritage sites, it can be done with appropriate devices (Caffo and Canale, 2014: 14). In heritage areas, objects and their stories can be accessed via digital tools such as mobile devices and tablets, and interaction can be established between the museum and people. (Hudson Smith et al., 2012: 1183; Rizvic, 2017: 50).

Digital Cultural Heritage Projects in Turkey and Europe

Some exemplary projects in the digitalization of cultural heritage are as follows:

Europe

CALIMERA (Cultural Applications: Local Institutions Mediating Electronic Resources): The project, which deals with the issue of digitalization on a very large scale, is carried out with the aim of digitalising and opening access to local cultural institutions (libraries, museums, archives) in Europe (Calimera, 2005: 26).

Pulman (Public Libraries Mobilizing Advanced Networks): It is a project initiated by European Union member and candidate member countries in May 2001 and aiming to develop cooperation among public libraries, museums and archives in these countries based on information technologies. The goal of the project is to increase the efficiency of public libraries, archives and museums (Pulman XT, 2002).

NINCH (National Initiative for Networked Cultural Heritage): It is a non-profit project that provides access to local cultural heritage. It was jointly initiated by the American Council and the Getty Information Institute in 1993 (NINCH, 2021).

ERPANET (Electronic Resources Preservation and Access Network): It is a project created by the European Commission aiming to establish an expandable European initiative, providing digital protection and access to cultural heritage and scientific objects (ERPANET, 2021).

InterPARES (International Research on Permanent Authentic Records in Electronic Systems) is a collaborative initiative of stakeholders to develop strategic, methodological and applied knowledge that defines best practices on digital preservation (InterPARES, 2021). Turkey joined this initiative in 2008.

CEDARS (Curl Exemplars in Digital Archives), The project aims to raise awareness of the importance of digital preservation, establish strategic frameworks for management policies, and promote appropriate methods for long-term preservation (Day, 1998).

CAMILEON (Creatieve Archiving at Michigan & Leeds: Emulating the Old on The New) is a project by the Universities of Michigan and Leeds that concluded in 2003 a technical set of strategies for the long-term preservation of digital materials (CAMILEON, 2021).

NEDLIB (Networked European Deposit Library) is a project carried out by 8 national libraries in Europe (Netherlands, France, Norway, Finland, Germany, Portugal, Switzerland, Italy). It was built on the creation of a digital network structure of these libraries (NEDLIB, 2021).

EUROPEANA: Another prominent initiative in the digitalization of cultural heritage products is the Europeana project, which enables access to Europe's cultural and scientific heritage via the Internet.

The mission of Europeana is explained as providing open access to cultural heritage in digital environment and encouraging the exchange of ideas and information (Europeana, 2016a). The overall aim of Europeana is to enable multicultural and multilingual environments to access Europe's rich heritage with the help of technological developments and new business models. (Eur-Lex, 2008).

Turkey

In the 1970s, manuscripts began to be digitalized in the National Library for the first time. Unlike museums, the digitalized manuscripts can be viewed by users and access to copies can be made at the same time. Some of the institutions that perform digitalization studies are the TBMM Library, General Directorate of State Archives, Atatürk Library, Islamic History, Art and Culture Research Center (IRCICA), Islamic Studies Center (ISAM), TRT Archive, Topkapı Museum, Vehbi Koç and Ankara Studies Center (VEKAM).

With Access IT ((Accelerate the Circulation of Culture Through Exchange of Skills in Information Technology), the necessary training and education services are provided in the countries within the scope of the project to transfer cultural and artistic works to the European Digital Library and to ensure wide and equal access to these works by Turkish and European citizens. AccesIT, 2011; Yılmaz, 2011: 118). This project includes digitization studies performed at the Ankara Anatolian Civilizations Museum. In the following process, a wide range of inventories consisting of manuscripts, objects, documents, photographs and maps from the National Library and Vehbi Koç Ankara Studies (VEKAM) were transferred to Europeana, the European Digital Library, with the LoCloud (Local Content in Europeana Cloud) project (Ülger and Külcü, 2016).

CONCLUSION

The protection of cultural heritage and its transfer to future generations have become the main responsibility of today's societies and the fundamental right of future generations to reach this heritage. With the development of digitalization day by day, the production of information, how it will be interpreted, how it will disseminate, and the way of consumption after access to information have begun to change over time. Developments in information and communication technologies have common responsibilities such as protecting the cultural heritage products of libraries, archives and museums, ensuring that they are accessible and transferring these products to future generations.Cultural heritage products that shed light on history, the past and the future are increasing day by day and the protection and storage conditions of valuable heritage products are starting to differentiate with the rapidly developing society. Disciplining the protection and transfer of cultural heritage with various laws and regulations undoubtedly plays an important role in the success of these actions.

Today, the advancement of technology has led to the development of devices that make the use of the internet more widespread in accordance with this technology. Digital technology is a term that covers any communication device or application that includes radio, television, cellular, telephone, computer and network hardware and software (Pocobelli et al., 2018). With these devices, people have been provided with easy access to all kinds of information they need over the internet. Individuals, organizations, communities are increasingly using digital technologies to document what they value and want to transfer to future generations. It is seen that digitization processes, which cover processes such as protection and renewal, maintenance, heritage management, interpretation, documentation and research, go beyond the traditional structure and take an international dimension blended with technology in order to ensure the sustainability of cultural assets and to increase their access. With digitization, people have started to access cultural heritage products more, regardless of time and place. Cultural heritage products, which include sites that are on the verge of extinction, monuments, traditions, epics, documents that shed light on history, travel books, stamps, photographs and many more, have started to open more access channels to users by being included in the axis of the digital world. Digitized cultural heritage items will not only serve as documents in the field of architectural preservation, but will contribute to many industries and business lines with their open accessibility.

REFERENCES

Abraham, J. (2015). The role of curiosity in making up digital content promoting cultural heritage. *Procedia: Social and Behavioral Sciences*, *184*, 259–265. doi:10.1016/j.sbspro.2015.05.089

Abrahamson, C. E. (1998). Storytelling as a pedagogical tool in higher education. *Education*, *118*(3), 440–452.

Aburamadan, R., Trillo, C., Udeaja, C., Moustaka, A., Awuah, K. G., & Makore, B. C. (2021). Heritage conservation and digital technologies in Jordan. *Digital Applications in Archaeology and Cultural Heritage*, *22*, e00197. doi:10.1016/j.daach.2021.e00197

AccessIT Türk Takımı. (n.d.). Accessed on June 14, 2021. http://www.accessit.hacettepe.edu.tr/index.php?kid=30&s=AccessIT%20AB%20Projesi%20Hakk%C4%B1nda

Addison, A. C. (2000). Emerging trends in virtual heritage. *IEEE MultiMedia*, *7*(2), 22–25. doi:10.1109/93.848421

Ardissono, L., Kuflik, T., & Petrelli, D. (2012). Personalization in cultural heritage: The road travelled and the one ahead. *User Modeling and User-Adapted Interaction*, *22*(1-2), 73–99. doi:10.100711257-011-9104-x

Arnold, D., & Geser, G. (2008). *EPOCH research agenda for the applications of ICT to cultural heritage*. EPOCH Project.

Azuma, R. (1993). Tracking requirements for augmented reality. *Communications of the ACM*, *36*(7), 50–51. doi:10.1145/159544.159581

Azuma, R., Baillot, Y., Behringer, R., Feiner, S., Julier, S., & MacIntyre, B. (2001). Recent advances in augmented reality. *IEEE Computer Graphics and Applications*, *21*(6), 34–47. doi:10.1109/38.963459

Azuma, R. T. (1997). A Survey of Augmented Reality. *Teleoperatorsand Virtual Environments*, *6*(4), 355–385. doi:10.1162/pres.1997.6.4.355

Basaraba, N. (2018). A communication model for non-fiction interactive digital narratives: A study of cultural heritage websites. *Frontiers of Narrative Studies*, *4*(1), 48–75. doi:10.1515/fns-2018-0032

Bautista, S. S. (2013). *Museums in The Digital Age: Changing Meanings of Place, Community, and Culture Lanham*. AltaMira Press.

Bellalouna, F. (2021). The Augmented Reality Technology as Enabler for the Digitization of Industrial Business Processes: Case Studies. *Procedia CIRP, 98*, 400–405. doi:10.1016/j.procir.2021.01.124

Bettington, J., Eberhard, K., Loo, R., & Smith, C. (Eds.). (2008). *Keeping archives*. Australian Society of Archivists Incorporated.

Bogicevic, V., Seo, S., Kandampully, J. A., Liu, S. Q., & Rudd, N. A. (2019). Virtual reality presence as a preamble of tourism experience: The role of mental imagery. *Tourism Management, 74*, 55–64. doi:10.1016/j.tourman.2019.02.009

Borneman, D., & Gibson, K. (2011). Digital storytelling: Meeting standards across the curriculum in a WWII/Holocaust unit. *School Library Monthly, 27*(7), 16–17.

Brayton, J. (2003). *The Meaning and Experience of Virtual Reality* (Ph.D. Dissertation). Dept of Sociology, University of New Brunswick.

Bruno, F., Bruno, S., De Sensi, G., Luchi, M. L., Mancuso, S., & Muzzupappa, M. (2010). From 3D reconstruction to virtual reality: A complete methodology for digital archaeological exhibition. *Journal of Cultural Heritage, 11*(1), 42–49. doi:10.1016/j.culher.2009.02.006

Burdea, G. C., & Coiffet, P. (2003). *Virtual Reality Technology* (2nd ed.). Wiley-Interscience. doi:10.1162/105474603322955950

Caffo, R. & Canale, D. (2014). *Digital Cultural Heritage and Tourism Recommendations for Cultural Institutions*. Version 1.0, 2 October 2014.

Caffo, R., Canale, D., Conticello, A., Natale, M. T., Petrangeli, P., & Piccininno, M. (2014). *Digital Cultural Heritage and Tourism Recommendations for Cultural Institutions*. Antenna International.

CAMILEON. (2021). *Dijital Curation Centre*. Accessed on June 14, 2021. https://www.dcc.ac.uk/resources/external/camileon-creative-archiving-michigan-and-leeds-emulating-old-new

Carmigniani, J., Furht, B., Anisetti, M., Ceravolo, P., Damiani, E., & Ivkovic, M. (2011). Augmented reality technologies, systems and applications. *Multimedia Tools and Applications, 51*(1), 341–377. doi:10.100711042-010-0660-6

Chiao, H. M., Chen, Y. L., & Huang, W. H. (2018). Examining the usability of an online virtual tour-guiding platform for cultural tourism education. *Journal of Hospitality, Leisure, Sport and Tourism Education, 23*, 29–38. doi:10.1016/j.jhlste.2018.05.002

Cirulis, A., De Paolis, L. T., & Tutberidze, M. (2015). Virtualization of digitalized cultural heritage and use case scenario modeling for sustainability promotion of national identity. *Procedia Computer Science, 77*, 199–206. doi:10.1016/j.procs.2015.12.384

Council of Europe. (2005). *Council of Europe Framework Convention on the Value of Cultural Heritage for Society*. Accessed on October 4, 2021 https://rm.coe.int/1680083746 >

Craig, A. B., Sherman, W. R., & Will, J. D. (2009). *Developing virtual reality applications foundations of effective design*. Morgan Kaufmann Publishers.

Day, M. (1998). *CEDARS: Digital preservation and metadata*. Conference: 6th DELOS Workshop: Preservation of Digital Information, Tomar, Portugal.

Dictionary, C. (2021). Accessed on October 1, 2021. https://dictionary.cambridge.org/dictionary/english/culture>

Elfadaly, A., Attia, W., Qelichi, M. M., Murgante, B., & Lasaponara, R. (2018). Management of Cultural Heritage Sites Using Remote Sensing Indices and Spatial Analysis Techniques. *Surveys in Geophysics*, *39*(6), 1347–1377. doi:10.100710712-018-9489-8

Emekli, G. (2012). *Kültür Mirasının Turizm Aracılığı ile Değerlendirilmesi: Kültürel Turizm ve İzmir. Buca İlçesinin Ekoturizm ve Kültür Turizmi Sektör Analizi Projesi, Kültür Turizmi Çalıştayı,8 Şubat 2012*. İzmir Kalkınma Ajansı-Buca Belediyesi, Buca.

ERPANET. (2021). Accessed on June 14, 20021. https://www.erpanet.org/about.php

Eur-Lex. (2008). *i2010: Digital libraries*. Accessed on June 19, 2021. http lex.europa.eu/legal-content/EN/TXT/?uri=URISERV%3Al24226i

Europeana. (2016). Accessed on June 19, 2021. http://www.europeana.eu/portal/

Farazis, G., Thomopoulos, C., Bourantas, C., Mitsigkola, S., & Thomopoulos, S. C. (2019). Digital approaches for public outreach in cultural heritage: The case study of iGuide Knossos and Ariadne's Journey. *Digital Applications in Archaeology and Cultural Heritage*, *15*, e00126. doi:10.1016/j.daach.2019.e00126

Ferdani, D., Pagano, A., & Farouk, M. (2014). *Terminology, Definitions and Types for Virtual Museums*. Retrieved from http://www.v-must.net/sites/default/files/D2.1c%20V_Must_TERMINOLOGY_V2014_FINAL.pdf

Floch, J., & Jiang, S. (2015). *One place, many stories digital storytelling for cultural heritage discovery in the landscape. In 2015 Digital Heritage* (Vol. 2). IEEE.

Franchi, E. (2017). *What is Cultural Heritage?* Available at https://www.khanacademy.org/humanities/art-history-basics/beginners-art- history/a/what-is-cultural-heritage

Gasimova, R. T., & Abbasli, R. N. (2020). Advancement of the search process for digital heritage by utilizing artificial intelligence algorithms. *Expert Systems with Applications*, *158*, 113559. doi:10.1016/j.eswa.2020.113559

Gomes, L., Bellon, O. R. P., & Silva, L. (2014). 3D reconstruction methods for digital preservation of cultural heritage: A survey. *Pattern Recognition Letters*, *50*, 3–14. doi:10.1016/j.patrec.2014.03.023

Gomez, D., Burdea, G., & Langrana, N. (1995). Integration of the Rutgers Master II in a Virtual Reality Simulation. *Virtual Reality Annual International Symposium*, 198-202. 10.1109/VRAIS.1995.512496

Gong, Y. (2021). Application of virtual reality teaching method and artificial intelligence technology in digital media art creation. *Ecological Informatics*, *63*, 101304. doi:10.1016/j.ecoinf.2021.101304

Gray, B., Young, A., & Blomfield, T. (2015). Altered Lives: Assessing the Effectiveness of Digital Storytelling as a Form of Communication Design. *Continuum, 29*(4), 635–649. doi:10.1080/1030431 2.2015.1025359

Guidelines, C. (2005). *Good practice guide.* Accessed on June 14, 2021. https://www.calimera.org/Countries/Turkey.aspx

Guttentag, D. A. (2010). Virtual reality: Applications and Implications for Tourism. *Tourism Management, 31*(5), 637–651. doi:10.1016/j.tourman.2009.07.003

Haddad, N. A. (2010). From Ground Surveying to 3D Laser Scanner: A Review of Techniques Used for Spatial Documentation of Historic Sites. *Journal of King Saud University, 23*(2), 109–118. doi:10.1016/j.jksues.2011.03.001

Hancock, M. (2018). *Culture is digital: executive summary, Department for Digital, Culture, Media and Sport.* Available at: www.gov.uk/government/publications/culture-is-digital/culture-is-digital

Hartley, J., & McWilliam, K. (Eds.). (2009). *Story circle.* Wiley-Blackwell. doi:10.1002/9781444310580

He, Z., Wu, L., & Li, X. (2018). When art meets tech: The role of augmented reality in enhancing museum experiences and purchase intentions. *Tourism Management, 68*, 127–139. doi:10.1016/j.tourman.2018.03.003

Hein, G. E. (1998). *Learning in the Museum.* Routledge.Holdsworth, D. (2007). *Instalment on Preservation Strategies for Digital Libraries Leeds University.* Version 1.0. Accessed on October 1, 2021. https://www.dcc.ac.uk/resource/curation-manual/chapters/preservationstrategies-digital-libraries

Heritage, C. (2002). Accessed on October 4, 2021. http://www.cultureindevelopment.nl/cultural_heritage/what_is_cultural_heritage

Hudson-Smith, A., Gray, S., Ross, C., Barthel, R., De Jode, M., Warwick, C., & Terras, M. (2012). Experiments with the internet of things in museum space: QRator. *Proceedings of the 2012 ACM Conference on Ubiquitous Computing*, 1183-1184. 10.1145/2370216.2370469

InterPARES. (2021). Accessed on June 14, 2021. http://www.interpares.org/background.htm

Jenny, S. (2017). *Enhancing Tourism with Augmented and Virtual Reality* [Unpublished doctoral dissertation]. Degree Programme in Business Information Technology Häme University of Applied Sciences.

Jin, V. (2011). Virtual Reality Technology in the Design of the Space Environment Research. In *2011 International Conference on Control, Automation and Systems Engineering (CASE)* (pp. 1-4). IEEE.

Johnson, L., Becker, S. A., Cummins, M., Estrada, V., Freeman, A., & Hall, C. (2016). *NMC horizon report: 2016 higher education.* Academic Press.

Johnston, R. S. (2014). *History in Your Hand: A Case Study of Digital History and Augmented Reality Using Mound 72* [Unpublished doctoral dissertation]. Graduate School Southern Illinois University Edwardsville.

Jung, T., Dieck, T. M. C., Lee, H., & Chung, N. (2016). Effects of Virtual Reality and Augmented Reality on Visitor Experiences in Museum. In Information and Communication Technologies in Tourism. New York: Springer International Publishing. doi:10.1007/978-3-319-28231-2_45

Katz, J., & Tokovinine, A. (2017). The past, now showing in 3D: An introduction. *Digital Applications in Archaeology and Cultural Heritage*, 6, 1–3. doi:10.1016/j.daach.2017.09.001

Kolivand, H., El Rhalibi, A., Sunar, M. S., & Saba, T. (2018). ReVitAge: Realistic virtual heritage taking shadows and sky illumination into account. *Journal of Cultural Heritage*, *32*, 166–175. doi:10.1016/j.culher.2018.01.020

Kuşçuoğlu, G. Ö., & Taş, M. (2017). Sürdürülebilir kültürel miras yönetimi. *Yalvaç Akademi Dergisi*, *2*(1), 58–67.

Lavoie, B. (2014). *The Open Archival Information System (OAIS) Reference Model: Introductory guide (2. bs)*. Digital Preservation Coalition.

MacDonald, L. (2006). *Digital heritage*. Routledge. doi:10.4324/9780080455303

Manuri, F., & Sanna, A. (2016). Survey on Applications of Augmented Reality. *ACSIJ Advances in Computer Science: an International Journal*, *5*(1), 18–27.

Marimon, D., Sarasua, C., Carrasco, P., Alvarez, R., Montesa, J., Adamek, T., Romero, I., Ortega, M., & Gascó, P. (2010). *MobiAR: Tourist Experiences through Mobile Augmented Reality*. Paper presented at the 2010 NEM Summit, Barcelona, Spain.

McKercher, B., & du Cros, H. (2012). *Cultural Tourism: The Partnership Between Tourism and Cultural Heritage Management*. Routledge. doi:10.4324/9780203479537

Merchán, M. J., Merchán, P., Salamanca, S., Pérez, E., & Nogales, T. (2019). Digital fabrication of cultural heritage artwork replicas. In the search for resilience and socio-cultural commitment. *Digital Applications in Archaeology and Cultural Heritage*, *15*, e00125. doi:10.1016/j.daach.2019.e00125

Merkx, C., & Nawijn, J. (2021). Virtual reality tourism experiences: Addiction and isolation. *Tourism Management*, *87*, 104394. doi:10.1016/j.tourman.2021.104394

MINERVA. (2021). Accessed on June 14, 2021. https://cordis.europa.eu/project/id/IST-2001-35461/it

NEDLİB. (2021). Accessed on June 14, 2021. http://www.ifs.tuwien.ac.at/~aola/publications/thesis-ando/NEDLIB.html

Nelson, T. (2016). *Impact of Virtual and Augmented Reality on Theme Parks* [Unpublished doctoral dissertation]. Master of Digital Media, Ryerson University.

Neuburger, L., Beck, J., & Egger, R. (2018). The 'Phygital' Tourist Experience: the Use of Augmented and Virtual Reality in Destination Marketing. In *Tourism Planning and Destination Marketing* (pp. 183–202). Emerald Publishing Limited. doi:10.1108/978-1-78756-291-220181009

NINCH. (2021). Accessed on June 14, 2021. https://www.ninch.org/about/mission.html

Nishanbaev, I. (2020). A web repository for geo-located 3D digital cultural heritage models. *Digital Applications in Archaeology and Cultural Heritage, 16*, e00139. doi:10.1016/j.daach.2020.e00139

Noh, Z., Sunar, M. S., & Pan, Z. (2009, August). A review on augmented reality for virtual heritage system. In *International conference on technologies for E-learning and digital entertainment* (pp. 50-61). Springer. 10.1007/978-3-642-03364-3_7

Oğuz, Ö. (2009). Somut Olmayan Kültürel Miras ve Kültürel İfade Çeşitliliği. *Milli Folklor, 82*, 6–12.

Oksaar, E. (2008). *"Kültürlerarası İletişim Bağlamında Kültür Kuramı"*, *Çev: Ayhan Selçuk*. Çizgi Kitabevi.

Özen, L., & Demirdelen, H. (2011). Access IT projesi müzelerde dijitalleştirme ve Europeana. *Türk Kütüphaneciliği, 25*(1), 132–136.

Özgan, S. Y. (2012). *Use Of Augmented Reality Technologies In Cultural Heritage Sites; Virtu(Re)Al Yenikapi* [Unpublished Master dissertation]. Istanbul Technical University Graduate School of Science Engineering And Technology, Istanbul, Turkey.

Pescarin, S. (2013). *Virtual Museums: From the Italian experience to a transnational network*. Academic Press.

Pescarin, S., Rizvic, S., & Selimovic, D. (2012). V-MUST. NET-The virtual museum transnational network. *Преглед НЦД, 21*, 47–56.

Portales, C., Rodrigues, J. M. F., Goncalves, A. R., Alba, E., & Sebastian, J. (2018). Digital cultural heritage. *Multimodal Technologies Interact, 2*(3), 58. doi:10.3390/mti2030058

Psomadaki, O. I., Dimoulas, C. A., Kalliris, G. M., & Paschalidis, G. (2019). Digital storytelling and audience engagement in cultural heritage management: A collaborative model based on the Digital City of Thessaloniki. *Journal of Cultural Heritage, 36*, 12–22. doi:10.1016/j.culher.2018.07.016

Pulman-XT. (2002). Türkiye Ulusal Toplantısı Sonuç Bildirgesi. *Türk Kütüphaneciliği, 16*(4), 461–464.

Rahaman, H., Champion, E., & Bekele, M. (2019). From photo to 3D to mixed reality: A complete workflow for cultural heritage visualisation and experience. *Digital Applications in Archaeology and Cultural Heritage, 13*, e00102. doi:10.1016/j.daach.2019.e00102

Rahaman. H., & Tan. B., (2009). Virtual Heritage: Reality and Criticism. *PUM 2009, Joining Languages, Cultures and Visions: CAADFutures*.

Remondino, F. (2011). Heritage recording and 3D modeling with photogrammetry and 3D scanning. *Remote Sensing, 3*(6), 1104–1138. doi:10.3390/rs3061104

Rizvić, S. (2017). How to Breathe Life into Cultural Heritage 3D Reconstructions. *European Review (Chichester, England), 25*(1), 39–50. doi:10.1017/S106279871600034X

Rizzi, A., Voltolini, F., Girardi, S., Gonzo, L., & Remondino, F. (2007). *Digital Preservation, Documentation and Analysis of Paintings, Monuments and Large Cultural Heritage With Infrared Technology, Digital Cameras and Range Sensors*. Paper presented at the XXI International CIPA Symposium, Athens, Greece.

Robin, B. R. (2008). Digital Storytelling: A Powerful Technology Tool for the 21st Century Classroom. *Theory into Practice*, *47*(3), 220–228. doi:10.1080/00405840802153916

Robinson, H. (2012). Remembering things differently: Museums, libraries and archives as memory institutions and the implications for convergence. *Museum Management and Curatorship*, *27*(4), 413–429. doi:10.1080/09647775.2012.720188

Roussou, M. (2002). Virtual heritage: From the research lab to the broad public. *Bar International Series*, *1075*, 93–100.

Scopigno, R., Callieri, M., Cignoni, P., Corsini, M., Dellepiane, M., Ponchio, F., & Ranzuglia, G. (2011). 3D models for cultural heritage: Beyond plain visualization. *Computer*, *44*(7), 48–55. doi:10.1109/MC.2011.196

Scopigno, R., Cignoni, P., Pietroni, N., Callieri, M., & Dellepiane, M. (2017). Digital fabrication techniques for cultural heritage: A survey. *Computer Graphics Forum*, *36*(1), 6–21. doi:10.1111/cgf.12781

Selmanovic, E., Rizvic, S., Harvey, C., Boskovic, D., Hulusic, V., Chahin, M., & Sljivo, S. (2018). VR Video Storytelling for Intangible Cultural Heritage Preservation. *Eurographics Workshop on Graphics and Cultural Heritage Conference*.

Shimray, S. R., & Ramaiah, C.K. (2019). Cultural Heritage Awareness among students of Pondicherry University: A Study. *Library Philosophy and Practice*, 1-10.

Steffen, J. H., Gaskin, J. E., Meservy, T. O., Jenkins, J. L., & Wolman, I. (2019). Framework of affordances for virtual reality and augmented reality. *Journal of Management Information Systems*, *36*(3), 683–729. doi:10.1080/07421222.2019.1628877

Thwaites, H., Santano, D., Esmaeili, H., & See, Z. S. (2019). A Malaysian cultural heritage digital compendium. *Digital Applications in Archaeology and Cultural Heritage*, *15*, e00116. doi:10.1016/j.daach.2019.e00116

Timothy, D. J. (2011). *Cultural Heritage and Tourism: An Introduction*. Cahnnel View Publications. doi:10.21832/9781845411787

UNESCO. (2001). *Universal Declaration on Cultural Diversity*. Accessed on October 6, 2021. https://www.refworld.org/docid/435cbcd64.html

UNESCO. (2003). *Report by the Governing Board on the Activities of the UNESCO Institute for Information Technologies in Education (2002-2003)*. UNESCO.

UNESCO. (2014). *Tangible Cultural Heritage*. Accessed on June 19, 2021. http://www.unesco.org/new/en/cairo/culture/tangible- cultural-heritage/

UNESCO (2017). *Convention for the Safeguarding of the Intangible Cultural Heritage*. UNESCO.

Van Krevelen, D. W. F., & Poelman, R. (2010). A survey of augmented reality technologies, applications and limitations. *The International Journal of Virtual Reality: a Multimedia Publication for Professionals*, *9*(2), 1–20. doi:10.20870/IJVR.2010.9.2.2767

Villalba, É. E., Azócar, A. L. S. M., & Jacques-García, F. A. (2021). State of the art on immersive virtual reality and its use in developing meaningful empathy. *Computers & Electrical Engineering, 93*, 107272. doi:10.1016/j.compeleceng.2021.107272

Virtual Museum Transitional Network. (2021). Retrieved from http://www.v-must.net/virtual-museums

Vrettakis, E., Kourtis, V., Katifori, A., Karvounis, M., Lougiakis, C., & Ioannidis, Y. (2019). Narralive–Creating and experiencing mobile digital storytelling in cultural heritage. *Digital Applications in Archaeology and Cultural Heritage, 15*, e00114. doi:10.1016/j.daach.2019.e00114

Wong, A. (2015). The whole story, and then some:'digital storytelling'in evolving museum practice. *MW2015. Museums and the Web, 2015*, 8–11.

Yagol, P. (2018). *Improving the User Knowledge and User Experience by using Augmented Reality in a Smart City context* [Unpublished doctoral dissertation]. Degree of Master of Science in Geospatial Technologies.

Yazmaları, T. (2016). *İstatistikler.* Accessed on June 19, 2021. https://www.yazmalar.gov.tr/istatistik.php

Yılmaz, B. (2011). Dijital Kütüphane Becerileri Konusunda Türkiye'de Durum: AccessIT Projesi Çerçevesinde Bir Değerlendirme. *Türk Kütüphaneciliği, 25*(1), 117–123.

Yılmaz, L. (2020). Mersin'de Somut Kültürel Miras Bilinci ve Koruma Üzerine Bir Değerlendirme. *Amisos, 5/8*, 156–177.

Zarnowski, A., Anna, B., & Banaszek, S. (2015). Application of technical measures and software in constructing photorealistic 3D models of historical building using ground-based and aerial (UAV) digital images. *Reports on Geodesy and Geoinformatics, 99*(1), 54–63. doi:10.2478/rgg-2015-0012

KEY TERMS AND DEFINITIONS

3D Reconstructions: Creation and development of three-dimensional images of objects in computer environment using special software.

Augmented Reality: Environments created by the interaction of virtual objects and real-world images.

Digital Cultural Heritage: Heritage that can be processed, modified, and shared in a virtual space of archaeological, historical, artistic, and cultural attractions.

Digital Heritage: Values produced directly from existing tangible resources or digitally.

Digital Storytelling: Combining traditional storytelling with technology using digital graphics, video, and audio narration.

Virtual Museum: An organized collection of all digitized artifacts and information resources in a virtual environment.

Virtual Reality: Environments structured on a virtual environment produced with various graphics, animations, and special sound effects, combined with human senses, and perceiving oneself as if one is a part of that environment.

APPENDIX: ADDITIONAL CASE STUDY

Virtual Museums Under V-Must.net Project

Museums play an important role in preserving cultural assets and transferring them to future generations. Virtual museums are an important and common form of use in the field of cultural heritage. Virtual museums are effective in disseminating cultural assets to large masses. Web-based virtual museums are low-cost, convenient for researchers, and have a significant potential in promoting cultures. Virtual Museum Transnational NETwork – V-MusT.net – It is a project that provides services to Virtual Museums and research in this field. The project, which consists of 18 partners from 13 different countries, was financed by the European Union fund. The project lasted 4 years between 2011-2014.

The V-Must.net project aims to provide cultural heritage with digital tools to develop Virtual Museums that are educational, entertaining, sustainable and easy to maintain. According to V-Must.net,

Figure 1. Defining virtual museums according to their content
Source: Virtual Museum Transitional Network, 2021

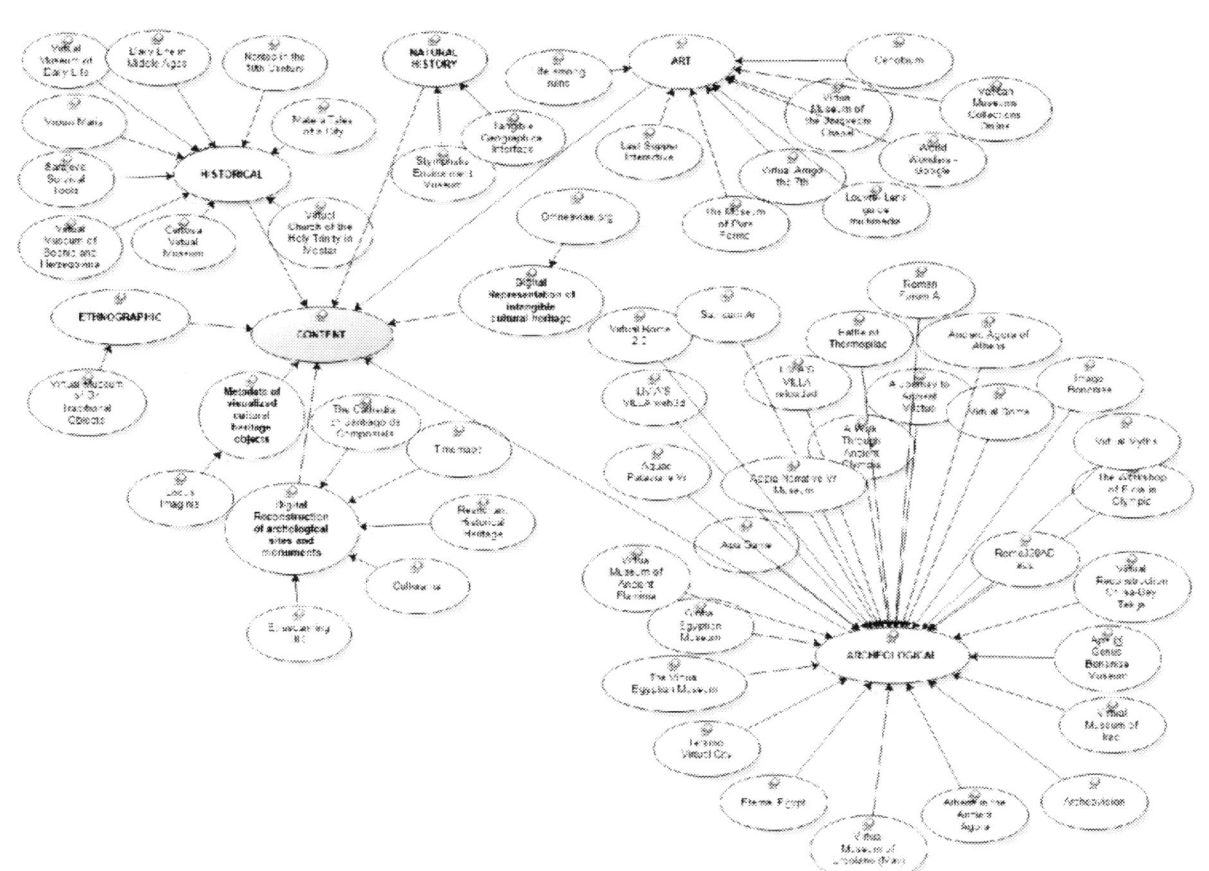

Virtual museum is a new communication model that aims to create an immersive, interactive way that personalizes cultural heritage resources. V-Must.net general strategies are: Changing the approach and perspective to virtual museums, establishing interdisciplinary working groups, using a holistic approach, identifying successful examples, integration of new researchers into the education system. The V-must. net project facilitates the creation, preservation and presentation of virtual museums. It also contributes to the creation, easy access, management and sustainability of digital content.

One of the first activities of V-Must.net was the attempt to define the categories and types of virtual museums. In the project, 8 main categories that can be used to define a virtual museum were determined: Content, interaction technology, duration, narration, level of immersion, sustainability level, format, scope (Pescarin, 2013). Virtual Museums can be defined according to their content (archaeology, art, etc.), type of interaction, duration, communication style, level of immersion, format, scope and sustainability level. (Ferdani, Pagano & Farouk, 2014: 12)

According to virtual museums contents are analyzed by the authors from the V-must.net website with the document analysis method through the Nvivo 11 program. As seen in Figure 1, virtual museums are classified as Art, Historical, Etnographic, Archeological, Metadata of visualized cultural heritage objects, Digital reconstruction of archeological sites and monuments, Natural history, Digital representation of intangible cultural heritage in the V-must.net project. According to the contents of the virtual museums on the website, it is seen that the museums are mostly within the scope of Archeological. People can visit these virtual museums without leaving their place of residence, feeling as if they were there.

While cultural heritage resources exhibited using digital tools in the world meet with consumers on digital platforms, it requires businesses to make some strategic decisions in this area. How can virtual museums be evaluated in terms of marketing strategy, especially in the recession period with the effect of health concerns during the pandemic process and the economic crisis afterwards? Despite all these negativities, it is predicted that virtual museums will be an important player in the sector and there will be serious investments in the future. Could virtual museums be an opportunity during the pandemic?

Source: This case study is prepared by the authors by compiling the information obtained from the web page given below and academic studies on this subject.
http://www.v-must.net/virtual-museums

Chapter 11
A Comprehensive Systematic Literature Review About Smartness in Tourism

Gizem Duran
Kırklareli University, Turkey

Selma Meydan Uygur
Ankara Hacı Bayram Veli University, Turkey

ABSTRACT

With the rapidly developing technology, the tourism experience has started to enrich and innovative/ personalized services and competitive advantage in tourism have started to gain importance. Smartness in tourism refers to tourism activities supported by technology. This study aims to classify the current literature on the subject of smartness in tourism. First of all, a qualitative research was carried out by explaining the concepts of smart tourism and smart tourism destination in the literature. Within the scope of the research, a qualitative research was conducted using systematic literature review method. In the research, 264 academic publications related to smartness in tourism were analyzed in terms of the destinations where they were applied, the scope of the journals they were published, the language of the publication, the methods and approaches, and suggestions were made for further studies.

INTRODUCTION

The widespread use of smartphones, numerous apps and other mobile devices, most notably in recent times, points to an unprecedented connection and an era in which the internet is accessible from anywhere (Gretzel et al., 2015a: p.182). The rapid advancement of technology, this significant increase in technology use, rising population density and consumption, pose a threat to cities and especially the tourism sector where the resource consumption is very intense, the environment and the people living in this environment. Increasing population density causes infrastructure insufficiency, blockage of transportation system, environmental pollution, lack of housing, reduction of agricultural areas, water

DOI: 10.4018/978-1-7998-8528-3.ch011

pollution, increase of carbon and greenhouse gas emissions and unemployment. On the other hand, there are problems brought by technology. The fact that the information is easily accessible also leads to abuse of this information, and dependence on technology restricts social shares and relationships. The tourism sector, however, is a sector where consumption is very intense and may cause some negativities due to the environmental damage in the construction of physical elements. With these growing problems, the need for researching new methods has emerged in order to obtain competitive advantage by producing solutions for these problems and the increasing demand of cities and tourism destinations.These developments bring on the agenda the concept of "smart", which refers to sustainability and technology.

The word smart was first recorded in 1968 as "mental, intelligence". When the concept was referred to as adjective, it was declared in 1972 as "acting smartly guided" (www.etymonline.com). According to Jasrotia and Gangotia (2018), smartness makes it easy to shape products, actions, processes and services in real time by uniting different stakeholders at the same time to optimize collective performance and competitiveness and create solutions and value for everyone. In the context of markets / economies, smartness refers to new forms of cooperation and technologies that support value creation, leading to innovation, entrepreneurship and competitiveness (Gretzel et al., 2015a: p.179). Based on these definitions, issues such as providing the fastest and easiest access to services for the well-being of all stakeholders and the society at these points where technology and consumption have come, creating a common experience involving all stakeholders, minimizing resource consumption and optimizing competitiveness open the way for smartness.

The smart concept required to integrate systems and processes to find solutions can be extended from micro-level goods and services to macro-level cities and nations (Khan et al., 2017: p.1). The concept of "smart city" emerges due to the complexity and management difficulties of the authorities in dealing with the rapid growth of the city population (Cacho et al., 2016: p.817). The term "smart" has been added to cities to define "efforts to use technology in an innovative way to achieve resource optimization, effective and fair governance, sustainability and quality of life (Gretzel et al., 2015a: p.179). In recent years, this concept and the concept of "smart tourism destination" (STD) arising from this concept continue to be increasingly popular in scientific literature and country politics. In order to understand these concepts, it is very important to reveal what is their strategic importance and reasons in planning tourism destinations with cities.

The main issue underlying the importance of these concepts is the need to make cities more efficient through innovative technologies (ICT) that can support the management, monitoring and functioning of cities in terms of better urban quality of service, reduction of environmental impacts and control of energy consumption (La Rocca, 2014: pp.272-273). In terms of tourism destination, in line with the development of the era, it is the integration of personalization (Buhalis and Amaranggana, 2015: p.381) into the said destination through ICT, which is the way to meet the demands of personalized goods and services in order to increase the quality of life of the tourists and improve their tourism experiences (Lamsfus et al., 2013: p.16).

Bringing smartness to tourism destinations means dynamically connecting their stakeholders through a technological platform where they can exchange real-time information about tourism activities (Buonincontri and Micera, 2016: p.288). When the literature is analyzed, it is understood that the concept of smart tourism destination is actually based on smart cities. For example; La Rocca (2014) states that while there are some difficulties in data sharing to manage the tourism phenomenon in urban areas, the smart city phenomenon promotes the smart tourism destination, while Cacho et al. (2016) states that the concept of smart tourism destination arises from the development of smart cities.

Since one of the challenges of the tourism sector is the presence of stakeholders with different interests and consequently, different preferences, the approach to smartness is deemed necessary for this sector as well (Buhalis and Amaranggana, 2015: p.378). The challenge that tourist cities have to face is their ability to find a balance between the promotion and conservation of their historical, cultural, architectural, regional, natural resources (La Rocca, 2014: p.278). For these reasons, smart cities and smart tourism destinations that have recently aimed at resource optimization are turning to the balanced distribution of resources in order to offer better efficiency, better sustainability, better quality of life for tourists and tourists (Khan et al., 2017: p.1). The benefits of smart tourism destinations not only serve tourists, but also serve citizens by improving the quality of their living environments through smart technologies. Indeed, sustainability is an important component of conceptualizing the smart tourism destination (Koo et al., 2016: p.377). As a result of these developments, it is observed that governments and public / private institutions are putting forward the concept of "smartness" by considering developing new policies and strategies that aim economic growth with the growing global sustainable development approach (Boes et al., 2015: p.392).

The most successful tourism experiences are tourism experiences that are created together with tourists and supported by high technology levels (Buonincontri and Micera, 2016: p.292). Having these high technology levels that will enrich the tourist experiences and establishing the process together with tourists as stakeholders can be considered as the basic building blocks that form the concept of "smart" in terms of tourism. According to La Rocca (2014), the new way to share these enriched experiences and feelings, which has radically changed the way to promote touristic cities, should be seen as part of city strategies. The new way that should be a part of these touristic city strategies is to integrate the cities into "smart" by integrating technological infrastructures such as Information Communication Technologies, cloud computing and the Internet of Things (IoT). The expression of Buonincontri and Micera (2016: p.286) that "Bringing smartness to tourism destinations requires the use of a technology platform where information about local resources, tourists, tourist actions and consumption habits can be integrated and used with various stakeholders" supports this idea.

In this chapter, it is aimed to provide a comprehensive understanding of the concept of smart tourism destination and to analyze scientific studies on the subject to date.

BACKGROUND

From Smart City to Smart Destination

The term smart city was first used in the 1990s. Over time, the importance of new Information and Communication Technologies has been emphasized, considering the modern infrastructures of cities (Albino, Berardi and Dangelico, 2015: p.1726). It is aimed to establish mechanisms that follow how certain infrastructure and superstructure systems work in the smart city, to collect data and to increase the quality and effectiveness of the services, to reduce costs and to provide effective control of resources through the collected data (Varol, 2017: p.45).

Many authors try to define the concept of "smart city" in the literature. In these definitions, the smart city has been handled from different angles. For example, considering the concept in terms of sustainability, while it is defined as reducing waste and unnecessary emissions by combining green cities with the technology of the future (Baidal et al., 2017: p.1581); using technology to optimize the use of scarce resources (Ercole, 2013: p.36) and the adoption of technology to optimize resource production and consumption (Gretzel et al; 2015b: p.559), when it is considered for the citizens it is defined as technology-based cities (Boes et al., 2015: p.391) and efforts to improve citizens' access to information (Junior et al., 2017: p.364).

In a study by La Rocca (2013), she described the smart city as similar to the above definitions; In a study conducted in 2014, according to the city planner's point of view, the concept of "smart city" provides better service quality of cities, reducing environmental impacts (pollution of emissions) and control of energy consumption through innovative technologies (ICT) that can support the management, monitoring and operation of cities. It emphasizes that it consists of making it more efficient.

From a different point of view, the smart city is expressed, as the places where existing traditional infrastructures are coordinated and integrated with new technologies (Chiappa and Baggio, 2015: p.2), learning and developing cities where personal data privacy and other ethical rules are also important (Çelik and Topsakal, 2017: p.152) are expressed as cities where visitors can access real-time information (Encalada et al., 2017: p.2). In addition, definitions in terms of sustainable development (Perfetto et al., 2016: p.251) and competitiveness (Kashima and Morita, 2017: p.76) have also started to appear in the literature.

The above-mentioned definitions, the concept of smart city, is directly related to Information and Communication Technologies, in summary, existing infrastructures integrate with technology and ensure sustainability, as a city that directs the focus directly to people and integrates people with people, institutions and people aims to maximize the interaction between people and institutions.

The smart city concept covers many sectors, including tourism (Guo et al., 2014: p.5). While Lamsfus et al. (2013), D'Amico (2013), Koo et al. (2013) are the first to define the concept of "smart tourism" based on the concept of smart city, Wang et al. (2013), La Rocca (2014), Boes and Buhalis (2015) have defined the concept of "smart tourism destination". The systems required for smart city and smart tourism destination formations should also be smart systems. In terms of tourism, smart systems represent next-generation information systems that promise to provide tourism consumers and service providers with more relevant information, more decision support, more mobility, and ultimately more enjoyable tourism experiences (Lamsfus et al., 2013: p.18). As La Rocca (2014) states, "smart city" and "smart tourism" are two closely connected concepts if the technological component is emphasized, and smart tourism for smart city in general refers to the intensive use of technology in tourism. According to Hunter et al. (2015), smart tourism rebuilds the social reality of digital tourism by making information exchange faster and more frequent, and thanks to smart tourism, people work together to build social ecosystems using information exchange with mobile devices connected to the internet. Göktaş Kulualp and Sarı (2020) "smart tourism is based on the adoption of technologies that collecting large amounts of data to create new values, such as smart devices, sensors, social media and mobile technologies."

The unique feature of the tourism industry is to address intangible products such as experience or services that reveal intense information that has more value than other industries. This has made the internet, a source of information, a central element of tourism (Chung et al, 2015: p.131). The implementation of the IoT in tourism means that tourists can use their mobile phones to explore their destination locations using on-site data collection and reporting (Jovicic, 2017: p.278). Over the past few years, tourist demand has changed rapidly, thanks to the widespread use of the internet and accessibility of new technologies. Touristic cities are expected to revise their strategies in this direction to preserve their attractiveness and promote their images in a "virtual" dimension (La Rocca, 2014: p.271). With the smart approach of cloud computing and end-user devices with the internet, tourists can actively engage with tourism service providers and collaborate in the creation of their own experiences (Buonincontri and Micera, 2016: p.286). This technology and new approaches to data collection, management and sharing constitute important steps for the parties in the implementation of smart tourism (Gretzel et al., 2015a: p.180).

According to La Rocca (2014), tourism can play an active role in promoting resources and attractions as a system for smart city and implementing sustainable service and infrastructure system. Therefore, harmonizing the potentials of smart cities with the tourism industry will not only contribute to the image and promotion of the city, but will also provide a sustainable service in the tourism industry, where resources can be consumed too much and quickly. In some studies, it is stated that the concept of smart tourism destination (STD) emerged with the application of smart tourism to cities or, in another respect, the implementation of tourism in smart cities (Tran et al., 2017: p.190; Kang et al., 2017: p.9846; Hernandez-Martin et al., 2017: p.45; Chiappa and Baggio, 2015: p.146; Buonincontri and Micera, 2016: p.288; Zhu et al., 2014).

Looking at the definitions of smart tourism destination in the literature, Boes et al. (2015) addressing the concept from three perspectives, tourists and wealth in terms of institutions and destinations; value in terms of profit and benefit, it is defined as the places that use existing technological tools and techniques that make it possible to provide demand and resources in terms of creating satisfaction and experiences together. Buonincantri and Micera (2016), by defining the smart tourism destination as a destination emerging with the use of new technology to increase the competitiveness of the destinations and to support tourism development projects, emphasizes that innovation is essential to be smart, and increasing competitiveness is an important factor for the formation of smart destinations. Gomes et al. (2017), by referring to a simpler definition, expresses smart tourism destinations in accordance with the age of social media as places where tourists interact more with the destination.

The concept of smart tourism refers to a much wider scope than the smart tourism destination. Hunter et al. (2015) emphasized that the concept of smart tourism defines the convergence of tourism with information technology, Li et al. (2017) defines it as a tour information service that can be found at the same time wherever taken by tourists throughout the tour process. Liburd et al. (2017) states that they aim to optimize service delivery, improve the quality of the experience consumed and use technology intensively to improve destination management.

Considering the smart tourism destination definitions above, in order to talk about smartness in destinations; enriching the tourist experience, applying technologies such as the IoT and Cloud Computing that facilitate access to services and provide faster information sharing, responding to the needs of stakeholders (tourists, tourism institutions and organizations, government, citizens, etc.), minimizing the use of resources, a sustainable society and it is understood that issues such as observing the destination, improving the quality of life for citizens and increasing the quality of travel experience for visitors should be at the forefront. On the other hand, it is seen that the concept of smart tourism has emerged by integrating and supporting the type of tourism applied in the destinations with intensive use of technology.

As Boes et al. (2016) pointed out, smartness uses the interconnectedness and interoperability of integrated technologies to produce innovative services, products and procedures to maximize the value of all stakeholders.

Smartness has long been perceived as complex ecosystems in the context of urban and tourism regions, where a wide range of stakeholders cooperate to create value for themselves and others (Boes et al., 2016: p.109). The smart tourism ecosystem (STE) can be defined as a tourism system that uses smart technology to create, manage and deliver smart tourism services / experiences, and is characterized by intense information sharing and co-creation. The collection, processing and modification of tourism-related data is a key function in STE and because of the conceptual roots in smart cities, STEs are typically considered to be smart destinations (Gretzel et al., 2015b: p.560). There are some discussions about the concept of STEs in the literature. For example, addressing smart tourism destinations with an ecosystem approach, Boes et al. (2016) defend that the complex structure of smart tourism can be resolved by focusing on the additional components of the ecosystem and while defining the concept of smart tourism destination with the ecosystem, Baidal et al. (2017) emphasizes that trying to explain the concept of smart tourism destination within the ecosystem based on global tourism remains quite simple and is not recommended. Instead, they argue that it would be more appropriate to define the key elements of integration of a destination in the tourism ecosystem, a key aspect of the level of smartness (Baidal et al., 2017: p.1583). STEs ensure that every stakeholder who contributes to enriching the tourism experience relates to Information and Communication Technology. STE, where the integration of stakeholders with each other is extremely important, creates a competitive advantage and threatens other destinations because it enriches its experience. In general, it is emphasized in the literature that key points are determined for STEs, and the lack of focus on the relationships and effects of the factors with each other is emphasized.

MAIN FOCUS OF THE CHAPTER

With the rapid advancement of technology, the transformation in industries becomes inevitable. The tourism industry is one of the service sectors where people-to-people interaction occurs most intensely. Tourists and visitors are now acting more consciously and keeping up with technological developments. Therefore, they expect their travel experiences to be enriched and customized in accordance with today's conditions. Tourism enterprises and destinations have begun to transform in order to meet these expectations, in accordance with the modern marketing approach and in order to maintain the level of competitiveness. Examples of this transformation are:

- Integration of systems used in businesses with technology,
- Widespread use of mobile applications for tourists,
- The increase of online reservations,
- The inclusion of virtual reality and augmented reality in the tourism industry,
- The ability to visit museums and exhibitions in virtual environments,
- The availability of internet access everywhere and instantly in the regions visited by tourists,
- Equipping the infrastructure and
- Superstructure systems in destinations with existing technological resources.

Likewise, academic studies in the field of tourism have turned to digital transformation in the tourism industry in parallel with this change. This chapter tries to explain the transformations in the field of tourism as a result of digitalization and compiles academic studies related to the smartness in tourism. For this purpose, by determining what the subject headings are being worked on, the gaps in the field can be seen, and new perspectives on smartness in tourism can be developed by considering the recommendations and results of the studies.

METHOD

The aim of this study is to analyze the academic literature about smartness in tourism. By classifying the studies related to smartness in tourism, the areas of research (destinations), the distribution of the study according to years, type, journal, congress, book and thesis / workshop in which they are published, the type of publication, the type of method, whether or not they apply the case method and the people they are directed to are examined under these headings.

The findings obtained in the research have both theoretical and practical contributions. Theoretically, this study systematically demonstrates the current knowledge of rationality research in tourism and is expected to guide future research. In practice, it is considered that the findings will attract the attention of specialists who are looking for suggestions on how to restructure the applications on the basis of destinations in order to increase the potential of the topic of smartness in tourism.

Qualitative research methods were used in the research and documentary scanning and publication scanning were used as data collection methods. Qualitative research is defined as the study in which qualitative information collection methods such as observation, interview and document analysis are used, and a qualitative process is followed to reveal perceptions and events in a realistic and holistic way in the natural environment (Yıldırım, 1999: p.10). Documentary scanning, while finding a specific purpose, involves finding resources, reading, taking notes and evaluating; publication screening is the listing of the sources published on the subject studied (Karasar, 2014). In this context, first of all, the definitions related to smart tourism destinations are included, and the meanings of different perspectives are discussed. Then for this study, all articles, conference articles and theses related to tourism-based smartness were determined and by the end of December 2019, Google Scholar, Science Direct and Scopus databases for articles and conference articles, for this data was collected from www.openthesis. org for theses and https://tez.yok.gov.tr web addresses. The process explained for the article scanning process was followed. First of all, the words "smart tourism", "smart destination" and "smart tourism destination" were searched in the "titles", "summaries" and "keywords" sections of the three databases mentioned to reach scientific studies on the subject. Journal selection is not only limited to the field of tourism, but all articles, conference papers and theses containing the words searched are included in the scope of the study. In this context, it has been paid attention to be included in the research, in which the researchers can be reached, all of which are not written in English. The articles, conference papers, theses and book chapters to be reached were determined to be directly related to the issue of smartness in tourism, which is the focus of this study. For this to happen, researchers have read the titles, abstracts and keywords in each article, conference article, thesis and book chapter. The collection of data covers the process from September 2018 to January 2020. In this process, a total of 264 academic literature published between 2010 and 2019 were included in the research.

FINDINGS

Classification Of Smartness Studies in Tourism

Distribution of Studies by Year

The first study on smartness in tourism belongs to 2010. a total of sixteen studies have been conducted in the first five years (0.4% (1) for 2010, 0.4% (1) for 2011), no articles for 2012, 2.6% (7) for 2013 and 2.6% (7 for 2014) and the number of studies has continued to increase (8% (21) for 2015, 8.7% (23) for 2016), 15.1% (40 for 2017), 21.2% (56 for 2018) and 41% for 2019 (108 pieces).

Figure 1. Distribution of studies by year

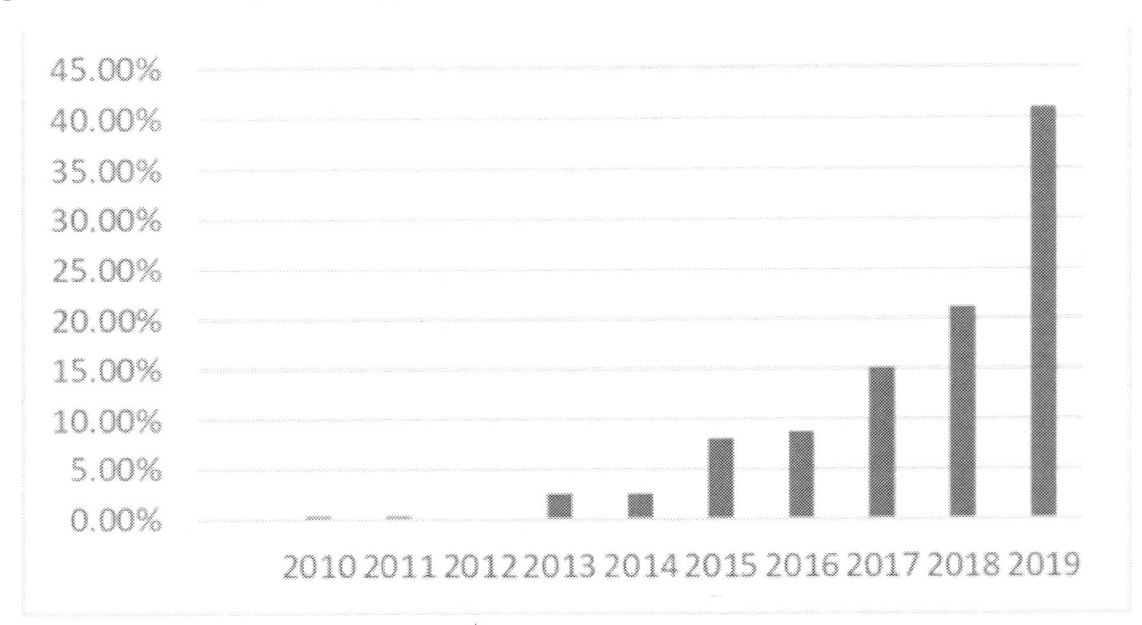

In Figure 1, it is understood that there was not much interest in the issue of smartness in tourism until 2013 and 2014. It is observed that after 2014, studies on the subject started to increase rapidly. It is understood that the interest in the subject has increased rapidly and will continue to increase with the rate of employment that reached 21.2% in 2018, reaching 41% in 2019.

Distribution of Studies by Type

The sources from which the studies are obtained consist of: journal publication, congress publication, book chapter, thesis and doctorate workshop. Accordingly, 66.3% of the studies are journal publications (175), 23.5% of the studies are congress publications (62), 8% of the studies are in the book chapter (21) and 2.2% of the studies are thesis and doctoral workshop (6).

Figure 2. Distribution of studies by type

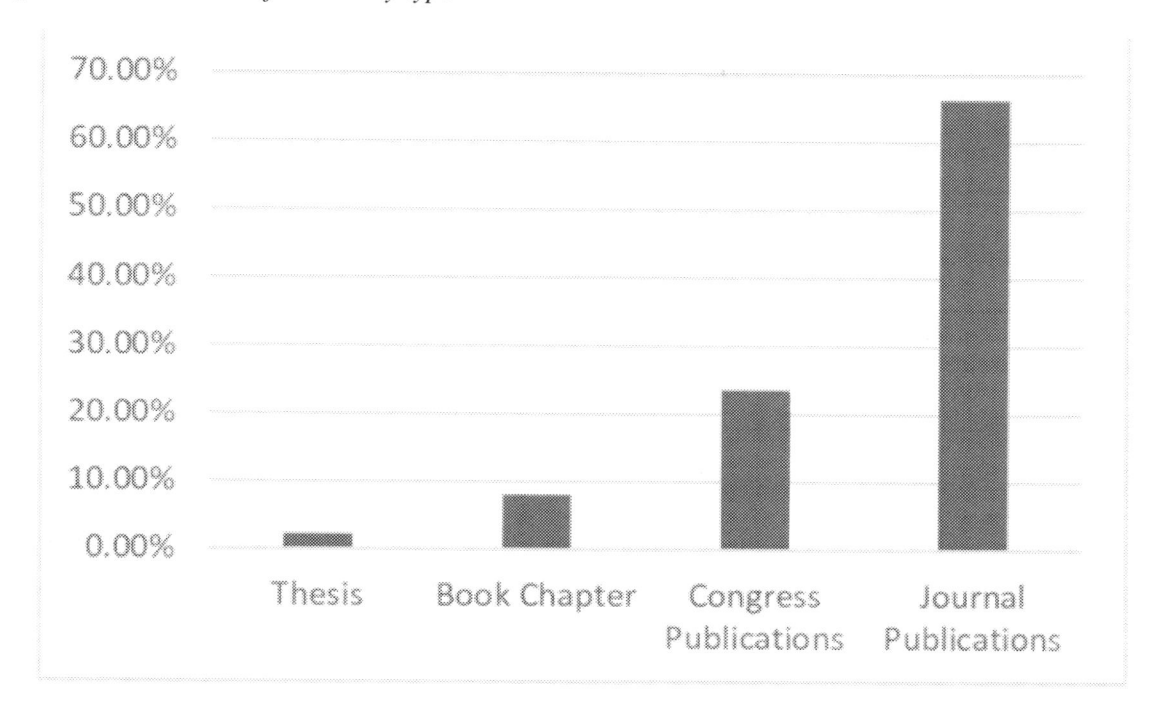

In this context, 264 studies have been reached in total, and there are 169 different sources in total (95 different journal sources, 56 different congresses and 18 different books). For example; 14 academic publications from the Sustainability journal, which is one of the sources used in the research, were examined. In this way, a total of 264 studies were reached.

Distribution of Studies according to the Journal Published

175 of the 264 studies obtained in total constitute journal publications, which indicates that journal publications represent 66.3% of the studies as a source (Figure 2). According to the review, the journal that publishes the most in terms of smartness in tourism has become the "Sustainability" journal with 14 studies. After this journal, "Journal of Destination Marketing & Management" with 8 studies and "Asia Pacific Journal of Tourism Research", "Current Issues in Tourism" with 7 studies and "Technological Forecasting and Social Change", "International Journal of Tourism Cities" with 4 studies and "Asia Pacific Journal of Information Systems" follow this journal, respectively. These seven journals, which make the most publications, make up 28% of journal resources. The reason why the rate is so low despite the fact that most studies are collected in these journals is the existence of many different journal resources that include a single study. These magazine resources with a single study have a total of 168, representing 72% of the journal publications.

SCI (Science Citation Index) of Journals Published by Studies

The studies obtained in the study were examined in terms of their status in the Social Science Citation Index (SSCI), which classifies the journals in which they are included. The review included SSCI journals, as well as journals in the Social Science Citation Index Expanded (SCI - E), which offers extended classification, and the Emerging Science Citation Index (Emergency SCI), which classifies journals of the quality that can be included in SSCI as a study, but not in SSCI. As a result of the examination, 69 of 95 different magazines are included in these scopes. Of these 69 journal sources, 30 of them (43.5%) were covered by SSCI (4 of them (5.8%) were also covered by SCI - E), 26 of them (37.7%) were covered by Emergency SCI, 9 of them (13%) were found to be within the scope of SCI - E.

Distribution of Studies according to the Congress Published

62 of the 264 studies reached constitute the works presented at the congress, which corresponds to 23.5% of the studies (Figure 2). The highest number of studies on smartness in tourism belongs to the 2018 IEEE 4th International Conference on Big Data Computing Service and Applications and ACM International Conference Proceeding Series. The work of these two congresses on the subject represents 9.6% of the total congress studies. These congresses are followed by The Third International Congress on Future of Tourism: Innovation, Entrepreneurship and Sustainability (Futourism 2019) and Twenty-Third Pacific Asia Conference on Information Systems congresses with two works (3.2% each). It is understood that there are many sources that have a single number of studies in congress publications as well as in journal publications. The congresses that include a single number of studies represent 84% of the total congress studies.

Distribution of Studies according to the Book Chapter in which it is Published

While conducting the research, a large number of book chapters on the subject of smartness in tourism were found in the sources where the data were collected, but there are 21 book chapters that can be accessed in this study since the contents of the chapters are not available. As a result of the examination, the books containing the most relevant sections were the 2 information studies, Information and Communication Technologies in Tourism (9.5%) and Smart Tourism as a Driver for Culture and Sustainability (9.5%). Books that contain a single number of studies constitute 81% of the book chapter studies in total.

Distribution of Studies by Thesis / Workshop Publication

During the research process, five theses related to smartness in tourism and one doctorate workshop were found. The institution that carries out the most thesis studies is Hameenlinna University Center (33.6%) with two studies; The institutions that included single study were determined as Umea School of Business and Economics (16.6%), NHTV Breda University of Apllied Sciences (16.6%) and Erciyes University Institute of Social Sciences (16.6%). The publication of the study carried out in the doctoral workshop is ENTER 2015 PhD Workshop Research Proposals (16.6%). These studies obtained as a result of the examination constitute 2.2% of the 264 studies (Figure 2).

Distribution of Studies by Publication Language

The analysis of the studies reached in this section is given according to the language published. Being a scientific and universal language, most of the studies were published in English with a rate of 88.6% (234 studies). In the languages of the studies studied, after English, respectively, 5.7% (15 studies) in Turkish, 1.9% (5 studies) Spanish, 0.7% Ukrainian and Portuguese (2 studies), 0.4% (one study) Indonesian, Chinese, Korean, French, Persian and Italian.

Distribution of Studies by Method Type

The studies obtained in this section are classified as qualitative, quantitative and mixed method users. According to Figure 3, the majority of the studies obtained in the study used qualitative methods with 179 studies (67.8%), followed by quantitative methods with 76 studies (28.8%) and mixed methods with 9 studies (3.4%).

Figure 3. Distribution of studies by method type

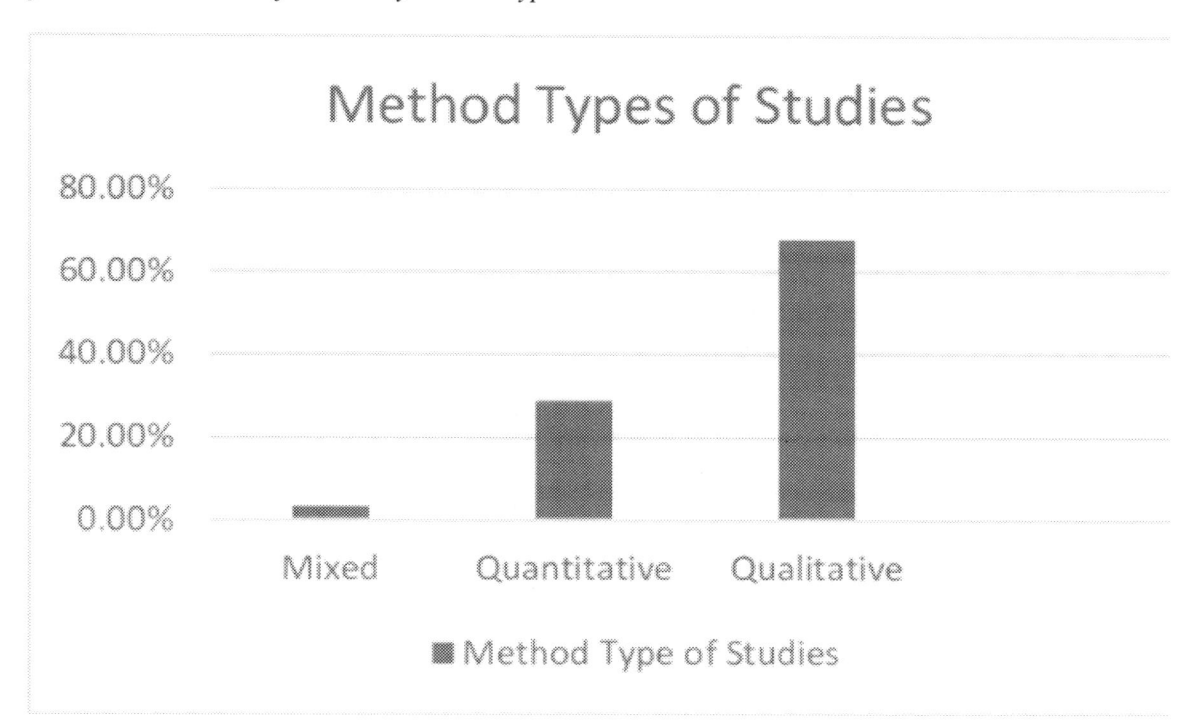

Techniques Applied in Qualitative Studies

In this section, where the data techniques applied in qualitative studies are analyzed, there are 57 (31.8%) studies that included only the literature review in order to create a conceptual framework from 179 qualitative studies on the subject of smartness in tourism. In addition to the literature review, one or more techniques were used in all 122 (68.2%) studies. In the Figure 4 below, the techniques determined in 122 studies involving one or more techniques are shown. Each technique is considered to be used in a single study to understand which technique is used and how often. In this way, the number of studies, which is actually 122, reaches 176. Accordingly, the most used technique is the case study method with 44.3% (78 times), followed by the project method with 10.2% (18 times), and the content analysis method with 8.5% (15 times). In qualitative studies, 36 different techniques have been identified, including the literature review method.

Figure 4. Techniques applied in qualitative studies

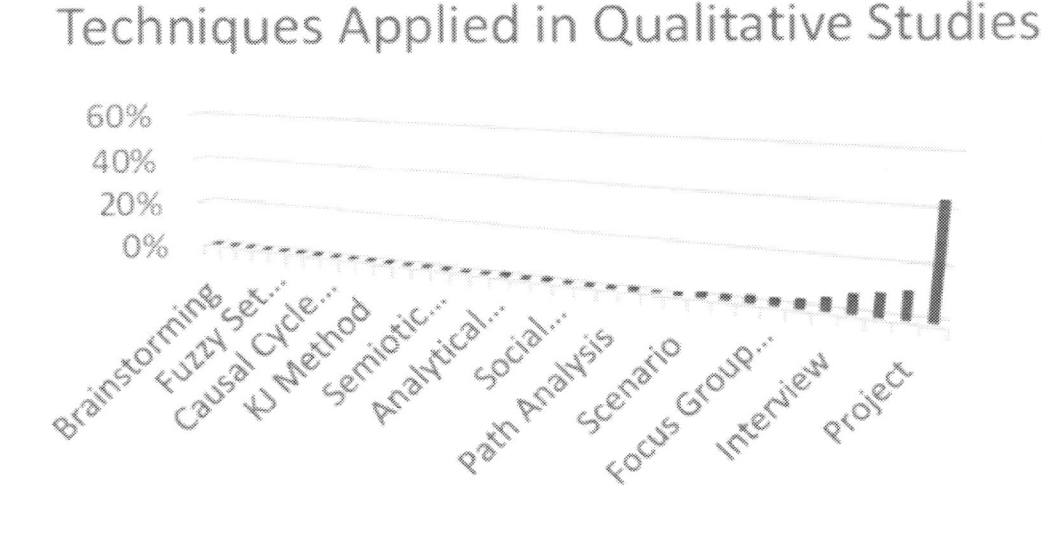

Theory, Approach and Models Applied in Qualitative Study

The theory, approach and models adopted in the qualitative studies examined were determined and shown in Table 1. While the 5 models in Table 1 were used once, it is seen that constructivism approach and pragmatic approach were used twice from 11 different approaches and the grounded theory from 10 different theories was used three times.

Table 1. Theory, approach and models applied in qualitative study

	Names of Theory, Approach, Model	**%**
Theory	Grounded Theory	%10
	Complexity Theory	%3,33
	Socio-technical Systems Theory	%3,33
	Triarchic Intelligence Theory	%3,33
	Complex Adaptive Systems Theory	%3,33
	Social Change Theory	%3,33
	Stakeholder Theory	%3,33
	Adaptive Structure Theory	%3,33
	Dynamic Talent Theory	%3,33
	Existence Theory	%3,33
Approach	Constructivism Approach	%6,70
	Pragmatic Approach	%6,70
	System Dynamics Approach	%3,33
	SERVQUAL Approach	%3,33
	Phonetic Approach	%3,33
	Design Science Research Approach	%3,33
	Methodological Approach	%3,33
	Interdisciplinary Approach	%3,33
	Fuzzy Logic Approach	%3,33
	Convolutional Neural Network Approach	%3,33
	Enomphenographic Approach	%3,33
Model	Buhalis' 6A Model of Tourism Destination	%3,33
	Baditas' Multifunctional Character Model of Tourist Cities	%3,33
	Intuitive Systematic Model	%3,33
	Five Spiral Model	%3,33
	Holistic Single Case Pattern	%3,33

Techniques Applied in Quantitative Studies

Table 2 shows the techniques included in a total of 76 quantitative studies obtained as a result of the research. In most of the studies, it was determined that more than one technique was applied and each technique was handled separately as in the other section. In this case, the number of studies actually increased from 76 to 185. A total of 52 different techniques were found to be used in quantitative research.

Table 2. Techniques applied in quantitative studies

Techniques	%	Techniques	%
Prototype	%1,1	Probabilistic Rough Sets	%0,6
K-fold Cross Validation	%0,6	Story Based Maturity Matrix	%0,6
UGC Data Analysis	%0,6	Core Intensive Prediction	%0,6
Epidemiological Modeling	%0,6	Spatial and Semantic Analysis	%0,6
Factor Analysis	%3,3	Likert Scael	%2,8
AHP	%1,1	Basic Component Analysis	%0,6
IPA	%0,6	Empirical Analysis	%0,6
Social Network Analysis	%0,6	Experiment	%0,6
Convolutional Neural Network	%0,6	PPR	%0,6
Deep Learning	%0,6	QPR	%0,6
Emotion Analysis	%0,6	Fitness and Kendalls' Measurements	%0,6
Post-hoc Analysis	%0,6	Easy Sampling Method	%0,6
Coexistence Analysis	%0,6	Multiple Regression and Correlation Analysis	%0,6
T Test	%0,6	Multiple Group Analysis	%0,6
Heckman's Prediction Procedure	%0,6	Content Analysis	%1,1
Ontological Analysis	%0,6	Interview	%2,8
Least Squares Method	%1,5	Scenario	%2,1
ANOVA	%2,1	Structural Equation Modeling	%4
Project	%3,3	Survey	%26,4
Case Study	%23,5	Mathematical Modeling	%0,6
Cluster-Outlier Analysis	%1,1	Algorithm	%0,6
Pearson Correlation	%1,1	SmartPLS	%0,6
Delphi Technique	%1,1	Counting Method	%0,6
Network Analysis	%0,6	Conditional Valuation Method	%0,6
Data Envelopment Analysis	%0,6	Kwong-Bai Method	%0,6
Simülation	%0,6	Whip Effect	%0,6

Theory, Approach and Models Applied in Quantitative Studies

The theory, approach and models adopted in the quantitative studies examined were determined and shown in Table 3. It is understood that 18 theories, 3 approaches and 3 models in Table 3 are used once.

Table 3. Theory, approach and models applied in quantitative studies

	Names of Theory, Approach and Model	%
Theory	Spectral Graphics Theory	%4,1
	Complexity Theory	%4,1
	Comparison Level Theory	%4,1
	Uses and Satisfaction Theory	%4,1
	Flow Theory	%4,1
	Self-Determination Theory	%4,1
	Cognitive Dissonance Theory	%4,1
	Rough Set Theory	%4,1
	Expectation-Confirmation Theory	%4,1
	Dann's Theory of Tourist Motivation	%4,1
	Extension and Construction Theory	%4,1
	Expectation Theor	%4,1
	Granular Computing Theory	%4,1
	Hedonic Theory	%4,1
	Supply Chain Management Theory	%4,1
	Rational Action Theory	%4,1
	Spill Theory	%4,1
	Social Practice Theory	%4,1
Approach	Bell's Museum Ecology	%4,1
	Fuzzy Logic Approach	%4,1
	Equation Modeling Approach	%4,1
Model	Three Way Decision Model	%4,1
	BBC Model	%4,1
	CCR Model	%4,1

Techniques Applied in Mixed Method Studies

In Figure 5, the techniques given in 9 studies that are determined to use mixed method as a result of the research are shown. In these studies, 12 different techniques were used. Among these techniques, the survey application is the most used technique with a rate of 33.3% (4 times), while the case study method with a rate of 25% (3 times); Structural equation model with 16.6% (2 times), project and prototype methods and interview technique with 8.3% (once), scenario, ontological analysis, sensitivity analysis, soft systems methodology, total system intervention and Google Analytics follows the methods.

Figure 5. Techniques used in mixed method studies

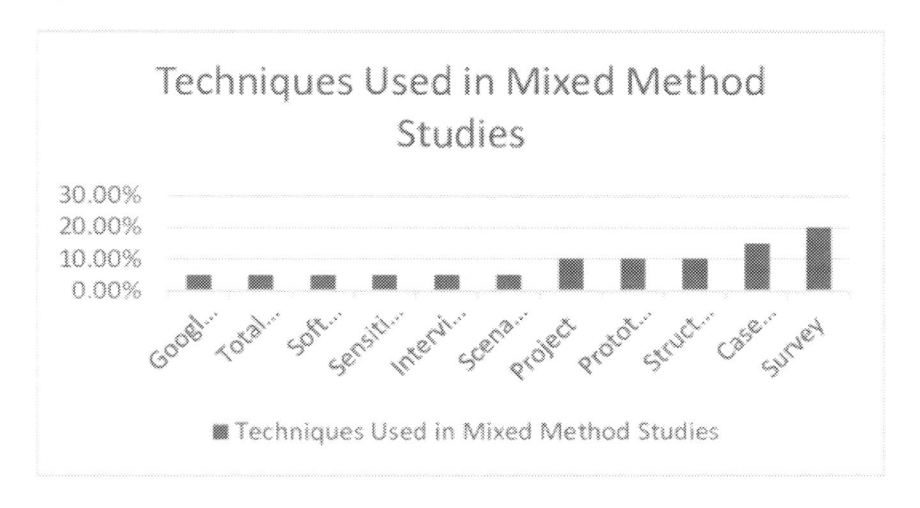

Distribution of the Studies according to the Case of Application or Not

As seen in Figure 6, 153 of the 264 studies obtained in the study have case studies. Accordingly, studies that carry out case studies represent 58% of the total, while studies that do not carry out case studies represent 42% of the total.

Figure 6. Distribution of the Studies According to the Case of Application or Not

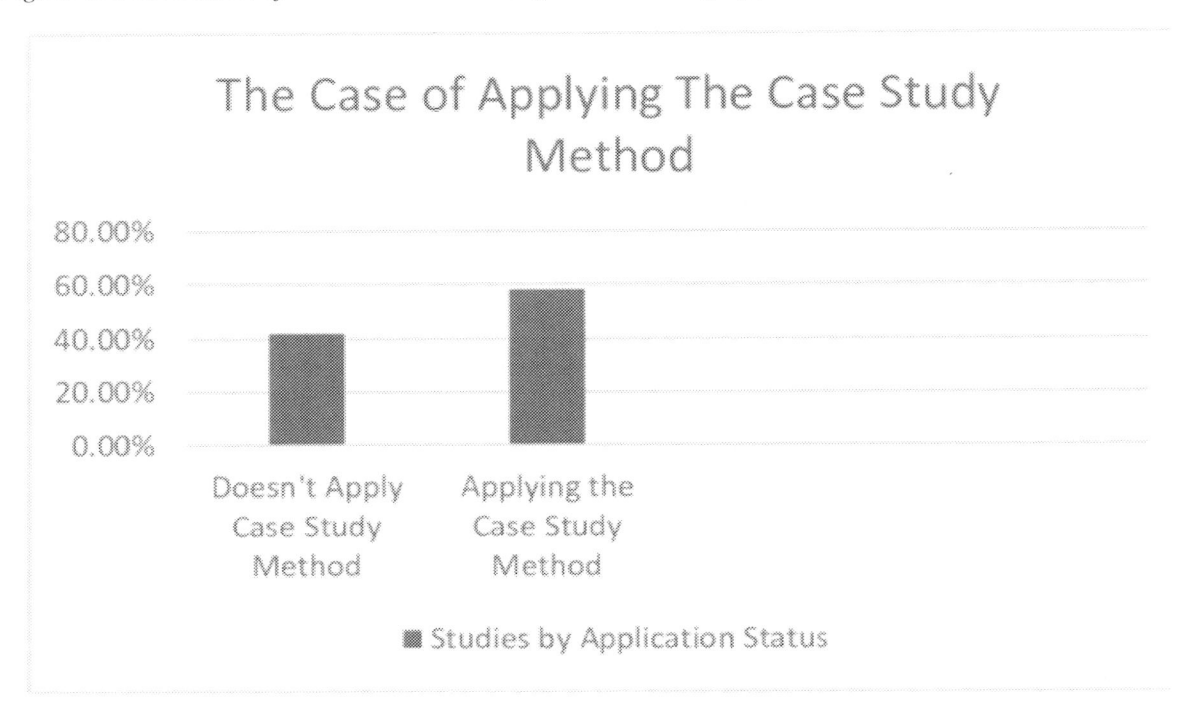

Distribution of the Studies according to the Destination of the Case Study

In this section, it is analyzed which destinations the 153 studies in total are among the studies that perform exemplary applications. However, since 39 of the 153 studies conducted multiple case studies, each destination in these 39 studies was counted to represent a separate study in order to make the analysis healthier. For example, while the congress titled "Smart Destination Branding: The Need for New" included multiple case studies covering the destinations of Indonesia and Malaysia, Indonesia and Malaysia destinations were counted as separate studies in order to understand how many times the destinations were subject to studies on the subject of smartness in tourism. Accordingly, when each destination is counted one by one, there are 192 studies in total.

Figure 7 shows the frequency of study of the destinations discussed in the case study. According to this, Spain, where the most case study application on tourism is smart, was Spain with 13.1% (25 studies). Spain compared to 11.1% (21 studies) Italy, compared to 10% (19 studies) in China, compared to 9.5% (18 studies), South Korea, compared to 5.8% (11 studies) and Turkey 3.6% Brazil, Portugal and Indonesia follow with rates (7 studies each).

Figure 7. Distribution of the studies according to the destination of the case study

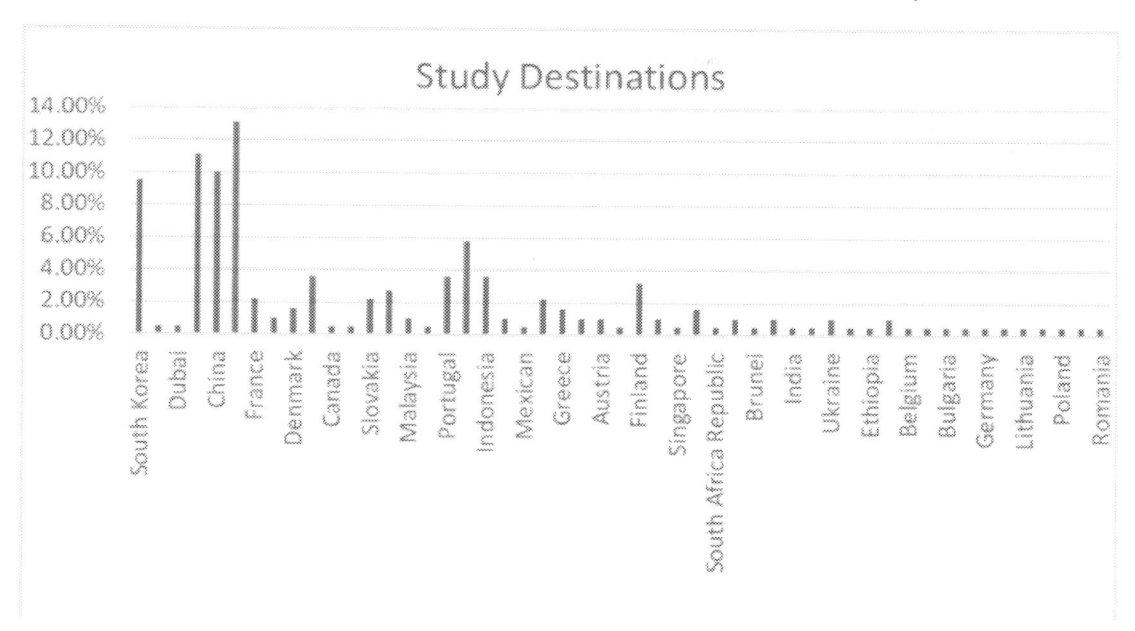

Distribution of Studies according to Persons Directed

It was determined that 103 studies were carried out by directing to one or more groups in 264 studies reached during the research process. These 103 studies were directed in the groups and they are classified in six sections: experts, tourists, citizens, social media users, smart device users and students.

Figure 8. Distribution of studies by persons directed

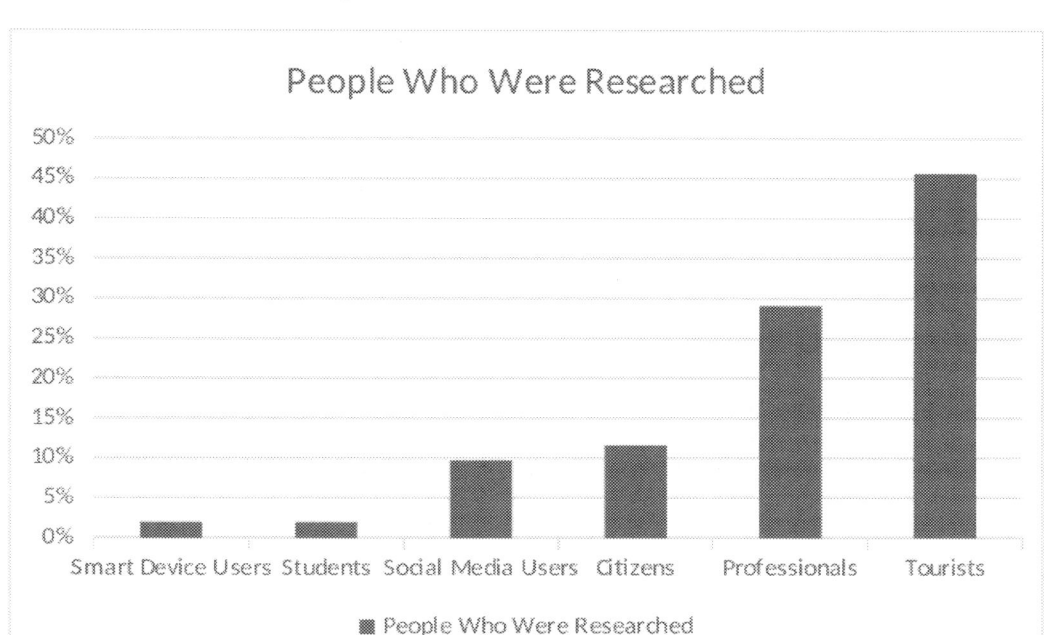

As seen in Figure 8, among 103 studies on smartness in tourism, the group that the research was directed most was the tourists with a ratio of 45.6% (47 studies). Experts of tourists with 29.1% (30 studies), citizens with 11.6% (12 studies), social media users with 9.7% (10 studies) and smart device users with 2% (2 studies each) and students follow.

When studies are examined, these perspectives are as follows; challenges of smart tourism, smart destinations as a competitive advantage for management, smart tourism destinations that contribute to sustainability, new smart tourism systems, smart tourism in terms of enriching the tourist experience, Big Data and IoT in tourism, smart tourism destinations for stakeholders, innovative products in tourism It is understood that smart tourists, the role of artificial intelligence in tourism and the impact of smart tourism on urban sustainability.

DISCUSSION

With the technology penetrating into every field and making progress and development day by day, it is expected that the interest of the Destination Management Organizations and the academic community will continue to increase in the following years. Applications to encourage future researches, personalized experiences, smart systems that can be used in places where tourist flow is intense, museums, smart infrastructures and the effects of their systems on citizens and tourists, what kind of activities are carried out to promote smart tourism destinations (gamification) etc.) and their effects.

When the studies are analyzed by type, they are gathered in 4 categories: book chapter, thesis, congress publication and journal publication (article). There are more books and book chapters on the subject of smartness in tourism, but what is available in the study has been examined. In this context, it can be said that books on the subject of smartness in tourism are presented comprehensively. When it is analyzed as a thesis study, it is seen that the subject is in its infancy. As the applications and advances in this field increase, the question marks on the subject will increase, and the academic issue will be addressed more frequently and from different perspectives and this will close the gap in the literature. The number of congresses in technology, big data, IoT and digitalization has increased in recent years. Therefore, the issue of smartness in tourism is increasingly discussed in congresses. When the congress publications are examined, it is seen that the main focus is on technology and digitalization rather than tourism. After this, depending on the technological developments in tourism, the main focus is expected to shift to tourism and the issues will be handled with a focus on tourism. As a type of studies, the journal publication (article) is predominant. When the magazines are examined, it is understood that magazines that bring tourism and technology together have emerged in recent years. This shows that the issue of smartness in tourism is one of the subjects that continues increasingly in the academic sense. As an example of these journals; Tourism Planning & Development (2004), Journal of Heritage Tourism (2006), Tourismos: An International Multidisciplinary Journal of Tourism (2006), GeoJournal of Tourism and Geosites (2008), Journal of Tourism History (2009), Tourism; The Journal of University of Lodz (2009), Journal of Hospitality and Tourism Technology (2010), Tourism Management Perspectives (2012), Journal of Hospitality, Leisure, Sport & Tourism Education (2012) and European Journal of Tourism Research (2019) shown.

Considering the journals in which the studies are published, it is understood that Sustainability magazine, which includes 14 studies, comes to the fore in terms of smartness in tourism. Magazines with works; SCI is divided into three categories: SCI - E and Emergency SCI. The studies reviewed were published in 95 different journals. As a result of the review, it was determined that 61 of these journals were covered by SCI, SCI - E and Emergency SCI. This shows that publications on the subject of smartness in tourism are published in qualified journals by 64.2%. This result shows that the subject has been accepted and taken into consideration by these journals which are accepted as scientific.

SOLUTIONS AND RECOMMENDATIONS

It has been determined that interest has increased since the year the subject was studied (2010). As the reason for the intensive increase in the related studies in the last two years, especially in 2010, understanding the importance of the concept of "smartness" in tourism as in other sectors, constantly updating the information due to the advances in technology and the purchasing behavior and awareness of those who experience touristic products and services. the level is thought to be changing. When the resource types of the studies examined are analyzed, it is understood that the important part is composed of articles. The necessity of the subject to be handled from different angles and presented as a book emerges.

In the research methods of the studies studied, there are qualitative, quantitative, and mixed methods, respectively, according to the rate of study. As can be seen here, conceptual studies are mostly dealt with, since the concept of smartness in tourism is a new phenomenon. In conceptual studies, in general, smart tourism, smart tourism destination, digitalization in tourism and their economic, environmental, and social dimensions were discussed with techniques such as case studies, interview, SWOT analysis and content analysis. In quantitative studies, the effects and results of these practices on the applications were investigated by using the survey technique (techniques such as social network analysis, factor analysis) from the researches on smart tourism practitioners and their experiences. The need to investigate smartness in tourism continues by applying different techniques suitable for the purpose, both qualitative and quantitative methods, because it expresses the technology applied intensely in the destinations of smartness in tourism, involves complex technological formations such as IoT, Cloud Computing and artificial intelligence, and concerns many stakeholders from tourists to destination management organizations.

Among the studies discussed, 152 of them, including multiple case studies, conducted case studies, and made examinations for destinations. According to the results of the implementation case studies carried out most of the first five destination, respectively: Spain, Italy, China, South Korea, and Turkey. It is thought that the fact that South Korea and China are more advanced than other countries in terms of technology and production, it is believed that there is more interest in the subject of smartness in tourism in these destinations and thus there are more publications on the subject. Spain and Italy are among the important tourism centers in the Mediterranean basin, and it is thought that government policies towards smart tourism destinations have been established and started to be implemented in both countries, as the interest in the subject is very intense and the studies are at high rates. Turkey also practices tourism policy, smart cities, and is considered an intense interest in this issue because of the academic literature and public works 2023 smart strategies.

As a result of the review, 113 of the 175 journal publications (64.5%) in which the studies were published are included in SCI, SCI-E and Emerging SCI. It was determined that a significant portion of these 113 journal publications (65 of them with 57.5%) SCI coverage, 37 of them (32.7%) emerging SCI coverage and 11 of them (9.8%) SCI-E coverage. This shows that the issue of smartness in tourism is on the way to become an internationally accessible and examinable subject. At the same time, acceptance of the subject for the scope of SCI, in which the publications of first-class journals are accepted, makes the subject even more important.

In future studies, smart systems related to the issue of smartness in tourism can be handled and examined in a wider scope. Information can be updated by adding new studies as a continuation of this study. In the coming years, another study that deals with new studies can be compared with another study. With the technology penetrating into every field and making progress and development day by day, it is expected that the interest of the Destination Management Organizations and the academic community will continue to increase in the following years.

FUTURE RESEARCH DIRECTIONS

Applications to encourage future researches, personalized experiences, smart systems that can be used in places where tourist flow is intense, museums, smart infrastructures and the effects of their systems on citizens and tourists, what kind of activities are carried out to promote smart tourism destinations (gamification) etc.) and their effects. At regular intervals (such as 5 years), positive and negative effects on all stakeholders for all touristic destinations can be explored. It is recommended to focus on researches especially on negative effects. This research can be repeated over time and it can be observed which topics are emphasized and which topics are gaining importance.

As smart technologies and the application of smartness in tourism are quite new, it has attracted great attention in the last 9 years and especially in the last 2 years as seen in the academic literature. Due to the rapid adoption of smart technologies and systems, it has begun to integrate into these systems in all countries and destinations. However, since most places are just beginning to understand and use the systems, it is normal for conceptual studies to understand the subject in academic literature. Systems are expected to become more functional in the coming years. In this context, focus topics will change in academic literature as well.

CONCLUSION

In this study, it is aimed to classify and analyze the current literature on the subject of smartness in tourism. Looking at the years of studies examined, it is understood that the first study on smartness in tourism belongs to 2010. While this initial study focuses on destination branding, it questions whether an exemplary destination is smart as well as sustainability. After 2010, the subject was handled again with smart guide systems for tourists in 2011, but in 2012, it could not find a place in a scientific study. The aim of developing a frame of the concept of "smart tourism destination" in 2013 and 2014 after 2012, the issue of smartness in tourism has been increasing more and more by 2020 after 2014 with different perspectives.

In current studies, the majority of research on smartness in tourism is conceptual and mainly focused on the development of tourism-related institutions and organizations and the integration of stakeholders to enrich the tourism experience. Smartness in tourism; tourists who are connected to each other and to the destination, are better informed and more actively involved in tourist activities; has become important because it will interact dynamically with the destination, create tourism products jointly with other stakeholders and add value to everyone to share experience and knowledge. A good tourism experience provides tourists with real-time and personal services and collects data for optimization of strategic management. Thus, smartness becomes a key role in tourism destination management and marketing.

There are several studies that try to explain the role, effects, results, practices, and the concept of smartness in terms of tourism. In this study, data has been collected and analyzed by researchers in order to analyze scientific studies on this subject. The importance of this research reveals the critical role of reasoning in tourism and the absence of a similar study on this subject.

ACKNOWLEDGMENT

This research received no specific grant from any funding agency in the public, commercial, or not-for-profit sectors.

REFERENCES

Albino, V., Berardi, U., & Dangelico, R. M. (2015). Smart cities: Definitions, dimensions, performance and initiatives. *Journal of Urban Technology*, *22*(1), 1723–1738. doi:10.1080/10630732.2014.942092

Baidal, J. A. I., Marco, A. C. B., Mazon, J. N., & Ivars, A. F. P. (2017). Smart destinations and the evolution of ICTs: A new scenario for destination management? *Current Issues in Tourism*, *20*, 1581–1600.

Boes, K., Buhalis, D., & Inversini, A. (2015). Conceptualising smart tourism destination dimensions. In I. Tussyadiah & A. Inversini (Eds.), *Information and communication technologies in tourism: 2015 proceeding of the international conference*. Springer International Publisher.

Boes, K., Buhalis, D., & Inversini, A. (2016). Smart tourism destinations: Ecosystems for tourism destination competitiveness. *International Journal of Tourism Cities*, *2*(2), 108–124. doi:10.1108/IJTC-12-2015-0032

Buhalis, D., & Amaranggana, A. (2015). *Information and communication technologies in tourism – smart tourism destinations enhancing tourism experience through personalization of services*. Springer International Publisher.

Buonincontri, P., & Micera, R. (2016). The experience co-creation in smart tourism destination: A multiple case analysis of European destinations. *Information Technology & Tourism*, *16*(3), 285–315. doi:10.100740558-016-0060-5

Cacho, A., Figueredo, M., Cassio, A., Araujo, M. V., Mendese, L., Lucas, J., Fairos, H., Coellho, J., Cacho, N., & Prolo, C. (2016). Social smart destination: A platform to analyze user generated content in smart tourism destinations. *New Advances in Information Systems and Technologies*, *1*, 817–826. doi:10.1007/978-3-319-31232-3_77

Çelik, P., & Topsakal, Y. (2017). Akıllı turizm destinasyonları: Antalya destinasyonunun akıllı turizm uygulamalarının incelenmesi [Smart tourism destinations: review of smart tourism applications of Antalya destination]. *Seyahat ve Otel İşletmeciliği Dergisi*, *14*(3), 149–166. doi:10.24010oid.369951

Chiappa, G. D., & Baggio, R. (2015). Knowledge transfer in smart tourism destinations: Analyzing the effects of a network structure. *Journal of Destination Marketing & Management, 4*(3), 145–150. doi:10.1016/j.jdmm.2015.02.001

Chung, N., Lee, H., Lee, S. J., & Koo, C. (2015). The influence of tourism website on tourists' behavior to determine destination selection: A case study of creative economy in Korea. *Technological Forecasting and Social Change, 96,* 130–143. doi:10.1016/j.techfore.2015.03.004

D'amico, G., Ercoli, S., & Bimbo, A. D. (2013). A framework for itinerary personalization in cultural tourism of smart cities. *AIHCI 2013: International Workshop on Intelligent User Interfaces,* 1.

Encalada, L., Portugal, I. B., Ferreira, C. C., & Rocha, J. (2017). Identifying tourist places of interest based on digital imprints: Towards a sustainable smart city. *Sustainability, 9*(12), 1–19. doi:10.3390u9122317

Ercole, E. (2013). Smart tourism: II ruolo dell' informazione social [Smart tourism: the role of social information]. *Annali del Tourismo, 2,* 35–48.

Göktaş Kulualp, H., & Sarı, Ö. (2020). Smart tourism, smart cities, and smart destinations as knowledge management tools. In E. Çeltek (Ed.), *Handbook of Research on Smart Technology Applications in the Tourism Industry* (pp. 371–390). IGI Global Disseminator of Knowledge. doi:10.4018/978-1-7998-1989-9.ch017

Gomes, E. L., Gandara, J. M., & Baidal, J. A. I. (2017). Is it important to be a smart tourism destination? public managers' understanding of destinations in the state of Parana. *Brazilian Journal of Tourism Research, 11*(3), 503–536.

Gretzel, U., Sigala, M., Xiang, Z., & Koo, C. (2015a). Smart tourism: Foundations and developments. *Electronic Markets, 25*(3), 179–188. doi:10.100712525-015-0196-8

Gretzel, U., Werthner, H., Koo, C., & Lamsfus, C. (2015b). Conceptual foundations for understanding smart tourism ecosystems. *Computers in Human Behavior, 50,* 558–563. doi:10.1016/j.chb.2015.03.043

Guo, Y., Liu, H., & Chai, Y. (2014). The embedding convergence of smart cities and tourism internet of things in China: An Advance Perspective. *Advances in Hospitality and Tourism Research, 2*(1), 54–69.

Hernandez-Martin, R., Rodriguez, Y. R., & Gahr, D. (2017). Functional zoning for smart destination management. *European Journal of Tourism Research, 17,* 43–58.

Hunter, W. C., Chung, N., Gretzel, U., & Koo, C. (2015). Constructivist research in smart tourism. *Asia Pacific Journal of Information Systems, 25*(1), 105–120. doi:10.14329/apjis.2015.25.1.105

Jasrotia, A., & Gangotia, A. (2018). Smart cities to smart destinations: A review paper. *Journal of Tourism Inteligence and Smartness, 1*(1), 47–56.

Jovicic, D. (2017). From the traditional understanding of tourism destination to the smart tourism destination. *Current Issues in Tourism, 20,* 276–282.

Junior, A. S., Filho, L. M., Garcia, F. A., & Simoes, J. M. (2017). Smart tourism destinations: A study based on the view of the stakeholders. *Revista Turismo em Analise, 28*(3), 358–379. doi:10.11606/issn.1984-4867.v28i3p358-379

Kang, K., Jwa, J. W., & Park, S. E. (2017). Smart audio tour guide system using TTS. *International Journal of Applied Engineering Research: IJAER, 12*(20), 9846.

Karasar, N. (2014). *Bilimsel araştırma yöntemi* [Scientific research method]. Nobel Academic Publishing.

Kashima, K., & Morita, Y. (2017). Conceptualizing smart tourism of Japan: A case study of smart tourism design on China and Thailand. *International Journal of Management and Applied Science, 3*(3), 76–78.

Khan, M. S., Woo, M., Nam, K., & Chathot, P. (2017). Smart city and smart tourism: A case of Dubai. *Sustainability, 9*(12), 1–24. doi:10.3390u9122279

Koo, C., Shin, S., Gretzel, U., Hunter, W. C., & Chung, N. (2016). Conceptualization of smart tourism destination competitiveness. *Journal of Information Systems, 26*(4), 367–384.

Koo, C., Shin, S., Kim, K., Kim, C., & Chung, N. (2013). Smart tourism of the Korea: A case study. *Pacific Asia Conference on Information Systems (PACIS 2013)*.

La Rocca, R. A. (2013). Tourism and city reflections about dimension of smart city. *Journal of Land Use, Mobility and Environment, 6*(2), 201–213.

La Rocca, R. A. (2014). The role of tourism planning the smart city, *Journal of Lnad Use. Mobility and Environment, 3*, 269–284.

Lamsfus, C., Sorzabal, A.A., Manzanera, T.E. & Vallejo, I.L. (2013). Theoretical framework for a tourism internet of things: smart destination. *Journal of Tourism and Human Mobility,* 15-22.

Li, Y., Hu, C., Huang, C., & Duan, L. (2017). The concept of smart tourism in the context of tourism information services. *Tourism Management, 58*, 293–300. doi:10.1016/j.tourman.2016.03.014

Liburd, J. J., Nielsen, T. K., & Heape, C. (2017). Co-designing smart tourism. *European Journal of Tourism Research, 17*, 28–42.

Perfetto, M. C., Sanchez, A. V., & Presenza, A. (2016). Managing a complex adaptive ecosystem: Towards a smart management of industrial heritage tourism. *Journal of Spatial and Organizational Dynamics, 4*(3), 243–264.

Tran, H. M., Huertas, A. & Moreno, A. (2017). A new framework for the analysis of smart tourism destinations a comparative case study of two Spanish destinations. *Actas del Seminario Internacional Destinos Turistos Inteligentes: Nuevos Horizantes En La Investigacion y Gestion del Turismo,* 190-214.

Varol, Ç. (2017). Sürdürülebilir gelişmede akıllı kent yaklaşımı [Smart city approach in sustainable development]. *Çağdaş Yerel Yönetimler, 26*(1), 43-58.

Wang, D., Li, X., & Li, Y. (2013). China's smart tourism destination initiative: A taste of the service-dominant logic. *Journal of Destination Marketing & Management, 2*(2), 59–61. doi:10.1016/j.jdmm.2013.05.004

Yıldırım, A. (1999). Nitel araştırma yöntemlerinin temel özellikleri ve eğitim araştırmalarındaki yeri ve önemi [The basic features of qualitative research methods and their place and importance in educational research]. *Eğitim ve Bilim, 23*(112), 7–17.

Zhu, W., Zhang, L. & Li, N. (2014). Challenges, function changing of government and enterprises in Chinese smart tourism. *e-Review of Tourism Research, 5,* 1-4.

ADDITIONAL READING

Chen, W. C., Chen, W. H., & Yang, S. Y. (2018). A big data and time series analysis technology-based multi-agent system for smart tourism. *Applied Sciences (Basel, Switzerland), 8*(6), 1–21. doi:10.3390/app8060947

Chung, H. C., Chung, N., & Nam, Y. (2017). A social network analysis of tourist movement patterns in blogs: Korean backpackers in Europe. *Sustainability, 9*(12), 1–19. doi:10.3390u9122251

Ghaderi, Z., Hatamifar, P., & Henderson, J. C. (2018). Destination selection by smart tourists: The case of Isfahan, Iran. *Asia Pacific Journal of Tourism Research, 23*(4), 385–394. doi:10.1080/10941665.2018.1444650

Graziano, T. (2014). Boosting innovation and development? The Italian smart tourism: a critical perspective. *European Journal of Geography, 5*(4:6), 6-18.

Jwa, J.W. (2018). Development of personalized travel products for smart tour guidance services. *International Journal of Engineering & Technology, 7*(3:33), 58-61.

Li, J., Xu, L., Tang, L., Wang, S., & Li, L. (2018). Big data in tourism research: A literature review. *Tourism Management, 68,* 301–323. doi:10.1016/j.tourman.2018.03.009

Lim, C., Mostafa, N., & Park, J. (2017). Digital omotenashi: Toward a smart tourism design systems. *Sustainability, 9*(12), 1–20. doi:10.3390u9122175

Pan, S. Y., Gao, M., Kim, H., Shah, K., Pei, S. L., & Chiang, P. C. (2018). Advances and challenges in sustainable tourism toward a green economy. *The Science of the Total Environment, 635,* 452–469. doi:10.1016/j.scitotenv.2018.04.134 PMID:29677671

Sederati, P. and Baktash, A. (2017). Adoption of smart glasses in smart tourism destination: a system thinking approach. *Tourism Travel and Research Association: Advancing Tourism Research Globally.* 13.

Zhang, Y., Yang, H., Zhang, C., & Li, N. (2018). A new way of being smart, creative computing and its applications in tourism. *42nd IEEE International Conference on Computer Software & Applications,* (pp. 45-50), Tokyo, Japan. 10.1109/COMPSAC.2018.10201

KEY TERMS AND DEFINITIONS

Digitalization: Digitalization is the process of transferring your accessible information and existing resources to digital media in a way that can be read by a computer, and it refers to the integration of technology into daily life and business life.

Innovative Technology: While technology undertakes the tasks of collecting, controlling, and transmitting information through devices, innovative technology refers to the realization of these processes such as Cloud Computing, Internet of Things, Big Data with the latest information systems.

Smart City: Smart City is existing infrastructures integrate with technology and ensure sustainability, as a city that directs the focus directly to people and integrates people with people, institutions and people aims to maximize the interaction between people and institutions.

Smart Tourism: Smart tourism refers to the formation that enables both tourists and residents to participate more effectively in tourism activities through information communication technologies by making digital tourism more social, accelerating information exchange and feedback, and providing more effective solutions to tourism problems.

Smart Tourism Destination: Smart tourism destination refers to the integration and support of the tourism type applied in the destinations with the intensive use of technology by aiming to enrich the tourist experience, implement innovative technologies that facilitate access to services and provide faster information sharing, respond to the needs of stakeholders (tourists, tourism institutions and organizations, government, citizens, etc.), minimize the use of resources, pursue a sustainable society and destination, citizens to improve the quality of life and the quality of the travel experience for visitors.

Smart Tourism Ecosystem: The smart tourism ecosystem (STE) defines as a tourism system that uses smart technology to create, manage and deliver smart tourism services / experiences, and is characterized by intense information sharing and co-creation.

Systematic Literature Review: A systematic literature review is a type of method that systematically examines the data, following a clearly defined protocol or plan, in which the criteria are clearly stated before the review is conducted to arrive at an answer to a question.

Chapter 12
Creative Destinations and the Rooster of Barcelos ("Galo de Barcelos")

Francisco Barbosa Gonçalves
Polytechnic Institute of Cávado and Ave, Portugal

Carlos Costa
University of Aveiro, Portugal

ABSTRACT

This chapter aims at understanding the Rooster of Barcelos (Galo de Barcelos) as local intangible cultural heritage, being the case study of a research leading to the proposal of this explanatory model for developing and implementing tourism creative destinations. The Barcelos Rooster is the result of two ancestral customs of this territory, namely handicrafts and the Jacobin legend of the miracle of the rooster. These two customs, eternalized in time, were associated by the intervention of tourism. In addition, handicrafts, the Camino de Santiago, gastronomy (roast rooster from this legend), wine (vinho verde) and the traditional market, and heritage associated with the Rooster of Barcelos emerge as the main tourist attractions of this territory. It might be concluded that the Rooster of Barcelos, as one of the main symbols of Portuguese tourism, local heritage, and tourism product honey pot has the potential to leverage the sustainable development of this territory as a creative tourist destination.

INTRODUCTION

The Rooster of Barcelos (*Galo de Barcelos*) emerged from two ancient customs of this territory, namely the rooster handicrafts and the Jacobean legend of the rooster's miracle. These two ancient customs were associated through the intervention of tourism. Moreover, the main tourist attractions of this territory appear to be the heritage linked to this symbol of the Portuguese tourism and Barcelos, namely the handicrafts, gastronomy (roast rooster of the Jacobean legend), wine (vinho verde), the Camino de Santiago and the traditional weekly market.

DOI: 10.4018/978-1-7998-8528-3.ch012

This article aims to analyse the Rooster of Barcelos (Galo de Barcelos) as a local intangible cultural heritage and the Model of Tourism Creative Destinations. This model proposes a tourism productive process of co-creation of creative experiences based on the interpretation of the territories, their visitors study (consumers of tourism destinations and products) and also the destination governance (Costa, 2001). In addition, it should be noted that the European Commission has set a number of guidelines for this decade. In particular the Commission wants tourism to be better integrated between urban generating poles and low density areas where tourist very often interact with handicraft producers and natural environments (Costa 2021). This calls for new models to approach tourism, and the creation of new agendas to this area (Duxbury and Richards, 2019).

It is argued this model is innovative as it proposes a productive process of co-creation, that puts together in a single plan the interpretation of destinations, governance and their visitors' study. It is also argued that Creative Tourism can work as a tool for the sustainable development of territories. It is also emphasized that Interpretation performed according to this model, contributes to the enrichment the overall quality of its visitors' experiences. Tourism has a strong association to the territory, as this is the main object of tourism consumption, but also because the endogenous resources of the territories are the basis of tourism development (Fazenda, 2014). In fact, a tourist destination is primarily a territory that attracts visitors, in fact, tourist companies depend a lot on geographical location, because the destinations are unique with removable products and resources (Brandão & Costa, 2014).

Regarding the methodology of this research, qualitative and quantitative methods were used, namely interviews with tourism-related subjects in this territory, and questionnaire surveys to its visitors, as well as a literature review and analysis of relevant documents for this study. The Creative Tourism, a theoretical framework is presented in section 1; the methodology of scientific research is presented in section 2; the Rooster of Barcelos is presented in section 3; and section 4 presents the results and final conclusions.

CREATIVE TOURISM: A THEORETICAL FRAMEWORK

The concept of Creative Tourism is defined by UNESCO (2006, p. 3), within the scope of the "Creative Cities Network", as a new generation of tourism stating: "creative tourism is travel directed toward an engaged and authentic experience, with participative learning in the arts, heritage, or special character of a place, and it provides a connection with those who reside in this place and create this living culture". Creative tourism is perceived as a form of cultural tourism, but different, because while cultural tourism is based on observing, watching and contemplating (visiting museums and art galleries), in turn, creative tourism is based on experience, participation and in learning. It satisfies self-actualization needs focused on developing skills based on intangible resources, including processes such as dancing, singing, producing handicrafts, painting, participating in festivals, but avoiding negative impacts generated by the consumption of the built space. It goes beyond the idea of tourism as an agglomeration of businesses and activities and moves into the concept of tourism as a holistic activity that calls for emotions and self-enrichment (Jelinčić and Senkic, 2019) capable of creating memorable experiences (Sterchele, 2020). It emerges in the context of the emergence of new phenomena, namely the experience economy, the sharing economy, globalization, the concept of intangible cultural heritage and the emerging paradigm of tourism as an instrument for the sustainable development of territories. In this sense, the concept of co-creation and the need to value creativity and innovation as critical factors of development and distinction of tourist destinations were brought to the centre of the debate (Ferreira, 2014).

Tourism being a tool for the sustainable development of territories brought to the centre of the debate several concepts, namely sustainability, accessibility, and the need to value creativity and innovation as critical factors for the development and distinction of tourist destinations. In this sense, according to Butler (1999), the theme of sustainable tourism emerged as discussions from the report "Our Common Future" presented by the UN Brundtland Commission. Within this report, the concept of sustainable development is defined as one that meets the needs of current generations without compromising the ability of future generations to meet their needs and aspirations. According to Hall (2011), the definition of the concept of sustainable tourism is a paradox because it can be perceived as one of the greatest success stories of tourism research and knowledge transfer, but it can also be perceived as a failure given the growing negative impacts of tourism growth, especially in the environmental sphere. However, sustainable tourism is based on an open and flexible strategy, adapted to the territorial and economic singularities of tourist destinations, and it aims at the development and planning of tourism activities that respect and preserve in the long-term the natural, cultural and social resources, contributing positively and equitably for economic development and comfort of receiving communities (Careto & Lima, 2006). Sustainable tourism is about involving local communities (Wisansing and Vongvisitsin, 2019) and make them live upon and care of the surrounding environment. By doing this, entrepreneurial activities may be developed in harmony with the environment (Matetskaya, Svyatunenko, and Gracheva, 2019), and local commerce may be developed in a sustainable and friendly way (Stoffelen, 2020).

MODEL OF TOURIST CREATIVE DESTINATIONS

Considering the objective of scientific research is to create models that explain and simplify reality so that we can position ourselves to take advantage of society in the future, we present the explanatory model of the process of development and implementation of Creative Tourism, in Figure 1 (Gonçalves, 2018). This model fits into the strategic management paradigm of Tourism, namely the "product-space" model (Costa, 2001), according to which the governance of a destination coordinates the network relations between the various stakeholders, and leads the production process to the co-creation, namely the process of inventorying endogenous resources in the framework elaborating a plan for the interpretation of tourist destinations and the study of their potential visitors. It also allows the establishment of closer relationships between the economics and management of tourism and the territories, which is essential for the creation of forms of sustainable tourism (Costa, 2020).

This model is divided into four blocks, namely the territory, the tourism production process, the interpretation and co-creation process, and the study of the tourist-emitting markets (visitors). A territory is a portion of space appropriated by a social group, according to the logic of political, administrative and economic power, and its own values of a cultural, affective, social, symbolic nature, daily living space, struggle for survival, belonging, identity, solidarity and affection. It is also a defined and delimited portion of terrestrial space, a space occupied, humanized, appropriate, lived, differentiated, unique, identity, organized, managed and ordered by social groups (Cavaco, 2013). It might be defined as a space of belonging to a community and a fusion between its physical base and the transformations that human occupation has been adding to it. It is expressed through its visual dimension, which is the landscape with all its natural and built elements, interactions and the immaterial dimension that culture adds to it (Umbelino, 2014).

A territory as a destination and potential tourist product presents itself as the main object of tourist consumption. In fact, the development of tourism always goes through the endogenous resources of the territories (Fazenda, 2014). Therefore, tourism has a strong association with the territory as tourism companies depend a lot on their geographical location, as tourist destinations are unique and with removable products and resources (Brandão & Costa, 2014). To sum up, a tourist destination is primarily a territory, and its development depends on the ability to create or value the territory, and on how this development is articulated and configured (Brito & Correia, 2006).

Figure 1. Explanatory model of the process of development and implementation of creative tourism
Source: Gonçalves, 2018

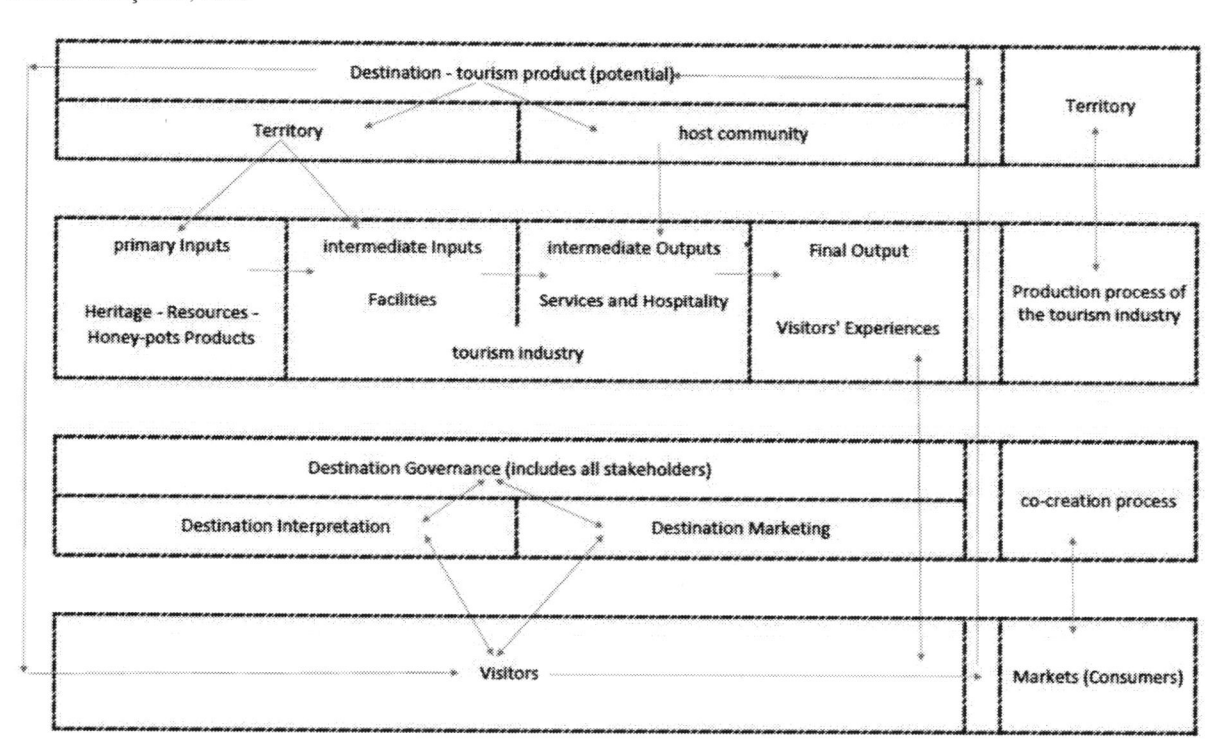

In Webster's dictionary the term "destination" designates the "place marked for the end of a trip", i.e., a territory where a visitor wishes to spend some time away from home. However, for Marketing and Economics a tourist destination is defined as "more than just a geographical place, it is an amalgam of products, services, natural resources, artificial elements and information with potential to attract visitors to a particular place" (Leiper, 1995; Bieger, 1998, cited in Manente & Minghetti 2006, p.229). In sum, a tourist destination is a territory with characteristics known to a enough potential visitors to justify their consideration as an entity, and to attract visitors regardless of the attractions of other places.

The productive process of Tourism includes the territory and its natural and cultural heritage. It must be transformed into tourism resources through human intervention and to be "consumed" by visitors. In this sense, this process, under this model, begins with the primary inputs, namely territory and its heritage (resources / raw materials) and other components (building materials, fuel and agricultural products) to be converted through human intervention, in intermediate inputs (tourism industry facilities: hotels, restaurants, souvenir shops, car rental companies, and other tourist attractions such as national parks, museums, galleries, historic sites, convention centres and media), which, in turn, are refined into intermediate outputs, services and hospitality, which are associated with tourism activities, such as hotels, tourism services, food services and festivals. However, receiving communities through services and hospitality (intermediate outputs) and visitors in the act of consuming services become components of the tourism product in the final output function. In this way, the production process takes place at the moment when visitors consume the destination, that is, the potential tourism product and co-create personal experience (Buhalis, 2000; Gonçalves, 2018; Smith, 1994; World Tourism Organization & European Travel Commission, 2011).

Tourism is a phenomenon that results from people traveling to outside their usual place of residence. According to the World Tourism Organization (WTO), not all travellers are visitors, as visitors are only tourism-related travellers, for example those who travel outside their usual environment for leisure, business or other reasons, and who do not engage in any paid activity at destinations. Visitors can be tourists (overnight) or hikers (not overnight at destination) and are the core element in the development of tourism products, destinations and activities in accordance with the Tourism Satellite Account. Visitors travel to territories with attractions that have the potential to attract them. Territories want to receive visitors because it is proven that Tourism contributes to its development, but also because it is an exporting and job-creating industry (Gonçalves, 2018; Silva, 2013; Smith, 1994; UNWTO, 2008).

In the scope of this model, it is argued that destinations must be interpreted efficiently and creatively so that tourism products are unique, memorable, authentic and creative experiences. Consequently, it is in the co-creation phase of this model that we intend to contribute to this area of knowledge by placing the emphasis on the interpretation of destinations to enrich the quality of tourism experiences (final output of the tourism product), and to make visitors satisfied, recommend the destination, repeat the experience and pass positive word-of-mouth to friends, relatives and acquaintances (one of the most effective destination marketing tools) (Barros & Gama, 2009; Buhalis, 1998; Buhalis, 2000). Therefore, it is proposed a productive process of co-creation of creative tourist experiences based on the interpretation and governance of destinations and the study of their potential visitors. One should argue here that this approach is innovative in bringing together the entire production-consumption process, that is, Interpretation, destination governance and the study of its visitors, but focusing on Interpretation rather than *Marketing*.

Under this model, Interpretation is presented as a tool that enables the visitor to experience the destination, including heritage, the territory's resources, local communities and living cultures. Therefore, this tool should serve for the visitors to experience the living cultures of the receiving communities, their heritage, including the intangible cultural heritage, and should work as an instrument for the development and implementation of creative tourism products and destinations (Buhalis, 2000; Costa, 2001; Costa, Panyik, & Buhalis, 2013; Costa, Costa, & Breda, 2014; Icomos, 2007; Smith, 1994).

The visitor is the core element of Tourism, because without visitors there are no destinations and tourist products or activities. We intend to explain how visitors can co-create, within a productive process, the final output of tourism products (tourist experiences, creative, unique and memorable tourist experiences) by "consuming" the destination (potential tourism product) and involving them with the receiving communities. In this context, it is argued that this productive process of co-creation takes place through the interpretation of destinations, but without devaluing the systematic study of visitors. Under this model, a territory which becomes a tourist destination (potential tourism product) is not only enough to attract visitors, it is necessary to make an inventory of the tangible and intangible natural and cultural heritage, in order to choose their potential tourism resources and attract visitors (Buhalis, 1998; Buhalis, 2000; Buhalis & Licata, 2002; Costa, 2014; Icomos, 2007; Knudson, *et al.,* 2003; Rosmaninho, 2009; Smith, 1994; Tilden, 2007).

In the scope of this innovative model, Interpretation acts as the voice of the members of the host communities, heritage, living cultures and intangible cultural heritage, where each stakeholder may be a co-creator of creative tourism destinations and products. To this end, it is recommended that the interpretation of tourist destinations should integrate the policy of strategic planning and management (concept of governance) and the study of its consumers (marketing of destinations) systematically and with the help of information and communication technologies (ICT) (Buhalis, 1998; Buhalis, 2000; Cooper, 2006; Costa, 2001; Costa, Panyik, & Buhalis, 2013). It should be emphasised that interpretation is a powerful tool to associate symbiotically tourists with destinations. By doing so, interpretation prompts the development of forms of sustainable tourism and make local communities more proud of their capital and heritage. The idea of turning experiences memorable is thus important from a psychological point of view and for the economic benefit of the local populations (Seyfi, Hall and Rasoolimanesh, 2019).

METHODOLOGY

The model used for the present study was adapted from Gonçalves (2018). In order to test this model, both qualitative and quantitative methods were used, namely interviews with tourism-related subjects in this territory, and questionnaire surveys to their visitors, as well as a literature review and analysis of relevant documents for this study.

The treatment of qualitative data obtained in the context of the interviews was carried out through a content analysis, which Bardin (1977, p. 19) defines as "a research technique, that aims at the objective, systematic and quantitative description of the content". "Therefore, to perform a content analysis, the texts must be read, annotated and coded, because the categories are generated from the readings, annotations and coding. Then, the categories are evaluated in relation to the relevance of the emerging taxonomy in relation to the empirical scenario from which they arose, as it is the reflection, questioning and assignment of codes and categories in the real world context (Jennings, 2005). After reading, annotating and coding the texts, the key ideas of each theme defined by each of the specific research objectives were systematized and quantified. Content analysis is one of the most powerful techniques in the empirical research carried out by the different Human and Social Sciences (Vala, 1986).

Regarding the data obtained through the survey surveys, 438 visitors from the territory of Barcelos Rooster were surveyed, and their data analysis was performed using the IBM SPSS Statistics version 19.0 statistical software since it is a quantitative data analysis (Pallant, 2007; Pestana & Gageiro, 1998). In this sense, this analysis is intended to help respond to the objectives of this research by expressing people's opinions, attitudes, and behaviours in quantitative terms (Altinay & Paraskevas, 2008).

According to Altinay & Paraskevas (2008, p. 89) "sampling is the process by which researchers select a subset or representative portion of the total population that can be studied for their topic, so that conclusions can be drawn about the entire population". Apparently, there are two main categories of sampling methods, namely probabilistic and non-probabilistic. In the scope of this investigation, the probabilistic sampling method was chosen because, according to Altinay & Paraskevas (2008), the choice of a probabilistic sample should aim to minimize the sampling error of the estimates of the most important variables of the study and, at the same time minimize the time and costs of carrying it out.

There are four ways to select a probabilistic sample: simple random sampling, systematic sampling, stratified sampling and cluster sampling. We then opted for the simple random sampling method since all members of the population under study are equally likely to be selected. Moreover, the right sample size depends on the level of sampling error one must prepare to tolerate (the degree of precision one wishes to achieve), and the level of confidence that the investigator needs to have in the data actually collected that is representative of the sample. population. Moreover, the non-probabilistic form of real-world tourism research is often quite difficult to obtain. And regarding sample size there is no accepted standard for defining a minimum percentage considered acceptable in terms of survey responses, but most researchers consider anything above 15% or 20% as acceptable, with 10% as the minimum acceptable (Altinay & Paraskevas, 2008).

In the context of the interviews, the selection of the interviewed subjects had as their sole criterion their relationship with tourism in Barcelos. Therefore, they were divided into four dimensions, namely the cultural dimension one (academics / opinion leaders), the cultural dimension two (material / responsible for cultural institutions / museums and local interpretative centres), the governance dimension (political-administrative). and finally, the economic dimension including all activities from the tourism satellite account (UNWTO, 2008). Thus, the group of subjects surveyed is composed of fourteen subjects from the economic dimension, seven from the governance (political-organizational) dimension, five from the cultural dimension one (academics / opinion leaders) and six from the cultural dimension two (material / institutions leaders). cultural / museums and local interpretive centres). Note that the respondents differ in other dimensions since they were not considered as a selection criterion. Briefly, these were the criteria adopted in this research.

CASE STUDY: THE ROOSTER OF BARCELOS (GALO DE BARCELOS)

This section aims at understanding the Rooster of Barcelos, its historical and morphological evolution. It emerges as an intangible cultural heritage of the community of this territory and it became one of the main symbols of the Portuguese tourism thanks to the political action of António Ferro, who was was responsible for the propaganda of Salazar's alt right regime.

This study can be divided in several phases according to the model of life cycle of a product (Buttler, 1980), namely the involvement phase: from ancient times to the 1940 exhibition as a piece of pottery and folk art; the development phase: from 1940 to 1960, as a piece of handicraft product and one of the symbols of the Portuguese tourism; the consolidation phase: after 1960, as a tradition arising from two customs, namely the piece of handicraft (tangible cultural heritage) and the Jacobean legend (intangible cultural heritage), and also the mark of a territory; the rejuvenation phase, in the 21st century, as intangible cultural heritage, a primary input and a honey pot product for the development of the tourism industry in Barcelos.

In the context of this chapter, it is argued that the tradition of the Rooster of Barcelos results from two ancient customs of this territory, namely the handcrafting of roosters and the Jacobean legend of the miracle of the rooster of Saint James, which were associated by tourism in the 1960s. This tradition as an intangible cultural heritage and a honey-pot product of this territory, and it appears to have potential to contribute to its sustainable tourism development. As it was stated before, creative tourism depends very much on the traditions since the consumers want to embark in memorable experiences (Seyfi, Hall and Rasoolimanesh, 2019; Sterchele, 2020).

The "protogalo" (old rooster) is the most ancient piece of this symbol, and the custom of making roosters and other domestic animals goes back to distant times. At those old times, the most common motifs were domestic animals, namely oxen, pigs, horses, roosters and chickens. But roosters predominated because they were traditionally associated with mythological virtues, namely the rooster crowed to herald Jesus Christ's deity and birth, as well as confirmed most of the miracles attributed to St. James along the Jacobean routes. In addressing the inspiring themes of figuration made in this territory, the ethnographer Rocha Peixoto states that the rooster exceeds in number and variety all other species of fauna, besides being the best treated bird in size of nobility, insistence of details and refinement of patterned. Moreover, the rooster stands for its dominating and manly customs, for being haughty, majestic, vigilant, but also for being celebrated in tales, superstitions and singing ceremonies. Its mythological, religious and popular importance is lost in distant times, because in the Greek symbolic the crowing of the rooster compels the demons to flee, awakens the dawn and causes men to rise (Rocha Peixoto, 1966).

In morphological terms, this "protogalo" presents the profile of a pinwheel, which was the most represented motif in the pinwheels of this territory. This "protogalo" is a 15 cm high "little rooster" with a small crest, a massive body and joined barbs, and has some archaisms, notably the non-serrated tail, the lack of paw representation and the underside of the tail (Mimoso, 2010).

António Ferro's Rooster: it was in the ambit of his political action (Salazar's alt right regime), in the 1940's, that the Rooster of Barcelos, as a piece of handicraft gained national and international dimension and became one of the symbols of the Portuguese tourism, becoming therefore important for the local economy. Thus, at the Portuguese World Exhibition in 1940, organized by António Ferro, this event presented many glazed and painted pieces to represent Barcelos handicraft, in the house of Portuguese Villages (Barcelos house). Many representative pieces of Barcelos' handicraft were made and taken in terms of folk art, even some of these pieces can be found at the Regional Ceramics Museum, but the piece of handicraft from Barcelos that had many admirers were the bestselling Rooster of Barcelos (Mimoso, 2010). Moreover, the handicrafts were considered by Estado Novo regime (Salazarism) as the quintessential achievement of the popular culture (Melo, 2001, p. 176).

According to Carlos Basto (Jornal de Barcelos, June 20, 1991), António Ferro's political action was decisive for the dissemination of the Rooster of Barcelos as one of the symbols of the Portuguese tourism. However, it is argued that painter Gonçalves Torres was the true creator of the current Rooster of Barcelos, an argument also corroborated by Macedo Correia (1965) who claims that the painter Gonçalves Torres gave to the Rooster of Barcelos the first touches of elegance.

Carlos Basto (Jornal de Barcelos, June 20, 1991) explains the success of the Rooster of Barcelos as follows: "in 1933, the Secretariat of National Propaganda was created, being the predecessor of the National Secretariat of Information, Popular Culture and Tourism (SNI) led by Antonio Ferro who, in September 1935, took to Geneva a memorable exhibition of Folk Arts, where the Rooster of Barcelos had its international debut, experiencing an unusual success. At the Paris International Exhibition, in 1937, the Portuguese stand was awarded with the Grand Prix, and the Barcelos handicrafts shone again thanks to its Rooster. These successes were repeated, in 1939, at the New York World Fairs and the San Francisco International Fairs, and the Rooster was re-imposed in the Double Centennial Exhibition in 1940. At the inauguration of the Museum of Popular Art, in Belém, in 1947, the Rooster of Barcelos was once again enthroned, by continuing its path to the success. In this sense, the Jornal de Barcelos, in its of April 2, 1959 edition, transcribed a telegram received from Paris, on March 26, 1959, with the following text: "the roosters of Barcelos flood Paris, announcing the spring". It was the internationalization of Rooster of Barcelos as one of the symbols of the Portuguese tourism.

The Rooster of Barcelos had a morphological evolution from the protogalo to the rooster of the 1940 Exhibition, thanks to the innovation of pottery production techniques. Hence, the latter cannot be classed as the current "Rooster of Barcelos", because at that time, as already mentioned, there were no large roosters, being the largest made in the pottery wheel was about 25 cm high. But it was from the mid-1950s onwards that colour black emerged as the background colour, which became a feature of the current Rooster of Barcelos. The emergence of black colour is due to the lack of chemical pigments during World War II, and because it is easy to obtain, using fish glue as a vehicle, and chimney soot as a pigment. Moreover, the techniques, prior to the 1930s, did not allow making roosters more than 15 cm high, and the pieces of handicraft of that time were mainly whistle toys. Consequently, the first large, decorative red roosters emerged from the 1930s and they might help in understanding the morphological evolution and innovation of production techniques. Its increased size implied a new manufacturing technique, as the clay (raw material) undergoes a sudden volumetric change at about 570°C (quartz inversion point) during baking in the oven which causes the rupture of bulky and massive pieces. Therefore, to make a rooster 20 cm high or even taller, it is necessary create a leak on the body to prevent it from breaking during the baking process. The pottery wheel and plaster casts emerged as innovative production techniques, making it possible to make roosters globular, and thus giving them one of the characteristics morphological characteristics of the current Rooster of Barcelos (Mimoso, 2010).

Barcelos Pottery Museum is a very important reference for local and national tourism, and may act in the future as an important driver for the preservation and promotion of the local handicrafts. It may also help to stimulate the development of the city of Barcelos (Zukin, 2020). The museum has a collection of representative roosters of all stages of its morphological evolution from which a photographic collection was made within the scope of this research. This Museum has a collection of roosters about 20 cm high which were offered by ethnologist Joaquim Sellès Paes de Villas Boas. These roosters, although newer, correspond to the description made by Leitão de Barros and Artur Maciel in the context of an exchange of missives, framed in the organization of an international congress in Estoril, at the end of September 1931, and for which the organizing committee (which included Antonio Ferro and Leitão de Barros) had decided to offer regional pieces of handicraft to the congressmen. Thus, in this letter, dated September 15, 1931, it could be read "Leitão de Barros had the idea of offering regional handicraft pieces from Barcelos and Famalicão, which were pieces of decorative regional handicraft only sold in street markets, namely oxen, red and roosters (Viana, 1988). This letter presents a valuable information by mentioning "red, primitive and large roosters and decorative regional handicraft pieces" because it shows that archaic roosters were already modelled in the decade prior to the 1940 Exhibition (without the serrated crest, which is a feature of the current Rooster of Barcelos) (Mimoso, 2010).

The testimony of the ethnologist and biologist Joaquim Rodrigues dos Santos Júnior, born in 1901, in Barcelos, appears to be a further evidence that the rooster of the 1940 Exhibition did not have the morphology of the current Rooster of Barcelos, because when referring to current pieces of handicraft, in "Life and Art of the Portuguese People" (published in 1940, after the exhibition of the Portuguese World), makes a special mention to the rooster of Barcelos pieces because it presents multiple forms or attitudes and a certain detail, in addition to a specially in modelling and painting, specifying the Barcelos statuary consisted of pieces of handicraft less than 20 cm high with whistles and toothpick holes (Mimoso, 2008).

The "Rooster of Tradition": in morphological terms, the current Rooster of Barcelos emerged in the mid-1950s. It is a modern, slender and different rooster, and it is characterized by its black background with red hearts and a slender and tall neck, a serrated crest and with a tail. An article and published in the Jornal de Barcelos in November 1957 signed by "M" might help to understand this morphological evolution of the Rooster of Barcelos. It can be read that the painter Gonçalves Torres has been trying to squeeze this Rooster for a long time and that the modern Rooster of Barcelos came out of his hands. It has gone from being naive to being smart but remains characteristically regional. Neither of the previous types has lost sales, as all continue to sell well, although the modern Roosters have been sold the most. Honour and glory to the painter Gonçalves Torres, who did not earn money from his input of adding the red hearts to the Rooster of Barcelos. Indeed, the painter Gonçalves Torres would have thought that the two key surfaces in the attractiveness of the Rooster of Barcelos were the crest and the tail, which could be highlighted and used as decoration supports. Accordingly, this redrawing of the rooster, perhaps an exercise to prove a point of view that would not expect great consequences date from 1955. Therefore, it was from this redesign with new shapes, new decoration and red hearts as central reason, that the Rooster de Barcelos has been presented itself as a tourist poster of Portugal in the French decoration magazines and in other countries. Perhaps Gonçalves Torres' redesign predates the vulgarization of red hearts, because there are "new look" roosters with classic decoration and archaic features. However, there are also roosters with archaic morphological characteristics, but decorated with punctuated designs involving hearts, thus evidencing the coexistence of the classic style and the modern style. Therefore, the red hearts were inspired by embroidery and jewellery from the region Minho and were introduced in the second half of the 1950s, and it remains a ubiquitous decorative theme. In the 1960s, the modern rooster reached its aesthetic heights, and in addition to black roosters, there were also white roosters (bridal roosters). However, due to their elegance, the roosters of this era became fragile and evolved in the opposite direction, making the neck shorter, the tail and crest cut-outs smaller and less numerous, thus becoming less airy but more robust (Mimoso, 2010).

The Rooster of Barcelos, a tradition invented and adapted by tourism, which might be evidenced by the documents found in the scope of this study, referring to the 1960s, show the existence of a controversy about the authorship of the Rooster of Barcelos. This controversy has dragged on over time and has come to the present days and can be explained by the ambition of financial gain with the registration of the patent "Galo de Barcelos". According to Mimoso (2010), there is evidence that the roosters of the Exhibition of 1940 were made in the pottery of the artisan Júlia Côta's father, a fact that was confirmed to us by herself. In addition, Jornal de Notícias published an article about the Rooster of Barcelos on May 5, 1991, which included an interview with artisan Maria Sineta, who claimed to be Domingos Côto (artisan Julia Côta's grandfather) the author of the first Rooster of Barcelos. In this regard, there is an article published in the Jornal de Barcelos, on July 14, 1960, entitled "Carta de Lisboa", demonstrating this controversy: "the subject, my friend, is of delicate development and more touchy now that the inventor - the age certificate (?) - of the Rooster of Barcelos appears".. and it continues… "if you know who is the author of the Rooster of Barcelos, who knows, you soon know that, as folk art, the piece is invalid", concluding, "the history of the Folks thing has no documents, always forged, and it only has to guide it what is called the evolution of the cultural complex". However, this controversy about the authorship of the Rooster of Barcelos is relevant in the scope of this study because it is the origin of the tradition of the Rooster of Barcelos. In this sense, the letter sent to the Civil Governor of Braga by the Mayor of Barcelos, Dr. Luís Fernandes de Figueiredo, published in the Jornal de Barcelos of June 9, 1960, with the following message: "someone strange to this municipal district wants to register the patent of the regional piece, known by the name of "Galo de Barcelos", in the Industrial Property Office". But to contest the patent registration and to claim the legitimate patrimonial right of the community of Barcelos on the Rooster of Barcelos, the mayor presented as argument, precisely, the Legend of the miracle of the Rooster of Barcelos. Therefore, this contestation of patent registration becomes a relevant historical fact as it is the first time that the rooster (handicraft) was associated with the rooster of the Jacobean legend of the Barcelos rooster miracle. However, the Civil Governor favourably accepted the defence presented by the Mayor of Barcelos City Council, whose document was published in the Jornal de Barcelos, on August 4, 1960, emerging then the tradition of the Rooster of Barcelos.

It is noted that the articles published on this theme, in the last two decades of the twentieth century, always associated the Rooster of the handicraft to the Rooster of the legend of the Camino of Santiago. For example, the Expresso Newspaper, in its February 26, 1983 issue, published an article entitled "The Power of the Rooster of Barcelos". In this article, "tourism" is pointed out as the "author" of the association between legend and the Rooster. The edition of the newspaper Comercio do Porto, March 9, 1986, devotes a page to the theme of "Origins of Ceramics in Portugal", which explains the origins of ceramics in this region, but highlights the Rooster of Barcelos in an article with the title "The Rooster of Barcelos", but exclusively dedicated to the "Legend of the miracle of the Rooster of Barcelos".

In Barcelos, tourism associated the rooster of the Jacobean legend to the rooster of handicrafts. This legend tells of one of the rooster miracles attributed to St. James along the paths of Santiago in medieval times. In the Archaeological Museum of Barcelos, there is a granite cross depicting this legend, representing the "miracle". Thus, the face of the cross, once turned to the gallows, features various figures, including a rooster, Jesus Christ and a pilgrim hanging from a rope, with St. James underneath holding his feet. The dating of this monument is not consensual, and the monument is inscribed in the fourteenth century, but some authors point out the sixteenth century, and others argue it is from the eighteenth century. As part of this study, the oldest documents found about this legend dated from the nineteenth century, namely an article by Amaral Ribeiro published in 1867 in the Descriptive News of Barcellos, and a book entitled Historical Memory of Villa de Barcellos, Barcellinhos and Villa Nova de Famelicão, by Domingos Joaquim Pereira, known as "Abbot of Louro", and which was published in 1867 by the typography of André J. Ferreira & Filho. Chapter XI of this book tells the story of the gallows of Barcelos and the allusive cross to this legend of the rooster. Also, Rocha Peixoto, an ethnographer who marked the nineteenth century, was one of the first authors to address the works of pottery that have originated the Rooster of Barcelos. Finally, Pires de Lima (1965), an ethnographer representative of the nationalist paradigm of the First Republic and the regime Estado Novo wrote a book about the legend of the rooster of Barcelos. It is noted that the Estado Novo used ethnography to legitimize the regime's nationalist ideology (Melo, 2001).

The argument of the existence of an "association forged" by tourism between the Jacobean legend and handicrafts was presented by Carlos Basto in the Jornal de Barcelos, on June 20, 1991, in an article entitled "The Rooster of Barcelos - What is its Identity? This argument is corroborated by Dr. Victor Pinho, historian and director of the municipal library of Barcelos, who in the interview in the scope of this study, he states that the "Rooster of Barcelos" represents a tradition of Barcelos' handicraft, whose authenticity comes from the fact of being produced for many years by local potters as a form of popular art expression. It adds that, only from the 90's of the twentieth century, the medieval Jacobean legend and the handicraft were associated, making the Rooster of Barcelos an icon of strength and popularity that needs to contextualize and find new forms of expression and dissemination, through marketing, by becoming the mark of this territory and one of the symbols of the Portuguese tourism from the 1950-60s.

In turn, the director of the Barcelos Pottery Museum states that the Rooster of Barcelos is an identity heritage of this territory because it has been represented over the centuries by the handcrafters of Barcelos and because there is no other producing centre with such a strong representation along the way that is known. It is argued that the later association with the Jacobean legend of the Barcelos rooster miracle made this identification with the Barcelos territory more decisive.

The Estado Novo regime, through Antonio Ferro's political action, made it a symbol of Portugal, reaching a national and international dimension, but never dissociating itself from its identity mark: "Galo de Barcelos". In short, tourism has made two customs of this community a tradition that, in turn, has become a heritage of this territory and one of the symbols of Portuguese tourism.

DISCUSSION OF RESULTS AND CONCLUSION

This chapter aimed at understanding the Rooster of Barcelos (Galo de Barcelos) as local intangible cultural heritage, being the case study of a research project leading to the proposal of an explanatory model for developing and implementing tourism creative destinations.

As the literature review demonstrates, creative tourism is perceived as a form of cultural tourism, but different, because it has developed from the intangible cultural heritage of the destination communities, it is based on experience, participation and in learning, it satisfies self-actualization needs focused on developing skills based on intangible resources, including processes such as dancing, singing, producing handicrafts, painting, participating in festivals. Creative tourism emerges in the context of new phenomena, namely the economy of experiences, the sharing economy, globalization, in the scope of the emerging paradigm of tourism being an instrument for the sustainable development of territories. Creative tourism practitioners should be aware of their theoretical and practical underpinnings so it can be properly developed (Carvalho, Costa, and Ferreira, 2019).

The chapter attempted to demonstrate that creative tourism plays a decisive role in linking the economics of the tourism sector (tourists) to the territory, as it is advocated by Costa (2020). Creative tourism ought to be used in order to associate tourism to the local communities because future tourism has to be sustainable and, thus, be closely developed with the local communities and economies (Remoaldo, Matos, Gôja, Alves, and Duxbury, 2020).

The literature review and the surveys carried out in this study led us to conclude that new tourism trends point out to searching for cultural destinations based on authenticity, identity and balance suiting the concept of new tourists, whose main motivations are discovering, learning and exploring different cultures in order to satisfying their needs, wishes and motivations. Therefore, it might be said that the Rooster of Barcelos has the potential to contribute for the sustainable development of this territory as a creative tourism destination, since it is one of the main symbols of Portuguese tourism, a local intangible cultural heritage, and it is also one of its main honey-pot products in attracting visitors to Barcelos.

The Rooster of Barcelos, as one of the main symbols of Portuguese tourism, representing the intangible cultural heritage and a honey-pot product of this territory, might contribute to the success of tourism industry, in Barcelos. Therefore, it might be concluded this case study can explain the proposal of this explanatory model for developing and implementing tourism creative destinations for the development and implementation of the creative tourism, that involves several elements, namely: territory, heritage, resources, products, and tourists experience as well as the host community culture.

REFERENCES

Altinay, L., & Paraskevas, A. (2008). *Planning Research in Hospitality and Tourism*. Elsevier, Ltd.

Bardin, L. (1977). *Análise de Conteúdo*. Presses Universitaires de France.

Barros, C., & Gama, R. (2009). Marketing territorial como instrumento de valorização dos espaços rurais: Uma aplicação na rede das Aldeias de Xisto. *Caderno de Geografia, 28/29*, 93–106.

Brandão, F., & Costa, C. (2014). Inovação em Turismo: Uma Abordagem Sistémica e Territorial. In Produtos e Competitividade do Turismo na Lusofonia (pp. 69–91). Lisboa: Escolar Editora.

Brito, C. H., & Correia, R. (2006). *A model for understanding the dynamics of territorial networks: the case of tourism in the Douro Valley*. Retrieved from https://bibliotecadigital.ipb.pt/handle/10198/5834

Buhalis, D. (1998). Strategic use of information technologies in the tourism industry. *Tourism Management, 19*(5), 409–421. doi:10.1016/S0261-5177(98)00038-7

Buhalis, D. (2000). Marketing the Competitive Destination of the future. *Tourism Management, 21*(July), 97–116.

Buhalis, D., & Licata, M. C. (2002). The future eTourism intermediaries. *Tourism Management, 23*(3), 207–220. doi:10.1016/S0261-5177(01)00085-1

Buttler, R. (1980). *The Tourism Area Life Cycle: Applications and Modifications*. Channel View Publications.

Carvalho, R., Costa, C., & Ferreira, A. (2019). Review of the theoretical underpinnings in the creative tourism research field. *Tourism & Management Studies, 15*(SI), 11–22.

Cavaco, C. (2013). Territórios de Turismo. *Revista Turismo & Desenvolvimento, 20*, 51–67.

Cooper, C. (2006). Knowledge management and tourism. *Annals of Tourism Research, 33*(1), 47–64. doi:10.1016/j.annals.2005.04.005

Costa, C. (2001). An Emerging Tourism Planning Paradigm? A Comparative Analysis Between Town and Tourism Planning. *International Journal of Tourism Research, 3*(3), 425–441. doi:10.1002/jtr.277

Costa, C. (2014). Gestão Estratégica do Turismo: Evolução Epistemológica dos Modelos e Paradigmas, e Tendências para o Futuro. In Turismo nos Países Lusófonos: Conhecimento, Estratégia e Territórios (pp. 19–40). Lisboa: Escolar Editora.

Costa, C. (2020). Tourism planning: A perspective paper. *Tourism Review, 75*(1), 198–202. doi:10.1108/TR-09-2019-0394

Costa, C. 2021, The impact of the COVID-19 outbreak on the tourism and travel sectors in Portugal: Recommendations for maximising the contribution of the European Regional Development Fund (ERDF) and the Cohesion Fund (CF) to the recovery. Report produced to the Directorate-General Regional and Urban Policy (DG REGIO), European Commission.

Costa, C., Costa, R., & Breda, Z. (2014). Produtos e Competividade do Turismo na Lusofonia - Vol II - Introdução. In Produtos e Competividade do Turismo na Lusofonia (pp. 13–15). Lisboa: Escolar Editora.

Costa, C., Panyik, E., & Buhalis, D. (2013). Towards a Conceptual Framework: An Introduction. In C. Buhalis, D. & Costa (Eds.), Trends in European Tourism Planning and Organisation (pp. 1–11). Channel View Publications.

Duxbury, N., & Richards, G. (2019). A research agenda for creative tourism. In N. Duxbury & G. Richards (Eds.), *A Research Agenda for Creative Tourism* (1st ed.). doi:10.4337/9781788110723

Fazenda, N. (2014). Turismo em Portugal: Reflexões para uma Política Nacional de Turismo. In C. Costa (Ed.), *Turismo nos Países Lusófonos: Conhecimento, Estratégia e Territórios* (pp. 293–312). Escolar Editora.

Ferreira, A. M. (2014). O Turismo como Fator de Regeneração e Desenvolvimento de Meios Urbanos e Rurais: Do Turismo Urbano ao Turismo Criativo. In Turismo nos Países Lusófonos: Conhecimento, Estratégia e Territórios (pp. 85–100). Lisboa: Escolar Editora.

Gonçalves, F. (2018). *A Interpretação do Património como fator de desenvolvimento do Turismo Cultural e Criativo. O caso do Galo de Barcelos*. Tese de Doutoramento, Universidade de Aveiro.

ICOMOS. (2007). *The Ename Charter*. ICOMOS.

Jelinčić, D. A., & Senkic, M. (2019). The value of experience in culture and tourism: the power of emotions. In N. Duxbury & G. Richards (Eds.), *A research agenda for creative tourism* (pp. 41–53). doi:10.4337/9781788110723.00012

Jennings, G. R. (2005). Interviewing: a Focus on Qualitative Techniques. In Tourism Research Methods: Integrating Theory with Practice (pp. 99–117). CAB International. doi:10.1079/9780851999968.0099

Knudson, D., Cable, T., & Beck, L. (2003). Interpretation of Cultural and Natural Resources. Venture Publishing, Inc.

Macedo, C. (1965). *As Louças de Barcelos*. Barcelos: Museu da Olaria.

Manente, M., & Minghetti, V. (2006). Destination Management Organizations and Actors. In C. Buhalis, D. & Costa (Eds.), Tourism Business Frontiers, Consumers, Products and Industry. Elsevier Ltd. doi:10.1016/B978-0-7506-6377-9.50032-8

Matetskaya, M., Svyatunenko, A., & Gracheva, O. (2019). The development of creative tourism in rural areas of Russia: issues of entrepreneurial ability, cooperation, and social inclusion. In N. Duxbury & G. Richards (Eds.), *A Research Agenda for Creative Tourism* (1st ed., pp. 137–150). Elgar Research Agendas. doi:10.4337/9781788110723.00021

Melo, D. (2001). *Salazarismo e Cultura Popular (1933 - 1958)*. Instituto de Ciências Sociais da Universidade de Lisboa.

Mimoso, J. M. (2008). *Uma História Natural do Galo de Barcelos*. Retrieved from http://www.historia.com.pt/barcelos/galo/textos/historia.htm

Mimoso, J. M. (2010). Origem e Evolução do Galo de Barcelos. *Olaria: Estudos Arqueológicos, Históricos e Etnológicos*, 143–159.

Pallant, J. (2007). *SPSS: Survival Manual*. Open University Press.

Pestana, M. H., & Gageiro, J. N. (1998). *Análise de Dados para Ciências Sociais - A Complementaridade do SPSS*. Edições Sílabo, Lda.

Pires de Lima, F. (1965). *A Lenda do Senhor do Galo de Barcelos e o Milagre do Enforcado*. Gabinete de Etnografia da FNAT.

Remoaldo, P., Matos, O., Gôja, R., Alves, J., & Duxbury, N. (2020). Management practices in creative tourism: Narratives by managers from international institutions to a more sustainable form of tourism. *Geosciences (Switzerland)*, *10*(46), 2–12. doi:10.3390/geosciences10020046

Rocha Peixoto. (1966). *As olarias de Prado*. Barcelos: Museu Regional de Cerâmica.

Rosmaninho, N. (2009). *Relatório da disciplina de Património e Identidade*. Universidade de Aveiro.

Seyfi, S., Hall, C. M., & Rasoolimanesh, S. M. (2019). Exploring memorable cultural tourism experiences. *Journal of Heritage Tourism*, *6631*(15), 3.

Silva, J. S. (2013). Turismo interno: A conceptualização e a cobertura estatística. *Revista Turismo & Desenvolvimento*, *20*, 151–165.

Smith, S. L. J. (1994). The tourism product. *Annals of Tourism Research*, *21*(3), 582–595. doi:10.1016/0160-7383(94)90121-X

Sterchele, D. (2020). Memorable tourism experiences and their consequences: An interaction ritual (IR) theory approach. *Annals of Tourism Research*, *81*(October), 1–13.

Stoffelen, A. (2020). Revitalising place-based commercial heritage: A Cultural Political Economy approach to the renaissance of lambic beers in Belgium. *International Journal of Heritage Studies*, *00*(00), 1–14. doi:10.1080/13527258.2020.1862275

Tilden, F. (2007). Interpreting our Heritage (4th ed.). The University of North Carolina Press. (Original publicado em 1957)

Umbelino, J. (2014). Os Valores do Território no Lazer e no Turismo. In Produtos e Competividade do Turismo na Lusofonia (pp. 203–216). Lisboa: Escolar Editora.

UNESCO. (2006). Towards Sustainable Strategies for Creative Tourism, Discussion Report of the Planning Meeting for 2008. UNESCO.

UNWTO. (2008). *Tourism Satellite Account: Recommended Methodological Framework 2008*. UNWTO.

Vala, J. (1986). A Análise de Conteúdo. In A. Santos Silva & J. Madureira Pinto (Eds.), *Metodologia das Ci~encias Sociais* (pp. 101–128). Edições Afrontamento.

Viana, A. (1988). *Gente e cousas d'Antre Minho e Lima*. Câmara Municipal de Viana do Castelo.

Wisansing, J., & Vongvisitsin, T. (2019). Local impacts of creative tourism initiatives. In N. Duxbury & G. Richards (Eds.), *A research agenda for creative tourism* (pp. 122–136). Elgar Research Agendas. doi:10.4337/9781788110723.00020

World Tourism Organization & European Travel Commission. (2011). Handbook on Tourism Product Development. Madrid: World Tourism Organization (UNWTO) and the European Travel Commission (ETC).

Zukin, S. (2020). The innovation Complex - Cities, Tech, and the New economy (1st ed.). Academic Press.

KEY TERMS AND DEFINITIONS

Creative Tourism: Phenomenon resulting from travel directed toward an engaged and authentic experience, with participative learning in the arts, heritage, providing a connection with those who reside in this place and create this living culture.

Interpretation of Heritage: Acts as the revelation and the voice of the members of communities and their heritage, living cultures and the intangible cultural heritage.

Model of Creative Destinations: It proposes and explain a tourism productive process of cocreation of creative experiences based on the interpretation of cultural heritage and territories, the study of their visitors and the destination governance.

Rooster of Barcelos (*Galo de Barcelos*)**:** It is a tradition, local cultural heritage, resulting from two ancient customs from Barcelos, namely Crafts of roosters and the legend of the rooster miracle in the Camino of Santiago, associated by tourism.

Tourism: It is a phenomenon resulting from people traveling outside their usual environment and their activities in the destination in accordance with the Tourism Satellite Account.

Tourist Destination: It designates the place marked for the end of a trip, a territory where a visitors wish to spend some time away from home, but being more than just a geographical place, being an amalgam of products, services, natural resources, artificial elements, and information with potential to attracting visitors.

Chapter 13
Cultural Tourism:
Use of Virtual Visits to Museums

Maria Gorete Dinis
GOVCOPP, Polytechnic Institute of Portalegre, Portugal

Adelaide Proença
VALORIZA, Polytechnic Institute of Portalegre, Portugal

Cláudia Batista
Polytechnic Institute of Portalegre, Portugal

Luís Barradas
Polytechnic Institute of Portalegre, Portugal

ABSTRACT

This chapter aims to know the experience of the public in the use of virtual visits to museums. For that, the authors developed a survey and gave it, through social media, between December 22, 2020 and January 5, 2021. Ninety-one valid responses were obtained. The results indicate that although most respondents say that they are aware of the possibility of carrying out virtual visits to museums, very few carry out this type of visit. One of the advantages most mentioned by respondents was the fact that it is not necessary to leave the house for the visit.

INTRODUCTION

The present-day impact that technology has caused on society is evident, changing the daily life of people and organizations. The new technologies shape our minds and lifestyle, as well as the type of services we have become accustomed to over time, transforming them, gaining new dynamics and images and adapting them to the public's taste.

Tourism is an important economic activity for any country and world economy and, due to its specific characteristics and strong dependence on information, this sector has been strongly affected by technological developments. Organizations have been incorporating technological advances, using them

DOI: 10.4018/978-1-7998-8528-3.ch013

to optimize their activity (Hassan, 2011). Buhalis (2003, p. 16) states that "the tourism industry uses information communication technologies (ICTs) for various functions, such as improving the efficiency of communication and management, improving the quality of services and differentiating products, providing new services and creating new products, reinventing and innovating new business practices, creating integrated experiences through partnerships with other suppliers and improving the distribution of tourism to the electronic market".

From the consumer's point of view, ICTs are revolutionizing the means and speed of access to information and the level of demand in terms of its quality. Currently, tourism consumers look for relevant information at all stages of the travel cycle and the Internet has been used as one of the main sources of information for the selection, planning and organization of their trips. In addition, the Internet, particularly social networks, has also been the stage for sharing the experiences of consumers, allowing for a beneficial level of involvement between consumers and between them and companies (Roque, Fernandes & Raposo, 2012).

VR is assumed by Barnes (2016) as one of the most important and popular technologies, but the adoption of virtual reality for the provision of tourism experiences has long been pointed out by Williams & Hobson (1995) as a technology that will have a significant impact on tourism and revolutionize the promotion and selling of the sector. The development of VR is comparable in importance with that of social media (Morris 2016) and is seen as an increasingly prominent tool for consumer marketing, mainly for tourism advertisers, because they can provide potential consumers, wherever they are located, with virtual experiences that allow them to have a realistic view in advance of their travel experience or product (Lo & Cheng, 2020). VR has evolved significantly in recent years and is no longer just a niche technology used only by gaming communities (Tussyadiah et al., 2018).

The beginning of 2020 proved to be troubled and full of challenges with the arrival of the COVID-19 pandemic. Because of it, the world was forced to adapt to this new reality (Frade, 2020). Museums worldwide have been particularly affected by the COVID-19 pandemic, with nearly 90% of them having been forced to close their doors in March 2020. Considering this world panorama, companies were advised to prepare their business for the digital age (Ferrão, 2020). According to a study developed by UNESCO (2020), the museum sector reacted very quickly to the COVID-19 crisis, developing its presence on the Internet, with a transformation being observed of many of the face-to-face museum activities planned for that year into the digital world. The same study reveals that virtual visits and the social networks were initiatives used by museums to keep in contact with their public, especially the "big museums" located in countries with better Internet access, but which can serve as inspiration for other museums (UNESCO, 2020). Given this pandemic context, with closed museums and restrictions on the movement of people inside and outside their countries, the public started to choose other alternatives to access cultural destinations and attractions, such as VR (Chen, 2020).

The theme of VR in tourism has been object of study in recent decades by some authors (e.g. Williams & Hobson, 1995; Guttentag, 2020; Huang et al., 2016; Tussyadiah et al., 2017). However, there have been rapid advances in this area and constraints imposed by certain contexts, such as the pandemic caused by COVID-19, which forced the population to stay at home and attractions, such as museums, to remain closed for long periods of time and adopt different strategies to reach the public, so this justifies the need to conduct new studies. In addition, museums face financial difficulties, accentuated by the pandemic, which makes it necessary to carry out studies to better understand the attitudes and behaviour of their audiences, so that they can make more informed and correct decisions. VR technology is constantly evolving and applying new VR innovations should be tested and analysed by advertisers (Lo & Cheng (2020).

The main objective of this chapter is to understand, on the one hand, the knowledge and experience of Portuguese public in the use of virtual visits to museums and, on the other hand, to ascertain whether the country's museums provide the public with the possibility of virtual visits to the museum. Considering that the study was carried out during the pandemic period caused by COVID-19, the aim will be to gain an understanding of the influence of the lived context, especially in terms of the use of virtual visits to museums.

To carry out the present study, a quantitative methodology was used. Data were collected using two instruments. For data collection, on the demand side, the questionnaire related to the use of virtual visits to museums was carried out, which was later shared on social media, in the period ranging from 22 December 2020 to 5 January 2021. The data were collected through the Wikipedia platform, according to the fields identified and that constitute the observation grid. The study was applied to the context of existing museums in Portugal, namely Lisbon and Porto, and the sample of the surveyed population also resides in the same country. Although the study was applied in this territory, the methodology used can be replicated in other geographic or public contexts.

The first part of the chapter focuses on the literature review, namely in cultural tourism and the importance and utilization of VR in tourism and museums. Subsequently, the methodology used for the study is described in more detail, and, finally, research findings are reported and discussed, and their implications for further research are highlighted.

BACKGROUND

Cultural Tourism and Museums

Cultural tourism is a phenomenon that has stood out and gained expression over the last decades, as a result of demographic, social and cultural trends. Therefore, cultural tourism has been characterized as a profitable and growing sector for the tourism industry (Lord, 2002). There are currently at least 40% of tourists in the world who can be classified as cultural tourists, and this is also one of the most important motivations for European tourists (CBI, 2021).

A cultural tourism product is created when a travel motivator meets the interests of the tourist (e.g. heritage, art or culture). Cultural tourism products can be created directly for visitors (e.g. a museum) or they can be inherent to the local community (e.g. landscapes, restaurants) (Lord, 2002).

Museums are seen as tourist attractions, since it is possible to find more concentrated knowledge that is sought by the tourist during the trip (Bauer, Shouhn & Oliveira, 2019). Museums have always had a direct relationship with tourism, being "recognized as having important cultural touristic attractions" (Gomes, 2001; Rodrigues, 2001; Barretto, 2008; De Varine, 2013, in Bauer et al., 2019).

According to a study published in a Portuguese newspaper, visitors to museums in Portugal "are indicated as being relatively young people (the average age is 41 years in the national audience and 43 years abroad), qualified in terms of education and professional occupation, those who go to the museum for the most diverse reasons and, usually, only once" (Canelas, 2016). Tourists are increasingly demanding and technological and are looking for more fulfilling experiences. Museums can capture diverse audiences, from local visitors to tourists who arrive at the destination and intend to deepen their "cultural life" (Bauer et al., 2019), and the new technologies and the digital empowerment of museums are crucial in attracting young generations and new public (Enhuber, 2015)

Museums are a way to motivate people to travel and to attract them. In some destinations, museums can even be a decisive and determining factor for the development of tourism, exerting a positive catalytic influence (Plaza, 2000; Richards, 2001; Camilo & Bahl, 2017). Currently, "consumers are increasingly demanding and discerning, not only wanting mutually beneficial relationship and excellent goods and services, but also positive experiences" (Conway & Leighton, 2012, p. 35). Thus, it is important to understand more deeply what drives tourists to travel and what to expect from the visit. On the other hand, traditional museums are also changing their approach, without ever losing sight of the reason for their existence. Thus, they are "gradually shifting toward the search for intelligent entertainment, as they are looking for the tools to make visits more of an 'experience'" (Mencarelli & Pulh, 2012, p. 149).

Technologies in Tourism

The world of travel was awakened by the Industrial Revolution, which gave rise to the first mass travel for leisure reasons. This was a significant technological advance that paved the way for tourism, making it what it is today (Hassan, 2011).

As Hassan (2011) says, today it is possible to see that the world has undergone several transformations, enabling evolution and progress. Access to technologies is increasingly necessary, since few people find themselves working without a computer or similar device nowadays, showing that ICTs are increasingly present in all activities of our daily lives. He also states that, as tourism is an important economic activity for most countries and the world economy, the sector is not indifferent to technological progress, ending up using them for a better expression of its activity. All these technological advances gave rise to new means of communication, such as the Internet, which have proven to be effective tools to promote tourism (Qi et al., 2010, in Marco, Gómez & Seville, 2018).

Therefore, technological development has been contributing to a significant increase in tourism, "as well as helping to increase the volume of tourism demand and supply" (Ramos, Rodrigues & Perna, 2009, p. 24). Thus, it can be seen that the tourism sector is dependent on the technological sector, in its various segments, and its growth depends mostly on the capacity for innovation and use of it to improve management and product development and improve communication, experiences and personalization of the service. In this way, professionals in the sector must be attentive and monitor all progress in order to make their businesses more competitive, ensuring their survival at national and global level (Ramos et al., 2009).

Technologies, specifically the Internet, have given museology a new opportunity, on the one hand by allowing access to museums by visitors who can be found anywhere in the world and on the other, it has allowed museums to go beyond their walls (Henriques, 2004). In this way, tourism stakeholders can explore the digital technologies to communicate local culture heritage or educate visitors on heritage preservation (Kang & Yang, 2020, in Bec et al., 2021), with three basic types of museum sites; electronic brochures, museums in the virtual world and the truly virtual (Henriques, 2004).

Although there are more and more museums adopting digital technologies and implementing them as a comprehensive and interactive learning experience (Kang & Yang, 2020, in Bec et al., 2021), there are curators who are still reluctant, as "there is not yet a real and shared awareness of how to make virtual and real contents interact and how to design the best experience for the public, aiming at cultural transmission" (Pietroni, 2018, p. 1)

Virtual Reality

VR has been defined as a computer-simulated environment with and within which people interact (Diemer et al., 2015). However, VR should be seen as more than a 3D representation; VR content should include graphics, sound effects and physical interfaces, so that the user feels committed to the activity, ensuring that they have a quality experience, which allows you to have sensations but also to interact and act in the virtual world, trying to make this experience as faithful as possible (Kim, 2005).

VR "is singled out as one of the most important contemporary technological developments to greatly impact the tourism industry" (Tussyadiah et al., 2018, p. 1). This technological aspect brings major changes in the world of tourism, since, by means of it, it becomes possible to be in an "interactive three-dimensional environment in real time, without displacement and in an immersive way" (Taufer, 2020, p. 916). In addition to being immersive, VR can also be categorized as non-immersive, that is, "when the user is partially transported to the virtual world, through a window [monitor or projection, for example], but continues to feel if predominantly in the real world" (Tori et al., 2006, in Taufer, 2020. p. 917).

VR can intervene in tourism through virtual tours, which can include the use of objects for a more interactive and immersive experience (Pestek & Sarvan, 2020). In addition to this, VR can also be used in heritage areas, hotels, museums, exhibitions in zoos, historical sites, for example. (Roussou, 2004; Tholos, 2009; Pestek & Sarvan, 2020). VR transports people to faraway places in an easy and accessible way, an imaginary world that seeks to be one acting as a simulation of the real world. VR is a constantly changing technology that can change our habits at any time, and which may be particularly relevant to the tourism sector, where a lot of experiences depend on visual stimulation (Guttentag, 2010). In the tourism sector, VR will continue to increase both in number and importance. There are six areas in which it can be particularly useful, and they are: planning and management, marketing, entertainment, education, accessibility, and heritage preservation (Guttentag, 2010). Museums have not been indifferent to this evolution, and have sought to adapt to these technological innovations, increasing the use of VR in museum environments. (Shehade & Lambert, 2020)

In their study, Tussyadiah et al. (2018) point out a synthesis of the benefits of VR in tourism contexts for customers and for businesses and destinations. Regarding the face-to-face visit to museums, there is free and immediate access, that is, the visitor can make the visit at any time of the day and also anywhere in the world, without having to travel, and it is thus being accessible for any type of visitors. In addition, the visit can be made without time and content restrictions, allowing the visitor to enjoy a different experience. Some authors (e.g. Sussmann & Vanhegan, 2000), consider that VR can replace the trip itself, thus contributing to environmental sustainability and to the preservation of heritage considered vulnerable or at risk but for others authors, VR can attract a greater audience for a later physical visit.

Currently, the world is facing the pandemic caused by COVID-19, which is having a strong impact on the tourism sector. The arrival of this virus implied several changes in the daily lives of people and organizations, leading to changes in various areas, such as health, social, economic and political. One of the measures implemented by countries, and also on people's own initiative, consisted of social isolation, people staying in their homes, and temporarily shutting down operations of museums and cultural institutions. The closure of museums in the lockdown period brought the digital issue to the forefront, as it allowed museums to remain in touch and be accessible to their users, and even reach new audiences (UNESCO, 2020).

In an attempt to circumvent the consequences of this situation, museums have developed their own projects, providing virtual visits to the museum through their own platform or have established a partnership with Google Arts & Culture. The Google Arts & Culture platform is an initiative first launched in 2011 by the Google company, which offers the possibility of exploring the art collections of the most famous museums in the world through street view technology so that the visitor can move inside the galleries with the aid of 360° vision. So that we can have a closer perception of reality, it is also possible to zoom in on any piece of art that one wanted to see in greater detail (FaberNovel, 2020).

Given the changes caused by COVID-19 in society and cultural institutions and taking into account that VR technology is rapidly evolving, VR tourism research needs to be constantly re-validated through continuous investigation (Guttentag, 2010).

METHODOLOGY

With this study we intend to approach virtual visits to museums from two perspectives. On the tourist demand side, the intention is to understand the knowledge and experience of the use of virtual visits to museums by the Portuguese and, on the tourist offer side, to ascertain the availability of a virtual visit service by museums in the two main cities of Portugal – Lisbon and Oporto.

In order to achieve the objectives stipulated in this investigation, a quantitative methodology was applied. It is called a quantitative study as the method is characterized by the use of quantification in the collection of information and treatment process (Dalfovo et al., 2008).

To collect data on the use of virtual museum visits, a questionnaire survey was carried out. Gil (1999) in Chaer (2011), considers that questionnaires can be defined as an "investigation technique consisting of a more or less high number of questions presented to people in writing, with the objective of knowing opinions, beliefs, feelings, interests, expectations, experienced situations etc." (p. 260). This questionnaire was developed and applied through the Google Forms platform.

For the preparation of this questionnaire, questions were defined. First, it was decided to ask questions related to the theme and, at the end, those of a personal nature. Thus, the questionnaire has 17 questions, divided into three sections. The first question was related to conducting virtual visits to museums (whether the respondent knows about the possibility of making virtual visits to museums), the second one concerns the characteristics of virtual visits to museums, and this section would only be answered if in the previous section there were "Yes" answers (questions about what the respondent knows or doesn't know about virtual visits and their experience). Finally, the third section refers to the individual's personal and professional characteristics: gender; age; residence; qualifications; profession and income.

The questionnaire has closed questions – multiple choice and ranking questions are used. There are also open questions, where the respondent can give their opinion, as the answer will depend, solely and exclusively, on their experience. The questionnaire was distributed through social networks, namely Facebook and Instagram, between December 22, 2020 and January 5, 2021. In addition to social networks, some requests for collaboration were made in person.

The selection technique used was snowball sampling. In this type of sampling, individuals from the population to be surveyed are not previously identified; the sample is made up of a person or group of people and increases with the links that these individuals have with other individuals, thus forming a network, and should end when there are no longer data that are considered new.

At the end of the application period, the questionnaires were analysed, and 91 questionnaires were considered valid. Data were extracted directly from Google Forms, which with its various features, allows all the information collected to be concentrated in a single document, allowing for a better, more detailed understanding of it. The data is analysed using SPSS 27.0 software. Univariate and bivariate were performed using contingency tables.

To obtain data on the supply side, an observation grid was created and applied to museums, with certain fields, covering aspects such as: the museum's identification and scope of action; the date of update of the data on the platform; conducting face-to-face and virtual visits; and the platform for providing the virtual visit. Data were collected in October 2021, through the Wikipedia platform, category "museums of Portugal by municipality". This category is made up of 15 subcategories, from which information on museums in the municipality of Lisbon and Porto was extracted. These municipalities in the country are the ones that offer the greatest number of museums, and the ones that present more information on the Wikipedia platform. 69 museums located in Lisbon and 27 in Porto were observed. Wikipedia is a free, web-based content encyclopedia, which has been freely available to the public since 2001, and where anyone can share their knowledge (Wikipedia, 2021). Its reputation has been increasing, having been ranked by the Alexa firm in 2021 as the 13th-most-popular site on the Internet (The Economist, 2021).

FINDINGS

In this section, the results obtained, firstly through the analyses carried out with the questionnaire data, are presented, and then with the data obtained through direct observation, seeking to respond to the objectives stipulated for the study.

In terms of characteristics of the questionnaire respondents, it can be seen that 81% are female and 19% male. About 47% of respondents are aged between 20 and 29 years, and most reside in Alto Alentejo (Portugal), i.e., 24% live in the municipalities of Sousel (24%), Marvão (18%) and Portalegre (15%). Regarding academic qualifications, 43% have completed secondary/professional education, 27% have undergraduate level, 13% have a master's degree and 13% have the third cycle of basic education. Respondents have several professions, with a highlight on students (31.8%), teachers (7%) and self-employed (5%), and incomes below €635 (41%) or between €635 and €1,000 per month (41%).

Regarding the respondents' knowledge of virtual visits to museums, about 75% said they know that it is possible; however, 81% of respondents mentioned that they never made a virtual visit. A detailed analysis of the data of respondents who have already made virtual visits to museums showed that 35% visited in the last three months, 35% in the last six months and 18% in the last 12 months. Only one respondent reported having a visit in 2019 and another in years prior to 2018. These results allow us to conclude that almost all respondents experienced a virtual visit to a museum during the COVID-19 pandemic period, in line with the study developed by the Network of European Museum Organizations, where it is stated that museums have seen an increase in virtual tours and online exhibitions.

The most visited museums by respondents were the Coach Museum (18%) and the National Tile Museum (11.8%) in Portugal and the Louvre Museum (11.8%). In Table 1, it is possible to observe the name of the other museums mentioned by the respondents, presenting a proportion of identical visitors in all museums (5.9%). About 50% of the museums visited are located in Portugal. The most used platforms to carry out these visits are the museum's website (53%), Google Arts and Culture (41%) and social networks (6%).

Table 1. Last museums visited virtually by the respondents

Museum visited virtually	Country	%
Frida Kahlo museum	Mexico	5.9%
Luz Museum	Portugal	5.9%
Rijstmuseum	Netherlands	5.9%
National Tile Museum	Portugal	11.8%
Coach Museum	Portugal	17.6%
Louvre Museum	France	11.8%
Versailles Palace	France	5.9%
Roman Galleries	Portugal	5.9%
Ethnology National Museum	Portugal	5.9%
Prado Museum	Spain	5.9%
Natural History and Science National Museum	Portugal	5.9%
Don't remember	——	11.8%
Total	——	**100%**

Source: Own elaboration

When asked about the reasons that led them to go online, about 41% of respondents indicated their interest in the exhibitions or in studying a specific topic, 29.4% mentioned knowing the museum, 23.5% mentioned that they made the visit to review or complement a previous visit and 23.5% stated that it was for entertainment. Regarding the respondents' degree of satisfaction with the virtual visit, it is possible to note that, on a scale of 0 to 5, around 65% were quite satisfied and 30% were fully satisfied.

The main advantages of virtual visits pointed out by respondents were the possibility of visiting without leaving the house (47%), getting new knowledge and expanding it (18%) and visiting with greater detail (12%). As a disadvantage, 37.5% of respondents reported not having the same resources or enjoying the same experience as the face-to-face visit, 25% indicated the impossibility of viewing certain details and 19% the absence of physical contact.

When asked whether the visit aroused the desire to visit the museum in person, 82% answered yes. Respondents who do not intend to visit the museum in person (18%) pointed out the fact that they were satisfied with the virtual visit (20%) or that they already knew the museum (20%) as the main reason.

In order to check if there is any age group of respondents that is more likely to carry out the same virtual visits to museums, we used preparation of contingency tables, and it was found that virtual visits are more used by older respondents with ages between 20 years and 50 years. However, it is also in the age group between 20 and 29 years that the largest number of respondents who never carried out a virtual visit are concentrated, around 45% of the total. These results indicate that although virtual visits are more common among young people, virtual visits to museums are still very little used by the Portuguese.

Figure 1. Those who realized a virtual visit to a museum vs. age of respondents
Source: Own elaboration

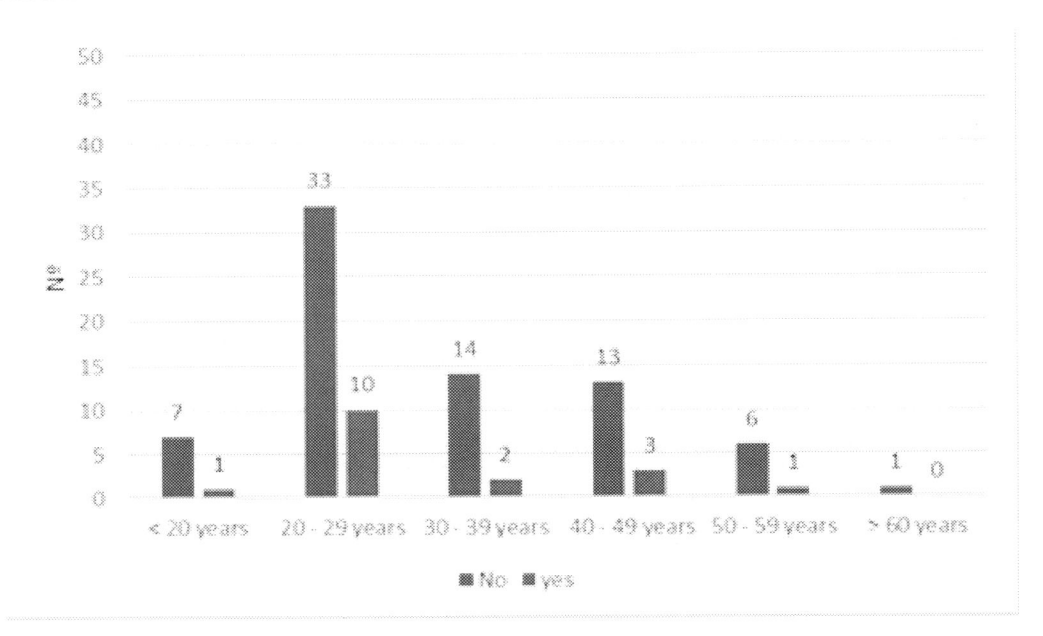

Cross tabulation is used to also understand the degree of satisfaction with the virtual visit to the museum depending on the platform that is used, and it was found that most of the respondents are satisfied or very satisfied with the virtual visit to the museum carried out through from its website. Respondents who use the Google Arts and Culture platform to carry out the visit also indicated that they were satisfied with the visit, as well as the respondent who accessed the museum through the social network (Figure 2).

Figure 2. Degree of visit satisfaction vs. platform used
Source: Own elaboration

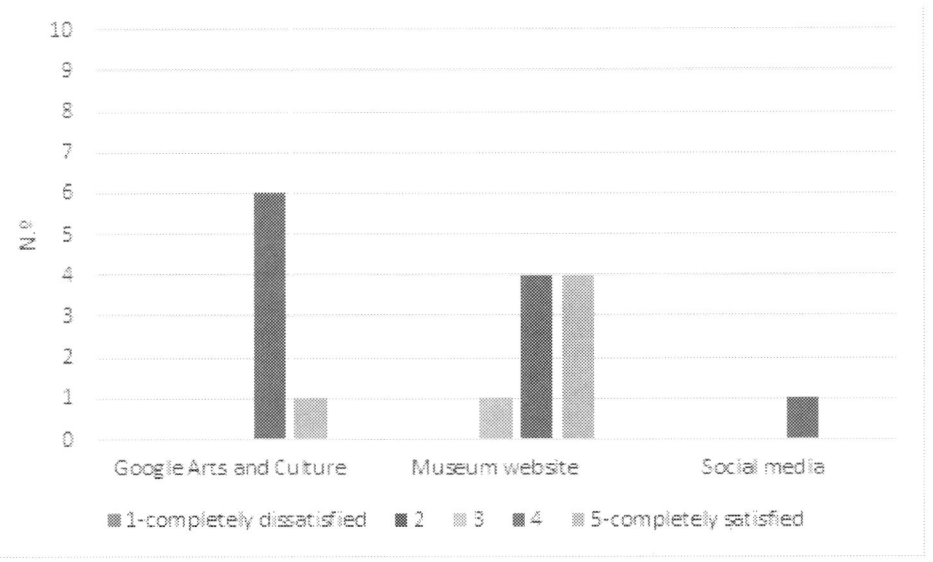

For the most part, the respondents indicated that they were aware of the possibility of carrying out virtual visits to museums; however, it was considered important to verify whether there is any relationship between this response and the respondents' municipality of residence. Observing Figure 3, it can be concluded that approximately 44.5% of respondents who responded that they had no knowledge of virtual tours are in the municipality of Sousel. On the other hand, most respondents (56%) who responded that they were aware of the visits reside in the municipalities of Portalegre, Marvão and Sousel. It is worth mentioning the fact that all respondents residing in the municipalities of Ponte de Sôr, Fronteira and Castelo indicated that they were aware of the existence of virtual visits to museums.

Figure 3. Knowledge of virtual visits to museums vs Municipality of residence
Source: Own elaboration

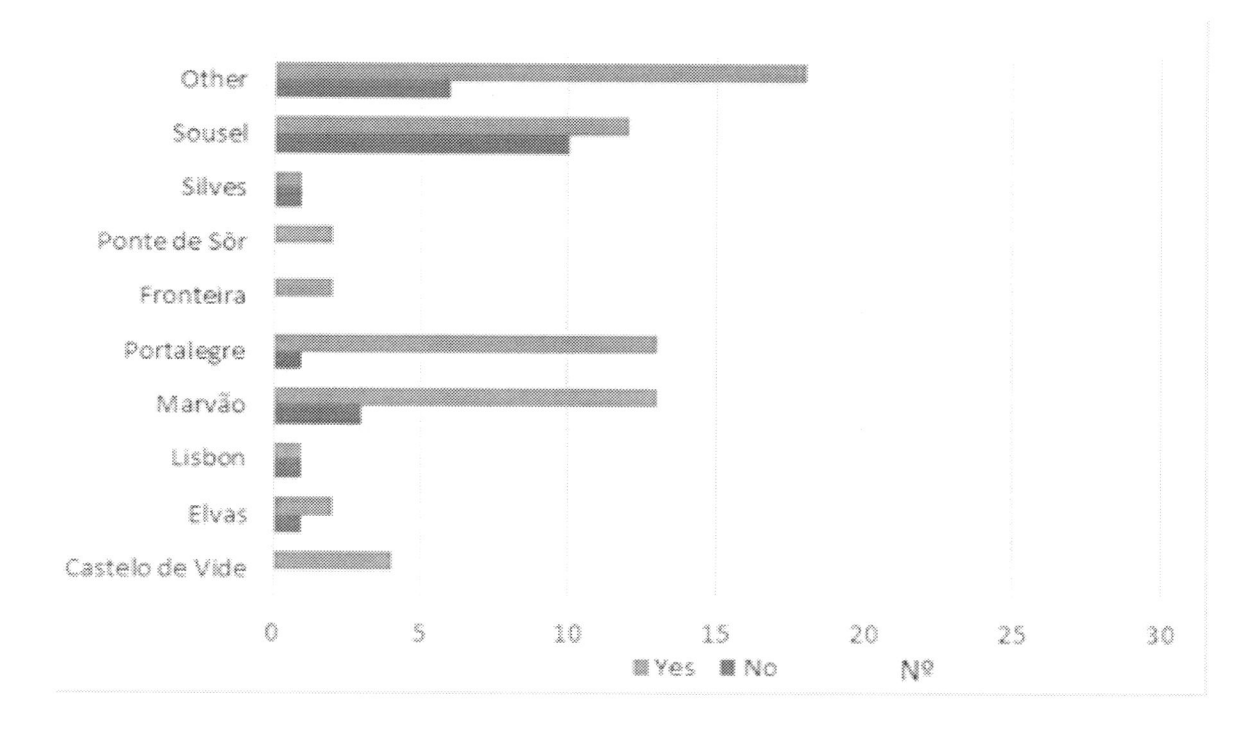

About 42% of respondents have a bachelor or master's degree and these correspond to the 50% of respondents who were aware of the possibility of conducting virtual visits. From the analysis performed, it was also found that 60% of respondents who said they did not know about virtual visits to museums have secondary or professional education.

Relating the profession to the time period that respondents mentioned having carried out the last virtual visit to museums, it appears that, in the last three to six months, in the midst of the pandemic caused by COVID-19, there was a greater use of virtual visits to museums, highlighting the respondents who are students.

Figure 4. Respondents' profession vs. when the virtual visit was made
Source: Own elaboration

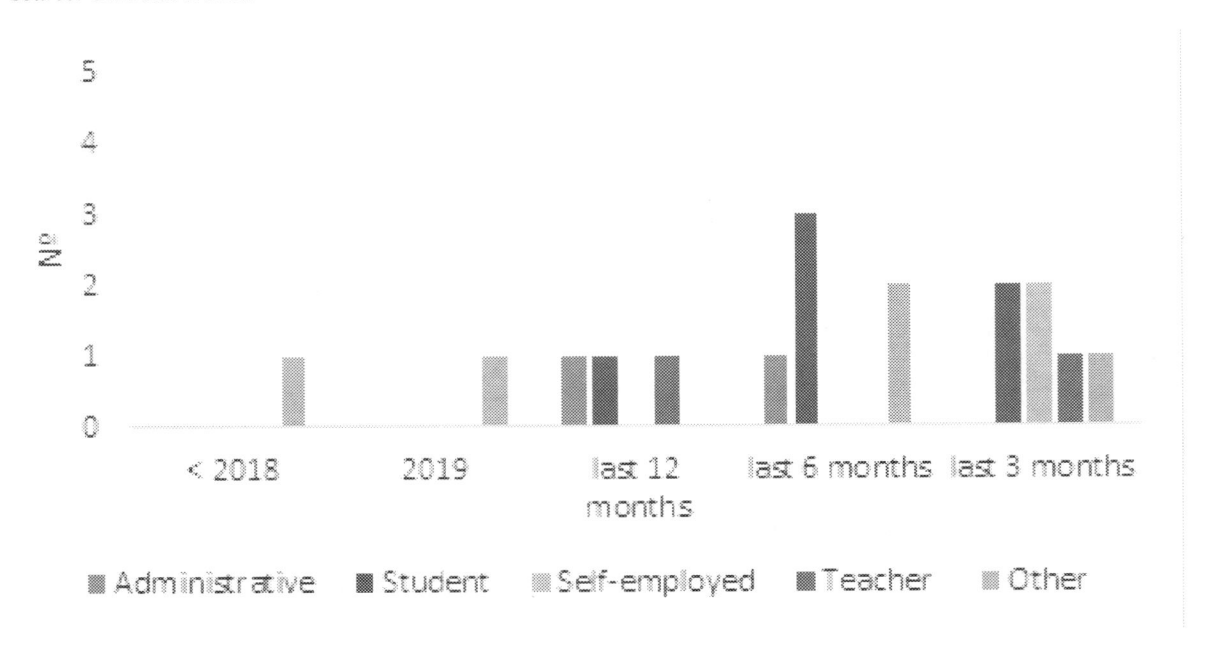

Through the analysis of data obtained through a questionnaire applied to the public residing in Portugal, it is possible to see that, although respondents have knowledge about virtual visits to museums, the number of respondents who carried out a virtual visit is still very small. This confirmation led researchers to try to understand, on the supply side, whether museums offer visitors a digital service, specifically, virtual tours. To this end, we analysed the information provided on the Wikipedia platform on the museums of Lisbon and Porto, in Portugal.

The results obtained allowed us to ascertain that most museums fit into the typology of cultural museums, consisting of collections and exhibitions. About 64% of museums report that they carry out in-person visits and some of them carry out guided tours. However, only 10% of museums explicitly mention that they provide a virtual visit service. The museums that indicated that this service was available also refer to the platform through which they can access the service, highlighting the platforms Wide, Google Arts & Culture and Zoom. Since about 81% of the information contained on the Wikipedia platform regarding these museums was updated in the years 2020 and 2021, it can be concluded that, even with restrictive measures for travel and face-to-face visits to museums imposed by the COVID-19 pandemic, there are still very few museums that provide information on the offer and carrying out of virtual tours.

With regard to museums located in the municipality of Porto, it was found that museums have areas of activity related to history, art, port wine, house museum and ethnography. All analysed museums carry out visits for the public and around 63% carry out guided tours. Only the Casa de Serralves Museum, the Serralves Contemporary Art Museum and the Puppet Museum indicate that they carry out virtual visits, through Google Arts & Culture and their own website, in the case of the Puppet Museum. The information provided on the Wikipedia platform was recently updated, in 2020 and 2021, in about 71% of museums, 19% in 2019, 4% in 2018 and 4% in 2017. Similarly, to the museums in Lisbon, it can be concluded that the offer of a virtual visit service in the museums of Porto is still very limited.

CONCLUSION

The development of ICTs has a great influence on the tourism sector, with implications at various levels, highlighting changes in tourism behaviour and consumption patterns, changes in the distribution channels of services and products and the possibility of offering new and different tourist experiences. Tourism consumers are currently more demanding and knowledgeable and tourism agents must therefore seek to provide unique and differentiating experiences.

Museums are one of the main attractions visited by consumers who travel for cultural reasons. Although the museum audience is diverse, the average age is around 40 years old. Thus, it is necessary for museums to provide the visitor with a remarkable experience, appealing to the different senses, so that they are satisfied, return at the next opportunity, and recommend the museum to friends and family. It is also important that museums innovate, modernize, and adopt technologies, so that they can conquer audiences of different generations, particularly the young audience.

Museums are including technologies in their development strategies, such as VR, and the COVID-19 pandemic has accelerated this process. Adoption of a service of virtual visits to the museum has been made available to the public, with the aim of bringing together and capturing new audiences. In this study, on the demand side, the questionnaire was applied to understand the use of virtual visits to museums by the Portuguese. The questionnaire was disseminated through social networks, mainly on Facebook and Instagram, and 91 responses were obtained.

The results obtained allowed us to conclude that the respondents know that it is possible to carry out virtual visits to museums; however, there are still very few people who have already carried out this type of visit. Respondents who have already made visits did so mainly in the last year, with the contribution of museums being closed and people having to stay at home, due to the COVID-19 pandemic. Carrying out the visit at any time and from home is one of the advantages most mentioned by the respondents. However, as a disadvantage, respondents also pointed out that the same resources are not available, and the experience is different from the face-to-face visit. It was found that younger audiences with a higher educational level tend to make more use of virtual visits, often doing so for study purposes or to get to know the museum.

From the point of view of the museums, the results revealed that in the two most populous municipalities and with the largest offer of museums in Portugal – Lisbon and Porto – most museums are visitable, but there is very little offer of a virtual tour service, the which means that, although this may have been boosted by the COVID-19 pandemic, the investment of museums in Portugal in this type of service is still very low.

Virtual visits are thus a solution that contributes to enriching visitors' experience, bringing them closer to the destination or tourist attraction. As such, the results of this study are important for destination management organizations and tourism stakeholders, as it validates the fact that virtual visits can serve as a marketing tool. Besides that, this study helps decision makers, mainly museums, to better understand the use of virtual visits by the public and better understand the online initiatives of their competitors.

FUTURE RESEARCH DIRECTIONS

Despite of the contributions of this study, like any investigation there are some limitations which should be addressed in future research. First, as a result of data collection procedure, the proportion of respondents from Alto Alentejo is quite high, which must be taken into account in terms of representativeness when interpreting the results. Thus, for future investigations, a more comprehensive territorial representation in terms of the sample is suggested, which can be obtained by extending the time period for the application of the questionnaire and with its dissemination in other contacts or social networks. It would be interesting to extend the study to other countries as well, beyond Portugal. Currently, it is still difficult to predict how consumers will react after the COVID-19 pandemic; however, although face-to-face visits exist or are reinforced, museums should consider maintaining hybrid systems, continuing to invest in online services. In this study, the information available on Wikipedia was used. Although this information had been updated recently, it is a collaborative platform. For future research, it would be desirable to compare this information with another source of information, namely with each museum. Thus, it would be interesting to consult museum managers on this topic, to understand their point of view regarding VR technology and the availability of virtual tours to the public.

REFERENCES

Barnes, S. (2016). *Understanding virtual reality in marketing: Nature, implications and potential.* Retrieved from https://bit.ly/3FSoN2b

Barretto, M. (2008). Os museus e a autenticidade no turismo. *Itinerarium, 1*(1), 42.

Bauer, J., Souhn, A., & Oliveira, B. (2019). Cultural Tourism: A study on museums and the internet. *Rev.Tur. Visão e Ação, 21*(3), 291–308.

Bec, A., Moyle, B., Schaffer, V., & Timms, K. (2021). Virtual reality and mixed reality for second chance tourism. *Tourism Management, 83*, 1–5. doi:10.1016/j.tourman.2020.104256

Buhalis, D. (2003). *eTourism: Information technology for strategic tourism management.* London: Pearson (Financial Times/Prentice Hall).

Camilo, I., & Bahl, M. (2017). Desenvolvimento do turismo baseado em elementos culturais. *Turismo e Sociedade, 10*(1). Advance online publication. doi:10.5380/tes.v10i1.52187

Canelas, L. (2016). *O visitante dos museus é jovem, tem formação e procura-os porque a arte lhe dá prazer. PUBLICO.* Retrieved from https://bit.ly/3aOlcni

CBI. (2021). *The European market potential for cultural tourism.* Retrieved from https://bityli.com/5j738

Chaer, G., Diniz, R. & Ribeiro, E. (2011). A Técnica do questionário a pesquisa educacional. *Araxá, 7*(7), 251–266.

Chen, A. (2020). Será que as Viagens Virtuais Vieram Para Ficar? *National Geographic.* Retrieved from: https://bit.ly/2YSPWS5

Conway, T., & Leighton, D. (2012). "Staging the past, enacting the present": Experiential marketing in the performing arts and heritage sectors. *Arts Marketing: An International Journal, 2*(1), 35–51. doi:10.1108/20442081211233007

Dalfovo, M., Lana, R., & Silveira, A. (2008). Métodos quantitativos e qualitativos: Um resgate teórico. *Revista Interdisciplinar Científica Aplicada, Blumenau, 2*(4), 1–13.

Diemer, J., Alpers, G. W., Peperkorn, H. M., Shiban, Y., & Mühlberger, A. (2015). The impact of perception and presence on emotional reactions: A review of research in virtual reality. Frontiers in Psychology, 6, 26. doi:10.3389/fpsyg.2015.00026

Enhuber, M. (2015). Art, space and technology: How the digitisation and digitalisation of art space affect the consumption of art - a critical approach. *Digital Creativity, 26*(2), 121–137. doi:10.1080/1462 6268.2015.1035448

FaberNovel. (2020). *Google Arts & Culture: Virtual visits to museums and monuments.* Retrieved from https://bit.ly/3ANLd0O

Ferrão, F. (2020). *Seis em cada 10 empresas a nível global aceleraram a sua transformação digital durante a pandemia.* Retrieved from https://bityli.com/lGwKc

Frade, R. (2020). *Tecnologia e Pandemia: Oportunidades e Ameaças.* Retrieved from https://bityli.com/geI9L

Guttentag, D. (2010). Virtual reality: Applications and implications for tourism. *Tourism Management, 31*(5), 637–651. doi:10.1016/j.tourman.2009.07.003

Hassan, H. (2011). *Tecnologias de Informação e Turismo: Faculdade de Letras da Universidade de Coimbra Hussein Hassan e-tourism* [Unpublished master's dissertation]. Faculdade de Letras da Universidade de Coimbra, Coimbra.

Henriques, R. (2004). *Virtual Museums and Cybermuseums: The Internet and Museums.* Retrieved from https://bit.ly/3mTkV8g

Huang, Y. C., Backman, K. F., Backman, S. J., & Chang, L. L. (2016). Exploring the Implications of Virtual Reality Technology in Tourism Marketing: An Integrated Research Framework. *International Journal of Tourism Research, 18*(2), 116–128. doi:10.1002/jtr.2038

Kim, G. (2005). *Designing Virtual Reality Systems: The Structured Approach.* Springer.

Lo, W., & Cheng, K. (2020). Does virtual reality attract visitors? The mediating effect of presence on consumer response in virtual reality tourism advertising. *Information Technology & Tourism, 22*(4), 537–562. doi:10.100740558-020-00190-2

Lord, B. (2002). *Cultural Tourism and Museums.* LORD Cultural Resources Planning and Management Inc.

Marco, J., Gómez, L., & Sevilha, C. (2018). Progress in information technology and tourism management: 30 years on and 20 years after the internet. *Tourism Management, 69*, 460–470. doi:10.1016/j.tourman.2018.06.002

Mencarelli, R., & Pulh, M. (2012). Museoparks and re-enchantment of the museum visits: An approach centred on visual ethnology. *Qualitative Market Research, 15*(2), 148–164.

Morris, C. (2016). *Virtual reality and the new sales experience.* Retrieved from https://bit.ly/3n5YpcK

Pestek, A. & Sarvan, A. (2020). Virtual Reality and modern tourism. *Journal of Tourism Futures*. DOI: doi:10.1108/JTF-01-2020-0004

Pietroni, E. (2019). Experience Design, Virtual Reality and Media Hybridization for the Digital Communication Inside Museums. *Applied System Innovation*, *2*(35), 35. Advance online publication. doi:10.3390/asi2040035

Plaza, B. (2000). Evaluating the influence of a large cultural artifact in the attraction of tourism: The Guggenheim Museum Bilbao case. *Urban Affairs Review*, *36*(2), 264–274. doi:10.1177/10780870022184859

Ramos, C., Rodrigues, L., & Perna, F. (2009). Sistemas e Tecnologias de Informação no Setor do Turismo. *Revista Turismo & Desenvolvimento*, *12*, 21–32.

Richards, G. (2001). *Cultural attractions and European tourism*. CAB International.

Roque, V., Fernandes, G., & Raposo, R. (2012). Identificação dos Media Sociais utilizados pelas organizações de gestão de destinos: o caso de estudo do destino turístico Serra da Estrela. Revista Turismo e Desenvolvimento, 17/18.

Roussou, M. (2004). Learning by doing and learning through play: An exploration of interactivity in virtual environments for children. *Computers in Entertainment*, *2*(1), 1–23.

Serra, J. (2008). *As tecnologias de Informação e comunicação no Turismo: - a emergência do e-tourism*. Universidade de Évora.

Shehade, M., & Lambert, S. T. (2020). Virtual Reality in Museums: Exploring the Experiences of Museum Professionals. *Applied Sciences (Basel, Switzerland)*, *10*(11), 4031. https://doi.org/10.3390/app10114031

Sussmann, S., & Vanhegan, H. (2000). Virtual reality and the tourism product: Substitution or complement? In H. R. Hansen, M. Bichler, & H. Mahrer (Eds.), *Proceedings of the 8th European Conference on Information Systems*, 2 (pp. 1077–1083). Academic Press.

Taufer, L., & Ferreira, L. T. (2019). Realidade Virtual no Turismo: Entretenimento ou uma mudança de paradigma? *Rosa dos Ventos – Turismo e Hospitalidade*, *11*(4), 908–921. doi:10.18226/21789061.v11i4p908

The Economist. (2021). *Wikipedia is 20, and its reputation has never been higher*. Retrieved from https://econ.st/3lLpYs3

Tholos. (2009). *Tholos virtual theater*. Retrieved from https://bit.ly/3peKaoF

Tussyadiah, P., Wang, D., Jung, T. M., & Dieck, M. C. (2018). Virtual reality, presence, and attitude change: Empirical evidence from Tourism. *Tourism Management*, *66*, 140–154.

United Nations Educational, Scientific and Cultural Organizations (UNESCO). (2020). *Museums around the world in the face of COVID-19*. UNESCO.

Wikipedia. (2009). *About*. Retrieved from https://bit.ly/3DHPDbk

Williams, P., & Hobson, J. P. (1995). Virtual reality and tourism: Fact or fantasy? *Tourism Management*, *16*(6), 423–427.

ADDITIONAL READING

Gonzalez-Rodrıguez, M. R., Dıaz-Fernandez, M. C., & Pino-Mejıas, M. A. (2020). *The impact of virtual reality technology on tourists' experience: a textual data analysis. In Soft Computing.* Springer-Verlag GmbH Germany.

Kargas, A., Karitsioti, N., & Loumos, G. (2020). Reinventing Museums in 21st Century: Implementing Augmented Reality and Virtual Reality Technologies Alongside Social Media's Logics. In G. Guazzaroni & A. Pillai (Eds.), *Virtual and Augmented Reality in Education, Art, and Museums* (pp. 117–138). IGI Global. doi:10.4018/978-1-7998-1796-3.ch007

Sylaiou, S., Mania, K., Karoulis, A., & White, M. (2010). Exploring the relationship between presence and enjoyment in a virtual museum. *International Journal of Human-Computer Studies*, 68(5), 243–253. doi:10.1016/j.ijhcs.2009.11.002

KEY TERMS AND DEFINITIONS

COVID-19: An infectious disease caused by a new species of coronavirus, called SARS-CoV-2. It appeared on December 31, 2019, in the city of Wuhan, China and spread to the rest of the world in 2020. In March of that year, it was declared a world pandemic by the World Health Organization.

Culture Tourism: This refers to the act of travel with the motivation of learning about the culture of a destination and experiencing its cultural heritage.

Museum: A non-profit institution whose objective is to conserve, investigate and communicate the material and immaterial heritage of a given location, for educational, leisure or tourism purposes.

Virtual Visit: An experience that allows the user to enjoy a simulation of an existing local or attraction through sequential videos or still images, and is able to incorporate other multimedia elements (e.g., sound).

Chapter 14
Cultural Tourism, Internet of Things, and Smart Technologies in Museums

Ümit Gaberli

College of Tourism and Hotel Management, Siirt University, Turkey

ABSTRACT

In this chapter, the author explores the application of the internet of things (IoT) in museums. IoT technology typically combines physical objects with hardware and software. For museums, the simplest example is 3D virtual tours, which need a computer and an internet connection. Today, however, museums have become more complicated with virtual and augmented technologies. Virtual and augmented reality devices, such as virtual reality (VR) glasses, and related applications, such as Google Arts and Culture, provide interactive museum tour experiences for visitors. For all these experiences, they only need to connect to the internet with their devices. Virtual museum tours range from history to space technologies. This chapter explores the nature of using IoT technologies in cultural tourism, especially in museums.

INTRODUCTION

Nowadays, many objects are connected thanks to the internet while IoT technologies have spread worldwide. They are applied in various sectors, including energy, manufacturing, logistics, education, health, and tourism. While the current COVID-19 pandemic has affected many sectors, one of the worst affected is tourism. IoT technologies have put a different complexion on the hospitality industry because of their tremendous potential to avoid physical contact. The use of IoT in smart museums, which is the focus of this chapter, is mainly related to visitor experiences. Mobile devices and wearable technologies, such as virtual or augmented reality glasses, have improved services in museums. The digital transformation accelerated by the COVID-19 pandemic means that business processes are conducted with fewer and fewer people while purely virtual activities have rapidly become popular, although they had previously not seemed likely in the near future. During the pandemic, many museums in Turkey started offering virtual tour services (e.g., İzmir Atatürk Museum, Museum of Troy, Republic Museum), which has started

DOI: 10.4018/978-1-7998-8528-3.ch014

a much bigger transformation. While this transformation makes museums accessible to larger masses, virtualization may also alienate traditional museum visitors. Nevertheless, given the new generation's technological ability and the pandemic situation, traditional museum visits will clearly differentiate with these new forms namely virtualization. One of the most important ways to understand this differentiation is by understanding the basic logic of IoT technology. This will allow us to predict changes in museology activities and museum visits, and identify how cultural tourism will evolve in this new context.

BACKGROUND: WHAT IS IOT?

Today, there is not yet a conceptual consensus about IoT (Wortmann & Flüchter, 2015). Weiser (1991) predicted that hardware and software items connected by cables, radio waves, and infrared would become very common, but he did not term it IoT. IoT began to improve after the Auto-ID Centre in the Massachusetts Institute of Technology (MIT) invented inter-company RFID (Radio Frequency Identification) infrastructure in 1999. In a presentation in 1999, Kevin Ashton became the first to mention IoT (Ashton, 2009) while Gershenfeld (1999) used a similar notion in his book "When Things Start to think" (Mattern & Floerkemeier, 2010).

The IoT paradigm emerged from the convergence of the three main visions indicated in Figure 1. Essentially, IoT is the capability of things to work interoperability and actively exchange information exchange according to predefined plans (Report, 2008, pp. 4). The following section describes these three basic visions that generate IoT.

Figure 1.
Source: Atzori et al., 2010: 3

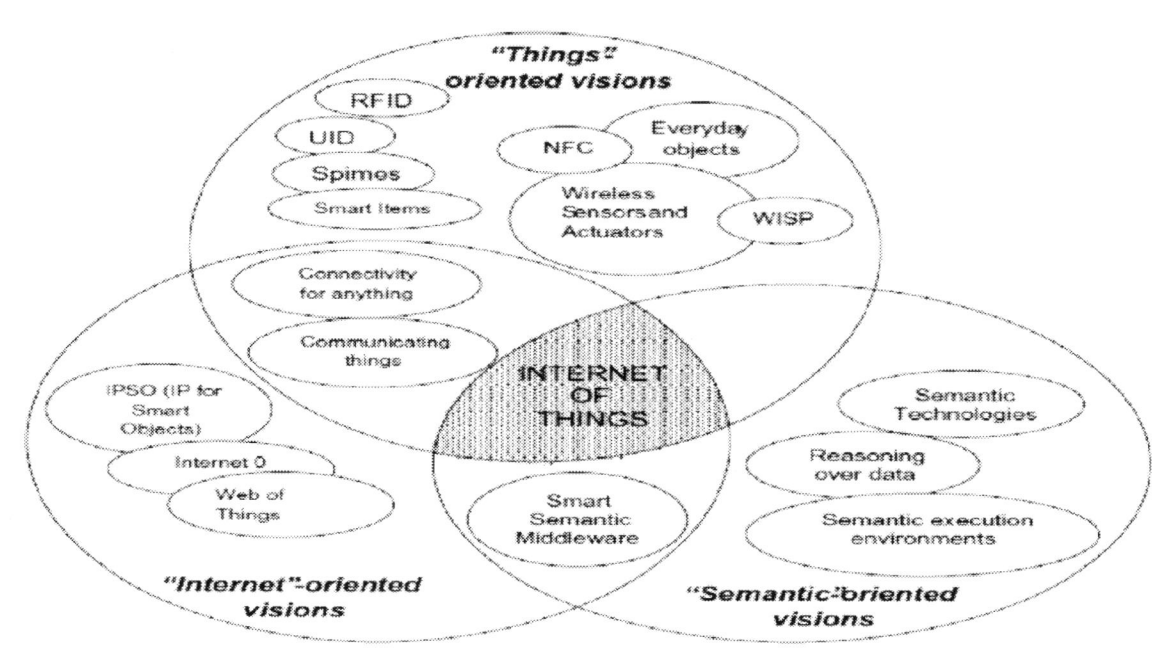

The first definition of IoT takes a things-oriented perspective. To understand this term, which is attributed to Auto-ID Labs (Atzori et al., 2010, pp. 3), it is first necessary to understand Automatic Identification and Data Capture (AIDC) technologies. AIDC technologies transfer or record data directly from a device/object to a computer using various methods, such as Optical Character Recognition (OCR), Voice Recognition, Biometric Systems, Barcode Systems, and Radio Frequency Identification (RFID). The things-oriented vision in Figure 1 is based on RFID technology.

RFID technology is a method for automatically and uniquely identifying things using radiofrequency waves. RFID technology requires a tag and reader. The tags can be programmed to receive, store, and share object information, such as an Electronic Product Code (EPC). For example, supply chain management data can be automatically recorded or changed by reading the labels on the products (EPCglobal, 2021). Today, barcode and EPC identification systems are used together, but the main aim is to standardize and enable their global use. Atzori et al. (2010) note that RFID tags are just one part of IoT. For example, Context Awareness has become technically feasible and cost-effective thanks to the development of small RFID tags, radio, and infrared beacons, and other devices. Context Awareness is also the basis of ubiquitous computing whereby computer systems can optimize operations to provide better service by recognizing the environmental conditions where people are. In short, ubiquitous computing technology allows us to connect the virtual and real worlds. (Sakamura, 2006, pp. 713). New generation communication technologies have also accelerated the expansion of IoT. For instance, near-field communication (NFC) technologies like Bluetooth enable data between electronic devices to exchange over short distances while wireless technologies, such as a wireless sensor and actuator network (WSAN) or a wireless identification and sensing platform (WISP), enable longer-distance communication. The adaptation of internet usage to these technologies has led to the IoT phenomenon.

These developments in turn relate to the second vision in Figure 1, the internet-oriented perspective, whereby smart things are integrated into the web. For example, RFIDs are integrated indirectly with an RFID reader with an embedded server, but devices are directly integrated with web technologies. While both methods can be used separately, nowadays they are mostly used together in a hybrid way. For this direct integration into the web, all devices must have an IP address or be IP-enabled to connect to the internet. Another requirement is that the devices in which the webserver is embedded must understand each other's languages, i.e., the web language (Zeng et al., 2011, pp. 427). This interoperability leads to the third vision, the semantic vision of semantic technologies. Hence, researcher reaches the intersection of the three visions in Figure 1, namely IoT.

To understand the semantic-oriented perspective, the researcher first needs to consider semantics. The word semantics expresses a range of ideas. Semantic technologies enable computers to think about data, programs, and infrastructure. Thanks to semantic web technology, computers can understand whatever the knowledge in the data or programs (Domingue et al., 2011, pp. 11-13).

MAIN FOCUS OF THE CHAPTER: IOT AND SMART TECHNOLOGIES IN DIFFERENT MUSEUM TYPES

The traditional role of museums has gradually changed. Weil (1999) summarizes the idea that "museums transform being about something into being for somebody" (Huang & Ng, 2020). Initially, museums were places of storage and preservation of cultural objects and materials (Spachos & Plataniotis, 2020) whereas their current role has three main purposes: cultural heritage preservation and conservation;

visitor experiences; cultural learning. Here, data processing is critical in many areas, from security to physical conditions or visitor experiences. Therefore, it is essential for the current role of the museums. For instance, presence detection sensors in museums can provide real-time data and give information about which artworks have more attention according to the dwell times. Furthermore, the researcher measures physical responses to work by measuring respiration and resting heart rate thanks to wireless IoT sensors (BEHRTECH, 2021).

Museums are not only places to preserve cultural heritage but also substantial tools for history and arts. Preserving museums from potential damage is thus a duty for future generations (Eltresy et al., 2019). But, today many works of art are stolen every year. The black market of these stolen pieces has a value between 6 and 8 billion dollars annually. Therefore, conserving museums is important in a more technological way. IoT technology offers various solutions for museum security. IoT sensors can be placed on doors and windows or inside and around artworks to set up warning systems for museum staff (BEHRTECH, 2021). Also, valuable artworks can be tracked during transportation using localization via public LPWAN (Low Power Wide Area Networks) technology (Aernouts et al., 2020). These kinds of location-based services are typical examples of IoT applications. Inside a museum, a Wireless Sensor Network (WSN) can control the microclimate, pollution, and lighting to reduce environmental damage (Eltresy et al., 2019). For example, sensors can be placed near water pipes, on the ceiling, or in sensitive areas for early warning of water leaks to prevent the museum from the flood (BEHRTECH, 2021). Even more specifically, Konev et al. (2019) applied IoT, Artificial Intelligence (AI), and Semantic Web technologies to a museum's microclimate parameters to choose the most suitable gallery for exhibiting each artwork. Localization also plays an important role in effectively identifying where the exhibition is, as well as improving visitor experience, in other words, the quality of service offered by the museum. For example, Maschio Angioino Castle in Naples, Italy, developed a talking museum project for its art exhibition. This describes the history of the objects in the exhibition using multimedia facilities, Bluetooth, and a Wireless Sensor Network (Amato et al., 2013).

Figure 2.
Source: Vallez et al., 2020: 9.

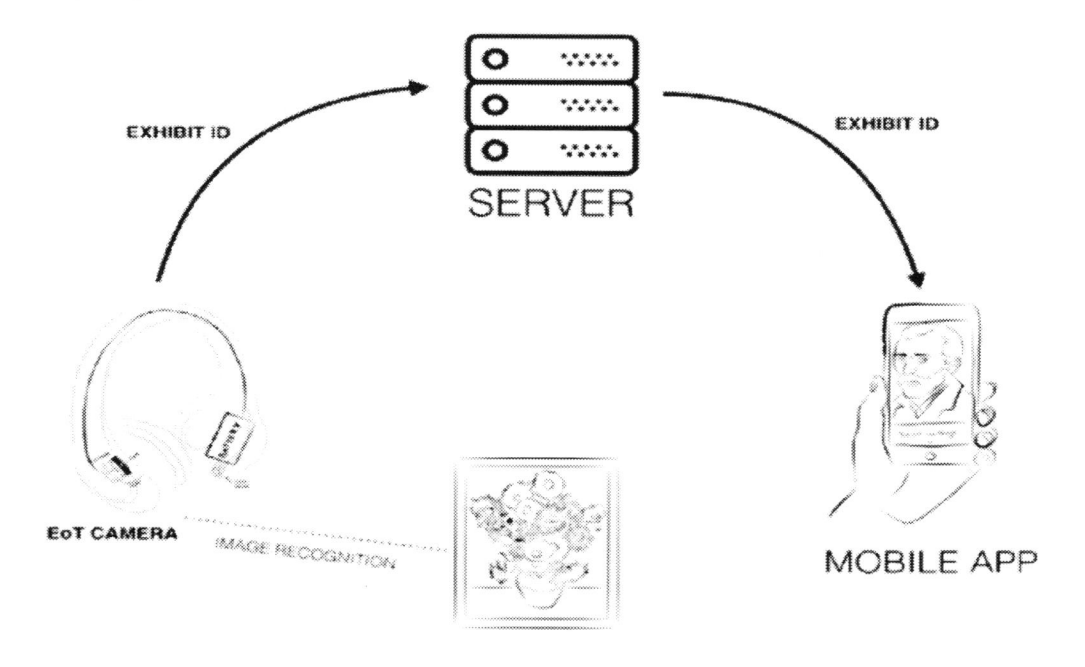

Similarly, Aletto (2016) proposed wearable devices designed to provide content related to works of art while Vallez et al. (2020) developed a multimedia museum guide for visitors (see Figure 2). This guide includes a headset connected to an application on the visitor's smartphone or other smart devices. The Eyes of Things (EoT) board has a Wi-Fi module that enables visitors to receive multimedia content thanks to the museum device and their smartphones or tablets (Vallez et al., 2020, pp. 9).

Using mobile and internet technologies, museums can also increase visitor satisfaction by creating a personalized service, especially in museums with multiple exhibitions and many visitors (Ivanov, 2019). However, these applications are not simply record-based descriptions of exhibits as in traditional museum information systems (Korzun et al., 2017). Given their mission to teach cultural heritage to future generations, museums are turning to IoT-based serious games to enable learning and interactive visitor experiences. For example, IoT card games help designers and practitioners conceptually to create a deeper interaction with the ideas of the visitors (Huang et al., 2020). On the other hand, museums design various energy-saving games with their visitors. For example, visitors are encouraged to use the stairs instead of the elevator during their visit. Stair use per visitor is measured with NFC tags and a smartphone app. At the end of the game, some commemorative prizes are offered to the visitors (Kotsopoulos et al., 2018, 2019).

Gamification is a much-debated concept in the digital media industry. Gamification differs from serious games. Serious games refer to the non-entertaining use of games, whereas gamification does not use all the elements of a game. It is unclear if it is an app, a game, or a gamified app (Deterding et al., 2011a). Gamification is linked to reality games and human-computer interactions (Deterding et al., 2011b). Gamified applications motivate users (Döpker et al., 2013). Bieszk-Stolorz et al. (2021) stated that the offering of gamified e-guides to visitors contributes positively to the cultural, environmental, and social sustainability of museums (Bieszk-Stolorz et al., 2021, pp. 4364). Also, Ha et al. (2021) investigated the effect of a mobile question-asking application on museum visitor groups' interactions. This research at two large museums in the American southwest indicates that the app encouraged sharing information among the group members. This research also shows the app provides informal learning.

The next section considers examples of smart museum applications for cultural learning and more attractive tour experiences in various types of museums. The aim is to determine the nature of using IoT technologies in cultural tourism, especially museums. Goode (1896) classified museums into two categories, of which the researcher focuses on the first in this chapter.

Table 1. Classification of museums

Category 1	Category 2
Museums of Art	**National Museums**
Historical Museums	Local, Provincial, or City Museums
Anthropological Museums	College and School Museums
National History Museums	Professional or Class Museums
Technological Museums	Museums of Cabinets for special research owned by societies or
Commercial Museums	individuals

Source: Goode, 1896

Virtual Tours, Virtual and Augmented Reality in Museums

IoT systems allow people to experience virtual tours in different museums around the world, such as the Louvre, Smithsonian National Museum of Natural History, the Dalí Theatre-Museum, the Vatican Museums, and the National Museum of the United States Air Force. These virtual tours only require an internet connection and a computer or smart device with Wi-Fi. Here, the researcher focuses on the Google Art Project. The Google Arts & Culture website includes many digital materials of artworks and museums. For instance, Bruegel's "The Fall of the Rebel Angels" (1562) can be experienced through virtual reality using VR glasses or as a 360-degree video. Google Arts & Culture also presents virtual reality videos from the Art Institute of Chicago, which has six of Monet's haystack paintings. You can experience a tour of these paintings while an expert gives you information about the artworks. Also, augmented reality enables visitors to participate in virtual reality scenes and interact with the real and virtual world simultaneously. One of the best examples of this kind of commercial museum is the Illusion 3D Art Museum in Kuala Lumpur, Malaysia. However, the interaction of these actual and virtual worlds causes some problems. For instance, real-time exhibition browsing does not accommodate late arrivals and offers limited support to temporarily disaggregated visitors (Chen et al., 2021).

Augmented Reality and Learning Process in Museums

Smart technologies are not only used for entertainment and improving visitor experiences in museums but also for education or learning about different subjects. A recent example is the Houston Space Center. This provides interactive mobile applications, such as location-aware audio tours, GPS-enabled maps, Space Center Houston selfie filters, interactive augmented reality and virtual reality lite experiences, a Space Center Houston event calendar, and take it home. For instance, location-aware audio stops tell you about space while you can explore the moon with augmented reality and watch the Saturn V rocket launch (Space Center Houston, 2021). Another example of a museum learning experience is the Ghosts in the Museum project. This enabled 183 children and adolescents in 25 groups to design and implement an Alternate Reality Game (ARG) application. The application is based on hunting clues using Einstein's 3D model with gamification guided by Einstein's ghost. In addition to contributing to the museum experience, it also contributes to creativity and scientific education (Carolei & Schlemme, 2015).

FUTURE OF THE CULTURAL TOURISM WITH SMART MUSEUMS

The spread of virtual technologies has significantly affected museum activities while the changes imposed by the COVID-19 pandemic have put a new complexion on cultural tourism.

The United Nations World Tourism Organization (UNWTO) defines cultural tourism as follows:

Cultural tourism is a type of tourism activity in which the visitor's essential motivation is to learn, discover, experience and consume the tangible and intangible cultural attractions/products in a tourism destination (World Tourism Organization, 2019).

Based on this definition, the researcher can argue that museums are critical for cultural tourism because they provide many tangible and intangible attractions and products. Also, museum activities have begun to undergo a radical change with the use of smart technologies and the COVID-19 pandemic. As McCall and Gray (2014) emphasize, traditional museology is collection-oriented and building-based whereas new museology redefines the relationship of museums to societies. Developments in smart technologies, such as the examples discussed in this chapter, have added a new dimension to museums that the researcher can call virtual museology. Many smart technologies are already in use and popular in museums. However, the relationship between museums, cultural activities, and tourism has changed after many were closed because of the pandemic and the increased free virtual tour opportunities. First, with this easy accessibility, museum visits have ceased to be a purely intellectual activity for some people as today's practices clearly show that cultural tourism and entertainment can be presented together. Thus, museum marketing strategies have changed radically due to the presentation of cultural heritage. In addition, virtual tours have increased tourism demand. For example, somebody who participates in a virtual museum tour just because they are interested in virtual technologies may then want to visit the country where the museum is. The World Tourism Organization (2021) summarizes these changes, transformations, and effects as follows:

The ability to virtually access and enjoy culture served a sense of comfort, as well as a source of inspiration for the travel of tomorrow (World Tourism Organization, 2021).

To conclude, although it is quite difficult to predict how cultural tourism will expand, smart museums can quickly increase market volume by increasing the motivation of individuals to participate in cultural tourism. In addition, because Virtual and Augmented Reality technologies offer realistic museum experiences from our homes, it may become possible to move cultural tourism to a completely virtual platform.

THE FINAL CONSIDERATION

Museology and tourism are in mutual interaction. These kinds of activities increase simultaneously and support each other (Hernández, 2018). In recent years, classical museums replaced by postmodern museums because of changes in the technological infrastructure of museums. The preparation of this radical change is the adaptation of IoT technology to many products. Widely use of virtual and augmented reality glasses has radically changed the content of museum activities, the way and quality of service, and visitor experiences. Today, museums in various regions of the world can be visited from our homes thanks to these kinds of virtual technologies. Also, the COVID-19 pandemic has reduced mobility and the tendency to virtual activities increased. Therefore, the spread of virtual tours has accelerated. This effect has the potential to reduce actual visitor numbers. Yet, adopting IoT technology to museums has also allowed visitors to visit museums minimizing contact with individuals in pandemic conditions. On the other side, according to the UNESCO report, about 90% of the museum institutions around the World have been affected by temporary closures because of COVID-19. Although some museums benefit from public subsidies, most are dependent on financial contributions from visitors and donors (UNESCO Report, 2020, pp. 4). Revenue loss during the pandemic proceeds from the revenue loss of tickets, shops, cafes, and other services. According to the NEMO Report survey, 44% of museums lose up to one thousand euros per week, 31% of museums lose up to five thousand euros per week, 18% lose up to thirty thousand euros per week, and 8% lose up to fifty thousand euros per week. Large museums such as the Rijksmuseum, the Vienna Kunsthistorisches Museum, and the Stedelijk Museum lose between one hundred and six hundred Euros per week. Also, many museums stated that they temporarily suspended their long-term infrastructure projects due to revenue losses. However, almost 70% of museums have increased their online presence because of closed due to social distancing measures and more than 40% of the museums stated that online visits have increased since the museums were closed (NEMO Report, 2020, pp. 7-14). Thus, the researcher can allege that the museum industry is faced with the dilemma of making technology investments or being suspended due to budget constraints. Therefore, in my opinion, future research should focus on this dilemma and its solutions.

REFERENCES

Aernouts, M., Lemic, F., Moons, B., Famaey, J., Hoebeke, J., Weyn, M., & Berkvens, R. (2020). A multimodal localization framework design for IoT applications. *Sensors (Basel)*, *20*(16), 4622. doi:10.339020164622 PMID:32824497

Alletto, S., Cucchiara, R., Del Fiore, G., Mainetti, L., Mighali, V., Patrono, L., & Serra, G. (2016). An indoor location-aware system for an IoT-based smart museum. *IEEE Internet of Things Journal*, *3*(2), 244–253. doi:10.1109/JIOT.2015.2506258

Amato, F., Chianese, A., Mazzeo, A., Moscato, V., Picariello, A., & Piccialli, F. (2013). The talking museum project. *Procedia Computer Science*, *21*, 114–121. doi:10.1016/j.procs.2013.09.017

Ashton, K. (2009). That 'internet of things' thing. *RFID Journal*, *22*(7), 97–114.

Atzori, L., Iera, A., & Morabito, G. (2010). The internet of things: A survey. *Computer Networks*, *54*(15), 2787–2805. doi:10.1016/j.comnet.2010.05.010

BERHTECH. (2021). https://behrtech.com/blog/smart-museums-6-artful-iot-applications-for-museums-and-galleries/

Bieszk-Stolorz, B., Dmytrów, K., Eglinskiene, J., Marx, S., Miluniec, A., Muszyńska, K., Niedoszytko, G., Podlesińska, W., Rostoványi, A., Swacha, J., Vilsholm, R. L., & Vurzer, S. (2021). Impact of the availability of gamified e-guides on museum visit intention. *Procedia Computer Science*, *192*, 4358–4366. doi:10.1016/j.procs.2021.09.212

Carolei, P., & Schlemme, E. (2015). Alternate reality game in museum: A process to construct experiences and narratives in hybrid context. *Proceedings of 7th International Conference on Education and New Learning Technologies*, 8037-8045.

Chen, W., Shan, Y., Wu, Y., Yan, Z., & Li, X. (2021). Design and evaluation of a distance-driven user interface for asynchronous collaborative exhibit browsing in an augmented reality museum. *IEEE Access: Practical Innovations, Open Solutions*, *9*, 73948–73962. doi:10.1109/ACCESS.2021.3080286

Deterding, S., Dixon, D., Khaled, R., & Nacke, L. E. (2011a). Gamification: Toward a definition. *CHI 2011 Gamification Workshop Proceedings*.

Deterding, S., Dixon, D., Khaled, R., & Nacke, L. E. (2011b). From game design elements to gamefulness: defining "gamification". *Proceedings of the 15th International Academic Mindtrek Conference: Envisioning Future Media Environments*, 9-15. 10.1145/2181037.2181040

Domingue, J., Fensel, D., & Hendler, J. A. (2011). Introduction to the semantic web technologies. In J. Domingue, D. Fensel, & J. A. Hendler (Eds.), *Handbook of semantic web technologies* (pp. 4–41). Springer. doi:10.1007/978-3-540-92913-0_1

Döpker, A., Brockmann, T., & Stieglitz, S. (2013). Use cases for gamification in virtual museums. *Proceedings of the Jahrestagung der Gesellschaft für Informatik 2013*, 2308–2321.

Eltresy, N. A., Dardeer, O. M., Al-Habal, A., Elhariri, E., Hassan, A. H., Khattab, A., Elsheakh, D. N., Taie, S. A., Mostafa, H., Elsadek, H. A., & Abdallah, E. A. (2019). RF energy harvesting IoT system for museum ambience control with deep learning. *Sensors (Basel)*, *19*(20), 4465. doi:10.339019204465 PMID:31618881

EPCglobal. (2021). https://web.archive.org/web/20070303054158/http://www.epcglobaltr.org/rfid.php

Gershenfeld, N. (1999). *When things start to think*. Henry Holt and Company, Inc.

Goode, G. B. (1896). On the classification of museums. *Science*, *3*(57), 154–161. doi:10.1126cience.3.57.154 PMID:17741599

Ha, J., Pérez Cortés, L. E., Su, M., Nelson, B. C., Bowman, C., & Bowman, J. D. (2021). The impact of a gamified mobile question-asking app on museum visitor group interactions: An ICAP framing. *International Journal of Computer-Supported Collaborative Learning*, *16*(3), 1–35. doi:10.100711412-021-09350-w

Hernández, H. (2018). Confluences between museology and tourism. *Revista Iberoamericana de Turismo*, *8*(4), 7–23.

Huang, H., & Ng, K. H. (2020). Designing for cultural learning and reflection using IoT serious game approach. *Personal and Ubiquitous Computing*, *2020*, 1–16.

Huang, H., Ng, K. H., Bedwell, B., & Benford, S. (2020). A Card-based internet of things game ideation tool for museum context. *Journal of Ambient Intelligence and Humanized Computing*, *2020*, 1–12.

Ivanov, R. (2019). An approach to developing internet of things (IoT)-based services for smart museums. *Digital Presentation and Preservation of Cultural and Scientific Heritage (DiPP)*, 8.

Konev, A., Khaydarova, R., Lapaev, M., Feng, L., Hu, L., Chen, M., & Bondarenko, I. (2019). CHPC: A complex semantic-based secured approach to heritage preservation and secure Iot-based museum processes. *Computer Communications*, *148*, 240–249. doi:10.1016/j.comcom.2019.08.001

Korzun, D., Varfolomeyev, A., Yalovitsyna, S., & Volokhova, V. (2017). Semantic infrastructure of a smart museum: Toward making cultural heritage knowledge usable and creatable by visitors and professionals. *Personal and Ubiquitous Computing*, *2*(2), 345–354. doi:10.100700779-016-0996-7

Kotsopoulos, D., Bardaki, C., Papaioannou, T. G., Lounis, S., & Pramatari, K. (2018). Agile user-centered design of an IoT-enabled gamified intervention for energy conservation. *IADIS International Journal on WWW/Internet*, *16*(1), 1–25.

Kotsopoulos, D., Bardaki, C., Papaioannou, T. G., Lounis, S., Stamoulis, G. D., & Pramatari, K. (2019). Designing a serious game to motivate energy savings in a museum: Opportunities & challenges. In *International Conference on Games and Learning Alliance* (pp. 572-584). Springer. 10.1007/978-3-030-34350-7_55

Mattern, F., & Floerkemeier, C. (2010). From the internet of computers to the internet of things. *Informatik-Spektrum*, *33*(2), 107–121. doi:10.100700287-010-0417-7

McCall, V., & Gray, C. (2014). Museums and the 'new museology': Theory, practice and organisational change. *Museum Management and Curatorship*, *29*(1), 19–35. doi:10.1080/09647775.2013.869852

NEMO Report. (2020). *Survey on the impact of the COVID-19 situation on museums in Europe Final Report.* Network of European Museum Organizations.

Report. (2008). *Internet of things in 2020: Roadmap for the future.* European Commission Information Society and Media.

Sakamura, K. (2006). Challenges in the age of ubiquitous computing: A case study of t-engine, an open development platform for embedded systems. *Proceedings of the 28th International Conference on Software Engineering*, 713-720. 10.1145/1134285.1134399

Space Center Houston. (2021). Date Accessed: 01.06.2021. https://spacecenter.org/

Spachos, P., & Plataniotis, K. N. (2020). BLE beacons for indoor positioning at an interactive IoT-based Smart Museum. *IEEE Systems Journal*, *14*(3), 3483–3493. doi:10.1109/JSYST.2020.2969088

UNESCO Report, . (2020). *Museums around the world in the face of covid-19.* UNESCO.

Vallez, N., Krauss, S., Espinosa-Aranda, J. L., Pagani, A., Seirafi, K., & Deniz, O. (2020). Automatic museum audio guide. *Sensors (Basel)*, *20*(3), 779. doi:10.339020030779 PMID:32023954

Weil, S. E. (1999). From being about something to being for somebody: The ongoing transformation of the american museum. *Daedalus*, *128*(3), 229–258.

Weiser, M. (1999). The computer for the 21st century. *Mobile Computing and Communications Review*, *3*(3), 3–11. doi:10.1145/329124.329126

World Tourism Organization. (2019). *Tourism definitions.* UNWTO.

World Tourism Organization. (2021). *UNWTO Inclusive Recovery Guide – Sociocultural Impacts of Covid-19, Issue 2: Cultural Tourism.* UNWTO.

Wortmann, F., & Flüchter, K. (2015). Internet of things: Technology and value added. *Business & Information Systems Engineering*, *57*(3), 221–224. doi:10.100712599-015-0383-3

Zeng, D., Guo, S., & Cheng, Z. (2011). The web of things: A survey. *Journal of Communication*, *6*(6), 424–438.

ADDITIONAL READING

Gaberli, Ü. (2019). Tourism in Digital Age: An Explanation for the Impacts of Virtual, Augmented and Mixed Reality Technologies on Tourist Experiences. *Journal of Tourism Intelligence and Smartness*, 2(2), 61–69.

Chapter 15
Digital Communication in Museums and Museological Spaces:
Diagnosis of Baixo Alentejo, Portugal

Victor Figueira
(iD) https://orcid.org/0000-0002-2936-0195
Polytechinc Institute of Beja, Portugal & CiTUR, Portugal

João Arnedo Rolha
Polytechnic Institute of Beja, Portugal

Bruno Barbosa Sousa
(iD) https://orcid.org/0000-0002-8588-2422
Polytechnic Institute of Cávado and Ave (IPCA), Portugal & CiTUR, Portugal

ABSTRACT

SMM (social media marketing) aims to produce content that users share in their various social media applications in order to increase brand exposure and broaden customer reach. There are numerous marketing techniques to apply in social media in order to involve the customer, some of which have costs and others that do not. Digitization was a real challenge for any museum, requiring cautious and well-planned action to be successful. In this sense, the nature of social networks demands the adoption of a constructivist perspective, that is, a perspective that involves affirmations of knowledge based on individual and collective experiences. Presently, being present in social networks presents itself as a high value advantage, allowing the exposure of the brand, product, or idea at a low cost to a large audience. This chapter aims to systematize some relational marketing best practices that are identified in the museums and museum spaces in "Baixo Alentejo" (Portugal). Specifically, some examples of relational marketing in terms of communication will be identified and analysed.

DOI: 10.4018/978-1-7998-8528-3.ch015

INTRODUCTION

Brand attachment studies have a vital importance for marketing and tourism (e.g. museums). There are few empirical studies that explicitly focus on the relation of brand attachment to other concepts, such as brand confidence, brand satisfaction, commitment and brand loyalty (Belaid & Temessek Behi, 2011; Sousa & Magalhães, 2019). For hospitality, such an approach can be very useful when operating within a global environment that sees companies often venture beyond their traditional geographical base into providing services to enhance tourist experience. Therefore, SMM (social media marketing) aims to produce content that users share in their various social media applications in order to increase brand exposure and broaden customer reach. There are numerous marketing techniques to apply in social media in order to involve the customer, some of which have costs and others do not. Digitization was a real challenge for any museum, requiring cautious and well-planned action to be successful. In this sense, the nature of social networks demands the adoption of a constructivist perspective, that is, a perspective that involves affirmations of knowledge based on individual and collective experiences. Presently, being present in social networks presents itself as a high value advantage, allowing to expose the brand, product, or idea, at a low cost, to a high audience. This chapter aims to systematize some relational marketing best practices that are identified in the museums and museum spaces in "Baixo Alentejo" (Portugal). Specifically, some examples of relational marketing in terms of communication will be identified and analysed.

TOURISM SEGMENTATION AND MUSEUMS

The study of consumer behavior has gathered particular interest in recent years in multiple contexts, notably with the development of the digital age (e.g. Pinto da Silva et al., 2019). Tourism is a multifaceted and geographically complex activity that increasingly generates new (and different) market segments with different individual interests. The term niche, in a marketing perspective, refers to two key inter-related ideas: that there is a place in the market for the product, and that there is an audience for that same product. This refers to a specific product capable of keeping up with the needs of a specific market segment (Sousa, Santos & Azevedo, 2020). Therefore, one should not look at the market in a simplistic and homogeneous way, since it represents a group of individuals with specific characteristics and needs.

In this way, niche markets emerge as a response to the growing demand for sophisticated and specialized tourism, such as museums. According to its classical meaning, the concept of heritage refers to the legacy we inherited from the past and that we transmit to future generations (Silva, 2000). Heritage is the "collecting" activity that results from the process of heritage formation. On the other hand, Faria and Almeida (2006, p. 124) consider that "heritage and identity are concepts that go hand in hand and whose diffusion runs in the same global channels", underlining that the identity of a people is based on its history and heritage milestones, both material and immaterial. For instance, it is widely accepted that destination image is an integral and influential part of the traveler's decision process and consequently travel behaviours (Vareiro et al., 2020).

In this context, trust has been studied for 30 years in several disciplines and continues to attract the interest of researchers in business-to-business (B2B) marketing (Akrout et al., 2016, p. 269). In relationship marketing, trust has been recognized as an important concept. According to some authors, trust is generally considered a fundamental to develop and maintain a long-term relationship (Sousa & Alves,

2019). This is an important concept in variety of relationships, whether interpersonal or interinstitutional, and consists of a factor to determine relationship quality. Trust is regarded as an essential key to maintaining continuity in the customer–provider relationship and trust likely leads to loyalty, irrespective of the magnitude of the level of the relationship between the company and its customers in specific tourism contexts (Yu et al., 2014).

Communication and Social Networks

The area of communication has become increasingly important over the years in our lives, in society, in companies and organizations, although it has not always been so. Lendrevie et al. (2015) recognize that today's role of communication is totally different given the pressure and strong competition that organizations face, and it plays a unique role in the success of an organization, a brand, a service or product. Prior to the dissemination of intended messages, communication has the function of designing, producing and disseminating them to achieve the intended targets. The choice of communication channels is also a fundamental task for the success of message transmission (Sousa et al., 2021). Kotler, Roberto and Lee (2002) consider that in order to develop strategic communication, it is essential to consider two main steps: the creation of messages and the selection of communication channels that best suit the specific case. Social media gives users the opportunity to interact with site content and other creators, enabling them to engage more with people (Weinreich (2011)). According to Kotler, Kartajaya and Setiawan (2017), social networks are considered "a powerful tool for consumer engagement" and have facilitated interaction between individuals, especially when it requires greater emotional involvement.

In a scenario of technological development, and change in the way people relate to brands, it is essential to adjust the communication strategies of companies that are required to be present in the most varied communication formats to reach the intended targets (Sousa et al., 2021). Social networks have already been perceived by companies as a great mechanism to help them reach their marketing goals and goals, especially in aspects such as customer engagement, customer relationship management and communication (Saxena & Khanna, 2013). In different contexts, companies look for ways to introduce social networks into the most diverse aspects of communicating with their customers, whether through interactivity, promotion, facilitating access to information, and even improving customer buying behavior (Zeng & Gerritsen, 2014). In this study, we will focus on four extremely successful social networks, such as Facebook, Instagram, Youtube and Twitter. The choice of these stands for its huge popularity worldwide as well as its ability to expand a business (Ferreira & Sousa, 2020). The Facebook is considered an attractive social network for digital marketing specialists and for online ads. These ads use social networks to connect customers to businesses, thereby creating new opportunities for customers to get to know their brands and products.

THE BAIXO ALENTEJO REGION

Baixo Alentejo (Lower Alentejo) is part of the extensive Alentejo Region, bordered to the north by the District of Évora, to the east by Spain, and to the south by the District of Faro. This subregion includes 13 Municipalities: Aljustrel, Almodôvar, Alvito, Barrancos, Beja, Castro Verde, Cuba, Ferreira do Alentejo, Mértola, Moura, Ourique, Serpa e Vidigueira – Figure 1.

Given its geographical, socioeconomic and cultural characteristics, Baixo Alentejo would at first sight benefit greatly from a route-based tourism development strategy. With approximately 8,544,6 km2, it is the largest Portuguese NUTS 3 region, comprising almost 10% of the national territory. It is, however, also one of the least populated. The population density of Baixo Alentejo is 14.77 inhabitants/km^2. The resident population of the area is 126,192 individuals.

Figure 1. Region of Baixo Alentejo - municipalities
Source: CIMBAL (s/d)

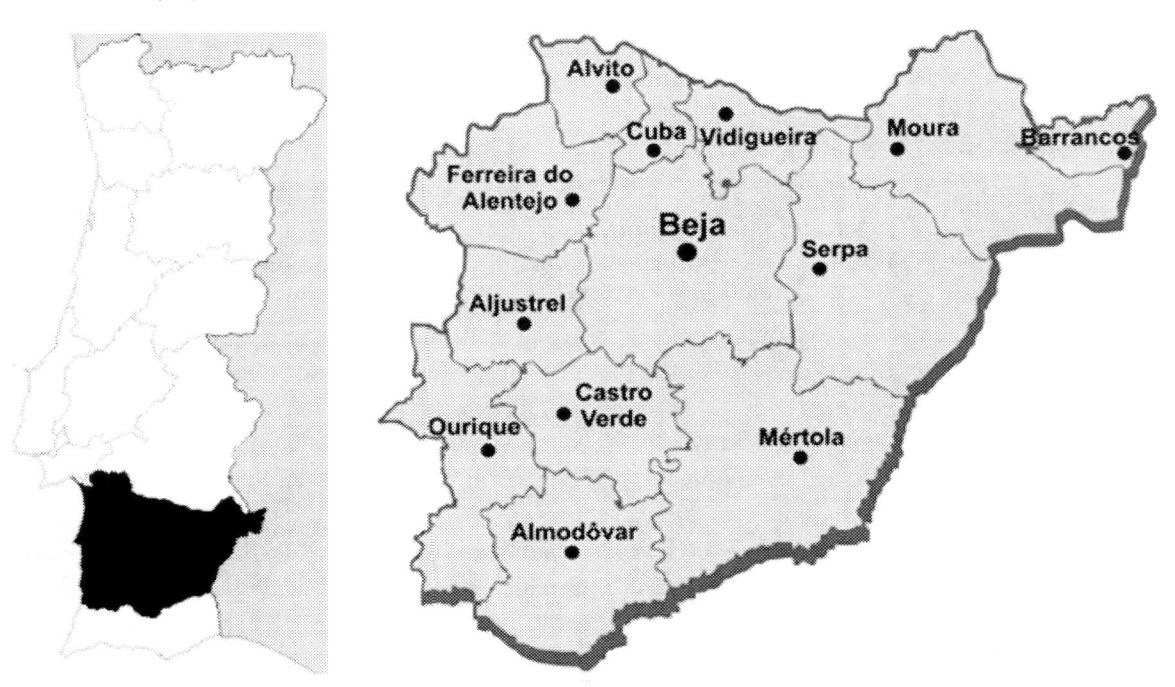

This subregion is strongly characterised not only by its cultural heritage, reflected in archaeological sites, castles, churches, old mines, museums and small towns and villages which, with their traditional constructions, reflect the diversity of cultural influences to which this region has been subjected, but also by its natural heritage, such as the Vale do Guadiana Nature Park and the Special Protection Areas (SPA) of Moura, Barrancos and Guadiana. The Guadiana river, considered to be one of the most important natural resources in Baixo Alentejo, is an international river of the Iberian Peninsula that originates in Spain, and when it reaches Portugal, in Alentejo, it follows the border line. The river is about 870 kilometres long, of which only 260 are in Portugal. It is thus a vast, mostly rural and agricultural territory, with distinctive natural features, a rich history, a unique tangible and intangible heritage and culture recognised by UNESCO, and an outstanding gastronomy, based on high-quality, certified and prize-winning products, such as olive oil, cheese, meat products and wines.

The completion of the Alqueva Dam, the largest artificial lake in Europe, and the construction of a complex network of secondary dams and irrigation systems have brought about a true "agricultural revolution", marked by a substantial expansion of olive grove plantations and olive oil factories, vineyards and wineries, as well as the introduction of new cultures and of advanced industrial production systems. Despite the wealth of its natural and cultural resources, the region of Alentejo (Table 1) is one of the least visited in the country, accounting for approximately 5,95% of overnight stays.

Table 1. Guests in Mainland Portugal - 2019

	Guests (thousands)	%
PORTUGAL	27,142.4	-
NORTH	5,873.0	21.63
CENTRE	4,118.7	15.17
LISBON	8,216.7	30.27
ALENTEJO	1,616.1	5.95
ALGARVE	5,064.1	18.65

Source: TRAVEL BI (2020)

Regarding the tourism activity in Baixo Alentejo, if we refer to Table 2, we can see that the largest number of tourists stays in the district capital, the city of Beja, and in Mértola, two of the main territories that aggregate a greater structure in light of the cultural and museological heritage available in this subregion.

Table 2. Guests in Baixo Alentejo - 2019

Geographic location	Average stay	Overnight stays (no.)			Guests (no.)		
		TOTAL	Portugal	Foreigners	TOTAL	Portugal	Foreigners
Baixo Alentejo	x	384617	287408	97209	216335	169064	47271
Aljustrel	x	14094	10600	3494	8510	6617	1893
Almodôvar	x	15228	13333	1895	11433	10679	754
Alvito	x	7621	5182	2439	4597	3031	1566
Barrancos	x	3452	2850	602	2196	1891	305
Beja	x	168264	116814	51450	88171	64052	24119
Castro Verde	x	20409	15308	5101	10622	8611	2011
Cuba	x	3815	2756	1059	1749	1557	192
Ferreira do Alentejo	x	23194	17783	5411	13566	11073	2493
Mértola	x	54687	39402	15285	31729	22743	8986
Moura	x	32510	28902	3608	20715	18569	2146
Ourique	x	12616	11166	1450	6615	5749	866
Serpa	x	16942	11966	4976	10089	8431	1658
Vidigueira	x	11785	11346	439	6343	6061	282

Source: adapted from INE (2019)

Alentejo, and more specifically Baixo Alentejo, is thus characterised as a region with huge potential in terms of its history and cultural, natural and heritage values. However, it still lacks a greater structuring of its offer, especially in the use of tools that allow a wider public to discover this region and its values.

Museums, Public Policies and the Future

Nowadays, there is a general perception that museums must perform multiple roles, contributing to public policies that, may or may not be, specifically in the field of culture, such as in the area of science, research, creativity, entrepreneurship, social integration, health and well-being, territorial cohesion, tourism development, sustainable development, among others (Legget 2017; Camacho 2020). The cultural sector itself certainly contributes to this perception, as there is a tendency to separate the various areas, with specific bodies assigned to the management of each area but with almost no communication between them.

Museology and museums have been a reflection of the existing vision and public policies that necessarily influence their way of acting from different angles. However, this vision has been changing in recent years, given the crises that the cultural sector, and specifically museums, have been experiencing. There is an increasing need for vision and strategic planning for this sector, establishing its own long-term priorities instead of following the oscillations of the government's political cycles, thus allowing a proper structuring and consolidation in view of the objectives that this sector should contribute to society.

At the municipal level, the cultural sector maintains the above-mentioned multifunctionality, encompassing several areas - cultural, immovable, mobile and intangible heritage, artistic expressions, traditional manifestations of culture, creative industries, spaces for socializing and sociability, networks of municipal facilities linked to these areas, municipal editing and communication, promotion of events, promotion of cultural tourism and, in a complementary way, education and training.

Table 3. Art galleries and other temporary exhibition spaces (no.) - 2019

Geographic location	Art galleries and other temporary exhibition spaces (no.)	Museums (no.)	Visitors (no.)	Operational museums (no.)
Baixo Alentejo	26	11	111183	23
Aljustrel	2	1	2497	2
Almodôvar	2	0	0	2
Alvito	1	0	0	1
Barrancos	3	1	x	1
Beja	4	2	30752	7
Castro Verde	2	2	x	3
Cuba	1	0	0	1
Ferreira do Alentejo	2	1	5863	1
Mértola	2	1	42900	1
Moura	1	1	6276	1
Ourique	0	0	0	0
Serpa	4	1	15796	2
Vidigueira	2	1	2037	1

Source: adapted from INE (2019)

The existence of several museological spaces in a given region are not enough, on their own, to guarantee the preservation of its cultural values and traditions. They need public policies that guarantee the continued investment that these facilities need to make, on an ongoing basis, so that they can achieve the purpose for which they were intended. Tourist demand for these facilities is increasing, but so is their demand regarding what they offer in terms of access and visit experience. The lack of investment and strategy applied to this sector does nothing to make it more visible. The use of social networks and other technologies has been gaining traction, especially in the promotion and dissemination of spaces like this, and Baixo Alentejo is no exception. Technology is constantly evolving and it is up to the public policies for the culture sector and, specifically, for museums to know how to transition to the digital world without losing their identity as physical spaces.

To conclude, it is important to mention that, in Portugal, in a legislative framework of change for museological and heritage entities under the Ministry of Culture, the "Future Museums Project Group" was created in February 2019. The main objective assigned to this group was to "create and propose the necessary tools for the implementation of management models". This group based its research and reflection on five axes: Management of Museums, Palaces and Monuments; Networks and Partnerships; Digital Transformation; Collections Management; Audiences and Mediation (Camacho, 2020).

It is considered important to highlight the group's main recommendations, specifying some of them as they are considered relevant:

- "Modernise and update internal IT equipment (hardware and software) by promoting electronic management, implementing the digitalisation of services, adapting public areas (e.g.: WIFI) to potential new technologies (e.g. Internet of Things) and ensuring conditions for technical support and maintenance of equipment and applications, in line with the Action Plan for Digital Transition. (T);
- Create a portal for Museums, Palaces and Monuments, updating and optimising their respective sites;
- Create a "Museums of the Future" helpline for restoration projects of Museums, Palaces and Monuments, taking into account their missions, objectives and strategies, geared towards investments with the implementation of technologies (e. g.: WIFI, augmented reality, virtual reality, interactive devices, among others), accessibilities and media content in languages that translate into actual perks in the visit experience for national and foreign visitors, through national (Digital Transition, Tourism and Culture) and/or EU funding. (T);
- Create a programme to systematically reinforce and expand the digitalisation of the collections of Museums, Palaces and Monuments;
- Ensure and increase digital access to collections and holdings;
- Develop a programme to use technology as a complementary means of interpretation;
- Create support, monitoring and evaluation mechanisms for Museums, Palaces and Monuments;
- Strengthen the establishment of partnerships in the area of digital communication;
- Promote pilot projects focused on transfers of knowledge and research;
- Ensure the recruitment of professionals with specialised digital skills and create regular training plans" (Camacho, 2020:62-63).

Although the referenced study is not geared towards small regional and local museum spaces, we can certainly take full advantage of its content and analysis so that we can ensure a tailored digital transition for each space and make the visit experience better and better.

The Museological Heritage of Baixo Alentejo: A Brief Summary

Like other museological spaces in other regions, in Baixo Alentejo these spaces seek to portray the history, traditions, people, ancestral activities, ways of working and living, as well as other aspects which can, in some way, show the richness of each of these municipalities regarding their tangible and intangible heritage. The influence of the many peoples that passed through this region, geographically dominated by plains and peneplains, of low altitude, with a strategic sea entry, privileged by the southernmost region of Portugal, Algarve, made possible the successive conquests and reconquests and the entry of several peoples, including the Romans, Visigoths, Muslims, among many others in its history, which led to the existence of many remnants, determining the way of being and acting of the Alentejo people (Correia, 2009). Most of these museological spaces include exhibitions and memories of the presence of these people from archaeological discoveries, aspects related to ethnography, sacred art and some traditions, in which the influences of Romanisation and Islamisation stand out (Torres,1993).

It is important to highlight the "Cante Alentejano", as a genuine form of musical expression, unique in the world, considered intangible heritage of humanity by UNESCO in 2014. The Alentejo Songbook is considered to be the country's largest by many authors (Nazaré, 1986; Marvão, 1997).

There are also some other singularities that should be mentioned and that determine the diversified richness of this region. These singularities include the influence of the "Islamic heritage" (Torres, 1987, 1992; Macias, 1996), which is very expressive in Mértola and is portrayed very well in the Islamic Festival that takes place every two years; the "southwest script", available at the Museum in Almodôvar, as an ancestral form of communication used between the peoples of Portugal and Spain for over 2500 years ago (Correia, 2014; Guerra, 2010); one of the most notable and preserved "tile collections" (Figure 2) in the country that can be observed in situ, with a tradition of 500 years of history - in this regard, Tadeia (2013:124) states that *"the Tiling is also a fundamental nucleus, not only for what is still in situ, covering the interior walls of the building of the Queen Leonor Museum, but also because it is part of the mobile collection, since the Queen Leonor Museum has an important collection of tiles from various convents and churches that have been demolished"*; the "Window of Mértola" (Figure 3), that depicts the story of a nun, Mariana Alcoforado of the Saint Clare Order, of the Convent of the Conception in Beja, who was given the authorship of the internationally known *Lettres Portugaises* (Portuguese Letters), five love letters dedicated to the French knight Noël Bouton, Marquis of Chamilly (Saramago, 1973; Borrela, 2019), the latter two are available in the Beja Regional Museum – Queen Leonor.

Figure 2. Chapter room – Beja Regional Museum
Source: DGPC

Figure 3. Window of Mértola – Beja Regional Museum
Source: MRBeja

Therefore, it is on this diversity that the existing offer in the several museological spaces of small and medium size, under municipal responsibility, is based.

METHODOLOGY AND CONTENSS: COMMUNICATION AND TECHNOLOGY IN THE MUSEOLOGICAL SPACES OF BAIXO ALENTEJO

In methodological terms, secondary research was carried out regarding the gathering of information on existing museological spaces in the mentioned region, as well as general information on the theme in question. Primary research was also carried out, with the proposal of carrying out an interview with each of the municipalities (13) in order to better ascertain the various dimensions of their reality, given that the study was only aimed at spaces at the municipal level, that is, under the responsibility of the municipalities of Baixo Alentejo. The study made it possible to evaluate the knowledge of several variables, namely, the media platforms and channels used; the way and means of promoting and publicising the space; whether or not a more accentuated promotion was carried out in view of the COVID-19 pandemic period; the potential use of certain types of technology, such as the Internet of Things (IoT) or others. It was in this context of qualitative analysis, but also quantitative, that the results obtained in the fieldwork carried out were interpreted. These results will be presented shortly.

Communication and Technology in Museological Spaces: Findings

As shown in Table 4 below, there are 45 museological spaces which are under the responsibility of each of the municipalities in Baixo Alentejo, with only 1 of them not being active at the time of this research, as it was undergoing refurbishment. There is only one municipality where no museological spaces have been identified - Ourique.

Regarding the media platforms used, it can be seen that the great majority of them, even for institutional reasons, use the municipality's official WEBSITE as their main platform, 95.55%. Only one of the spaces has its own site. All other platforms only see residual use: FACEBOOK, 22%, 4 of them with their own pages; INSTAGRAM and TWITTER, 4.4% and YOUTUBE, 2.2%. It should be noted that these last three platforms are used only for museums, and not in a generalist manner.

Thus, we can see that almost all the spaces use only and/or simultaneously the municipality's official website for their promotion, which can be reductive considering the target audience to be reached. The complexity of the municipalities' web pages, with their institutional needs and obligations regarding the information displayed, often does not facilitate the necessary path to reach the desired information, which makes it unfeasible or time consuming for potential visitors to get to know it.

Being municipal spaces, but whose promotion should be focused on their visitors, it should be expected the existence of individualized platforms to better identify their product. However, only 1 of the museums has its own website, and only 4 of them have Facebook pages. These are the museums that complement their promotion efforts with other identified platforms such as Instagram, YouTube or Twitter. All the others are dependent on the structuring and management of information carried out by the municipal media platforms.

Table 5 refers to the form of communication of each one of these spaces, in times of pandemic, and potential use of innovative technologies such as the Internet of things or others.

Table 4. Municipal museological spaces in Baixo Alentejo - 2021

Geographic location	Name of the Museological Space	Communication channels used	Active (Y/N)
Municipality/Baixo Alentejo			
Aljustrel	Aljustrel Municipal Museum	Official WEBSITE of the Municipality Official FACEBOOK of the Municipality	Y
	Rural Nucleus of Ervidel	Official WEBSITE of the Municipality Official FACEBOOK of the Municipality	Y
Almodôvar	Southwest Script Museum	Official WEBSITE of the Municipality FACEBOOK	Y
	Manuel Vicente Guerreiro Ethnographic Museum	Official WEBSITE of the Municipality	Y
	Severo Portela Museum	Official WEBSITE of the Municipality	Y
Alvito	Cante-Alvito Museum Centre	Official WEBSITE of the Municipality	Y
Barrancos	Municipal Museum of Archaeology and Ethnography of Barancos / Barrancos	Official WEBSITE of the Municipality Official FACEBOOK of the Municipality	Y
Beja	Jorge Vieira Museum	House of Arts (Casa das Artes) – Beja	Official WEBSITE of the Municipality	Y
	Museum Centre of Sembrano Street	Official WEBSITE of the Municipality	Y
	Beja Regional Museum – Queen Leonor	Official WEBSITE of the Municipality	Y
	Visigothic Museum	Official WEBSITE of the Municipality	Y
Castro Verde	Treasure of the Royal Basilica of Our Lady of the Conception – Castro Verde	Official WEBSITE of the Municipality FACEBOOK	Y
	Lamps (lucerna) Museum in Castro Verde	Official WEBSITE of the Municipality	Y
	Rural Life Museum	Official WEBSITE of the Municipality Official FACEBOOK of the Municipality	Y
	Aivados Museum Centre – Community Village	Official WEBSITE of the Municipality	Y
Cuba	Quinta da Esperança House-Museum	WEBSITE; FACEBOOK; INSTAGRAM; TWITTER	Y
	Christopher Colon Centre	Official WEBSITE of the Municipality	Y
Ferreira do Alentejo	Ferreira Municipal Museum	Official WEBSITE of the Municipality FACEBOOK; INSTAGRAM	Y
	Museum Centre: NAS - Religious Art Nucleus	Official WEBSITE of the Municipality	Y
	Museum Centre: House of Wine and Singing - Zé Lélito Tavern	Official WEBSITE of the Municipality	Y
	Museum Centre: Municipal Archives	Official WEBSITE of the Municipality	Y
	Museum Centre: Roman Villa Archaeological Site of Monte da Chaminé	Official WEBSITE of the Municipality	Y

Continued on following page

Table 4. Continued

Geographic location	Name of the Museological Space	Communication channels used	Active (Y/N)
Municipality/Baixo Alentejo			
Mértola	Museum Centre of Alcáçova and Islamic House	Official WEBSITE of the Municipality	Y
	Islamic Art Museum Centre	Official WEBSITE of the Municipality	Y
	Religious Art Museum Centre	Official WEBSITE of the Municipality	Y
	Paleochristian Basilica Museum Centre	Official WEBSITE of the Municipality	Y
	Castle Museum Centre	Official WEBSITE of the Municipality	Y
	Roman House Museum Centre	Official WEBSITE of the Municipality	Y
	Museum Centre of Mértola's Main Church	Official WEBSITE of the Municipality	Y
	Miner's House Museum Centre - São Domingos Mine	Official WEBSITE of the Municipality	Y
	Weaving Workshop Museum Centre	Official WEBSITE of the Municipality	Y
	Museum Centre of Ermida and Necropolis of S. Sebastian	Official WEBSITE of the Municipality	Y
	Blacksmith's Forge Museum Centre	Official WEBSITE of the Municipality	Y
	Mértola House Museum Centre	Official WEBSITE of the Municipality	Y
	Alcaria do Javazes Museum Centre	Official WEBSITE of the Municipality	Y
	Monastery Museum Centre	Official WEBSITE of the Municipality	Y
Moura	Olive Oil Museum: Lagar (olive press) of Varas de Fojo	Official WEBSITE of the Municipality	Y
	Alberto Gordillo Museum – Contemporary Jewellery	Official WEBSITE of the Municipality	Y
	Municipal Museum	Official WEBSITE of the Municipality	Y
	Religious Art Museum / St Peter's Church	Official WEBSITE of the Municipality	Y
Ourique	x	x	X
Serpa	Archeology Museum	Official WEBSITE of the Municipality / Official FACEBOOK of the Municipality	Y
	Serpa Ethnographic Museum	Official WEBSITE of the Municipality / Official FACEBOOK of the Municipality	N
Vidigueira	Quinta da Esperança – Museum-house and Cultural Space	FACEBOOK; INSTAGRAM; YOUTUBE; TWITTER	Y
	Vidigueira Municipal Museum	Official WEBSITE of the Municipality	Y
	Marmelar Exhibition Centre	Official WEBSITE of the Municipality	Y

Source: Own elaboration.

Table 5. Communication and use of technologies in museological spaces - 2021

Name of the Museum	Use of digital media platforms for promotion	Communication Strengthening in times of pandemic	Use of technologies: Internet of Things	Use of other technologies
Aljustrel Municipal Museum	√	X	X	X
Rural Nucleus of Ervidel	√	X	X	X
Southwest Script Museum	√	X	X	Interactive panel
Manuel Vicente Guerreiro Ethnographic Museum	√	X	X	X
Severo Portela Museum	√	X	X	X
Cante-Alvito Museum Centre	√	X	X	X
Municipal Museum of Archeology and Ethnography of Barancos /Barrancos	√	√	X	X
Jorge Vieira Museum I House of Arts (Casa das Artes) – Beja	√	X	X	X
Museum Centre of Sembrano Street	√	X	X	X
Beja Regional Museum – Queen Leonor	√	X	X	X
Visigothic Museum	√	X	X	X
Treasure of the Royal Basilica of Our Lady of the Conception – Castro Verde	√	X	X	X
Lamps (lucernas) Museum in Castro Verde	√	X	X	X
Rural Life Museum	√	X	X	X
Aivados Museum Centre – Community Village	√	X	X	X
Quinta da Esperança House-Museum	√	X	X	QR code
Christopher Colon Centre	√	X	X	X
Ferreira Municipal Museum	√	√	X	X
Museum Centre: NAS - Religious Art Nucleus	√	√	X	Holography
Museum Centre: House of Wine and Singing - Zé Lélito Tavern	√	√	X	X
Museum Centre: Municipal Archives	√	√	X	X
Museum Centre: Roman Villa Archaeological Site of Monte da Chaminé	√	√	X	X
Museum Centre of Alcáçova and Islamic House	√	X	X	Museum App
Islamic Art Museum Centre	√	X	X	Museum App
Religious Art Museum Centre	√	X	X	Museum App
Paleochristian Basilica Museum Centre	√	X	X	Museum App
Castle Museum Centre	√	X	X	Museum App
Roman House Museum Centre	√	X	X	Museum App

Continued on following page

Table 5. Continued

Name of the Museum	Use of digital media platforms for promotion	Communication Strengthening in times of pandemic	Use of technologies: Internet of Things	Use of other technologies
Museum Centre of Mértola's Main Church	√	X	X	Museum App
Miner's House Museum Centre - São Domingos Mine	√	X	X	Museum App
Weaving Workshop Museum Centre	√	X	X	Museum App
Museum Centre of Ermida and Necropolis of S. Sebastian	√	X	X	Museum App
Blacksmith's Forge Museum Centre	√	X	X	Museum App
Mértola House Museum Centre	√	X	X	Museum App
Alcaria do Javazes Museum Centre	√	X	X	Museum App
Monastery Museum Centre	√	X	X	Museum App
Olive Oil Museum: Lagar (olive press) of Varas de Fojo	√	√	X	X
Alberto Gordillo Museum – Contemporary Jewellery	√	√	X	X
Municipal Museum	√	√	X	X
Religious Art Museum / St Peter's Church	√	√	X	X
Archeology Museum	√	√	X	Interactive panels
Serpa Ethnographic Museum	√	X	X	X
Quinta da Esperança – Museum-house and Cultural Space	√	√	X	X
Vidigueira Municipal Museum	√	X	X	X
Marmelar Exhibition Centre	√	X	X	X

Information regarding all museums in Baixo Alentejo exists and is available on digital platforms, particularly in the municipalities' websites.

We can see that only 26.66% of museums felt the need to strengthen their promotion/dissemination during this pandemic period as a way of connecting with their followers, thus maintaining their interest in the work that is being developed in each museum.

Some technologies are used to complement the visit, such as interactive panels, QR CODES to identify certain objects and spaces, an APP with information about the museums that can speed up their accessibility and, lastly, a holographic historical figure that interacts with visitors.

As for the use of technology associated with the Internet of Things, none of the spaces showed any signs of using this technology.

The structuring, organisation and management of municipal museological spaces is by no means easy. Each of them has its own organisation that depends on the executive bodies' decisions regarding their respective municipalities, with different views on how these spaces should be integrated within the context of tourism-oriented municipalities. The management of the staff assigned to these spaces may also prove to be a complex factor, due to their rotation with other departments.

The situation arising from the communication aspects in the museums in Baixo Alentejo is also largely due to the financial issues of each of the regions and the size of these spaces. The vast majority of these spaces are small, making it difficult to get the necessary means for their projection. However, digital media can bridge this gap and, if well structured, allow these spaces to be known and promoted all over the world, because of the Internet.

CONCLUSIONS, LIMITATIONS AND NEXT STEPS

The present chapter focused on understanding the importance of relational marketing and digital communication, specifically reflecting on constructs such as brand attachment, in the influence of tourists (as consumers), taking the museums contexts. The region of Baixo Alentejo is in itself a historical region in its designation. However, this designation continues to be recognised and accepted for the purposes of the administrative division of the territory. It is a sparsely populated region where many towns are located at great distances from each other, resulting in an extensive territorial dispersion. For instance, and according to Sousa, Castro, Luís and Lopes (2021), in particular, the preliminary approach allowed the perception from a marketing perspective that feelings of place identity, in the emotional dimension of the journey, and the satisfaction with the experience may increase and consequently can reinforce the loyalty to the destination (in Alentejo, Portugal contexts). These contribute to tourist satisfaction and loyalty. The research suggests that this rationale is suitable for spiritual tourism. This study is a preliminary contribution towards a greater understanding regarding the relationship between the local affection and behavioural intentions in specific contexts of religious and spiritual tourism, considering the particular case of Portugal (Alentejo). Therefore, the municipalities have made an effort to preserve their history and traditions by creating museological spaces that perpetuate these memories. However, the fact that these are public entities with certain types of organisational characteristics means that institutional communication is often carried out in a more scattered manner, due to the numerous public responsibilities that these entities are bound to.

The museological spaces have, from the outset, a set of constraints arising from the governance itself, from the human and financial resources allocated to them and from their dependence on the City Council's size and vision. In terms of tourist offer, this dependence may be an unfavourable factor since the structuring of a tourism product based on all this cultural wealth may not be carried out in the best possible way, due to the lack of conditions for its proper planning.

Regarding communication and technologies of the museological spaces in Baixo Alentejo, at the municipal level, we were able to observe, in this study, that all of them now have a digital space, mostly through the institutional website of each of their respective municipality. The use of other platforms is almost incipient, with Facebook being the one that shows more use. It is worth highlighting the fact that these spaces maintained their activity even during the pandemic period, although little or nothing was done to strengthen their communication during this period. However, there is a need to promote the creation of their own platforms that allow these spaces to target their visitors in a more efficient way. We can also see a total absence of any technology associated with the Internet of Things. However, there is still some use of other technologies, which are associated with interactive panels, the creation of an app, holographic effects and qr codes.

There is still a long way to go to provide these spaces with the necessary functionalities to keep up with the technological advances in their way of communicating. This will not solely rely on who manages these spaces but, above all, on the public policies that will be implemented in this respect and, particularly, in the cultural sector.

Although in 2016 the Baixo Alentejo Museums Network was created, which combines in the same place what all of these museological spaces have to offer, this network still follows along the same lines of the institutional bodies, ending up having little visibility and projection regarding its promotion.

In a future research work, we intend to carry out a more comprehensive study that will include all the cultural spaces, both public and private, in order to make a more complete characterisation of the art's state in the region, thus creating a tourist product based on the people's identity of Baixo Alentejo.

In conclusion, through this study, it was possible to observe that a good and consistent SMM strategy, based on improving brand attachment, satisfaction, commitment and, ultimately, loyalty, have an influence on tourists' behaviour and the extent of its relationship with the museums. Thus, social networks potential as a relational marketing tool for tourism must continue to be explored. In terms of limitations, while developing this study, it was possible to identify a main limitation regarding the fact that the methodology design selected for the study, considering its characteristics, does not made it possible to generalize the results obtained (i.e. Alentejo case study).

This study stands on a preliminary and exploratory research having a qualitative approach method on which conclusions derive from the researchers' perspective. For future research, it would be interesting to work with the insights of this study and to direct some attention to the limitation identified above trying to overcome it. Therefore, it is suggested a broader application of this study to the reality of museums management in Portugal. In fact, it would be appropriate to consider conducting a research that would have into consideration more examples of good relational marketing practices in museums in order to complement the findings and conclusions of this research. To get different perspectives of the subject, there is also, for example, the possibility of conducting this study through other qualitative and detailed methodologies like the development of focus groups or in-depth interviews.

REFERENCES

Akrout, H. (2014). Relationship quality in cross-border exchanges: A temporal perspective. *Journal of Business-To-Business Marketing*, *21*(3), 145–169. doi:10.1080/1051712X.2014.952179

Akrout, H., Diallo, M. F., Akrout, W., & Chandon, J.-L. (2016). Affective trust in buyer-seller relationships: A two-dimensional scale. *Journal of Business and Industrial Marketing*, *31*(2), 260–273. doi:10.1108/JBIM-11-2014-0223

Alves, G. M., Sousa, B. M., & Machado, A. (2020). The Role of Digital Marketing and Online Relationship Quality in Social Tourism: A Tourism for All Case Study. In J. Santos & Ó. Silva (Eds.), *Digital Marketing Strategies for Tourism, Hospitality, and Airline Industries* (pp. 49–70). IGI Global. doi:10.4018/978-1-5225-9783-4.ch003

Andersen, P. (2007). *What is Web 2.0? Ideas, technologies and implications for education.* JISC.

Andreasen, A. R. (1995). *Marketing social change: Changing behavior to promote health, social development, and the environment.* Jossey-Bass.

Atwal, G., & Williams, A. (2017). Luxury brand marketing–the experience is everything! In *Advances in luxury brand management* (pp. 43–57). Palgrave Macmillan. doi:10.1007/978-3-319-51127-6_3

Becken, S., Simmons, D. G., & Frampton, C. (2003). Energy use associated with different travel choices. *Tourism Management, 24*(3), 267–277. doi:10.1016/S0261-5177(02)00066-3

Belaid, S., & Temessek Behi, A. (2011). The role of attachment in building consumer-brand relationships: An empirical investigation in the utilitarian consumption context. *Journal of Product and Brand Management, 20*(1), 37–47. doi:10.1108/10610421111108003

Berthon, P., Pitt, L., Parent, M., & Berthon, J. P. (2009). Aesthetics and ephemerality: Observing and preserving the luxury brand. *California Management Review, 52*(1), 45–66. doi:10.1525/cmr.2009.52.1.45

Bigné, J., Andreu, L., & Gnoth, J. (2005). The theme park experience: An analysis of pleasure, arousal and satisfaction. *Tourism Management, 26*(6), 833–844. doi:10.1016/j.tourman.2004.05.006

Borrela, L. (2019). *Cartas de Soro Mariana Alcoforado*. Lisbonpress.

Brenner, L., & Aguilar, A. G. (2002). Luxury tourism and regional economic development in Mexico. *The Professional Geographer, 54*(4), 500–520. doi:10.1111/0033-0124.00346

Camacho, C. (2020). *Grupo de Projeto Museus no Futuro: Relatório Final*. Direção-Geral do Património Cultural.

Chen, A., & Peng, N. (2014). Examining Chinese consumers' luxury hotel staying behavior. *International Journal of Hospitality Management, 39*, 53–56. doi:10.1016/j.ijhm.2014.01.002

Comunidade Intermunicipal do Baixo Alentejo – CIMBAL. (n.d.). *Caracterização do Baixo Alentejo*. CIMBAL

Correia, M. (2009). *A Cidade de Beja – Património Histórico, Cultural e Linguístico*. Universidade da Beira Interior, Dissertação de Mestrado.

Correia, V. (2014). *A escrita do Sudoeste da Península Ibérica. In Portvgalia, Nova Série* (Vol. 35). DCTP-FLUP.

Creswell, J. W., & Creswell, J. D. (2017). *Research design: Qualitative, quantitative, and mixed methods approaches*. Sage publications.

Dalgic, T., & Leeuw, M. (1994). Niche marketing revisited: Concept, applications and some European cases. *European Journal of Marketing, 28*(4), 39–55. doi:10.1108/03090569410061178

Echtner, C. M., & Jamal, T. B. (1997). The disciplinary dilemma of tourism studies. *Annals of Tourism Research, 24*(4), 868–883. doi:10.1016/S0160-7383(97)00060-1

Faria, M., & Almeida, R. (2006). A problemática da "identidade" e o lugar do "património" num mundo crescentemente cosmopolita. *Comunicação e Cultura, 1*, 117–133.

Ferreira, J., & Sousa, B. (2020) Experiential Marketing as Leverage for Growth of Creative Tourism: A Co-creative Process. Advances in Tourism, Technology and Smart Systems. Smart Innovation, Systems and Technologies, 171, 567-577. doi:10.1007/978-981-15-2024-2_49

Fortune. (2007). Luxury goes mass market. *Fortune Magazine*.

Goes, C. (1998). *Beja. XX Séculos de História de uma Cidade, I e II volumes*. Câmara Municipal de Beja.

Guerra, A. (2010). - Algumas observações sobre a Escrita do Sudoeste. *Xelb, 10*, 103–113.

Han, Y. J., Nunes, J. C., & Drèze, X. (2010). Signaling status with luxury goods: The role of brand prominence. *Journal of Marketing*, *74*(4), 15–30. doi:10.1509/jmkg.74.4.015

Hennig-Thurau, T., Gwinner, K. P., & Gremler, D. D. (2002). Understanding relationship marketing outcomes: An integration of relational benefits and relationship quality. *Journal of Service Research*, *4*(3), 230–247. doi:10.1177/1094670502004003006

Hung, K. P., Huiling Chen, A., Peng, N., Hackley, C., Amy Tiwsakul, R., & Chou, C. L. (2011). Antecedents of luxury brand purchase intention. *Journal of Product and Brand Management*, *20*(6), 457–467. doi:10.1108/10610421111166603

Instituto Nacional de Estatística – INE. (2019). *Statistical Yearbook of Alentejo Region – 2018*. INE.

Instituto Nacional de Estatística – INE. (2019). *Estatísticas Regionais*. INE.

Kimpakorn, N., & Dimmitt, N. (2007). Employer branding: The perspective of hotel management in the Thai luxury hotel industry. *Australasian Marketing Journal*, *15*(3), 49.

Koch, K. D. (2011). Luxury Tourism–Does This Market Segment Still Work? In *Trends and issues in global tourism 2011* (pp. 179–185). Springer. doi:10.1007/978-3-642-17767-5_19

Kotler, P., & Armstrong, G. (2001). *Principles of Marketing* (9th ed.). Prentice-Hall.

Kotler, P., Kartajaya, H., & Setiawan, I. (2017). *Marketing 4.0: Mudança do tradicional para o digital*. Conjuntura Actual Editora.

Kotler, P., & Roberto, E. L. (1992). *Marketing Social: Estratégias para alterar o comportamento público*. Campus.

Kotler, P., Roberto, N., & Lee, N. (2002). *Social Marketing: Improving the quality of life*. SAGE Publications.

Legget, J. (2017). Museums and Public Policy: An Introduction. *Museum International*, *69*(275–276), 6–9. doi:10.1111/muse.12169

Lendrevie, J., Lévy, J., Dionísio, P., & Rodrigues, J. V. (2015). *Mercator da Língua Portuguesa: Teoria e Prática do Marketing* (16th ed.). Publicações D. Quixote.

Li, X., Sanders, K., & Frenkel, S. (2012). How leader–member exchange, work engagement and HRM consistency explain Chinese luxury hotel employees' job performance. *International Journal of Hospitality Management*, *31*(4), 1059–1066. doi:10.1016/j.ijhm.2012.01.002

Macias, S. (1996). *Mértola Islâmica. Estudo histórico-arqueológico do bairro da alcáçova (séculos XII-XIII)*. Mértola, Campo Arqueológico de Mértola.

Marshall, C., & Rossman, G. B. (2014). *Designing qualitative research*. Sage publications.

Marvão, A. (1997). *Estudos sobre o Cante Alentejano*. INATEL.

Mohsin, A., & Lockyer, T. (2010). Customer perceptions of service quality in luxury hotels in New Delhi, India: An exploratory study. *International Journal of Contemporary Hospitality Management*, *22*(2), 160–173. doi:10.1108/09596111011018160

Narteh, B., Agbemabiese, G. C., Kodua, P., & Braimah, M. (2013). Relationship marketing and customer loyalty: Evidence from the Ghanaian luxury hotel industry. *Journal of Hospitality Marketing & Management, 22*(4), 407–436. doi:10.1080/19368623.2012.660564

Nazaré, J. (1986). *Momentos Vocais do Baixo Alentejo*. Imprensa Nacional-Casada Moeda.

Palmatier, R. W., Dant, R. P., Grewal, D., & Evans, K. R. (2006). Factors influencing the effectiveness of relationship marketing: A meta-analysis. *Journal of Marketing, 74*(4), 136–153. doi:10.1509/jmkg.70.4.136

Park, K. S., Reisinger, Y., & Noh, E. H. (2010). Luxury shopping in tourism. *International Journal of Tourism Research, 12*(2), 164–178. doi:10.1002/jtr.744

Pinto da Silva, F., Brandão, F., & Sousa, B. (2019). Towards socially sustainable Tourism in cities: local community perceptions and development guidelins. *Enlightening Tourism. A Pathmaking Journal, 9*(2), 168-198.

Prayag, G. (2008). Image, Satisfaction and Loyalty: The Case of Cape Town. Anatolia. *An International Journal of Tourism and Hospitality Research, 19*(2), 205–224. doi:10.1080/13032917.2008.9687069

Saramago, A. (1973). *Convento de Sóror Mariana Alcoforado: Real Mosteiro de Nossa Senhora da Conceição*. Colares.

Saxena, A., & Khanna, U. (2013). Advertising on social network sites: A structural equation modelling approach. *Vision (Basel), 17*(1), 17–25. doi:10.1177/0972262912469560

Silva, E. P. (2000). Património e identidade. Os desafios do turismo cultural. *Antropológicas, 4*, 217–224.

Silva, M. (2018). *As Lettres Portugaises na Literatura Portuguesa Contemporânea: Reescritas*. Universidade de Lisboa, Faculdade de Letras, Tese de Doutoramento.

Sousa, B., & Alves, G. (2019). The role of relationship marketing in behavioural intentions of medical tourism services and guest experiences. *Journal of Hospitality and Tourism Insights, 2*(3), 224–240. doi:10.1108/JHTI-05-2018-0032

Sousa, B.; Malheiro, A. & Veloso, C. M. (2019). O Marketing Territorial como Contributo para a Segmentação Turística: Modelo conceptual no turismo de shopping. *International Journal of Marketing, Communication and New Media, 5*, 93-116.

Sousa, B. B., Castro, C., Luís, M. E., & Lopes, P. (2021). Religious and Spiritual Tourism: From Its Origins to Alentejo (Portugal). In Global Development of Religious Tourism (pp. 44-64). IGI Global.

Sousa, B. B., & Magalhães, F. C. (2019). An Approach on Attachment in Public Marketing and Higher Education Management Contexts. In C. Machado & J. Davim (Eds.), *Higher Education and the Evolution of Management, Applied Sciences, and Engineering Curricula* (pp. 151–171). IGI Global. doi:10.4018/978-1-5225-7259-6.ch006

Sousa, B. B., Magalhães, F. C., & Soares, D. B. (2021). The Role of Relational Marketing in Specific Contexts of Tourism: A Luxury Hotel Management Perspective. In Building Consumer-Brand Relationship in Luxury Brand Management (pp. 223-243). IGI Global. doi:10.4018/978-1-7998-4369-6.ch011

Tadeia, H. (2013). *Contributos para o estudo da colecção de pintura do Museu Rainha D. Leonor – Beja*. Universidade Aberta, Dissertação de Mestrado.

Torres, C. (1987). *Cerâmica islâmica portuguesa.* Mértola, Campo Arqueológico de Mértola.

Torres, C. (1992). *Povoamento antigo no Baixo Alentejo. Alguns problemas de topografia histórica. Arqueologia Medieval, n.º 1/fevereiro.* Edições Afrontamento.

TRAVEL BI. (n.d.). Turismo em Números – 2019. *Turismo de Portugal.*

Vareiro, L., Sousa, B. B., & Silva, S. S. (2020). The importance of museums in the tourist development and the motivations of their visitors: An analysis of the Costume Museum in Viana do Castelo. *Journal of Cultural Heritage Management and Sustainable Development, 11*(1), 39–57. doi:10.1108/JCHMSD-05-2020-0065

Vigneron, F., & Johnson, L. W. (2004). Measuring perceptions of brand luxury. *Journal of Brand Management, 11*(6), 484–506. doi:10.1057/palgrave.bm.2540194

Weinreich, N. K. (2011). *Hands-on social marketing: a step-by-step guide to designing change for good* (2nd ed.). SAGE Publications.

Yu, J. Y. (2009). A cross-cultural study on participation intention to medical tourism among Korean, Chinese and Japanese visitors in Korea. *The Korean Academic Society of Tourism, 33*(3), 187–204.

Zeng, B., & Gerritsen, R. (2014). What do we know about social media in tourism? A review. *Tourism Management Perspectives, 10*, 27–36. doi:10.1016/j.tmp.2014.01.001

KEY TERMS AND DEFINITIONS

Consumer Behavior Online: The study of individuals, groups, or organizations and all the activities associated with the purchase, use and disposal of goods and services, including the consumer's emotional, mental, and behavioral responses that precede or follow these activities in the online environment.

Digital Marketing: Is the marketing of products or services using digital technologies, mainly on the Internet, but also including mobile phones, display advertising, and any other digital medium.

E-Satisfaction: The contentment of a consumer with respect to his or her prior purchasing experiences with a given retail-oriented website.

E-WOM: Is any positive or negative statement made by potential, actual or a former customer which is available to a multitude of people via the internet.

Museum: A building in which objects of historical, scientific, artistic, or cultural interest are stored and exhibited.

Online Relationship: Is an integrative and multidimensional concept, such as relationship quality in an offline context.

Social Media: Social media are interactive computer-mediated technologies that facilitate the creation and sharing of information, ideas, career interests and other forms of expression via virtual communities and networks.

Social Networks: Is a social structure composed of persons or organizations, connected by one or several types of relationships, which share common values and goals.

Chapter 16
Using New Tools to Attract Visitors to Museums and Heritage Sites

Lia Bassa
Budapest Metropolitan University, Hungary

Melanie Kay Smith
Budapest Metropolitan University, Hungary

Árpád Ferenc Papp-Váry
Budapest Metropolitan University, Hungary

ABSTRACT

This chapter discusses the ways in which museums and heritage sites have adapted to the need to create technology-based experiences in recent decades culminating in the intensive online provision during the COVID period. The aim of both online and live visits should be as inclusive as possible of different audiences, stimulating interesting, rich, multi-cultural experiences that encourage re-visitation or at least recommendation to others. Ideally, sites should create meaningful as well as memorable experiences. This process includes several aspects and is very complex requiring the combination and harmonisation of education, heritage interpretation, marketing skills, and local initiatives. This chapter uses case studies to analyse the extent to which museums are rising to these challenges above, including the principles of the so-called 'new museology', the need for more innovative technology to create visitor experiences, and COVID-19.

INTRODUCTION

A large number of recent publications and conferences have investigated how to present museum exhibitions and attractions to tourists, including built, natural, tangible and intangible heritage. In 2021, this became a double-edged intention and post-COVID-19, tourism attractions will be wanting to gain back

DOI: 10.4018/978-1-7998-8528-3.ch016

their previous numbers of visitors as well as those who are more eager than ever to leave their homes. Before COVID-19, over-tourism and crowd management was a major concern for many attractions, but now they have experienced significant losses and will want to compensate.

On the other hand, during COVID, museum and heritage site visitors experienced various well-developed digital programmes, such as streamed guided tours, exhibitions of objects, 3D presentations and on-line events which they previously never had the opportunity to see. The on-line experiences offered by the closed institutions may have been so attractive and exceptional that now visitors want to make the effort to spend money and time to visit a site in person. So, it may mean that the online programmes have raised an interest in certain sites or experiences which tourists formerly did not know about or had no time or intention to visit. Indeed, Choi and Kim (2021) suggest that COVID-19 created a trigger for museums to expand their participants, especially from local communities. However, there is not much data about the effects of online museum and heritage site visitation during COVID-19 and what could be expected afterwards. King, Smith, Wilson, and Williams (2021) undertook an analysis of 88 online exhibitions in the UK and concluded that more work needs to be done in order to understand fully how digital exhibitions work for audiences, especially the impact of the presentation methods.

This paper discusses the ways in which museums and heritage sites have adapted to the need to create technology-based experiences in recent decades culminating in the intensive online provision during the COVID-19 period. Systematic reviews of literature about the use of technology in heritage sites and museums show that a number of techniques or tools are used, such as VR (virtual reality), AR (augmented reality), robots, QR codes, location detects like GPS, animation and games. Many of these are assisted by mobile devices like telephones, tablets, iPods and interactive display screens (Chen, Duan & Wang, 2021). The aim of both on-line and live visits should be as inclusive as possible of different audiences, stimulating interesting, rich, multi-cultural experiences that encourage re-visitation or at least recommendation to others. Ideally, sites should create meaningful as well as memorable experiences. This process includes several aspects and is very complex requiring the combination and harmonisation of education, heritage interpretation, marketing skills and local initiatives. The process connects changes in cultural heritage experiences with teaching methods as well as with the new approaches and tools of site interpretation of tourist attractions. Marini and Agostino (2021) suggest that digital technologies should enable new systems of interactions between museums and their visitors in a more 'humanized' way. In the future, Choi and Kim (2021) predict that museums will co-create new products along with visitors meaning that users will become producers and consumers at the same time.

This chapter uses case studies to analyse the extent to which museums are rising to the challenges above, including the principles of the so-called 'new museology', the need for more innovative technology to create visitor experiences and more latterly, COVID-19.

BACKGROUND

Heritage Preservation and Education

Cultural heritage is of primary importance in a person's development and in his/her surroundings, including the construction of the local communities. If heritage protection is incorporated in the educational development of children from the very beginning, it will contribute to the formation of their direct environment and communities having a common history and past. It is also important to identify and outline what information and data should be incorporated in school teaching and in the actual life-long education of people. Obviously, different user groups have different requirements concerning cultural education and the role of institutions like museums.

It is an undeniable fact that we inherit our genes, inner and outer qualities, family names, environment, ethnic roots and history of our nation, just as we are also part of a language, religion and rituals, with moral, social, dressing, gastronomic and living standards, building up and communicating altogether something called CULTURE (Bassa, 2014). Its representation appears in various forms in the institutional framework of what we call museums. The process of safeguarding, preservation and presentation also include the maintenance of intangible heritage (legends, traditions, dances, music, etc.), requiring harmonized actions on behalf of local people, which ultimately lead them to have and feel common identity and awareness of heritage preservation, assuring the continuity of their culture and ultimately their civilization.

Examples of how different scientific fields transfer heritage knowledge include geography – sites and people and their interrelation; history – social development; art – perception of the environment; languages – cognitive characteristics; literature – legends, folktales, plays, philosophy, religion. The representation of all of these fields should and could appear in exhibitions. It is also clear that besides the accomplishment of properly educating youth, the bearers of a given culture are responsible for adequately protecting all kinds of heritage values in order to have something to transmit to future generations. The elements of the past (built, natural, tangible, intangible) can be locally unique and exceptional, so it must be the task of nations, leading bodies and local communities (including families) to safeguard them for the sustainable future of their living spaces. The discovery, scientific documentation, protection, sustainable application and publication of local heritage require that activities related to the above must be regulated by law, while the actual tasks are to be distributed efficiently, under the control of the authorities (Bassa & Kiss, 2011).

The process of heritage education starts by understanding the concept of heritage responsibilities. Jansen-Verbeke, Priestley, and Russo (2008) interpreted heritage as a creation of the mind, a pure mental construction of a set of values presently given to the past in order to build a future. Heritage preservation means (re)creating cultural identities of places and people. Although heritage protection is undertaken by experts, teaching by schools and awareness raising by families, the three aspects together set up the personal development of individuals, and the common heritage of a group contributes to community building that leads to the wish to not only safeguard joint heritage but also make it known to others, i.e. to show it to visitors, foreigners, namely, to tourists. This process can efficiently be done, if in the eyes of children, heritage is an inherent part of their environment, including the preservation of traditions (celebrations, events) and respect for man-made artifacts. This should be the aim taking local attributes and sensitivity into consideration (Bassa, 2011).

Internal and External Communication in Museums

An important question is how people can get acquainted properly with cultural heritage in the context of museums. There are a number of levels and opportunities, covering various intensities and areas of communication, such as the following:

- The adequate education of the main role players: teachers, trainers
- The establishment of resource centres

- Information provision in reports, at forums conferences, by social media, at competitions, Exhibitions, calls (all gathering a huge amount of information)
- Promotional objects (making and selling them in cultural institutions, at local sites)
- Traveling, tourism – getting to know other cultures, traditions (Bassa, 2014).

In order to attract visitors to museums and heritage sites, the communication process must be considered. One of the starting points can be to follow the pattern of a communication process, as museums or sites are the senders of the experience, their contents are the message, and the public is the receiver and the target is to accomplish this act in the optimum way. One communication process theory that could be applied here refers to Roman Jakobson's (1972) basic model of constitutive dimensions of the communication act there is a "Sender" or source of information (about a representation of the past such as an object, custom, site, etc.) who wants to send a "Message" (here: meaning and knowledge) to an identified target audience, the "Receiver" (here: the visitors). The Message must correspond to a given "Context" (place and time of presented values), whereas the "Code" is to set up in the way (technical tools) that the "Contact" or means of information or knowledge transfer could be realized between the sender and the receiver, as seen in the well-known figure below.

Context

Message

Sender ------------ Receiver

Contact

Code

In the case of teaching or educational presentations of a museum or site visit, the application of this process appears in a way that cultural heritage experiences are connected to education or edutainment (sending an educational message using an entertaining method). Chen, Duan, and Wang (2021) recommend collaborative learning and interaction between learners in an educational context, as well as designing learning experiences that correspond (more) closely with the learning process of the users.

Target Groups in the Case of Museums

With regard to museums, it is important to point out that target groups include not only visitors, but also supporters (sponsors), the parliament/government (the authorities), the owner and professional partners. These all have different expectations and needs, as summarized by István Piskóti (2003, 2004) in his museum marketing studies.

Many types of segmentation are possible among visitors on the basis of demography, geography, sociography or psychography. Of all these, geographical segmentation usually includes categories such as locals, residents of the region (with a travel time between 50 minutes and two hours), visiting relatives and friends, individual tourists/hikers, group visitors, school groups and foreign visitors.

Table 1.

Target group	Expectations, needs
Visitors	Exhibition with the appropriate topic, new information, knowledge, exciting exhibition tours and guided tours, interesting and pleasant pastime, entertainment, good accessibility, the opportunity to buy souvenirs and collect information, etc.
Supporters	The provision of information and professional services, marketing/PR value for businesses (publicity, image building, etc.), cooperation in the field of marketing, protection of community and cultural values, maintenance of respect for and the preservation of traditions, events
Parliament, government	Interest in the preservation of national/local cultural values, professional standards, provision of performances, observance of laws
Owner	Efficient, problem-free, transparent operation, management within a given budget, property preservation and enrichment of cultural values
Professional partners	Provision of information, cooperation in research, education, the implementation of events, programmes, tourism organization and city image building

The farther a visitor comes from, the more relevant the following questions are:

Does the tourist travel to that destination in a general sense and visit that museum just because he/she is already there? Or is the museum so interesting or special that the tourist travels there because of it? In the latter case, does he/she also look around at the destination site too?

Previous studies of museum visitor or audience segmentation focused on motivations, behaviour and background, among others. In her study of online users, Villaespesa (2019) identified six segments: professional researcher, personal interest information-seeker, student researcher, inspiration-seeker, casual browser, and visit planner. These segments were used to make recommendations for multiple kinds of online experiences.

The New Museology and Interactive Technology

The museum environment has changed considerably in recent decades as visitors' expectations, preferences and demands have been shaped significantly by new technology and digital entertainment. Museums have been forced to compete with numerous other leisure opportunities, thus the size of museum audiences has been decreasing (Kelly, 2005). In order to counterbalance this decline as well as the more recent impacts of COVID-19, museums have been forced to examine their approach to attracting, entertaining and retaining visitors. As described by Choi and Kim (2021) museums have recently been transformed into user-centred institutions.

The so-called new museology from the late 1990s was based on the idea that the role of museums in society needed to change (McCall & Gray, 2014). Archer et al. (2016) showed that first time visitors to museums often feel disorientated, overwhelmed or confused and can struggle with the 'habitus' of a museum (i.e. they are not sure how to behave or what to do or not do). They may think that 'there would be no-one like them there' (a "mismatch of habitus", ibid.p.989) and that they would not be made to feel welcome (Dawson, 2014). There can be linguistic and educational barriers too. Papadimitriou et al. (2017, p.272) describe how "as we approached the new millennium, museums became more self-reflecting and socially conscious, focusing on questions of wider public participation and interaction". Museums had to change their focus to the needs and interests of people rather than concentrating on artifacts or collections (Hudson, 1998).

Researchers proved that leisure and entertainment are strong motivations to visit museums (Packer & Ballantyne, 2002), whereas learning as a motivation turned out to be secondary (Tomiuc, 2014). Kotler and Kotler (2000) mention the competition that many museums faced from other forms of entertainment, for example, shopping malls, cinemas, sports, restaurants, cafes, science and technology centres as well as a whole range of online entertainment. This has intensified with the advent of social media and the ubiquitous popularity of the mobile phone and tablet-based entertainment, especially with young people. They note that museums need to adapt and position themselves differently, creating a new image and identity to attract new segments like young professional people or families with children. It is also important to consider that many young people may not even physically visit a museum these days (which was especially true during the COVID-19 period). Papadimitriou et al. (2017) suggest that most museums now have more online or virtual visitors than physical ones and Dal Falco and Vassos (2017, p.3978) suggest that "a virtual museum experience may be a highly inclusive alternative to a more traditional visit".

For those who do choose to visit, museums can function as social spaces providing opportunities for family time and meetings between friends. Thus, they play a crucial role in promoting social wellbeing (Chatterjee & Noble, 2013). For this reason, many museums now contain cafes, restaurants and shops which may even be visited independently of the museum collections or exhibitions. The new museology aims to place the visitor at the centre of a museum's function to represent the past in new ways, which can mean allowing people to select those objects that are most interesting for them, to re-interpret them and to tell their own stories (Hooper-Greenhill, 2007). Sheng and Cheng (2012) analysed the visitor expectations of frequent museum visitors and identified five different types of visitor expectations: ease and fun; cultural entertainment; self-determination; historical remembrance and escapism. The analysis showed that most visitors arrive at museums with the expectation of ease and fun. If the visitors enjoy their visit and feel in some way transformed by it, then they will share their positive experiences in social media and it can become a memorable experience too (Packer & Ballantyne, 2016). Within museum design, different spatial arrangements and less thematic or chronological placement of exhibits can help to encourage interaction and multiple visits (Papadimitriou et al., 2017). Claisse et al. (2017) emphasise the importance of tangible interaction and the creation of multisensory and immersive experiences.

Clearly, the type of museum is likely to affect visitor expectations and experiences. Burcaw (1997) defined three types of museums, including museums that collect and exhibit works of art; museums that collect memories of human history, and museums of science and technology. Interactivity and other possibilities of interpretation appear in different forms in each type of museum. Interactive experiences have clearly become almost essential in many museums, especially for young people. According to Addis et al. (2005) 'edutainment' based on new technologies enriches and transforms the experience, as these tools offer flexibility, interactivity and previously unexplored capabilities. Falk et al. (2004) emphasise that interactive experiences promote 'learning by doing' and encourage conversation, communication and co-creation. Deeper experiences can be created by using Bradburne's (2002) notion of hands-on, minds-on, and hearts-on attributes including touching objects by hands, but also spiritually engaging themes and content that impacts on emotions in an exhibition. Many research studies have been undertaken in a museum context, analysing the application of multisensory devices and their effect on visitor experience. This can include the releasing of different kinds of scents (Lai, 2015) or touchable art pieces and replicas. Visitors can try on costumes or role play. Dolcos and Cabeza (2002) believe sensory effects tend to become more embedded in people's memory.

In summary, the methodologies for creating meaningful experiences during a visit must include several aspects:

- **The analysis of the application** and visitor reflections of recent technological and digital developments introduced at given attractions;
- **The variety of tools** afforded by the institutions and its exhibitions which are also in harmony with local traditions;
- **New educational methods** to be applied that involve and engage participants and comply with their age and cultural background;
- The arriving **tourists should be prepared**, their interest raised for the experience they will be offered (not surprised by the theme, type of site, time of the visit etc.).

The above approaches also involve the development of behavioural culture and the evaluation of the environment and the identification of local roots and values, including common responsibility for the site. These actions should result in well-developed awareness of identity, open minds for cultural heritage preservation and thirst for knowing the colourful diversity of the world (hence the latest UNESCO Convention on the Protection and Promotion of the Diversity of Cultural Expressions).

Case Studies

Three case studies will be presented in this section which have been carefully chosen to illustrate various points that have been raised above about heritage preservation and cultural continuity; education and edutainment as approaches or methods of engaging visitors, especially young visitors; and interactive tools and techniques that are used for delivering the main message of museums. Comments from short interviews with the museums' directors and visitors' feedback in the form of reviews will also be briefly included as well as some analysis of the external marketing of the museums.

The three cases were selected to illustrate different kinds of museums: the first two are located in Hungary. The first used to be a traditional industrial museum, the second was created for modern exhibitions and the third is an example of general 'good practice' in the UK, where the 'new museology' was implemented much earlier than in Hungary.

Central Museum of Mining, Sopron, Hungary

The Central Museum of Mining is a museum of mining heritage in a historic Hungarian town, where young visitors form the main target segment and should understand and enjoy an exhibition about the past life of miners using innovative experience creations in a country museum. The exhibition was formed using an interactive presentation and workshop space. It includes the presentation of restored and operating models that innovatively represent the development of mining machines, the changes in the operating resources ranging from using water, animal energy to various mechanical energy productions. For supporting pedagogical programs, a modern technology assisted, energy saving light controlled installation called *light-bridge* was designed that contributes to the provision of the cultural historical background knowledge of the exhibition. The system presents the exhibited objects so that it drives the attention of the visitors towards the presented tools, their history, use and the inter-relationships between them.

The development builds on the museum's strong museum pedagogical activities, but the info-communication tools, software, and technologies that are incorporated in these newly developed spaces not only strengthen young people's digital competencies but help bridge the digital gap that often exists between adults and their children. The target audience of the development is wide, as it ranges from children to interested elderly people. Accordingly, the professional program by which they are addressed is also really rich and diverse. Educators have a special and emphasized importance throughout the program: the museum counts on them in content design, and equally want to support their work by offering innovative, non-formal learning opportunities. Priority is given to the issue of equal opportunities: on the ground floor the workshop is physically barrier-free and equipped with special development toys for the visually impaired. In the spirit of info-communicational accessibility, the web content is developed with a view designed for the visually impaired, and brochure written in Braille, pictograms are also placed there to help people with disabilities navigate. An induction loop was introduced into the rooms for the development of the hearing impaired. In addition, the mobile tools needed are assured by the museum for the visitors to access interactive content and to eliminate social and economic inequalities.

There is an establishment of two specific elements of the exhibition: the digital stock catalogue and coin display. The digital stock catalogue is the digital record of the museum's collection where not only objects, but historical photos and maps are recorded and can be searched on a touch screen by the visitors. The digital coin display presents the most valuable pieces of the museum's numismatic collection, provided with scientific descriptions and magnified coin pictures from several sides. Both systems are barrier-free: there is a text-to-speech program for the blind and visually impaired and a magnifying view also helps their information provision.

The automated, QR code-controlled exhibition guide operating in the exhibition can also be connected to the new investments: it is an installation providing cultural-historical background materials making the interrelations explicit for the exhibits in a way that the attention of the visitors is drawn on the presented tool and parallelly, there is a video presentation of pre-recorded, historical materials that used to be accessible only for researchers until now. The descriptions to each exhibit are available by the capturing of its QR codes which produce further pictures and sounding materials that can be accessed by all visitors with the help of their smart phone This is supported by a special system characterised by the sounding presentation, the projected materials (animation, video) as well as the demonstrations, operating machines etc. to be watched are time-synchronised, so that the knowledge provided with the additional multimedia contents can be acquired more simply and efficiently.

A further element of the same project was a newly created community area for presentations, film projections and museum pedagogical workshops within the museum itself where more expressive and interactive programs can be carried out for the school children or other groups of visitors due to the multimedia equipment set procured in the framework of the same project. Whereas further information provision for visitors is implemented by an interactive information board where the most important data of the museum can be found and – with the help of a sounding map – the facts of each exhibition can also be retrieved.

Another interesting aspect of digital development is where young visitors are introduced to the different themes of the museum using separate tools (e.g. a question bank, a picture database, video library and task collection). They have the possibility to use them as games and acquire knowledge at the same time. It is especially enjoyed by younger age groups as they have to move and look around the exhibition halls thoroughly while solving and completing the task as quickly as possible. In this way, spatial orientation, the recognition and use of symbols, and abstract logical thinking can be developed simultaneously. The outcome of this new development was that the children brought here by their school have returned with their family in numerous cases proving that the aim of the exhibition has been achieved: their interest is raised!

Museums have been changing quite a lot recently as they are now service providing institutions as stated by the former director of the Mining Museum, Erzsébet Bircher. A Hungarian development strategy can only take place if they are awarded special funding for it. The main change is the behaviour towards museum pedagogy that has changed very positively. Today, they are not only supporting school programs but are also inventing and supplementing. The tendency is strengthened by the current COVID induced - online program that will certainly affect the way of future visits. Only EU funded development could achieve digital tool procurements, online, multilingual guiding, QR code supplied information provision, info-communication counters for research even in the museum's film archives.

The Director described that they have offers for various age groups: "we satisfy the curiosity and creativity of the youngest ones by giving them Lego bricks to build their own mine which develops their motor skills, 3D vision and the understanding of the mine structure. We also have an 'experience mine' which is a playground with our machine models including the basic mining tools. The teenagers are proficient in the digital space and have some basic knowledge, although the difference in their knowledge can be great, so flexibility from the simplest games to complex ones is offered at almost the same level as the adult tasks. As for pensioners, they are split: one group of them has digital literacy whereas the other do not even want to deal with it in the museum, so we must take care not to exclude them from the experiences with e.g. built-in projection or assistance of the staff".

The primary task of the museum is to provide an experience and not just intrinsic knowledge. The visitors have to enjoy their stay therefore its length and quantity should be limited and well planned (no crowds and exhaustion). If edutainment is well done, the child comes back with the family.

Sample Reviews from TripAdvisor

Although there were only 42 reviews at the same of writing this paper (from 2019 pre-COVID), the comments were mostly positive. Visitors commented on the friendliness of the staff, who also respond to visitor reviews. There were many references to 'learning' and to the interactive nature of the experience which is enjoyed very much by children. The museum was considered to be well presented, informative and entertaining, e.g. "The working models of old mining "machines" are fun for kids and adults"; "children friendly 'hands on'; with "interesting exhibits". Visitors also commented on the heritage value of the museum stating that "it is worth visiting before we completely forget about the hard work of our grandfathers' generation". One of the comments summarised well the aims of the museum to attract and engage several generations simultaneously "At last. This is a museum where the kids and parents, boys and girls, young or older have fun".

The Marketing Communications

The Central Museum of Mining (Központi Bányászati Múzeum) is listed on the https://sopronimuzeum. hu/ website summarizing the city's museums in the exhibition ('kiállítás') menu, along with ten other attractions. One of these is the Brennberg Memorial House of Mining (Brennbergi Bányászati Emlékház)

– it is a few kilometres from Sopron but has a similar theme. It is also interesting that only 8 attractions from Sopron appear on the English-language website, and these do not include the Central Museum of Mining, which may indicate that they are not expecting many foreign visitors. The main page of sopronimuzeum.hu itself is not easy to follow, as one news item is listed after another.

In addition, the museum also has its own website kbm.hu, where kbm is the abbreviation of the Hungarian name of the institution (Központi Bányászati Múzeum). The website cannot be considered up to date, as the logo celebrates the 50th anniversary of the museum, but the two years in the logo are 1957 and 2007. The website was probably completed around that time or even earlier. The page predominantly includes textual information, and even that is difficult to read as it uses small font. There are hardly any pictures in it. There is also a blog available from the website, which uses the engine of blog.hu, therefore its structure is in accordance with blog.hu. In this case, it has several advantages, because it gives a much more modern impression than the website itself. The first post on the blog was created on 3 April 2015, and it has been quite active for a couple of years, although it was updated irregularly: there were weeks when 7 posts were published, and there were months with no posts. It is currently in the latter state, as no new content has been published since June 2019.

The Central Museum of Mining has its own Facebook page as well with about 2,200 followers. At the same time, this cannot be considered very active, because content is published weekly or fortnightly, mostly in connection with professional topics. They also made a 3-minute film about the museum which can be viewed on YouTube, inviting people to the 2020 Museums Night ('Múzeumok Éjszakája') event. However, only 500 people have viewed it. It seems, therefore, that the museum has had more success on-site reaching a range of visitors of different ages than it has online, although more research would be needed to confirm this point.

World Heritage Wine Museum Tokaj, Hungary

The most recent attraction of this new museum is a Sensorium, an interactive meeting with a piece of art, based on the experiment in the Tate Gallery, London. The majority of information in this section comes from an interview with the World Heritage Wine Museum Manager, Mrs Katalin Bősze. She explained that the task of the Tokaj Museum is to collect, preserve and present the historical, geographical and natural richness of the World Heritage Site. In 1962, the local history collection received a license to operate, and in 1985, they could move into the most beautiful Greek merchant dwelling house in the city, as a museum presenting the local traditions, history, archaeology and ethnography, supplemented by natural treasures representing a huge amount of growing heritage. The solution came in 2015. An almost collapsing building - which was also built in the 1790s, first as a brewery and then in the 18th century was transformed into a Jewish educational centre and finally, at the end of the 19th century, it became a museum. Thus, the city has got 2 museum buildings, under one maintainer and in one organizational unit, although the permanent exhibitions of the two buildings are complementary. The new building, named the World Heritage Wine Museum, awaits visitors with a thematic exhibition presenting the greatest offerings from the Tokaj-Hegyalja region.

Due to the characteristics of the buildings, a completely different presentation concept prevails in the two exhibitions. While the so-called 'mother museum' presents and transfers information and knowledge according to the statutes of the classical museum, the new building is representative of the 21st century and uses modern tools. The World Heritage Wine Museum uses only a few objects and inscription information. A 1-1 Audio Guide is located next to the entrance in each room. This audio exhibition guide provides detailed information on the exhibits and themes in the hall, thus almost replacing live exhibition guides. The topic is taught in a fun way with the help of various technical tools and games. On the virtual cooking table, the process of preparing 6 regional dishes is shown. In another room, there are 40 scents of wine available from the cellar to the glass for the visitors. The visitors can also learn about the minerals of volcanic soil using a digital microscope. QR codes are also there providing additional information. Unfortunately, the thick walls of the building result in a frequent reception problem, however, a recent tender brought significant changes in this respect. The museum has a permanent exhibition of the Tokaj-Hegyalja quarry, which was presented in the cellar using new tools of technology. A number of educational materials on the topic of the exhibition are available through its 4 touch screen TV sets. Again, for the children, interesting games and puzzles have been uploaded. The inner branch of the exhibition presents an ore mine. The image of life shown there comes to life with the help of virtual glasses. For example, the users may experience a mining disaster.

How do visitors receive these innovations? It depends on age. Older people prefer the traditional museum presentation. However, they try the new tools out of curiosity, but the emotional experience is provided to them through sight. For young people, the wine museum is the "peak". For them, these tools are familiar, objects are used regularly in their daily lives, which also includes playing programs. The visitors decide themselves what they want to try from the rich offer. If a group arrives, the staff suggests what would be appropriate and beneficial for their visit. Visitors prefer experiences based on new technologies but non-digital experiences may also be similarly popular, although this is age dependent. The current museum exhibition trend is that a few objects are used to emphasize and highlight the essence, to show what the message is. Today's people do not like to read and get tired of a lot of information which they cannot absorb. People need the new, the astonishing, the attention-grabbing irrespective of whether it is a digital or non-digital experience. Studies have shown that visitors prefer to have fun rather than study in a museum. For families, a visit to the museum is a leisure program. They are not forced to come and this already applies to school visits. They come if the museum provides them with a meaningful and entertaining exhibition / museum pedagogical program. Its income is also depending on their success.

The most prominent technological invention of the museum is an innovative presentation of a painting that created edutainment for both young and adult visitors. It focuses on sensory learning which starts even before birth and continues throughout brain development and includes the five senses (sight, hearing, touch, smell and taste). The historic painting is presented – on request – by using the five senses that help visitors to feel the atmosphere of it, to better understand the intentions of the painter. Interested visitors from all backgrounds could learn about culture by creating a special journey through art, landscape and history inspired by a painting of a landscape and historical event which is presented in an innovative way in an activity zone. Before seeing the painting, visitors are invited to get into the atmosphere of the picture by activating their senses. The room is filled with a complex fragrance (artificially produced and scientifically mixed by an expert) that is related to the picture (smells of a spring landscape, river, forest). In the room, tangible objects are placed, such as materials on a table that can be found in the picture. Wood, metal, leather, felt objects, stone, tile are all materials typical of the age, related to the natural landscape and the inn of the painting and the lifestyle of that given time or event or are characteristic of the environment. The visitor can take them in their hands and touch them several times. By feeling the materials, they can travel back in time. This painting is linked to meals, fruits, food, feasts. The visitors can join them by tasting the snacks and drinks prepared for them on the table in order to evoke similar flavours. Meanwhile contemporary music can be heard in the background in connection with the painting, as well as sounds of movements, activity, and speech as if it were coming from the painting. Only after this, the painting is unveiled for the visitors who can now view it. By using multi-sensory experiences - touching, tasting, listening to or reading materials - visitors receive a complete knowledge about the age of the painter and/or the painting, as well as gaining an unforgettable experience. This method is more than a one-time experience, it is a learning process that goes beyond the simple acquirement practice. Visitors play an active role in the procedure that could also be re-imagined the next time they viewed an artwork. This 'journey' to the world of an art piece will certainly be both memorable and meaningful for them.

Sample Reviews from TripAdvisor

There were only 28 reviews from TripAdvisor at the time that the paper was written, some of which were from 2020 when the museum was briefly re-opened. It was referred to as a "brilliant modern museum" which visitors found "interesting, well-designed and -executed" and they enjoyed the "interactive displays, videos and activities". This also included games and an opportunity to drive virtually around Tokaj. Sensory experiences were especially enjoyed with the "smell-test" game and the chance to "try different smells".

The Marketing Communications

In connection with the branding of the Museum, there is an immediate difficulty that has not yet been resolved: to what extent the World Heritage Wine Museum should be communicated separately from the Tokaj Museum (Tokaji Múzeum). This question is also demonstrated by the fact that the Wine Museum also has its own website, but it also has a page on the Tokaj Museum's website. There is a similar oddity in connection with the Facebook page: there is one profile for Tokaji Múzeum (Tokaj Museum) and Világörökségi Bormúzeum (World Heritage Wine Museum) together, and there is another called Bormúzeum Tokaj (Wine Museum Tokaj), but we may not see much activity, if we look at any of them. Moreover, not many posts appeared during the COVID pandemic, either.

What is currently one of the museum's best advertising activities is a travel blogger, Balázs Gyémánt, who took a 36-hour tour of the wine region around Mád and Tokaj in 2020. As part of this, he visited the museum, and made photos and videos to present the experience; for example, how you can ride a bicycle in the museum or get in a car and travel the wine region using a simulator. As he writes in the blog, "The museum educates and entertains, and it takes a minimum of 1 hour to walk around."

Norwich Castle Museum (Norfolk, UK)

"Norwich Castle is an iconic Norman Castle offering outstanding collections and displays of archaeology, decorative and fine art, natural history and much more" (Museums of Norfolk, 2021). It won the Sandford Award for Heritage in 2017 for its "Inspirational surroundings for a range of learning programs tailored to the educational requirements of school groups at all levels". It provides a family experience and opportunity for extending school education as well as offering positive experiences for tourists. The Learning Team of Norwich Castle describes their activities with the following words: "We are committed to engaging and inspiring young people with our fabulous collections to enable them to take an active role in Norfolk Museum Service and to enrich their lives and those of others" (Norwich Castle, https://www.museums.norfolk.gov.uk/).

The manner of communicating contents (the message) is designed (code) and implemented (context) by an appropriately trained staff in order to assure the best channel for the target audience. Norwich Castle places emphasis upon introducing and attracting children to museums and transmitting heritage. Although this is a small town in Britain, a group of local people are proud to present their past to visitors (for example, in Wymondham Heritage House where the history of the settlement is presented – in chronological order – using school children's drawings). They design exhibitions in schools, in a local house, bakery or anywhere where a local specialty can be presented, made and sold.

In the autumn of 2017, the exhibitions of the Castle offered family visitors the following educative games and entertainment within the permanent historic presentations of the Castle:

- Medieval soldier board at the entrance, the child goes behind it and his face appears for having a picture taken of him in armour;
- Continuous projection about the development of the landscape;
- Building an arch of foam blocks to find out how supportive it is;
- A small sling on a table for shooting a target;
- The flying buttress in a touchable, moving model to check its function;
- Creating a wooden bridge from pencil size logs;
- Wall decorations (reliefs) produced as touchable replicas
- Pre-printed sheets of simplified exhibit drawings for colouring with pencils on a table for the youngest visitors;
- Chariot ride for children with the help of an interactive video;
- Diorama of animals with buttons to push for identifying, hearing, touching and smelling the animals;
- Puppets, books illustrating natural life – an area for playing with them;
- Toy corner;
- Food corner with children's menu (select five items from the offer);
- Shop with scientific and children's books, toys, replicas;
- Presenters in costumes explain their historic roles;
- Weapons available for touching, with their functions being explained by guides dressed in contemporary costumes;
- Historic handicrafts taught by paper cutting and gluing.

In the last four activities including the shop, well-trained and friendly staff members provide explanations and give instructions by adapting them to the listeners' age and knowledge.

In addition to that, currently, we have to take into account that this generation has been taking part in a period of distance online learning because of the COVID-19 period. The museums are still not open but they provide young visitors with activities for their holidays, for example, the Castle Museum organized an Easter holiday programme at Gressenhall Farm where children could create nature diaries, spot wildlife, learn about different animals' habitats, learn how to create bee-friendly gardens and play games outdoors.

The main programs are organized for school visits to be booked in advance by schools as a part of their education. This museum has a 'course' (regular visits) for Learning Outside the Classroom Quality Badge holders and organizes programs for all school age groups. The aims and learning outcomes are to

- Develop awareness of the changing uses of Norwich Castle;
- Meet costumed characters who will bring the subjects to life;
- Complete a study of a site that is important in the locality;
- Link the exhibition to the National Curriculum 2014, History Programme of Study (A study of an aspect of history or a site dating from a period beyond 1066 that is significant in the locality.);
- A plan, in the near future, to offer a sort of historic carousel of four activities: three activities led by characters in costumes and one a teacher-led exploration of The Square Box on the Hill (local name of the Castle) exhibition;
- Investigate Norwich Castle's time as a Royal Palace, so that children join a character in a costume to explore the magnificent keep;
- Meet and talk with a nineteenth century prisoner and find out about his crime, his experiences in the prison and about his later life;
- Spend some time with a Victorian curator, so as to discover more about the castle as a museum;
- Visit the Square Box on the Hill exhibition and watch not only the Castle's past but also its future.

At the end of the visit, while they are waiting for the parents to take their coats from the cloakroom, children can sit down and watch a video animation about the construction of the Castle.

Sample Reviews from TripAdvisor

Norwich Castle scores highly in its reviews (average of 4.5/5) and there are significantly more reviews than for the previous two case studies (which are located in rural Hungary). Altogether, there are 2,233 reviews, but here, we selected reviews from 2019 (pre-COVID) to give an indication of what visitors value most about the attraction. Many visitors were delighted, e.g. "the castle is a total joy and an amazing time capsule of facts, learning and entertainment" and "the exhibits are fun and interactive for children and very informative for adults. Many people found the attraction rather expensive but often spent longer there than they intended to (several hours) because there was so much to do: "this place could keep adults and children informed and amused all day". They liked the "amazing and thoroughly interesting" museum. The heritage value for children was mentioned "good for children to learn about and remember this city was once England's second city mostly for its history in trade". Dressing up experiences were mentioned "Fun to dress up as convict and take photos" and "the grandchildren liked dressing up as Vikings". People also highlighted how much they enjoyed the cafe.

The Marketing Communications

As mentioned above, the Norwich Castle Museum goes further with the concept of an experience-based museum and the same is true for their marketing communications. They have more than 11,200 followers on Facebook, posting content 4-5 times a week, which may be a little more than ideal, but obviously the rich collection gives them an opportunity for such content marketing.

The museum also has its own Youtube channel, which has only 160 subscribers, but it is clear that they find it an important platform. This is where a video was published during the COVID-19 pandemic, enabling visitors to take a virtual tour of the castle with a tour guide. https://www.youtube.com/watch?v=4cANXKSYy00

The Norwich Castle Museum does not have its own page, it only has a subpage on the https://www.museums.norfolk.gov.uk website. It features a special option 'Museums from home', where they emphasize that "Even when our museums are closed, we are always open online… You can join a virtual tour, find learning resources, and discover family activities all from the comfort of home."

In connection with Norwich Castle itself, there is a wealth of content that engages the visitors of the website, for example: "Adopt an object at Norwich Castle", "Castle Writers goes digital! – A brand new resource inspired by our collections to develop your creative writing" and "Learning at Norwich Castle – Award-winning programmes for schools and all ages".

DISCUSSION

The three case studies are clearly rather different from one another, both in terms of type and use of technological techniques and tools. As stated by Burcaw (1997) the type of museum clearly affects visitors' expectations and experiences. However, there are also some similarities. The methods used by all of the chosen museums reflect well the principles of the new museology where the user is placed at the centre of experience design (Choi & Kim, 2021), different segments of visitors are targeted with different activities (Villaespesa, 2019) and the interactions are very 'humanized' (Marini & Agostino, 2021).

The museum of mining places emphasis on education which is delivered through informal, digital methods. Access and equal opportunities are also a priority, including for those with special needs. Several digital tools are used such as QR codes, multi-media content (e.g. animation, videos), as well as games. All age groups are carefully considered in the creation of experience. One interesting point is that school visits inspire and encourage children to return with their family and that technology is used to try to bridge digital gaps between adults and children. Although the second museum is based on wine, it still aims to educate and attract families as well. Several technological tools are used to create virtual reality and multi-sensory experiences. Visitors are invited to engage in co-created journeys and emphasis is placed on interaction and play. The third case study also focuses on education and families, but it aims to create positive experiences for tourists too. Heritage is also transmitted beyond the walls of the attraction with outreach work and virtual tours. Experiences are not all digital either, but include costumed interpretation, creative workshops and outdoor activities.

It can be seen that the museums in this study are using many of the technological tools that were identified by Chen, Duan, and Wang (2021), such as virtual reality, QR codes, animation and games. However, they are also using off-line and live methods, such as costumed interpretation and outdoor games. Some of the museums have also clearly realised the importance of multi-sensory experiences (Dolcos & Cabeza, 2002; Lai, 2015; Claisse et al., 2017). Clearly, during the COVID-19 lockdown periods, emphasis was placed rather on the on-line experiences. Indeed, it is possible in these case studies that COVID-19 acted as a trigger for the museums to expand their audiences (Choi & Kim, 2021), but more research would be needed to prove this and to evaluate the success of on-line experiences. Although previous researchers have suggested that leisure and entertainment are strong motivations to visit museums (Packer & Ballantyne, 2002; Tomiuc, 2014) and that most visitors arrive with expectations of fun (Sheng & Cheng, 2012), education and learning are still clearly important in the museums researched in this chapter. The approach to education includes many elements of interaction between learners (including from different generations) and takes the learning process of users into consideration

(Chen, Duan & Wang, 2021). The museums also clearly function as social spaces (Chatterjee & Noble, 2013), especially for families.

CONCLUSION

Post-Covid, most leisure attractions will be competing for the newly liberated visitors who have been starved of cultural and travel experiences. Although some of them may have enjoyed online museum and heritage site visits, the majority will be debating how to spend their precious leisure time, especially with the knowledge that another lockdown could be imminent. Previous research has shown the visitors are not necessarily looking for education in their leisure time and are not able or willing to digest and absorb extensive information. On the other hand, museums and heritage sites are some of the few cultural spaces that still endeavour to provide informal and life-long learning through leisure experiences. With this purpose in mind, it has become increasingly challenging to engage younger visitors without making use of the latest technological developments and tools to create appropriate experiences for this age group. The Hungarian case study research shows that this process often requires the support of funding programs (e.g. EU) or nation-wide strategies that support more creative museum pedagogy. The UK example already demonstrates how museum or heritage site activities are closely connected to the national curriculum.

On the other hand, the case study research suggests that visitors are also happy to experience museums and heritage sites via more traditional, non-digital methods, too. This could include multi-sensory experiences, craft-making or costumed role-play, for example. One of the key aims is to take the experience from being passive and simply looking at the site, listening to the guides and buying post cards to wanting to become (inter)actively involved at cultural attractions, for example, by taking part in events, producing a souvenir or obtaining a personalised digital image that can be taken home and will provide permanent access to the memories of the visited site.

It has become clear that a modern museum not only needs new types of exhibitions using the latest tools, but the new era is also represented by the interactions and marketing communication between institutions and visitors. Communications, marketing and segmentation can play an important role in targeting visitors who are primarily interested in the museum or who may want to visit the wider environment, too. Websites, social media pages, review sites and blogs play an important role in positioning cultural attractions within a country or region's tourism. The case studies show that it is important to maintain an updated website, an active social media page or even a YouTube platform. Inviting bloggers or travel writers could also help to raise the profile of lesser-known museums, especially in the countryside. However, further research is needed to evaluate the impacts of such activities on the users.

Overall, this paper has shown the importance of heritage education and cultural continuity in a museum context and explored ways to (re)present this to the public using entertaining and innovative methods and tools. The case studies highlight both the successes and challenges of implementing the so-called 'new' museology and museum pedagogy in different contexts suggesting some improvements for both communication and experience creation in the future.

LIMITATIONS

The limitations of the research are that the case study data did not manage to capture the experiences of visitors during the COVID-19 lockdown periods or to compare their on-line experiences with their previous or subsequent off-line ones. It was also not possible to assess whether on-line experiences will encourage more people to visit museums and to expand audiences at local, national or international level. It would also be useful to undertake more research on the museum communication process pre-, during and post visit using a range of media tools, such as videos, social media or review sites. It remains to be seen whether on-line museums have generated more interest in the long term, but it is hoped that at least some positive experiences and good practices have been created as a result.

REFERENCES

Addis, M., Martinez, K., Lewis, P., Stevenson, J., & Giorgini, F. (2005). *New ways to search, navigate and use multimedia museum collections over the web.* https://www.archimuse.com/mw2005/papers/addis/addis.html

Archer, L., Dawson, E., Seakins, A., & Wong, B. (2016). Disorientating, fun or meaningful? Disadvantaged families' experiences of a science museum visit. *Cultural Studies of Science Education, 11*(4), 917–939. doi:10.100711422-015-9667-7

Bassa, L. (2011). Why Is It Important? World Heritage, Tourism, Teaching. Academia Budapestiensis Communicationis et Negotii Annales Tomus III, 24-35.

Bassa, L. (2014). How to raise the interest of students for culture? Educating heritage for contributing sustainability. *The 7th International Conference on Heritage and Sustainable Development.*

Bassa, L., & Kiss, F. (2011). Preservation of Traditional Craftsmanship Practices. *Conference on Sharing Cultures 2011, 2nd International Conference on Intangible Heritage.*

Bradburne, J. M. (2002). Museums and their languages: Is interactivity different for fine art as opposed to design? *Interactive Learning in Museums of Art and Design.* http://media.vam.ac.uk/media/documents/legacy_documents/file_upload/5758_file.pdf

Burcaw, G. E. (1997). *Introduction to museum work.* AltaMira Press.

Chatterjee, H. J., & Noble, G. (2013). *Museums, health and wellbeing.* Ashgate Publishing Ltd.

Chen, S., Duan, A., & Wang, J. (2021). Using Digital Technologies in Museum Learning Activities to Enhance Learning Experience: A Systematic Review. *Bulletin of the Technical Committee on Learning Technology, 21*(2), 32–36.

Choi, B., & Kim, J. (2021). Changes and Challenges in Museum Management after the COVID-19 Pandemic. *Journal of Open Innovation, 7*(148), 148. Advance online publication. doi:10.3390/joitmc7020148

Claisse, C., Ciolfi, L., & Petrelli, D. (2017). Containers of Stories: Using co-design and digital augmentation to empower the museum community and create novel experiences of heritage at a house museum. *The Design Journal, 20*(1), S2906–S2918. doi:10.1080/14606925.2017.1352801

Dal Falco, F., & Vassos, S. (2017). Museum Experience Design: A Modern Storytelling Methodology. *The Design Journal*, *20*(1), S3975–S3983. doi:10.1080/14606925.2017.1352900

Dawson, E. (2014). "Not Designed for Us": How Science Museums and Science Centers Socially Exclude Low-Income, Minority Ethnic Groups. *Science Education*, *98*(6), 981–1008. doi:10.1002ce.21133 PMID:25574059

Dolcos, F., & Cabeza, R. (2002). Event-related potentials of emotional memory: Encoding pleasant, unpleasant, and neutral pictures. *Cognitive, Affective & Behavioral Neuroscience*, *2*(3), 252–263. doi:10.3758/CABN.2.3.252 PMID:12775189

Falk, J. H., Scott, C., Dierking, L., Rennie, L., & Jones, M. C. (2004). Interactives and visitor learning. *Curator (New York, N.Y.)*, *47*(2), 171–198. doi:10.1111/j.2151-6952.2004.tb00116.x

Gyémánt, B. (2020). *Mád és Tokaj – 36 órában* [Mád and Tokaj in 36 hours]. https://balazsutazik.blog.hu/2020/07/06/mad_es_tokaj_36_oraban?fbclid=IwAR3SEDBwk2Oq8tUC2LGO3fuHdsKRxYpALE5YKxpodd7qY_On9GRy8DXJTiI

Hooper-Greenhill, E. (2007). *Museums and education: Purpose, pedagogy, perfomance*. Routledge. doi:10.4324/9780203937525

Hudson, K. (1998). The museum refuses to stand still. *Museum International*, *50*(1), 43–50. doi:10.1111/1468-0033.00135

Jakobson, A. R. (1972). *Hang – Jel – Vers* [Sounds, Signs, Poems]. Gondolat Kiadó.

Jansen-Verbeke, M., Priestley, G. K., & Russo, A. R. (Eds.). (2008). *Cultural Resources for Tourism Patterns, Processes and Policies*. Nova Science Publishers.

Kelly, L. (2005). Evaluation, research and communities of practice: Program evaluation in museums. *Archival Science*, *4*(1–2), 45–69. doi:10.100710502-005-6990-x

King, E., Smith, M. P., Wilson, P. F., & Williams, M. A. (2021). Digital Responses of UK Museum Exhibitions to the COVID-19 Crisis, March-June 2020. *Curator (New York, N.Y.)*, *64*(3), 487–504. doi:10.1111/cura.12413 PMID:34230675

Kotler, N., & Kotler, P. (2000). Can museums be all things to all people? Missions, goals, and marketing's role. *Museum Management and Curatorship*, *18*(3), 271–287. doi:10.1080/09647770000301803

Lai, M. K. (2015). Universal scent blackbox: engaging visitors communication through creating olfactory experience at art museum. In *Proceedings of the 33rd Annual International Conference on the Design of Communication*. Limerick, Ireland: ACM. 10.1145/2775441.2775483

Marini, C., & Agostino, D. (2021). Humanized museums? How digital technologies become relational tools. *Museum Management and Curatorship*, 1–18. Advance online publication. doi:10.1080/09647775.2021.1969677

McCall, V., & Gray, C. (2014). Museums and the 'new museology': Theory, practice and organisational change. *Museum Management and Curatorship*, *29*(1), 19–35. doi:10.1080/09647775.2013.869852

Navarrete, T. (2019). Digital heritage tourism: Innovations in museums. *World Leisure Journal, 61*(3), 200–214. doi:10.1080/16078055.2019.1639920

Packer, J., & Ballantyne, R. (2002). Motivational factors and the visitor experience: A comparison of three sites. *Curator (New York, N.Y.), 45*(3), 183–198. doi:10.1111/j.2151-6952.2002.tb00055.x

Papadimitriou, N., Plati, M., Markou, E., & Catapoti, D. (2017). Identifying Accessibility Barriers in Heritage Museums: Conceptual Challenges in a Period of Change. *Museum International, ICOM, 68,* 271–272.

Piskóti, I. (2003). Múzeumi marketing - a múzeumok integrálása a turizmus rendszerébe [Museum marketing – integrating museums into tourism]. *Magyar Múzeumok, 25*(2), 33–36.

Piskóti, I. (2004). Múzeumi marketing. In L. Dinya, E. Hetesi, & Z. Veres (Eds.), Nonbusiness marketing és menedzsment: civil szervezetek, alapítványok, politika, kultúra, karitatív szervezetek, közigazgatás, közüzemek, nonprofitok [Non-business marketing and management] (pp. 401-416). Jogi és Üzleti Kiadó Kft.

Sheng, C. W., & Cheng, M. C. (2012). A study of experience expectations of museum visitors. *Tourism Management, 33*(1), 53–60. doi:10.1016/j.tourman.2011.01.023

Tomiuc, A. (2014). Navigating culture. Enhancing visitor museum experience through mobile technologies. From Smartphone to Google Glass. *The Journal of Medical Research, 7*(3), 33–47.

Villaespesa, E. (2019). Museum Collections and Online Users: Development of a Segmentation Model for the Metropolitan Museum of Art. *Visitor Studies, 22*(2), 233–252. doi:10.1080/10645578.2019.1668679

ADDITIONAL READING

Gretzel, U., Fuchs, M., Baggio, R., Hoepken, W., Law, R., Neidhardt, J., Pesonen, J., Zanker, M., & Xiang, Z. (2020). e-Tourism beyond COVID-19: A call for transformative research. *Information Technology & Tourism, 22*(2), 187–203. doi:10.100740558-020-00181-3

Neuhofer, B., Buhalis, D., & Ladkin, A. (2014). A typology of technology-enhanced tourism experiences. *International Journal of Tourism Research, 16*(4), 340–350. doi:10.1002/jtr.1958

Recupero, A., Talamo, A., Triberti, S., & Modesti, C. (2019). Bridging Museum Mission to Visitors Experience: Activity, Meanings, Interactions, Technology. *Frontiers in Psychology, 10,* 2092. doi:10.3389/fpsyg.2019.02092 PMID:31551900

KEY TERMS AND DEFINITIONS

Access: The process of making museums more open, welcome, understandable, and appealing to a wider range of visitors (e.g., of different ages, educational backgrounds, and socio-demographic groups).

Augmented Reality: Improving or enhancing reality by overlaying virtual images onto real objects or sites.

Co-Creation: Museum curators and educators work interactively with their visitors to create experiences.

Communication: The processes through which museums convey messages to existing or potential visitors (e.g., via heritage interpretation techniques, digital tools, marketing).

Heritage: The cultural dimensions that connect people to their collective past as well as the process by which history is selected, interpreted, and represented.

New Museology: A new approach to museum practice that began in the late 1980s which considered the role of museums in wider social and political processes, aiming to become more inclusive and accessible and placing visitors at the centre of experience creation.

Virtual Reality: Using digital tools to simulate reality or to create experiences that are more fantastical than reality.

Chapter 17
An Exploratory Study on the Role of Websites in Gastronomy Museum Dialogic Communication

Eray Polat

Gumushane University, Turkey

ABSTRACT

Rooted in the dialogic communication model, the main objective of this study is to analyse the interactivity level of websites of gastronomy museums in Turkey. Thus, it will be unearthed whether gastronomy museums are progressing towards more dialogic or are staying informative systems with the relationship with their target audience. Via content analysis on websites, two questions were sought: (1) What kind of tools are utilized to present information? (2) What tools or resources are utilized on websites to interact with virtual visitors? The data were analysed by comparing private and public museums. The results indicate that the websites of gastronomy museums in Turkey have a medium level of interaction in presenting information and a low level of interaction in the tools available to virtual visitors. And thus, it can be said that museums use their websites for one-way communication, which are not fit for dialogic communication. This is valid for both private and public museums. Managerial implications were discussed, and future research directions are presented.

INTRODUCTION

The Internet has become not only an indispensable means of our life at present but also an integral part of our culture and has a significant impact on our lifestyle. The said impacts have changed the ways of communication, such as the means, form, and time of communication that people establish with each other and with organizations and the number of tools serving for this purpose have increased. The websites have a significant place among these tools.

DOI: 10.4018/978-1-7998-8528-3.ch017

The websites were considered as a tool providing one-way information (Web 1.0) to its users in the beginning stages of their emergence. Today, Web 2.0 technologies provide the opportunity to establish symmetrical, bidirectional, and interactive communication between its users and the organizations. In this context, websites have become one of the most necessary tools for organizations to communicate dialogically with their target audiences.

During recent years, museums have received their share of such changes (Camarero et al., 2016) and began to change their communication channels and models to effectively respond to ongoing dynamic, social, and technological progress and increase visitor engagement (Najda-Janoszka & Sawczuk, 2021). The relationship between the museums and their visitors has become more participatory and interactive through the ability of the museums to access many tools such as video channels, blogs, podcasts, social media sites, tags, forums, especially with the development of Web 2.0 technologies (Capriotti & Pardo Kuklinski, 2012; López et al., 2010). In this context, dialogic communication has gained an important position in terms of online communication strategy in museums as in entire organizations at present (Capriotti et al., 2016).

Interestingly, when the studies examining the position of museums in terms of dialogic communication are reviewed (Capriotti et al., 2016; Capriotti & Pardo Kuklinski, 2012; Lopatovska, 2015; Pallas & Economides, 2008), it has been observed that gastronomy museums have not been addressed as the research subject in the studies. In the studies conducted concerning gastronomy museums, it is seen that the issues such as the impact of such museums on tourist motivation (Kim et al., 2020; Park et al., 2020) or the number of various characteristics of gastronomy museums in a particular country [e.g., Turkey (Akyürek & Erdem, 2019); Italy (Garibaldi & Pozzi, 2021)] are prevalently discussed.

Considering this limitation, the overall purpose of the study is to analyse the degree of interactivity applied on the websites of gastronomy museums and to evaluate whether these digital platforms have become more interactive.

INTERACTIVITY AND DIALOGIC COMMUNICATION

In the early stages of the Internet (Web 1.0), users had the opportunity to statically view and read the content on the webpage without any interaction (like, comment, answers, etc.) with the page content (Handsfield et al., 2009). Therefore, solely one-way communication from organizations to users was concerned (Capriotti & Pardo Kuklinski, 2012). However, this has changed radically with the introduction of the period referred to as Web 2.0. This period, enabled the users to comment on, change and update the content as well as reading it (Curran et al., 2007). Thus, the level of interaction between websites and users has increased and the opportunity for two-way, symmetrical communication has emerged (Capriotti et al., 2021). A comparison between Web 2.0 and Web 1.0 can be seen in Table 1.

Table 1. Difference between Web 1.0 and Web 2.0

	Web 1.0	Web 2.0
Mode of usage	Read	Write and contribute
Unit of content	Page	Record
State	Static	Dynamic
How-to content is viewed	Web browser	Browser, RSS readers, Mobile devices, etc.
Creation of content	By web site authors	By everyone

Source: (Curran et al., 2007)

The internet, facilitating the interaction with an unlimited number of individuals simultaneously, is an especially important and necessary tool for organizations to establish and sustain a dialogue with their target audiences (Ingenhoff & Koelling, 2009). Moreover, the internet has a significant position for organizations to create dialogic communication with their target audiences as a result of the opportunities developed through Web 2.0 (Kent & Taylor, 1998). McAllister-Spooner (2009) argued that websites constitute one of the first stages in terms of the function of establishing a relationship in the process of public relations and emphasized its necessity from the aspect of dialogic communication. Furthermore, Kent and Taylor (1998) suggested that the strategic design, implementation, and management of websites provide organizations with an opportunity to develop dialogic relationships with their target audiences.

The concept of dialogic theory is often associated with Martin Buber, the philosopher. Buber considered interpersonal communication as an intersubjective process in which the parties establish a relationship based on openness and respect (Taylor & Kent, 2014). Dialogue is the foundation of such a relationship and implicitly focuses on ethics. In other words, for a dialogic relationship to exist, the parties must perceive their communication as the main purpose of the relationship rather than a tool (Kent & Taylor, 1998, 2002). In this context, Kent and Taylor (1998; p.325) define dialogic communication as "any negotiated idea and exchange of views" and argue that it is shaped based on two principles: (a) the desire to achieve mutually satisfactory positions through dialogue; (b) emphasis on co-creating shared meaning rather than achieving the absolute truth claimed by either party. In this regard, dialogic communication involves comprehending the past and the present and focuses on the shared future (Kent & Taylor, 2002).

Interaction is one of the cornerstones of dialogic communication (Guillory & Sundar, 2014) and is used by organizations to achieve the engagement of their target audiences in an appropriate manner (Taylor & Kent, 2014). As is mentioned earlier, the internet is the most important tool today in terms of ensuring interaction between organizations and their target audiences through the tools provided by Web 2.0 technologies (López et al., 2010). Therefore, it has been the subject of various studies as it forms the basis of dialogic communication between an organization and its target audiences in different fields (Morehouse & Saffer, 2018; Wirtz & Zimbres, 2018). In such studies (Cristobal-Fransi et al., 2017, 2020; Guillory & Sundar, 2014; Heinze & Hu, 2006; Oh, 2021; Sundar et al., 2003), the level of interaction between both parties was analysed and the tools and resources utilized by the websites to encourage and facilitate the interaction were examined.

Under dialogic communication, the organizations communicating with their target audiences through websites are expected to consider such websites not only as a platform used to disseminate information online but also as a medium where they establish relationships and interact with their target audiences utilizing various tools or resources (Capriotti et al., 2021). The first approach aims to convey the information unilaterally from the organization to the user to influence or persuade them. The latter involves utilizing tools or resources suitable for the purposes such as facilitating two-way communication and increasing the level of interaction on the website are used (Moreno & Capriotti, 2009).

The studies measuring the level of interaction on the websites have focused on assessing two key aspects (Capriotti et al., 2016; Capriotti & Moreno, 2007): (1) The manner visitors access the information on the website and the level they interact with such information (through the analysis of the tools used to present the information on the websites); (2) The manner of the use of the resources and tools available on the websites to facilitate and increase the organization's interaction with virtual visitors (by examining the interaction resources or tools provided by the organization to its virtual visitors). The results obtained by most of the studies (Aced-Toledano & Lalueza, 2018; Gonçalves, 2020; McAllister-Spooner & Kent, 2009; Taylor et al., 2001) reveal that organizations still use their websites, similar to the early stages of the internet, to provide solely one-way information. In most cases, organizations are still in the early stages of their transition to the model of the dialogical website.

DIALOGIC COMMUNICATION, INTERACTIVITY, AND GASTRONOMY MUSEUMS

The wide range of new opportunities in the fields of communication and public relations offered by the Internet has enabled organizations to change the manner they communicate and interact with their target audiences (Capriotti & González-Herrero, 2013). Undoubtedly, museums have also been affected by this change and have begun to actively develop their online presence to increase and improve the interaction of visitors with their virtual and physical collections (Lopatovska, 2015).

In the early years of the internet, museums provided general information on their websites regarding the opening times, ticket prices, event calendars, maps, and directions (López et al., 2010). Although these were in the form of one-way communication, they enabled museums to be noticed easily and quickly in a wide environment (Marty, 2007) and served to fulfil their mission. While these are invaluable to visitors, the development of tools known as Web 2.0 has created new possibilities for museums to communicate and interact with their target audiences (Dawson, 2008). Through such opportunities, the museums have been able to establish more collaborative, versatile and dialogic communication with their target audiences and could co-create content and discuss and assess them (Capriotti et al., 2016).

In many studies (Capriotti & Pardo Kuklinski, 2012; Garibaldi, 2015; Lopatovska, 2015; López et al., 2010; Najda-Janoszka & Sawczuk, 2021), it was found that the museums have tried to use different tools to establish a highly interactive and collaborative relationship with their target audiences. There are two main analyses regarding such tools as was mentioned earlier: analysis of the level of interaction of the tools used for the provision of information and the analysis of resources and tools used on websites to increase the organization's interaction with virtual visitors (Capriotti et al., 2016). In this manner, the purpose of the museums to use websites can be determined (with the orientation of one-way communication and solely to provide information or to ensure dialogic communication).

To the best of our knowledge, although the museums of art, history or natural history have been examined in such studies concerning such subject, there has not been much study or analysis related to gastronomy museums. However, with the increasing importance of gastronomy tourism, the museums of gastronomy have become popular destinations for tourists. (Kim et al., 2020). For instance, Guinness Storehouse in Ireland hosted 1.7 million visitors in 2019 (Garibaldi & Pozzi, 2021).

Although gastronomy museums are an important determinant for tourists' travel decisions, this is not the only function. These museums, like all others, have undertaken functions such as collecting, protecting, exhibiting, providing research and recreation opportunities (Williams, 2013). However, unlike nature and history museums, they focus on the product and interpretation. They tell the story of the food, its preparation, celebrations, and social and cultural meanings. They can be warehouses for tools and machinery used in agriculture, food production, cooking and food serving. They can display plant species, raw materials and finished products, cookbooks, historical documents and images about rural life (Garibaldi & Pozzi, 2021). Thus, they can play a crucial role in displaying the gastronomic culture of the society they belong to.

In recent years, museums need to be able to attract and engage with new visitors to ensure economic sustainability (Kotler & Kotler, 2000). This situation forces gastronomy museums to adapt their management and organizational processes and implement new practices (Antón et al., 2018). In this context, technology-based innovations and also Web 2.0 technologies have become one of the most important instruments of museum management in recent years (Agostino et al., 2020). In the future of gastronomy museums, applications in which the museum story is interactively combined with technology will take an important place (Williams, 2013). Because, as mentioned before, these technologies offer the opportunity to interact with numerous individuals at the same time and can do this 7/24 without the limitations of space. Further, these technologies are used to (i) raise awareness for museum exhibitions and events, (ii) engage visitors before, during, and after their visit, and (iii) explore museum service failures investigating unfavourable visitor evaluations (Leoni & Cristofaro, 2021b). All of these facilitate the sustainability of interactivity. Besides, the audience-oriented museum concept, a leading concept in the literature of museum management in recent years (Najda-Janoszka & Sawczuk, 2021), argues that museums should interact with their visitors both on-site and on-line (Agostino et al., 2020). Moreover, when problems such as pandemics (e.g., COVID-19) emerging suddenly are encountered, the online presence of museums may be the single option to open their doors to the visitors.

With the adoption of Web 2.0 technologies, museums have become places where visitors can be emotionally stimulated (Leoni & Cristofaro, 2021a) and have unforgettable experiences (Antón et al., 2018), rather than a site where culturally interesting objects are collected, preserved and displayed. Mandarano analyses museum communication under two headings, inside and outside. Thanks to these technologies, the level of interaction of both inside and outside communication increases. Inside communication tools are illustrative panels, audio guides, multimedia stations or applications where visitors can temporarily access museum services (direction, guidance, etc.) with software downloaded to mobile phones or tablets (Leoni & Cristofaro, 2021a). Outside communication tools can be considered as communication tools that enable visitors to access and engage the services offered by the museum remotely (Hume, 2015; van Hage et al., 2010). All these tools can transform visitors from being passive viewers and readers into active participating players (Sylaiou et al., 2010) as 'prosumers' (Garibaldi, 2015).

The internet has become one of the critical tools for museums in both inside and outside communication. However, in this circumstance, the following question comes to mind: If people can access digital collections of museums from anywhere they want, why should they come to the museum in person? However, studies have shown that museum websites increase physical participation in the museum (Marty, 2007). Therefore, the virtual presence of online museums is critical and this also binding for the actual gastronomy museums.

PURPOSE OF THE RESEARCH

In this study, the level of interaction established by the gastronomy museums in Turkey with their virtual visitors through their institutional websites is assessed. At the same time, this situation is addressed comparatively based on the ownership (public or private museum) status of museums. To achieve this aim, firstly, how information is presented on websites, and secondly, the resources used by the websites to interact with their visitors will be analysed. Thus, it will be determined whether these platforms are positioned as a medium with a high level of interaction (dialogic model) or whether they are used as an informational medium adopting a one-way approach.

METHODOLOGY

The population of the research is the gastronomy museums in Turkey. Accordingly, the website of the Ministry of Culture and Tourism, with the web address of www.muze.gov.tr, providing detailed information about the museums' assets in Turkey, was visited to determine the gastronomy museums. It has been found that there was only one museum within the scope of the study after examining 349 museums one by one taking place on the website. Subsequently, the studies in the literature providing information about gastronomy museums in Turkey were reviewed and it was figured out that there were 27 museums according to the latest study conducted by Akyürek & Erdem (2019). All these museums have been recorded in the database. Afterwards, with a Google search whether different museums not mentioned by Akyürek & Erdem (2019) existed and two more museums were identified as a result. In total, 29 museums were addressed within the scope of the research. However, when the websites of these museums are examined, it has been determined that the websites of eight museums are not available or such pages cannot be viewed in the internet browser. Therefore, 21 museums could be examined in the research. Among these, seven of them belong to various public organizations (referred to as public museums), and 14 of them belong to private organizations or various foundations and associations (referred to as private museums).

This research builds on the previous one (Capriotti et al., 2016). The researchers analysed that the interactivity level of major international art museums' websites. Thus, the author formulated three research questions (RQs) to achieve the overall aim of the research;

- RQ1: What kind of tools is utilized to present information on the websites of the gastronomy museums in Turkey?
- RQ2: What tools or resources do the gastronomy museums utilize on their websites to interact with virtual visitors?
- RQ3: Does the level of interaction differ on the websites of the public and private museums? Content analysis was conducted on the websites to answer these RQs.

For the RQ1, the category of Presentation of Information Tools enables us to identify the tools utilized by the museums to present information for their activities. Therefore, three types of resources have been identified according to their level of interaction: (1) Expositive: Mainly involves presenting information to a passive visitor. These consist of the subcategories referred to as "Graphic" (written text, photo or graphic) and "Audio-Visual" (audio and video items). (2) Hyper-textual: These are the links directing to another website with additional information or another section on the same website when the content on the museum website is clicked to interact more with the expositive resources. (3) Participative: They are tools assisting an active and participative visitor to learn by interacting with it. This category consists of "interactive" (such as interactive graphics and/or infographics that allow interacting with information) and "immersive" (virtual tours used to visit the museum in a virtual environment) resources (Table 2).

For the RQ2, the category of Resources for Virtual Visitor Interaction was utilized. This tool, enabling us an assessment of the type and level of interaction between the museum and virtual visitors, consists of five dimensions and a total of 20 sub-titles. The dimensions are considered according to the level of participation that the website allows the user: "connecting" (visitors can participate in events at a very low level and send certain information); "sharing" (visitors can have a low level of participation in events and share information on different sites); "reviewing" (visitors can participate in events at a moderate level and comment); "participating" (visitors can participate in events with a high level of interaction) and "collaborating" (visitors can participate in events at a very high level and create their own spaces). Each dimension consisted of 3 to 5 sub-titles (Table 3).

Table 2. Resources of presentation of information tools

Types of tools		Tools
Expositive	Graphic	Texts/Photos/Images
	Audio-Visual	Audio/Video
Hyper-textual	Links	External links
Participative	Interactive	Interactive resources
	Immersive	Virtual visits

Table 3. Resources for virtual visitor interaction

Dimensions	Tools
Connecting	Content syndication Subscription forms Registration (sign up/registration) Mobile alerts
Sharing	Tools/buttons for tagging information Tools/buttons for linking information to external sites Tools/buttons for sharing information in social networks
Reviewing	Polling/voting Surveys Open-ended questions Message board/commenting box Online guestbook
Participating	Contests/competitions Sweepstake Coupons, barcodes, QR codes Individual or collective games
Collaborating	Tools for creating a personal gallery Uploading tools (texts, images, videos, podcasts) Tools for experiments (simulations, reconstructions, etc.) Tools for the co-creation of content or displays

After the categories of analysis were defined, a Likert scale was applied by assigning a weighted value according to the interaction level of both resources [Presentation of Information Tools (RQ1) and Resources for Virtual Visitor Interaction (RQ2)] to understand the interaction level of the museums with the visitors (1-5 points; 1=very low-level interaction, 5=very high-level interaction). These scores were multiplied with the scores prepared by the dichotomous "yes/no" structure and indicating the presence (=1) or absence (=0) of each resource or tool, and valid scores were obtained. The average scores were then calculated. Finally, the differences were examined by addressing the results separately according to the type of ownership (public and private museums).

To determine the "interaction level" of websites related to the Presentation of Information Tools (RQ1), resource types are assigned weighted values in terms of interaction potential: "Graphics" 1 point (very low interaction); "Audio-Visual" 2 points (low interaction), "Links" 3 points (moderate interaction); "Interactive" 4 points (high interaction) and "Immersive" 5 points (very high interaction) (Table 4).

Table 4. Level of interactivity presentation of information tools and resources for virtual visitor interaction

Resources for the Presentation of Information	Interactivity scale (Likert Scale)	Value assigned (VA)	Presence(P) NO-YES	Valid Score (VS)	Result (level of interactivity)
Graphics	Very low	1 point	0-1	VA * P	
Audio-visual	Low	2 points	0-1	VA * P	=Mean(X) (Total VS/5)
Links	Mean	3 points	0-1	VA * P	
Interactive	High	4 points	0-1	VA * P	
Immersive	Very high	5 points	0-1	VA * P	
Resources for Virtual Visitor Interaction	**Interactivity scale (Likert Scale)**	**Value assigned (VA)**	**Presence (P) NO-YES**	**Valid Score (VS)**	**Result (level of interactivity)**
Connecting	Very low	1 point	0-1	VA * P	
Sharing	Low	2 points	0-1	VA * P	=Mean(X) (Total VS/5)
Reviewing	Mean	3 points	0-1	VA * P	
Participating	High	4 points	0-1	VA * P	
Collaborating	Very high	5 points	0-1	VA * P	

To understand the level of interaction of websites concerning Resources for Virtual Visitor Interaction (RQ2), weighted values were assigned to each of the sub-dimensions according to the level of interaction: "Connecting" 1 point (very low interaction); "Sharing" 2 points (low interaction); "Reviewing" 3 points (moderate interaction); "Participating" 4 points (high interaction) and "Collaborating" 5 points (very high interaction) (Table 4).

The results obtained by calculating the mean value of the sum of the weighted values of each resource will reveal the level of interaction of the websites. The interaction level is in the range of 0-3 points and consists of three levels: "low/weak level interaction" (0-1 points), "moderate level interaction" (1.01-2 points) and "high-level interaction" (2.01-3 points).

The forms used in the reviews and the method followed were previously utilized and applied by Capriotti et al. (2016) to examine the websites of 100 art museums around the world and have been proposed as a valid method. Therefore, it is assumed that the form and method are valid. The analysis of the data was conducted utilizing Microsoft Excel.

RESULTS

Among the seven public museums studied, solely one has its website, in others; the museum website is located under the museum tab on the web page of the public institution. When the private museums are concerned, it has been observed that nine museums have their web pages and the web pages of the remaining five museums are available as tabs on the web page of the institution. While 10 museums have their websites in total, the remaining 11 museums do not have. The results obtained to find answers to the research questions after the examinations are presented in the following parts of the study.

Among the gastronomy museums, 10 of them do not focus on a specific type of food. 11 of them focus on a prominent food. Among these, the most prominent food is olives and olive oil (n: 5). The other museums involve food such as honey (n: 2) and chocolate, aromatic herbs, ice cream and wine.

Presentation of Information Tools

As seen in Table 5, graphic resources are used as the most basic information presentation tool in both public and private museums (100%). Another significant tool for presenting information is external links (76%). However, interactive resources are available on more than half of the websites (57%). Nonetheless, it has been observed that audio-visual items (28.5%) and immersive resources (9.5%) are scarce on websites.

The utilization of graphic resources does not differ according to the ownership types of museums and they are at a sufficient level in both. While public museums are more adequate than private museums in terms of using audio-visual items, it can be argued that both types of museums are insufficient in terms of the availability of immersive resources. However, it can be suggested that private museums are more adequate in terms of external links and interactive resources.

Table 5. Presentation of information tools

Types of tools		Tools	All	Public	Private
Expositive	Graphic	Texts/Photos/Images	100%	100%	100%
	Audio-Visual	Audio/Video	28.5%	42.8%	21%
	Hyper-textual	External links	76%	28.5%	100%
Participative	Interactive	Interactive resources	57%	28.5%	71.4%
	Immersive	Virtual visits	%9.5	28.5%	0

The results for the assessment of the interaction level of the resources and tools used by the museums in the presentation of information are shown in Table 6. Accordingly, the resources used by the gastronomy museums in Turkey to provide information to their visitors have a mean score of 1.32 and present a moderate level of interaction. When the results are assessed according to the ownership type of the museums, a moderate level of interaction has been observed in both types of museums. The situation in public museums is remarkably close to the lower mid-range. Private museums have a higher level of interaction with their visitors in terms of the presentation of information. The fact that these museums are much more sufficient than public museums, especially in terms of hypertextual and interactive resources, has been effective in that manner. Although public museums provide opportunities for their visitors in terms of immersive resources, they are below the overall average due to being insufficient from the aspect of other resources.

Table 6. Level of interactivity in the presentation of information by gastronomy museums

Resources for the Presentation of Information	Value (V)	Presence (P)			Scores (P*V)			Level of interactivity ([P/5]/museums no.)		
		All	Public	Private	All	Public	Private	All	Public	Private
Graphic	1p	21	7	14	21	7	14	1.32	1.05	1.45
Audio–visual	2p	6	3	3	12	6	6			
Hyper-textual	3p	16	2	14	48	6	42			
Interactive	4p	12	2	10	48	8	40			
Immersive	5p	2	2	-	10	10	-			
Total					139	37	102			

Resources for Virtual Visitor Interaction

Analysis conducted concerning RQ2 shows which interaction tools carry more weight within the dimension and thus which best describe the dimension. While presence indicates the number of museums that have such a tool; the per cent values (%) indicate the weight of each in the dimension of which they are a part (Table 7).

Table 7. Resources for virtual visitor interaction

Dimensions	Tools	Total	
		Presence	%
Connecting	Content syndication Subscription forms Registration (sign up/registration) Mobile alerts	7 6 7 -	35 30 35 -
	Total	20	100
Sharing	Tools/buttons for tagging information Tools/buttons for linking information to external sites Tools/buttons for sharing information in social networks	- 5 17	- 22.7 77.3
	Total	22	100
Reviewing	Polling/voting Surveys Open-ended questions Message board/commenting box Online guestbook	- - - 4 7	- - - 36.3 63.7
	Total	11	100
Participating	Contests/competitions Sweepstake Coupons, barcodes, QR codes Individual or collective games Contests/competitions	- - - - -	- - - - -
	Total	-	-
Collaborating	Tools for creating a personal gallery Uploading tools (texts, images, videos, podcasts) Tools for experiments (simulations, reconstructions, etc.) Tools for the co-creation of content or displays	- - - -	- - - -
	Total	-	-

The results reveal that museum websites utilize limited resources to interact with their visitors. The most striking point among these results is that the museums do not utilize any resources in the dimensions of participating and collaborating. Moreover, because of the absence of some resources from other dimensions, it was revealed that 14 of the 20 resources were not utilized by any museum. There is a relatively equal distribution among the resources that defining the connecting dimension, except for mobile alerts. The sharing dimension is largely defined by the sharing tool in social networks (77.3%). While it is observed that resources in the reviewing dimension are used less respectively; online guestbook is utilized the most among these (63.7%).

The results in Table 8 show the proportion of museums in each dimension that have at least one resource. Accordingly, the results regarding the five dimensions identified show that most museums (80.9%) utilize low-level interaction resources (Sharing). Connecting, a very low-level interaction resource is utilized on approximately 62% of websites. The reviewing resource has the lowest usage rate (33.3%) and only private museums (50%) benefit from this resource. When the ownership type is concerned, it has been observed that private museums benefit more from resources providing high interaction than public museums.

Table 8. Dimensions of resources for virtual visitor interaction level of interactivity in the resources for virtual visitor interaction

Dimension	All	Public	Private
Connecting	61.9%	28.5%	78.5%
Sharing	80.9%	42.8%	100%
Reviewing	33.3%	-	50%
Participating	-	-	-
Collaborating	-	-	-

The results concerning the assessment of Resources for Virtual Visitor Interaction (Table 9) of the museums reveal that the gastronomy museums in Turkey have a low level of interaction (0.65 out of 3). The results have generally emerged under the weight of sharing and reviewing resources. The absence of resources in the participating and collaborating dimensions can be considered as the primary source of low-level interaction.

Table 9. Level of interactivity in the resources for virtual visitor interaction

Resources for Virtual Visitor Interaction	Value (V)	Presence (P)			Scores (P*V)			Level of interactivity ([P/5]/museums no.)		
		All	Public	Private	All	Public	Private	All	Public	Private
Connecting	1p	13	2	11	13	2	11	0.65	0.23	0.85
Sharing	2p	17	3	14	34	6	28			
Reviewing	3p	7	-	7	21	0	21			
Participating	4p	-	-	-	-	-	-			
Collaborating	5p	-	-	-	-	-	-			
Total					68	8	60			

When the results are examined according to the ownership type of the museums, a low level of interaction is found in both museum types. The level of interaction in public museums is lower and closer to the lower limit (close to zero). The interaction level of private museums is approximately 0.60 points higher than public museums and is close to the upper limit (0.85). This is due to the presentation of more resources to the visitors by such museums, especially in the dimension of reviewing, which has a higher level of interaction.

DISCUSSION

Gastronomy tourism has created significant touristic mobility in recent years. Destinations strive to offer different opportunities to get a share of such mobility. Different destinations benefit from gastronomy museums as a tool that emerged in this context and can significantly increase the quality of the tourist experience (Kim et al., 2020). It has been observed that many gastronomy museums have been established or are in the process of being established in Turkey in line with these efforts (Akyürek & Erdem, 2019).

On the other hand, in recent years, museums have begun to actively develop their online presence to increase and improve visitor accessibility and interaction with their virtual and physical collections (Boutsiouki & Polydora, 2019; Lopatovska, 2015). In this context, well-designed websites assist museums in terms of increasing their online competitiveness, attracting visitors and facilitating dialogic communication with them. In this study, the level of interaction of the museums was assessed by analysing the resources utilized by the gastronomy museums in Turkey in presenting information (expositive, hyper-textual and participative resources) and interacting with visitors (based on the dimensions of connecting, sharing, reviewing, participating, and collaborating). In addition, this assessment was made comparatively based on the ownership status of the museums such as private or public. The research indicates certain results and differences.

Regarding the results on Presentation of Information Tools (RQ1), it can be argued that all museums benefit from expositive sources such as texts, photos, or images to present information on their websites which is a significant result of the study. The fact that these resources are effective and easy to apply in attracting the attention of users (Wang & Yang, 2020) increases their use. Hyper-textual resources, which have moderate interaction in the presentation of information, are available in museums. This means that museums also use different sites to present information. It can be suggested that museums are very inadequate in terms of resources providing a high level of interaction. It is found that private museums benefit more from highly interactive resources when the ownership status of the museums was examined. While public museums are sufficient in terms of expositive resources, private museums are also sufficient in terms of hypertextual and interactive resources in addition to expositive resources. For instance, while all the private museums examined have the hyper-textual resource, solely two out of nine public museums present it. Similarly, Wang & Yang (2020) examined the activities of organizations on Twitter in terms of dialogic communication and determined that non-profit organizations use Twitter only to inform and retain their visitors while for-profit organizations use it in a manner suitable for dialogic communication.

The results obtained from the Likert scale designed by Capriotti et al. (2016) suggest that museums are moderately sufficient in terms of presenting the information. Accordingly, it can be argued that the gastronomy museums in Turkey are more adequate than either the art museums around the world (Capriotti et al., 2016; López et al., 2010), in Spain (Capriotti & Pardo Kuklinski, 2012) or Italy (Garibaldi,

2015) or the archaeological museums in Greece (Boutsiouki & Polydora, 2019). At the same time, these results are generally in line with the results obtained at the level of different organizations (McAllister-Spooner & Kent, 2009; Taylor et al., 2001; Wang & Yang, 2020).

When the dimensions of resources for virtual visitor interaction (RQ2) were examined, it has been found that the sharing dimension, the second-lowest in terms of interaction level, is used more frequently than the others. The most important reason for this result is that this dimension is related to information sharing on social media. Websites largely allow sharing information about museums on social media. This may attract more visitors to websites, as 87% of young internet users in Turkey are register on social media (Andı et al., 2020). In addition, the fact that social media ranks second after TV as a source of receiving news in the country (Andı et al., 2020) may facilitate the spread of developments regarding museums to a wider scope. Finally, considering social media is one of the most important sources of information and evaluation for tourism in general and gastronomy tourism in particular (Yu & Sun, 2019), the competence of the museums in this scope becomes more important.

Connecting ranks, the second, and this dimension is the resource providing the least interaction to the visitors. The reviewing resource is used by up to one-third of the museums. Participating and collaborating resources, enabling the highest level of interaction, are not used by any museum. This result is slightly different from the results obtained by analysis of RQ1 (presentation of information tools) and the websites providing a moderate level of interaction in terms of presenting information, provide a low level of interaction in terms of the virtual visitor experience. Another point that should be emphasized is that private museums involve resources with a high level of interaction when they are examined in terms of the resources they offer to virtual visitors. For instance, while the reviewing resource is not utilized by public museums, half of the private museums provide a said resource to their visitors. The absence of this resource in public museums prevents visitors from sharing their experiences with other people visiting the website. However, these comments have a great impact on decision processes as reliable sources of information for other people. Moreover, it keeps the users commenting on the website in touch with the museum and increases their chances of revisiting the website (Antón et al., 2019). In addition, through such comments, deficiencies can be considered from the perspective of visitors from many different segments and of those with high education levels visiting the museums and improvements can be made accordingly (Sheng & Chen, 2012).

The results obtained from the Likert scale reveal that museums are quite inadequate in terms of the interaction level provided to their virtual visitors. This applies to both public and private museums. Accordingly, it can be argued that the tools referred to as Web 2.0, offering a more interactive and participatory environment to the visitors, are not used sufficiently on the websites. The results are consistent with previous studies (Garibaldi, 2015; López et al., 2010). Capriotti et al. (2016) suggested that the art museums are more adequate in their study addressing the art museums around the world.

The results of two indicators (tools for the presentation of information and virtual visitor interaction) designed to determine the level of interaction of museums is presented in Figure 1 for each museum and by type of ownership (some points have more than one museum). According to the results obtained, it has been observed that museums have a medium level of interaction in terms of the presentation of information, low level of interaction in terms of the resources provided to virtual visitors, and private museums are more adequate when the resources provided to virtual visitors are concerned. There is no museum providing a high level of interaction in both dimensions. However, solely one museum has the values close to a high level of interaction (presentation of information point=2; interaction with virtual visitors=2.4). The number of museums with a low level of interaction in both dimensions is seven (33.3%). Among these, while five of them are public museums (55.5%); two are private museums (14.3%). Finally, the number of museums providing an interaction level above the medium level in terms of both dimensions is six (27.2%) [two public museums (22.2%); four private museums (28.6%)].

Figure 1. The interactivity levels of the museums analysed

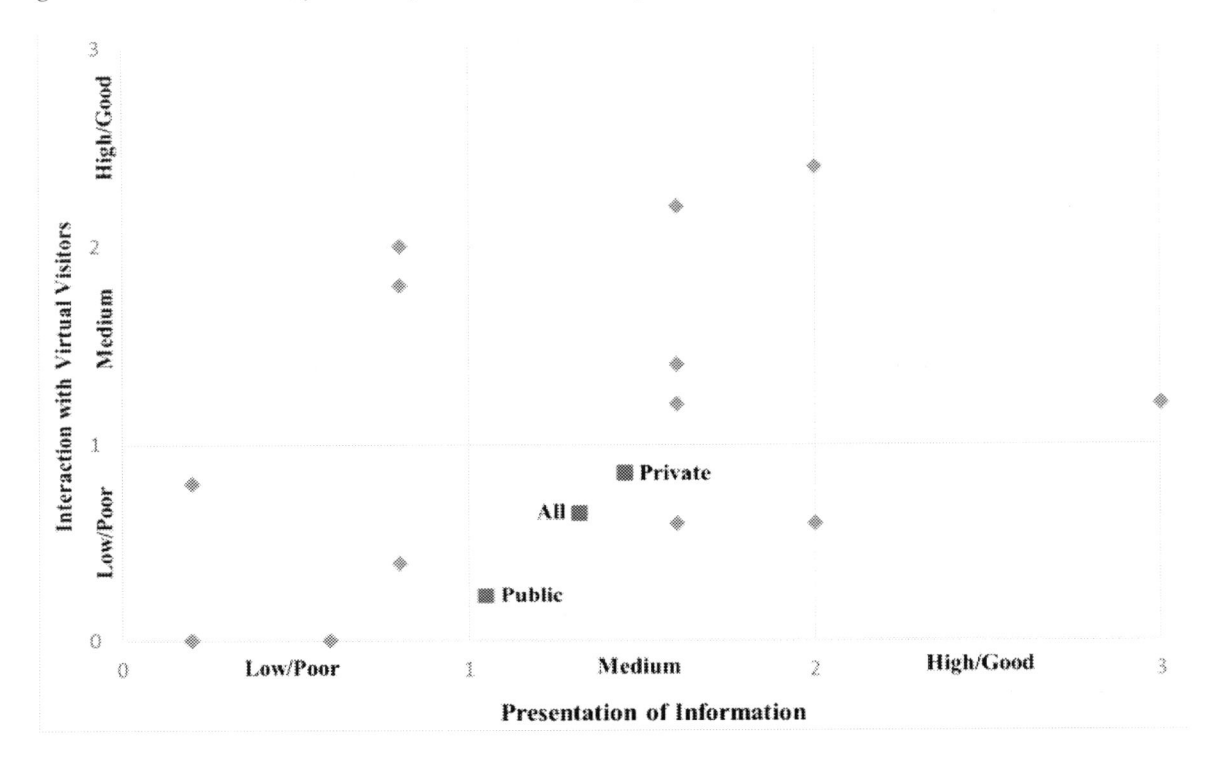

Briefly stated, the holistic analysis of interaction indicators reveals that the websites of gastronomy museums in Turkey do not have a high level of interaction with visitors, do not fully benefit from the opportunities provided by Web 2.0 technologies on their websites, and as such, they do not present a basis appropriate for dialogic communication. In other words, gastronomy museums in Turkey mostly use websites as a medium to display multimedia content and provide one-sided information. Although this result is more adequate in terms of indicators, also applicable to private museums.

CONCLUSION AND FUTURE RESEARCH

To the best of our knowledge, this study is the first in terms of assessing the websites of gastronomy museums from a perspective of dialogic communication. In previous studies, although the websites of different museums such as art, natural history and archaeology have been analysed, less emphasis was made on gastronomy museums. However, today the gastronomy museums, especially valued by tourists seeking a different and authentic experience (Kim et al., 2020), with websites adapted to dialogic communication, can reinforce their presence, reach wider markets, and increase the number of on-site visitors as in art and history museums (Pallud & Straub, 2014).

Managerial Implications

This research reveals that gastronomy museums in Turkey do not benefit from opportunities sufficiently provided by the internet. In addition, surprisingly it has been figured out that among 29 gastronomy museums in Turkey, eight of them do not even have a website. Since websites are the most required and effective tools for dialogic communication, it is particularly important for museums to take the necessary actions to eliminate said deficiency.

Our results suggest several implications for museum management. Although the websites of gastronomy museums contain basic information, materials that offer emotional experiences such as video and photo galleries need to be increased. This will increase the number of visits, the time spent on the site, and therefore the site traffic in general.

Secondly, museums may offer opportunities for other transactions (purchase of products, gastronomy books, ticket sales, etc.) on the Internet. In online transactions, special offers or products sold only online can be used as incentives. These can not only increase traffic on the site but can improve visitor services and increase the number of users.

Thirdly, the establishment of opportunities to increase visitor interaction on websites is quite easy through the technology used at present. For instance, designing the websites in such a manner enabling the comments of the visitors or the online chats with the authorized persons with knowledge on gastronomy to provide significant opportunities for establishing interactive and one-to-one relationships with visitors. In addition, considering that the human voice increases the quality of the tourist experience (Kang & Gretzel, 2012), the inclusion of podcasts on the websites can increase visitor interaction.

Fourthly, providing visitors with information about gastronomy that they can use in their daily lives may increase the frequency of visits to the website. Because, in various studies (Kim et al., 2020; Park et al., 2020) it has been concluded that one of the most important motivations for museum visits is education and learning. This information should be able to offer visits to the website an enjoyable experience. At the same time, visitors should be able to co-create this information and contribute to the content like a curator.

All of this increases the level of dialogic communication of websites. Museums that improve the level of interaction with their visitors can also ensure their economic sustainability. Further, this can contribute to the preservation of the gastronomic element that constitutes the museum theme and the related social activities by transferring them from generation to generation.

Limitations and Future Research

The results presented in this study were obtained by analysing whether the tools that can increase the dialogic communication capacities of the websites are available on the websites. To better understand the impact of the factors ensuring the dialogic communication on gastronomy museum visitors, more research is required. In this manner, the visitors' perspective on the factors ensuring the dialogic communication can be revealed especially in gastronomy museums. In addition, the roles of these factors in achieving the mission of museums have not been analysed in this research. Future research could examine the assessments made by the museum professionals and staff to gain a more comprehensive overview of the relationship between museums and the factors of dialogic communication. Moreover, how highly interactive online visits to museums and co-creation activities affect on-site visits to museums or how online and on-site visits will be integrated are also interesting research questions that await answers for gastronomy museums. As gastronomy museums become more aware of the opportunities provided by the factors to increase dialogic communication, the adoption rate of the aforementioned tools will increase and new studies will be required to identify the innovative practices that best fit the museum's goals. Finally, as far as the author has reviewed, the author could not encounter any study about gastronomy museums in other countries in the literature. The studies conducted in different countries will enable us to benchmark and implement good practices in other countries.

This research received no specific grant from any funding agency in the public, commercial, or not-for-profit sectors.

REFERENCES

Aced-Toledano, C., & Lalueza, F. (2018). Monologues in the conversational era: Assessing the level of dialogic communication that big firms are reaching on social media. *El Profesional de la Información*, *27*(6), 1270–1280. doi:10.3145/epi.2018.nov.10

Agostino, D., Arnaboldi, M., & Lampis, A. (2020). Italian state museums during the COVID-19 crisis: From onsite closure to online openness. *Museum Management and Curatorship*, *35*(4), 362–372. doi:10.1080/09647775.2020.1790029

Akyürek, S., & Erdem, B. (2019). Gastronomy museums as sustainable hangouts in gastronomy tourism: A gastronomy museum proposal for Gümüşhane City, Turkey. *Turizam*, *23*(1), 17–33. doi:10.5937/turizam23-20717

Andı, S., Aytaç, S. E., & Çarkoğlu, A. (2020). Internet and social media use and political knowledge: Evidence from Turkey. *Mediterranean Politics*, *25*(5), 579–599. doi:10.1080/13629395.2019.1635816

Antón, C., Camarero, C., & Garrido, M.-J. (2018). Exploring the experience value of museum visitors as a co-creation process. *Current Issues in Tourism*, *21*(12), 1406–1425. doi:10.1080/13683500.2017.1373753

Antón, C., Camarero, C., & Garrido, M.-J. (2019). What to Do After Visiting a Museum? From Post-consumption Evaluation to Intensification and Online Content Generation. *Journal of Travel Research*, *58*(6), 1052–1063. doi:10.1177/0047287518793040

Boutsiouki, S., & Polydora, A. (2019). Is the museum going digital? Experiences from the websites of Greek museums. In V. Katsoni & T. Spyriadis (Eds.), *Cultural and Tourism Innovation in the Digital Era Proceedings Book* (pp. 229–245). Springer.

Camarero, C., Garrido, M. J., & San José, R. (2016). Efficiency of Web Communication Strategies: The Case of Art Museums. *International Journal of Arts Management*, *18*(2), 42–62.

Capriotti, P., Carretón, C., & Castillo, A. (2016). Testing the level of interactivity of institutional websites: From museums 1.0 to museums 2.0. *International Journal of Information Management*, *36*(1), 97–104. doi:10.1016/j.ijinfomgt.2015.10.003

Capriotti, P., & González-Herrero, A. (2013). Managing media relations in museums through the Internet: A model of analysis for online pressrooms in museums. *Museum Management and Curatorship, 28*(4), 413–429. doi:10.1080/09647775.2013.831246

Capriotti, P., & Moreno, Á. (2007). Corporate citizenship and public relations: The importance and interactivity of social responsibility issues on corporate websites. *Public Relations Review, 33*(1), 84–91. doi:10.1016/j.pubrev.2006.11.012

Capriotti, P., & Pardo Kuklinski, H. (2012). Assessing dialogic communication through the Internet in Spanish museums. *Public Relations Review, 38*(4), 619–626. doi:10.1016/j.pubrev.2012.05.005

Capriotti, P., Zeler, I., & Camilleri, M. A. (2021). Corporate Communication Through Social Networks: The Identification of the Key Dimensions for Dialogic Communication. In M. A. Camilleri (Ed.), *Strategic Corporate Communication in the Digital Age* (pp. 33–51). Emerald Publishing Limited. doi:10.1108/978-1-80071-264-520211003

Cristobal-Fransi, E., Daries, N., Martin-Fuentes, E., & Montegut-Salla, Y. (2020). Industrial Heritage 2.0: Internet Presence and Development of the Electronic Commerce of Industrial Tourism. *Sustainability, 12*(15), 5965. doi:10.3390u12155965

Cristobal-Fransi, E., Daries-Ramon, N., Mariné-Roig, E., & Martin-Fuentes, E. (2017). Implementation of Web 2.0 in the snow tourism industry: Analysis of the online presence and e-commerce of ski resorts. *Spanish Journal of Marketing - ESIC, 21*(2), 117–130.

Curran, K., Murray, M., & Christian, M. (2007). Taking the information to the public through Library 2.0. *Library Hi Tech, 25*(2), 288–297. doi:10.1108/07378830710755036

Dawson, B. (2008). Facilitating Innovation: Opportunity in Times of Change. *Museum Management and Curatorship, 23*(4), 313–331. doi:10.1080/09647770802517316

Garibaldi, R. (2015). The use of Web 2.0 tools by Italian contemporary art museums. *Museum Management and Curatorship, 30*(3), 230–243. doi:10.1080/09647775.2015.1043329

Garibaldi, R., & Pozzi, A. (2021). Food museums as cultural institutions and tourist attractions: Evidence from Italy. *Journal of Gastronomy and Tourism, 5*(2), 83–94. doi:10.3727/216929720X15968961037935

Gonçalves, G. (2020). Are hospitals our friends? An exploratory study on the role of Facebook in hospital organizations' dialogic communication. *Health Marketing Quarterly, 37*(3), 265–279. doi:10.1080/07359683.2020.1805898 PMID:32835646

Guillory, J. E., & Sundar, S. S. (2014). How Does Web Site Interactivity Affect Our Perceptions of an Organization? *Journal of Public Relations Research, 26*(1), 44–61. doi:10.1080/1062726X.2013.795866

Handsfield, L. J., Dean, T. R., & Cielocha, K. M. (2009). Becoming Critical Consumers and Producers of Text: Teaching Literacy with Web 1.0 and Web 2.0. *The Reading Teacher, 63*(1), 40–50. doi:10.1598/RT.63.1.4

Heinze, N., & Hu, Q. (2006). The evolution of corporate web presence: A longitudinal study of large American companies. *International Journal of Information Management, 26*(4), 313–325. doi:10.1016/j.ijinfomgt.2006.03.008

Hume, M. (2015). To Technovate or Not to Technovate? Examining the Inter-Relationship of Consumer Technology, Museum Service Quality, Museum Value, and Repurchase Intent. *Journal of Nonprofit & Public Sector Marketing*, *27*(2), 155–182. doi:10.1080/10495142.2014.965081

Ingenhoff, D., & Koelling, A. M. (2009). The potential of Web sites as a relationship building tool for charitable fundraising NPOs. *Public Relations Review*, *35*(1), 66–73. doi:10.1016/j.pubrev.2008.09.023

Kang, M., & Gretzel, U. (2012). Effects of podcast tours on tourist experiences in a national park. *Tourism Management*, *33*(2), 440–455. doi:10.1016/j.tourman.2011.05.005

Kent, M., & Taylor, M. (1998). Building Dialogic Relationships Through the World Wide Web. *Public Relations Review*, *24*(3), 321–334. doi:10.1016/S0363-8111(99)80143-X

Kent, M., & Taylor, M. (2002). Toward a dialogic theory of public relations. *Public Relations Review*, *28*(1), 21–37. doi:10.1016/S0363-8111(02)00108-X

Kim, S., Park, E., & Xu, M. (2020). Beyond the authentic taste: The tourist experience at a food museum restaurant. *Tourism Management Perspectives*, *36*, 100749. doi:10.1016/j.tmp.2020.100749

Kotler, N., & Kotler, P. (2000). Can museums be all things to all people? Missions, goals, and marketing's role. *Museum Management and Curatorship*, *18*(3), 271–287. doi:10.1080/09647770000301803

Leoni, L., & Cristofaro, M. (2021a). Technology adoption in small Italian museums: An empirical investigation. *Il Capitale Culturale - Studies on the Value of Cultural Heritage*, *23*, 57–87.

Leoni, L., & Cristofaro, M. (2021b). To adopt or not to adopt? A co-evolutionary framework and paradox of technology adoption by small museums. *Current Issues in Tourism*, 1–22. doi:10.1080/13683500.2020.1870941

Lopatovska, I. (2015). Museum website features, aesthetics, and visitors' impressions: A case study of four museums. *Museum Management and Curatorship*, *30*(3), 191–207. doi:10.1080/09647775.2015.1042511

López, X., Margapoti, I., Maragliano, R., & Bove, G. (2010). The presence of Web 2.0 tools on museum websites: A comparative study between England, France, Spain, Italy, and the USA. *Museum Management and Curatorship*, *25*(2), 235–249. doi:10.1080/09647771003737356

Marty, P. F. (2007). Museum Websites and Museum Visitors: Before and After the Museum Visit. *Museum Management and Curatorship*, *22*(4), 337–360. doi:10.1080/09647770701757708

McAllister-Spooner, S. M. (2009). Fulfilling the dialogic promise: A ten-year reflective survey on dialogic Internet principles. *Public Relations Review*, *35*(3), 320–322. doi:10.1016/j.pubrev.2009.03.008

McAllister-Spooner, S. M., & Kent, M. L. (2009). Dialogic Public Relations and Resource Dependency: New Jersey Community Colleges as Models for Web Site Effectiveness. *Atlantic Journal of Communication*, *17*(4), 220–239. doi:10.1080/15456870903210113

Morehouse, J., & Saffer, A. J. (2018). A bibliometric analysis of dialogue and digital dialogic research: Mapping the knowledge construction and invisible colleges in public relations research. *Journal of Public Relations Research*, *30*(3), 65–82. doi:10.1080/1062726X.2018.1498343

Moreno, A., & Capriotti, P. (2009). Communicating CSR, citizenship and sustainability on the web. *Journal of Communication Management (London)*, *13*(2), 157–175. doi:10.1108/13632540910951768

Najda-Janoszka, M., & Sawczuk, M. (2021). Interactive communication using social media – the case of museums in Southern Poland. *Museum Management and Curatorship*, *36*(6), 1–20. doi:10.1080/09 647775.2021.1914135

Oh, J. (2021). Quantity vs. quality of interactions: The combinatory effects of website interactivity and need for cognition on anti-smoking message perceptions and smoking attitudes. *Mass Communication & Society*, 1–30. Advance online publication. doi:10.1080/15205436.2021.1925299

Pallas, J., & Economides, A. A. (2008). Evaluation of art museums' web sites worldwide. *Information Services & Use*, *28*(1), 45–57. doi:10.3233/ISU-2008-0554

Pallud, J., & Straub, D. W. (2014). Effective website design for experience-influenced environments: The case of high culture museums. *Information & Management*, *51*(3), 359–373. doi:10.1016/j.im.2014.02.010

Park, E., Kim, S., & Xu, M. (2020). Hunger for learning or tasting? An exploratory study of food tourist motivations visiting food museum restaurants. *Tourism Recreation Research*, 1–15. doi:10.1080/0250 8281.2020.1841374

Sheng, C.-W., & Chen, M.-C. (2012). A study of experience expectations of museum visitors. *Tourism Management*, *33*(1), 53–60. doi:10.1016/j.tourman.2011.01.023

Sundar, S. S., Kalyanaraman, S., & Brown, J. (2003). Explicating Web Site Interactivity: Impression Formation Effects in Political Campaign Sites. *Communication Research*, *30*(1), 30–59. doi:10.1177/0093650202239025

Sylaiou, S., Mania, K., Karoulis, A., & White, M. (2010). Exploring the relationship between presence and enjoyment in a virtual museum. *International Journal of Human-Computer Studies*, *68*(5), 243–253. doi:10.1016/j.ijhcs.2009.11.002

Taylor, M., & Kent, M. L. (2014). Dialogic Engagement: Clarifying Foundational Concepts. *Journal of Public Relations Research*, *26*(5), 384–398. doi:10.1080/1062726X.2014.956106

Taylor, M., Kent, M. L., & White, W. J. (2001). How activist organizations are using the Internet to build relationships. *Public Relations Review*, *27*(3), 263–284. doi:10.1016/S0363-8111(01)00086-8

van Hage, W. R., Stash, N., Wang, Y., & Aroyo, L. (2010). Finding Your Way through the Rijksmuseum with an Adaptive Mobile Museum Guide. In *The Semantic Web: Research and Applications* (pp. 46–59). Springer. doi:10.1007/978-3-642-13486-9_4

Wang, Y., & Yang, Y. (2020). Dialogic communication on social media: How organizations use Twitter to build dialogic relationships with their publics. *Computers in Human Behavior*, *104*, 106183. doi:10.1016/j.chb.2019.106183

Williams, E. (2013). Food museums. In K. Albala (Ed.), *Routledge International Handbook of Food Studies* (pp. 229–237). Routledge.

Wirtz, J. G., & Zimbres, T. M. (2018). A systematic analysis of research applying 'principles of dialogic communication' to organizational websites, blogs, and social media: Implications for theory and practice. *Journal of Public Relations Research, 30*(1–2), 5–34. doi:10.1080/1062726X.2018.1455146

Yu, C.-E., & Sun, R. (2019). The role of Instagram in the UNESCO's creative city of gastronomy: A case study of Macau. *Tourism Management, 75,* 257–268. doi:10.1016/j.tourman.2019.05.011

ADDITIONAL READING

Chen, Y.-R. R., Hung-Baesecke, C.-J. F., & Chen, X. (2020). Moving forward the dialogic theory of public relations: Concepts, methods and applications of organization-public dialogue. *Public Relations Review, 46*(1), 101878. doi:10.1016/j.pubrev.2019.101878

Christians, C. G. (1988). Dialogic communication theory and cultural studies. *Studies in Symbolic Interaction, 9,* 3–31.

Kent, M., & Taylor, M. (1998). Building Dialogic Relationships Through the World Wide Web. *Public Relations Review, 24*(3), 321–334. doi:10.1016/S0363-8111(99)80143-X

Kent, M. L., & Taylor, M. (2021). Fostering Dialogic Engagement: Toward an Architecture of Social Media for Social Change. *Social Media + Society, 7*(1).

Pang, A., Shin, W., Lew, Z., & Walther, J. (2018). Building relationships through dialogic communication: Organizations, stakeholders, and computer-mediated communication. *Journal of Marketing Communications, 24*(1), 68–82. doi:10.1080/13527266.2016.1269019

Park, E., Kim, S., & Xu, M. (2020). Hunger for learning or tasting? An exploratory study of food tourist motivations visiting food museum restaurants. *Tourism Recreation Research,* ●●●, 1–15. doi:10.1080/02508281.2020.1841374

Sommerfeldt, E. J., & Yang, A. (2018). Notes on a dialogue: Twenty years of digital dialogic communication research in public relations. *Journal of Public Relations Research, 30*(3), 59–64. doi:10.1080/1062726X.2018.1498248

Taylor, M., Kent, M. L., & Xiong, Y. (2019). Dialogue and Organization-Public Relationships. In B. R. Brunner (Ed.), *Public Relations Theory* (pp. 79–96). John Wiley & Sons, Inc.

KEY TERMS AND DEFINITIONS

Dialogic Communication: Any exchange of ideas and views that are mutually negotiated and tend to co-create a common meaning rather than a certain truth claimed by each party.

Gastronomy: (1) The science and art of eating and drinking that examines the relationship between culture and food. (2) Healthy, well-arranged, pleasant, and delicious cuisine, food order, and system.

Gastronomy Museum: A space or institution that engages with a particular food or drink and tells its story, its preparation, or its social and cultural ties; where tools and machinery used in agricultural production, cooking and food service are stored, exhibited, and researched.

Interactivity: Versatile and interactive communication and relationship in which both parties can negotiate directly.

Museum: A space or institution where works of art or science found in excavations are unearthed, stored, researched, and exhibited according to the collections.

Web 1.0: A web technology that was used in the early stages of the Internet, in which the user communicates with the other computer in one direction.

Web 2.0: It is the second-generation internet service. It defines social communication sites, wikis, communication tools and the system created by internet users jointly and by sharing.

Chapter 18
Serendipitous Cultural Tourist

Mahmut Baltaci

https://orcid.org/0000-0001-7509-3094

Silifke Tasucu Vocational School, Selcuk University, Turkey

A. Celil Cakici

Tourism Faculty, Mersin University, Turkey

ABSTRACT

Factors such as technological developments, increasing population growth, social opportunities, the right to paid vacation, increase in leisure time, increase in income level have provided tourism development and rapid acceleration in recent years. In addition, factors such as culture and education level have gained importance in the development of tourism. The prominence of cultural values in the destination management is proportional to the satisfaction of the tourists coming to the region. The aim of this chapter is to explain and give knowledge about the "serendipitous cultural tourist" typology, which is one of the types of tourists who do not come for cultural motivations. Although tourists do not participate in tourism for cultural purposes, the fact that they visit cultural attractions causes them to be named as cultural tourist type. Destination management organizers providing better service and more detailed information to the tourists improve the likelihood of them visiting the destination again.

INTRODUCTION

With technological developments, leisure time of individuals has increased as well as their disposible incomes and they desire to leave the routine has revealed the need for touristic experience. With the return of touristic experiences to routine, aslternative and special interest tourism types such as cultural tourism, sport tourism, cycling tourism, ecological tourism and agro-tourism have emerged (Yun et al., 2007).

Since the 1980s, cultural tourism has become a popular form of tourism that has a common agreement among tourism authorities to create a positive image for destinations, affirm national pride, prolong the length of stay of visitors and even rivive endangered traditions (Qi et al., 2018, p. 217). According to many studies, a significant percentage of tourists are seeking cultural experiences, such as visiting cultural attractions unrelated to the sea, sand and the sun, and participating in various cultural activities.

DOI: 10.4018/978-1-7998-8528-3.ch018

World Tourism Organization estimates that cultural tourism currently accounts for 37% of all touristic trips, with demand having increased by 15% per year (McKercher, 2002; Richards, 1996). American Travel Industry Association estimates that two-thirds of U.S. Adults visit a cultural or heritage site or tourist destination while traveling (Silberberg, 1995). Based on these data, it has been suggested that cultural tourists represent a new type of mass tourist seeking meaningful travel experiences (McKercher & Du Cros, 2003).

Cultural tourism is a sub-set of tourism (Mishra, 2013). The range of possible uses of the term is so vast, that no single widely accepted definition of cultural tourism emerged (Dolnicar, 2002; Hughes, 2002). United Nations World Tourism Organization defines cultural tourism as "Movements mainly aimed at cultural motivations such as study tours, performing arts and cultural tours, travel to festivals and other events, visits to places and monuments, studying nature, folklore or arts, and travel for pilgrimage" (WTO, 1985).

Cultural tourism means different things to different people (Hughes, 1996; McKercher & Du Cros, 2003; Stebbins, 1996). Bonink and Richards (1992) came up with two main approaches by reviewing the current definitions of cultural tourism. The first is the areas and monuments approach, which is clearly related to a product-based definition of culture and focuses on defining the type of tourist attractions visited by cultural tourists. The second is the conceptual approach that attempts to explain the causes and meanings attributed to cultural tourism activity and are clearly related to the process-based definitions of culture. For example; cultural tourism covers all aspects of travel (McIntosh et al., 2009, p. 268). The contextual role of culture shapes the tourist's experience of a situation in general, without a specific focus on the uniqueness of a particular cultural identity (Mishra, 2013, p. 45).

Various tourist typologies appear in cultural tourism. The most common tourist typologies are explained by McKercher (2002); (1) purposeful cultural tourists are those who have a deep cultural experience and their major reason of visit is learning about culture or heritage; (2) sightseeing cultural tourists visit mainly for culture or heritage. However, their experience is shallower and entertainment-orientated; (3) casual cultural tourists are those whose cultural reason plays a limited role in the decision of the visit and subsequently they visit in a shallow manner; (4) incidental cultural tourists participate in cultural tourism activities, although cultural tourism plays little or no meaningful role in their destination decision-making process. They also have shallow experiences; (5) serendipitous cultural tourists visit cultural attractions and have a deep experience even if at the beginning cultural tourism plays little or no role in the decision making of visiting a destination.

Serendipitous cultural tourists were firstly described by McKercher (2002). Fortunately, the cultural tourist represents an outlier. Cultural tourism factors play little or no role in the decision to visit a destination for this person, but have a profound experience when participating in cultural tourism (McKercher, 2002, p. 33). McKercher (2017) created a framework showing that the needs of tourists can be accommodated through a general-specific process. The cultural needs of serendipitous tourists seem to be general, because cultural tourism is not important in terms of their motivation. However, in some cases (e.g. Poland), it seems that fortunate tourists have certain cultural needs.

Studies show that serendipitous cultural tourists are rarely investigated (Morita & Johnston, 2018). Depending on the target content, they can be found at high frequencies. However, the portrait of serendipitous cultural tourists remains unclear in detail. Clarifying the portrait is important for cultural tourism marketers and destination marketing organizations as marketers need to understand and anticipate causes and behaviors to successfully identify the appropriate marketing mix (Croes & Semrad, 2015; Morita, 2014; Vong, 2016). The scarcity of studies remains insufficient to understand the serendipitous cultural tourist. More study is important to understand serendipitous tourists and development cultural tourism more.

TOURISM AND CULTURE

Tourism

Tourism is a social and cultural phenomenon that has turned into important economic outputs for cities and regions around the world. In both developed and developing countries, tourism is one of the fastest growing sectors of the economy and an important source of employment and investment (Wearing et al., 2009). Tourism, which is estimated to provide approximately 200 million jobs, directly employs 74 million people with related activities (Butcher, 2005, p. 6).

Tourism has become an important internationalized component of capitalist economies (Britton, 1991, p. 451). World Tourism Organization (WTO) has estimated that the worldwide international movement will increase from 25 million in 1950 to 846 million in 2006 (average annual growth of 6.5%) and to 1.6 billion in 2020 (*UNWTO Tourism Highlights, 2007 Edition*).

The significant increase in tourism after the Second World War was largely the result of various economic, technological, social and political changes that occurred in developing countries (Graburn, 1989; Urry, 1990). Especially, the significant growth in international tourism in the post-war period, it prompted Crick (1989, p. 310) to describe tourism as "the largest non-wartime movement of the human population". Similarly, Butcher (2005, p. 5) states as a suggestion that "Over the last century and a half the achieve- ment of the industry has been nothing less than the democratisation of leisure travel, from the few deemed worthy, and wealthy enough to partake, to an everyday activity for the majority in developed societies."

The most dramatic increase in tourism occurred in the last two decades of the twentieth century, making it "an essential feature of mass consumer culture and modern life" (Britton, 1991, p. 451). The twentieth century wittnessed a sudden collapse of the upper-class monopoly on tourism and the rise of active middle-class participation in tourism. Tourism today is a surprisingly large-scale phenomenon, representing one of the largest peacetime movements of people, goods, services and money in human history. International tourism is the largest item in foreign trade and is seen by many countries as the main source of capital for future economic development (Greenwood, 1972).

People travel for pleasure. They seek to return to the familiar and known, as well as discovering and experiencing new places. Some tourists are motivated to learn about other people and cultures, while others travel to gain insight into the self. Of course, most people want to take a "vacation". Every year, hundreds of millions of people around the world leave their homes for varying periods of time to experience the transience, movement and perhaps excitement of "distance", "being there". Tourism has expanded in recent years, both in scope and importance, to become a major social, cultural and economic phenomenon. (Wearing et al., 2009, p. 1) In short, tourists travel to learn and participate in folklore, traditions, scenic landscapes and historical sites and other activities such as nature, adventure, sports, festivals, crafts and sightseeing (MacDonald & Jolliffe, 2003).

Culture

Culture is a complex and multidimensional phenomenon that is difficult to define and the hundreds of different definitions presented in the literature reflect this (Reisinger & Turner, 2003, p. 4). According to Tylor (1871, p. 1), culture is "that complex whole which includes knowledge, belief, art, morals, law, custom, and many other abilities and habits acquired by man as a member of society". Hofstede (1997) defines culture as "knowledge, experience, beliefs, values, attitudes, meanings, hierarchies, religion, concepts of time, roles, spatial relations, concepts of the universe, material objects and cumulative accumulation acquired by a group of people over generations through individual and group effort". Cultures are inseparable, giving a chance to constantly interact and communicate with each other. Of course, this trend will play a role in strongly determining the formation and development of cultural tourism (Csapó, 2012, p. 202).

Culture is what people think (attitudes, beliefs, ideas, and values), what people do (normative behavior patterns or lifestyle), and what people produce (arts, artifacts, cultural products). (Mbaiwa & Sakuze, 2009) Therefore, culture consists of processes (people's ideas and lifestyles) and the products of these processes (buildings, artifacts, art, traditions and atmosphere) (Richards, 2001).

Richards (2019) identifies culture as one of the most important content providers for tourism experiences that have shifted from a somewhat elite location to representing what is authentically "local". Culture consists of explicit or implicit patterns for behaviors acquired and transmitted by symbols that constitute the distinctive achievements of human groups. The core of culture consists of traditional ideas and especially the values attached to them. Cultural systems can be thought of as products of action on the one hand and as conditioning elements of subsequent action on the other (Kroeber & Kluckhohn, 1952, p. 181).

In modern societies, culture has evolved over time by defining people as singular and differentiated social groups. This slow transformation in the creation of the cultural identity of diverse communities is now struggling against the rapid and in some ways inhumane emergence of a globalization that imposes standardization from the dominant societies of the twenty-first century, resulting in the loss of people's cultural diversity (González Santa Cruz et al., 2020, p. 485).

Culture and Tourism

Culture and tourism have always been inextricably linked. Cultural sights, attractions and events provide an important motivation for travel, and travel creates culture in itself. However, in recent years, with the close relationship between culture and tourism, cultural tourism has emerged as a form of consumption (Richards, 2013, p. 12) Culture is an important part of tourism as a product and is one of the factors that can increase the competitiveness of a tourism destination (Yun et al., 2007, p. 101).

It is possible to look at culture from two perspectives. One perspective explains culture as an ideological entity encompassing values, norms, customs, and traditions. The other perspective explains culture as a combination of ideological and material elements, such as what and how people eat, wear, and use (Reisinger & Turner, 2003, p. 10). Tourism studies focus either on the ideological aspects of culture or on a combination of the ideological and material aspects of culture. For example; Reisinger and Turner (2003) analyzed the social psychology of tourist behavior and analyzed the social psychology of tourist behavior. He stated that he was investigating the perceptions of Australia's qualifications.

Tourists also bring their own culture to their holiday environments. This culture is the individual's own and of the country they come from. Tourists' culture guides tourists' behavior. At the same time, here it is faced the culture of the host country (Jafari, 1987). According to Jafari (1987), the behavior of all participants involved in the tourism process creates a different "tourism culture" that is different from their routine and everyday culture. Tourists behave differently when they are away from home because they are in a different mood and "game" mode. Hosts treat tourists differently because they offer hospitality services. However, both groups preserve remnants of their respective cultures while in contact. Therefore, tourism culture should be analyzed in relation to "residue culture", which explains how tourists from different cultures behave.

CULTURAL TOURISM: THEORETICAL AND CONCEPTUAL FRAMEWORK

Definition of Cultural Tourism

Cultural tourism is a term with various meanings. According to anthropologists and sociologists, cultural tourism is a term closely related to "ethnic tourism" and is often used in relation to tourism's impact on developing societies (Tighe, 1985, p. 234). According to Wood (1984, p. 361), uniqueness of ethnic tourism should be defined by focusing directly on individuals living a cultural identity marketed to tourists. Cultural tourism, on the other hand, can be defined as situations where the role of culture is contextual, where its role is to shape the tourist's experience of a situation in general without a particular focus on the uniqueness of a particular cultural identity. The focus here is more specifically on buildings, vehicles, food stalls, clothing, etc., rather than the tangible cultural activities of people. According to any tourist, any of these types of tourism can be either primary or secondary to another form of tourism (Wood, 1984, p. 361).

For many tourists, traveling to experience different cultures is synonymous with cultural tourism. They consume the different sights, sounds, tastes and smells of a foreign culture. On the other hand, academics and tourism marketers define cultural tourism as a distinct product category that differs from other tourism activities or attractions by consuming the tangible and intangible cultural heritage of a destination (Yun et al., 2007).

Cultural tourism refers to a tourism industry that is owned, controlled, accepted and desired by local people, meeting their socio-cultural and economic needs (McIntosh, 2004). It is based on local cultural products, artifacts and host populations in target areas. Therefore, cultural tourism is a form of tourism built around cultural resources (Mbaiwa, 2004). Cultural tourism is not just about visiting places and monuments, it also includes consuming the way of life of the places visited. Cultural tourism includes both heritage tourism (related to works of the past) and arts tourism (related to contemporary cultural production) (Richards, 2001). The benefits of cultural tourism include that visitors experience local cultures, thereby enhancing their awareness, understanding and appreciation of local cultures (McIntosh, 2004).

Cultural tourism is a type of tourism activity where the main motivation of the visitor is to learn, discover, experience and consume the tangible and intangible cultural attractions or products in a tourism destination. These attractions or products are relevant to a set of distinctive material, intellectual, value systems, beliefs and traditions, spiritual and emotional characteristics of a society that includes art and architecture, historical and cultural heritage, culinary heritage, literature, music, creative industries and living cultures with lifestyles (Richards, 2018, p. 13).

Silberberg (1995, p. 361) defines cultural tourism as 'visits outside the host community motivated by wholly or partly interest in the historical, artistic, scientific or lifestyle/heritage offerings of a community, region, group or institution'. According to this definition, cultural attractions are; museums, galleries, festivals, architecture, heritage sites, artistic performances and attractions related to food, dress, language and religion. According to Stebbins (1996), "Cultural tourism is a type of special interest tourism based on seeking and participating in new and profound cultural experiences, whether aesthetic, intellectual, emotional or psychological." However, a somewhat narrower definition can often be used. Cultural tourism generally relates to excursions that include visits to places such as museums, art galleries, historical and archaeological sites, festivals, architecture, artistic performances and heritage sites (Hughes, 1996; Stebbins, 1996).

It can be said that cultural tourism is a social phenomenon and takes a lot of place in academic studies, which is related to the increase in leisure travel after World War II. Travel in Europe has helped the increase in cultural understanding and rebuild fragmented economies. In the 1960s and 1970s, consumption continued to increase with the increase in individuals' incomes, while international travel and cultural consumption also increased. In the 1980s, the influx of international tourists to landmarks and attractions received enough attention that the label "cultural tourism" was added to an emerging niche market. Early academic studies on cultural tourism also surfaced during this period, and the World Tourism Organization made the first description of the phenomenon (Richards, 2013, p. 12).

According to World Tourism Organization (1985), cultural tourism is expressed as one of the old new forms of tourism in which individuals act with cultural motivations such as "study tours, art and cultural tours, travels for festivals and other events, visits to historical ruins and monuments, travels for nature, folklore and art, and pilgrimage" (McKercher, 2020). Cultural tourism, by definition, consists of a wide range of cultural activities ranging from the dedication of leisure time cultural trips to participatory learning. McKercher and Du Cros (2003, p. 6) explored a range of motivational, experiential, aspirational, and operational definitions and found that cultural tourism includes four elements: tourism, use of cultural heritage assets, consumption of experiences and products, and tourists.

In the early 1980s, the evaluation of cultural assets as a touristic product had a very important place due to reasons such as creating a positive image for destinations, providing competitive advantage among destinations, prolonging the stay of visitors and reviving forgotten traditions (Qi et al., 2018).

Cultural tourism is no longer considered a 'niche' or 'special interest' form of tourism and emerges as an 'an umbrella term for a set of culturally oriented tourism typologies and various activities' (Wearing et al., 2009). To operate successfully in cultural tourism market segment, a precise definition of cultural tourists or their underlying motivations and expectations is necessary. The more information available in advance about this tourist segment, the easier the choice of subsequent marketing measures are. In general, cultural tourists are portrayed as a highly attractive market segment, which explains some of the excitement shown by, for example, cultural politicians and tourist operators about this tourism segment (Hausmann, 2007, p. 175).

Tourism global market in the 21st century creates an organic and interdependent system in which supply and demand sides experience significant changes in terms of time and space, as well as quantitative and qualitative aspects or components. Newer and newer regions and tourism products may be included in international and domestic tourism trends. In the ever-increasing competitive environment, only a tourism destination that can provide a quality standard will be able to survive (Csapó, 2012, p. 224). In other words, in order for the cultural tourism potential of a destination to be named and developed, touristic products and tourism services offered must have the originality that reflects that geography, that is, a cultural management specific to that destination and an ongoing cultural life (Bachleitner & Zins, 1999, p. 200).

Cultural tourists refer to those who attend at least one cultural event, regardless of their travel motivation (McKercher, 2002). Although market differentiation using only demographic and travel profiles is insufficient for the selection of subsequent marketing metrics. Instead, it is important to emphasize that there are different degrees of consumer motivation to undertake cultural tourism and therefore different types of cultural tourists can be identified. McKercher (2002), classifies cultural tourists as high, modest and low motivated according to their willingness to participate in cultural tourism. Each group may have different reasons for visiting a destination. Four types of cultural tourists are depicted (McKercher & Du Cros, 2003; Silberberg, 1995). These; highly motivated tourists are the type of tourists whose main motivation is to experience the cultural product. Partially motivated tourists; it is a type of tourist that is partly cultural tourism and partly motivated for purposes such as visiting relatives, friends and peers. Tourists motivated in the second plan from the cultural element; is the type of tourist who consider cultural tourism activities as a second-order activity that complements their basic motivation. Serendipitous tourists; it is the type of tourist whose main purpose is not to be in a cultural tourism activity, but who exhibits compulsory purchasing behavior with the request of friends.

Since ancient times cultural tourism has been a motivation for travel, albeit for a very small minority of general public, to experience a different culture. The Grand Tour was once considered an essential part of the education of 'aristocrats'. Such travelers are currently fully allocated to the segment of cultural tourism. These are for example; are "highly motivated" people who travel to a destination specifically to see museums, cultural sights, churches or festivals. The main purpose of visiting a destination is culture in all its different forms (Hausmann, 2007, p. 176).

The second group includes people who are only "partially" motivated by culture. These individuals travel to a destination both for its cultural opportunities and, for example, to visit friends or for certain city amenities and attractions. The third group includes people for whom culture is "additional" to another main travel motivation. For example, the primary motivation for visiting a particular destination will be business-related and/or attending a convention. However, they will also visit heritage sites, museums or other cultural events. Therefore, the main purpose of a journey is not cultural and includes various motives. Finally, there are the 'accidental cultural tourists'. This group includes people who do not plan to visit a heritage site or any other cultural property, but are traveling to a destination, for example because it rains and outdoor activities are postponed, or because visiting friends take them with them. In such cases, the visit of cultural sites is not planned but accidental.

Silberberg (1995, pp. 362-363) explained this situation through concentric segments. The first segment consists of "highly motivated" tourists, who travel to a destination for its cultural resources and experiences and make up 15% of the tourism market. The second segment is called "partially", which includes tourists visiting a destination for cultural and secondary reasons such as business and visiting friends/relatives, and this group accounts for approximately 30% of the tourist market. The third segment is called "helpful" tourists. Tourists in this segment visit a destination for non-cultural reasons, but are happy to participate in cultural tourism. They make up about 20% of the tourist market. The fourth segment is "accidental cultural tourists"; people who do not intend to visit a cultural attraction or event but do so unintentionally. They also make up about 20% of the market. There are also tourists who are excluded from these conditions. These tourists do not participate in any cultural activities under any circumstances and they constitute about 15% of the tourism market.

McKercher (2002) collected tourist types in five different typologies. According to him, different types of tourists may seek qualitatively different experiences. These differences can be expected to reflect the way they respond to communicative calls. McKercher has segmented the cultural tourism market according to two main dimensions: The importance of cultural motives in the decision to visit a destination and the depth of experience (Figure 1);

1. Purposeful cultural tourist: Learning about the culture or heritage of the other is an important reason to visit a destination and this type of cultural tourist has a deep cultural experience.
2. Sightseeing cultural tourist: Learning about the other's culture or heritage is an important reason to visit a destination, but this type of tourist has a shallower, leisure-oriented experience.
3. Casual cultural tourist: Cultural tourism reasons play a limited role in the decision to visit a destination and this type of cultural tourist occupies the destination shallowly.
4. Incidental cultural tourist: Cultural tourism does not play a meaningful role in the decision-making process on destination. However, while in the destination, the person will participate in cultural tourism activities by having a shallow experience.
5. Serendipitous cultural tourist: Cultural tourism plays little or no role in the decision to visit a destination, but while there, this tourist visits cultural attractions and has a deep experience at the end.

Figure 1. McKercher's typology
Source: McKercher, 2002

	SHALLOW EXPERIENCE	DEEP EXPERIENCE
HIGH INVOLVEMENT	Sightseeing cultural tourist	Purposeful cultural tourist
LOW INVOLVEMENT	Casual cultural tourist / Incidental cultural tourist	Serendipitous cultural tourist

Cultural tourists actively seek personal, "authentic" and "intimate" experiences in destinations, and in their interactions with host cultures and communities. Most cultural tourists seek some form of authenticity, either in terms of self-improvement or in terms of the sites, communities and activities they are involved in. Tourists' experiences, activities and desires related to their pursuit of cultural interaction show that the travel experience is more than just sightseeing, and it is about participation, experience and learning (Wearing et al., 2009, pp. 31-32). Focusing on tourism cultures created and shaped by travel and mobility shows that tourism experiences are complex and tourism is a multidimensional experience (Wearing et al., 2009, p. 32).

It has been argued that cultural tourists in the tourism market as a whole are more homogeneous, older, better educated and wealthier than the travelling individuals (Richards, 1996), they stay longer, spend more and are more active than other tourists (Richards, 1996; Silberberg, 1995). Cultural tourists are also considered to be more ethical than others. In addition, the increasing number of women in cultural tourism are economically more important than before (Hausmann, 2007). In parallel with the investigation of the origins of tourists, the concept of cultural distance has been defined in relation to their willingness to engage in cultural activities (McKercher, 2002). Cultural distance refers to the tendency that tourists exhibit according to their degree of interest in a destination's culture. It depends on the cultural background of the tourists. The more diverse the destination's cultural background, the more tourists will be interested in the destination's culture in terms of cultural exploration (Morita, 2014).

A SPESIFIC SEGMENT: SERENDIPITOUS CULTURAL TOURIST

Definition of Serendipitous Cultural Tourist

When tourism researches are examined, many typologies have been determined according to the behaviors, motivations, interests, travel preferences and experiences of the tourists (Stylianou-Lambert, 2011; Uriely, 2005). Researchers consider the depth of experience at destinations as a classification factor, beyond culture being the most important for visitors' travel choice. Van der Ark and Richards (2006) recognize that the level of enjoyment of the cultural experience depends on the cultural capital provided by the visitor, mainly on his or her personal characteristics, and even on the specific tourism product chosen by the visitors, which defines the experience characteristics of each particular vacation.

Typology is used in marketing as a tool to understand what and how people consume (Swarbrooke & Horner, 2007). One of the typologies is the "serendipitous cultural tourist" typology. To understand this typology, it is necessary to first investigate the origin of the word "serendipity". "Serendipity" (Seymore, 2009), the process of finding something valuable that was not initially sought, has also played an important role in tourism. Within their holiday motivation, tourists have desires for serendipitous experiences (Meng & Tung, 2016, p. 441). These desires are important for the satisfaction of tourists.

McKercher's (2002, p. 29) typology reveals that cultural tourists differ greatly from each other on the basis of their participation in and propensity to experience cultural attractions. For these reasons, they are also sensitive to different forms of marketing communication. The Foote, Cone, and Belding (FCB) Grid can be used to detail differences that reflect the way they respond to communication calls.

McKercher (2002) states that different types of tourists may seek qualitatively different experiences or engage in different levels of attraction. It can also be assumed that these differences reflect the way they respond to communication calls (Figure 2).

Purposeful cultural tourists are highly involved in a particular cultural attraction. They are also highly motivated to achieve a specific goal and gain a deep cultural experience. They need to understand the meaning of the wider cultural connections of attraction for the experience to take place. Thus, they follow the learn-feel-do path of persuasion. These tourists are also emotionally sensitive about cultural issues, and that means the marketer may try to persuade them emotionally first. Then they would be more interested in processing attraction information. In this case, persuasion follows the feel-learn-do route.

Sightseeing cultural tourists are similar to purpose tourists. They are highly interested in a particular cultural destination and also highly motivated to reach the destination, but their experience is light and shallow. These tourists are sensitive to information, they want to learn and know all the facts of the attraction. However, they do not seek deep understanding like purposeful cultural tourists. The way of persuasion is learn-feel-do.

Casual cultural tourists and incidental cultural tourists have a moderate or low level of cultural attraction. They are not sensitive to deep cultural experiences. They travel not primarily for attraction, but for other reasons. However, they can visit the attraction if the persuasive strategy is appropriate. The usual strategy is the best for them: 'come and try'. These tourists are therefore sensitive to the usual strategy that follows the do-learn-feel hierarchy.

Serendipitous cultural tourists have low participation. They do not care about the target at all. However, they are prone to deep experience and if someone manage to persuade them to participate they will intensely experience the cultural object. It can be assumed that serendipitous tourists follow the do-feel-learn hierarchy.

Figure 2. McKercher's typology and the four hierarchy-of-effect types of message perception
Source: Vaughn, 1980: 31

	SHALLOW EXPERIENCE	DEEP EXPERIENCE
HIGH INVOLVEMENT	Sightseeing cultural tourist LEARN-FEEL-DO Informative strategy	Purposeful cultural tourist LEARN-FEEL-DO FEEL-LEARN-DO Informative strategy Affective strategy
LOW INVOLVEMENT	Casual cultural tourist Incidental cultural tourist DO-LEARN-FEEL Habitual strategy	Serendipitous cultural tourist DO-FEEL-LEARN Satisfaction strategy

John (2001) defined the word serendipity as "the accidental (and happy) discovery of important new information". The word "serendipity" was first coined by Horace Walpole in 1754 from a fairy tale called The Three Princes of Serendip, where three princes "always accidentally and prudently discover what they were not looking for."

Serendipity is defined in various encyclopedic sources as 'the natural ability of some people to find interesting or valuable things by chance', 'a putative ability to find valuable or pleasant things that they are not looking for' and 'to make happy and unexpected discoveries by accident or chance' (Huang et al., 2014). Cary (2004), used the word 'accidentally' to describe the moment when the tourist forgets that she/he is a tourist. The tourist moment covered by a spontaneous experience is a moment of self-discovery, of social belonging, of being on the border between being a tourist and not being a tourist, and such an experience can only happen by accident. According to these definitions, 'accidental' in the context of travel is the ability or tendency to accidentally make unexpected discoveries and find interesting or valuable things during one's journey, including self-discovery (Huang et al., 2014, p. 172).

McKercher (2002) defined an 'serendipitous' tourist type in the cultural tourist typology. 'Serendipitous cultural tourist' refers to those who are not motivated by cultural tourism but have intense experience in the cultural attractions they visit. Serendipitous cultural tourists differ from 'accidental cultural tourists' who are also not motivated by cultural tourism but have only a shallow experience in the area. As such, the concept of "serendipitous" refers not only to the element of surprise and unexpectedness, but also to the ability to find pleasure and meaning in accidental discoveries, and are more meaningful and memorable because they are accidental.

McKercher (2002), stated that the serendipitous cultural tourist is the 'unusual' type and indeed the definition of the serendipitous cultural tourist is a new addition to his cultural tourist typology, which has different tourist characteristics from other types of tourists. Morita and Johnston (2018), mentioned in their study that serendipitous cultural tourists want to see places that local people do not recommend, and stated that McKercher's (2017) needs are compatible with the idea that their needs are general and unspecified according to the culture.

McKercher (2017) has recently established a framework that shows that the needs of tourists can be located along a general and specific continuum. The cultural needs of serendipitous tourists seem to be general, because cultural tourism is not important for their motivation. However, in some cases (e.g. in Poland) accidental tourists seem to have certain cultural needs. The inconsistency in knowledge level and the difference in specificity of needs indicate that the serendipitous subtype is more complex than that shown in McKercher's (2002) five-cell matrix.

According to Kantanen and Tikkanen (2006), if culture serendipitously persuades tourists to visit a fascinating attraction destination and experience a cultural attraction, they tend to have deep experiences. If they are satisfied with their experience, Foote, Cone and Belding (FCB) may change their position in the guide and move into the sightseeing cultural tourist group. Naturally, a habit-forming process can take place among these tourists (Figure 3).

Figure 3. FCB (Foote, Cone and Belding) Grid
Source: Vaughn, 1980: 30

	THINK	FEEL
HIGH INVOLVEMENT	INFORMATIVE STRATEGY LEARN-FEEL-DO	AFFECTIVE STRATEGY FEEL-LEARN-DO
LOW INVOLVEMENT	HABITUAL STRATEGY DO-LEARN-FEEL	SATISFACTION STRATEGY DO-FEEL-LEARN

The strategy for improving the cultural experience of accidental cultural tourists should be quite different. Many are returning visitors for reasons other than culture. Destination management's aim will be to persuade them to experience cultural activities that they do not plan to do. This requires extensive social awareness. Destination management organizers, front desk staff, and cultural site managers should maximize their knowledge of community-maintained cultural sites so that maximum word-of-mouth can occur. Enhanced knowledge of convenience is important, as the serendipitous cultural tourist segment has somewhat substitutable experience needs (Morita & Johnston, 2018).

Nguyen and Cheung (2014) aimed to identify and categorize the profiles of cultural tourists coming with package tours in their study in the city of Hue, Vietnam. They say that the findings of accidental tourists are interesting, that those who visit the city of Hue, although they have no cultural intentions, are interested in cultural values and gain deep experience. It was also found that their knowledge about Hue and Vietnam increased and they are satisfied about the trip.

Silberberg (1995) suggested that the motivation levels of tourists who benefit from and consume cultural products and services differ from each other at certain points, and grouped this diversity under four headings as highly motivated tourists, partially motivated tourists, secondarily motivated tourists from culture, and accidental tourists.

McKercher and du Cros (2003) tested a previously developed cultural tourist typology with a wider range of travel-related characteristics, demographic characteristics, awareness level, and motivational variables. In the research, the importance given to cultural tourism in the selection of the tourism region and the depth of the cultural tourism experience were used as the main determinants. In this direction, five different types of cultural tourists have been identified. These are purposeful cultural tourist, sightseeing cultural tourist, casual cultural tourist, accidental cultural tourist and serendipitous cultural tourist. Significant differences were found between these types of tourists in terms of the cultural experience sought. The findings obtained from the research indicated that cultural tourists do not travel for the sole purpose of gaining cultural experience. On the contrary, they travel for the purposes of leisure, enjoyment, and increasing the travel experience. Again, according to the findings obtained from the research, it has been found that most of the cultural tourists are motivated to travel for purposes such as relaxing, having fun, having a good time with family or friends.

Nyaupane, White, and Burduk (2006) aimed to make motivation-based segmentation to understand tourists visiting cultural heritage sites in Arizona, USA. Data for this study were collected through a postal survey from a representative sample of 671 tourists visiting three cultural heritage sites. Three separate sections were found using cluster analysis based on cultural history and learning motives. These are: (1) 'culture-focused', (2) 'culture-attentive', and (3) 'culture appreciative' tourists. These groups differed significantly in behavior, experience, and interpretation. It has been found that culture-focused tourists stay longer in their destination, consider archaeological sites as their primary activity and attach more importance to interpretation. In addition, culture-focused groups are more satisfied with their trips, appreciate the preservation of archaeological resources, and are more focused on learning.

DIGITALIZATION AND FUTURE OF CULTURAL TOURISM

Digitalization has had a profound impact on various industries and has created competition in the marketplace where organizations operate to deliver and extract value (Ammirato et al., 2019). Digitalization enables people to better address the needs and expectations of stakeholders (Nambisan et al., 2019). Digitalization has created new job opportunities in many industries as well as in cultural tourism (Bouwman et al., 2018; Nambisan et al., 2017).

Firms operating in cultural tourism are increasingly aware of the benefits of digital technologies for improving internal operations and a way to meet new market demands. On the other hand, digitalization guides entrepreneurs with appropriate and innovative business models. Digitalization renews many business processes in cultural tourism, both on demand and supply (Ammirato et al., 2021).

From a tourist perspective, ICT-based solutions can aid decision-making along with the tourism experience lifecycle, support the realization of travel-related activities, and enrich the cultural experience of travel (Ammirato et al., 2015). Digital technologies can assist cultural tourists with many functionalities to respond to specific and potential constraints such as the risk of epidemics (i.e. Covid-19). Recent advances in mobile technologies and the Internet of Things (IoT) have increased the innovation of business models by leveraging context awareness, ubiquity and pervasiveness (Felicetti et al., 2019).

From a supply point of view, the huge stream of data captured by sensors, devices, cameras and travel stages across cultural tourism destinations, one of the digital initiatives generated by cultural tourists, provides a promising basis for developing the ability of tourism companies to customize their product and service offerings (Ardito et al., 2019). In this sense, digitalization allows the production and simultaneous consumption of cultural services, paves the way for new ways of offering value to tourists, and offers cultural tourism services that are more sensitive to consumers' expectations and needs. Such emerging opportunities make it possible to design a new wave of business models in which cultural tourism stakeholders can interact with digital initiatives in an efficient value creation cycle. Mobile applications become attractive in the cultural travel market, not only to support cultural tourists while carrying out their travel activities, but also for digital enterprises as the core business providers of marketplaces, namely "cyber-intermediaries" (Runfola et al., 2013).

Digitalization has had a dramatic impact on the rise of the active and participatory cultural tourism experience and has greatly influenced travel in tourism. Various studies have highlighted how digital technologies positively affect the attractiveness of cultural destinations, thanks to the opportunities provided by knowledge sharing and co-creation (Porter & Heppelmann, 2014). The emergence of social networking platforms has profoundly affected the way tourists interact with other tourists. The "social web environment" has made possible new mechanisms of interaction, cooperation and "social experience" among tourists that foster electronic word-of-mouth, dissemination of opinions about places, services and tourism operators (Volpentesta & Felicetti, 2012). Sharing activities and social interactions includes any activity that accompanies cultural travelers through the tourism experience and makes them feel part of a community (Liu et al., 2019). More recently, the Internet of Things, geo-reference data and big data combined with mobile-based technologies and artificial intelligence represent key elements to deliver customized and proactive cultural tourism experiences and realize the transition to smart and competitive destinations (Femenia-Serra & Ivars-Baidal, 2021).

As tourists are "digital active" travelers, the success of cultural tourism and cultural tourist products strategically depends on the capacity of digital technology to integrate complex travel information to the traveler's needs, anywhere and anytime. Therefore, smartphone applications are strategically important for the success of cultural travel and cultural tourism in general (Ammirato et al., 2018). In order to best meet these challenging requirements of cultural travel management, tourists use information and/or digital technologies, namely web-based services (Akoumianakis et al., 2011; Runfola et al., 2013) and smartphone applications and are self-motivated (Gupta et al., 2018).

The evolution of cultural travels (Niemczyk, 2013), which has become more evident and diversified in cultural contents, motivations and experiences, has created a demand for travel-related services and has attracted digital businesses seeking potential customers. On the other hand, Ammirato et al. (2015) proposed a cultural tourism lifecycle model and described digital technologies that support tourists at lifecycle stages such as dreaming, booking experience, and recall. Chang and Shen (2018) have deepened the role of social networking features for mobile cultural tourism services.

In the light of the above, the importance of digitalization has once again become important for cultural tourism. With the development of technology, digitalization in tourism has increased and it has saved time and space in tourism as in many areas. Providing diversity for the promotion of cultural values is important for the development of cultural tourism.

CONCLUSION

In order to get a bigger share from world tourism, to compete and to take place in the tourism market, countries have revealed their current potentials and created various strategies. Countries that want to put aside the sea, sand and the sun trio have put forward the concept of alternative tourism in order to make world tourism sustainable. Cultural tourism, which is one of the alternative tourism types, is shaped according to the changing tourism trends and the differing expectations of the tourists.

Cultural tourism is taking a bigger place in the tourism market day by day. It includes many different areas within cultural tourism. Archaeological sites and museums, architectural places, artistic galleries, festivals, sculptures, music and dance events, theater performances, religious festivals take an important place in cultural tourism. Market segmentation of cultural tourists in cultural tourism is easy. Cultural tourists are travelers who tend to stay in destinations longer, participate more in activities, and travel frequently. Cultural tourists have more distinctive behaviors than other types of tourists. They differ from other types of tourists according to their education levels, age groups and professional knowledge. The facts that they are more educated, over 50 years old and from professional occupational groups push them to participate in tourism more consciously.

In this chapter, it is aimed to give detailed information about the serendipitous tourist type, which is included in the cultural tourist typologies. However, due to the limited number of studies, serendipitous cultural tourist type is explained according to available sources. The chapter is of great importance in terms of digitalization and guiding future of cultural tourism studies.

REFERENCES

Akoumianakis, D., Vidakis, N., Akrivos, A., Milolidakis, G., Kotsalis, D., & Vellis, G. (2011). Building 'flexible' vacation packages using collaborative assembly toolkits and dynamic packaging: The case study of the eKoNES. *Journal of Vacation Marketing*, *17*(1), 17–30. doi:10.1177/1356766710391132

Ammirato, S., Felicetti, A. M., Della Gala, M., Raso, C., & Cozza, M. (2018). Smart tourism destinations: can the destination management organizations exploit benefits of the ICTs? Evidences from a multiple case study. *Working Conference on Virtual Enterprises*.

Ammirato, S., Felicetti, A. M., & Gala, M. D. (2015). Rethinking tourism destinations: Collaborative network models for the tourist 2.0. *International Journal of Knowledge-Based Development*, *6*(3), 178–201. doi:10.1504/IJKBD.2015.072800

Ammirato, S., Felicetti, A. M., Linzalone, R., & Carlucci, D. (2021). Digital business models in cultural tourism. *International Journal of Entrepreneurial Behavior & Research*.

Ammirato, S., Linzalone, R., & Volpentesta, A. P. (2019). Business Model innovation in Travel Industry: Implications for Integrated Bus Transportation Services. *Proceedings of IFKAD2019-International Forum of Knowldege Asset Dynamics*.

Ardito, L., Cerchione, R., Del Vecchio, P., & Raguseo, E. (2019). *Big data in smart tourism: challenges, issues and opportunities*. Taylor & Francis.

Bachleitner, R., & Zins, A. H. (1999). Cultural tourism in rural communities: The residents' perspective. *Journal of Business Research*, *44*(3), 199–209. doi:10.1016/S0148-2963(97)00201-4

Bonink, C., & Richards, G. (1992). Cultural Tourism in Europe. A Transnational Research Initiative of the Atlas Consortium. ATLAS, University of North London.

Bouwman, H., Nikou, S., Molina-Castillo, F. J., & de Reuver, M. (2018). The impact of digitalization on business models. *Digital Policy, Regulation and Governance*.

Britton, S. (1991). Tourism, capital, and place: Towards a critical geography of tourism. *Environment and Planning. D, Society & Space*, *9*(4), 451–478. doi:10.1068/d090451

Butcher, J. (2005). *The moralisation of tourism: sun, sand... and saving the world?* Routledge. doi:10.4324/9780203987025

Cary, S. H. (2004). The tourist moment. *Annals of Tourism Research*, *31*(1), 61–77. doi:10.1016/j.annals.2003.03.001

Chang, S. E., & Shen, W.-C. (2018). Exploring smartphone social networking services for mobile tourism. *International Journal of Mobile Communications, 16*(1), 63–81. doi:10.1504/IJMC.2018.088273

Crick, M. (1989). Representations of international tourism in the social sciences: Sun, sex, sights, savings, and servility. *Annual Review of Anthropology, 18*(1), 307–344. doi:10.1146/annurev.an.18.100189.001515

Croes, R., & Semrad, K. J. (2015). The relevance of cultural tourism as the next frontier for small island destinations. *Journal of Hospitality & Tourism Research (Washington, D.C.), 39*(4), 469–491. doi:10.1177/1096348013491599

Csapó, J. (2012). The role and importance of cultural tourism in modern tourism industry. *Strategies for tourism industry-micro and macro perspectives*, 201-232.

Dolnicar, S. (2002). *Activity-based market sub-segmentation of cultural tourists*. Academic Press.

Felicetti, A. M., Volpentesta, A. P., & Ammirato, S. (2019). Analyzing app-based food information services: The case of Olive Oil sector. *VINE Journal of Information and Knowledge Management Systems, 50*(3), 427–453. doi:10.1108/VJIKMS-05-2019-0062

Femenia-Serra, F., & Ivars-Baidal, J. A. (2021). Do smart tourism destinations really work? The case of Benidorm. *Asia Pacific Journal of Tourism Research, 26*(4), 365–384. doi:10.1080/10941665.2018.1561478

González Santa Cruz, F., Pemberthy Gallo, L. S., López-Guzmán, T., & Pérez Gálvez, J. C. (2020). Tourist segmentation in an intangible heritage setting: The Holy Week processions in the city of Popayán, Colombia. *Journal of Heritage Tourism, 15*(5), 485–499. doi:10.1080/1743873X.2019.1692854

Graburn, N. (1989). Tourism: The sacred journey. In Hosts and guests, the anthropology of tourism. University of Philadelphia Press.

Greenwood, D. J. (1972). Tourism as an agent of change: A Spanish Basque case. *Ethnology, 11*(1), 80–91. doi:10.2307/3773161

Gupta, A., Dogra, N., & George, B. (2018). What determines tourist adoption of smartphone apps? An analysis based on the UTAUT-2 framework. *Journal of Hospitality and Tourism Technology, 9*(1), 50–64. doi:10.1108/JHTT-02-2017-0013

Hausmann, A. (2007). Cultural tourism: Marketing challenges and opportunities for German cultural heritage. *International Journal of Heritage Studies, 13*(2), 170–184. doi:10.1080/13527250601121351

Hofstede, G. H. (1997). *Cultures and organisations: Software of the mind*. McGraw-Hill.

Huang, W.-J., Norman, W. C., Hallo, J. C., Mcgehee, N. G., Mcgee, J., & Goetcheus, C. L. (2014). Serendipity and independent travel. *Tourism Recreation Research, 39*(2), 169–183. doi:10.1080/02508281.2014.11081765

Hughes, H. L. (1996). Redefining cultural tourism. *Annals of Tourism Research, 23*(3), 707–709. doi:10.1016/0160-7383(95)00099-2

Hughes, H. L. (2002). Culture and tourism: A framework for further analysis. *Managing Leisure, 7*(3), 164–175. doi:10.1080/1360671022000013701

Jafari, J. (1987). Tourism models: The sociocultural aspects. *Tourism Management, 8*(2), 151–159. doi:10.1016/0261-5177(87)90023-9

John, M. (2001). *A dictionary of epidemiology.* Oxford University Press.

Kantanen, T., & Tikkanen, I. (2006). Advertising in low and high involvement cultural tourism attractions: Four cases. *Tourism and Hospitality Research, 6*(2), 99–110. doi:10.1057/palgrave.thr.6040049

Kroeber, A. L., & Kluckhohn, C. (1952). *Culture: A critical review of concepts and definitions. Papers. Peabody Museum of Archaeology & Ethnology.* Harvard University.

Liu, H., Wu, L., & Li, X. (2019). Social media envy: How experience sharing on social networking sites drives millennials' aspirational tourism consumption. *Journal of Travel Research, 58*(3), 355–369. doi:10.1177/0047287518761615

MacDonald, R., & Jolliffe, L. (2003). Cultural rural tourism: Evidence from Canada. *Annals of Tourism Research, 30*(2), 307–322. doi:10.1016/S0160-7383(02)00061-0

Mbaiwa, J. E. (2004). Prospects of basket production in promoting sustainable rural livelihoods in the Okavango Delta, Botswana. *International Journal of Tourism Research, 6*(4), 221–235. doi:10.1002/jtr.477

Mbaiwa, J. E., & Sakuze, L. K. (2009). Cultural tourism and livelihood diversification: The case of Gcwihaba Caves and XaiXai village in the Okavango Delta, Botswana. *Journal of Tourism and Cultural Change, 7*(1), 61–75. doi:10.1080/14766820902829551

McIntosh, A. J. (2004). Tourists' appreciation of Maori culture in New Zealand. *Tourism Management, 25*(1), 1–15. doi:10.1016/S0261-5177(03)00058-X

McIntosh, R., Goeldner, C., & Ritchie, J. (2009). *Tourism: Principles, practices, philosophies. Hoboken.* Wiley.

McKercher, B. (2002). Towards a classification of cultural tourists. *International Journal of Tourism Research, 4*(1), 29–38. doi:10.1002/jtr.346

McKercher, B. (2017). Do attractions attract tourists? A framework to assess the importance of attractions in driving demand. *International Journal of Tourism Research, 19*(1), 120–125. doi:10.1002/jtr.2091

McKercher, B. (2020). Cultural tourism market: A perspective paper. *Tourism Review, 75*(1), 126–129. doi:10.1108/TR-03-2019-0096

McKercher, B., & Du Cros, H. (2003). Testing a cultural tourism typology. *International Journal of Tourism Research, 5*(1), 45–58. doi:10.1002/jtr.417

Meng, Y. T., & Tung, V. W. S. (2016). Travel Motivations of Domestic Film Tourists to the Hengdian World Studios: Serendipity, Traverse, and Mimicry. *Journal of China Tourism Research, 12*(3-4), 434–450. doi:10.1080/19388160.2016.1266068

Mishra, A. (2013). A Study of the Factors Influencing Cultural Tourists' Perception and Its Measurement with Reference to Agra. *IUP Journal of Marketing Management, 12*(4).

Morita, T. (2014). *Spoiled for choice! Which sites shall we visit: destination choice of heritage attractions in New Zealand's Bay of Islands.* Auckland University of Technology.

Morita, T., & Johnston, C. S. (2018). Are they all "serendipitous"? *International Journal of Tourism Research, 20*(3), 378–387. doi:10.1002/jtr.2189

Nambisan, S., Lyytinen, K., Majchrzak, A., & Song, M. (2017). Digital Innovation Management: Reinventing innovation management research in a digital world. *Management Information Systems Quarterly, 41*(1), 223–238. doi:10.25300/MISQ/2017/41:1.03

Nambisan, S., Wright, M., & Feldman, M. (2019). The digital transformation of innovation and entrepreneurship: Progress, challenges and key themes. *Research Policy, 48*(8), 103773. doi:10.1016/j.respol.2019.03.018

Nguyen, T. H. H., & Cheung, C. (2014). The classification of heritage tourists: A case of Hue city, Vietnam. *Journal of Heritage Tourism, 9*(1), 35–50. doi:10.1080/1743873X.2013.818677

Niemczyk, A. (2013). Cultural tourists:"An attempt to classify them. *Tourism Management Perspectives, 5,* 24–30. doi:10.1016/j.tmp.2012.09.006

Nyaupane, G. P., White, D. D., & Budruk, M. (2006). Motive-based tourist market segmentation: An application to native American cultural heritage sites in Arizona, USA. *Journal of Heritage Tourism, 1*(2), 81–99. doi:10.2167/jht010.0

Porter, M. E., & Heppelmann, J. E. (2014). How smart, connected products are transforming competition. *Harvard Business Review, 92*(11), 64–88.

Qi, S., Wong, C. U. I., Chen, N., Rong, J., & Du, J. (2018). Profiling Macau cultural tourists by using user-generated content from online social media. *Information Technology & Tourism, 20*(1-4), 217–236. doi:10.100740558-018-0120-0

Reisinger, Y., & Turner, L. W. (2003). *Cross-cultural behaviour in tourism: Concept and analysis.* Elsevier.

Richards, G. (1996). *Cultural tourism in Europe.* Cab International.

Richards, G. (2001). *Cultural attractions and European tourism.* Cabi. doi:10.1079/9780851994406.0000

Richards, G. (2013). Cultural tourism. In *Routledge handbook of leisure studies* (pp. 505–514). Routledge.

Richards, G. (2018). Cultural tourism: A review of recent research and trends. *Journal of Hospitality and Tourism Management, 36,* 12–21. doi:10.1016/j.jhtm.2018.03.005

Richards, G. (2019). Culture and tourism: Natural partners or reluctant bedfellows? A perspective paper. *Tourism Review.*

Runfola, A., Rosati, M., & Guercini, S. (2013). New business models in online hotel distribution: Emerging private sales versus leading IDS. *Service Business, 7*(2), 183–205. doi:10.100711628-012-0150-1

Seymore, S. B. (2009). Serendipity. *North Carolina Law Review, 88,* 185.

Silberberg, T. (1995). Cultural tourism and business opportunities for museums and heritage sites. *Tourism Management, 16*(5), 361–365. doi:10.1016/0261-5177(95)00039-Q

Stebbins, R. A. (1996). Cultural tourism as serious leisure. *Annals of Tourism Research, 23*(4), 948–950. doi:10.1016/0160-7383(96)00028-X

Stylianou-Lambert, T. (2011). Gazing from home: Cultural tourism and art museums. *Annals of Tourism Research, 38*(2), 403–421. doi:10.1016/j.annals.2010.09.001

Swarbrooke, J., & Horner, S. (2007). *Consumer behaviour in tourism*. Routledge. doi:10.4324/9780080466958

Tighe, A. J. (1985). Cultural tourism in the USA. *Tourism Management, 6*(4), 234–251. doi:10.1016/0261-5177(85)90001-9

Tylor, E. B. (1871). *Primitive culture: Researches into the development of mythology, philosophy, religion, art and custom* (Vol. 2). J. Murray.

UNWTO Tourism Highlights. (2007). doi:10.18111/9789284413539

Uriely, N. (2005). The Tourist Experience. *Annals of Tourism Research, 32*(1), 199–216. doi:10.1016/j.annals.2004.07.008

Urry, J. (1990). Tourist gaze: travel, leisure and society. *Tourist gaze: Travel, leisure and society.*

Van der Ark, L. A., & Richards, G. (2006). Attractiveness of cultural activities in European cities: A latent class approach. *Tourism Management, 27*(6), 1408–1413. doi:10.1016/j.tourman.2005.12.014

Vaughn, R. (1980). How advertising works: A planning model. *Journal of Advertising Research.*

Volpentesta, A. P., & Felicetti, A. M. (2012). Identifying opinion leaders in time-dependent commercial social networks. *Working Conference on Virtual Enterprises.* 10.1007/978-3-642-32775-9_57

Vong, F. (2016). Application of cultural tourist typology in a gaming destination–Macao. *Current Issues in Tourism, 19*(9), 949–965. doi:10.1080/13683500.2013.842543

Wearing, S., Stevenson, D., & Young, T. (2009). Tourist cultures: Identity, place and the traveller. *Sage (Atlanta, Ga.).*

Wood, R. E. (1984). Ethnic tourism, the state, and cultural change in Southeast Asia. *Annals of Tourism Research, 11*(3), 353–374. doi:10.1016/0160-7383(84)90027-6

WTO. (1985). *Identification and Evaluation of Those Components of Tourism Services which Have a Bearing on Tourist Satisfaction and which Can.* World Tourism Organization.

YunD.MacDonaldR. M.MacEachernM.HennesseyS. (2007). Typology of cultural tourists: an island study. doi:10.2139/ssrn.1617362

Chapter 19
Virtual Reality:
The Groundbreaking Smart Technology for the Tourism and Service Industry

Aruditya Jasrotia

https://orcid.org/0000-0002-8274-5609

Amity University, Noida, India

ABSTRACT

Virtual reality, also known as computer-based reality, is an advanced technology that has the capability to upsurge destination accessibility and to increase the popularity of lesser-known destinations. The objective of the current study is to understand the latest trends in virtual reality and to discover the future scope of implementation of virtual reality in the tourism industry across the world. The potential and the employment of virtual reality is not entirely understood and comprehended by many destinations. The present study identifies that there is a continuous development in popularity of virtual reality, and it is the need of the hour today. This disruptive technology has led to the phenomenon of virtual tourism, which gives people a preview and understanding of what they will experience if they visit a place physically. Virtual reality is becoming an outstanding way to showcase information and to gain relevant response from the tourists to enhance the services and overall tourist experience in the tourism destination.

INTRODUCTION

Disruptive technologies like artificial intelligence, robotics, internet, cloud technology, etc. have changed the tourism business from dreaming moments to experiencing moments, as a result it is also changing our life style and travel decision making. Meta-searches, virtual reality and virtual tours are becoming popular. The generation Y (people born between mid-1990s to 2000s) and generation Z (born between mid to late 1990s to early 2010) who are living in technology are becoming more comfortable with virtual reality and due to this, there will be new opportunities in future to utilize it in different ways for additional revenue generation. The dawn of the 21st century presented new innovative and interactive technologies, which has changed various sectors and industries, including the tourism industry completely (Buhalis & Law, 2008). Because of the advanced computer technologies several tourism processes, procedures

DOI: 10.4018/978-1-7998-8528-3.ch019

and methods have changed (Owen, Buhalis, & Pletinckx, 2004). The mobile-based tour guides (Bellotti, Berta, De Gloria, & Margarone, 2002), audio guides (Gebbensleben, Dittmann, & Vielhauer, 2006) and virtual reality supported museums (Jacobson & Vadnal, 2005) are some of the examples of advanced technologies involved in delivery of tourism services.

Tourism and technology are growing together in the present ecosystem and it can provide the greatest passive engagements on platforms. Virtual tours can help not only in tour planning but also in marketing of a particular destination. Within a few years, "seeing the world" could take on a whole new meaning. The Covid-19 pandemic has contributed to this shift in the favor of virtual tourism and it's no longer a choice but a necessity. It's also a fact that it's too early to say how virtual tourism will shape the tourism industry, but the idea of interacting virtually with locals and experiencing new places without actually travelling is interesting for the modern tourist. In a short period of time, the tourism industry has advanced in the area of application of computers. Information and Communication Technologies (ICT), can provide unimaginable opportunities, if they are used in an effective manner (Mariani, Baggio, Buhalis, & Longhi, 2014). For example, ICT can affect tourism related business as cultural heritage organizations like museums can use it to collect visitors' feedbacks, ideas, preferences in order to improve their services in future (Cappa et al., 2020). According to Jung and Han (2014) in order to achieve destination competitiveness, we need to invest innovative technologies. Virtual reality is beneficial for both the supply side and the demand side of tourism. With the help of information communication technology, it also enhances the visitor's experience. The true potential of the implementation of virtual reality is not yet known and understood. Researchers and academicians have been discussing the impact of technology on tourism since the 90s.

Virtual Reality (VR) has enhanced the relationship between tourists and destinations as it is a tool capable of providing information to the customers and motivating them to travel to a particular destination. These days a vast number of companies are reaching their target customers through interactive and sophisticated presentations such as engaging 360-degree virtual tours. Virtual reality creates a new level of extraordinary tour experience and services. The tourism experience, particularly offered in the form of audio and visual methods plays in important part in persuading the tourists to visit a destination. Virtual tours can assist in maintain sustainability and safeguarding fragile tourism attractions (natural and man-made) by ensuring that tourists are at a safe distance from the attraction. Virtual Reality is now being considered as an instrument to endorse a tourism attraction but, it is important to understand where and how to use it effectively. The objectives of this paper are; (1) To understand the current trends in virtual reality and (2) To explore the future scope of the implementation of Virtual Reality in the tourism industry across the globe. The next section provides a detailed review of literature on the topic of the study. After the literature review, contemporary trends regarding the usage of virtual reality in tourism industry are explained in depth. The final part of the study presents the conclusion and future implications. The rationale behind this study is the need to recognize the current scenario of virtual reality and to comprehend how it can revolutionize tourism industry globally. After the outbreak of Covid-19 pandemic, the virtual reality is no longer a choice. It has become a necessity which needs to be adopted by us in various industries and our daily lives. The study also seeks to the find answer to the big question that is, 'How will virtual reality transform and revolutionize the tourism industry?'

THEORETICAL BACKGROUND

Information Technology in Tourism Industry

Information technology (IT) is the employment of internet and computers for storage, retrieval, transmission, and manipulation of data (Daintith, John, 2009), or information which is often used in the setting of a business or other enterprise. Information technology is a part of the larger term, information and communications technology (ICT). This terminology is frequently used as another word for networks and computers. Information communication technology also includes information dispersal technologies like telephones and televisions. Tourism is a very much dependable on information technology (Nua Internet Surveys, 1998). In other words, all the activities from the creation, assembling, analyzing, implementation and dispersal of information are significant in the tourism industry. Technology is no longer a trend, it's a way of life now. The tourism products are insubstantial and they cannot be showcased or investigated during the purchase process. Moreover, the products in tourism industry are consumed later but purchased before the actual consumption happens. Tourism product is presented in the form of information to the customer. Therefore, information has a vital part in persuading the potential tourist. Williams (1993) suggested that tourists need an extensive variety of information regarding the destination, including, approachability, available, attractions, and events. This information needs to be conveyed at the right time and the most effective manner. Fulfilling the tourist's needs leads to successful business. Hence, it's clear that the tourism industry is intensively impacted by advances in information technology (Bennett, 1991). Technology has been engaged in tourism operations for a while but in many cases the use of latest and improved technology gives viable advantage to service providers over others. Use of ICT in tourism has also led to the rise of smart tourism destinations. Huang (2012) mentioned that smart tourism destinations focus and take care of the personal needs of the tourist by combining ICT with casual culture. Smart tourism destinations also establish smartness by installing suitable tourism applications within the destinations (Cohen, 2012). Information technology is playing a more crucial role in smoothening the relationships between various components of tourism. Tourism merchandises and products are becoming more dependent on information technology; this will become more so in the future. Digitalization of individuals in general has been a facilitator of the easy implementation of technologies like virtual reality for tourism. Almost everyone these days owns a smartphone, has access to internet and other technologies. Social networking websites are getting more popular and important in tourism business and marketing. They have emerged as a rich source of information by creating virtual destination environments that offer pictures, audios, videos, and other prospects for sharing unique tourism experiences (Fatemeh Mostafavi Shirazi, 2018; Gaberli, 2019). Technologically equipped customers now have higher expectations than ever before; they want everything right and they want everything right away. Online bookings, tourism websites, mobile apps, media advertisements etc. are various forms of information technology and it has revolutionized the day-to-day activities in tourism industry. The new generation of information technology is changing rapidly and it is fast, reliable and affordable.

VIRTUAL REALITY

From the utilization of virtual reality in corporate communications, to showcasing tourists the videos of destinations to attract them, there are obvious close links between VR and Information communication technology, especially in context of tourism industry. Many researchers have indicated that virtual reality in future will turn out to be an additional support for tourism products (Standing, C., Vasudavan, T., & Borbely, S., 1998). Consequently, it is significant to comprehend the present and future consequences of virtual reality in the tourism industry. The commonly accepted definition for VR is the use of computer-generated 3D environment, that the user can navigate and interact with, resulting in real-time simulation of one or more of the user's five senses (Burdea & Coiffet, 2003; Gutierrez, Vexo, & Thalmann, 2008; Guttentag, 2010). Virtual reality includes a 3D environment produced by a computer which is termed as the virtual environment (VE). A user can steer and intermingle with the virtual environment which results in instantaneous simulation of various senses of users (Guttentag, 2010). A significant feature of Virtual Reality is that the users can participate in a completely fictitious environment created by the computer system, which makes them temporarily forget the actual world (Cawood and M. Fiala, 2007). Virtual reality technology can now also help to attain feedback from the tourists through audio or touch-screen. This is done by simulating real-life surroundings in a non-natural environment. Steuer (1993) argues that the feeling of being present in an environment similar to reality is the key component of virtual reality which is produced with the help of both natural or artificial tools. In other words, through virtual reality the person discovers himself surrounded with the data entered or in the artificially created environment without leaving the actual place. Virtual tourism changes the types of content available by including visual, audio, and interactive materials for the tourists. It makes the learning experience more participatory (Craig Saper, 2008). The participants are able to hear, see, feel, interact and manipulate the environment which makes the experience more realistic. Another important thing to notice is that language is not a barrier in this environment. Virtual reality can allow us to do all these things we can't actually do with the simulative power of computers and smartphones (Giuseppe Riva, 2020).

According to Paquet, H. L. Viktor (2005) and R. Cheong (1995) virtual reality presents real-life like immersion into the tourism attraction, which also prevents the risk of any damage to the tourist sites. This can be immensely helpful in the case of tourist sites that have a delicate environment and aren't appropriate for masses. Cheong (1995) explains virtual reality as a computer-created experience that provides an entry into a different dimension. In short, Virtual Reality helps to provide tailored or enhanced experiences to the tourists which might not be possible at the actual destination (Wagler and Hanus 2018). This enhanced experience also compels and motivates the viewer to visit the destination in real. Virtual reality (VR) also acts as a communication medium in this era which has revalorized the communication process (F. Biocca and Levy, 2013) and is also being used in the field of robotics.

VIRTUAL TOUR/TOURISM

It has been argued by McKeown, P. G., & Watson, R. T. (1996) that even before theme parks were created the tourism industry created many illegitimate or artificial environments in order to attract tourists. Kalin (1998) suggested that, consumers tend to get more attracted to simulated environments as they provide guaranteed fun and are relatively less expensive. One of the popular destinations to adapt this technology is Disney. Disney World is one such leading destination which offers many virtual experiences for families and thousands of tourists visit Disney World throughout the year. Another example of such destinations is the Cinepolis complex in Connecticut, USA. Virtual Reality helps in creating personalized and tailored tourism experiences to the tourists which are called as virtual tours. A virtual tour includes visiting a computer-generated environment of an existing location, which includes sequence of videos or still images. A virtual tour may also include other elements like sound, music, and text (Cho et al., 2002, Weber et. al, 2019). The term "virtual tour" is usually used to denote various videos and photographic-based media. Virtual theme parks and entertainment centers are coming up throughout the world, especially in western countries. These sites are smaller, cheaper and adaptable according to the wishes of customers. Virtual Reality has the potential to contribute to sustainability by making certain processes sustainable, and by encouraging people to adopt more sustainable lifestyles. Virtual tours can be used by geographically dispersed people to understand the need for travel and reduce their carbon footprint.

CONTEMPORARY TRENDS IN VIRTUAL REALITY

Destination Promotion through Virtual Reality

Virtual Reality can play a pivotal role in promoting a destination and attracting more tourist. One of the latest projects related to Virtual Reality is "Mission 828". This project was launched recently in order to create an amazing Virtual Reality-experience at Burj Khalifa. Burj Khalifa is amongst the most visited places in Dubai. The users can get the experience of "Mission 828" with the help of six virtual reality pods placed at Level 124 and 125 of Burj Khalifa. The visitors get the feeling of ascending and descending the tower in exciting ways (Inition, 2018). This whole experience is also interactive which makes more satisfying. "Mission 828" is an apt example of application of virtual reality in the tourism industry, in order to attract more visitors. Another important example is "Mars 2117" in Virtual Reality. The UAE (United Arab Emirates) is also working on strategies to develop the first city on planet Mars within the next 100 years. Computer-generated images were displayed during The World Government Summit in Dubai to give the visitors an idea of how the city on Mars could look like. Moreover, the results of the 'Try Before You Fly' scheme launched by Thomas Cook in 2015, indicate that in the initial three months it generated around $17,000 and a 40% return on investment on flights and hotel bookings (Neil C. Hughes, 2016). Through implementing virtual reality in the field of marketing, tourism destinations can shape the decision-making process of potential tourists. According to Kim, et. al, (2018) destination marketing organizations can equip the sensory apparatuses of the virtual reality with sound, effects, pictures and videos, in order to influence potential tourists. It is also advised that tourism marketing organizations should enable the user's connection with Virtual Reality by offering the experience and content that is meticulously linked and significant for potential visitors.

Virtual Reality in Destination Management

Virtual Reality can provide an alternative way of access to various heritage sites which are in danger. This will minimize the impacts of visitors' and enhance the involvement of the tourists in various activities (Ab Aziz, K., & Siang, T. G., 2014). Let's take the example of Taj Mahal, India. Considering the negative impacts of pollution and increasing crowd on Taj Mahal, Virtual Reality experience can be used to give a breathtaking 360-degree view of Taj Mahal while actually staying far away from the place. This is just an example of what Virtual Reality can enable in the near future. On an average, the Ajanta and Ellora caves (India) are visited by between 3,000 and 5,000 people every day (Madhu Jain, 1987). Virtual Reality can perform a significant part in giving the experience of being in the caves without even visiting the place as these caves need immediate attention and preservation. The efficient use of Virtual Reality can be witnessed in Troy Museum located in Canakkale, Turkey, where various audio-video technologies make the experience wholesome and memorable. This enables a respectful immersion into the history and art of the place without leaving a negative impact on the tourism attraction. Hence, Virtual Reality can be used to create astounding and renowned tourist attractions even more striking and to preserve the heritage sites. A virtual environment for cultural heritage is reasonable and sustainable not only because it respects the local cultural heritage, but also it enhances the knowledge of the tourists (Bonini, 2008).

Selling Hotels through Virtual Reality

According to Forbes Magazine, more than half of all digital commerce globally will be made through mobile devices in 2020. This shift toward mobiles has spread across the Asia Pacific region with 72% of purchases expected to be made via mobiles in 2020. (Michelle Evans, 2020). This means that online sales will increase in future. Now the question arises can we use Virtual Reality in online sales? According to experts, Virtual Reality platforms, will be used in future by customers for booking a hotel room, a table at a restaurant or for entrance to visit a monument. Virtual reality can be implemented in promotion, market research, online sale, and public relations.

Virtual Reality enables full interaction with marketing messages. It includes wearing a headset, which helps to avoid disturbance while experiencing the content related to marketing (Barnes, 2016). Also, Virtual Reality technology connects with the customer as its direct and engages the customer in a virtual environment. Displaying hotel rooms online through 360-degree videos is popular among hotels these days and it's attracting the interest of many tourists. Various hotels are providing 360-degree videos on their websites or YouTube which can be seen through Virtual Reality headsets. Anchor Associates equips customers with Google headsets made with cardboard at reasonable prices (Mandelbaum, 2015). Virtual Reality can increase online sales by showing images of hotels. Indeed, Virtual Reality can help the customers to make sound decisions before booking a hotel room. A potential customer can explore the room from various angles, check the view and other expects relating to his stay, before actually booking the room. Due to the easy availability of technology Virtual Reality videos can be easily captured with special cameras and mobile phones. Due to this reason, hotel owners and customers are getting very much interested in virtual reality. Hotels like Marina del Rey Hotel in Los Angeles, art'otel Amsterdam, Hotel de Paris Monte Carlo, Lotte Hotel Seoul, Strand Palace Hotel in London, The Oberoi Amarvilas Agra in India are offering fascinating Virtual Reality contents (Rashad Aghayev, 2017).

Virtual Reality in Online Travel Agencies

Virtual Reality is an innovative way of getting a preview of destinations. Virtual Reality can generate an enhanced and comprehensive image of a tourism destination and help tourists in making accurate predictions about a place before the trip. This enables the tourists to make a decision whether to undertake the journey or not. There are a few Online Travel Agency (OTA) platforms where virtual reality technology is being used. Some of the popular OTA's like Booking.com and Expedia are curious about virtual reality (Rashad Aghayev, 2017). They are working on projects to create Virtual Reality versions of content. Before making the decision of booking a tour, customers can check out the destination virtually before actually spending the money. Now, the travel company Expedia is working on a "try before you buy" project for hotel demonstrations. This enables the users to walk around a hotel room, open doors and also to check out the view from the balcony. Till now, only a few Expedia offices have been providing a demo version of this Virtual Reality experience.

Virtual Reality content requires comparatively higher bandwidth than static content. Therefore, creating such platform and content can be quite costly. But, with new technologies affordable options are also available in market. Petrangeli, Swaminathan, Hosseini (2017) suggested enhancing virtual reality performance using HTTP/2. They also suggested that spatially tiling the video can save bandwidth. Future will show how OTAs will use Virtual Reality in the best possible way.

Bookings through Virtual Reality

Raymond and Bergeron (1997) proposed the idea that tour operators and travel agents must employ the Global-Distribution-System (GDS) as elementary infrastructure. Global Distribution System provides important information to the travel agents. Amadeus is one of the biggest user-friendly GDS. It always tries to look deep into the future and project important trends. Amadeus tries to execute ideas that helps the customers to do things more effectively, creatively and easily to deliver value. The sub company of Amadeus, 'Navitaire' announced the foremost "Virtual Reality Search and Booking Experience" (Roman Egger, 2017). This user interactive program involves virtual reality glasses and distinct gloves. The users can select the wanted tourism destination from a virtual globe. The tourists are able to perform a wide range of activities, including for searching for flights, car-rentals, booking hotels and buying tickets. The payment options are also available and users can book directly via credit card.

CONCLUSION

Virtual Reality is one of those developing technologies that has the power to influence the travel decision making choices of prospective travelers. It can be used in tourism industry for destination management, entertainment purposes, marketing and preservation. Virtual Reality is a very powerful tool for marketing and promoting destinations. Various studies have shown that Virtual Reality can stimulate the travel related decisions of tourists. The desire for travelling to a place seen on Virtual Reality is higher because Virtual Reality allows the viewer to establish more realistic expectations of the destination. Potential tourists are able to get a clear and realistic perception of the place. Virtual reality is surely a very effective and path-breaking technological intervention in the tourism marketing scape. As we understand, tourism is very dynamic discipline that is very responsive to technological changes. Precise, pertinent and appropriate information is necessary in order to make travel decisions. Virtual reality provides the same in an effective and efficient manner. Virtual tours are the most frequently used technologies of virtual tourism. The main benefit of virtual tours is the opportunity of unlimited consumption of tourist attractions as per the needs of the tourists.

Moreover, intangible products can be experienced virtually by the tourist in very innovative and interactive ways in the virtual environment. In other words, it reduces elements of uncertainty and supplies tangible information. As we become more familiar with newer facets of virtual reality, more options to use them will emerge bringing additional benefits. With time the technology is progressing and we can surely expect the travel industry to utilize Virtual Reality's amazing capabilities. The acknowledgement of potential impacts of virtual tours on tourists and the establishment of communication culture in virtual tourism will lead to the conversion of tourism industry into a people-oriented digital economy. This is a conceptual study; therefore, empirical testing is required in the area to continue subject related explorations. Virtual reality in this era is an emerging and magnificent field and in order to ensure destination promotion and preservation, tourism destinations must capitalize Virtual Reality technologies.

FUTURE IMPLICATIONS

Modern tourists are looking for reliable, timely and relevant data and information to make their travel choices. Since, the products in tourism industry are mostly intangible, unstable and fragile, the information given to the tourists is considered as the key product. This puts more pressure on virtual reality to provide precise and appropriate information to the tourists. In order to create a virtual environment, authorities and business owners must accurately record the whole site three dimensionally (Jung, 2019). In this rapidly developing technology, advanced and special recording cameras and tools have been developed. Moreover, 3D pictures and videos can be easily recorded by smart phones these days. It's a popular trend among tourists to record 3D pictures/videos and sharing them on social media. This ultimately leads to more flow of tourists to the site, as they get motivated by watching the 3D pictures and videos. In the imminent future, there will be very few tourists who will not see the tourism destination prior to the actual visit, through virtual tours. Consequently, future tourist experiences will be more cognizant and sensible because of the diffusion of AR and VR technologies throughout tourism industry, like in areas such as cultural, heritage, educational, religious and adventure tourism etc. Nevertheless, it is clear that increasing virtuality will increase the demand for tourism activities.

Although, Virtual Reality seems to be an auspicious, innovative and pioneering technology, it's still in the developing stage. Therefore, challenges and issues might emerge in future which can hamper the applicability and functionality of this technology. Tourism organisations and travel agents need to be aware of its benefits and potential drawbacks and should preferably aim for increasing gains and minimizing expenses. Virtual reality will also emerge as a new tool for heritage site presentation and preservation. Further, Virtual Reality can be employed to improve and promote sustainable tourism in selected regions. This technology will reduce the number of visits to tourism destinations, which will minimize the dangerous effects on environment, culture and heritage. Therefore, Virtual Reality will probably work for the progress of widely popular, sustainable tourism in near future. In addition to this, Virtual Reality could be used as a means prepare a replica of fragile or endangered tourism destinations that are inaccessible for the tourists. The implementation of digital and virtual technology, may enhance the visibility, engagement, and access to art consumers, especially in Asian countries, which will challenge the traditional boundaries. In the future, tourists should be considered as the key part to integrate tourism information resources and reinforce the creation of intelligent tourism post Covid-19. Virtual reality in travel and tourism has been trending during the Covid-19 pandemic because of the ongoing lockdown. Numerous virtual conferences, workshops, seminars, tours etc. are being organized in the tourism industry. Researchers and professionals are looking forward to virtual reality in helping tourism destinations recover from Covid-19.

REFERENCES

Aghayev, R. (2017). *VR-The Future of Selling Hotel Rooms*. Available at: http://www.virtual-reality-in-tourism.com/Virtual Reality-future-selling-hotel-rooms/

Aziz, K. A., & Siang, T. G. (2014). Virtual Reality and Augmented Reality combination as a holistic application for heritage preservation in the Unesco World Heritage Site of Melaka. *International Journal of Social Science and Humanity*, 4(5), 333–338. doi:10.7763/IJSSH.2014.V4.374

Barnes, S. (2016). *Understanding virtual reality in marketing: nature, implications and potential*. Academic Press.

Bellotti, F., Berta, C., De Gloria, A., & Margarone, M. (2002). User testing a hypermedia tour guide. *IEEE Pervasive Computing*, 1(2), 33–41. doi:10.1109/MPRV.2002.1012335

Bennett, M., & Radburn, M. (1991). *Information technology in tourism: the impact on the industry and supply of holidays*. Academic Press.

Biocca, F., & Levy, M. R. (Eds.). (2013). *Communication in the age of virtual reality*. Routledge. doi:10.4324/9781410603128

Bonini, E. (2008). Building virtual cultural heritage environments: the embodied mind at the core of the learning processes. *International Journal of Digital Culture and Electronic Tourism, 1*(2-3), 113-125.

Buhalis, D. (1996). Information and telecommunication technologies as a strategic tool for tourism enhancement at destination regions. Information and communication technologies in tourism, 131-142. doi:10.1007/978-3-7091-7598-9_16

Buhalis, D., & Law, R. (2008). Progress in information technology and tourism management: 20 years on and 10 years after the Internet—The state of eTourism research. *Tourism Management*, 29(4), 609–623. doi:10.1016/j.tourman.2008.01.005

Burdea, G., & Coiffet, P. (2003). *Virtual reality technology*. Academic Press.

Cappa, F., Rosso, F., & Capaldo, A. (2020). Visitor-sensing: Involving the crowd in cultural heritage organizations. *Sustainability*, 12(4), 1445. doi:10.3390u12041445

Cawood, S., & Fiala, M. (2008). *Augmented reality: A practical guide*. Academic Press.

Cheong, R. (1995). The virtual threat to travel and tourism. *Tourism Management*, 16(6), 417–422. doi:10.1016/0261-5177(95)00049-T

Cho, Y. H., Wang, Y., & Fesenmaier, D. R. (2002). Searching for experiences: The web-based virtual tour in tourism marketing. *Journal of Travel & Tourism Marketing*, 12(4), 1–17. doi:10.1300/J073v12n04_01

Cohen, B. (2012). What exactly is a smart city. *Co. Exist*, 19.

Daintith, J. (Ed.). (2009). *"IT", A Dictionary of Physics*. Oxford University Press.

Egger, R. (2017). *Booking via VR?* Available at: http://www.virtual-reality-in-tourism.com/booking-via-Virtual Reality/

Evans, M. (2020). *5 Stats You Need To Know About Digital Consumers In 2020*. Available at: https://www.forbes.com/sites/michelleevans1/2020/02/04/5-stats-you-need-to-know-about-digital-consumers-in-2020/#6412f4335b0f

Gaberli, Ü. (2019). Tourism in Digital Age: An Explanation for the Impacts of Virtual, Augmented and Mixed Reality Technologies on Tourist Experiences. *Journal Of Tourism Intelligence and Smartness*, 2(2), 61–69.

Gare, A. (2020). *The Palgrave Encyclopedia of the Possible*. Palgrave.

Gebbensleben, S., Dittmann, J., & Vielhauer, C. (2006). February. Multimodal audio guide for museums and exhibitions. In *Multimedia on Mobile Devices II* (Vol. 6074, p. 60740S). International Society for Optics and Photonics. doi:10.1117/12.641404

Gutierrez, M., Vexo, F., & Thalmann, D. (2008). *Stepping into virtual reality*. Springer Science & Business Media. doi:10.1007/978-1-84800-117-6

Guttentag, D. A. (2010). Virtual reality: Applications and implications for tourism. *Tourism Management*, 31(5), 637–651. doi:10.1016/j.tourman.2009.07.003

Han, D. I. D., Weber, J., Bastiaansen, M., Mitas, O., & Lub, X. (2019). Virtual and augmented reality technologies to enhance the visitor experience in cultural tourism. In *Augmented reality and virtual reality* (pp. 113–128). Springer. doi:10.1007/978-3-030-06246-0_9

Huang, X. K., Yuan, J. Z., & Shi, M. Y. (2012, December). Condition and key issues analysis on the smarter tourism construction in China. *International Conference on Multimedia and Signal Processing*, 444-450. 10.1007/978-3-642-35286-7_56

Hughes. (2016). *How Virtual Reality Is About to Transform the Travel Industry*. Available at: https://www.inc.com/neil-c-hughes/how-virtual-reality-is-ab-transform-the-travel-industry.html

Inition. (2018). *VR Experience at the top of Burj Khalifa*. Available at: https://www.inition.co.uk/case_study/Virtual Reality-experience-top-burj-khalifa/

Jacobson, J., & Vadnal, J. (2005). The virtual pompeii project. In *E-Learn: World Conference on E-Learning in Corporate, Government, Healthcare, and Higher Education* (pp. 1644-1649). Association for the Advancement of Computing in Education (AACE).

Jain, M. (1987). *Cave paintings of Ajanta and Ellora become a tragic monument to archaeological neglect*. Available at: https://www.indiatoday.in/magazine/heritage/story/19870315-cave-paintings-of-ajanta-and-ellora-become-a-tragic-monument-to-archaeological-neglect-798635-1987-03-15

Jung, T. (2019). *Augmented Reality and Virtual Reality. The Power of AR and VR for Business*. Springer Nature Switzerland AG.

Jung, T.H., & Han, D.I. (2014). Augmented Reality (AR) in Urban Heritage Tourism. *e-Review of Tourism Research*, 5.

Kalin, S. (1998). Conflict resolution. *CIO WebBusiness Magazine*. htttp://www.cio.com/archive/webBusiness/020198_Sales_content.html

Kim, M. J., Lee, C. K., & Jung, T. (2020). Exploring consumer behavior in virtual reality tourism using an extended stimulus-organism-response model. *Journal of Travel Research*, *59*(1), 69–89. doi:10.1177/0047287518818915

Mandelbaum. (2015). *Are Virtual Reality Concierges Coming?* Available at: https://www.hospitalitynet.org/opinion/4073212.html

Mariani, M., Baggio, R., Buhalis, D., & Longhi, C. (Eds.). (2014). Tourism management, marketing, and development: Volume I: the importance of networks and ICTs. Springer.

McKeown, P. G., & Watson, R. T. (1997). *Metamorphosis: A guide to the world wide web & electronic commerce*. John Wiley & Sons, Inc.

Nua Internet Surveys. (1998). *Datamonitor: Travel Will be Largest Online Product By 2002*. Available on http://www.nua.net/surveys/

Owen, R., Buhalis, D., & Pletinckx, D. (2004). December. Identifying technologies used in Cultural Heritage. VAST, 155-163.

Paquet, E., & Viktor, H. L. (2005). Long-term preservation of 3-D cultural heritage data related to architectural sites. *Proceedings of the ISPRS Working Group*, *4*, 1–8.

Petrangeli, S., Swaminathan, V., Hosseini, M., & De Turck, F. (2017). Improving virtual reality streaming using http/2. *Proceedings of the 8th ACM on Multimedia Systems Conference*, 225-228. 10.1145/3083187.3083224

Raymond, L., & Bergeron, F. (1997). Global distribution systems: A field study of their use and advantages in travel agencies. *Journal of Global Information Management*, *5*(4), 23–32. doi:10.4018/jgim.1997100103

Saper, C. (2008). Folkvine. org as a model of virtual tourism. *International Journal of Digital Culture and Electronic Tourism*, *1*(2-3), 209–224. doi:10.1504/IJDCET.2008.021408

Shirazi, S. F. M. (2018). Social Network Sites and Virtual Tourism Experience. In *Quality Services and Experiences in Hospitality and Tourism*. Emerald Publishing Limited. doi:10.1108/S2042-144320180000009008

Standing, C., Vasudavan, T., & Borbely, S. (1998). Re-engineering travel agencies with the world wide web. *Electronic Markets*, *8*(4), 40–43. doi:10.1080/10196789800000055

Steuer, J. (1992). Defining virtual reality: Dimensions determining telepresence. *Journal of Communication*, *42*(4), 73–93. doi:10.1111/j.1460-2466.1992.tb00812.x

Wagler, A., & Hanus, M. D. (2018). Comparing virtual reality tourism to real-life experience: Effects of presence and engagement on attitude and enjoyment. *Communication Research Reports*, *35*(5), 456–464. doi:10.1080/08824096.2018.1525350

Williams, P. (1993). Information technology and tourism: a dependent factor for future survival. *World Travel and Tourism Review, 3*, 200-205.

KEY TERMS AND DEFINITIONS

Digitalization: The use of digital technologies to improve processes and to provide value-producing opportunities.

Global Distribution System: A computer-based reservation system used for reserving airline tickets, rental cars, hotels, and other travel-related services.

Information Communication Technology: An umbrella term that comprises communication devices or applications including mobile phones, computers, network hardware, software, the Internet, satellite systems and many more.

Meta-Research: A research that uses the methods of science to study science itself.

Simulated: The imitation of the operation of a real-world process or system over time.

Virtual Environment: A simulated environment produced through computer-generated images.

Virtual Reality: A simulated experience that can be similar or entirely different from the real world.

Virtual Tourism: A simulation of an existing tourism destination or attraction location which is constructed by a sequence of videos or images.

Chapter 20
Social Media and Cultural Tourism

Murat Koçyiğit
https://orcid.org/0000-0002-2250-415X
Necmettin Erbakan University, Turkey

Büşra Küçükcivil
https://orcid.org/0000-0001-6719-8160
Necmettin Erbakan University, Turkey

ABSTRACT

The development of digital communication technologies and the increase in the use of digital platforms by individuals have increased the tendency towards touristic activities. Cultural tourism, which is carried out for certain purposes within the diversity of tourism, is one of the rising tourism activities of recent times. In this context, tourism management benefits from social media platforms as a tool in marketing their products and services related to cultural tourism. Social media platforms are important here for two aspects. The first of these is the use of social media by tourism management in the marketing of products and services by organizing individual and mass cultural tours and communicating with target audiences. The second is that individuals benefit from social media platforms in participating in cultural tourism and decision making. In this direction, it is important to evaluate conceptually the relationship between social media platforms, one of the most important digital communication technologies, and cultural tourism.

INTRODUCTION

Social media, which emerged as a result of technological developments, has become an inseparable part of individuals' lives. Individuals benefit from these platforms in the decision process of any touristic activity. In this respect, the actors of the cultural tourism sector should also actively use social media platforms and communicate with their target audiences on these platforms, and market their products and services to them.

DOI: 10.4018/978-1-7998-8528-3.ch020

On the other hand, the importance of social media platforms, which are effective in the promotion and marketing of touristic product attractions, is increasing day by day for both tourism businesses and consumers. Social media platforms, which are the most important source of information for tourists who are motivated by the desire to experience the culture of a destination, have also become an important tool of intercultural communication. Moreover, it can be stated that the recognition and awareness of cultural tourism, which is a type of tourism that aims to recognize and share all products of tangible and intangible cultural heritage, has increased through social media platforms. The necessity of taking into account the preferences of tourists in cultural tourism, which is a complex phenomenon, draws attention to the connection of the concept with social media. In this respect, it is important to associate social media with the concept of cultural tourism because of its features such as developing relationships, raising awareness, impressiveness, creating content for interests, mediating intercultural interaction and showing different cultures to other users. The aim of this study is to reveal the relationship between social media and cultural tourism in today's world, which is under the influence of digitalization, in line with the literature. In this context, the relationship between social media and cultural tourism has been conceptually examined in this study. In this direction, in this study, it has been tried to explain how individuals use social networks and social media environments related to cultural tourism and how they benefit from these environments and why cultural tourism companies need to exist strategically in these environments. In the study, various platforms and applications related to social media and social networks are included. In addition, it has been mentioned about what cultural tourism means conceptually, its types, activities, sources, and reasons. Finally, the priority issues in the marketing of cultural tourism through social media are discussed.

SOCIAL MEDIA CONCEPT: A BRIEF OVERVIEW

Social media is a group of internet-based applications that build on the ideological and technological foundations of Web 2.0 and allows users to create and share content (Kaplan, & Haenlein, 2010, p. 61). Social media defines the online resources that people use to share content such as videos, photos, images, text, ideas, insights, humor, gossip, and news. These resources include blogs, vlogs, social networks, message boards, podcasts, general bookmarks, and wikis (Drury, 2008, p. 274). Social media has transformed individuals into content publishers beyond being content readers. These platforms allow people to share and interact with each other (Evans, 2008, p. 33). It is characterized as a collection of websites and applications designed to create and develop online communities for networking and information sharing. Talking and sharing things with individuals on social media is not different from the situation in real life. The only difference is that these interactions take place online (Osborne-Gowey, 2014, p. 55). Social media is a new type of media that has the characteristics of participation, openness, conversation, community, and connectedness. These concepts, which express the characteristics of social media tools, were explained by Mayfield as follows (2008, p. 5):

- Participation: Social media encourages contributions and feedback from anyone interested. It blurs the line between media and audience.
- Openness: Most social media services are open to feedback and participation. It encourages voting, commenting, and information sharing. There are no barriers to access and use the content.

- Conversation: Social media is about two-way communication while traditional media is about content conveyed or distributed to the audience.
- Community: Social media allows communities to form quickly and communicate effectively. In this way, communities share common areas such as photography, a political issue, a favorite TV show.
- Connectedness: Many of the social media platforms provide links to other sites, resources, and users and thus develop by making use of the links.

Social media platforms provide important advantages to brands as they have features such as improving the relations of businesses with their consumers, promoting brand awareness, increasing brand loyalty. The effective use of social media platforms makes it possible for individuals to talk positively, develop relationships based on trust, influence consumers, and create a mutually beneficial relationship. On these platforms, businesses should not over-commercialize their sites and accounts and should be open to consumer insights and criticisms. Effective use of social media platforms enables businesses to reach and support millions of consumers around the world. On the other hand, it can be said that these platforms provide businesses with an economical and viable strategy (McLennan, & Howell, 2010, pp: 16-17). The increase in the number of users of social media platforms every day has led to an increase in the time users spend on these platforms. At the same time, this situation necessitated the communication strategies of businesses to be based on a social media-based strategy (Pavlik, 2008). This also applies to businesses, organizations, and actors operating in the tourism industry. In this context, the social networking platforms popularly used by individuals, institutions, and brands are as follows: Twitter, Facebook, Instagram, YouTube, Flickr, MySpace, Wikipedia, Google+, Second Life, Pinterest, LinkedIn, etc. (Drury, 2008; Evans, 2008; Macarthy, 2015). In this study, social media platforms (blogs, microblogs, wikis, forums, social networks) used by tourism companies are explained. On the other hand, YouTube, Twitter, Facebook, Instagram, Flickr, TripAdvisor, and Foursquare platforms, which are among the types of social networks, are also briefly explained.

Blogs: It is derived from the words web and log. A blog is a website where information is displayed in chronological order, with the most up-to-date information at the top. It is possible to categorize blogs in different ways. Many blog administrators categorize blogs according to their topics. Within this classification, it is possible to list the main categories such as academic, arts, entertainment, finance, food, career and business, technology, politics, personal, and sports (Newson et al., 2009).

Microblogs: Social networks combined with instant messaging, where a limited number of content/updates are distributed online. The leading application in the category of microblogs is Twitter (Mayfield, 2008, p. 6). Microblogs have easier, faster, and instantly accessible features than traditional blogging. These features have made microblogging an increasingly popular form of social interaction and communication as people begin to use it to search and share information and daily developments (Safko, & Brake, 2009, p. 264).

Wikis: It is a type of website that allows multiple users to add and remove content, edit and make changes (Newson et al., 2009). Wikis, everyone can edit and update are websites where information sharing is based on cooperation (Koçyiğit, 2017, p. 103).

Forums: Forums are online discussion sites where people engage in conversations on related topics through posted messages. Forums differ from chat rooms in that the messages are generally longer and chat rooms happen in real-time, more like a phone call, versus a forum discussion that functions more like an email conversation. According to estimates, it is believed that there are millions of internet forums.

Forums are similar to blogs in that they provide digital meeting places for people interested in common topics. These platforms may also be called message boards, bulletin boards, discussion boards, chain discussions, or discussion groups (Quesenberry, 2019, p. 126).

Social Networks: They are online communities where common interests and activities are shared. It offers the user a variety of interaction possibilities, from a simple chat to multiple video conferences and the forwarding of e-mail messages to participation in blogs and discussion groups (Miguéns et al., 2008, p. 1). The social network is a hub between businesses and their customers. These networks represent a new type of customer-focused interaction that combines marketing, public relations, product development, sales, and customer relations into a single community. It defines how we join each network, our position in them, and also determines our ability to gain friends and followers (Solis, 2010, pp. 7-8). On the other hand, social networks are the most widely used platforms by users as follows:

- **YouTube:** It is a platform where video sharing is carried out on the Internet. While individuals upload their videos here, they also watch videos shared by others. Video sharing sites such as YouTube are places where businesses can promote themselves and where consumers can spot mistakes and pass on bad customer experiences to others (Brown, 2009, p. 164). In this direction, YouTube is an effective visual and audio content-sharing platform in the promotion of cultural tourism destinations.

- **Twitter:** It is a microblogging and social networking service that allows its users to send and receive text-based, micro mail instant messages called Tweets (Safko, & Brake, 2009, p. 264). In the 21st century, Twitter has proven that it is no longer a temporary social network and has a lasting reputation. So much so that this platform has become a source of breaking news as it a mainstream channel. Search.twitter.com is also a very useful channel in terms of showing what users are saying about each other (Seitel, 2016, p. 212).

- **Facebook:** It is one of the most visited social networks in the world, with over one billion users on desktop and mobile devices. On Facebook, one of the leading social networks, it is almost impossible for businesses not to have a target audience. It is an application used in the context of branding, marketing and influencing target audiences (Macarthy, 2015). As an effective travel motivation tool, Facebook has also become a tool that enables users to gain new cultural experiences and raise their cultural levels.

- **Instagram:** It is a social networking application used by over a billion people worldwide to share photos, videos, and messages (ConnectSafely, 2021). This application allows posts to be published on other social networks. It has created a change in people's lives in sharing photos, shopping, promoting, and much more (Safko, 2012, p. 43). Thanks to these features, Instagram can also increase the interest in destinations such as museums, heritage sites, artistic performances, and festivals, which are among the cultural attractions.

- **Flickr:** It is a website that helps users to deliver their visual content to their target audience via the web, mobile devices, email, Flickr website, RSS feeds, external blogs, or any other technological method (Safko, & Brake 2009, p. 494). Flickr is a platform where both amateur and professional photographers can showcase their work, comment on photos, connect with individuals and groups, and subscribe to others' photo feeds via RSS (Morris, 2010, p. 14). In this context, Flickr is an effective content-sharing platform where people can convey their cultural tourism experiences and motivations to other users through various visuals.

- **TripAdvisor:** TripAdvisor, the world's largest travel platform, helps millions of travelers' month to have the best trip of their lives, all time. Travelers around the world can use the TripAdvisor site and app to browse millions of reviews and opinions on accommodation, restaurants, experiences, airlines, and cruises. Travelers visit TripAdvisor whenever they want to compare low prices on hotels, flights, and cruises, book popular attractions and tours and book a table at great restaurants (TripAdvisor, 2017).
- **Foursquare:** It is an application that can be used on mobile phones and lists restaurants, bars, and shops near the user's location (Seitel, 2016, p. 217). The comments and information shared by the person who checks in on Foursquare are seen by the people on their friend list. Users can associate their Foursquare accounts with other social media accounts such as Facebook and Twitter, and have their actions on Foursquare appear on other social media environments they are users of. Foursquare also allows for social suggestions through tips, which are small pieces of text associated with a place. Hints are intended to suggest possible events for that place (Lindqvist et al., 2011, p. 2410).

In this direction, social media tools and social networks enable individuals to be aware of events taking place at the local and global levels. These environments not only enable individuals to be aware of events but also encourage them to communicate and interact with other people and institutions related to their special interests. Therefore, these tools are dialogue tools. Discussing the necessity of tourism enterprises to use these tools in communicating and interacting with their target audience is an unnecessary issue for the conditions of today's century. Because, as stated by Boniface (2003), tourism is a major component of the modern world. Therefore, modern methods should be used for tourism in the modern world. While the approach here is humane and holistic, the most up-to-date and sophisticated technology should be used (pp. 3-4).

In this context, the world has become a global village through social media platforms. Thanks to these tools, the cultures of people and societies have come closer to each other and a state of familiarity has emerged. So much so that individuals both decide on the touristic activity they want to perform and maybe see a photo of a touristic place they can never go to in their life. Moreover, individuals can listen to ethnic music belonging to a different culture that they may never listen to live. In this context, social media platforms also have an aspect of showing and teaching different cultures to others. This situation can directly affect the desire of individuals to participate in one of the various types of cultural tourism, or it can lead the individual to the idea of orienting to another cultural tourism activity. As stated by Komito and Bates (2009), new information and communication technologies are often at the center of the transnational process (p. 233). Therefore, it is important for tourism companies, organizations, and actors to have an effective presence on these platforms to bring world citizens closer to each other. It can be stated that social media platforms, whose importance is increasing day by day in terms of intercultural interaction, bring cultures and people closer to each other. This situation can increase the motivation of individuals with different cultures to get to know each other's cultures, lifestyles, and beliefs. These issues can be a supporting factor for tourism mobility by increasing the demand for cultural tourism.

CULTURAL TOURISM AND RELATED CONCEPTS

Cultural tourism, which consists of four elements like tourism, tourist, use of cultural heritage assets, consumption of experiences and products (McKercher, & Du Cros, 2012, p. 6), is broadly defined as travel motivated by the desire to experience the culture of a destination (Cole, 2008, p. 61). The World Tourism Organization has made two definitions for cultural tourism, narrow and broad. In the narrow sense, cultural tourism includes the movements of individuals for cultural motivations, such as study tours, performing arts and cultural tours, festivals and other cultural events, trips to regions and monuments, nature, folklore, art, and pilgrimages. In a broad sense, cultural tourism is all the activities of individuals in which they meet their needs for diversity, tend to raise their cultural level, and lead to new knowledge, experience, and encounters. Because culture is subjective, definitions of cultural tourism are either too broad or too narrow. This situation limits the practical use of the concept in the field (Pedersen, 2002, pp. 23-24). ATLAS Cultural Tourism Project, on the other hand, expresses cultural tourism definitions as technical (narrow) and conceptual (broad). According to the technical definition, cultural tourism is all movements of individuals outside their normal place of residence to specific cultural attractions such as museums, heritage sites, artistic performances, and festivals. According to the conceptual definition, cultural tourism is the cultural movement of individuals by going to other regions from their places of permanent residence in order to gain new knowledge and experience satisfying their cultural needs (Richards, & Bonink, 1995, p. 174). Cultural tourism is a type of trip that aims to share and recognize all products of tangible and intangible cultural heritage, covering natural areas, monumental or civil architectural structures, art products, collections, cultural identities, traditions, and different languages (Dedehayır, 2012). Hausmann (2007) outlines some common points in most definitions of cultural tourism as follows. Cultural tourism is a form of special interest tourism. Tourists participating in cultural tourism are not different from other tourists due to their limited time and budget. Cultural tourism is the use of heritage sites and their opportunities and value to visitors. Cultural tourists, like other tourists, want to benefit from a variety of cultural services and experiences. In addition, since cultural tourism is a complex phenomenon, the preferences of tourists should be taken into consideration as a priority in cultural tourism (pp. 173-174).

Cultural tourism encompasses all aspects of travel where people learn about each other's lifestyles and thoughts. Tourism is a tool to develop cultural relations and international cooperation. The development of cultural factors within a nation is a way of increasing the resources used to attract visitors. In many countries, tourism is associated with the policy of cultural relations. The channels through which a country offers itself to tourists are its cultural factors. These are the entertainment, food, drink, hospitality, architecture, handicraft products of a country, and other features of a nation's way of life. Successful tourism is not just a matter of having better transportation and hotels. It is a matter of creating a certain national mood following traditional lifestyles and projecting a positive image of the benefits to tourists of such goods and services (Goeldner, & Ritchie, 2003, p. 262). What is needed to live in harmony in a world of countless diversity and different cultures; depends on people to know, respect, and understand what is different from them. In this respect, cultural tourism has a privileged place (Boniface, 2003, p. 3).

There are types of cultural tourism that are important in introducing and integrating different societies and their cultural elements. Cultural tourism types are as in Table 1.

Table 1. Types of cultural tourism

Types of Cultural Tourism	Tourism Products, Activities
Heritage Tourism	•Natural and cultural heritage • Material (built heritage, architectural sites, world heritage sites, national and historical memorials) • Non-material (literature, arts, folklore) • Cultural heritage sites (museums, collections, libraries, theatres, event locations, memories connected to historical persons)
Thematic Routes	• Wide range of themes and types (spiritual, industrial, artistic, gastronomic, architectural, linguistic, vernacular, minority)
City Tourism	• "Classic" city tourism, sightseeing • Cultural Capitals of Europe • "Cities as creative spaces for cultural tourism"
Ethnic Tourism	• Local cultures' traditions • Ethnic diversity
Event Tourism	• Cultural festivals and events (music festivals and events, fine arts festivals and events)
Religious Tourism	• Visiting religious sites and locations with religious motivation • Visiting religious sites and locations without religious motivation (desired by the architectural and cultural importance of the sight) • Pilgrimage routes
Creative Tourism	• Traditional cultural and artistic activities (performing arts, visual arts, cultural heritage, and literature) • As well as cultural industries (printed works, multimedia, the press, cinema, - audiovisual and phonographic productions, craft, design and cultural tourism)

Source: (Csapó, 2012, pp. 209-210).

Heritage Tourism: Its built heritage includes living lifestyles, antiquities, and modern art and culture. Heritage tourism is a type of cultural tourism that encompasses all elements of the human past and associated visitor experiences and desires (Timothy, 2011).

Thematic Routes: It means a route that connects natural or artificial attractions based on a theme and is accessible by a form of transport. The purpose of these routes is education, entertainment, interest, collaboration, and keeping up with trends (Nagy, 2012, p. 48).

City Tourism: It is a term that expresses the effects of various urban tourism activities of individuals on society, economy, and environment. It is based on the overall characteristics of the city and the attractiveness of its tourism resources (Wang, & Pei, 2014, p. 463).

Ethnic Tourism: It is the type of tourism where traditions of local, different, and exotic people are market. This type of tourism consists of visiting local houses and villages, watching dances and ceremonies, and shopping for primitive items and antiques valuable in art history (Smith, 1989, p. 4).

Event Tourism: Event tourism, which revitalizes the natural and physical tourism resources in destinations and creates an image, is defined as the systematic planning, development, and marketing of activities as a tourism attraction (Getz, & Wicks, 1993).

Religious Tourism: It is a type of tourism that individuals perform partially or fully motivated by religious reasons (Rinschede, 1992, p. 52).

Creative Tourism: These are the trips that teach the participants the art, cultural heritage and unique character of a region, establish close relations with the people of the region, and provide authentic experiences by interactively teaching the living culture (UNESCO, 2006, pp. 2-3).

These types of cultural tourism are the choices that individuals make among alternatives in line with their reasons for participating in cultural tourism. Individuals participate in the mentioned cultural tourism types with some tourism activities. According to Smith (2003, p. 31), cultural tourism activities vary according to activity areas and topics. Accordingly, cultural tourism activities and topics are as follows: "Heritage sites *(archaeological sites, whole towns, monuments, museums)*, performing arts venues *(theatres, concert halls, cultural centres)*, visual arts *(galleries, sculpture parks, photography museums, architecture)*, festivals and special events *(music festivals, sporting events, carnivals)*, religious sites *(cathedrals, temples, pilgrimage destinations, spiritual retreats)*, rural environments *(villages, farms, national parks, ecomuseums)*, indigenous communities and traditions *(tribal people, ethnic groups, minority cultures)*, arts and crafts *(textiles, pottery, painting, sculpture)*, language *(learning or practice)*, gastronomy *(wine tasting, food sampling, cookery courses)*, industry and commerce *(factory visits, mines, breweries and distilleries, canal trips)*, modern popular culture *(pop music, shopping, fashion, media, design, technology)*, special interest activities *(painting, photography, weaving)*".

Another classification of cultural tourism activities is expressed as cultural resources by Swarbrooke (1999). According to Swarbrooke, cultural tourism resources are as follows: "Sites associated with historic events and famous people, modern popular culture *(film locations, TV locations)*, traditional food and drinks, themed trails and itineraries, special interest holidays, sport and leisure activities *(participant, spectator, traditional games and sports)*, traditional crafts, arts *(theatres, art galleries)*, types of architecture, language *(indigenous dominant language, minority and regional languages, language schools)*, religious sites *(shrines, churches, cathedrals)*, industry and commerce *(workplace visits, farm attractions, famous shops, markets, leisure shopping complexes)*, festivals and special events *(folklore, performing arts, sporting, special interest)*, heritage attractions *(museums and heritage centers, castles, stately homes and ancient monuments, historic gardens, historic landscape, historic villages, and townscapes)*" (p. 307).

Cultural tourism types, activities, and resources have become the main reasons, even the purpose of travel. Cultural travelers set out with the desire to learn something new and to have experiences that will enrich their lives along the way. Thus, meeting and mingling with different cultural elements open new horizons for the traveler's feelings and thoughts (Dedehayır, 2012). Individuals participate in cultural tourism activities to receive education on various subjects and to have different cultural experiences. In addition, some individuals are involved in cultural tourism activities between business trips and holidays (Lohmann ve Mundt, 2002, p. 219). As can be seen, cultural tourism offers its participants great opportunities for seasonal expansion and diversification of products, ranging from entertainment (such as music or film festivals) to educational entertainment (such as exhibitions and events) and education (such as language courses) (Vos et al., 2008, p. 220).

Of course, the profiles of tourists engaged in so many different types of cultural tourism, activities, and causes are likely to be quite different in many ways (Smith, 2003, p. 31). According to Silberberg (1995, p. 363), cultural tourists consist of individuals with the following characteristics: Those who earn more than other tourists and spend more money during their travels, spend more time in that region during their travels, prefer hotels and motels more, have a higher probability of shopping, have a higher level of education, are more women than men, and are more advanced in age than other tourists. The classification made by McKercher and Du Cros (2012, p. 39), for the characteristics of cultural tourists is as follows:

- The Purposeful Cultural Tourist: This group is related to cultural tourism, and they travel for cultural tourism and seek a deep cultural tourism experience.
- The Sightseeing Cultural Tourist: These tourists travel for cultural tourism purposes but have a shallow experience.
- The Serendipitous Cultural Tourist: These tourists are those who do not travel for cultural reasons but have a deep cultural tourism experience after participating.
- The Casual Cultural Tourist: For these tourists, cultural tourism is a weak reason for travel, and the resulting experience at the end of the trip is shallow.
- The Incidental Cultural Tourist: These tourists do not travel for cultural reasons but still get experiences by participating in some activities.

Cultural tourists interact with cultural tourism activities in different ways, and they can all exist simultaneously. The mixes and interactions of tourist types vary according to various aspects of cultural tourism, travel planning, motivations, tastes, preferences, and experiences of tourists (Wall, & Mathieson, 2006, pp. 267-269). As can be seen, cultural tourists act under the influence of different elements and different motivation levels.

Cultural tourism is a developing and beneficial type of tourism (Hughes, 2002, p. 172). It arouses excitement and attracts more and more interest in cultural tourists. The development of this type of tourism provides economic benefits and creates employment opportunities for societies with unique cultural, historical, and natural resources. Cultural tourism does not only provide economic benefits when applied with the right strategy, but also is an empowering tool in terms of cultural and social values (Dogget, 1993). Cultural tourism is the oldest of the new tourism phenomena. People have been traveling for cultural tourism reasons since the Romans. But they had never been recognized as a separate group of travelers before. Visiting historical sites, cultural sites, attending special events and festivals, or visiting museums has always been a part of tourism experiences. In this sense, it is possible to state that all travels of individuals contain a cultural element (McKercher, & Du Cros, 2012, p. 1).

Individuals have participated in cultural tourism activities in a planned or unplanned way since ancient times. Cultural tourism activities are a significant part of the tourism industry today. In this respect, cultural tourism enterprises should establish strategic communication with their target audiences and direct them to cultural tourism activities. In this regard, cultural tourism companies must use social media to communicate and interact with their target audience. Social media tools are significant for cultural tourists to convey their experiences and views to cultural tourism companies and other people. In addition, these tools have essential features and advantages for tourism companies to market their products and services to their target audiences and learn their feelings and thoughts about themselves.

SOCIAL MEDIA AND CULTURAL TOURISM: A CONCEPTUAL OVERVIEW

The emergence of social media platforms has been an important development for the marketing approach. Businesses perform social media marketing thanks to these platforms. Through social media platforms, businesses interact with their consumers and have the opportunity to listen to them. Thus, it has created an advantage for businesses to discover new ways of interacting with their customers (Smith, & Zook, 2011, p. 4). Social media platforms emphasize collectivity rather than individuality. On these platforms, users come together and start talking among themselves about various topics. Accordingly, a business should use social media platforms for marketing purposes to communicate effectively with social media users and online communities about its products and services. Social media marketing involves listening to communities and engaging with them as representatives of the company (Weinberg, 2009, p. 3). Moreover, social media marketing is a form of digital marketing that consists of any effort made on behalf of the use of social media platforms such as Facebook, Instagram, and Twitter to promote a business and increase web traffic and leads. Businesses should be in social media environments that create an advantage for them in line with their goals, target audiences, wishes, and needs (Schaffner, 2019). Social media marketing is an effective powerhouse for businesses to promote their websites, products, or services through online social channels. On the other hand, social media platforms offer businesses the ability to communicate with a large community that cannot be reached through traditional media channels in terms of online reputation management (Weinberg, 2009, p. 4). Businesses use social media marketing to create new product designs together with customers, listen to the market and observe customer impressions, connect and maintain a constant dialogue with vendors and partners in their value chains. However, businesses aim to interact with their customers and serve their customers through social media platforms by using social networks as advertising and messaging platforms (Nair, 2011, p. 47).

Social media platforms are a force for businesses to communicate with consumers and raise awareness. These sites inherently connect people with similar backgrounds and interests, hub pages dedicated to products and services are often invoked either by fans or by marketers/businesses out a desire to create strong associations between individuals and products (Weinberg, 2009, p. 149). Many businesses operating in the good and service sector interact with their consumers through social media platforms and manage these platforms in line with various strategies. Tourism is one of these sectors.

Due to the increasing popularity of Web 2.0 applications and social networks, many tourism businesses such as hotels, airlines, travel agencies have adopted the internet as a part of their marketing and communication strategies. Thus, internet technologies have become an important tool for the tourism industry (Buhalis, & Law, 2008, p. 611). Nowadays, it has become almost impossible to think of a tourism marketing effort without the internet. The trend in internet usage in the last five years provides more opportunities for user-based content production, especially thanks to social media platforms. In this direction, although most of the tourism businesses now have social network accounts such as Facebook, Twitter, YouTube, and TripAdvisor, they maintain their existence in digital media with many social media platforms such as blogs, forums, and wikis. Thanks to social media platforms, tourists can exchange their ideas with other users about tourism businesses, cultural destinations, accommodation, restaurants, and hotels. Thus, tourists can benefit from social media platforms to a great extent when they decide on their touristic activities (Parker, 2012, p. 1).

Social media platforms are influential in the travel experience of tourists in three contexts. The first is pre-experience based on other people's travel stories before traveling. The second is the experience during travel or stay shared in real-time. The third is to share post-experience comments, evaluations, and feelings. These issues form the foundation on which the specialized Travel 2.0 tourism websites (TripAdvisor, WAYN, Tripwolf, Travelblog, Trivago, etc.) build on their success. In particular, social networks, which can be interpreted as the beginning of a new trend in some countries and seen as a new phenomenon, are used more in travel and tourism (Milano et al., 2011). In this context, one of the most important roles of social media is to encourage users and travelers to post and share their travel experiences, reviews, and opinions by enabling them to serve as a source of information for others. Because digital technologies have contributed to fundamental changes in the tourism industry and provide a better understanding of the travel decision-making process, tourist behavior during vacation and post-holiday activities. Accordingly, social media marketing mostly focuses on improving relations in social media and adapting to the needs of tourists. Social media platforms are also considered as one of the important competitive tools in terms of tourism marketing. Tourism businesses should engage tourists with integrated multi-channel communication and encourage them to talk about good experiences and give advice to other users. Accordingly, real-time interaction with travelers on social media platforms has huge implications for the travel industry (Živković et al., 2014, pp. 760-761).

Social media platforms continue to affect the tourism industry socially and economically. These platforms fundamentally change the way tourists search, find, read and trust, and also generate information about tourism destinations. Social media platforms are influencing the marketing and promotion processes in the tourism industry and offer new ways for tourism organizations to restructure and implement new business models and operations such as service development, marketing, networking and knowledge management (Zeng, & Gerritsen, 2014, p. 33). In this respect, social media and social networking environments provide businesses and brands with opportunities such as providing access to the target market, branding, developing relationships, improving business processes, getting higher in search engine rankings, selling when the opportunity arises, and reducing advertising costs (Zimmerman, & Sahlin, 2010, pp: 15-21), seems to offer especially economic opportunities for tourism companies.

With benefits for both businesses and users, social media platforms have facilitated access to communities and networks that would otherwise be nearly impossible to find and join. There is mutual interaction of users on these platforms. In this context, they make it easier for businesses to interact with their consumers. Moreover, thanks to these platforms, businesses can learn what their consumers are thinking and talking about (Linden, & Linden, 2017, p. 188). In this respect, sharing tourism-related content on social media platforms contributes significantly to touristic destinations and values. The use of mass media is very important in the realization of promotional activities for tourism. Social media has become one of the most effective mass media tools of recent times. People share photos and videos of the places they travel to through social media platforms. On these platforms that offer interaction, users can easily recognize touristic areas (Çakmak, & Altaş, 2018, p. 402).

Social media platforms offer ample opportunities to the tourism industry and businesses and individuals who participate or have the thought of participating in tourism activities in terms of influencing tourism activities. In this respect, it is important for businesses operating in the tourism industry to use these platforms with a wide variety of content to benefit from the wide possibilities of social media platforms. Businesses need to constantly update their social media accounts in terms of their structural features. This is important in terms of responding to the wishes and needs of the consumer. It is a requirement for tourism businesses to give timely feedback to social media platforms, taking into account the positive and negative comments made by the followers. In this way, customers and businesses, who are important elements in the tourism industry, will have access to the desired, successful tourism events and their benefits (Aktan, & Koçyiğit, 2016, p. 70).

In terms of the relationship between social media and tourism, all of the above mentioned also apply to cultural tourism. Individuals can reach all activities included in cultural tourism through social media tools. There is a two-way situation here. While cultural tourism companies reach their target audiences with social media, cultural tourists also get information about cultural tourism activities and make decisions through social media. In this sense, it is understood that more attention has been drawn to the concept of cultural tourism with social media. Social media has led to the revival of cultural tourism and, accordingly, to the use of these platforms by cultural tourism companies for marketing purposes (Ülgen, 2020, pp. 75-76).

Culture and tourism have always been inextricably linked. Cultural sites, attractions and events provide an important motivation for travel, and travel itself creates culture. However, in recent years, the link between culture and tourism has been more clearly defined as cultural tourism as a specific form of consumption (Richards, 2018, p. 12). In this respect, looking at the OECD report on the link between culture and tourism in terms of marketing cultural tourism, tourism and culture were considered separate aspects of destinations for most of the 20th century. Cultural resources were largely seen as part of the cultural heritage of destinations, forming the basis for the education of local populations and local or national cultural identities. On the other hand, tourism was largely regarded as a leisure-related activity separate from daily life and the culture of local people. This understanding changed towards the end of the 20th century. Because the role of cultural assets in attracting tourists and distinguishing differences has become more apparent. In particular, from the 1980s, cultural tourism began to be seen as the main source of economic development for many destinations (OECD, 2009, p. 19). For example, according to the European Union, cultural tourism is an important tool of economic and social development in Europe. In this context, cultural consumption has grown and cultural tourism has become an increasingly important form of cultural consumption, financed by the local, national and international levels. Therefore, the cultural tourism market in Europe has become increasingly competitive (Mikaeili, & Aytuğ, 2019, p. 115). In addition, developed countries have diversified tourism in order to maximize its contribution to the country's economy by spreading tourism to twelve months of the year, and one of the most prominent of these tourism types is cultural tourism (Bakır, & Çelik, 2020, p. 325).

Advances in the internet and social media have deeply affected the communication and marketing understanding of the cultural tourism sector. Today's cultural tourism operators are faced with a wide variety of media with rich content and travelers with a high level of interaction. In this environment, social media provides clear credentials for organizations and allows consumers to tell their side of the story with the possibility of posting online reviews about a particular product/service. Social networking sites offer innovative ways to develop customer relationship management strategies and engagement that can directly impact the company's credibility, influence, reputation and word of mouth advertising. In this regard, social media will continue to be an important force guiding conversations on digital platforms in cultural tourism in the foreseeable future. Social media offers cultural tourism operators the opportunity to conduct investigations to determine the reactions, behaviors and interactions of tourists. This opportunity also offers opportunities to identify the dynamics that affect individuals and groups involved in cultural tourism. Because the emergence and rapid development of social networks and social media environments has made the communication between cultural tourism companies and cultural tourists a two-way interactive. Therefore, the use of social media by these two parties has begun to directly affect many aspects of the industry. The power of the tourist in social media influences the cultural tourism market (Munar, & Jacobsen, 2014; Inversini et al., 2015; Richards, 2018; Liu et al., 2021).

Social media, which facilitates interaction between those interested in cultural tourism, is an important component of this sector. In this context, social media has an increasing importance in the field of cultural tourism. So much so that these environments have become primary sources of information in the field of cultural tourism. Therefore, in such an environment, it is impossible for those interested in the marketing of cultural tourism to remain indifferent to the importance of social media. On the subject, it is argued that there is important evidence that individuals frequently use the internet and social media to be aware of cultural activities. At the point of participating in cultural tourism activities, the use of social media by individuals may vary. Individuals benefit from social media at different stages and in different ways, including before, during and after the activity. Before deciding on cultural tourism activities, individuals pay attention to the sharing of information, videos, photos and comments in these environments. In this sense, social media platforms are important for users to make decisions regarding cultural tourism activities. Individuals make great use of social media for research, discovery, planning and finally sharing (Xiang, & Gretzel, 2010; Timothy, 2011, Samoladas et al., 2016, p. 169; Amaro, & Duarte, 2017; Li et al., 2019).

It is known that the changes in the field of communication and marketing have a direct impact on the cultural tourism sector. From this point of view, it is a necessity for businesses operating in the cultural tourism sector to adapt to current conditions in today's world where digital developments and changes are experienced. In this respect, outdated communication models should be left in the past and new ones should be adopted instead. It is now almost impossible for cultural tourists not to share their experiences on social media. In this respect, it is quite possible to comment on any cultural tourism business (whether this business is in social media or not). Of course, the mere presence of cultural tourism businesses in social media environments is not a sufficient condition in terms of benefiting them. The important thing is that they can exist in these environments with a successful strategy in the long run (Kyriakou, 2016, pp. 480-481).

The fact that social media has an important role in the decision-making process of the consumer in the field of cultural tourism, as in many areas, provides cultural tourism enterprises with the opportunity to reach more target audiences at lower costs with the use of the right strategy. It is argued that cultural tourists are greatly influenced by the information and interactions on social media platforms in their purchasing activities related to cultural tourism. Therefore, communicators and marketers in the field have to know how to use social media tools effectively in order to influence their target audiences. In this respect, cultural tourism marketers can facilitate the information flow process through social media, and this influence makes a significant contribution to their marketing and sales efforts. Since individuals use social media platforms for many reasons such as obtaining information, purchasing, influencing, sharing their travel experiences, cultural tourism marketers should use these media in a planned manner in order to achieve corporate goals. Because the sharing of content that appeals to the market on platforms such as Twitter, Facebook, Instagram and YouTube about cultural tourism encourages individuals to cultural tourism. These environments provide important data to companies in order to reveal the potential of cultural tourists, who are consumers of cultural tourism (Icoz et al., 2018; Kalvet et al., 2020; Mele et al., 2021).

Cultural tourism is a huge opportunity and a growing trend. At least 40% of all tourists worldwide are considered cultural tourists. In this context, judging by the evaluation of generations within the scope of cultural tourism, initially, the interest of the baby boom generation in cultural tourism was quite high. This generation often traveled in groups, preferring to visit important cultural and tourist attractions such as museums and monuments. This generation has contributed to the growth and strengthening of cultural tourism. Generations Y and Generation Z, who are the next generations after them, are driven by demands that appeal to a more popular and everyday culture that is more original, unique, small-scale, and based on personal experiences. These generations like to create their way of traveling to a place and prefer to travel on their own. It can be said that cultural tourists are well-educated and have a command of technology in terms of personal characteristics. In terms of demographic characteristics, although cultural tourists still mostly consist of retirees, it is seen that the rate of young people has increased recently (CBI Ministry of Foreign Affairs, 2021). Cultural tourism companies should definitely benefit from social media environments, especially in attracting young people's attention to cultural tourism. Social media has become an integral part of life for this segment and is a very valuable source of information for them. In this respect, social media environments offer insights into their needs, as well as inspiration and suggestions on how to transform standardized services into personalized experiences (Kowalczyk-Anioł, & Nowacki, 2020).

Young tourists, who are likely to be better educated and more frequent travelers, are an important demographic segment of the cultural tourism industry (McDonnell, & Burton, 2005, p. 19). It is seen that the presence of young people in cultural tourism has increased. In addition, according to Digital 2021 age-related social media usage statistics, it was determined that the highest age percentages were between 18-24, 25-34, and 35-44 (We are Social, 2021). All this information reveals the necessity of tourism businesses to give importance to cultural tourism marketing focused on the young generation in social media. As this generation grows with fast and direct access to information provided by digital technology, these usage patterns will continue to affect how tourism services are delivered. Because young people refer to online resources such as websites and social media rather than offline resources at the stage of determining their tourism activities (OECD, 2020, p. 62). However, in a study conducted, individuals between the ages of 25-38 see the internet and social networks as an important source of information about cultural tourism and a travel motivation tool (Koçyiğit, 2016, p. 25).

According to the Digital 2021 report, the continuous increase in the percentages of social media usage rates of world citizens from 2016 to 2021 (We are Social, 2021) makes it necessary for tourism companies to use these platforms in their marketing policies. Regarding the subject, Van Gorp (2012), states that, in general, tourists use tools such as travel agencies, brochures, guidebooks for the trips they plan to make, but they also use the internet and social media today (p. 3). It is seen that the popularity of social media platforms among tourism consumers continues to increase. In this direction, tourism businesses should not ignore the increasing popularity of social media and the role of travelers in the travel planning process. (Leung et al., 2013, p. 18). In this respect, cultural tourism businesses need to exist with an effective communication strategy on social media platforms. In today's competitive conditions, this has become a necessity regardless of any characteristic of the target audience. Social media platforms, which are also an important travel motivation tool in terms of cultural tourism, seem to be an impressive source of information. In this direction, it can be said that thanks to these features of social media platforms, which are an important tool in terms of destination awareness intercultural interaction and societies get to know each other more closely. In terms of the relationship between social media and cultural tourism, it is seen that both concepts have inclusive features today (in the digital age). In addition, it can be said that social media is seen as an important tool that helps to increase the attractiveness of cultural tourism.

FUTURE RESEARCH DIRECTIONS

It is recommended that researchers who will conduct future studies on social media and cultural tourism conduct qualitative or quantitative research to reveal the thoughts of followers regarding the marketing of products and services of any cultural tourism business(s) through social media.

CONCLUSION

Cultural tourism activities, which have existed since ancient times, are considered as an area of activity in which the tourism industry should act strategically, with the effect of the digital age. Social media platforms are one of the important factors for the development of this field of activity in the context of communication and marketing. In particular, the fact that cultural tourists generally consist of educated, sophisticated individuals and are good at using technology, in addition to the fact that there is an increase in the use of social media by world citizens' day by day, shows that social media environments are effective in the decision-making of individuals for cultural tourism activities. It is no longer possible for cultural tourism businesses to remain indifferent to these factors. In this context, it is important for cultural tourism businesses take part in social media and social networking platforms and to manage their processes strategically to both learn the emotions and thoughts of consumers in the virtual environment and guide their policies by measuring the pulse of the sector.

Cultural tourists have different purposes and motivations than other types of tourists. For example, the fact that cultural tourism can be done in all seasons of the year without fitting into a narrow framework like sea tourism is a very important advantage for it cultural tourism. The presence of cultural tourism with rich content such as cultural heritage, thematic routes, cities, ethnicities, events, religions and creative activities can be an advantage for businesses operating in the tourism sector. In this respect, cultural tourism businesses should use both traditional media and social media in combination for their target audiences in order to gain a competitive advantage in a challenging competitive environment. Therefore, it can be stated that social media is a little more important than traditional media in order to allow two-way communication and interaction. On the other hand, tourism businesses should use the pluralism and reciprocity qualities of social media platforms to serve their business purposes. Successfully applying this pluralism and reciprocity strategy to a well-defined target audience segmentation in line with company objectives can make individuals volunteer ambassadors of the business.

As a result, although the target audience of cultural tourism still consists of middle-aged and older people, the introduction of technology into the lives of individuals more and more, the emergence of virtual assistants, and the increase in the use of social media platforms have brought some changes. One of these changes is the increased interest in culture, art, and festivals. Individuals participate in cultural tourism activities whenever they find time and financial means and use social media platforms as an important source of cultural information. Recently, the increase in the interest of the young generation in cultural tourism has revealed the necessity for businesses operating in the tourism sector to maintain a successful communication and marketing policy on digital platforms. Therefore, it is important for all types of tourism that all generations use digital communication tools intensively. Because, social media platforms, which have become the most important information source and travel motivation tool of individuals, should be used as a very effective tool by tourism businesses. In this direction, it has become a necessity to benefit from the advantages of social media platforms. On the other hand, social media platforms have a great role in shaping the perceptions of tourists and travelers towards cultural tourism destinations and increasing the attractiveness of these destinations. As a result of the conceptual evaluation of social media and cultural tourism, the positive effect of social media on cultural tourism cannot be denied. In this direction, it is important for future studies to emphasize the quantitative and qualitative relationship between both concepts.

ACKNOWLEDGMENT

No financial support has been received for this study.

REFERENCES

Aktan, E., & Koçyiğit, M. (2016). Sosyal medyanın turizm faaliyetlerindeki rolü üzerine teorik bir inceleme. *Dumlupınar Üniversitesi Sosyal Bilimler Dergisi*, (Special Issue), 62–73.

Amaro, S., & Duarte, P. (2017). Social media use for travel purposes: A cross cultural comparison between Portugal and the UK. *Information Technology & Tourism*, *17*(2), 161–181. doi:10.100740558-017-0074-7

Bakır, Z. N., & Çelik, H. C. (2020). Kitle ve kültür turizmi bağlamında JollyTur ve EtsTur seyahat acentelerine ait internet reklamlarının içerik analizi. *Akdeniz Üniversitesi İletişim Fakültesi Dergisi*, (33), 318–337. doi:10.31123/akil.695931

Boniface, P. (2003). *Managing quality cultural tourism*. Routledge.

Brown, R. (2009). *Public relations and the social web how to use social media and web 2.0 in communications*. Kogan Page Publishers.

Buhalis, D., & Law, R. (2008). Progress in information technology and tourism management: 20 years on and 10 years after the Internet—The state of eTourism research. *Tourism Management*, *29*(4), 609–623. doi:10.1016/j.tourman.2008.01.005

Çakmak, V., & Altaş, A. (2018). Sosyal medya etkileşiminde tren yolculukları: Doğu Ekspresi ile ilgili YouTube paylaşım videolarının analizi. *Journal of Tourism and Gastronomy Studies*, *6*(1), 390–408.

CBI Ministry of Foreign Affairs. (2021). Retrieved from https://www.cbi.eu/market-information/tourism/cultural-tourism/market-potential

Cole, S. (2008). *Tourism, culture and development: Hopes, dreams and realities in East Indonesia*. Channel View Publications.

ConnectSafely. (2021). *Parent's guide to Instagram*. Retrieved from https://www.connectsafely.org/instagram/

Csapó, J. (2012). The role and importance of cultural tourism in modern tourism industry. In M. Kasimoğlu & H. Aydın (Eds.), *Strategies for tourism industry – micro and macro perspectives* (pp. 201–232). InTech. doi:10.5772/38693

Dedehayır, H. (2012). *Sürdürülebilir kültür turizmi. Çevre ve Kültür Değerlerini Koruma ve Tanıtma Vakfı*. Retrieved from https://www.cekulvakfi.org.tr/makale/surdurulebilir-kultur-turizmi

Dogget, L. (1993). Multi-cultural tourism development offers a new dimension in travel. *Business America*, *114*(18), 8–10.

Drury, G. (2008). Opinion piece: Social media: Should marketers engage and how can it be done effectively? *Journal of Direct, Data and Digital Marketing Practice, 9*(3), 274–277. doi:10.1057/palgrave.dddmp.4350096

Evans, D. (2008). *Social media marketing: An hour a day.* Wiley Publishing.

Getz, D., & Wicks, B. (1993). Editorial. *International Journal of Festival Management and Event Tourism, 1*(1), 1–3. PMID:12287128

Goeldner, C. R., & Ritchie, J. R. B. (2003). *Tourism principles, practices, philosophies.* John Wiley & Sons.

Hausmann, A. (2007). Cultural tourism: Marketing challenges and opportunities for German cultural heritage. *International Journal of Heritage Studies, 13*(2), 170–184. doi:10.1080/13527250601121351

Hughes, H. L. (2002). Culture and tourism: A framework for further analysis. *Managing Leisure, 7*(3), 164–175. doi:10.1080/13606710022000013701

Icoz, O., Kutuk, A., & Icoz, O. (2018). Social media and consumer buying decisions in tourism: The case of Turkey. *Pasos Revista de Turismo y Patrimonio Cultural, 16*(4), 1051–1066. doi:10.25145/j.pasos.2018.16.073

Inversini, A., Xiang, Z., & Fesenmaier, D. R. (2015). New media in travel and tourism communication: Toward a new paradigm. In L. Cantoni & J. A. Danowski (Eds.), *Communication and Technology* (pp. 497–512). De Gruyter. doi:10.1515/9783110271355-029

Kalvet, T., Olesk, M., Tiits, M., & Raun, J. (2020). Innovative tools for tourism and cultural tourism impact assessment. *Sustainability, 12*(18), 7470. doi:10.3390u12187470

Kaplan, A. M., & Haenlein, M. (2010). Users of the world, unite! The challenges and opportunities of social media. *Business Horizons, 53*(1), 59–68. doi:10.1016/j.bushor.2009.09.003

Koçyiğit, M. (2016). The role of religious tourism in creating destination image: The case of Konya Museum. *International Journal of Religious Tourism and Pilgrimage, 4*(7), 21–30.

Koçyiğit, M. (2017). *Dijital halkla ilişkiler ve online kurumsal itibar yönetimi.* Eğitim Yayınevi.

Komito, L., & Bates, J. (2009). Virtually local: Social media and community among Polish nationals in Dublin. *Aslib Proceedings: New Information Perspective, 61*(3), 232–244. doi:10.1108/00012530910959790

Kowalczyk-Anioł, J., & Nowacki, M. (2020). Factors influencing Generation Y's tourism-related social media activity: The case of Polish students. *Journal of Hospitality and Tourism Technology, 11*(3), 543–558. doi:10.1108/JHTT-03-2019-0049

Kyriakou, D., Belias, D., Vassiliadis, L., Koustelios, A., Bregkou, M., & Varsanis, K. (2016). Social media and tourism: A digital investment for Thessaly? In V. Katsoni & A. Stratigea (Eds.), *Tourism and culture in the age of innovation* (pp. 471–483). Springer. doi:10.1007/978-3-319-27528-4_32

Leung, D., Law, R., Van Hoof, H., & Buhalis, D. (2013). Social media in tourism and hospitality: A literature review. *Journal of Travel & Tourism Marketing, 30*(1-2), 3–22. doi:10.1080/10548408.2013.750919

Li, C., Guo, S., Wang, C., & Zhang, J. (2019). Veni, vidi, vici: The impact of social media on virtual acculturation in tourism context. *Technological Forecasting and Social Change, 145*, 513–522. doi:10.1016/j. techfore.2019.01.013

Linden, H., & Linden, S. (2017). *Fans and fan cultures: Tourism, consumerism and social media.* Palgrave Macmillan. doi:10.1057/978-1-137-50129-5

Lindqvist, J., Cranshaw, J., Wiese, J., Hong, J., & Zimmerman, J. (2011). I'm the mayor of my house: Examining why people use Foursquare - a social-driven location sharing application. *Proceedings of the SIGCHI conference on human factors in computing systems*, 2409-2418. 10.1145/1978942.1979295

Liu, Y., Zhang, R., & Yao, Y. (2021). How tourist power in social media affects tourism market regulation after unethical incidents: Evidence from China. *Annals of Tourism Research, 91*, 103296. doi:10.1016/j. annals.2021.103296

Lohmann, M., & Mundt, J. W. (2002). Maturing markets for cultural tourism: Germany and the demand for the 'cultural' destination. In R. Voase (Ed.), *Tourism in western Europe a collection of case histories* (pp. 213–225). CABI Publishing. doi:10.1079/9780851995724.0213

Macarthy, A. (2015). *500 Social media marketing tips: Essential advice, hints and strategy for business: Facebook, Twitter, Pinterest, Google+, YouTube, Instagram, LinkedIn, and More.* Academic Press.

Mayfield, A. (2008). *What is social media. iCrossing e-book.* Retrieved from https://icrossing.co.uk/ ideas/fileadmin/uploads/ebooks/what_is_social_media_icrossing_ebook.pdf

McDonnell, I., & Burton, C. (2005). The marketing of Australian cultural tourist attractions: A case study from Sydney. In M. Sigala & D. Leslie (Eds.), *International cultural tourism: Management, implications and cases* (pp. 16–25). Elsevier. doi:10.1016/B978-0-7506-6312-0.50005-4

McKercher, B., & Du Cros, H. (2012). *Cultural tourism: The partnership between tourism and cultural heritage management.* Routledge. doi:10.4324/9780203479537

McLennan, A., & Howell, G. V. J. (2010). Social networks and the challenge for public relations. *Asia Pacific Public Relations Journal, 11*(1), 11–19.

Mele, E., Kerkhof, P., & Cantoni, L. (2021). Analyzing cultural tourism promotion on Instagram: A cross-cultural perspective. *Journal of Travel & Tourism Marketing, 38*(3), 326–340. doi:10.1080/1054 8408.2021.1906382

Miguéns, J., Baggio, R., & Costa, C. (2008). Social media and tourism destinations: TripAdvisor case study. *Advances in Tourism Research, 26*(28), 1–6.

Mikaeili, M., & Aytuğ, H. K. (2019). Evaluation of Iran's cultural tourism potential from the European Union perspective: Jolfa Region. In *Cultural sustainable tourism* (pp. 115–130). Springer. doi:10.1007/978-3-030-10804-5_12

Milano, R., Baggio, R., & Piattelli, R. (2011). *The effects of online social media on tourism websites.* 18th International Conference on Information, Technology and Travel & Tourism, Innsbruck, Austria. 10.1007/978-3-7091-0503-0_38

Morris, T. (2010). *All a Twitter: A personal and professional guide to social networking with Twitter.* Que Publishing.

Munar, A. M., & Jacobsen, J. K. S. (2014). Motivations for sharing tourism experiences through social media. *Tourism Management, 43,* 46–54. doi:10.1016/j.tourman.2014.01.012

Nagy, K. (2012). Heritage tourism, thematic routes and possibilities for innovation. *Club of Economics in Miskolc, 8*(1), 46–53.

Nair, M. (2011). Understanding and measuring the value of social media. *Journal of Corporate Accounting & Finance, 22*(3), 45–51. doi:10.1002/jcaf.20674

Newson, A., Houghton, D., & Patten, J. (2009). *Blogging and other social media: Exploiting the technology and protecting the enterprise.* A Gower Book.

OECD. (2009). *The impact of culture on tourism.* OECD.

OECD. (2020). *OECD Tourism trends and policies 2020.* OECD.

Osborne-Gowey, J. (2014). What is social media. *Fisheries (Bethesda, Md.), 39*(2), 55–55. doi:10.1080/03632415.2014.876883

Parker, R. D. (2012). The evolving dynamics of social media in internet tourism marketing. *Journal of Tourism Research & Hospitality, 1*(1). Advance online publication. doi:10.4172/2324-8807.1000e102

Pavlik, J. (2008). *Mapping the consequences of technology on public relations.* Retrieved from https://instituteforpr.org/mapping-technology-consequences/

Pedersen, A. (2002). *World heritage manuals managing tourism at world heritage sites: A practical manual for world heritage site managers.* UNESCO World Heritage Centre.

Quesenberry, K. A. (2019). *Social media strategy: Marketing, advertising, and public relations in the consumer revolution.* Rowman & Littlefield Publishers.

Richards, G. (2018). Cultural tourism: A review of recent research and trends. *Journal of Hospitality and Tourism Management, 36,* 12–21. doi:10.1016/j.jhtm.2018.03.005

Richards, G., & Bonink, C. (1995). Marketing cultural tourism in Europe. *Journal of Vacation Marketing, 1*(2), 172–180. doi:10.1177/135676679500100205

Rinschede, G. (1992). Forms of religious tourism. *Annals of Tourism Research, 19*(1), 51–67. doi:10.1016/0160-7383(92)90106-Y

Safko, L. (2012). *The social media bible: Tactics, tools & strategies for business success.* John Wiley & Sons.

Safko, L., & Brake, D. K. (2009). *The social media bible: Tactics, tools, and strategies for business success.* John Wiley & Sons, Inc.

Samoladas, I., Zilianakis, C., Lazaridou, K., Papadopoulou, K., Tsolaki, E., & Nerantzaki, D. M. (2016). Citizen perspectives on the development of local cultural resources: The case of the municipality of serres. In V. Katsoni & A. Stratigea (Eds.), *Tourism and culture in the age of innovation* (pp. 157–170). Springer. doi:10.1007/978-3-319-27528-4_11

Schaffner, A. (2019). *Social media marketing workbook 2019: How to leverage the power of Facebook advertising, Instagram marketing, YouTube and SEO to explode your business and personal brand.* Independently Published.

Seitel, F. P. (2016). *Halkla ilişkiler uygulaması* (S. Mengü, Trans.). Nobel Akademik Yayıncılık.

Silberberg, T. (1995). Cultural tourism and business opportunities for museums and heritage sites. *Tourism Management, 16*(5), 361–365. doi:10.1016/0261-5177(95)00039-Q

Smith, M. K. (2003). *Issues in cultural tourism studies.* Routledge. doi:10.4324/9780203402825

Smith, P. R., & Zook, Z. (2011). *Marketing communications integrating offline and online with social media.* Kogan Page.

Smith, V. L. (1989). *Hosts and guests: The anthropology of tourism.* University of Pennsylvania Press. doi:10.9783/9780812208016

Solis, B. (2010). *Engage: The complete guide for brands and businesses to build, cultivate, and measure success in the new web.* John Wiley & Sons.

Swarbrooke, J. (1999). *Sustainable Tourism Management.* CABI Publishing.

Timothy, D. J. (2011). *Cultural heritage and tourism: An introduction.* Channel View Publications. doi:10.21832/9781845411787

Tripadvisor. (2017). Retrieved from https://tripadvisor.mediaroom.com/tr-about-us

Ülgen, Y. (2020). *Sosyal medyadaki yeni kanaat önderlerinin kültür turizmi alanında tüketici karar verme sürecine etkisi: Instagram üzerine bir inceleme* (Master's dissertation). İstanbul Üniversitesi.

UNESCO. (2006). *Towards Sustainable Strategies for Creative Tourism: Discussion Report of the Planning Meeting for 2008, International Conference on Creative Tourism.* Retrieved from https://unesdoc.unesco.org/images/0015/001598/159811e.pdf

Van Gorp, B. (2012). Guidebooks and the representation of 'other' places. In M. Kasimoğlu & H. Aydin (Eds.), *Strategies for tourism industry – micro and macro perspectives* (pp. 3–32). InTech.

Vos, K., Rulle, M., & Jansen-Verbeke, M. (2008). Cultural heritage and the rejuvenation of spa towns. Evidence from four European cities. In M. Jansen-Verbeke, G. K. Priestley, & A. P. Russo (Eds.), *Cultural resources for tourism: Patterns, processes, policies* (pp. 215–230). Nova Science Publishers.

Wall, G., & Mathieson, A. (2006). *Tourism: Change, impacts, and opportunities.* Pearson Education.

Wang, Z. X., & Pei, L. (2014). A systems thinking-based grey model for sustainability evaluation of urban tourism. *Kybernetes, 43*(3/4), 462–479. doi:10.1108/K-07-2013-0137

We are Social Digital. (2021). Retrieved from https://wearesocial.com/digital-2021

Weinberg, T. (2009). *The new community rules: Marketing on the social web*. O'Reilly Media.

Xiang, Z., & Gretzel, U. (2010). Role of social media in online travel information search. *Tourism Management*, *31*(2), 179–188. doi:10.1016/j.tourman.2009.02.016

Zeng, B., & Gerritsen, R. (2014). What do we know about social media in tourism? A review. *Tourism Management Perspectives*, *10*, 27–36. doi:10.1016/j.tmp.2014.01.001

Zimmerman, J., & Sahlin, D. (2010). *Social media marketing all-in-one for dummies*. Wiley Publishing. doi:10.1002/9781118257661

Živković, R., Gajić, J., & Brdar, I. (2014). The impact of social media on tourism. *Sinteza*, 758-761.

ADDITIONAL READING

Aktan, E., & Koçyiğit, M. (2016). Sosyal medyanın turizm faaliyetlerindeki rolü üzerine teorik bir inceleme. *Dumlupınar Üniversitesi Sosyal Bilimler Dergisi*, (Special Issue), 62–73.

Evans, D. (2008). *Social media marketing: An hour a day*. Wiley Publishing.

Goeldner, C. R., & Ritchie, J. R. B. (2003). *Tourism principles, practices, philosophies*. John Wiley & Sons.

Hughes, H. L. (2002). Culture and tourism: A framework for further analysis. *Managing. Leisure (Waterloo, Ont.)*, *7*(3), 164–175.

Koçyiğit, M. (2016). The role of religious tourism in creating destination image: The case of Konya Museum. *International Journal of Religious Tourism and Pilgrimage*, *4*(7), 21–30.

Linden, H., & Linden, S. (2017). *Fans and fan cultures: Tourism, consumerism and social media*. Palgrave Macmillan. doi:10.1057/978-1-137-50129-5

McKercher, B., & Du Cros, H. (2012). *Cultural tourism: The partnership between tourism and cultural heritage management*. Routledge. doi:10.4324/9780203479537

Smith, M. K. (2003). *Issues in cultural tourism studies*. Routledge. doi:10.4324/9780203402825

KEY TERMS AND DEFINITIONS

Cultural Tourism: It is the visits of individuals, motivated to a certain extent, to discover and learn about the historical, artistic, scientific, cultural assets, life, and thinking styles of a society or region.

Culture: It is the whole of material and spiritual values specific to a society.

Intercultural Communication: Intercultural communication, which is one of the popular concepts of recent times with the effect of tourism and many factors, is a field where the similar and different aspects of individuals from different cultures are examined based on communication.

Social Media: It is a communication technology that allows two-way and simultaneous information sharing via Web 2.0.

Social Media Marketing: Brands and businesses can use the features of social media and social networking environments and the shares of their target audiences on this platform for their purposes in the name of marketing policies.

Tourism: It is a field that deals with the temporary travels of individuals and their purchasing activities within the scope of the holiday, entertainment, education, religion, sports, and various activities.

Chapter 21
Social Media Analytics:
Opportunities and Challenges for Cultural Tourism Destinations

Časlav Kalinić

Faculty of Sciences, University of Novi Sad, Serbia

Miroslav D. Vujičić

Faculty of Sciences, University of Novi Sad, Serbia

ABSTRACT

The rise of social media allowed greater people participation online. Platforms such as Facebook, Twitter, Instagram, or TikTok enable visitors to share their thoughts, opinions, photos, locations. All those interactions create a vast amount of data. Social media analytics, as a way of application of big data, can provide excellent insights and create new information for stakeholders involved in the management and development of cultural tourism destinations. This chapter advocates for the employment of the big data concept through social media analytics that can contribute to the management of visitors in cultural tourism destinations. In this chapter, the authors highlight the principles of big data and review the most influential social media platforms – Facebook, Twitter, Instagram, and TikTok. On that basis, they disclose opportunities for the management and marketing of cultural tourism destinations.

INTRODUCTION

The emergence of social media in the first decade of the 21st century created the opportunity for studying socio-economic processes in a new way, especially since it allowed more people to engage in online content co-creation. Opinions, attitudes, ideas, and emotions of a large portion of the world population became publicly available through tracking of their posts, conversations, shopping habits, online movement, etc. The number of social media users is growing together with the availability and growth in numbers of devices that allow internet access, such as personal computers, mobile phones, and tablets. Furthermore, the number of social media and user-generated content continues to grow and impact the travel industry (Browning et al., 2013; Xiang and Gretzel, 2010; Narangajavana Kaosiri et al., 2019). This

DOI: 10.4018/978-1-7998-8528-3.ch021

growth encouraged the development of new approaches to understanding this socio-economic phenomenon in various fields (Wood et al., 2013; George et al., 2014; Batrinca and Treleaven, 2014). The big data concept is one of them, and it allows tourism organizations and destinations to gain new insight into their past, present, and future visitors. Social media analytics, as a field of big data application, offers them new possibilities in formulating marketing strategies, as well as ways of communication with tourists.

With this chapter, we advocate for the employment of a big data concept through social media analytics that can contribute to the management of visitors in cultural tourism destinations. Basic principles of big data are highlighted followed by the review of indicators of analytic capabilities of most influential social media platforms – Facebook, Twitter, Instagram, and TikTok. On that basis, we disclose opportunities and challenges for stakeholders in the cultural tourism destination landscape. The chapter extends the ongoing discussion on the role of big data and social media analytics approach in the domain of tourism management and marketing.

SOCIAL MEDIA

Although there is no single definition of social media, various terms are used to closer define social media, depending on research purpose and perspective. Among them are web 2.0 (Constantinides, Fountain, 2008; Constantinides, 2008), social websites (Akehurst, 2009; Kim et al., 2010), platforms for social communication (Jansen et al., 2009), etc. The additional term that helps define social media is user-generated content (Dhar and Chang, 2009; Dotan and Zaphiris, 2010; O'Connor, 2010). However, most of the authors use the term social media (Kaplan and Haenlein, 2010; Thevenot, 2007; Smith, 2009; Xiang and Gretzel, 2010; Para-Lopez et al., 2011; Mangold and Faulds, 2009; Leung et al., 2013; Jin et al., 2010; Hanna et al., 2011; Cha et al., 2010). Kaplan and Haenlein (2010, 61) are focusing on platform and content and consider social media ''a group of online applications that are based on ideological and technological foundations of web 2.0, and which facilitate creation and exchange of user-generated content''. However, it is a broad term that includes platforms such as social networks, blogs, microblogs, social news, platforms for multimedia sharing, review websites, and others (Gundecha and Liu, 2012; Kaplan and Haenlein, 2010). Social networks are the most widespread subgroup of social media, with Facebook as a typical representative. Boyd and Ellison (2007, p.211) define social network sites as "web-based services that allow individuals to (1) construct a public or semi-public profile within a bounded system, (2) articulate a list of other users with whom they share a connection, and (3) view and traverse their list of connections and those made by others within the system". With the emergence of social media and web 2.0 technologies, communication is not one-way anymore, meaning that users are active participants, generating large amounts of data every day.

There are approximately 4.2 billion users of social media worldwide as of the beginning of 2021, with a significant 13% user base growth during 2020. The social media platform with by far the most active users is Facebook, counting for almost 2.7 billion active users. Other social media that are the focus of this paper, Instagram, Twitter, and TikTok have 1.1 billion, 380 million, and 800 million respectively (Haenlein et al., 2020). People use these platforms to keep up with friends, news, or just as a pastime. Despite the ubiquity of social media platforms, the market potential is still increasing, as not only user figures but also user engagement continues to grow. Users spend one in every three minutes online networking, while the average daily time spent online is also on the rise. The average number of social media accounts per person has also risen from three to more than eight. The major driver of this trend is anytime, anywhere access that smartphones are facilitating, resulting in most people networking via mobile. That trend is even stronger with younger age groups such as Millennials and Gen Z (Haenlein et al., 2020). Smartphone apps, as well as mobile web access, have facilitated the constant presence of mobile-first or mobile-only platforms such as Twitter, Instagram, or TikTok. In addition, they have heightened the profile of location-based services and enabled users to comfortably access visual blogging sites including Tumblr and Pinterest via tablet. Accordingly, mobile has become the first screen, giving a new meaning to the term ''second screening'', which denotes simultaneous use of multiple screens.

Social media platform Twitter has proven especially popular as users can run a direct commentary through live-tweeting and direct short-form discussion. Social media buzz based on online user mentions and interactions is a relevant tool for measuring user engagement before, during, and after a certain event. On the other hand, Instagram, which started as a platform for online photo sharing, follows similar usage patterns as Twitter. It offers excellent social integration, which allows users to share their content on Facebook, Twitter, and other platforms. Similarly, Instagram increasingly propagates video upload as well as live streaming (Kemp, 2021).

When it comes to tourists, there is a widespread opinion that older generations are more likely to be interested in culture and history, and participate in various forms of cultural tourism. Yet, the research suggests that Millennials are taking over the cultural tourism landscape and becoming the dominant cohort in this form of tourism (Kim and Chung, 2019, Tesin et al., 2020). In a generation breakdown of travelers from the United States, Millennials showed the highest interest in culture, with their average psychographic intensity score was 70.3, compared to 68.6 and 63.8 of Generation X and Baby Boomers, respectively. It is of no surprise that Millennials are most likely to use mobile phones for travel planning (83.5% of the respondents), which is significantly more than Generation X (61.2%), while only 32.8% of Baby Boomers plan on using mobile phones for the same purpose. They also prefer using social media as means for travel planning, namely Facebook (46.5%), Instagram (22.1%), and Twitter (20.7%). The same social media is a trusted source for 35.8% (Facebook), 9.8% (Twitter), and 7.9% (Instagram) of Generation X respondents. Percentages are even lower for Baby Boomers and account for 14.5% (Facebook), 2.3% (Twitter), and 1.1% (Instagram) of the respondents. It also has to be noted that the percentage of Baby Boomers who have social media account is quite lower as well (statista.com, 2017).

Concept of Big Data Analytics

Cognizant of previously stated, the key characteristic of social media analytics is a focus on data. As a consequence, a new perspective of communication mix emerged, influencing how organizations communicate with users. Social medial analytics comprises of analysis of structured and unstructured data, acquired on social media. It is quite difficult to collect and analyze such data with conventional methods, therefore a new approach is needed. One of the solutions is the big data approach, which allows collection and analysis of data of unprecedented volume, depth, and scope, intending to solve everyday problems. The term itself was coined in the mid-90s, but the wider use is seen only after 2011. One of the definitions of big data states that it is ''a term that describes large volumes of high velocity, complex and variable data that require advanced techniques and technologies to enable the capture, storage, distribution, management, and analysis of the information.'' (Gandomi and Haider, 2015, 138). Although the term itself associates with the size or volume, there are three main characteristics of big data or 3Vs: Volume, Velocity, and Variety (Chen et al., 2012). Volume refers to the amount of data, which is expressed in terabytes, petabytes, and zettabytes (He and Chen, 2014; Erevelles et al., 2016). This is a dynamic category, so the precise definition of threshold is not possible. First, because different types of data occupy different amount of space (e.g. text vs. video), and secondly due to constant technology improvement which allows faster speed and higher storage volume. Velocity, as a characteristic of big data, refers to the speed of collection and analysis of data. Higher penetration of mobile device usage results in a surge in available data, which can be demographic, or geolocation data, or can represent shopping habits and come from different sources. When it comes to variety, the heterogeneous nature of databases comprises structured, semi-structured, and unstructured data spanning across various types of data such as numerical, text, audio, photo, or video (Mariani, 2019).

Figure 1. Big data analytics
Source: Gandomi and Haider, 2015

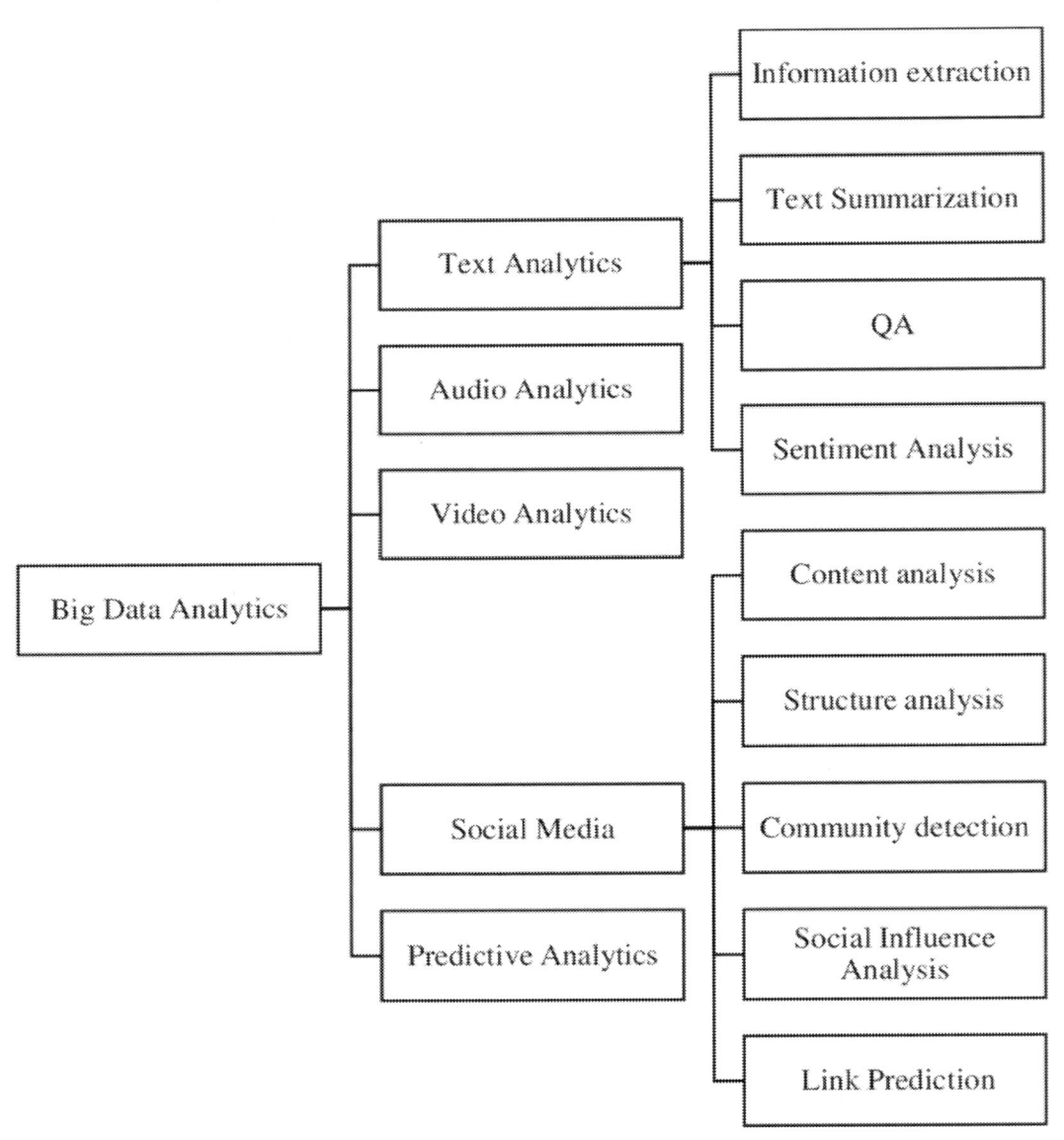

The aim of the big data approach to analytics is the generation of new information that adds up to traditional statistical research methods. Such an approach allows organizations to have better insight into their business, improve the decision-making process as well as better understand consumers which provides the foundation for better relations with them. Although big data offers unprecedented opportunities for both professionals and researchers, it also brings challenges, such as storage, management, and processing (Kaisler et al., 2013; Hashem et al., 2015; Rodrigues-Mazahua et al., 2016). Social media as a source can provide data in several ways (Figure 1.). Based on that, social media analytics can roughly be divided into two subcategories: content analysis and structure analysis (Gandomi and Haider, 2015). The former analyzes user-generated content that includes reviews, photos, video, text, etc. The latter one aims to extract information from relations between network entities (people, organizations, etc.) (Kang et al., 2021).

Although tourism is not oriented toward technology in its nature, development in information and communication technologies (ICT) influences the way it functions (Khan et al., 2020), with said influence primarily being driven by consumers. Therefore, the application of ICT in tourism represents a new era in the development of this industry and can contribute to increased consumer satisfaction. The majority of tourists search for information and make reservations online (Grønflaten, 2009; Pan et al., 2013; Gavilan et al., 2018). In the application of ICT, one of the most important trends is the use of social media, both from the supply (destinations, tourism providers, etc.) and demand side (tourists). Many users today harness the power of social media in various phases of trip planning (Lo et al., 2011; Tussyadiah et al., 2011; Yoo and Gretzel, 2010; Schmallegger and Carson, 2008). For example, the use of social media can influence user's travel preferences (McCarthy et al., 2010; Ladhari and Michaud, 2015; Tham et al., 2019), while the probability of making a reservation is significantly determined by online reviews (Sparks and Browning, 2011; Gavilan et al., 2018). On the supply side, marketing is one of the most important factors that benefit from social media use. However, for it to be successful, social media must be actively monitored to gain better insights about users, simultaneously spotting opportunities for improvement of services and products (Litvin et al., 2018; Pantelidis, 2010; Xiang et al., 2017, Ghermandi et al., 2020). Besides that, social media enable direct communication with the users, which can help better understand their preferences and needs (Huang et al., 2011; Raletic Jotanovic et al., 2016; Yang et al., 2018).

Social Media Analytics

Hereinafter we discuss social media analytics methods and their application to tourism destinations with the focus on cultural tourism settings. Since social media enabled and induced people to share their opinions, locations, and emotions publicly, analyzing such data represents the unobtrusive way of gathering important information, thus benefiting cultural tourism destinations in many ways (Cuomo et al., 2021). First, as a massive source of user-generated content, social media allows destination management to better understand the characteristics of the transmitted image of the destination and its assets by online users (Marine-Roig and Clave, 2016; Molinillo et al., 2018). The same data is a valuable source when it comes to destinations' reputation, branding, image as well as analyzing tourists' perceptions, experiences, and behavior (Koltringer and Dickinger, 2015; Lu and Stepchenkova, 2015; Stankov and Gretzel, 2020; Seyfi et al., 2020). Manual processing of this data has many limitations, therefore automation is necessary. This is when text analysis is used most often, where techniques such as natural language processing help with semantic analysis (Li et al., 2015; Le et al., 2020). Through information extraction that can produce results in the form of keywords, informing the decision-makers which terms are most associated with their destination (after identifying relevant keywords). Moreover, although those keywords provide helpful insight such as that museum at the main square is the most mentioned sight at the destination, they have limited value without the negative, positive or neutral context of the term. Sentiment analysis (opinion mining) can solve this problem by analyzing people's opinions toward products, events or places, and determine the valence and strength of the sentiment. Keywords can also be grouped into categories, so they can refer to sights, history, accommodation, transportation, etc. (Koltringer, Dickinger, 2015). Eventually, these steps can determine whether the museum was mentioned favorably; whether the queue was too long, or it sparked a positive experience. All this can provide decision-makers with information about how the destination is projected to the tourists versus how it is perceived by them (Ćulić et al., 2021).

Structure analysis is concerned with intelligence extraction from relationships among the participating entities on social media. Visualization is the technique most commonly used, through the utilization of network and activity graphs, to show connections, as well as interactions between nodes (likes, comments, shares, retweets, etc.). This can benefit decision-makers in many ways. It offers insight into the popularity of certain posts based on likes and shares, with post reach that specifies the number of people who have seen the post, while the number of comments indicates user engagement. Further analysis can provide information on destination social media accounts, and help better understand users through the post format and content, or time of the day or week it is most effective to engage with users (Kalinić and Vujičić, 2019). Community detection is also a technique often used when performing structure analysis. It extracts particular communities within a larger network, by uncovering existing behavioral patterns. User segmentation is the main benefiter of this process and allows decision-makers to formulate optimal targeted communication and marketing strategies with the users (Kalinić and Lesjak, 2019).

The Role of Social Media Platforms in Marketing of Cultural Tourism Destinations

The role and functions of SNSs for tourism operations have been widely discussed in tourism literature (Leung et al., 2013). Being one of the major trends attracting the global interest of marketers (Baethge et al. 2016), SNSs offer many new resources and opportunities for improving and reengineering operations of travel and tourism organizations (Hvass and Munar 2012; Minazzi 2015; Zeng and Gerritsen 2014) that are usually responsible for managing visitors' activities in cultural tourism destinations.

To improve marketing effectiveness, successful organizations need to develop marketing strategies adjusted accordingly to reflect the new realities represented in an overflow of new social media platforms (Shao et al., 2012; Mariani et al., 2016) The role of social media platforms for travel destination in general, is especially vital for inbound marketing and content marketing strategies (Vujičić et al., 2019). Furthermore, social media platforms can be used by stakeholders at cultural tourism destinations to dissimilate word of mouth electronically (Zhang et al., 2017; Litvin et al., 2018). In that context, Tham and colleagues (2019) suggest that organizations could extend opportunities for communicating visitors' experiences through social media use, while also engaging them more and involving industry partners to build desirable destination images.

Different social media strategy approaches were found in the comparative international analysis of US and EU countries (Stankov et al., 2018). Similarly, the research of Zeng and Gerritsen (2014) confirms that there are differences between countries in social media usage. The study of Milwood et al.

(2013) found that the USA widely embraces the most popular social media whereas Swiss destination marketing organizations are more cautious about social media adoption. Similar practices will probably continue in the future, as social media approaches are not only driven by organizational structure and overall organizational competencies but also by the dynamic and innovative nature of social media itself.

In the following section, we review indicators of Facebook analytics capabilities as a separate paragraph. After that, a review of Twitter, Instagram, and TikTok analytic capabilities will follow.

Review of Indicators of Facebook Analytics Capabilities

Every Facebook Page has a unique structure to start from. It is a "blank paper" that needs to be filled out by the given organization. Based on the review of the studies on the business usage of Facebook (e.g. Mariani et al., 2016; Hays et al., 2013; Hsu, 2012; Kwok and Yu, 2013; Munar and Jacobsen, 2014; Roque and Raposo, 2016; Sabate et al., 2014; Lee et al., 2020, Molina et al., 2020) and advances in Facebook usability, in the following text, we will explain some basic characteristics of Pages and posts that organizations should consider when analyzing visitor engagement. These characteristics are not conclusive but are offered to spark consideration and to add to the constantly open debate which is necessary concerning the dynamic nature of this social medium.

When visiting a Page, if the visitor has not landed from an official destination website, there is always a question of Page authenticity. Simple Google search or search using a Facebook internal search engine will often result in various unofficial destination Pages (Dwivedi et al., 2011). Therefore, complete authenticity can be guaranteed by Facebook when Page is manually verified with the assignation of a special verification sign next to Page's title (Facebook Developers, 2019). Regarding content communication, Facebook Pages can be enriched by using Page Tabs. Besides standard Tabs, such as (,,About", ,,Photos, ,,Videos", etc) businesses can make custom Tabs containing different types of apps, welcoming messages, polls, showcase videos, reservation forms, etc. Generally, custom Facebook Tabs can create a much richer visitors experience and add value to the standard Facebook Page (Pitre, 2015). If a business pays attention merely to the main Page News Feed (Page Wall) that can be considered as neglecting and limiting the full potential of this platform for spreading of the information and collaboration with the tourists (Hsu 2012; Zouganeli et al., 2011).

Facebook, as a democratic SNS medium, provides options for user-generated content, posting, and expressing opinions on the official Pages. Even though organizations should promote tourist participation (Belanche et al., 2010), customer dissatisfaction can be a matter of concern (Sparks and Bradley, 2017). For some types of Page categories, visitors' ratings and reviews section can be enabled. Looking for and reading other consumers' reviews is a common travel-related Internet activity. (Zhao et al., 2019). A Page's star rating is the average of all public star ratings (star ratings that are shared publicly) that the Page has received (Facebook, 2020). In digital marketing, "calls for action" words are often used as a motivation to take a desirable action when visiting websites (Eisenberg and Eisenberg, 2006). The "Call-to-action" feature on Facebook Page is a button at the top of the page that links to any destination on or off Facebook and can help Pages to drive business objectives. Currently, there are seven calls for action available: book now, contact us, use the app, play game, shop now, sign up and watch the video (Facebook for Business, 2020).

There is no general agreement on posting frequency of content. The frequent posting provides new content, keeps visitors engaged, and allows greater interaction with the fans (Zarrella and Zarrella, 2010). However, high posting frequency does not necessarily guarantee high engagement rates. For example, the Australian Tourism Commission advises organizations to be cautious with the number of posts, putting attention to well-planned posts, as opposed to quantity (South Australian Tourism Commission, 2015). A study by Mariani and colleagues (2016) for the regional DMOs in Italy found that high post frequency has a negative impact on user engagement. Facebook users' news feeds (i.e. Walls) are constantly filled with content coming from multiple sources, such as other users' profiles, Facebook Pages liked by users, sponsored content. On average, only about 17% of a business Page's post shows up on fans' walls (Hubspot, 2015). Facebook uses a complex ranking algorithm based on machine learning to select and rank the content that shows up in the user's news feed. Before every post to Facebook Page, an organization usually has to choose: what it will post (link, photo, video, status, or event), the time of day when content should be posted and the day of the week to post (Mariani et al., 2018; Kalinić and Vujičić, 2019). One of the determinants of internet advertising effectiveness can be the length of the message. According to Mariani et al. (2018), lengthy messages that involve paying close attention can reduce direct response to it.

Review of Basic Indicators of Twitter Analytics Capabilities

Twitter is a microblogging platform where users share their thoughts, news, information, and humor in 280 (initially 140) or fewer characters of text. It makes global communication cheap and measurable. Profiles are (usually) public, so anyone in the world can see what somebody writes unless they elect to make the profile private. It has somewhat different dynamics and structure than Facebook, so users "follow" each other to keep tabs on and converse with people. The connections between users are asynchronous, which means that if one user "follows" another, it does not imply a connection in the other direction. It is also quite simplified meaning there is a character limit to posts, no complicated profiles, etc. Because of this, Twitter has become a top choice for professionals that want a social / semi-work-related network through which they can share work news alongside personal news. There are on average 6000 tweets per second summing to around 500 million tweets per day, which produce a lot of data. Twitter agreed to provide the Library of Congress (US) with every public tweet sent and is continuing to supply it on an ongoing basis. Considering all this, Twitter has become social media with quite fast dynamics and positioned itself as an excellent news source. Certain characteristics of Twitter have contributed to it, such as the use of hashtags. They help with marking a topic of a tweet, and since Twitter is monitoring hashtags, make the tweet easier to discover. This allows Twitter's algorithm to recognize trending topics, which is of great benefit to cultural tourism destinations in general since the grouping of keywords is partly done by the social media itself (Philander & Zhong, 2016). It also gives great insight into what topic is popular at the moment, so they can decide how the next tweet is going to stand out in the crowd or is it going along the mainstream in the first place. Due to Twitter specifics, which force users to share their content concisely, there is on average one to two hashtags per tweet.

The functionalities of the Twitter platform for stakeholders at destinations are reflected in the possibility of creating a business account through which they can perform marketing activities. The basic components of a business account primarily include the Twitter username, which is displayed with the prefix @ and allows the user to mark the business page, as well as mention the account in the user's posts. It generally contains some components of the official name and is shorter than it. Above the Twitter username is an account name that can be changed as needed. Below that, organizations are allowed to fill in a short text of up to 160 characters where they can provide basic information about their facility, or more often the brand. The location of the organization, as well as the official website, are also visible below this text. Business accounts also include a profile photo, which is a smaller format, and which is also shown on every post. In addition, the photo in the account header is larger and allows you to upload not only image content but also dynamic animations and videos. When it comes to tweets, business accounts are allowed to pin a post they consider important, so that it appears at the top of the profile, and serves to convey information to users regardless of when they visit the profile, and to whether in the meantime there were more posts on the same profile (Twitter, 2020).

The rate at which technology is progressing saw many devices and tools shrinking in size. One of those devices is GPS. Originally intended for military use, it is now a mandatory part of mobile phones, from the market point of view. It has numerous functions, like navigation, but social media facilitated its use differently. With geotagging options people are now sharing their location on social media, ''checking in'', and not only that. Geolocation tag is not an isolated function. It can be used when writing a post on social media, uploading a photo or a video, or expressing an opinion. In that regard, it gives a spatial dimension to the aforementioned user-generated content, allowing connection with the precise location of the user. Since tourism implies movement, it is of the highest priority to analyze tourist flows, especially with the possibility of combining with different types of data (Shao et al., 2017; Vu et al., 2018). One of the techniques that best communicate the cross-referenced geospatial and online data and which is most often used for analyzing Twitter data is a heat map. In the case of tourism, it can show where tourists take photos, thus revealing the most attractive sights, or combined with tweets or posts, indicate tourists' experiences on certain locations.

The functionalities of Twitter for performing organizations' marketing activities on this social media platform enable targeting potential consumers according to the language they use, gender, interests, devices they use, behavior, location as well as keywords. Carrying out these activities may aim, among other things, to increase the number of followers, spread awareness about the brand or products and services, engage users in tweets, as well as redirect to the official website of the organization. This social media platform enables business accounts and certain analytical functionalities, which primarily concern the tweets these accounts post, as well as information about the followers of these accounts, and are available to administrators on individual accounts (Twitter, 2020).

Other examples of how an organization, focusing on promoting cultural aspects and values of a destination, can extract insights from Twitter data are brand sentiment, or what people think about their product. In addition, network and relationships, finding influencers, or which market segment is still untapped is also at organizations' disposal. Moreover, they can gain insights into patterns in product consumption, i.e. where, when, and what people are consuming. Tweets can also be polls, which can at the same time encourage more engagement from the followers as well as provide valuable insights regarding followers' opinions about any topic relevant to the organization.

Review of Basic Indicators of Instagram Analytics Capabilities

Following the path of GPS, cameras became a standard part of mobile phones too. That created a space for the birth of another social media platform. Instagram is a mobile photo-sharing platform, launched in 2010. It allows users to share their experiences through photos and short videos, through simple mechanics while at the same time maintaining high quality. The platform features a set of tools that enables users to take, edit and upload their photos in numerous ways without having to leave the application. Unlike Facebook and Twitter, it does not allow text-only posts. In addition, the app has an easy integration option to immediately share photos to other social media such as Facebook and Twitter. On the other hand, hashtags are similarly important as on Twitter. Furthermore, Instagram's character limit is set to 2200, allowing users to post more than a couple. Since the focus is on the photo, hashtags can refer to various topics, including but not limited to location, emotion, editing technique, and content of the photo itself (Highfiels and Leaver, 2014). It follows Twitter's network mechanics with followers rather than friends. Analytics capabilities are to the most extent similar to ones available with Facebook and Twitter (Manikonda et al., 2014). It allows basic user statistics, which includes frequency of posting or followers, as well as network structure analysis. The content analysis differs from the aforementioned social media. It is focused on hashtags, geolocation, and comments (Giannoulakis and Tsapatsoulis, 2016). Photo analysis requires different techniques and technologies for acquiring, analyzing, and most importantly storing the data. Still, photo analysis (Hochman and Schwartz, 2012) can provide tourism organizations with invaluable insights into users' habits regarding the use of filters and visual styles of photos they are posting. Tourism implies visiting a certain place, and motivations for travel can vary (Vujičić et al., 2020). However, the certainty is that Instagram's focus on photos has facilitated destinations visibility. Good marketing strategy can communicate not only great views of the places, but also tell stories, transfer emotions, and experiences to the followers.

Instagram functionalities for organizations that carry out marketing activities on this social media platform, enable the creation of a business account, provide insight into followers and posts, as well as further activities on the platform through the promotion of posts. All these functionalities are available within the Instagram application for mobile phones. As in the case of consumer accounts, business users can also connect to an existing account on Facebook, adding information such as an address, phone number, or email to their business account. This information is displayed at the top of the business account, which can display the specified info. This allows potential consumers to contact organizations, or get directions to the site. Organizations are also allowed to verify their account, after which a blue verification sign will be displayed on their account, similar to other platforms. The call to action allows for the creation of a button that can contain one of four different options such as "buy", "order", "schedule" and "book". Also, Instagram introduced the possibility of directly purchasing products and services on its platform. Business accounts provide the opportunity to gain information about the gender, age, and location of users who interact with the site. In addition, user insights provide information on how users interact with the account through the "likes" format, comments, and saved posts, as well as through various parameters that indicate the popularity of posts regarding the time, location, or topic markers (Instagram for Business, 2020).

Review of Tiktok Analytic Capabilities

TikTok is one of the most recent social media platforms, thus will receive more attention in this chapter. It is the global version, launched in August 2018, of Chinese platform Douyin, founded in 2016 by a company called ByteDance. Since then, it has become one of the most popular social media platforms with around 800 million active users, while its' app has been the most downloaded in 2020. It is particularly popular among younger generations, with two-thirds of the user base comprising of females, while more than 93% of users are under 30 years old (Du et al., 2020). It differs from other social media platforms, such as Facebook, Twitter, or Instagram in several ways. Primarily, TikTok is a platform focused on videos, rather short ones 15 to 60 seconds long, thus providing entertainment and personalized content appealing to young people, and an effective tool for attracting tourists. The spread of genuine, user-generated material is encouraged by simple editing tools. TikTok allows users to make a short video with background music and a range of special effects, stickers, and filters. TikTok also provides editing and recording templates for various life circumstances (e.g., travel, anniversary, etc.) for users to utilize. Those videos are frequently created based on some sound element, which can be snatched from songs, speech from movies or TV episodes, or sound elements created and posted by other users, thus making sound a crucial component for connecting information on the platform. Users may search for certain sound components and view all of the material created with that sound. In that regard, TikTok is considered closer to Vine, a now-defunct platform for short video sharing, than to the stories of Instagram, Facebook, and Twitter. The platform is a place for creativity, and a virtual playground so that it is viewed more as creative than social media (Bresnick, 2019).

The next distinction between TikTok and other social media platforms is that TikTok is essentially algorithm-driven, as opposed to other social media applications that are based on friends and followers. This implies that a TikTok video from a person with no followers can rapidly gain traction when it shows in the feeds of other users. While TikTok allows users to follow others, those relationships are less likely to be social ties from the offline world. As a result, TikTok is less of a social network in the classic sense. Instead, it is more akin to an entertainment site like YouTube, where consumers watch content created by people they don't necessarily need to know. Because very little is known about the algorithm that runs TikTok, consumers might frequently experience increased uncertainty over content success (Haenlein et al., 2020).

TikTok's content is presented in two distinct forms. The "Following" feed, which displays the content of individuals the user is following, and the "For You" feed, which displays content picked by an artificial intelligence system that is likely to be relevant to the user. Furthermore, unlike social networking applications like Facebook, Instagram, Twitter, and Tumblr, which provide a feed for scrolling, TikTok delivers content one video at a time, with the user having to swipe up for the next video. The video in the display will loop until the user swipes up or taps the screen to pause it (Haenlein et al., 2020).

Similar to other social media platforms, individuals may tag others in the comments using hashtags, and TikTok is no exception. Hashtags show on the video screen alongside the user's name and can be clicked on to find other videos with that same hashtag. Discover also displays trending hashtags and a search box for searching hashtags, videos, sounds, and people. Users engage with content by responding to the video with a video of their own. The original video displays on the screen in a tiny box, allowing the audience to view both the original and the reaction. This activates the duet option, which divides the screen for synchronized, or comparison performance. Digital co-creation appears to be one of the app's distinguishing characteristics that have contributed to its success, enabling users to create their films alongside influencers and TikTok stars (Anderson, 2020).

Shorter videos, spanning 15 to 60 seconds, are more effective at catching viewer attention. They enable mobile phone use and sharing during short breaks (Wright, 2017). As a result of the growing need to consume faster and shorter content, video-sharing services such as Instagram, and TikTok have emerged. Tourists' perceptions of travel videos are established first via their regular consumption of TikTok travel and other relevant videos. The positive experiences created by leisure consumption are transferred to the tourism environment, involving and leading tourists in the making of travel videos. Based on knowledge of tourists' video content preferences, tourism marketers can create and develop content campaigns particular to a place or develop trip video templates with representative music by knowing visitors' video content preferences (Du et al., 2020). For tourism businesses, TikTok as such is a platform where travelers share their experiences, which subsequently influences the destination image and travel motives of other potential visitors. Therefore, destination marketing companies could encourage travelers to share experiences via social media platforms (Stankov et al., 2019). Although DMOs focused on cultural tourism products and sights would be especially eager to explore this opportunity, the TikTok platform is still growing in commercial sense and capabilities for businesses.

In terms of functionalities for service providers in cultural tourism setting, TikTok offers similar opportunities for businesses as other major social media platforms. It includes the creation of a business account, provides insight into followers and posts, as well as further activities on this social network through the promotion of posts. However, due to the nature of the platforms where users are compelled to actively participate rather than just observe, tourism providers need to take a more proactive approach to communication with users. That means that businesses are allowed to create several options for their advertisements, with the platform offering in-feed ads, appearing on users' feeds, or topview ads, that appear as soon as they open the app. Businesses are also encouraged to start branded hashtag challenges, one of the features that proved to be quite popular and generated over 25 billion views as of December 2019. It is already showcasing the great potential for tourism providers as one of the most popular hashtags to follow is #TikTokTravel which in combination with location-specific hashtags can further focus the content on the specific destinations. As an example, #TravelChallenge is a very popular hashtag with over 184M views and many users mentioning this in the content they share on the platform. Therefore, certain companies created a contest to get users to share away content and possibly win a trip around the world as the official TikTok creator for that company (Gonzalo, 2020).

The platform also advises businesses to focus on audio and music content, which is also one of the platform's characteristics. Although creating such content requires significant efforts from businesses, the platform allows for integration with other social media platforms, to increase the reach of such content. TikTok also offers analytical capabilities similar to other major social media platforms. The platform offers three main points of analytics. First are insights on account that include metrics on the number of followers. Then, businesses are also able to gain more knowledge regarding the content, i.e. the trending videos and sounds. Tourism providers, DMOs, as well as cultural organizations such as museums, galleries, NGOs may want to also monitor what content is being created and shared with a hashtag specific to their city, area, state, or province. Finally, capabilities include analytics of account followers that allow businesses to gain more insight into target audience segments. In addition, it is possible to perform real-time monitoring of several metrics and track campaigns through the use of pixels. However, the platform is still in its infancy and remains yet to be thoroughly used from an advertising standpoint (TikTok for Business, 2021).

DISCUSSION AND CONCLUSION

The application of big data analytics to social media is being used by a growing number of organizations. They enable them to assess the impact of social media on business objectives, evaluate the size, engagement, and growth of the online audience, the type of online comments, and the presence of their consumers on other platforms (Lepkowska-White, 2017). Tourism destinations are still struggling to measure the exact number of visitors. In that regard, social media can serve as an excellent additional source that can provide data about tourists visits and flows (e Silva et al., 2018). Not only that, it approaches the market on a granular level, while at the same time maintaining a reach of mass media. Different social media platforms, such as Facebook, Twitter, Instagram, and TikTok each with their specifics, offer cultural tourism destinations opportunities to analyze their prospective visitors and provide them with insights regarding behavioral patterns and travel habits in various phases of trip planning (Zhang et al., 2019; Van der Zee and Bertocchi, 2018; Pesce et al., 2019). Social media analytics may also provide tourist feedback on organizations' products and services, as well as their satisfaction and opinions with various aspects of those products and services. Organizations may leverage that knowledge to better tailor new products and services for the target segments, thus enabling value co-creation in the cultural tourism landscape (Duan et al., 2016; Lin et al., 2018). In addition, social media analytics can facilitate organizations to understand problems customers might have experienced but are not willing to express offline during their visit. This could allow organizations to swiftly address and resolve problems, and bring visitors back (Dolan et al., 2019).

The democratization of communication and increased participation brought by social media makes it difficult for organizations to stand out in the crowd. It instigated the need for intermediaries in information dissemination, thus giving a rise to influencer marketing (Gretzel, 2017). Although celebrity endorsements were traditionally used by tourism organizations to influence destination image and awareness, social media has produced a new kind of influencers who amassed their followership with relevant and engaging content (Jerslev, 2016). Tourism organizations engage with influencers to improve brand advocacy and awareness, reach new audiences, and improve sales conversion, and they are usually employed to promote and create content, launch and review products and services as well as cover events (Lou and Yuan, 2019). That presents a new set of challenges for cultural tourism organizations, primarily pertaining to influencer discovery and choice. Social media analytics can provide optimal methods, such as structure analysis and community detection, to choose the right individual(s) (Lagrée et al., 2018). Depending on their marketing goals, organizations can decide to work with a celebrity with a high number of followers, thus increasing visibility, or a content creator and micro-influencer, with higher relevance, resulting in higher user engagement. In the case of the latter, Instagram has proven to be a particularly popular platform (Jin et al., 2019). Although influencer marketing can provide more return on investment than traditional promotion, measuring the returns and overall campaign success remains difficult, since the campaigns are done through third parties (influencers). Nevertheless, influencer marketing has become widespread, especially in the tourism industry, to the degree that evidenced the emergence of influencer marketplaces platforms that cater to this specific form of social media marketing for cultural tourism destinations (Gretzel, 2017).

Cultural tourism destinations are very sensitive ecosystems that are evolving and changing in time. Tourism at such destinations brings its advantages but also challenges. The first one is additional pressure on the site. Overtourism can not only deteriorate the state of the physical buildings and urban landscape but also negatively influence the local population, their culture and endanger the unique values of the destination (Adie et al., 2020). On the other hand, globalization can also bring benefits to the community. Social media, as one of the trends, allows destinations to showcase their values and heritage at the global market. If properly utilized, it can further enhance and promote these aspects, without necessarily losing authenticity. The structure of social media platforms allows different destinations to compete in a system that is the same for everyone. That is why big data analytics is an excellent way of grasping the world of social media. It can provide information about tourists, their needs, and answer the questions where, why, when, and how. It can help cultural destinations with the issue of tourist flow both in the online and offline world. Most importantly it can put nontangible aspects such as nonmaterial cultural heritage or brand image into commercial perspective by providing measurement (Qiu and Zhang, 2021).

On the other hand, the propositions made in this paper highlight some important challenges of social media and big data analysis of cultural tourism destinations. These fall under the general constraints experienced by tourism providers in their endeavor to adopt new technologies. Wasan (2014) categorizes these constraints as internal (i.e. operational, financial, and human resources) and external (i.e. market forces, legislation, policies and standards, customer and technology-driven) barriers. Most importantly, the key challenge for the adoption of big data analysis based on social media indicators rests in the scope of existing internal limitations. Tourism providers in the cultural landscape must carefully choose which social media channels they wish to use. Each platform requires the acquisition of new skills and resources because identical content cannot simply be shared on different platforms. Financial and human resources, as well as time, may quickly become an issue, especially for smaller tourism providers.

Furthermore, the choice of the right platform should not be the first step in establishing social media presence but rather the matter of target group that tourism providers want to reach, as well as how they want to approach them. Only after that, tourism providers should decide which platform offers the best opportunities for achieving the goals. Monitoring of social media activities and especially analytics require developing or hiring personnel with the optimal skills (Haenlein et al., 2020). Although social media platforms provide analytical capabilities for organizations, platforms are the ones that control what kind of analysis and insights are provided. In case that organizations may need to take advantage of advanced analytical techniques and methods to gain deeper knowledge, they need to invest significant resources either to build in-house solutions or to acquire custom-made solutions and services tailored to their need (Xiang et al., 2017). This is because the rapid growth of social media sources combined with big data technology presents particularly interesting problems pertinent to the collection and storage of data that is quickly increasing in speed and volume, especially concerning the increased use of videos and associated visual analytics. Next, the challenge for organizations in the cultural tourism landscape is syndicating/fusing data gathered from multiple social media platforms to obtain meaningful insights. Capturing consumer online journey is increasingly difficult due to the ever-growing number of platforms and tourists' social media accounts, yet it is important to determine the benefits of each platform (Park et al., 2015; Gandomi and Heider, 2015; Miah et al., 2017; Sivarajah et al., 2017).

Another challenge is pertinent to external factors. Getting high levels of engagement and visibility is becoming increasingly difficult, even with the right choice of platform and optimal strategy. Artificial intelligence algorithms, which determine the content a person sees on their feed, are increasingly driving the dynamics of social media platforms. In addition, these algorithms are trade secrets and represent the competitive advantage of the platforms, so tourism providers participating on those platforms can never completely know and understand how they work (Dwivedi et al., 2019; De Bruyn et al., 2020).

It is important to remember that social media platforms are operating in their own best interests. As a result, tourism providers are vulnerable to the strategic decisions of those businesses, which may have a significant impact on them. Even slight changes in platform mechanics, functionalities, or algorithms can severely affect tourism providers' efforts. However, tourism providers using social media platforms to engage with tourists, especially if they dedicated significant resources, do not have a favorable perception towards the uncertainty of strategic goals they set to achieve through said platforms, especially with the increased use of artificial intelligence. In this way, they have the leverage to counterbalance the platforms' advanced position (Puntoni et al., 2021). Furthermore, the increased deployment of artificial intelligence in social media analytics, and automated decisions raise an issue with human resources, more precisely cultural organizations involved in tourism need to find the right way to blend human and machine capabilities (Davenport et al., 2020).

Another important issue pertaining to the use of big data analytics in social media is protecting the privacy of the users. Interestingly, the more advanced analytical methods and technologies are applied, the more privacy becomes an issue. This is especially the case with social media platforms, where users leave a vast digital footprint, through sharing personal opinions, photos, videos, and other content related to their lives. Regarding privacy, the issue of social identification requires organizations employing social media analytics to carefully approach data acquisition, analytics, and storage, and to have policies adhering to current privacy regulations (Olteanu et al., 2019).

This chapter examines the application of the big data concept through social media analytics and demonstrates its contribution to the stakeholders and management of cultural tourism destinations. The chapter makes three main contributions to the body of knowledge. First, it analyzes the concept of big data, its key characteristics, and its techniques. Second, it analyzes major social media platforms and examines their analytic capabilities. Lastly, it outlines examples of opportunities and challenges of the application of big data analytics through the use of social media, thus indicating how the organizations involved in cultural tourism destinations can benefit from its adoption. The chapter extends the ongoing discussion on the role of big data and social media analytics approach in the domain of tourism management and marketing.

REFERENCES

Adie, B. A., Falk, M., & Savioli, M. (2019). Overtourism as a perceived threat to cultural heritage in Europe. *Current Issues in Tourism*, *23*(14), 1737–1741. doi:10.1080/13683500.2019.1687661

Akehurst, G. (2009). User generated content: The use of blogs for tourism organisations and tourism consumers. *Service Business*, *3*(1), 51–61. doi:10.100711628-008-0054-2

Anderson, K. E. (2020). Getting acquainted with social networks and apps: It is time to talk about TikTok. *Library Hi Tech News*, *37*(4), 7–12. doi:10.1108/LHTN-01-2020-0001

Baethge, C., Klier, J., & Klier, M. (2016). Social commerce—State-of-the-art and future research directions. *Electronic Markets*, *26*(3), 269–290. Advance online publication. doi:10.100712525-016-0225-2

Batista e Silva, F., Marín Herrera, M. A., Rosina, K., Ribeiro Barranco, R., Freire, S., & Schiavina, M. (2018). Analysing spatiotemporal patterns of tourism in Europe at high-resolution with conventional and big data sources. *Tourism Management*, *68*, 101–115. doi:10.1016/j.tourman.2018.02.020

Batrinca, B., & Treleaven, P. C. (2014). Social media analytics: A survey of techniques, tools and platforms. *AI & Society*, *30*(1), 89–116. Advance online publication. doi:10.100700146-014-0549-4

Belanche, D., Casalo, L. V., Flavian, C., & Guinaliu, M. (2010). Online social networks in the travel sector. *International Journal of Electronic Marketing and Retailing*, *3*(4), 321–340. doi:10.1504/IJEMR.2010.036880

Boyd, D. M., & Ellison, N. B. (2007). Social network sites: Definition, history, and scholarship. *Journal of Computer-Mediated Communication*, *13*(1), 210–230. doi:10.1111/j.1083-6101.2007.00393.x

Bresnick, E. (2019). *Intensified Play: Cinematic study of TikTok mobile app*. from https://www.researchgate.net/publication/335570557_Intensified_Play_Cinematic_study_of_TikTok_mobile_app

Browning, V., So, K. K. F., & Sparks, B. (2013). The influence of online reviews on consumers' attributions of service quality and control for service standards in hotels. *Journal of Travel & Tourism Marketing, 30*(1-2), 23–40. doi:10.1080/10548408.2013.750971

Cha, M., Haddadi, H., Benevenuto, F., & Gummadi, K. P. (2010). Measuring user influence in Twitter: The million follower fallacy. International Association for the Advancement of Artificial Intelligence Conference on Weblogs and Social Media.

Chen, H., Chiang, R. H. L., & Storey, V. C. (2012). Business Intelligence and Analytics: From Big Data To Big Impact. *Management Information Systems Quarterly, 36*(4), 1165–1188. doi:10.1145/2463676.2463712

Constantinides, E. (2008). The empowered customer and the digital myopia. *Business Strategy Series, 9*(5), 215–223. doi:10.1108/17515630810906710

Constantinides, E., & Fountain, S. (2008). Web 2.0: Conceptual foundations and marketing issues. *Journal of Direct, Data and Digital Marketing Practice, 9*(3), 231–244. doi:10.1057/palgrave.dddmp.4350098

Ćulić, M., Vujičić, M. D., Kalinić, Č., Dunjić, M., Stankov, U., Kovačić, S., Vasiljević, Đ. A., & Anđelković, Ž. (2021). Rookie tourism destinations—The effects of attractiveness factors on destination image and revisit intention with the satisfaction mediation effect. *Sustainability (Switzerland), 13*(11), 5780. doi:10.3390u13115780

Cuomo, M. T., Tortora, D., Foroudi, P., Giordano, A., Festa, G., & Metallo, G. (2021). Digital transformation and tourist experience co-design: Big social data for planning cultural tourism. *Technological Forecasting and Social Change, 162*, 120345. doi:10.1016/j.techfore.2020.120345

Davenport, T., Guha, A., Grewal, D., & Bressgott, T. (2020). How artificial intelligence will change the future of marketing. *Journal of the Academy of Marketing Science, 48*(1), 24–42. doi:10.100711747-019-00696-0

De Bruyn, A., Viswanathan, V., Beh, Y. S., Brock, J. K.-U., & von Wangenheim, F. (2020). Artificial Intelligence and Marketing: Pitfalls and Opportunities. *Journal of Interactive Marketing, 51*, 91–105. doi:10.1016/j.intmar.2020.04.007

Dhar, V., & Chang, E. (2009). Does chatter matter? The impact of user-generated content on music sales. *Journal of Interactive Marketing, 23*(4), 300–307. doi:10.1016/j.intmar.2009.07.004

Dolan, R., Seo, Y., & Kemper, J. (2019). Complaining practices on social media in tourism: A value co-creation and co-destruction perspective. *Tourism Management, 73*, 35–45. doi:10.1016/j.tourman.2019.01.017

Dotan, A., & Zaphiris, P. (2010). A cross-cultural analysis of Flickr users from Peru, Israel, Iran, Taiwan and the UK. *International Journal of Web Based Communities, 6*(3), 284–302. doi:10.1504/IJWBC.2010.033753

Du, X., Liechty, T., Santos, C. A., & Park, J. (2020). 'I want to record and share my wonderful journey': Chinese Millennials' production and sharing of short-form travel videos on TikTok or Douyin. *Current Issues in Tourism*, 1–13. Advance online publication. doi:10.1080/13683500.2020.1810212

Duan, W., Yu, Y., Cao, Q., & Levy, S. (2016). Exploring the Impact of Social Media on Hotel Service Performance. *Cornell Hospitality Quarterly, 57*(3), 282–296. doi:10.1177/1938965515620483

Dwivedi, M., Yadav, A., & Venkatesh, U. (2011). Use of social media by national tourism organizations: A preliminary analysis. *Information Technology & Tourism, 13*(2), 93–103. doi:10.3727/109830 512X13258778487353

Dwivedi, Y. K., Hughes, L., Ismagilova, E., Aarts, G., Coombs, C., Crick, T., ... Williams, M. D. (2019). Artificial Intelligence (AI): Multidisciplinary perspectives on emerging challenges, opportunities, and agenda for research, practice and policy. *International Journal of Information Management, 101994.* Advance online publication. doi:10.1016/j.ijinfomgt.2019.08.002

Eisenberg, B., & Eisenberg, J. (2006). *Call to Action: Secret Formulas to Improve Online Results.* Thomas Nelson.

Erevelles, S., Fukawa, N., & Swayne, L. (2016). Big Data consumer analytics and the transformation of marketing. *Journal of Business Research, 69*(2), 897–904. doi:10.1016/j.jbusres.2015.07.001

Facebook. (2020). *How is a Page's star rating determined? Facebook.* https://www.facebook.com/help/500762053364226

Facebook Developers. (2019). *Page. Facebook Developers.* https://developers.facebook.com/docs/graph-api/reference/page

Facebook for Business. (2020). *Facebook Pages: Calls to Action' Facebook for Business.* https://www.facebook.com/business/news/call-to-action-button

Gandomi, A., & Haider, M. (2015). Beyond the hype: Big data concepts, methods and analytics. *International Journal of Information Management, 35*(2), 137–144. doi:10.1016/j.ijinfomgt.2014.10.007

Gavilan, D., Avello, M., & Martinez-Navarro, G. (2018). The influence of online ratings and reviews on hotel booking consideration. *Tourism Management, 66,* 53–61. doi:10.1016/j.tourman.2017.10.018

George, G., Haas, M. R., & Pentland, A. (2014). Big Data and Management. *Academy of Management Journal, 57*(2), 321–326. doi:10.5465/amj.2014.4002

Ghermandi, A., Camacho-Valdez, V., & Trejo-Espinosa, H. (2020). Social media-based analysis of cultural ecosystem services and heritage tourism in a coastal region of Mexico. *Tourism Management, 77,* 104002. doi:10.1016/j.tourman.2019.104002

Giannoulakis, S., & Tsapatsoulis, N. (2016). Evaluating the descriptive power of Instagram hashtags. *Journal of Innovation in Digital Ecosystems, 3*(2), 114–129. doi:10.1016/j.jides.2016.10.001

Gonzalo, F. (2020). *Why TikTok Matters For Travel Brands.* https://fredericgonzalo.com/en/2020/01/06/why-tiktok-matters-for-travel-brands/

Gretzel, U. (2017). Influencer marketing in travel and tourism. In *Advances in social media for travel, tourism and hospitality* (pp. 147–156). Routledge. doi:10.4324/9781315565736-13

Grønflaten, Ø. (2009). Predicting travelers' choice of information sources and information channels. *Journal of Travel Research, 48*(2), 230–244. doi:10.1177/0047287509332333

Gundecha, P., & Liu, H. (2012). Mining social media: A brief introduction. Tutorials in Operations Research, 1(4). doi:10.1287/educ.1120.0105

Haenlein, M., Anadol, E., Farnsworth, T., Hugo, H., Hunichen, J., & Welte, D. (2020). Navigating the New Era of Influencer Marketing: How to be Successful on Instagram, TikTok, & Co. *California Management Review, 63*(1), 5–25. doi:10.1177/0008125620958166

Hanna, R., Rohm, A., & Crittenden, V. L. (2011). We're all connected: The power of the social media ecosystem. *Business Horizons, 54*(3), 265–273. doi:10.1016/j.bushor.2011.01.007

Hashem, I. A. T., Yaqoob, I., Anuar, N. B., Mokhtar, S., Gani, A., & Khan, S. U. (2015). The rise of "big data" on cloud computing: Review and open research issues. *Information Systems, 47*, 98–115. doi:10.1016/j.is.2014.07.006

Hays, S., Page, S. J., & Buhalis, D. (2013). Social media as a destination marketing tool: Its use by national tourism organizations. *Current Issues in Tourism, 16*(3), 211–239. doi:10.1080/13683500.2012.662215

He, W., & Chen, Y. (2014). Using Blog Mining as an Analytical Method to Study the Use of Social Media by Small Businesses. *Journal of Information Technology Case and Application Research, 16*(2), 91–104. doi:10.1080/15228053.2014.943092

Highfield, T., & Leaver, T. (2014). A methodology for mapping Instagram hashtags. *First Monday, 20*(1). Advance online publication. doi:10.5210/fm.v20i1.5563

Hochman, N., & Schwartz, R. (2012). Visualizing Instagram: Tracing cultural visual rhythms. In *Proceedings of the workshop on Social Media Visualization (SocMedVis) in conjunction with the sixth international AAAI conference on Weblogs and Social Media (ICWSM–12)* (pp. 6-9). AAAI.

Hsu, Y. L. (2012). Facebook as international eMarketing strategy of Taiwan hotels. *International Journal of Hospitality Management, 31*(3), 972–980. doi:10.1016/j.ijhm.2011.11.005

Huang, L., Yung, C. Y., & Yang, E. (2011). How do travel agencies obtain a competitive advantage?: Through a travel blog marketing channel. *Journal of Vacation Marketing, 17*(2), 139–149. doi:10.1177/1356766710392737

Hubspot. (2015). *How to engage fans on Facebook. Hubspot.* http://cdn1.hubspot.com/hub/53/How-to-Engage-Fans-on-Facebook-04.pdf

Hvass, K. A., & Munar, A. M. (2012). The takeoff of social media in tourism. *Journal of Vacation Marketing, 18*(2), 93–103. doi:10.1177/1356766711435978

Instagram for Business. (2020). *Creating a Business Profile on Instagram.* https://business.instagram.com/blog/creating-a-business-profile-on-instagram/

Jansen, B. J., Zhang, M., Sobel, K., & Chowdury, A. (2009). Twitter power: Tweets as electronic word of mouth. *Journal of the American Society for Information Science and Technology, 60*(11), 2169–2188. doi:10.1002/asi.21149

Jerslev, A. (2016). Media times in the time of the microcelebrity: Celebrification and the YouTuber Zoella. *International Journal of Communication, 10*, 19.

Jin, S. V., Muqaddam, A., & Ryu, E. (2019). Instafamous and social media influencer marketing. *Marketing Intelligence & Planning*, *37*(5), 567–579. doi:10.1108/MIP-09-2018-0375

Jin, X., Gallagher, A., Cao, L., Luo, J., & Han, J. (2010). The wisdom of social multimedia: using Flickr for prediction and forecast. In: *Proceedings of the International Conference on Multimedia*. ACM. 10.1145/1873951.1874196

Kaisler, S., Armour, F., Espinosa, J. A., & Money, W. (2013). Big Data: Issues and Challenges Moving Forward. *2013 46th Hawaii International Conference on System Sciences*, 995–1004. 10.1109/HICSS.2013.645

Kaisler, S., Armour, F., Espinosa, J. A., & Money, W. (2013) Big data: issues and challenges moving forward. *6th Hawaii International Conference on System Sciences*, 995–1004. 10.1109/HICSS.2013.645

Kalinić, Č., & Lesjak, M. (2019). Connecting with iGeneration: Importance of Social Media for Hotel Promotion. In *The Contemporary Trend in Tourism and Hospitality 2019* (pp. 26–33). University of Novi Sad, Faculty of Sciences, Department for Geography, Tourism and Hotel Management.

Kalinić, C., & Vujičić, M. (2019). A subnational assessment of hotel social media metrics - The case of Serbia. *Geographica Pannonica*, *23*(2), 87–101. Advance online publication. doi:10.5937/gp23-19968

Kang, S., Kim, W. G., & Park, D. (2021). Understanding tourist information search behaviour: The power and insight of social network analysis. *Current Issues in Tourism*, *24*(3), 403–423. doi:10.1080/13683500.2020.1771290

Kaplan, A. M., & Haenlein, M. (2010). Users of the world, unite! The challenges and opportunities of Social Media. *Business Horizons*, *53*(1), 59–68. doi:10.1016/j.bushor.2009.09.003

Kemp, S. (2021). *Digital 2021 - We Are Social*. https://wearesocial.com/digital-2021

Khan, I., Melro, A., Amaro, A. C., & Oliveira, L. (2020). Internet of Things prototyping for cultural heritage dissemination. *Journal of Digital Media & Interaction*, *3*(7), 20–35.

Kim, S., & Chung, J. (2019). Enhancing visitor return rate of national museums: Application of data envelopment analysis to millennials. *Asia Pacific Journal of Tourism Research*, *25*(1), 76–88. doi:10.1080/10941665.2019.1578812

Kim, W. G., Jeong, O. R., & Lee, S. W. (2010). On social Web sites. *Information Systems*, *35*(2), 215–236. doi:10.1016/j.is.2009.08.003

Költringer, C., & Dickinger, A. (2015). Analyzing destination branding and image from online sources: A web content mining approach. *Journal of Business Research*, *68*(9), 1836–1843. doi:10.1016/j.jbusres.2015.01.011

Kwok, L., & Yu, B. (2013). Spreading Social Media Messages on Facebook an Analysis of Restaurant Business-to-Consumer Communications. *Cornell Hospitality Quarterly*, *54*(1), 84–94. doi:10.1177/1938965512458360

Ladhari, R., & Michaud, M. (2015). EWOM effects on hotel booking intentions, attitudes, trust, and website perceptions. *International Journal of Hospitality Management, 46*, 36–45. doi:10.1016/j.ijhm.2015.01.010

Lagrée, P., Cappé, O., Cautis, B., & Maniu, S. (2018). Algorithms for online influencer marketing. *ACM Transactions on Knowledge Discovery from Data, 13*(1), 1–30. doi:10.1145/3274670

Le, T. H., Arcodia, C., Novais, M. A., & Kralj, A. (2020). Proposing a systematic approach for integrating traditional research methods into machine learning in text analytics in tourism and hospitality. *Current Issues in Tourism*. Advance online publication. doi:10.1080/13683500.2020.1829568

Lee, M., Hong, J. H., Chung, S., & Back, K. J. (2020). Exploring the Roles of DMO's Social Media Efforts and Information Richness on Customer Engagement: Empirical Analysis on Facebook Event Pages. *Journal of Travel Research, 60*(3), 670–686. doi:10.1177/0047287520934874

Lepkowska-White, E. (2017). Exploring the Challenges of Incorporating Social Media Marketing Strategies in the Restaurant Business. *Journal of Internet Commerce, 16*(3), 323–342. doi:10.1080/15332861.2017.1317148

Leung, D., Law, R., van Hoof, H., & Buhalis, D. (2013). Social media in tourism and hospitality: A literature review. *Journal of Travel & Tourism Marketing, 30*(1-2), 22. doi:10.1080/10548408.2013.750919

Li, G., Law, R., Vu, H. Q., Rong, J., & Zhao, X. (2015). Identifying emerging hotel preferences using Emerging Pattern Mining technique. *Tourism Management, 46*, 311–321. doi:10.1016/j.tourman.2014.06.015

Lin, S., Yang, S., Ma, M., & Huang, J. (2018). Value co-creation on social media. *International Journal of Contemporary Hospitality Management, 30*(4), 2153–2174. doi:10.1108/IJCHM-08-2016-0484

Litvin, S. W., Goldsmith, R. E., & Pan, B. (2018). A retrospective view of electronic word-of-mouth in hospitality and tourism management. *International Journal of Contemporary Hospitality Management, 30*(1), 313–325. doi:10.1108/IJCHM-08-2016-0461

Lo, I. S., McKercher, B., Lo, A., Cheung, C., & Law, R. (2011). Tourism and online photography. *Tourism Management, 32*(4), 725–731. doi:10.1016/j.tourman.2010.06.001

Lou, C., & Yuan, S. (2019). Influencer marketing: How message value and credibility affect consumer trust of branded content on social media. *Journal of Interactive Advertising, 19*(1), 58–73. doi:10.1080/15252019.2018.1533501

Lu, W., & Stepchenkova, S. (2015). User-Generated Content as a Research Mode in Tourism and Hospitality Applications: Topics, Methods, and Software. *Journal of Hospitality Marketing & Management, 24*(2), 119–154. doi:10.1080/19368623.2014.907758

Mangold, W., & Faulds, D. (2009). Social media: The new hybrid element of the promotion mix. *Business Horizons, 52*(4), 357–365. doi:10.1016/j.bushor.2009.03.002

Manikonda, L., Hu, Y., & Kambhampati, S. (2014). *Analyzing user activities, demographics, social network structure and user-generated content on Instagram.* arXiv preprint arXiv:1410.8099.

Mariani, M. (2019). Big Data and analytics in tourism and hospitality: A perspective article. *Tourism Review*, *75*(1), 299–303. doi:10.1108/TR-06-2019-0259

Mariani, M. M., Di Felice, M., & Mura, M. (2016). Facebook as a destination marketing tool: Evidence from Italian regional Destination Management Organizations. *Tourism Management*, *54*, 321–343. doi:10.1016/j.tourman.2015.12.008

Marine-Roig, E., & Anton Clavé, S. (2016). A detailed method for destination image analysis using user-generated content. *Information Technology & Tourism*, *15*(4), 341–364. Advance online publication. doi:10.100740558-015-0040-1

McCarthy, L., Stock, D., & Verma, R. (2010). How travelers use online and social media channels to make hotel-choice decision. *Cornell Hospitality Report*, *10*(18), 4–18.

Miah, S. J., Vu, H. Q., Gammack, J., & McGrath, M. (2017). A Big Data Analytics Method for Tourist Behaviour Analysis. *Information & Management*, *54*(6), 771–785. doi:10.1016/j.im.2016.11.011

Milwood, P., Marchiori, E., & Zach, F. (2013). A comparison of social media adoption and use in different countries: The case of the United States and Switzerland. *Journal of Travel & Tourism Marketing*, *30*(1-2), 165–168. doi:10.1080/10548408.2013.751287

Minazzi, R. (2015). *Social media marketing in tourism and hospitality*. Springer International Publishing. doi:10.1007/978-3-319-05182-6

Molina, A., Gómez, M., Lyon, A., Aranda, E., & Loibl, W. (2020). What content to post? Evaluating the effectiveness of Facebook communications in destinations. *Journal of Destination Marketing & Management*, *18*, 100498. doi:10.1016/j.jdmm.2020.100498

Molinillo, S., Liébana-Cabanillas, F., Anaya-Sánchez, R., & Buhalis, D. (2018). DMO online platforms: Image and intention to visit. *Tourism Management*, *65*, 116–130. doi:10.1016/j.tourman.2017.09.021

Munar, A. M., & Jacobsen, J. K. S. (2014). Motivations for sharing tourism experiences through social media. *Tourism Management*, *43*, 46–54. doi:10.1016/j.tourman.2014.01.012

Narangajavana Kaosiri, Y., Callarisa Fiol, L. J., Moliner Tena, M. Á., Rodríguez Artola, R. M., & Sánchez García, J. (2017). User-Generated Content Sources in Social Media: A New Approach to Explore Tourist Satisfaction. *Journal of Travel Research*. Advance online publication. doi:10.1177/0047287517746014

O'Connor, P. (2010). Managing a Hotel's Image on TripAdvisor. *Journal of Hospitality Marketing & Management*, *19*(7), 754–772. doi:10.1080/19368623.2010.508007

Olteanu, A., Castillo, C., Diaz, F., & Kıcıman, E. (2019). Social Data: Biases, Methodological Pitfalls, and Ethical Boundaries. *Frontiers in Big Data*, *2*(13), 13. doi:10.3389/fdata.2019.00013 PMID:33693336

Pan, B., Zhang, L., & Law, R. (2013). The complex matter of online hotel choice. *Cornell Hospitality Quarterly*, *54*(1), 74–83. doi:10.1177/1938965512463264

Pantelidis, I. S. (2010). Electronic meal experience: A content analysis of online restaurant comments. *Cornell Hospitality Quarterly*, *51*(4), 483–491. doi:10.1177/1938965510378574

Park, K., Nguyen, M. C., & Won, H. (2015). Web-based collaborative big data analytics on big data as a service platform. In *International Conference on Advanced Communication Technology, ICACT* (pp. 564–567). Institute of Electrical and Electronics Engineers Inc. 10.1109/ICACT.2015.7224859

Parra-Lopez, E., Bulchand-Gidumal, J., Gutierrez-Tano, D., & Diaz-Armas, R. (2011). Intentions to use social media in organizing and taking vacation trips. *Computers in Human Behavior, 27*(2), 640–654. doi:10.1016/j.chb.2010.05.022

Pesce, D., Neirotti, P., & Paolucci, E. (2019). When culture meets digital platforms: Value creation and stakeholders' alignment in big data use. *Current Issues in Tourism, 22*(15), 1883–1903. doi:10.1080/1 3683500.2019.1591354

Philander, K., & Zhong, Y. Y. (2016). Twitter sentiment analysis: Capturing sentiment from integrated resort tweets. *International Journal of Hospitality Management, 55*, 16–24. doi:10.1016/j.ijhm.2016.02.001

Pitre, A. (2015). *How to Create Custom Tabs for Your Facebook Business Page. Hubspot.* https://blog.hubspot.com/blog/tabid/6307/bid/26330/How-to-Create-Custom-Tabs-for-Facebook-Business-Pages.aspx

Puntoni, S., Reczek, R. W., Giesler, M., & Botti, S. (2021). Consumers and Artificial Intelligence: An Experiential Perspective. *Journal of Marketing, 85*(1), 131–151. doi:10.1177/0022242920953847

Qiu, Q., & Zhang, M. (2021). Using Content Analysis to Probe the Cognitive Image of Intangible Cultural Heritage Tourism: An Exploration of Chinese Social Media. *ISPRS International Journal of Geo-Information, 10*(4), 240. doi:10.3390/ijgi10040240

Raletić Jotanović, S., Sudarević, T., Katić, A., Kalinić, M., & Kalinić, Č. (2016). Environmentally responsible purchasing - Analysis of the ex-Yugoslavian republics. *Applied Ecology and Environmental Research, 14*(3), 559–572. Advance online publication. doi:10.15666/aeer/1403_559572

Rodríguez-Mazahua, L., Rodríguez-Enríquez, C. A., Sánchez-Cervantes, J. L., Cervantes, J., García-Alcaraz, J. L., & Alor-Hernández, G. (2016). A general perspective of Big Data: Applications, tools, challenges and trends. *The Journal of Supercomputing, 72*(8), 3073–3113. doi:10.100711227-015-1501-1

Roque, V., & Raposo, R. (2016). Social media as a communication and marketing tool in tourism: An analysis of online activities from international key player DMO. *Anatolia An International Journal of Tourism and Hospitality Research, 27*(1), 58–70. doi:10.1080/13032917.2015.1083209

Sabate, F., Berbegal-Mirabent, J., Cañabate, A., & Lebherz, P. R. (2014). Factors influencing popularity of branded content in Facebook fan pages. *European Management Journal, 32*(6), 1001–1011. doi:10.1016/j.emj.2014.05.001

Schmallegger, D., & Carson, D. (2008). Blogs in tourism: Changing approaches to information exchange. *Journal of Vacation Marketing, 14*(2), 99–110. doi:10.1177/1356766707087519

Seyfi, S., Hall, C. M., & Rasoolimanesh, S. M. (2020). Exploring memorable cultural tourism experiences. *Journal of Heritage Tourism, 15*(3), 341–357. doi:10.1080/1743873X.2019.1639717

Shao, H., Zhang, Y., & Li, W. (2017). Extraction and analysis of city's tourism districts based on social media data. *Computers, Environment and Urban Systems, 65*, 66–78. doi:10.1016/j.compenvurbsys.2017.04.010

7

Shao, J., Rodriguez, M. D., & Gretzel, U. (2012). Riding the social media wave: strategies of DMOs who successfully engage in social media marketing. In M. Sigala, E. Christou, & U. Gretzel (Eds.), *Social media in travel, tourism and hospitality: theory, practice and cases* (pp. 87–98). Ashgate Publishing.

Sivarajah, U., Kamal, M. M., Irani, Z., & Weerakkody, V. (2017). Critical analysis of Big Data challenges and analytical methods. *Journal of Business Research, 70,* 263–286. Advance online publication. doi:10.1016/j.jbusres.2016.08.001

Smith, T. (2009). The social media revolution. *International Journal of Market Research, 51*(4), 559–561. doi:10.2501/S1470785309200773

South Australian Tourism Commission. (2015). *Social Media Hints and Tips for the Tourism Industry.* https://www.tourism.sa.gov.au/assets/documents/Industry/Social_Media_Hints_and_Tips.pdf

Sparks, B. A., & Bradley, G. L. (2017). A "Triple A" Typology of Responding to Negative Consumer-Generated Online Reviews. *Journal of Hospitality & Tourism Research (Washington, D.C.), 41*(6), 719–745. doi:10.1177/1096348014538052

Sparks, B. A., & Browning, V. (2011). The impact of online reviews on hotel booking intentions and perception of trust. *Tourism Management, 32*(6), 1310–1323. doi:10.1016/j.tourman.2010.12.011

Stankov, U., & Gretzel, U. (2020). Tourism 4.0 technologies and tourist experiences: A human-centered design perspective. *Information Technology & Tourism, 22*(3), 1–12. doi:10.100740558-020-00186-y

Stankov, U., Jovanović, T., Pavluković, V., Kalinić, C., Drakulić-Kovačević, N., & Cimbaljević, M. (2018). A regional survey of current practices on destination marketing organizations' Facebook Pages: The case of EU and US. *Geographica Pannonica, 22*(2), 81–96. Advance online publication. doi:10.5937/22-16673

Stankov, U., Kennell, J., Morrison, A. M., & Vujičić, M. D. (2019). The view from above: The relevance of shared aerial drone videos for destination marketing. *Journal of Travel & Tourism Marketing, 36*(7), 808–822. doi:10.1080/10548408.2019.1575787

Statista. (2017). https://www.statista.com/study/12393/social-networks-statista-dossier/

Tešin, A., Kovačić, S., Pivac, T., Vujičić, M. D., & Obradović, S. (2020). From children to seniors: Is culture accessible to everyone? *International Journal of Culture, Tourism and Hospitality Research, 15*(2), 183–201. doi:10.1108/IJCTHR-08-2019-0142

Tham, A., Mair, J., & Croy, G. (2019). Social media influence on tourists' destination choice: Importance of context. *Tourism Recreation Research, 45*(2), 161–175. doi:10.1080/02508281.2019.1700655

Thevenot, G. (2007). Blogging as a social media. *Tourism and Hospitality Research, 7*(3), 287–289. doi:10.1057/palgrave.thr.6050062

TikTok For Business. (2021). *Marketing on TikTok.* https://www.tiktok.com/business/en/

Tussyadiah, I., Park, S., & Fesenmaier, D. R. (2011). Assessing the effectiveness of consumer narratives for destination marketing. *Journal of Hospitality & Tourism Research (Washington, D.C.), 35*(1), 64–78. doi:10.1177/1096348010384594

Twitter. (2020). *Establish your Twitter presence*. https://business.twitter.com/en/basics/create-a-twitter-business-profile.html

Van der Zee, E., & Bertocchi, D. (2018). Finding patterns in urban tourist behaviour: A social network analysis approach based on TripAdvisor reviews. *Information Technology & Tourism, 20*(1–4), 153–180. doi:10.100740558-018-0128-5

Vu, H. Q., Li, G., Law, R., & Zhang, Y. (2018). Tourist Activity Analysis by Leveraging Mobile Social Media Data. *Journal of Travel Research, 57*(7), 883–898. doi:10.1177/0047287517722232

Vujičić, M. D., Kalinić, Č., & Vasiljević, Đ. A. (2019). Presence of Hotels in Serbia on Major Social Media Platforms. In *The Contemporary Trend in Tourism and Hospitality 2019* (pp. 9–16). University of Novi Sad, Faculty of Sciences, Department for Geography, Tourism and Hotel Management.

Vujičić, M. D., Kennell, J., Morrison, A., Filimonau, V., Papuga-Štajner, I., & Stankov, U. (2020). Fuzzy Modelling of Tourist Motivation: An Age-Related Model for Sustainable, Multi-Attraction, Urban Destinations. *Sustainability, 12*(20), 8698. doi:10.3390u12208698

Wasan, P. (2014). Sustainable Technology in Hospitality Industry. In V. Jauhari (Ed.), Managing Sustainability in the Hospitality and Tourism Industry Paradigms and Directions for the Future (pp. 101–135). Apple Academic Press.

Wood, S. A., Guerry, A. D., Silver, J. M., & Lacayo, M. (2013). Using social media to quantify nature-based tourism and recreation. *Scientific Reports, 3*(1), 2976. doi:10.1038rep02976 PMID:24131963

Wright, C. (2017). Are Beauty Bloggers More Influential than Traditional Industry Experts? *Journal of Promotional Communications, 5*(3), 303–322. http://promotionalcommunications.org/index.php/pc/article/view/113

Xiang, Z., Du, Q., Ma, Y., & Fan, W. (2017). A comparative analysis of major online review platforms: Implications for social media analytics in hospitality and tourism. *Tourism Management, 58*, 51–65. doi:10.1016/j.tourman.2016.10.001

Xiang, Z., & Gretzel, U. (2010). Role of social media in online travel information search. *Tourism Management, 31*(2), 179–188. doi:10.1016/j.tourman.2009.02.016

Yang, Y., Mao, Z., & Tang, J. (2018). Understanding Guest Satisfaction with Urban Hotel Location. *Journal of Travel Research, 57*(2), 243–259. doi:10.1177/0047287517691153

Yoo, K. H., & Gretzel, U. (2010). Antecedents and impacts of trust in travel-related consumer-generated media. *Information Technology & Tourism, 12*(2), 139–152. doi:10.3727/109830510X12887971002701

Zarrella, D., & Zarrella, A. (2010). *The Facebook marketing book*. O'Reilly Media, Inc.

Zeng, B., & Gerritsen, R. (2014). What do we know about social media in tourism? A review. *Tourism Management Perspectives, 22*, 68–85. doi:10.1016/j.tmp.2014.01.001

Zhang, K., Chen, Y., & Li, C. (2019). Discovering the tourists' behaviors and perceptions in a tourism destination by analyzing photos' visual content with a computer deep learning model: The case of Beijing. *Tourism Management, 75*, 595–608. doi:10.1016/j.tourman.2019.07.002

Zhang, T., Abound Omran, B., & Cobanoglu, C. (2017). Generation Y's positive and negative eWOM: Use of social media and mobile technology. *International Journal of Contemporary Hospitality Management*, *29*(2), 732–761. doi:10.1108/IJCHM-10-2015-0611

Zhao, Y., Xu, X., & Wang, M. (2019). Predicting overall customer satisfaction: Big data evidence from hotel online textual reviews. *International Journal of Hospitality Management*, *76*, 111–121. Advance online publication. doi:10.1016/j.ijhm.2018.03.017

Zouganeli, S., Trihas, N., & Antonaki, M. (2011). Social media and tourism: The use of Facebook by the European national tourism organizations. *Tourism Today (Nicosia)*, *11*, 110–121.

ADDITIONAL READING

Batrinca, B., & Treleaven, P. C. (2014). Social media analytics: A survey of techniques, tools and platforms. *AI & Society*, *30*(1), 89–116. Advance online publication. doi:10.100700146-014-0549-4

Cuomo, M. T., Tortora, D., Foroudi, P., Giordano, A., Festa, G., & Metallo, G. (2021). Digital transformation and tourist experience co-design: Big social data for planning cultural tourism. *Technological Forecasting and Social Change*, *162*, 120345. doi:10.1016/j.techfore.2020.120345

Del Vecchio, P., Mele, G., Ndou, V., & Secundo, G. (2018). Creating value from social big data: Implications for smart tourism destinations. *Information Processing & Management*, *54*(5), 847–860. doi:10.1016/j.ipm.2017.10.006

Gandomi, A., & Haider, M. (2015). Beyond the hype: Big data concepts, methods and analytics. *International Journal of Information Management*, *35*(2), 137–144. doi:10.1016/j.ijinfomgt.2014.10.007

Gerrard, D., Sykora, M., & Jackson, T. (2017). Social media analytics in museums: Extracting expressions of inspiration. *Museum Management and Curatorship*, *32*(3), 232–250. doi:10.1080/09647775.2 017.1302815

Gretzel, U. (2018). Tourism and social media. The Sage handbook of tourism management, 2, 415-432.

Mariani, M. (2019). Big Data and analytics in tourism and hospitality: A perspective article. *Tourism Review*, *75*(1), 299–303. doi:10.1108/TR-06-2019-0259

Pesce, D., Neirotti, P., & Paolucci, E. (2019). When culture meets digital platforms: Value creation and stakeholders' alignment in big data use. *Current Issues in Tourism*, *22*(15), 1883–1903. doi:10.1080/1 3683500.2019.1591354

Sigala, M., & Gretzel, U. (Eds.). (2017). *Advances in social media for travel, tourism and hospitality: New perspectives, practice and cases*. Routledge. doi:10.4324/9781315565736

Xiang, Z., Du, Q., Ma, Y., & Fan, W. (2017). A comparative analysis of major online review platforms: Implications for social media analytics in hospitality and tourism. *Tourism Management*, *58*, 51–65. doi:10.1016/j.tourman.2016.10.001

KEY TERMS AND DEFINITIONS

Big Data Analytics: An approach to the analysis of large volumes of high velocity, complex and variable data from a multitude of sources that require advanced techniques and technologies.

Content Analysis: The analysis of user-generated content in various forms originating from the vast digital footprint users leaves on social media platforms.

Cultural Tourism: A form of tourism whose main appeal includes attractions such as heritage sites, arts, and cultural events, and related experiences, aiming to satisfy tourists' cultural needs.

Facebook: The most widely used social media platform, and more precisely social network with 2.6 billion users.

Instagram: Mobile-first photo-sharing platform focused on visual content, with 1 billion users. Very popular for sharing travel experiences.

Social Media Platform: Platforms that are built on the foundation of Web 2.0 technologies, which enables interaction and publishing of user-generated content.

Structure Analysis: Analysis of social media platforms that aims to extract information from relations between network entities.

TikTok: The most recent, Chinese social media platform relying on artificial intelligence for content discovery. Popular with younger generations.

Tourism Providers: Any type of government, private, or civic organization that participate in the tourism industry from the supply side, offering core or supplementary products and services.

Twitter: Microblogging platform with a simple interface where users communicate through short text posts limited to 240 characters (tweets). Established as a good news source due to its fast dynamics.

Chapter 22
Integrating Big Data to Smart Destination Heritage Management

Kubra Ozer
Istanbul University, Turkey

Mehmet Altug Sahin
https://orcid.org/0000-0003-1048-1963
Istanbul University, Turkey

Gurel Cetin
Istanbul University, Turkey

ABSTRACT

New technological requirements and needs of today's world are forcing cities to transform into smart cities and smart destinations in tourism cases. Smart destinations are focused on enhancing the tourist experience while also supporting the decision-making process, sustaining effective usage of resources, and maintaining sustainability. Big data has started to act as a reliable resource that assists these processes and offers alternative solution methods. Improvements in the usage of big data within the framework of smart destination management systems will also provide new insights and understandings about heritage sites and their management. Istanbul and the Sultanahmet region, which were included in the UNESCO World Heritage List, form the main domain of this chapter. This research aims to reveal any significant differences between Istanbul Wi-Fi data, Sultanahmet Wi-Fi data, and Istanbul Arrivals data. Kruskal-Wallis Test was conducted for comparing these data sets for 28 countries, and recommendations are presented.

INTRODUCTION

Cultural heritage plays a crucial role in defining the national identity, sustainable development, and compatibility of creative industries (Borissova, 2018). As the cultural heritage gives an identity to a

DOI: 10.4018/978-1-7998-8528-3.ch022

region, it also brings values that will guide lives in the changing world. Cultural heritage has also been regarded as one of the main motivations of tourism. According to the UNESCO definition, cultural heritage is classified under three main headings (UNWTO, 2016):

- Tangible cultural heritage: movable cultural heritage (paintings, sculptures, coins, manuscripts), immovable cultural heritage (monuments, archaeological sites, and so on), underwater cultural heritage (shipwrecks, underwater ruins, and cities),
- Intangible cultural heritage: oral traditions, performing arts, rituals,
- Natural heritage: natural sites with cultural aspects such as cultural landscapes, physical, biological, or geological formations.

According to the UNWTO, "Tourism and Cultural Synergies" report, it is estimated that cultural tourism accounts for approximately 40% of foreign tourists (UNWTO, 2016). . Heritage tourists travel to visit historic sites, monuments, landmarks, museums, art galleries, theatres, festivals, concerts, performances (McNulty & Koff, 2014);

Cultural heritage is expected to cultivate urban innovation, liveability, and socio-economic prosperity, which form the basis of smart city approaches. At the same time, smart cities tend to move toward more "trendy" trends in urban development such as liveability, inclusion, accessibility, and openness, and cultural heritage is expected to contribute to these goals (Angelidou, 2016).

"Smart" has been widely accepted and used as a term to describe technological, economic, and social developments supported by technologies (big data, radio frequency identification, internet of things, near field communication, etc.) (Gretzel, Sigala et al., 2015). Smart cities are a model that drives cities towards technology and innovation. Cities aim to increase welfare, efficiency, and competitiveness by becoming smart. While potential applications and approaches exist, cultural heritage offers numerous integration opportunities in the smart city context. At the intersection of cultural heritage and smart cities, it is necessary to bring the two disciplines together in order to enrich the existing knowledge base. The distinguishing feature of smart cities is their main role as a means of facilitating, organizing, and enabling people's access to information with the increasing use of technology (Angelidou, 2016).

The International Organization for Standardization (ISO) 37120 (2014) defines the smart city as a new model that uses next-generation communication technologies such as the Internet of Things (IoT), cloud computing, big data, and integrated geographic information systems, which will facilitate the planning, management, construction and smart services of the city. Smart city transformation requires an integrated framework based on the city's existing social, economic, organizational, and competitive assets. The development and operation of a strategic framework help to deliver efficient urban planning and scarce resources. Taken from a tourist perspective, the smart city means a smart destination.

Smart destinations focus on improving an understanding of how emerging technologies can be better used to create value for tourism stakeholders and tourists. Bringing smart applications to life in a city fronted by tourist activities will help position the city as a smart destination. Improving the tourism experience will also affect the image and identity of the destination, enhancing the competitive advantage in the market. Simultaneously, smart applications that will facilitate the availability of tourist services offered in the destination and offer a high-quality experience to tourists will positively impact the image and economy of the destination.

Smart tourism involves multiple components and layers such as smart experience, smart business ecosystem, and smart destination. These components are supported by layers that collect, exchange, and process data with the involvement of Information and Communication Technologies (ICTs) (Gretzel, Sigala, et al., 2015). ICTs driven by investment-oriented economic growth are developing rapidly and generating big data on many levels, which supports the development of smart destinations (Wu et al., 2018).

Research on big data is gaining attention from tourism scholars too. Even though the first research published on big data applications in tourism goes back to 2007, and is still at an early stage, continuing growth in publications is easily observed (J. Li et al., 2018). One of the first publications in this regard was conducted by Ahas et al. (2007), which focused on using mobile positioning data for revealing the seasonality of foreign tourists' space consumption.

The emergence of big data triggered a transformation in tourism research from traditional data to the use of big data, which is more informative and structure-complex. Tourism research in big data has mainly focused on three data sources, with each generating big data. The first one is users, which generate User-Generated Content (UGC). These data can be presented on online platforms using texts or photos. The second one is the devices that generate the device data. These devices produce data from GPS, mobile roaming, Bluetooth, radio frequency identification (RFID), and wireless fidelity (Wi-Fi). The third one is operations that generate transaction data. These data include web search, webpage visiting, online booking, and purchasing (J. Li et al., 2018). Considering the importance of sustainability of cultural heritage, the destination (e.g., carrying capacity), and visitor experience (e.g., queue management) integration of big data to heritage management in smart destinations is a viable strategy.

Istanbul was included in the UNESCO World Heritage List in 1985 as four regions. These regions: The Sultanahmet Urban Archeological Site, which includes the Hippodrome, Hagia Sophia, Hagia Irene, The Small Hagia Sophia Mosque and Topkapı Palace; Suleymaniye Preservation Area, which includes the Suleymaniye Mosque and its surroundings; Zeyrek Preservation Area, which includes Zeyrek Mosque and its surrounding (UNESCO, n.d.). As an important tourist attraction with its cultural value, Sultanahmet area in Turkey has been selected as the domain of this study. Many of its historical sites – such as Topkapı Palace and Hagia Sophia – are listed amongst the historical landmarks of Istanbul. It attracts millions of visitors and is one of the most visited locations in Turkey. Due to these visits by tourists, significant data on various levels have been generated; however, these data are in fragmented forms and could not be analyzed. Therefore, our study aims to collect and analyze the data generated from Wi-Fi devices of Istanbul Metropolitan Municipality to make suggestions regarding tourism and related activities.

In this chapter, the literature review is presented in the background section. This section provides the relevant information and literature review on smart cities and destinations, big data and Wi-Fi data, cultural heritage in tourism, and related areas. In the second section, the research topic is being addressed. Information about the characteristics of the study areas -Istanbul and Sultanahmet-, the research methodology, and the conducted research findings are shared. Solutions and recommendations section builds on our research findings and reveals statistically significant differences between data sets. The possible reasons for these differences are shared with the readers. The conclusion section provides an overview and insights based upon the findings of the research. Limitations of the research and recommendations on the future research directions are shared in the next sections.

BACKGROUND

Smart Cities and Destinations

The term smart, which was first used around the 90s (Albino et al., 2015), has been used in technology as a term to emphasize the special capabilities, intelligence, and connectivity of devices (Gretzel, Werthner, et al., 2015). Smart city has been regarded as a city that has the capability of using advanced Information and Communication Technologies (ICTs) to optimize resource production and consumption (Gretzel, Werthner, et al., 2015). The development of ICTs has made cities more accessible and enjoyable for both residents and visitors (Buhalis & Amaranggana, 2013). However, in time, the smart city has expanded its focus, and the definition became multifaceted. The quality of people and communities is now mentioned in smart city definitions, as well as ICTs (Albino et al., 2015). The smart city concept captures the informative and transformative changes presented by new technologies, but also takes social factors into consideration in today's environment (Nam & Pardo, 2011). Giffinger and Gudrun (2010) have identified six main components of a smart city as smart economy, smart mobility, smart environment, smart people, smart living, smart governance; which can also be associated with touristic destinations in urban areas (Gretzel, Sigala, et al., 2015). Then Lombardi et al. (2012) associated these components with urban life aspects, respectively with industry, logistics, and sustainability, efficiency and sustainability, education, security and quality, e-democracy.

Numerous countries and cities started smart city programs that implement data-driven online platforms to enhance their decision-making processes. Singapore collects urban life data and provides information on an online platform that shares information with residents and private enterprises in real-time. Dubai created 22 government entities and developed smart services such as vehicle registration, tracking visa status. Seoul proposed and running an urban plan that can provide 14 services via smart services. Estonia launched an initiative for developing a green technology-based smart city (Lee et al., 2020). The vision and priorities in achieving a smart status might differ from city to city. Yet, the integrated development of hard (resources, energy, environment, mobility, building, healthcare) and soft (entertainment, education culture, public admin, public safety, economy) aspects of a smart city needs to be achieved (Albino et al., 2015; Neirotti et al., 2014).

Smart cities' main focus is on establishing improvements in residents' life quality, where smart tourism destinations aim to enhance the tourist experience. Innovative practices implemented by smart tourism destinations do not just solely favor tourists, but also residents too (Boes et al., 2016). Smart cities aim to meet the demands of their citizen by providing a new generation of services, and smart tourism acts as one of them (Zeng et al., 2020). Smart tourism plays an important role in building an infrastructure in smart city's application systems (Guo et al., 2014). The integration of all the actors in smart tourism destinations needs to be accomplished. The value co-creation process in these destinations will generate a collaborative ecosystem, where different components can be inter-linked (Boes et al., 2016).

A technological platform where stakeholders are able to communicate and share information with each other is a requirement for a touristic destination to become smart. This platform should provide multiple touchpoints that are accessible from various devices. Thus, users can become both the user and the creator of this information and exchange their experiences with others. The main objective of these systems should focus on the enhancement of the tourism experience, the effective usage of resources, and maintaining its sustainability (Buhalis & Amaranggana, 2013).

Development of a smart destination can be achieved with the implementation of a comprehensive framework that adopts service-dominant logic; where smart contributors (people, ICT, leadership) play a role at the first stage, smart process (economic, social, and technological actors) at the second, and smart outcomes (smart innovations) at the third. In the first stage, each individual contributor plays a unique role in bringing the smartness concept into a destination. People (human and social capital), ICTs (IoT, big data, cloud, and edge computing), and leadership (participatory governance, policies, and regulations) concepts need to be enhanced and developed to sustain a reliable smart system. In the second stage, the smart process is intended to develop a value co-creation ecosystem between social, technological, and economic actors. In the final stage, smart innovations should be presented as an outcome of these systems with the integration of the aforementioned six components of a smart city (smart economy, smart mobility, smart environment, smart people, smart living, smart governance) and 6A components (attractions, accessibility, amenities, available packages, activities, ancillary services) of a tourism destination introduced by Buhalis (2000) (Boes et al., 2016).

Big Data and Wi-Fi

The sustainable development of a smart destination requires a knowledge-based and data-driven approach. The demand for a more personalized and co-created tourist experience is pushing smart destinations towards an integration between business models and big data (Vecchio et al., 2018). Therefore, it can be stated, big data has become an important resource as a knowledge generator for tourism destinations, which aids decision-makers in developing more effective solutions (Fuchs et al., 2014).

Big data provides alternative solution methods to traditional solutions based on databases (Bello-Orgaz et al., 2016). However, the quick approval from the public and private sectors and the fast evolution of big data left little time for academia to establish a common understanding of this subject. The consensus on the definition and characteristics of big data has not been still achieved (Gandomi & Haider, 2015). Ward and Barker (2013) analyzed big data definitions of companies such as Microsoft, Gartner, IBM, etc., and concluded that; size, complexity, and technologies are the three assertion topics encountered among these definitions. Mostly, size reflects the importance of the volume of these data sets, while complexity underlines the importance of structure, behavior, and permutation. Technologies exhibit the tools and technologies required to process them.

Other researches carried out in the big data field also pointed out various definitions of big data shared some characteristics too. Volume, Velocity, and Variety are some of the shared characteristics of big data information (De Mauro et al., 2016; Kitchin & McArdle, 2016). Laney (2001) mentioned the changes observed in traditional data management principles from the perspective of e-commerce and introduced these aforementioned three characteristics (Volume, Velocity, and Variety) that form 3V's of big data. Laney also noted that by focusing on a new approach to data management and with the collaboration of these information assets, businesses could provide better solutions and eventually achieve greater results. Later, Gantz and Reinsel (2011) stated that big data is not a thing but a dynamic activity in many IT borders. Their definition of big data introduced a new characteristic into consideration, Value. Even though there are other terms offered as characteristics of big data such as exhaustivity, resolution, indexicality, relationality, extensionality, veracity, scalability (Kitchin & McArdle, 2016); Volume, Velocity, Variety, and Value (4V's) have been accepted and considered as the four characteristics of big data by the majority. These V's can be described as follows (M. Chen et al., 2014; Hashem et al., 2015);

- Volume refers to the amount of collected data. Data generated and collected from different sources expands to a large scale and becomes increasingly big.
- Velocity refers to the rapid generation of big data and the speed of data transfer. Big data analysis should be conducted without delays to maximize the obtained value.
- Variety refers to the different types of data (videos, images, audios, texts, etc.) collected from various types of data sources (web pages, mobile applications, companies' databases, etc.).
- Value refers to exploring the hidden value of these data sets and their rapid generation.
- It should be noted that big data is an involving topic, and the future definition and characteristics might differ from what it is today (Gandomi & Haider, 2015).

Big data can be classified according to their aspects shown in Figure 1. Web and social media platforms (blogs, Facebook, Instagram), machine-generated data from hardware or software (computers, medical devices), sensing devices, transactions (financial data), devices that connect through Internet of Things (smartphones, tablets) can be classified as data sources of big data. Big data content can be in structured (SQL managed), semi-structured or unstructured (text messages) formats. Big data can be stored in document-oriented (MongoDB, CouchDB), column-oriented (MariaDB), graph-based (OrientDB), key-value (Oracle NoSQL Database) databases. Cleaning (identifying incomplete data), normalizing (minimizing redundancy), and transforming (making data suitable for analysis) are some of the processes of data staging. Data can be processed by using a batch or a real time data (Hashem et al., 2015)

Figure 1. Big data classification
Source: Hashem et al., 2015

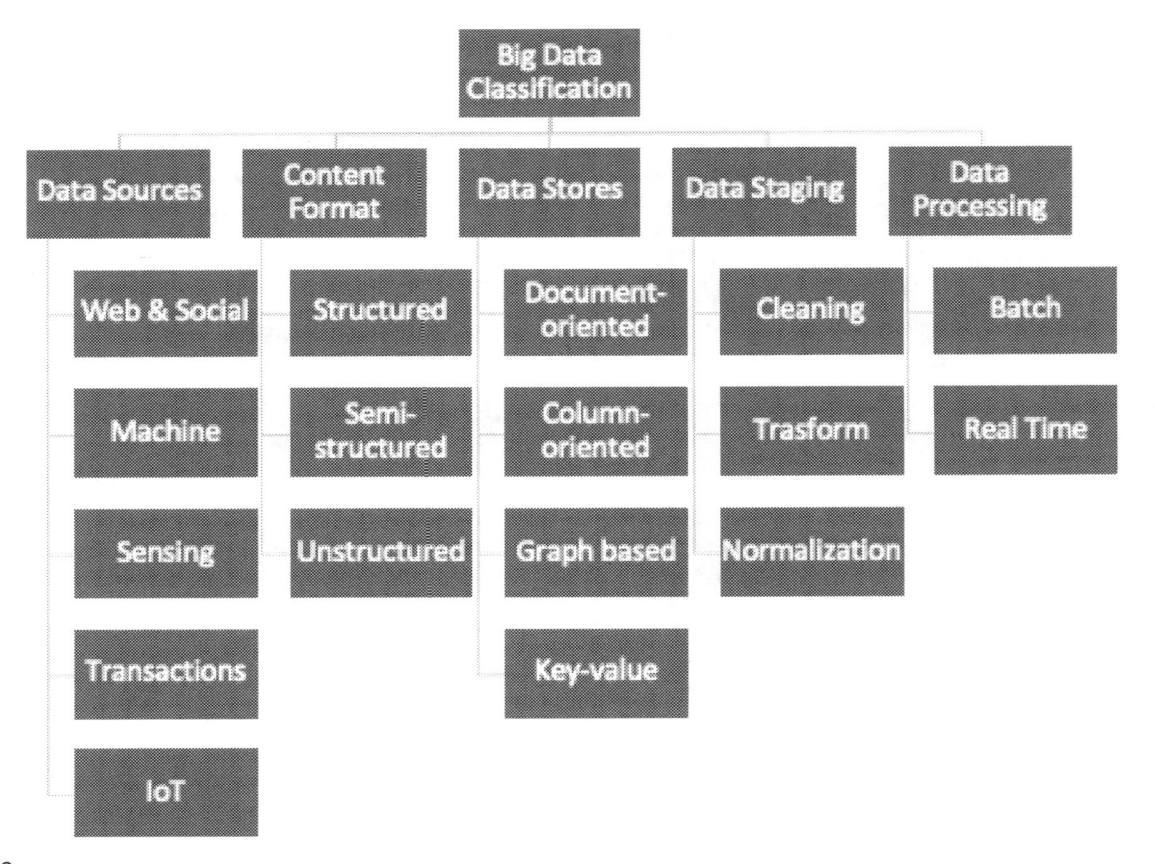

Data acquired from various systems play a vital role in the modern world. For example, IoT data shows the potential to provide improvement in both interactions and communicants between users, products, environments and ensure better services as a result of this co-created value chain. The continuing development of these systems and the competitive environment create the necessity for the cities to undergo a transformation, where they will be forced to become smarter and eventually turn into a Smart City (Vicini et al., 2012).

Big data mainly consists of two sub-processes, data management, and analytics. Data management process involves data acquisition, storage, and preparation of big data, which builds a basic structure for the next step, big data analytics. Big data analytics focus on analyzing the preprocessed data, unveiling the intelligence it contains, and making use of this information (Gandomi & Haider, 2015). Big data acquired from reliable resources should be analyzed using big data analytics, which integrates these data into various processes and infrastructures such as tourist demand forecasts, crowd monitoring, etc. (Zeng et al., 2020). Also, the integration of social big data analysis into smart destination management systems will provide value creation opportunities on decision-making processes, enhancing tourist experience, building data-driven business models, developing a new product/service, and creating an ecosystem at destination levels while providing insight on tourist profiles, socio-demographics, preferences, etc. As a result of this integration, a smart destination can achieve effective management, marketing, and policy-making decisions that can better meet the specified tourist needs (Vecchio et al., 2018).

The role and importance of tourism-related community websites and social media platforms where photographs, opinions, and reviews can be shared, has expanded in recent years (Chareyron et al., 2015). Big data generated from these platforms act as an important tool for enhancing the decision-making process of a tourism destination. Information on tourists' behavior, interest, and experience can be gathered from social media shares, and the touristic demand predictions can be run if sufficient data can be collected. Destination management organizations can make the best use of this processed data (Miah et al., 2017).

A tourism destination can reach reliable knowledge by applying Business Intelligence methods such as data identification and preparation, database modeling and data warehousing, and data mining. Data mining plays a crucial role in identifying trends and patterns of huge data by implementing classification, estimation, prediction, clustering, and association rules techniques (Fuchs et al., 2014).

As it was noted before, Wi-Fi contributes to the production of big data as one of the device data (J. Li et al., 2018). Modern smartphones provide Wi-Fi services that are being enabled by default (Bonne et al., 2013), and these devices are continuously searching for available networks (Ramos et al., 2021). When the mobile phone is connected to the Wi-Fi service, it provides the opportunity to track the beneficiaries of these services without requiring additional permission (Bonne et al., 2013). Wi-Fi data provides various data collection and analysis advantages for tourism destinations, such as being a low-cost alternative, collecting data in a homogenous style and providing accuracy at geolocation (Ramos et al., 2021).

Wi-Fi has received attention from scholars in various fields, including tourism, in recent years. Wi-Fi has been suggested as an important tourism infrastructure for wine tourism, especially in rural areas, that enables wineries to have social interaction and create a real-time promotion of both the destination and the brands (Pelet et al., 2019). The use of Wi-Fi as a tracking device at mega-events has also been proposed in research conducted by Bonne et al. (2013). They presented it as a low-cost choice and noted that it doesn't require the active cooperation of its users. Yet, Wi-Fi still stands as one of the less explored areas in tourism social media analysis (Z. Chen et al., 2021).

Cultural Heritage and Digitalization

Heritage is defined as "contemporary product shaped from history" (Loulanski, 2006). Heritage is the most valuable asset that we have inherited from our ancestors and that we must pass on to future generations intact (UNWTO, 2015). While heritage is increasingly perceived as people-oriented in a social context, it has been attributed more as a public and common legacy to all humanity than private property (Loulanski, 2006).

The topic of cultural heritage has been of interest to many disciplines including geography, history, sociology, anthropology, archaeology, and tourism. As well as the subject being multidisciplinary and complex combined with social factors contributed to the development of the concept of cultural heritage (Snis et al., 2021). From the perspective of tourism research, cultural tourism is defined as visits made by people outside the host community, partly for the purpose of seeing the historical, artistic, scientific, or lifestyle/heritage of a community, region, group, or institution (Silberberg, 1995).

Tourism is one of the fastest-growing industries in the world, and culture is one of the fastest-growing elements of international tourism. Since ancient times, people have traveled to areas of natural and cultural heritage. Interaction between World Heritage sites and tourism has increased with the enactment of the World Heritage Convention in the early 1970s. The reason for this is that it considers these places as the most valuable and symbolic destination in the world internationally (UNWTO, 2015).

The management of cultural heritage is a particularly complex process as preservation of the "old" must go hand in hand with the innovation of something "new" and smart (Al-hagla, 2010). This ongoing digitalization of society also embraces dimensions of integration, equality, citizen needs, sustainability, and quality of life are of increasing importance for city transformation (Josefsson & Steinthorsson, 2021). Cultural tourism research focused on big data knowledge is expected to provide new insights on the development of cultural tourism chains (D. Li & Li, 2020).

INTEGRATING BIG DATA TO SMART DESTINATION HERITAGE MANAGEMENT

Characterization of the Study Area

The historical development of Istanbul stretches from 2000 BC to 1453 AD, and this period continues within the walls of the historical peninsula (İstanbullu Dincer & Ertugral, 2000). The historical peninsula is geographically surrounded by the Golden Horn in the north, the Sea of Marmara in the south, the Bosphorus in the east, and the Byzantine walls in the west. It was the administrative center of great empires such as Rome, Byzantium, and Ottoman.

Istanbul is represented on the UNESCO World Heritage List by four main areas: Sultanahmet Urban Archaeological Site, Suleymaniye Conservation Area, Zeyrek Conservation Area, and Land Walls Conservation Area. Sultanahmet Urban Archeological Site includes Hippodrome of Constantine, Hagia Sophia, Hagia Irene, Little Hagia Sophia, and Topkapı Palace (Istanbul Directorate of Culture and Tourism, n.d.). These areas mentioned above are located in Fatih region, which recorded the highest overnight stays in both 2019 and 2020 amongst 39 regions of Istanbul (Istanbul Directorate of Culture and Tourism, 2020)

The Sultanahmet Urban Archaeological Site, located within the historic peninsula, is noted as a historical, cultural, religious, commercial center. The Sultanahmet Urban Archaeological Site is a large partition of Istanbul's historical development, as well as a focus for tourism. It has also often been the subject of research in academic studies due to the region being an important center in many areas. After the Istanbul Museum-City Project launch in 2004, museumization was adopted as a common strategy for the regeneration of Istanbul's historical peninsula (Aykaç, 2019). The area that will be transformed into a museum neighborhood was selected as Sultanahmet. Topkapi Palace, Turkish and Islamic Arts Museum, Great Palace Mosaics Museum, Istanbul Archaeological Museum, Istanbul Museum of The History of Science & Technology in Islam, Hagia Irene Museum, Basilica Cistern, Serefiye Cistern attract great attention from tourists.

According to the results of the survey conducted by the Tourism Development and Education Foundation (TUGEV), Istanbul Congress and Visitors Bureau (ICVB), and Fatih Municipality with 5,096 foreign visitors coming to Istanbul, the most visited places in Istanbul are the Blue Mosque (Sultanahmet Mosque). 53.8%), Hagia Sophia (46.4%), Topkapi Palace (28%), Grand Bazaar (20.7%), Istiklal Street (18.1%), Galata Tower (14.9%), Basilica Cistern (13.3%), Islands (11.8%). Five of these visitor attractions are located in the Sultanahmet area.

Research Methodology

Wi- Istanbul Metropolitan Municipality (IBB) provides a free-of-charge "ibbWiFi" service that can be accessed from public places such as squares, parks, sports, and cultural facilities. Isttelkom, a center that develops solutions in Information Technologies for Istanbul, describes "ibbWiFi" as a solution partner within the smart urban approach of IBB. It is stated that the "ibbWiFi" system has over 1.5 million single users, with at least 2.500 local and over 150 foreign new users each day (Isttelkom, n.d.) IBB collects these Wi-Fi connection data while associating the device with the country it is used and obtains this information. Data obtained from IBB constitute the main data of our research.

In our research, three sets of monthly recorded data from March 2019 to February 2020 were used. Istanbul Wi-Fi, the number of Wi-Fi connections recorded from 1.083 hotspots through Istanbul, forms the first data set of our research. A total of 162.022 Wi-Fi connections from 134 countries were recorded through this aforementioned period.

Sultanahmet Wi-Fi forms our second data set. The surroundings of Sultanahmet Urban Archeological Site and its cultural heritage sites were taken into consideration while determining the related Wi-Fi hotspots. In the selection process of appropriate Wi-Fi hotspots for the Sultanahmet area, we eliminated Istanbul Wi-Fi hotspots that don't provide services in predetermined Sultanahmet Urban Archeological Site and cannot be reached within walking distance. As shown in Figure 2, these sites were marked with red boxes, and the surrounding Wi-Fi hotspots are shown with the star embed red circles. Sultanahmet Square and Sultanahmet Mosque, Spice (Egyptian) Bazaar, Gulhane, and Sultanahmet tram stations are the examples of 19 Wi-Fi hotspots used in the analysis. Sultanahmet Wi-Fi data from 19 Wi-Fi hotspots were extracted from the main data set, Istanbul Wi-Fi, for obtaining the related data. After all, a total of 64.327 Wi-Fi connections from 125 countries were taken into analysis.

Figure 2. Sultanahmet cultural heritage sites and Wi-Fi hotspots

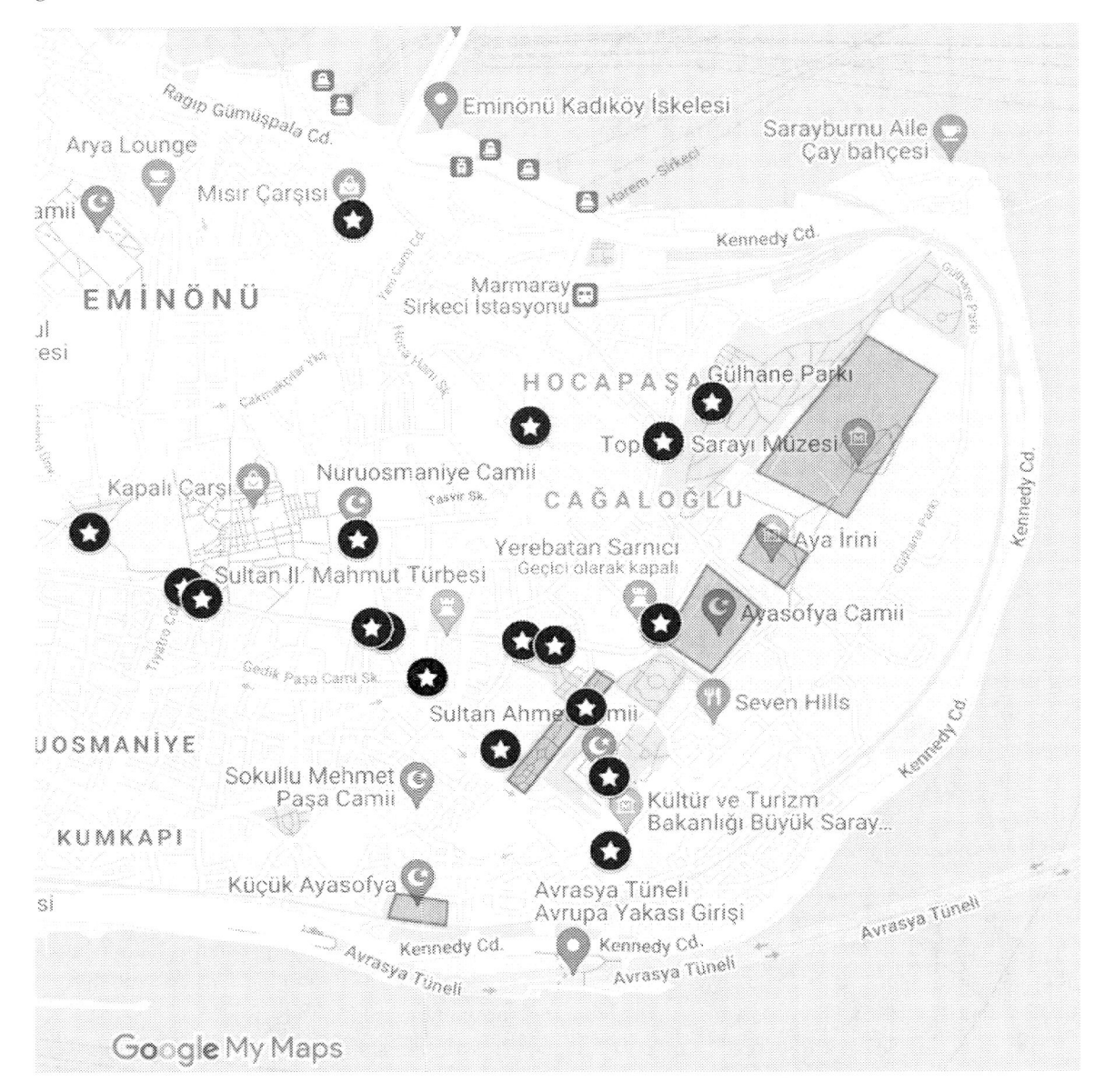

The last set of data forms the arrivals of international tourists to Istanbul from various border gates. This data set was acquired from Ministry of Culture and Tourism of Republic of Turkey. From March 2019 to February 2020, a total of 14.982.210 international tourist arrivals from 201 countries were recorded for Istanbul province. The comparisons between these data sets were run by using a Kruskal-Wallis Test, a non-parametric comparison test between two or more variables, in SPSS 24 program.

Findings

The monthly and annual figures of these data sets were divided into related totals and converted into ratios. Based on these calculations, 20 countries providing the highest percentages over the annual data, separately for all three data sets, were included in the analysis. As a result, Russia, Germany, Iran, England, Italy, France, Ukraine, Saudi Arabia, Bosnia and Herzegovina, United Arab Emirates, Azerbaijan, Tunisia, Algeria, Spain, Netherlands, United States of America, Romania, Belgium, Iraq, Lebanon, Greece, Switzerland, China, Kuwait, Jordan, Israel, Turkmenistan, and Libya -a total of 28- forms the main focus group. Table 1 shows the list of counts and the percentiles of these countries with their related data sets.

Table 1. Annual Istanbul Wi-Fi, Sultanahmet Wi-Fi and Istanbul arrivals data

	Istanbul Wi-Fi				Sultanahmet Wi-Fi				Istanbul Arrivals		
1	Russia	18.095	11,17%	1	Russia	8.300	12,90%	1	Germany	1.121.035	7,48%
2	Germany	14.226	8,78%	2	England	5.791	9,00%	2	Iran	933.807	6,23%
3	Iran	10.914	6,74%	3	Germany	4.186	6,51%	3	Russia	741.349	4,95%
4	England	10.747	6,63%	4	Italy	3.964	6,16%	4	Iraq	670.314	4,47%
5	Italy	6.768	4,18%	5	France	3.046	4,74%	5	France	514.349	3,43%
6	France	6.393	3,95%	6	Ukraine	2.313	3,60%	6	England	495.370	3,31%
7	Ukraine	5.329	3,29%	7	Iran	1.937	3,01%	7	United States of America	461.976	3,08%
8	Saudi Arabia	4.816	2,97%	8	Spain	1.705	2,65%	8	Saudi Arabia	460.141	3,07%
9	Bosnia and Herzegovina	4.011	2,48%	9	Bosnia and Herzegovina	1.657	2,58%	9	China	353.628	2,36%
10	United Arab Emirates	3.847	2,37%	10	Algeria	1.651	2,57%	10	Kuwait	343.116	2,29%
11	Tunisia	3.644	2,25%	11	United Arab Emirates	1.440	2,24%	11	Jordan	326.701	2,18%
12	Azerbaijan	3.526	2,18%	12	Romania	1.431	2,22%	12	Ukraine	326.312	2,18%
13	Algeria	3.369	2,08%	13	United States of America	1.327	2,06%	13	Israel	318.539	2,13%
14	Spain	3.162	1,95%	14	Saudi Arabia	1.279	1,99%	14	Netherlands	296.789	1,98%
15	Netherlands	2.968	1,83%	15	Netherlands	1.134	1,76%	15	Italy	284.873	1,90%
16	United States of America	2.867	1,77%	16	Belgium	1.071	1,66%	16	Turkmenistan	272.358	1,82%
17	Romania	2.698	1,67%	17	Tunisia	1.056	1,64%	17	Algeria	270.852	1,81%
18	Belgium	2.509	1,55%	18	Azerbaijan	1.038	1,61%	18	Lebanon	249.582	1,67%
19	Iraq	2.493	1,54%	19	Greece	905	1,41%	19	Libya	247.937	1,65%
20	Lebanon	2.478	1,53%	20	Switzerland	835	1,30%	20	Azerbaijan	242.537	1,62%
	TOTAL	162.022	100,00%		TOTAL	64.237	100,00%		TOTAL	14.982.210	100,00%

In our case, each of our data sets has entries for the period of 12 months (March 2019-February 2020) for each predetermined country. Due to the low sample size, we decided to conduct a non-parametric test for comparing Istanbul Wi-Fi data with Sultanahmet Wi-Fi data and Istanbul Wi-Fi data with Istanbul Arrivals data. As we aim to search for a significant difference between these data sets, we conducted the Kruskal-Wallis Test, a non-parametric test that compares the overall difference between two or more groups (Salkind & Frey, 2020).

Data processing was carried out to run the analysis mentioned above. The raw data received from IBB was processed into monthly actual data for each of the 20 countries. Then, this monthly actual data was transformed into monthly relative data for each data set. Afterwards, Kruskal-Wallis Test was conducted using these processed relative data sets. The significant results of pairwise comparisons of the data sets are shared in Table 2 as a result of the conducted analyzes, and non-significant results are excluded.

Table 2. Pairwise comparisons of data sets

Countries	Sample 1-Sample 2	Test Statistic	Std. Error	Std. Test Statistic	Sig.	Adj. Sig.[a]
Germany	Sultanahmet Wi-Fi-Istanbul Wi-Fi	-14,917	4,301	-3,468	0,001	0,002
Lebanon	Sultanahmet Wi-Fi-Istanbul Wi-Fi	-15,667	4,301	-3,642	0,000	0,001
Iran	Sultanahmet Wi-Fi-Istanbul Wi-Fi	-17,583	4,301	-4,088	0,000	0,000
England	Istanbul Arrivals-Istanbul Wi-Fi	-13,583	4,301	-3,158	0,002	0,005
Russia	Istanbul Arrivals -Istanbul Wi-Fi	-15,917	4,301	-3,701	0,000	0,001
Ukraine	Istanbul Arrivals -Istanbul Wi-Fi	-13,750	4,301	-3,197	0,001	0,004
Italy	Istanbul Arrivals -Istanbul Wi-Fi	-14,333	4,301	-3,332	0,001	0,003
Bosnia and Herzegovina	Istanbul Arrivals -Istanbul Wi-Fi	-17,583	4,301	-4,088	0,000	0,000
United Arab Emirates	Istanbul Arrivals -Istanbul Wi-Fi	-19,000	4,301	-4,417	0,000	0,000
Tunisia	Istanbul Arrivals -Istanbul Wi-Fi	-16,417	4,301	-3,817	0,000	0,000
United States of America	Istanbul Wi-Fi-Istanbul Arrivals	17,583	4,301	4,088	0,000	0,000
Romania	Istanbul Arrivals -Istanbul Wi-Fi	-14,917	4,301	-3,468	0,001	0,002
Iraq	Istanbul Wi-Fi-Istanbul Arrivals	14,583	4,301	3,391	0,001	0,002
Greece	Istanbul Wi-Fi-Istanbul Arrivals	-13,083	4,301	-3,042	0,002	0,007
Switzerland	Istanbul Arrivals -Istanbul Wi-Fi	-12,417	4,301	-2,887	0,004	0,012
China	Istanbul Wi-Fi-Istanbul Arrivals	20,500	4,301	4,766	0,000	0,000
Kuwait	Istanbul Wi-Fi-Istanbul Arrivals	13,333	4,301	3,100	0,002	0,006
Jordan	Istanbul Wi-Fi-Istanbul Arrivals	10,833	4,301	2,519	0,012	0,035
Israel	Istanbul Wi-Fi-Istanbul Arrivals	15,500	4,301	3,604	0,000	0,001
Turkmenistan	Istanbul Wi-Fi-Istanbul Arrivals	17,583	3,851	4,565	0,000	0,000
Belgium	Istanbul Arrivals -Istanbul Wi-Fi	-13,583	4,301	-3,158	0,002	0,005
Libya	Istanbul Wi-Fi-Istanbul Arrivals	13,750	4,301	3,197	0,001	0,004

As a result of the analysis, significant differences ($p<0,05$) between Sultanahmet Wi-Fi data and Istanbul Wi-Fi data were recorded for Germany, Lebanon and Iran. On the other hand, significant differences ($p<0,05$) between Istanbul Arrivals and Istanbul Wi-Fi for England, Russia, Ukraine, Italy, Bosnia and Herzegovina, United Arab Emirates, Tunisia, United States of America, Romania, Iraq, Greece, Switzerland, China, Kuwait, Jordan, Israel, Turkmenistan, Belgium, Libya were observed. France, Spain, Saudi Arabia, Algeria, Netherlands and Azerbaijan didn't show any significant differences for pairwise comparisons of these data sets.

SOLUTIONS AND RECOMMENDATIONS

Significant differences for Germany (Sultanahmet Wi-Fi usage: 6,51% - Istanbul Wi-Fi: 8,78%), Iran (Sultanahmet Wi-Fi usage: 3,01% - Istanbul Wi-Fi: 6,74%) and Lebanon (Sultanahmet Wi-Fi usage: 0,97% - Istanbul Wi-Fi: 1,53%) were observed as a result of the analysis. It should also be noted that a significant difference between Istanbul Arrivals and Istanbul Wi-Fi wasn't found for these countries. The observed lower percentages for the usage of Sultanahmet Wi-Fi reveals a possible reason for this scenario; visiting Sultanahmet area is not a primary focus of their travel for a portion of these international tourist group. This insight reveals that the decisions and strategies regarding Sultanahmet area should be taken under these circumstances. Yet, this scenario must be analyzed and supported by other researches and data that also question this case.

Also, significant differences between Istanbul Wi-Fi and Istanbul Arrival were found, creating two groups. Countries with higher Istanbul Wi-Fi scores forms the first group, while the vice-versa situation forms the second. England (Istanbul Wi-Fi usage: 6,63% - Istanbul Arrival: 3,31%), Russia (Istanbul Wi-Fi usage: 11,17% - Istanbul Arrival: 4,95%), Ukraine (Istanbul Wi-Fi usage: 3,29% - Istanbul Arrival: 2,18%), Italy (Istanbul Wi-Fi usage: 4,18% - Istanbul Arrival: 1,90%), Bosnia and Herzegovina (Istanbul Wi-Fi usage: 2,48% - Istanbul Arrival: 0,37%), United Arab Emirates (Istanbul Wi-Fi usage: 2,37% - Istanbul Arrival: 0,21%), Tunisia (Istanbul Wi-Fi usage: 2,25% - Istanbul Arrival: 1,14%), Romania (Istanbul Wi-Fi usage: 1,67% - Istanbul Arrival: 0,94%), Greece (Istanbul Wi-Fi usage: 1,38% - Istanbul Arrival: 0,75%), Switzerland (Istanbul Wi-Fi usage: 1,42% - Istanbul Arrival: 0,91%), Belgium (Istanbul Wi-Fi usage: 1,55% - Istanbul Arrival: 0,95%), creates the first group with higher Istanbul Wi-Fi scores. This outcome might mean that the international tourists traveling to Istanbul from these countries tend to use technology more frequently and benefit from its opportunities. Since this group is expected to benefit from the use of technology in their travels, a technological infrastructure should be used for sharing promotional materials with them. Information on trips, museums, exhibitions, offers can be presented using these connections from Istanbul Wi-Fi hotspots.

United States of America (Istanbul Wi-Fi usage: 1,77% - Istanbul Arrival: 3,08%), Iraq (Istanbul Wi-Fi usage: 1,54% - Istanbul Arrival: 4,47%), China (Istanbul Wi-Fi usage: 0,30% - Istanbul Arrival: 2,36%), Kuwait (Istanbul Wi-Fi usage: 0,58% - Istanbul Arrival: 2,29%), Jordan (Istanbul Wi-Fi usage: 1,26% - Istanbul Arrival: 2,18%), Israel (Istanbul Wi-Fi usage: 0,44% - Istanbul Arrival: 2,13%), Turkmenistan (Istanbul Wi-Fi usage: 0,001% - Istanbul Arrival: 1,82%), Libya (Istanbul Wi-Fi usage: 0,27% - Istanbul Arrival: 1,65%) forms the second group. This group has lower scores in Istanbul Wi-Fi data. The difference between Istanbul Arrivals and Istanbul Wi-Fi raises the questions if the Wi-Fi service promotion is utilized, international tourists from these countries prefer to use these technological services and Wi-Fi services are provided in their native languages. The usage of Wi-Fi should be encouraged for this group of international tourists by running promotional materials starting from their arrival in Istanbul.

CONCLUSION

The management of tourism at world heritage sites plays an important role that extends far beyond remaining competitive in the international tourism market. Such sites have an immeasurable inherent value in the expression and sense of identity of a host community. They play an essential role in public education, and when managed properly, help to protect natural and cultural values and improve the quality of life for residents and visitors alike. As such, their integrity and authenticity must be conserved, so that the values they represent are available to current and future generations (UNWTO, 2015).

Tourism management departments can use big data for sustaining improvements on the quality of tourism scenic spots, competitiveness of tourism attractions, promoting the urbanization of tourism, and regional economic levels (D. Li & Li, 2020).

In this study, we aimed to find significant differences between Istanbul Wi-Fi data and Sultanahmet Wi-Fi data, Istanbul Wi-Fi data, and Istanbul Arrival data. We revealed significant differences between Istanbul Wi-Fi and Sultanahmet Wi-Fi usage rates of international tourists from Germany, Iran, and Lebanon. This tourist group's usage frequency of Wi-Fi from Sultanahmet area is lower than Istanbul in general. Even though this scenario must be analyzed thoroughly, it might mean this group is less likely to travel to Sultanahmet area.

Comparison analysis between Istanbul Wi-Fi and Istanbul Arrival has shown us significant differences occurred for two groups of countries. The first group has a higher frequency rate of Wi-Fi usage in Istanbul. This group of international tourists is more likely to welcome Wi-Fi technology and use it the fullest. Second group has shown a lower frequency rate of Wi-Fi usage in Istanbul. The reasons of this lower frequency can be explained with multiple reasons such as low promotion of this service, a tourist profile that resists the use of technology, and language barriers.

Wi-Fi data collected by smart destinations can be used to reveal new insights on identifying tourist profiles, destination preferences, possible routes and many other subjects. This newly acquired information will support smart destinations in building their tourism strategies and supporting their decision-making processes. The conducted analysis should be integrated with relevant data acquired from other resources or researches. Thus, the decision-making process of heritage management sites can be supported with a systematic data-driven approach. This approach to big data and big data analytics will make the best use of decision-making processes with the optimized data and solutions they offer.

LIMITATIONS

Our research focused on a specific period due to Covid-19 and its effects. The emergence of this crisis negatively affected tourism movements and activities, causing an inability to collect the data and a decrease in the relevant data. Also, the retrieved Wi-Fi data set and the conducted analysis offered a certain level of insight, which puts a limitation on the analysis. In order to perform deeper analysis and gather a better understanding of tourist profiles and related issues, other data sets supporting the Wi-Fi sets should be integrated.

FUTURE RESEARCH DIRECTIONS

Smart destinations, that can identify the applications used by tourists using the provided Wi-Fi services, will be able to develop customized marketing efforts. Detection of both application usage and duration of use will provide enhanced information about tourist needs and preferences for smart destinations. Also, due to the increasing importance of social media, marketing efforts can be canalized through these channels. Personalized marketing plays a critical role in achieving and maintaining success. Future researches should focus on addressing these issues.

In addition, these analyses should also be conducted with a larger data set and supported with other related analyzes. Tourist profiles using these Wi-Fi services should be identified and the main reasons behind the use/resistance to using should be emphasized.

REFERENCES

Ahas, R., Aasa, A., Mark, Ü., Pae, T., & Kull, A. (2007). Seasonal tourism spaces in Estonia: Case study with mobile positioning data. *Tourism Management*, *28*(3), 898–910. Advance online publication. doi:10.1016/j.tourman.2006.05.010

Al-hagla, K. S. (2010). Sustainable urban development in historical areas using the tourist trail approach: A case study of the Cultural Heritage and Urban Development (CHUD) project in Saida, Lebanon. *Cities (London, England)*, *27*(4), 234–248. Advance online publication. doi:10.1016/j.cities.2010.02.001

Albino, V., Berardi, U., & Dangelico, R. M. (2015). Smart cities: Definitions, dimensions, performance, and initiatives. *Journal of Urban Technology*, *22*(1), 3–21. Advance online publication. doi:10.1080/1 0630732.2014.942092

Angelidou, M. (2016). Four European Smart City Strategies. *International Journal of Social Science Studies*, *4*(4). Advance online publication. doi:10.11114/ijsss.v4i4.1364

Aykaç, P. (2019). Musealisation as a strategy for the reconstruction of an idealised Ottoman past: Istanbul's Sultanahmet district as a 'museum-quarter.'. *International Journal of Heritage Studies*, *25*(2), 160–177. Advance online publication. doi:10.1080/13527258.2018.1475407

Bello-Orgaz, G., Jung, J. J., & Camacho, D. (2016). Social big data: Recent achievements and new challenges. *Information Fusion*, *28*, 45–59. Advance online publication. doi:10.1016/j.inffus.2015.08.005 PMID:32288689

Boes, K., Buhalis, D., & Inversini, A. (2016). Smart tourism destinations: Ecosystems for tourism destination competitiveness. *International Journal of Tourism Cities*, *2*(2), 108–124. Advance online publication. doi:10.1108/IJTC-12-2015-0032

Bonne, B., Barzan, A., Quax, P., & Lamotte, W. (2013). WiFiPi: Involuntary tracking of visitors at mass events. *2013 IEEE 14th International Symposium on a World of Wireless, Mobile and Multimedia Networks, WoWMoM 2013*. 10.1109/WoWMoM.2013.6583443

Borissova, V. (2018). Cultural heritage digitization and related intellectual property issues. *Journal of Cultural Heritage*, *34*, 145–150. Advance online publication. doi:10.1016/j.culher.2018.04.023

Buhalis, D. (2000). Marketing the competitive destination of the future. *Tourism Management*, *21*(1), 97–116. Advance online publication. doi:10.1016/S0261-5177(99)00095-3

Buhalis, D., & Amaranggana, A. (2013). Smart Tourism Destinations. Information and Communication Technologies in Tourism 2014. doi:10.1007/978-3-319-03973-2_40

Chareyron, G., Da-Rugna, J., & Raimbault, T. (2015). Big data: A new challenge for tourism. *Proceedings - 2014 IEEE International Conference on Big Data, IEEE Big Data 2014*. 10.1109/BigData.2014.7004475

Chen, M., Mao, S., & Liu, Y. (2014). Big data: A survey. *Mobile Networks and Applications*, *19*(2), 171–209. Advance online publication. doi:10.100711036-013-0489-0

Chen, Z., Alfred, R., & Eboy, O. V. (2021). Modeling Tourism Using Spatial Analysis Based on Social Media Big Data: A Review. *Lecture Notes in Electrical Engineering*, *724*, 437–451. Advance online publication. doi:10.1007/978-981-33-4069-5_36

De Mauro, A., Greco, M., & Grimaldi, M. (2016). A formal definition of Big Data based on its essential features. Library Review, 65(3). doi:10.1108/LR-06-2015-0061

Del Vecchio, P., Mele, G., Ndou, V., & Secundo, G. (2018). Creating value from Social Big Data: Implications for Smart Tourism Destinations. *Information Processing & Management*, *54*(5), 847–860. Advance online publication. doi:10.1016/j.ipm.2017.10.006

Fuchs, M., Höpken, W., & Lexhagen, M. (2014). Big data analytics for knowledge generation in tourism destinations - A case from Sweden. *Journal of Destination Marketing & Management*, *3*(4), 198–209. Advance online publication. doi:10.1016/j.jdmm.2014.08.002

Gandomi, A., & Haider, M. (2015). Beyond the hype: Big data concepts, methods, and analytics. *International Journal of Information Management*, *35*(2), 137–144. Advance online publication. doi:10.1016/j.ijinfomgt.2014.10.007

Gantz, J., & Reinsel, D. (2011). Extracting Value from Chaos State of the Universe: An Executive Summary. *IDC IView*.

Giffinger, R., & Gudrun, H. (2010). *Smart cities ranking: an effective instrument for the positioning of the cities? ACE: Architecture, City and Environment*. doi:10.5821/ace.v4i12.2483

Gretzel, U., Sigala, M., Xiang, Z., & Koo, C. (2015). Smart tourism: Foundations and developments. *Electronic Markets*, *25*(3), 179–188. Advance online publication. doi:10.100712525-015-0196-8

Gretzel, U., Werthner, H., Koo, C., & Lamsfus, C. (2015). Conceptual foundations for understanding smart tourism ecosystems. *Computers in Human Behavior*, *50*, 558–563. Advance online publication. doi:10.1016/j.chb.2015.03.043

Guo, Y., Liu, H., & Chai, Y. (2014). The embedding convergence of smart cities and tourism internet of things in China: An advance perspective. *Advances in Hospitality and Tourism Research*, *2*(1), 54–69.

Hashem, I. A. T., Yaqoob, I., Anuar, N. B., Mokhtar, S., Gani, A., & Ullah Khan, S. (2015). The rise of "big data" on cloud computing: Review and open research issues. In Information Systems (Vol. 47). doi:10.1016/j.is.2014.07.006

ISO. (2014). *ISO 37120 - Sustainable development of communities - Indicators for city services and quality of life*. ISO.

Istanbul Directorate of Culture and Tourism. (2020). *Istanbul Tourism Statistics Report*. Author.

İstanbullu Dincer, F. F., & Ertugral, S. M. (2000). Kültürel Mirasın Korunması ve İstanbul ilindeki Tarihi Yapıların Turizm Amaclı Kullanımı Üzerine Bir Deneme. *Anatolia: Turizm Araştırmaları Dergisi, 11*(2), 69–78.

Isttelkom. (n.d.). *We are laying the foundations of smart cities*. https://isttelkom.istanbul/en/yusuf-kotil-we-are-laying-the-foundations-of-smart-cities

Josefsson, M. Y., & Steinthorsson, R. S. (2021). Reflections on a SMART urban ecosystem in a small island state: The case of SMART Reykjavik. *International Journal of Entrepreneurship and Small Business, 42*(1–2), 93. Advance online publication. doi:10.1504/IJESB.2021.112260

Kitchin, R., & McArdle, G. (2016). What makes Big Data, Big Data? Exploring the ontological characteristics of 26 datasets. *Big Data & Society, 3*(1). Advance online publication. doi:10.1177/2053951716631130

Laney, D. (2001). 3D Data Management: Controlling Data Volume, Velocity, and Variety. *Application Delivery Strategies, 949*(February).

Lee, P., Hunter, W. C., & Chung, N. (2020). Smart tourism city: Developments and transformations. *Sustainability (Switzerland), 12*(10), 3958. Advance online publication. doi:10.3390u12103958

Li, D., & Li, K. (2020). Research on Big Data System Based on Cultural Tourism in Dongguan. In K. Li, W. Li, H. Wang, & Y. Liu (Eds.), Communications in Computer and Information Science: Vol. 1205 CCIS (pp. 320–332). Springer. doi:10.1007/978-981-15-5577-0_24

Li, J., Xu, L., Tang, L., Wang, S., & Li, L. (2018). Big data in tourism research: A literature review. *Tourism Management, 68*, 301–323. Advance online publication. doi:10.1016/j.tourman.2018.03.009

Lombardi, P., Giordano, S., Farouh, H., & Yousef, W. (2012). Modelling the smart city performance. Innovation: The European Journal of Social Science Research, 25(2). doi:10.1080/13511610.2012.660325

Loulanski, T. (2006). Revising the Concept for Cultural Heritage: The Argument for a Functional Approach. *International Journal of Cultural Property, 13*(2). Advance online publication. doi:10.1017/S0940739106060085

McNulty, R., & Koff, R. (2014). *Cultural Heritage Tourism*. Partners for Livable Communities. https://www.americansforthearts.org/sites/default/files/culturalheritagetourism.pdf

Miah, S. J., Vu, H. Q., Gammack, J., & McGrath, M. (2017). A Big Data Analytics Method for Tourist Behaviour Analysis. *Information & Management, 54*(6), 771–785. Advance online publication. doi:10.1016/j.im.2016.11.011

Nam, T., & Pardo, T. A. (2011). Conceptualizing smart city with dimensions of technology, people, and institutions. *ACM International Conference Proceeding Series*. 10.1145/2037556.2037602

Neirotti, P., De Marco, A., Cagliano, A. C., Mangano, G., & Scorrano, F. (2014). Current trends in smart city initiatives: Some stylised facts. *Cities (London, England), 38*, 25–36. Advance online publication. doi:10.1016/j.cities.2013.12.010

Pelet, J. É., Barton, M., & Chapuis, C. (2019). Towards the implementation of digital through Wi-Fi and IoT in wine tourism: Perspectives from professionals of wine and tourism. In M. Sigala & R. N. S. Robinson (Eds.), *Management and Marketing of Wine Tourism Business: Theory, Practice, and Cases* (pp. 207–236). Palgrave Macmillan., doi:10.1007/978-3-319-75462-8_11

Ramos, V., Yamaka, W., Alorda, B., & Sriboonchitta, S. (2021). High-frequency forecasting from mobile devices' bigdata: An application to tourism destinations' crowdedness. *International Journal of Contemporary Hospitality Management, 33*(6), 1977–2000. Advance online publication. doi:10.1108/IJCHM-10-2020-1170

Salkind, N. J., & Frey, B. B. (2020). Statistics for people who (think they) hate statistics (7th ed.). SAGE Publications, Inc.

Silberberg, T. (1995). Cultural tourism and business opportunities for museums and heritage sites. *Tourism Management, 16*(5), 361–365. Advance online publication. doi:10.1016/0261-5177(95)00039-Q

Snis, U. L., Olsson, A. K., & Bernhard, I. (2021). Becoming a smart old town – How to manage stakeholder collaboration and cultural heritage. *Journal of Cultural Heritage Management and Sustainable Development, 11*(4), 627–641. Advance online publication. doi:10.1108/JCHMSD-10-2020-0148

UNESCO. (n.d.). *Historic Areas of Istanbul*. World Heritage List. https://whc.unesco.org/en/list/356/

UNWTO. (2015). *Tourism at World Heritage Sites – Challenges and Opportunities: International tourism seminar*. UNWTO. 10.18111/9789284416608

UNWTO. (2016). *UNWTO congress to discuss the links between cultural heritage and creative tourism*. Press Release. https://www.unwto.org/archive/europe/press-release/2016-11-23/unwto-congress-discuss-links-between-cultural-heritage-and-creative-tourism

Vicini, S., Bellini, S., & Sanna, A. (2012). How to co-create internet of things-enabled services for smarter cities. *SMART 2012, The First International*.

Ward, J. S., & Barker, A. (2013). *Undefined By Data: A Survey of Big Data Definitions*. Academic Press.

Wu, Y., Zhang, W., Shen, J., Mo, Z., & Peng, Y. (2018). Smart city with Chinese characteristics against the background of big data: Idea, action and risk. *Journal of Cleaner Production, 173*, 60–66. Advance online publication. doi:10.1016/j.jclepro.2017.01.047

Zeng, D., Tim, Y., Yu, J., & Liu, W. (2020). Actualizing big data analytics for smart cities: A cascading affordance study. *International Journal of Information Management, 54*, 102156. Advance online publication. doi:10.1016/j.ijinfomgt.2020.102156

KEY TERMS AND DEFINITIONS

Big Data: Data obtained from variety of sources and demonstrate the characteristics of high volume, high velocity, and high veracity that can be used in creating value by using analytical methods.

Cultural Heritage: Tangible and intangible heritage assets that is passed down from past generations.

Smart: Technological, economic, and social developments supported by technologies.

Smart City: City aiming to optimize resource production and consumption, expand the life quality of people and the community using its the capability of using advanced ICTs.

Smart Destination: Smart city that adopts the aim of enhancing the tourist experience via using advanced ICTs and technological tools.

Smart Destination Management: Smart destination that adopts and utilizes strategic decisions on organizational and operational levels in tourism-related areas.

Wi-Fi: A system that enables the internet connection from various devices without using wires.

Chapter 23
Post–Pandemic Re–Positioning in a Cultural Tourism City:
From Overtourism to E–Tourism

Monica Coronel
Corvinus University of Budapest, Hungary

Árpád Ferenc Papp-Váry
Budapest Metropolitan University, Hungary

Ivett Pinke-Sziva
Corvinus University of Budapest, Hungary

Zombor Berezvai
 https://orcid.org/0000-0001-7807-2977
Corvinus University of Budapest, Hungary

Melanie K. Smith
 https://orcid.org/0000-0003-4557-9901
Budapest Metropolitan University, Hungary

ABSTRACT

The aim of the chapter is to provide recommendations for cities that are aiming to reposition themselves in the post-pandemic period in terms of image, product development, and the attraction of different segments of visitors. It is aimed at those readers who seek to understand the role that digital tools can play in the information provision and promotion of cities, especially for younger tourists who may have been more attracted by night-time activities in the pre-COVID period and who could be redirected to other activities or areas in future strategies. A case study of Budapest is presented that is typical of a European cultural tourism destination that has also suffered from overtourism in recent years. Primary data is used to identify tourists' preferred activities in the destination as well as their choice of digital tools for finding information and optimizing experiences. Both theory and primary data are used to make recommendations for repositioning cultural cities post pandemic with the assistance of appropriate digital tools.

DOI: 10.4018/978-1-7998-8528-3.ch023

INTRODUCTION

Cultural cities that were suffering from overtourism before COVID-19 may be exploring ways to re-position themselves in the post-pandemic period. Overtourism can be defined as "the impact of tourism on a destination, or parts thereof, that excessively influences perceived quality of life of citizens and/or quality of visitors' experiences in a negative way" (UNWTO, 2018, p.4). This deterioration had been experienced in numerous cities and various solutions were being sought to address issues and problems ranging from overcrowding, price increases and resident discontent to visitor behaviour, flow management and decreasing satisfaction. The arrival of the COVID-19 pandemic abruptly ended concerns about overtourism in terms of visitation, but it also afforded an opportunity to re-think future tourism strategies.

One element of future strategies could be the re-positioning of destinations to create a different image or to attract alternative segments of visitors. This can include *real repositioning* with changes to services offered as well as *psychological repositioning* to change tourists' perceptions of the destination (Crompton, 2009). The aim might be to attract segments for whom culture and heritage are primary or core motivations or tourists who are interested in off-the-beaten-track activities outside crowded city centers. The use of new technology can be central to this process, as it encourages independent exploration and can help to manage visitor experiences and flows.

The following sections provide an overview of the overtourism phenomenon in cultural tourism cities including its causes and consequences. A case study of Budapest is presented which is typical of a European cultural tourism destination that has also suffered from overtourism in recent years. Primary data is used to identify tourists' preferred activities in the destination as well as their choice of digital tools for finding information and optimizing experiences. One of the proposed solutions to overtourism is the diversification of the product into activities that attract smaller numbers of more educated tourists (e.g. cultural, creative or off-the-beaten-track experiences). Both theory and primary data are used to make recommendations for re-positioning cultural cities post-pandemic with the assistance of appropriate digital tools.

Overall, the main aim of the chapter is to provide recommendations for cities that are aiming to re-position themselves in the post-pandemic period in terms of image, product development and the attraction of different segments of visitor. It is aimed at those readers who seek to understand the role that digital tools can play in the information provision and promotion of cities, especially for younger tourists who may have been more attracted by night-time activities in the pre-COVID period and who could be re-directed to other activities or areas in future strategies.

BACKGROUND

Overtourism in Cultural Cities

Overtourism in cultural cities has become one of the major challenges of the past decade for tourism management and many authors view it as being inextricably connected to issues of sustainability (Capocchi, Vallone, Pierotti, & Amaduzzi, 2019). Although tourist resorts have struggled with over-crowding for decades as a result of mass package tourism, it was somewhat unexpected that cultural cities attracting mainly independent travellers would suffer from a similar phenomenon. Budget airlines and cheap, freely available accommodation through Airbnb and such platforms have accelerated this problem. Today, it is common for tourism in cities to be blamed (rightly or wrongly) for a range of impacts from night noise (Dirksmeier & Helbrecht, 2015; Pinkster & Boterman, 2017), to party and alcohol tourism (Füller & Michel, 2014; Pixová & Sládek, 2017; Smith et al., 2017; Sommer & Helbrecht, 2017); anti-social behaviour (Rouleau, 2017); congestion and overcrowding of public spaces (García-Hernández, de la Calle-Vaquero, & Yubero, 2017; Vianello, 2017); littering (Sommer & Helbrecht, 2017); gentrification (Gravari-Barbas & Guinand, 2017); and house price rises and displacement of residents because of Airbnb (Mermet, 2017; Wachsmuth & Weisler, 2018). A number of case studies have also emerged in recent years documenting the growing protests and resistance of local residents in tourism cities (Colomb & Novy, 2017; Pinkster & Boterman, 2017; Pixová & Sládek, 2017; Smith, Pinke-Sziva, & Olt., 2019; Vianello, 2017). As stated by Butler (2018), overtourism is not the same as overcrowding or mass tourism, it instead represents a situation where visitors overload the available facilities and services and become a serious inconvenience for local residents in destinations.

Although many cities still attract tourists who are predominantly interested in cultural and heritage attractions, they often arrive with multiple motivations and engage in more *omniverous* experiences (Du Cros & McKercher, 2015; Peterson, 1992; Smith & Richards, 2013; Van der Ark & Richards, 2006). It can also no longer be assumed that culturally-motivated tourists are good for a city because they are educated (Smith & Richards, 2013), even if there are examples of cultural tourism impacting positively on resident wellbeing (Tokarchuk, Gabriele, & Maurer, 2017). It is well documented that culturally-motivated tourism can have negative consequences if it is not managed well (Du Cros & McKercher, 2015). In some cases, this has led to undesirable forms of overtourism. Several authors have documented the phenomenon where (city and cultural) tourists want to *live like a local* (Russo & Richards, 2016), engage in *authentic* and *back-of-house* experiences (McKercher, 2020) and *real* destinations and their people (Wolfram & Burnhill, 2012). The search for authentic local neighbourhood experiences can create borderless interactions between tourists and residents or a "blending of practices" (Lim & Bouchon, 2017, p.14) which can sometimes have negative consequences as shown above.

Re-Positioning Cultural Tourism Cities Post-Covid-19

There has been a plethora of studies in the post-COVID-19 period that focus on the impacts of the pandemic on tourism as well as proposed solutions to development in the future. Sharma, Thomas and Paul (2021) identify two major themes that emerge from the post-COVID-19 literature, which are resilience and transformation in the new global economy and other studies that use the crisis to help define new tourism development pathways. Even more specifically, some authors have studied cities that previously suffered from overtourism in Central and Eastern Europe (also the context for this chapter). For example, Kowalczyk-Anioł, Grochowicz, and Pawlusinski (2021) discuss the post-COVID-19 strategies being used in Kracow in Poland, such as re-orientating and promoting activities to the domestic market. Even before COVID-19, the city had tried to change its tourist image and limit the negative effects of the night-time economy in its historic center.

Although the new strains of the COVID-19 pandemic have resulted in a slower return to tourism development than hoped, future strategies for cultural cities that were previously suffering from overtourism could include *de*-marketing a city (e.g. as a party destination) and *re*-marketing or re-positioning it as a cultural tourism or special interest destination including off-the-beaten-track activities. The notion of off-the-beaten-track experiences in cities is not new (Maitland, 2007; Maitland & Newman, 2014), but could play an even more important role in diversification of urban tourism activities after COVID-19.

It is important to consider the ways in which repositioning of a destination and its products or activities can be approached, as well as examining which tools might be used to do so.

Kotler (2000) emphasises that positions are determined by a combination of the image that a service supplier would like to convey as well the way in which that image is perceived by the relevant stakeholders. Kaczynski, Havitz, and McCarville (2005) assert the importance of communication in this process for which they advocate social marketing. A positioning strategy should aim to create the desired brand image in the minds of consumers (Qu, Kim, & Im, 2011). Therefore, re-positioning involves the need to change the current image of the city for the desired one. Re-positioning strategies should take into consideration the important role that both the Internet and social media play nowadays as information sources and consequently as image formation drivers (Llodrà-Riera, Martínez-Ruiz, Jiménez-Zarco, & Izquierdo-Yusta, 2015). Web 2.0 allows travellers to get information from peers and to publish content about their own travel experiences through a wide range of online platforms such as travel communities, social media, forums, blogs and online reviews (ibid., 2015). The latter are seen as the most reliable information sources (Marine-Roig & Ferrer-Rosell, 2018).

The most important goal of a destination repositioning strategy according to Chacko and Marcell (2008) is to find the right mix of segments, to offer memorable experiences for them and to communicate this effectively with consistent messages. In the case of cities struggling with overtourism, the key objective is to find those segments who appreciate the city and its residents and to find experiences that support the unique values of the city (over its cheap, party characteristics, for example). Medway and Warnaby (2014) developed a de-marketing typology which included several measures. For example, selective passive place de-marketing which uses segmentation and positioning strategies to attract certain markets and avoid others (e.g. attracting cultural tourists rather than party tourists). The authors also suggest certain strategies that re-direct tourists to alternative places, which this data demonstrated could be possible (e.g. towards off-the-beaten-track activities outside the city center).

As Trout and Rivkin (2009) point out, repositioning can be essential because of 3C-s: Competition, Change and Crisis. This model can also be adapted to the world of tourism. Competition is steadily growing with more and more destinations entering the race of tourist destinations, making it increasingly important to highlight distinctive, unique advantages. One of the drivers of change is digitalisation: tourists find information online before they make a decision and being online all the time in the city is also a priority for them, not least to share their experiences with their acquaintances on social media. Aspects such as *instagrammability* are increasingly important, with data showing that 40% of the new generation consider this to be a top priority when choosing their latest destination (Adweek.com, 2018; Forbes.com, 2018). This outranks aspects such as the cost of travel and accommodation, local cuisine and whether cheap alcohol is available in the city. What is most surprising, perhaps, is that tourist attractions rank last, i.e. they are the least important for the new generation, although it is difficult to take a good Insta-photo without attractions! Finally, the crises include overtourism, which inevitably means that destinations need to rethink themselves and find a more sustainable way forward. Of course, the COVID-19 pandemic is an even greater challenge, but it is also an opportunity to re-think about what the city wants to offer in the first place when tourists return and to whom.

Séraphin, Zaman, Olver, Bourliataux-Lajoinie, and Dosquet (2019) suggest that destinations that have been suffering from overtourism could brand each region as Special Interest Tourism areas by focusing on a particular type of experience that they want to offer to visitors. Matoga and Pawłowska (2018) discuss the phenomenon of off-the-beaten-track tourism in European historical cities and categorise it as exploring urban space beyond traditional tourism centers; seeking less visited cultural and heritage sites; thematic sightseeing; experiencing the *authentic* side of the city; and visiting places where the everyday life of inhabitants takes place. These are often places that have not been specifically constructed for tourists, hence their appeal (Judd, 2003). Lim and Bouchon (2017, p.14) emphasise that the role of technology in the creation of these experiences is proving to be more and more important as it offers "the possibility to escape from the serialization of tourism spaces, through unique and off the beaten track experiences". Matoga and Pawłowska (2018) also state that off-the-beaten-track tourism is related to various forms of collaborative consumption, including virtual communities (e.g. planning, advice, reviews) and the sharing economy (e.g. transport, accommodation, catering).

The Role of Digital Tools in E-Tourism

In recent years, information and communication technology (ICT) "has been an important enabler, catalyst and, in some cases, disruptor for travel and tourism" (Gretzel et al, 2020, p.188). ICT has been found to significantly change the tourism experience, therefore it is considered an instrument to transform a conventional tourism experience into a so-called *technology-enhanced experience*. Such experience-enhancing technologies include interactive websites, interactive ordering systems (e-Table technology), interactive mobile platforms (iPads), diverse social media channels, and mobile applications (Neuhofer, Buhalis, & Ladkin, 2014).

Tourism marketing and management have benefited from the interactivity between tourism enterprises and consumers. In this context, e-tourism brings about the interplay of tourism actors (e.g., transport, travel agencies, tour operators, airlines, and hospitality), the business area (management, marketing, and finance), and ICT and other technologies (social media, big data, and mobile technologies). The deep impact of e-tourism on creating dynamic networks, changing consumer behavior and leveraging stakeholder capabilities to co-create meaningful immersive experiences seems to be aligned with sustainability goals (Pohjola, Lemmetyinen, & Dimitrovski, 2020). As a result of the pandemic, ICT has become a major player in every aspect of our daily life. The pandemic might thus become an opportunity to develop e-tourism in the short and long term.

The notion of smart tourism is partly characterized by personal technologies which are used to create meaningful and memorable experiences (Gretzel, Sigala, Xiang, & Koo, 2015). Several authors have highlighted the importance of smart experiences (e.g. Buhalis & Amaranggana, 2015; Gretzel et al., 2015) which imply technology-mediated tourist experiences which create data as well as improving quality. Internet access in destinations is essential for tourists when planning their trips and smart phones and their apps have revolutionized travel from anticipation, through purchase, to the actual travel experience and even in the management of subsequent memories (Dickinson et al., 2014; Liberato, Alen, & Liberato, 2018). Huang, Goo, Nam, and Yoo (2017) examine the mechanism of how travelers use technologies in planning their trips and enhancing satisfaction. The results suggest that when designing a website or app for travel planning, it is important to pay attention to informativeness, accessibility, interactivity, and personalization, because these attributes will ultimately lead to overall satisfaction of travel experience. Gretzel (2018) differentiates between e-tourism and smart tourism, where e-tourism spans all phases of the tourism experience (pre-, during and post-travel), whereas smart tourism is much more focused on experiences within the destination, its physical and other attributes and the wider organizational and institutional frameworks that support them. The research in this chapter focuses mainly on e-tourism because most of the latest tourism strategies have not yet been implemented because of COVID-19 and it was not possible to examine the wider context.

Context for the Research: Budapest – A Cultural Tourism Destination in Hungary

The context for the research is the Hungarian capital city Budapest. Before the pandemic, in 2019, Budapest was ranked at the top of the list of tourist destinations in Europe (European Best Destinations, 2019). The city was mainly promoted as a heritage and cultural tourism destination for the first twenty years of the post-socialist period (1990-2010) and research showed that the city was mainly perceived as a cultural tourism destination by visitors (Puczkó, Rátz, & Smith, 2007; Smith & Puczkó, 2010). Nevertheless, the number of tourists coming for nightlife and cheap alcohol grew steadily from E.U. accession onwards and reached a peak by 2019 resulting in an undesirable form of overtourism centred around the so-called *party district*. Research on overtourism in Budapest by Pinke-Sziva, Smith, Olt, and Berezvai (2019) showed that younger international tourists (below the age of 39) enjoy pubs, bars, ruin pubs, clubs and discos the most, whereas older visitors prefer cultural attractions. However, even younger visitors were well educated and cited culture as a major motivation for visiting, which means that the two segments are not so easy to differentiate.

The Hungarian Tourism Agency (Magyar Turisztikai Ügynökség), the highest level organisation in Hungarian tourism, published its *National Tourism Development Strategy 2030* in 2017. As described in this document in connection with Budapest:

In the short term (1-3 years) the goal is to provide renewed, quality marketing communication based on Budapest's heritage and culture, attracting high spending segments who value the offered range of experiences based on cultural and historical heritage (spas), the specific culture and history (museums), the arts (concerts, opera, architecture), civic leisure activities (cafés, wine bars) and gastronomy – in essence, "haute culture". (Magyar Turisztikai Ügynökség, 2017, p. 104)

The strategy also highlighted that "it is important to consciously brand Budapest as a proud, elegant, vibrant, 'premium' European capital, worthy of its historic role, rather than being considered as a destination for 'party tourists'" (Magyar Turisztikai Ügynökség, 2017, p. 40). The strategy also pointed out that besides increasing the number of tourists in Hungary, the average per capita spending of tourists must be increased as well. In this context, the strategy identified four product development opportunities:

1. *Health tourism and especially medical tourism, where the length of stay is longer, the unit of expenditure per day is higher and the patient is often accompanied by relatives or family members;*
2. *Within cultural tourism, top quality cultural attractions offering a unique experience, 'high culture'. (World-class opera performances, concerts, exhibitions, which are attractions that generate travel decisions even on an international scale);*
3. *MICE tourism, which also attracts guests with a typically higher per capita spending, often arriving with their family members;*
4. *The high-end section of gastronomy and wine tourism, as it offers a significantly higher price level than the average price level of other restaurants in the destination.* (Magyar Turisztikai Ügynökség, 2017, p. 40)

In addition to the above-mentioned *National Tourism Development Strategy 2030*, prepared by the Hungarian Tourism Agency in 2017, the strategic document *Budapest Tourism Development Strategy*

2027 was created by Budapest Brand Nonprofit Plc. (Budapest Brand Zrt), a company belonging to the Municipality of Budapest. The document states that "The combination of the 19th century milieu with party culture creates a unique atmosphere" (Budapest Brand Zrt, 2021). In fact, this is a top priority in terms of attraction development and supply development: "A particularly important element of this is party tourism, which has become one of Budapest's most characteristic hallmarks. It is important to retain party tourism, but in a way that eliminates its disturbing elements (tourists behaving in an unacceptable way and the illegal economy that relies on them)" (Budapest Brand Zrt, 2021). The latter quotation suggests a slight contradiction between the national strategy and the city one. It seems that party tourists are valued more at city level, which is a more realistic view of the pre-COVID-19 situation. On the other hand, the national strategy suggests that tourism development and marketing should shift towards segments who appreciate high culture and fine dining and are willing to spend more money on it. Indeed, in 2018, the Hungarian Tourism Agency launched the campaign *Budapest, Spice of Europe* in order to establish the new city's brand and target high profile visitors. The main goal was expressing Budapest's character: historical heritage, cultural life, premier quality gastronomy, flourishing fashion and more (Kovács, 2018).

(OVER)TOURISM IN BUDAPEST BEFORE COVID-19

Research Method

A questionnaire was designed by the authors for tourists to Budapest to enquire about their tourism activities and preferences and their attitude toward experiences outside the core tourist area of Budapest (i.e. off-the-beaten-track experiences). This information was deemed useful for discovering how far tourists are prepared to undertake activities outside of the crowded center and to potentially improve visitor flows. The survey was undertaken in April 2019 (pre-COVID-19) and it was distributed in various locations close to cultural attractions in the city. The survey resulted in 614 valid responses. Of these, 44% could be described as *cultural tourists* based on their preferred activities (e.g. heritage sites, museums and galleries), whereas 32% were *party tourists* (mostly attracted by bars, pubs and clubs). Data was also collected in the questionnaire about the tools that they used for finding information about the destination before their visit.

In order to explore the use of digital tools, image and experiences of the city further, qualitative interviews also took place in autumn 2019 and the spring of 2020 (before the COVID-19 pandemic crisis) with 95 tourists using targeted sampling focusing on different age groups (18-25, 26-38, 39-54 and above 55). The questions focused on their image or perception of Budapest (pre- and after-visit); their main reason for visiting; their experiences in the city, and how they could be improved; the role of digital tools in pre-trip planning and in creating experiences on-site. Content analysis was used with open-coding. This paper mainly focuses on responses from the respondents under 39 years old (54 interviewees), as these account for the majority of party tourists:

- Y1 (18-25 years old): 32 respondents, with an average age of 22. Their nationality varied, participants mainly came from Europe, followed in number by people from Asia and America, respectively.

- Y2 (26-38 years old): 22 respondents, with an average age of 28. The majority of respondents were from Europe, while a smaller number took a long-haul trip from Asia, America and Africa.

Findings

Questionnaire Data

The questionnaire revealed the preferred reasons for visiting Budapest. As shown in Figure 1 atmosphere and gastronomy (including food and wine) were the top-rated activities for all tourists. Visiting heritage sites (importance: 5.64 on a 1-7 scale) was rated higher than enjoying pubs, clubs, and bars (4.89). However, the latter activity shows the largest standard deviation indicating that the younger the tourists are, the more they are interested in pubs, clubs, and bars.

*Figure 1. Importance of different activities during the visit to Budapest (1: not important at all – 7: very important). Note: * indicates significant differences on 5% level based on ANOVA; error bars show the 95% confidence intervals.*

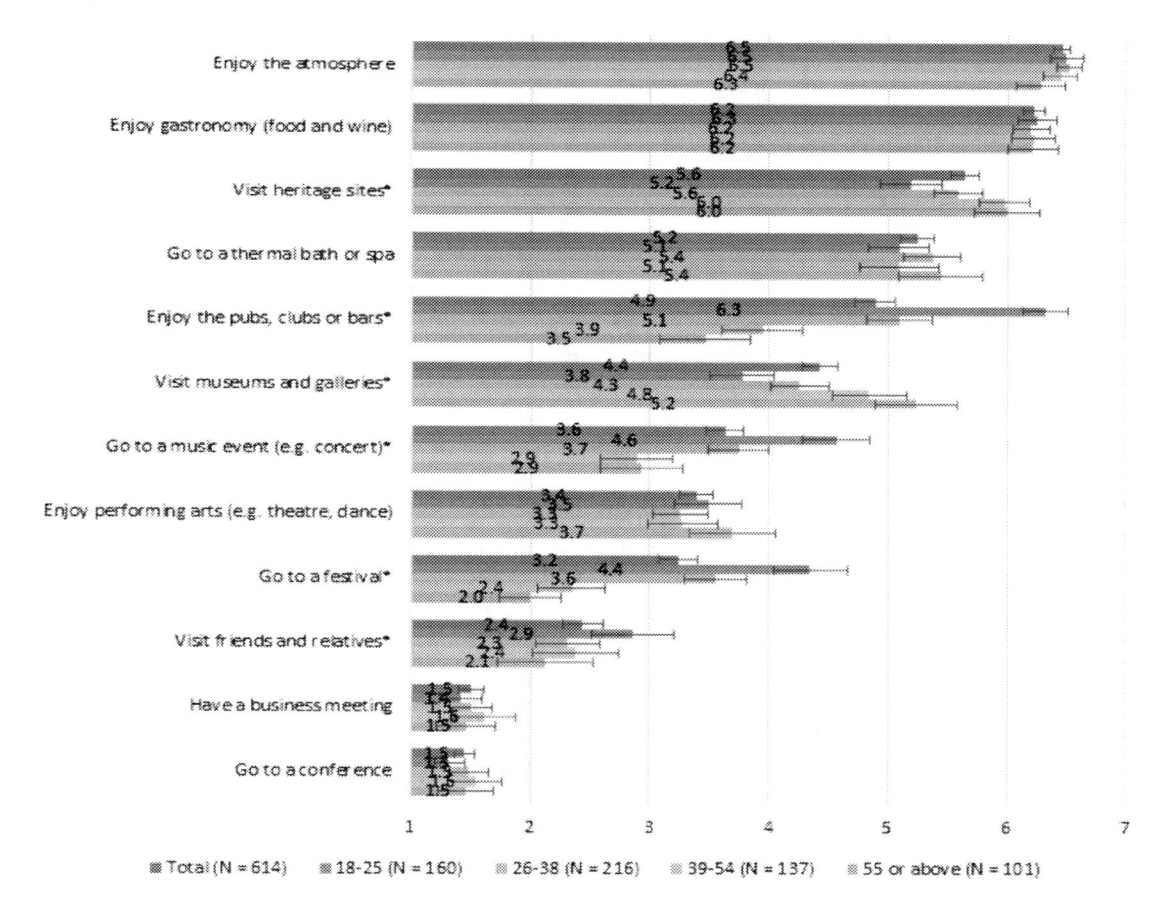

Regarding off-the-beaten-track activities, respondents were asked to indicate the attractiveness of 14 different programs using a multiple-choice question.

Figure 2. Percentage of respondents interested in the suggested off-the-beaten-track activities/programs
Note: Error bars show the 95% confidence intervals.

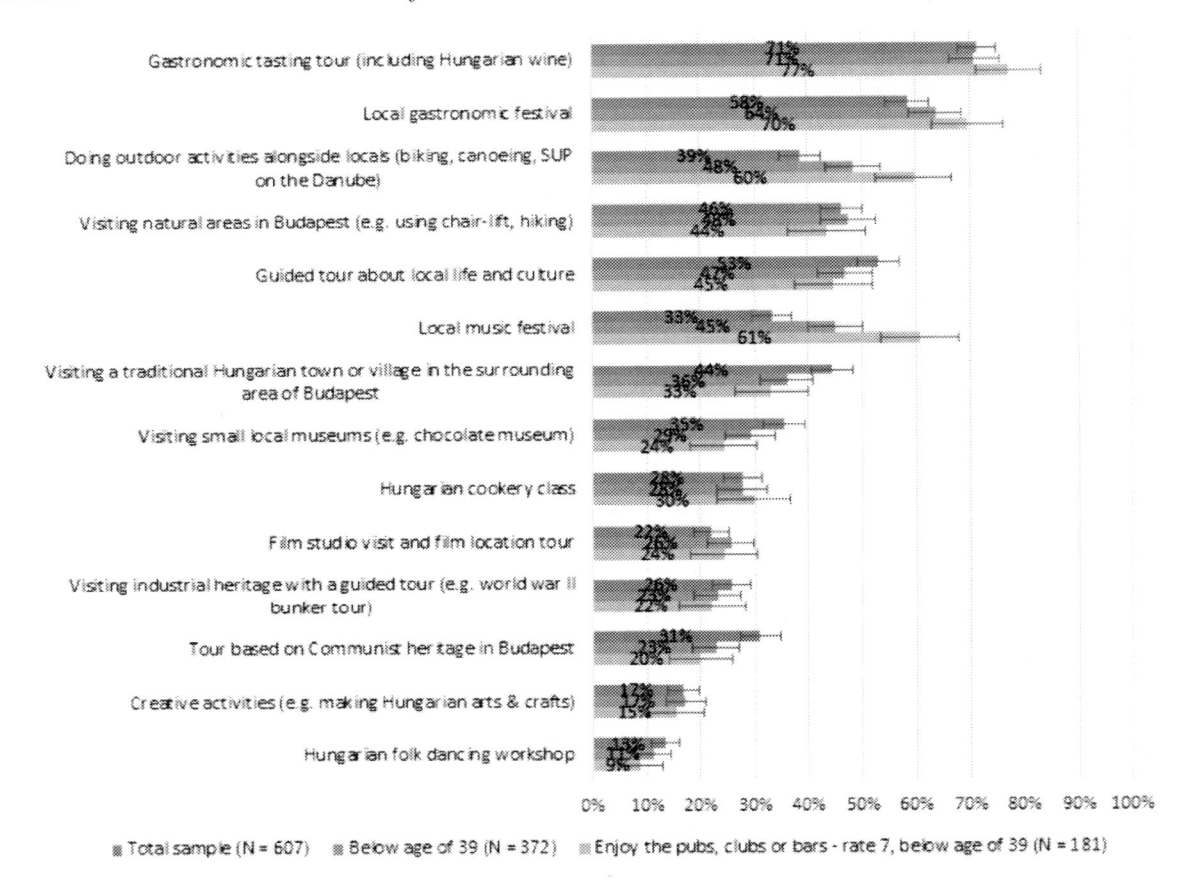

As depicted in Figure 2, the questionnaire findings revealed that younger and older generations have similar interests in terms of several activities (e.g. guided tours, gastronomy). Traditional cultural activities such as visiting local museums, heritage tours and folk dancing workshops are generally the least popular options for all of the tourists regardless of age. Creative and interactive activities were not rated very highly either. Visiting natural areas close to Budapest was rated highly (almost every second tourist is interested in this possibility) and it is liked almost equally by all tourist segments. Thirdly, outdoor activities in natural areas are highly rated by party tourists (60% of them indicated that they would like to try them), which shows a potential way to encourage them to undertake activities outside the city center. However, young party tourists are more attracted by music and festivals than older ones. Furthermore, results suggest that (regardless of age) the majority (more than 70%) of the tourists are willing to travel more than 45 minutes to reach an attraction and spend between 16 and 60 euros on it.

A question about the digital channels used for finding information revealed that TripAdvisor is the most utilized planning tool for all tourists. Figure 3 demonstrates that younger tourists clearly prefer online tools, mainly TripAdvisor, Facebook and Instagram, while older tourists tend to use more offline tools (accommodation and tourist information centers).

Figure 3. Most Important information sources for tourists when planning their trip to Budapest (percentage of respondents, multiple-choice) Note. * indicates significant differences (on 5% level) between below and above 39 age groups; error bars show the 95% confidence intervals.

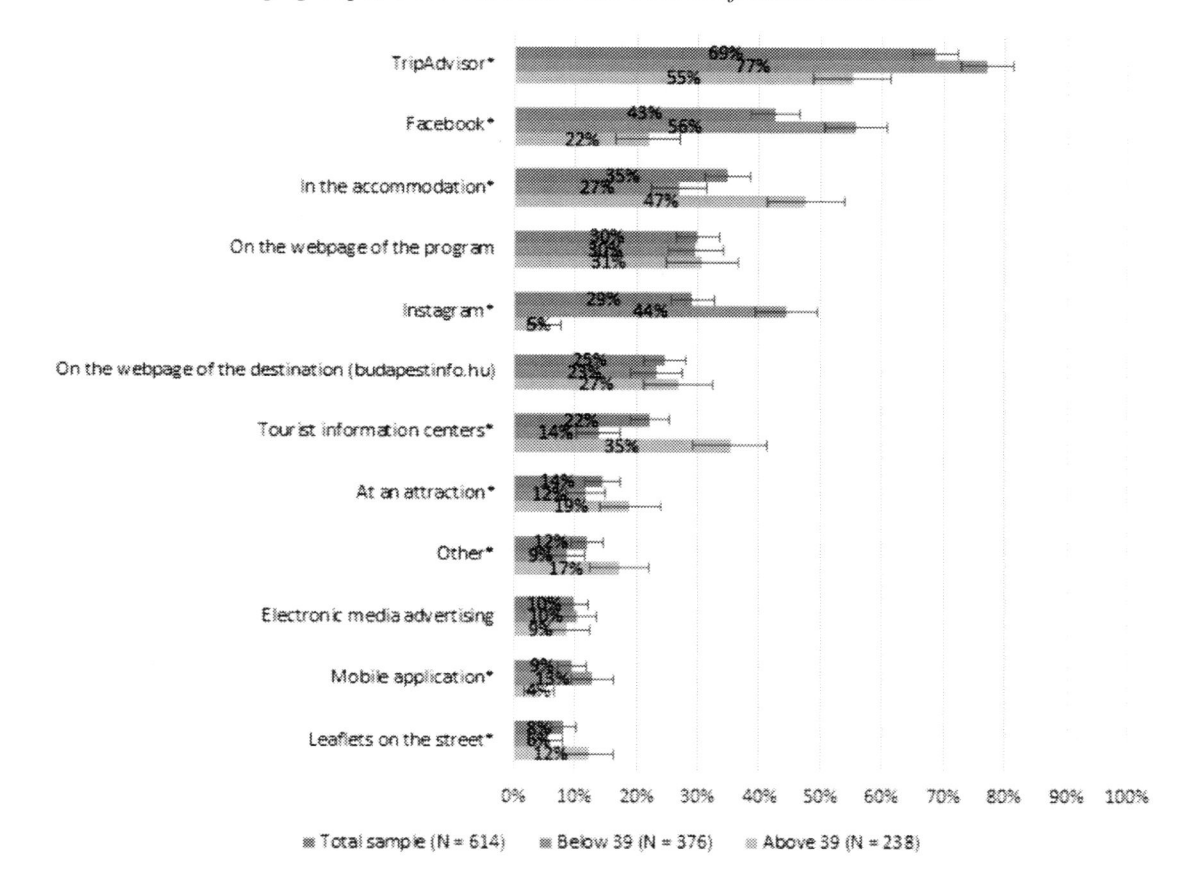

Interview Data

Results revealed that attachment to smart phones is strong among the under 39s. Moreover, it was found that attachment increases conversely to the age. For example, participants from Y1 group were more attached to their smart phone than participants from Y2 group. Participants of both groups acknowledged the usefulness of digital tools to improve their travel experience. Digital tools are seen as a *means* to make the trip memorable, since they facilitate or promote experiences according to the particular interests.

Pre-Travel

Before travelling, social media was shown to play a key role for the under-39 segment when it comes to travel motivation. Respondents came to Budapest mainly encouraged by word-of-mouth (WOM) or e-WOM (social media posts). In fact, many of them had friends who had travelled to Budapest or were living in the city. Many of the participants claimed they had seen pictures of the *beautiful scenery* or had heard about the *affordable prices*. Therefore, whenever they had the opportunity (i.e. break, holiday or vacation), they visited the city:

"I heard great reviews of the city, we saw lots of picture of it and we fell in love with it" (34 year old, German male)

Some of my friends are studying here and a couple of my friends have travelled here, and they were like 'this is an amazing city, you should just travel'... whenever I saw the pictures of it my friends posted in social accounts, I was like 'yeah...' (21 year old, Belorussian female)

In this context, social media i.e. Instagram is among the main online digital sources they used to find information about Budapest:

To be honest I only saw some Facebook and Instagram posts, mostly videos and I just thought: it can be the time of my life here (29 year old, German male).

I use Instagram too: I put the city, like the hashtag of the city and I see all the places, for some bar, pubs, to see some places (26 year old, Italian female)

They also used search engines as well as online travel guides/blogs which include reviews i.e. TripAdvisor:

I just googled. I typed Budapest and looked at all the information about it (33 year old, Belgium respondent)

I received information from bloggers, read many of them before I came here (26 year old, Swedish female)

Lonely Planet and TripAdvisor and also Google (36 year old, Chinese male)

I mostly used Google and searched through it: 'Best places to visit in Budapest'. Also TripAdvisor and they had like a fun list of bunch places like 10- 25 places you must visit (25 year old, Albanian male)

As it can be seen, e-WOM is fundamental for the younger age groups when it comes to collecting information about a destination and making a decision.

During the Trip

Regarding the tools used during the trip, for both age groups (18-25, 26-38) the main source is Google Maps, followed by social media and online travel guides/blogs:

Mostly the map, Google Maps, and the social media (24 year old, Russian female)

My cell phone: using Google Maps for locations, Instagram and Facebook, blogs to read other people's experiences here (27 year old, South African male)

I have searched on TripAdvisor for reviews of certain restaurants (26 year old, Dutch male)

The most common uses of digital tools during the trip are for posting in social media, for taking pictures and for finding places.

I use my cell phone for Google Maps and posting on facebook and instagram and I also have my camera with me always for taking photos during the visits (29 year old, German male)

I use my phone to call sometimes, also for the GPS. It is easy. Every day I post pictures on social media. I use Facebook. I take a lot of pictures (33 year old, Belgium respondent)

Apart from sightseeing, culture, food and drinks; interviewees from under-39 group, specially the younger group (18-25 years old), considered as interesting experiences those that were unexpected and off-the-beaten-track:

The most interesting experience that I had definitely is the Adventurous Caving Tour. I found the information about this tour in my hostel registration office. And I would say it is the best thing that happened while being in the city. In the tour I met a few more people who were travelling in Budapest. I also learned about myself more (23 year old, Latvian female)

I prefer less touristic places like the abandoned factory in Ferencváros. I was attending the Képzőművészeti Egyetem before. So I am an artist, and I like Epreskert. It is an artistic area of the university. That place is special for me, it is not a popular touristic place (24 year old, Czech male)

There were a lot of interesting buildings such as 'Paloma' which I found by accident. Beautiful space that is open to customers and creators [...] But there are plenty of interesting places that Google will not suggest to you, and I have to admit I really love all these places like small businesses for instance (24 year old, Polish female)

Once I was just exploring my social media and I saw an event on Facebook. It was about hiking so I put interested button and I joined this sport association and I havd a great time with international guys and we also explored different hills of Budapest (22 year old, Azerbaijani female)

As can be seen, for both age groups interesting experiences involve meeting people, either locals or foreigners:

Going out and talking to local people (26 year old, German female)

I met many new interesting people and went out having some fun at night (26 year old, Swedish female)

Post-Travel

In the post-trip stage, digital tools also played an important role by allowing respondents to share the lived experience (e-WOM). Furthermore, they help in the recollection and remembrance of past travel experiences.

I think it is pretty good. I was enjoying the moment, while being in the city. - In the evenings at the hostel I was sharing some photos with my friends on Instagram. I am doing that cause I really want to introduce my friends, family and other followers to beautiful places. I am always writing a caption to my pictures - with some interesting facts that I didn't know before or some historical facts about places that I have visited (23 year old, Latvian female)

I take a lot of pics but I post them always after the holiday, after the trip (26 year old, Italian female)

I share the experience mostly the same day at night (26 year old, Dutch male)

Interviewees were asked what they would improve about their experience in Budapest, too. The most highlighted issues concerned language barriers, as many websites, signs, menus and monument descriptions are in Hungarian. There is limited information about public transport in English (e.g. stops, timetables, connections). The solutions recommended by the respondents are mainly based on different applications in order to facilitate the navigation throughout the city and find detailed information at each point.

So Hungarian... the language is so different... So I can only use the Google Translate. The translation between English and Hungarian is not so correct sometimes digitally So I am really confused what kind of place, what kind of food that is (32 year old, Chinese female)

CONCLUSION

This chapter demonstrates the dilemma that faces many cultural cities in Europe post-COVID-19 which suffered from overtourism but are now in a position of undertourism. It may be the case that their main traffic and revenue was derived from young party tourists in the pre-COVID-19 period, but this created undesirable impacts for local resident quality of life as well as being detrimental to the city's image. While not wanting to alienate or exclude existing lucrative tourist markets (i.e. those enjoying the city's nightlife), re-positioning strategies still aim to create a desired image as a destination that offers high culture and fine dining instead.

Post-COVID-19, strategies may include re-positioning cultural cities in order to attract different markets or those with motivations that are more closely connected to cultural activities or that cause minimal disturbance for residents. Re-positioning strategies should aim to create a desired image in the minds of consumers, for example, shifting from the idea that cultural cities are a mere backdrop for party or alcohol tourism. New technology and especially social media play a pivotal role in this process, especially for younger generations whose primary or only source of information may be derived from social media word-of-mouth rather than official marketing channels. Cities may need to offer some new experiences in order to provide the *instagrammable* moments that young travellers are looking for,

for example, off-the-beaten-track. However, care must be taken that these new offers do not encroach too much on residential spaces and compromise local quality of life. This is challenging in cases where tourists want to visit *authentic* local neighbourhoods and interact with local people as part of their urban cultural experience.

SOLUTIONS AND RECOMMENDATIONS

The research in this chapter suggests that some of the younger party tourists could be re-directed towards other activities which do not require a larger budget but which take place outside of the city centre and further away from local neighbourhoods. The data showed that young party tourists are most attracted by gastronomy as well as music and festivals. Since festivals (including gastronomy and music festivals) could be organized outside the city center, it might create an opportunity to ease the burden of overtourism in central areas. Festivals can represent an opportunity to eat, drink and party to music but away from resident neighbourhoods. Visiting natural areas outside Budapest was also popular with all age groups. It therefore represents another opportunity worth considering within a repositioning strategy. Although it is predominantly a daytime rather than a night-time activity, picnics, barbecues, or wine tasting in natural areas could also allow tourists to socialise and party without great disturbance for local residents.

This chapter examined some of the tools that are used by tourists in the process of e-tourism (i.e. to find information pre- and during the visit). In terms of reaching younger segments with offers of alternative or off-the-beaten-track activities, younger tourists clearly prefer online tools like TripAdvisor, Facebook and Instagram. When interviewees were asked about what they would improve about their experiences, the majority mentioned language or transport information. It is important to note in any repositioning strategy that the levels of English and other language translations are even lower outside of the capital city and that public transport can be limited. For this reason, off-the-beaten-track information provision may need to be almost entirely digital.

LIMITATIONS OF THE RESEARCH

Although the questionnaire was undertaken with a representative sample of tourists, the research was only conducted in the English and Hungarian languages which may have limited the responses because of linguistic barriers. The sample of interviewees was relatively small and the questions only referred to e-tourism, so insights were not gained into some of the important trends relating to smart tourism (e. g. visitor flow management, experience creation). Although some of the results might be generalisable to other European historic cities that have suffered from overtourism, many of the listed attractions, activities and experiences are only relevant to this city.

FUTURE RESEARCH DIRECTIONS

Emerging trends in the post-COVID-19 urban tourism literature include a focus on smart cities, sustainability and resilience. In addition to e-tourism, future research should consider a smart tourism approach in which the wider organizational and institutional frameworks are taken into consideration. This might include, for example, research that measures or monitors the implementation of tourism management or marketing strategies such as those designed by the Hungarian Tourism Agency, Budapest Brand Zrt or similar agencies in other cities. Tourists might be questioned further about their experiences *in situ* once they have opted for some of the cultural, creative or off-the-beaten-track activities suggested in this research. Local residents also need to be consulted about their experiences of new forms of tourism or new segments of tourists and the extent to which they are involved in or affected by these developments. Clearly, smart tourism involves not only technology but an integrated approach which includes multiple stakeholders. Only then can urban destinations move beyond the current situation of having shifted from overtourism to undertourism post-COVID-19 towards a more sustainable, smart and resilient future.

Overall, these findings might provide some useful insights for other cultural tourism cities in Europe suffering from a concentration of party tourists in central areas. The exploration of off-the-beaten-track possibilities within a repositioning strategy enhanced by digital tools could provide a fruitful way forward post-COVID-19. Future research might focus on uptake and experiences of the suggested off-the-beaten-track activities and long-term image development of the city, as well as the implications for resident wellbeing in former overtourism areas.

REFERENCES

Adweek.com. (2018, May 11). *How Influencers Are Turning the Business of Travel on Its Head.* Retrieved September 17, 2019, from https://www.adweek.com/digital/how-influencers-are-turning-the-business-of-travel-on-its-head/

Budapest Brand Zrt. (2021). *Találkozunk Budapesten - Budapesti Turizmusfejlesztési Stratégia 2021–2027* [Meet us in Budapest - Budapest Tourism Development Strategy 2021-2027]. Municipality of Budapest.

Buhalis, D., & Amaranggana, A. (2015). Smart tourism destinations enhancing tourism experience through personalisation of services. In I. Tussyadiah & A. Inversini (Eds.), *ENTER 2015 Proceedings* (pp. 377–390). Springer-Verlag. doi:10.1007/978-3-319-14343-9_28

Butler, R. W. (2018). Challenges and opportunities. *Worldwide Hospitality and Tourism Themes, 10*(6), 635–641. doi:10.1108/WHATT-07-2018-0042 PMID:30591573

Capocchi, A., Vallone, C., Pierotti, M., & Amaduzzi, A. (2019). Overtourism: A Literature Review to Assess Implications and Future Perspectives. *Sustainability, 11*(12), 3303. doi:10.3390u11123303

Chacko, H. E., & Marcell, M. H. (2008). Repositioning a Tourism Destination. *Journal of Travel & Tourism Marketing, 23*(2-4), 223–235. doi:10.1300/J073v23n02_17

Colomb, C., & Novy, J. (2017). *Protest and Resistance in the Tourist City.* Routledge., doi:10.4324/9781315719306

Crompton, J. L. (2009). Strategies for implementing repositioning of leisure services. *Managing Leisure, 14*(2), 87–111. doi:10.1080/13606710902752497

Dirksmeier, P., & Helbrecht, I. (2015). Resident perceptions of new urban tourism: A neglected geography of prejudice. *Geography Compass, 9*(5), 276–285. doi:10.1111/gec3.12201

Du Cros, H., & McKercher, B. (2015). *Cultural Tourism.* Routledge.

European Best Destinations. (2019). *European Best Destinations 2019*. Retrieved October 14, 2019, from https://www.europeanbestdestinations.com/european-best-destinations-2019/

Forbes.com. (2018, January 24). *Here's How Much Instagram Likes Influence Millennials' Choice Of Travel Destinations*. Retrieved September 19, 2019, from https://www.forbes.com/sites/andrewarnold/2018/01/24/heres-how-much-instagram-likes-influence-millennials-choice-of-travel-destinations/#7d3c8f1a4eba

Füller, H., & Michel, B. (2014). 'Stop Being a Tourist!' New Dynamics of Urban Tourism in Berlin-Kreuzberg. *International Journal of Urban and Regional Research*, *38*(4), 1304–1318. doi:10.1111/1468-2427.12124

García-Hernández, M., de la Calle-Vaquero, M., & Yubero, C. (2017). Cultural heritage and urban tourism: Historic city centres under pressure. *Sustainability*, *9*(8), 1346. doi:10.3390u9081346

Gravari-Barbas, M., & Guinand, S. (2017). *Tourism and Gentrification in Contemporary Metropolises*. Routledge., doi:10.4324/9781315629759

Gretzel, U. (2018). From smart destinations to smart tourism regions. *Investigaciones Regionales – Journal of Regional Research, 42*, 171-184.

Gretzel, U., Fuchs, M., Baggio, R., Hoepken, W., Law, R., Neidhardt, J., Pesonen, J., Zanker, M., & Xiang, Z. (2020). e-Tourism beyond COVID-19: A call for transformative research. *Information Technology & Tourism*, *22*(2), 187–203. doi:10.100740558-020-00181-3

Gretzel, U., Sigala, M., Xiang, Z., & Koo, C. (2015). Smart Tourism: Foundations and Developments. *Electronic Markets*, *25*(3), 179–188. doi:10.100712525-015-0196-8

Huang, C. D., Goo, J., Nam, K., & Yoo, C. W. (2017). Smart Tourism Technologies in Travel Planning: The Role of Exploration and Exploitation. *Information & Management*, *54*(6), 757–770. doi:10.1016/j.im.2016.11.010

Judd, D. R. (2003). *The Infrastructure of Play: Building the Tourist City*. Taylor & Francis., doi:10.4324/9781315699585

Kaczynski, A. T., Havitz, M. E., & McCarville, R. E. (2005). Altering Perceptions Through Repositioning: An Exercise in Framing. *Leisure Sciences*, *27*(3), 241–261. doi:10.1080/01490400590930871

Kotler, P. (2000). *Marketing management, millennium edition*. Prentice Hall.

Kovács, Z. (2018). Here's how Hungary's the 'Spice of Europe' will shake up Europe's tourism. *About Hungary*. Retrieved October 14, 2019, from https://abouthungary.hu/blog/heres-how-hungarys-the-spice-of-europe-will-shake-up-europes-tourism/

Kowalczyk-Anioł, J., Grochowicz, M., & Pawlusinski, R. (2021). How a Tourism City Responds to COVID-19: A CEE Perspective (Kraków Case Study). *Sustainability*, *13*(14), 7914. doi:10.3390u13147914

Liberato, P., Alen, E., & Liberato, D. (2018). Smart tourism destination triggers consumer experience: The case of Porto. *European Journal of Management and Business Economics*, *27*(1), 6–25. doi:10.1108/EJMBE-11-2017-0051

Lim, S. E. Y., & Bouchon, F. (2017). Blending in for a life less ordinary? Off the beaten track tourism experiences in the global city. *Geoforum, 86*, 13–15. doi:10.1016/j.geoforum.2017.08.011

Llodrà-Riera, I., Martínez-Ruiz, M. P., Jiménez-Zarco, A. I., & Izquierdo-Yusta, A. (2015). A multidimensional analysis of the information sources construct and its relevance for destination image formation. *Tourism Management, 48*, 319–328. doi:10.1016/j.tourman.2014.11.012

Magyar Turisztikai Ügynökség. (2017). *Nemzeti Turizmusfejlesztési Stratégia 2030* [National Tourism Development Strategy 2030]. https://mtu.gov.hu/documents/prod/mtu_strategia_2030.pdf

Maitland, R. (2007). Cultural Tourism and the Development of New Tourism Areas in London. In G. Richards (Ed.), *Cultural Tourism: Global and Local Perspectives* (pp. 113–128). Haworth Press.

Maitland, R., & Newman, P. (2014). *World tourism cities: Developing tourism off the beaten track.* Routledge. doi:10.4324/9780203886564

Marine-Roig, E., & Ferrer-Rosell, B. (2018). Measuring the gap between projected and perceived destination images of Catalonia using compositional analysis. *Tourism Management, 68*, 236–249. doi:10.1016/j.tourman.2018.03.020

Matoga, L., & Pawłowska, A. (2018). Off-the-beaten-track tourism: A new trend in the tourism development in historical European cities. A case study of the city of Krakow, Poland. *Current Issues in Tourism, 21*(14), 1644–1669. doi:10.1080/13683500.2016.1212822

McKercher, B. (2020). Cultural tourism market: A perspective paper. *Tourism Review, 75*(1), 126–129. doi:10.1108/TR-03-2019-0096

Medway, D., & Warnaby, G. (2014). What's in a name? Place branding and toponymic commodification. *Environment & Planning, 46*(1), 153–167. doi:10.1068/a45571

Mermet, A. (2017). Airbnb and tourism gentrification: Critical insights from the exploratory analysis of the 'Airbnb syndrome' in Reykjavík. In M. Gravari-Barbas & S. Guinand (Eds.), *Tourism and Gentrification in Contemporary Metropolises* (pp. 52–74). Routledge., doi:10.4324/9781315629759-3

Neuhofer, B., Buhalis, D., & Ladkin, A. (2014). A typology of technology-enhanced tourism experiences. *International Journal of Tourism Research, 16*(4), 340–350. doi:10.1002/jtr.1958

Peterson, R. A. (1992). Understanding Audience Segmentation from Elite and Mass to Omnivore and Univore. *Poetics, 21*(4), 243–258. doi:10.1016/0304-422X(92)90008-Q

Pinke-Sziva, I., Smith, M. K., Olt, G., & Berezvai, Z. (2019). Overtourism and the night-time economy: A case study of Budapest. *International Journal of Tourism Cities, 5*(1), 1–16. doi:10.1108/IJTC-04-2018-0028

Pinkster, F. M., & Boterman, W. R. (2017). When the spell is broken: Gentrification, urban tourism and privileged discontent in the Amsterdam canal district. *Cultural Geographies, 24*(3), 457–472. doi:10.1177/1474474017706176 PMID:29278248

Pixová, M., & Sládek, J. (2017). Touristification and awakening civil society in post-socialist Prague. In C. Colomb & J. Novy (Eds.), *Protest and Resistance in the Tourist City* (pp. 73–89). Routledge., doi:10.4324/9781315719306-11

Pohjola, T., Lemmetyinen, A., & Dimitrovski, D. (2020). Value Co-creation in Dynamic Networks and E-Tourism. In Z. Xiang, M. Fuchs, U. Gretzel, & W. Höpken (Eds.), *Handbook of e-Tourism* (pp. 1–23). Springer., doi:10.1007/978-3-030-05324-6_92-1

Puczkó, L., Rátz, T., & Smith, M. K. (2007). Old City, New Image: Perception, Positioning and Promotion of Budapest. *Journal of Travel & Tourism Marketing*, *22*(3-4), 21–34. doi:10.1300/J073v22n03_03

Qu, H., Kim, L. H., & Im, H. H. (2011). A model of destination branding: Integrating the concepts of the branding and destination image. *Tourism Management*, *32*(3), 465–476. doi:10.1016/j.tourman.2010.03.014

Rouleau, J. (2017). Every (nocturnal) tourist leaves a trace: Urban tourism, nighttime landscape, and public places in Ciutat Vella, Barcelona. *Imaginations*, *7*, 58–71. doi:10.17742/IMAGE.VOS.7-2.3

Russo, A. P., & Richards, G. (Eds.). (2016). *Reinventing the local in tourism: Producing, consuming and negotiating place*. Channel View Publications., doi:10.21832/9781845415709

Séraphin, H., Zaman, M., Olver, S., Bourliataux-Lajoinie, S., & Dosquet, F. (2019). Destination branding and overtourism. *Journal of Hospitality and Tourism Management*, *38*, 1–4. doi:10.1016/j.jhtm.2018.11.003

Sharma, G. D., Thomas, A., & Paul, J. (2021). Reviving tourism industry post-COVID-19: A resilience-based framework. *Tourism Management Perspectives*, *37*, 100786. doi:10.1016/j.tmp.2020.100786 PMID:33391988

Smith, M., & Puczko, L. (2010). Out with the old, in with the new? Twenty years of post-socialist marketing in Budapest. *Journal of Town & City Management*, *1*(3), 288–299.

Smith, M. K., Egedy, T., Csizmady, A., Olt, G., Jancsik, A., & Michalkó, G. (2017). Non-Planning and Tourism Consumption in Budapest's Inner City. *Tourism Geographies*, *20*(3), 524–548. doi:10.1080/14616688.2017.1387809

Smith, M. K., Pinke-Sziva, I., & Olt, G. (2019). Overtourism and Resident Resistance in Budapest. *Tourism Planning & Development*, *16*(4), 376–392. doi:10.1080/21568316.2019.1595705

Smith, M. K., & Richards, G. (2013). *The Routledge Handbook of Cultural Tourism*. Routledge. doi:10.4324/9780203120958

Sommer, C., & Helbrecht, I. (2017). Seeing like a tourist city: How administrative constructions of conflictive urban tourism shape its future. *Journal of Tourism Futures*, *3*(2), 157–170. doi:10.1108/JTF-07-2017-0037

Tokarchuk, O., Gabriele, R., & Maurer, O. (2017). Development of city tourism and well-being of urban residents: A case of German Magic Cities. *Tourism Economics*, *23*(2), 343–359. doi:10.1177/1354816616656272

Trout, J., & Rivkin, S. (2009). *Repositioning: Marketing in an Era of Competition, Change and Crisis*. McGraw-Hill Education.

UNWTO. (2018). *'Overtourism'? Understanding and Managing Urban Tourism Growth beyond Perceptions*. UNWTO.

Van der Ark, L. A., & Richards, G. (2006). Attractiveness of the cultural activities in European cities: A latent class approach. *Tourism Management*, *27*(6), 1408–1413. doi:10.1016/j.tourman.2005.12.014

Vianello, M. (2017). The No Grandi campaign: Protests against cruise tourism in Venice. In C. Colomb & J. Novy (Eds.), *Protest and Resistance in the Tourist City* (pp. 171–190). Routledge., doi:10.4324/9781315719306-16

Wachsmuth, D., & Weisler, A. (2018). Airbnb and the rent gap: Gentrification through the sharing economy. *Environment & Planning A. Economy and Space*, *50*(6), 1147–1170. doi:10.1177/0308518X18778038

Wolfram, G., & Burnill, C. (2012). The Tactical Tourist – Growing Self-awareness and Challenging the Strategists: Visitor-Groups in Berlin. In M. K. Smith & G. Richards (Eds.), *The Routledge Handbook of Cultural Tourism* (pp. 361–368). Routledge. doi:10.4324/9780203120958-60

ADDITIONAL READING

Bouchon, F., & Rauscher, M. (2019). Cities and tourism, a love and hate story; towards a conceptual framework for urban overtourism management. *International Journal of Tourism Cities*, *5*(4), 598–619. doi:10.1108/IJTC-06-2019-0080

Coca-Stefaniak, J. A. (2019). Marketing smart tourism cities–a strategic dilemma. *International Journal of Tourism Cities*, *5*(4), 513–518. doi:10.1108/IJTC-12-2019-163

Huettermann, M., Thimm, T., Hannich, F., & Bild, C. (2019). Requirements for future digital visitor flow management. *Journal of Tourism Futures*, *5*(3), 241–258. doi:10.1108/JTF-03-2019-0023

Iwanicki, G., Dłużewska, A., & Smith, M. K. (2016). Assessing the level of popularity of European stag tourism destinations. *Quaestiones Geographicae*, *35*(3), 15–29. doi:10.1515/quageo-2016-0023

Malet Calvo, D., Nofre, J., & Geraldes, M. (2017). The Erasmus Corner: Place-making of a sanitised nightlife spot in the Bairro Alto (Lisbon, Portugal). *Leisure Studies*, *36*(6), 778–792. doi:10.1080/02614367.2016.1271821

Pappalepore, I., Maitland, R., & Smith, R. (2014). Prosuming creative urban areas. Evidence from East London. *Annals of Tourism Research*, *44*, 227–240. doi:10.1016/j.annals.2013.11.001

Richards, G. (2019). Culture and tourism: natural partners or reluctant bedfellows? A perspective paper. *Tourism Review*, *75*(1), 232-234. . doi:10.1108/TR-04-2019-0139

Richards, G. (2021). *Re-Thinking Cultural Tourism*. Edward Elgar Publishing Ltd. doi:10.4337/9781789905441

KEY TERMS AND DEFINITIONS

Cultural Tourism: Act of visiting a destination mainly attracted by the local culture i.e. lifestyle, heritage, language, etc.

Digital Tools: Refers to both the electronic devices and the computerized and internet technologies used by them; usually employed in tourism to find information and optimize experiences.

E-Tourism: Use of technologies to accomplish a series of tasks related to the tourism activity: pre-, during and post-travel.

Image: Perception about a city or tourist destination in the visitor's mind.

Off the Beaten Track: Unconventional and unusual activities. In the case of tourist destinations, it refers to non-touristy places, or places that are not part of the mainstream.

Overtourism: Saturation of visitors affecting the quality of life of local citizens.

Party Tourist: A tourist whose main motivation at the destination is visiting bars, pubs, and clubs.

Re-Positioning: Act of replacing the current brand image in the consumer's mind by the desired brand image from the supply side.

Smart Tourism: Comprises the use of technologies within the tourism activity in order to enhance experiences at the destination.

Undertourism: Reduction in the number of visitors to a minimum level.

Chapter 24
Innovation in Sustainability of Tourism After the COVID–19 Pandemic

Buket Buluk Eşitti

https://orcid.org/0000-0001-5646-6166

Çanakkale Onsekiz Mart University, Turkey

ABSTRACT

The tourism industry includes air, sea, and land transportation; food supply chain; accommodation; entertainment; recreation; etc. services. Hence, tourism businesses are proposing changes, and post-COVID tourists will not be the same as pre-COVID ones. Innovative solutions regarding safety and hygiene measures as well as the proximity of medical facilities will be of key importance in meeting the tourist expectations and sustainability of the tourism industry. In addition, it is possible to state that the COVID-19 pandemic has affected the whole world. This situation caused the economic balances of countries to deteriorate and some sectors to be adversely affected. The most affected sector is undoubtedly the tourism industry. Innovation has gained more importance in the tourism industry in the context of sustainability of tourism with the COVID-19 pandemic process. In this context, this chapter aimed to examine how innovation can contribute to the sustainability of post-COVID tourism.

INTRODUCTION

Defined as the "Novel Coronavirus Disease", "Covid-19" is a group of viruses first defined in Wuhan, China, 1 December 2019, as a result of research completed on a specific group of patients with symptoms such as fever, cough, shortness of breath (Pal et al., 2020). The Covid-19 virus was first detected in seafood and people in the animal market in the Wuhan region. Afterwards, it spread through person-to-person transmission to other cities in Hubei, with Wuhan being the first, and from there to other provinces in China and other world countries (Zhu, Wei & Niu, 2020).

The World Health Organization (WHO) defines the official name of the Covid-19 virus as "SARS-CoV-2 (Severe Acute Respiratory Syndrome-Coronavirus-2)" (Lopes et al., 2020). The term "Covid-19"

DOI: 10.4018/978-1-7998-8528-3.ch024

is used by the WHO to describe the disease state caused by the coronavirus. On January 30, 2020, Covid-19 was declared as a "global health emergency" by the WHO, and on March 11, 2020, the virus was declared as a "pandemic" (Ali, 2020).

It is obvious that there is a close relationship between pandemics and tourism (Henderson & Ng, 2004). While the spread of diseases from the origin country to other countries may be the issue due to tourism movements, the measures taken to prevent the risk of transmission as a result of the spread of the pandemic may cause tourism movements to be adversely affected. It is stated that Covid-19 pandemic has some differences in terms of its effects and spread on world economies that have faced various pandemics in the past. It is also stated that Covid-19 pandemic, which spreads very rapidly from China to the whole world, brought all industries to the point of completion in the economic context, but it affected the tourism industry quite significantly compared to other industries. National and international travel restrictions, which countries had to apply, stopped tourist movements, and the tourism industry had to face a "sudden" and "indefinite" crisis before the season (Pacific Asia Travel Association, 2020).

The Covid-19 vaccine, which started to be applied in the UK for the first time in December 2020, is currently being applied all over the world. It has been emphasized that the discovery of the vaccine and the initiation of vaccination are a very important development for the immunization of communities, stopping the Covid-19 pandemic, reviving the global economy, and resuming travel and tourism activities (OECD, 2020a).

Although it is difficult, it is necessary to start tourism after the Covid-19 pandemic, to manage it in a controlled way, in short, to ensure sustainability in tourism (Gössling, Scott & Hall, 2020). Otherwise, closing the borders and dealing with the Covid-19 epidemic, in the long run, is not a viable solution. On the contrary, it has to be foreseen that the economic crisis that will follow may lead to worse results than all the negative effects of the Covid-19 pandemic. As it is known, tourism, by its nature, is a industry that requires touching, feeling, in other words, experiencing it. This feature of tourism adds value to human relations. Kıvılcım (2020) examined the possible effects of the Covid-19 pandemic on the tourism industry and tried to predict possible tourist behaviors based on the World Tourism Organization (UNWTO) data and the struggles against the pandemic in the world. In the study, she stated that contactless transactions will come to the fore in the tourism industry, digitalization will become widespread, predicts that social distance tours and more isolated holiday preferences will increase. In order to prevent the Covid-19 pandemic and other possible future viruses and to ensure the continuity of tourism, innovation needs to be integrated into every possible area of the tourism industry (Wyman, 2020). In this context, this chapter aims to examine the subject of innovation in sustainability of tourism after Covid-19 pandemic. From this point, firstly, the subject of the impact of Covid-19 pandemic on the tourism industry will be explained to the readers. This will be followed by the innovation subject in the sustainability of tourism which covers the social, economic, political, and environmental aspects of the sector. The chapter concludes with recommendations for future research and conclusion.

BACKGROUND

The pandemic, known as Covid-19, has made it mandatory to take measures such as travel restrictions, quarantines and social distance rules all over the World (Wasdani & Prasad, 2020). It caused serious disruptions in the global economy in a short time. Tourism is a sector where human relations are intensely experienced. For this reason, it was one of the sectors most affected by the Covid-19 pandemic, and tourism activities came to a standstill (Economic Commission for Latin America and the Caribbean (ECLAC), 2020).

It is predicted that the digitalization process, which has been on the rise so far in tourism industry, will gain further momentum along with the Covid-19 pandemic process. According to the report prepared in cooperation with Skift Research & McKinsey & Company, digitalization in the tourism industry will become even more important during and after the Covid-19 pandemic (OECD, 2020b). It is also stated that in the report, radical changes have been underway for a long time in the way customers research and purchase travel products and services digitally. In response to the Covid-19 pandemic, recent trends point to an increasing shift to mobile and digital for certain activities, such as congresses, which are particularly important in the tourism sector. Especially consumers and businesses stand out for five years in digital adoption in about eight weeks, it is emphasized that as the Covid-19 pandemic spreads, customer behaviors and preferred interactions will change significantly. It is foreseen that these behaviors will continue to change, but the increase in the use of digital services will be permanent. 75 percent of first-time users of digital channels in travel and tourim sectors say they will continue to use them when things return to "normal". Therefore, investing in digital can be considered as the first phase in which travel and tourism businesses, such as hospitality establishments, plan to grow again following Covid-19 pandemic.

Özaltın Türker (2020) aimed to determine the possible effects of the Covid-19 pandemic, which emerged in the city of Wuhan, China and affected the whole world, on the tourism industry, through the lecturers who teach in the area of tourism in Turkey. It is possible to summarize the basic concepts that emerged as a result of the study, in which the data obtained were subjected to content analysis, as "hygiene and trust demand", "social distance", "individual tourism instead of mass tourism", "nature tourism", "new standards" and "digitalization".

Alan (2020) aimed to reveal the impact of digitalization and the reflections of digital transformation on service innovations in the Covid-19 pandemic. It was determined that the fields of activity that are most affected by digital service innovations in the service industry are related to business management services such as human resources applications and e-commerce platforms that aim to serve customers. As a result of the study, it was also revealed that the digitalization trend is high, especially in the "health", "education" and "tourism" industries.

Finally, based on the Covid-19 pandemic process, it can be stated that smart technologies will take their place in the new tourism understanding, which is basically a sector that minimizes human contact, adopts automation and innovation, as indispensable elements that will make life easier (Sharifi & Khavarian-Garmsir, 2020). Considering the health concern that has arisen with Covid-19, the tourism sector must be prepared for the newly digitalized visitor profile. As a result of the technology era, today's tourists are seen to be individuals who are not alien to technology and use smart technologies compared to ten years ago.

Smartphone applications can directly affect the quality of supply and demand in destinations. In particular, it is seen that destinations that prioritize innovation and automation, which are called Smart tourism destinations, enter a period in which they will gain a competitive advantage in the tourism sector. In essence, Smart tourism refers to the efforts made in a destination to integrate data from government/organizational resources, physical infrastructure, social connections, and human bodies/minds into tourist experiences and business practices using advanced technologies and innovations with a focus on sustainability, efficiency, and enrichment of tourist experiences. (Gretzel et al., 2015: 181). For instance, it is possible for visitors to see a gladiator fight taking place in Rome just like in the arena via augmented reality with smartphone apps. In addition, contactless hotel management is increasing its importance in the hospitality industry day by day (Jiang & Wen, 2020).

According to Lee, Hunter and Chung (2020) it is certain that Industry 4.0, artificial intelligence, internet-based information services, augmented reality and robots will make life easier and increase the travel experience, even if they do not replace humans in tourism. It is known that smart tourist guides have been put into practice in many tourism regions of Spain such as Barcelona and Malaga and in Rome. It is seen that similar applications are also in question for Istanbul. In the new tourism approach, it is predicted that smart applications in destinations will continue to be an important tool in visitor satisfaction.

It is possible to say that after the Covid-19 pandemic, the tourism industry will transition to a high rate of digital age and a period of complete isolation will begin (Wyman, 2020). The world is being prepared for a period in which contactless transactions will be made, the robot era will begin, and social distance, hygiene and sanitation will be at the forefront. There will be sterile kitchens in the hotels and restaurants, disinfected transportation vehicles and hotel rooms, which are important components of the tourism sector, an increase in the demand for masks and gloves by tourism personnel and tourists, new technological systems in bellboy services, contactless use in-room door cards and similar innovations will become widespread. Although the financial burden of all these is high, it appears as a new marketing technique. Now, instead of the all-inclusive system, everything hygienic system will be offered. All these indicate that a new era will begin in tourism (Orîndaru et al., 2021).

As a result, it is seen in the recent literature that the concepts and applications will gain more importance in terms of the tourism industry during and after the Covid-19 pandemic (Arenas, Goh & Urueña, 2019; Gretzel et al., 2020) such as "innovation", "e-transformation", "digitalization", "new technological systems", "smart technologies", "smart tourism applications", "new technological systems" and etc.

MAIN FOCUS OF THE CHAPTER

During a global crisis, the tourism and hospitality industry usually takes the strongest punch, being one of the strong pillars of the modern socio-economic system (Ocheni et al., 2020). Especially now, when this industry is closely correlated to the origin of the Covid-19 crisis, it can be expected an even greater downturn. The question that no one seems to have an answer is how the changes in the industry are going to affect the rules of the game. According to Polyzos et al., (2020), these changes will affect almost every aspect of the tourist's activities which they want to realize. In response to this, it can be also stated that tourism industry will inevitably have to move forward with bold, innovative ideas that include wider technology adoption. A comprehensive literature review shows that limited number of previous studies have a clear focus on the effects of innovation in sustainability of tourism after Covid-19 pandemic (Adam & Alarifi, 2021). The tourism industry has entered a period in which border crossings with facial recognition are discussed and contactless applications are started in every field with the Covid-19 pandemic process. It is noteworthy that hotels are trying to keep up with this transformation with many technological applications from online check-in processes to contactless door entrances. In fact, experts state that digitality will be the main element in new hotel investments. In addition, it is stated that new ways and more efficient use of scarce resources should be ensured in subjects such as travel, tourist flow and management, thanks to technologies such as tourism, artificial intelligence, big data, blockchain, and the internet of things (IoT) (Wang et al., 2021). Therefore, it can be stated that the importance of digital technologies in the tourism industry is better understood in this process, and the digital innovation infrastructure should be further developed in ifferent tourism services such as accommodation services, tour operators, travel agencies, transportation services and other tourism services. All these points out that innovation has an important role in sustainability of tourism after Covid-19 pandemic (Susanto & Kiswantoro, 2021). Below each of these important developments will be discussed how innovation may affect the sustainability of tourism after Covid-19 pandemic in addition to the impact of Covid-19 pandemic on the tourism industry.

The Impact of Covid-19 Pandemic on the Tourism Industry

As of December 2019, when Covid-19 emerged, it is seen that travel movements were stopped gradually (Chakraborty & Maity, 2020). While restrictions were imposed on travel movements in the countries affected by the virus in the first stage, almost all international flights were suspended with the spread of the virus. In line with the assessment of World Tourism Organization (UNWTO) (2021), it is stated that the damage done to tourism industry by Covid-19 pandemic has increased eight times of the global economic crisis in 2009.

UNWTO (2020) stated that international tourism movements in July 2020 decreased by 81 percent compared to July 2019, and decreased by 79 percent in August. In line with this result, it is understood that the rate of loss in international tourism movements reached 70 percent during the eight-month period. As a result of these data, it is stated that the number of international travels decreased by 700 million in the eight-month period compared to the same period of 2019. The loss of international tourism income in the same period amounted to 730 billion dollars.

The decline in the tourism industry has also been examined by the World Economic Cooperation and Development Organization (OECD). In the OECD report, in which the Covid-19 pandemic is defined as an "unprecedented crisis", it is stated that if the Covid-19 pandemic couldn't be brought under control by December 2020, the decline in the tourism industry might be at the level of 80 percent (OECD, 2020b).

UNWTO (2021) announced that due to Covid-19 pandemic, the number of people traveling internationally in 2020 decreased by 74 percent compared to 2019. However, the Covid-19 pandemic caused a financial loss of 1.3 trillion dollars on the tourism industry in 2020, and this loss was eleven times more than the loss recorded during the global economic crisis in 2009. The region where the number of tourists decreased the most in 2020 was Asia and the Pacific with a rate of 84 percent. The number of tourists in Europe, which is stated to have decreased by 71 percent in 2020 compared to 2019, decreased by more than 500 million.

According to the OECD report, in which it is stated that there will be a recovery starting from certain regions, primarily Europe, within the scope of global tourism industry, during the period after the Covid-19 pandemic and the recovery will be faster in OECD countries where the share of the domestic tourism market in the tourism economy is 75 percent. The report also indicates that countries with a high number of facilities and employment, especially in the tourism industry, will have a higher chance of recovery (OECD, 2020b).

The Covid-19 pandemic has also negatively affected employment in the tourism industry. In line with the research conducted by the World Travel and Tourism Council (WTTC) (2020), it has been predicted that the number of employees who have the potential to lose their job in the tourism industry worldwide due to the Covid-19 pandemic will be between 98 and 197.5 million. It was also stated that the contribution of the tourism industry to the gross domestic product of the countries in the global sense will be lost at the level of 5.5 trillion dollars. In addition, in the research conducted by WTTC

(2020), it was stated that 98.2 million workers could be unemployed with a global employment loss of 30 percent in the best scenario. Also, it is predicted that the decrease in tourism employment will cause 37 to 121 million people to lose their jobs, and according to the worst scenario, 197.5 million people will be unemployed with a 60 percent decrease in tourism employment worldwide.

WTTC (2020) emphasized that the loss to be caused by the pause in the domestic tourism movements of the countries due to Covid-19 pandemic also will be quite high together with international tourism with a decrease of 30 percent in the global tourism industry's contribution to gross domestic product, a loss of 2.6 trillion dollars may occur. In addition a 39 percent decrease in tourism industry's contribution to gross domestic product and a loss of 3.4 trillion dollars may be in question. It is also predicted that another loss option could be realized as 5.5 trillion dollars with a decrease of 62 percent in tourism industry's contribution to gross domestic product.

Innovation in Sustainability of Tourism after Covid-19 Pandemic

Pandemics will continue to be a part of life today and in the future as they were yesterday (Brachman, 2003). Therefore, the basic question to be asked should not be about whether pandemics will occur in the future, but how prepared mankind is for these pandemics. Because human beings' excessive intervention in nature, interacting with or consuming many new living species, and not taking necessary precautions despite knowing that new pandemics will occur, increase concerns about the future. It is precisely for these reasons that a new type of Coronavirus called Covid-19 has entered the life of human beings (Shereen et al., 2020). Today, the whole world is making great efforts to combat this virus, and despite this, hundreds of thousands of people have already lost their lives, the economic problem of the century has emerged, and the number of unemployed, unhappy and worried about the future has increased. Undoubtedly, Covid-19 pandemic has affected all sectors to a greater or lesser extent. However, perhaps the biggest damage has been done to the tourism sector. Because people's anxieties and worries, which started with psychological reasons, have also been the cause of a lot of problems that have reached the dimensions that will change social, economic, cultural and political life over time (Poudel & Subedi, 2020).

The tourism industry consists of small, medium and large enterprises (Tsiotsou & Goldsmith, 2012). Although global pandemics affected all tourism enterprises, it was mostly small-scale enterprises that suffered the most from this process. It is very difficult for these enterprises, which are not very competent in financial matters, to survive as they cannot stock the product and transfer it to the next year. Researching how the economies of small businesses in the USA are affected by Covid-19 pandemic, Bartik et al. (2020) concluded that it is difficult for small-scale accommodation and food & beverage businesses to survive if the crisis lasts longer than four months. Therefore, as stated above, the cost of the crisis increases as the duration of the crisis increases. Despite all this, many proposals are being developed in order for the industry to come out of this crisis with the least damage, to revitalize it, to serve effectively and to ensure sustainability in tourism. Ways to be more sustainable in tourism must include; primarily social and political structure, reorganizing living conditions (eco-villages, eco-municipality, and sustainable cities), re-evaluating economic sectors or business practices (permaculture, green building, use of sustainable agricultural products), using science to develop new technologies (green technologies, renewable energy, and sustainable fission and fusion power) or designing systems in a flexible and reversible way and adjusting individual lifestyles that conserve natural resources.

It is thought that the fact that the world is in a difficult process has caused some measures to be taken about how to fight this process (Han et al., 2020). Situations where it is necessary not to enter crowded environments and to avoid close contact allow people to do their work through online services. It is thought that digitalization will increase in the tourism industry with the spread of online transactions as of this process. National and international meeting, conference, seminar, congress etc. organizations will be held mostly online, museums that are closed to visitors will be able to be visited online, and some tourism centers will be able to be seen with digital tours. Digital applications, digital infrastructure and digital workforce opportunities will be increased in agency activities such as reservation, tour sales and ticketing. Mobile software can be created to provide contactless transactions. It will be possible to progress faster and easier with the inclusion of technology in people's lives so intensely (Anderson, Rainie & Vogels, 2021).

It is also stated that health checks before stay and travel will become more frequent (Gostin, Cohen & Shaw, 2021). Biological passport systems will be implemented. Considering the developments in the health services of the countries after Covid-19 pandemic, the construction of new hospitals, the increase of bed capacities, devices and equipment, the development of new treatment methods and the treatment with artificial intelligence show that there will be different alternatives in health tourism. This situation will lead to an increase in competition and thus both to provide an exchange rate advantage and to lower prices (Alsunaidi et al., 2021).

While the travel industry uses digital instruments very well, especially in the field of marketing, it is seen that the situation is different in innovation studies (Jalonen, 2012). The travel industry is relatively more disadvantaged than other industries in the field of innovation, due to the low proportion of large enterprises, the real-time travel product, very complex and many stakeholders. Shrinking margins also makes it harder to focus on innovation, that is, future success. Because of all these, it is seen that companies operating in the field of travel generally do not have a corporate innovation strategy and a structured innovation process (Teece, 2010).

Innovations often appear to consist of personal effort, the rapid untested presentation of ideas inspired by competitors or other stakeholders (Kibert et al., 2012). It is noteworthy that hotels stand out in examples of innovation in the travel sector, and that better experiences are tried to be offered to guests, generally with equipment and technological innovations. For instance, in a hotel in Vienna, the room door can be opened with a smartphone, while guests can find their room more easily with the illuminated directions on the walls.

It is stated that experts see the greatest technological impact in the travel industry in the widespread use of artificial intelligence (Bulchand-Gidumal, 2020). They also state that it should not be forgotten that bots can become the backbone of communication with touristic consumers. Although it is a matter of curiosity to what extent this technology can fill the expertise of travel professionals, it is stated that it is necessary to make sure that travel agencies that can touch touristic consumers in any case and can detect and solve problems that they are not even aware of yet, will not break away from this race.

On the other hand, virtual reality, which has emerged in recent years but has not yet been fully embraced by touristic consumers can watch 360-degree travel videos on some sites, for example, by putting a mobile phone in glasses for 3-5 dollars today, but few people have this opportunity (Pasanen et al., 2019). It is not difficult to foresee that the tourism companies using this technology to add value can gain a significant advantage, and that the concept of physicalization, that is, the combination of the physical with the digital space, will be heard more frequently after the Covid-19 pandemic process. However, it is stated that virtual life without going to a holiday destination and even experiences such as time travel are possible with such applications. Information technologies can open new horizons in the tourism sector, and it is possible to gain experiences such as the direction in which touristic consumers will walk, the vibrations of the sensors in their shoes, directing them to their rooms, to the right door in airports, or to the most interesting objects for them in museums (Wyman, 2020).

It is stated that as in most sectors, Covid-19 pandemic has further accelerated the need for digitalization and 4.0 technologies in the tourism industry (Lau, 2020). In this sense, it is possible to say that technological development and social networks will become even more essentials tools to obtain information, organize trips, share opinions among businessmen and tourists, build customer loyalty, show products and services, and improve online reputation among others. Besides, it is stated that the arrival of 5G and other technological innovations will allow the appearance of autonomous robots much more powerful and operational in terms of speed, latency and hyperconnectivity, which will revolutionize transport, logistics and hotels (Tourism Innovation Summit, 2021).

Consequently, it is possible to say that both before and during the Covid-19 pandemic, the travel and hospital industry was seen by consumers to be lagging behind banking and financial services, telecommunications and retail industries in the innovative use of technology. Because a consumer's experiences in one industry will affect expectations in another, it can be stated that so hospitality and travel businesses need to pay attention to new and innovative trends emerging in diverse sectors in the context of sustaibability of tourism industry (Patni, 2020).

Another important factor is flexibility in the context of sustainability of tourism industry after Covid-19 pandemic (Persson-Fischer & Liu, 2021). In this industry, flexibility is what businesses are going to highlight through cancellation policies, service rates, schedule modifications, etc. Also, new practices and policies are expected in nearly every aspect of the guests' experience. It is possible to say that it is a good time to explore technological innovations that will ensure the industry are well placed and to ensure whole travel ecosystem is in the strongest position (McKinsey&Company, 2020).

SOLUTIONS AND RECOMMENDATIONS

Gössling, Scott and Hall (2020) stated that the Covid-19 pandemic created an opportunity to reconsider the global tourism industry in line with sustainable development goals, but the crisis was so great, the industry needed to be revived as soon as the Covid-19 pandemic ended. Niewiadomski (2020), who advocates the view that the transformation of tourism into a more economic, fairer, more social and more sustainable post-covid tourism will depend on all stakeholders, is the first great power that can effectively stop or even reverse globalization and time-space pressure. He also mentioned that the Covid-19 pandemic has suspended the entire travel and tourism industry. According to the researcher, although the price that the world has paid for this is huge, the processes of deglobalization due to the Covid-19 pandemic present a unique opportunity for the tourism industry to restructure in line with the principles of sustainability. Considering the factors affecting the sustainability of tourism after the Covid-19 pandemic, it seems to be some of the most important factors are "digitalization", "e-transformation" "innovation", "smart technologies", "new technological systems" (Gössling, 2020; Gretzel et al., 2020; Lee, Hunter & Chung, 2020). Paying attention to the following elements and integrating these elements into the tourism industry can increase the experience of touristic consumers and create a perception that tourism is successfully sustained after the Covid-19 pandemic. These recommendations can be applied more broadly to global tourism markets:

- In order for the tourism industry to recover after the Covid-19 pandemic process, instead of adopting strategies based on returning to the norms of the past, it should be focused on how to look forward and adapt to the transformations of the future through "innovation", "e-transformation" and "digitalization".
- It is necessary to turn the perception and understanding of tourism into a fairer and more egalitarian focus, to question the consumption pattern and capitalist approach that requires mass growth in a touristic geography, and to support innovative methods for a more sustainable growth of the tourism industry.
- Fighting Covid-19 pandemic and other possible future viruses in order to ensure the sustainability of tourism and to integrating technologies into every possible area of the industry required. In this sense, virtual reality can be used. Although virtual reality cannot replace real tourism, it can be used to eliminate possible risks during pandemic periods. For example, in a pandemic period like today, with the help of virtual reality, theme parks, archaeological sites, museums or any attraction with intense human movements can be easily visited.
- It can be stated that in the wake of global economic recovery evidenced by the loosening of lockdowns and commencement of complete internal air travels, there is a need for concerted policies that will increase tourist arrivals, broaden clean energy use and ensure economic and environmental sustainability. Due to the Covid-19 pandemic has affected energy consumption patterns and impacted globalization, it can be stated that tourism industry should rethink innovation for sustainable recovery strategies.

FUTURE RESEARCH DIRECTIONS

Tourism industry can be expected to overcome and provide sustainability of tourism industry without harming to the extent that it offers tourists new experiences via innovative tourism practices (Sigala, 2020). In this context, some factors should be brought together at the creation of innovative tourism practices. However, in the current literature, it is seen that researches on the subject are quite limited. Related literature points out that among the success and sustainability factors of the tourism industry after the Covid-19 pandemic, there are factors such as "innovation", "e-transformation" and "digitalization". Therefore, it is important to investigate the factors affecting the success and sustainability of the tourism industry (Abbas et al., 2021). In addition, it is important to investigate how these factors can take place in the tourism sector and to examine successful practices. Finally, the satisfaction of tourists participating in these tourism activities, their views on these practices and the impacts of these practies in sustainability of tourism may be another research subjects. Understanding the experiences of tourists and help tourism industry managers and marketers to create practices that increase tourist satisfaction and contribute sustainability of tourism after Covid-19 pandemic (Sigala, 2020).

CONCLUSION

The tourism industry, whose importance is increasing day by day as an economic phenomenon, is an important tool in creating income, business and tax revenues and alleviating balance of payments problems (FaladeObalade & Dubey, 2014). The demand elasticity of the tourism industry is quite high. It is affected more rapidly by events such as political problems, pandemics, and economic crises compared to other industries. In this context, the Covid-19 virus, which emerged in December 2019 and has continued to spread globally since then, is an event that adversely affects the tourism industry as well as human health. Economic losses in the tourism industry, increase in unemployment, changes in daily life, decreases in travel activities, decreases in accommodation preferences, losses in transportation are the leading ones (Del Rio-Chanona et al., 2020).

It is stated that after the Covid-19 pandemic, the use of technology will increase and life will change digitally in the tourism industry (BW Bureau, 2020). In this context, hotels are expected to integrate technologies such as reservation engines, mobile applications, digital concierge services, automatic check-in/out and keyless entry systems into the tourism recovery process after Covid-19 pandemic. For example, Crowne Plaza Greater Noida, a business hotel in Noida (India), has decided to create a VR Experience Center and a sales channel called WAVE to deliver global distribution and post-pandemic virtual experience to its customers through the virtual reservation process. For this reason, it has been stated that the technological infrastructure in question is important for the post-pandemic operation (Hotelierindia, 2020).

It is also stated in the literature that people's attitudes towards tourism and risk level perceptions are negatively affected after the Covid-19 pandemic (Samdin et al., 2021). It is thought that people who travel in the tourism industry, where tourists feel anxiety around the world, travel is unsafe and tourism plans especially for big cities are reduced, will prefer more family and shorter vacations (Nazneen et al., 2020: 3). From this point of view, it is possible to say that isolation will be at the forefront by starting the digitalization period to a large extent in the tourism industry. In many places, an all-inclusive system will be offered instead of an all-inclusive system with elements such as sterilized kitchens, disinfectants, masks, and gloves, on holidays where robotization, contactless transactions will be made, and social distance, hygiene and sanitation will be prioritized (Kıvılcım, 2020: 25). It is also stated that in tourism destinations with changing perspectives, hygiene and cleanliness, as well as medical facility equipment and population density will affect the travel decisions of tourists (Wen et al., 2020: 9).

Again, it is seen that the idea of projecting 3D animations on restaurant tables in the food and beverage businesses with the intention of making the wait more enjoyable has garnered the attention of diners (Margetis et al., 2013). Even if it will not increase sales at first, it is stated that diners will certainly enjoy an unforgettable experience that will be shared with their acquaintances, which can then transform into more clients in the medium or long term. In this context, it is possible to say that user experience consists of designing and planning products or services while thinking about the feelings that businesses want to awaken in users.

Another innovative strategy with proven results is gamification (Xu, Weber & Buhalis, 2013). Gamification consists of introducing game dynamics in apps or products in order to make the user experience more enjoyable, simple and unforgettable. It uses game methods to digitally interact with consumers and motivate them to lead or achieve specific goals. This significantly improves the overall experience as it makes the entire visit to a particular tourism company's site much more fun, engaging and interactive. (Xi & Hamari, 2020).

Due to Covid-19 pandemic, not only are people restricted in the places they can visit, but they are also not motivated to get back out there and start exploring (Riazi et al., 2021). Therefore, to avoid shutting down completely due to Covid-19 pandemic, many museums and other sites have developed travel and tourism games to peak people's interests and motivate them to start coming back (Watson, 2020). While this is not a new concept for the sector, incorporating digital tools and social media requires a new and innovative approach (Watson, 2020).

As a result, it can be stated that after the Covid-19 pandemic, innovation, digitalization, smart tourism applications, e-transformation, smart technologies, new technological systems will gain more importance in terms of sustainability of tourism industry and will come to the fore in the preferences and travel decisions of tourists.

REFERENCES

Abbas, J., Mubeen, R., Iorember, P. T., Raza, S., & Mamirkulova, G. (2021). Exploring the impact of COVID-19 on tourism: Transformational potential and implications for a sustainable recovery of the travel and leisure industry. *Current Research in Behavioral Sciences*, *2*, 100033. doi:10.1016/j. crbeha.2021.100033

Adam, N. A., & Alarifi, G. (2021). Innovation practices for survival of small and medium enterprises (SMEs) in the COVID-19 times: The role of external support. *Journal of Innovation and Entrepreneurship*, *10*(1), 1–22. doi:10.118613731-021-00156-6 PMID:34075328

Alan, H. (2020). COVID-19 Pandemic and digitalization of service organizations: A trademark approach. *Turkish Studies*, *15*(6), 31–47.

Ali, I. (2020). The covid-19 pandemic: Making sense of rumor and fear: Op-ed. *Medical Anthropology*, *39*(5), 376–379. doi:10.1080/01459740.2020.1745481 PMID:32212931

Alsunaidi, S. J., Almuhaideb, A. M., Ibrahim, N. M., Shaikh, F. S., Alqudaihi, K. S., Alhaidari, F. A., Khan, I. U., Aslam, N., & Alshahrani, M. S. (2021). Applications of big data analytics to control CO-VID-19 pandemic. *Sensors (Basel)*, *21*(7), 2282. doi:10.339021072282 PMID:33805218

Anderson, J., Rainie, L., & Vogels, E. A. (2021, February 19). *Experts say the 'new normal' in 2025 will be far more tech-driven, presenting more big challenges.* https://www.pewresearch.org/internet/2021/02/18/experts-say-the-new-normal-in-2025-will-be-far-more-tech-driven-presenting-more-big-challenges/

Arenas, A. E., Goh, J. M., & Urueña, A. (2019). How does IT affect design centricity approaches: Evidence from Spain's smart tourism ecosystem. *International Journal of Information Management*, *45*, 149–162. doi:10.1016/j.ijinfomgt.2018.10.015

Bartik, A. W., Bertrand, M., Cullen, Z. B., Glaeser, E. L., Luca, M., & Stanton, C. T. (2020). *How are small businesses adjusting to Covid-19? Early evidence from a survey.* National Bureau of Economic Research. https://www.nber.org/papers/w26989.pdf

Brachman, P. S. (2003). Infectious diseases-past, present, and future. *International Journal of Epidemiology*, *32*(5), 684–686. doi:10.1093/ije/dyg282 PMID:14559728

Bulchand-Gidumal, J. (2020). Impact of artificial intelligence in travel, tourism, and hospitality. In *Handbook of e-Tourism* (pp. 1–20). Springer. doi:10.1007/978-3-030-05324-6_110-1

Bureau, B. W. (2020, March 25). *Crowne plaza greater noida launches world's first hotel VR experience center.* BW Hotelier. http://bwhotelier.businessworld.in/article/CrownePlaza-Greater-Noida-launches-World-s-First-Hotel-VR-Experience-Center/09-03-2020-185809/

Chakraborty, I., & Maity, P. (2020). COVID-19 outbreak: Migration, effects on society, global environment and prevention. *The Science of the Total Environment, 728,* 138882. doi:10.1016/j.scitotenv.2020.138882 PMID:32335410

Del Rio-Chanona, R. M., Mealy, P., Pichler, A., Lafond, F., & Farmer, J. D. (2020). Supply and demand shocks in the COVID-19 pandemic: An industry and occupation perspective. *Oxford Review of Economic Policy, 36*(1, Supplement_1), 94–137. doi:10.1093/oxrep/graa033

Economic Commission for Latin America and the Caribbean (ECLAC). (2020). *The impact of the COVID-19 pandemic on the tourism sector in Latin America and the Caribbean, and options for a sustainable and resilient recovery.* United Nations Publication.

FaladeObalade, T. A., & Dubey, S. (2014). Managing tourism as a source of revenue and foreign direct investment inflow in a developing country: The Jordanian experience. *International Journal of Academic Research in Economics and Management Sciences, 3*(3), 16–42.

Gostin, L. O., Cohen, I. G., & Shaw, J. (2021). Digital health passes in the age of COVID-19: Are "vaccine passports" lawful and ethical? *Journal of the American Medical Association, 325*(19), 1933–1934. doi:10.1001/jama.2021.5283 PMID:33825831

Gössling, S. (2020). Technology, ICT and tourism: From big data to the big picture. *Journal of Sustainable Tourism,* 1–10.

Gössling, S., Scott, D., & Hall, M. C. (2020). Pandemics, tourism and global change: A rapid assessment of COVID-19. *Journal of Sustainable Tourism, 29*(1), 1–20. doi:10.1080/09669582.2020.1758708

Gretzel, U., Sigala, M., Xiang, Z., & Koo, C. (2015). Smart tourism: Foundations and developments. *Electronic Markets, 25*(3), 179–188. doi:10.100712525-015-0196-8

Gretzel, U., Fuchs, M., Baggio, R., Hoepken, W., Law, R., Neidhardt, J., Pesonen, J., Zanker, M., & Xiang, Z. (2020). e-Tourism beyond COVID-19: A call for transformative research. *Information Technology & Tourism, 22*(2), 187–203. doi:10.100740558-020-00181-3

Han, E., Tan, M. M. J., Turk, E., Sridhar, D., Leung, G. M., Shibuya, K., Asgari, N., Oh, J., García-Basteiro, A. L., Hanefeld, J., Cook, A. R., Hsu, L. Y., Teo, Y. Y., Heymann, D., Clark, H., McKee, M., & Legido-Quigley, H. (2020). Lessons learnt from easing COVID-19 restrictions: An analysis of countries and regions in Asia Pacific and Europe. *Lancet, 396*(10261), 1525–1534. doi:10.1016/S0140-6736(20)32007-9 PMID:32979936

Henderson, J. C., & Ng, A. (2004). Responding to crisis: Severe acute respiratory syndrome (SARS) and hotels in Singapore. *International Journal of Tourism Research, 6*(6), 411–419. doi:10.1002/jtr.505

Hotelierindia. (2020, March 2). *From social distancing to contactless check-in and dining-Interactive technology will be key in dealing with pandemic issues.* https://www.hotelierindia.com/business/10763-from-social-distancing-to-contactlesscheck-in-and-dining-interactive-technology-will-be-key-in-dealing-with

Jalonen, H. (2012). The uncertainty of innovation: A systematic review of the literature. *Journal of Management Research*, *4*(1), 1.

Jiang, Y., & Wen, J. (2020). Effects of COVID-19 on hotel marketing and management: A perspective article. *International Journal of Contemporary Hospitality Management*, *32*(8), 2563–2573. doi:10.1108/IJCHM-03-2020-0237

Kıvılcım, B. (2020). Probable effects of COVID-19 (New Coronavirus) pandemic on tourism sector. *International Journal of Western Black Sea Social and Humanities Sciences*, *4*(1), 17–27.

Kibert, C. J., Thiele, L., Peterson, A.. & Monroe, M. (2012). *The ethics of sustainability*. University of Florida Press.

Lau, A. (2020). New technologies used in COVID-19 for business survival: Insights from the Hotel Sector in China. *Information Technology & Tourism*, *22*(4), 497–504. doi:10.100740558-020-00193-z

Lee, P., Hunter, W. C., & Chung, N. (2020). Smart tourism city: Developments and transformations. *Sustainability*, *12*(10), 3958. doi:10.3390u12103958

Lopes, R. D., Macedo, A. V. S., Moll-Bernardes, R. J., Feldman, A., Arruda, G. D. A. S., de Souza, A. S., ... de Souza, O. F. (2020). Continuing versus suspending angiotensin-converting enzyme inhibitors and angiotensin receptor blockers: Impact on adverse outcomes in hospitalized patients with severe acute respiratory syndrome coronavirus 2 (SARS-CoV-2)—The Brace Corona Trial. *American Heart Journal*, *226*, 49–59. doi:10.1016/j.ahj.2020.05.002 PMID:32502882

Margetis, G., Grammenos, D., Zabulis, X., & Stephanidis, C. (2013). iEat: An interactive table for restaurant customers' experience enhancement. In *International Conference on Human-Computer Interaction* (pp. 666-670). Springer.

McKinsey & Company. (2020, February 10). *The travel industry turned upside down insights, analysis and actions for travel executives.* https://www.mckinsey.com/~/media/mckinsey/industries/travel%20logistics%20and%20infrastructure/our%20insights/the%20travel%20industry%20turned%20upside%20down%20insights%20analysis%20and%20actions%20for%20travel%20executives/the-travel-industry-turned-upside-down-insights-analysis-and-actions-for-travel-executives.pdf

NazneenS.HongX.Ud DinN. (2020, May 5). COVID-19 crises and tourist travel risk perceptions, SSRN: https://ssrn.com/abstract=3592321 doi:10.2139/ssrn.3592321

Niewiadomski, P. (2020). COVID-19: From temporary DeGlobalisation to a re-discovery of tourism? *Tourism Geographies*, *22*(3), 651–656. doi:10.1080/14616688.2020.1757749

Ocheni, S. I., Agba, A. O., Agba, M. S., & Eteng, F. O. (2020). Covid-19 and the tourism industry: Critical overview, lessons and policy options. *Academic Journal of Interdisciplinary Studies*, *9*(6), 114–114. doi:10.36941/ajis-2020-0116

OECD. (2020a, February 10). *Rebuilding tourism for the future: COVID-19 policy responses and recovery.* https://read.oecd-ilibrary.org/view/?ref=137_137392-qsvjt75vnh&title=Rebuilding-tourism-for-the-future-COVID-19-policy-response-and-recovery&_ga=2.144837364.1583123711.1622917893-726322868.1622392034

OECD. (2020b, February 15). *Tourism policy responses.* https://read.oecd-ilibrary.org/view/?ref=124_124984-7uf8nm95se&title=Covid19_Tourism_Policy_Responses

Orîndaru, A., Popescu, M. F., Alexoaei, A. P., Căescu, Ş. C., Florescu, M. S., & Orzan, A. O. (2021). Tourism in a post-COVID-19 era: Sustainable strategies for industry's recovery. *Sustainability, 13*(12), 6781. doi:10.3390u13126781

Pal, M., Berhanu, G., Desalegn, C., & Kandi, V. (2020). Severe acute respiratory syndrome coronavirus-2 (SARS-CoV-2): An update. *Cureus, 12*(3), e7423. doi:10.7759/cureus.7423 PMID:32337143

Pasanen, K., Pesonen, J., Murphy, J., Heinonen, J., & Mikkonen, J. (2019). Comparing tablet and virtual reality glasses for watching nature tourism videos. In *Information and Communication Technologies in Tourism* (pp. 120–131). Springer.

Patni, A. (2020, April 22). *COVID 19 and innovation in the hospitality industry.* https://www.linkedin.com/pulse/covid-19-innovation-hospitality-industry-arihant-patni/

Persson-Fischer, U., & Liu, S. (2021). The impact of a global crisis on areas and topics of tourism research. *Sustainability, 13*(2), 906. doi:10.3390u13020906

Polyzos, S., Samitas, A., & Spyridou, A. E. (2020). Tourism demand and the COVİD-19 pandemic: An LSTM approach. *Tourism Recreation Research*, 1–13.

Poudel, K., & Subedi, P. (2020). Impact of COVID-19 pandemic on socioeconomic and mental health aspects in Nepal. *The International Journal of Social Psychiatry, 66*(8), 748–755. doi:10.1177/0020764020942247 PMID:32650687

Özaltın Türker, G. (2020). How Covid-19 pandemic affects tourism sector? An evaluation from tourism academics perspective. *International Journal of Social Sciences and Education Research, 6*(2), 207–224. doi:10.24289/ijsser.760790

Pacific Asia Travel Association (PATA). (2020, April 22). *COVID-19 and the tourism sector: A comparison of policy responses in Asia Pacific.* https://static1.squarespace.com/static/5f24290fd0d0910ecab2b02e/t/5fd03d335ec17a4c668ae0ed/1607482699608/COVID19-TourismSector-APAC-11Nov.pdf

Riazi, N. A., Wunderlich, K., Gierc, M., Brussoni, M., Moore, S. A., Tremblay, M. S., & Faulkner, G. (2021). You can't go to the park, you can't go here, you can't go there: Exploring parental experiences of COVID-19 and its impact on their children's movement behaviours. *Children (Basel, Switzerland), 8*(3), 219. doi:10.3390/children8030219 PMID:33809221

Samdin, Z., Abdullah, S. I. N. W., Khaw, A., & Subramaniam, T. (2021). Travel risk in the ecotourism industry amid COVID-19 pandemic: Ecotourists' perceptions. *Journal of Ecotourism*, 1–29. doi:10.1080/14724049.2021.1938089

Sharifi, A., & Khavarian-Garmsir, A. R. (2020). The COVID-19 pandemic: Impacts on cities and major lessons for urban planning, design, and management. *The Science of the Total Environment, 749*, 142391. doi:10.1016/j.scitotenv.2020.142391 PMID:33370924

Shereen, M. A., Khan, S., Kazmi, A., Bashir, N., & Siddique, R. (2020). COVID-19 infection: Origin, transmission, and characteristics of human coronaviruses. *Journal of Advanced Research*, *24*, 91–98. doi:10.1016/j.jare.2020.03.005 PMID:32257431

Sigala, M. (2020). Tourism and COVID-19: Impacts and implications for advancing and resetting industry and research. *Journal of Business Research*, *117*, 312–321. doi:10.1016/j.jbusres.2020.06.015 PMID:32546875

Susanto, D. R., & Kiswantoro, A. (2021). Tourism branding: A strategy of regional tourism sustainability post COVID-19 in Yogyakarta. *IOP Conference Series. Earth and Environmental Science*, *704*(1), 012003. doi:10.1088/1757-899X/1108/1/012003

Teece, D. J. (2010). Business models, business strategy and innovation. *Long Range Planning*, *43*(2-3), 172–194. doi:10.1016/j.lrp.2009.07.003

Tourism Innovation Summit (TIS). (2021, April 19). *Travel & Tourism after Covid-19*. https://www.tisglobalsummit.com/travel-tourism-after-covid-19/

Tsiotsou, R. H., & Goldsmith, R. E. (2012). *Strategic marketing in tourism services*. Emerald Group Publishing.

UNWTO (World Tourism Organization). (2020, April 19). *International tourism highlights*. https://www.e-unwto.org/doi/pdf/10.18111/9789284421152

UNWTO (World Tourism Organization). (2021, April 14). *International tourism down 70% as travel restrictions impact all regions*. https://www.unwto.org/taxonomy/term/347

Wang, Q., Su, M., Zhang, M., & Li, R. (2021). Integrating digital technologies and public health to fight Covid-19 pandemic: Key technologies, applications, challenges and outlook of digital healthcare. *International Journal of Environmental Research and Public Health*, *18*(11), 6053. doi:10.3390/ijerph18116053 PMID:34199831

Wasdani, K. P., & Prasad, A. (2020). The impossibility of social distancing among the urban poor: The case of an Indian slum in the times of COVID-19. *Local Environment*, *25*(5), 414–418. doi:10.1080/13549839.2020.1754375

Watson, T. (2020, April 14). *Gamification in tourism-benefits & use cases*. https://skywell.software/blog/gamification-in-tourism-benefits-use-cases

Wen, J., Kozak, M., Yang, S., & Liu, F. (2020). COVID-19: Potential effects on Chinese Citizens' lifestyle and travel. *Tourism Review*, *76*(1), 74–87. doi:10.1108/TR-03-2020-0110

WTTC (World Travel & Tourism Council). (2020, April 14). *More than 197m travel & tourism jobs will be lost due to prolonged travel restrictions, according to new research from WTTC*. https://wttc.org/News-Article/More-than-197m-Travel-Tourism-jobs-will-be-lost-due-to-prolonged-travel-restrictions

Wyman, O. (2020, March 5). *To recovery & beyond the future of travel & tourism in the wake of Covid-19*. https://www.oliverwyman.com/content/dam/oliver-wyman/v2/publications/2020/To_Recovery_and_Beyond-The_Future_of_Travel_and_Tourism_in_the_Wake_of_COVID-19.pdf

Xi, N., & Hamari, J. (2020). Does gamification affect brand engagement and equity? A study in online brand communities. *Journal of Business Research*, *109*, 449–460. doi:10.1016/j.jbusres.2019.11.058

Xu, F., Weber, J., & Buhalis, D. (2013). Gamification in tourism. In *Information and Communication Technologies in Tourism* (pp. 525–537). Springer.

Zhu, H., Wei, L., & Niu, P. (2020). The novel coronavirus outbreak in Wuhan, China. *Global Health Research and Policy*, *5*(1), 1–3. doi:10.118641256-020-00135-6 PMID:32226823

ADDITIONAL READING

Breier, M., Kallmuenzer, A., Clauss, T., Gast, J., Kraus, S., & Tiberius, V. (2021). The role of business model innovation in the hospitality industry during the COVID-19 crisis. *International Journal of Hospitality Management*, *92*, 102723. doi:10.1016/j.ijhm.2020.102723

Cooke, P., & Nunes, S. (2021). Post-Coronavirus regional innovation policies: From mega to giga and beyond through sustainable spatial planning of global tourism. *European Planning Studies*, 1–19. doi:10.1080/09654313.2021.1936463

Graziano, T. (2021). Smart Technologies, Back-to-the-village rhetoric, and tactical urbanism: Post-COVID planning scenarios in Italy. *International Journal of E-Planning Research*, *10*(2), 80–93. doi:10.4018/IJEPR.20210401.oa7

Mohanty, P., Hassan, A., & Ekis, E. (2020). Augmented reality for relaunching tourism post-COVID-19: Socially distant, virtually connected. *Worldwide Hospitality and Tourism Themes*, *12*(6), 753–760. doi:10.1108/WHATT-07-2020-0073

Nunes, S., & Cooke, P. (2021). New global tourism innovation in a post-coronavirus era. *European Planning Studies*, *29*(1), 1–19. doi:10.1080/09654313.2020.1852534

Pasca, M. G., Renzi, M. F., Di Pietro, L., & Mugion, R. G. (2021). Gamification in tourism and hospitality research in the era of digital platforms: A systematic literature review. *Journal of Service Theory and Practice*, *31*(5), 691–737. Advance online publication. doi:10.1108/JSTP-05-2020-0094

Sharma, A., Shin, H., Santa-María, M. J., & Nicolau, J. L. (2021). Hotels' COVID-19 innovation and performance. *Annals of Tourism Research*, *88*, 103180. doi:10.1016/j.annals.2021.103180

Sharma, G. D., Thomas, A., & Paul, J. (2021). Reviving tourism industry post-COVID-19: A resilience-based framework. *Tourism Management Perspectives*, *37*, 100786. doi:10.1016/j.tmp.2020.100786 PMID:33391988

Shen, S., Sotiriadis, M., & Zhang, Y. (2020). The influence of smart technologies on customer journey in tourist attractions within the smart tourism management framework. *Sustainability*, *12*(10), 4157. doi:10.3390u12104157

KEY TERMS AND DEFINITIONS

Artificial Intelligence (AI): An artificial operating system that is unique to human intelligence and is expected to exhibit higher cognitive functions or autonomous behaviors such as perception, learning, connecting plural concepts, thinking, reasoning, problem solving, communication, inference and decision making.

Augmented Reality (AR): It is the live or indirect physical view of the real-world environment and its contents, enhanced by computer-generated sound, image, graphics and GPS data.

Big Data: It is the form of the data that has been analyzed, classified, and transformed into a meaningful and processable form.

Blockchain: A distributed database system that provides encrypted transaction tracking.

Bot: A group of software agents specially developed to perform actions on the internet.

COVID-19: A virus that was first identified on January 13, 2020 as a result of research conducted in a group of patients who developed respiratory symptoms (fever, cough, shortness of breath) in Wuhan Province of China in late December.

Digitalization: The use of digital technologies to change a business model and provide new revenue and value-producing opportunities; it is the process of moving to a digital business.

E-Transformation: An expression that defines the process of creating solutions for social and sectoral needs with the integration of digital technologies and, accordingly, the development and change of business practices and culture.

Innovation: Adapting and applying new creative ideas or inventions to economic fields. In other words, the process of creative solutions presented for the solution of visibly open needs.

Internet of Things (IoT): A communication network in which physical objects are connected with each other or with larger systems.

Sustainability: It is to make the life of humanity permanent while ensuring the continuity of production and diversity. In other words, it is the ability to meet human needs without compromising the needs of future generations.

Chapter 25
Cultural Heritage and Digitalization in City Branding

Oya Yildirim
Cukurova University, Turkey

A. Celil Çakici
Mersin University, Turkey

ABSTRACT

In today's competitive global environment, cities are striving to stand out and be attractive to investors, visitors, and residents. City branding is an important tool to differentiate the city from its competitors and to be preferred by visitors. Every city has its own characteristics resulting from its historical development, the influence of its geography, and its social, cultural, and economic past. Therefore, the tangible and intangible cultural heritage of cities is vital for their promotion and branding. This study aims to show the importance of their cultural heritage, which is the most fundamental feature to differentiate themselves from their competitors in city branding. It is emphasized that the cultural events organized in cities or the assets specific to cities, most of which are on the UNESCO World Heritage List, have a significant impact on city branding. In addition, the chapter explains the impact of digitalization, which is one of the most important developments of our time, on city branding and cultural heritage.

INTRODUCTION

Tourism is a significant industry in the development of a city due to its economic, social and cultural contributions. In tourism, destination marketing has gained the upper hand over national marketing, both theoretically and practically. Destination marketing can also include marketing of regions, cities and towns. In city marketing, the concept of city branding, which can be expressed as the promotion of the city and the presentation of an image developed in accordance with its resources, has an important place. One of the most crucial steps in city branding is the need to create an identity for the city. Each city has unique characteristics, and these unique qualities determine the identity of the city. In other words, while creating the city brand, the positive, distinctive, original and local cultural heritage of the

DOI: 10.4018/978-1-7998-8528-3.ch025

city is leveraged. Accordingly, cultural heritage emerges as an attractive element of city branding, the importance of which is constantly growing (Apostolakis, 2003; Hall & Piggin, 2002; Iliachenko, 2005; Kavaratzis & Ashworth, 2007).

Cultural heritage is one of the most key attractions in cultural tourism. People are paying more and more attention to different cultures and cultural heritage. The tendency to adapt to nature and highlight unique visual values is also increasing (World Travel & Tourism Council, 2021). This trend has also significantly increased cultural tourism (Zhang & Yang, 2011). On the other hand, negative aspects such as the complexity of social life, stress, destruction of nature, environmental pollution, noise and traffic problems increase people's search for peace. This situation directs people to historical cities that meet these needs and at the same time have rich opportunities in terms of cultural heritage. Historical cities are going to digitalise to meet today's demands, protect their valuable cultural heritage, and facilitate access to these values.

Digitalization and/or technology can have a positive impact on the competitiveness of cities. Awareness and the ability to compete are crucial requisites for cities to have a say in the global arena. For this reason, cities that have competed within the borders of their country have ceded their place to brand cities that can compete globally and strive to create a strong image for themselves with their cultural heritage, originality, and difference to have an advantage in this race. Brand cities make these differences even more visible with the advantages of technology. By digitising various archival materials and museum collections, they protect both their cultural heritage and lay the groundwork for the unhindered accessibility and use of cultural heritage.

This study aims to explain the importance of cultural heritage, which is the main feature that makes cities different from their competitors, in city branding and the impact of digitalization in this context, based on the literature. In the study, it is aimed to contribute to local managers and destination management organizations that want to make their cities a successful brand. Adding the Covid-19 pandemic that the entire world has faced in recent years to developments in technology, understanding and leveraging the benefits of digitalization will go a long way in helping city managers and tourism marketers. To this end, the chapter, which is designed as a literature review, first explains the basic concepts involved in the process of city branding. Then it highlights the role of tangible and intangible cultural heritage in city branding and finally discusses the relationship between cultural heritage and city branding in the digital age.

CONCEPTS IN THE PROCESS OF CITY BRAND FORMATION

A tourism destination is a geographical area or a region where the tourists are located in the local community (Tinsley & Lynch, 2001). Such destinations are mostly cities. The effort to make any city distinguishable from its competitors in the eyes of potential visitors is defined as city marketing. This can be achieved by developing a city brand. The city brand formation process involves the application of basic stages of product branding (Kavaratzis & Ashworth, 2005) and concepts such as brand and branding, brand identity, brand image and brand positioning should be understood in this process (Ma et al., 2021, p.3). Cities that have successful branding can attract tourists.

Brand and Branding

The concept of brand can be explained with different approaches in terms of business, consumer and brand owner (Blain et al., 2005; Kotler, 1997; Randall, 2000; Wood, 2000). A brand is a consumer's conception of a product and can mean something different from the product itself. (Blackston, 2000). In other words, a brand is a name, term, sign, symbol, shape, or combination of designs that identifies the goods and services of a seller or group of sellers and aims to distinguish them from the offerings of competitors (Wood, 2000). A brand is not just a name, but an entity that gives identity and personality to the product. It is shaped by consumers' perceptions and guides them in their product preferences (Aaker, 1996). Branding, on the other hand, is the practice of giving a specific name to one or more products of a seller, the process of meaning attribution and awarding meaning to identity (Pillai & Bagavathi, 2000). Many things we see around us today, such as clothes, cars, skyscrapers, movies, entertainment centres, hotels, bridges, towers, countries, regions, and cities can also be a brand. Egypt, for example, is known for her pyramids. Moreover, cities with rich cultural heritage are the most influential brands in the tourism industry. Rome has become a brand city with its historical and religious buildings (Colosseum, Trevi Fountain, Pantheon, etc.), London with its Big Ben bell tower, Moscow with St. Basil's Cathedral and Prague with its cultural attractions (Charles Bridge, Powder Tower, Astronomical Clock, etc.). The "Eiffel Tower" has an important contribution to the tourist attraction. (Kaypak, 2013).

Brand Identity

A brand should have an identity that distinguishes it from others, just like a person. Brand identity encompasses the meaning of the brand and all its cultural and social aspects. Brand identity is the set of associations that enable the brand strategy to be developed and easily remembered (Aaker, 1996). Brand identity can also be defined as the combination of the visual and verbal elements, and all the values it evokes in the consumer's mind. For example, in branding a city, the brand identity should reflect what a city wants to be.

The themes that shape the identity of the city in the branding process are the characteristics of the city from the past and the current activities. In other words, historical and cultural features are important in shaping the city's identity, which is an essential part of its image. For example, the texture of Paris based on art and culture, which dates back to centuries, has increased interest in the city, and Paris has become a "cultural and art centre", leading to attract more tourist year after year, with the exception of the Covid-19 period. Rome, Prague and Vienna are the cities that have developed in parallel with their cultural heritage based on identities. Today, when casinos and entertainment centres are mentioned, the first thing that comes to mind is Las Vegas or Monte Carlo, and when cinema is mentioned, Cannes or Hollywood (Demir, 2006). For this reason, today it is of great importance to give cities an identity, and in this context, it is necessary to highlight the various values of social and cultural heritage associated with the city. Moreover, it is inevitable to digitise these cultural values in order to adapt to today's conditions, in which technology is developing rapidly and the Covid-19 pandemic is affecting the whole world, and to keep up with the competition.

Brand Image

From the consumer's perspective, brand image, which encompasses both brand associations and perceptions of quality and value, is at the heart of the brand concept. Brand image expresses the perception level of the brand and is the sum of the meaning that consumers ascribe to the product or what they understand from the product. To put it more clearly, a brand image is the perception of the product which includes all the elements such as the product personality, emotions, and associations in the mind (Karavatzis & Ashworth, 2005).

One of the most important points in the process of city branding is the image of the city. City image is the perception, belief, association, impression or ideas conveyed about a city (Alhempud & Armstrong, 1996). Brand city image, on the other hand, refers to the perception of a city preferred by tourists as a result of branding activities. The perception of Paris as the city of lovers and Milan as the city of fashion or Rio de Janeiro with its carnival (Anholt, 2005) are well-known examples of branding activities that lead to a brand image of cities.

Cultural events also contribute significantly to the image of cities. The Edinburgh Festival, the Cannes Film Festival or the Notting Hill Carnival could be cited. Such major events shape the image of the host community or city and create a positive trend in terms of its potential to be visited by tourists (Hall, 1992, p.14). For this reason, it is necessary to identify the city's opportunities, analyze its current image and the characteristics of the target audience, shape the desired city image and manage this process.

Positioning of Brand Character

Another important issue in branding is brand positioning. Brand positioning, which expresses the benefits and promises of a brand and the place it occupies in the minds of its current and potential customers compared to its competitors, is a fundamental point in determining brand identity (Goeldner et al., 2000). Brand positioning can be defined as an essential part of brand identity and brand equity that can communicate with target consumers and show that it offers more advantages rather than other competing brands (Aaker, 1996).

Brand positioning determines which "personality and identity elements" are remembered by consumers and provide brand awareness (Kapferer, 1992, p.96). Positioning is about how a product becomes embedded in people's minds and is central to creating brand character (Mariotti, 1999, p.47). Terms used to express the brand character of cities are generally tolerant, peaceful, mystical, hospitable and soothing. After a tourism destination has selected its target markets, it should create a brand character and try to position itself in those markets. The answer to how a city is positioned as a tourism destination includes infrastructure development, investment, services and human capital, cultural heritage, and marketing, all of which form the basis of tourist attractions (Johns & Mattsson, 2005). In order to position itself properly in the market, a city should build an image that differentiates it from other cities with which it competes and ensure that the image it builds is compatible with the requirements of its target market (Kastenholz, 2002, p.83). At this point, the importance of the concept of differentiation becomes clear.

City Branding

City branding is defined as creating a consistent brand identity for the city and differentiating the city brand through positive image development (Cai, 2002, p.722) and can be a powerful weapon in global competition. Cities that have deeper meaning and higher emotional value than their competitors are the brand cities. Moreover, people can spend more money to travel to these cities. Branding means creating an identity, and along with the quality that distinguishes one city from another, it is the perceived uniqueness (Kaypak, 2013).

Being a tourism brand has many benefits for a city. Branding increases the rate of repeat visitors to the city and enables it by creating an emotional connection with customers (Oppermann, 2000). In the model of destination branding, three dimensions are mentioned in relation to the historical, cultural and natural characteristics of the region. These dimensions are local customs, geographical location and scenic features. They reflect the original characteristics that distinguish and define the city (Iliachenko, 2005, p.6).

Just like product branding, there are also studies that examine place branding in order to choose one place over another (Keller, 1998). Place branding is used for cities as a new type of branding. Today, experts agree that marketing can be applied to cities and destinations and these cities can be marketed like goods and services by commercial companies. Cities can be marketed in many different dimensions, such as cityscape and architecture, regional geography, and local values. Tourism usually considers the cultural values and local identities of cities and regions when marketing them (Rainisto, 2003).

A city brand can be considered as a set of marketing activities. These activities can help the city become a branded city and are preferred as follows (Pike, 2009):

- Creates a name, symbol, logo, word, sign, or other graphic material that defines and distinguishes a city from others;
- Provides for the consistent delivery of a beautiful city-specific holiday experience;
- Serves to create an emotional connection between the visitor and the city and strengthen existing bonds;
- Reduces the cost and risk of finding customers.

City branding can also be considered as a development, recognition and image project supported by a unique symbol to distinguish the city from others (Kaypak, 2013). Today, many cities such as London, New York, Paris, Rome, Amsterdam, Barcelona and Hong Kong have branded themselves with their local identities and distinguishing features (Varlı, 2011, p.1).

CITY BRANDING AND CULTURAL HERITAGE

The cultural, historical and natural values of regions and cities are fundamental to the promotion and branding of cities. Urban structures, architecture, trees, parks, libraries and places of worship reflect the traces of people's experiences, work and personal history (Kaya et al., 2007). In this regard, these unique values that constitute cultural heritage should be prioritized in branding a city.

In order to explain the concept of cultural heritage, it is first necessary to explain the concepts of culture and heritage, which form the basis of the concept. For this reason, firstly, explanations on the concepts of culture and heritage are given below, and then the concept of cultural heritage is explained and focused on tangible and intangible cultural heritage.

Culture and Cultural Heritage

Culture can be defined differently depending on the discipline. Culture is the learned patterns of behavior that are shared and passed on by members of a society and are in a process of change; it is a way of life that results from the outcomes of these patterns including beliefs, values, attitudes, and materials (Kempner, 1976). Culture, a concept that encompasses everything that people who are members of a society have and share, is a complex whole. In this regard, culture has two dimensions: tangible and intangible. All man-made tools, devices and structures belong to the tangible elements of culture: practices, expressions, values, knowledge and skills are examples of intangible cultural elements.

Heritage refers to the transmission of something from one generation to the next and thus the values of past societies extend to the present (Nuryanti, 1996). Cultural heritage, on the other hand, includes material and spiritual cultural elements created by previous generations and passed down from generation to generation (Cetin, 2010, p.183). Cultural heritage comes from the past and gives people a sense of belonging to a place. Therefore, cultural heritage is also something that completes people (Tweed & Sutherland, 2007).

Indispensable tools and equipment that meet the needs of daily life have been produced as a defence and life mechanism against economic and intellectual-religious impulses; this type of production provided some material evidence to document information about past lives. These goods constitute the common cultural heritage of mankind (Ozgunel, 2007). Cultural heritage, a particularly broad concept, can be divided into two groups: tangible and intangible cultural heritage.

Tangible Cultural Heritage

Tangible cultural heritage consists of movable cultural heritage such as paintings, sculptures, coins and manuscripts; immovable cultural heritage such as monuments and archaeological sites; underwater cultural heritage such as shipwrecks, underwater ruins and cities (United Nations Educational, Scientific and Cultural Organization [UNESCO], 2021). UNESCO (1972) divided tangible cultural heritage into three parts in the Convention Concerning the Protection of the World Cultural and Natural Heritage.

Monuments: Exceptional universal architectural works of history, art and science, masterpieces of sculpture and painting, archaeological elements and structures, inscriptions, caves and combinations of elements.

Groups of buildings: Ensembles of separate or combined buildings that are of exceptional value from a historical, artistic, or scientific point of view because of their architecture, harmony and location on the land.

Sites: Artifacts of outstanding universal value from a historical, aesthetic, ethnological or anthropological point of view, or joint works of nature and man, and areas including archaeological sites.

According to another typology, tangible cultural heritage includes scientific heritage with plants, animals, rocks and natural habitats and cultural heritage with local and fine arts, customs and traditions, and spoken language (Nuryanti, 1996). Natural areas with cultural aspects such as physical, biological or geological formations have become areas that carry the development of societies over time. These areas, which have existed for many years, are attractive to people for their natural beautyand are considered and valued by the tourism industry as tourist attractions. Consequently, both natural and cultural assets are also part of the tangible cultural heritage (Ahunbay, 2011).

Intangible Cultural Heritage

Intangible cultural heritage includes oral and auditory traditions, rituals, etc., that have been passed down from one generation to the next over many years. In the Convention for the Safeguarding of the Intangible Cultural Heritage, adopted on 17 October 2003, this term refers to "the practices, representations, expressions, knowledge and skills, - as well as the instruments, objects, artifacts and cultural spaces associated with that communities, groups and, in some cases, individuals recognize as part of their cultural heritage" (UNESCO, 2003). In other words, intangible cultural heritage is not physical and invisible, but it is the values that make up a society. These consist of elements such as traditional, historical, spiritual, religious values, beliefs, music, language, theater, songs, dances, performances, festivals, nursery rhymes, stories and poems (Kozak, 2014, p.49). UNESCO (2003) identified the specific areas of intangible cultural heritage and adopted the Convention for the Safeguarding of the Intangible Cultural Heritage at its 32nd General Conference on 17 October 2003 to protect folk culture and traditions in the face of globalization. The areas designated by UNESCO are:

- Oral traditions and expressions, including language as a carrier of intangible cultural heritage. For example, myths, legends, fairy tales, epics, stories, laments, lullabies, and folk songs.
- Performing arts, such as theater rehearsals, folk music and folk dance performances.
- Social practices, rituals and festivals; transitional customs and traditions such as birth, marriage and death; all kinds of traditional gatherings such as festivals, holidays, anniversaries; and traditional practices and beliefs based on these
- Knowledge and practices related to nature and the universe; folk medicine and folk meteorology developed by people in the traditional culture structure.
- Traditional craftsmanship; traditional trades such as coppersmithing, tinsmithing and blacksmithing, which are learned in a master-apprentice relationship and are not based on mass production.

The Role of Cultural Heritage in City Branding

In a globalised world, countries, regions and cities face great competition and increasingly use marketing and branding techniques to attract tourists (Rizzi & Dioli, 2010, p.40). Increasing competition between cities has caused marketing expenditures to focus on local development strategies.

The most important part of regional marketing is city marketing (Matlovicova et al., 2010, p.215). City marketing is the effort to make a city distinct from its competitors in the eyes of potential visitors; this is possible through the creation of a city brand (Kavaratzis & Ashworth, 2005). A city has the potential to become a city brand depending on factors such as financial capabilities, cultural and historical heritage, appearance, climate, ease of access, differences from other cities, and marketing and communication activities carried out for the city (Sahin, 2010).

In the process of becoming a city brand, tangible and intangible cultural heritage occupy an important place along with other characteristics of cities. Due to the fact that tourism grows, the diversification of people's demands, the growing interest in unique personal experiences and differences, and the desire to be privileged, people are turning away from the typical sea, sun and sand holiday and are orienting towards a more sophisticated holiday. The shift in focus in the tourism industry from product to consumer orientation also creates a need for a unique experience. To satisfy this need for experience, people's attention has been turned to cultural heritage tourism. The uniqueness of cultural heritage resources has given cities a special place in the tourism industry. Moreover, cultural heritage sites are also very successful in disseminating information to tourists (Apostolakis, 2003). Therefore, these areas play an important role in raising the profile of cities.

City branding is a particularly popular phenomenon in the field of tourism. One of the most important reasons for this is that a city brand strengthens nations both economically and culturally. In addition to their contribution to the country, city branding also adds economic, social, cultural and artistic value to the local people. When cities have a strong brand, they sell their other goods and services much more easily, attract people and investment, and draw attention to the wealth of information about different cities (Sahin, 2010). Barcelona, New York, Helsinki, Oregon, Rio de Janeiro, Singapore, Stockholm, Paris, San Francisco, London, Sydney, Toronto, and Amsterdam are among the most successful cities in the world in this regard (Yavuz, 2007).

A good example of this is Amsterdam, which has prioritized both city tourism and cultural tourism, making it one of the most prosperous city brands in the world. Its rich historical heritage and culture, business acumen, openness to change, quality of life and innovation set Amsterdam apart from other major European cities. Its cultural contribution to the world is that Amsterdam is a source of inspiration, with world-class museums such as the Vincent Van Gogh Museum or the Rijks Museum. While preserving the values of its history, Amsterdam has managed to incorporate innovation into its identity. Amsterdam prides itself on combining the old with the new. The presence of creative, innovative and commercial elements in the historical sites has helped the city reach its current position (Kavaratzis & Ashworth, 2007). The biggest factor that makes global brands such as Paris, London and Rome a city brand is that they created their urban characteristics several centuries ago and incorporated the reflections of these characteristics into the structure of the city (Sahin, 2010, p.62).

In the Macao region, which has many cultural assets, an economic development policy has been introduced, including cultural tourism. This policy attempts to create an image as a heritage tourism destination. The studies have found that 99.3% of tourists who come to Macau-a casino centre-visit historical and religious sites, and the survey respondents have indicated that the primary motivation for 40.3% of them is cultural heritage. In addition, eight out of ten people are described as cultural tourists (Zhang & Yang, 2011). 92.3% of those who visit Troy and the region due to their interest in history, culture and heritage (Aksu, 2004).

Cities are a combination of people, culture, historical heritage and material value. The attractiveness of the quality of life, its culture and atmosphere, liveability, investment capacity and values are among the required qualifications of cities (Kotler et al., 1993). Every city that concentrates on natural and cultural heritage has important advantages in becoming a city brand and can grow with its own resources. In other words, when it comes to branding a city, the historical, geographical, cultural and economic features of the city emerge as an important branding infrastructure. Cities with a historical past very often use these features in promotion or in the creation of a city brand. All cities with historical monuments have potential in this regard. Cities possessing one of the Seven Wonders of the World, such as the Egyptian pyramids and the Great Wall of China, are usually branded with the names of these marvelous structures (Varlı, 2011).

Cultural heritage sites clearly exhibit brand character and their importance in the tourism industry. It is reported that the number of visitors increased after these sites were granted the statusof World Heritage Site. Accordingly, it can be said that cultural heritage is an important component of society and people's well-being. Preservation of cultural heritage not only contributes to a healthy environment of the buildings, but also helps to define the character of the city through society and its cultural identities

(Tweed & Sutherland, 2007). Each of the cities that make up a country may have different aspects that come to the fore. Therefore, it can be difficult to create a consistent perception for a country in people's minds, and cities can be one step ahead of countries. This is particularly evident in tourism. For example, people frequently do not go to France or Italy for vacation, but to Paris or Venice. Similarly, many people who are not familiar with Turkey know Istanbul, which was the European Capital of Culture in 2010 (European Capital of Culture Grant Scheme Programme, 2009). Due to the high awareness of Antalya, it can even be observed that some tourists ask where Turkey is located in Antalya.

The Cultural heritage sites on the World Heritage List (WHL) should be protected and preserved. However, this situation leads to an increase in the number of visitors to the heritage sites (Bandarin, 2005). As a result, exceeding the carrying capacity brings several negative impacts, such as damage to cultural heritage sites and disruption of some services (Boyd & Timothy, 2006). Digitization, both in protecting and opening cultural heritage sites to visitors, can play an important role in passing on cultural heritage to future generations with less degradation, as it can mitigate the physical pressure on these sites. This situation can pave the way for all kinds of sustainable contributions to destinations by the tourism industry.

CITY BRANDING AND CULTURAL HERITAGE IN THE DIGITAL AGE

The widespread use of technology has influenced many aspects of life, changing people's lifestyles, communication habits and even travel styles (Li et al., 2018). In tourism literature, there are studies that confirm the increasingly widespread use of technology and even highlight the benefits of using information and communication technology (ICT) in tourism (Dickinson et al., 2016; Law et al., 2013; Marasco et al., 2018). From this point of view, this section highlights the contribution of digitalization in the areas of city branding and cultural heritage in terms of cities and tourism.

Digitalization and City Branding

Digitalization has three main components: Data generation, data connectivity, and data analysis. Nowadays, more and more data are being generated by technological devices and the number of devices collecting this data is increasing. The data connection (internet) makes this data accessible worldwide. Data analytics is the rapid development of new methods to analyze and visualize data (Finger & Razaghi, 2017). For this reason, digitalization has allowed people to access to more information and creativity in less time and at a lower cost. (Winden & Carvalho, 2017). Therefore, digitalization has been integrated and validated in all aspects of daily life, such as security, childcare, smart home, e-health and online reservation services (Gray & Rumpe, 2015) On the one hand, the amount of data produced in cities is increasing exponentially, on the other hand, cities want to benefit from these technological developments in order to increase the quality of life in the city and strengthen all promotional activities (advertising, personal selling, public relations, sales promotion and direct marketing). Cities need to keep up with changing technological conditions in order to become a brand city by increasing their competitiveness and market share against emerging strong brand cities. Digitalization is seen as the infrastructure to modernize and compete for cities and has long been at the heart of cities' innovation policies. (Parks & Rohracher, 2019, p.56). Moreover, the necessity of adopting new technologies that allow contactless approaches during the COVID-19 pandemic process comes to the fore (Allam, 2020), and it is predicted that the economic problems created by the pandemic will create 21st century cities shaped by technological innovations (Allam & Jones, 2020).

Cities are trying new digital solutions to overcome tourism-related challenges or stand out from other cities in global competition (Winden & Carvalho, 2017, p.18). To this end, cities are being transformed into smart cities with digital city systems. Various infrastructures are being equipped with data collection devices such as sensors and cameras. In this way, it is possible to collect data on everything from many sources such as buildings, energy networks, and transport infrastructures. The collected data will enable more efficient operation and management of urban infrastructures with applications such as "smart water", "smart waste", and "smart transportation" (Finger & Razaghi, 2017).

The application areas of digitalization in a branded tourist city are highlighted with examples such as digital travel guides, digital museum archives, virtual tours, smart mobility, smart tourism, and smart cities (Gray & Rumpe, 2015). The digital transformation that can be observed in many areas is also experienced in cultural tourism. It is noted that this transformation has greatly affected the tourist journey and completely changed the demand structure in the travel industry. For example, in Italy, which relies heavily on its cultural heritage, digital tourism accounts for a quarter of the total national tourism value and is constantly growing (Cuomo et al., 2020). Therefore, the careful consideration of digital transformation and the inclusion of digital solutions in their city branding strategy are inevitable for cities that want to be ahead of the competition.

Digitalization and Cultural Heritage

Many studies acknowledge the impact of digitalization on the increasing attractiveness of cities and cultural spaces, characterized by intense knowledge sharing and co-creation of value (Akehurst, 2009; Da Costa Liberato et al., 2018; Allam & Jones, 2021). There are many areas where cities can benefit from digitalization. In the area of cultural heritage, we are currently witnessing an increasing interaction between digital technologies and virtual spaces with material and tangible experiences taking place in the virtual world (Affleck & Kvan, 2008). For example, cultural heritage assets such as art objects and historical relics are digitized, and digital libraries are created. The Central Institute for the Union Catalogue of Italian Libraries and Bibliographic Information has developed several digital cultural heritage (DCH) projects in Italy and organized international conferences to present and discuss DCH policy (Caffo, 2014). The European portal has contained Europe's online digital library and archive since 2008. There are more than 50 million digital works on this portal, with more than 3,000 institutions contributing (Stewart, 2017). Another application is the Open Heritage 3D (www.openheritage.eu), a data sharing network that makes three-dimensional DCH data open and accessible. Recent developments in 3D surveying and web technologies have made an important contribution to the digital preservation and dissemination of cultural heritage. The CyArk project, which is creating 3D digital models of more than 200 different cultural heritage sites on seven continents, is a good example (Nishanbaev, 2020). Especially since the mid-1990s, memory institutions such as museums and libraries have increased their investments in the digitization of their collections (Astle & Muir, 2012). In this way, while preventing the damage of cultural heritage assets, it is also possible to reach a wider audience (Gray & Rumpe, 2015, p.1319). The use of digital technologies in tourism promotes intercultural dialogue. Creating the concept of a common cultural and historical heritage region through the digitization of cultural heritage will accelerate the rapprochement of people living in cross-border regions (European Union [EU], 2021).

Cities also benefit from new opportunities such as new forms of transport services, including autonomous vehicles, sensors and cameras to control traffic (Allam & Jones, 2021, p.1).

In 2018, the European Commission launched the "European Smart Tourism Capital" competition and encouraged cities to develop innovative projects. In order for a city to be recognized as a European Smart Tourism Capital, it must ensure accessibility, sustainability and digitalization, and use cultural heritage and creativity to enrich the visitor experience. Although the competition is only open to member countries, the criteria of the competition are a source of inspiration for cities striving to become smart tourism destinations and brand cities. In the category of digitalization, there are WeChat Mini Program, Alipay, Virtual Reality Program Helsinki 2020 applications; in the category of cultural heritage and creativity, the Löyly Sauna and The Oodi Library are some of the applications that earned Helsinki the title of European Smart Tourism Capital in 2019. Gothenburg (Sweden) is committed to using digital trends to solve problems such as traffic and transport to improve the experience for citizens and tourists alike; Malaga (Spain), on the other hand, was named the European Smart Tourism Capital 2020 for integrating the concepts of sustainability, accessibility, innovation and culture into its holistic smart tourism strategies. In addition, Karlsruhe (Germany) ranked first in 2020 (EU, 2021) for its outstanding achievements in cultural heritage and creativity. It is clear that sustainable and accessible cities that combine their cultural heritage with digitalization will make a difference and will be the city brand candidates of the future.

Realizing this, cities have started to consider digital environments as well as rebranding in their tourism plans by developing online marketing strategies. For example, "Tuscany+" acts as a bilingual digital tour guide in the Tuscany valley by collecting necessary information from Wikipedia and Google (Kounavis et al., 2012).

FUTURE RESEARCH DIRECTIONS

The concept of smart tourism will shape the future of tourism. The four main components of smart tourism are accessibility, sustainability, digitalization, and cultural heritage and creativity (EU, 2021). It is also believed that in the future, depending on the developments in wireless technologies (5G and 6G), there will be countless opportunities that will have a great role and impact on cities (Allam & Jones, 2021). In a world where communication and interaction have developed so much, it is predicted that smart cities will play a bigger role in the future than they do today in city branding studies. Cities that can successfully implement smart tourism practices will provide competitive advantages and play an important role in building a sustainable future. In particular, developing cities that lack sufficient technological infrastructure may struggle to compete with branded cities in the future, which could lead to a decline in tourism revenue. On the other hand, while it is known that the interest in cultural heritage has increased in recent years, it is also believed that the studies dealing with city branding, cultural heritage, and digital transformation are insufficient.

CONCLUSION

The importance of tourism as an industry is increasing day by day in every aspect and in those areas where competition is intense at international and regional level. While the importance of tourism is increasing, the main motive that directs people to tourism is the desire to understand different historical and cultural values and experience these attractions. In this context, one of the most important product components is cultural heritage (Kozak, 2014). The tendency towards individual and/or small group tours has increased the importance of urban and cultural tourism (Varlı, 2011).

Visitors' preference for a destination is realized by choosing among many alternatives. In order for cities to be successful in a competitive environment, they need to be different and creative. History and culture are the most important sources of attraction of a city. The key characteristic of cities with international recognition is that they occupy a historically significant position and welcome tourists with an effective presentation about a reflection of their cultural values. Successful and interesting cities can preserve the cultural values of the locals without losing them and present these values as an element that can attract tourists (Ozdemir, 2008). Cities try to differentiate themselves through the physical characteristics of their superstructure investments. However, as these features can be easily copied, they are far from sufficiently motivating tourists (Yavuz, 2007). As a result, the use of cities' natural, historical and cultural values becomes more important, and the city brand can be used as a symbol, logo, or emblem that reflects cultural heritage. Cities will be able to differentiate themselves through these unique qualities and create a unique brand image, and only with such an image, they can be successfully marketed as a brand (Iliachenko, 2005).

Many cities today, such as Paris, Rome, New York, Amsterdam and Barcelona have become a "city brand". In becoming a city brand, the events organized in the cities (festivals, cultural events, sports organizations, etc.) or the city-specific symbols (Eiffel Tower, Statue of Liberty, Great Wall of China, Taj Mahal, Big Ben, Tower of Pisa, etc.) have a significant impact. The factor that stands out at this point is that many of these symbols can be found on UNESCO WHL. There are so many cities and places to visit in the world that these places are known worldwide, regardless of country or geography.

Brand cities should be functional and provide visible benefits. This shows that cities provide functional destinations, jobs, industry, transportation, recreational attractions, restaurants, cultural heritage, diversity and the amenities they offer to tourists (Pfefferkorn, 2005). At this point, it is vital for cities to use technology and digital applications effectively. It is inevitable that cities will benefit from digitalization in managing urban infrastructure systems and metropolitan areas to provide better urban services.

While cultural heritage is essential for the branding of cities, tourism, on the other hand, is an effective and positive force for the protection of natural and cultural heritage. Tourism can reveal the economic aspects of cultural heritage and make them available for conservation by creating resources, educating the public and influencing policy. For this reason, it is necessary to highlight the natural and cultural heritage, cultural diversity and vibrant cultures that are a great attraction for cities. Moreover, these values need to be preserved for future generations and managed with the participation and cooperation of representatives of local communities, conservationists, tourism operators, property owners, decision-makers, national development planners and site managers. Therefore, the most important task for countries is to pave the way for branding their cities. In doing so, they need to develop creative and proper strategies that both protect their cultural heritage and make it more accessible through digital developments.

REFERENCES

Aaker, D. A. (1996). *Building strong brands*. The Free Press.

Affleck, J., & Kvan, T. (2008). A virtual community as the context for discursive interpretation: A role in cultural heritage engagement. *International Journal of Heritage Studies, 14*(3), 268–280. doi:10.1080/13527250801953751

Ahunbay, Z. (2011). *Tarihi çevre koruma ve restorasyon.* Yem Publishing.

Akehurst, G. (2009). User generated content: The use of blogs for tourism organisations and tourism consumers. *Service Business, 3*(1), 51–61. doi:10.100711628-008-0054-2

Aksu, M. (2004). *A research to determine to relationship between presented cultural heritage in destinations and tourists: The case of Troia* [Unpublished master's dissertation]. University of Canakkale Onsekiz Mart, Canakkale, Turkey.

Alhempud, A., & Armstrong, E. (1996). Image of tourism attracations in Kuwait. *Journal of Travel Research Spring, 34*(4), 76-80.

Allam, Z. (2020). Underlining the role of data science and technology in supporting supply chains, political stability and health networks during pandemics. In Surveying the Covid-19 Pandemic and its Implications. Elsevier.

Allam, Z., & Jones, D. S. (2020). Pandemic stricken cities on lockdown. Where are our planning and design professionals? *Land Use Policy, 97*, 104805. doi:10.1016/j.landusepol.2020.104805 PMID:32508374

Allam, Z., & Jones, D. S. (2021). Future (post-COVID) digital, smart and sustainable cities in the wake of 6G: Digital twins, immersive realities and new urban economies. *Land Use Policy, 101*(105201), 1–13. doi:10.1016/j.landusepol.2020.105201

Anholt, S. (2005). How the world sees the world's cities. *Place Branding, 2*(1), 18–31. doi:10.1057/palgrave.pb.5990042

Apostolakis, A. (2003). The convergence process in heritage tourism. *Annals of Tourism Research, 30*(4), 795–812. doi:10.1016/S0160-7383(03)00057-4

Astle, P. J., & Muir, A. (2002). Digitization and preservation in public libraries and archives. *Journal of Librarianship and Information Science, 34*(2), 67–79. doi:10.1177/096100060203400202

Bandarin, F. (2005). Foreword. In D. Harrison & M. Hitchcock (Eds.), *The politics of world heritage: Negotiating tourism and conservation.* Channel View Publications.

Blackston, M. (2000). Observations: Building brand equity by managing the brand's relationships. *Journal of Advertising Research, 32*(3), 79–83. doi:10.2501/JAR-40-6-101-105

Blain, C., Levy, S. E., & Ritchie, J. R. B. (2005). Destination branding: Insights and practices from destination management organizations. *Journal of Travel Research, 43*(4), 328–338. doi:10.1177/0047287505274646

Boyd, S. W., & Timothy, D. J. (2006). Marketing issues and world heritage sites. In A. Leask & A. Fyal (Eds.), *Managing world heritage sites* (pp. 55–67). Butterworth-Heinemann. doi:10.1016/B978-0-7506-6546-9.50013-7

Cai, L. A. (2002). Cooperative branding for rural destinations. *Annals of Tourism Research, 29*(3), 720–742. doi:10.1016/S0160-7383(01)00080-9

Cetin, T. (2010). Perception of cultural heritage and tourism in Cumalıkızık village. *Milli Folklor Journal, 22,* 181–190.

Cuomo, M. T., Tortora, D., Foroudi, P., Giordano, A., Festa, G., & Metallo, G. (2020). Digital transformation and tourist experience co-design: Big social data for planning cultural tourism. *Technological Forecasting and Social Change, 162*(120345), 1–9.

Da Costa Liberato, P. M., Alén-González, E., & de Azevedo Liberato, D. F. V. (2018). Digital technology in a smart tourist destination: The case of Porto. *Journal of Urban Technology, 25*(1), 75–97. doi:10.1080/10630732.2017.1413228

Demir, C. (2006). Kent kimliği geliştirme sürecinde mekansal model tasarımı ve kent plancılarının rolü. *TMMOB Şehir Plancıları Odası Yayını, 3,* 117–122.

Dickinson, J. E., Hibbert, J. F., & Filimonau, V. (2016). Mobile technology and the tourist experience: (Dis)connection at the campsite. *Tourism Management, 57,* 193–201. doi:10.1016/j.tourman.2016.06.005

European Union (EU). (2021). *2020 European capitals of smart tourism.* https://smarttourismcapital.eu

Finger, M., & Razaghi, M. (2017). Conceptualizing "Smart Cities". *Informatik Spektrum, 4*(1), 6–13. doi:10.100700287-016-1002-5

Goeldner, C. R., Ritchie, J. R., & Mcintosh, R. (2000). *Tourism; Principles, practices, philosophies.* John Wiley & Sons.

Hall, C. M. (1992). *Hallmark tourist events.* Belhaven Press. https://openheritage.eu/oh-project/

Istanbul 2010 European Capital of Culture Grant Scheme Programme. (2009). https://www.ab.gov.tr/43388_en.html

Johns, N., & Mattsson, J. (2005). Destination development through entrepreneurship: A comparison of two cases. *Tourism Management, 26*(4), 605–616. doi:10.1016/j.tourman.2004.02.017

Kapferer, J. N. (1992). *Strategic brand management.* The Free Press.

Kastenholz, E. (2002). *The role and marketing implications of destination images on tourist behavior: The case of Northern Portugal* [Unpublished doctoral dissertation]. Aveiro University.

Kavaratzis, M., & Ashworth, G. J. (2005). City branding: An effective assertion of identity or a transitory marketing trick? *Tijdschrift voor Economische en Sociale Geografie, 96*(5), 506–514. doi:10.1111/j.1467-9663.2005.00482.x

Kaya, E., Senturk, H., Danıs, O., & Simsek, S. (2007). *Modern kent yönetimi.* Okutan Publishing.

Kaypak, S. (2013). Branding cities on process of globalization and "brand cities". *Cukurova University Faculty of Economics and Administrative Sciences, 14*(1), 335–355.

Keller, K. L. (1998). *Strategic brand management.* Prentice Hall.

Kempner, T. (1976). *A handbook of management.* Penguin Books Inc.

Kotler, P. (1997). *Marketing management.* Prentice Hall.

Kotler, P., Haider, D. H., & Rein, I. (1993). *Marketing places.* The Free Press.

Kounavis, C. D., Kasimati, A. E., & Zamani, E. D. (2012). Enhancing the tourism experience through mobile augmented reality: Challenges and prospects. *International Journal of Engineering Business, 4*, 1–6. doi:10.5772/51644

Kozak, M. (Ed.). (2014). *Sürdürülebilir turizm.* Detay Publishing.

Law, R., Leung, D., Au, N., & Lee, H. A. (2013). Progress and development of information technology in the hospitality industry evidence from Cornell Hospitality Quarterly. *Cornell Hospitality Quarterly, 54*(1), 10–24. doi:10.1177/1938965512453199

Li, J., Pearce, P. L., & Low, D. (2018). Media representation of digital-free tourism: A critical discourse analysis. *Tourism Management, 69*, 317–329. doi:10.1016/j.tourman.2018.06.027

Ma, W., Jong, M., Hoppe, T., & Bruijne, M. (2021). From city promotion via city marketing to city branding: Examining urban strategies in 23 Chinese cities. *Cities (London, England), 116*(103269), 1–16. doi:10.1016/j.cities.2021.103269

Marasco, A., De Martino, M., Magnotti, F., & Morvillo, A. (2018). Collaborative innovation in tourism and hospitality: A systematic review of the literature. *International Journal of Contemporary Hospitality Management, 30*(6), 2364–2395. doi:10.1108/IJCHM-01-2018-0043

Mariotti, J. L. (1999). *Smart things to know about brands and branding.* Capstone Publishing Limited.

Matlovicova, K., Nemethyova, B., & Matlovic, R. (2010). City branding of Bratislava: History and the present. *Indian Journal of Engineering and Materials Sciences, 2*(2), 215–234.

Nishanbaev, I. (2020). A web repository for geo-located 3D digital cultural heritage models. *Digital Applications in Archaeology and Cultural Heritage, 16*(e00139), 1–9. doi:10.1016/j.daach.2020.e00139

Nuryanti, W. (1996). Heritage and postmodern tourism. *Annals of Tourism Research, 23*(2), 249–260. doi:10.1016/0160-7383(95)00062-3

Oppermann, M. (2000). Tourism destination loyalty. *Journal of Travel Research, 39*(1), 78–84. doi:10.1177/004728750003900110

Ozdemir, G. (2008). *Destinasyon pazarlaması.* Detay Publishing.

Ozgunel, C. (2007). *Kent ve planlama geçmişi korumak geleceği tasarlamak.* İmge Publishing.

Parks, D., & Rohracher, H. (2019). From sustainable to smart: Re-branding or re-assembling urban energy infrastructure? *Geoforum, 100*, 51–59. doi:10.1016/j.geoforum.2019.02.012

Pfefferkorn, J. W. (2005). *The branding of cities.* Syracuse University.

Pike, S. (2009). Destination brand positions of a competitive set of near-home destinations. *Tourism Management, 30*(6), 857–866. doi:10.1016/j.tourman.2008.12.007

Pillai & Bagavathi. (2000). *Modern marketing: Principles and practices.* S. Chand Publishing.

Randall, G. (2000). *Branding: A practical guide to planning.* Kogan Page Limited.

Rizzi, P., & Dioli, İ. (2010). From strategic planning to city branding: Some empirical evidence in İtaly. *Pasos Revista de Turismo i Patrimonio Cultural, 8*(3), 39–49. doi:10.25145/j.pasos.2010.08.033

Sahin, G. (2010). *The importance of being a brand city in tourism: The Example of Istanbul* [Unpublished master's dissertation]. University of Ankara, Ankara, Turkey.

Stewart, J. (2017). *Free digital archives Europeana collections*. https://mymodernmet.com/free-digital-archiveseuropeana-collections/

Tinsley, R., & Lynch, P. (2001). Small tourism business networks and destination development. *International Journal of Hospitality Management, 4*(20), 367–378. doi:10.1016/S0278-4319(01)00024-X

Tweed, C., & Shutherland, M. (2007). Built cultural heritage and sustainable urban development. *Landscape and Urban Planning, 83*(1), 62–69. doi:10.1016/j.landurbplan.2007.05.008

United Nations Educational, Scientific and Cultural Organization. (1972). *Convention Concerning the Protection of the World Cultural and Natural Heritage*. Author.

United Nations Educational, Scientific and Cultural Organization. (2003). *Text of the Convention for the Safeguarding of the Intangible Cultural Heritage*. Author.

United Nations Educational, Scientific and Cultural Organization. (2021). *What is meant by "cultural heritage"?* http://www.unesco.org/new/en/culture/themes/illicit-trafficking-of-cultural-property/unesco-database-of-national-cultural-heritage-laws/frequently-asked-questions/definition-of-the-cultural-heritage/

van Winden, W., & de Carvalho, L. (2017). *Cities and digitalization: How digitalization changes cities: Innovation for the urban economy of tomorrow*. Amsterdam University of Applied Sciences.

Varlı, B. (2011). *The analysis of communication-based activities in the process of city: İstanbul 2010 European capital of culture* [Unpublished master's dissertation]. University of Kocaeli, Kocaeli, Turkey.

Wood, L. (2000). Brands and equity: Definition and management. *Management Decision, 38*(9), 662–669. doi:10.1108/00251740010379100

World Travel & Tourism Council. (2021). *Sustainable development goals*. https://wttc.org/Initiatives/Sustainable-Growth

Yavuz, M. C. (2007). *Identity building process in international destination branding: A Case for the city of Adana* [Unpublished doctoral dissertation]. University of Cukurova, Adana, Turkey.

Zhang, M. Y. W., & Yang, Y. (2011). On life cycle of cultural heritage engineering tourism: A case study of Macau. *System Engineering Procedia, 1*, 351–357. doi:10.1016/j.sepro.2011.08.053

ADDITIONAL READING

Caffo, R. (2014). Digital cultural heritage projects: Opportunities and future challenges. *Procedia Computer Science, 38*, 12–17. doi:10.1016/j.procs.2014.10.003

Gray, J., & Rumpe, B. (2015). Models for digitalization. *Software & Systems Modeling*, *14*(4), 1319–1320. doi:10.100710270-015-0494-9

Hall, C. M., & Piggin, R. (2002). World heritage sites: Managing the brand. In A. Fyall, B. Garrod, & A. Leask (Eds.), *Managing visitor attractions: New directions* (pp. 203–219). Butterworth-Heinemann.

Iliachencko, E. Y. (2005, September). *Exploring culture, history and nature as tourist destination branding constructs: The case of a Peripheral Region in Sweden* [Paper presentation]. The 14th Nordic Symposium in Tourism and Hospitality Research, Akureyri, Iceland.

Kavaratzis, M., & Ashworth, G. J. (2007). Partners in coffeeshops, canals and commerce: Marketing the city of Amsterdam. *Cities (London, England)*, *24*(1), 16–25. doi:10.1016/j.cities.2006.08.007

Rainisto, S. K. (2003). *Success factors of place marketing: A study of place marketing practices in Northern Europe and The United States* [Unpublished doctoral dissertation]. University of Helsinki, Helsinki, Finland.

KEY TERMS AND DEFINITIONS

Brand: A name or sign used to identify a product and distinguish it from its competitors.

Brand Identity: The whole of the features that determine the brand or the combination of the visual and verbal elements of the brand and all the values it evokes in the consumer's mind.

Brand Image: The belief formed in the mind of the consumer from the experiences and hearings about a brand and the impression about that brand.

Brand Positioning: The place and value a brand takes in the minds of consumers compared to its competitors, taking into account its benefits and promises.

Branding: To introduce an object or product, to name and mark to distinguish it from similar ones.

City Branding: Where a city is differentiated from other cities by highlighting its original features.

Digital Cultural Heritage: Tangible and intangible cultural heritage assets that are recorded and displayed on a screen by electronic means.

Digitization: The process of creating digital copies of original materials in analogue media using a scanner, camera, or other electronic device.

Compilation of References

Aaker, D. A. (1996). *Building strong brands*. The Free Press.

Abbas, J., Mubeen, R., Iorember, P. T., Raza, S., & Mamirkulova, G. (2021). Exploring the impact of COVID-19 on tourism: Transformational potential and implications for a sustainable recovery of the travel and leisure industry. *Current Research in Behavioral Sciences, 2*, 100033. doi:10.1016/j.crbeha.2021.100033

Abraham, J. (2015). The role of curiosity in making up digital content promoting cultural heritage. *Procedia: Social and Behavioral Sciences, 184*, 259–265. doi:10.1016/j.sbspro.2015.05.089

Abrahamson, C. E. (1998). Storytelling as a pedagogical tool in higher education. *Education, 118*(3), 440–452.

Aburamadan, R., Trillo, C., Udeaja, C., Moustaka, A., Awuah, K. G., & Makore, B. C. (2021). Heritage conservation and digital technologies in Jordan. *Digital Applications in Archaeology and Cultural Heritage, 22*, e00197. doi:10.1016/j.daach.2021.e00197

Accenture Digitization Index. (2015). *Accenture digitization index Turkey results*. Turkish Science Foundation.

AccessIT Türk Takımı. (n.d.). Accessed on June 14, 2021. http://www.accessit.hacettepe.edu.tr/index.php?kid=30&s=AccessIT%20AB%20Projesi%20Hakk%C4%B1nda

Aced-Toledano, C., & Lalueza, F. (2018). Monologues in the conversational era: Assessing the level of dialogic communication that big firms are reaching on social media. *El Profesional de la Información, 27*(6), 1270–1280. doi:10.3145/epi.2018.nov.10

Ackerman, F., & Heinzerling, L. (2002). Pricing the Priceless: Cost-Benefit Analysis of Environmental Protection. *University of Pennsylvania Law Review*.

Ackoff, R. L. (1989). From data to wisdom. *Journal of Applied Systems Analysis, 16*(1), 3–9.

Adam, N. A., & Alarifi, G. (2021). Innovation practices for survival of small and medium enterprises (SMEs) in the COVID-19 times: The role of external support. *Journal of Innovation and Entrepreneurship, 10*(1), 1–22. doi:10.118613731-021-00156-6 PMID:34075328

Addis, M., Martinez, K., Lewis, P., Stevenson, J., & Giorgini, F. (2005). *New ways to search, navigate and use multimedia museum collections over the web*. https://www.archimuse.com/mw2005/papers/addis/addis.html

Addison, A. C. (2000). Emerging trends in virtual heritage. *IEEE MultiMedia, 7*(2), 22–25. doi:10.1109/93.848421

Adie, B. A., Falk, M., & Savioli, M. (2019). Overtourism as a perceived threat to cultural heritage in Europe. *Current Issues in Tourism, 23*(14), 1737–1741. doi:10.1080/13683500.2019.1687661

Adweek.com. (2018, May 11). *How Influencers Are Turning the Business of Travel on Its Head*. Retrieved September 17, 2019, from https://www.adweek.com/digital/how-influencers-are-turning-the-business-of-travel-on-its-head/

Aernouts, M., Lemic, F., Moons, B., Famaey, J., Hoebeke, J., Weyn, M., & Berkvens, R. (2020). A multimodal localization framework design for IoT applications. *Sensors (Basel)*, *20*(16), 4622. doi:10.339020164622 PMID:32824497

Affleck, J., & Kvan, T. (2008). A virtual community as the context for discursive interpretation: A role in cultural heritage engagement. *International Journal of Heritage Studies*, *14*(3), 268–280. doi:10.1080/13527250801953751

Aghayev, R. (2017). *VR-The Future of Selling Hotel Rooms*. Available at: http://www.virtual-reality-in-tourism.com/ Virtual Reality-future-selling-hotel-rooms/

Agostino, D., Arnaboldi, M., & Lampis, A. (2020). Italian state museums during the COVID-19 crisis: From onsite closure to online openness. *Museum Management and Curatorship*, *35*(4), 362–372. doi:10.1080/09647775.2020.1790029

Agrafiotis, P., Drakonakis, G., Georgopoulos, A., & Skarlatos, D. (2017). *The effect of underwater imagery radiometry on 3D reconstruction and orthoimagery*. International Society for Photogrammetry and Remote Sensing. doi:10.5194/isprs-archives-XLII-2-W3-25-2017

Ahas, R., Aasa, A., Mark, Ü., Pae, T., & Kull, A. (2007). Seasonal tourism spaces in Estonia: Case study with mobile positioning data. *Tourism Management*, *28*(3), 898–910. Advance online publication. doi:10.1016/j.tourman.2006.05.010

Aho, S. K. (2001). Towards a general theory of touristic experiences: Modelling experience. *Tourism Review*, *56*(3), 33–37. doi:10.1108/eb058368

Ahunbay, Z. (2011). *Tarihi çevre koruma ve restorasyon*. Yem Publishing.

Akehurst, G. (2009). User generated content: The use of blogs for tourism organisations and tourism consumers. *Service Business*, *3*(1), 51–61. doi:10.100711628-008-0054-2

Akergar, R. (2012). *Big data and tourism*. Technomathematics Research Foundation.

Akkurt, M. (2019*). Simulation of Internet of Things Applications with Cupcarbon: Smart City Examples* (Master Thesis). Kocaeli University Institute of Science and Technology, Kocaeli.

Akoumianakis, D., Vidakis, N., Akrivos, A., Milolidakis, G., Kotsalis, D., & Vellis, G. (2011). Building 'flexible'vacation packages using collaborative assembly toolkits and dynamic packaging: The case study of the eKoNES. *Journal of Vacation Marketing*, *17*(1), 17–30. doi:10.1177/1356766710391132

Akram, W., & Kumar, R. (2017). A study on role and applications of augmented reality in tourism: Its challanges and future prospects. *International Journal of Advanced Research in Computer Science*, *8*(8), 168–172. doi:10.26483/ijarcs.v8i8.4633

Akrout, H. (2014). Relationship quality in cross-border exchanges: A temporal perspective. *Journal of Business-To-Business Marketing*, *21*(3), 145–169. doi:10.1080/1051712X.2014.952179

Akrout, H., Diallo, M. F., Akrout, W., & Chandon, J.-L. (2016). Affective trust in buyer-seller relationships: A two-dimensional scale. *Journal of Business and Industrial Marketing*, *31*(2), 260–273. doi:10.1108/JBIM-11-2014-0223

Aksu, M. (2004). *A research to determine to relationship between presented cultural heritage in destinations and tourists: The case of Troia* [Unpublished master's dissertation]. University of Canakkale Onsekiz Mart, Canakkale, Turkey.

Aktan, E., & Koçyiğit, M. (2016). Sosyal medyanın turizm faaliyetlerindeki rolü üzerine teorik bir inceleme. *Dumlupınar Üniversitesi Sosyal Bilimler Dergisi*, (Special Issue), 62–73.

Akyıldız, N. A., & Olğun, T. N. (2020). Somut olmayan kültürel mirasın Anadolu'da tarihî yerleşimlerin korunması ve sürdürülebilirliği bağlamında değerlendirilmesi [Evaluation of the intangible cultural heritage in the context of conservation and sustainability of historical settlements in Anatolia]. *Milli Folklor, 32*(16), 234–243.

Akyürek, S., & Erdem, B. (2019). Gastronomy museums as sustainable hangouts in gastronomy tourism: A gastronomy museum proposal for Gümüşhane City, Turkey. *Turizam, 23*(1), 17–33. doi:10.5937/turizam23-20717

Alaeddinoğlu, F. (2007). Van halkının turisti ve turizmi algılama şekli [Van community's perception of tourists and tourism]. *Coğrafi Bilimler Dergisi, 5*(1), 1–16.

Alaei, A. R., Becken, S., & Stantic, B. (2019). Sentiment analysis in tourism: Capitalizing on big data. *Journal of Travel Research, 58*(2), 175–191. doi:10.1177/0047287517747753

Alagöz, G., Çalık, İ., & Güneş, E. (2018). Kültürel miras turizmi açısından Erzincan bakır işleme sanatının mevcut durumu ve sürdürülebilirliği [Current situation and sustainability of erzincan copper processing art in terms of cultural heritage tourism]. *Dumlupınar Üniversitesi Sosyal Bilimler Dergisi, 55*, 174–191.

Alan, H. (2020). COVID-19 Pandemic and digitalization of service organizations: A trademark approach. *Turkish Studies, 15*(6), 31–47.

Albino, V., Berrardi, U., & Dangalico, R. M. (2015). Smart cities definitions; performance and initiatives. *Journal of Urban Technology, 22*(1), 3–21. doi:10.1080/10630732.2014.942092

Al-hagla, K. S. (2010). Sustainable urban development in historical areas using the tourist trail approach: A case study of the Cultural Heritage and Urban Development (CHUD) project in Saida, Lebanon. *Cities (London, England), 27*(4), 234–248. Advance online publication. doi:10.1016/j.cities.2010.02.001

Alhempud, A., & Armstrong, E. (1996). Image of tourism attracations in Kuwait. *Journal of Travel Research Spring, 34*(4), 76-80.

Ali, I. (2020). The covid-19 pandemic: Making sense of rumor and fear: Op-ed. *Medical Anthropology, 39*(5), 376–379. doi:10.1080/01459740.2020.1745481 PMID:32212931

Alivizatou, M. (2021). Digital ıntangible heritage: Inventories, virtual learning and participation. *Heritage & Society, 12*(2-3), 116–135. doi:10.1080/2159032X.2021.1883950

Allam, Z. (2020). Underlining the role of data science and technology in supporting supply chains, political stability and health networks during pandemics. In Surveying the Covid-19 Pandemic and its Implications. Elsevier.

Allam, Z., & Jones, D. S. (2020). Pandemic stricken cities on lockdown. Where are our planning and design professionals? *Land Use Policy, 97*, 104805. doi:10.1016/j.landusepol.2020.104805 PMID:32508374

Allam, Z., & Jones, D. S. (2021). Future (post-COVID) digital, smart and sustainable cities in the wake of 6G: Digital twins, immersive realities and new urban economies. *Land Use Policy, 101*(105201), 1–13. doi:10.1016/j.landusepol.2020.105201

Alletto, S., Cucchiara, R., Del Fiore, G., Mainetti, L., Mighali, V., Patrono, L., & Serra, G. (2016). An indoor location-aware system for an IoT-based smart museum. *IEEE Internet of Things Journal, 3*(2), 244–253. doi:10.1109/JIOT.2015.2506258

Alqahtani, H., Liu, C. Z., Thorne, M., & Kang, Y. (2019). An agent-based intelligent HCI information system in mixed reality. *Proceedings 28th International Conference On Information Systems Development*, 226-235.

Alsunaidi, S. J., Almuhaideb, A. M., Ibrahim, N. M., Shaikh, F. S., Alqudaihi, K. S., Alhaidari, F. A., Khan, I. U., Aslam, N., & Alshahrani, M. S. (2021). Applications of big data analytics to control COVID-19 pandemic. *Sensors (Basel)*, *21*(7), 2282. doi:10.339021072282 PMID:33805218

Altinay, L., & Paraskevas, A. (2008). *Planning Research in Hospitality and Tourism*. Elsevier, Ltd.

Alves, G. M., Sousa, B. M., & Machado, A. (2020). The Role of Digital Marketing and Online Relationship Quality in Social Tourism: A Tourism for All Case Study. In J. Santos & Ó. Silva (Eds.), *Digital Marketing Strategies for Tourism, Hospitality, and Airline Industries* (pp. 49–70). IGI Global. doi:10.4018/978-1-5225-9783-4.ch003

Alzua-Sorzabal, A., Linaza, M., & Abad, M. (2007). An experimental usability study for Augmented Reality technologies in the tourist sector. *IENTER*, 231-242.

Alzueta, E., Perrin, P., Baker, F. C., Caffarra, S., Usuga, D. R., Yuksel, D., & Lasprilla, J. C. A. (2021). How the COVID-19 pandemic has changed our lives: A study of psychological correlates across 59 countries. *Journal of Clinical Psychology*, *77*(3), 556–570. doi:10.1002/jclp.23082 PMID:33128795

Amaro, S., & Duarte, P. (2017). Social media use for travel purposes: A cross cultural comparison between Portugal and the UK. *Information Technology & Tourism*, *17*(2), 161–181. doi:10.100740558-017-0074-7

Amato, F., Chianese, A., Mazzeo, A., Moscato, V., Picariello, A., & Piccialli, F. (2013). The talking museum project. *Procedia Computer Science*, *21*, 114–121. doi:10.1016/j.procs.2013.09.017

Ammirato, S., Felicetti, A. M., Della Gala, M., Raso, C., & Cozza, M. (2018). Smart tourism destinations: can the destination management organizations exploit benefits of the ICTs? Evidences from a multiple case study. *Working Conference on Virtual Enterprises*.

Ammirato, S., Felicetti, A. M., Linzalone, R., & Carlucci, D. (2021). Digital business models in cultural tourism. *International Journal of Entrepreneurial Behavior & Research*.

Ammirato, S., Felicetti, A. M., & Gala, M. D. (2015). Rethinking tourism destinations: Collaborative network models for the tourist 2.0. *International Journal of Knowledge-Based Development*, *6*(3), 178–201. doi:10.1504/IJKBD.2015.072800

Ammirato, S., Linzalone, R., & Volpentesta, A. P. (2019). Business Model innovation in Travel Industry: Implications for Integrated Bus Transportation Services. *Proceedings of IFKAD 2019-International Forum of Knowldege Asset Dynamics*.

Andersen, P. (2007). *What is Web 2.0? Ideas, technologies and implications for education*. JISC.

Anderson, J., Rainie, L., & Vogels, E. A. (2021, February 19). *Experts say the 'new normal' in 2025 will be far more tech-driven, presenting more big challenges*. https://www.pewresearch.org/internet/2021/02/18/experts-say-the-new-normal-in-2025-will-be-far-more-tech-driven-presenting-more-big-challenges/

Anderson, E. (2010). *The imperative of integration*. Princeton University Press. doi:10.1515/9781400836826

Anderson, K. E. (2020). Getting acquainted with social networks and apps: It is time to talk about TikTok. *Library Hi Tech News*, *37*(4), 7–12. doi:10.1108/LHTN-01-2020-0001

Andı, S., Aytaç, S. E., & Çarkoğlu, A. (2020). Internet and social media use and political knowledge: Evidence from Turkey. *Mediterranean Politics*, *25*(5), 579–599. doi:10.1080/13629395.2019.1635816

Andreasen, A. R. (1995). *Marketing social change: Changing behavior to promote health, social development, and the environment*. Jossey-Bass.

Angelidou, M. (2016). Four European Smart City Strategies. *International Journal of Social Science Studies*, *4*(4). Advance online publication. doi:10.11114/ijsss.v4i4.1364

Angelidou, M., Karachaliou, E., Angelidou, T., & Stylianidis, E. (2017). Cultural Heritage In Smart City Environments. *The International Archives of the Photogrammetry, Remote Sensing and Spatial Information Sciences, XLII-2*(W5), 27–32. doi:10.5194/isprs-archives-XLII-2-W5-27-2017

AngelidouM.StylianidisE. (2020). Cultural Heritage In Smart City Environments: The Update. *ISPRS Annals of the Photogrammetry, Remote Sensing and Spatial Information Sciences, V-2–2020*, 957–964. doi:10.5194/isprs-annals-V-2-2020-957-2020

Angelo, J. (2000). The link flight trainer. *ASME Landmarks*, 12.

Anholt, S. (2005). How the world sees the world's cities. *Place Branding, 2*(1), 18–31. doi:10.1057/palgrave.pb.5990042

Antón, C., Camarero, C., & Garrido, M.-J. (2018). Exploring the experience value of museum visitors as a co-creation process. *Current Issues in Tourism, 21*(12), 1406–1425. doi:10.1080/13683500.2017.1373753

Antón, C., Camarero, C., & Garrido, M.-J. (2019). What to Do After Visiting a Museum? From Post-consumption Evaluation to Intensification and Online Content Generation. *Journal of Travel Research, 58*(6), 1052–1063. doi:10.1177/0047287518793040

Apostolakis, A. (2003). The convergence process in heritage tourism. *Annals of Tourism Research, 30*(4), 795–812. doi:10.1016/S0160-7383(03)00057-4

Arat, T., & Baltacıoğlu, S. (2016). Sanal gerçeklik ve turizm. *Selçuk Üniversitesi Sosyal Bilimler Meslek Yüksek Okulu Dergisi, 19*(1), 103–118.

Arbib, M., & Fellous, J. M. (2004). Emotions: From brain to robot. *Trends in Cognitive Sciences, 8*(12), 553–561. doi:10.1016/j.tics.2004.10.004 PMID:15556025

Archer, L., Dawson, E., Seakins, A., & Wong, B. (2016). Disorientating, fun or meaningful? Disadvantaged families' experiences of a science museum visit. *Cultural Studies of Science Education, 11*(4), 917–939. doi:10.100711422-015-9667-7

Ardissono, L., Kuflik, T., & Petrelli, D. (2012). Personalization in cultural heritage: The road travelled and the one ahead. *User Modeling and User-Adapted Interaction, 22*(1-2), 73–99. doi:10.100711257-011-9104-x

Ardito, L., Cerchione, R., Del Vecchio, P., & Raguseo, E. (2019). Big data in smart tourism: Challenges, issues and opportunities. *Current Issues in Tourism, 22*(15), 1805–1809. doi:10.1080/13683500.2019.1612860

Ardito, L., Cerchione, R., Del Vecchio, P., & Raguseo, E. (2019). *Big data in smart tourism: challenges, issues and opportunities.* Taylor & Francis.

Arenas, A. E., Goh, J. M., & Urueña, A. (2019). How does IT affect design centricity approaches: Evidence from Spain's smart tourism ecosystem. *International Journal of Information Management, 45*, 149–162. doi:10.1016/j.ijinfomgt.2018.10.015

Argyropoulos, V., & Stratigea, A. (2019). Sustainable management of underwater cultural heritage: The route from discovery to engagement—Open issues in the Mediterranean. *Heritage, 2*(2), 1588–1613. doi:10.3390/heritage2020098

Arkas News. (2020). *Dünyanın En Eski Batığı Türkiye'de Keşfedildi.* Arkas News (E.T.31.05.2021): https://arkasnews.com/dunyanin-en-eski-batigi-turkiyede-kesfedildi/

Arnold, D., & Geser, G. (2008). *EPOCH research agenda for the applications of ICT to cultural heritage.* EPOCH Project.

Ashton, K. (2009). That 'Internet of Things' Thing. *RFID Journal.* Retrieved 05.05.2021 from https://www.rfidjournal.com/articles/pdf?4986

Ashton, K. (2009). That 'internet of things' thing. *RFID Journal, 22*(7), 97–114.

Ashworth, G. J. (1994). From history to heritage–from heritage to identity.: In search of concepts and models. In G. J. Ashworth & P. J. Larkham (Eds.), *From history to heritage–from heritage to identity. Building a new heritage: Tourism, culture and identity in the new Europe* (pp. 13–30). Routledge.

Astle, P. J., & Muir, A. (2002). Digitization and preservation in public libraries and archives. *Journal of Librarianship and Information Science, 34*(2), 67–79. doi:10.1177/096100060203400202

Atwal, G., & Williams, A. (2017). Luxury brand marketing–the experience is everything! In *Advances in luxury brand management* (pp. 43–57). Palgrave Macmillan. doi:10.1007/978-3-319-51127-6_3

Atzori, L., Iera, A., & Morabito, G. (2010). The internet of things: A survey. *Computer Networks, 54*(15), 2787–2805. doi:10.1016/j.comnet.2010.05.010

Aykaç, P. (2019). Musealisation as a strategy for the reconstruction of an idealised Ottoman past: Istanbul's Sultanahmet district as a 'museum-quarter.'. *International Journal of Heritage Studies, 25*(2), 160–177. Advance online publication. doi:10.1080/13527258.2018.1475407

Aynur, H. (2012). Türkiye Yazmaları Toplu Kataloğu [Collective catalog of Turkey manuscripts], DİA, İstanbul. *Türkiye Diyanet Vakfı Yayınları, 41*, 597–598.

Azis, N., Amin, M., Chan, S., & Aprilia, C. (2020). How smart tourism technologies affect tourist destination loyalty. *Journal of Hospitality and Tourism Technology, 11*(4), 603–625. doi:10.1108/JHTT-01-2020-0005

Aziz, K. A., & Siang, T. G. (2014). Virtual Reality and Augmented Reality combination as a holistic application for heritage preservation in the Unesco World Heritage Site of Melaka. *International Journal of Social Science and Humanity, 4*(5), 333–338. doi:10.7763/IJSSH.2014.V4.374

Azuma, R. (1993). Tracking requirements for augmented reality. *Communications of the ACM, 36*(7), 50–51. doi:10.1145/159544.159581

Azuma, R. T. (1997). A survey of augmented reality. *Presence (Cambridge, Mass.), 6*(4), 355–385. doi:10.1162/pres.1997.6.4.355

Azuma, R., Baillot, Y., Behringer, R., Feiner, S., Julier, S., & MacIntyre, B. (2001). Recent advances in augmented reality. *IEEE Computer Graphics and Applications, 21*(6), 34–47. doi:10.1109/38.963459

Bachi, V., Fresa, A., Pierotti, C., & Prandoni, C. (2014). The Digitization Age: Mass Culture Is Quality Culture. Challenges for Cultural Heritage and Society. In M. Ioannides, N. Magnenat-Thalmann, E. Fink, R. Žarnić, A.-Y. Yen, & E. Quak (Eds.), *Digital Heritage. Progress in Cultural Heritage: Documentation, Preservation, and Protection* (pp. 786–801). Springer International Publishing. doi:10.1007/978-3-319-13695-0_81

Bachleitner, R., & Zins, A. H. (1999). Cultural tourism in rural communities: The residents' perspective. *Journal of Business Research, 44*(3), 199–209. doi:10.1016/S0148-2963(97)00201-4

Bader, A., Baldauf, M., Leinert, S., Fleck, M., & Liebrich, A. (2012). Mobile tourism services and technology acceptance in amature domestic tourism market: the case of Switzerland. In M. Fuchs, F. Ricci, & L. Cantoni (Eds.), *Information and communication technologies in tourism 2012* (pp. 296–307). Springer. doi:10.1007/978-3-7091-1142-0_26

Baethge, C., Klier, J., & Klier, M. (2016). Social commerce—State-of-the-art and future research directions. *Electronic Markets, 26*(3), 269–290. Advance online publication. doi:10.100712525-016-0225-2

Bağçı, E., & İçöz, O. (2019). Digitalized tourism through Z and Alpha generation. *Güncel Turizm Araştırmaları Dergisi*, *3*(2), 232–256.

Baidal, J. A. I., Marco, A. C. B., Mazon, J. N., & Ivars, A. F. P. (2017). Smart destinations and the evolution of ICTs: A new scenario for destination management? *Current Issues in Tourism*, *20*, 1581–1600.

Bail, C. A. (2014). The cultural environment: Measuring culture with big data. *Theory and Society*, *43*(3–4), 465–482. doi:10.100711186-014-9216-5

Bak, S. (2007). Domestic and International Cultural Tourism in the Context of Intangible Heritage. In Safeguarding Intangible Heritage and Sustainable Cultural Tourism: Opportunities and Challenges. Bangkok: UNESCO Bangkok.

Baker, K., & Verstockt, S. (2017). Cultural heritage routing: A recreational navigation-based approach in exploring cultural heritage. *Journal on Computing and Cultural Heritage*, *10*(4), 1–20. doi:10.1145/3040200

Bakır, Z. N., & Çelik, H. C. (2020). Kitle ve kültür turizmi bağlamında JollyTur ve EtsTur seyahat acentelerine ait internet reklamlarının içerik analizi. *Akdeniz Üniversitesi İletişim Fakültesi Dergisi*, (33), 318–337. doi:10.31123/akil.695931

Balasaraswathi, M., Srinivasan, K., Udayakumar, L., Sivasakthiselvan, S., & Sumithra, M. G. (2020). Big data analytic of contexts and cascading tourism for smart city. *Materials Today: Proceedings*. Advance online publication. doi:10.1016/j.matpr.2020.10.132

Bal, H. (1991). *Turizmin Kırsal Toplumda Aile İçi İlişkilere Etkisi* [The effect of tourism on family relations in rural society]. Doğa İnsan Yayınları.

Bandarin, F. (2005). Foreword. In D. Harrison & M. Hitchcock (Eds.), *The politics of world heritage: Negotiating tourism and conservation*. Channel View Publications.

Baran, H. (2020). Technological development and art and design as a digital medium. *International Journal of Scientific and Technological Research.*, *6*(13), 36–45.

Bardin, L. (1977). *Análise de Conteúdo*. Presses Universitaires de France.

Barnes, S. (2016). *Understanding virtual reality in marketing: nature, implications and potential*. Academic Press.

Barnes, S. (2016). *Understanding virtual reality in marketing: Nature, implications and potential*. Retrieved from https://bit.ly/3FSoN2b

Barretto, M. (2008). Os museus e a autenticidade no turismo. *Itinerarium*, *1*(1), 42.

Barros, C., & Gama, R. (2009). Marketing territorial como instrumento de valorização dos espaços rurais: Uma aplicação na rede das Aldeias de Xisto. *Caderno de Geografia*, *28/29*, 93–106.

Bartik, A. W., Bertrand, M., Cullen, Z. B., Glaeser, E. L., Luca, M., & Stanton, C. T. (2020). *How are small businesses adjusting to Covid-19? Early evidence from a survey*. National Bureau of Economic Research. https://www.nber.org/papers/w26989.pdf

Basaraba, N. (2018). A communication model for non-fiction interactive digital narratives: A study of cultural heritage websites. *Frontiers of Narrative Studies*, *4*(1), 48–75. doi:10.1515/fns-2018-0032

Başer, G., Doğan, O., & Al-Turjman, F. (2019). Smart Tourism Destination in Smart Cities Paradigm: A Model for Antalya. In F. Al-Turjman (Ed.), *Artificial Intelligence in IoT. Transactions on Computational Science and Computational Intelligence* (pp. 63–83). Springer.

Bassa, L. (2011). Why Is It Important? World Heritage, Tourism, Teaching. Academia Budapestiensis Communicationis et Negotii Annales Tomus III, 24-35.

Bassa, L. (2014). How to raise the interest of students for culture? Educating heritage for contributing sustainability. *The 7th International Conference on Heritage and Sustainable Development*.

Bassa, L., & Kiss, F. (2011). Preservation of Traditional Craftsmanship Practices. *Conference on Sharing Cultures 2011, 2nd International Conference on Intangible Heritage*.

Batista e Silva, F., Marín Herrera, M. A., Rosina, K., Ribeiro Barranco, R., Freire, S., & Schiavina, M. (2018). Analysing spatiotemporal patterns of tourism in Europe at high-resolution with conventional and big data sources. *Tourism Management*, *68*, 101–115. doi:10.1016/j.tourman.2018.02.020

Batı, U. (2017). *Markethink ya da Farkethink: Deneyimsel pazarlama ve duyusal markalama*. Kitap Kulübü.

Batrinca, B., & Treleaven, P. C. (2014). Social media analytics: A survey of techniques, tools and platforms. *AI & Society*, *30*(1), 89–116. Advance online publication. doi:10.100700146-014-0549-4

Baudrillard, J. (1994). *Simulacra ve simulation*. University of Michigan press.

Bauer, J., Souhn, A., & Oliveira, B. (2019). Cultural Tourism: A study on museums and the internet. *Rev.Tur. Visão e Ação*, *21*(3), 291–308.

Bautista, S. S. (2013). *Museums in The Digital Age: Changing Meanings of Place, Community, and Culture Lanham*. AltaMira Press.

Bec, A., Moyle, B., Schaffer, V., & Timms, K. (2021). Virtual reality and mixed reality for second chance tourism. *Tourism Management*, *83*, 1–5. doi:10.1016/j.tourman.2020.104256

Bec, A., Moyle, B., Timms, K., Schaffer, V., Skavronskaya, L., & Little, C. (2019). Management of immersive heritage tourism experiences: A conceptual model. *Tourism Management*, *72*, 117–120. doi:10.1016/j.tourman.2018.10.033

Becken, S., Simmons, D. G., & Frampton, C. (2003). Energy use associated with different travel choices. *Tourism Management*, *24*(3), 267–277. doi:10.1016/S0261-5177(02)00066-3

Belaid, S., & Temessek Behi, A. (2011). The role of attachment in building consumer-brand relationships: An empirical investigation in the utilitarian consumption context. *Journal of Product and Brand Management*, *20*(1), 37–47. doi:10.1108/10610421111108003

Belanche, D., Casalo, L. V., Flavian, C., & Guinaliu, M. (2010). Online social networks in the travel sector. *International Journal of Electronic Marketing and Retailing*, *3*(4), 321–340. doi:10.1504/IJEMR.2010.036880

Belhi, A., Bouras, A., & Foufou, S. (2017). Digitization and preservation of cultural heritage: The CEPROQHA approach. *11th International Conference on Software, Knowledge, Information Management and Applications (SKIMA)*, 1–7. 10.1109/SKIMA.2017.8294117

Bellalouna, F. (2021). The Augmented Reality Technology as Enabler for the Digitization of Industrial Business Processes: Case Studies. *Procedia CIRP*, *98*, 400–405. doi:10.1016/j.procir.2021.01.124

Bello-Orgaz, G., Jung, J. J., & Camacho, D. (2016). Social big data: Recent achievements and new challenges. *Information Fusion*, *28*, 45–59. Advance online publication. doi:10.1016/j.inffus.2015.08.005 PMID:32288689

Bellotti, F., Berta, C., De Gloria, A., & Margarone, M. (2002). User testing a hypermedia tour guide. *IEEE Pervasive Computing*, *1*(2), 33–41. doi:10.1109/MPRV.2002.1012335

Bencheva, N. & Manevsky, N. (2019). Digital transformation of the tourism industry. *Knowledge - International Jorunal, 34*(1), 165-168.

Bencheva, N., & Manevsky, N. (2019). Digital transformation of the tourist industry. *Knowledge International Journal, 34*(1), 165–168.

Benckendorff, P. J., Xiang, Z., & Sheldon, P. (2019). *Tourism information technology*. CABI. doi:10.1079/9781786393432.0000

Bennett, M., & Radburn, M. (1991). *Information technology in tourism: the impact on the industry and supply of holidays*. Academic Press.

BERHTECH. (2021). https://behrtech.com/blog/smart-museums-6-artful-iot-applications-for-museums-and-galleries/

Berlin. (2021). *Augmented Reality by Highsnobiety*. Visit in Berlin (E.T.07.06.2021): https://www.visitberlin.de/en/event/berlin-berlin-augmented-reality-highsnobiety

Berryman, D. R. (2012). Augmented Reality: A Review. *Medical Reference Services Quarterly, 31*(2), 212–218. doi:10.1080/02763869.2012.670604 PMID:22559183

Berthon, P., Pitt, L., Parent, M., & Berthon, J. P. (2009). Aesthetics and ephemerality: Observing and preserving the luxury brand. *California Management Review, 52*(1), 45–66. doi:10.1525/cmr.2009.52.1.45

Bestwestern. (2018). *Innovative companies*. Retrieved from: https://www.bestwestern.com/en_US/about/press-media/2018-press-release/bw-named-one-of-top-10-most-innovative-companies.html

Bettington, J., Eberhard, K., Loo, R., & Smith, C. (Eds.). (2008). *Keeping archives*. Australian Society of Archivists Incorporated.

Bhatt, G. D., & Grover, V. (2005). Types of information technology capabilities and their role in competitive advantage: An empirical study. *Journal of Management Information Systems, 22*(2), 253–277. doi:10.1080/07421222.2005.11045844

Bieszk-Stolorz, B., Dmytrów, K., Eglinskiene, J., Marx, S., Miluniec, A., Muszyńska, K., Niedoszytko, G., Podlesińska, W., Rostoványi, A., Swacha, J., Vilsholm, R. L., & Vurzer, S. (2021). Impact of the availability of gamified e-guides on museum visit intention. *Procedia Computer Science, 192*, 4358–4366. doi:10.1016/j.procs.2021.09.212

Bigné, J., Andreu, L., & Gnoth, J. (2005). The theme park experience: An analysis of pleasure, arousal and satisfaction. *Tourism Management, 26*(6), 833–844. doi:10.1016/j.tourman.2004.05.006

Bilişim ve Bilgi Güvenliği İleri Teknolojiler Araştırma Merkezi. (n.d.). *Müze Ulusal Envanter Sistemi Projesi* [Museum National Inventory System Project]. https://b3lab.org/sayfa/mues_muze_ulusal_envanter_sistemi_projesi-32

Bimber, O., & Raskar, R. (2019). *Spatial augmented reality: merging real and virtual worlds*. AK Peters/CRC Press.

Binkhorst, E., & Den Dekker, T. (2009). Agenda for co-creation tourism experience research. *Journal of Hospitality Marketing & Management, 18*(2/3), 311–327. doi:10.1080/19368620802594193

Biocca, F., & Levy, M. R. (Eds.). (2013). *Communication in the age of virtual reality*. Routledge. doi:10.4324/9781410603128

Blackston, M. (2000). Observations: Building brand equity by managing the brand's relationships. *Journal of Advertising Research, 32*(3), 79–83. doi:10.2501/JAR-40-6-101-105

Blain, C., Levy, S. E., & Ritchie, J. R. B. (2005). Destination branding: Insights and practices from destination management organizations. *Journal of Travel Research, 43*(4), 328–338. doi:10.1177/0047287505274646

Boboc, R., Duguleană, M., Voinea, G., Postelnicu, C., Popovici, D., & Carrozzino, M. (2019). Mobile augmented reality for cultural heritage: Following the footsteps of Ovid among different locations in Europe. *Sustainability*, *11*(4), 1167. doi:10.3390u11041167

Boden. (2015). https://www.nfcw.com/2015/04/28/335007/starwood-guests-unlock-hotel-rooms-with-apple-watch-app/

Boes, K., Buhalis, D., & Inversini, A. (2015). Conceptualising smart tourism destination dimensions. In I. Tussyadiah & A. Inversini (Eds.), *Information and communication technologies in tourism: 2015 proceeding of the international conference*. Springer International Publisher.

Boes, K., Buhalis, D., & Inversini, A. (2016). Smart tourism destinations: Ecosystems for tourism destination competitiveness. *International Journal of Tourism Cities*, *2*(2), 108–124. doi:10.1108/IJTC-12-2015-0032

Bogicevic, V., Seo, S., Kandampully, J. A., Liu, S. Q., & Rudd, N. A. (2019). Virtual reality presence as a preamble of tourism experience: The role of mental imagery. *Tourism Management*, *74*, 55–64. doi:10.1016/j.tourman.2019.02.009

Boniface, P. (2003). *Managing quality cultural tourism*. Routledge.

Bonini, E. (2008). Building virtual cultural heritage environments: the embodied mind at the core of the learning processes. *International Journal of Digital Culture and Electronic Tourism*, *1*(2-3), 113-125.

Bonink, C., & Richards, G. (1992). Cultural Tourism in Europe. A Transnational Research Initiative of the Atlas Consortium. ATLAS, University of North London.

Bonne, B., Barzan, A., Quax, P., & Lamotte, W. (2013). WiFiPi: Involuntary tracking of visitors at mass events. *2013 IEEE 14th International Symposium on a World of Wireless, Mobile and Multimedia Networks, WoWMoM 2013*. 10.1109/WoWMoM.2013.6583443

Borissova, V. (2018). Cultural heritage digitization and related intellectual property issues. *Journal of Cultural Heritage*, *34*, 145–150. Advance online publication. doi:10.1016/j.culher.2018.04.023

Borneman, D., & Gibson, K. (2011). Digital storytelling: Meeting standards across the curriculum in a WWII/Holocaust unit. *School Library Monthly*, *27*(7), 16–17.

Bornhorst, T., Ritchie, J. B., & Sheehan, L. (2010). Determinants of tourism success for DMOs & destinations: An empirical examination of stakeholders' perspectives. *Tourism Management*, *31*(5), 572–589. doi:10.1016/j.tourman.2009.06.008

Borras, J., Morena, A., & Valls, A. (2014). Intelligent tourism recommender systems: A survey. *Expert Systems with Applications*, *41*(16), 7370–7389. doi:10.1016/j.eswa.2014.06.007

Borrela, L. (2019). *Cartas de Soro Mariana Alcoforado*. Lisbonpress.

Boulaalam, O., Aghoutane, B., El Ouadghiri, D., Moumen, A., & Malinine, M. L. C. (2018). Proposal of a big data system based on the recommendation and profiling techniques for an intelligent management of moroccan tourism. *Procedia Computer Science*, *134*, 346–351. doi:10.1016/j.procs.2018.07.200

Boutsiouki, S., & Polydora, A. (2019). Is the museum going digital? Experiences from the websites of Greek museums. In V. Katsoni & T. Spyriadis (Eds.), *Cultural and Tourism Innovation in the Digital Era Proceedings Book* (pp. 229–245). Springer.

Bouwman, H., Nikou, S., Molina-Castillo, F. J., & de Reuver, M. (2018). The impact of digitalization on business models. *Digital Policy, Regulation and Governance*.

Boyd, D. M., & Ellison, N. B. (2007). Social network sites: Definition, history, and scholarship. *Journal of Computer-Mediated Communication*, *13*(1), 210–230. doi:10.1111/j.1083-6101.2007.00393.x

Boyd, S. W., & Timothy, D. J. (2006). Marketing issues and world heritage sites. In A. Leask & A. Fyal (Eds.), *Managing world heritage sites* (pp. 55–67). Butterworth-Heinemann. doi:10.1016/B978-0-7506-6546-9.50013-7

Brachman, P. S. (2003). Infectious diseases-past, present, and future. *International Journal of Epidemiology, 32*(5), 684–686. doi:10.1093/ije/dyg282 PMID:14559728

Bradburne, J. M. (2002). Museums and their languages: Is interactivity different for fine art as opposed to design? *Interactive Learning in Museums of Art and Design.* http://media.vam.ac.uk/media/documents/legacy_documents/file_upload/5758_file.pdf

Brandão, F., & Costa, C. (2014). Inovação em Turismo: Uma Abordagem Sistémica e Territorial. In Produtos e Competitividade do Turismo na Lusofonia (pp. 69–91). Lisboa: Escolar Editora.

Brayton, J. (2003). *The Meaning and Experience of Virtual Reality* (Ph.D. Dissertation). Dept of Sociology, University of New Brunswick.

Breazeal, C., Buchsbaum, D., Gatenby, D., & Blumberg, B. (2005). Learning from and about others by robots. *Artificial Life, 11*(1-2), 31–62. doi:10.1162/1064546053278955 PMID:15811219

Brenner, L., & Aguilar, A. G. (2002). Luxury tourism and regional economic development in Mexico. *The Professional Geographer, 54*(4), 500–520. doi:10.1111/0033-0124.00346

Bresnick, E. (2019). *Intensified Play: Cinematic study of TikTok mobile app.* from https://www.researchgate.net/publication/335570557_Intensified_Play_Cinematic_study_of_TikTok_mobile_app

Brice, Q. (1996). Salvage and the underwater cultural heritage. *Marine Policy, 20*(4), 337–342. doi:10.1016/0308-597X(96)00022-X

Brito, C. H., & Correia, R. (2006). *A model for understanding the dynamics of territorial networks: the case of tourism in the Douro Valley.* Retrieved from https://bibliotecadigital.ipb.pt/handle/10198/5834

Britton, S. (1991). Tourism, capital, and place: Towards a critical geography of tourism. *Environment and Planning. D, Society & Space, 9*(4), 451–478. doi:10.1068/d090451

Brooks, C., & McCormack. (2020). *Driving digital transformation in higher education.* Retrieved form https://www.educause.edu/ecar/research-publications/driving-digital-transformation-in-higher-education/2020/defining-digital-transformation

Brown, M. (2003). *Virtual reality training manual.* Retrieved from: https://oxford.universitypressscholarship.com/view/10.1093/acprof:oso/9780195167962.001.0001/acprof-9780195167962-chapter-11

Browning, V., So, K. K. F., & Sparks, B. (2013). The influence of online reviews on consumers' attributions of service quality and control for service standards in hotels. *Journal of Travel & Tourism Marketing, 30*(1-2), 23–40. doi:10.1080/10548408.2013.750971

Brown, R. (2009). *Public relations and the social web how to use social media and web 2.0 in communications.* Kogan Page Publishers.

Bruno, F., Barbieri, L., Mangeruga, M., Cozza, M., Lagudi, A., Čejka, J., Liarokapis, F., & Skarlatos, D. (2019). Underwater augmented reality for improving the diving experience in submerged archaeological sites. *Ocean Engineering, 190*, 106487. doi:10.1016/j.oceaneng.2019.106487

Bruno, F., Bruno, S., De Sensi, G., Luchi, M. L., Mancuso, S., & Muzzupappa, M. (2010). From 3D reconstruction to virtual reality: A complete methodology for digital archaeological exhibition. *Journal of Cultural Heritage, 11*(1), 42–49. doi:10.1016/j.culher.2009.02.006

Bruno, F., Lagudi, A., Muzzupappa, M., Lupia, M., Cario, G., Barbieri, L., Passaro, S., & Saggiomo, R. (2016). Project VISAS: Virtual and augmented exploitation of submerged archaeological sites-overview and first results. *Marine Technology Society Journal, 50*(4), 119–129. doi:10.4031/MTSJ.50.4.4

Bryson, G., Bell, M., & Lysaker, P. (1997). Affect recognition in schizophrenia: A function of global impairment or a specific cognitive deficit. *Psychiatry Research, 71*(2), 105–113. doi:10.1016/S0165-1781(97)00050-4 PMID:9255855

Budapest Brand Zrt. (2021). *Találkozunk Budapesten - Budapesti Turizmusfejlesztési Stratégia 2021–2027* [Meet us in Budapest - Budapest Tourism Development Strategy 2021-2027]. Municipality of Budapest.

Buhalis D. & Yovcheva, Z. (2013). Augmented reality in tourism: 10 Unique applications explained, digital tourism think tank reports and best practice. *Digital Tourism Think Tank*, 1-12.

Buhalis, D. (1996). Information and telecommunication technologies as a strategic tool for tourism enhancement at destination regions. Information and communication technologies in tourism, 131-142. doi:10.1007/978-3-7091-7598-9_16

Buhalis, D. (2000). Marketing the Competitive Destination of the future. *Tourism Management, 21*(July), 97–116.

Buhalis, D. (2003). *eTourism: Information technology for strategic tourism management.* London: Pearson (Financial Times/Prentice Hall).

Buhalis, D. (2015). *Working definitions of Smartness and Smart tourism destination.* http: buhalis.blogspot.com/2014/12/working-definitions-of-smartness-and.html

Buhalis, D., & Amaranggana, A. (2013). Smart Tourism Destinations. Information and Communication Technologies in Tourism 2014. doi:10.1007/978-3-319-03973-2_40

Buhalis, D., & Amaranggane, A. (2015). Smart Tourism Destinations Enhancing Tourism Experience through Personalisation of Services. In Proceedings of Information and Communication Technologies in Tourism (pp. 377-389). Springer International Publishing. doi:10.1007/978-3-319-14343-9_28

Buhalis, D. (1998). Strategic use of information technologies in the tourism industry. *Tourism Management, 19*(5), 409–421. doi:10.1016/S0261-5177(98)00038-7

Buhalis, D. (1999). Tourism on the Greek Islands: Issues of peripherality, competitiveness and development. *International Journal of Tourism Research, 1*(5), 341–358. doi:10.1002/(SICI)1522-1970(199909/10)1:5<341::AID-JTR201>3.0.CO;2-0

Buhalis, D. (2000). Marketing the competitive destination of the future. *Tourism Management, 21*(1), 97–116. Advance online publication. doi:10.1016/S0261-5177(99)00095-3

Buhalis, D., & Amaranggana, A. (2014). Smart Tourism Destinations. In Z. Xiang & I. Tussyadiah (Eds.), *Information and Communication Technologies in Tourism* (pp. 553–564). Springer.

Buhalis, D., & Amaranggana, A. (2014). Smart tourism destinations. In Z. Xiang & I. Tussyadiah (Eds.), *Information and communication technologies in tourism 2014 Springer* (pp. 553–564).

Buhalis, D., & Amaranggana, A. (2015). *Information and communication technologies in tourism – smart tourism destinations enhancing tourism experience through personalization of services.* Springer International Publisher.

Buhalis, D., & Law, R. (2008). Progress in information technology and tourism management: 20 years on and 10 years after the Internet—The state of eTourism research. *Tourism Management, 29*(4), 609–623. doi:10.1016/j.tourman.2008.01.005

Buhalis, D., & Licata, M. C. (2002). The future eTourism intermediaries. *Tourism Management, 23*(3), 207–220. doi:10.1016/S0261-5177(01)00085-1

Bulchand-Gidumal, J. (2020). Impact of artificial intelligence in travel, tourism, and hospitality. In *Handbook of e-Tourism* (pp. 1–20). Springer. doi:10.1007/978-3-030-05324-6_110-1

Buonincontri, P., & Micera, R. (2016). The Experience Co-Creation in Smart Tourism Destinations: A Multiple Case Analysis of European Destination. *Information Technology & Tourism, 16*(3), 285–315. doi:10.100740558-016-0060-5

Burcaw, G. E. (1997). *Introduction to museum work.* AltaMira Press.

Burdea, G., & Coiffet, P. (2003). *Virtual reality technology.* Academic Press.

Burdea, G. C., & Coiffet, P. (2003). *Virtual Reality Technology* (2nd ed.). Wiley-Interscience. doi:10.1162/105474603322955950

Bureau, B. W. (2020, March 25). *Crowne plaza greater noida launches world's first hotel VR experience center.* BW Hotelier. http://bwhotelier.businessworld.in/article/CrownePlaza-Greater-Noida-launches-World-s-First-Hotel-VR-Experience-Center/09-03-2020-185809/

Burnett, A., Yates, T., & Crane, R. (2007). Rights and the reality of healthcare charging in the United Kingdom. *Medicine, Conflict, and Survival, 23*(4), 297–304. doi:10.1080/13623690701596775 PMID:17987981

Butcher, J. (2005). *The moralisation of tourism: sun, sand... and saving the world?* Routledge. doi:10.4324/9780203987025

Butler, R. (1993). Alternative tourism: The thin edge of the wedge. In V. Smith & W. Eadington (Eds.), *Tourism alternatives: Potential and problems in the development of tourism* (pp. 31–36). University of Pennsylvania Press.

Butler, R. W. (2018). Challenges and opportunities. *Worldwide Hospitality and Tourism Themes, 10*(6), 635–641. doi:10.1108/WHATT-07-2018-0042 PMID:30591573

Buttler, R. (1980). *The Tourism Area Life Cycle: Applications and Modifications.* Channel View Publications.

Büyükkuru, M., & Aslan, Z. (2016). The effect of communication skills of tourist guides on tourists' tour experiences: A research in Nevsehir. *Mustafa Kemal University Journal of Social Sciences Institute, 13*(34), 338–354.

Büyükuslu, A. R. (2018). *Dijital dönüşüm.* D&R Yayınevi.

Cacho, A., Figueredo, M., Cassio, A., Araujo, M. V., Mendese, L., Lucas, J., Fairos, H., Coellho, J., Cacho, N., & Prolo, C. (2016). Social smart destination: A platform to analyze user generated content in smart tourism destinations. *New Advances in Information Systems and Technologies, 1*, 817–826. doi:10.1007/978-3-319-31232-3_77

Caffo, R. & Canale, D. (2014). *Digital Cultural Heritage and Tourism Recommendations for Cultural Institutions.* Version 1.0, 2 October 2014.

Caffo, R., Canale, D., Conticello, A., Natale, M. T., Petrangeli, P., & Piccininno, M. (2014). *Digital Cultural Heritage and Tourism Recommendations for Cultural Institutions.* Antenna International.

Cai, L. A. (2002). Cooperative branding for rural destinations. *Annals of Tourism Research, 29*(3), 720–742. doi:10.1016/S0160-7383(01)00080-9

Çakmak, V., & Altaş, A. (2018). Sosyal medya etkileşiminde tren yolculukları: Doğu Ekspresi ile ilgili YouTube paylaşım videolarının analizi. *Journal of Tourism and Gastronomy Studies, 6*(1), 390–408.

Calin, R. A. (2018). Virtual reality, augmented reality and mixed reality-trends in pedagogy. *Social Sciences and Education Research Review, 5*(1), 169–179.

Camacho, C. (2020). *Grupo de Projeto Museus no Futuro: Relatório Final*. Direção-Geral do Património Cultural.

Camarero, C., Garrido, M. J., & San José, R. (2016). Efficiency of Web Communication Strategies: The Case of Art Museums. *International Journal of Arts Management, 18*(2), 42–62.

Cameron, D., Gregory, C., & Battaglia, D. (2012). Nielsen personalizes the mobile shopping app if you build the technology, they will come. *Journal of Advertising Research, 52*(3), 333–338. doi:10.2501/JAR-52-3-333-338

CAMILEON. (2021). *Dijital Curation Centre*. Accessed on June 14, 2021. https://www.dcc.ac.uk/resources/external/camileon-creative-archiving-michigan-and-leeds-emulating-old-new

Camilleri, M. A. (2020). The Use of data-driven technologies for customer-centric marketing. *International Journal of Big Data Management, 1*(1), 50–63. doi:10.1504/IJBDM.2020.106876

Camilo, I., & Bahl, M. (2017). Desenvolvimento do turismo baseado em elementos culturais. *Turismo e Sociedade, 10*(1). Advance online publication. doi:10.5380/tes.v10i1.52187

Canadi, M., Höpken, W., & Fuchs, M. (2010). Application of QR codes in online travel distribution. In U. Gretzel, R. Law, & M. Fuch (Eds.), Information and communication technologies in tourism 2010 (pp. 137-148). Springer. doi:10.1007/978-3-211-99407-8_12

Canelas, L. (2016). *O visitante dos museus é jovem, tem formação e procura-os porque a arte lhe dá prazer. PUBLICO*. Retrieved from https://bit.ly/3aOlcni

Caneparo, L. (2001). Shared virtual reality for design and management: The Porta Susa project. *Automation in Construction, 10*(2), 217–228. doi:10.1016/S0926-5805(99)00032-1

Capocchi, A., Vallone, C., Pierotti, M., & Amaduzzi, A. (2019). Overtourism: A Literature Review to Assess Implications and Future Perspectives. *Sustainability, 11*(12), 3303. doi:10.3390u11123303

Cappa, F., Rosso, F., & Capaldo, A. (2020). Visitor-sensing: Involving the crowd in cultural heritage organizations. *Sustainability, 12*(4), 1445. doi:10.3390u12041445

Capriotti, P., Carretón, C., & Castillo, A. (2016). Testing the level of interactivity of institutional websites: From museums 1.0 to museums 2.0. *International Journal of Information Management, 36*(1), 97–104. doi:10.1016/j.ijinfomgt.2015.10.003

Capriotti, P., & González-Herrero, A. (2013). Managing media relations in museums through the Internet: A model of analysis for online pressrooms in museums. *Museum Management and Curatorship, 28*(4), 413–429. doi:10.1080/09647775.2013.831246

Capriotti, P., & Moreno, Á. (2007). Corporate citizenship and public relations: The importance and interactivity of social responsibility issues on corporate websites. *Public Relations Review, 33*(1), 84–91. doi:10.1016/j.pubrev.2006.11.012

Capriotti, P., & Pardo Kuklinski, H. (2012). Assessing dialogic communication through the Internet in Spanish museums. *Public Relations Review, 38*(4), 619–626. doi:10.1016/j.pubrev.2012.05.005

Capriotti, P., Zeler, I., & Camilleri, M. A. (2021). Corporate Communication Through Social Networks: The Identification of the Key Dimensions for Dialogic Communication. In M. A. Camilleri (Ed.), *Strategic Corporate Communication in the Digital Age* (pp. 33–51). Emerald Publishing Limited. doi:10.1108/978-1-80071-264-520211003

Caragliu, A., Del Bo, C., & Nijkamp, P. (2011). Smart cities in Europe. *Journal of Urban Technology, 18*(2), 65–82. doi:10.1080/10630732.2011.601117

Carmigniani, J., Furht, B., Anisetti, M., Ceravolo, P., Damiani, E., & Ivkovic, M. (2011). Augmented reality technologies, systems and applications. *Multimedia Tools and Applications, 51*(1), 341–377. doi:10.100711042-010-0660-6

Carolei, P., & Schlemme, E. (2015). Alternate reality game in museum: A process to construct experiences and narratives in hybrid context. *Proceedings of 7th International Conference on Education and New Learning Technologies*, 8037-8045.

Carrozzino, M., & Bergamasco, M. (2010). Beyond virtual museums: Experiencing immersive virtual reality in real museums. *Journal of Cultural Heritage*, *11*(4), 452–458. doi:10.1016/j.culher.2010.04.001

Carvalho, R., Costa, C., & Ferreira, A. (2019). Review of the theoretical underpinnings in the creative tourism research field. *Tourism & Management Studies*, *15*(SI), 11–22.

Cary, S. H. (2004). The tourist moment. *Annals of Tourism Research*, *31*(1), 61–77. doi:10.1016/j.annals.2003.03.001

Casillo, M., Clarizia, F., D'Aniello, G., De Santo, M., Lombardi, M., & Santaniello, D. (2020). CHAT-Bot: A cultural heritage aware teller-bot for supporting touristic experiences. *Pattern Recognition Letters*, *131*, 234–243. doi:10.1016/j.patrec.2020.01.003

Castiglione, A., Colace, F., Moscato, V., & Palmieri, F. (2018). CHIS: A big data infrastructure to manage digital cultural items. *Future Generation Computer Systems*, *86*, 1134–1145. doi:10.1016/j.future.2017.04.006

Catlin-Legutko, C. (2012). *Interpretation: Education, Programs, and Exhibits Stacy*. Altamira Press.

Cavaco, C. (2013). Territórios de Turismo. *Revista Turismo & Desenvolvimento*, *20*, 51–67.

Cawood, S., & Fiala, M. (2008). *Augmented reality: A practical guide*. Academic Press.

CBI Ministry of Foreign Affairs. (2021). Retrieved from https://www.cbi.eu/market-information/tourism/cultural-tourism/market-potential

CBI. (2021). *The European market potential for cultural tourism*. Retrieved from https://bityli.com/5j738

Čejka, J., Zsíros, A., & Liarokapis, F. (2020). A hybrid augmented reality guide for underwater cultural heritage sites. *Personal and Ubiquitous Computing*, 1–14.

Çelik, P., & Topsakal, Y. (2017). Akıllı turizm destinasyonları: Antalya destinasyonunun akıllı turizm uygulamalarının incelenmesi. *Seyahat ve Otel İşletmeciliği Dergisi*, *14*(3), 149–166. doi:10.24010oid.369951

Çelik, P., & Topsakal, Y. (2019). *Endüstri 4.0 ve Akıllı turizm*. Detay Yayıncılık.

Çeltek, E. (2021). Gamification: Augmented Reality, Virtual Reality Games and Tourism Marketing Applications. In *Gamification for Tourism* (pp. 237–279). Channel View Publications. doi:10.21832/9781845418236-014

Centobelli, P., & Ndou, V. (2019). Managing customer knowledge through the use of big data analytics in tourism research. *Current Issues in Tourism*, *22*(15), 1862–1882. doi:10.1080/13683500.2018.1564739

Çetin, T. (2010). Cumalıkızık köyünde kültürel miras ve turizm algısı [Perception of cultural heritage and tourism in Cumalıkızık village]. *Milli Folklor*, *22*(87), 181–190.

Cetin, T. (2010). Perception of cultural heritage and tourism in Cumalıkızık village. *Milli Folklor Journal*, *22*, 181–190.

Cha, M., Haddadi, H., Benevenuto, F., & Gummadi, K. P. (2010). Measuring user influence in Twitter: The million follower fallacy. International Association for the Advancement of Artificial Intelligence Conference on Weblogs and Social Media.

Chacko, H. E., & Marcell, M. H. (2008). Repositioning a Tourism Destination. *Journal of Travel & Tourism Marketing*, *23*(2-4), 223–235. doi:10.1300/J073v23n02_17

Chaer, G., Diniz, R. & Ribeiro, E. (2011). A Técnica do questionário a pesquisa educacional. *Araxá*, *7*(7), 251–266.

Chakraborty, I., & Maity, P. (2020). COVID-19 outbreak: Migration, effects on society, global environment and prevention. *The Science of the Total Environment, 728*, 138882. doi:10.1016/j.scitotenv.2020.138882 PMID:32335410

Chang, G., & Caneday, L. (2011). Web-based GIS in tourism information search: Perceptions, tasks, and trip attributes. *Tourism Management, 32*(6), 1435–1437. doi:10.1016/j.tourman.2011.01.006

Chang, S. E., & Shen, W.-C. (2018). Exploring smartphone social networking services for mobile tourism. *International Journal of Mobile Communications, 16*(1), 63–81. doi:10.1504/IJMC.2018.088273

Chapman, P., Roussel, D., Drap, P., & Haydar, M. (2008). Virtual exploration of underwater archaeological sites: visualization and interaction in mixed reality environments. In *The 9th International Symposium on Virtual Reality, Archaeology and Intelligent Cultural Heritage*. Braga, Portugal: VAST 2008.

Chareyron, G., Da-Rugna, J., & Raimbault, T. (2015). Big data: A new challenge for tourism. *Proceedings - 2014 IEEE International Conference on Big Data, IEEE Big Data 2014*. 10.1109/BigData.2014.7004475

Chatterjee, H. J., & Noble, G. (2013). *Museums, health and wellbeing*. Ashgate Publishing Ltd.

Chavan, S. R. (2014). Augmented reality vs. virtual reality: Differences and similarities. *International Journal of Advanced Research in Computer Engineering and Technology, 5*(6), 1947–1752.

Chen, A. (2020). Será que as Viagens Virtuais Vieram Para Ficar? *National Geographic*. Retrieved from: https://bit.ly/2YSPWS5

Chen, A., & Peng, N. (2014). Examining Chinese consumers' luxury hotel staying behavior. *International Journal of Hospitality Management, 39*, 53–56. doi:10.1016/j.ijhm.2014.01.002

Chen, H., Chiang, R. H. L., & Storey, V. C. (2012). Business Intelligence and Analytics: From Big Data To Big Impact. *Management Information Systems Quarterly, 36*(4), 1165–1188. doi:10.1145/2463676.2463712

Chen, H., Chiang, R. H., & Storey, V. C. (2012). Business intelligence and analytics: From big data to big impact. *Management Information Systems Quarterly, 36*(4), 1165–1188. doi:10.2307/41703503

Chen, M., Mao, S., & Liu, Y. (2014). Big data: A survey. *Mobile Networks and Applications, 19*(2), 171–209. Advance online publication. doi:10.100711036-013-0489-0

Chen, S., Duan, A., & Wang, J. (2021). Using Digital Technologies in Museum Learning Activities to Enhance Learning Experience: A Systematic Review. *Bulletin of the Technical Committee on Learning Technology, 21*(2), 32–36.

Chen, W., Shan, Y., Wu, Y., Yan, Z., & Li, X. (2021). Design and evaluation of a distance-driven user interface for asynchronous collaborative exhibit browsing in an augmented reality museum. *IEEE Access: Practical Innovations, Open Solutions, 9*, 73948–73962. doi:10.1109/ACCESS.2021.3080286

Chen, Z., Alfred, R., & Eboy, O. V. (2021). Modeling Tourism Using Spatial Analysis Based on Social Media Big Data: A Review. *Lecture Notes in Electrical Engineering, 724*, 437–451. Advance online publication. doi:10.1007/978-981-33-4069-5_36

Cheong, R. (1995). The virtual threat to travel and tourism. *Tourism Management, 16*(6), 417–422. doi:10.1016/0261-5177(95)00049-T

Chiao, H.-M., Chen, Y.-L., & Huang, W.-H. (2018). Examining the usability of an online virtual tour-guiding platform for cultural tourism education. *Journal of Hospitality, Leisure, Sport and Tourism Education, 23*, 29–38. doi:10.1016/j.jhlste.2018.05.002

Chiappa, G. D., & Baggio, R. (2015). Knowledge transfer in smart tourism destinations: Analyzing the effects of a network structure. *Journal of Destination Marketing & Management, 4*(3), 145–150. doi:10.1016/j.jdmm.2015.02.001

Choi, B., & Kim, J. (2021). Changes and Challenges in Museum Management after the COVID-19 Pandemic. *Journal of Open Innovation, 7*(148), 148. Advance online publication. doi:10.3390/joitmc7020148

Cho, Y. H., Wang, Y., & Fesenmaier, D. R. (2002). Searching for experiences: The web-based virtual tour in tourism marketing. *Journal of Travel & Tourism Marketing, 12*(4), 1–17. doi:10.1300/J073v12n04_01

Chung, N., Lee, H., Ham, J., & Koo, C. (2021). Smart Tourism Cities' Competitiveness Index: A Conceptual Model. In *Information and Communication Technologies in Tourism 2021* (pp. 433–438). Springer. doi:10.1007/978-3-030-65785-7_42

Chung, N., Lee, H., Kim, J., & Koo, C. (2018). The role of augmented reality for experience-influenced environments: The case of cultural heritage tourism in Korea. *Journal of Travel Research, 57*(5), 627–643. doi:10.1177/0047287517708255

Chung, N., Lee, H., Lee, S. J., & Koo, C. (2015). The influence of tourism website on tourists' behavior to determine destination selection: A case study of creative economy in Korea. *Technological Forecasting and Social Change, 96*, 130–143. doi:10.1016/j.techfore.2015.03.004

Cirulis, A., De Paolis, L. T., & Tutberidze, M. (2015). Virtualization of digitalized cultural heritage and use case scenario modeling for sustainability promotion of national identity. *Procedia Computer Science, 77*, 199–206. doi:10.1016/j.procs.2015.12.384

Cizel, B., & Ajovic, E. (2019). Smart tourism Ecosystem Impacts. In D. Gursoy & R. Nunkoo (Eds.), *The Routledge Handbook of Tourism Impacts- Theoretical and Applied Perspectives* (pp. 403–417). Taylor and Francis. doi:10.4324/9781351025102-30

Claisse, C., Ciolfi, L., & Petrelli, D. (2017). Containers of Stories: Using co-design and digital augmentation to empower the museum community and create novel experiences of heritage at a house museum. *The Design Journal, 20*(1), S2906–S2918. doi:10.1080/14606925.2017.1352801

Claveria, O., Monte, E., & Torra, S. (2015). A new forecasting approach for the hospitality industry. *International Journal of Contemporary Hospitality Management, 27*(7), 1520–1538. doi:10.1108/IJCHM-06-2014-0286

Clawson, M., & Knetsch, J. L. (1966). *Economics of outdoor recreation.* Johns Hopkins Press.

Coates, C. (2021). *Virtual Reality is a big trend in museums, but what are the best examples of museums using VR?* Museum Next (E.T: 6.10.21): https://www.museumnext.com/article/how-museums-are-using-virtual-reality/

Cohen, B. (2012). What exactly is a smart city. *Co. Exist, 19*.

Cohen, B. (2018). *Blockchain cities and the smart cities wheel.* https://medium.com/iomob/blockchain-cities-and-the-smart-cities-wheel-9f65c2f32c36

Colace, F., De Santo, M., Greco, L., Lemma, S., Lombardi, M., Moscato, V., & Picariello, A. (2014). A context-aware framework for cultural heritage applications. *2014 Tenth International Conference on Signal-Image Technology and Internet-Based Systems*, 469–476. 10.1109/SITIS.2014.14

Cole, S. (2008). *Tourism, culture and development: Hopes, dreams and realities in East Indonesia.* Channel View Publications.

Collins, L., Eylott, S., Leedale, J., & Graham, T. N. (2015). Alaska steve: Using virtual reality to enhance a 2nd platforming game. *Proceedings Annual Symposium on Computer-Human Interaction in Play*, 767-770.

Colomb, C., & Novy, J. (2017). *Protest and Resistance in the Tourist City.* Routledge., doi:10.4324/9781315719306

Comunidade Intermunicipal do Baixo Alentejo – CIMBAL. (n.d.). *Caracterização do Baixo Alentejo.* CIMBAL

ConnectSafely. (2021). *Parent's guide to Instagram.* Retrieved from https://www.connectsafely.org/instagram/

Constantinides, E. (2008). The empowered customer and the digital myopia. *Business Strategy Series, 9*(5), 215–223. doi:10.1108/17515630810906710

Constantinides, E., & Fountain, S. (2008). Web 2.0: Conceptual foundations and marketing issues. *Journal of Direct, Data and Digital Marketing Practice, 9*(3), 231–244. doi:10.1057/palgrave.dddmp.4350098

Consumerlab, E. (2017). TV and media 2017. *A Consumer-Driven Future of Media, 9.*

Convento de Cristo. (2021). Retrieved from: http://www.conventocristo.gov.pt

Conway, T., & Leighton, D. (2012). "Staging the past, enacting the present": Experiential marketing in the performing arts and heritage sectors. *Arts Marketing: An International Journal, 2*(1), 35–51. doi:10.1108/20442081211233007

Cook. (2020). *Thomascook.* Retrieved from: https://www.thomascook.com/

Cooper, C. (2006). Knowledge management and tourism. *Annals of Tourism Research, 33*(1), 47–64. doi:10.1016/j.annals.2005.04.005

Corea, F. (2019). Introduction to Data. In F. Corea (Ed.), *An Introduction to Data: Everything You Need to Know About AI, Big Data and Data Science* (pp. 1–5). Springer International Publishing. doi:10.1007/978-3-030-04468-8_1

Correia, M. (2009). *A Cidade de Beja – Património Histórico, Cultural e Linguístico.* Universidade da Beira Interior, Dissertação de Mestrado.

Correia, V. (2014). *A escrita do Sudoeste da Península Ibérica. In Portvgalia, Nova Série* (Vol. 35). DCTP-FLUP.

Coşkun, V., Özdenizci, B., & Ok, K. (2013). A survey on near field communication (NFC) technology. *Wireless Personal Communications, 71*(3), 2259–2294. doi:10.100711277-012-0935-5

Cosovic, M., & Brkic, B. R. (2019). Game-based learning in museums—Cultural heritage applications. *Information (Basel), 11*(22), 3–13.

Costa, C. (2014). Gestão Estratégica do Turismo: Evolução Epistemológica dos Modelos e Paradigmas, e Tendências para o Futuro. In Turismo nos Países Lusófonos: Conhecimento, Estratégia e Territórios (pp. 19–40). Lisboa: Escolar Editora.

Costa, C. 2021, The impact of the COVID-19 outbreak on the tourism and travel sectors in Portugal: Recommendations for maximising the contribution of the European Regional Development Fund (ERDF) and the Cohesion Fund (CF) to the recovery. Report produced to the Directorate-General Regional and Urban Policy (DG REGIO), European Commission.

Costa, C., Costa, R., & Breda, Z. (2014). Produtos e Competividade do Turismo na Lusofonia - Vol II - Introdução. In Produtos e Competividade do Turismo na Lusofonia (pp. 13–15). Lisboa: Escolar Editora.

Costa, C., Panyik, E., & Buhalis, D. (2013). Towards a Conceptual Framework: An Introduction. In C. Buhalis, D. & Costa (Eds.), Trends in European Tourism Planning and Organisation (pp. 1–11). Channel View Publications.

Costa, C. (2001). An Emerging Tourism Planning Paradigm? A Comparative Analysis Between Town and Tourism Planning. *International Journal of Tourism Research, 3*(3), 425–441. doi:10.1002/jtr.277

Costa, C. (2020). Tourism planning: A perspective paper. *Tourism Review, 75*(1), 198–202. doi:10.1108/TR-09-2019-0394

Cotteler, M., & Sniderman, B. (2017). *Forces of change: Industry 4.0.* Deloitte Touche Tohmatsu Limited.

Council of Europe. (2005). *Council of Europe Framework Convention on the Value of Cultural Heritage for Society.* Accessed on October 4, 2021 https://rm.coe.int/1680083746 >

Cox, C. (2003). *The use of computer graphics and virtual reality for visual impact assessments* (Doctoral dissertation). University of Nottingham.

Craig, A. B., Sherman, W. R., & Will, J. D. (2009). *Developing virtual reality applications foundations of effective design.* Morgan Kaufmann Publishers.

Craig-Smith, S., & French, C. (1994). *Learning to live with tourism.* Pitman.

Cranmer, E. & Jung, T. (2017). The value of augmented reality from a business model perspective. *e-Review of Tourism Research*, 8.

Cranmer, E., Jung, T., & Miller, A. (2016). Implementing Augmented Reality to Increase Tourist Attraction Sustainability. In *AR VR Innovate.* Dublin: Perspectives on Business Realities of AR and VR Conference.

Cranmer, E., Tom Dieck, M., & Fountoulaki, P. (2020). Exploring the value of augmented reality for tourism. *Tourism Management Perspectives*, *35*, 100672. doi:10.1016/j.tmp.2020.100672

Creswell, J. W., & Creswell, J. D. (2017). *Research design: Qualitative, quantitative, and mixed methods approaches.* Sage publications.

Crick, M. (1989). Representations of international tourism in the social sciences: Sun, sex, sights, savings, and servility. *Annual Review of Anthropology*, *18*(1), 307–344. doi:10.1146/annurev.an.18.100189.001515

Cristobal-Fransi, E., Daries-Ramon, N., Mariné-Roig, E., & Martin-Fuentes, E. (2017). Implementation of Web 2.0 in the snow tourism industry: Analysis of the online presence and e-commerce of ski resorts. *Spanish Journal of Marketing - ESIC, 21*(2), 117–130.

Cristobal-Fransi, E., Daries, N., Martin-Fuentes, E., & Montegut-Salla, Y. (2020). Industrial Heritage 2.0: Internet Presence and Development of the Electronic Commerce of Industrial Tourism. *Sustainability*, *12*(15), 5965. doi:10.3390u12155965

Croes, R., & Semrad, K. J. (2015). The relevance of cultural tourism as the next frontier for small island destinations. *Journal of Hospitality & Tourism Research (Washington, D.C.)*, *39*(4), 469–491. doi:10.1177/1096348013491599

Crompton, J. L. (2009). Strategies for implementing repositioning of leisure services. *Managing Leisure*, *14*(2), 87–111. doi:10.1080/13606710902752497

Crytek. (2019). Retrieved from: https://www.crytek.com/

Csapó, J. (2012). The role and importance of cultural tourism in modern tourism industry. *Strategies for tourism industry-micro and macro perspectives*, 201-232.

Csapó, J. (2012). The role and importance of cultural tourism in modern tourism industry. In M. Kasimoğlu & H. Aydın (Eds.), *Strategies for tourism industry – micro and macro perspectives* (pp. 201–232). InTech. doi:10.5772/38693

Ćulić, M., Vujičić, M. D., Kalinić, Č., Dunjić, M., Stankov, U., Kovačić, S., Vasiljević, Đ. A., & Anđelković, Ž. (2021). Rookie tourism destinations—The effects of attractiveness factors on destination image and revisit intention with the satisfaction mediation effect. *Sustainability (Switzerland)*, *13*(11), 5780. doi:10.3390u13115780

Cuomo, M. T., Tortora, D., Foroudi, P., Giordano, A., Festa, G. & Metallo, G. (2021). Digital transformation and tourist experience co-design: Big social data for planning cultural tourism. *Technological Forecasting and Social Science, 162,* Article Number: 120345.

Cuomo, S., De Michele, P., Galletti, A., & Piccialli, F. (2015). A cultural heritage case study of visitor experiences shared on a social network. *2015 10th International Conference on P2P, Parallel, Grid, Cloud and Internet Computing (3PGCIC),* 539–544.

Cuomo, M. T., Tortora, D., Foroudi, P., Giordano, A., Festa, G., & Metallo, G. (2021). Digital transformation and tourist experience co-design: Big social data for planning cultural tourism. *Technological Forecasting and Social Change, 162,* 120345. doi:10.1016/j.techfore.2020.120345

Cuomo, S., Colecchia, G., Cola, V. S., & Chirico, U. (2021). A virtual assistant in cultural heritage scenarios. *Concurrency and Computation, 33*(3), e5331. doi:10.1002/cpe.5331

Curran, K., Murray, M., & Christian, M. (2007). Taking the information to the public through Library 2.0. *Library Hi Tech, 25*(2), 288–297. doi:10.1108/07378830710755036

D'amico, G., Ercoli, S., & Bimbo, A. D. (2013). A framework for itinerary personalization in cultural tourism of smart cities. *AIHCI 2013: International Workshop on Intelligent User Interfaces,* 1.

da Costa Liberato, P. M., Alén-González, E., & de Azevedo Liberato, D. F. V. (2018). Digital technology in a smart tourist destination: The case of Porto. *Journal of Urban Technology, 25*(1), 75–97. doi:10.1080/10630732.2017.1413228

Daghestani, L. (2013). *The design, implementation and evaluation of a desktop virtual reality for teaching numeracy concepts via virtual manipulatives* (Doctoral dissertation). University of Huddersfield.

Daintith, J. (Ed.). (2009). *"IT", A Dictionary of Physics.* Oxford University Press.

Dal Falco, F., & Vassos, S. (2017). Museum Experience Design: A Modern Storytelling Methodology. *The Design Journal, 20*(1), S3975–S3983. doi:10.1080/14606925.2017.1352900

Dalfovo, M., Lana, R., & Silveira, A. (2008). Métodos quantitativos e qualitativos: Um resgate teórico. *Revista Interdisciplinar Científica Aplicada, Blumenau, 2*(4), 1–13.

Dalgic, T., & Leeuw, M. (1994). Niche marketing revisited: Concept, applications and some European cases. *European Journal of Marketing, 28*(4), 39–55. doi:10.1108/03090569410061178

Dalton, R., Lynch, P., & Lally, A. M. (2009). *Towards an Understanding of Experience Concept Development in Tourism Service Design.* RIKON Group.

Damari, R. P. (2013). Searching for smart city definition: A comprehensive proposal. *International Journal of Computers and Technology, 11*(5), 2544–2551. doi:10.24297/ijct.v11i5.1142

Davenport, T., Guha, A., Grewal, D., & Bressgott, T. (2020). How artificial intelligence will change the future of marketing. *Journal of the Academy of Marketing Science, 48*(1), 24–42. doi:10.100711747-019-00696-0

Davidde, B. (2004). Methods and strategies for the conservation and museum display in situ of underwater cultural heritage. *Archaeologia Maritima Mediterranea, 1,* 137–150.

Dawson, B. (2008). Facilitating Innovation: Opportunity in Times of Change. *Museum Management and Curatorship, 23*(4), 313–331. doi:10.1080/09647770802517316

Dawson, E. (2014). "Not Designed for Us": How Science Museums and Science Centers Socially Exclude Low-Income, Minority Ethnic Groups. *Science Education, 98*(6), 981–1008. doi:10.1002ce.21133 PMID:25574059

Day, M. (1998). *CEDARS: Digital preservation and metadata.* Conference: 6th DELOS Workshop: Preservation of Digital Information, Tomar, Portugal.

De Bruyn, A., Viswanathan, V., Beh, Y. S., Brock, J. K.-U., & von Wangenheim, F. (2020). Artificial Intelligence and Marketing: Pitfalls and Opportunities. *Journal of Interactive Marketing, 51,* 91–105. doi:10.1016/j.intmar.2020.04.007

De Mauro, A., Greco, M., & Grimaldi, M. (2016). A formal definition of Big Data based on its essential features. Library Review, 65(3). doi:10.1108/LR-06-2015-0061

Deacon, H., Dondolo, L., Mrubata, M., & Prosalendis, S. (2004). *The subtle power of intangible heritage: Legal and financial instruments for safeguarding intangible heritage.* HSRC Publishing.

Dedehayır, H. (2012). *Sürdürülebilir kültür turizmi. Çevre ve Kültür Değerlerini Koruma ve Tanıtma Vakfı.* Retrieved from https://www.cekulvakfi.org.tr/makale/surdurulebilir-kultur-turizmi

Del Rio-Chanona, R. M., Mealy, P., Pichler, A., Lafond, F., & Farmer, J. D. (2020). Supply and demand shocks in the COVID-19 pandemic: An industry and occupation perspective. *Oxford Review of Economic Policy, 36*(1, Supplement_1), 94–137. doi:10.1093/oxrep/graa033

Del Vecchio, P., Mele, G., Ndou, V., & Secundo, G. (2018a). Open innovation and social big data for sustainability: Evidence from the tourism industry. *Sustainability, 10*(9), 3215. doi:10.3390u10093215

Del Vecchio, P., Mele, G., Ndou, V., & Secundo, G. (2018b). Creating value from Social Big Data: Implications for Smart Tourism Destinations. *Information Processing & Management, 54*(5), 847–860. doi:10.1016/j.ipm.2017.10.006

Deligiannis, K., Raftopoulou, P., Tryfonopoulos, C., Platis, N., & Vassilakis, C. (2020). Hydria: An Online Data Lake for Multi-Faceted Analytics in the Cultural Heritage Domain. *Big Data and Cognitive Computing, 4*(2), 7. doi:10.3390/bdcc4020007

Deligöz, K. (2014). *A study on determining the effect of experiential marketing practices on brand preference (the case of coffee world and Starbucks)* (Master Thesis). Atatürk University, Erzurum, Turkey.

Demir, C. (2006). Kent kimliği geliştirme sürecinde mekansal model tasarımı ve kent plancılarının rolü. *TMMOB Şehir Plancıları Odası Yayını, 3,* 117–122.

Demirezen, B. (2019). A Literature Review on the Availability of Augmented Reality and Virtual Reality Technology in the Tourism Sector. *International Journal of Global Tourism Research, 3*(1), 1–26.

Demunter, C. (2017, June 21). Tourism statistics: Early Adopters of Big Data. *Sixth UNWTO International Conference on Tourism Statistics Measuring Sustainable Tourism.*

Depuit, J. (1848). On the measurement of utility of public works. *International Economics Papers, 2.*

Deterding, S., Dixon, D., Khaled, R., & Nacke, L. E. (2011a). Gamification: Toward a definition. *CHI 2011 Gamification Workshop Proceedings.*

Deterding, S., Dixon, D., Khaled, R., & Nacke, L. E. (2011b). From game design elements to gamefulness: defining "gamification". *Proceedings of the 15th International Academic Mindtrek Conference: Envisioning Future Media Environments,* 9-15. 10.1145/2181037.2181040

Dewailly, J. M. (1999). Sustainable tourist space: From reality to virtual reality? *Tourism Geographies Journal, 1*(1), 41–55. doi:10.1080/14616689908721293

Dhar, V., & Chang, E. (2009). Does chatter matter? The impact of user-generated content on music sales. *Journal of Interactive Marketing, 23*(4), 300–307. doi:10.1016/j.intmar.2009.07.004

Dickinson, J. E., Hibbert, J. F., & Filimonau, V. (2016). Mobile technology and the tourist experience: (Dis) connection at the campsite. *Tourism Management, 57*, 193–201. doi:10.1016/j.tourman.2016.06.005

Dictionary, C. (2021). Accessed on October 1, 2021. https://dictionary.cambridge.org/dictionary/english/culture>

Diemer, J., Alpers, G. W., Peperkorn, H. M., Shiban, Y., & Mühlberger, A. (2015). The impact of perception and presence on emotional reactions: A review of research in virtual reality. Frontiers in Psychology, 6, 26. doi:10.3389/fpsyg.2015.00026

Dierking, L. D., Falk, J. H., & Storksdieck, M. (2013). 34 learning from neighboring fields: conceptualizing outcomes of environmental education within the framework of free-choice learning experiences. In International Handbook of Research on Environmental Education. Routledge.

Dilek, S. (2017). *Internet of Things Based Remote Healthcare Monitoring Application* (Master Thesis). Gazi University Institute of Social Sciences, Ankara.

Dimitropoulos, K., Manitsaris, S., Tsalakanidou, F., Nikolopoulos, S., Denby, B., Al Kork, S., ... Grammalidis, N. (2014, January). Capturing the intangible an introduction to the i-Treasures project. In *Proceedings international conference on computer vision theory and applications (VISAPP)* (pp. 773-781). IEEE.

Dirksmeier, P., & Helbrecht, I. (2015). Resident perceptions of new urban tourism: A neglected geography of prejudice. *Geography Compass, 9*(5), 276–285. doi:10.1111/gec3.12201

Doğan, K., & Arslantekin, S. (2016). Big data: Its importance, structure, and current status. *Ankara DTCF Journal, 56*(1), 15–36.

Dogget, L. (1993). Multi-cultural tourism development offers a new dimension in travel. *Business America, 114*(18), 8–10.

Dokmetas, G. (2016). *Internet of Things with Arduino and Raspberry PI, (1 st. Edition).* Dikeyeksen Publications.

Dolan, R., Seo, Y., & Kemper, J. (2019). Complaining practices on social media in tourism: A value co-creation and co-destruction perspective. *Tourism Management, 73*, 35–45. doi:10.1016/j.tourman.2019.01.017

Dolcos, F., & Cabeza, R. (2002). Event-related potentials of emotional memory: Encoding pleasant, unpleasant, and neutral pictures. *Cognitive, Affective & Behavioral Neuroscience, 2*(3), 252–263. doi:10.3758/CABN.2.3.252 PMID:12775189

Dolgos, G. (2018). *Tourism industry benefit greatly from big data.* Retrieved from https://www.tourismreview.com/tourism-industry-relies-more-on-the-big-data-news10492

Dolnicar, S. (2002). *Activity-based market sub-segmentation of cultural tourists.* Academic Press.

Domingue, J., Fensel, D., & Hendler, J. A. (2011). Introduction to the semantic web technologies. In J. Domingue, D. Fensel, & J. A. Hendler (Eds.), *Handbook of semantic web technologies* (pp. 4–41). Springer. doi:10.1007/978-3-540-92913-0_1

Döpker, A., Brockmann, T., & Stieglitz, S. (2013). Use cases for gamification in virtual museums. *Proceedings of the Jahrestagung der Gesellschaft für Informatik 2013*, 2308–2321.

Dorsi, S. (2016). *Travel industry – wearables don't offer much.* Retrieved form https://www.tourismreview.com/hotel-of-the-future-would-include-lots-of-technologynews10616

Dotan, A., & Zaphiris, P. (2010). A cross-cultural analysis of Flickr users from Peru, Israel, Iran, Taiwan and the UK. *International Journal of Web Based Communities, 6*(3), 284–302. doi:10.1504/IJWBC.2010.033753

Dou, J., Qin, J., Jin, Z., & Li, Z. (2018). Knowledge graph based on domain ontology and natural language processing technology for Chinese intangible cultural heritage. *Journal of Visual Languages and Computing*, *48*, 19–28. doi:10.1016/j.jvlc.2018.06.005

Doulamis, N., Doulamis, A., Ioannidis, C., Klein, M., & Ioannides, M. (2017). Modelling of static and moving objects: Digitizing tangible and intangible cultural heritage. In *Mixed reality and gamification for cultural heritage* (pp. 567–589). Springer. doi:10.1007/978-3-319-49607-8_23

Dragoni, M., Tonelli, S., & Moretti, G. (2017). A knowledge management architecture for digital cultural heritage. *Journal on Computing and Cultural Heritage*, *10*(3), 1–18. doi:10.1145/3012289

Driver, F., & Martins, L. (2006). Shipwreck and salvage in the tropics: The case of HMS Thetis, 1830–1854. *Journal of Historical Geography*, *32*(3), 539–562. doi:10.1016/j.jhg.2005.10.010

Dromgoole, S. (2013). Reflections on the position of the major maritime powers with respect to the UNESCO Convention on the Protection of the Underwater Cultural Heritage 2001. *Marine Policy*, *38*, 116–123. doi:10.1016/j.marpol.2012.05.027

Drummond, M. F., O'Brien, B., & Stoddart, G. L. (2005). *Methods for the economic evaluation of health care programs*. Oxford University Press.

Drury, G. (2008). Opinion piece: Social media: Should marketers engage and how can it be done effectively? *Journal of Direct, Data and Digital Marketing Practice*, *9*(3), 274–277. doi:10.1057/palgrave.dddmp.4350096

Du Cros, H., & McKercher, B. (2015). *Cultural Tourism*. Routledge.

Duan, W., Yu, Y., Cao, Q., & Levy, S. (2016). Exploring the Impact of Social Media on Hotel Service Performance. *Cornell Hospitality Quarterly*, *57*(3), 282–296. doi:10.1177/1938965515620483

Dubey, A. K. (2017). *Future technology and service industry: A case study of travel and tourism industry*. Informatic-journal.com

Durmaz, C., Bulut, Y., & Tankuş, E. (2018). The integration of virtual reality into tourism: Application in the hotels with five star in Samsun. *Turkish Journal of Marketing*, *3*(1), 32–49. doi:10.30685/tujom.v3i1.27

Du, X., Liechty, T., Santos, C. A., & Park, J. (2020). 'I want to record and share my wonderful journey': Chinese Millennials' production and sharing of short-form travel videos on TikTok or Douyin. *Current Issues in Tourism*, 1–13. Advance online publication. doi:10.1080/13683500.2020.1810212

Duxbury, N., & Richards, G. (2019). A research agenda for creative tourism. In N. Duxbury & G. Richards (Eds.), *A Research Agenda for Creative Tourism* (1st ed.). doi:10.4337/9781788110723

Dwivedi, M., Yadav, A., & Venkatesh, U. (2012). Use of social media by national tourism organizations: A preliminary analysis. *Information Technology & Tourism*, *13*(2), 93–103. doi:10.3727/109830512X13258778487353

Dwivedi, Y. K., Hughes, L., Ismagilova, E., Aarts, G., Coombs, C., Crick, T., ... Williams, M. D. (2019). Artificial Intelligence (AI): Multidisciplinary perspectives on emerging challenges, opportunities, and agenda for research, practice and policy. *International Journal of Information Management*, *101994*. Advance online publication. doi:10.1016/j.ijinfomgt.2019.08.002

Echtner, C. M., & Jamal, T. B. (1997). The disciplinary dilemma of tourism studies. *Annals of Tourism Research*, *24*(4), 868–883. doi:10.1016/S0160-7383(97)00060-1

Economic Commission for Latin America and the Caribbean (ECLAC). (2020). *The impact of the COVID-19 pandemic on the tourism sector in Latin America and the Caribbean, and options for a sustainable and resilient recovery.* United Nations Publication.

Egger, R. (2017). *Booking via VR?* Available at: http://www.virtual-reality-in-tourism.com/booking-via-Virtual Reality/

Egger, R., & Jooss, M. (2010). mTourism. Wiesbaden: Gabler Springer.

Egger, I., Lei, S. I., & Wassler, P. (2020). Digital free tourism–An exploratory study of tourist motivations. *Tourism Management, 79*, 104098. doi:10.1016/j.tourman.2020.104098

Eisenberg, B., & Eisenberg, J. (2006). *Call to Action: Secret Formulas to Improve Online Results.* Thomas Nelson.

Elazhary, H. (2019). Internet of Things (IoT), Mobile Cloud, Cloudlet, Mobile IoT, IoT Cloud, Fog, Mobile Edge, and Edge Emerging Computing Paradigms. *Disambiguation and Research Directions Journal of Network and Computer Applications, 128*, 105–140. doi:10.1016/j.jnca.2018.10.021

Electronic Resources Preservation and Access Network (ERPANET). (2021). Retrieved 07.05.2021, from https://www.erpanet.org/

Elfadaly, A., Attia, W., Qelichi, M. M., Murgante, B., & Lasaponara, R. (2018). Management of Cultural Heritage Sites Using Remote Sensing Indices and Spatial Analysis Techniques. *Surveys in Geophysics, 39*(6), 1347–1377. doi:10.100710712-018-9489-8

Eltresy, N. A., Dardeer, O. M., Al-Habal, A., Elhariri, E., Hassan, A. H., Khattab, A., Elsheakh, D. N., Taie, S. A., Mostafa, H., Elsadek, H. A., & Abdallah, E. A. (2019). RF energy harvesting IoT system for museum ambience control with deep learning. *Sensors (Basel), 19*(20), 4465. doi:10.339019204465 PMID:31618881

Emekli, G. (2012). *Kültür Mirasının Turizm Aracılığı ile Değerlendirilmesi: Kültürel Turizm ve İzmir. Buca İlçesinin Ekoturizm ve Kültür Turizmi Sektör Analizi Projesi, Kültür Turizmi Çalıştayı, 8 Şubat 2012.* İzmir Kalkınma Ajansı-Buca Belediyesi, Buca.

Encalada, L., Portugal, I. B., Ferreira, C. C., & Rocha, J. (2017). Identifying tourist places of interest based on digital imprints: Towards a sustainable smart city. *Sustainability, 9*(12), 1–19. doi:10.3390u9122317

Enhuber, M. (2015). Art, space and technology: How the digitisation and digitalisation of art space affect the consumption of art - a critical approach. *Digital Creativity, 26*(2), 121–137. doi:10.1080/14626268.2015.1035448

EPCglobal. (2021). https://web.archive.org/web/20070303054158/http://www.epcglobaltr.org/rfid.php

Epstein, J. M. (1995). Global positioning system (GPS): Defining the legal issues of its expanding civil use. *Journal of Air Law and Commerce, 61*(1), 243–285.

Erbaş, Ç., & Demirer, V. (2014). Eğitimde artırılmış gerçeklik uygulamaları: Google Glass örneği. *Journal of Instructional Technologies and Teacher Education, 3*(2), 8–16.

Ercole, E. (2013). Smart tourism: Il ruolo dell' informazione social [Smart tourism: the role of social information]. *Annali del Tourismo, 2*, 35–48.

Erevelles, S., Fukawa, N., & Swayne, L. (2016). Big Data consumer analytics and the transformation of marketing. *Journal of Business Research, 69*(2), 897–904. doi:10.1016/j.jbusres.2015.07.001

ERPANET. (2021). Accessed on June 14, 20021. https://www.erpanet.org/about.php

Ertürk, N. (2020). Preservation of digitized intangible cultural heritage in museum storage. *Milli Folklor, 16*(128), 100–110.

Eschner, K. (2017). The Bizarre Story of 'Vasa,' the Ship That Keeps On Giving. *Smithsonian Magazine*. https://www.smithsonianmag.com/smart-news/bizarre-story-vasa-ship-keeps-giving-180964328/

Esen, F., & Türkay, B. (2017). Big data applications in tourism industries. *Journal of Tourism and Gastronomy Studies*, *5*(4), 92–115. doi:10.21325/jotags.2017.140

Etymology Dictionary. (2021). Virtual. *Online Etymology Dictionary*. https://www.etymonline.com/search?q=virtual

EU. (2021). https://smarttourismcapital.eu

Eur-Lex. (2008). *İ2010: Digital libraries*. Accessed on June 19, 2021. http lex.europa.eu/legal-content/EN/TXT/?uri=URISERV%3Al24226i

European Best Destinations. (2019). *European Best Destinations 2019*. Retrieved October 14, 2019, from https://www.europeanbestdestinations.com/european-best-destinations-2019/

European Commission. (2016*). İ-treasures: capturing the intangible cultural heritage and learning the rare know-how of living human treasures*. https://ec.europa.eu/digital-single-market/en/blog/i-treasures-capturing-intangible-cultural-heritage-and-learning-rare-know-how-living-human

European Commission. (2021). *European Capitals of Smart Tourism*. Retrieved on 18.06.2021, https://smart-tourism-capital.ec.europa.eu/competition-winners-2020/malaga/malaga-winner-2020-european-capitals-smart-tourism_en

European Union (EU). (2021). *2020 European capitals of smart tourism*. https://smarttourismcapital.eu

Europeana. (2016). Accessed on June 19, 2021. http://www.europeana.eu/portal/

Evans, D. (2011). *How the next evolution of the internet is changing everything*. https://www.cisco.com/c/dam/en_us/about/ac79/docs/innov/IoT_IBSG_0411FINAL.pdf

Evans, M. (2020). *5 Stats You Need To Know About Digital Consumers In 2020*. Available at: https://www.forbes.com/sites/michelleevans1/2020/02/04/5-stats-you-need-to-know-about-digital-consumers-in-2020/#6412f4335b0f

Evans, D. (2008). *Social media marketing: An hour a day*. Wiley Publishing.

FaberNovel. (2020). *Google Arts & Culture: Virtual visits to museums and monuments*. Retrieved from https://bit.ly/3ANLd0O

Facebook Developers. (2019). *Page. Facebook Developers*. https://developers.facebook.com/docs/graph-api/reference/page

Facebook for Business. (2020). *Facebook Pages: Calls to Action' Facebook for Business*. https://www.facebook.com/business/news/call-to-action-button

Facebook. (2020). *How is a Page's star rating determined? Facebook*. https://www.facebook.com/help/500762053364226

FaladeObalade, T. A., & Dubey, S. (2014). Managing tourism as a source of revenue and foreign direct investment inflow in a developing country: The Jordanian experience. *International Journal of Academic Research in Economics and Management Sciences*, *3*(3), 16–42.

Falk, J. H., Scott, C., Dierking, L., Rennie, L., & Jones, M. C. (2004). Interactives and visitor learning. *Curator (New York, N.Y.)*, *47*(2), 171–198. doi:10.1111/j.2151-6952.2004.tb00116.x

Farazis, G., Thomopoulos, C., Bourantas, C., Mitsigkola, S., & Thomopoulos, S. C. (2019). Digital approaches for public outreach in cultural heritage: The case study of iGuide Knossos and Ariadne's Journey. *Digital Applications in Archaeology and Cultural Heritage*, *15*, e00126. doi:10.1016/j.daach.2019.e00126

Faria, M., & Almeida, R. (2006). A problemática da "identidade" e o lugar do "património" num mundo crescentemente cosmopolita. *Comunicação e Cultura, 1*, 117–133.

Fazenda, N. (2014). Turismo em Portugal: Reflexões para uma Política Nacional de Turismo. In C. Costa (Ed.), *Turismo nos Países Lusófonos: Conhecimento, Estratégia e Territórios* (pp. 293–312). Escolar Editora.

Felicetti, A. M., Volpentesta, A. P., & Ammirato, S. (2019). Analyzing app-based food information services: The case of Olive Oil sector. *VINE Journal of Information and Knowledge Management Systems, 50*(3), 427–453. doi:10.1108/VJIKMS-05-2019-0062

Femenia-Serra, F., & Ivars-Baidal, J. A. (2021). Do smart tourism destinations really work? The case of Benidorm. *Asia Pacific Journal of Tourism Research, 26*(4), 365–384. doi:10.1080/10941665.2018.1561478

Femenia-Serra, F., Neuhofer, B., & Ivars-Baidal, J. A. (2019). Towards a conceptualisation of smart tourists and their role within the smart destination scenario. *Service Industries Journal, 39*(2), 109–133. doi:10.1080/02642069.2018.1508458

Ferdani, D., Pagano, A., & Farouk, M. (2014). *Terminology, Definitions and Types for Virtual Museums.* Retrieved from http://www.v-must.net/sites/default/files/D2.1c%20V_Must_TERMINOLOGY_V2014_FINAL.pdf

Fereidouni, M. A., & Kawa, A. (2019). Dark side of digital transformation in tourism. In *Asian Conference on Intelligent Information and Database Systems.* Springer. 10.1007/978-3-030-14802-7_44

Ferhat, S. (2016). Dijital dünyanın gerçekliği, gerçek dünyanın sanallığı bir dijital medya ürünü olarak sanal gerçeklik. *Trt Akademi, 1*(2), 724–746.

Ferrão, F. (2020). *Seis em cada 10 empresas a nível global aceleraram a sua transformação digital durante a pandemia.* Retrieved from https://bityli.com/lGwKc

Ferreira, A. M. (2014). O Turismo como Fator de Regeneração e Desenvolvimento de Meios Urbanos e Rurais: Do Turismo Urbano ao Turismo Criativo. In Turismo nos Países Lusófonos: Conhecimento, Estratégia e Territórios (pp. 85–100). Lisboa: Escolar Editora.

Ferreira, J., & Sousa, B. (2020) Experiential Marketing as Leverage for Growth of Creative Tourism: A Co-creative Process. Advances in Tourism, Technology and Smart Systems. Smart Innovation, Systems and Technologies, 171, 567-577. doi:10.1007/978-981-15-2024-2_49

Fes, N. (2018). *Hotel 4.0 - what the hotel of the future looks like.* Retrieved from https://www.tourismreview.com/hotel-of-the-future-would-include-lots-of-technologynews10616

Finger, M., & Razaghi, M. (2017). Conceptualizing "Smart Cities". *Informatik Spektrum, 4*(1), 6–13. doi:10.100700287-016-1002-5

First. (2020). Retrieved from: https://firstairlines.jp/

Flayinglab. (2020). Retrieved from: https://www.flyinglab.aero/en/about/

Fletcher-Tomenius, P., & Forrest, C. (2000). Historic wreck in international waters: Conflict or consensus? *Marine Policy, 24*(1), 1–10. doi:10.1016/S0308-597X(99)00019-6

Floch, J., & Jiang, S. (2015). *One place, many stories digital storytelling for cultural heritage discovery in the landscape. In 2015 Digital Heritage* (Vol. 2). IEEE.

Forbes.com. (2018, January 24). *Here's How Much Instagram Likes Influence Millennials' Choice Of Travel Destinations.* Retrieved September 19, 2019, from https://www.forbes.com/sites/andrewarnold/2018/01/24/heres-how-much-instagram-likes-influence-millennials-choice-of-travel-destinations/#7d3c8f1a4eba

Fortune. (2007). Luxury goes mass market. *Fortune Magazine.*

Fortune. (2021). *One year later: 15 ways life has changed since the onset of the COVID pandemic.* https://fortune.com/2021/03/09/covid-pandemic-how-life-has-changed-coronavirus-one-year-later-march-2020/

Fotis, J., Buhalis, D., & Rossides, N. (2011). Social media impact on holiday travel planning: The case of the Russian and the FSU markets. *International Journal of Online Marketing, 1*(4), 1–19. doi:10.4018/ijom.2011100101

Frade, R. (2020). *Tecnologia e Pandemia: Oportunidades e Ameaças.* Retrieved from https://bityli.com/geI9L

Franchi, E. (2017). *What is Cultural Heritage?* Available at https://www.khanacademy.org/humanities/art-history-basics/beginners-art- history/a/what-is-cultural-heritage

Frank, R. H. (2000). Why is Cost-Best Analysis So Controversial. *Journal of Legal Studies,* In Kwangseon, H. (2016). Cost-benefit analysis: Its usage and critiques. *Journal of Public Affairs, 16*(1), 75–80.

Frank, R. H., & Sunstein, C. R. (2002). Why cost –Benefit Analysis and Relative Position. *The University of Chicago Law Review. University of Chicago. Law School,* (68), 323–374.

Freina, L., & Canessa, A. (2015). Immersive vs desktop virtual reality in game based learning. *European Conference on Games Based Learning,* 195.

Frey, B. S., & Briviba, A. (2021). A policy proposal to deal with excessive cultural tourism. *European Planning Studies, 29*(4), 601–618. doi:10.1080/09654313.2021.1903841

Fritz, F., Susperregui, A., & Linaza, M. T. (2005). Enhancing Cultural Tourism Experiences with Augmented Reality Technologies. *The 6th International Symposium on Virtual Reality, Archaeology and Cultural Heritage VAST,* 1-6.

Fuchs, M., Höpken, W., & Lexhagen, M. (2014). Big data analytics for knowledge generation in tourism destinations - A case from Sweden. *Journal of Destination Marketing & Management, 3*(4), 198–209. Advance online publication. doi:10.1016/j.jdmm.2014.08.002

Füller, H., & Michel, B. (2014). 'Stop Being a Tourist!' New Dynamics of Urban Tourism in Berlin-Kreuzberg. *International Journal of Urban and Regional Research, 38*(4), 1304–1318. doi:10.1111/1468-2427.12124

Funk, J. B., Baldacci, H. B., Pasold, T., & Baumgardner, J. (2004). Violence exposure in real-life, video games, television, movies, and the internet: Is there desensitization? *Journal of Adolescence, 27*(1), 23–39. doi:10.1016/j.adolescence.2003.10.005 PMID:15013258

Gaberli, Ü. (2019). Tourism in Digital Age: An Explanation for the Impacts of Virtual, Augmented and Mixed Reality Technologies on Tourist Experiences. *Journal Of Tourism Intelligence and Smartness, 2*(2), 61–69.

Gajdošík, T., Maráková, V., & Kučerová, J. (2020). From mass tourists to smart tourists: A perspective article. *Tourism Review, 76*(1), 47–50. doi:10.1108/TR-07-2019-0285

Gajdošík, T., & Orelová, A. (2020). Smart Technologies for Smart Tourism Development. In *Computer Science On-line Conference.* Springer.

Gandhi, R. D., & Patel, D. S. (2018). Virtual reality–opportunities and challenges. *Virtual Reality (Waltham Cross), 5*(1), 482–490.

Gandomi, A., & Haider, M. (2015). Beyond the hype: Big data concepts, methods and analytics. *International Journal of Information Management, 35*(2), 137–144. doi:10.1016/j.ijinfomgt.2014.10.007

Gantz, J., & Reinsel, D. (2011). Extracting Value from Chaos State of the Universe: An Executive Summary. *IDC IView.*

Gao, H. (2021). Big data development of tourism resources based on 5G network and internet of things system. *Microprocessors and Microsystems*, *80*, 103567. doi:10.1016/j.micpro.2020.103567

Garau, C. (2014). Smart paths for advanced management of cultural heritage. *Regional Studies, Regional Science*, *1*(1), 286–293. doi:10.1080/21681376.2014.973439

García-Hernández, M., de la Calle-Vaquero, M., & Yubero, C. (2017). Cultural heritage and urban tourism: Historic city centres under pressure. *Sustainability*, *9*(8), 1346. doi:10.3390u9081346

Gare, A. (2020). *The Palgrave Encyclopedia of the Possible*. Palgrave.

Garg, R., Rahman, Z., & Qureshi, M. N. (2014). Measuring customer experience in banks: Scale development and validation. *Journal of Modelling in Management*, *9*(1), 87–117. doi:10.1108/JM2-07-2012-0023

Garibaldi, R. (2015). The use of Web 2.0 tools by Italian contemporary art museums. *Museum Management and Curatorship*, *30*(3), 230–243. doi:10.1080/09647775.2015.1043329

Garibaldi, R., & Pozzi, A. (2021). Food museums as cultural institutions and tourist attractions: Evidence from Italy. *Journal of Gastronomy and Tourism*, *5*(2), 83–94. doi:10.3727/216929720X15968961037935

Garipağaoğlu-Uğur, N. (2020). İçsel ve Dışsal Motivasyon Araçlarının Örgütsel Bağlılığa Etkisi: Turizm Sektöründe Bir Araştırma. *IBAD Sosyal Bilimler Dergisi*, 95-115.

Gartner. (2020). *Gartner glossary*. Retrieved from https://www.gartner.com/en/information-technology/glossary/digitalization

Gasimova, R. T., & Abbasli, R. N. (2020). Advancement of the search process for digital heritage by utilizing artificial intelligence algorithms. *Expert Systems with Applications*, *158*, 113559. doi:10.1016/j.eswa.2020.113559

Gavilan, D., Avello, M., & Martinez-Navarro, G. (2018). The influence of online ratings and reviews on hotel booking consideration. *Tourism Management*, *66*, 53–61. doi:10.1016/j.tourman.2017.10.018

Gebbensleben, S., Dittmann, J., & Vielhauer, C. (2006). February. Multimodal audio guide for museums and exhibitions. In *Multimedia on Mobile Devices II* (Vol. 6074, p. 60740S). International Society for Optics and Photonics. doi:10.1117/12.641404

General, A. (2015). *Transforming our world: the 2030 agenda for sustainable development*. UN.

Georgakopoulos, V. (2008). Food safety training: A model HACCP instructional technique. *TOURISMOS: An International Multidisciplinary Journal of Tourism*, *5*(1), 55–72.

George, G., Haas, M. R., & Pentland, A. (2014). Big Data and Management. *Academy of Management Journal*, *57*(2), 321–326. doi:10.5465/amj.2014.4002

Gershenfeld, N. (1999). *When things start to think*. Henry Holt and Company, Inc.

Getz, D., & Wicks, B. (1993). Editorial. *International Journal of Festival Management and Event Tourism*, *1*(1), 1–3. PMID:12287128

Ghermandi, A., Camacho-Valdez, V., & Trejo-Espinosa, H. (2020). Social media-based analysis of cultural ecosystem services and heritage tourism in a coastal region of Mexico. *Tourism Management*, *77*, 104002. doi:10.1016/j.tourman.2019.104002

Giannoulakis, S., & Tsapatsoulis, N. (2016). Evaluating the descriptive power of Instagram hashtags. *Journal of Innovation in Digital Ecosystems*, *3*(2), 114–129. doi:10.1016/j.jides.2016.10.001

Giffinger, R., & Gudrun, H. (2010). *Smart cities ranking: an effective instrument for the positioning of the cities? ACE: Architecture, City and Environment*. doi:10.5821/ace.v4i12.2483

Gigante, G., & Tomassini, G. (1993). *Deformations of complex structures on a real lie algebra in complex analysis and geometry*. Springer.

Girvan, C. (2018). What is a virtual world? definition and classification. *Educational Technology Research and Development*, *66*(5), 1087–1100. doi:10.100711423-018-9577-y

Global. (2020). Retrieved from: https://www.turizmglobal.com/sanal-gerceklik-vr-jolly-tur-tarafindan-acentecilik-sektorune-girdi/

GlobalData Technology. (2018). *Top 6 technology trends to watch out for in the travel and tourism industry in 2018*. Retrieved on 18.06.2021, https://www.globaldata.com/top-6-technology-trends-watch-travel-tourism-industry-2018/

Goeldner, C. R., & Ritchie, J. R. B. (2003). *Tourism principles, practices, philosophies*. John Wiley & Sons.

Goeldner, C. R., Ritchie, J. R., & Mcintosh, R. (2000). *Tourism; Principles, practices, philosophies*. John Wiley & Sons.

Goes, C. (1998). *Beja. XX Séculos de História de uma Cidade, I e II volumes*. Câmara Municipal de Beja.

Goetz, J., Kiesler, S., & Powers, A. (2003). Matching robot appearance and behavior to tasks to improve human-robot cooperation, *Proceedings of the IEEE International Symposium on Robot and Human Interactive Communication*. 10.1109/ROMAN.2003.1251796

Göktaş Kulualp, H., & Sarı, Ö. (2020). Smart tourism, smart cities, and smart destinations as knowledge management tools. In E. Çeltek (Ed.), *Handbook of Research on Smart Technology Applications in the Tourism Industry* (pp. 371–390). IGI Global Disseminator of Knowledge. doi:10.4018/978-1-7998-1989-9.ch017

Gomes, E. L., Gandara, J. M., & Baidal, J. A. I. (2017). Is it important to be a smart tourism destination? public managers' understanding of destinations in the state of Parana. *Brazilian Journal of Tourism Research*, *11*(3), 503–536.

Gomes, L., Bellon, O. R. P., & Silva, L. (2014). 3D reconstruction methods for digital preservation of cultural heritage: A survey. *Pattern Recognition Letters*, *50*, 3–14. doi:10.1016/j.patrec.2014.03.023

Gomez, D., Burdea, G., & Langrana, N. (1995). Integration of the Rutgers Master II in a Virtual Reality Simulation. *Virtual Reality Annual International Symposium*, 198-202. 10.1109/VRAIS.1995.512496

Gonçalves, F. (2018). *A Interpretação do Património como fator de desenvolvimento do Turismo Cultural e Criativo. O caso do Galo de Barcelos*. Tese de Doutoramento, Universidade de Aveiro.

Gonçalves, G. (2020). Are hospitals our friends? An exploratory study on the role of Facebook in hospital organizations' dialogic communication. *Health Marketing Quarterly*, *37*(3), 265–279. doi:10.1080/07359683.2020.1805898 PMID:32835646

Gong, Y. (2021). Application of virtual reality teaching method and artificial intelligence technology in digital media art creation. *Ecological Informatics*, *63*, 101304. doi:10.1016/j.ecoinf.2021.101304

González Santa Cruz, F., Pemberthy Gallo, L. S., López-Guzmán, T., & Pérez Gálvez, J. C. (2020). Tourist segmentation in an intangible heritage setting: The Holy Week processions in the city of Popayán, Colombia. *Journal of Heritage Tourism*, *15*(5), 485–499. doi:10.1080/1743873X.2019.1692854

Gonzalo, F. (2020). *Why TikTok Matters For Travel Brands*. https://fredericgonzalo.com/en/2020/01/06/why-tiktok-matters-for-travel-brands/

Goode, L. (2019). Get Ready to Hear a Lot More About 'XR'. *Wired.* https://www.wired.com/story/what-is-xr/

Goode, G. B. (1896). On the classification of museums. *Science, 3*(57), 154–161. doi:10.1126cience.3.57.154 PMID:17741599

Google Arts& Culture. (2021). https://artsandculture.google.com/

Gössling, S. (2020). Technology, ICT and tourism: From big data to the big picture. *Journal of Sustainable Tourism,* 1–10.

Gössling, S., Scott, D., & Hall, M. C. (2020). Pandemics, tourism and global change: A rapid assessment of COVID-19. *Journal of Sustainable Tourism, 29*(1), 1–20. doi:10.1080/09669582.2020.1758708

Gostin, L. O., Cohen, I. G., & Shaw, J. (2021). Digital health passes in the age of COVID-19: Are "vaccine passports" lawful and ethical? *Journal of the American Medical Association, 325*(19), 1933–1934. doi:10.1001/jama.2021.5283 PMID:33825831

Grabosky, P. (2001). The prevention and control of economic crime. In Corruption and Anticorruption. Canberra: Asia Pacific Press.

Graburn, N. (1989). Tourism: The sacred journey. In Hosts and guests, the anthropology of tourism. University of Philadelphia Press.

Gravari-Barbas, M., & Guinand, S. (2017). *Tourism and Gentrification in Contemporary Metropolises.* Routledge., doi:10.4324/9781315629759

Gray, B., Young, A., & Blomfield, T. (2015). Altered Lives: Assessing the Effectiveness of Digital Storytelling as a Form of Communication Design. *Continuum, 29*(4), 635–649. doi:10.1080/10304312.2015.1025359

Graziano, T., & Privitera, D. (2020). Cultural heritage, tourist attractiveness and augmented reality: Insights from Italy. *Journal of Heritage Tourism, 15*(6), 666–679. doi:10.1080/1743873X.2020.1719116

Greenfield, D. N. (1999). *Virtual addiction: Sometimes new technology can create new problems.* Retrieved from: http://www.virtual-addiction.com/pdf/ nature_internet_addiction.pdf

Greenwood, D. J. (1972). Tourism as an agent of change: A Spanish Basque case. *Ethnology, 11*(1), 80–91. doi:10.2307/3773161

Gretzel, U. (2018). From smart destinations to smart tourism regions. *Investigaciones Regionales – Journal of Regional Research, 42,* 171-184.

Gretzel, U. (2011). Intelligent systems in tourism: A social science perspective. *Annals of Tourism Research, 38*(3), 757–779. doi:10.1016/j.annals.2011.04.014

Gretzel, U. (2017). Influencer marketing in travel and tourism. In *Advances in social media for travel, tourism and hospitality* (pp. 147–156). Routledge. doi:10.4324/9781315565736-13

Gretzel, U., Fuchs, M., Baggio, R., Hoepken, W., Law, R., Neidhardt, J., Pesonen, J., Zanker, M., & Xiang, Z. (2020). e-Tourism beyond COVID-19: A call for transformative research. *Information Technology & Tourism, 22*(2), 187–203. doi:10.100740558-020-00181-3

Gretzel, U., & Jamal, T. (2009). Conceptualizing the creative tourist class: Technology, mobility, and tourism experiences. *Tourism Analysis, 14*(4), 471–481. doi:10.3727/108354209X12596287114219

Gretzel, U., Reino, S., Kopera, S., & Koo, C. (2015). Smart tourism challenges. *Journal of Tourism, 16*(1), 41–47.

Gretzel, U., Sigala, M., Koo, C., & Lensfus, C. (2015). Smart tourism for understanding smart tourism ecosystems. *Computers in Human Behavior*, *50*, 558–563. doi:10.1016/j.chb.2015.03.043

Gretzel, U., Sigala, M., Yiang, Z., & Koo, C. (2015). Smart tourism foundations and developments. *Electronic Markets*, *25*(3), 179–188. doi:10.100712525-015-0196-8

Grønflaten, Ø. (2009). Predicting travelers' choice of information sources and information channels. *Journal of Travel Research*, *48*(2), 230–244. doi:10.1177/0047287509332333

Guan, Z. (2021). Digital rescue protection of representative inheritors of intangible cultural heritage in the information age. *Journal of Physics: Conference Series*, *1744*(4), 042124. doi:10.1088/1742-6596/1744/4/042124

Güdüm, S. (2016). Sanal yaşamlar ve bilgisayar oyunlarinda pazarlanan şiddet. *Journal of International Social Research*, *9*(42), 1986. doi:10.17719/jisr.20164216306

Guerra, A. (2010). - Algumas observações sobre a Escrita do Sudoeste. *Xelb*, *10*, 103–113.

Guidelines, C. (2005). *Good practice guide*. Accessed on June 14, 2021. https://www.calimera.org/Countries/Turkey.aspx

Guillory, J. E., & Sundar, S. S. (2014). How Does Web Site Interactivity Affect Our Perceptions of an Organization? *Journal of Public Relations Research*, *26*(1), 44–61. doi:10.1080/1062726X.2013.795866

Gülcan, B. (2010). Body of Cultural Tourism in Turkey and Need of Product Differentiation Based on Tangible Cultural Assets. *Journal of Business Studies*, *2*(1), 99–120.

Gundecha, P., & Liu, H. (2012). Mining social media: A brief introduction. Tutorials in Operations Research, 1(4). doi:10.1287/educ.1120.0105

Güney, D. (2015). *The effect of experiential marketing on customer loyalty: An application for boutique hotels in Muğla* (Master Thesis). Muğla Sıtkı Koçman University, Muğla, Turkey.

Guo, Y., Liu, H., & Chai, Y. (2014). The embedding convergence of smart cities and tourism internet of things in China: An advance perspective. *Advances in Hospitality and Tourism Research*, *2*(1), 54–69.

Guo, Y., Liu, H., & Chai, Y. (2014). The embedding convergence of smart cities and tourism internet of things in China: An Advance Perspective. *Advances in Hospitality and Tourism Research*, *2*(1), 54–69.

Gupta, A., Dogra, N., & George, B. (2018). What determines tourist adoption of smartphone apps? An analysis based on the UTAUT-2 framework. *Journal of Hospitality and Tourism Technology*, *9*(1), 50–64. doi:10.1108/JHTT-02-2017-0013

Gutierrez, M., Vexo, F., & Thalmann, D. (2008). *Stepping into virtual reality*. Springer Science & Business Media. doi:10.1007/978-1-84800-117-6

Guttentag, D. A. (2010). Virtual reality: Applications and implications for tourism. *Tourism Management*, *31*(5), 637–651. doi:10.1016/j.tourman.2009.07.003

Güzel, T., & Sucaklı, G. (2020). Müze turizminde artırılmış gerçeklik teknolojisi uygulamaları; Dünya ve Türkiye örnekleri. *Journal of Tourism Research Institute*, *1*(2), 71–82.

Gyémánt, B. (2020). *Mád és Tokaj – 36 orában* [Mád and Tokaj in 36 hours]. https://balazsutazik.blog.hu/2020/07/06/mad_es_tokaj_36_oraban?fbclid=IwAR3SEDBwk2Oq8tUC2LGO3fuHdsKRxYpALE5YKxpodd7qY_On9GRy8DXJTiI

Haddad, N. A. (2010). From Ground Surveying to 3D Laser Scanner: A Review of Techniques Used for Spatial Documentation of Historic Sites. *Journal of King Saud University*, *23*(2), 109–118. doi:10.1016/j.jksues.2011.03.001

Haenlein, M., Anadol, E., Farnsworth, T., Hugo, H., Hunichen, J., & Welte, D. (2020). Navigating the New Era of Influencer Marketing: How to be Successful on Instagram, TikTok, & Co. *California Management Review*, *63*(1), 5–25. doi:10.1177/0008125620958166

Ha, J., Pérez Cortés, L. E., Su, M., Nelson, B. C., Bowman, C., & Bowman, J. D. (2021). The impact of a gamified mobile question-asking app on museum visitor group interactions: An ICAP framing. *International Journal of Computer-Supported Collaborative Learning*, *16*(3), 1–35. doi:10.100711412-021-09350-w

Halac, H. H., & Ogulmus, V. (2021). Digital Storage of Cultural Heritage Data: Openheritage3D Example. *The Turkish Online Journal of Design, Art and Communication*, *11*(2), 521–540.

Halaç, H. H., & Öğülmüş, V. (2021). Kültürel miras verilerinin dijital olarak depolanması: Openherıtage3d örneği [Digital storage of cultural heritage data: Openheritage3d example]. *The Turkish Online Journal of Design Art and Communication*, *11*(2), 521–540.

Halaweh, M. (2013). Emerging technology: What is it. *Journal of Technology Management & Innovation*, *8*(3), 108–115. doi:10.4067/S0718-27242013000400010

Hall, C. M. (1992). *Hallmark tourist events*. Belhaven Press. https://openheritage.eu/oh-project/

Han, D. (2016). *The Development of a Qualıty Function Deployment (QFD) Model for the Implementation of A Mobile Augmented Reality (AR) Tourism Application in the Context of Urban Heritage Tourism* (PhD thesis). Department of Food and Tourism Management, The Manchester Metropolitan University.

Hancock, M. (2018). *Culture is digital: executive summary, Department for Digital, Culture, Media and Sport*. Available at: www.gov.uk/government/publications/culture-is-digital/culture-is-digital

Han, D. I. D., Weber, J., Bastiaansen, M., Mitas, O., & Lub, X. (2019). Virtual and augmented reality technologies to enhance the visitor experience in cultural tourism. In *Augmented reality and virtual reality* (pp. 113–128). Springer. doi:10.1007/978-3-030-06246-0_9

Handsfield, L. J., Dean, T. R., & Cielocha, K. M. (2009). Becoming Critical Consumers and Producers of Text: Teaching Literacy with Web 1.0 and Web 2.0. *The Reading Teacher*, *63*(1), 40–50. doi:10.1598/RT.63.1.4

Han, E., Tan, M. M. J., Turk, E., Sridhar, D., Leung, G. M., Shibuya, K., Asgari, N., Oh, J., García-Basteiro, A. L., Hanefeld, J., Cook, A. R., Hsu, L. Y., Teo, Y. Y., Heymann, D., Clark, H., McKee, M., & Legido-Quigley, H. (2020). Lessons learnt from easing COVID-19 restrictions: An analysis of countries and regions in Asia Pacific and Europe. *Lancet*, *396*(10261), 1525–1534. doi:10.1016/S0140-6736(20)32007-9 PMID:32979936

Hanna, R., Rohm, A., & Crittenden, V. L. (2011). We're all connected: The power of the social media ecosystem. *Business Horizons*, *54*(3), 265–273. doi:10.1016/j.bushor.2011.01.007

Hannewijk, B., Vinella, F. L., Khan, V. J., Lykourentzou, I., Papangelis, K., & Masthoff, J. (2020). Capturing the city's heritage on-the-go: Design requirements for mobile crowdsourced cultural heritage. *Sustainability*, *12*(6), 2–20. doi:10.3390u12062429

Hansson, S. O. (2007). Philosophical problems in cost- benefit analysis. *Economics and Philosophy*, *23*(2), 163–183. doi:10.1017/S0266267107001356

Han, Y. J., Nunes, J. C., & Drèze, X. (2010). Signaling status with luxury goods: The role of brand prominence. *Journal of Marketing*, *74*(4), 15–30. doi:10.1509/jmkg.74.4.015

Harrison, C., Eckman, B., Hamilton, R., Hartswick, P., Kalagnanam, J., Paraszczak, J., & Williams, P. (2010). Foundations for smarter cities. *IBM Journal of Research and Development*, *54*(4), 1–16. doi:10.1147/JRD.2010.2048257

Hartley, J., & McWilliam, K. (Eds.). (2009). *Story circle.* Wiley-Blackwell. doi:10.1002/9781444310580

Hashem, I. A. T., Yaqoob, I., Anuar, N. B., Mokhtar, S., Gani, A., & Khan, S. U. (2015). The rise of "big data" on cloud computing: Review and open research issues. *Information Systems, 47,* 98–115. doi:10.1016/j.is.2014.07.006

Hassan, H. (2011). *Tecnologias de Informação e Turismo: Faculdade de Letras da Universidade de Coimbra Hussein Hassan e-tourism* [Unpublished master's dissertation]. Faculdade de Letras da Universidade de Coimbra, Coimbra.

Hausmann, A. (2007). Cultural tourism: Marketing challenges and opportunities for German cultural heritage. *International Journal of Heritage Studies, 13*(2), 170–184. doi:10.1080/13527250601121351

Hayashi, Y., & Morisugi, H. (2000). International comparison of background concept and methodlogy of transportation project appraisal. *Transport Policy, 7*(1), 73–88. doi:10.1016/S0967-070X(00)00015-9

Hays, S., Page, S. J., & Buhalis, D. (2013). Social media as a destination marketing tool: Its use by national tourism organizations. *Current Issues in Tourism, 16*(3), 211–239. doi:10.1080/13683500.2012.662215

Hein, G. E. (1998). *Learning in the Museum.* Routledge.Holdsworth, D. (2007). *Instalment on Preservation Strategies for Digital Libraries Leeds University.* Version 1.0. Accessed on October 1, 2021. https://www.dcc.ac.uk/resource/curation-manual/chapters/preservationstrategies-digital-libraries

Heinze, N., & Hu, Q. (2006). The evolution of corporate web presence: A longitudinal study of large American companies. *International Journal of Information Management, 26*(4), 313–325. doi:10.1016/j.ijinfomgt.2006.03.008

Heinzerling, L., & Ackerman, F. (2002). *Pricing the priceless: Cost-Benefit analysis of environmental protection.* Georgetown Environmental Law and Policy Institute.

Heldal, I. (2007). Supporting participation in planning new roads by using virtual reality systems. *Virtual Reality (Waltham Cross), 11*(2), 145–159. doi:10.100710055-006-0061-3

Henderson, J. C., & Ng, A. (2004). Responding to crisis: Severe acute respiratory syndrome (SARS) and hotels in Singapore. *International Journal of Tourism Research, 6*(6), 411–419. doi:10.1002/jtr.505

Hennig-Thurau, T., Gwinner, K. P., & Gremler, D. D. (2002). Understanding relationship marketing outcomes: An integration of relational benefits and relationship quality. *Journal of Service Research, 4*(3), 230–247. doi:10.1177/1094670502004003006

Henriette, E., Feki, M., & Boughzala, I. (2016). Digital transformation challenges. In *Proceedings of the Tenth Mediterranean Conference on Information Systems* (p. 33). Paphos, Cyprus: Academic Press.

Henriques, R. (2004). *Virtual Museums and Cybermuseums: The Internet and Museums.* Retrieved from https://bit.ly/3mTkV8g

Henser, D. A., Rose, M. J., Ortuzar, J. D., & Rizzi, L. I. (2009). Estimating the willingness to pay and value of risk reduction for car occupants in the road. *Transportation Research Part A, Policy and Practice, 43*(7), 692–707. doi:10.1016/j.tra.2009.06.001

Hensher, D. A., & Greene, W. H. (2003). Mixed logit models: The state of practice. *Transportation, 30*(2), 133–176. doi:10.1023/A:1022558715350

Heritage, C. (2002). Accessed on October 4, 2021. http://www.cultureindevelopment.nl/cultural_heritage/what_is_cultural_heritage

Hernández, H. (2018). Confluences between museology and tourism. *Revista Iberoamericana de Turismo, 8*(4), 7–23.

Hernandez-Martin, R., Rodriguez, Y. R., & Gahr, D. (2017). Functional zoning for smart destination management. *European Journal of Tourism Research, 17*, 43–58.

He, W., & Chen, Y. (2014). Using Blog Mining as an Analytical Method to Study the Use of Social Media by Small Businesses. *Journal of Information Technology Case and Application Research, 16*(2), 91–104. doi:10.1080/1522805 3.2014.943092

He, Z., Wu, L., & Li, X. (2018). When art meets tech: The role of augmented reality in enhancing museum experiences and purchase intentions. *Tourism Management, 68*, 127–139. doi:10.1016/j.tourman.2018.03.003

Highfield, T., & Leaver, T. (2014). A methodology for mapping Instagram hashtags. *First Monday, 20*(1). Advance online publication. doi:10.5210/fm.v20i1.5563

Hiltzic, M. (2018). Self driving car deaths raise the questions: Is society ready for us to take our hands off the wheel? *Los Angeles times.* www.latimes.com/business/ la-fi-hiltzik/la-fi-hiltzic-self-drive-20180403.-story.html

Hjalager, A. M. (2010). A review of innovation research in tourism. *Tourism Management, 31*(11), 1–12. doi:10.1016/j.tourman.2009.08.012

Hjalager, A. M. (2015). 100 Innovations that Transformed Tourism. *Journal of Travel Research, 54*(1), 3–21. doi:10.1177/0047287513516390

Hochman, N., & Schwartz, R. (2012). Visualizing Instagram: Tracing cultural visual rhythms. In *Proceedings of the workshop on Social Media Visualization (SocMedVis) in conjunction with the sixth international AAAI conference on Weblogs and Social Media (ICWSM–12)* (pp. 6-9). AAAI.

Hoehle, H., & Venkatesh, V. (2015). Mobile application usability: Conceptualization and instrument development. *Management Information Systems Quarterly, 39*(2), 435–472. doi:10.25300/MISQ/2015/39.2.08

Hofstede, G. H. (1997). *Cultures and organisations: Software of the mind.* McGraw-Hill.

Höjer, M., & Wangel, J. (2015). Smart Sustainable Cities: Definition and Challenges. In L. M. Hilty & B. Aebischer (Eds.), *Proceedings of ICT Innovations for Sustainability, Advances in Intelligent Systems and Computing* (pp. 333–349). Springer. https://webunwto.s3.eu-west-1.amazonaws.com/s3fs-public/2020-01/final_nursultan_declaration_unwto_urban.pdf

Holler, J., Tsiatsis, V., Mulligan, C., Avesand, S., Karnouskos, S., & Boyle, D. (2014). *From machine-to-machine to the Internet of things: Introduction to a new age of intelligence.* Academic Press.

Hong, M., Jung, J. J., Piccialli, F., & Chianese, A. (2017). Social recommendation service for cultural heritage. *Personal and Ubiquitous Computing, 21*(2), 191–201. doi:10.100700779-016-0985-x

Hooijdonk, R. (2015). *Technology trends 2030.* Retrieved from https://www.richardvanhooijdonk.com/en/keynote/trends2030/

Hooper-Greenhill, E. (2007). *Museums and education: Purpose, pedagogy, perfomance.* Routledge. doi:10.4324/9780203937525

Hotelierindia. (2020, March 2). *From social distancing to contactless check-in and dining-Interactive technology will be key in dealing with pandemic issues.* https://www.hotelierindia.com/business/10763-from-social-distancing-to-contactlesscheck-in-and-dining-interactive-technology-will-be-key-in-dealing-with

Hsu, L. (2012). Web 3D simulation-based application in tourism education: A case study with second life. *Journal of Hospitality, Leisure, Sport and Tourism Education, 11*(2), 113–124. doi:10.1016/j.jhlste.2012.02.013

Hsu, Y. L. (2012). Facebook as international eMarketing strategy of Taiwan hotels. *International Journal of Hospitality Management, 31*(3), 972–980. doi:10.1016/j.ijhm.2011.11.005

Huaman, K. (2018). *The history of virtual reality: An escape to different worlds.* Retrieved from: https://www.colocationamerica.com/blog/history-of-virtual-reality

Huang, C. D., Goo, J., Nam, K., & Yoo, C. W. (2017). Smart Tourism Technologies in Travel Planning: The Role of Exploration and Exploitation. *Information & Management, 54*(6), 757–770. doi:10.1016/j.im.2016.11.010

Huang, H. M., Rauch, U., & Liaw, S. S. (2010). Investigating learners' attitudes toward virtual reality learning environments: Based on a constructivist approach. *Computers & Education, 55*(3), 1171–1182. doi:10.1016/j.compedu.2010.05.014

Huang, H., & Ng, K. H. (2020). Designing for cultural learning and reflection using IoT serious game approach. *Personal and Ubiquitous Computing, 2020*, 1–16.

Huang, H., Ng, K. H., Bedwell, B., & Benford, S. (2020). A Card-based internet of things game ideation tool for museum context. *Journal of Ambient Intelligence and Humanized Computing, 2020*, 1–12.

Huang, J. (2013). Chasing provenance: Legal dilemmas for protecting states with a verifiable link to underwater culture heritage. *Ocean and Coastal Management, 84*, 220–225. doi:10.1016/j.ocecoaman.2012.11.007

Huang, J. (2014). Maritime archaeology and identification of historic shipwrecks: A legal perspective. *Marine Policy, 44*, 256–264. doi:10.1016/j.marpol.2013.09.017

Huang, L., Yung, C. Y., & Yang, E. (2011). How do travel agencies obtain a competitive advantage?: Through a travel blog marketing channel. *Journal of Vacation Marketing, 17*(2), 139–149. doi:10.1177/1356766710392737

Huang, W.-J., Norman, W. C., Hallo, J. C., Mcgehee, N. G., Mcgee, J., & Goetcheus, C. L. (2014). Serendipity and independent travel. *Tourism Recreation Research, 39*(2), 169–183. doi:10.1080/02508281.2014.11081765

Huang, X. K., Yuan, J. Z., & Shi, M. Y. (2012, December). Condition and key issues analysis on the smarter tourism construction in China. *International Conference on Multimedia and Signal Processing*, 444-450. 10.1007/978-3-642-35286-7_56

Huang, Y. C., Backman, S. J., & Backman, K. F. (2010). The impacts of virtual experiences on people's travel intentions. In U. Gretzel, R. Law, & M. Fuchs (Eds.), *ENTER 2010.* Springer-Verlag. doi:10.1007/978-3-211-99407-8_46

Huang, Y., Backman, K., Backman, S., & Chang, L. (2016). Exploring the implications of virtual reality technology in tourism marketing: An integrated research framework. *International Journal of Tourism Research, 18*(2), 116–128. doi:10.1002/jtr.2038

Hubspot. (2015). *How to engage fans on Facebook. Hubspot.* http://cdn1.hubspot.com/hub/53/How-to-Engage-Fans-on-Facebook-04.pdf

Hudson, K. (1998). The museum refuses to stand still. *Museum International, 50*(1), 43–50. doi:10.1111/1468-0033.00135

Hudson-Smith, A., Gray, S., Ross, C., Barthel, R., De Jode, M., Warwick, C., & Terras, M. (2012). Experiments with the internet of things in museum space: QRator. *Proceedings of the 2012 ACM Conference on Ubiquitous Computing*, 1183-1184. 10.1145/2370216.2370469

Hughes, N. C. (2016). *How virtual reality is about to transform the travel industry.* https://www.inc.com/neil-c-hughes/how-virtualreality-is-ab-transform-the-travel-industry.html

Hughes. (2016). *How Virtual Reality Is About to Transform the Travel Industry.* Available at: https://www.inc.com/neil-c-hughes/how-virtual-reality-is-ab-transform-the-travel-industry.html

Hughes, H. L. (1996). Redefining cultural tourism. *Annals of Tourism Research, 23*(3), 707–709. doi:10.1016/0160-7383(95)00099-2

Hughes, H. L. (2002). Culture and tourism: A framework for further analysis. *Managing Leisure, 7*(3), 164–175. doi:10.1080/1360671022000013701

Hu, I.-L., Chang, C.-C., & Lin, Y.-H. (2021). Using big data and social network analysis for cultural tourism planning in Hakka villages. *Tourism and Hospitality Research, 21*(1), 99–114. doi:10.1177/1467358420957061

Hume, M. (2015). To Technovate or Not to Technovate? Examining the Inter-Relationship of Consumer Technology, Museum Service Quality, Museum Value, and Repurchase Intent. *Journal of Nonprofit & Public Sector Marketing, 27*(2), 155–182. doi:10.1080/10495142.2014.965081

Hung, K. P., Huiling Chen, A., Peng, N., Hackley, C., Amy Tiwsakul, R., & Chou, C. L. (2011). Antecedents of luxury brand purchase intention. *Journal of Product and Brand Management, 20*(6), 457–467. doi:10.1108/10610421111166603

Hunter, W. C., Chung, N., Gretzel, U., & Koo, C. (2015). Constructivist Research in Smart Tourism. *Asia Pacific Journal of Information Systems, 25*(1), 105–120. doi:10.14329/apjis.2015.25.1.105

Hvass, K. A., & Munar, A. M. (2012). The takeoff of social media in tourism. *Journal of Vacation Marketing, 18*(2), 93–103. doi:10.1177/1356766711435978

Hwang, J. S., Liu, C., Li, G., & Park, S. T. (2020). A Study on Problem Solution of Culture Tourism Festival Through Big Data Analysis. *International Journal of Emerging Multidisciplinary Research, 4*(3), 17–21. doi:10.22662/IJEMR.2020.4.3.020

Hwang, J., Kim, H., & Kim, W. (2019). Investigating motivated consumer innovativeness in the context of drone food delivery services. *Journal of Hospitality and Tourism Management, 38*, 102–110. doi:10.1016/j.jhtm.2019.01.004

Icaros. (2019). https://www.icaros.com/en/about/

ICCROM Working Group. (1990). *Heritage and Society.* http://cif.icomos.org/pdf_docs/Documents%20on%20line/Heritage%20definitions.pdf

ICOMOS Türkiye. (2013). *ICOMOS Türkiye Mimari Mirası Koruma Bildirgesi* [ICOMOS Turkey Architectural Heritage Protection Declaration]. http://www.icomos.org.tr/Dosyalar/ICOMOSTR_tr0784192001542192602.pdf

ICOMOS. (2007). *The Ename Charter.* ICOMOS.

Icoz, O., Kutuk, A., & Icoz, O. (2018). Social media and consumer buying decisions in tourism: The case of Turkey. *Pasos Revista de Turismo y Patrimonio Cultural, 16*(4), 1051–1066. doi:10.25145/j.pasos.2018.16.073

İHA. (2021). *Antalya kıyılarında 3 yılda 125 batık bulundu.* NTV (E.T.31.05.2021): https://www.ntv.com.tr/galeri/sanat/antalya-kiyilarinda-3-yilda-125-batik-bulundu,7OmiL1LhOUSqcOP7ZZoKiQ/VzW1wCFDnkGpcI8R7Ea_JA

Ilgar, R. (2011). Çanakkale Boğazı Batıkları. *Türk Bilimsel Derlemeler Dergisi, 4*(2), 63–68.

ILO. (2020). *The impact of COVID-19 on the tourism sector. ILO Sectoral Briefs Mayıs 2020.* https://www.ilo.org/wcmsp5/groups/public/---ed_dialogue/--sector/documents/briefingnote/wcms_741468.pdf

Immersion, V. R. (2021). *What is virtual reality in travel?* VR for Tourism (E.T.02,05.2021): https://immersionvr.co.uk/about-360vr/vr-for-tourism/

INA. (2021). *Mediterranean.* Institute of Nautical Archaeology (E.T.31.05.2021): https://nauticalarch.org/about/

Ingenhoff, D., & Koelling, A. M. (2009). The potential of Web sites as a relationship building tool for charitable fundraising NPOs. *Public Relations Review, 35*(1), 66–73. doi:10.1016/j.pubrev.2008.09.023

Inition. (2018). *VR Experience at the top of Burj Khalifa.* Available at: https://www.inition.co.uk/case_study/Virtual Reality-experience-top-burj-khalifa/

Instagram for Business. (2020). *Creating a Business Profile on Instagram.* https://business.instagram.com/blog/creating-a-business-profile-on-instagram/

Instituto Nacional de Estatística – INE. (2019). *Estatísticas Regionais.* INE.

Instituto Nacional de Estatística – INE. (2019). *Statistical Yearbook of Alentejo Region – 2018.* INE.

Intellias.com. (2020). Retrieved on 15.06.2021, https://www.intellias.com/from-smart-cities-to-smart-tourism/

Internetworldstats. (2021). Retrieved on 15.06.2021, https://www.internetworldstats.com/stats.htm

InterPARES. (2021). Accessed on June 14, 2021. http://www.interpares.org/background.htm

Inukollu, V. N., Keshamoni, D. D., Kang, T., & Inukollu, M. (2014). Factors influencing quality of mobile apps: Role of mobile app development life cycle. *International Journal of Software Engineering and Its Applications, 5*(5), 15–34. doi:10.5121/ijsea.2014.5502

Inversini, A., Xiang, Z., & Fesenmaier, D. R. (2015). New media in travel and tourism communication: Toward a new paradigm. In L. Cantoni & J. A. Danowski (Eds.), *Communication and Technology* (pp. 497–512). De Gruyter. doi:10.1515/9783110271355-029

I-Scoop. (2010). *Industry 4.0: the fourth industrial revolution – guide to Industry 4.0.* https://www.i-scoop.eu/industry-4-0/#origins-and-history-of-industry-40

ISO. (2014). *ISO 37120 - Sustainable development of communities - Indicators for city services and quality of life.* ISO.

Istanbul 2010 European Capital of Culture Grant Scheme Programme. (2009). https://www.ab.gov.tr/43388_en.html

Istanbul Directorate of Culture and Tourism. (2020). *Istanbul Tourism Statistics Report.* Author.

İstanbullu Dincer, F. F., & Ertugral, S. M. (2000). Kültürel Mirasın Korunması ve İstanbul ilindeki Tarihi Yapıların Turizm Amaclı Kullanımı Üzerine Bir Deneme. *Anatolia: Turizm Araştırmaları Dergisi, 11*(2), 69–78.

Isttelkom. (n.d.). *We are laying the foundations of smart cities.* https://isttelkom.istanbul/en/yusuf-kotil-we-are-laying-the-foundations-of-smart-cities

Ivanov, R. (2019). An approach to developing internet of things (IoT)-based services for smart museums. *Digital Presentation and Preservation of Cultural and Scientific Heritage (DiPP), 8.*

Ivanov, S., & Webster, C. (2019). Conceptual framework of the use of robots, artificial intelligence and service automation in travel, tourism, and hospitality companies. In S. Ivanov & C. Webster (Eds.), *Robots, artificial intelligence, and service automation in travel, tourism and hospitality* (pp. 7–37). Emerald Publishing Limited. doi:10.1108/978-1-78756-687-320191002

Ivanov, S., Webster, C., & Berezina, K. (2017). Adoption of robots and service automation by tourism and hospitality companies. *Revista Turismo & Desenvolvimento, 27*(28), 1501–1517.

Jacobsen, J. K. S., & Munar, A. M. (2012). Tourist information search and destination choice in a digital age. *Tourism Management Perspectives, 1,* 39–47. doi:10.1016/j.tmp.2011.12.005

Jacobson, J., & Vadnal, J. (2005). The virtual pompeii project. In *E-Learn: World Conference on E-Learning in Corporate, Government, Healthcare, and Higher Education* (pp. 1644-1649). Association for the Advancement of Computing in Education (AACE).

Jafari, J. (1987). Tourism models: The sociocultural aspects. *Tourism Management, 8*(2), 151–159. doi:10.1016/0261-5177(87)90023-9

Jain, M. (1987). *Cave paintings of Ajanta and Ellora become a tragic monument to archaeological neglect.* Available at: https://www.indiatoday.in/magazine/heritage/story/19870315-cave-paintings-of-ajanta-and-ellora-become-a-tragic-monument-to-archaeological-neglect-798635-1987-03-15

Jakobson, A. R. (1972). *Hang – Jel – Vers* [Sounds, Signs, Poems]. Gondolat Kiadó.

Jalonen, H. (2012). The uncertainty of innovation: A systematic review of the literature. *Journal of Management Research, 4*(1), 1.

Jansen, B. J., Zhang, M., Sobel, K., & Chowdury, A. (2009). Twitter power: Tweets as electronic word of mouth. *Journal of the American Society for Information Science and Technology, 60*(11), 2169–2188. doi:10.1002/asi.21149

Jansen-Verbeke, M., Priestley, G. K., & Russo, A. R. (Eds.). (2008). *Cultural Resources for Tourism Patterns, Processes and Policies.* Nova Science Publishers.

Jara, A. J., Sun, Y., Song, H., Bie, R., Genooud, D., & Bocchi, Y. (2015). Internet of Things for cultural heritage of smart cities and smart regions. *2015 IEEE 29th International Conference on Advanced Information Networking and Applications Workshops,* 668–675.

Jasrotia, A., & Gangotia, A. (2018). Smart cities to smart tourism destinations: A review paper. *Journal of Tourism Intelligence and Smartness, 1*(1), 47-56.

Jasrotia, A., & Gangotia, A. (2018). Smart cities to smart destinations: A review paper. *Journal of Tourism Inteligence and Smartness, 1*(1), 47–56.

Jasrotia, A., & Gangotia, A. (2018). Smart cities to smart tourism destinations: A review. *Journal of Tourism Intelligence and Smartness, 1*(1), 47–56.

Jelinčić, D. A., & Senkic, M. (2019). The value of experience in culture and tourism: the power of emotions. In N. Duxbury & G. Richards (Eds.), *A research agenda for creative tourism* (pp. 41–53). doi:10.4337/9781788110723.00012

Jennings, G. R. (2005). Interviewing: a Focus on Qualitative Techniques. In Tourism Research Methods: Integrating Theory with Practice (pp. 99–117). CAB International. doi:10.1079/9780851999968.0099

Jenny, S. (2017). *Enhancing Tourism with Augmented and Virtual Reality* [Unpublished doctoral dissertation]. Degree Programme in Business Information Technology Häme University of Applied Sciences.

Jerslev, A. (2016). Media times in the time of the microcelebrity: Celebrification and the YouTuber Zoella. *International Journal of Communication, 10,* 19.

Jiang, Y., & Balaji, M. S. (2021). Getting unwired: What drives travellers to take a digital detox holiday? *Tourism Recreation Research, 2021,* 1–17. doi:10.1080/02508281.2021.1889801

Jiang, Y., & Wen, J. (2020). Effects of COVID-19 on hotel marketing and management: A perspective article. *International Journal of Contemporary Hospitality Management, 32*(8), 2563–2573. doi:10.1108/IJCHM-03-2020-0237

Jinendra, D. R., Bhagyashri, J. R., Pranav, G. Y., Seema, V. U., & Parag, A. N. (2012). Smart travel guide: Application for Android mobile. *International Journal of Electronics, Communication and Soft Computing Science & Engineering*, 2, 115–120.

Jingen Liang, L., & Elliot, S. (2020). A systematic review of augmented reality tourism research: What is now and what is next? *Tourism and Hospitality Research*.

Jin, J., Gubbi, J., Marusic, S., & Palaniswami, M. (2014). An information framework for creating a smart city through Internet of things. *IEEE Internet of Things Journal*, *1*(2), 112–121. doi:10.1109/JIOT.2013.2296516

Jin, S. V., Muqaddam, A., & Ryu, E. (2019). Instafamous and social media influencer marketing. *Marketing Intelligence & Planning*, *37*(5), 567–579. doi:10.1108/MIP-09-2018-0375

Jin, V. (2011). Virtual Reality Technology in the Design of the Space Environment Research. In *2011 International Conference on Control, Automation and Systems Engineering (CASE)* (pp. 1-4). IEEE.

Jin, X., Gallagher, A., Cao, L., Luo, J., & Han, J. (2010). The wisdom of social multimedia: using Flickr for prediction and forecast. In: *Proceedings of the International Conference on Multimedia*. ACM. 10.1145/1873951.1874196

John, M. (2001). *A dictionary of epidemiology*. Oxford University Press.

Johns, N., & Mattsson, J. (2005). Destination development through entrepreneurship: A comparison of two cases. *Tourism Management*, *26*(4), 605–616. doi:10.1016/j.tourman.2004.02.017

Johnson, L., Becker, S. A., Cummins, M., Estrada, V., Freeman, A., & Hall, C. (2016). *NMC horizon report: 2016 higher education*. Academic Press.

Johnston, R. S. (2014). *History in Your Hand: A Case Study of Digital History and Augmented Reality Using Mound 72* [Unpublished doctoral dissertation]. Graduate School Southern Illinois University Edwardsville.

Josefsson, M. Y., & Steinthorsson, R. S. (2021). Reflections on a SMART urban ecosystem in a small island state: The case of SMART Reykjavik. *International Journal of Entrepreneurship and Small Business*, *42*(1–2), 93. Advance online publication. doi:10.1504/IJESB.2021.112260

Jovicic, D. (2017). From the traditional understanding of tourism destination to the smart tourism destination. *Current Issues in Tourism*, *20*, 276–282.

Jovicic, D. Z. (2019). From the traditional understanding of tourism destination to the smart tourism destination. *Current Issues in Tourism*, *22*(3), 276–282. doi:10.1080/13683500.2017.1313203

Joy of Museums Virtual Tours. (2021). *National Museum of Singapore – Virtual Tour*. Joy of museums virtual tours. Virtual Tours of Museums, Art Galleries, and Historic Sites (E.T. 07.06.2021): https://joyofmuseums.com/museums/asia-museums/singapore-museums/national-museum-of-singapore/

Judd, D. R. (2003). *The Infrastructure of Play: Building the Tourist City*. Taylor & Francis., doi:10.4324/9781315699585

Jung, T. & Han, D.D. (2014). Augmented reality (AR) in urban heritage tourism. *e-Review of Tourism Research*, 5, 1-7.

Jung, T., Dieck, T. M. C., Lee, H., & Chung, N. (2016). Effects of Virtual Reality and Augmented Reality on Visitor Experiences in Museum. In Information and Communication Technologies in Tourism. New York: Springer International Publishing. doi:10.1007/978-3-319-28231-2_45

Jung, T.H., & Han, D.I. (2014). Augmented Reality (AR) in Urban Heritage Tourism. *e-Review of Tourism Research*, 5.

Jung, T. (2019). *Augmented Reality and Virtual Reality. The Power of AR and VR for Business.* Springer Nature Switzerland AG.

Jung, T. H., & tom Dieck, M. C. (2017). Augmented reality, virtual reality and 3D printing for the co-creation of value for the visitor experience at cultural heritage places. *Journal of Place Management and Development, 10*(2), 140–151. Advance online publication. doi:10.1108/JPMD-07-2016-0045

Jung, T., Chung, N., & Leue, M. C. (2015). The determinants of recommendations to use augmented reality technologies: The case of a Korean theme park. *Tourism Management, 49*(August), 75–86. doi:10.1016/j.tourman.2015.02.013

Jung, T., Dieck, T. M. C., Lee, H., & Chung, N. (2016). Effects of Virtual Reality and Augmented Reality on Visitor Experiences in Museum. In A. Inversini & R. Schegg (Eds.), *Information and Communication Technologies in Tourism.* Springer International Publishing.

Jung, T., Tom Dieck, M. C., Moorhouse, N., & Tom Dieck, D. (2017). Tourists' experience of virtual reality applications. *IEEE International Conference on Consumer Electronics*, 208-210.

Junior, A. S., Filho, L. M., Garcia, F. A., & Simoes, J. M. (2017). Smart tourism destinations: A study based on the view of the stakeholders. *Revista Turismo em Analise, 28*(3), 358–379. doi:10.11606/issn.1984-4867.v28i3p358-379

Kaczynski, A. T., Havitz, M. E., & McCarville, R. E. (2005). Altering Perceptions Through Repositioning: An Exercise in Framing. *Leisure Sciences, 27*(3), 241–261. doi:10.1080/01490400590930871

Kaisler, S., Armour, F., Espinosa, J. A., & Money, W. (2013). Big Data: Issues and Challenges Moving Forward. *2013 46th Hawaii International Conference on System Sciences*, 995–1004. 10.1109/HICSS.2013.645

Kalaycı, T. E. (2009), Wireless Sensor Networks and Applications. XI. In *Academic Informatics Conference Proceedings* (pp. 37-46). Harran University.

Kalin, S. (1998). Conflict resolution. *CIO WebBusiness Magazine.* htttp://www.cio.com/archive/webBusiness/020198_Sales_content.html

Kalinić, Č., & Lesjak, M. (2019). Connecting with iGeneration: Importance of Social Media for Hotel Promotion. In *The Contemporary Trend in Tourism and Hospitality 2019* (pp. 26–33). University of Novi Sad, Faculty of Sciences, Department for Geography, Tourism and Hotel Management.

Kalinić, C., & Vujičić, M. (2019). A subnational assessment of hotel social media metrics - The case of Serbia. *Geographica Pannonica, 23*(2), 87–101. Advance online publication. doi:10.5937/gp23-19968

Kalvet, T., Olesk, M., Tiits, M., & Raun, J. (2020). Innovative tools for tourism and cultural tourism impact assessment. *Sustainability, 12*(18), 7470. doi:10.3390u12187470

Kang, K., Jwa, J. W., & Park, S. E. (2017). Smart audio tour guide system using TTS. *International Journal of Applied Engineering Research: IJAER, 12*(20), 9846.

Kang, M., & Gretzel, U. (2012). Effects of podcast tours on tourist experiences in a national park. *Tourism Management, 33*(2), 440–455. doi:10.1016/j.tourman.2011.05.005

Kang, S., Kim, W. G., & Park, D. (2021). Understanding tourist information search behaviour: The power and insight of social network analysis. *Current Issues in Tourism, 24*(3), 403–423. doi:10.1080/13683500.2020.1771290

Kantanen, T., & Tikkanen, I. (2006). Advertising in low and high involvement cultural tourism attractions: Four cases. *Tourism and Hospitality Research, 6*(2), 99–110. doi:10.1057/palgrave.thr.6040049

Kapferer, J. N. (1992). *Strategic brand management.* The Free Press.

Kaplan, A. M., & Haenlein, M. (2010). Users of the world, unite! The challenges and opportunities of social media. *Business Horizons*, *53*(1), 59–68. doi:10.1016/j.bushor.2009.09.003

Karadag, D. K. (2019). *Developing Content Management Systems for Museums in Turkey Within the Frame of Digital Cultural Heritage Management's Digital Curation Applications* (Master Thesis). Hacettepe University Institute of Social Sciences, Department of Information and Records Management.

Karaman, E. E., & Karaman, A. (2019). Smart Hotel Management and Tourism 4.0. In Digital Tourism: The New Future of the Industry (pp. 41-62). Eğitim Publication.

Karasar, N. (2014). *Bilimsel araştırma yöntemi* [Scientific research method]. Nobel Academic Publishing.

Kardasz, P., Doskocz, J., Hejduk, M., Wiejkut, P. & Zarzycki, H. (2016). Drones and possibilities of their using. *Journal of Civil & Environmental Engineering, 6*, Article Number: 233.

Karen, S., & David, G. (2010). *Ethics and game design: Teaching values through play*. IGI Global.

Kasapakis, V., Gavalas, D., & Galatis, P. (2016). Augmented reality in cultural heritage: Field of view awareness in an archaeological site mobile guide. *Journal of Ambient Intelligence and Smart Environments*, *8*(5), 501–514. doi:10.3233/AIS-160394

Kashima, K., & Morita, Y. (2017). Conceptualizing smart tourism of Japan: A case study of smart tourism design on China and Thailand. *International Journal of Management and Applied Science*, *3*(3), 76–78.

Kastenholz, E. (2002). *The role and marketing implications of destination images on tourist behavior: The case of Northern Portugal* [Unpublished doctoral dissertation]. Aveiro University.

Katsoni, V. (Ed.). (2015). Cultural tourism in a digital era. In *First International Conference IACuDiT*. Springer. 10.1007/978-3-319-15859-4

Katz, J., & Tokovinine, A. (2017). The past, now showing in 3D: An introduction. *Digital Applications in Archaeology and Cultural Heritage*, *6*, 1–3. doi:10.1016/j.daach.2017.09.001

Kaur, M. J., & Maheshwari, P. (2016). Smart tourist for dubai city. In *2016 2nd International Conference on Next Generation Computing Technologies (NGCT)* (pp. 30-34). IEEE. 10.1109/NGCT.2016.7877385

Kaur, K., & Kaur, R. (2016). Internet of Things to promote tourism: An insight into smart tourism. *International Journal of Recent Trends in Engineering & Research*, *2*, 357–361.

Kavaratzis, M., & Ashworth, G. J. (2005). City branding: An effective assertion of identity or a transitory marketing trick? *Tijdschrift voor Economische en Sociale Geografie*, *96*(5), 506–514. doi:10.1111/j.1467-9663.2005.00482.x

Kayabaşı, Y. (2005). Virtual reality and use for education. *The Turkish Online Journal of Educational Technology*, *4*(3), 151–158.

Kaya, E., Senturk, H., Danıs, O., & Simsek, S. (2007). *Modern kent yönetimi*. Okutan Publishing.

Kayıkçı, M. Y., & Bozkurt, A. K. (2018). Generation Z and Alpha in digital age, artificial intellegence and reflections on tourism. *Sosyal Bilimler Metinleri*, *1*, 54–64.

Kaypak, S. (2013). Branding cities on process of globalization and "brand cities". *Cukurova University Faculty of Economics and Administrative Sciences*, *14*(1), 335–355.

Kazandzhieva, V. (2021). Enhancing the competitiveness of destination Bulgaria through digital transformation in tourism. *Economic Studies Journal*, *30*(2), 177–198.

Kelly, L. (2005). Evaluation, research and communities of practice: Program evaluation in museums. *Archival Science*, *4*(1–2), 45–69. doi:10.100710502-005-6990-x

Kemp, S. (2021). *Digital 2021 - We Are Social*. https://wearesocial.com/digital-2021

Kempner, T. (1976). *A handbook of management*. Penguin Books Inc.

Kent, M., & Taylor, M. (1998). Building Dialogic Relationships Through the World Wide Web. *Public Relations Review*, *24*(3), 321–334. doi:10.1016/S0363-8111(99)80143-X

Kent, M., & Taylor, M. (2002). Toward a dialogic theory of public relations. *Public Relations Review*, *28*(1), 21–37. doi:10.1016/S0363-8111(02)00108-X

Keshab, M. C. (2018). *Digitization study in industry: Requirements and considerations* (Master Thesis). Stavanger University Faculty of Science and Technology, Norway.

Khan, I., Melro, A., Amaro, A. C., & Oliveira, L. (2020). Internet of Things prototyping for cultural heritage dissemination. *Journal of Digital Media & Interaction*, *3*(7), 20–35.

Khan, M. S., Woo, M., Nam, K., & Chathot, P. (2017). Smart city and smart tourism: A case of Dubai. *Sustainability*, *9*(12), 1–24. doi:10.3390u9122279

Kibert, C. J., Thiele, L., Peterson, A., & Monroe, M. (2012). *The ethics of sustainability*. University of Florida Press.

Kılıç, A. (2019). *Internet of Things and Suggestions for Food and Beverage Sector, A Sample Practice* (Master Thesis). Haliç University Graduate Education Institute Management Information Systems, Istanbul.

Killian, T., Hennigs, N., & Langner, S. (2012). Do Millennials read books or blogs? Introducing a media usage typology of the internet generation. *Journal of Consumer Marketing*, *29*(2), 114–124. doi:10.1108/07363761211206366

Kim, E., Lin, J. S., & Sung, Y. (2013). To app or not to app: Engaging consumers via branded mobile apps. *Journal of Interactive Advertising*, *13*(1), 53–65. doi:10.1080/15252019.2013.782780

Kim, G. (2005). *Designing Virtual Reality Systems: The Structured Approach*. Springer.

Kim, M. J., Lee, C. K., & Jung, T. (2020). Exploring consumer behavior in virtual reality tourism using an extended stimulus-organism-response model. *Journal of Travel Research*, *59*(1), 69–89. doi:10.1177/0047287518818915

Kimpakorn, N., & Dimmitt, N. (2007). Employer branding: The perspective of hotel management in the Thai luxury hotel industry. *Australasian Marketing Journal*, *15*(3), 49.

Kim, S., & Chung, J. (2019). Enhancing visitor return rate of national museums: Application of data envelopment analysis to millennials. *Asia Pacific Journal of Tourism Research*, *25*(1), 76–88. doi:10.1080/10941665.2019.1578812

Kim, S., Park, E., & Xu, M. (2020). Beyond the authentic taste: The tourist experience at a food museum restaurant. *Tourism Management Perspectives*, *36*, 100749. doi:10.1016/j.tmp.2020.100749

Kim, W. G., Jeong, O. R., & Lee, S. W. (2010). On social Web sites. *Information Systems*, *35*(2), 215–236. doi:10.1016/j.is.2009.08.003

King, E., Smith, M. P., Wilson, P. F., & Williams, M. A. (2021). Digital Responses of UK Museum Exhibitions to the COVID-19 Crisis, March-June 2020. *Curator (New York, N.Y.)*, *64*(3), 487–504. doi:10.1111/cura.12413 PMID:34230675

Kır, S. (2014). *Test drives in the context of experiential marketing* (Master Thesis). Selçuk University, Konya, Turkey.

Kitchin, R., & McArdle, G. (2016). What makes Big Data, Big Data? Exploring the ontological characteristics of 26 datasets. *Big Data & Society, 3*(1). Advance online publication. doi:10.1177/2053951716631130

Kıvılcım, B. (2020). Probable effects of COVID-19 (New Coronavirus) pandemic on tourism sector. *International Journal of Western Black Sea Social and Humanities Sciences, 4*(1), 17–27.

Knudson, D., Cable, T., & Beck, L. (2003). Interpretation of Cultural and Natural Resources. Venture Publishing, Inc.

Kocabaş, G., & Kopurlu, S. B. (2010). An Ex-Post–Benefit Analysis of Bolu Mountain Tunnel Project. *Ege Academic Review, 10*(4), 1279–1287. doi:10.21121/eab.2010419612

Koch, K. D. (2011). Luxury Tourism–Does This Market Segment Still Work? In *Trends and issues in global tourism 2011* (pp. 179–185). Springer. doi:10.1007/978-3-642-17767-5_19

Koçyiğit, M. (2016). The role of religious tourism in creating destination image: The case of Konya Museum. *International Journal of Religious Tourism and Pilgrimage, 4*(7), 21–30.

Koçyiğit, M. (2017). *Dijital halkla ilişkiler ve online kurumsal itibar yönetimi*. Eğitim Yayınevi.

Kolivand, H., El Rhalibi, A., Sunar, M. S., & Saba, T. (2018). ReVitAge: Realistic virtual heritage taking shadows and sky illumination into account. *Journal of Cultural Heritage, 32*, 166–175. doi:10.1016/j.culher.2018.01.020

Költringer, C., & Dickinger, A. (2015). Analyzing destination branding and image from online sources: A web content mining approach. *Journal of Business Research, 68*(9), 1836–1843. doi:10.1016/j.jbusres.2015.01.011

Komito, L., & Bates, J. (2009). Virtually local: Social media and community among Polish nationals in Dublin. *Aslib Proceedings: New Information Perspective, 61*(3), 232–244. doi:10.1108/00012530910959790

Konev, A., Khaydarova, R., Lapaev, M., Feng, L., Hu, L., Chen, M., & Bondarenko, I. (2019). CHPC: A complex semantic-based secured approach to heritage preservation and secure Iot-based museum processes. *Computer Communications, 148*, 240–249. doi:10.1016/j.comcom.2019.08.001

Konstantakis, M., Alexandridis, G., & Caridakis, G. (2020). A personalized heritage-oriented recommender system based on extended cultural tourist typologies. *Big Data and Cognitive Computing, 4*(2), 12. doi:10.3390/bdcc4020012

Konstantinova, S. (2019). Digital Transformation in Tourism. *Knowledge International Journal, 35*(1), 188–193.

Koo, C., Gretzel, U., Hunter, W. C., & Chung, N. (2015). Editorial The Role of IT in Tourism. *Asia Pacific Journal of Information Systems, 25*(1), 99–102. doi:10.14329/apjis.2015.25.1.099

Koo, C., Shin, S., Gretzel, U., Hunter, W. C., & Chung, N. (2016). Conceptualization of smart tourism destination competitiveness. *Journal of Information Systems, 26*(4), 367–384.

Koo, C., Shin, S., Kim, K., Kim, C., & Chung, N. (2013). Smart tourism of the Korea: A case study. *Pacific Asia Conference on Information Systems (PACIS 2013)*.

Korkmaz, H. U. (2021). Cultural Heritage and Creativity For "Smart Tourism": A Qualitative Research on Konya. *Journal of Vocational and Social Scinces of Turkey, 3*(5), 132–143.

Korzun, D., Varfolomeyev, A., Yalovitsyna, S., & Volokhova, V. (2017). Semantic infrastructure of a smart museum: Toward making cultural heritage knowledge usable and creatable by visitors and professionals. *Personal and Ubiquitous Computing, 2*(2), 345–354. doi:10.100700779-016-0996-7

Kotler, N., & Kotler, P. (2000). Can museums be all things to all people? Missions, goals, and marketing's role. *Museum Management and Curatorship, 18*(3), 271–287. doi:10.1080/09647770000301803

Kotler, P. (1997). *Marketing management*. Prentice Hall.

Kotler, P. (2000). *Marketing management, millennium edition*. Prentice Hall.

Kotler, P., & Armstrong, G. (2001). *Principles of Marketing* (9th ed.). Prentice-Hall.

Kotler, P., Haider, D. H., & Rein, I. (1993). *Marketing places*. The Free Press.

Kotler, P., Kartajaya, H., & Setiawan, I. (2017). *Marketing 4.0: Mudança do tradicional para o digital*. Conjuntura Actual Editora.

Kotler, P., & Roberto, E. L. (1992). *Marketing Social: Estratégias para alterar o comportamento público*. Campus.

Kotler, P., Roberto, N., & Lee, N. (2002). *Social Marketing: Improving the quality of life*. SAGE Publications.

Kotsopoulos, D., Bardaki, C., Papaioannou, T. G., Lounis, S., & Pramatari, K. (2018). Agile user-centered design of an IoT-enabled gamified intervention for energy conservation. *IADIS International Journal on WWW/Internet, 16*(1), 1–25.

Kotsopoulos, D., Bardaki, C., Papaioannou, T. G., Lounis, S., Stamoulis, G. D., & Pramatari, K. (2019). Designing a serious game to motivate energy savings in a museum: Opportunities & challenges. In *International Conference on Games and Learning Alliance* (pp. 572-584). Springer. 10.1007/978-3-030-34350-7_55

Kotsopoulos, K. I., Chourdaki, P., Tsolis, D., Antoniadis, R., Pavlidis, G., & Assimakopoulos, N. (2019). An authoring platform for developing smart apps which elevate cultural heritage experiences: A system dynamics approach in gamification. *Journal of Ambient Intelligence and Humanized Computing*, •••, 1–17. doi:10.100712652-019-01505-w

Kounavis, C. D., Kasimati, A. E., & Zamani, E. D. (2012). Enhancing the tourism experience through mobile augmented reality: Challenges and prospects. *International Journal of Engineering Business, 4*, 1–6. doi:10.5772/51644

Kovács, Z. (2018). Here's how Hungary's the 'Spice of Europe' will shake up Europe's tourism. *About Hungary*. Retrieved October 14, 2019, from https://abouthungary.hu/blog/heres-how-hungarys-the-spice-of-europe-will-shake-up-europes-tourism/

Kowalczyk-Anioł, J., Grochowicz, M., & Pawlusinski, R. (2021). How a Tourism City Responds to COVID-19: A CEE Perspective (Kraków Case Study). *Sustainability, 13*(14), 7914. doi:10.3390u13147914

Kowalczyk-Anioł, J., & Nowacki, M. (2020). Factors influencing Generation Y's tourism-related social media activity: The case of Polish students. *Journal of Hospitality and Tourism Technology, 11*(3), 543–558. doi:10.1108/JHTT-03-2019-0049

Kozak, M. (Ed.). (2014). *Sürdürülebilir turizm*. Detay Publishing.

Kranenburg, R. V. (2008). The Internet of Things: A critique of ambient technology and the all-seeing network of RFID. Institute of Network Cultures.

Kroeber, A. L., & Kluckhohn, C. (1952). *Culture: A critical review of concepts and definitions. Papers. Peabody Museum of Archaeology & Ethnology*. Harvard University.

Kuchelmeister, V. (2018). The Virtual (Reality) Museum of Immersive Experiences. *Electronic Visualisation and the Arts*, 203-210.

Kuflik, T., Wecker, A. J., Lanir, J., & Stock, O. (2015). An integrative framework for extending the boundaries of the museum visit experience: Linking the pre, during and post visit phases. *Information Technology & Tourism, 15*(1), 17–47. doi:10.100740558-014-0018-4

Kuntay, O. (2004). *Sürdürülebilir turizm planlaması* [Sustainable tourism planning]. Alp Yayınevi.

Kurtar, C. (2012). *Urban Cultural Heritage Management and Its Relationship with Recreation: The Case of Ankara Hamamönü* (Master's Thesis). Ankara University Institute of Social Sciences, Department of Geography, Human and Economic Geography.

Kuşçuoğlu, G. Ö., & Taş, M. (2017). Sürdürülebilir kültürel miras yönetimi. *Yalvaç Akademi Dergisi, 2*(1), 58–67.

Kutup, N. (2016). *Internet of Things; 4H Connection with Anywhere, Everyone, Anytime, Any object.* Internet Conference in Turkey.

Kwangseon, H. (2016). Cost-benefit analysis: Its usage and critiques. *Journal of Public Affairs, 16*(1), 75–80. doi:10.1002/pa.1565

Kwok, A. O., & Koh, S. G. (2020). COVID-19 and extended reality (XR). *Current Issues in Tourism*, 1–6.

Kwok, L., & Yu, B. (2013). Spreading Social Media Messages on Facebook an Analysis of Restaurant Business-to-Consumer Communications. *Cornell Hospitality Quarterly, 54*(1), 84–94. doi:10.1177/1938965512458360

Kyriakou, D., Belias, D., Vassiliadis, L., Koustelios, A., Bregkou, M., & Varsanis, K. (2016). Social media and tourism: A digital investment for Thessaly? In V. Katsoni & A. Stratigea (Eds.), *Tourism and culture in the age of innovation* (pp. 471–483). Springer. doi:10.1007/978-3-319-27528-4_32

La Rocca, R. A. (2013). Tourism and city reflections about dimension of smart city. *Journal of Land Use, Mobility and Environment, 6*(2), 201–213.

La Rocca, R. A. (2014). The role of tourism planning the smart city, *Journal of Lnad Use. Mobility and Environment, 3*, 269–284.

Ladhari, R., & Michaud, M. (2015). EWOM effects on hotel booking intentions, attitudes, trust, and website perceptions. *International Journal of Hospitality Management, 46*, 36–45. doi:10.1016/j.ijhm.2015.01.010

Lagrée, P., Cappé, O., Cautis, B., & Maniu, S. (2018). Algorithms for online influencer marketing. *ACM Transactions on Knowledge Discovery from Data, 13*(1), 1–30. doi:10.1145/3274670

Lai, M. K. (2015). Universal scent blackbox: engaging visitors communication through creating olfactory experience at art museum. In *Proceedings of the 33rd Annual International Conference on the Design of Communication.* Limerick, Ireland: ACM. 10.1145/2775441.2775483

Lamsfus, C., Sorzabal, A.A., Manzanera, T.E. & Vallejo, I.L. (2013). Theoretical framework for a tourism internet of things: smart destination. *Journal of Tourism and Human Mobility,* 15-22.

Laney, D. (2001). 3D Data Management: Controlling Data Volume, Velocity, and Variety. *Application Delivery Strategies, 949*(February).

Lau, A. (2020). New technologies used in COVID-19 for business survival: Insights from the Hotel Sector in China. *Information Technology & Tourism, 22*(4), 497–504. doi:10.100740558-020-00193-z

Lavoie, B. (2014). *The Open Archival Information System (OAIS) Reference Model: Introductory guide (2. bs).* Digital Preservation Coalition.

Lawn, J. (2004). Innovation. *Food Management, 39*(7), 30–42. PMID:10164554

Law, R., Leung, D., Au, N., & Lee, H. A. (2013). Progress and development of information technology in the hospitality industry evidence from Cornell Hospitality Quarterly. *Cornell Hospitality Quarterly, 54*(1), 10–24. doi:10.1177/1938965512453199

Lee, H., Lee, J., Chung, N., & Koo, C. (2018). Tourists' happiness: Are there smart tourism technology effects? *Asia Pacific Journal of Tourism Research*, 23(5), 486–501. doi:10.1080/10941665.2018.1468344

Lee, J., Kao, H. A., & Yang, S. (2014). Service innovation and smart analytics for industry 4.0 and big data environment. *Procedia CIRP*, 16, 3–8. doi:10.1016/j.procir.2014.02.001

Lee, M., Hong, J. H., Chung, S., & Back, K. J. (2020). Exploring the Roles of DMO's Social Media Efforts and Information Richness on Customer Engagement: Empirical Analysis on Facebook Event Pages. *Journal of Travel Research*, 60(3), 670–686. doi:10.1177/0047287520934874

Lee, P., Hunter, W. C., & Chung, N. (2020). Smart tourism city: Developments and transformations. *Sustainability (Switzerland)*, 12(10), 3958. Advance online publication. doi:10.3390u12103958

Lee, S. J. (2017). A review of audio guides in the era of smart tourism. *Information Systems Frontiers*, 19(4), 705–715. doi:10.100710796-016-9666-6

Legget, J. (2017). Museums and Public Policy: An Introduction. *Museum International*, 69(275–276), 6–9. doi:10.1111/muse.12169

Legoland. (2018). Retrieved from: https://www.legoland.com

Lendrevie, J., Lévy, J., Dionísio, P., & Rodrigues, J. V. (2015). *Mercator da Língua Portuguesa: Teoria e Prática do Marketing* (16th ed.). Publicações D. Quixote.

Leoni, L., & Cristofaro, M. (2021a). Technology adoption in small Italian museums: An empirical investigation. *Il Capitale Culturale - Studies on the Value of Cultural Heritage, 23*, 57–87.

Leoni, L., & Cristofaro, M. (2021b). To adopt or not to adopt? A co-evolutionary framework and paradox of technology adoption by small museums. *Current Issues in Tourism*, 1–22. doi:10.1080/13683500.2020.1870941

Lepkowska-White, E. (2017). Exploring the Challenges of Incorporating Social Media Marketing Strategies in the Restaurant Business. *Journal of Internet Commerce*, 16(3), 323–342. doi:10.1080/15332861.2017.1317148

Le, T. H., Arcodia, C., Novais, M. A., & Kralj, A. (2020). Proposing a systematic approach for integrating traditional research methods into machine learning in text analytics in tourism and hospitality. *Current Issues in Tourism*. Advance online publication. doi:10.1080/13683500.2020.1829568

Leung, D., Law, R., Van Hoof, H., & Buhalis, D. (2013). Social media in tourism and hospitality: A literature review. *Journal of Travel & Tourism Marketing*, 30(1-2), 3–22. doi:10.1080/10548408.2013.750919

Li, D., & Li, K. (2020). Research on Big Data System Based on Cultural Tourism in Dongguan. In K. Li, W. Li, H. Wang, & Y. Liu (Eds.), Communications in Computer and Information Science: Vol. 1205 CCIS (pp. 320–332). Springer. doi:10.1007/978-981-15-5577-0_24

Liberato, P., Alen, E., & Liberato, D. (2018). Smart tourism destination triggers consumer experience: The case of Porto. *European Journal of Management and Business Economics*, 27(1), 6–25. doi:10.1108/EJMBE-11-2017-0051

Liburd, J. J., Nielsen, T. K., & Heape, C. (2017). Co-designing smart tourism. *European Journal of Tourism Research*, 17, 28–42.

Li, C., Guo, S., Wang, C., & Zhang, J. (2019). Veni, vidi, vici: The impact of social media on virtual acculturation in tourism context. *Technological Forecasting and Social Change*, 145, 513–522. doi:10.1016/j.techfore.2019.01.013

Li, C., Wang, D., & Zhang, Y. (2011). iFeel3: a haptic device for virtual reality dental surgery simulation. *International Conference on Virtual Reality and Visualization*, 179-184. 10.1109/ICVRV.2011.32

Li, G., Law, R., Vu, H. Q., Rong, J., & Zhao, X. (2015). Identifying emerging hotel preferences using Emerging Pattern Mining technique. *Tourism Management, 46*, 311–321. doi:10.1016/j.tourman.2014.06.015

Li, J. (2021). Digital Protection and Inheritance of Intangible Cultural Heritage in the Era of Big Data. *Cyber Security Intelligence and Analytics: 2021 International Conference on Cyber Security Intelligence and Analytics (CSIA2021)*, 1, 24–30. 10.1007/978-3-030-70042-3_4

Li, J., Pearce, P. L., & Low, D. (2018). Media representation of digital-free tourism: A critical discourse analysis. *Tourism Management, 69*, 317–329. doi:10.1016/j.tourman.2018.06.027

Li, J., Xu, L., Tang, L., Wang, S., & Li, L. (2018). Big data in tourism research: A literature review. *Tourism Management, 68*, 301–323. doi:10.1016/j.tourman.2018.03.009

Lim, S. E. Y., & Bouchon, F. (2017). Blending in for a life less ordinary? Off the beaten track tourism experiences in the global city. *Geoforum, 86*, 13–15. doi:10.1016/j.geoforum.2017.08.011

Lim, V., Frangakis, N., Tanco, L. M., & Picinali, L. (2018). PLUGGY: A pluggable social platform for cultural heritage awareness and participation. In M. Ioannides, J. Martins, R. Žarnić, & V. Lim (Eds.), *Advances in Digital Cultural Heritage* (pp. 117–129). Springer. doi:10.1007/978-3-319-75789-6_9

Linden, H., & Linden, S. (2017). *Fans and fan cultures: Tourism, consumerism and social media.* Palgrave Macmillan. doi:10.1057/978-1-137-50129-5

Lindqvist, J., Cranshaw, J., Wiese, J., Hong, J., & Zimmerman, J. (2011). I'm the mayor of my house: Examining why people use Foursquare - a social-driven location sharing application. *Proceedings of the SIGCHI conference on human factors in computing systems*, 2409-2418. 10.1145/1978942.1979295

Line, N. D., Dogru, T., El-Manstrly, D., Buoye, A., Malthouse, E., & Kandampully, J. (2020). Control, use and ownership of big data: A reciprocal view of customer big data value in the hospitality and tourism industry. *Tourism Management, 80*, 104106. doi:10.1016/j.tourman.2020.104106

Lin, S., Yang, S., Ma, M., & Huang, J. (2018). Value co-creation on social media. *International Journal of Contemporary Hospitality Management, 30*(4), 2153–2174. doi:10.1108/IJCHM-08-2016-0484

Litvin, S. W., Goldsmith, R. E., & Pan, B. (2018). A retrospective view of electronic word-of-mouth in hospitality and tourism management. *International Journal of Contemporary Hospitality Management, 30*(1), 313–325. doi:10.1108/IJCHM-08-2016-0461

Liu, H., Wu, L., & Li, X. (2019). Social media envy: How experience sharing on social networking sites drives millennials' aspirational tourism consumption. *Journal of Travel Research, 58*(3), 355–369. doi:10.1177/0047287518761615

Liu, Y.-Y., Tseng, F.-M., & Tseng, Y.-H. (2018). Big Data analytics for forecasting tourism destination arrivals with the applied Vector Autoregression model. *Technological Forecasting and Social Change, 130*, 123–134. doi:10.1016/j.techfore.2018.01.018

Liu, Y., Zhang, R., & Yao, Y. (2021). How tourist power in social media affects tourism market regulation after unethical incidents: Evidence from China. *Annals of Tourism Research, 91*, 103296. doi:10.1016/j.annals.2021.103296

Li, X., & Law, R. (2020). Network analysis of big data research in tourism. *Tourism Management Perspectives, 33*, 100608. doi:10.1016/j.tmp.2019.100608

Li, X., Sanders, K., & Frenkel, S. (2012). How leader–member exchange, work engagement and HRM consistency explain Chinese luxury hotel employees' job performance. *International Journal of Hospitality Management, 31*(4), 1059–1066. doi:10.1016/j.ijhm.2012.01.002

Li, Y., Hu, C., Huang, C., & Duan, L. (2017). The concept of smart tourism in the context of tourism information services. *Tourism Management*, *58*, 293–300. doi:10.1016/j.tourman.2016.03.014

Llodrà-Riera, I., Martínez-Ruiz, M. P., Jiménez-Zarco, A. I., & Izquierdo-Yusta, A. (2015). A multidimensional analysis of the information sources construct and its relevance for destination image formation. *Tourism Management*, *48*, 319–328. doi:10.1016/j.tourman.2014.11.012

Lohmann, M., & Mundt, J. W. (2002). Maturing markets for cultural tourism: Germany and the demand for the 'cultural' destination. In R. Voase (Ed.), *Tourism in western Europe a collection of case histories* (pp. 213–225). CABI Publishing. doi:10.1079/9780851995724.0213

Lo, I. S., McKercher, B., Lo, A., Cheung, C., & Law, R. (2011). Tourism and online photography. *Tourism Management*, *32*(4), 725–731. doi:10.1016/j.tourman.2010.06.001

Lombardi, P., Giordano, S., Farouh, H., & Yousef, W. (2012). Modelling the smart city performance. Innovation: The European Journal of Social Science Research, 25(2). doi:10.1080/13511610.2012.660325

Lonne, T. (2020). *Deep Diving: Rules, Recommendations And Fun Facts*. Divein.com (E.T.25.05.2021): https://www.divein.com/articles/deep-diving/#:~:text=In%20Recreational%20diving%2C%20the%20maximum,to%2018%20meters%20and%20beyond

Lopatovska, I. (2015). Museum website features, aesthetics, and visitors' impressions: A case study of four museums. *Museum Management and Curatorship*, *30*(3), 191–207. doi:10.1080/09647775.2015.1042511

Lopes, E. R., Simões, J. T., & Nunes, M. R. (2020). Cultural Tourism and Heritage Resources: evolution of visitors to a municipality. In Heritage Tourism: The past as an experience. Pelotas.

Lopes, R. D., Macedo, A. V. S., Moll-Bernardes, R. J., Feldman, A., Arruda, G. D. A. S., de Souza, A. S., ... de Souza, O. F. (2020). Continuing versus suspending angiotensin-converting enzyme inhibitors and angiotensin receptor blockers: Impact on adverse outcomes in hospitalized patients with severe acute respiratory syndrome coronavirus 2 (SARS-CoV-2)—The Brace Corona Trial. *American Heart Journal*, *226*, 49–59. doi:10.1016/j.ahj.2020.05.002 PMID:32502882

Lopez de Avila, A. (2015). Smart Destinations: XXI Century Tourism. Proceedings on Information and Communication Technologies in Tourism, 4-6.

Lopez de Avila, A. (2015). Smart destinations: XXI century tourism. *Proceedings of the ENTER2015*.

López, X., Margapoti, I., Maragliano, R., & Bove, G. (2010). The presence of Web 2.0 tools on museum websites: A comparative study between England, France, Spain, Italy, and the USA. *Museum Management and Curatorship*, *25*(2), 235–249. doi:10.1080/09647771003737356

Lord, B. (2002). *Cultural Tourism and Museums*. LORD Cultural Resources Planning and Management Inc.

Lou, C., & Yuan, S. (2019). Influencer marketing: How message value and credibility affect consumer trust of branded content on social media. *Journal of Interactive Advertising*, *19*(1), 58–73. doi:10.1080/15252019.2018.1533501

Loulanski, T. (2006). Revising the Concept for Cultural Heritage: The Argument for a Functional Approach. *International Journal of Cultural Property*, *13*(2). Advance online publication. doi:10.1017/S0940739106060085

Loureiro, S., Guerreiro, J., & Ali, F. (2020). 20 years of research on virtual reality and augmented reality in tourism context: A text-mining approach. *Tourism Management*, *77*, 104028. doi:10.1016/j.tourman.2019.104028

Loverlock, C., & Wirtz, J. (2006). *Marketing de serviços: pessoas, tecnologia e resultados*. Pretice Hall.

Lo, W., & Cheng, K. (2020). Does virtual reality attract visitors? The mediating effect of presence on consumer response in virtual reality tourism advertising. *Information Technology & Tourism, 22*(4), 537–562. doi:10.100740558-020-00190-2

Löwgren, J., & Stolterman, E. (2004). *Thoughtful interaction design: A design perspective on information technology.* MIT Press.

Lu, C. H. (2018). Uav-based photogrammetry for the application on geomorphic change-the case stydy of Penghu Kuibishan geopark, Taiwan. In *Proceedings of the IEEE International Geoscience and Remote Sensing Symposium* (pp. 7840-7842). IEEE.

Lu, J., Wang, M., Mao, Z., & Hu, L. (2015). Goodbye maps, hello apps? Exploring the influential determinants of travel app adoption. *Current Issues in Tourism, 18*(11), 1059–1079. doi:10.1080/13683500.2015.1043248

Lu, W., & Stepchenkova, S. (2015). User-Generated Content as a Research Mode in Tourism and Hospitality Applications: Topics, Methods, and Software. *Journal of Hospitality Marketing & Management, 24*(2), 119–154. doi:10.1080/19368623.2014.907758

Macarthy, A. (2015). *500 Social media marketing tips: Essential advice, hints and strategy for business: Facebook, Twitter, Pinterest, Google+, YouTube, Instagram, LinkedIn, and More.* Academic Press.

MacDonald, L. (2006). *Digital heritage.* Routledge. doi:10.4324/9780080455303

MacDonald, R., & Jolliffe, L. (2003). Cultural rural tourism: Evidence from Canada. *Annals of Tourism Research, 30*(2), 307–322. doi:10.1016/S0160-7383(02)00061-0

Macedo, C. (1965). *As Louças de Barcelos.* Barcelos: Museu da Olaria.

Machado, L. P., & Almeida, A. (2010). *Inovação e Novas Tecnologias.* SPI Sociedade Portuguesa de Informação.

Macias, S. (1996). *Mértola Islâmica. Estudo histórico-arqueológico do bairro da alcáçova (séculos XII-XIII).* Mértola, Campo Arqueológico de Mértola.

Magnenat-Thalmann, N., Papagiannakis, G., Ponder, M., Molet, T., Kshirsagar, S., Cordier, F., & Thalmann, D. (2002). LifePlus: Revival of life in ancient Pompeii. *Proc. VSMM (Virtual Systems and Multimedia).* http://george.papagiannakis.org/wp-content/uploads/2011/10/Proc.-of-Virtual-Systems-and-Multimedia-VSMM02-Gyeongju-2002-Papagiannakis.pdf

Magyar Turisztikai Ügynökség. (2017). *Nemzeti Turizmusfejlesztési Stratégia 2030* [National Tourism Development Strategy 2030]. https://mtu.gov.hu/documents/prod/mtu_strategia_2030.pdf

Mahsereci, N. (2013). *Türkiye'de kazılmış arkeolojik batıklar.* Bilim ve Gelecek (E.T: 31.05.2021): https://bilimvegelecek.com.tr/index.php/2013/09/01/turkiyede-kazilmis-arkeolojik-batiklar/

Maitland, R. (2007). Cultural Tourism and the Development of New Tourism Areas in London. In G. Richards (Ed.), *Cultural Tourism: Global and Local Perspectives* (pp. 113–128). Haworth Press.

Maitland, R., & Newman, P. (2014). *World tourism cities: Developing tourism off the beaten track.* Routledge. doi:10.4324/9780203886564

Mandal, S. (2013). Brief introduction of virtual reality and its challenges. *International Journal of Scientific and Engineering Research, 4*(4), 304–309.

Mandelbaum. (2015). *Are Virtual Reality Concierges Coming?* Available at: https://www.hospitalitynet.org/opinion/4073212.html

Manente, M., & Minghetti, V. (2006). Destination Management Organizations and Actors. In C. Buhalis, D. & Costa (Eds.), Tourism Business Frontiers, Consumers, Products and Industry. Elsevier Ltd. doi:10.1016/B978-0-7506-6377-9.50032-8

Mangold, W., & Faulds, D. (2009). Social media: The new hybrid element of the promotion mix. *Business Horizons*, *52*(4), 357–365. doi:10.1016/j.bushor.2009.03.002

Manikonda, L., Hu, Y., & Kambhampati, S. (2014). *Analyzing user activities, demographics, social network structure and user-generated content on Instagram.* arXiv preprint arXiv:1410.8099.

Manjari, R. M. E. (2018). *Introducing tourism 4.0: What is it and how do we get here?* Retrieved from http://forbil.org/id/article/211/introducing-tourism-40-what-is-it-and-howdo-we-get-here

Manuri, F., & Sanna, A. (2016). A survey on applications of augmented reality. *ACSIJ Advances in Computer Science: An International Journal*, *5*(1), 19–28.

Manuri, F., & Sanna, A. (2016). Survey on Applications of Augmented Reality. *ACSIJ Advances in Computer Science: an International Journal*, *5*(1), 18–27.

Marasco, A., Buonincontri, P., Van Niekerk, M., Orlowski, M., & Okumus, F. (2017). Exploring the role of next-generation virtual technologies in destination marketing. *Journal of Destination Marketing & Management*, *9*, 138–148. doi:10.1016/j.jdmm.2017.12.002

Marasco, A., De Martino, M., Magnotti, F., & Morvillo, A. (2018). Collaborative innovation in tourism and hospitality: A systematic review of the literature. *International Journal of Contemporary Hospitality Management*, *30*(6), 2364–2395. doi:10.1108/IJCHM-01-2018-0043

Maraslı, F., & Cıbuk, M. (2015). RFID Technology and Application Areas. *BEU. Journal of Science*, *4*(2), 249–275.

Marco, J., Gómez, L., & Sevilha, C. (2018). Progress in information technology and tourism management: 30 years on and 20 years after the internet. *Tourism Management*, *69*, 460–470. doi:10.1016/j.tourman.2018.06.002

Margetis, G., Grammenos, D., Zabulis, X., & Stephanidis, C. (2013). iEat: An interactive table for restaurant customers' experience enhancement. In *International Conference on Human-Computer Interaction* (pp. 666-670). Springer.

Mariani, M., Baggio, R., Buhalis, D., & Longhi, C. (Eds.). (2014). Tourism management, marketing, and development: Volume I: the importance of networks and ICTs. Springer.

Mariani, M. (2019). Big data and analytics in tourism and hospitality: A perspective article. *Tourism Review*, *75*(1), 299–303. doi:10.1108/TR-06-2019-0259

Mariani, M. M., Di Felice, M., & Mura, M. (2016). Facebook as a destination marketing tool: Evidence from Italian regional Destination Management Organizations. *Tourism Management*, *54*, 321–343. doi:10.1016/j.tourman.2015.12.008

Marimon, D., Sarasua, C., Carrasco, P., Alvarez, R., Montesa, J., Adamek, T., Romero, I., Ortega, M., & Gascó, P. (2010). *MobiAR: Tourist Experiences through Mobile Augmented Reality.* Paper presented at the 2010 NEM Summit, Barcelona, Spain.

Marine-Roig, E., & Anton Clavé, S. (2016). A detailed method for destination image analysis using user-generated content. *Information Technology & Tourism*, *15*(4), 341–364. Advance online publication. doi:10.100740558-015-0040-1

Marine-Roig, E., & Ferrer-Rosell, B. (2018). Measuring the gap between projected and perceived destination images of Catalonia using compositional analysis. *Tourism Management*, *68*, 236–249. doi:10.1016/j.tourman.2018.03.020

Marini, C., & Agostino, D. (2021). Humanized museums? How digital technologies become relational tools. *Museum Management and Curatorship*, 1–18. Advance online publication. doi:10.1080/09647775.2021.1969677

Mariotti, J. L. (1999). *Smart things to know about brands and branding*. Capstone Publishing Limited.

Marr, B. (2020). *Robots and drones are now used to fight COVID-19*. Retrieved from https://www.forbes.com/sites/bernardmarr/2020/03/18/how-robots-and-drones-are-helping-to-fight-coronavirus/#f29aee32a12e

Marriott. (2018). https://hotel-development.marriott.com/wp-content/uploads/2018/11/Marriott-Hotels-NoAm-November-2018-One-Pager.pdf

Marshall, C., & Rossman, G. B. (2014). *Designing qualitative research*. Sage publications.

Marty, P. F. (2007). Museum Websites and Museum Visitors: Before and After the Museum Visit. *Museum Management and Curatorship, 22*(4), 337–360. doi:10.1080/09647770701757708

Marvão, A. (1997). *Estudos sobre o Cante Alentejano*. INATEL.

Ma, S., Kirilenko, A. P., & Stepchenkova, S. (2020). Special interest tourism is not so special after all: Big data evidence from the 2017 Great American Solar Eclipse. *Tourism Management, 77*, 104021. doi:10.1016/j.tourman.2019.104021

Masseno, M. D., & Santos, C. (2018). Smart tourism destinations privacy risks on data protection. *Revista Eletronica Sapere Aude, 1*(1), 125–149.

Matetskaya, M., Svyatunenko, A., & Gracheva, O. (2019). The development of creative tourism in rural areas of Russia: issues of entrepreneurial ability, cooperation, and social inclusion. In N. Duxbury & G. Richards (Eds.), *A Research Agenda for Creative Tourism* (1st ed., pp. 137–150). Elgar Research Agendas. doi:10.4337/9781788110723.00021

Matlovicova, K., Nemethyova, B., & Matlovic, R. (2010). City branding of Bratislava: History and the present. *Indian Journal of Engineering and Materials Sciences, 2*(2), 215–234.

Matoga, L., & Pawłowska, A. (2018). Off-the-beaten-track tourism: A new trend in the tourism development in historical European cities. A case study of the city of Krakow, Poland. *Current Issues in Tourism, 21*(14), 1644–1669. doi:10.1080/13683500.2016.1212822

Mattern, F., & Floerkemeier, C. (2010). From the internet of computers to the internet of things. *Informatik-Spektrum, 33*(2), 107–121. doi:10.100700287-010-0417-7

Ma, W., Jong, M., Hoppe, T., & Bruijne, M. (2021). From city promotion via city marketing to city branding: Examining urban strategies in 23 Chinese cities. *Cities (London, England), 116*(103269), 1–16. doi:10.1016/j.cities.2021.103269

Mayfield, A. (2008). *What is social media. iCrossing e-book*. Retrieved from https://icrossing.co.uk/ideas/fileadmin/uploads/ebooks/what_is_social_media_icrossing_ebook.pdf

Mazuryk, T., & Gervautz, M. (1996). *Virtual reality-history, applications, technology and future*. Technical Report TR-186-2-96-06. Vienna: Institute of Computer Graphics Vienna University of Technology.

Mbaiwa, J. E. (2004). Prospects of basket production in promoting sustainable rural livelihoods in the Okavango Delta, Botswana. *International Journal of Tourism Research, 6*(4), 221–235. doi:10.1002/jtr.477

Mbaiwa, J. E., & Sakuze, L. K. (2009). Cultural tourism and livelihood diversification: The case of Gcwihaba Caves and XaiXai village in the Okavango Delta, Botswana. *Journal of Tourism and Cultural Change, 7*(1), 61–75. doi:10.1080/14766820902829551

McAllister-Spooner, S. M. (2009). Fulfilling the dialogic promise: A ten-year reflective survey on dialogic Internet principles. *Public Relations Review, 35*(3), 320–322. doi:10.1016/j.pubrev.2009.03.008

McAllister-Spooner, S. M., & Kent, M. L. (2009). Dialogic Public Relations and Resource Dependency: New Jersey Community Colleges as Models for Web Site Effectiveness. *Atlantic Journal of Communication, 17*(4), 220–239. doi:10.1080/15456870903210113

McCall, V., & Gray, C. (2014). Museums and the 'new museology': Theory, practice and organisational change. *Museum Management and Curatorship, 29*(1), 19–35. doi:10.1080/09647775.2013.869852

McCarthy, L., Stock, D., & Verma, R. (2010). How travelers use online and social media channels to make hotel-choice decision. *Cornell Hospitality Report, 10*(18), 4–18.

McCraken, S. (2018). *Hoteliers share insights on the industry's future.* Retrieved from http://www.hotelnewsnow.com/Articles/283839/Hoteliers-shareinsights-on-the-industrys-future

McDonnell, I., & Burton, C. (2005). The marketing of Australian cultural tourist attractions: A case study from Sydney. In M. Sigala & D. Leslie (Eds.), *International cultural tourism: Management, implications and cases* (pp. 16–25). Elsevier. doi:10.1016/B978-0-7506-6312-0.50005-4

McIntosh, A. J. (2004). Tourists' appreciation of Maori culture in New Zealand. *Tourism Management, 25*(1), 1–15. doi:10.1016/S0261-5177(03)00058-X

McIntosh, R., Goeldner, C., & Ritchie, J. (2009). *Tourism: Principles, practices, philosophies. Hoboken.* Wiley.

McKeown, P. G., & Watson, R. T. (1997). *Metamorphosis: A guide to the world wide web & electronic commerce.* John Wiley & Sons, Inc.

McKercher, B. (2002). Towards a classification of cultural tourists. *International Journal of Tourism Research, 4*(1), 29–38. doi:10.1002/jtr.346

McKercher, B. (2017). Do attractions attract tourists? A framework to assess the importance of attractions in driving demand. *International Journal of Tourism Research, 19*(1), 120–125. doi:10.1002/jtr.2091

McKercher, B. (2020). Cultural tourism market: A perspective paper. *Tourism Review, 75*(1), 126–129. doi:10.1108/TR-03-2019-0096

McKercher, B., & Du Cros, H. (2003). Testing a cultural tourism typology. *International Journal of Tourism Research, 5*(1), 45–58. doi:10.1002/jtr.417

McKercher, B., & du Cros, H. (2012). *Cultural Tourism: The Partnership Between Tourism and Cultural Heritage Management.* Routledge. doi:10.4324/9780203479537

McKinsey & Company. (2020, February 10). *The travel industry turned upside down insights, analysis and actions for travel executives.* https://www.mckinsey.com/~/media/mckinsey/industries/travel%20logistics%20and%20infrastructure/our%20insights/the%20travel%20industry%20turned%20upside%20down%20insights%20analysis%20and%20actions%20for%20travel%20executives/the-travel-industry-turned-upside-down-insights-analysis-and-actions-for-travel-executives.pdf

McLennan, A., & Howell, G. V. J. (2010). Social networks and the challenge for public relations. *Asia Pacific Public Relations Journal, 11*(1), 11–19.

McNulty, R., & Koff, R. (2014). *Cultural Heritage Tourism.* Partners for Livable Communities. https://www.americans-forthearts.org/sites/default/files/culturalheritagetourism.pdf

Medway, D., & Warnaby, G. (2014). What's in a name? Place branding and toponymic commodification. *Environment & Planning, 46*(1), 153–167. doi:10.1068/a45571

Mele, E., Kerkhof, P., & Cantoni, L. (2021). Analyzing cultural tourism promotion on Instagram: A cross-cultural perspective. *Journal of Travel & Tourism Marketing, 38*(3), 326–340. doi:10.1080/10548408.2021.1906382

Melo, D. (2001). *Salazarismo e Cultura Popular (1933 - 1958)*. Instituto de Ciências Sociais da Universidade de Lisboa.

Mencarelli, R., & Pulh, M. (2012). Museoparks and re-enchantment of the museum visits: An approach centred on visual ethnology. *Qualitative Market Research, 15*(2), 148–164.

Meng, Y. T., & Tung, V. W. S. (2016). Travel Motivations of Domestic Film Tourists to the Hengdian World Studios: Serendipity, Traverse, and Mimicry. *Journal of China Tourism Research, 12*(3-4), 434–450. doi:10.1080/19388160.20 16.1266068

Meral, K. (2021). *Strategic Social Media Marketing and Data Privacy. In Management Strategies to Survive in a Competitive Environment: How to Improve Company Performance.* Springer.

Mercan, S. O., & Kazancı, M. (2019). Destination Selection for Cultural Values: A Research on Local Visitors to Çanakkale. *Academic Journal of Tourism, 02*, 115–125.

Merchán, M. J., Merchán, P., Salamanca, S., Pérez, E., & Nogales, T. (2019). Digital fabrication of cultural heritage artwork replicas. In the search for resilience and socio-cultural commitment. *Digital Applications in Archaeology and Cultural Heritage, 15*, e00125. doi:10.1016/j.daach.2019.e00125

Merkx, C., & Nawijn, J. (2021). Virtual reality tourism experiences: Addiction and isolation. *Tourism Management, 87*, 104394. doi:10.1016/j.tourman.2021.104394

Mermet, A. (2017). Airbnb and tourism gentrification: Critical insights from the exploratory analysis of the 'Airbnb syndrome' in Reykjavík. In M. Gravari-Barbas & S. Guinand (Eds.), *Tourism and Gentrification in Contemporary Metropolises* (pp. 52–74). Routledge., doi:10.4324/9781315629759-3

Mersin. (2020). Retrieved from: https://vr.mersin.bel.tr/

Mesároš, P., Mandičák, T., Mesárošová, A., Hernandez, M., Kršák, B., Sidor, C., & Delina, R. (2016). Use of Augmented Reality and Gamification techniques in tourism. *e-Review of Tourism Research, 13*(1/2), 366-381.

Meyer, É., Grussenmeyer, P., Perrin, J.-P., Durand, A., & Drap, P. (2007). A web information system for the management and the dissemination of Cultural Heritage data. *Journal of Cultural Heritage, 8*(4), 396–411. doi:10.1016/j.culher.2007.07.003

Miah, S. J., Vu, H. Q., Gammack, J., & McGrath, M. (2017). A Big Data Analytics Method for Tourist Behaviour Analysis. *Information & Management, 54*(6), 771–785. doi:10.1016/j.im.2016.11.011

Middleton, V. (2001). *Marketing in Travel and Tourism* (3rd ed.). Taylor & Francis.

Miguéns, J., Baggio, R., & Costa, C. (2008). Social media and tourism destinations: TripAdvisor case study. *Advances in Tourism Research, 26*(28), 1–6.

Mihelj, M., Novak, D., & Beguš, S. (2014). *Virtual reality technology and applications*. Springer. doi:10.1007/978-94-007-6910-6

Mikaeili, M., & Aytuğ, H. K. (2019). Evaluation of Iran's cultural tourism potential from the European Union perspective: Jolfa Region. In *Cultural sustainable tourism* (pp. 115–130). Springer. doi:10.1007/978-3-030-10804-5_12

Mikropoulos, T. A., & Bellou, J. (2006). The unique features of educational virtual environments. *International Association for Development of the Information Society, 1*, 122–128.

Milano, R., Baggio, R., & Piattelli, R. (2011). *The effects of online social media on tourism websites. 18th International Conference on Information, Technology and Travel & Tourism*, Innsbruck, Austria. 10.1007/978-3-7091-0503-0_38

Milliyet. (2021). *Marmara Denizi'nde keşfedildi! 3,5 metrede gemi batığı*. Milliyet (E.T: 10.10.2021): https://www.milliyet.com.tr/galeri/marmara-denizinde-kesfedildi-3-5-metrede-gemi-batigi-6610713/1

Mills, A., & Gibson, L. (1998). *Health economies for developing countries: A survival kit*. HEFP working paper 01/88.

Milwood, P., Marchiori, E., & Zach, F. (2013). A comparison of social media adoption and use in different countries: The case of the United States and Switzerland. *Journal of Travel & Tourism Marketing, 30*(1-2), 165–168. doi:10.108 0/10548408.2013.751287

Mimoso, J. M. (2008). *Uma História Natural do Galo de Barcelos*. Retrieved from http://www.historia.com.pt/barcelos/galo/textos/historia.htm

Mimoso, J. M. (2010). Origem e Evolução do Galo de Barcelos. *Olaria: Estudos Arqueológicos, Históricos e Etnológicos*, 143–159.

Minazzi, R. (2015). *Social media marketing in tourism and hospitality*. Springer International Publishing. doi:10.1007/978-3-319-05182-6

MINERVA. (2021). Accessed on June 14, 2021. https://cordis.europa.eu/project/id/IST-2001-35461/it

Miorandi, D., Sicari, S., De Pellegrini, F., & Chlamtac, I. (2012). Internet of Things: Vision, Applications and Research Challenges. *Ad Hoc Networks, 10*(7), 1497–1516. doi:10.1016/j.adhoc.2012.02.016

Mishra, A. (2013). A Study of the Factors Influencing Cultural Tourists' Perception and Its Measurement with Reference to Agra. *IUP Journal of Marketing Management, 12*(4).

Mitchell, R., Hall, C. M., & McIntosh, A. (2009). Wine tourism and consumer behaviour. In *Wine tourism around the world* (pp. 115–135). Routledge. doi:10.4324/9780080521145-6

Mitroulis, D., & Kitsios, F. (2019). Evaluating digital transformation strategies: A MCDA analysis of Greek tourism smes. In *Proceedings of the European Conference on Innovation and Entrepreneurship*, (pp. 667-676), Kalamata, Greece: Academic Press.

Mnhn. (2020). Retrieved from: https://www.mnhn.fr/en/explore/virtual-reality/journey-into-the-heart-of-evolution

Mohanty, P., Hassan, A., & Ekis, E. (2020). *Augmented reality for relaunching tourism post-COVID-19: socially distant, virtually connected*. Worldwide Hospitality and Tourism Themes.

Mohsin, A., & Lockyer, T. (2010). Customer perceptions of service quality in luxury hotels in New Delhi, India: An exploratory study. *International Journal of Contemporary Hospitality Management, 22*(2), 160–173. doi:10.1108/09596111011018160

Molina, A., Gómez, M., Lyon, A., Aranda, E., & Loibl, W. (2020). What content to post? Evaluating the effectiveness of Facebook communications in destinations. *Journal of Destination Marketing & Management, 18*, 100498. doi:10.1016/j.jdmm.2020.100498

Molinillo, S., Liébana-Cabanillas, F., Anaya-Sánchez, R., & Buhalis, D. (2018). DMO online platforms: Image and intention to visit. *Tourism Management, 65*, 116–130. doi:10.1016/j.tourman.2017.09.021

Molz, J. G. (2012). *Travel connections: Tourism, technology, and togetherness in a mobile world*. Routledge. doi:10.4324/9780203123096

Moorhouse, N., Jung, T., & tom Dieck, M. (2019). Tourism marketers perspectives on enriching visitors city experience with augmented reality: An exploratory study. In Augmented reality and virtual reality (pp. 129-144). Cham: Springer.

Mooter, N. (2014). *Cost- Benefit Analysis in Practice-A study of the way Cost-Benefit Analysis is perceived by key individuals in the Dutch CBA practice for spatial-infrastructure projects* [Unpublished master dissertation]. University of Delft.

Moptil. (2019). Retrieved from: http://www.moptil.com/sites_lindos

Morehouse, J., & Saffer, A. J. (2018). A bibliometric analysis of dialogue and digital dialogic research: Mapping the knowledge construction and invisible colleges in public relations research. *Journal of Public Relations Research, 30*(3), 65–82. doi:10.1080/1062726X.2018.1498343

Moreno, A., & Capriotti, P. (2009). Communicating CSR, citizenship and sustainability on the web. *Journal of Communication Management (London), 13*(2), 157–175. doi:10.1108/13632540910951768

Morita, T. (2014). *Spoiled for choice! Which sites shall we visit: destination choice of heritage attractions in New Zealand's Bay of Islands.* Auckland University of Technology.

Morita, T., & Johnston, C. S. (2018). Are they all "serendipitous"? *International Journal of Tourism Research, 20*(3), 378–387. doi:10.1002/jtr.2189

Morosan, C., & DeFranco, A. (2014). Understanding the actual use of mobile devices in private clubs in the US. *Journal of Hospitality and Tourism Technology, 5*(3), 278–298. doi:10.1108/JHTT-07-2014-0022

Morris, C. (2016). *Virtual reality and the new sales experience.* Retrieved from https://bit.ly/3n5YpcK

Morris, T. (2010). *All a Twitter: A personal and professional guide to social networking with Twitter.* Que Publishing.

MUES. (2021). *Müze ulusal envanter sistemi* [Museum national inventory system]. https://mues.kultur.gov.tr/giris

Muhanna, M. A. (2015). Virtual reality and the CAVE: Taxonomy, interaction challenges and research directions. *Journal of King Saud University-Computer and Information Sciences, 27*(3), 344–361. doi:10.1016/j.jksuci.2014.03.023

Munar, A. M., & Jacobsen, J. K. S. (2014). Motivations for sharing tourism experiences through social media. *Tourism Management, 43*, 46–54. doi:10.1016/j.tourman.2014.01.012

Museums and Heritage. (2021). *London museums join augmented reality art trail to tempt visitors back after reopening.* Museums and Heritage Advisor (E.T.07.06.2021): https://advisor.museumsandheritage.com/news/london-museums-join-augmented-reality-art-trail-to-tempt-visitors-back-after-reopening/

Musil, S., & Pigel, G. (1994). Can tourism be replaced by virtual reality technology? In *Information and Communications Technologies in Tourism.* Springer. doi:10.1007/978-3-7091-9343-3_14

Muti, S. R. (2019). *Using Internet of Things and Big Data in Production Systems* (Master's Thesis). Gebze Technical University Social Sciences Institute, Gebze.

Mutlu, E. (2017). Education in Museums with New Generation Technologies. *National Education, 214*. https://dergipark.org.tr/en/download/article-file/441171

Nabben, A., Wetzel, E., Oldani, E., Huyeng, J., Boel, M., & Fan, Z. (2016). Smart technologies in tourism: Case study on the influence of iBeacons on customer experience during the 2015 SAIL Amsterdam Event. In *Proceedings of the International Tourism Student Conference* (pp. 1-32). Madrid, Spain: Academic Press.

Nacak, E. (2020). *The Use of Digital Interactive Narrative Methods in the Context of Cultural Heritage* (Master's Thesis). Akdeniz University Institute of Social Sciences, Department of Tourism Guidance, Antalya.

Nagy, K. (2012). Heritage tourism, thematic routes and possibilities for innovation. *Club of Economics in Miskolc, 8*(1), 46–53.

Nair, M. (2011). Understanding and measuring the value of social media. *Journal of Corporate Accounting & Finance, 22*(3), 45–51. doi:10.1002/jcaf.20674

Najda-Janoszka, M., & Sawczuk, M. (2021). Interactive communication using social media – the case of museums in Southern Poland. *Museum Management and Curatorship, 36*(6), 1–20. doi:10.1080/09647775.2021.1914135

Nambisan, S., Lyytinen, K., Majchrzak, A., & Song, M. (2017). Digital Innovation Management: Reinventing innovation management research in a digital world. *Management Information Systems Quarterly, 41*(1), 223–238. doi:10.25300/MISQ/2017/41:1.03

Nambisan, S., Wright, M., & Feldman, M. (2019). The digital transformation of innovation and entrepreneurship: Progress, challenges and key themes. *Research Policy, 48*(8), 103773. doi:10.1016/j.respol.2019.03.018

Nam, T., & Pardo, T. A. (2011). Conceptualizing smart city with dimensions of technology, people, and institutions. *ACM International Conference Proceeding Series.* 10.1145/2037556.2037602

Narangajavana Kaosiri, Y., Callarisa Fiol, L. J., Moliner Tena, M. Á., Rodríguez Artola, R. M., & Sánchez García, J. (2017). User-Generated Content Sources in Social Media: A New Approach to Explore Tourist Satisfaction. *Journal of Travel Research.* Advance online publication. doi:10.1177/0047287517746014

Narteh, B., Agbemabiese, G. C., Kodua, P., & Braimah, M. (2013). Relationship marketing and customer loyalty: Evidence from the Ghanaian luxury hotel industry. *Journal of Hospitality Marketing & Management, 22*(4), 407–436. doi:10.1080/19368623.2012.660564

Navarrete, T. (2019). Digital heritage tourism: Innovations in museums. *World Leisure Journal, 61*(3), 200–214. doi:10.1080/16078055.2019.1639920

Nazaré, J. (1986). *Momentos Vocais do Baixo Alentejo.* Imprensa Nacional-Casada Moeda.

NazneenS.HongX.Ud DinN. (2020, May 5). COVID-19 crises and tourist travel risk perceptions, SSRN: https://ssrn.com/abstract=3592321 doi:10.2139/ssrn.3592321

NEDLİB. (2021). Accessed on June 14, 2021. http://www.ifs.tuwien.ac.at/~aola/publications/thesis-ando/NEDLIB.html

Negruşa, A., Toader, V., Sofică, A., Tutunea, M., & Rus, R. (2015). Exploring gamification techniques and applications for sustainable tourism. *Sustainability, 7*(8), 11160–11189. doi:10.3390u70811160

Neirotti, P., De Marco, A., Cagliano, A. C., Mangano, G., & Scorrano, F. (2014). Current trends in smart city initiatives: Some stylised facts. *Cities (London, England), 38*, 25–36. Advance online publication. doi:10.1016/j.cities.2013.12.010

Nelson, T. (2016). *Impact of Virtual and Augmented Reality on Theme Parks* [Unpublished doctoral dissertation]. Master of Digital Media, Ryerson University.

NEMO Report. (2020). *Survey on the impact of the COVID-19 situation on museums in Europe Final Report.* Network of European Museum Organizations.

Nepal, G. C., & Shiqi, T. (2017). Issues and challenges. *Virtual Reality Multimedia Communication.* Retrieved from: http: http://web.tecnico.ulisboa.pt/ist188480/cmul/issues.html

Neuburger, L., Beck, J., & Egger, R. (2018). The 'phygital' touristexperience: the use of augmentedand virtual reality in destination marketing. Tourism Planning and Destination Marketing, 1(2), 188–202.

Neuburger, L., Beck, J., & Egger, R. (2018). The 'Phygital' TouristExperience: theUse of Augmentedand Virtual Reality in Destination Marketing. In *Tourism Planning andDestination Marketing* (pp. 183–202). Emerald Publishing Limited. doi:10.1108/978-1-78756-291-220181009

Neuhofer, B., Buhalis, D., & Ladkin, A. (2014). A typology of technology-enhanced tourism experiences. *International Journal of Tourism Research*, *16*(4), 340–350. doi:10.1002/jtr.1958

Neves, J. M. (2012). The attractiveness of Portugal as a tourist destination, by mature domestic travellers. *World Review of Entrepreneurship, Management and Sustainable Development*, *8*(1), 37–52. doi:10.1504/WREMSD.2012.044486

Newson, A., Houghton, D., & Patten, J. (2009). *Blogging and other social media: Exploiting the technology and protecting the enterprise*. A Gower Book.

Nguyen, T. H. H., & Cheung, C. (2014). The classification of heritage tourists: A case of Hue city, Vietnam. *Journal of Heritage Tourism*, *9*(1), 35–50. doi:10.1080/1743873X.2013.818677

Nguyen, T. T., Camacho, D., & Jung, J. E. (2017). Identifying and ranking cultural heritage resources on geotagged social media for smart cultural tourism services. *Personal and Ubiquitous Computing*, *21*(2), 267–279. doi:10.100700779-016-0992-y

NHM. (2021). *Virtual Museum: 14 ways to expṣore from home*. Natural History Museum (E.T: 20.05.2021): https://www.nhm.ac.uk/visit/virtual-museum.html

Niccolucci, F., & Cantone, F. (2002, April). Legend and virtual reconstruction: Porsenna's mausoleum in x3d. In CAA (pp. 57-62). Academic Press.

Niemczyk, A. (2013). Cultural tourists:"An attempt to classify them. *Tourism Management Perspectives*, *5*, 24–30. doi:10.1016/j.tmp.2012.09.006

Niewiadomski, P. (2020). COVID-19: From temporary DeGlobalisation to a re-discovery of tourism? *Tourism Geographies*, *22*(3), 651–656. doi:10.1080/14616688.2020.1757749

NINCH. (2021). Accessed on June 14, 2021. https://www.ninch.org/about/mission.html

NINCH. (2021). http://www.ninch.org/about/

Nishanbaev, I. (2020). A web repository for geo-located 3D digital cultural heritage models. *Digital Applications in Archaeology and Cultural Heritage*, *16*, e00139. doi:10.1016/j.daach.2020.e00139

Nitch, V., & Popp, M. (2014). Emotions in Robot Psychology. *Biological Cybernetics*, *2*(9), 418–427.

No, E., & Kim, J. (2014). Determinants of the adoption for travel information on smartphone. *International Journal of Tourism Research*, *16*(6), 534–545. doi:10.1002/jtr.1945

Noh, Z., Sunar, M. S., & Pan, Z. (2009, August). A review on augmented reality for virtual heritage system. In *International conference on technologies for E-learning and digital entertainment* (pp. 50-61). Springer. 10.1007/978-3-642-03364-3_7

North, M. M., North, S. M., & Coble, J. R. (1997). Virtual reality therapy: an effective treatment for psychological disorders. *Virtual Reality In Neuro-Psycho-Physiology*, 59-70.

Nua Internet Surveys. (1998). *Datamonitor: Travel Will be Largest Online Product By 2002*. Available on http://www.nua.net/surveys/

Nuryanti, W. (1996). Heritage and postmodern tourism. *Annals of Tourism Research*, *23*(2), 249–260. doi:10.1016/0160-7383(95)00062-3

Nyaupane, G. P., White, D. D., & Budruk, M. (2006). Motive-based tourist market segmentation: An application to native American cultural heritage sites in Arizona, USA. *Journal of Heritage Tourism, 1*(2), 81–99. doi:10.2167/jht010.0

O'Connor, P. (2010). Managing a Hotel's Image on TripAdvisor. *Journal of Hospitality Marketing & Management, 19*(7), 754–772. doi:10.1080/19368623.2010.508007

Ocheni, S. I., Agba, A. O., Agba, M. S., & Eteng, F. O. (2020). Covid-19 and the tourism industry: Critical overview, lessons and policy options. *Academic Journal of Interdisciplinary Studies, 9*(6), 114–114. doi:10.36941/ajis-2020-0116

OECD, Organization for Economic Cooperation and Development. (2009). Temple Stay Programme, Korea, The impact of culture. OECD.

OECD. (2009). *The impact of culture on tourism*. OECD.

OECD. (2020). *OECD Tourism trends and policies 2020*. OECD.

OECD. (2020a, February 10). *Rebuilding tourism for the future: COVID-19 policy responses and recovery*. https://read.oecd-ilibrary.org/view/?ref=137_137392-qsvjt75vnh&title=Rebuilding-tourism-for-the-future-COVID-19-policy-response-and-recovery&_ga=2.144837364.1583123711.1622917893-726322868.1622392034

OECD. (2020b, February 15). *Tourism policy responses*. https://read.oecd-ilibrary.org/view/?ref=124_124984-7uf8nm95se&title=Covid19_Tourism_Policy_Responses

Oğuz, M. Ö. (2013). Terim Olarak Somut Olmayan Kültürel Miras [Intangible cultural heritage as a term]. *Milli Folklor, 25*(100), 5–13.

Oğuz, Ö. (2009). Somut Olmayan Kültürel Miras ve Kültürel İfade Çeşitliliği. *Milli Folklor, 82*, 6–12.

Oh, J. (2021). Quantity vs. quality of interactions: The combinatory effects of website interactivity and need for cognition on anti-smoking message perceptions and smoking attitudes. *Mass Communication & Society*, 1–30. Advance online publication. doi:10.1080/15205436.2021.1925299

Ohlan, R. (2018). Role of information technology in hotel industry. *International Journal of Scientific Research in Computer Science, Engineering and Information Technology, 3*(2), 277–281.

Okhrimenko, I., Sovık, I., Pyankova, S., & Lukyanova, A. (2019). Digital transformation of the socio-economic system: Prospects for digitalization in society. *Revista Espacios, 40*(38), 26–35.

Oksaar, E. (2008). *''Kültürlerarası İletişim Bağlamında Kültür Kuramı''*, Çev: Ayhan Selçuk. Çizgi Kitabevi.

Ölçer Özünel, E. (2011). Kültür turizminde "yöresel" ve "otantik" olanı sorgulamak ve tüketilmiş mekânları yeniden üretmek üzerine [Questioning the locality and authenticity in cultural tourism and arguing the space consuming]. *Turkish Studies, 6*(4), 255–262.

Olshavsky, R. W., & Granbois, D. H. (1979). Consumer Decision Making - Fact or Fiction? *The Journal of Consumer Research, 6*(2), 93–100. doi:10.1086/208753

Olteanu, A., Castillo, C., Diaz, F., & Kıcıman, E. (2019). Social Data: Biases, Methodological Pitfalls, and Ethical Boundaries. *Frontiers in Big Data, 2*(13), 13. doi:10.3389/fdata.2019.00013 PMID:33693336

Öngider, M. U., & Yazıcı, S. (2020). 360° sanal gerçeklik videolarının turistlerin seyahat motivasyonuna etkisi üzerine deneysel bir araştırma. *Türk Turizm Araştırmaları Dergisi, 4*(1), 121–136. doi:10.26677/TR1010.2020.303

OpenHeritage. (2021). https://openheritage3d.org/about

Oppermann, M. (2000). Tourism destination loyalty. *Journal of Travel Research*, *39*(1), 78–84. doi:10.1177/004728750003900110

Orîndaru, A., Popescu, M. F., Alexoaei, A. P., Căescu, Ş. C., Florescu, M. S., & Orzan, A. O. (2021). Tourism in a post-COVID-19 era: Sustainable strategies for industry's recovery. *Sustainability*, *13*(12), 6781. doi:10.3390u13126781

Osborne-Gowey, J. (2014). What is social media. *Fisheries (Bethesda, Md.)*, *39*(2), 55–55. doi:10.1080/03632415.2014.876883

Otto, J. E., & Ritchie, T. (1996). The service experience in tourism. *Tourism Management*, *17*(3), 165–174. doi:10.1016/0261-5177(96)00003-9

Outman, J. L., & Outman, E. M. (2003). *Industrial Revolution: Almanac*. Thomson Learning.

Owen, R., Buhalis, D., & Pletinckx, D. (2004). December. Identifying technologies used in Cultural Heritage. VAST, 155-163.

Özaltın Türker, G. (2020). How Covid-19 pandemic affects tourism sector? An evaluation from tourism academics perspective. *International Journal of Social Sciences and Education Research*, *6*(2), 207–224. doi:10.24289/ijsser.760790

Özdemir, M. (2021). Virtual Reality (VR) and Augmented Reality (AR) Technologies for Accessibility and Marketing in the Tourism Industry. In *ICT Tools and Applications for Accessible Tourism* (pp. 227-301). IGI Global.

Ozdemir, G. (2008). *Destinasyon pazarlaması*. Detay Publishing.

Özen, L., & Demirdelen, H. (2011). Access IT projesi müzelerde dijitalleştirme ve Europeana. *Türk Kütüphaneciliği*, *25*(1), 132–136.

Özgan, S. Y. (2012). *Use Of Augmented Reality Technologies In Cultural Heritage Sites; Virtu(Re)Al Yenikapi* [Unpublished Master dissertation]. Istanbul Technical University Graduate School of Science Engineering And Technology, Istanbul, Turkey.

Ozgunel, C. (2007). *Kent ve planlama geçmişi korumak geleceği tasarlamak*. İmge Publishing.

Özgüneş, R. E., & Bozok, D. (2017). Turizm sektörünün sanal rakibi (mi?): Arttırılmış gerçeklik. *Uluslararası Türk Dünyası Turizm Araştırmaları Dergisi*, *2*(2), 146–160.

Oztemiz, S. (2016). *Open Access to Digitalized Cultural Heritage Products in Turkey: A Model Proposal* (PhD Thesis). Hacettepe University Institute of Social Sciences, Department of Information and Records Management.

Öztemiz, S. (2016). Türkiye'de dijitalleştirilen kültürel miras ürünlerine açık erişim: bir model önerisi [Open Access to digitized cultural heritage products in Turkey: A model offer] (Yayınlanmamış Doktora Tezi). Hacettepe Üniversitesi Sosyal Bilimler Enstitüsü, Bilgi ve Belge Yönetimi Anabilim Dalı, Ankara.

Öztemiz, S., & Yılmaz, B. (2017). Kültürel bellek kurumlarında dijitalleştirme: Kültürel miras ürünlerine yönelik uygulamalar üzerine bir araştırma [Digitization in cultural memory institutions: A study on applications for cultural heritage products]. *Ankara Üniversitesi Dil ve Tarih-Coğrafya Fakültesi Dergisi*, *57*(1), 493–523. doi:10.1501/Dtcfder_0000001524

Pacific Asia Travel Association (PATA). (2020, April 22). *COVID-19 and the tourism sector: A comparison of policy responses in Asia Pacific*. https://static1.squarespace.com/static/5f24290fd0d0910ecab2b02e/t/5fd03d335ec17a4c668a e0ed/1607482699608/COVID19-TourismSector-APAC-11Nov.pdf

Packer, J., & Ballantyne, R. (2002). Motivational factors and the visitor experience: A comparison of three sites. *Curator (New York, N.Y.)*, *45*(3), 183–198. doi:10.1111/j.2151-6952.2002.tb00055.x

Pai, C. K., Liu, Y., Kang, S., & Dai, A. (2020). The role of perceived smart tourism technology experience for tourist satisfaction, happiness and revisit intention. *Sustainability*, *12*(16), 6592. doi:10.3390u12166592

Painter, A. (2015). *The New Philadelphia Augmented Reality Tour App*. Cultural Heritage Informatics Initiative (E.T. 07.06.2021): http://chi.anthropology.msu.edu/2015/11/new-philadelphia-app/

Pallant, J. (2007). *SPSS: Survival Manual*. Open University Press.

Pallas, J., & Economides, A. A. (2008). Evaluation of art museums' web sites worldwide. *Information Services & Use*, *28*(1), 45–57. doi:10.3233/ISU-2008-0554

Pallud, J., & Straub, D. W. (2014). Effective website design for experience-influenced environments: The case of high culture museums. *Information & Management*, *51*(3), 359–373. doi:10.1016/j.im.2014.02.010

Pal, M., Berhanu, G., Desalegn, C., & Kandi, V. (2020). Severe acute respiratory syndrome coronavirus-2 (SARS-CoV-2): An update. *Cureus*, *12*(3), e7423. doi:10.7759/cureus.7423 PMID:32337143

Palmatier, R. W., Dant, R. P., Grewal, D., & Evans, K. R. (2006). Factors influencing the effectiveness of relationship marketing: A meta-analysis. *Journal of Marketing*, *74*(4), 136–153. doi:10.1509/jmkg.70.4.136

Pan, B., Zhang, L., & Law, R. (2013). The complex matter of online hotel choice. *Cornell Hospitality Quarterly*, *54*(1), 74–83. doi:10.1177/1938965512463264

Pantelidis, I. S. (2010). Electronic meal experience: A content analysis of online restaurant comments. *Cornell Hospitality Quarterly*, *51*(4), 483–491. doi:10.1177/1938965510378574

Pantelidis, S. V. (2009). Reasons to Use virtual reality in education and training courses and a model to determine when to use virtual reality. *Themes in Science and Technology Education*, *2*(1), 58–70.

Papadimitriou, N., Plati, M., Markou, E., & Catapoti, D. (2017). Identifying Accessibility Barriers in Heritage Museums: Conceptual Challenges in a Period of Change. *Museum International, ICOM*, *68*, 271–272.

Papagiannakis, G., Schertenleib, S., O'Kennedy, B., Arevalo, P. M., Magnenat, T. N., Stoddart, A., & Thalmann, D. (2005). Mixing virtual and real scenes in the site of ancient Pompeii. *Journal of Visualization and Computer Animation*, *16*(1), 11–24. doi:10.1002/cav.53

Papangelis, K., Chamberlain, A., & Liang, H. N. (2016, September). New directions for preserving intangible cultural heritage through the use of mobile technologies. In *Proceedings of the 18th International Conference on Human-Computer Interaction with Mobile Devices and Services(MobileHCI '16)* (pp. 964-967). Adjunct. 10.1145/2957265.2962643

Paquet, E., & Viktor, H. L. (2005). Anthropometric calibration of virtual mannequins through cluster analysis and content-based retrieval of 3-D body scans. *IEEE Instrumentationand Measurement Technology Conference Proceedings*, *2*, 1458-1463. 10.1109/IMTC.2005.1604392

Paquet, E., & Viktor, H. L. (2005). Long-term preservation of 3-D cultural heritage data related to architectural sites. *Proceedings of the ISPRS Working Group*, *4*, 1–8.

Park, E., Kim, S., & Xu, M. (2020). Hunger for learning or tasting? An exploratory study of food tourist motivations visiting food museum restaurants. *Tourism Recreation Research*, 1–15. doi:10.1080/02508281.2020.1841374

Parker, R. D. (2012). The evolving dynamics of social media in internet tourism marketing. *Journal of Tourism Research & Hospitality*, *1*(1). Advance online publication. doi:10.4172/2324-8807.1000e102

Park, K. S., Reisinger, Y., & Noh, E. H. (2010). Luxury shopping in tourism. *International Journal of Tourism Research*, *12*(2), 164–178. doi:10.1002/jtr.744

Park, K., Nguyen, M. C., & Won, H. (2015). Web-based collaborative big data analytics on big data as a service platform. In *International Conference on Advanced Communication Technology, ICACT* (pp. 564–567). Institute of Electrical and Electronics Engineers Inc. 10.1109/ICACT.2015.7224859

Park, S., & Huang, Y. (2017). Motivators and inhibitors in booking a hotel via smartphones. *International Journal of Contemporary Hospitality Management, 29*(1), 161–178. doi:10.1108/IJCHM-03-2015-0103

Park, S., Xu, Y., Jiang, L., Chen, Z., & Huang, S. (2020). Spatial structures of tourism destinations: A trajectory data mining approach leveraging mobile big data. *Annals of Tourism Research, 84*, 102973. doi:10.1016/j.annals.2020.102973

Parks, D., & Rohracher, H. (2019). From sustainable to smart: Re-branding or re-assembling urban energy infrastructure? *Geoforum, 100*, 51–59. doi:10.1016/j.geoforum.2019.02.012

Parra-Lopez, E., Bulchand-Gidumal, J., Gutierrez-Tano, D., & Diaz-Armas, R. (2011). Intentions to use social media in organizing and taking vacation trips. *Computers in Human Behavior, 27*(2), 640–654. doi:10.1016/j.chb.2010.05.022

Parsons, T. D., & Rizzo, A. A. (2008). Affective outcomes of virtual reality exposure therapy for anxiety and specific phobias: A meta-analysis. *Journal of Behavior Therapy and Experimental Psychiatry, 39*(3), 250–261. doi:10.1016/j.jbtep.2007.07.007 PMID:17720136

Parviainen, P., Tihinen, M., Kääriäinen, J., & Teppola, S. (2017). Tackling the digitalization challenge: How to benefit from digitalization in practice. *International Journal of Information Systems and Project Management, 5*(1), 63–77.

Pasanen, K., Pesonen, J., Murphy, J., Heinonen, J., & Mikkonen, J. (2019). Comparing tablet and virtual reality glasses for watching nature tourism videos. In *Information and Communication Technologies in Tourism* (pp. 120–131). Springer.

Pate, J., & Adegbija, T. (2018). AMELIA: An application of the Internet of Things for aviation safety. 15th IEEE Annual Consumer Communications & Networking Conference, 1-6.

Patel, K., & McCarthy, M. (2000). *Digital transformation: the essentials of e-business leadership.* McGraw-Hill Professional.

Patni, A. (2020, April 22). *COVID 19 and innovation in the hospitality industry.* https://www.linkedin.com/pulse/covid-19-innovation-hospitality-industry-arihant-patni/

Pavlidis, G. (2019). Recommender systems, cultural heritage applications, and the way forward. *Journal of Cultural Heritage, 35*, 183–196. doi:10.1016/j.culher.2018.06.003

Pavlik, J. (2008). *Mapping the consequences of technology on public relations.* Retrieved from https://instituteforpr.org/mapping-technology-consequences/

Pedersen, A. (2002). *World heritage manuals managing tourism at world heritage sites: A practical manual for world heritage site managers.* UNESCO World Heritage Centre.

Pelet, J. É., Barton, M., & Chapuis, C. (2019). Towards the implementation of digital through Wi-Fi and IoT in wine tourism: Perspectives from professionals of wine and tourism. In M. Sigala & R. N. S. Robinson (Eds.), *Management and Marketing of Wine Tourism Business: Theory, Practice, and Cases* (pp. 207–236). Palgrave Macmillan., doi:10.1007/978-3-319-75462-8_11

Pelton, L. F., & Pelton, T. W. (2011). Outreach workshops, applications, and resources. In D. Lary (Ed.), *Pacific crystal centre for science, mathematics, and technology literacy: lessons learned* (pp. 113–129). Sense Publishers. doi:10.1007/978-94-6091-506-2_7

Pence, H. E. (2010). Smartphones, smart objects, and augmented reality. *The Reference Librarian, 52*(2), 136–145. doi:10.1080/02763877.2011.528281

Perfetto, M. C., Sanchez, A. V., & Presenza, A. (2016). Managing a complex adaptive ecosystem: Towards a smart management of industrial heritage tourism. *Journal of Spatial and Organizational Dynamics*, *4*(3), 243–264.

Persson-Fischer, U., & Liu, S. (2021). The impact of a global crisis on areas and topics of tourism research. *Sustainability*, *13*(2), 906. doi:10.3390u13020906

Pescarin, S. (2013). *Virtual Museums: From the Italian experience to a transnational network*. Academic Press.

Pescarin, S., Rizvic, S., & Selimovic, D. (2012). V-MUST. NET-The virtual museum transnational network. *Преглед НЦД*, *21*, 47–56.

Pesce, D., Neirotti, P., & Paolucci, E. (2019). When culture meets digital platforms: Value creation and stakeholders' alignment in big data use. *Current Issues in Tourism*, *22*(15), 1883–1903. doi:10.1080/13683500.2019.1591354

Pestana, M. H., & Gageiro, J. N. (1998). *Análise de Dados para Ciências Sociais - A Complementaridade do SPSS*. Edições Sílabo, Lda.

Pestek, A. & Sarvan, A. (2020). Virtual Reality and modern tourism. *Journal of Tourism Futures*. Doi:10.1108/JTF-01-2020-0004

Peterson, R. A. (1992). Understanding Audience Segmentation from Elite and Mass to Omnivore and Univore. *Poetics*, *21*(4), 243–258. doi:10.1016/0304-422X(92)90008-Q

Petrangeli, S., Swaminathan, V., Hosseini, M., & De Turck, F. (2017). Improving virtual reality streaming using http/2. *Proceedings of the 8th ACM on Multimedia Systems Conference*, 225-228. 10.1145/3083187.3083224

Pfefferkorn, J. W. (2005). *The branding of cities*. Syracuse University.

Philander, K., & Zhong, Y. Y. (2016). Twitter sentiment analysis: Capturing sentiment from integrated resort tweets. *International Journal of Hospitality Management*, *55*, 16–24. doi:10.1016/j.ijhm.2016.02.001

Philbin-Briscoe, O., Simon, B., Mudur, S., Poullis, C., Rizvic, S., Boskovic, D., . . . Skarlatos, D. (2017). A serious game for understanding ancient seafaring in the Mediterranean sea. In *2017 9th international conference on virtual worlds and games for serious applications (VS-games)* (pp. 1-5). IEEE.

Piccialli, F., Benedusi, P., Carratore, L., & Colecchia, G. (2020). An IoT data analytics approach for cultural heritage. *Personal and Ubiquitous Computing*, *24*(3), 1–8. doi:10.100700779-019-01323-z

Piccialli, F., & Jung, J. E. (2017). Understanding customer experience diffusion on social networking services by big data analytics. *Mobile Networks and Applications*, *22*(4), 605–612. doi:10.100711036-016-0803-8

Pietroni, E. (2019). Experience Design, Virtual Reality and Media Hybridization for the Digital Communication Inside Museums. *Applied System Innovation*, *2*(35), 35. Advance online publication. doi:10.3390/asi2040035

Pike, S. (2009). Destination brand positions of a competitive set of near-home destinations. *Tourism Management*, *30*(6), 857–866. doi:10.1016/j.tourman.2008.12.007

Pillai & Bagavathi. (2000). *Modern marketing: Principles and practices*. S. Chand Publishing.

Pindžo, R., & Brjaktarović, L. (2018). Digital transformation of tourism. *TISC-Tourism International Scientific Conference Vrnjačka Banja*, *3*(1), 340-355.

Pine, B. J., & Gilmore, J. H. (1998). *Welcome to the experience economy*. Academic Press.

Pinke-Sziva, I., Smith, M. K., Olt, G., & Berezvai, Z. (2019). Overtourism and the night-time economy: A case study of Budapest. *International Journal of Tourism Cities*, *5*(1), 1–16. doi:10.1108/IJTC-04-2018-0028

Pinkster, F. M., & Boterman, W. R. (2017). When the spell is broken: Gentrification, urban tourism and privileged discontent in the Amsterdam canal district. *Cultural Geographies*, 24(3), 457–472. doi:10.1177/1474474017706176 PMID:29278248

Pinto da Silva, F., Brandão, F., & Sousa, B. (2019). Towards socially sustainable Tourism in cities: local community perceptions and development guidelins. *Enlightening Tourism. A Pathmaking Journal*, 9(2), 168-198.

Pires de Lima, F. (1965). *A Lenda do Senhor do Galo de Barcelos e o Milagre do Enforcado*. Gabinete de Etnografia da FNAT.

Piro, G., Cianci, I., Grieco, L. A., Boggia, G., & Camarda, P. (2014). Information centric services in smart cities. *Journal of Systems and Software*, 88, 169–188. doi:10.1016/j.jss.2013.10.029

Piskóti, I. (2004). Múzeumi marketing. In L. Dinya, E. Hetesi, & Z. Veres (Eds.), Nonbusiness marketing és menedzsment: civil szervezetek, alapítványok, politika, kultúra, karitatív szervezetek, közigazgatás, közüzemek, nonprofitok [Non-business marketing and management] (pp. 401-416). Jogi és Üzleti Kiadó Kft.

Piskóti, I. (2003). Múzeumi marketing - a múzeumok integrálása a turizmus rendszerébe [Museum marketing – integrating museums into tourism]. *Magyar Múzeumok*, 25(2), 33–36.

Pitre, A. (2015). *How to Create Custom Tabs for Your Facebook Business Page. Hubspot*. https://blog.hubspot.com/blog/tabid/6307/bid/26330/How-to-Create-Custom-Tabs-for-Facebook-Business-Pages.aspx

Pixová, M., & Sládek, J. (2017). Touristification and awakening civil society in post-socialist Prague. In C. Colomb & J. Novy (Eds.), *Protest and Resistance in the Tourist City* (pp. 73–89). Routledge., doi:10.4324/9781315719306-11

Plaza, B. (2000). Evaluating the influence of a large cultural artifact in the attraction of tourism: The Guggenheim Museum Bilbao case. *Urban Affairs Review*, 36(2), 264–274. doi:10.1177/10780870022184859

Pohjola, T., Lemmetyinen, A., & Dimitrovski, D. (2020). Value Co-creation in Dynamic Networks and E-Tourism. In Z. Xiang, M. Fuchs, U. Gretzel, & W. Höpken (Eds.), *Handbook of e-Tourism* (pp. 1–23). Springer., doi:10.1007/978-3-030-05324-6_92-1

Polyzos, S., Samitas, A., & Spyridou, A. E. (2020). Tourism demand and the COVİD-19 pandemic: An LSTM approach. *Tourism Recreation Research*, 1–13.

Portales, C., Lerma, J. L., & Perez, C. (2009). Photogrammetry and augmented reality for cultural heritage applications. *The Photogrammetric Record*, 24(128), 316–331. doi:10.1111/j.1477-9730.2009.00549.x

Portales, C., Rodrigues, J. M. F., Goncalves, A. R., Alba, E., & Sebastian, J. (2018). Digital cultural heritage. *Multimodal Technologies Interact*, 2(3), 58. doi:10.3390/mti2030058

Porter, M. E., & Heppelmann, J. E. (2014). How smart, connected products are transforming competition. *Harvard Business Review*, 92(11), 64–88.

Poudel, K., & Subedi, P. (2020). Impact of COVID-19 pandemic on socioeconomic and mental health aspects in Nepal. *The International Journal of Social Psychiatry*, 66(8), 748–755. doi:10.1177/0020764020942247 PMID:32650687

Pradhan, M. K., Oh, J., & Lee, H. (2018). Understanding travelers' behavior for sustainable smart tourism: A technology readiness perspective. *Sustainability*, 10(11), 4259. doi:10.3390u10114259

Praveen. (2021). Retrieved from: https://amt.parsons.edu/~praveen/thesis/html/wk05_1.html

Prayag, G. (2008). Image, Satisfaction and Loyalty: The Case of Cape Town. Anatolia. *An International Journal of Tourism and Hospitality Research*, 19(2), 205–224. doi:10.1080/13032917.2008.9687069

Prentice, R. C., Witt, S. F., & Hamer, C. (1998). Tourism as experience: The case of heritage parks. *Annals of Tourism Research*, 25(1), 1–24. doi:10.1016/S0160-7383(98)00084-X

Psomadaki, O. I., Dimoulas, C. A., Kalliris, G. M., & Paschalidis, G. (2019). Digital storytelling and audience engagement in cultural heritage management: A collaborative model based on the Digital City of Thessaloniki. *Journal of Cultural Heritage*, 36, 12–22. doi:10.1016/j.culher.2018.07.016

Puczkó, L., Rátz, T., & Smith, M. K. (2007). Old City, New Image: Perception, Positioning and Promotion of Budapest. *Journal of Travel & Tourism Marketing*, 22(3-4), 21–34. doi:10.1300/J073v22n03_03

Pulman-XT. (2002). Türkiye Ulusal Toplantısı Sonuç Bildirgesi. *Türk Kütüphaneciliği*, 16(4), 461–464.

Puntoni, S., Reczek, R. W., Giesler, M., & Botti, S. (2021). Consumers and Artificial Intelligence: An Experiential Perspective. *Journal of Marketing*, 85(1), 131–151. doi:10.1177/0022242920953847

Purcell, K., Entner, R., & Henderson, N. (2010). *The rise of apps culture, internet and American life project.* Retrieved from https://www.pewresearch.org/internet/2010/09/14/the-rise-of-apps-culture/

Put-van den Beemt, W., & Smith, R. (2016). Smart tourism tools: linking technology to the touristic resources of a city. *Smart Tourism Congress Barcelona*, 1–12.

Qi, S., Wong, C. U. I., Chen, N., Rong, J., & Du, J. (2018). Profiling Macau cultural tourists by using user-generated content from online social media. *Information Technology & Tourism*, 20(1-4), 217–236. doi:10.100740558-018-0120-0

Qiu, Q., & Zhang, M. (2021). Using Content Analysis to Probe the Cognitive Image of Intangible Cultural Heritage Tourism: An Exploration of Chinese Social Media. *ISPRS International Journal of Geo-Information*, 10(4), 240. doi:10.3390/ijgi10040240

Quan, S., & Wang, N. (2004). Towards a structural model of the tourist experience: An illustration from food experiences in tourism. *Tourism Management*, 25(3), 297–305. doi:10.1016/S0261-5177(03)00130-4

Quesenberry, K. A. (2019). *Social media strategy: Marketing, advertising, and public relations in the consumer revolution.* Rowman & Littlefield Publishers.

Qu, H., Kim, L. H., & Im, H. H. (2011). A model of destination branding: Integrating the concepts of the branding and destination image. *Tourism Management*, 32(3), 465–476. doi:10.1016/j.tourman.2010.03.014

Quora. (2020). *What is the difference between scuba diving and deep diving?* Quora (E.T. 25.05.2021): https://www.quora.com/What-is-the-difference-between-scuba-diving-and-deep-diving

Rahaman. H., & Tan. B., (2009). Virtual Heritage: Reality and Criticism. *PUM 2009, Joining Languages, Cultures and Visions: CAADFutures.*

Rahaman, H., Champion, E., & Bekele, M. (2019). From photo to 3D to mixed reality: A complete workflow for cultural heritage visualisation and experience. *Digital Applications in Archaeology and Cultural Heritage*, 13, e00102. doi:10.1016/j.daach.2019.e00102

Rainey, A. (2018). *Using Technology in parks and recration: A new spectrum of reality.* Retrieved from: http://greenplayllc.com/wp-content/uploads/2018/06/AR-VR-Edited-F2.pdf

Raletić Jotanović, S., Sudarević, T., Katić, A., Kalinić, M., & Kalinić, Č. (2016). Environmentally responsible purchasing - Analysis of the ex-Yugoslavian republics. *Applied Ecology and Environmental Research*, 14(3), 559–572. Advance online publication. doi:10.15666/aeer/1403_559572

Ramaswamy, V. (2009). Co-creation of value - towards an expanded paradigm of value creation. *Marketing Review St. Gallen*, *6*(6), 11–17. doi:10.100711621-009-0085-7

Ramos, C., Rodrigues, L., & Perna, F. (2009). Sistemas e Tecnologias de Informação no Setor do Turismo. *Revista Turismo & Desenvolvimento*, *12*, 21–32.

Ramos, V., Yamaka, W., Alorda, B., & Sriboonchitta, S. (2021). High-frequency forecasting from mobile devices' bigdata: An application to tourism destinations' crowdedness. *International Journal of Contemporary Hospitality Management*, *33*(6), 1977–2000. Advance online publication. doi:10.1108/IJCHM-10-2020-1170

Ranasinghe, N., Jain, P., Karwita, S., Tolley, D., & Do, E. Y. L. (2017). Ambiotherm: enhancing sense of presence in virtual reality by simulating real-world environmental conditions. *Proceedings of the CHI Conference on Human Factors in Computing Systems*, 1731-1742.

Randall, G. (2000). *Branding: A practical guide to planning*. Kogan Page Limited.

Raymond, L., & Bergeron, F. (1997). Global distribution systems: A field study of their use and advantages in travel agencies. *Journal of Global Information Management*, *5*(4), 23–32. doi:10.4018/jgim.1997100103

Read, M. (2013). Socio-economic and environmental cost-benefit analysis for tourism products-A protype tool to make holidays more sustainable. *Tourism Management Perspectives*, (8), 114–125.

Rebenitsch, L., & Owen, C. (2016). Review on cybersickness in applications and visual displays. *Virtual Reality (Waltham Cross)*, *20*(2), 101–125. doi:10.100710055-016-0285-9

Reif, J., & Schmücker, D. (2020). Exploring new ways of visitor tracking using big data sources: Opportunities and limits of passive mobile data for tourism. *Journal of Destination Marketing & Management*, *18*, 100481. doi:10.1016/j.jdmm.2020.100481

Reisinger, Y., & Turner, L. W. (2003). *Cross-cultural behaviour in tourism: Concept and analysis*. Elsevier.

Relevant. (2020). Retrieved from: https://www.relevent.com/work/marriott/teleporter

Remoaldo, P., Matos, O., Gôja, R., Alves, J., & Duxbury, N. (2020). Management practices in creative tourism: Narratives by managers from international institutions to a more sustainable form of tourism. *Geosciences (Switzerland)*, *10*(46), 2–12. doi:10.3390/geosciences10020046

Remondino, F. (2011). Heritage recording and 3D modeling with photogrammetry and 3D scanning. *Remote Sensing*, *3*(6), 1104–1138. doi:10.3390/rs3061104

Report. (2008). *Internet of things in 2020: Roadmap for the future*. European Commission Information Society and Media.

Retro Futuro. (2021). *Pompeii. Voice from the past*. Retro Futuro (E.T.07.06.2021): https://pompeii.refutur.com/en/

Riazi, N. A., Wunderlich, K., Gierc, M., Brussoni, M., Moore, S. A., Tremblay, M. S., & Faulkner, G. (2021). You can't go to the park, you can't go here, you can't go there: Exploring parental experiences of COVID-19 and its impact on their children's movement behaviours. *Children (Basel, Switzerland)*, *8*(3), 219. doi:10.3390/children8030219 PMID:33809221

Ricci, F., Rokach, L., & Shapira, B. (2015). Recommender systems: introduction and challenges. In *Recommender systems handbook* (pp. 1–34). Springer. doi:10.1007/978-1-4899-7637-6_1

Richards, G. (1996). *Cultural tourism in Europe*. Cab International.

Richards, G. (2001). *Cultural attractions and European tourism*. CAB International.

Richards, G. (2013). Cultural tourism. In *Routledge handbook of leisure studies* (pp. 505–514). Routledge.

Richards, G. (2018). Cultural tourism: A review of recent research and trends. *Journal of Hospitality and Tourism Management, 36*, 12–21. doi:10.1016/j.jhtm.2018.03.005

Richards, G. (2019). Culture and tourism: Natural partners or reluctant bedfellows? A perspective paper. *Tourism Review*.

Richards, G., & Bonink, C. (1995). Marketing cultural tourism in Europe. *Journal of Vacation Marketing, 1*(2), 172–180. doi:10.1177/135676679500100205

Rinschede, G. (1992). Forms of religious tourism. *Annals of Tourism Research, 19*(1), 51–67. doi:10.1016/0160-7383(92)90106-Y

Rizvić, S. (2017). How to Breathe Life into Cultural Heritage 3D Reconstructions. *European Review (Chichester, England), 25*(1), 39–50. doi:10.1017/S106279871600034X

Rizzi, A., Voltolini, F., Girardi, S., Gonzo, L., & Remondino, F. (2007). *Digital Preservation, Documentation and Analysis of Paintings, Monuments and Large Cultural Heritage With Infrared Technology, Digital Cameras and Range Sensors*. Paper presented at the XXI International CIPA Symposium, Athens, Greece.

Rizzi, P., & Dioli, İ. (2010). From strategic planning to city branding: Some empirical evidence in İtaly. *Pasos Revista de Turismo i Patrimonio Cultural, 8*(3), 39–49. doi:10.25145/j.pasos.2010.08.033

Robin, B. R. (2008). Digital Storytelling: A Powerful Technology Tool for the 21st Century Classroom. *Theory into Practice, 47*(3), 220–228. doi:10.1080/00405840802153916

Robinson, H. (2012). Remembering things differently: Museums, libraries and archives as memory institutions and the implications for convergence. *Museum Management and Curatorship, 27*(4), 413–429. doi:10.1080/09647775.2012.720188

Rocha Peixoto. (1966). *As olarias de Prado*. Barcelos: Museu Regional de Cerâmica.

Rockonit. (2020). Retrieved from: https://rockonit.weebly.com/blog/how-augmented-reality-is-revolutionizing-the-hospitality-industry

Rodrigues, J. M., Ramos, C. M., Cardoso, P. J., & Henriques, C. (2017). Handbook of research on technological developments for cultural heritage and eTourism applications. IGI Global.

Rodríguez-Mazahua, L., Rodríguez-Enríquez, C. A., Sánchez-Cervantes, J. L., Cervantes, J., García-Alcaraz, J. L., & Alor-Hernández, G. (2016). A general perspective of Big Data: Applications, tools, challenges and trends. *The Journal of Supercomputing, 72*(8), 3073–3113. doi:10.100711227-015-1501-1

Rogers, Y., Sharp, H., & Preece, J. (2011). *Interaction design: beyond human-computer interaction*. John Wiley & Sons.

Roque, V., Fernandes, G., & Raposo, R. (2012). Identificação dos Media Sociais utilizados pelas organizações de gestão de destinos: o caso de estudo do destino turístico Serra da Estrela. Revista Turismo e Desenvolvimento, 17/18.

Roque, M. (2015). As humanidades digitais no cruzamento entre museus e turismo. *Revista Internacional de Ciências Humanas, 4*(2), 179–194. doi:10.37467/gka-revhuman.v4.748

Roque, V., & Raposo, R. (2016). Social media as a communication and marketing tool in tourism: An analysis of online activities from international key player DMO. *Anatolia An International Journal of Tourism and Hospitality Research, 27*(1), 58–70. doi:10.1080/13032917.2015.1083209

Rosmaninho, N. (2009). *Relatório da disciplina de Património e Identidade*. Universidade de Aveiro.

Rouleau, J. (2017). Every (nocturnal) tourist leaves a trace: Urban tourism, nighttime landscape, and public places in Ciutat Vella, Barcelona. *Imaginations, 7*, 58–71. doi:10.17742/IMAGE.VOS.7-2.3

Rouse, M. (2016). *Internet of Things (IoT).* https://internetofthingsagenda.techtarget.com/definition/Internet-of-ThingsIoT

Roussou, M. (2002). Virtual heritage: From the research lab to the broad public. *Bar International Series, 1075,* 93–100.

Roussou, M. (2004). Learning by doing and learning through play: An exploration of interactivity in virtual environments for children. *Computers in Entertainment, 2*(1), 10–29. doi:10.1145/973801.973818

Roussou, M. (2004). Learning by doing and learning through play: An exploration of interactivity in virtual environments for children. *Computers in Entertainment, 2*(1), 1–23.

Runfola, A., Rosati, M., & Guercini, S. (2013). New business models in online hotel distribution: Emerging private sales versus leading IDS. *Service Business, 7*(2), 183–205. doi:10.100711628-012-0150-1

Russo, A. P., & Richards, G. (Eds.). (2016). *Reinventing the local in tourism: Producing, consuming and negotiating place.* Channel View Publications., doi:10.21832/9781845415709

Sabate, F., Berbegal-Mirabent, J., Cañabate, A., & Lebherz, P. R. (2014). Factors influencing popularity of branded content in Facebook fan pages. *European Management Journal, 32*(6), 1001–1011. doi:10.1016/j.emj.2014.05.001

Safko, L. (2012). *The social media bible: Tactics, tools & strategies for business success.* John Wiley & Sons.

Safko, L., & Brake, D. K. (2009). *The social media bible: Tactics, tools, and strategies for business success.* John Wiley & Sons, Inc.

Sağlık Bakanlığı, T. C. (2021). *Covid 19 nedir?* [Whats Covid 19]. https://covid19.saglik.gov.tr/TR-66300/covid-19-nedir-.html

Sahin, G. (2010). *The importance of being a brand city in tourism: The Example of Istanbul* [Unpublished master's dissertation]. University of Ankara, Ankara, Turkey.

Sakamura, K. (2006). Challenges in the age of ubiquitous computing: A case study of t-engine, an open development platform for embedded systems. *Proceedings of the 28th International Conference on Software Engineering,* 713-720. 10.1145/1134285.1134399

Salkind, N. J., & Frey, B. B. (2020). Statistics for people who (think they) hate statistics (7th ed.). SAGE Publications, Inc.

Samara, D., Magnisalis, I., & Peristeras, V. (2020). Artificial intelligence and big data in tourism: A systematic literature review. *Journal of Hospitality and Tourism Technology, 11*(2), 343–367. Advance online publication. doi:10.1108/JHTT-12-2018-0118

Sambhanthan, A., & Good, A. (2013). Critical success factors for positive user experience in hotel websites: Applying Herzberg's two factor theory for user experience modeling. *International Journal of E-Services and Mobile Applications, 5*(1), 1–25. doi:10.4018/jesma.2013010101

Samdin, Z., Abdullah, S. I. N. W., Khaw, A., & Subramaniam, T. (2021). Travel risk in the ecotourism industry amid COVID-19 pandemic: Ecotourists' perceptions. *Journal of Ecotourism,* 1–29. doi:10.1080/14724049.2021.1938089

Samoladas, I., Zilianakis, C., Lazaridou, K., Papadopoulou, K., Tsolaki, E., & Nerantzaki, D. M. (2016). Citizen perspectives on the development of local cultural resources: The case of the municipality of serres. In V. Katsoni & A. Stratigea (Eds.), *Tourism and culture in the age of innovation* (pp. 157–170). Springer. doi:10.1007/978-3-319-27528-4_11

Sanchez-Vives, M. V., & Slater, M. (2005). From presence to consciousness through virtual reality. *Nature Reviews. Neuroscience, 6*(4), 332–339. doi:10.1038/nrn1651 PMID:15803164

Saper, C. (2008). Folkvine. org as a model of virtual tourism. *International Journal of Digital Culture and Electronic Tourism*, *1*(2-3), 209–224. doi:10.1504/IJDCET.2008.021408

Saramago, A. (1973). *Convento de Sóror Mariana Alcoforado: Real Mosteiro de Nossa Senhora da Conceição*. Colares.

Satar, İ., & Güneş, G. (2014). *Türkiye'de somut olmayan kültürel mirasın korunmasında kültür turizmin önemi* [The importance of cultural tourism in the protection of intangible cultural heritage in Turkey] [Paper Presentation]. Quo Vadis: Sosyal Bilimler – Artvin Çoruh Üniversitesi Hopa Uluslararası Sosyal Bilimler Konferansı.

Saxena, A., & Khanna, U. (2013). Advertising on social network sites: A structural equation modelling approach. *Vision (Basel)*, *17*(1), 17–25. doi:10.1177/0972262912469560

Schaffner, A. (2019). *Social media marketing workbook 2019: How to leverage the power of Facebook advertising, Instagram marketing, YouTube and SEO to explode your business and personal brand*. Independently Published.

Schmallegger, D., & Carson, D. (2008). Blogs in tourism: Changing approaches to information exchange. *Journal of Vacation Marketing*, *14*(2), 99–110. doi:10.1177/1356766707087519

Schmitt, B. H. (2003). *Competitive Advantage Through The Customer Experience*. www.exgroup.com

Schmitt, B. H. (1999). *Experiential marketing: How to get customers to sense, feel, think, act, relate to your company and brands*. The Free Press.

Schweibenz, W. (2012). Museum exhibitions-The real and the virtual ones: An account of a complex relation. *Uncommon Culture*, 38-52.

Scopigno, R., Callieri, M., Cignoni, P., Corsini, M., Dellepiane, M., Ponchio, F., & Ranzuglia, G. (2011). 3D models for cultural heritage: Beyond plain visualization. *Computer*, *44*(7), 48–55. doi:10.1109/MC.2011.196

Scopigno, R., Cignoni, P., Pietroni, N., Callieri, M., & Dellepiane, M. (2017). Digital fabrication techniques for cultural heritage: A survey. *Computer Graphics Forum*, *36*(1), 6–21. doi:10.1111/cgf.12781

Segittur. (2020). Retrieved from www.segittur.es

Seitel, F. P. (2016). *Halkla ilişkiler uygulaması* (S. Mengü, Trans.). Nobel Akademik Yayıncılık.

Seker, S. (2018). *5G Internet of Things and Our Health* (1st ed.). Hayykitap Publications.

Selmanovic, E., Rizvic, S., Harvey, C., Boskovic, D., Hulusic, V., Chahin, M., & Sljivo, S. (2018). VR Video Storytelling for Intangible Cultural Heritage Preservation. *Eurographics Workshop on Graphics and Cultural Heritage Conference*.

Selstad, L. (2007). The social anthropology of the tourist experience. Exploring the middle role. *Scandinavian Journal of Hospitality and Tourism*, *7*(1), 19–33. doi:10.1080/15022250701256771

Selvam, A., Yap, T., Tzen-Vun, N., Tong, H., Hau, L., & Ho, C. C. (2016). Augmented reality for information retrieval aimed at museum exhibitions using smartphones. *Journal of Engineering and Applied Sciences (Asian Research Publishing Network)*, *100*(3), 635–639.

Séraphin, H., Zaman, M., Olver, S., Bourliataux-Lajoinie, S., & Dosquet, F. (2019). Destination branding and overtourism. *Journal of Hospitality and Tourism Management*, *38*, 1–4. doi:10.1016/j.jhtm.2018.11.003

Serra, J. (2008). *As tecnologias de Informação e comunicação no Turismo: - a emergência do e-tourism*. Universidade de Évora.

Seyfi, S., Hall, C. M., & Rasoolimanesh, S. M. (2019). Exploring memorable cultural tourism experiences. *Journal of Heritage Tourism*, *6631*(15), 3.

Seyitoğlu, Z. (2019). *Changing customer experience in digital public relations in Turkey: Chatbot applications* (Master Thesis). Istanbul Kultur University, İstanbul, Turkey.

Seymore, S. B. (2009). Serendipity. *North Carolina Law Review, 88*, 185.

Shao, H., Zhang, Y., & Li, W. (2017). Extraction and analysis of city's tourism districts based on social media data. *Computers, Environment and Urban Systems, 65*, 66–78. doi:10.1016/j.compenvurbsys.2017.04.010

Shao, J., Rodriguez, M. D., & Gretzel, U. (2012). Riding the social media wave: strategies of DMOs who successfully engage in social media marketing. In M. Sigala, E. Christou, & U. Gretzel (Eds.), *Social media in travel, tourism and hospitality: theory, practice and cases* (pp. 87–98). Ashgate Publishing.

Sharifi, A., & Khavarian-Garmsir, A. R. (2020). The COVID-19 pandemic: Impacts on cities and major lessons for urban planning, design, and management. *The Science of the Total Environment, 749*, 142391. doi:10.1016/j.scitotenv.2020.142391 PMID:33370924

Sharma, G. D., Thomas, A., & Paul, J. (2021). Reviving tourism industry post-COVID-19: A resilience-based framework. *Tourism Management Perspectives, 37*, 100786. doi:10.1016/j.tmp.2020.100786 PMID:33391988

Sharples, S., Cobb, S., Moody, A., & Wilson, J. R. (2008). Virtual reality induced symptoms and effects (VRISE): Comparison of head mounted display (HMD). *Desktop and Projection Display Systems Displays, 29*(2), 58–69. doi:10.1016/j.displa.2007.09.005

Shaw, G., Bailey, A., & Williams, A. M. (2011). Service dominant logic and its implications for tourism management: The co-production of innovation in the hotel industry. *Tourism Management, 32*(2), 207–214. doi:10.1016/j.tourman.2010.05.020

Shehade, M., & Lambert, S. T. (2020). Virtual Reality in Museums: Exploring the Experiences of Museum Professionals. *Applied Sciences (Basel, Switzerland), 10*(11), 4031. https://doi.org/10.3390/app10114031

Sheng, C. W., & Cheng, M. C. (2012). A study of experience expectations of museum visitors. *Tourism Management, 33*(1), 53–60. doi:10.1016/j.tourman.2011.01.023

Shen, S., Sotiriadis, M., & Zhang, Y. (2020). The influence of smart technologies on customer journey in tourist attractions within the smart tourism management framework. *Sustainability, 12*(10), 4157. doi:10.3390u12104157

Sheoran, S. K. (2017). Big data: A big boon for tourism sector. *International Journal of Research in Advanced Engineering and Technology, 3*, 10–13.

Shereen, M. A., Khan, S., Kazmi, A., Bashir, N., & Siddique, R. (2020). COVID-19 infection: Origin, transmission, and characteristics of human coronaviruses. *Journal of Advanced Research, 24*, 91–98. doi:10.1016/j.jare.2020.03.005 PMID:32257431

Shimray, S. R., & Ramaiah, C.K. (2019). Cultural Heritage Awareness among students of Pondicherry University: A Study. *Library Philosophy and Practice*, 1-10.

Shirazi, S. F. M. (2018). Social Network Sites and Virtual Tourism Experience. In *Quality Services and Experiences in Hospitality and Tourism*. Emerald Publishing Limited. doi:10.1108/S2042-144320180000009008

Siang, T., Aziz, K., & Ahmad, Z. (2020). Developing a Framework for Augmented Reality Mobile Application Success and World Heritage Sites Sustainability. *International Journal of Advance Science and Technology, 29*(108), 287–296.

Sigala, M. (2020). Tourism and COVID-19: Impacts and implications for advancing and resetting industry and research. *Journal of Business Research, 117*, 312–321. doi:10.1016/j.jbusres.2020.06.015 PMID:32546875

Sigalat-Signes, E., Calvo-Palomares, R., Roig-Merino, B., & García-Adán, I. (2020). Transition towards a tourist innovation model: The smart tourism destination: Reality or territorial marketing? *Journal of Innovation & Knowledge*, *5*(2), 96–104. doi:10.1016/j.jik.2019.06.002

Silberberg, T. (1995). Cultural tourism and business opportunities for museums and heritage sites. *Tourism Management*, *16*(5), 361–365. doi:10.1016/0261-5177(95)00039-Q

Silva, E. P. (2000). Património e identidade. Os desafios do turismo cultural. *Antropológicas*, *4*, 217–224.

Silva, J. S. (2013). Turismo interno: A conceptualização e a cobertura estatística. *Revista Turismo & Desenvolvimento*, *20*, 151–165.

Silva, M. (2018). *As Lettres Portugaises na Literatura Portuguesa Contemporânea: Reescritas*. Universidade de Lisboa, Faculdade de Letras, Tese de Doutoramento.

Silverman, H., & Ruggles, D. F. (2007). Cultural Heritage and Human Rights. In Cultural Heritage and Human Rights. Springer.

Simsek, E. (2019). *Edge Computing Based Intelligent Visual Perception Analysis for the Internet of Things* (Master's Thesis). Ataturk University Institute of Science and Technology, Erzurum.

Singh, S. (2019). The Onwards March of Technology and Its Impact on the World of Tourism. In D. Gursoy & R. Nunkoo (Eds.), *The Routledge Handbook of Tourism Impacts- Theoretical and Applied Perspectives* (pp. 418–427). Francis and Taylor. doi:10.4324/9781351025102-31

Sites in 3D. (2021). *360 Derece Panoramik Fotagraflarla Sanal Turlar*. 3D Mekanlar (E.T. 16.05.2021): http://www.3dmekanlar.com/index.html

Sivarajah, U., Kamal, M. M., Irani, Z., & Weerakkody, V. (2017). Critical analysis of Big Data challenges and analytical methods. *Journal of Business Research*, *70*, 263–286. Advance online publication. doi:10.1016/j.jbusres.2016.08.001

Slater, M., Gonzalez, L. C., Haggard, P., Vinkers, C., Gregory-Clarke, R., Jelley, S., Watson, Z., Breen, G., Schwarz, R., Steptoe, W., Szostak, D., Halan, S., Fox, D., & Silver, J. (2020). The ethics of realism in virtual and augmented reality. *Frontiers in Virtual Reality*, *1*(1), 84–96. doi:10.3389/frvir.2020.00001

Smirnov, A., Kashevnik, A., Balandin, S. I., & Laizane, S. (2013). Intelligent mobile tourist guide. In S. Balandin, S. Andreev, & Y. Koucheryavy (Eds.), *Internet of things, smart spaces, and next generation networking*. Springer. doi:10.1007/978-3-642-40316-3_9

Smith, M. K. (2003). *Issues in cultural tourism studies*. Routledge. doi:10.4324/9780203402825

Smith, M. K., Egedy, T., Csizmady, A., Olt, G., Jancsik, A., & Michalkó, G. (2017). Non-Planning and Tourism Consumption in Budapest's Inner City. *Tourism Geographies*, *20*(3), 524–548. doi:10.1080/14616688.2017.1387809

Smith, M. K., Pinke-Sziva, I., & Olt, G. (2019). Overtourism and Resident Resistance in Budapest. *Tourism Planning & Development*, *16*(4), 376–392. doi:10.1080/21568316.2019.1595705

Smith, M. K., & Richards, G. (2013). *The Routledge Handbook of Cultural Tourism*. Routledge. doi:10.4324/9780203120958

Smith, M., & Puczko, L. (2010). Out with the old, in with the new? Twenty years of post-socialist marketing in Budapest. *Journal of Town & City Management*, *1*(3), 288–299.

Smith, P. R., & Zook, Z. (2011). *Marketing communications integrating offline and online with social media*. Kogan Page.

Smith, S. L. J. (1994). The tourism product. *Annals of Tourism Research, 21*(3), 582–595. doi:10.1016/0160-7383(94)90121-X

Smith, T. (2009). The social media revolution. *International Journal of Market Research, 51*(4), 559–561. doi:10.2501/S1470785309200773

Smith, V. L. (1989). *Hosts and guests: The anthropology of tourism.* University of Pennsylvania Press. doi:10.9783/9780812208016

Snis, U. L., Olsson, A. K., & Bernhard, I. (2021). Becoming a smart old town – How to manage stakeholder collaboration and cultural heritage. *Journal of Cultural Heritage Management and Sustainable Development, 11*(4), 627–641. Advance online publication. doi:10.1108/JCHMSD-10-2020-0148

Snyder, K. (2017). *Oceans Have More Historical Artifacts Than All Museums Combined.* Clipperton Project (E.T: 25.05.2021): https://www.clippertonproject.com/oceans-have-more-historical-artifacts-than-all-museums-combined/

Soares, T. C. (2009). *Características do Turismo de Experiência: Estudos de caso em Belo Horizonte e Sabará sobre inovação e diversidade na valorização dos clientes.* Minas Gerais–UFMG.

Soava, G. (2015). Development prospects of the tourism industry in the digital age. *Revista Tinerilor Economist, 1*, 101–116.

Solis, B. (2010). *Engage: The complete guide for brands and businesses to build, cultivate, and measure success in the new web.* John Wiley & Sons.

Sommer, C., & Helbrecht, I. (2017). Seeing like a tourist city: How administrative constructions of conflictive urban tourism shape its future. *Journal of Tourism Futures, 3*(2), 157–170. doi:10.1108/JTF-07-2017-0037

Sousa, B. B., Castro, C., Luís, M. E., & Lopes, P. (2021). Religious and Spiritual Tourism: From Its Origins to Alentejo (Portugal). In Global Development of Religious Tourism (pp. 44-64). IGI Global.

Sousa, B. B., Magalhães, F. C., & Soares, D. B. (2021). The Role of Relational Marketing in Specific Contexts of Tourism: A Luxury Hotel Management Perspective. In Building Consumer-Brand Relationship in Luxury Brand Management (pp. 223-243). IGI Global. doi:10.4018/978-1-7998-4369-6.ch011

Sousa, B.; Malheiro, A. & Veloso, C. M. (2019). O Marketing Territorial como Contributo para a Segmentação Turística: Modelo conceptual no turismo de shopping. *International Journal of Marketing, Communication and New Media, 5*, 93-116.

Sousa, B. B., & Magalhães, F. C. (2019). An Approach on Attachment in Public Marketing and Higher Education Management Contexts. In C. Machado & J. Davim (Eds.), *Higher Education and the Evolution of Management, Applied Sciences, and Engineering Curricula* (pp. 151–171). IGI Global. doi:10.4018/978-1-5225-7259-6.ch006

Sousa, B., & Alves, G. (2019). The role of relationship marketing in behavioural intentions of medical tourism services and guest experiences. *Journal of Hospitality and Tourism Insights, 2*(3), 224–240. doi:10.1108/JHTI-05-2018-0032

South Australian Tourism Commission. (2015). *Social Media Hints and Tips for the Tourism Industry.* https://www.tourism.sa.gov.au/assets/documents/Industry/Social_Media_Hints_and_Tips.pdf

Soydas, M. E., & Saclı, Ç. (2019). Big Data and Tourism 4.0. In Digital Tourism: The New Future of the Industry (pp. 91-101). Education Publishing.

Space Center Houston. (2021). Date Accessed: 01.06.2021. https://spacecenter.org/

Spachos, P., & Plataniotis, K. N. (2020). BLE beacons for indoor positioning at an interactive IoT-based Smart Museum. *IEEE Systems Journal, 14*(3), 3483–3493. doi:10.1109/JSYST.2020.2969088

Sparks, B. A., & Bradley, G. L. (2017). A "Triple A" Typology of Responding to Negative Consumer-Generated Online Reviews. *Journal of Hospitality & Tourism Research (Washington, D.C.)*, *41*(6), 719–745. doi:10.1177/1096348014538052

Sparks, B. A., & Browning, V. (2011). The impact of online reviews on hotel booking intentions and perception of trust. *Tourism Management*, *32*(6), 1310–1323. doi:10.1016/j.tourman.2010.12.011

Spennemann, D. (2007). Extreme cultural tourism from Antarctica to the Moon. *Annals of Tourism Research*, *34*(4), 898–918. doi:10.1016/j.annals.2007.04.003

Standing, C., Vasudavan, T., & Borbely, S. (1998). Re-engineering travel agencies with the world wide web. *Electronic Markets*, *8*(4), 40–43. doi:10.1080/10196789800000055

Stankov, U., & Gretzel, U. (2020). Tourism 4.0 technologies and tourist experiences: A human-centered design perspective. *Information Technology & Tourism*, *22*(3), 1–12. doi:10.100740558-020-00186-y

Stankov, U., Jovanović, T., Pavluković, V., Kalinić, C., Drakulić-Kovačević, N., & Cimbaljević, M. (2018). A regional survey of current practices on destination marketing organizations' Facebook Pages: The case of EU and US. *Geographica Pannonica*, *22*(2), 81–96. Advance online publication. doi:10.5937/22-16673

Stankov, U., Kennell, J., Morrison, A. M., & Vujicic, M. D. (2019). The view from above: The relevance of shared aerial drone videos for destination marketing. *Journal of Travel & Tourism Marketing*, *36*(7), 808–822. doi:10.1080/10548408.2019.1575787

Statista. (2017). https://www.statista.com/study/12393/social-networks-statista-dossier/

Statista. (2021). Retrieved on 15.06.2021, https://www.statista.com

Stebbins, R. A. (1996). Cultural tourism as serious leisure. *Annals of Tourism Research*, *23*(4), 948–950. doi:10.1016/0160-7383(96)00028-X

Steffen, J. H., Gaskin, J. E., Meservy, T. O., Jenkins, J. L., & Wolman, I. (2019). Framework of affordances for virtual reality and augmented reality. *Journal of Management Information Systems*, *36*(3), 683–729. doi:10.1080/07421222.2019.1628877

Stelick, A., Penano, A. G., Riak, A. C., & Dando, R. (2018). Dynamic context sensory testing–A proof of concept study bringing virtual reality to the sensory booth. *Journal of Food Science*, *83*(8), 2047–2051. doi:10.1111/1750-3841.14275 PMID:30044500

Sterchele, D. (2020). Memorable tourism experiences and their consequences: An interaction ritual (IR) theory approach. *Annals of Tourism Research, 81*(October), 1–13.

Steuer, J. (1992). Defining Virtual Reality: Dimensions Determining Telepresence. *Journal of Communication*, *42*(4), 73–93. doi:10.1111/j.1460-2466.1992.tb00812.x

Stewart, J. (2017). *Free digital archives Europeana collections*. https://mymodernmet.com/free-digital-archiveseuropeana-collections/

Stoffelen, A. (2020). Revitalising place-based commercial heritage: A Cultural Political Economy approach to the renaissance of lambic beers in Belgium. *International Journal of Heritage Studies*, *00*(00), 1–14. doi:10.1080/13527258.2020.1862275

Stolterman, E., & Fors, A. C. (2004). Information technology and the good life. In B. Kaplan, D. P. Truex, D. Wastell, A. T. Wood-Harper, & J. I. DeGross (Eds.), *Information systems research* (pp. 687–692). Springer. doi:10.1007/1-4020-8095-6_45

Stylianou-Lambert, T. (2011). Gazing from home: Cultural tourism and art museums. *Annals of Tourism Research, 38*(2), 403–421. doi:10.1016/j.annals.2010.09.001

Sucaklı, G., & Güzel, T. (2020). Augmented Reality Technology Applications in Museum Tourism; World and Turkey Examples. *Journal of Tourism Research Institute., 1*(2), 71–82.

Sukanthasirikul, K., & Trongpanich, W. (2016). Cultural Tourism experience on customer satisfaction: Evidence from Thailand. *Journal of Economic and Social Development, 3*(1), 17–25.

Suler, J. (2004). Computer and Cyberspace "Addiction". *International Journal of Applied Psychoanalytic Studies, 1*(4), 359–362. doi:10.1002/aps.90

Sundar, S. S., Kalyanaraman, S., & Brown, J. (2003). Explicating Web Site Interactivity: Impression Formation Effects in Political Campaign Sites. *Communication Research, 30*(1), 30–59. doi:10.1177/0093650202239025

Susanto, D. R., & Kiswantoro, A. (2021). Tourism branding: A strategy of regional tourism sustainability post CO-VID-19 in Yogyakarta. *IOP Conference Series. Earth and Environmental Science, 704*(1), 012003. doi:10.1088/1757-899X/1108/1/012003

Sussmann, S., & Vanhegan, H. (2000). Virtual reality and the tourism product: Substitution or complement? In H. R. Hansen, M. Bichler, & H. Mahrer (Eds.), *Proceedings of the 8th European Conference on Information Systems, 2* (pp. 1077–1083). Academic Press.

Swarbrooke, J. (1999). *Sustainable Tourism Management.* CABI Publishing.

Swarbrooke, J., & Horner, S. (2007). *Consumer behaviour in tourism.* Routledge. doi:10.4324/9780080466958

Syafina, I., Juni, M. H., İbrahim, F., & Abdul Manaf, R. (2017). Valuation of Impacts in Cost Benefit Analysis. *International Journal of Public Health and Clinical Sciences, 4*(4), 51–60.

Sylaiou, S., Mania, K., Karoulis, A., & White, M. (2010). Exploring the relationship between presence and enjoyment in a virtual museum. *International Journal of Human-Computer Studies, 68*(5), 243–253. doi:10.1016/j.ijhcs.2009.11.002

T.C. Kültür ve Turizm Bakanlığı. (2014). *Müzeler Ulusal Envanter Sistemi (MUES)* [Museum National Inventory System]. https://kvmgm.ktb.gov.tr/TR-98489/muzeler-ulusal-envanter-sistemi-mues.html

T.C. Kültür ve Turizm Bakanlığı. (2021a). *Somut olmayan kültürel mirasın korunması sözleşmesi hakkında* [On the convention for the protection of the intangible cultural heritage]. https://aregem.ktb.gov.tr/TR-50837/somut-olmayan-kulturel-mirasin-korunmasi-sozlesmesi-hak-.html

T.C. Kültür ve Turizm Bakanlığı. (2021b). *Somut olmayan kültürel miras ulusal envanteri* [National inventory of intangible cultural heritage]. https://aregem.ktb.gov.tr/TR-159257/somut-olmayan-kulturel-miras-ulusal-envanteri.html

T.C. Kültür ve Turizm Bakanlığı. (2021c). *Somut olmayan kültürel miras envanter çalışmaları* [Intangible cultural heritage inventory works]. https://aregem.ktb.gov.tr/TR-50839/somut-olmayan-kulturel-miras-envanter-calismalari.html

Tadeia, H. (2013). *Contributos para o estudo da colecção de pintura do Museu Rainha D. Leonor – Beja.* Universidade Aberta, Dissertação de Mestrado.

Tarssanen, S., & Kylänen, M. (2007). A Theoretical Model for Producing Experiences – A Touristic Perspective. In *Lapland Centre of Expertise for the Experience Industry* (pp. 134–154). Lapland University Press.

Taufer, L., & Ferreira, L. T. (2019). Realidade Virtual no Turismo: Entretenimento ou uma mudança de paradigma? *Rosa dos Ventos – Turismo e Hospitalidade, 11*(4), 908–921. doi:10.18226/21789061.v11i4p908

Tavitiyaman, P., Qu, H., Tsang, W. S. L., & Lam, C. W. R. (2021). The influence of smart tourism applications on perceived destination image and behavioral intention: The moderating role of information search behavior. *Journal of Hospitality and Tourism Management*, *46*, 476–487. doi:10.1016/j.jhtm.2021.02.003

Taylor, M., & Kent, M. L. (2014). Dialogic Engagement: Clarifying Foundational Concepts. *Journal of Public Relations Research*, *26*(5), 384–398. doi:10.1080/1062726X.2014.956106

Taylor, M., Kent, M. L., & White, W. J. (2001). How activist organizations are using the Internet to build relationships. *Public Relations Review*, *27*(3), 263–284. doi:10.1016/S0363-8111(01)00086-8

TDK. (2021). https://sozluk.gov.tr/

Teece, D. J. (2010). Business models, business strategy and innovation. *Long Range Planning*, *43*(2-3), 172–194. doi:10.1016/j.lrp.2009.07.003

Tekin, O., Bideci, M., & Aydın, A. (2017). Comparison of Mobile Guide Applications and Competence of Professional Tourist Guides in Transfer of Cultural Heritage (The Case of Konya Mevlana Museum). *Eurasia International Tourism Congress: Current Issues, Trends, and Indicators (EITOC-2015)*.

Terras, M. (2015). Opening Access to Collections: The Making and Using of Open Digitized Cultural Content. *Online Information Review*, *39*(5), 1–30. doi:10.1108/OIR-06-2015-0193

Tešin, A., Kovačić, S., Pivac, T., Vujičić, M. D., & Obradović, S. (2020). From children to seniors: Is culture accessible to everyone? *International Journal of Culture, Tourism and Hospitality Research*, *15*(2), 183–201. doi:10.1108/IJCTHR-08-2019-0142

Tham, A., Mair, J., & Croy, G. (2019). Social media influence on tourists' destination choice: Importance of context. *Tourism Recreation Research*, *45*(2), 161–175. doi:10.1080/02508281.2019.1700655

The Economist. (2021). *Wikipedia is 20, and its reputation has never been higher*. Retrieved from https://econ.st/3lLpYs3

Thevenot, G. (2007). Blogging as a social media. *Tourism and Hospitality Research*, *7*(3), 287–289. doi:10.1057/palgrave.thr.6050062

Tholos. (2009). *Tholos virtual theater*. Retrieved from https://bit.ly/3peKaoF

Thomas, P. Y. (2011). Cloud computing. *The Electronic Library*, *29*(2), 214–224. doi:10.1108/02640471111125177

Throsby, D. (1997). Seven questions in the economics of cultural heritage. In M. Hutter & I. Rizzo (Eds.), *Economic Perspectives on Cultural Heritage* (pp. 13–30). Macmillan. doi:10.1007/978-1-349-25824-6_2

Thwaites, H., Santano, D., Esmaeili, H., & See, Z. S. (2019). A Malaysian cultural heritage digital compendium. *Digital Applications in Archaeology and Cultural Heritage*, *15*, e00116. doi:10.1016/j.daach.2019.e00116

Tighe, A. J. (1985). Cultural tourism in the USA. *Tourism Management*, *6*(4), 234–251. doi:10.1016/0261-5177(85)90001-9

TikTok For Business. (2021). *Marketing on TikTok*. https://www.tiktok.com/business/en/

Tilden, F. (2007). Interpreting our Heritage (4th ed.). The University of North Carolina Press. (Original publicado em 1957)

Time. (2021). *These 29 numbers show how the covid-19 pandemic changed our lives over the last year*. https://time.com/5947302/covid-19-data/

Timothy, D. J. (2011). *Cultural Heritage and Tourism: An Introduction*. Cahnnel View Publications. doi:10.21832/9781845411787

Tinsley, R., & Lynch, P. (2001). Small tourism business networks and destination development. *International Journal of Hospitality Management, 4*(20), 367–378. doi:10.1016/S0278-4319(01)00024-X

Toedt, M. (2016). *Hospitality net - beacons - top or flop for the hospitality industry?* Retrieved from https://www.hospitalitynet.org/news/4073267.html

Tokarchuk, O., Gabriele, R., & Maurer, O. (2017). Development of city tourism and well-being of urban residents: A case of German Magic Cities. *Tourism Economics, 23*(2), 343–359. doi:10.1177/1354816616656272

tom Dieck, M., & Jung, T. (2018). A theoretical model of mobile augmented reality acceptance in urban heritage tourism. *Current Issues in Tourism, 21*(2), 154–174. doi:10.1080/13683500.2015.1070801

Tomiuc, A. (2014). Navigating culture. Enhancing visitor museum experience through mobile technologies. From Smartphone to Google Glass. *The Journal of Medical Research, 7*(3), 33–47.

Topsakal, Y. (2018). Disabled-friendly mobile services in the context of smart tourism: Recommendations for Turkey 4.0. *Journal of Tourism Intelligence and Smartness, 1*(1), 1–13.

Topsakal, Y., Yüzbaşıoğlu, N., Çelík, P., & Bahar, M. (2018b). Tourism 4.0 - tourist 5.0: Why the human revolution is one number bigger than industrial revolutions? *Journal of Tourism Intelligence and Smartness, 1*(2), 1–11.

Topsakal, Y., Yüzbaşıoğlu, N., & Çuhadar, M. (2018a). Industrial revolutions and tourism: Turkey tourism 4.0 swot analysis and proposal for adaptation process. *Süleyman Demirel Üniversitesi İktisadi ve İdari Bilimler Fakültesi Dergisi, 23*, 1623–1638.

Torres, C. (1987). *Cerâmica islâmica portuguesa*. Mértola, Campo Arqueológico de Mértola.

Torres, C. (1992). *Povoamento antigo no Baixo Alentejo. Alguns problemas de topografia histórica. Arqueologia Medieval, n.º 1/fevereiro*. Edições Afrontamento.

Tosun, N., & Saglık, E. (2019). Internet of Things and Tourism 4.0. In Digital Tourism: The New Future of the Industry (pp. 91-101). Education Publishing House.

Tourism Innovation Summit (TIS). (2021, April 19). *Travel & Tourism after Covid-19*. https://www.tisglobalsummit.com/travel-tourism-after-covid-19/

Tran, H. M., Huertas, A. & Moreno, A. (2017). A new framework for the analysis of smart tourism destinations a comparative case study of two Spanish destinations. *Actas del Seminario Internacional Destinos Turísticos Inteligentes: Nuevos Horizantes En La Investigacion y Gestion del Turismo*, 190-214.

TRAVEL BI. (n.d.). Turismo em Números – 2019. *Turismo de Portugal*.

Travis, R. (2010). Bioshock in the cave: ethical education in plato and in video games. In K. Schrier & D. Gibson (Eds.), *Ethics and game design*. IGI Global. doi:10.4018/978-1-61520-845-6.ch006

Tripadvisor. (2017). Retrieved from https://tripadvisor.mediaroom.com/tr-about-us

TripAdvisor. (2021). *Request Developer API*. Retrieved from https://developer-tripadvisor.com/content-api/request-api-access/

Trout, J., & Rivkin, S. (2009). *Repositioning: Marketing in an Era of Competition, Change and Crisis*. McGraw-Hill Education.

Tsaur, S., Chiu, Y., & Wang, C. (2006). The visitors behavioral consequences of experiential marketing: An empirical study on Taipei zoo. *Journal of Travel & Tourism Marketing, 21*(1), 47–64. doi:10.1300/J073v21n01_04

Tsiotsou, R. H., & Goldsmith, R. E. (2012). *Strategic marketing in tourism services.* Emerald Group Publishing.

Tulane. (2021). *What's the difference between AR and VR?* Tulane University (E.T: 6.10.21): https://sopa.tulane.edu/blog/whats-difference-between-ar-and-vr

Tung, V. W., & Ritchie, J. R. (2011). Exploring the essence of memorable tourism experiences. *Annals of Tourism Research, 38*(4), 1367–1386. doi:10.1016/j.annals.2011.03.009

Türkan, T. (2006). Televizyon Haber Yayıncılığında Tabloidleşme Olgusu: ATV ve Kanal 7 Haber Bültenlerinin Karşılaştırılması (Doktora tezi). Ege Üniversitesi Sosyal Bilimler Enstitüsü, İzmir.

Türker, A., & Çelik, İ. (2012). Somut olmayan kültürel miras unsurlarının turistik ürün olarak geliştirilmesine yönelik alternatif öneriler [Alternative proposals for tourist product development of ıntangible cultural heritage elements]. *Yeni Fikir Dergisi,* (12), 86–98.

Türkiye Kültür Portalı. (2021). *Kültür atlası.* https://www.kulturportali.gov.tr/portal/halk-bilimi-ve-kultur-atlasi

Türkiye Yazma Eserler Kurumu Başkanlığı (TYEKB). (2021a). http://www.yazmalar.gov.tr/

Türkiye Yazma Eserler Kurumu Başkanlığı (TYEKB). (2021b). *Basit tarama* [Simple scan]. http://www.yazmalar.gov.tr/basit-arama?q=yazma

Türkiye Yazma Eserler Kurumu Başkanlığı (TYEKB). (2021c). *Keşfu'z-Zunûn 'an-Esâmî'l-Kutubi ve 'l-Fünûn.* http://www.yazmalar.gov.tr/eser/kesfuz-zun%C3%BBn-an-esam%C3%AEl-kutubi-ve-l-fun%C3%BBn/126743

Türkmendağ, Z., & Tuna, M. (2021). Empowering leadership and knowledge management: The mediating role of followers' technology use. *Journal of Organizational Change Management.* doi:10.1108/JOCM-11-2020-0364

Tussyadiah, I. P., Wang, D., & Jia, C. H. (2017). *Virtual reality and attitudes toward tourism destinations. In Information and communication technologies in tourism.* Springer.

Tussyadiah, I., Park, S., & Fesenmaier, D. R. (2011). Assessing the effectiveness of consumer narratives for destination marketing. *Journal of Hospitality & Tourism Research (Washington, D.C.), 35*(1), 64–78. doi:10.1177/1096348010384594

Tussyadiah, P., Wang, D., Jung, T. M., & Dieck, M. C. (2018). Virtual reality, presence, and attitude change: Empirical evidence from Tourism. *Tourism Management, 66,* 140–154.

Tuyed. (2016). http://www.tuyed.org.tr/turizmde-insansi-robotlar-devri/

Tüzel, B. (2020). Covid-19 salgını sürecinde el sanatları geleneği deneyimleri [The experiences of traditional craftsmanship in the process of covid-19 pandemic]. *Milli Folklor, 16*(127), 87–100.

Tüzünkan, D. (2019). Turizm 4.0. In O. İçoz & M. Uysal (Eds.), *Turizm Ansiklopedisi - Türkiye: Turizmin ve Ağırlama Endüstrisinin Temel Kavramları* (p. 521). Detay Yayıncılık.

Tweed, C., & Shutherland, M. (2007). Built cultural heritage and sustainable urban development. *Landscape and Urban Planning, 83*(1), 62–69. doi:10.1016/j.landurbplan.2007.05.008

Twitter. (2020). *Establish your Twitter presence.* https://business.twitter.com/en/basics/create-a-twitter-business-profile.html

Tylor, E. B. (1871). *Primitive culture: Researches into the development of mythology, philosophy, religion, art and custom* (Vol. 2). J. Murray.

Tzima, S., Styliaras, G., Bassounas, A., & Tzima, M. (2020). Harnessing the potential of storytelling and mobile technology in intangible cultural heritage: A case study in early childhood education in sustainability. *Sustainability*, *12*(22), 2–22. doi:10.3390u12229416

Uğur, N. (2020). *Effects of Internet on Tourism Marketing: An Empirical Analysis About Online Tourism. In Tools and Techniques for Implementing International E-Trading Tactics for Competitive Advantage.* IGI Global.

Ülgen, Y. (2020). *Sosyal medyadakï yenï kanaat önderlerïnïn kültür turïzmï alanında tüketïcï karar verme sürecïne etkïsï: Instagram üzerïne bïr inceleme* (Master's dissertation). İstanbul Üniversitesi.

Umbelino, J. (2014). Os Valores do Território no Lazer e no Turismo. In Produtos e Competividade do Turismo na Lusofonia (pp. 203–216). Lisboa: Escolar Editora.

UNDP. (2018). *Channel17 Partnership for the Goals.* https://pacificfilmfoundation.org/partnerships17?gclid=EAIaIQ obChMIpKLNvbSw8QIVCdTtCh0MWATrEAAYAyAAEgKPy_D_BwE

UNEP & UNWTO. (2005). *Making tourism more sustainable: a guide for policy makers.* Author.

UNESCO (2017). *Convention for the Safeguarding of the Intangible Cultural Heritage.* UNESCO.

UNESCO Report, . (2020). *Museums around the world in the face of covıd-19.* UNESCO.

UNESCO Türkiye Milli Komisyonu. (2021). *Somut Olmayan Kültürel Miras Listelerinde Türkiye* [Turkey on Intangible Cultural Heritage Lists]. https://www.unesco.org.tr/Pages/126/123/UNESCO-%C4%B0nsanl%C4%B1%C4%9F%C4%B1n-Somut-Olmayan-K%C3%BClt%C3%BCrel-Miras%C4%B1-Temsil%C3%AE-Listesi

UNESCO. (1972). *Convention for the Protection of the Cultural and Natural Heritage.* www.unesco.org.tr

UNESCO. (1990). *Third medium-term plan (1990-1995).* UNESCO, General Conference, 25th session. https://unesdoc. unesco.org/ark:/48223/pf0000084697

UNESCO. (2001). *UNESCO Universal Declaration on Cultural Diversity.* https://www.refworld.org/docid/435cbcd64.html

UNESCO. (2001). *Universal Declaration on Cultural Diversity.* Accessed on October 6, 2021. https://www.refworld. org/docid/435cbcd64.html

UNESCO. (2001a). *Submerged Archaeologıcal Sıtes: Commercıal Exploıtatıon Compared To Long-Term Protectıon.* http://www.unesco.org/new/en/culture/themes/underwater-cultural-heritage/2001-convention/

UNESCO. (2001b). *Protection of the Underwater Cultural Heritage.* Underwater Cultural Heritage. http://www.unesco. org/new/en/culture/themes/underwater-cultural-heritage/2001-convention/#:~:text=The%20UNESCO%20Convention%20 on%20the,protect%20their%20submerged%20cultural%20heritage.&text=provides%20widely%20recognized%20practical%20rules,research%20of

UNESCO. (2003). *Charter on the Preservation of Digital Heritage.* http://portal.unesco.org/en/ev.php-URL_ID=17721&URL_DO=DO_TOPIC&URL_SECTION=201.html

UNESCO. (2003). *Convention for the Safeguarding of the Intangible Cultural Heritage.* http://www.unesco.org/culture/ ich/doc/src/00009-TR-PDF.pdf

UNESCO. (2003). *Report by the Governing Board on the Activities of the UNESCO Institute for Information Technologies in Education (2002-2003).* UNESCO.

UNESCO. (2003). *Somut Olmayan Kültürel Mirasın Korunması Sözleşmesi* [Convention for the Safeguarding of the Intangible Cultural Heritage]. https://ich.unesco.org/doc/src/00009-TR-PDF.pdf

UNESCO. (2005). *Venice Charter 1964*. https://www.international.icomos.org/charters/venice_e.htm

UNESCO. (2006). Towards Sustainable Strategies for Creative Tourism, Discussion Report of the Planning Meeting for 2008. UNESCO.

UNESCO. (2006). *Towards Sustainable Strategies for Creative Tourism: Discussion Report of the Planning Meeting for 2008, International Conference on Creative Tourism*. Retrieved from https://unesdoc.unesco.org/images/0015/001598/159811e.pdf

UNESCO. (2014). *Tangible Cultural Heritage*. Accessed on June 19, 2021. http://www.unesco.org/new/en/cairo/culture/tangible- cultural-heritage/

UNESCO. (2020a). *Culture & covid-19 impact & response tracker*. https://en.unesco.org/sites/default/files/issue_1_en_culture_covid-19_tracker.pdf

UNESCO. (2020b). *RESILIART Artists and Creativity beyond Crisis*. https://en.unesco.org/news/resiliart-artists-and-creativity-beyond-crisis#

UNESCO. (2020c). *UNESCO supports culture and heritage during COVID-19's shutdown*. https://whc.unesco.org/en/news/2099

UNESCO. (2021a). *Dünya miras listesi* [World heritage list]. http://whc.unesco.org/en/list/&order=country#alphaT

UNESCO. (2021b). *Dünya miras listesi (Türkiye)* [World heritage list (Turkey)]. http://whc.unesco.org/en/statesparties/tr

UNESCO. (2021c). *Cutting Edge | Bringing cultural tourism back in the game*. https://en.unesco.org/news/cutting-edge-bringing-cultural-tourism-back-game

UNESCO. (2021c). *Purpose of the lists of intangible cultural heritage and of the register of good safeguarding practices*. https://ich.unesco.org/en/purpose-of-the-lists-00807

UNESCO. (2021d). *Browse the lists of intangible cultural heritage and the register of good safeguarding practices*. https://ich.unesco.org/en/lists

UNESCO. (n.d.). *Historic Areas of Istanbul*. World Heritage List. https://whc.unesco.org/en/list/356/

UNESCO. (n.d.). *What is meant by "cultural heritage"?* http://www.unesco.org/new/en/culture/themes/illicit-trafficking-of-cultural-property/unesco-database-of-national-cultural-heritage-laws/frequently-asked-questions/definition-of-the-cultural-heritage/

United Nations (UN). (2007). *Indicators of Sustainable Development: Guidelines and Medhodologies*. UN Publishing.

United Nations Educational, Scientific and Cultural Organization. (1972). *Convention Concerning the Protection of the World Cultural and Natural Heritage*. Author.

United Nations Educational, Scientific and Cultural Organization. (2003). *Text of the Convention for the Safeguarding of the Intangible Cultural Heritage*. Author.

United Nations Educational, Scientific and Cultural Organization. (2021). *What is meant by "cultural heritage"?* http://www.unesco.org/new/en/culture/themes/illicit-trafficking-of-cultural-property/unesco-database-of-national-cultural-heritage-laws/frequently-asked-questions/definition-of-the-cultural-heritage/

United Nations Educational, Scientific and Cultural Organizations (UNESCO). (2020). *Museums around the world in the face of COVID-19*. UNESCO.

UNWTO (World Tourism Organization). (2020, April 19). *International tourism highlights.* https://www.e-unwto.org/doi/pdf/10.18111/9789284421152

UNWTO (World Tourism Organization). (2021, April 14). *International tourism down 70% as travel restrictions impact all regions.* https://www.unwto.org/taxonomy/term/347

UNWTO Tourism Highlights. (2007). doi:10.18111/9789284413539

UNWTO. (2004). *Tourism Market Trends.* World Tourism Organisation.

UNWTO. (2007). *A Practical Guide to Tourism Destination Management.* Madrid, Spain: World Tourism Organization. Retrieved from https://www.e-unwto.org/doi/abs/10.18111/9789284412433

UNWTO. (2008). *Tourism Satellite Account: Recommended Methodological Framework 2008.* UNWTO.

UNWTO. (2015). *Tourism at World Heritage Sites – Challenges and Opportunities: International tourism seminar.* UNWTO. 10.18111/9789284416608

UNWTO. (2016). *UNWTO congress to discuss the links between cultural heritage and creative tourism.* Press Release. https://www.unwto.org/archive/europe/press-release/2016-11-23/unwto-congress-discuss-links-between-cultural-heritage-and-creative-tourism

UNWTO. (2018). *'Overtourism'? Understanding and Managing Urban Tourism Growth beyond Perceptions.* UNWTO.

UNWTO. (2019). *8th UNWTO Global Summit on Urban Tourism Smart Cities, Smart Destinations. Top Incredible Robots that Actually Exist.* https://www.youtube.com/watch?v=ZgtpUd5TsIg

UNWTO. (2019). Retrieved from http://www.unwto.org

UNWTO. (2021). *Tourist numbers down 83% but confidence slowly rising.* https://www.unwto.org/news/tourist-numbers-down-83-but-confidence-slowly-rising

Uriely, N. (2005). The Tourist Experience. *Annals of Tourism Research, 32*(1), 199–216. doi:10.1016/j.annals.2004.07.008

Urry, J. (1990). Tourist gaze: travel, leisure and society. *Tourist gaze: Travel, leisure and society.*

Vala, J. (1986). A Análise de Conteúdo. In A. Santos Silva & J. Madureira Pinto (Eds.), *Metodologia das Ci~encias Sociais* (pp. 101–128). Edições Afrontamento.

Vallez, N., Krauss, S., Espinosa-Aranda, J. L., Pagani, A., Seirafi, K., & Deniz, O. (2020). Automatic museum audio guide. *Sensors (Basel), 20*(3), 779. doi:10.339020030779 PMID:32023954

Van der Ark, L. A., & Richards, G. (2006). Attractiveness of cultural activities in European cities: A latent class approach. *Tourism Management, 27*(6), 1408–1413. doi:10.1016/j.tourman.2005.12.014

Van der Zee, E., & Bertocchi, D. (2018). Finding patterns in urban tourist behaviour: A social network analysis approach based on TripAdvisor reviews. *Information Technology & Tourism, 20*(1–4), 153–180. doi:10.100740558-018-0128-5

Van Gorp, B. (2012). Guidebooks and the representation of 'other' places. In M. Kasimoğlu & H. Aydin (Eds.), *Strategies for tourism industry – micro and macro perspectives* (pp. 3–32). InTech.

van Hage, W. R., Stash, N., Wang, Y., & Aroyo, L. (2010). Finding Your Way through the Rijksmuseum with an Adaptive Mobile Museum Guide. In *The Semantic Web: Research and Applications* (pp. 46–59). Springer. doi:10.1007/978-3-642-13486-9_4

Van Krevelen, D. W. F., & Poelman, R. (2010). A survey of augmented reality technologies, applications and limitations. *The International Journal of Virtual Reality: a Multimedia Publication for Professionals, 9*(2), 1–20. doi:10.20870/IJVR.2010.9.2.2767

Van Loon, R., Gosens, T., & Rouwendal, J. (2014). Cultural Heritage and Attractiveness of Cities: Evidence from Recreation Trips. *Journal of Cultural Economics, 38*(3), 253–285. doi:10.100710824-014-9222-5

Van Wee, B. (2007). Rail Infrastructure: Challenges for Cost-Benefit Analysis and Other ex-ante Evaluations. *Transportation Planning and Technology, 30*(1), 31–48. doi:10.1080/03081060701207995

van Winden, W., & de Carvalho, L. (2017). *Cities and digitalization: How digitalization changes cities: Innovation for the urban economy of tomorrow.* Amsterdam University of Applied Sciences.

Vareiro, L., Sousa, B. B., & Silva, S. S. (2020). The importance of museums in the tourist development and the motivations of their visitors: An analysis of the Costume Museum in Viana do Castelo. *Journal of Cultural Heritage Management and Sustainable Development, 11*(1), 39–57. doi:10.1108/JCHMSD-05-2020-0065

Vargün, Ö., & Nuhoğlu, M. (2019). Kültürel miras eğitiminde bilgi iletişim teknolojilerinin rolü ve mobil uygulamalar [The role of ICT in cultural heritage education and evaluation of mobile communication vehicle]. *UNIMUSEUM, 2*(2), 45–53.

Varlı, B. (2011). *The analysis of communication-based activities in the process of city: İstanbul 2010 European capital of culture* [Unpublished master's dissertation]. University of Kocaeli, Kocaeli, Turkey.

Varol, Ç. (2017). Sürdürülebilir gelişmede akıllı kent yaklaşımı [Smart city approach in sustainable development]. *Çağdaş Yerel Yönetimler, 26*(1), 43-58.

Vaughn, R. (1980). How advertising works: A planning model. *Journal of Advertising Research.*

Viana, A. (1988). *Gente e cousas d'Antre Minho e Lima.* Câmara Municipal de Viana do Castelo.

Vianello, M. (2017). The No Grandi campaign: Protests against cruise tourism in Venice. In C. Colomb & J. Novy (Eds.), *Protest and Resistance in the Tourist City* (pp. 171–190). Routledge., doi:10.4324/9781315719306-16

Vicini, S., Bellini, S., & Sanna, A. (2012). How to co-create internet of things-enabled services for smarter cities. *SMART 2012, The First International.*

Vigneron, F., & Johnson, L. W. (2004). Measuring perceptions of brand luxury. *Journal of Brand Management, 11*(6), 484–506. doi:10.1057/palgrave.bm.2540194

Villaespesa, E. (2019). Museum Collections and Online Users: Development of a Segmentation Model for the Metropolitan Museum of Art. *Visitor Studies, 22*(2), 233–252. doi:10.1080/10645578.2019.1668679

Villalba, É. E., Azócar, A. L. S. M., & Jacques-García, F. A. (2021). State of the art on immersive virtual reality and its use in developing meaningful empathy. *Computers & Electrical Engineering, 93*, 107272. doi:10.1016/j.compeleceng.2021.107272

Virtual Museum Transitional Network. (2021). Retrieved from http://www.v-must.net/virtual-museums

Visitqatar. (2021). Retrieved on 18.06.2021, https://www.visitqatar.qa/en/plan-your-trip/travel-tips

Vlahakis, V., Ioannidis, N., Karigiannis, J., Tsotros, M., Gounaris, M., Stricker, D., Gleue, T., Daehne, P., & Almeida, L. (2002). Archeoguide: An augmented reality guide for archaeological sites. *Computer Graphics in Art History and Archaeology, 22*(5), 52–60. doi:10.1109/MCG.2002.1028726

Volpentesta, A. P., & Felicetti, A. M. (2012). Identifying opinion leaders in time-dependent commercial social networks. *Working Conference on Virtual Enterprises*. 10.1007/978-3-642-32775-9_57

Vong, F. (2016). Application of cultural tourist typology in a gaming destination–Macao. *Current Issues in Tourism*, *19*(9), 949–965. doi:10.1080/13683500.2013.842543

Vos, K., Rulle, M., & Jansen-Verbeke, M. (2008). Cultural heritage and the rejuvenation of spa towns. Evidence from four European cities. In M. Jansen-Verbeke, G. K. Priestley, & A. P. Russo (Eds.), *Cultural resources for tourism: Patterns, processes, policies* (pp. 215–230). Nova Science Publishers.

Vrettakis, E., Kourtis, V., Katifori, A., Karvounis, M., Lougiakis, C., & Ioannidis, Y. (2019). Narralive–Creating and experiencing mobile digital storytelling in cultural heritage. *Digital Applications in Archaeology and Cultural Heritage*, *15*, e00114. doi:10.1016/j.daach.2019.e00114

VRfocus. (2018). Retrieved from https://www.vrfocus.com/2018/05/the-oriental-science-fiction-valley-is-chinas-first-vr-theme-park/

VRon. (2019). *Multi-user VR across industries made simple.* https://vr-on.com/stage-vr- collaboration.html

VRS - Virtual Reality Society. (2017). *Headsight first motion tracking HMD.* Retrieved from https://www.vrs.org.uk/virtual-reality/history.html

Vu, H. Q., Li, G., Law, R., & Zhang, Y. (2018). Tourist Activity Analysis by Leveraging Mobile Social Media Data. *Journal of Travel Research*, *57*(7), 883–898. doi:10.1177/0047287517722232

Vujičić, M. D., Kalinić, Č., & Vasiljević, Đ. A. (2019). Presence of Hotels in Serbia on Major Social Media Platforms. In *The Contemporary Trend in Tourism and Hospitality 2019* (pp. 9–16). University of Novi Sad, Faculty of Sciences, Department for Geography, Tourism and Hotel Management.

Vujičić, M. D., Kennell, J., Morrison, A., Filimonau, V., Papuga-Štajner, I., & Stankov, U. (2020). Fuzzy Modelling of Tourist Motivation: An Age-Related Model for Sustainable, Multi-Attraction, Urban Destinations. *Sustainability*, *12*(20), 8698. doi:10.3390u12208698

Wachsmuth, D., & Weisler, A. (2018). Airbnb and the rent gap: Gentrification through the sharing economy. *Environment & Planning A. Economy and Space*, *50*(6), 1147–1170. doi:10.1177/0308518X18778038

Wade, M. (2015). *A conceptual framework for digital business transformation.* Retrieved from https://www.imd.org/contentassets/d0a4d992d38a41ff85de509156475caa/framework

Wadhwa, V. (2015). How The Cutting Edge of Virtual Reality Is Making The Real World Seem Boring. *The Washington Post.* Retrieved from https://www.washingtonpost.com/news/innovations/wp/2015/10/21/how-the-cutting-edge-of-virtual-reality-is-making-the-real-world-seem-boring/

Wagler, A., & Hanus, M. D. (2018). Comparing virtual reality tourism to real-life experience: Effects of presence and engagement on attitude and enjoyment. *Communication Research Reports*, *35*(5), 456–464. doi:10.1080/08824096.2018.1525350

Wall, G., & Mathieson, A. (2006). *Tourism: Change, impacts, and opportunities.* Pearson Education.

Walls, A. R., Okumus, F., Wang, Y. R., & Kwun, D. J. W. (2011). An epistemological view of consumer experiences. *International Journal of Hospitality Management*, *30*(1), 10–21. doi:10.1016/j.ijhm.2010.03.008

Wang, D., Li, X. R., & Li, Y. (2013). China's "smart tourism destination" initiative: A taste of the service-dominant logic. *Journal of Destination Marketing & Management*, *2*(2), 59–61. doi:10.1016/j.jdmm.2013.05.004

Wang, D., Park, S., & Fesenmaier, D. (2012). The Role of Smartphones in Mediating the Tourism Experience. *Journal of Travel Research*, *51*(4), 371–387. doi:10.1177/0047287511426341

Wang, D., Xiang, Z., & Fesenmaier, D. (2014). Smartphone use in everyday life and travel. *Journal of Travel Research*, *55*(1), 1–12.

Wang, H. Y., & Wang, S. H. (2010). Predicting mobile hotel reservation adoption: Insight from a perceived value standpoint. *International Journal of Hospitality Management*, *29*(4), 598–608. doi:10.1016/j.ijhm.2009.11.001

Wang, J., Xie, C., Huang, Q., & Morrison, A. M. (2020). Smart tourism destination experiences: The mediating impact of arousal levels. *Tourism Management Perspectives*, *35*, 100707. doi:10.1016/j.tmp.2020.100707

Wang, N. (2014). Research on construction of smart tourism perception system and management platform. *Advances in Social Science, Education and Humanities Research*, *30*, 1745–1748. doi:10.4028/www.scientific.net/AMM.687-691.1745

Wang, Q., Su, M., Zhang, M., & Li, R. (2021). Integrating digital technologies and public health to fight Covid-19 pandemic: Key technologies, applications, challenges and outlook of digital healthcare. *International Journal of Environmental Research and Public Health*, *18*(11), 6053. doi:10.3390/ijerph18116053 PMID:34199831

Wang, X., Li, X. R., Zhen, F., & Zhang, J. (2016). How smart is your tourist attraction? Measuring tourist preferences of smart tourism attractions via a FCEM-AHP and IPA Approach. *Tourism Management*, *54*, 309–320. doi:10.1016/j.tourman.2015.12.003

Wang, Y., & Fesenmaier, D. R. (2004). Towards understanding members' general participation in and active contribution to an online travel community. *Tourism Management*, *25*(6), 709–722. doi:10.1016/j.tourman.2003.09.011

Wang, Y., & Yang, Y. (2020). Dialogic communication on social media: How organizations use Twitter to build dialogic relationships with their publics. *Computers in Human Behavior*, *104*, 106183. doi:10.1016/j.chb.2019.106183

Wang, Z. X., & Pei, L. (2014). A systems thinking-based grey model for sustainability evaluation of urban tourism. *Kybernetes*, *43*(3/4), 462–479. doi:10.1108/K-07-2013-0137

Ward, J. S., & Barker, A. (2013). *Undefined By Data: A Survey of Big Data Definitions*. Academic Press.

Wasan, P. (2014). Sustainable Technology in Hospitality Industry. In V. Jauhari (Ed.), Managing Sustainability in the Hospitality and Tourism Industry Paradigms and Directions for the Future (pp. 101–135). Apple Academic Press.

Wasdani, K. P., & Prasad, A. (2020). The impossibility of social distancing among the urban poor: The case of an Indian slum in the times of COVID-19. *Local Environment*, *25*(5), 414–418. doi:10.1080/13549839.2020.1754375

Watson, T. (2020, April 14). *Gamification in tourism-benefits & use cases*. https://skywell.software/blog/gamification-in-tourism-benefits-use-cases

We are Social Digital. (2021). Retrieved from https://wearesocial.com/digital-2021

Wearing, S., Stevenson, D., & Young, T. (2009). Tourist cultures: Identity, place and the traveller. *Sage (Atlanta, Ga.)*.

Weber, J. (2014). Augmented reality gaming: A new paradigm for tourist experiences. *Information and Communication Technologies in Tourism*, 57-67.

Weil, S. E. (1999). From being about something to being for somebody: The ongoing transformation of the american museum. *Daedalus*, *128*(3), 229–258.

Weinberg, T. (2009). *The new community rules: Marketing on the social web*. O'Reilly Media.

Weinreich, N. K. (2011). *Hands-on social marketing: a step-by-step guide to designing change for good* (2nd ed.). SAGE Publications.

Weiser, M. (1999). The computer for the 21st century. *Mobile Computing and Communications Review*, *3*(3), 3–11. doi:10.1145/329124.329126

Weiss, P. L., Rand, D., Katz, N., & Kizony, R. (2004). Video capture virtual reality as a flexible and effective rehabilitation tool. *Journal of Neuroengineering and Rehabilitation*, *1*(1), 1–12. doi:10.1186/1743-0003-1-12 PMID:15679949

Wen, J., Kozak, M., Yang, S., & Liu, F. (2020). COVID-19: Potential effects on Chinese Citizens' lifestyle and travel. *Tourism Review*, *76*(1), 74–87. doi:10.1108/TR-03-2020-0110

Westerman, G., Calmejane, C., & Bonnet, D. (2011). Digital transformation: A roadmap for billion-dollar organizations. MIT Center for Digital Business.

Weyermuller, A., Jung, P., Rosa, M., & Kehl, L. (2015). A Indústria Criativa Verde e adaptação ambiental: O Turismo Criativo como Materialização. *Revista do Instituto de Ciências Sociais Aplicadas-Gestão e Desenvolvimento*, *12*(2), 83–96.

Whistler, C. T. (2018). Fantasy and reality: Tiepolo's poetic language at Wutzburg, Verona and Madrid. *Verona Illustrata*, *7*(3), 30–43.

WHO. (2006). *Guidelines for conducting cost benefit analysis of household energy and health interventions.* https://www.who.int/indoorair/publications/

WHO. (2021a). *Archived: WHO timeline - COVID-19.* https://www.who.int/news/item/27-04-2020-who-timeline---covid-19

WHO. (2021b). *WHO Coronavirus (COVID-19) dashboard.* https://covid19.who.int/

Wikipedia. (2009). *About.* Retrieved from https://bit.ly/3DHPDbk

Wikipedia. (2021). https://en.wikipedia.org/wiki/Technology

Williams, P. (1993). Information technology and tourism: a dependent factor for future survival. *World Travel and Tourism Review*, *3*, 200-205.

Williams, A. (2006). Tourism and hospitality marketing: Fantasy, feeling and fun. *International Journal of Contemporary Hospitality Management*, *18*(6), 482–495. doi:10.1108/09596110610681520

Williams, A. P., & Hobson, J. P. (1995). Virtual Reality and Tourism: Fact or Fantasy? *Tourism Management*, *16*(6), 423–427. doi:10.1016/0261-5177(95)00050-X

Williams, E. (2013). Food museums. In K. Albala (Ed.), *Routledge International Handbook of Food Studies* (pp. 229–237). Routledge.

Williams, P., & Hobson, J. P. (1995). Virtual reality and tourism: Fact or fantasy? *Tourism Management*, *16*(6), 423–427.

Wirtz, J. G., & Zimbres, T. M. (2018). A systematic analysis of research applying 'principles of dialogic communication' to organizational websites, blogs, and social media: Implications for theory and practice. *Journal of Public Relations Research*, *30*(1–2), 5–34. doi:10.1080/1062726X.2018.1455146

Wisansing, J., & Vongvisitsin, T. (2019). Local impacts of creative tourism initiatives. In N. Duxbury & G. Richards (Eds.), *A research agenda for creative tourism* (pp. 122–136). Elgar Research Agendas. doi:10.4337/9781788110723.00020

Wojciechowski, R., Walczak, K., White, M., & Cellary, W. (2004). Building virtual and Augmented Reality Museum Exhibitions. *Proceedings of the Ninth International Conference on 3D Web Technology-Web3D*, 135-144. 10.1145/985040.985060

Wolfram, G., & Burnill, C. (2012). The Tactical Tourist – Growing Self-awareness and Challenging the Strategists: Visitor-Groups in Berlin. In M. K. Smith & G. Richards (Eds.), *The Routledge Handbook of Cultural Tourism* (pp. 361–368). Routledge. doi:10.4324/9780203120958-60

Wolwort, K. (2019). *5 Major challenges for the VR industry*. The Innovation Enterprise Channels. Retrieved from https://channels.theinnovationenterprise.com/articles/5-major-challenges-of-vr-industry

Wong, A. (2015). The whole story, and then some: 'digital storytelling' in evolving museum practice. *MW2015. Museums and the Web, 2015*, 8–11.

Wood, L. (2000). Brands and equity: Definition and management. *Management Decision, 38*(9), 662–669. doi:10.1108/00251740010379100

Wood, R. E. (1984). Ethnic tourism, the state, and cultural change in Southeast Asia. *Annals of Tourism Research, 11*(3), 353–374. doi:10.1016/0160-7383(84)90027-6

Wood, S. A., Guerry, A. D., Silver, J. M., & Lacayo, M. (2013). Using social media to quantify nature-based tourism and recreation. *Scientific Reports, 3*(1), 2976. doi:10.1038rep02976 PMID:24131963

World Itineraries. (2020). *Augmented reality ingites museum experiences. A Luxury Travel Blog*. World Itineraries (E.T. 2021.05.20): https://worlditineraries.co/2020/08/12/augmented-reality-ignites-museum-experiences/

World Tourism Organisations (WTO). (2004). *Indicators of Sustainable Development for Tourism Destination: A Guide Book*. WTO Publishing.

World Tourism Organization & European Travel Commission. (2011). Handbook on Tourism Product Development. Madrid: World Tourism Organization (UNWTO) and the European Travel Commission (ETC).

World Tourism Organization. (1998). *Guide for Local Authorities on Developing Sustainable Tourism*. WTO.

World Tourism Organization. (2019). *Tourism definitions*. UNWTO.

World Tourism Organization. (2021). *UNWTO Inclusive Recovery Guide – Sociocultural Impacts of Covid-19, Issue 2: Cultural Tourism*. UNWTO.

World Travel & Tourism Council. (2021). *Sustainable development goals*. https://wttc.org/Initiatives/Sustainable-Growth

Wortmann, F., & Flüchter, K. (2015). Internet of things: Technology and value added. *Business & Information Systems Engineering, 57*(3), 221–224. doi:10.100712599-015-0383-3

Wright, C. (2017). Are Beauty Bloggers More Influential than Traditional Industry Experts? *Journal of Promotional Communications, 5*(3), 303–322. http://promotionalcommunications.org/index.php/pc/article/view/113

WTO. (1985). *Identification and Evaluation of Those Components of Tourism Services which Have a Bearing on Tourist Satisfaction and which Can*. World Tourism Organization.

WTTC (World Travel & Tourism Council). (2020, April 14). *More than 197m travel & tourism jobs will be lost due to prolonged travel restrictions, according to new research from WTTC*. https://wttc.org/News-Article/More-than-197m-Travel-Tourism-jobs-will-be-lost-due-to-prolonged-travel-restrictions

WTTC. (2019). *Travel & tourism economic impact 2019 world*. https://www.slovenia.info/uploads/dokumenti/raziskave/raziskave/world2019.pdf

Wu, Y., Zhang, W., Shen, J., Mo, Z., & Peng, Y. (2018). Smart city with Chinese characteristics against the background of big data: Idea, action and risk. *Journal of Cleaner Production, 173*, 60–66. Advance online publication. doi:10.1016/j.jclepro.2017.01.047

Wyman, O. (2020, March 5). *To recovery & beyond the future of travel & tourism in the wake of Covid-19*. https://www.oliverwyman.com/content/dam/oliver-wyman/v2/publications/2020/To_Recovery_and_Beyond-The_Future_of_Travel_and_Tourism_in_the_Wake_of_COVID-19.pdf

Xiang, Z., Du, Q., Ma, Y., & Fan, W. (2017). A comparative analysis of major online review platforms: Implications for social media analytics in hospitality and tourism. *Tourism Management, 58*, 51–65. doi:10.1016/j.tourman.2016.10.001

Xiang, Z., & Gretzel, U. (2010). Role of social media in online travel information search. *Tourism Management, 31*(2), 179–188. doi:10.1016/j.tourman.2009.02.016

Xi, N., & Hamari, J. (2020). Does gamification affect brand engagement and equity? A study in online brand communities. *Journal of Business Research, 109*, 449–460. doi:10.1016/j.jbusres.2019.11.058

Xu, F., Tian, F., Buhalis, D., & Weber, J. (2013). Marketing tourism via electronic games: understanding the motivation of tourist players. In *2013 5th International Conference on Games and Virtual Worlds for Serious Applications (VS-GAMES)* (pp. 1-8). IEEE.

Xu, F., Weber, J., & Buhalis, D. (2013). Gamification in tourism. In *Information and Communication Technologies in Tourism* (pp. 525–537). Springer.

Xu, J. (2020). Research on the Construction of Cultural Tourism Market in Shenyang Based on Big Data. *Journal of Physics: Conference Series, 1621*(1), 012104. doi:10.1088/1742-6596/1621/1/012104

Yagol, P. (2018). *Improving the User Knowledge and User Experience by using Augmented Reality in a Smart City context* [Unpublished doctoral dissertation]. Degree of Master of Science in Geospatial Technologies.

Yalçınkaya, P., Atay, L., & Karakaş, E. (2018). Akıllı turizm uygulamaları. *Gastroia: Journal of Gastronomy and Travel Research, 2*(2), 34–52.

Yalçınkaya, P., Atay, L., & Korkmaz, H. (2018). An evaluation on smart tourism. *China-USA Business Review, 17*(6), 308–315.

Yallop, A., & Seraphin, H. (2020). Big data and analytics in tourism and hospitality: Opportunities and risks. *Journal of Tourism Futures, 6*(3), 257–262. doi:10.1108/JTF-10-2019-0108

Yang, Y., Mao, Z., & Tang, J. (2018). Understanding Guest Satisfaction with Urban Hotel Location. *Journal of Travel Research, 57*(2), 243–259. doi:10.1177/0047287517691153

Yarmaci, N., Keleş, M., & Ergil, B. (2017). Diving of underwater tourism current status, Problems and suggestions for the development: A case study of Kaş. *Güncel Turizm Araştırmaları Dergisi, 1*(1), 66–87.

Yavuz, M. C. (2007). *Identity building process in international destination branding: A Case for the city of Adana* [Unpublished doctoral dissertation]. University of Cukurova, Adana, Turkey.

Yazıcı, S., & Ayazlar, G. (2019). Cloud Computing and Tourism 4.0. In Digital Tourism: The New Future of the Industry (pp. 63-82). Education Publisher.

Yazmaları, T. (2016). *İstatistikler*. Accessed on June 19, 2021. https://www.yazmalar.gov.tr/istatistik.php

Yengin, D., & Bayrak, T. (2017). *Sanal Gerçeklik-VR*. Der Yayınları.

Yigit, A. Y., Ulvi, A., & Varol, F. (2020). 3D Documentation of Cultural Heritage with Augmented Reality Application: The Case of Chashma-Ayup Tomb in Uzbekistan. *Journal of Tourism and Gastronomy Studies*, *8*(4), 3155–3172.

Yıldırım, G., & Ozbek, O. (2019). Tourist Guidance and Interactive Technologies in Museums. In Digital Tourism: The New Future of the Industry (pp.165-174). Education Publisher.

Yıldırım, A. (1999). Nitel araştırma yöntemlerinin temel özellikleri ve eğitim araştırmalarındaki yeri ve önemi [The basic features of qualitative research methods and their place and importance in educational research]. *Eğitim ve Bilim*, *23*(112), 7–17.

Yıldırım, Y. (2019a). Endüstri 4.0'a kapsamlı bir bakış: 2011'den bugüne. *Bilgi Dünyası*, *20*(2), 217–249. doi:10.15612/BD.2019.754

Yıldırım, Y. (2019b). Industry 4.0, Marketing and Value Triplication. In A. Y. H. A. N. Fatih (Ed.), *Several Dimension of Innovation, Technology and Industry 4.0* (pp. 127–141). Peter Lang Pub.

Yıldırım, Y. (2020). Farklı disiplinlerde endüstri 4.0. *OPUS–Uluslararası Toplum Araştırmaları Dergisi*, *15*(21), 756–789. doi:10.26466/opus.624938

Yıldız, S. (2019). The Rise of Robot Guides in the Tourist Guiding Profession. *Süleyman Demirel University Visionary Journal*, *10*(23), 164–177.

Yılmaz, B. (2011). Dijital Kütüphane Becerileri Konusunda Türkiye'de Durum: AccessIT Projesi Çerçevesinde Bir Değerlendirme. *Türk Kütüphaneciliği*, *25*(1), 117–123.

Yılmaz, L. (2020). Mersin'de Somut Kültürel Miras Bilinci ve Koruma Üzerine Bir Değerlendirme. *Amisos*, *5/8*, 156–177.

Yin, C., Jung, T., & Lee, M. (2021). Mobile Augmented Reality Heritage Applications: Meeting the Needs of Heritage Tourists. *Sustainability*, *13*(5), 2523. doi:10.3390u13052523

Yin, X., & Li, J. (2021). Development of cultural tourism platform based on FPGA and convolutional neural network. *Microprocessors and Microsystems*, *80*, 103579. doi:10.1016/j.micpro.2020.103579

Yoo, C. W., Goo, J., Huang, C. D., Nam, K., & Woo, M. (2017). Improving travel decision support satisfaction with smart tourism technologies: A framework of tourist elaboration likelihood and self-efficacy. *Technological Forecasting and Social Change*, *123*, 330–341. doi:10.1016/j.techfore.2016.10.071

Yoo, K. H., & Gretzel, U. (2010). Antecedents and impacts of trust in travel-related consumer-generated media. *Information Technology & Tourism*, *12*(2), 139–152. doi:10.3727/109830510X12887971002701

Yovcheva, Z., & Buhalis, D. (2013). Augmented Reality in Tourism: 10 Unique Applications Explained. *Digital Tourism Think Tank*, 1-12.

Yovcheva, Z., Buhalis, D., & Gatzidis, C. (2012). Overview of Smartphone Augmented Reality Applications for Tourism. *e-Review of Tourism Research (eRTR)*, *10*(2), 63-66.

Yu, C.-E., & Sun, R. (2019). The role of Instagram in the UNESCO's creative city of gastronomy: A case study of Macau. *Tourism Management*, *75*, 257–268. doi:10.1016/j.tourman.2019.05.011

Yücel, D. M. (2016). Farklı Bir Olay Yeri Olarak Sanal Gerçek. *Kırıkkale Üniversitesi Sosyal Bilimler Dergisi*, *6*(2), 407–421.

Yu, J. Y. (2009). A cross-cultural study on participation intention to medical tourism among Korean, Chinese and Japanese visitors in Korea. *The Korean Academic Society of Tourism*, *33*(3), 187–204.

YunD.MacDonaldR. M.MacEachernM.HennesseyS. (2007). Typology of cultural tourists: an island study. doi:10.2139/ssrn.1617362

Yung, R., & Khoo, L. C. (2019). New realities: A systematic literature review on virtual reality and augmented reality in tourism research. *Current Issues in Tourism, 22*(17), 2056–2081. doi:10.1080/13683500.2017.1417359

Yüzbaşıoğlu, N., Çelik, P., Topsakal, Y., & Bahar, M. (2018). Industry 4.0 and smart tourism: Antalya destination smart tourist guide application development. *Proceedings of the Innovation and Global Issues in Social Sciences III*.

Zamora, T. (2008). The impact of commercial exploitation on the preservation of underwater cultural heritage. *Museum International, 60*(4), 18–30. doi:10.1111/j.1468-0033.2008.00662.x

Zarnowski, A., Anna, B., & Banaszek, S. (2015). Application of technical measures and software in constructing photorealistic 3D models of historical building using ground-based and aerial (UAV) digital images. *Reports on Geodesy and Geoinformatics, 99*(1), 54–63. doi:10.2478/rgg-2015-0012

Zarrella, D., & Zarrella, A. (2010). *The Facebook marketing book*. O'Reilly Media, Inc.

Zeng, B., & Gerritsen, R. (2014). What do we know about social media in tourism? A review. *Tourism Management Perspectives, 10*, 27–36. doi:10.1016/j.tmp.2014.01.001

Zeng, D., Guo, S., & Cheng, Z. (2011). The web of things: A survey. *Journal of Communication, 6*(6), 424–438.

Zeng, D., Tim, Y., Yu, J., & Liu, W. (2020). Actualizing big data analytics for smart cities: A cascading affordance study. *International Journal of Information Management, 54*, 102156. Advance online publication. doi:10.1016/j.ijinfomgt.2020.102156

Zhang, J., & Dong, L. (2021). Image monitoring and management of hot tourism destination based on data mining technology in big data environment. *Microprocessors and Microsystems, 80*, 103515. doi:10.1016/j.micpro.2020.103515

Zhang, K., Chen, Y., & Li, C. (2019). Discovering the tourists' behaviors and perceptions in a tourism destination by analyzing photos' visual content with a computer deep learning model: The case of Beijing. *Tourism Management, 75*, 595–608. doi:10.1016/j.tourman.2019.07.002

Zhang, M. Y. W., & Yang, Y. (2011). On life cycle of cultural heritage engineering tourism: A case study of Macau. *System Engineering Procedia, 1*, 351–357. doi:10.1016/j.sepro.2011.08.053

Zhang, T. (2020). Co-creating tourism experiences through a traveler's journey: A perspective article. *Tourism Review, 75*(1), 56–60. doi:10.1108/TR-06-2019-0251

Zhang, T., Abound Omran, B., & Cobanoglu, C. (2017). Generation Y's positive and negative eWOM: Use of social media and mobile technology. *International Journal of Contemporary Hospitality Management, 29*(2), 732–761. doi:10.1108/IJCHM-10-2015-0611

Zhao, Y., Xu, X., & Wang, M. (2019). Predicting overall customer satisfaction: Big data evidence from hotel online textual reviews. *International Journal of Hospitality Management, 76*, 111–121. Advance online publication. doi:10.1016/j.ijhm.2018.03.017

Zhong, R. Y., Wang, L. H., & Xuan, X. (2017). IoT-enabled real-time machine status monitoring approach for cloud manufacturing. *Procedia CIRP, 63*, 709–714. doi:10.1016/j.procir.2017.03.349

Zhu, W., Zhang, L. & Li, N. (2014). Challenges, function changing of government and enterprises in Chinese smart tourism. *e-Review of Tourism Research, 5*, 1-4.

Zhu, H., Wei, L., & Niu, P. (2020). The novel coronavirus outbreak in Wuhan, China. *Global Health Research and Policy*, *5*(1), 1–3. doi:10.118641256-020-00135-6 PMID:32226823

Zimmerman, J., & Sahlin, D. (2010). *Social media marketing all-in-one for dummies.* Wiley Publishing. doi:10.1002/9781118257661

Živković, R., Gajić, J., & Brdar, I. (2014). The impact of social media on tourism. *Sinteza*, 758-761.

Zouganeli, S., Trihas, N., & Antonaki, M. (2011). Social media and tourism: The use of Facebook by the European national tourism organizations. *Tourism Today (Nicosia)*, *11*, 110–121.

Zukin, S. (2020). The innovation Complex - Cities, Tech, and the New economy (1st ed.). Academic Press.

About the Contributors

Lídia Oliveira has a degree in Philosophy from the University of Coimbra (1990), a Master's degree in Educational Technology from the University of Aveiro, in partnership with the University of Valenciennes (France) and Mons (Belgium) (1995), and a PhD in Sciences and Technologies of Communication from the University of Aveiro (2002). She has been a professor in the Department of Communication and Art (http://www.ua.pt) at the University of Aveiro since 1995 until the present. Her main scientific interest is in cyberculture studies. Her areas of interest are: New Media & Cultural Heritage, Internet of Things & Cultural Tourism, Science and Technologies of Communication, ICT and Education, Multimedia, Social Network Analysis, Sociology of Communication, Information Systems, Digital Libraries, Time Studies, Science Communication, Communication in the Scientific Community (theoretical and empirical studies). She has published both nationally and internationally in peer review journals, book chapters, and conferences proceedings.

* * *

Orhan Akova is a Full Professor in the Department of Tourism Management at Istanbul University, Turkey. He obtained his Ph.D. and Master's degree in Tourism Management (Turkey). He specializes in tourism studies. His research interests include the socio-cultural impacts of tourism, sustainable tourism, and management in tourism.

Mehmet Altug Sahin is a Research Assistant at the Faculty of Economics Tourism Management Department, Istanbul University. He holds Ph.D. and Master's Degree in Tourism Management. His research interests include accounting, revenue management, big data and social media in tourism and related areas.

Mahmut Baltaci is a full-time lecturer at the Vocational School of Tasucu, department of Tourism and Travel Services at Selcuk University, Turkey. He has published articles, book chapters and conference papers about tourism. He is one of the editors of a textbook called "Basic Kitchen Techniques and Management". His research interests are travel marketing and management, tourist behaviors, gastronomy, tour guiding. He is also a member of Turkey Tourist Guide Association as a tourist guide. Dr. Mahmut Baltacı https://orcid.org/ 0000-0001-7509-3094.

Huseyin Baran received his PhD in Arts and Graphic Arts from the Ankara Hacettepe University in Turkey 2021. In 2005 his BsD in Painting and Sculpture from Eskisehir Anatolian University in Turkey.

In 2011, he was hired as academician by University of Duzce for Art and Architecture Faculty in Turkey. He works as an Art Director in visual communication in Duzce University and also lectures at the faculty of Art and Architecture Faculty. He writes and presents widely on issues of visual design, 3D drawing techniques, Reality Technologies.

Zuleyhan Baran received her PhD in Tourism and Hotel Management from the University of Sakarya in Turkey 2017. In 2003 her BsD in Food Engineering in Engineering Faculty from University of Gaziantep. In 2009, she was hired as academician by University of Duzce in Turkey and is currently Erasmus Coordinator and assistant manager of Akcakoca Vocational School for the Akcakoca campus of University of Duzce. She writes and presents widely on issues of gastronomy, tourism, QFD and halal food.

Lia Bassa (Budapest, 1954) graduated as an English/French teacher for linguistics and literature 1978, Ph.D. in English literature 1982. Assistant professor TUB, establishing a post graduate course for technical interpretation being a professional consecutive and simultaneous interpreter all through her career. Senior consultant of the Hungarian National Committee of UNESCO World Heritage (2000-2004). Assistant professor TUB, Department of Information and Knowledge Management (2004-2007). Managing Director of the Foundation for Information Society, researcher of UNESCO World Heritage Information Management Research Centre (2005-). Author of numerous heritage related articles. Invited lecturer of culture, heritage and communication, responsible for World Heritage MA education at the Budapest Metropolitan University (2010-).

Cláudia Batista, born in the municipality of Marvão, completed in 2020, the Superior Professional Technical Course (CTsP) in Tourism and Tourism Information. Currently, she attends the Tourism Degree at the Polytechnic Institute of Portalegre (2020/2023). She is interested in the areas of culture and languages. In the future, she intends to follow the path of scientific research in Portugal, although he would like to experience other professional contexts related to the area of Tourism in Portugal and abroad.

Zombor Berezvai is an Assistant Lecturer at Corvinus University of Budapest and the Chief Economist of the Hungarian Competition Authority. He graduated as an economist from Eötvös Loránd University and started his career at Procter & Gamble. His main research interests include retail innovation, transportation, and cultural tourism.

Buket Buluk Eşitti graduated from Akdeniz University, Alanya Faculty of Business, Department of Tourism Management (2013). In 2014, she started to work as a Research Assistant at Çanakkale Onsekiz Mart University, Faculty of Tourism. She received her master's degree from Çanakkale Onsekiz Mart University, Institute of Social Sciences, Department of Tourism Management (2016). She received her PhD degree from Çanakkale Onsekiz Mart University, School of Graduate Studies, Department of Tourism Management (2020). She is currently working at Çanakkale Onsekiz Mart University, Faculty of Tourism, Department of Tourism Management as Research Assistant Doctor. Her main fields of study area are; Behavioral Sciences, Tourism Marketing, Tourism Management, Travel Agency, Sustainable Tourism and E-Tourism.

A. Celil Cakici is a full-time professor at the Faculty of Tourism at Mersin University, Turkey. He has published many articles, book chapters, and conference papers besides a course book on Meeting Management. He is one of the editors of a textbook called "Tourism Guidance" and also edited a course book named "General Tourism". His research interests are marketing issues, research methods and business statistics. He has also contributed to national and international journals and academic conferences by refereeing the articles and papers. Additionally, he is a member of the Accreditation Council of Tourism Education at university level in Turkey. Prof. Dr. A. Celil ÇAKICI ORCİD: https://orcid.org/0000-0002-9192-1969.

İsmail Çalık is a lecturer at Gümüşhane University, Faculty of Tourism, Department of Tourism Management and Vice Dean at the same faculty. Çalık's research areas are sustainable tourism, intangible cultural heritage and tourism, occupational health and safety in tourism, tourism and traditional handicrafts and halal tourism. Çalık has many books and articles on Gümüşhane province and the Eastern Black Sea Region.

Gurel Cetin is a professor in Faculty of Economics at Istanbul University. He earned his Ph.D from business administration from Istanbul University in 2012, since then he has been teaching tourism and marketing courses in several institutions. His research interests include entrpreneurship, sustainable development, tourism, and marketing.

Aybuke Ceyhun Sezgin worked as an Assistant Professor at Gazi University in Turkey, Faculty of Tourism, Department of Gastronomy and Culinary Arts in the 2012-2018 list. In 2018, she received the title of Associate Professor in the field of Tourism at Ankara Hacı Bayram Veli University, Faculty of Tourism, Department of Gastronomy and Culinary Arts. She is still working as an Associate Professor at Ankara Hacı Bayram Veli University, Faculty of Tourism in Turkey. Tourism, articles published in journals, articles published in national and international congresses, articles published in gastronomy and food perspective indexed journals. She is on the scientific committees of international and national conferences, congresses, and symposiums.

Monica Coronel is a PhD student of the Doctoral School of Business and Management, Tourism Specialization. Areas of interest: Destination branding, destination image, destination image on Social Media, Destination Promotional Videos and Image of long-haul destinations.

Carlos Costa is Full Professor, Head of the Department (School) of Economics, Management, Industrial Engineering and Tourism (DEGEIT) of the University of Aveiro, and Tourism Expert at the European Commission. He is Editor-in-Chief of the Journal of Tourism & Development (Revista de Turismo e Desenvolvimento) (SCOPUS), and Associate Editor of several renown international journals. Carlos is the leader of the PhD Tourism Programme of the University of Aveiro and is head of the Tourism Research Centre of the University of Aveiro. He holds a PhD and MSc in Tourism Management (University of Surrey, UK), and a BSc in Urban and Regional Planning (University of Aveiro, Portugal).

Maria Gorete Ferreira Dinis holds a Ph.D. in Tourism, an MA in Innovation, Planning and Development, and a BSc in Tourism Management and Planning from the University of Aveiro. She is coordinator and professor of the BSc in Tourism at the Polytechnic Institute of Portalegre (PIP) / School of Education and Social Sciences. She is a full member of the Research Unit Governance, Competitiveness, and Public Policies and collaborating member of Centre for Tourism Research, Development and Innovation (CITUR). She is also a member of the editorial and scientific boards of international journals, as well as a member of the scientific committees of international tourism conferences. During recent years, she has published several scientific articles and presented communications in areas such as management of tourist destinations, tourism indicators, media and tourism, ICT applied to tourism and Big data in tourism.

Ahmet Erdem is a research assistant at the School of Tourism and Hotel Management/Department of Tourism Management, Harran University, Turkey. His research area includes smart tourism. Dr. Erdem has published many articles, conference papers, and book chapters in these fields.

Victor Figueira is an Assistant Professor at the Polytechnic Institute of Beja (IPBeja) in the area of Tourism, Environment and Sustainable Development. PhD in Tourism by the University of Évora and is now currently linked to several projects, national and international concerning social, cultural and other related to social sustainability of rural communities, tourism and regional development and social responsibility in tourism. He is a member of IPBeja team who cooperates with the Tourism Observatory of Alentejo and also the Scientific Coordinator of the project for certification of the Alentejo and Ribatejo Regional Tourism destination. Presently, he is coordinator of the Tourism Lab at IPBeja's Technology and Management School. He is also member of the Governance, Competitiveness and Public Policy research unit (GOVCOPP), where he integrates the Tourism and Development group and also in Centre for Tourism Research, Development and Innovation (CiTUR).

Umit Gaberli is an Assistant Professor of Recreation Management at Siirt University, College of Tourism and Hotel Management, Turkey. He holds a B. A and PhD. in Economics from Ege University, Turkey. His areas of research include tourism economics, technological change in tourism, and recreation.

Francisco Gonçalves has a PhD in Tourism from the University of Aveiro and is Assistant Professor and director of the Tourism management degree at the Polytechnic Institute of Cávado e Ave (Barcelos – Portugal). He is also member of the Research Unit on Governance, Competitiveness and Public Policy (GOVCOPP) of the University of Aveiro. He is author and co-author of papers presented in national and international conferences or published in scientific journals.

Onur Icoz is Associate Professor of Tourism Management at the Department of Travel Management, Faculty of Tourism, Adnan Menderes University, Kusadasi-Aydın, Turkey. He gained his PhD in Tourism Management from Dokuz Eylul University in 2013, became Asssociate Professor in 2021. His research interests include Marketing in Tourism, Social Media Marketing, Sport Tourism and Destination Branding.

Orhan Icoz is Professor of Tourism Management at the Department of Tourism Guidance, School of Applied Sciences, Yasar University, Izmir, Turkey. He gained his PhD in Tourism Management from Dokuz Eylul University in 1987, became full professor in 1997. His research interests include Economics of Travel and Tourism, Tourism and Hospitality Marketing, Travel and Tourism Market Research, Tourism Planning and Policy.

Füsun İstanbullu Dinçer was born in Istanbul. She graduated from Saint Benoît French Girls High School in 1977. After completing her undergraduate education, she completed her master's degree in 1985 and Ph.D. degree in 1988 at the Faculty of Economics of Istanbul University. She became Assistant Professor in 1992, Associate Professor in 1994 and Professor in 2000. She is the Head of the Department of Tourism Management at the Faculty of Economics of Istanbul University. She has published many books and conference papers presented in Turkey and abroad. She speaks French and English. Her areas of expertise are tourism economy, travel management, tourist products and alternative tourism types, European Union and tourism policies, tourism ethics and philosophy. ORCID: 0000-0003-2338-2462.

Aruditya Jasrotia is currently working as an Assistant Professor in Amity Institute of Travel and Tourism at Amity University, Noida, India. He completed his Ph.D. in Travel and Tourism Management from Central University of Jammu, India. His areas of expertise are Smart Tourism, Smart Tourism Destinations, Smart Cities, Tourism Technologies, Urban Planning, and Sustainable Tourism.

Časlav Kalinić is a research associate at the University of Novi Sad, Faculty of Sciences, Department of Geography, Tourism and Hotel Management. His main research areas include social media analytics, digital marketing, artificial intelligence, and big data analytics in the tourism and hospitality industry. Prior to work in academia, he has acquired extensive international experience in the tourism industry, including experience with domestic and EU-funded project management within both government and NGO sectors. In addition, he has worked in a consultative capacity for an accommodation booking platform. He currently participates in COST action LEAD-ME.

Elif Esma Karaman graduated from Atatürk University, Faculty of Tourism, Department of Food and Beverage Management in 2012-2016. She completed her master's degree in tourism management and hotel management at Atatürk University Faculty of Tourism in 2016-2019. In 2019, she started her doctorate education at Ankara Hacı Bayram Veli University, Faculty of Tourism, Department of Gastronomy and Culinary Arts, and continues. She also works as a lecturer in the culinary department of the hotel and restaurant services program at Artvin Coruh University Vocational School.

Murat Koçyiğit, completed his undergraduate education in Selcuk University, Faculty of Communication, Public Relations and Publicity Department in 2008. In the same year, he started his master's degree in the Department of Public Relations and Publicity at Selcuk University Social Sciences Institute and graduated from the master's program in 2011. In 2015, he completed his Ph.D. program in the Department of Public Relations and Publicity at Selcuk University Social Sciences Institute. He has been working as an Assistant Professor at Necmettin Erbakan University, Faculty of Tourism since 2015, and has been appointed as Assistant Professor in 2015. He received the title of Associate Professor in 2018. He has scientific studies on digital communication, Web 2.0, semantic web, digital culture, digital transformation, digital public relations, social network marketing, and transmedia.

Büşra Küçükcivil completed her primary and secondary education from open education. Later, Büşra Küçükcivil graduated from Selçuk University, Faculty of Communication, Department of Public Relations and Publicity in 2011. She received her master's degree from Selcuk University, Social Sciences Institute, Public Relations and Publicity Department in 2017. She started her doctorate education in Selcuk University, Social Sciences Institute, Public Relations and Publicity Department in 2018 and she is still continuing this education. The author works as a research assistant at Necmettin Erbakan University, Faculty of Social Sciences and Humanities, Department of Public Relations and Advertising. Büşra Küçükcivil's fields of work are communication studies and public relations.

Eunice Ramos Lopes has an Advanced Training Course in Tourism by the Department of Economics, Management, Industrial Engineering and Tourism from University of Aveiro; a PhD in Antropology (Specialization in Politics and Images of Culture and Museology) awarded by the New University of Lisbon; a MSc in Heritage and Museology awarded by the New University of Lisbon and a BA degree in Conservation and Restoration awarded by the School of Technology of Tomar. She is an Adjunt Professor at the Polytechnic Institute of Tomar (IPT), at the Management School of Tomar (ESGT). She lectures in the Culture and Tourism Bachelor degree and in the Development of Cultural Tourism Products Master degree. Presently, she is the coordinator of the higher education courses of Tourism at the IPT. She is a researcher at the Network Research Center in Anthropology (CRIA-FCSH – UNL), and member of the Research Unit Governance, Competitiveness and Public Policies (GOVCOPP) of the University of Aveiro. She is also member of the editorial and scientific boards of a few academic national and international journals, as well member of the organizing and scientific committees of international tourism conferences. Research areas include tourism, cultural tourism, anthropology, heritage, museology, events, and networks.

Seda Ozdemir Akgul is an Assistant Professor in the Department of Tourism Management in Faculty of Tourism at Selcuk University. She received her Bachelor's degree at Istanbul University and Master's degree in Tourism Management from Gazi University, Turkey. She holds a doctorate from the Department of Tourism Management at Gazi University and Selcuk University, Turkey. Her research interests revolve around consumer behavior in travel and tourism, destination marketing and management, particularly in the areas of special interest tourism, smart tourism, tourist experiences and sustainable tourism. The majority of her research involves the use of qualitative data analysis. ORCID: 0000-0003-4482-4119.

Kubra Ozer is a master's student of Tourism Management, Istanbul University Social Science Institute. Her research interests include smart tourism, cultural tourism, utilizing big data in tourism, and destination marketing.

Árpád Ferenc Papp-Váry is the dean of the Faculty of Tourism, Business and Communication at the Budapest Metropolitan University, Hungary. He is also the head of the Commerce and Marketing BSc programme and vocational programme, the Marketing MSc programme (running from 2019), and the Digital Marketing executive MBA postgraduate programme. At the same time, he is research associate of the Urban Marketing and Geostrategy Centre of John von Neumann University, Kecskemét, Hungary. Besides university education, Árpád regularly holds training sessions and provides branding consultancy for cities, companies and professionals. He is serving as Vice President of the Hungarian Marketing Association. His teaching and research areas are country branding, city branding, personal branding, sports branding and branded entertainment. Árpád is the author of six books and several hundred publications, most of which are available online at www.papp-vary.hu.

Eray Polat received his MS in Tourism and Hotel Management in 2015; PhD in Tourism Management in 2019 and both from the Balikesir University, Turkey. He is working at the Gumushane University as

Assistant Professor and is currently the Head of the Department of Gastronomy and Culinary Arts. His research areas are generally on job insecurity, ethics, consumer behaviour in tourism.

Adelaide Proença is a Ph.D. in Education Sciences. Master in Probabilities and Statistics by the Faculty of Science of the University of Lisbon. Adjunct Professor at the School of Education and Social Sciences of the Polytechnic Institute of Portalegre. Collaborating researcher of VALORIZA (Research Centre for the valorisation of endogenous resources).

João José Severo Arnedo Rolha is a invited professor of Tourism at the Polytechnic Institute of Beja (Portugal). PhD Candidate in Tourism, at the Faculdad de Turismo y Finanzas from the University of Seville, Spain.

Paulo Alexandre Gomes Santos is an Adjunct Professor at the Polytechnic Institute of Tomar. He works in the area(s) of Engineering Sciences and Technologies with emphasis on Electrical, Electronic and Computer Engineering. Various publications in the field of ICT. https://orcid.org/0000-0002-5604-8009.

Ferhat Şeker is a research assistant at the Department of Tourism Management, Faculty of Business, Adana Alparslan Türkeş Science and Technology University, Turkey. His research area includes behavioural intentions and tourist experience. Dr. Şeker has published many articles, conference papers, and book chapters in these fields.

João Tomaz Simões completed, in 2020, the Title of Specialist in Tourism and Leisure, and is currently developing his Doctoral Thesis in Tourism at the Institute of Geography and Spatial Planning of the University of Lisbon, in partnership with Estoril Higher Institute for Tourism and Hotel Studies (ESHTE). He completed his master's degree in Cultural Tourism Product Development at the School of Management of the Polytechnic of Tomar in 2012 and a Degree in Tourism in 2008 from the Higher Institute of Languages and Administration (ISLA – Santarem). Since 2011, he has been a Specialized Technician of Tourism Training and Planning, since 2019, Guest Professor at the Polytechnic Institute of Tomar. Since 2020, he is a Researcher at Techn&Art Center (Center for Technology, Restoration and Enhancement of the Arts) and researcher at ISLA UI&D Management, Tourism, and Marketing.

Bruno Sousa is a Professor in Polytechnic Institute of Cavado and Ave (IPCA, Portugal) Head of Master Program - Tourism Management - PhD Marketing and Strategy. He was Market Analist at Sonae Distribuição – Modelo e Continente, S.A. (2006 to 2009) and he was Marketing Assistant - Jornal O Jogo at Controlinveste (2005) - Best Paper Award in Strategic Marketing & Value Creation (International Conference on Innovation and Entrepreneurship in Marketing and Consumer Behaviour 2020) Teaching Award of the School of Economics and Management of the University of Minho 2015/2016 - Best Thesis in Tourism Award - ICIEMC 2015 - Management Graduation, University of Minho Award - Best performance (2006) - Merit Scholarship for Students in Public Higher Education Awards of Merit Scholarship by University of Minho in 2001/02 - 2002/03 - 2003/04 Rresearch centre: CiTUR and Applied Management Research Unit (UNIAG). He is author or co-author of several papers and her research interests include tourism management, marketing and strategy. Editorial board member of several peer reviewed scientific journals and ad-hoc reviewer of several peer-reviewed scientific journals. Member of the scientific committee of several national and international congresses and conferences.

Yunus Topsakal received his BA from Bilkent University, School of Applied Technology and Management, Department of Tourism and Hotel Management in 2011, and his MA from Akdeniz University, Institute of Social Sciences, Tourism Management and Hotel Management Program in 2013, and his PhD in 2017, again from Akdeniz University Tourism Management.

Zafer Türkmendağ is an Assistant Professor at the Faculty of Tourism, Atatürk University, Turkey. He holds a BA and MA in tourism management. He holds his PhD in tourism management in 2019 from the Gazi University, Turkey. His research interests include tourism technology, tourism marketing and management, sustainable tourism and accessible tourism. He has certificates on software development (Middle East Technical University) and hotel management system (Oracle Opera 5.0).

Nihan Garipağaoğlu Uğur has been in the tourism sector since 1989. She started her career in the front office in hotel. She worked in food service in London and after back to Turkey, became a flight attendant in International Airlines. She continued her professional life in Limousine service as a sales manager in Istanbul. She used to run a travel agency for a long time as a general manager. She pursued her career as an operational manager in a hotel & casino's sales agency. She had a master's degree in tourism management from Istanbul Medeniyet University. Her thesis was about organizational commitment. She is still an ongoing Ph.D. in tourism management at Istanbul University in Turkey. She is interested in recreational activities, organizational commitment, tourism management, gamification in tourism.

Miroslav Vujičić is associate professor at the University of Novi Sad, Faculty of Sciences, Department of Geography, Tourism and Hotel Management. Main field of interest is decision making processes, project management, product development, cultural tourism and has proficiency skills in data gathering, analysis and interpretation of mathematical and statistical methods. He has published 29 research papers at Scopus indexed journals and has more than 304 citations in Scopus database. Programme Leader, BA Hons tourism. RVP for Eastern Europe in ITSA network. Department coordinator for international affairs and students and staff mobility. Member of Department Accreditation team has experience in creating study programs, managing quality assurance. He is main evaluator for impact assessment of European Capital of Culture Novi Sad 2022. He is experienced project manager and researcher (EXtremeClimTwin, Green SCENT, CULTURWB, DiCultYouth, euCULTher, LEAD-ME).

Oya Yildirim is a Lecturer in the Department of Accommodation Management, School of Karataş Tourism and Hotel Management at Cukurova University, Turkey. She is also the assistant manager in the same school. She gained her PhD in Tourism Management from Mersin University in 2018. She has published 16 international and national articles, 16 conference papers and 2 book chapters. Her research interests are tourism marketing, sustainable tourism, special interest tourism, event and gastronomic tourism.

Fisun Yüksel, (BA in Tourism and Hotel Management, Dokuz Eylül University; MSc in Tourism Management, Sheffield Hallam University, Ph.D. at Sheffield Hallam University). She is a professor at the faculty of Tourism and Hospitality Management, Adnan Menderes University, fisun.yuksel@adu.edu.tr). She has published articles on destination management, planning and marketing, tourist satisfaction and complaint management, and tourism research in prestigious scientific journals, including *Annals of Tourism Research*, *Tourism Management*, *Journal of Hospitality and Tourism Research*, *Journal of*

Travel and Tourism Marketing, *Journal of Vocation Marketing* and the *Journal of Travel and Tourism Research*. Her recent research areas include big data, information and communication technology (ICT), smart tourism and artificial intelligence.

Index

M

N

O

P

R

S

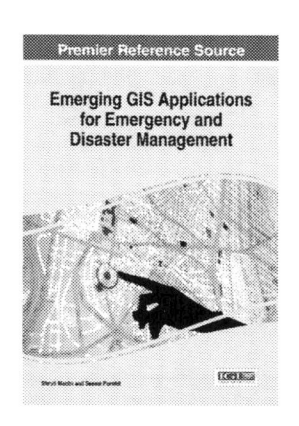   

Printed in the United States
by Baker & Taylor Publisher Services